CASSELL CAREERS ENCYCLOPEDIA

FOURTEENTH EDITION

CASSELL CAREERS ENCYCLOPEDIA

FOURTEENTH EDITION

KATHERINE LEA

CASSELL

ACKNOWLEDGEMENT

CLCI reproduced by agreement with the Careers and Occupational Information Centre (COIC), Sheffield.

Cassell
Wellington House
125 Strand
London WC2R 0BB

127 West 24th Street
New York, NY 10011

First edition 1952
Second edition 1958
Third edition 1963
Fourth edition 1965
Fifth edition 1967
Sixth edition 1969
Seventh edition 1970
Eighth edition 1975
Ninth edition 1978
Tenth edition 1980
Eleventh edition 1984
Twelfth edition 1987
Thirteenth edition 1992
Fourteenth edition 1997

British Library Cataloguing-in-Publication Data
A catalogue record for this book is available from the British Library.

ISBN 0-304-33740-4 (hardback)

Designed and typeset by Ben Cracknell Studios

Printed and bound in Great Britain by Martins the Printers, Berwick-on-Tweed

Contents

Introduction

Over the last 45 years the *Careers Encyclopedia* has become established as an authoritative careers reference resource providing well-researched and accurate careers information from an independent and impartial viewpoint. It provides comprehensive information on careers, qualifications, and employment trends for people and organisations interested and concerned with work and training in the UK. It is of particular interest to young people between 14 and 22, their parents, their teachers and advisers, and increasingly it is a valuable resource for adults who may be contemplating a change of career.

The *Encyclopedia* deals with work and occupations in the widest sense, covering jobs and careers ranging from unskilled to professional work, and is not limited in any way by type or level of work. Occupations are examined within the relevant sector of employment. The *Encyclopedia* gives an outline sketch of each occupation and area of employment; what is happening to them and information on employment trends; what the work is like and what kinds of skills are needed. It describes recruitment and entry patterns, the relevant education and training, and how to obtain further information.

This fourteenth edition of the *Careers Encyclopedia* has been completely revised with a small amount of restructuring to incorporate minor changes in the classification system. New chapters have been added to reflect areas of growing significance or concern. Once again the revision has been a team effort, giving the benefit of a wider range of experience and knowledge. I enlisted the help of many colleagues in the careers field – experienced careers advisers from the schools and further and higher education sectors, careers information officers, and members of the professional Careers Writers' Association, to check the previous text for accuracy and content and where necessary update and rewrite. Without their committed help this fourteenth edition would not have been possible, so grateful thanks are due to Cathy Avent, Barbara Buffton, Antonia Clark, Beryl Dixon, Alison Dixon, Neil Harris, Fiona Hindle, Mark Hornby, Paul Kingston, Viv Neale, Joan Llewelyn Owens, Sara Morgan-Evans, Hilary Nickell, Marcus Offer, Philip Schofield, Helen Steadman, Judith Stewart, and Pam Thompson.

We could not have done the revision, though, without the help of over 700 professional institutions, professional bodies, lead bodies, industry training organisations, trade associations, and major employers, who painstakingly checked the text, allowed us to quote from their text, supplied new statistical information, new material and guidelines, and identified further sources of help when we had difficulty tracking down statistical material. Many of these, although not all, are listed in 'Appendix 1: Useful Addresses' for further information. It is impossible to thank them all individually but we would like to record our thanks and appreciation for their help.

One of the aims of the thirteenth edition was to map as many occupations, areas of work and preparation for them as possible, and to show how these are changing. This approach has been continued and extended in the fourteenth edition, and we have included some new occupations and taken account of trends and developments in the 1990s.

Wherever possible, we have tried to look ahead and sketch in the possible prospects within each occupation, but this is becoming increasingly difficult against a background of economic, educational, social, political and technological change. Some of the changes will be short-term, others long-term, but until one can view them with hindsight it is sometimes impossible to identify what may be just a temporary blip and what is a significant trend.

We have included the most up-to-date statistics, where these have been collected, as the figures can often illustrate a situation more clearly and economically than long descriptions. However, statistics often take years to be published so some of these statistics inevitably come from the early rather than the mid-1990s. Some of the more general statistical sources used have been identified in 'Appendix 2: Bibliography', but we have also used other specialist sources.

This edition continues to use the Careers Library Classification Index (CLCI) produced by the Careers and Occupational Information Centre (COIC) (part of the Choice and Careers Division of the Department for Education and Employment) as the basic structure for the *Encyclopedia*. The CLCI groups similar careers together and enables the user to identify easily other careers in the same field or related areas and thus explore the similarities and differences between them and see how they match the user's interests. Users in schools familiar with CLCI should find this structure helpful and details are given in 'Appendix 3'. COIC are planning some minor revision of CLCI in 1996, but details were unavailable at the time of writing this introduction. There is also a detailed alphabetical index to help users find their way round the *Encyclopedia*.

Although the *Careers Encyclopedia* broadly uses CLCI it is not always possible to fit material into the rigid categories that any classification imposes. This *Encyclopedia* is concerned to give the overview of a particular area of work or industry and this does not always fit neatly into one category. It is difficult for example to draw the line between engineering and manufacturing industries in a classification system particularly when they employ scientists, engineers and technologists from a wide range of disciplines. So there will be anomalies. Moreover, although the occupational categories of CLCI are widely used, the general categories covering for example *Higher Education* or *Working Overseas* are less familiar, so I have not assigned a CLCI category to the general chapters.

I have continued to incorporate cross-references in the text so that a particular aspect of a career can be pursued within a different context. If the cross-reference is in small capitals, it is a chapter title, or a section heading in a chapter. Other searches can be made using the alphabetical index at the back.

The occupational chapters are preceded by a number of general chapters and these have been expanded and extended in the fourteenth edition. Some of the general chapters provide a social commentary on what is happening in the world of work and I have tried to keep them factual and free of bias. However, I am concerned about the human suffering caused by downsizing, delayering, rightsizing, cutbacks and mass redundancies. Also, the leaner, slimmer workforce may be more competitive and efficient, but even for those in work there are still fears about keeping their jobs, future restructuring, reorganisation, mergers, privatisation, or whatever, and many employees are now working longer and longer hours to try to keep up with the sheer volume of work.

So, to reflect these concerns in the *Careers Encyclopedia* and provide a source of help, I expanded 'The World of Work' chapter, introduced a new chapter on 'Changing Your Career', which can be read separately, wrote a new chapter on 'The Job Search', and incorporated practical job-hunting information into 'Working Overseas'. Chapters dealing with the disadvantaged – those with special needs and women – have been extended, and there is a new chapter on student finance which, as well as surveying the current situation, gives practical guidance and information.

My other major concern in the general chapters was to rationalise the educational changes and vocational maze. These topics are impossible to simplify, but I have introduced new chapters specifically on vocational qualifications and general vocational qualifications, and in these I have tried to provide both a general introduction as well as review what is happening. The 'Education and Qualifications' chapter has been restructured and rewritten and incorporates a brief guide to the Dearing Report and developments on the Higher Still programme. I would like to record special thanks to all the educational bodies for all the helpful material they sent, their lengthy telephone calls explaining what was happening, and allowing me to quote from their literature (both published and unpublished). Despite interactive computer programmes, the Internet, etc., vocational preparation, guidance and training for young people remains as important as ever, so this section has been slightly expanded and turned into a stand-alone chapter.

Professional bodies usually phrase entry requirements for careers in terms of GCSE/GCE. Usually this is followed by the catch-all phrase 'or equivalent'. Sometimes other qualifications such as SCE, GNVQ/GSVQ or BTEC/SCOTVEC are specifically mentioned by name, but all too often they are ignored. In this *Encyclopedia*, wherever possible we have listed the alternatives giving A-levels/H Grades and/or GCSE/SCE (grades A–C/1–3), etc., but where the professional body does not spell out the equivalents we have not done so either. Although GNVQ and GSVQ are equivalent, many professional bodies based in England do not mention GSVQ, and its omission does not reflect any bias by the editor or careers team! Details of all qualifications are covered in the chapter on qualifications.

Terminology is always a problem, and a few examples need clarification. Both the names European Union (EU) and European Community (EC) are used in the *Careers Encyclopedia*. EU is the general term used since Maastricht to describe the EC and its member states. It is still correct to refer to EC institutions. Youth Training (YT) is the current (1996) umbrella term, but it is marketed under different brand names by different TEC/LECs. YT is currently used throughout the *Encyclopedia* but the name may change again post-Dearing to incorporate 'National' into the title.

Although this is the most detailed and comprehensive careers encyclopedia in the UK, there is a limit to the number of topics that can be covered in any one book, so I have included an extensive *address list* as *Appendix 1* and a *bibliography* as *Appendix 2* so that users can obtain further information. When sending off to professional bodies, employing organisations or institutions for further information, a stamped addressed envelope is always appreciated.

This *Encyclopedia* is as accurate and as up-to-date as we could make it. Most of the material was thoroughly revised during the period December 1995–May 1996 by my colleagues and myself, and where possible I have incorporated any late changes received at the proof stage into the appropriate chapters. However, it is impossible to keep up with all the changes. For example, between 26 February 1996 and 30 April 1996, 18 new agencies were launched in the Home Civil Service and Northern Ireland Civil Service; there were three agency mergers affecting Forensic Science, Service Children's Education, and Statistical services; the Social Security Resettlement Agency ceased to exist; and a number of Laboratories such as the Laboratory of the Government Chemist and the Transport Research Laboratory were sold; and other changes are in the pipeline! These changes affected chapters across the *Encyclopedia*.

Change is endemic and careers information can become out-of-date very quickly, so it is essential for anyone considering a career to verify the factual information given, particularly regarding entry requirements, courses and training.

Katherine Lea
Editor
June 1996

How to use the Careers Encyclopedia

The *Careers Encyclopedia* is divided into a number of chapters.

The first eleven chapters cover general topics. All of these can be read as stand-alone chapters, although you may need to read related general chapters to get the full picture.

Chapters one to seven cover the world of work starting with a general introduction, 'The World of Work', in chapter one and particular aspects of the world of work in the next six chapters – 'Working Overseas', 'Women at Work', 'Work for those with Special Needs', 'Preparing for Work', 'The Job Search' (which is a detailed guide to finding vacancies) and 'Changing your Career'.

Chapters eight, nine and ten cover education and qualifications. Chapter eight is a broad overview of 'Education and Qualifications' from age 14 up to postgraduate level. Chapter nine specifically covers 'General National Vocational Qualifications and General Scottish Vocational Qualifications', while chapter ten covers 'National Vocational Qualifications and Scottish Vocational Qualifications'.

Chapter eleven covers 'Student Financial Support' for both degree and postgraduate qualifications.

All the other chapters give detailed information on specific careers within broad occupational groups.

Three Appendices cover: sources of further information in 'Useful Addresses'; a detailed bibliography; and the Careers Library Classification Index (CLCI).

If you are interested in a broad category of work then the relevant chapters can be found from the contents list on page v. The occupational chapters have been classified and arranged using the CLCI, which provides a framework for grouping together related careers. The Classified Index in Appendix 3 relates the CLCI categories to the chapters and entries in the *Encyclopedia*. Those familiar with CLCI will find this approach useful.

Each occupational chapter is divided into sections and these are listed in the chapter contents at the start of each chapter. These sections describe individual careers and industries, and provide information about the type of work performed, recruitment and entry, and qualifications and training. Background information and employment trends for the occupations and industries covered are also given in the chapter.

If you already have some idea of the job or career you are interested in and want to locate it in the *Encyclopedia*, the easiest way to do this is to look for the job title in the alphabetical index starting on page 737 which gives the relevant page numbers.

Some careers fall within more than one occupational group and cross-references are given where necessary both in the alphabetical index and in the text of each chapter.

Each chapter also contains references to professional organisations who can provide further information; their addresses and telephone numbers can be found in Appendix 1 on page 688. These organisations usually provide information free of charge but would appreciate a stamped addressed envelope.

If you want to read more about careers and courses, you will find a bibliography in Appendix 2 on page 726. This gives details of some general careers reference books and series of books and booklets on particular occupations.

Abbreviations

In the text we have had to use frequent abbreviations or terminology. Some of the more common ones are listed below.

A-level	Advanced level, GCE
BA	Bachelor of Arts
BSc	Bachelor of Science
BEd	Bachelor of Education
BTEC	Business and Technology Education Council
CBI	Confederation of British Industry
CLCI	Careers Library Classification Index
COIC	Careers and Occupational Information Centre
Coll	College
CFE	College of Further Education
CT	College of Technology
CSYS	Certificate of Sixth-Year Studies in Scotland
CTC	City Technology College
DfEE	Department for Education and Employment
EC	European Community
ECCTIS	(*originally* Educational Counselling and Credit Transfer Information Service)
EU	European Union
ERASMUS	European Community Action Scheme for the Mobility of University Students
EURES	European Employment Services
FE	Further Education
ft	full-time
GCE	General Certificate of Education (A-level only)
GCSE	General Certificate of Secondary Education
GNVQ	General National Vocational Qualification
GSVQ	General Scottish Vocational Qualification
H grade	Higher Grade examinations and awards in Scotland
HEFCE	Higher Education Funding Council for England
HMSO	(*formerly* Her Majesty's Stationery Office, but full title not used now)
HNC	Higher National Certificate awarded by BTEC/SCOTVEC
HND	Higher National Diploma awarded by BTEC/SCOTVEC
IES	Institute for Employment Studies
IT	Information Technology
LEA	Local Education Authority
LEC	Local Enterprise Companies (in Scotland)
MA	Master of Arts
MBA	Master of Business Administration
MSc	Master of Science
NAFE	Non-Advanced Further Education
NC	National Certificate awarded by BTEC/SCOTVEC *or* National Curriculum, depending on context
NCVQ	National Council for Vocational Qualifications
ND	National Diploma awarded by BTEC/SCOTVEC
NFER	National Foundation for Educational Research in England and Wales
NVQ	National Vocational Qualification
PhD	Doctor of Philosophy
pt	part-time
QTS	Qualified Teacher Status
RSA	Royal Society of Arts
SCAA	School Curriculum and Assessment Authority
SCE	Scottish Certificate of Education
SCOTVEC	Scottish Vocational Educational Council
SOCRATES	EU programme on student mobility (*see* ERASMUS)
SVQ	Scottish Vocational Qualification
TEC	Training and Enterprise Council
TTA	Teacher Training Agency
UCAS	Universities and Colleges Admissions Service
Yr	Year
YT	Youth Training

Contents

The World of Work

Background

In recent years we have been undergoing a massive restructuring of our economy. This is having a fundamental effect upon the careers of people who have all or much of their working lives ahead of them. The permanent and progressive full-time career with a single employer is fast being replaced by the 'portfolio career' of many varied jobs with a succession of employers. Some of these jobs are likely to be on a self-employed basis. This means that individuals can no longer expect employers to provide them with a career, but must take charge of their own careers. What has led to this change?

We are in the middle of a post-industrial revolution. This is as profound as the industrial revolution of the eighteenth and nineteenth centuries. However, there is one major difference. The industrial revolution was relatively gradual, with the changes absorbed over almost a century. It is likely that our revolution will take no more than a single working generation. This has given us too little time to adapt easily to all the changes involved.

Under the circumstances, it is not surprising that in recent years we have been unable to match exactly the supply and demand for the thousands of different skills we use in our economy. Like many developed countries, we have had high unemployment at the same time as serious skill shortages.

The industrial revolution was based on a move away from agriculture to the mass manufacture of low-value-added goods. Many of these were exported to our colonies, few of which had any manufacturing capability. After the Second World War our colonies were given their independence. Not only did it become easier for them to buy from suppliers outside Britain, but many developed their own manufacturing capability. Captive customers were lost and new overseas competitors entered the world market. We not only lost many of our traditional overseas markets, but for a time failed to compete with overseas suppliers even at home. A huge restructuring of our economy became inevitable.

Our post-industrial revolution is based on a move towards the development and production of high value-added goods, often exploiting the latest science and technology. We have shifted from a skill-based to a knowledge-based economy. In 1983 the number of 'white-collar' knowledge jobs overtook 'blue-collar' jobs for the first time, and the gap continues to widen.

With improved transport and communications worldwide, and the removal of trade barriers between countries, business has become more international. Our goods and services must sell in global markets. To compete effectively, our employers have had to cut costs, improve quality, and become more flexible so that they can rapidly adapt to changing market circumstances.

Population growth, and the changing age-profile of our population, are also having a major impact on the number of jobs, patterns of employment, and on social welfare such as pensions and unemployment benefit.

The future of employment

Changes in the type, range and variety of jobs and occupations which make up the world of employment are not new. Indeed, they have probably been near-continuous since primitive people first began to cultivate the land as well as hunt for food. The nature of the changes, the number of the changes which have taken place in any one period of time, and the speed of change have up to recent times been such that they could be relatively easily absorbed by society, causing few long-term difficulties in themselves – even though for many people work could be intermittent and poorly paid. Some of the necessary adaptations were obviously difficult and even painful for particular individuals and groups, especially during each economic recession, but transitions have been made, new occupations and work have replaced the old.

But the pace and magnitude of change, accelerating over the past two centuries, has now reached a stage where technological innovation, social, economic and political factors have interacted and combined to have a cumulative and massive worldwide impact on the pattern of employment.

While Britain and many other developed countries have entered a post-industrial revolution, in other parts of the world countries are moving swiftly from agriculture-based economies to ones based on manufacturing.

It is difficult to pinpoint the start of our post-industrial revolution, but a major shift in employment patterns was starting to become apparent in the 1960s. However, the main effects have been felt in the 1980s and 1990s. The changes have been both quantitative and qualitative.

Until recently there were predictions that we were moving towards a leisure-based economy, in which people would have less work and enjoy more leisure. However, there are no signs of this. It should also be recognised that most people need employment not only to meet their physical needs but also to satisfy psychological needs.

Work is becoming increasingly complex and demands ever higher levels of skills and knowledge. This had led to a huge increase in further and higher education as well as in vocational training initiatives. However, our education and training attainments so far remain behind those of such competitor nations as Germany and the USA. The job market is placing ever-growing importance on good academic and vocational qualifications. Those who have no such qualifications face a bleak future. Moreover, the pace of change is constantly accelerating. People at work will need to constantly acquire new skills and update their knowledge. Lifelong learning will be an essential part of the career of the future.

The size and shape of the employment market

The size and shape of the employment market is affected by population changes; government policy; growing overseas competition; quantitative and qualitative changes in consumer demand at home and abroad; innovation and the adoption of new technology, processes and working practices; swings in the economy; the decline of old industries and the rise of new ones; changes in education policy and practice; investment in training; UK and European law; social change; and much else. With so many interdependent variables, it is hard to see a clear picture.

In the century between the censuses of 1891 and 1991 the UK population grew from 34.264 million to 56.467 million, an increase of 65%. In the same period the number of people who were economically active nearly doubled from 14.7 million to 28.1 million. The growth rates of both the population and the economically active were not constant over this period, as can be seen by looking at the figures over the last 40 years.

In the 20 years between the 1951 census and that of 1971, the population increased by almost 5.3 million. Because of a sharp fall in 'live births' from 1965 to 1977 (the so-called 'demographic timebomb') the population rose by only 33,000 between 1971 and 1981. With a recovery in the birth-rate underway, the population in the decade to 1991 rose by a further 619,000.

Now, with the recovery in the birth-rate, the Office for National Statistics (previously Office of Population Censuses and Surveys) predicts that by 2001 our population will have risen by yet another 3.2 million. Hence, in 50 years (little more than a working generation) the UK population will have risen by 9.5 million – from just over 50.2 million to just over 59.7 million – an increase of 18.9%.

During some periods the civilian workforce (which includes the employed, self-employed, and unemployed, but excludes HM Forces) has increased even faster than the population. For instance, between 1971 and 1991 the population rose by 952,000, but the workforce grew by 1.6 million – from 25.5 million to 27.1 million. Subsequently, because the school-leaving age was raised from 15 to 16 in 1972, and more men retired than entered employment, the number of men in the workforce fell by almost 100,000. However, 1.7 million women joined the workforce. Between 1991 and 1994 the workforce increased by a further 1.8 million and is expected to grow by almost another 0.8 million by 2001.

The overall trend in employment has been upwards for a long time, although this pattern is sometimes masked by the effects of regular recessions. The UK economy tends to go from boom to recession and back again about every five years, with particularly deep recessions on alternate cycles. Similar cycles occur in other countries, and politicians of both the right and left have so far proved powerless to break this pattern.

The employment market has three broad sectors: the primary and utilities sector, which include agriculture, fishing, mining, and energy and water supply; the secondary sector, which includes manufacturing and construction; and the tertiary sector, which includes public services, distribution and transport, and business and miscellaneous services.

At the beginning of the nineteenth century, employment in the UK was divided just about equally between the three sectors. By 1993, employment in the primary and utilities sector had fallen to under 4% of the workforce. In the secondary sector the proportion rose to well over 50% of the total by 1951. It remained relatively steady until the early 1960s but has since declined, and by 1993 was barely a quarter of the workforce. Tertiary-sector employment has continued to expand proportionately throughout the period, to almost 72% of the total by 1993. Not all of these are new jobs. While the number of jobs in the service industries has increased significantly in recent years, a small proportion of these were transferred (by subcontracting) from manufacturing.

According to the Institute for Employment Research (IER) at Warwick University, the percentage of employees in each of the main sectors in 1993 was as follows:

	%
Primary and utilities	3.7
Manufacturing	
Engineering	7.8
Other	10.8
Construction	5.8
Public services	
Health and Education	18.1
Public administration	6.9

Distribution and Transport	
Retailing	9.4
Other distribution	6.6
Transport and communications	5.9
Hotels and catering	5.5
Business and miscellaneous services	
Banking and business	9.9
Professional	4.8
Other	4.9

The broad categories of work of employees and the self-employed in 1993 were spread as follows:

	%
Managers and administrators	16.6
Professionals	9.1
Associate professional/technical	9.3
Clerical and secretarial	16.2
Sales	7.3
Personal and protective services	9.3
Craft and skilled manual	13.7
Plant and machine operators	10.2
Others	8.4

Employment in the primary sector, particularly agriculture, has been in decline since the industrial revolution, and this brought people off the land and into the factories. However, output has continued to grow, through mechanisation, better disease and pest control, artificial fertilisers, improved plant and animal breeding and other measures. Small farms have been integrated into bigger units, so allowing the more efficient use of machines. This process has been supported and subsidised by the government and the European Common Agricultural Policy.

The water and power companies have similarly rationalised over the years and made better use of new technology and processes, enabling them to cut their workforce. Recent privatisation has also led these companies to seek further efficiencies, and so reduce staffing further.

Job-loss in the primary sector has been a fairly gradual process, and the people released have been absorbed relatively easily by growth in other sectors. Projections indicate that employment in this sector will continue to fall by 2.8% a year until the year 2000.

In the manufacturing sector, there has been a similar change in the pattern of employment. This is not simply the result of short-term economic recession and low aggregate demand, but one of structural change. Just as the industrial revolution shifted labour-intensive working from the land to the factories, so the post-industrial revolution is moving people out of manufacturing into the service industries. The Science Policy Research Unit at Sussex University has shown that, since 1965, any growth in industrial output has not been accompanied by growth in employment, and even that, since 1973, the reverse has been the case within the EC. Even in the years 1965–73, when there was a relatively high growth rate (an annual average of 6%), there was virtually no parallel growth in the number of jobs.

Industries can survive only by adapting to the new levels of competition. The alternative is to make a deliberate decision to move out of areas of production where competition with other countries is most intensive, and invest in industries and products based on new, complex technologies and 'high-value-added' products.

In the UK companies have adapted to greater competition by improving the quality of their output and becoming more efficient. This has involved introducing new technology, especially automated systems and processes, stripping out layers of management, and other measures. As a result they employ fewer people but with generally higher levels of skill.

Some businesses, particularly those based on the mass-production of low-value-added goods, have largely closed down or moved their manufacturing to low cost areas, mainly in the Indian sub-continent and the Far East. Although new businesses have developed to exploit the latest science and technology and produce high-value-added goods, these businesses generally need fewer people than the old.

Manufacturing, then, is unlikely to absorb more than a small proportion of those coming onto the labour market. However, within the overall picture of continuing job losses, there are already shortages of technician and professional skills, and the larger, and permanent job losses are amongst the semi-skilled and unskilled, and single-skilled craftworkers (*see also* MANUFACTURING INDUSTRIES). Department for Education and Employment statistics indicate a total fall in employment in the manufacturing sector of 32.4% between 1981 and 1995. The Institute for Employment Research (IER) predicts that manufacturing employment will continue to fall by 1.1% a year until 2001. However, employment in construction is expected to grow by an average of 1.3% a year over the same period.

The tertiary sector divides into public service (which in addition to the Civil Service and local government and the NHS, includes private-sector jobs in health and public administration); distribution, transport and communications; and business and other services. These have been the huge growth areas in recent years, more than compensating for job losses in other sectors of the economy.

Although much depends on government policy, it is unlikely that there will be any further growth in public administration and defence. On the other hand there are likely to be small increases in health and education. Overall, the IER expects public-service employment to increase by 1% a year up to 2001.

Retailing and other distribution has seen a major growth in employment. It is predicted to grow by another 120,000 jobs between 1993 and 2001 (up 5%). Although hotels and catering suffered during the recession, they are expected to have created 280,00 extra jobs (up nearly 21%) by 2001. On the other hand, transport and communications are expected to lose 80,000 jobs because of new technology and reorganisation.

Business and other services include retailing, hotels and catering, transport and communications. Collectively these have seen a massive growth over the past few decades in spite of job losses during the recession as well as the shedding of many junior clerical jobs in banking through computerisation. However, employment in this sector is now expected to grow by 2.6% a year – which will mean 1.1 million new jobs between 1993 and 2001.

Over the whole economy, the IER expects employment to have grown by more than 6% between 1993 and 2001 – an average annual growth of 0.6% or about 200,000 new jobs a year.

The greatest growth, by type of work, is expected among managers and administrators, the professional occupations, and associate professional and technical workers. There is also expected to be job growth in the skilled construction trades, retail sales, and in both protective and personal services.

In most of these areas women are expected to take the majority of the extra jobs. It is predicted that they will take 70% of the new jobs for managers and administrators, 60% of the jobs for professionals, 65% of those for associate professional and technical workers, and almost 80% of the jobs for personal and protective services. In retail sales male employment is expected to fall, with women taking all the new jobs. By 2001 women are expected to hold over two-thirds of all sales jobs.

On the other hand, further job losses are expected among plant and machine operators; skilled trades in the engineering industry; agricultural occupations; low-skill manual workers such as refuse collectors, farmworkers, cleaners and labourers; and to a lesser extent, clerical and secretarial workers.

As can be seen, growth is mainly in the high-skill high-knowledge occupations. However, narrow technical skills and specialist knowledge will not be enough in the careers of the future. Employers are placing more and more emphasis on flexibility and teamworking, customer care, quality, and innovation. This means that workers will need a wide portfolio of additional skills.

The impact of technological development

In the long history of technological advance, change has been largely incremental, with one development building on others, and the effects therefore progressive and not immediately disruptive. However, there have been occasional innovatory breakthroughs which have rapid, and quite dramatic effects on human development: the wheel, the printing press, gunpowder, the steam engine, radio, splitting the atom, the computer, and the discovery of the structure of DNA.

From amongst the very many technological advances of the twentieth century, semiconductor technology, or microelectronics, was probably the most significant in terms of innovation, with all the potential to make really fundamental changes throughout society in a relatively short space of time. Optical fibres and laser technology together have raised still further the potential of microelectronics, particularly in communications.

Other technologies, though, already promise more such changes in the future. Biotechnology is now having a growing impact in many areas and will probably have as great an impact as microelectronics in the next few years.

Microelectronics makes possible faster, more efficient, more reliable and usually less labour-intensive ways of doing progressively more tasks, and of doing sophisticated tasks that previously were completely impossible or not cost-effective. Microelectronics brings together the previously separate technologies of (tele)communications, broadcasting and computing, to create many new ways of capturing, transmitting, managing and exploiting information, in order to analyse, monitor, present, and use it in many more, and more sophisticated ways. Used to convert voice and for example fax to the same digital signals that transmit computer data, it is integrating all forms of communication, so information can be transmitted flexibly between different kinds of equipment. Worldwide communication has become all but instantaneous. Microelectronics, with its supporting technologies, has created near-'intelligent' systems to carry out more sophisticated medical and scientific tasks; robots to paint, weld and assemble; and a global financial market through information systems.

Information Technology (IT) is the application of microelectronic systems to information-processing, and it has taken the computer and computer-based systems into almost every possible environment: home, school, office, factory, shop, construction site, studio, farm, car and briefcase. Different IT systems, separated by office wall or by oceans, can now be linked together using various methods of 'networking'. Text, full-colour moving images and sound can be combined and manipulated in 'multimedia' presentations using conventional personal computers. Retail outlets can use Electronic Funds Transfer at Point of Sale (EFTPoS) systems, and computerised stock-control systems to increase their operating efficiency.

Manufacturing organisations are increasingly installing Computer-Aided Design (CAD) systems in their design studios, and Computer Numerical Control (CNC) systems in their production areas. Some manufacturing companies are even moving towards total Computer Integrated Manufacture (CIM), with computerised control of all functions, from the creation of the initial design to final product distribution.

IT has destroyed many of the jobs it created earlier in the technological process, such as data preparation as a separate skill. The use of optical scanners to 'capture' data from printed documents has led to the loss of some jobs, and voice recognition systems may cost more. The need for large numbers of applications programmers may have peaked. However, as more and more computers come into business and household use, many new jobs are being created in computing. The business world now employs people who combine computer skills with an understanding of their employers' specialist business and who can select, modify and implement software packages, work on projects, and solve problems inside the user-department or organisation. (*See* INFORMATION TECHNOLOGY AND COMPUTER WORK.)

In traditional areas of manufacturing, the most obvious job losses arise from the increasing levels of automation, where because the technology is improving all the time even greatly increased sales do not create enough jobs to balance out the losses. The classic example was the all-electronic telephone exchange which needed only one out of the 26 needed to make an electromechanical exchange. Automation is not the only job loser, however. Where and when microprocessors replace components in existing products, not only are there fewer parts to put together, and fewer assembly processes, but fewer items have to be held in stock. Further, since the new components are smaller, less warehouse space is required and fewer transport systems are needed. Fewer stages in manufacturing mean fewer supervisory and administrative staff to link them.

The next stages in developing IT business systems link manufacturer, or other supplier (e.g. tour and airline operators) directly to their retail outlet via what are called 'value added networks'. This is amongst the developments which let firms 'strip out' whole layers of staffing. Here, according to the Institute of Employment Studies (IES, formerly the Institute of Manpower Studies), 'line' managers, rather than the travelling sales personnel, are becoming the point of contact. More, the information generated from direct, on-line ordering by customers can be used to set up automated stock-control systems, notifying component and raw materials requirements plus the size of the production run in the plant itself.

Automating the office has had a considerable impact on employment. Whole layers of junior clerical staff have been removed in such areas as banking, insurance and other industries which used to generate large amounts of paper. However, as employers have made increasing use of the data-processing capability of computers, they have created a smaller number of higher-level jobs.

Any additional increase in efficiency in information flow within organisations, via the increasing use of sophisticated software packages serving nearly all commercial requirements, was expected to lead to a cut in the number of managerial, administrative and even professional staff. But this does not appear to have happened yet. Contrary to these expectations, computers have created jobs at these levels. However, as 'intelligent systems' become more widespread, these could replace some junior and middle-ranking specialists.

Information technology is only one area of considerable technological impact. Research is leading to the development of many new materials that in turn are leading to improvements in performance, and reduction in production costs in many manufacturing processes. In many cases the development of new materials make possible the development of completely new products. The new materials that it is currently thought will have the greatest impact on manufacturing industry in the 1990s will be ceramics with increased heat or wear resistance, and polymer compounds with weight-saving applications in industries such as aerospace. Technological advance has also led to many developments in 'biotechnology' – the industrial application of biological processes or systems. Many of these developments involve 'genetic engineering'; examples range from the genetic modification of yeast to improve bread making, or the creation of growth hormones to increase milk yields in cows, through to creating new strains of animals, bacteria and plants with 'desirable' characteristics. The ethical and social implications of genetic engineering have led to considerable public interest in the issue. Currently much biotechnology work is still at the research and development phase, although genetically engineered products are now being introduced to the market. Its industrial impact is slowly becoming apparent. (*See also* BIOTECHNOLOGY *in* MANUFACTURING INDUSTRIES.)

The changing pattern of work

Business restructuring – changes in the management structure – smaller operating units – project teamworking – flexible workforce of core and peripheral workers – 'hot-desking' – contracting-out or 'outsourcing' work – management redundancy – longer working hours and increased levels of stress – less job security and more job changing

Business restructuring

Many manual workers have been replaced by machines, and many routine clerical workers by computers. On the other hand, the use of increasingly complex technology has created large numbers of jobs for specialists of many kinds. Technology has had a major impact on jobs. However, work is changing in even more fundamental ways.

The major stimulus for changes in the way work is carried out is competition, especially from overseas. This competition is not based solely on costs. Customers also want innovative products and services which are tailored to their needs. They expect their suppliers to be flexible. They will no longer tolerate faults and late deliveries. They want better and consistent quality. They want deliveries which are always on time. If companies cannot compete on these terms, they are very likely to go out of business.

Businesses have had to restructure, with some merging or taking over others. This is likely to be a continuing process. They need to cut costs and this includes shedding any surplus staff (sometimes called 'downsizing' or, even more euphemistically, 'rightsizing').

However, the remaining staff must be of a high calibre and must be more effective than before. There must be innovators to develop new products. Staff must make the most efficient use they can of plant, machinery, tools, materials and energy. It is no longer good enough to have quality-control checks to spot and reject faulty goods: quality must be built-in and the manufacturing process must aim for 'zero defects'. Quality is everybody's responsibility.

Because it costs money to hold stocks of raw materials and finished goods, 'just-in-time' manufacturing is becoming normal. At the same time there must be efficient systems to ensure goods are always delivered at the time promised. An automotive assembly plant may, for instance, require suppliers to deliver components once an hour around the clock. If a single delivery is missed, the whole plant can come to a halt. All this means that the workforce must be highly skilled, highly trained, and highly motivated.

Changes in the management structure

One reason many companies used to be unable to respond as quickly to changing customer needs as their overseas competitors was the management structure. There were too many layers of management between the policy-makers at the top and the first-line supervisors who actually made things happen. It took too long for information and ideas to be passed up and down the organisation, with each layer wanting to have its say. It was exceedingly difficult to make changes in such a cumbersome system. Then it was realised that our competitors had more streamlined and flexible structures. For example, the Ford Motor Company used to have more than 15 levels of management between the Chairman and the first-line supervisor – while Toyota in Japan had only five.

In recent years companies have been cutting out tiers of management, a process often called 'delayering'. A survey by the Institute of Management (IM) found that 58% of organisations stripped out layers of management in the previous five years, and most expect further delayering up to the end of the century.

Smaller operating units

Many large organisations are breaking down their activities into smaller operating units. Research suggests that, irrespective of industry, employing more than 500 or so people under one roof leads to unpredictable and substantial problems. The theory that big operations result in cost savings and greater efficiency is giving way to a belief that smaller units are more innovative, more flexible and more productive. Moreover, companies are pushing decision-making 'down-the-line' to people who are closer to the customer.

A nationwide survey was carried out in mid-1995 by the Harris Research Centre for the Institute of Personnel and Development and Templeton College Oxford. This found that in the last five years 85% of employees had been affected by the introduction of new technology, 79% by new working practices, 75% by restructuring, 57% by redundancies/layoffs and 30% by takeover or merger. Experience of redundancy/layoffs was highest in organisations with more than 500 employees (61%) and among managers (69%).

Project teamworking

More change lies ahead. Traditional jobs involve working in one place and being responsible for a clear set of duties laid down in a 'job description'. People usually work in a specific 'department' and report to one person, their immediate boss. If they are supervisors or managers, they will also have a number of people reporting to them. However, departmental functions are increasingly being handed over to multidisciplinary project teams drawn from several functional areas. A team is formed when a project starts and disbanded when it ends. Team members are chosen solely on the basis of the expertise and skills needed to do that particular job. Individuals may move from one project to another and sometimes work on two or more at once. Team leaders are selected for the level of expertise they can bring to the specific project, so a leader on one team may be an ordinary member of another.

As individuals gain experience on a variety of projects, and become more expert, they are likely to be better rewarded, but not necessarily promoted. With much-flattened corporate structures, career development opportunities in many organisations are now very limited. Progression increasingly involves moving between employers.

Flexible workforce of core and peripheral workers

Work rarely flows evenly through organisations. It can vary from season to season and between boom and recession. Employers are therefore seeking a 'flexible workforce' that can quickly respond to change. The use of overtime working and temps provides some flexibility, but not enough. Employers want working time to exactly match the amount of work to be done. To do this, employers are starting to organise their workers into two groups: core workers and peripheral workers.

The core group consists of full-time people with a high level of expertise and skills which are specific to the business. The peripheral group is made up of temporary staff, freelance workers, people on short-term contracts, those who are contracted only to do a particular piece of work, and others. Many of those in the peripheral group will be self-employed or working as employees of work-contracting companies.

The 'flexible workforce' of core and peripheral workers was being discussed by the forerunners of the Institute of Employment Studies (IES) and the Institute for Employment Research (IER) in the early 1980s. Although this pattern of working has been slow to take off, 750,000 people are already employed by 'temp agencies' in the UK, and work-contracting company Manpower has already become the largest employer in the USA. Flexible working will become far more widespread in the next few years according to the fourth Annual Survey of Long Term Employment Strategies published in late 1995 by the Institute of Management (IM) and Manpower plc.

The survey found that four out of five large employers expect 90% of their staff to remain core employees over the next year, but only 47% expect this to be so in four years time. Over half say that at least a quarter of their staff will be 'complementary to the core workforce' within four years.

Almost nine in ten of these larger employers already use part-time and temporary staff, almost three-quarters are contracting work out, and more than half use flexible working. Over the next four years 80% of employers expect an increase in flexible working and 70% in contracting-out. About two-thirds expect substantial increases in teleworking, part-time work and the use of temporary staff. The authors observe that the survey confirms the trend away from the traditional patterns of full-time core employment towards a wholly flexible employment market.

Moreover, the survey reported that although half of Britain's employers had restructured since the start of 1994, four in ten intended further restructuring within the next twelve months and over 70% expect more within the next four years.

'Hot-desking'

Because offices are expensive and usually empty for more hours than they are in use, employers are now finding ways to reduce the office space they use. In some cases they are persuading employees to work from home. When these staff do need to come into the office, they book and are allocated a workspace only for the hours needed – a process sometimes called 'hot desking'. In some companies most personal offices, and even personal desks, have gone.

Contracting-out or 'outsourcing' work

Employers are also increasingly concentrating on their core business. This means that they are contracting-out (also called 'outsourcing') work to other firms. For example, instead of operating their own canteens, running their own fleet of delivery vehicles, and employing their own office cleaners, this work is handed over to specialist subcontractors. This means that organisations are employing fewer people, although of course there are new opportunities in the subcontracting firms.

Management redundancy

The effects of the existing changes on people's careers have been dramatic, and are likely to become more so as the pace of change accelerates. During the late 1980s and early 1990s many people lost their jobs, some as the result of the recession but many more because of a fundamental restructuring of their organisations. For perhaps the first time, because of 'delayering', large numbers of managers were made redundant. Although overall employment was rising, many of those who had lost their jobs entered lower-grade posts, self-employment, part-time work, and other less secure forms of employment than they had been used to. *See* CHANGING YOUR CAREER; THE JOB SEARCH; *and* ADMINISTRATION, BUSINESS MANAGEMENT AND OFFICE WORK.

Longer working hours and increased levels of stress

In many companies that delayered, the surviving managers have found themselves working longer hours of (usually unpaid) overtime. An Institute of Management (IM) survey, *Finding the Time*, published in March 1995, reported that the individual workloads of almost half the managers surveyed had 'greatly increased' in the preceding two years. One in five reported working over 15 hours overtime a week. Only 5% of managers did no overtime at all.

Fewer than half of the managers in the survey felt that there was a sensible balance between their work and personal life, and 60% said they would like to spend more time with family and friends. The increase in management overtime was not attributed to economic recovery but to company restructuring.

In a separate survey of almost 1,000 senior managers, *Managers under Stress*, the IM found 77% thought the hours they work was to some extent stressful. Most (77%) were also anxious or very anxious about the demands of their work on their relationship with their family, and 74% about how it affected their relationship with their partner. Moreover, 71% of the managers were worried about redundancy through further restructuring and so were under more stress.

The IM further points out that although some people can cope with high levels of pressure for short periods, and may even thrive on it, stress has considerable costs. It is estimated that British employers lose 40 million working days a year, at a cost of £7 billion, due to stress-related sickness.

The British workforce as a whole works the longest average hours in the European Union (EU). This is in spite of having the shortest basic average working week of 37.5 hours. The reason for this discrepancy is that UK employers are already more dependent on overtime working than any of their counterparts in the EU. Recent data from Eurostat, the European Commission's statistical office, shows that the average British working week for full-time staff in 1992 was 43.4 hours (including overtime) – three hours more than the EU average. Portugal had the next-longest working week at 41.3 hours. At the other end of the scale, Belgian employees worked only 38.2 hours a week. Apart from the UK, only the poorer European economies with a high proportion of agricultural workers continue to work over 40 hours a week.

Weekly full-time hours worked in the EU

	1983	1992
United Kingdom	42.3	43.4
Portugal	-	41.3
Spain	-	40.6
Greece	41.0	40.5
Ireland	40.2	40.4
France	39.7	39.7
Germany	40.9	39.7
Luxembourg	40.0	39.7

Netherlands	41.0	39.4
Denmark	40.5	38.8
Italy	39.2	38.5
Belgium	38.6	38.2
European Union	-	40.3

In ten years, average working hours have risen in no EU countries except Ireland and the UK. In Ireland the average increase has been less than quarter of an hour a week, in Britain it is over an hour. Surprisingly, this increase has affected British working women far more than men. Male workers have seen an average weekly increases of under 15 minutes, women of almost an hour and a half. British women now work 40.2 hours a week, the longest hours of any women in the EU.

According to the Confederation of British Industry, Britain's employers use overtime more than their European counterparts because the UK came out of the last recession before other EU countries. It says people tend to work longer hours in a thriving economy. However, the facts do not support this argument. In 1990, in the depths of recession, the total amount of overtime worked by operatives in manufacturing industry exceeded 12 million hours a week; by January 1995 it averaged 9.58 million hours. This drop is partly explained by the fact that the number of operatives in manufacturing was cut by a third. However, the proportion of operatives doing overtime fell from 37.7% in 1990 to 34.2% in 1994; and the average overtime per person increased by only 12 minutes a week, from 9.4 to 9.6 hours over the same period.

In practice, Britain has had consistently long working hours. The percentage of operatives in manufacturing doing overtime, and the average hours of overtime worked per head, has remained remarkably constant for over 30 years. There is plenty of evidence that white-collar overtime (where most jobs now are), has shown large recent increases. However, at present no statistics are maintained for white-collar overtime, much of which is also unpaid.

Less job security and more job-changing

Few employers are now willing to offer a job for life. Moreover, because they have flattened their management structures, they can offer only limited career development prospects. To secure advancement, people will probably have to move from employer to employer. It has already been predicted that the average person will have eight job changes during their career – and that half of these moves will be involuntary. People are now advised to think of portability, not stability, in their careers.

All this has changed the basis of the unwritten understanding which used to exist between employers and their employees. If you worked hard and were loyal to your employer, the employer in return gave you job security and career development opportunities. This was often known as the 'psychological contract'. Employers have unilaterally broken this contract, and not yet replaced it with something people can believe in.

The IES argues in its 1995 report, *Careers in Organisations: Issues for the Future*, that we need a new psychological contract. It says that employers should ask their employees to identify with the business goals of the enterprise, to have the flexibility to switch to new roles or tasks, be able and willing to retrain, and have the ability to find a job elsewhere if they are no longer required. In return, people can expect their employer to provide employability through continuing development, choice of career paths and job roles, the ability to plan for their financial security, choice in their life/work balance, information about job options, and processes that allow for real negotiation. How such a 'psychological contract' can actually be achieved, and have real credibility with the average person, is very far from clear.

Sources of further information

The Institute of Employment Studies; Institute for Employment Research; Department for Education and Employment (for *Labour Market Quarterly Report* and the monthly *Labour Market Trends* – which now incorporates *Employment Gazette*).

Education, training and lifelong learning

Most careers are already in knowledge-based white-collar occupations. The need for young people to be educated to their full potential is even more important than before. In recent years our graduate output has risen sharply, and already a third of school-leavers are entering degree courses in higher education. This is about the same proportion as in France, Germany and the Netherlands. Even so, the Confederation of British Industry would like to see UK graduate output rise to 40%.

However, in overall terms of education and vocational training, Britain is lagging badly. In the 1995 World Competitiveness Report from the World Economic Forum, the UK was placed 24th in the world for the quality of its skills, down from 21st place a year earlier. Moreover, what the forum described as our 'inadequate educational system' ranked 35th in the world.

We are failing particularly badly at school-leaving level. In 1995 the National Institute of Economic Research produced a report, *Productivity, Education and Training*. This showed that the proportion of 16-year-olds reaching GCSE grade C or better (or equivalent) in mathematics, a science and the national language is 27% in Britain, 62% in Germany and 66% in France. The proportion gaining a comparable upper-secondary qualification (A-level or equivalent) is 29% in Britain, 48% in France and 68% in Germany.

We do no better with vocational qualifications. In Britain 64% of the workforce has no vocational qualifications at all. In France the proportion is 53%, the Netherlands 35%, Germany 26% and Switzerland only 23%.

Young people who leave school without academic qualifications and who do not actively seek a vocational qualification are increasingly likely to have difficulty finding a job of any kind.

In the past many higher-level careers, particularly in the professions and in management, recruited trainees mainly from school-leavers with A-levels or their equivalent. However, as jobs have become more complex, and graduate supply has increased, many posts have become mainly or entirely graduate entry. This process accelerated in the late 1980s when the numbers of school-leavers fell dramatically because of a plummeting birth-rate 16 years earlier. At the same time graduate output remained relatively constant because a higher proportion of school-leavers went on into higher education. The result was that it became easier to recruit graduates than A-level school-leavers.

Because many graduates are now entering jobs once filled by school-leavers, there have been fears that many graduates will be underemployed. In practice this is rare as long as graduates make the most of the opportunities available. Graduates are expected to work with far lower levels of supervision than school-leavers, and to be self-starters who manage their own work. This means that they can develop the jobs given to them in ways which school-leavers could not, and put their own stamp on them.

There are far fewer traditional graduate jobs than there were, especially management traineeships. The vast majority of graduates go into substantive posts and are expected to make an early contribution to the business of the organisation. Some companies have two graduate entry streams: a management trainee scheme for a small number of 'high flyers' destined for senior management; and a larger 'direct entry' stream for substantive posts.

Graduate recruiters are now rarely satisfied with a degree on its own. Courses vary substantially in their intellectual rigour. It is also widely felt that standards are not consistent between the various institutions. Consequently employers are starting to favour specific institutions and types of course.

Moreover, recruiters expect graduates to have some general work-related skills as one of their selection criteria. Because these skills can be applied in any job, they are usually described as 'transferable skills'. These skills include: teamworking, leadership, social skills, good oral and written communications, problem-solving, business awareness, numeracy, the ability to prioritise work, effective time management, computer literacy and ideally, a foreign language.

Training in transferable skills is now being built into a slowly growing number of degree courses. However, these skills are also becoming important to school-leavers and even more so to anyone already in work. Because people are increasingly likely to have to move between various employers during their career (voluntarily and involuntarily), to have a portfolio of skills and expertise which can be applied in any job is a vital asset.

Computer literacy is becoming ever more important at work. Because constantly updated information is increasingly easy to access on databases and from the Internet worldwide, there will be less emphasis on memorised knowledge in the future, and more on how to access and interpret information for decision-making. It is already predicted that this will also have a profound effect on education in the future.

Employers are investing less in training for long-term needs, but are probably spending more on training people for the job in hand. The emphasis in both government training schemes and employer schemes is very much on skills (or 'competencies' in the new jargon) rather than knowledge. This is particularly true in those organisations which train people for the National or Scottish Vocational Qualifications (NVQs and SVQs).

Employers generally feel that there are now too many qualifications and that there is a need for rationalisation. It seems likely therefore that there will be changes in the next few years.

Because the pace of change is constantly accelerating, and organisations are having to adapt faster than ever before, it is now widely accepted that people will need to undertake lifelong training. Many professional institutions already expect their members to undertake a given number of days a year in Continuing Professional Education (CPE).

Until relatively recently training was 'given' to employees by the employer. Today, this is largely only true of training for the job in hand. Those who hope to make career progress are increasingly expected by their employers to identify their own training and career development needs, and then to ask for appropriate training and work experience. People are expected to take charge of their own careers.

Self-employment and new ways of working

Cooperatives – franchising – self-employment – women returners and career breaks – job-sharing – working from home – teleworking – voluntary work – managament buy-outs – support and assistance – further information

For 40 years all the trends were towards more people gaining their incomes through employment with an organisation – commercial and industrial companies, local authorities, central government and so on. The push towards larger units for economy of scale made it increasingly difficult for small traders of all kinds to survive: the supermarket and large store crowded out the small local shop; in industries from electronics to textiles, in banking and publishing, and so on, the number of individual companies declined severely. Interest in traditional crafts declined, and the income to be made by providing services such as window-cleaning were not comparable with the pay provided by companies short of labour. Planning and redevelopment did not allow much space for small units.

During the last ten years it has been recognised that small and medium-sized firms are able to create proportionally more new jobs than big firms. Planners have begun to take account of the needs of new, small concerns. New building has largely been concentrated on industrial estates, often situated out of city centres, which provide concentrations of small units for service and light industrial businesses.

However, even where the traditions of self-employment or partnership survived – mainly in the professions, such as accountancy, law, architecture, general medical practice – the trend has been to larger units: few 'own practice' GPs remain, many working from health centres in partnerships.

Even so, the self-employment tradition has not died out. Surprisingly, perhaps, modern technology has brought a revival. For example, many computer specialists work independently and very successfully from home – providing consultancy and problem-solving services, and maintaining technical databases. New technology is making it easier for people to work from home. This enables employers to reduce office space and employees to avoid commuting. However, employers have not yet fully worked out how to motivate home workers and control the quality of their output. Moreover, the workplace is a 'social' meeting place for employees, and many home workers can feel isolated.

Part-time working has grown considerably. The proportion of those who work part-time increased from 15% in 1971 to 20.9% in 1984 and 21.4% in 1990. In 1995 6.2 million people (24% of the workforce) were employed part-time. Women make up the majority of part-time employees, numbering about 5 million. Another 1.5 million people do temporary, 'contract', seasonal, and casual work, and this also is predicted to increase sharply by the end of the century. Firms want to operate in future with as small a 'core' of permanent employees as possible, and draw both expertise and physical labour from a large pool of part-time, contract, temporary staff as and when needed. The 'demographic trough' (arising from a drop in live births until 1977, leading to a shortage of school-leavers entering the employment market) made employers aware of the skills and experience of the 50-plus age group. In the early 1990s some large organisations in the retail sector were tapping into this pool of experienced labour. However, this has not taken off as much as had been hoped. Casual and voluntary work are also useful ways of bridging between jobs, can lead to more permanent work, add skills and experience, and at the very least help keep up the habit of working.

Cooperatives

Cooperatives are businesses set up by a group, or team, of people who each have an equal stake and equal (managerial) responsibility. After some rather spectacular early failures, they are growing in numbers, although they still have major problems in finding finance. In 1991 there were about 1,400 cooperatives in the UK. Some are formed by groups of employees to take over a firm in financial trouble, but most are brand-new cooperative businesses. The main areas for co-operatives are in building, entertainment, retail/catering, and printing, but others are in crafts, engineering (e.g. making central heating systems), manufacturing (e.g. clothing, garden products), community services (e.g. a village shop). While the failure rate for cooperatives is well below that of conventional businesses the managerial problems are said to be tougher than in a conventional business, and made more complicated by consensus decision-making.

Franchising

Franchising is also expanding, and franchise turnover is estimated to reach £10.5 billion by 1997. Currently in excess of 180,000 jobs have been created by over 400 franchise systems with more than 25,000 units. Franchise system owners (franchisers) sell the right to operate a proven branded business system to a network of individuals (franchisees) to operate in accordance with the system through operating units which they own and run. Many high-street names have expanded as franchises, and there is a wide range of choice from retailing/catering to van-based franchises, for example pizza and fried-chicken houses, print shops, parcel delivery, home maintenance and cleaning, drain-cleaning and plumbing.

Investment levels vary from £3,000 to £200,000, although a small number require significantly more. Banks will normally lend up to two-thirds for sound schemes. Prospective franchisees should check that the franchiser is able to provide ethical contracts, operations manuals, and sound training in the practical skills required for managing the business together with ongoing support, in return for which a management service fee will be paid.

Franchisees need sound business skills as in any other business, together with a commitment to invest a lot of hard work, often at unsocial hours over long periods of time. Franchisees should also take professional advice from banks, lawyers, accountants, etc. to check out the franchise offer before investing. Existing franchisees should be contacted, and a list should be available from the franchiser.

Self-employment

In 1995 about 3.3 million (13%) of the workforce was self-employed (17.7% men and 7.5% women), against 2.8 million in 1986 (11%), and only 8% in 1971. Between 1981 and 1989 self-employment rose by a staggering 57%.

Self-employed, spring 1995	(thousands)
Total	3,264
Manual	1,507
Non-manual	1,756
Managers and administrators	810
Professional occupations	386
Associated professional and technical	344
Clerical	106
Craft and related	936
Personal and protective services	116
Selling	125
Plant and machinery	245
Other occupations	194

High levels of uncertainty about full-time jobs, not surprisingly, have brought a revival of interest in what are now often called alternatives to full employment. Organisations of all kinds, both companies and central and local government, are trying to reduce the numbers they employ in full-time jobs, so the alternatives are clearly going to be important to many people. It has been recognised, not only in Britain but in other developed countries like Germany and the USA, that most new jobs are created by small and medium-sized businesses. The government therefore is encouraging people to start up on their own with a range of financial assistance and practical advice, e.g. through Local Enterprise Agencies; Training and Enterprise Councils (in England and Wales); Local Enterprise Companies (in Scotland); Business Links (England and Wales) and Business Shops (Scotland).

The conventional advice to people who want to work independently is that it is better to gain a skill or some kind of expertise, preferably through formal training, and then gain fairly extensive experience and build contacts, by working for an organisation which can give this, before even thinking of starting out alone. This is, of course, still essential for anyone who wants to practise as a solicitor, a GP, a chartered accountant. To do skilled electrical work, computer programming, hairdressing, nursing, chiropody, osteopathy, fashion design, or make musical instruments independently, for example, also needs fairly extensive technical training first.

But with high unemployment, people without prior training or experience are also being encouraged to consider self-employment, including school-leavers and new graduates.

It is possible to build a business on relatively straightforward skills possibly built up from a long-standing hobby or interest – babysitting, delivery/despatch rider services, making/selling sandwiches – the main criteria for reasonable success are a gap in the market, business sense (and training), and very hard work. Self-employment is, though, still risky, for people of any age, training or experience. Some experience of employment, and/or a family background in self-employment or running almost any kind of business is still useful. Starting a business while still working part-time is a halfway house which provides at least some financial security.

Like any kind of work, going into business alone or with others takes particular qualities. Self-employed people have to be self-starters, to have initiative and drive. They should not need anyone to tell them what to do next, or to be supervised, so they need to be able to organise and plan their own time efficiently and effectively. They have to be prepared to work long, and probably very irregular, hours to build up the business.

It is relatively easy to think of ideas for a business, but the possible market has to be researched thoroughly to make sure there is a real gap to be filled, that a service or product will sell at a price that will bring in an income. Good advice, on finance and financial planning (even for the smallest enterprise), detailed research and analysis, and careful preparation and planning can make a real difference between success and failure. Marketing and public relations advice can be expensive, but well worth having. Funding and enough money to live on while the business is being built up have to be arranged, and probably somewhere suitable from which to run the business. A (written) business plan is essential, both to see that nothing has been forgotten, but more crucially to gain any financial or other support.

An unexpected hazard for the newly self-employed is the time taken by administration – much of which must be done to satisfy the taxman, HM Customs and Excise (VAT), and the law. You need to be well organised in how you handle paperwork.

Women returners and career breaks

Almost half of the UK workforce are women (more than 12 million). Two-thirds of them are married, which means almost one in three of all workers is a married woman. Women tend to be better educated, and more flexible (of choice or necessity) than men. Women returning to work (eight out of ten return within five years), are therefore often better equipped than men for the new forms of flexible, 'knowledge'-based job.

Most women have a career break, perhaps to have children, or for other family reasons, e.g. caring for a dependent adult. A major problem for a woman returning to the world of work is lack of confidence in her own ability. Training aimed specifically at women returners can help a woman overcome fears of inadequacy and ease the transition back to work. Such courses are provided by the government-funded training system, which is delivered by a national network of Training and Enterprise Councils (TECs) in England and Wales and Local Enterprise Companies in Scotland. In addition, short introductory courses in less-traditional occupations are available in some parts of the country. The local TEC or LEC should be contacted for information on the courses they provide.

Opportunities for women to reassess their abilities or to enhance existing skills are also being offered via courses such as the Higher Introductory Technology Engineering Conversion Course (HITECC), details of which can be found via the local educational advisory service. Many HITECC courses have now dropped the 'HITECC' title as the conversion element in the first year was causing a problem with mandatory awards, and they are now more frequently referred to as Extended Engineering Technology courses. These courses are for those without the traditional entry qualifications for an engineering degree – male or female, although one or two may be for women only. Details of these courses can also be obtained from the local careers service, prospectuses and directories.

The Educational Guidance Service for Adults (EGSA) can also help with counselling which may lead to preparatory or refresher courses. Not all areas will have a local Educational Advisory Service or an Educational Guidance Service for Adults. Universities and colleges around the country offer women-only courses.

Women in high-level posts in science and engineering have particular problems returning to work after a career break. Their existing knowledge is likely to have become redundant, the day-to-day jargon will have changed, and they will lack experience of current working practices.

Moreover, those who come from the academic world are often rejected because they have no recent publications to their credit.

The Daphne Jackson Fellowships, launched in 1985, enable highly qualified engineers and scientists to return to their careers after a break taken for family reasons. The fellowships are funded by charitable trusts, industry and universities. The Daphne Jackson Fellowship Trust, based in the Department of Physics at the University of Surrey, aims to provide at least five new fellowships a year. A typical fellowship lasts two years on a flexible part-time basis. It includes retraining and updating as well as a guided research or development project. The fellowships are open to both sexes, although so far only women have applied for them.

The need to provide training within school hours is now becoming better understood. Whilst women returning to work often have a longer period at work than they did before their career break, many still carry on a dual role of worker/family manager. This often means that women returners take up part- time, or lower-status jobs with less earning potential compared with their previous employment. It is estimated that four out of every five new jobs in the next five years will be taken up by women; therefore flexibility must be a major consideration for employers and trainers.

The provision of childcare facilities is a major factor in a woman's decision to return to training or the workplace. The absence of accessible childcare for pre-school and school-age children during term-time and holidays can prevent women from taking jobs that demand full-time commitment. Subject to a range of conditions, women have the right to return to their previous employment after a break to have a baby, although not necessarily in the same job. Some employers and professional organisations have extended these rights, and made provision for career breaks in law, engineering, health, architecture, the trade unions, accountancy, banking, the Civil Service, local authorities, and in some major retailers, and industrial organisations.

Job-sharing

Although not exclusive to women, job-sharing can prove an attractive route to return to work. Flexibility is the keynote here, and can have advantages in that the employees may decide how to split the time in the workplace. It is also a way in which professional and management skills can be employed by women returners who might not otherwise be able to commit themselves to the full-time requirements of a post. Job-sharing is being seen as an accepted mode of employment by employers, and even more so by the voluntary sector, where job-sharers may contribute more than one particular set of skills. Job-sharing may demand a certain compromise in methods of work, etc., so it is important for those employed in this way to be able to relate well to each other. Job-sharers can also apply for a senior post which is unlikely to be offered on a part-time basis. This gives them better prospects and a higher salary as well as the chance to use professional and management skills.

Working from home

Working from home can offer some practical advantages in that it is not necessary to rush to meet that train or catch that bus, there is no bad weather to contend with, and it is easier to schedule domestic duties into the daily work routine (although this should not be used as an excuse for not working).

Working at home demands certain qualities that those who are accustomed to taking instructions may have to learn. Motivating oneself, organising a proper routine, and being able to ignore the call of other work are important self-disciplines. Very often working at home can be a solitary affair, and may take some time to adjust to. There are myriad choices in the type of work that can be carried on from home, from traditional 'outworker' employment in, for instance, sewing, or garment finishing, to component assembly or the use of 'new technology' – computers or word processors.

The type of work chosen may affect the status of the home itself. It is important to discover if there are any specific restrictions in a lease, or whether the building society has any objections to plans. The addition of an extension to a property may require planning permission from the local authority, and may also have to comply with building regulations. The environmental health department of the local authority might also take an interest if they receive complaints about noise or fumes.

It is usual for homeworkers to negotiate their levels of pay with the company they are working for, but it is important when deciding a price to take account of hidden costs: electricity, telephone, and other materials that may not necessarily be supplied.

Employment protection in terms of benefits for a homeworker can be affected by the number of hours worked. The Trades Union Congress can advise on finding the trade union that represents a particular type of work.

Teleworking

Teleworking is the name given to home-based Information Technology (IT) businesses. A number of factors have given an impetus to the idea of working at home in IT. Growing pressure on companies to reduce overheads not only in terms of labour costs, but also in expensive urban office space, coincides with initiatives in rural development. A recent Industrial Society survey revealed that a growing number of staff in the 50-plus age group taking early retirement were considering acquiring IT skills to be able to freelance from home. Home-based IT work lends itself to the activities of a variety of people, from freelance journalists and computer programmers (fifteen years ago there were 200 freelance software programmers throughout Britain, now there are almost 20,000), to those involved in the world of finance and insurance. The appeal of living and working at home, especially if the home is situated in the pleasant environs of the countryside, is for many preferable to commuting. It was estimated that by 1995, 2 million people would be teleworking, saving 21.78 million (20%) commuter days.

The Rural Development Commission has been active in promoting and supporting the idea of 'telecottages' (translated from the Swedish *telestuga* where the concept has its origins). In rural communities the telecottage is envisaged as an IT centre which will offer a range of IT services to the local community and small businesses. Telecottages are basically workshops equipped with computers, electronic mailing facilities, fax, photocopiers, desktop publishing, and other database facilities, which it is hoped might lead to rural England becoming a main national location for IT activities. Plans are currently underway in Rural Development Areas for county-based groups of telecottages, jointly funded by the public and private sector. It is hoped eventually that banks, insurance companies, retail and manufacturing groups will increase their use of contract IT 'distance' workers in telecottage-style businesses. There are also a number of highly successful telecottages in the Highlands and Islands of Scotland. Although still in its early stages, the idea is catching on, and may indeed prove particularly attractive to rural areas, providing employment opportunities to soften the impact of the contraction in agricultural employment. The social impact of growth in this area is yet to be assessed.

Voluntary work

Voluntary work (paid or unpaid) may provide a route to return to work, or a satisfying way of contributing to community activity. With more than 168,000 registered charities in the UK, it is almost impossible to gauge how many people are involved in this type of work. Suffice to say that there is always a call for the volunteer.

Most jobs in the voluntary sector will be part-time and unpaid but may still demand a reasonably heavy commitment. In health and social services, volunteers may find themselves providing befriending services that require no specialist skills, other than the ability to offer support or companionship. Other opportunities may be found with conservation groups locally and nationally, in community projects, and in fundraising. Paid work in the voluntary sector can be as diverse as working as a trainer for Guide Dogs for the Blind, or in administration duties for Age Concern. Some jobs may include residential work, and require specialist skills. Training may be provided or supplemented by the organisation concerned.

Management buy-outs

A recent trend has been for groups of employees to buy the business in which they work. This can happen because an owner is retiring or selling-up, the business is in the hands of the receiver, or because the organisation is being transferred from the public to the private sector.

The scheme can be attractive both to the owners and to the employees. The 'sellers' know the business is going into the hands of people who understand the product, the systems, and the customers. Moreover, they are people who will have committed their money (and often their home) to the business. They have a vested interest in success. The employees in their turn become 'stakeholders' in the business which employs them and which they well understand. They are most likely to know where savings can be made, quality improved and so on.

However, there are risks, although these are rarely as great as starting a business from scratch. Few employees have enough money to buy a company, so they necessarily have to borrow, often on the security of their house. If the business fails, they may lose their home. On the other hand, management buy-outs are sometimes spectacularly successful, with the shareholders sharing considerable wealth.

Support and assistance

A considerable number of schemes, agencies, etc. have been introduced in the last few years to offer support, information and training to help people of all ages so that they can set up in business either on their own or with others. A list of some of the most useful/helpful are given below, and it is possible to gain financial support, training, and help with planning, preparing a business plan, obtaining suitable premises, etc.

Finance

The government's Business Start-Up Programme (formerly the Enterprise Allowance scheme) is the most straightforward form of financial support for people starting up on their own in a new business (other government schemes provide for e.g. expansion). Funds for the programme are administered by the Training and Enterprise Councils (TECs) in England and Wales, and the Local Enterprise Companies (LECs) in Scotland. TECs and LECs are in a better position to direct training to take account of perceived local needs, and therefore the programmes vary from region to region, as do the criteria for joining the programme.

Funds are made available to those who have been unemployed (or given notice of redundancy) for a minimum period, and candidates must have access to a predetermined amount of funds to put into their business. Again, amounts required vary from region to region, but typically might be £1,000, which could simply be an overdraft facility – and some banks also provide free banking and some counselling. This is a change from the old MSC provision of £40 per week for a year for all who took up the scheme. Previously the survival rate was considered to be good with the majority of businesses still trading after three years. Under the new administration of the start-up programme the effect of the changes has yet to be statistically assessed.

Other support

Some local authorities, some national schemes (e.g. the Prince of Wales' Youth Business Trust), and a network of about 350 local/regional enterprise agencies (funded by local authorities and/or private sponsors), give various levels of support ranging from straightforward information, advice and counselling, or help with preparing a business plan, through to actually providing workspaces and/or some funding. Some schemes are geared to particular groups, e.g. young people from Afro-Caribbean and Asian backgrounds. Some local authorities provide help in the form of rate relief, etc.

Training

Government funds for training are administered by the 82 Training and Enterprise Councils (TECs) and 23 Local Enterprise Companies (LECs), who support a range of courses for people going into self-employment, or starting new businesses. Many of these are put on by local consultancies and by FE colleges and, for more 'ambitious' schemes (i.e. people wanting to employ 12 or more people), at universities. A special scheme for graduates is put on by Cranfield, Durham, Stirling and Warwick Universities.

The Small Firms Service

The Small Firms Service provided by the Department for Education and Employment operates through 13 Small Firms Centres located around the country, and is backed by 200 Area Counselling Offices. The service provides information and counselling to owners and managers of small businesses, and offers guidance on a wide range of business topics to those planning to start up on their own.

Business development

Launched in January 1988 the Department of Trade and Industry (DTI) Enterprise Initiative seeks to encourage self-help for independent firms with fewer than 500 employees. This takes the form of a series of 'Initiatives' in areas such as design, marketing, quality, etc. Firms are put in touch with 'managing bodies' such as the Design Council or Institute of Marketing. Consultants from these bodies work with firms to improve/update areas of their business. The consultant's fees are supported in part by the DTI. First contact for these services should be made through local DTI regional offices.

Further information

The British Franchise Association, United Kingdom Co-operative Council (UKCC), Industrial Common Ownership Movement (ICOM), Industrial Common Ownership Finance (ICOF), Rural Development Commission (RDC), Crafts Council (for advice and help on all aspects of craft practice), Business in the Community, Small Firms Service (Freephone Enterprise), DTI regional offices (local directory), Business Links and Business Shops (local directory), TECs and LECs offices (local directory), Enterprise Agency regional offices (local directory), job centres for Department of Employment schemes, local library or careers service for addresses of any local support schemes, Trades Union Congress (TUC), the Low Pay Unit, National Council for Voluntary Organisations, National Youth Agency, the Volunteer Centre UK, local volunteer bureaux and councils, Welsh Development Agency.

Working Overseas

Contents

Background

Men and women have migrated from place to place in search of better living conditions, food and work, fame and fortune, or simply adventure, something new and different, since prehistoric times. Motives for moving may change, but the 'greener grass' syndrome is still common.

According to the most recent (1993) statistics, about 212,500 people (163,900 in 1984) migrated abroad, to the EC and rest of the world (figures do not include those going to Eire). Of these 76,700 (40,500 in 1984) left for work reasons, and 14,000 (4,000 in 1984) for formal study. Some 68,900 (50,800 in 1984) were professionals/managers, with about 43,800 (34,500 in 1984) involved in manual/clerical work.

Unfortunately, despite all the talk of a 'global village' it is possibly getting more, rather than less, difficult to up stakes and earn an income elsewhere, even though most of the world welcomes tourists, and anyone with money to invest. There are real problems and pitfalls in either trying to make a new life and career overseas and even finding work abroad on a shorter-term basis.

Opportunities for British nationals to live and work in other countries change all the time, with political, economic and social changes. In general, fewer countries are prepared to welcome any Briton with unquestioning open arms. Unemployment is a worldwide phenomenon, and governments have to give priority in the job market to their own nationals. Most countries legislate for this, just as Britain has legislation which restricts the rights of both Commonwealth citizens and foreign nationals to live and work in Britain. The countries to which Britons have traditionally migrated, such as New Zealand, Australia and Canada, are increasingly selective in their choice of migrants and are equally unwilling to let visitors work except under agreed schemes. The United States has long had strict legislation along similar lines. Other former colonial and developing countries, mainly for nationalist, political and social reasons, are now equally reluctant to have people of European origin permanently holding senior positions. The exception, of course, is that UK membership of the EU makes it legally possible for British nationals to work freely in any member country. To obtain reasonable work in a European country, though, usually means being completely fluent in the language, not something that the many who went out to English-speaking countries in the past had to worry about. And any Briton trying for a job in Europe still has to compete with nationals who will often be preferred by local employers.

As in Britain, opportunities in other countries are increasingly limited to people with expertise, skills, training and/or experience to sell, skills which countries, and employers there, may need to buy from abroad, including the UK, just as they buy goods. (The alternative is to have enough money to start a business and create jobs.) The skills may not always be the obvious ones, and each country's needs are likely to change over time. For example, although Australia will consider anyone who is qualified, there is a continuing need there for physiotherapists, secondary teachers of Japanese or mathematics, and therapeutic radiographers.

It is likely that, as in Britain, there will be more such shortages, since the fall in the birth-rate since the 1960s affects most Western countries. However, like Britain, most Western countries are (1996) only now beginning to emerge from the throes of recession, with an unemployment problem of their own. Consequently, opportunities for non-nationals may well be reduced.

But without skills which are sought after, the chances to work in other countries are few, except on a casual basis, or as a volunteer. Even countries which may be short of labour in particular industries are reluctant to import unskilled people because of the political and social problems this can bring, or else they can't afford them. Except in special circumstances, it is not normally possible to be trained in foreign countries at the state's – or any organisation's – expense. There are, however, various specific schemes which allow training or work experience in Europe. These are detailed below under SHORT-TERM OPPORTUNITIES AND TEMPORARY WORK. Of course, within the EU, unskilled people may still work wherever they want to, provided work is available.

Most careers literature emphasises that the people who gain most from working in other countries are those who have thought through their reasons for wanting to do so, and have matched realistic opportunities to their own personal priorities. It is all too easy to be carried away by the excitement of jetting off into the unknown, or thinking personal or other problems can be solved just by going abroad, and to forget practicalities. Thoroughly researching the opportunities, thinking through what happens if plans don't work out, what the opportunities would be for returning to a career in the UK, etc. are just as crucial – if not more so – for anyone who is considering going overseas as for finding a career or job in Britain.

It is fair to decide that living in South America (or wherever) is a good idea, but while professional practices may vary from country to country, actual daily life in a bank, as an accountant or a teacher, in construction or engineering, is fundamentally the same the world over. Someone who doesn't enjoy teaching in England is most unlikely to find the job itself any more congenial in another country, even if the climate or the income is better. Equally, it is wrong to assume that it is possible to gain experience of a wider range of occupations overseas than at home in Britain. In fact, the reverse is often the case, since in many countries there are just as likely to be the same kinds of restrictions – qualifications, nationality, for example – as in Britain.

Planning to work overseas for a finite period, and planning to make a career abroad permanently, either by a single move from Britain to another country, or by choosing work which involves working in other countries, or by working for an organisation which sends employees to work overseas, imply quite different sorts of motivation and intention. Moreover, the opportunities are quite different in each case.

Emigrating

Emigrating implies a decision to make a total change of lifestyle, and not just the work situation. People seldom decide to move to another country solely on the basis of work – although of course unemployment may force some to look for permanent work abroad even though they would prefer to live in Britain. Permanent emigration suggests a desire to live in a different political, economic, social or even physical climate – to look for a differently structured society, to earn more money, to escape from a situation.

Emigrants need marketable training and skills, and usually fairly extensive experience of the work too. Countries accepting permanent immigrants as such are now relatively few: with the exception of Europe, the opportunities for English-speaking nationals to go to and live permanently in the traditional places, such as Australia, New Zealand and Canada, are now very restricted. Permanent residence in the United States is difficult, but not impossible, although it usually means having a job to go to. In general, it has to be assumed that immigration quotas are being reduced, although any organisation seriously short of people with specific skills is unlikely to have problems in getting round them.

While in theory a trial period working in the country in question is a good idea, in practice this is not always possible, since there are also very strict limitations on short-term work permits in many non-EU/EEA countries including, for example, Australia. Many countries now also expect immigrants to have jobs before entry, and some (e.g. New Zealand) that they also have somewhere to live (and this does not mean having enough money to buy or rent property after arrival). It is, therefore, extremely important to use the most up-to-date information on the details of immigration laws and regulations from the appropriate authorities, before making any plans.

Further information

The high commissions/embassies in the UK should have information both on immigration regulations and of the skills currently in short supply.

Working permanently overseas

Working permanently overseas for organisations which employ people in countries other than Britain is an alternative to emigrating. These are opportunities, however, which rarely offer the chance to spend an entire working career in a single place, and are therefore not ideal for those who want a settled life in one place. It means being happy to move from place to place fairly often, enjoying new experiences, change, and differing surroundings, over an entire working life. There are other disadvantages to this kind of life: choice of country is not always up to the individual, and may mean unpleasant climatic conditions, political instability, and so on. As with any nomadic existence, organising family life, even with substantial support from the employing organisation, can be difficult, especially when it comes to children's schooling.

Many of the traditional opportunities to work permanently or regularly abroad are declining, with economic, political, social or technological change, although others are opening up.

The decline of the merchant fleet, for example, means fewer opportunities to travel the world in the merchant navy. THE ARMED FORCES, including the Royal Navy, do not, generally, go so far afield so often or for so long now (with the exception of the Falklands). The media, generally, has fewer foreign correspondents stationed permanently in individual countries, because jet travel makes it much easier to send people out to where the news is at any one time, but this does make some journalists more peripatetic. However, INTERPRETING and TRANSLATING (*see in* LANGUAGES) still take people to other countries, on a permanent or semi-permanent basis, for short stays or single events.

The Diplomatic Service *(see in* CENTRAL GOVERNMENT) continues to give a comparatively small number of people the opportunity to work overseas for a large part of their careers.

Professional sportsmen/women live international lives, on world circuits, playing for foreign clubs, or just competing in the growing number of international events.

The entertainment business allows people to spend a proportion of their working lives working abroad. Broadcasters, radio and television engineers, technicians and librarians are employed by the Ministry of Defence to entertain service personnel on their own radio and television stations around the world.

EDUCATION AND TEACHING is still a major way of working abroad, especially teaching English as a foreign language (TEFL), in both state and private schools, in language schools and in (the equivalent of) higher and further education, in a wide range of countries, but usually on contract rather than in permanent employment. Teachers are also employed by the Ministry of Defence to teach the children of service personnel in primary schools in many areas abroad where the Armed Forces are based.

THE CONSTRUCTION INDUSTRY is increasingly international, with major British firms competing for business building, e.g., airports, industrial plant, power stations, roads, hospitals, and schools, worldwide, and sending out managers, engineers, etc., often for the length of a contract, which may be years. Such contracts also involve the firms which make equipment, machinery, etc.

MINING AND ENERGY INDUSTRIES search for and exploit reserves in more and more remote parts of the world, which gives work for, e.g. geologists, and mining and drilling experts. Opportunities, though, fluctuate with the price and demand for oil, minerals, etc.

Some multinational companies give appropriately qualified UK personnel the chance to work elsewhere. Mostly, though, they are committed to employing people in the countries where they are based. Exceptions are, for example, that large multinationals may concentrate research and development operations in particular countries, and therefore scientists of all nationalities are recruited for these units, and some large multinationals do move around production staff. It is always worth asking firms if they have the kind of organisational structure which allows employees to transfer from one country to another, or whether it is possible to apply direct to subsidiaries in other countries.

UK-based industrial and commercial firms giving the best opportunities to work abroad on a long-term basis are mainly those whose operations are international because their business demands it rather than because they happen to have subsidiaries or branches in a large number of countries. Firms selling internationally – particularly heavy capital equipment, aircraft and telecommunications – have international sales teams. FREIGHT FORWARDING *(see in* THE TRANSPORT INDUSTRY), and firms in THE TRAVEL INDUSTRY may also send trained, experienced staff to work in overseas offices, or on trips/tours abroad. Tourist firms also employ, but mainly on a seasonal basis, couriers and resort representatives.

The EU is slowly turning more occupations into 'European' careers, and qualifications are being harmonised. PATENT WORK, for example *(see in* THE LEGAL SYSTEM), is becoming a European profession. Accountants and lawyers/financial experts qualified professionally and linguistically to work in more than one European country are in demand.

European institutions employ nationals of all member states, including the UK.

Scientists are recruited Europe-wide for a still fairly small number of collaborative ventures, e.g. CERN – the European Organisation for Nuclear Research in Geneva (physicists, computer scientists, electrical engineers) – and labs working for the European Space Agency.

Politicians can make a career in the European Parliament.

Developing countries may recruit – either directly or via, e.g. ODA, or charities, for development and/or research – agricultural experts, people with qualifications in construction and surveying, teachers and other education specialists, engineers, business experts, qualified medical and paramedical people.

Overseas development, the relatively small number of international organisations, and bodies like the British Council, provide work for a comparatively small number of people.

The British Council

The British Council (founded 1934) promotes educational, cultural and technical cooperation between Britain and other countries and is Britain's principal agency for cultural relations overseas, with offices in over 100 countries. Its work is designed to establish long-term and worldwide partnerships for Britain and improve international understanding.

However, the structure of the Council is changing to adopt a more commercial approach in the way it organises itself and its activities. Budgetary cuts in 1996 are likely further to affect the organisation; probably resulting in reductions in staff, and possibly in the scale of its activities. In 1994/95 the Council had total receipts of £426 million. Of this 33% came from government grants and was used to carry out the Council's main activities; 27% was earned as revenue from services to clients and customers including income earned from teaching centres, administration of British examinations, management of contract work and from library fees; 40% came from agencies such as Britain's Overseas Development Administration and the World Bank who contracted the Council to act as agents in managing specific projects or programmes.

The Council's unique strength as an international cultural organisation lies in its extensive overseas network of offices through which it seeks to achieve its five core objectives which are: to promote international partnerships in educational and scientific fields; to extend the use and improve the teaching of English; to demonstrate the vitality and excellence of British arts; to extend Britain's contribution to overseas development; and to promote, in response to overseas demand, the use of British goods and services in education and training.

The UK has an international reputation for the quality and diversity of its education. The Council brings together its knowledge of education in Britain and its understanding of the needs of overseas countries by:

1 procuring education and training for governments, funding agencies, institutions and individuals;
2 providing information about British institutions and courses through its network around the world;
3 managing training programmes for over 100 clients, in institutions, industry, commerce and government;
4 helping UK universities and colleges in their international activities, including student recruitment;
5 supporting joint international research and teaching projects;
6 enriching education provision in the UK by supporting the teaching and learning of modern foreign languages and promoting the international dimension in all sectors of the curriculum;
7 organising international seminars and summer schools in the UK and overseas on topics such as medicine, the environment, English language teaching and public administration; and
8 promoting collaboration and consortia involving Britain and other European institutions.

Working closely with the British scientific community, the Council promotes British expertise overseas by: supporting partnerships in joint scientific and medical research and training; providing information on British research, education and training services; demonstrating the excellence of British science, technology and engineering; and supporting overseas development, particularly human resource and institutional development.

Twenty per cent of the world's population uses English, and the number is constantly increasing. The Council promotes Britain's leading role in servicing this demand. It also supports the role of English in development as the universal language of technology, information, and international communications. The Council does this by: providing advisory services for teachers and learners in state education systems; training in Council centres in English language skills and applications; providing British books and examinations; monitoring quality standards for language courses for overseas students in the UK; and presenting the diversity of British culture and life by promoting British studies.

Additionally, the Council has over 185 libraries and resource centres around the world. The information they provide supports the Council's work in cultural cooperation and development. The role of the Council's library and information services includes: providing access to the English language and all aspects of British education, culture and ideas; promoting British books and publishing through book fairs, exhibitions and market surveys; and managing projects in libraries, books and information on behalf of international clients.

The Council presents the vitality and excellence of Britain's arts and literature worldwide. Examples of this work include: arranging international tours by British drama, dance and music companies; exhibiting British painting, sculpture and photography; enabling writers and literary critics to take part in overseas readings and workshops; and promoting British films to international film festivals.

The Council manages contracts on behalf of bilateral and multilateral agencies, national governments and other organisations, which involve: providing training, in the UK and overseas from short study visits and on-the-job training to academic courses; providing consultants to design, implement and evaluate development programmes and projects; supplying equipment, books and information.

Development through aid is designed to promote the socio-economic development of the less wealthy countries. Priorities include poverty reduction through the encouragement of human resource development, health and population policies, care for the environment, economic reform, the role of women in development, open and accountable government, and enhanced productive capacity.

The Council's ability to match professional resources to the development agenda enable it to add value to aid investments and contribute to sustainable impact.

Partnership with business and industry is a growing aspect of the Council's work. Association with the Council provides opportunities for companies operating internationally to: make and maintain contact with decision-makers; build links in local communities; assist in the development of healthy economies; promote corporate image; and participate in influential exhibitions and seminars.

Recruitment and entry

There are five groups of British Council Staff:

1 UK appointed staff (who work in the UK and/or overseas);
2 teachers of English as a foreign language (for Council teaching centres abroad);
3 teachers and lecturers in all disciplines (who work in educational institutions overseas);
4 consultants to act as team leaders/project managers for Council-managed projects overseas;
5 local staff (in overseas offices).

Vacancies in the UK (Group 1)

From time to time the Council runs exercises to fill general posts at various levels in its offices in London and Manchester, with occasional vacancies occurring in the offices in Edinburgh, Cardiff and Belfast: there are also outposted staff in a number of university centres throughout the UK. The qualifications and experience required vary according to the types of post under recruitment, ranging from school-leavers with less than one year's work experience to people with significant work experience in a particular field. There are also occasional opportunities for recruitment to specialised/specialist posts (e.g. in arts, information technology, professional finance, academic specialisms, or information science). Almost all such vacancies are advertised on a fixed-term contract basis. The Council does not run general recruitment campaigns aimed specifically at school-leavers, graduates or any other groups, nor does it operate a graduate trainee scheme or offer work placements/experience to school or other students. Its staff does not include interpreters or translators.

Vacancies are advertised in the national press and/or sometimes through job centres. Use is most frequently made of *The Guardian* and/or professional journals. Manchester-based posts are usually advertised in the *Manchester Evening News*. An application form and other information relating to specific posts/exercises are sent to anyone responding to press advertisements, but the Council does not accept speculative applications.

Vacancies overseas (Groups 1–5)

The Council used to recruit staff to an Overseas Career Service: such staff would be expected to spend up to two-thirds of their career overseas. This no longer happens: recruitment for UK-based posts overseas is normally on an initial fixed-term contract, with possibilities for renewal in accordance with operational requirements, business needs and performance. The procedures for advertisement and application are as set out above.

Teachers of English as a Foreign Language (Group 2) are recruited for the Council's Direct Teaching Operations (DTOs) in countries throughout the world. For most DTOs, the minimum criteria include a recognised TEFL qualification (RSA DipTEFL, PGCE TEFL, or their equivalent), plus at least two years' teaching experience, preferably obtained overseas. Appointments are generally on fixed-term contracts of two years.

Advisers and lecturers (Group 3) in a variety of subjects (mainly ELT, British Literature, British Studies, Maths, Science and Health); qualified schoolteachers (usually secondary) in a variety of subjects (mainly English, Maths, Science, CDT, Agricultural Science, Art, Geography and Home Economics). All these are selected for institutions, overseas governments, schools, etc.; and occasionally Head and Deputy Headteachers are recruited for International Schools. These posts are frequently linked to projects funded by British or multilateral aid agencies, or where the Council acts as a recruiting agent. Appointments are on fixed-term contract. All these vacancies are advertised, most frequently in *The Guardian* and *The Times Educational Supplement*.

People with project management experience overseas (Group 4) are sometimes recruited as consultants/contractors on projects being managed by the Council on behalf of agencies such as the Overseas Development Administration, the World Bank and the European Commission. Development and Training Services (DATS) in Manchester maintains a database of people interested in such assignments.

The majority of the employees in Council Offices overseas are on local contracts (Group 5). Such posts are normally advertised in the local press and filled, very often by local nationals, on local terms. Recruitment is handled entirely through the local office: the Country Director is the point of information about such opportunities as there may be. Addresses may be found in *Whitaker's Almanac* or the *Statesman's Year Book*.

Group 1 vacancies: contact Corporate Personnel, Recruitment (London office), or Personnel Services, Corporate Personnel (Manchester office); Group 2 vacancies: contact Central Management of Direct Teaching, Recruitment (London office); Group 3 vacancies: contact Overseas Appointments Services (Manchester office); Group 4 vacancies: contact Development and Training Services, Marketing and Production Unit (Manchester office).

International organisations

The main international organisations which employ British nationals are the United Nations and its agencies.

The United Nations

The United Nations has few professional posts, and these take considerable expertise in fields related to the work of the UN. Junior professional staff normally have an honours degree or its equivalent, and for higher-level professional posts they generally have recognised standing in their fields.

The UN administers its own development programme and also participates in a joint programme with a number of specialised agencies. The UN itself deals with industrial and economic development, social services (including housing and community development) and natural-resource development (other than agriculture). Demand is always for senior expert advisers, who are normally expected to have the highest professional standing and at least fifteen years' experience in their fields; more junior candidates are seldom nominated.

Economists (*see in* CENTRAL GOVERNMENT), with substantial governmental experience at home or overseas, are employed to advise on economic planning, programming and development problems.

In development of mineral resources, experts employed include geologists, mining engineers, seismologists, geophysicists, geochemists, hydrologists and hydrogeologists (*see in* THE MINING AND ENERGY INDUSTRIES).

In public finance, experts help, e.g., to set up government accounts, to establish central banks, with taxation and insurance problems, in fiscal aspects of trade policy and with ways of attracting capital investment.

Data processing experts (*see in* INFORMATION TECHNOLOGY AND COMPUTER WORK) advise on using computers in government organisational, financial, management and personnel administration.

STATISTICIANS advise on the organisation of, for example, population surveys. (*See* MATHEMATICS, STATISTICS AND ECONOMICS.)

Other experts and advisers are employed on transport, electric power, planning (especially low-cost housing) (*see in* LAND USE PROFESSIONS), social welfare, community development, public administration, and promoting and developing tourism. The UN employs a few specialists in energy conservation, land survey and mapping, cartographers, and museum and library staff.

Administrative vacancies in the UN are few and far between, and are normally filled by reassigning existing staff. Posts in the office of public information take substantial professional experience in the use of the media even for junior posts, with preference for people able to work in more than one language. Some posts in the office are filled on a rotating basis through secondment from professional services in member states.

The office of legal affairs has only a small staff (with a low turnover), all of whom have specialised in public international law.

Translators/precis-writers translate into their mother tongues (English, French, Spanish, Russian or Chinese) – English translators have to be able to work in French with a sound background in one other language, and the few Arabic translators must translate from English and French into Arabic. All translators are graduates of a university where the language of instruction was their mother tongue. Interpreters must have a university degree and a thorough knowledge of at least three of the above languages.

The UN also has a few social welfare workers, a number of posts for computer programmers (with degrees in economics or accounting plus at least three years' experience), qualified librarians (with a reading knowledge of several languages).

The UN field service personnel working in the field missions include security officers, vehicle mechanics, radio technicians and operators, and male secretaries. They may have to move from mission to mission in any part of the world at any time. Clerical and secretarial staff are generally recruited locally, except for the headquarters staff, who are chosen from among successful competitors in examinations held in New York (minimum requirements are a typing speed of about 50 wpm and a stenographic speed of about 100 wpm in the candidate's mother tongue, and secretaries and typists should preferably be at least bilingual). There is a special need for high-speed conference typists in the six official languages working in large typing pools during the period of the meetings of the general assembly (mid-September to mid-December). They are required to work night shifts as well as overtime at various times.

UN guides are recruited in New York (candidates from other countries must pay their own travel expenses), and all are under the age of 30, with a good secondary education and attractive speaking voices, fluent in English and preferably other languages as well.

In its Secretariat functions throughout the world, the United Nations had 10,115 posts funded by the regular budget, with another 4,831 posts funded outside the budget, for instance, by individual countries. Thus in total, the UN Secretariat throughout the world numbers 14,188 people. Together with the many United Nations funds and programmes, such as those noted above, the total reaches more than 53,000 people. However, the UN faces a considerable budget crisis. The General Assembly recommended that the UN's $1.3 billion annual budget be cut in 1996/97.

Worse, cumulative withholding by member states as well as late payment by others has contributed to a major financial crisis. Even if this were all paid up, the UN would still have to make reductions in services, in staff, and in what it can do for member states. In view of these difficulties, recruitment (with the exception of a small number of specialist staff) is unlikely for the foreseeable future.

UN Agencies

UN agencies recruit more closely to specialist interests, which are fairly obvious from their titles.

For example, the Food and Agricultural Organisation employs highly qualified technical personnel specialising in various fields of agriculture irrigation engineering, forestry, fisheries, nutrition, economics, and statistics.

The list of experts needed by the UN agencies is endless, but it is emphasised that some skills are not suitable: there is little demand for industrial executives, for example, and very few posts for civil and mechanical engineers except in, e.g., dam or highway design, and it is extremely rare for the UN to employ retired officers from the Armed Forces, however extensive their foreign experience.

UN agencies include: the Food and Agricultural Organisation (FAO) in Rome, UNESCO, and the Industrial Development Organisation (UNIDO) in Paris. Other bodies include the General Agreement on Tariffs and Trade (GATT) in Geneva, the International Court of Justice in The Hague, the International Maritime Organisation (IMO) in London, the International Atomic Energy Agency (IAEA) in Vienna, the World Bank (which comprises the International Bank for Reconstruction and Development, the International Development Association, and the International Finance Corporation) and the International Monetary Fund (IMF) in Washington, the International Civil Aviation Organisation (ICAO) based in Montreal, the International Labour Organisation (ILO) in Geneva, the International Telecommunication Union (ITU) also in Geneva, the Universal Postal Union (UPU) in Berne, the World Health Organisation (WHO) and the World Meteorological Organisation (WMO), both in Geneva, the World Intellectual Property Organisation (WIPO), also in Geneva, and the International Fund for Agricultural Development (IFAD), based in Rome.

Most posts in international organisations are either administrative, in the organisation's secretariat (and this normally includes e.g. translators and interpreters), or in professional, highly expert work carrying out the aims of the organisation. With few exceptions (mainly amongst linguistic staff and, in some organisations, secretarial personnel), international organisations try to keep a balance of staff among the member states of the organisation, as far as possible.

The World Bank

The World Bank (whose official name is The International Bank for Reconstruction and Development), together with the International Development Association and the International Finance Corporation provides both financial and technical help to improve the living standards of developing member countries. Almost every country in the world is a member of the Bank.

The Washington-based Bank has a common administrative staff, but operational staff work either for IBRD and IFC or for the IDA. Most posts are permanent, calling for a combination of good academic and technical qualifications, and several years' professional experience (preferably in less-developed countries), often with specialisation in depth across a broad range of related activities.

Project officers are professionally qualified specialists who handle the investigation of schemes put forward for loan approval – increasingly these are agriculturists, agricultural engineers (including irrigation engineers) and agricultural credit specialists, although there are also posts for power, telecommunications and water-supply engineers, road, ports and railway engineers, specialists in education (agricultural, technical and general secondary), and school-building architects. Economists (with an advanced degree and appropriate applied experience) are also employed in substantial numbers, in the projects departments, in the five area departments which handle the Bank's day-to-day relations with its member countries, and in the economics department itself, which makes special economic and financial studies on general and specific problems of interest to the Bank. Specialists in promoting and analysing new investment proposals, company legislation and finance, raising new issues and so on, are also in demand.

The Bank recruits young professionals who have little or no professional experience as such under a special programme – the upper age limit is 30 and a first- or good second-class honours degree (in theory in any discipline, although there is in fact a preference for economics), and some (preferably relevant) experience in finance, economics or development are required.

Recruitment and entry

Technical personnel for most of these organisations are recruited in Britain via the Overseas Appointments and Contracts Department. Exceptions are more general posts in the UN (for which application must be made direct to the New York headquarters).

Working in the European Union

Member states, EU and EEA – professional qualifications – vocational qualifications – educational qualifications – income tax – transferring social benefits

The European Economic Community was established by the Treaty of Rome in 1957. In 1985, the EU heads of government committed themselves to completing a single 'common' market by 31 December 1992, and the commitment was defined in the package of Treaty reforms included in the Single European Act.

The Act defines the single market as 'an area without internal frontiers...'. All barriers to trade are effectively removed and community legislation allows the free movement of goods, services, capital and persons. In short, the Treaty of Rome guarantees the freedom for every national of a member state to work, to seek work, to set up business or to provide services in any member state. Community citizens then may not be discriminated against simply on grounds of nationality. A British citizen working in a member state enjoys the same entitlements to pay, working conditions, housing, social security, vocational training, income tax and trade union membership as a national of that country. In addition, families and immediate dependants entitled to join them have similar rights.

Having said that, in practice, finding a job is not necessarily as easy as it sounds. The recession has been harsh, unemployment is high, and above all, overseas employers require those applying for jobs to be fluent in the country's first language: English, though widely spoken, is not sufficient. Conditions of employment are a matter of agreement between the employer and employee, and it's as well to bear in mind that employment rights in other EU/EEA countries differ to those found in the UK. Those seeking work overseas need to check any contracts thoroughly, and treat any request to provide money as an 'indemnity' with great suspicion – very often this practice is illegal.

Member states, EU and EEA

There are 15 full member states: Austria, Belgium, Denmark, Finland, France, Germany, Greece, Ireland, Italy, Luxembourg, Netherlands, Portugal, Spain, Sweden and United Kingdom.

Iceland, Liechtenstein and Norway have agreed with the member states of the EU to participate in a European Economic Area (EEA).

EU/EEA nationals can enter another member state for up to three months to look for work or set up in business without the need for a work permit. However, if an individual's intention is to stay for longer than three months, a residence permit is required. These are usually issued for a five- or ten-year period and are renewable. Depending on the country, permits are issued by the town hall of the town/city of residence. Procedures vary from country to country. Some involve a great deal of bureaucracy, whilst others are comparatively straightforward (*see* Documentation *sections under* THE EU FACTFILE *below*).

Although the idea of 'free movement' is enshrined in the legislation, it is always a good idea to contact the embassy/consulate of the host country to check on up-to-date entry routines/requirements before venturing abroad.

To work in an EU/EEA country you must have a full EU/UK passport. A British Visitors passport or Excursion document will not suffice. You may also be asked to prove that you have adequate means for the duration of your stay, and the cost of the return journey back to the UK.

Conditions vary within the individual EU member states. They still have strong identities with widely differing customs and needs. Similarly, employment requirements differ from country to country, depending on specific skill shortages. For example, Belgium, an extremely cosmopolitan country, has a constant need for English-speaking people to work in technical and administrative jobs; Denmark and Spain have high unemployment rates and jobs there are difficult to find; France is particularly good for seasonal work on farms or in the hospitality industry; Germany needs skilled tradespeople and professionals; Greece has vacancies in the tourism industry, au-pair work and education; secretaries and teachers of English are in demand in Italy.

Professional qualifications

By 1988 a directive had been agreed to enable a professional from one member state to become a member of the equivalent profession, if it is regulated in another member state, without having to requalify. A fully qualified professional in one member state is deemed to be fully qualified in another, subject to two safeguard provisions designed to maintain professional standards. These safeguards deal with the length of education and training a professional has received, and the content of education and training in a given profession between two member states. Professionals who wish to practise in another member state may have to either take an aptitude test or undergo an 'adaptation period' (not exceeding three years in the host country). Incoming professionals can choose between the two.

However, in certain circumstances a member state may specify 'aptitude' or 'adaptation', though not both. The UK professions to which this exception applies are the legal professions, patent agents, patent attorneys, accountants and auditors. The DTI produce a booklet *Europe Open for Professions* which gives a good guide to issues of comparability, and lists professions regulated in the UK for the purposes of the directive. The list shows the designated authority responsible. In the UK this may be either a state department, or a professional body. For detailed information on comparability, professionals should contact their own professional body.

Vocational qualifications

Until 1992 each member state had a 'Comparability Co-ordination' unit organised under the CEDEFOP programme which sought to compare non-professional qualifications in each member state. The information produced is now dated, and unfortunately there is no easily accessed point of reference for those who wish to compare their qualifications. However, a number of jobs and trades are covered by directives requiring member states to recognise qualifications and experience obtained elsewhere in the Community. Member states (in the UK, the Certification Unit of British Chambers of Commerce) issue a Certificate of Experience to a worker who meets the requirements of the directive covering their job area (there is a small charge for this). The Certificate may be accepted in other member states in place of their own national qualifications for that job. Further information on Certificates of Experience can be obtained from the DTI (Relations Division 1), or the Certification Unit of British Chambers of Commerce.

Educational qualifications

The National Academic Recognition Information Centres (NARIC) form a European network providing advice and information on recognition of academic qualifications. The UK NARIC has produced an *International Guide to Qualifications in Education*. In the UK, the NARIC Centre is open to telephone enquiries from the public, 2–5pm Monday to Friday (0161-957 7000).

Income tax

Income earned from employment in another country may be liable for UK income tax depending on length of time spent working overseas, and the circumstances of employment. The UK has double taxation agreements with all EU/EEA countries, therefore tax is not payable twice on the same income. Methods of collecting income tax vary from country to country. Check with the local tax office or the EU Unit of the Inland Revenue, and when abroad, with the local tax office in the host country.

Transferring social benefits

It is possible to receive UK social benefits such as unemployment and sickness benefit for up to three months whilst you look for work in EU/EEA countries. Check with your local social security office, or contact the Overseas Contributions section of the Contributions Agency. They can provide advice about benefits and healthcare cover. A brief summary of conditions applicable to each member state is covered below. However, conditions can change very rapidly. It is very important to check on current information with embassies of host countries and other bodies.

Looking for work

There are a number of ways of job-seeking before travelling abroad. The UK National Vacancy System (NATVACS) currently available at JobCentres, is expected to be replaced in the near future, with an expanded scheme. NATVACS facilitates an overseas search of particular areas of employment of the potential host country. The Employment Service Jobfinder Service on ITV Teletext p. 368 is currently available, and contains overseas employment information. In addition, the Overseas Placing Unit of the Employment Service provides advice and guidance to people who want to work abroad. They publish a *Working In* series of very useful factsheets.

EURES

The EURES Network (European Employment Services) facilitates the circulation of vacancies and up-to-date information on living and working conditions in each EU/EEA member state via a computer network. The network is accessed by about 450 trained Euroadvisers who specialise in practical issues regarding working in EU/EEA countries. Euroadvisers can be contacted via local Employment Services offices.

Professional bodies, associations, trade unions

Many have established links with their EU/EEA opposite numbers, and can assist with advice and information, and some with placements/exchanges overseas.

Press and publications

National newspapers in the UK carry overseas job vacancies. These may be for UK companies with offices overseas, or foreign firms advertising in this country. The same is true for other EU/EEA countries' press. Foreign daily/weekly nationals can be purchased in this country at larger newsagents, or may be available on subscription. There are a number of specialist and professional journals/periodicals produced in host countries (*see under* THE EU FACTFILE *below*). The equivalent UK Yellow Pages of the host country (these are normally available in this country in larger libraries) can be a good source of addresses of companies for speculative contact. A letter addressed to a contact name is likely to get a more positive response than one just addressed to the Human Resources Manager, so it's wise to enquire by telephone first in order to get a contact name. It can also be useful to advertise as a job-seeker in the press of member states via an agency in the UK such as Powers International in London.

Employment agencies

These can be a useful source, especially for those seeking temporary work. Check if the agency normally charges the employer or the employee for their services. In some EU/EEA countries employment agencies are prohibited. Contact the Federation of Recruitment and Employment Services Ltd (FRES). For a small charge they can provide a list of appropriate agencies in the EU and elsewhere abroad. The CEPEC Recruitment Guide lists recruitment agencies and search consultants in the UK. The guide may be available in local libraries, or purchased direct from CEPEC Ltd.

Self-employment

Form E101 (exemption certificate) is required for some self-employed contracts abroad. Eligibility requires that an individual has been self-employed for at least three months. E101 confirms self-employed status and confirms the individual continues to contribute to the UK social security scheme. The E101 is issued on application to the Department of Social Security Overseas Branch when a contract start date is decided. It is usually obtainable within about a week. It is also necessary (unless already registered self-employed) to declare (on form CF11) the intention to become self-employed.

Seasonal/casual employment

Traditional seasonal work such as fruit-picking and hotel work is available in most EU/EEA countries.

Education, training and work experience schemes

The Central Bureau

The Central Bureau incorporates the UK Centre for European Education (UKCEE), and forms part of THE BRITISH COUNCIL (*see above*). It is the UK national office for information, advice and support on all forms of educational visits and exchanges, and is the UK National Agency for many of the European Union education and training programmes. As well as running a wide range of schemes to promote international cooperation in education, the Bureau also publishes information guides and newsletters, and answers more than 30,000 enquiries every year on all types of educational visits and exchanges. The principle task of the Bureau is to strengthen the learning and teaching of modern foreign languages, and to promote awareness of the European dimension in education. This is done by forging links between students and educationalists and their counterparts abroad. The Bureau can provide further information on a number of major initiatives which involve cooperation between EU countries. These include the following.

The European Commission programmes: SOCRATES, LEONARDO, Inter-University Co-operation Programmes

ERASMUS (which promoted student mobility and funding cooperation in higher education) and LINGUA (which promoted foreign language competence in the EU, staff-training and educational exchanges) enabled the movement of some 280,000 students and 35,000 teaching staff within the EU. From 1995 these initiatives have been absorbed into the expanded SOCRATES programme.

Inter-University Co-operation Programmes (ICPs) operate under the European Commission's educational exchange programmes. In 1995 about 100,000 places annually were available, and the Commission's target is to increase the number of places to enable 10% of all European students to participate in study abroad.

Vocational programmes such as PETRA, FORCE, EUROTECNET, COMETT, and IRIS dealt with training, research, exchanges and study visits for students, trainers and industry personnel, and now operate under the banner of the new LEONARDO programme. An important element of LEONARDO is the opportunity it provides for periods of work placement experience (or stage) abroad.

Eastern European programmes: TEMPUS

Beyond the boundaries of the 15 member states, the TEMPUS programme seeks to encourage the development of higher education in Eastern Europe. Interaction with EU member states is assisted through joint activities and mobility, such as exchanges involving both higher education and industry.

Other associations and organisations

FEDORA is an EU-sponsored association to link together those involved in student guidance in higher education.

CEDEFOP is an EU organisation sponsoring a programme of vocational training initiatives and harmonisation of vocational qualifications, based in Thessalonika, Greece.

EURYDICE, an EU education information network based in Brussels, publishes papers on the educational systems of member states.

Further information

The Central Bureau for Educational Visits and Exchanges; The Employment Service, Overseas Placing Unit; The European Commission.

The EU factfile

AUSTRIA

Job-seeking

JobCentre equivalent: (Arbeitsmarktservice-stelle). Addresses: in local telephone directory. HQ: Bundesministerium Für Arbeit und Soziales, Stubenring 1, A-1010 Wien. Austria's international JobCentre: (Arbeitsmarktverwaltung) (*see* Addresses). Access to job vacancies throughout Austria. Samsomat: self-service computer-accessed information on local job opportunities, from which individuals can arrange their own interviews with prospective employers.

Private agencies: can be useful source of employment opportunities. Addresses in local directory.

Media: job adverts in newspapers: *Kurier*, *Standard*, *Presse*.

Documentation

Residence permit: (EWR Lichtbildausweis) available from Polizei or Gendarmerie-Wachzimmer when employer confirms three months-plus contract. Application forms from: Fremdenpolizeiliches Buro (*see* Addresses). Also register with local aliens administration office (Polizei or Gendarmerie-Wachzimmer) within eight days of arrival.

Self-employment

Check current registration requirements with Austrian Embassy.

Income tax

In Austria check with the Bundesministerium für Finanzen (*see* Addresses).

Conditions

Legislation covers income agreements. Collective wage agreements are common for all sectors. *Working week*: maximum 40 hours/8 hours per day. *Holidays*: minimum four weeks after six months' service.

Addresses

Austrian Embassy, 18 Belgrave Mews West, London SW1X 8HU 0171-235 3731.
British Embassy, Jauresgasse 12, A-1030, Vienna.
Anglo-Austrian Society, 46 Queen Anne's Gate, London SW1H 9AU 0171-222 0366.
British Council, Schenkenstrasse 4, A-1010 Vienna.
Arbeitsmarktverwaltung, EURO BIZ, Sudtiroler Platz 14-16, A-6020, Innsbruck.
Fremdenpolizeiliches Buro, Wasagasse 22, A-1090, Vienna.
Budesministerium für Finanzen, Himmelpfortgasse 4-8, A-1010, Vienna.
Fremdenpolizeiliches Buro, Wasagasse 22, A-1090 Vienna.

BELGIUM

Job-seeking

JobCentre equivalent: in Flanders, Vlaamse Dienst voor Arbeidsbemiddeling (VDAB); in Wallonia, Office de la Formation Professionelle de l'Emploi (FOREM); in Brussels, Office Regional Bruxellois et de l'Emploi (BGDA/ORBEM. Addresses: in Belgian telephone directory.

Private agencies: (Aanwervingsbureaus) offer permanent work, whilst Interimairies or Tijdelijke Abeid offer temporary work. Agencies listed in Yellow Pages (Pages D'or/Gouden Gids).

The T-Service, run by the Belgian employment service also arranges temporary work (offices in every city) (*see* Addresses).

Media: job adverts in newspapers: *Le Soir* and *La Libre Belgique* (French); *De Standaad*, *Het Nieuwsblad*, *De Gazet Van Antwerpen* and *Het Laatste Nieuws* (Dutch); as well as French- and Dutch-language dailies. *The Bulletin* is a weekly English-language journal.

The European Commission based in Brussels is a major employer.

Documentation

Temporary residence permit: (Certificate d'Immatrianlation) valid three months. A temporary residence permit may be renewed for a further three months before a Certificate d'Inscription au Registre d'Etrangers (CIRE) is issued. Individuals must register at local town hall (*maison communale/gemeentehuis*) within eight days of arrival.

Self-employment

There is a compulsory social security scheme for the self-employed which individuals must join within 90 days, unless exempt for up to twelve months by paying UK NI and holding a E101.

Income tax

Income tax (Impôt des Personnes Physiques/ Personenbelasting) is assessed annually. Employer is required to withhold a percentage of monthly income to offset against tax bill at year end. This is known as the Precompte Professional, or Bedrijfsvoorheffing.

Conditions

There exist separate laws for temporary and permanent work. Extensive rights are gained after twelve months' service. Construction workers are not allowed to be employed on a temporary basis. Legal minimum wage for most employment sectors. All employees automatically receive a pay rise every six months linked to the rise in cost of living. *Working week*: 40 hours maximum. Overtime and Sunday working only permitted by special agreement between employer and trade union. *Holidays*: 20 days paid leave in year following 'reference' calendar year. Holiday bonus 85% of one month's salary in agreed employment sector, or two days' paid holiday for each month worked. Statutory rights exist for time off for births, marriages, divorce, deaths, religious festivals, and study.

Addresses

Belgian Embassy, 103 Eaton Square, London SW1W 9AB. 0171-470 3700.
British Embassy, rue d'Arlon, 85 Aarlenstraat, 1040, Bruxelles.
VDAB Head Office, Keizerslaan 11, 1000 Bruxelles.
FOREM, Boulevard de l'Empereur 5, 1000 Bruxelles.
ORBEM/BGDA Head Office, Boulevard Anspach 65, 1000 Bruxelles.
(T-Service) T-Interim, Lemonnierlaan 129-131 1000, Bruxelles.

DENMARK

Job-seeking

JobCentre equivalent: (*arbejdsformidling* (AF)). Addresses: in telephone directory (*navnbogen*) or Yellow Pages (De Gule Sider). HQ: Arbejdsmarkedsstyrelsen, Blegdamsvej 56, Box 2722, DK-2100 Kobenhavn 0. Also a list of JobCentres is available from the Danish Embassy.

Private agencies: (*vikarbureauer*) listed under heading in De Gule Sider. Further information on job-hunting provided by a Youth Information Service programme 'Use It' (*see* Addresses).

Media: job adverts in newspapers: *Politiken*, *Berlingske Tidende* (Sunday issue best), *Jyllands – Posten*, *Borsen*.

Documentation

Residence permit: (*opholdstilladelse*) apply to local police station, or Directorate for Aliens (*see* Addresses). Requirements: having a job which meets government guidelines on hours/salary. Staying in Denmark (non-tourist): requires a personal code certificate number (*personnummer*) which is needed when dealing with Danish authorities. *Personnummer* issued by civil register authorities Folkeregisteret (*see* Addresses). At the same time a social security certificate (*sygesikringsbevis*) is issued which provides access to the public hospital service.

Self-employment

Advice on self-employment available from Danish Employment Service (Arbejdsmarkedsstyrelsen – address above).

Income tax

Income tax (*indkomstskat*) deducted at source; payable to both central/local government. When starting work individuals must obtain a tax card (*skattekort*). Without a *skattekort* stating level of liability, employer must deduct 60% of earnings until one is obtained from local town hall (*radhus*). In Denmark contact local tax office (*skatteforvaltningen*) or Ministry of Taxes (Told og Skattestyrelsen – *see* Addresses).

Conditions

Working week: 37–39 hours set by collective agreement. *Holidays*: minimum of 5 weeks plus 13 days public holiday. *Holiday pay*: (*feripenge*) 12.5% of wages earned during previous year paid by employer to national holiday fund. Employer must ensure employees receive a *feriegiro-kort*, which shows entitlement to holiday pay. Card can be cashed at any post office in Denmark. Further information from FerieGiro (*see* Addresses).

Addresses

Royal Danish Embassy, 55 Sloane Street, London SW1X 9SR. 0171-333 0200.
British Embassy, Kastelsvej 36, 2100 Kobenhavn.
British Council, Gammel Mont 12, 3, 1117 Kobenhavn K.

(Aliens): **Direktorate fur Udlaendinge**, Ryesgade 53, 2100 Kobenhavn.

(Folkeregisteret): **CPR Kontoret**, Datavej 20, Postboks 269, 3460 Birkerod.

(Income Tax): **Told og Skattestyrelsen**, Amaliegade 11, 1256, Kobenhavn K.

'Use It' Youth Information Kobenhavn, Radhusstraede 13, 1466 Kobenhavn K.

FerieGiro, Arbejdsmarkedets Feriefond, Kongens Voenge, 3400 Hillerod.

FINLAND

Job-seeking

JobCentre equivalent: employment offices throughout the country provide nationwide job information. Euro-counsellors in larger municipalities. Self-service terminals enable access to job information. Trained psychologists available to answer questions on choice of profession and education.

Private agencies: addresses in local telephone directory.

Media: job adverts in newspapers: *Helsingin Sanomat*, especially Sunday edition.

Documentation

Residence permit: granted automatically with job/practice/business. Apply at local police station with certificate from employer. For employment lasting less than one year a permit is issued valid one year. Permanent employment: permit valid five years. Moving to Finland: individuals must submit a notice of moving for stays longer than one month. Application forms available at Finnish Post Offices; complete and return within three days of arrival. Subsequent moves to other addresses require new notice. *Population register*: individuals must be entered on the population register in the place of residence. Applications (with residence permit) to municipal or city authority. Once on the register a Finnish social security number is issued.

Seasonal/temporary work/traineeships

Seasonal work: on Finnish farms for those between 18 and 30 years is organised via the International Farm Experience Programme (*see* Addresses), applications three months before departure date. *Temporary work*: Finnish Family Programme (summer) – for those aged 18–23 to teach English to Finnish families (*see* Addresses). *Traineeships* for students 18–30 years old; information available from Finnish Center for International Mobility and Exchange (*see* Addresses).

Self-employment

Advice on self-employment available from Finnish Employment Service. Courses exist on self-employed skills. Possibility of start-up subsidies.

Income tax

Employed less than six months: employer holds 35% of salary at source. No requirement to submit a formal tax declaration. Those employed more than six months: taxed the same as Finnish citizen; tax on income earned in Finland and abroad, and on any property owned abroad. In Finland contact Helsinki Tax Bureau (*see* Addresses).

Conditions

Temporary contracts end without notice when period of employment ends. Otherwise employer gives two months' notice, employees one month. *Minimum salary*: recorded in contract. *Overtime*: with employee's consent. *Holidays*: usually 4–5 weeks per year.

Addresses

Finnish Embassy, 38 Chesham Place, London SW1X 8HW. 0171-235 9531.

British Embassy, Itainen Puistotie 17, 00140, Helsinki.

Ministry of Labour, International Employment Service, Fabianinkatu 32, 00100 Helsinki.

Central Bureau for Educational Visits, Seymour Mews House, Seymour Mews, London W1H 9PE. 0171-389 4004.

The Finnish Center for International Mobility and Exchange, Hakaniemenkatu 2, 00530, Helsinki.

Helsinki Tax Bureau, Haapaniemenkatu, 7–9, 00530 Helsinki, Finland.

FRANCE

Job-seeking

JobCentre equivalent: Agence Nationale pour l'Emploi (ANPE). Offices throughout the country. Addresses: French telephone directory and Yellow Pages (Les Pages Jaunes). HQ: ANPE, Le Galilee, 4 rue Galilee, 95198, Noisy-Le-Grand.

Private agencies: (Agences de Travail Temporaire) cover temporary work only. To register with these a French social security number is required. Apply to local Caisse d'Assurance Maladie.

Media: job adverts in newspapers: *France Soir*, *Le Monde*, and *Le Figaro*. French 'Minitel' computer database service available to all telephone subscribers in France, holds job vacancies.

Documentation

Residence permit: (*carte de sejour*). Apply to local Commissariat de Police or town hall (*mairie*) within one week of arrival, if work has been arranged before leaving UK. If not, as soon as you find work. The *carte de sejour* is valid for the period of contracted employment if the contract is less than twelve months. If longer, issued for five years, and automatically renewable. This becomes invalid if you leave France for more than six months. Contact: French Embassy, or in France, Section Service de Resortissants CEE, in the region in which you are living.

Self-employment

Establishing a firm: contact Agence Nationale pour la Creation d'Entreprise (l'ANCE) of the region. *Trade/cottage industry*: contact local Chambre de Commerce et d'Industrie, or local Chambre des Métiers.

Income tax

No PAYE system. Tax assessed on earnings in one year is payable in the following year. Income tax can be paid monthly/quarterly as an advance on assessment. Further information from French Fiscal Attaché (*see* Addresses). In France, contact local tax office (Centre des Impôts).

Conditions

Statutory minimum wage: Salaire Minimum Interprofessionel de Croissance (SMIC). *Pay*: monthly, sometimes on 13/14-monthly cycle. *Working week*: 39 hours, maximum basic overtime of 9 hours per week. *Holidays*: 30 days (5 weeks).

Addresses

French Embassy, 58 Knightsbridge, London SW1 0171-201 1000.
French Consulate, PO Box 520, 21 Cromwell Road, London SW7 20N 0171 838 2000; and 11 Randolph Cresc., Edinburgh, EH3 7TT 0131-225 7954.
French Fiscal Attaché, 5th Floor, Kingsgate House, 115 High Holborn, London WC1V 6JJ 0171-831 9048.
British Embassy, 35 rue du Fauboug St Honore, 75008, Paris.
British Council, 9 rue Constantine, 75007, Paris.

GERMANY

Job-seeking

JobCentre equivalent: (*Arbeitsamt*) 800 offices throughout the country. Addresses: Yellow Pages (Gelbe Seiter).

Private agencies: addresses in Gelbe Seiter.

Media: job adverts in newspapers: *Hamburger Abendblatt*, *Berliner Morgenpost*, *Die Welt*, *BZ*, *Suddeutsche Zeitung*, *Frankfurter Allgemeine Zeitung*. Weeklies: *Die Zeit*, *Welt am Sonntag*.

Seasonal work

Contact Euroadviser, or write (in German) to Zentralstelle fur Arbeitsvermittlung (ZAV) (*see* Addresses).

Documentation

Residence permit: *Aufenthaltsgenehmigung* or *Aufenthaltserlaubnis*. Residence Registration Office (Einwohnermeldeamt/Meldestelle). Other than hotel accommodation: register at Meldestelle (in town hall) and update subsequent moves at local Meldestelle. Requirements: Passport, lease/rental agreement, application form. Those who intend to stay longer than three months must register with the Foreign Nationals Authority (Auslanderbehorde). Requirements: proof of employment, two passport photos, copy of residents registration and passport (addresses of Meldestelle and Auslanderbehorde in local telephone directory under Stadtverwaltung).

Self-employment:

Self-employed: (*selbständig*) in construction, must register as a meister at a Handwerkskammer (handicraft chamber) and a Gewerbemeldestelle (local trades registration office), or obtain exemption on grounds of equivalent status. Requirements for exemption: copy of qualifications/ Certificate of Experience, apply to Handswerkskammer. For further information in Germany, contact your local JobCentre or Handswerkskammer. Those who work self-employed in the construction industry must register at the Handswerkskammer. Failure to do so can result in large fines.

Income tax

Those who work more than 183 days may be liable for German income tax and must register with the local German tax office (Finanzamt). Check with UK Inland Revenue, or in Germany, with local Finanzamt.

Conditions

Working week: usually 36–40 hours. The construction industry, especially in the former East Germany, is booming; however, there are many problems associated with working there and individuals should proceed with caution.

Addresses

German Embassy, 23 Belgrave Square, London SW1X 8PZ. 0171-824 1300.
British Embassy, Friedrich Ebert Allee 77, D-53113 Bonn.
German Consulate General, 16 Eglington Crescent, Edinburgh EH1Z 5DG. 0131-337 2323.
(Immigration and legislation): **Bundesverwattingsamt**, Marzellenstrasse 50–56,50668 Köln.
British Chamber of Commerce, Heumarkt 14, 50667 Köln.
(Seasonal work): **Zentralstelle fur Arbeitsvermittlung (ZAV)**, Feuerbachstrasse 42–46, D-60325 Frankfurt am Main.

GREECE

Job-seeking

JobCentre equivalent: Organisimos Apasholisseos Ergatikou Dynamikou (OAED). *Addresses*: Telephone directory (*tilepfonikos odigos*). *HQ*: OAED, Eures (SEDOC), Ethnikis Antistasis 8, 16610 A Kalamaki.

Private agencies: those allowed to operate are called Grafia Evresseos Ergassias, listed in Greek Yellow Pages (Chryssos odigos).

Media: job adverts in newspapers: *Ta Nea*, *Eleftheros Tipos*, *Eleftherotipia Apogevmatini*. English-language newspaper: *Athens News*, Lekka Street 23–25, 105 62, Athens.

Documentation

Residence permit: residence permits are usually issued for six months, then renewed for five years. Register with local police within eight days of arrival. A longer stay requires a residence permit. Those intending to work/look for work for between three and twelve months may be issued with a temporary permit. Outside of Athens: register with local police station (*astynomia*). In Athens: register with Aliens Dept. Office (Grafio Tmimatos Allodapon) (*see* Addresses).

Self-employment

Check current registration requirements with Greek Embassy, or in Greece any AOED office.

Income tax

Income tax (*foros issodimatos*) deducted monthly, adjusted annually. Contact Ministry of Finance (Ypourgio Ikonomikon) (*see* Addresses).

In Greece contact local tax office (*efories*).

Conditions

Legal minimum wage for most sectors. *Working week*: 40 hours, overtime and Sunday working restricted. *Holidays*: four weeks after one year's service plus eleven days statutory public holidays.

Addresses

Greek Embassy, 1a Holland Park, London W11 3TP. 0171-229 3850.
British Embassy, 1 Ploutarchou Street, 106 75 Athens.
British Council, Filikis Etrairias 17, Kolonaki Square, 106 73 Athens.
Information on Greek companies: **Emborika & Viomichaniko Epimelitino Athinon, (EBEA)**, Akadimias 7–9, 106 71, Athens; **Aliens Department Office (Grafio Tmimatos Allodapon)**, 173 Alexandras Avenue, Athens.
Ypourgio Ikonomikon Tmima Diethon Scheseon, Sinn Street 2–4, 101 84 Athens.

IRELAND

Job-seeking

JobCentre equivalent: FAS Office (Foras Aiseanna Saothair). Addresses: in Yellow Pages equivalent (Golden Pages). HQ: FAS, 27–33 Upper Baggott Street, Dublin 4.

Private agencies: licensed by the Department of Enterprise and Employment. List of agencies available from: Employment Agencies Section, Department of Enterprise & Employment.

Media: job adverts in newspapers: *Irish Independent*, *Irish Times*, *Irish Press*, *Cork Examiner.*

Documentation

There are no restrictions to EU nationals who wish to live and work in Ireland.

Self-employment

Check current registration requirements with Irish Embassy. In Ireland, check with local FAS office.

Income tax

Income tax is deducted at source. Further information from the Revenue Commissioners (*see* Addresses).

Conditions

No minimum wage. *Working week*: maximum 48hrs/9 hours per day. *Holidays*: minimum of 15 days after 8 months' service but most receive more than this.

Addresses

Embassy of the Republic of Ireland, 17 Grosvenor Place, London SW1X 7HR. 0171-235 2171.
British Embassy, 33 Merrion Road, Dublin 4.
British Council, Newmont House, 22–24 Lower Mount Street, Dublin 2.
Chamber of Commerce in Ireland, 22 Merrion Square, Dublin 2.
Employment Agencies Section, Department of Enterprise & Employment, Davitt House, 65a Adelaide Road, Dublin 2.
The Revenue Commissioners, Dublin Castle, Dublin 2.

ITALY

Job-seeking

JobCentre equivalent: Sezione Circoscrizionale per l'Impiego e il Collocamento in Agricoltura (SCICA). Offices throughout the country. Addresses: of local SCICA in telephone directory under SCICA or Ufficio di Collocamento, or Ufficio del Lavoro e della Massima Occupazione.

Private agencies: None.

Media: Job adverts in newspapers: *Corriere Della Sera*, *La Republica*, *La Stampa*, *Il Sole/24 Ore*, and *Italia Oggi*. Two English-language periodicals (fortnightly) covering Rome area: *Wanted in Rome* and *Metropolitan*. Expat' magazine: *The Informer* (monthly). Subscription: Buro Service, Via le Tigli 2, 20020 Arese, Milano. English Yellow Pages directory contains listings for English-speaking professionals, businesses, organisations, and services. Available from newsagents and bookshops; Rome, Florence, Bologna, Milan.

Documentation

Residence permit: (*permesso di soggiorno*). Report to local police HQ (*questura*) or, in small towns, *commissariato*, within seven days of arrival. The *permesso* enables a stay in Italy for up to three months. After three months apply for extension; renewals through local police or the *questura* in large towns and cities. All renewals on special document paper (*carta bollata*) purchased from tobacconists (*tobacocherie*).

Workers registration card; (*libretto di lovoro*) needed for most types of work. Check with employer or town hall (*municipio*) whether this is required. If it is required it is kept by employer, or individual if unemployed.

Self-employment

Check current registration requirements with Italian Consulate Office, in UK or, in Italy: Camera di Commercio, Industria, Agricoltura e Artigianato (CCIAA).

Income tax

Income tax (Imposta sul Reddito delle Persone Fisiche (IRPEF)) is deducted at source. Starting work: requires tax number (*codice fiscale*) from local tax office (Ufficio Imposte Diretto).

Conditions

Most employment sectors have their own legal minimum wage, set every three years. *Pay*: some sectors divide the annual salary into 14, 15, or 16 payments. Extra month's pay (13th month) in December. *Working week*: maximum 48 hours. Voluntary overtime paid at 130/150% per hour (many unions have agreed overtime bans). *Holidays*: 25–30 days depending on length of service, plus 10 days public holidays.

Addresses

Italian Embassy, 14 Three Kings Yard, London W1 0171-312 2200.
Italian Consulate General, 38 Eaton Place, London SW1 0171-235 9371; and 32 Melville Street, Edinburgh EA3 7HA 0131-226 3631.
British Embassy, Via XX, Settembre 80a, 00187 Roma

LUXEMBOURG

Job-seeking

JobCentre equivalent: l'Administration de l'Emploi. Addresses: in telephone directory (Annuaire Telephonique) or Yellow Pages (Ligne Bleue). HQ: l'Administration de l'Emploi, 38a rue Philippe II, Boite Postal 23, L-2010 Luxembourg.

Private agencies: (Agences de Travail) addresses in Ligne Bleue.

Media: job adverts in newspapers: *Luxembourger Wort*, *Tageblatt*, and *Republican Lorrain*. *Luxembourg News* is an English-language weekly.

Documentation

Residence permit: register with local authority (*administration communale*) and apply for an identity card (*carte identité*) valid five years and serves as a residence permit. Central Luxembourg Office: Accueil des Etrangers, 9 rue Chimay, L-1333, Luxembourg.

Self-employment

Check current registration requirements with Luxembourg embassy, or l'Administration de l'Emploi.

Income tax

Income tax (Impôts sur le Revenue) deducted at source monthly. Annual tax return to balance any excess/underpayment. In Luxembourg contact Administration des Contributions et des Accises (*see* Addresses).

Conditions

Legal minimum wage: fixed twice yearly. *Working week*: maximum 48hrs/10hrs per day. *Holidays*: minimum 25 days after three months' service.

Addresses

Luxembourg Embassy, 27 Wilton Crescent, London SW1X 8SD 0171-235 6961.
British Embassy, 14 Boulevard Roosevelt, L-2450, Luxembourg.
British Chamber of Commerce for Luxembourg, BP2740, L-2740, Luxembourg.
Chambre du Commerce du Grande Duche de Luxembourg, 7 rue Alcide de Gaspers, L-2981, Luxembourg.
Administration des Contributions et des Accises, 45 Boulevard Roosevelt, L-2982, Luxembourg.

NETHERLANDS

Job-seeking

JobCentre equivalent: Arbeidsbureau (AB). AB offices throughout the country. Addresses: in telephone directory and Yellow Pages (Goudon Gids), or list from Central Bureau Voor de Arbeidsvoorziening, Visseringlaan 26, Postbus 415, 2280 AK Rijswijk. Before using the service individuals must: obtain '3-monthly EU Jobseeker stamp' on passport from police; obtain a social insurance (SOFI) number from local tax office. This is required by prospective employers and temporary employment agencies.

Temporary agencies: (Uitzendbureau) for temporary employment for maximum of six months/1000 hours of work. Possible to extend up to one year. 1500 agencies specialise in particular fields of employment. Addresses in Gouden Gids. Temporary agencies require: current CV, residence permit, and if applicable work permit, bank/GIRO number, proof of identity, SOFI number.

Short-term/seasonal employment: apply with six weeks notice to National Office of Employment (*see* Addresses). Other opportunities: bulb-picking, June–October, pay depends on productivity; and farm experience, for those aged 18–21 with a minimum of two years' training or with a practical background in agriculture/horticulture for three- to twelve-month placement (*see* Addresses).

Media: job adverts in newspapers: *De Telegraph*, *Het Algemeen Dagblad*, *De Volksrant*.

Documentation

Contact Netherlands Embassy before leaving the UK. If intending to live in the Netherlands obtain a copy of *New Arrivals to the Netherlands: A General Guide*, available from

British Consulate General (*see* Addresses). *Registration procedure*: register with local Foreign Police Registration Office (Vreemdelingenpolitie) within eight days of arrival. Present passport to look for work under European free movement legislation. Those with a non-temporary work contract must present passport, contract, two non-machine passport-type photos, and a fee. Some with temporary contracts will have to report back for renewal, another fee may be payable. First time job-seekers: must obtain a SOFI number from the local tax office (Belastingdienst), present passport and police permit. *Residence permit*: (Verblijfsvergunning) apply to town hall (Stadhuis) or community office (Gemeente). Requirements: passport, police permit, SOFI number, two photos, full version of birth certificate, proof of permanent address from landlord. On leaving the Netherlands permanently, individuals must deregister with police and town hall.

Self-employment

Check current registration requirements with Royal Netherlands Embassy.

Income tax

Income tax: in the Netherlands contact tax authority (Rijksbelastingen) (*see* Addresses).

Conditions

A two-month probationary period is usual. Either party can terminate without reason. Legislation and policy includes: income agreements, minimum wages, maximum working hours, rest periods, shiftwork and collective wage agreements. Netherlands also has minimum wage and youth wage legislation (revised twice yearly).

Addresses:

Royal Netherlands Embassy, 38 Hyde Park Gate, London SW7 5DP. 0171-584 5040.
British Embassy, Lange Voorhout 10, 25144 ED The Hague.
British Consulate General, Koningslaan 44, 1075 AF Amsterdam.
The Tax Authority (Rijksbelastingen), Stationplein 74, 2515 BX The Hague.
(Short-term work): **National Office of Employment**, Afd: IAD, Eures, PO Box 415, 2280 AK Rijseijk.
(Bulb-picking): **Koninklijke Algemene Vereniging voor Bloembollencultuur 'Bloembollencentrum'**, Postbus 175, 2180 AD Hillegom.
(Farm experience): **International Farm Experience Programme**, National Federation of Young Farmers Clubs, Stoneleigh Park, Kenilworth, Warwickshire CV8 2LJ.

PORTUGAL

Job-seeking

JobCentre equivalent: (Centro do Emprego) administered by the Ministerio de Emprego e Seguranco Social. Addresses: in telephone directory (Lista Telefonika) and Yellow Pages (Paginas Amareles).

Private agencies: Most are based in Lisbon and Oporto. Listed in Paginas Amareles under Pessoal Temporario (temporary), and Pessoal Recrutamento e Seleccao (personnel recruitment and selection).

Media: job adverts in newspapers: *Diario de Noticias*, *Correio da Manha*, *Publico*, *Jornal de Noticias*.

Documentation

Residence permit: (*autorizacao de residencia*) from Foreigners department of the Ministry of Internal Affairs (Servicio de Estrangeiros e Fronteiras (SEF)). *Identity card*: (*bilhete de identidad*) must be carried at all times. Application forms for this from any British Consulate office in Portugal. Completed forms to local parish council (*junta de freguesia*). Individuals should register with British Consul on arrival.

Self-employment

The self-employed are classed as small businesses. A licence may be needed to practise. Contact Portuguese Embassy, or in Portugal, local office of Labour Inspectorate (Inspeccao-general do Trabalho).

Income tax

Income tax: (Imposto Sobre O Rendimento das Pessoas Singulares (IRS)). Self-assessed annually. Returns and payments by 31 May each year. Those paying Portuguese income tax require a fiscal number from the Cartao de Contribuinte which issues a temporary number to begin with. Further information: Direccao-Geral das Contribuicoes e Impostos (DGCI) (*see* Addresses).

Conditions:

All full-time employees receive 13th month extra month salary at Christmas, and 14th month extra at end of June. *Working week*: 44 hours legal maximum. Overtime limit two hours daily/200 hours annually. Overtime rates, 150% first hour, 175% thereafter. *Holidays*: 22 days plus 12 days public obligatory, plus two days optional.

Addresses

Portuguese Embassy, 11 Belgrave Square, London SW12 8PP. 0171-235 5331.
British Embassy, Rua Sao Domingos a Lapa 35-37, 1200 Lisboa.
Portuguese Consulate-General, Silver City House, 62 Brompton Road, London SW3 0171 581 8722.
The Portuguese Consulate, 25 Bernard Street, Edinburgh 0131-555 2080.
DGCI, Rua D Duarte 4, 100 Lisboa.

SPAIN

Job-seeking

JobCentre equivalent: (Oficina de Empleo) are run by the Instituto Nacional de Empleo (INEM). Offices throughout the country. Addresses: telephone directory (*la guia telefonica*).

Private agencies: (Empresas de Trabajo Temporal) cover temporary placings only. Addresses in Yellow Pages (Paginas Amarillas).

Media: job adverts in newspapers: *El Pais*, *ABC*, *El Mundo*, *Diario 16*, *La Vanguardia*, and *Ya*. *Lookout* is an English-language newspaper circulated on the Costa del Sol.

Documentation

Residence permit: (*targeta de residencia*) apply to local police station within fifteen days of arrival. A *gestor* can handle a variety of administration problems including residence permits. *Gestorias* offices are listed in Paginas Amarillas. Prices for their services vary.

Self-employment

If setting up in business, register with local police. Also register with the British Consulate on arrival. Advice on self-employment available from Spanish Consulate (*see* Addresses) before travelling.

Income tax

Income tax (Impuesto Sobre La Renta de las Personas Fisicas (IRPF or *La renta*) is deducted at source, though assessed annually. In Spain contact local tax office or Ministerio de Economia y Hacienda (*see* Addresses).

Conditions

Minimum wage fixed annually by government. Extra payrolls in summer and at Christmas (*pagas extraordinarias*). Employment contracts for indefinite periods. *Working week*: 40 hours. Overtime with employee's consent, but maximum of 80 hours per year, paid at minimum of 175% of hourly rates. *Holidays*: 30 days including Sat and Sun, plus twelve days obligatory national public holidays, plus two days regional public holidays. Paid leave for marriage and maternity.

Addresses

Spanish Embassy, 24 Belgrave Square, London SW1X 8QA. 0171-235 5555.

British Consulate General, Centro Colon, Maques de la Ensenada 16, 2 28004, Madrid.

Spanish Consulate General, 20 Draycott House, London SW3 2RZ. 0171-589 8989.

British Chamber of Commerce in Spain, Plaza Santa Barbera 10, 28010, Madrid.

Ministerio de Economia y Hacienda, C/Alcala 11, Madrid.

SWEDEN

Job-seeking

JobCentre equivalent: (*arbetsformedlingen*) 380 offices throughout the country. Major employment office: Arbetsformedlingen City, Vasagatan 28–34, 101 30 Stockholm, Sweden. Major international office: International Employment Office, Sergels Torg 12, Box 7763, S-10396 Stockholm, Sweden.

Private agencies: (*arbetsformedlingar*) addresses in Yellow Pages, mostly supply office staff. Union agencies supply salaried employees such as engineers.

Media: job adverts in newspapers: *Dagens Nyheter*, *Svenska Dagbladet*, *Dagens Industri*, local regional papers. Employment magazines: *Platsjournalen* and *Nytt jobb* available in employment offices, and via (free) subscription. In Sweden, 'Af-direct' is a free telephone line (English/Swedish) supplying information about vacancies throughout the country. Accessible 9am–7pm weekdays.

Documentation

Residence permit: apply at local police station with proof of employment. If employment is permanent, a residence permit is granted for five years, otherwise for the period of employment.

Self-employment

Check current registration requirements with Swedish Embassy or in Sweden with British–Swedish Chamber of Commerce (*see* Addresses).

Income tax

Most important taxes are local income tax and national tax levied on capital. In Sweden contact Local Tax Office Farsta (*see* Addresses).

Conditions

No statutory minimum wage. *Working week*: 40 hours maximum, or as set by collective agreement. *Holidays*: at least 25 days per year, additional days by collective agreement.

Addresses

Swedish Embassy, 11 Montague Place, London W1H 2AL. 0171-724 2101.

British Embassy, Skarpogatan 6–8, Box 27819, Stockholm.

British–Swedish Chamber of Commerce, Nybrogalan 75, S-11440, Stockholm.

Stockholm Information Service, Box 7542, 103 93, Stockholm.

Local Tax Office Farsta, Box 70297, Folkungagaten, 107 22, Stockholm.

Working for the European Community

The European Community is made up of a number of semi-independent 'bodies', each with separate responsibilities (and recruiting separately). The management of the European Union is entrusted to the Commission which sees that the provisions of the European Treaties are observed and carried out properly, and is also the 'executive' body of the Communities, initiating policy.

The other institutions and bodies are: the Council of the European Union, the European Parliament, the European Court of Justice, the European Court of Auditors, the Economic and Social Committee, and the Committee of the Regions. Between them they employ about 28,000 staff, including: about 8,400 executive/administrative staff, 2,800 linguistic staff, about 5,600 executive assistants, 9,800 secretarial and clerical staff, and about 1,400 service and manual workers.

The majority of jobs (about 18,600) are with the Commission. Most Commission staff work in Brussels, with about 2,000 located in Luxembourg, and a further 600 work in the Commission's offices all over the world in diplomatic, political, technical assistance, or information functions. About 3,500 staff are engaged in research and development, principally in its R&D framework programmes. About 2,000 specialist staff work on research at the different locations of the Commission's Joint Research Centre (JRC): in Ispra (Italy), Karlsruhe (Germany), Seville (Spain), Petten (the Netherlands) and Geel (Belgium).

The Commission is divided into a number of services, and 24 'directorates general', and these indicate the scope of the work. The services include legal, interpreting/conference, statistical, customs union, translation, security, consumer policy and 'spokesman'. The directorates general cover external relations; economic and financial affairs; internal market and industrial affairs; competition; employment, social affairs and industrial relations; agriculture; transport; development; personnel and administration; information, communication and culture; environment, consumer protection and nuclear safety; science, research and development; telecommunications, information industries and innovation; fisheries; financial institutions and company law; regional policy; energy; credit and investments; budgets; financial control; customs union and indirect taxation; coordination of structural policies; enterprise policy, distributive trades, tourism and cooperatives.

All posts are tightly graded and classified:

Category A officials have a university education, deal with policy formation and administration, and advisory work, often political in character. The category divides into 'career brackets' running from A3 (head of division), A4 or 5 (head of specialised service) through the main career brackets A4 to 7. A8 is a new assistant-administrator grade for trainees. In some cases they may also have management or supervisory duties for the work of category B staff. In areas where policy is already developed (e.g. agriculture, trade policy and development), they often have considerable autonomy and responsibility for carrying out Community legislation.

Translators and interpreters are on a parallel structure to category A. Translation (with a few exceptions) is a self-contained unit in personnel and administration. Each division translates into one language, and is further divided into groups specialising in translating material in specified fields. Translators work exclusively into their mother tongue. A 'reviser's' main function is to check translations produced by less-experienced staff. One group deals with terminology and computer applications, and the legal service has its own team of legally qualified translators.

The interpretation–conferences service provides interpreters for all meetings held by the Brussels Commission, the Council of Ministers, the Economic and Social Committee, and the European Investment Bank – which involves servicing over 8,000 meetings a year.

There are various recognised routes for graduates to gain jobs. The EU holds regular 'generalist' competitions for the recruitment of graduates with a degree in any subject, into general administration. Candidates need to have a working knowledge of an EU language other than their own. They participate in a community-wide written and oral test and, if successful, are invited to an interview in Brussels. There is no immediate assurance of a job: names are placed on a 'reserved list' which forms the basis of subsequent selection. Although any subject is acceptable, law or economics, preferably with a European Studies bias, are still the most useful disciplines for a career in the European Community institutions. The government provides help to all British candidates for competitions, whether or not they are civil servants, by offering seminars and reading lists and giving advice and support in the lobbying process for those on the 'reserved list'.

There may also be bursaries for postgraduate courses in European Studies. Another possible way in is the *stagiaire* programme, a short training scheme designed to give new graduates up to five months' work experience in EU institutions, in either an administrative or a linguistic capacity – not, however, a guarantee of a permanent job. These opportunities exist at the Commission, the Council, the Parliament, and at the Economic and Social Committee. Recruitment procedures vary considerably since each institution makes its own arrangements.

Some countries have their own graduate training schemes. The British Civil Service, for instance, selects up to 30 graduates a year for the 'European Fast-Stream'. Help is given to these recruits to prepare for the EU recruitment competitions, entering into the administrative A grade. They are offered a programme of relevant work experience in British government departments as well as related training, including language training, EU study visits and courses on European issues. Although European success is not guaranteed, a career in the British Civil Service is assured. (*See also* CENTRAL GOVERNMENT.) Graduates and final-year undergraduates from all disciplines are eligible, providing they hold or expect to hold a first- or second-class honours degree. For entry into A8 competitions, there is an upper age limit of 32 and often a limit to the number of years after graduation during which application may be made – usually three. A7 posts require at least two years' experience after graduation, relevant to the institutions' activities. The age limit for the Commission's competition is 35, but this can be relaxed in certain circumstances such as having taken time off to have a baby. Although administrators do need to be able to work effectively in both French and English, the institutions do offer good language-training facilities to new recruits.

Category B post-holders are responsible for executive tasks, assisting in the implementation of policy, and in internal management, notably in budgetary and financial affairs or personnel work, computing or librarianship.

Category C posts are mainly secretarial and clerical, whilst Category D employees deal with service and manual tasks, such as messengers, drivers, catering, and workshop staff.

Recruitment and entry

The Commission recruits via open competitions to fill existing or future vacancies as and when needed. The Commission has said that there is a shortfall of British applicants.

All staff must have a thorough working knowledge of one Community 'working language' (which can be their mother tongue). A satisfactory knowledge of a second EU language is required, though formal language qualifications are not a prerequisite (nor is fluency). Successful candidates may be offered intensive language training on recruitment.

For category A posts, a university degree is required, preferably in the subject area of the post(s) in question, e.g. economics, law, finance, administration, agriculture, social science, statistics, computer science or languages. For e.g. scientific posts, the requirement may be more specific, e.g. in nuclear sciences. Interpreters must be able to work in at least three Community languages. Entry to A7 requires at least two years' relevant experience after graduating, with an upper age limit of 35. For A8, no experience is required, but candidates must have graduated within the previous three years, and be under 32.

Category B posts need proof of advanced secondary education as well as some relevant experience, normally in administration, accounting, archives, documentation, computing, or statistics. Upper age limit 35.

Category C posts need proof of secondary education, with training and/or experience in typing/secretarial work, general office/clerical assistant work, childcare or telex/telephone work. C-grade recruitment may be organised on a language basis for typists and secretarial officers, with separate competitions for each of the official EU languages. Upper age limit 35.

Category D staff must have completed the basic course of compulsory national education. The Commission also recruits graduates as temporary trainees – called *stagiaires* – to work for three to five months, which can help in gaining a permanent post later on.

Qualifications and training

Throughout their careers, staff can take advantage of extensive training opportunities – courses in economics, law, computing, word processing, negotiating techniques, and management development, and seminars for secretaries, are examples. Translators and interpreters are given additional training as and when needed. Almost all training helps with career development, preparing staff for possible future moves.

Other 'bodies'

The Council of Ministers

The Council of Ministers coordinates policies and activities of the member states and of the Community. The Council is supported by a secretariat of 2,360 staff, of whom about 280 are A-grade administrators and 530 LA-grade translators.

The European Parliament

The European Parliament is the directly elected body considering and giving opinion on Commission proposals. As a result of the Treaty of Maastricht, the Parliament has the right of co-decision with the Council in certain areas. In these areas, legislation cannot be adopted if the Parliament does not approve it. It also has a direct role in the appointment of the Commission. Parliament meets in Strasbourg and Brussels. Its secretariat is located in Luxembourg. There are 420 A-grade officials in a staff of 3,800.

The Court of Justice

The Court of Justice sees Community law is implemented, checks the legality of Community actions, and deals with references by national courts for preliminary rulings on matters of Community law. Based in Luxembourg, the court has 750 permanent staff including 120 A grades. Most court staff need a legal background.

The Court of Auditors

The Court of Auditors, responsible for supervising the EU's budget, is also based in Luxembourg. It employs 450 staff, of whom 200 are A-grade officials.

The Economic and Social Committee

The Economic and Social Committee is made up of representatives of the various areas of economic and social activity throughout the Community, giving opinion on Commission proposals in its area of responsibility.

Further information

The European Commission, and the other institutions listed above.

Short-term opportunities and temporary work

This may simply be a way of financing an extended working vacation 'to see the world', a way of having an enjoyable time before settling down to a 'serious' career or before starting a full-time course, e.g. for a degree. International work camps, working on an Israeli kibbutz (perhaps also learning Hebrew), taking a 'working holiday' in Australia, or seasonal tourist-based work are all possibilities. Or this may be part of a career plan – gaining extra experience, faster promotion, fluent use of one or more languages. Another choice is to do some form of service to an underdeveloped country, although this now usually means having a needed skill. Making sure that a period abroad will be a career advantage, and that it will not mean missing opportunities – just by coming back to the UK at the wrong time of year, for instance – is very important, though.

One alternative is to choose a career in which regular, if short, periods abroad are usual or can be arranged relatively easily. They range from SELLING (*see in* BUYING, SELLING AND RELATED CAREERS) to film-making, and also include, e.g., academic work – university staff regularly spend periods abroad, studying, doing research, on sabbatical leave, advising developing countries, external examining, lecturing, on British Council business. Some opportunities exist to work for overseas governments on short-term contracts to fill particular gaps in their services, and for which local candidates with the right qualifications are not yet available. The international and other institutions and organisations described above also have limited numbers of openings for people to work on short-term contracts. These vary from year to year, often according to demand.

Other organisations recruiting on a short-term basis include four independent voluntary societies which send suitably qualified volunteers overseas in response to requests from developing countries. The main areas of work are education, health, technical trades, crafts and engineering, agriculture, social, community and business development. All volunteers are now skilled and/or qualified people: teachers, doctors, nurses (including nurse tutors), electricians, accountants, civil engineers, builders and building craftworkers, technical education trainers, agricultural experts, water engineers, mechanics, medical lab technicians, small enterprise managers, etc.

These societies are *Skillshare Africa* (mainly southern Africa, some West Africa and Asia), the *United Nations Association International Service* (mainly Latin America, Africa and the Middle East), the *CIIR Overseas Programme* (same areas as UN), and *Voluntary Service Overseas* (mainly Africa, Asia, the Caribbean, Papua New Guinea, and the Pacific).

The minimum period of service is normally two years, and some people stay for three or four. While people are recruited for specific work, they usually get involved in many other activities. Volunteers are generally expected to train local people to take over their work and keep the project going after volunteers go home.

Other organisations sending volunteers abroad – again mainly appropriately qualified people in fairly small numbers (mostly they recruit local people or spend through local organisations) – include *Oxfam, Save the Children Fund,* and *Christian Aid.*

Overseas Development Administration (ODA)

The ODA manages Britain's programme of aid to developing countries. As ODA, in partnership with the country concerned, focuses on practical ways of meeting their most pressing needs, the range of skills required is vast and changes all the time.

The people who work under the British aid programme are drawn from a very wide range of backgrounds and professions, and the following list, although not exhaustive, gives an idea of the variety of professional disciplines from which experienced people may be needed: agriculture, architecture, education, engineering, finance, fisheries, forestry, health and population, management, social development, and surveying.

The minimum requirement for most vacancies with the aid programme is usually a professional qualification, such as a good first degree, coupled with two or three years' relevant experience, preferably in a developing country.

Successful applicants are usually offered assignments of up to two or three years' duration. This can either be as a technical cooperation officer employed by ODA on loan to the relevant overseas government or as a supplemented officer, under contract to the overseas government, whose local salary is supplemented by ODA to bring it up to the appropriate UK level.

Consultants, either registered self-employed or working for consultancy companies, who specialise in areas where ODA needs immediate expert advice, are also used. This type of appointment can last for anything from a few days to several months.

Further information

The organisations mentioned above.

Contents

Women at Work

Setting the scene

'Why should half of our population go through life like a hobbled horse in a steeplechase?' asked John Major at the launch in October 1991 of Business in the Community's Opportunity 2000. At that point over 60 leading employers had joined the scheme and pledged to boost opportunities for women at all levels within their organisations by the year 2000.

By November 1995 membership of Opportunity 2000 had risen to 293. Many improvements have taken place since its inception, but further improvement is vital. 'Women really are beginning to break through the glass ceiling', said Lady Howe, chairman, at the launch of Opportunity's fourth-year report.

In recent years many more women than men have entered the labour force. Today 12.1 million women are economically active and 70% of all women of working age are at work or seeking work. For women with higher qualifications this figure rises to 80%.

Women account for 45% of the total labour force, the highest in any country except Denmark, and will account for 1.3 million of the projected total rise of 1.6 million in the labour force by 2006. The forecast is that the majority of jobs in the next few years will be taken by women with family responsibilities; at present 68% of working women are married or cohabiting. It is normal for a woman to work full-time until the birth of her first child and she is far more likely than her mother to return to work after the birth.

More women than men are employed in non-manual occupations: 85% of all female employees and 92% of female part-time employees are in service sectors of industrial divisions; 18% (14% male) of full-time employees are in banking, finance and insurance, etc.; 16% (15% male) are in distribution, hotels and restaurants; 47% (29% male) are in 'other services' including transport, communication, public administration and health; 25% of women work in clerical and secretarial occupations, 31% in managerial and professional (about 33% of whom are employed in associated professional and technical occupations as, for example, health associate professionals such as nurses or scientific technicians).

Over 80% of part-timers and 54% of temporary employees are women. A large proportion of those who work part-time are sales or checkout assistants or in other sales occupations. Catering and health and related occupations form other important sources of part-time employment. Part-time working in management is possible, too. Women are very much in a minority in areas such as the chemical industry, air transport and electrical and electronic engineering.

In its *Occupational Assessment, 1994–2001*, the Institute of Employment Research at Warwick University says that the labour force is projected to rise steadily over this period. Most of the additional jobs are expected to be taken by women and to be part-time. Male full-time employment is expected to decline. The growth of the service sector has benefited job prospects for women while the decline in primary and manufacturing industries has led to the loss of full-time jobs for men.

There will be a growth in high-skill, white-collar employment (especially for women) and a decline in low-skilled, manual jobs. Considerable growth is projected for personal and protective services. This reflects the growth expected in services such as leisure, tourism, health and education. Another projection is an increase of over 600,000 managerial jobs, with especially large increases for women.

Fewer women than men become self-employed, but the number has risen by 84% since 1981. In 1990 only 7% of women in employment were self-employed, although more than double the figure for 1979 (3%). Altogether, over 400,000 additional self-employed persons were projected between 1994 and 2001.

How do self-employed women fare? *Women in the Workforce*, published by the Industrial Society in 1990, maintained that female entrepreneurs showed a greater success rate than men in keeping their businesses going. They had moved into fields such as market research, advertising, PR, publishing, design, computer software, management consultancy, and so on.

Arline Woutersz, National President of the British Association of Women Entrepreneurs, comments: 'Women build on concrete, not sand. They do not take out large bank loans. And they don't buy Porsches.'

Women's pay rose appreciably in the early 1970s as a result of the Equal Pay Act, but they still tend to lose out. In April 1994 women's average hourly earnings (excluding overtime) were 75.9% of men's, and their average weekly earnings (including overtime) 72.2%.

Women and education

Today, girls are more likely than boys to leave school with a qualification. In all the first assessment tests they matched or outperformed boys. In 1993/94 48% of girls achieved five or more GCSE grade A–C compared with 39% of boys. More girls than boys stay on in full-time education or training after 16. Latest figures show that 31% of 17-year-olds achieved two or more A- or AS-levels compared with 26% of boys.

Women are now in a majority in higher education. In 1995 there were 123,926 female applicants accepted onto university degree courses compared with 116,784 males. Unfortunately, girls are to a great extent shunning maths, science and technology at higher levels. Twice as many boys as girls take A-level maths, and in physics and technology the proportions are over 3:1 and 4:1 respectively. In engineering there are seven times as many men as women graduates; in physical sciences twice as many; and in maths and computing science three times as many. There are proportionately more women than men students enrolled in higher education to study medicine, dentistry, biological sciences and languages.

Today's young women are, however, much better educated than their mothers. In spring 1993 over four-fifths of women aged 16 to 24 had some sort of educational qualification compared with just over three-fifths of those in their forties and just under half of those in their fifties.

Women at the top

Despite their increased qualifications, women are sadly under-represented in top jobs in business.

Women certainly do better if employed by companies subscribing to Opportunity 2000. The percentage of women directors in member organisations has doubled in one year from 8 to 16%, while the percentage of women in senior management was up from 12 to 17% and middle managers from 24 to 28%.

It is difficult to arrive at a precise figure for the country as a whole. The National Management Salary Survey, published by the Institute of Management in April 1995, revealed that the number of female managers was up to 10.7% from 9.5%, while the number of women in the boardroom had reached a new peak of 3%. The most popular jobs for women were in personnel and marketing, with the least popular being research and development, manufacturing and production.

Although there had been but a modest increase in the number of female directors in the past 12 months, the number employed by companies in the over-£600-million turnover range continued to rise. The 1993 survey noted that, for the first time, the database included one female director in this turnover range, which number had doubled by 1994. The current survey showed a further increase – five of the 31 female directors covered by the survey being employed by five different companies with a sales turnover in excess of £600 million. Two of the five were personnel directors, two marketing directors, and the fifth concerned with general management and administration.

In a survey *Women on the Board of Britain's Top 200 Companies*, published by Ashridge Management Research Group, 1993, Viki Holton, senior researcher, revealed that 49 (25% of *The Times* Top 200 companies surveyed) had women directors.

This was a disappointingly small proportion of the total population of directors. A statistic that had remained constant was that just over 80% of women directors were non-executive, holding part-time appointments. Only eleven women identified in the 1993 survey were executive directors, and only one of those had the most senior job in the company.

Specialist backgrounds of the women directors identified in the Ashridge Survey included law, information technology and, in particular, finance. Five of the eleven had finance responsibilities or a financial background.

Over half the companies with women directors were Opportunity 2000 campaigners: Rank Xerox UK, ICI, Kingfisher, British Airways, the Post Office and J Sainsbury were among the founding companies who launched the campaign in 1992.

The factors that hold women back

What does hold women back? It may be the conflicting demands of work and marriage, perhaps the problem of a two-career family. Who gives in if one is asked to move to another part of the country? Often women find it necessary to postpone having children until established in a career. And when children arrive, more problems occur. According to the Equal Opportunities Commission, domestic responsibilities result in 23% of women in their late twenties remaining outside the labour market, compared with virtually none of their male counterparts.

Jo Gardiner, campaign manager of the Industrial Society, mentions a number of other factors, including sex stereotyping (perpetuated through media, advertising and press images); the assumption that women's skills are different from men's, and the expectation that they will bear the primary caring responsibility. Practical issues include: the long-hours culture prevalent in many organisations; the lack of affordable, accessible child and eldercare facilities; and the assumption that choosing flexible or discontinuous working patterns means lacking commitment.

Having a family can certainly finish a woman's hopes of a senior management career unless the employer is understanding, provides career breaks with an opportunity to keep in touch, and guarantees that a job at the same level as before will be available when the woman returns.

Happily, there are more employers such as this. Opportunity 2000 reported in 1995 that there had been considerable rises in the numbers of members offering flexible hours, homeworking, job-sharing, and paternity leave.

Part-time working is more generally acceptable, too. In 1994 the ban on working part-time in the police was lifted. Now officers up to the rank of superintendent are able to work part-time, allowing them to combine their police work with family and educational commitments.

In 1992 we commented that one of the reasons for women failing to progress was that they tended to miss out on training. That is not so true now. The Labour Force Survey shows that in 1994 15% of women of working age received training or education, compared with 14% of men. Occupational groups receiving the most training were professionals (31% females, 26% males) and associate professional and technical (29% females, 26% males).

But the playing field is still not level. The Equal Opportunities Commission says there is a clear gender difference in the nature of employment-related training undertaken, with the traditional segregation in occupations still evident.

Women can be their own worst enemies. Some do not set their sights high enough. Women are very much in the majority in teaching but under-represented in senior positions. Researchers at Manchester School of Management found that women teachers suffered from lack of confidence and self-esteem. They needed help to develop more positive attitudes. However, their share of promotions is increasing: in 1992/93 77% of senior positions in primary schools were held by women, compared with 63% in 1985/86, and 37% in secondary schools compared with 31% six years earlier. Women are also well-represented on school governing bodies.

Women in the workplace

The Civil Service is an equal-opportunity employer – Women under-represented in top local government posts – Women in the NHS – Women and the law – Not enough women scientists and engineers – Women in information technology – Women in business – Part-time employment increases in retailing – A changing climate in hotel and catering – The BBC a model employer – Only three women edit national newspapers – No discrimination against women in public relations – Women in the air – The police and the prison service – Women today

The Civil Service is an equal-opportunity employer

Where do the best opportunities lie for women? Some would mention the Civil Service. Women form 51.3% of non-industrial staff, but the numbers of women entering and working in the Civil Service in science, engineering and technology are still low compared to men. Of the Professional and Technology group entrants 10% were women in 1994 and about 2% of current staff.

In 1984 a programme of action on equal opportunities for women was launched. Today, 47% of the first management level in the Service are women, compared with 29% in 1984.

Now nearly 10% of posts in the top three grades are filled by women (4% in 1984) compared with the current private-sector average of 3–4%. Departments with the highest ratio of women in grades 1–7 are Crown Prosecution Service, Crown Office, Department of Health, Office of Public Censuses and Surveys, and Lord Chancellor's Department.

While women form nearly 50% of the executive officer grade – the first management level – there is significant under-representation of women at higher executive level. There is a fall in the proportion of women in clerical work at the administrative assistant level from 79% in 1984 to 70% in 1994.

Women are well represented in administration but less so in other disciplines. Numbers recorded in engineering, science and research have fallen, but 419 women (at grade 7 equivalent or above) work in the government legal service. Women form 13% of total qualified accountants; 20% of economists in economist posts; and there are 222 women in the government statistical service.

A few more women have been appointed to the very top jobs. Jenny Bacon was in 1995 appointed director-general of the Health and Safety Executive, which has 4,700 staff (including 228 women inspectors) and a budget of £190 million. The other women permanent secretaries are Stella Rimington, head of MI5; Valerie Strachan, who heads Customs and Excise; Barbara Mills, Director of Public Prosecutions; and Ann Bowtell in the Department of Social Security.

A Civil Service benchmark has been set up to achieve at least 15% women in the top three grades by the year 2000.

Among initiatives to achieve equality of opportunity are 46 workplace nurseries and over 120 holiday play schemes; enhanced maternity leave; career breaks lasting up to five years with formal keeping-in-touch schemes; a wider range of flexible working patterns, including part-time working, job-sharing and term-time working.

The proportion of women working part-time has more than trebled over ten years from 6 to 18%, (49,000 in all). This is no bar to promotion. At grade 3 (senior management) today, 62 women work part-time compared with three in 1984.

Until 1972 women in the Diplomatic Service had to resign on marriage. The effect of this change is beginning to be felt. The majority of women (one-third of the total staff) are still employed in the more junior grades but numbers of those who reach the senior grades are expected to increase considerably. Of the 2,000 people who applied for the 1995 fast-stream intake, 21 have been accepted, of whom 12 are women.

There are now women ambassadors to the Holy See, Dublin, Beirut, Cote d'Ivoire, Usbekistan, Belarus and Bwanda. The youngest, Jessica Pearce, 38, was to take up her post in Belarus in January 1996.

Women under-represented in top local-government posts

Women outnumber men in local government (67% of the workforce), but the top echelons are still dominated by men. In 1995 there were only 30 women chief executives, 5% of the total. In 1993 there were just six.

A Local Government Management Board survey shows that, in 1995, women chief officers formed 7% of the total (6% in 1993); deputy chief officers 11% (10% in 1993). The greatest number of women chief officers were found in social services (20%); education (15%); legal services (16%); libraries (18%); IT/computer services (14%).

The representation of women reflects their representation in the professions generally, with 62% of teaching professionals being women; and 69% of librarians/related professions.

This continuing under-representation of women has led the LGMB to set up a Women's Leadership Programme. This is targeted on women managers who do not currently occupy chief executive, chief officer and similar posts, and who are seeking further development. This is a companion to the Top Managers Programme, which is targeted on women and men chief executives and chief officers.

What is being done to help women below management level to prepare for the next stage of their career? The situation is patchy; each local authority is to a large extent a law until itself. Only 25 belong to Opportunity 2000 and they, one must assume, pursue good equal opportunities policies.

Many authorities use the Springboard programme, which helps women to make career plans. Birmingham City Council and others have introduced work-shadowing schemes. These allow women employees to shadow senior managers, to see how a woman can succeed in such an area. Glasgow City Council, unhappy that women were still significantly under-represented at all levels above clerical and junior administrative posts, despite positive action, carried out a survey to discover the remaining barriers to women's development and progress.

METRA (The Metropolitan Authorities Recruitment Agency) does a great deal to help local authorities to exploit the full potential of their existing workforce. They have produced a directory of the achievements of the best authorities and a number of publications, including *Do it! Walk the Talk*, advising employers how to change the gender culture in the workplace.

METRA's director, Carl Gilleard, says, 'The conclusion we have drawn is that it isn't sufficient just to have equal opportunities policies in place. We need to look at the working culture of the organisation, and that has to change. It is one of the most invisible glass ceilings but one of the most difficult to penetrate because it is to do with tradition and attitudes and working practices.'

Women in the NHS

Another public-sector employer, the Health Service, is the largest civilian employer in Europe. About four in five of its 1.5 million employees are women.

The Department of Health was the first government department to sign up for Opportunity 2000, and a ministerial campaign was launched in June 1991 to put women's employment issues on the main NHS managerial agenda. This set a number of goals, and by 1995 achievements were as follows:

- Women were appointed to 38% (i.e. 85 out of 219) chief executive/general manager posts in the 33 months period to 31 March 1995.
- 28% of chief executive or general manager posts were held by women; this represented an increase of 10% in the five-year period from September 1989 to December 1994.
- 47.5% of senior manager posts were held by women at 30 September 1994, an increase of 16.4% in the five-year period from September 1989.
- The number of women directors of finance had almost quadrupled, from 23 in December 1992 to 84 at 31 December 1994.
- 38.6% of non-executive posts were filled by women, exceeding the 1994 goal of 35%. The number of women chairing NHS Trusts had risen from 8% in the first wave to 30.6% in the fourth wave.
- The proportion of women consultants increased by 5% in a ten-year period, from 12% in 1983 to 17% in 1993. Although overall progress on Goal 3 fell short of the target, higher percentages of women in the junior grades suggested that this percentage was set to rise further.
- 72% of nurse executive director posts were now filled by women. The gap between men and women is closing, and both are taking less time to reach posts at senior nurse level.

A revised set of goals has been agreed by ministers for achievement in the next three-year period to 30 September 1998. These include increasing the numbers of women in general management posts; of qualified woman accountants to 40%; and of women consultants to 22% by 30 September 1998; and increasing representation of women as members of authorities and trusts to 44% and of women chairmen to 30%.

The NHS also intends to provide systematic programmes allowing women aspiring to management positions to go through a career development centre with a view to establishing their own personal development needs.

Still only a few women consultants

Though women represent 50% of those entering medical school, they are still very much under-represented in consultant posts. In *Doctors and their Careers: a New Generation* published by the Policy Studies Institute in 1994,

Dr Isobel Allen gives many reasons. Here we can refer to only a few.

The book is a study of doctors qualifying in 1986. Many felt that the medical career structure and the way careers were organised were major factors not only in preventing women from maximising their contribution to medicine but also in inhibiting the progress of those unable to follow a straight career structure.

Although equal proportions of men and women were working in general practice at the time of the interviews, it appeared that men qualifying in 1986 were more than twice as likely as the women to have reached GP principal grade. In a 1988 study it was found that equal proportions of men and women were working as registrars and senior registrars in hospital medicine; in the 1994 study 34% of men and only 17% of the 1986 women were working as registrars. In some ways, women were doing less well than a few years earlier.

Half the men and three-quarters of the women complained of long hours and on-call responsibilities. They also felt that the constant uprooting and geographical mobility essential for young doctors were a strain, particularly if they were married, and even more so when there were dual careers. Marriage and children were often thought of as constraints upon the careers of women doctors.

Women also found themselves discriminated against, losing jobs because of their sex. They were asked questions at interviews which the men were never asked. Did they intend to marry? Did they intend to have children?

Women doctors were more likely than men to want to work less than full-time. And it has to be remembered that in medicine, a part-time post often involves longer hours than a full-time post in another type of career.

Initiatives to help women doctors

The Department of Health has introduced a number of initiatives designed to help overcome the obstacles faced by women doctors. Junior doctors' hours have been reduced. There are some part-time postgraduate training facilities, a shorter training time for specialist practice, and a certain number of part-time career posts. But not nearly enough.

Of women in 1986 only 5% had part-time training posts and only 3% were currently in a part-time training post, considerably lower percentages than for women qualifying in 1966.

Dr Allen found almost universal support among both sexes for more to be done to help women doctors to continue working while they had small children. Help should also be given to those who wanted to return to work after a break, with opportunities to rise to senior positions. It was a waste of resources to ignore the fact that women had special needs.

Women dentists and their problems

Women form about one quarter of just over 25,000 dentists on the dental register. Like men, the majority are in general dental practice, which provides greater flexibility and the possibility of part-time work.

One of the difficulties women face is that no part-time posts exist in the hospital service. There are reports of men being interviewed for posts that women had been told were filled and a reluctance to consider women because their career patterns do not fit the male norm. In general practice, they are now legally obliged to provide emergency cover for their patients. For those with young children, particularly single parents, this can be difficult.

According to a ten-year review published in 1985 of the provision of dental care by women dentists, postponing having children until a woman is more established in practice and has consolidated her skills is an emerging pattern.

Dentists as well as doctors have a keeping-in-touch scheme for anyone taking a career break. Maternity allowances mean that those working in the NHS can take 13 weeks' paid leave when it most suits them.

There are now two female professors in dentistry: Dorothy Geddes and Edwina Kidd.

Women and the law

There seems little room at the top for women lawyers. In 1992 Barbara Mills was appointed as director of public prosecutions, but women are still poorly represented in the higher reaches of the law. There are twelve male Lords of Appeal in Ordinary, no women; five male heads of divisions, no women; 31 male Lords Justices of Appeal, one woman; 88 male high court judges, 7 women; 485 male circuit judges, 29 women; 843 male recorders, 54 women; 291 male assistant recorders, 50 women; 288 male district judges, 33 women; 620 male deputy district judges, 98 women; 43 metropolitan stipendiary magistrates, 9 women; 36 male provincial stipendiary magistrates, 4 women; 60 male assistant recorders in training, 15 women.

The percentage of women solicitors on the Roll maintained by the Law Society has grown from 26% in July 1991 to 29% (24,447 out of 79,919). The proportion of women applicants accepted onto university law degree courses continues to rise (now about 53%). Once they qualify, 78% go into private practice, but of 26,110 partners only 3,706 are women. Six per cent of women go into commerce and industry and 10% into the public sector (more in both cases than men). Out of a total of 75 members of the Council of the Law Society, just eight are women, and there are 11 women presidents of local law societies (total 125).

In 1994, out of a total of 1,445 called to the Bar, 629 (43%) were women. Of 8,498 practising barristers on 1 October 1995, 1,900 were women. On the same date there were 4,346 men and 57 women Queen's Counsel in independent practice in England and Wales.

At a London Law Fair, a woman solicitor and a woman barrister emphasised that if women were to make their mark in the law they must make themselves very visible, be flexible, and plan their careers as did men. After about four years they usually had to decide whether to have children and when, and how they were going to cope on their return. It was essential to organise reliable childcare. You could not leave a meeting halfway through or walk out of court in order to collect your children from school.

Both branches of the profession are anxious to improve women's prospects. There is a growth of part-time work, and part-time articles are now possible for trainee solicitors. In 1977 the Association of Women Solicitors pioneered refresher courses to assist women returning to practice, and a Law Society working party on women's careers has made several recommendations.

But in 1995 the Association reported very slow progress. The admission of women had gone up tremendously, but by a certain age many dropped out because of children. However, draft maternity clauses had been introduced, and anti-discrimination measures, which have now become a practice rule.

The Association of Women Barristers has about 400 members. Susan Ward, its vice-president, says, 'I think there is a significant degree of prejudice and inequality both in the type of work that women get and opportunities they get for career advancement. But I don't think it is necessarily any greater than in any other profession or life in general.'

The Association has set up a dialogue between themselves and the Bar Council and the Lord Chancellor's Department, aimed at increasing the number of women selected for judicial appointments. They are also trying to get more women appointed as Queen's Counsel. A new student group advises women students coming into the profession, and speakers are sent to universities to talk about equal opportunities.

The Lord Chancellor himself, at a day on 'Women and the Law' set up under the aegis of the Law Society and the Bar Council in April 1995, emphasised that all judicial appointments were made solely on merit. He added that he had taken steps to encourage applications from women and to ensure that all who applied for judicial office were considered fairly.

Not enough women scientists and engineers

Women are still very much under-represented in science and engineering. The figures below are taken from the Labour Force Survey of Spring 1994:

	women in workforce	% of total
scientists		
chemists	6,253	19
biological scientists and biochemists	19,557	36
physicists, geologists, etc.	3,994	24
other natural scientists	9,689	39
engineers		
civil, structural, etc.	2,226	3
mechanical	1,772	3
electrical	447	1
electronic	373	2
software	8,305	14
chemical	938	11
design and development	3,246	4
process and production	609	3
planning and quality control	8,225	13
other, and technologists	5,705	9
pharmacists, pharmacologists	*18,451*	*59*
ophthalmic opticians	*3,120*	*39*

The Institute of Physics reports that out of a total of 3,000 undergraduates, 16–17% are women. The Royal Society of Chemistry says that the percentage of female chemistry graduates in the old universities is increasing (1994 26.6%; 1988 22.2%), and that the percentage of females achieving higher degrees in chemistry is smaller than at first degree but is still increasing.

Moves to encourage women into science and engineering

Every effort is being made to persuade more girls to pursue careers in these fields. The Women Into Science and Engineering campaign (WISE) was launched in 1984 by the Engineering Council and the Equal Opportunities Commission. Since then the numbers of women studying engineering in higher education have risen from 7%, to 15% in 1995.

The government is promoting the role of women in science, engineering and technology, too, and a development unit within the Department of Trade and Industry provides advice to individuals and to employers.

Its 1995 publication *Making the Most* includes case studies of six organisations which are making the most of women specialists and highlights the business benefits which this is bringing to them. At the launch of the booklet, Ian Taylor, Science and Technology Minister, said, 'Too few of our bright young women choose careers in science and engineering. And for those who have, too many have been unable to fulfil their potential due to working policies and practices which are unfavourable to those with family responsibilities.'

We few . . .

Though things haven't necessarily been easy for them, many outstanding women have broken through the glass ceiling to achieve considerable success.

In 1994 Jennie Poulton was the winner of the Young Women Engineer of the Year Award, sponsored by the Institution of Electronics and Electrical Incorporated Engineers (IEEIE). Apprenticed to GEC Telecommunications, she obtained her HNC in Telecommunications in 1987. Now 29, she is Senior Project Manager at GPT Strategic Communications Systems, and is managing the communications contract for the Hong Kong Mass Transport Corporation extension to the new airport.

Civil engineering has tended to be thought of as male-dominated, but women do rise to the top in construction companies like Tarmac or Ove Arup, and many successfully manage large construction projects both at home and overseas. For example, Josephine Parker is Control Manager, Provinces, Thames Water Utilities and through Red R, the engineering for emergency relief organisation, she has been to Sarajevo and Afghanistan, reinstalling their water supplies.

Women scientists too have made their mark. Dianne Edwards, Professor of Geology at University College, Wales, is a leading authority on fossil research. Jocelyn Bell Burnell, Professor of Physics at the Open University, was involved in the discovery of pulsars, and Kay Davies, the Professor of Genetics at Oxford, played a crucial role in targeting the gene responsible for Duchenne muscular dystrophy. Women also successfully combine science with management skills to carve out very successful careers in industry. For example, Dr Eileen Read, who obtained a PhD in Physics at Lancaster, is now Director and General Manager of GEC-Marconi Infra-Red (the UK's largest supplier of Infra-Red detectors) and was voted European Woman of Achievement in the Business Section for 1995.

Meteorology is another field in which women seem to excel. Eleven of the 35 trained Met Office forecasters are women, Suzanne Charlton on the BBC being one of the best-known.

Women in information technology

The relatively new field of information technology (IT), with no traditional barriers to break down, seemed in the early 1960s to promise so much for women. Latest information about how well or badly they are faring is found in *Riding The Whirlwind*, 1995 Skills Trends Report produced by Philip Virgo, IT Strategy Services Director of Winsafe Ltd, for the Institute of Data Processing Management, Computer Weekly 500 Club, and the Women into IT Foundation.

Singapore, the most advanced society in the use of IT, is the only nation where women make up the majority (55%) of the professional (analysts and programmers) IT workforce. This compares with only 21–22% in the UK over the past two or three years.

The proportion of girls entering UK computer science courses was only 17% in 1994. The reasonable assumption is that the low proportion of women actually working in IT is likely to be due to 'endemic stereotyping' in the UK education system rather than discrimination on the part of employers. However, the UK IT industry does not appear to discriminate as consciously against women as it does against anyone over 40 and/or those taking a career break, whatever the reason.

The best firms do not discriminate. One such is Rank Xerox, mentioned in *Making the Most* referred to earlier. Rank Xerox won the 1992 Women in Business Award acknowledging their commitment to tackling the culture change that was vital to creating an environment where all employees could aspire to their full potential.

Among initiatives introduced are: improved maternity benefits; career breaks; five days' annual paid emergency childcare leave to meet unexpected emergencies; and flexible working to enable men and women to respond to the family impact of more couples with dual incomes.

The Skills Trends Report comments that one of the world's leading facilities management operations has identified that many of its most effective accounts managers are women: their problem is the low proportion of women who apply for jobs. An interesting finding is that in their CVs women often tend to understate their achievements, while men exaggerate.

A May 1995 salary survey sample by Computer Economics, covering 34,000 individuals from over 500 computer installations, showed a continuing fall in the proportion of women in programming and operations and an equal continuing rise among those in systems posts. This increased the trend for the proportion of women to be higher the nearer the job was to applications (customer/user support or systems analysis) rather than technical support of operations. Female earnings were less than those of males in the same type of post, ranging from 67% to 97% of the male salaries.

There have been slight improvements in recent years. In 1995 women represented 9.6% of those in all types of IT management, as opposed to 8.9% in 1994.

Women in business

More women managers in banking

In March 1995 total employment in all banks, merchant as well as the retail sector, was 376,600, of whom 224,000 (59.5%) were women (88% in the retail sector). In managerial jobs the ratio was 2.5 men to one woman.

Fifteen banks have joined the Opportunity 2000 initiative. Their target is to have at least 30% of women in managerial posts by 2000. A number of retail banks are well on target.

There are scarcely any women at board level and these are mostly non-executive. However, N. M. Rothschild, the merchant bank, has two women directors: Caroline Banszky (Finance) and Penelope Curtis (Compliance).

While there are still pathetically few women in senior management and not really very many branch managers, retail banks report increasing numbers at senior clerical and junior management level. With the aid of development programmes and accelerated training, it is hoped that they will rise to senior management.

The Midland reports that 11% of their branches are now run by women, and from 1992, women in management have increased from 21.5% to 23.4%. There have also been marginal increases in the number of women in senior management positions (now 6% of the total).

Among other examples of progress are an increase in women managers working part-time (100 at July 1995), and a continued increase in job-sharing: now over 1,000 jobs (including 20 women managers).

Women outnumber men in building societies

Like banks, building societies have a large female workforce (about 75%), mostly concentrated in the clerical grades. Many are part-timers, particularly in the branches, as opposed to head office or administration centres. Some of the larger companies take up to 40% of women into graduate entry, but women do not, in general, rise as high as men, though they are often to be found as department heads in the larger societies.

The Building Societies Association has no figures for the numbers of women chief executives. It is thought to be very few. Britain's biggest society, the Halifax, reports that at assistant manager level about 60% of staff are women, at middle management 28.6% (up from 19.7% in 1991/92) and in senior management 11.4% (up from 5.4%). Since the merger with the Leeds, Prue Leith has joined the board as a non-executive director.

Initiatives to assist staff include enhanced maternity pay and leave; adoption leave; paternity leave; and a childcare information service.

Well-qualified women to increase their share of City jobs

When we come to other financial sectors, Amin Rajan and Penny Van Eupen, the writers of *Winning People*, published in 1994, revealed that the City had lost 50,000 jobs since 1990. However, assuming that the economy would grow at an average rate of 2% a year and that the City's international competitiveness would remain virtually constant, they forecast that institutions would create 5,000 new jobs by 1996 and 21,000 by 1998. Job growth would be confined to two distinct pockets: those areas most closely associated with financial markets and those professional and business services which served City institutions as well as multinational clients.

Staff whose share of employment in the City would be increased were: graduates; holders of A-levels and vocational qualifications; female staff; ethnic minorities; and part-time, temporary and short-contract staff.

Women accountants not reaching the top as often as men

Despite record numbers of women entering the accountancy profession, few are making it to the top, according to a survey released in January 1995 by the Chartered Institute of Management Accountants. Men are twice as likely to become directors or partners.

The survey shows that 36% of students in the six accountancy bodies are women and concludes that 'any barriers to women entering the profession have been largely overcome'. Fourteen per cent of accountants registered with the six bodies are women, compared with 4% in 1980.

Many women are attracted to the profession because it allows them to work from home. The CIMA study maintains that as the proportion of women accountants rises, employers will have to become more flexible about working hours and family-related issues. Isobel Boyer, one of the authors of the survey, says, 'There are plenty of women who are partners in the big six practices but statistical evidence shows that they are not proportional to men. People would say there is still a glass ceiling which it is difficult to penetrate. Of course there are some high-profile very successful women.

'Most of these successful women have neither taken a career break nor worked part-time, and they are also exceptionally competent. However, we interviewed one woman working part-time as a partner in a regional practice, on a three-day basis. She can spend time with her family when she needs to and resume full-time work later on. This is a very positive example of what can be done.'

Part-time employment increases in retailing

Retailing is another career in which there has been a continued growth in female employment since the 1970s. There has also been a growth of part-time working, to 48% of the labour force, and of these 80% are female.

Retailers are finding management positions hard to fill, according to *The Retail Labour Market Report 1995* compiled by the National Retail Training Council and published by the British Retail Consortium. Projections for 2001 are that employment for managers will increase and more women will take these positions.

With a few notable exceptions, retail management has been dominated by men. Many retailers are trying to improve the representation of women in management. Nine of the UK's biggest retailers were among those who signed up for Opportunity 2000. Included in those who have recorded a quantifiable improvement in employment prospects for women is Boots the Chemist. Among those short-listed for a top-level commitment award was Marks and Spencer for its Family Care Policy which incorporates enhanced maternity policies and a new concept of Dependency Leave.

J Sainsbury has appointed three women directors: Rosemary Thorne (Finance), Judith Evans (Corporate Personnel), and Angela Megson (responsible for buying cheese, frozen food, dairy food and deli). Sainsbury also has 110 women store managers or deputy store managers, and 15 women in senior management. Two of these last are part-timers, and there are 23 part-timers in middle management and 422 in junior management.

A changing climate in hotel and catering

Another sector employing large numbers of women, many of them part-time, is hotel and catering.

The Hotel and Catering Research Centre at Huddersfield University states that between 66 and 75% of the students on hotel and catering courses at undergraduate level are women. Females represent about 46% of management, predominating in institutional catering but forming less than 20% of management in hotels.

The climate is changing, however. There are now more than a handful in important positions today, but they need tremendous determination. 'They have to be better than men in every respect', says Roy Hayter, who writes on the industry. Dagmar Woodward is general manager of the Mayfair Hotel in London. Sue Harrison is catering director of the House of Commons. Zoe Jenkins, a graduate of Huddersfield, is banqueting manager at the Dorchester. Traditionally, food and beverages tended to be a male domain, while women went into the accommodation and housekeeping side.

There are outstanding women chefs today, too. Sally Clarke's eponymous restaurant in Kensington is highly successful.

Contract catering remains a good field for women

In contract catering women have always fared better. Gardner Merchant is now in partnership with a French company, Sodexho. The total workforce is 115,000, 90% being female. Over 50% of those in management are women, and there are six or so women managing business units, one level below the board. The person in charge of such a division may be employing 2,000 people, and have a turnover of £10–15 million.

Several companies in the industry, including Gardner Merchant, are taking positive steps to encourage women with children to return to work. Help varies but may include career breaks, childcare vouchers, workplace creches, job-sharing, part-time working, and working hours to fit in with school hours and holidays.

The BBC a model employer

Increasing numbers of women work in the media.

In 1995 women made up 47% of staff employed by the BBC, an increase of 4% since 1991.

The Corporation, a founder member of Opportunity 2000, aims to improve the representation of women at all levels of management. It aims, for example, to increase the percentage of women at senior executive level from 21% in 1995 to 30% in the year 2000 and at senior and middle management level from 27% and 33% respectively in 1995 to 40% in 2000.

Women's representation in management and production grades has improved steadily. By 1995 there were four women on the BBC Board of Management: Jane Drabble, Director of Education; Liz Forgan, Managing Director, Network Radio; Patricia Hodgson, Director of Policy and Planning; and Margaret Salmon, Director of Personnel.

And, of course, it is no longer a novelty to see women foreign correspondents reporting from war and disaster zones.

The BBC's first equal opportunities officer was appointed in 1986, followed by equality specialists in most directorates. The BBC runs a number of women-only courses, including women in management, career development, operational awareness and on-air presentation skills, as well as mentoring schemes. It is monitoring both the workforce and recruitment to establish whether barriers exist for women and in which areas they are under-represented.

The BBC has introduced a number of initiatives to help working parents, including a total of 270 nursery places for children under five at nine locations, holiday and half-term play schemes for children aged from five to 12, flexible working, career breaks, parent support groups, and a telephone advice service offering guidance on parenting issues.

Only three women edit national newspapers

We can find only three women editing national papers: Bridget Rowe at the *People*; Tessa Hilton at the *Sunday Mirror* and Sue Douglas at the *Sunday Express*. Several women have edited the colour magazines produced by the nationals, and in 1995 Emma Soames, editor of the *Telegraph Magazine*, was voted Editor of the Year at the Society of Magazine Editors awards.

According to a survey by Women in Journalism, launched in June 1995, men still dominate the top jobs in Fleet Street, with the ratio of women to men in policy- and decision-making roles in national newspapers currently standing at a meagre 20:80.

Eve Pollard, formerly editor of the *Sunday Express* and chairman of this new organisation, comments, 'Half the people entering journalism these days are women, yet our survey shows how few women actually make it to the top. Hard news, leader and comment writing, and policy-making are still a male preserve.'

Women do little better in the regions. The Guild of Newspaper Editors has 423 members. Two of its 40 women members edit national papers, 33 regional weekly papers, while two are between jobs and one is retired.

Newspapers give maternity leave and may in the odd case consider part-time working on return, but one gains the impression that, although there is equal pay, there are no equal opportunities initiatives as such. Journalists are journalists, whatever their sex.

In periodical publishing, trade, technical and business magazines tend to be edited by men, and consumer magazines (many aimed specifically at women) by women. Miller Freeman (formerly Morgan Grampian) publishes 66 magazines. Fourteen are edited by women. One woman is managing director of three magazines, and on nine the advertising manager is a woman.

When we consider the glossy magazine groups, perhaps it is the men who have grounds for asking for an equal opportunities initiative to be targeted at them. Among IPC's 78 periodicals, the vast majority of editors and advertising managers, plus a fair number of publishers, are women. IPC now has two women on the board: Linda Lancaster-Gage, Managing Director of the specialist group, and Sly Grice, Group Advertising/Sales Manager.

No discrimination against women in public relations

Almost as many women as men work as public relations practitioners (44% of members of the Institute of Public Relations are female).

The Institute calls PR a very attractive area for women to enter because there is no discrimination. Rosemary Brook, 1996 President of the IPR, has gone on record as saying that there is no glass ceiling for women in PR. Now running her own company, Brook Wilkinson Public Relations, she was formerly chairman of Edelmann Public Relations, the largest independent agency in the world.

While all areas are open to everyone, consumer public relations tends to be dominated by women and high tech by men; healthcare by women, government affairs and lobbying by men. Business-to-business is fairly evenly balanced.

Women in the air

While in recent years scarcely any occupation is thought to be unsuitable for women, there are still a few in which it is unusual to find them. Air transport is an outstanding case.

The Civil Aviation Authority reported on 1 December 1995, that the total number of females with commercial pilots' licences was 296, compared with 12,140 males. Of these there were nine female helicopter pilots and 416 males. This is certainly better than four years earlier, when there were only 54 women with commercial pilots' licences.

This minority keeps growing. British Airways employs about 50 women pilots. In March 1993, First Officer Barbara Harmer became its first woman supersonic pilot, when she operated a Concorde. Vacancies for Concorde pilots arise rarely. There are just 20 Captains, 17 First Officers and 17 Flight Engineers on Concorde out of a total 3,500 flight crew.

In July 1989 the RAF announced that women would become eligible to fly as pilots and navigators in non-combat roles. Not until 1992 were women cleared to fly in all roles, including combat.

The first female jet pilot was Flight Lieutenant Jo Salter. She flies a Tornado GRIB on 617 Squadron, RAF Lossiemouth. Having passed her weapons training, she is now qualified to go into combat.

In December 1995, the number of female pilots fully qualified and posted to squadrons was twelve. There were 17 qualified navigators. Five more women had qualified as pilots but not yet qualified on a particular aircraft type. In addition, 19 pilots and 16 navigators were being trained.

The police and the prison service

Women in the police have for many years performed the same duties as men, but not until August 1995 did a woman reach the rank of Chief Constable. Then Pauline Clare, who joined as a cadet, took over as Chief Constable of Lancashire. Another first was notched up the following month, when Superintendent Judy Davison took up a post as commander and became one of three senior officers in the City of London force. There are still only six other women officers of equivalent rank in England and Wales.

There is nothing new about women working as prison officers, but a recent trend is the appointment of women to become governors of male prisons. There are now nine women 'governing governors'. Five are in charge of male prisons, four in charge of female prisons, and one working at headquarters.

Women today

Life today may be slightly easier for women who want to get into the jobs which were previously a man's preserve, but it is still not easy, particularly if they aim at the heights. Combining a career, marriage and children involves choice and poses dilemmas. The strains can be enormous.

Work for those with Special Needs

Contents

Background

It is important to identify the terminology in general use when discussing the educational, employment and training opportunities available to people with special needs, and to clearly define the difference between disability and handicap (two terms which are often used synonymously but which most emphatically do not have the same meaning).

The World Health Organisation provides the following definitions:

- *Health Condition.* A disease, disorder or injury.
- *Impairment.* The change in normal structure or functioning brought about by a disease, disorder or injury.
- *Disability.* The reduction or loss of ability to perform a specific task which is caused by the health condition or impairment.
- *Handicap.* The disadvantage(s) which occur(s) in a particular context as a result of the disability or impairment. This includes the negative attitudes of others.

The following example may serve to clarify the difference between disability and handicap.

a Mary is blind. She has a guide dog. She is handicapped.
b Mary is blind. She has a guide dog. She has a disability.

The second sentence (b) is correct. Mary is registered blind and does have a guide dog. However, she attended a specialist college at which she received training in independent living skills and learnt how to operate a switchboard and audio-typing. As a result she lives alone in her own flat, works in a local company and is able to travel on public transport with the aid of her guide dog. There are obviously some areas of work which Mary could not attempt – any driving job would be impossible – but within her current work and social environment Mary is not actually handicapped by her disability. She can work, live and socialise independently.

When advising clients with special needs on opportunities available to them, it is essential to keep these differences in mind, as a disability may not be a handicap if an individual is given adequate training, skills, and in some cases adapted equipment, in order to be able to function effectively in the workplace.

Types of disability

Disabilities can be broadly divided into three groups: physical, sensory and mental. In all groups the range of the disability can be tremendous. A hearing impairment can mean anything from slight hearing loss in one ear, virtually corrected by hearing aids, through to no usable hearing. The implications of the effect which a disability will have on employment will frequently be affected by the level of the disability itself. The way in which a disability is dealt with will also vary tremendously from person to person, and when discussing opportunities open to people with disabilities it is essential to consider how the disability affects the particular individual in question.

The way in which individuals become disabled also varies. Many people are born with disabilities and will possibly have received specialist help in terms of education and training from the first. However, people also become disabled through the effects of illness or accident, and this can have a traumatic effect on their lives, families and careers. Often people need to come to terms with the emotional effects of disability before they begin to consider the need for retraining, which is often essential.

Further and higher education

Many people, particularly those who have been born with or who develop special needs during their school life, will continue their education either at a local college or at one of the many specialist colleges available.

Since 1 December 1994, the Special Educational Needs Code of Practice has been in force. This Code requires that all agencies involved with young people with special educational needs work together to ensure that the best-quality next step can be achieved for each individual. In addition, from the age of 14, the Code requires that the local education authority call annual review meetings for each young person with identified special educational needs and that a transition plan be formulated which clearly outlines the options open to the individual in their progression from compulsory education into further education, training or employment. The LEA *must* invite the careers service to be present at or contribute to these meetings. (NB Prior to the age of 14, it is the school's responsibility to arrange annual reviews.)

Colleges of further education used to come within the control of local education authorities, but they are now funded by the Further Education Funding Council (FEFC), which is responsible for ensuring that the colleges provide facilities for students with special educational needs or disabilities. This support may take the form of a percentage of support teacher/lecturer time within college or the provision of specialist assistance and/or equipment, e.g. magnified computer screens for the visually impaired or the provision of a communicator for hearing-impaired students. Information on the type of support and funding available can be obtained from the college direct. Most colleges have a student services officer or a special educational needs co-ordinator who will be able to offer advice. If a student with a disability or special educational needs is thinking of applying to a college of further education it is advisable to contact the college/colleges as early as possible to ensure that they have time to assess the level of support which will be required by the student and put mechanisms into place to ensure that this can be provided.

In addition to providing support on mainstream courses, many colleges offer courses specifically designed to meet the needs of students with special needs. Courses may be academic or vocational and range from courses designed to help those with moderate or severe learning difficulties to acquire independent living skills, through to courses specifically offering office skills to people with hearing impairments. The best source of information on the range of courses available locally would be the Special Needs Careers Officer, usually based at the local careers office.

As well as courses offered at local colleges of further education there are a great many specialist colleges which offer further education and training to people with specific disabilities. These colleges are frequently run by charities such as the Royal National Institute for the Deaf (RNID), the Royal National Institute for the Blind (RNIB), the Royal Society for Mentally Handicapped Children and Adults (MENCAP), etc. These colleges offer specialist vocational education and training; and as they are, in the main, residential, they also give the opportunity for people to acquire independent living skills. The fees charged by these colleges are frequently necessarily high because of the high staff-to-student ratios and the expensive specialist equipment they use. Courses may be paid for in a variety of ways and students may be funded by their local education authority or by the Further Education Funding Council. In many cases, for students with disabilities, funding will come from a variety of sources, for example, the educational element being funded by the FEFC with the care element coming from social services (who may well use the individual's benefits as part of the funding) and any medical support being financed by the local health authority. Many colleges offer courses under the Youth Credit and Training for Work schemes. In some cases it is possible to claim Income Support in addition to the YC allowance, but each case would need to be discussed individually with the Department of Social Security. Mobility and Attendance Allowances are unaffected by YC, TFW or attendance at college.

If an individual is contemplating application to a residential college it is *essential* to contact the named liaison officer for the FEFC within the local authority. Applications for funding can be complex and time-consuming, and an early start is vital. Residential placement would only be considered once it had been established that no local provision could adequately meet the individual's needs.

Students with disabilities who attend courses of higher education (degrees, HNDs, etc.) are entitled to the usual mandatory awards and may apply for discretionary awards. In addition to this they can claim the Disabled Students Allowance if they are in receipt of a mandatory award. This allowance is to pay for additional costs incurred on going on the course because of the disability. It is not a travel allowance. In 1995/96 the following allowances could be paid at the discretion of the local authority (they decide whether a cost was necessarily incurred): up to £1,215 p.a. for any cost; up to £4,850 p.a. for non-medical helpers; up to £3,650 (per course) for major items of specialist equipment.

Training

As mentioned above, vocational training can be done either locally or at one of the specialist colleges and can be paid for in the ways outlined.

For people who have recently become disabled a period of assessment may be necessary before they can embark on any formal training, not least because they may need to totally rethink their ideas on employment and careers plans. Employment Rehabilitation Centres, originally on fixed sites, but now moving towards a mobile service, offer assessments. Rehabilitation courses used to be offered at the centres, but there are now moves to contract-out this service to other agencies, e.g. the RNIB offer a residential assessment course for those who have recently become blind, at RNIB Manor House, Torquay; and Action for the Blind offer a similar facility on a part-time day basis at Lewisham College in London.

Youth Credits and Training for Work provision are the responsibility of TECs (Training Enterprise Councils). TECs have given a quota of training weeks, with appropriate additional funding, to selected Training Providers for people with special training needs (not necessarily disabilities). These needs could be emotional, academic or as a result of a disability or a combination of these. It is up to the Special Needs Careers Officer in the area to 'endorse' these trainees, i.e. decide on what level of additional support and funding is needed and complete the appropriate documentation. It may be that a trainee needs additional help as a direct result of a disability, e.g. a visually impaired trainee may need a personal reader or a specially adapted typewriter in these circumstances. The TEC is expected to provide the additional support or equipment required for the trainee to complete their training to an appropriate NVQ level. Training for Work is also open to adults with disabilities and also offers the specialist support and equipment provision outlined above. Both types of training can incorporate extended induction and assessment periods for people with disabilities, part-time hours and attendance at the specialist colleges as described above.

Currently, YC allowance is £29.50 p.w. at 16 and £35.00 at 17, but many TECs have topped up this basic minimum. TFW allowance is £10.00 in addition to benefits. People with disabilities are in the target group for YC and TFW and, depending on the regulations of the local TEC, may not have to meet age or length of unemployment restrictions for entry onto training. The local TEC offices, Employment Services Office or Careers Office should have details on the availability of training locally and give details of the practices of the local TEC.

Employment services

The *Special Needs Careers Officer* (SNCO) is usually based at the Careers Office. General brief is to provide advice and information on opportunities in education, training and employment available for people with special needs. SNCOs usually deal with clients in full-time education, those in training or those moving into employment.

Disability Employment Advisors (DEAs) used to be known as DROs (Disablement Resettlement Officers). Based at the Employment Services Offices (old Job Centres) they administer the Disabled Workers Registration Scheme and the schemes designed to assist job seekers with disabilities.

The *Placing, Assessment and Counselling Team* (PACT) (formerly the Disablement Advisory Service) offer information and advice to people with disabilities, and to employers and training providers. It is part of the Employment Service.

The following are a number of special schemes designed to assist people with special needs in finding and keeping employment; they come under the umbrella of Access to Work.

Registering as disabled

The Employment Service keep a register of people with disabilities who are available or in work. In order to register, the person must be 'a person who, on account of injury, disease or congenital deformity is substantially handicapped in obtaining or keeping employment or in undertaking work on his own account of a kind which apart from that injury, disease or deformity would be suited to his age, experience and qualification'. The person must be likely to remain disabled for at least the following twelve months. Registration is entirely voluntary and those who register are given a green registration card. NOTE this is *not* the same as registering with the local authority or social services. It is *not* necessary to have registered as disabled to use the Access to Work facilities.

Access to work scheme

This scheme can be used to access various sorts of help:

- a communicator for those who are deaf or have a hearing impairment – this includes providing a communicator for a job interview;
- a part-time reader or assistant at work for those who are blind or have a visual impairment;
- a support worker (who may be an existing employee) for someone who needs practical help, either at work or getting work;
- adaptations to equipment, or new equipment to meet individual needs;
- alterations to premises or a working environment;
- adaptations to a car, or help towards taxi fares or other transport costs if a disabled employee cannot use public transport to get to work.

The DEA will be able to consider other proposals which could enable a person with a disability to work more effectively. Access to help under the Access to Work scheme is available for up to five years and up to a total of £21,000.

Job introduction scheme

The JIS is available to those people with a disability who, in the opinion of the DEA, need some time with an employer to demonstrate their ability to do the job. It is a payment of £45.00 per week for a six-week trial period paid to the company taking on the disabled worker.

Jobs in supported employment

These are available for people with disabilities who are unable to obtain or retain jobs in the open market. They include Supported Placements, Remploy Interwork, Remploy factories and workshops run by local authorities or voluntary organisations. Details are available from the local DEA.

Disabled working allowance

This is a tax-free benefit aimed at those who have a disability which puts them at a disadvantage in the job market and who are currently working or about to start work. It is a means-tested benefit which is payable to those who are working or who are due to start work for more than 16 hours each week. The period of employment must be expected to last at least five weeks. The term 'work' includes employment and self-employment, but only paid work qualifies. Unpaid or voluntary work does not count. People who claim must be in receipt of one of the following benefits: Attendance Allowance, Disability Living Allowance, Mobility Allowance,

War Disablement Pension including Constant Attendance Allowance or a mobility supplement, Industrial Injuries Disablement Benefit including Constant Attendance Allowance or an invalid three-wheeler from the DSS. Or, for at least one day in the eight weeks before a claim is made the individual must be in receipt of one of the following benefits: Invalidity Benefit, Severe Disablement Allowance, Income Support including a Disability Premium or Higher Pension Premium, Community Charge Benefit including a Disability Premium or Higher Pension Premium or Housing Benefit which includes a Disability Premium or Higher Pension Premium.

Those with more than £16,000 in savings are excluded from DWA. Savings of between £3,000 and £16,000 will affect the amount of DWA paid. Those in receipt of Family Credit are excluded from claiming DWA. Housing Benefit and Community Charge Benefit may be affected by the receipt of DWA.

DWA is paid for six-month periods and will not be affected by the person ceasing to work or reducing their working hours during that period. A fresh claim form will have to be completed every six months.

For the purposes of DWA the term disability covers Mental Disability, Fits and Comas, Exhaustion and Pain, Seeing, Hearing, Communicating with People, Getting Around, Using your Hands, Reaching with your Arms and Building up your Strength (after illness/accident). More information on the details of these definitions can be obtained from the DSS.

Claim forms and information packs are available from the DSS. Claim forms are also available from the Post Office.

Bars to employment

When discussing employment with people with special needs the starting-point should always be the individual and his or her aspirations. Gone are the days when blind people were only considered suitable to become switchboard operators. With advances in technology and training there are a greater number of jobs open to people with disabilities than ever before. However, it is still important to be realistic when discussing employment and to be aware of the implications on job choice of some disabilities. The Armed Forces, Police Force, Fire Service and Civil Aviation Authority (for a pilot) give very stringent medicals to all applicants, and people with an illness, impairment or disability will probably find themselves barred from these areas of work. Epilepsy and diabetes are a bar to working in driving or joining the Civil Service or Armed Forces. The CASCAID Unit, County Hall, Glenfield, Leicester LE3 8RF (moving to Loughborough late 1996) produce a very useful booklet entitled *Health and Occupational Choice* which gives information on the major types of disability and suggests points for consideration when discussing job choice.

Where to get further education and/or training

As mentioned above, there are a great number of courses of education and training open to people with special needs offered at both local colleges and specialist colleges. Information on what is available in a local area is best sought from the Special Needs Careers Officer based at the Careers Office or from the Disablement Employment Adviser based at the local Employment Services Office. Applications to local colleges are usually made direct but applications to specialist, residential colleges frequently need to be made via the SNCO or DEA because of the funding implications involved. Below is a list of *some* of the major colleges offering specialist help. It is not an exhaustive list and anyone considering making an application to one of these colleges would be best advised to approach their SNCO or DEA initially. The list is simply intended to give examples of the type of training available, and inclusion or exclusion is not intended to imply any comment on quality.

- Banstead Place Assessment and Further Education Centre (Banstead, Surrey) offers assessment and further education to people with physical disabilities aged between 16 and 25 years. Courses are tailored to individual needs and can include independence training as well as vocational and further education courses. Banstead is also a mobility centre offering assessment and tuition for disabled drivers. It is controlled by the Queen Elizabeth Foundation for the Disabled.
- Dilston Hall (Corbridge, Northumberland) offers vocational, academic and independence courses for people with mental disabilities/learning difficulties. It is run by MENCAP.
- Finchale Training College (Durham, County Durham) offers vocational training for people with all types of disability and attempts to help them regain confidence via employment skills. Run by an independent charity.
- RNIB College Loughborough (Loughborough, Leicestershire) offers vocational further education and training to people with visual disabilities. Can also offer retraining and basic skills courses to those who have recently become blind.
- Doncaster College for the Deaf (Doncaster, South Yorkshire) offers further education, pre-vocational and vocational training to the deaf and hearing-impaired. Run by the Charity Commission.
- Chalfont Centre for Epilepsy (Gerrards Cross, Buckinghamshire) offers assessment, treatment and rehabilitation for people with epilepsy. Run by the National Society for Epilepsy.
- The Richmond Fellowship run a variety of projects, residential units and training workshops for the rehabilitation and training of people suffering from mental illness.

Further information

There are a vast range of organisations offering advice and information to people with special needs, their carers and associated professionals. Some offer employment advice and placing services as well as help and advice to students with disabilities. A few of the major ones are listed below. This cannot be an exhaustive list but *The Disability Rights Handbook* provides lists of the organisations in great detail. It also provides extensive information on benefits and services available for people with disabilities. *The Disability Rights Handbook* is updated annually. It is available from The Disability Alliance ERA, Universal House, 88–94 Wentworth Street, London, E1 7SA. Telephone 0171-247 8776.

Royal National Institute for the Blind, 224 Great Portland Street, London W1N 6AA. 0171-388 1266.

Royal National Institute for the Deaf, 105 Gower Street, London WC1E 6AH. 0171-387 8033.

British Diabetic Association, 10 Queen Anne Street, London W1M 0BD. 0171-232 1531.

Royal Association for Disability and Rehabilitation (RADAR), 25 Mortimer Street, London W1N 8AB. 0171-637 5400.

MIND (National Association for Mental Health), 22 Harley Street, London W1N 2ED. 0171-637 0741.

MENCAP (Royal Society for Mentally Handicapped Children and Adults), 123 Golden Lane, London EC1Y 0RT. 0171-454 0454.

Richmond Fellowship, 8 Addison Road, Kensington, London W14 8DL.

Skill (National Bureau for Students with Disabilities), 336 Brixton Road, London SW9 7AA. 0171-274 0565.

SCOPE, 12 Park Crescent, London W1N 4EQ. 0171-636 5020.

Preparing for Work

Background

Advising and informing young people on their futures in a rapidly changing and often difficult employment situation is not getting easier. Traditional patterns of career development are changing significantly and probably permanently, and there is no way that careers advisers can promise all young people reasonable, satisfying careers for life, however well they are prepared.

Finding and negotiating the complex route from school into a reasonable future is a difficult process. Every young adult wants something different from and in their work, has different interests, and has different aptitudes and abilities to offer. Some people are ambitious while others are not; not all young people are content to go through a lengthy training. Everyone can do something reasonably well; most people have their own unique package of abilities, aptitudes and skills, some or all of which will make the basis of a sound start in adult life. The problem is to find a way of relating interests, talents and abilities to the realities of the world of work and employment. Being 'good' at science at school does not necessarily mean having to become a scientist: scientific abilities such as logical thinking, observation, deduction, imagination and curiosity are qualities that can be useful in many other occupations.

Deciding on personal career priorities remains as important as ever because recruiters for jobs and training schemes, and course admissions tutors, prefer to choose the people who are well motivated, and who can show their interest in and knowledge of the job or course, as well as having the right aptitudes and qualifications.

Thinking and finding out about ideas for study and/or work has to start early, especially as it is important to make sure essential and/or useful subjects are studied, but deciding should be left as long as possible. Being flexible and prepared to change ideas or direction if necessary, and having alternative plans and ideas to follow up, should be part of strategic planning for everyone. Accident, chance, luck and impulse will still inevitably play their part in career decisions on the next step on the education/training/careers path, but anyone who wants to make the most of the available opportunities is going to give more time to intelligent planning and preparation.

Coping with change

It is probably no longer sensible to plan in terms of 'choosing a career'. The idea that in the more stable past most people stayed in a single occupation for all of their working lives is something of a myth. People have always changed the kind of work they do, often more than once in a working lifetime, as new opportunities have arisen, and as they themselves have developed. The difference now is that it will no longer be a matter of having the choice of doing something different, but of having to switch occupations several times in a lifetime, and accept the inevitability of change.

Few of today's school-leavers can therefore expect to find a single occupation to follow through for all of their working lives. Their 'careers' will almost certainly be made up of several different, even if related, kinds of work, periods of retraining, periods of temporary work and/or self-employment, and perhaps 'unemployment' too. They need to be prepared for this, both in their thinking and in their educational and vocational preparation.

Most people have the necessary potential, capabilities, interests and even motivation to take them successfully into any of a number of different occupations – which means not being obsessive about one. Young people should now try to think in terms of a broad range of possible areas of work, or higher/further education or training, as a first step after school, rather than latch onto a single, narrow fixed idea about a career, job or employer, or course. It is worth learning about 'families' or groups of work and training, to see the relationship between one area of work and another, and how it is possible to acquire skills that help in transferring between occupations and areas of work.

Lifelong learning

Preparing for a different future, keeping options open and being flexible means it makes sense for young people to take as much advantage as they can of all available education – school, college, and university – and training. This is not just because there will be fewer opportunities for the least and unqualified – and rather more for those who have greater educational, and preferably vocational, preparation. A good educational background and sound basic training at whatever level should also make it easier to adapt to change as it comes. Every young person should go on learning full-time for as long as they benefit from it and stay interested, keeping their studies as broadly based as possible. With few exceptions, it is not good strategy to turn down educational opportunities, especially for an immediate job with no real long-term prospects and/or proper training. Lifelong learning – not just for young people – is seen as the key to getting and keeping work and developing a satisfying career in the future. The government's National Education and Training Targets set levels of qualification in the population generally, to aim at for the end of the decade, in the country as a whole.

Formal qualifications now earn an interview, but not a job, if they ever did. Acquiring extra, potentially useful skills is another way of becoming more employable and insuring against future change. Some experience of using a computer is an obvious example: keyboard skills may be needed in many jobs that are not simply 'office work', and the ability to use and understand word processors and spreadsheets, databases and multimedia systems, or to use electronic mail and the Internet, will enhance employability in many careers. It is always worth trying to improve on mathematical or statistical skills. Even the most elementary training in business skills could be useful, and so is the ability to use one or more languages within the context of a chosen area of work. Everyone should learn to drive, and have a valid driving licence.

Careers education

Careers education programmes are designed to support students during their transition from school to the world of work, and they have been a feature of secondary school life for many years. Schools have developed facilities for careers education to become part of the whole curriculum, and for students to be able to use a wide range of careers information. Most of those teachers involved view careers work as being far more than just another subject on the timetable. Their interpretation of careers education owes as much to the development of self-awareness and coping with 'life skills' as it does to simply giving careers information. Appropriate professional organisations, publications and teaching materials have evolved. Few, however, of the designated careers teachers have had specialist off-the-job training in careers work, and for most, the job of coordinating careers education programmes and maintaining careers libraries is only one part of their duties, which usually include administration and the teaching of other 'subjects'.

The 1990s has so far been a period of significant change in careers education and guidance. Following the Education Reform Act of 1988 and the resulting National Curriculum for all pupils between five and 16 in England and Wales, careers education and guidance was recognised as a major 'cross-curricular theme' to form an essential part of the 'whole curriculum' of each pupil. Elements of the theme include adequate access to information and to guidance, recording personal achievement, future planning and experience of work. Though the implementation of this idea in practice has proved more difficult than might at first have been anticipated, commitment to it continues – for example, the School Curriculum and Assessment Authority (*Looking Forward*, 1995) outlined a variety of ways in which careers education objectives may be realised through the teaching of other subjects. In addition, the developmental aspect of careers education has been recognised by the increasing concern, supported by government funding through more than one initiative, to encourage careers education at very much younger ages and Key Stages than the traditional 14–16 year group. Nowadays the emphasis is on a 14–19 programme in most cases, with preparatory work being done in the primary school to encourage pupils, even at Key Stage 1, to understand themselves and develop their capabilities, and investigate careers and opportunities, though implementation of their career plans may yet be a long way off.

One reason for the heightened awareness of the importance of careers education and guidance for young people was the interest taken in the subject by the Confederation of British Industry – first in the report *Towards a Skills Revolution* (1989) and then in two other reports in 1993, *Routes for Success* and *A Credit to Your Career*. These argued that 'putting individuals first' and encouraging them to develop their skills and knowledge throughout their working lives was an important way of rectifying the defects of the current education and training system. They proposed the concept of 'careership' and urged that funding for education and training be channelled through individuals rather than providers, using a system of credits for young people aged 16+. This implied an improved careers guidance programme – one of the four main building blocks for the concept of careership – if individuals were to be empowered to make effective use of the credits available. The government followed suit with legislation and funding initiatives, including additional money for careers guidance in Years 9 and 10. Young people at this age are now 'entitled' to individual and group careers guidance as well as reliable and adequate careers information.

Careers information

Information resources and media improved by leaps and bounds in the first half of the 1990s. Rapid developments in information technology – particularly the use of multimedia systems, networking of computer equipment, and the increased use of the Internet – enabled schools to use a wide variety of information technology in connection with careers education. Systems available in school careers rooms can now allow pupils almost immediate access to vast quantities of up-to-date information on courses and careers. Typical uses are programs that match a student's interest or skill profile, derived from a self-assessment questionnaire, to a database of occupations or courses, and provide a list of options that may be of interest to that individual. Information retrieval systems – usually databases of courses or occupations – are also widely used; and, increasingly, dedicated word processors that tutor the user through the preparation of an action plan, a record of achievement or a curriculum vitae, and others that teach the skills of job searching and handling interviews. Psychometric testing facilities using the computer, either to administer and score or to prepare a report on the test results for the user, are also increasingly common. Government money, in the form of the Careers Library Information Initiative, has been used to improve school careers libraries in particular and has led in many cases to a much wider use of information technology. Meanwhile printed reference books are equally attractively presented and widely available.

Work experience and related skills

Work experience has become a central feature of many school and college courses, and the number of school pupils undertaking some form of work experience as part of their course has increased considerably. Having, and keeping up, interests outside academic study and/or working life is also crucial. Employers and course admissions tutors like candidates to be 'rounded' personalities with a range of interests. Learning to run a club, organise some kind of activity for a group, producing a magazine or newspaper, or being involved regularly in a spare-time activity, can be a substitute for, or a valuable addition to, work experience. Such experience also helps in developing the all-important social skills, of learning to work closely with other people (especially where you work in a team), and communicate effectively with them, and in finding out about your personal interests.

Training and Enterprise Councils (*see also below*) share considerable interest and involvement in Education and Business Partnerships between local schools, colleges, industries and commercial organisations, as well as numerous related initiatives. Secondment of teachers to industry and vice versa, the organising of work experience and work shadowing schemes, and the running of 'Industry Days' in schools have been some of the concerns and achievements of these Partnerships.

Vocational guidance

Careers services, previously provided by local education authorities, provide individual careers guidance to young people and anyone else in, or leaving, full- or part-time education. Careers advisers normally have a specialist training at postgraduate level in vocational guidance, and spend much of their time interviewing young people about their career plans after leaving the education system as well as offering support to those who are starting work or work-based training for the first time. Some services offer guidance to adults as well, though this may not be free and will be in addition to the guidance work they are required to do by law. Individual guidance to young people and their parents, however, remains free.

Recent changes mean that careers services have now been re-formed as careers companies, owned by a variety of organisations, including, in England and Wales, some private companies or training providers, and under contract to the Department for Education and Employment to deliver much the same services as before. The new situation is governed by the Trade Union Reform and Employment Rights Act 1993. Apart from changes in appearance of some of the literature and some careers centres, members of the public are not likely to notice a great difference, since the changes are largely at the level of management, organisational structure and policy. The changes have been less drastic in Scotland, where the services are still generally run by partnerships between the local education authority and the local enterprise councils. In England and Wales, each careers company may have different owners: sometimes a Training and Enterprise Council or Education Business Partnership may have joined with the former careers service management to run the service; sometimes the service may be run quite separately from the TEC by another organisation altogether. In yet other cases, the new careers company is simply the old management who made a successful bid to run the service themselves as a private limited company. Whatever the ownership, the requirements on it are the same as far as statutory clients are concerned, and the service given to them is likely to be similar in essentials.

The new qualifications framework

As an increasing proportion of post-GCSE/SCE students have chosen to remain in full-time education, the traditional distinctions between 'academic' and 'vocational' options are gradually declining. A-levels and Scottish Higher courses are still popular choices, but students now have a range of alternatives to choose from, and their own schools are offering them many of those alternatives. Many students entering a degree course do so with vocational qualifications rather than A-levels/Highers.

There are now important new qualifications such as the General National Vocational Qualification schemes which offer a significant enhancement of the 'applied' but education-based route to various career areas such as art and design, business or leisure and tourism. They exist at several levels, spanning different abilities and the age range 14–19, and, by using project-based work and assessment of competence, offer real alternatives for many students for whom the more academic forms of study are unappealing or unsuitable. GNVQ at level 3 is now deemed to be an alternative entry qualification for higher education, particularly in related subject areas.

GNVQs are essentially the school- or college-based version of the work-based National Vocational Qualification framework for assessment of competencies, developed in most occupations and industries over the first half of the decade. Assessment is not work-based, but competence must be demonstrated against set benchmarks ('performance criteria') and the assessment concerns itself with what a person can do as well as with what they know.

Options for school-leavers therefore at present now fall into three distinct pathways: the academic, via GCSE and A/AS-level qualifications and courses; the applied, via GNVQs; and the vocational, work-based, alternative of National (or Scottish) Vocational Qualifications (NVQ/SVQs).

New National Certificates and Diplomas are currently proposed for England, Wales and Northern Ireland (Dearing, 1996) which may then be obtained by any of these three routes, provided certain key skills are covered. The National Certificate would be available at intermediate and advanced levels, with a possible foundation level to be developed later on. At advanced level this would require the achievement of two A-level passes or a GNVQ Advanced, or a full NVQ at level 3 plus competence at level 3 in the three key skills of communication, application of number and information technology. The proposed National Advanced Diploma is similar but would require, in addition, four broadly defined areas of study to be pursued to a level equivalent to that resulting from taking one year's full-time A-level study (or the same in terms of GNVQ or NVQ levels). Significant changes in the ways study is organised and qualifications are awarded are therefore particularly likely to affect the 16–19 age group of students in the last years of the century.

In Scotland, the revised starting date of 1998 for the Higher Still Development Programme should bring GSVQ within the mainstream of the Scottish educational system, and the differences between academic and vocational courses will blur.

See also EDUCATION AND QUALIFICATIONS; and the chapters on NVQ/SVQS; and GNVQ/GSVQS.

Training for Work: Youth Training and Youth Credits

There are at present three main routes into employment: academic, leading to A/AS-levels or Highers; general vocational, leading to GNVQ/GSVQs; or work-based training, leading to NVQ/SVQ 2/3.

The Training and Enterprise Councils (TECs) in England and Wales (Northern Ireland has its own programme), and the Local Enterprise Companies (LECs) in Scotland are primarily responsible for managing the work-based training route – Training for Work – as youth training, and employment training for adults, are now jointly described. Each TEC or LEC contracts with training providers (FE colleges, private training organisations, etc.) to deliver training. Schemes in each local TEC or LEC area may be called something different – e.g. 'New Horizons', 'Traineeship', etc. – but are similar in essentials. There will be quality assurance criteria applied to ensure that training delivered is of a certain standard.

The wide range of work-based youth training on offer locally is open to anyone aged 16 or 17 if there is a suitable place they can take up before the age of 25. Such young people are guaranteed a place if they have left full-time education, are not in a job and want to train. This guarantee can be extended to over-18s who have special needs of various kinds (including disability, pregnancy, a language difficulty, a care order or custodial sentence or similar problems) and who have been unable to start or complete their training because of these. Trainees are paid a training allowance during the programme unless already employed, and training can be converted to a modern apprenticeship (*see below*) if available.

Youth credits

In 1991 the White Paper *Education and Training for the 21st Century* floated the idea of training credits, following suggestions from the CBI as described above. The idea of routing the funding for training for work through the individual rather than the provider, seemed to offer a way of galvanising the providers who would now be part of a market, competing to provide what young people and their employers wanted, in the way they wanted. Training credits became 'Youth Credits' – entitlements to 'purchase' approved forms of training up to a specified value, typically at least £1,000 but varying according to the type and length of training undertaken and the needs of the young person. The main purpose was to expand and improve the training of young people, by motivating the individual to train and to train to higher standards, encouraging employers to invest in training, establishing an efficient market in training, and in particular, improving individual choice.

Youth Credits are the mechanism by which school- or college-leavers get into modern apprenticeships, or work-based youth training, leading to NVQ level 2 (or other appropriate outcome for those with special needs). Like 'Youth Training' opportunities which they purchase, they may be known by another local name in your area. They may be used equally by employed or unwaged young people. The arrangements for their use may differ from one area to another, in the same way as their name. An actual 'credit card' is probably less likely than a form to fill out, and the administrative transfer of funds, when you accept a training place with an accredited company or organisation.

In 1995 there were approximately 245,000 young people in Youth Training/Youth Credits in England and Wales. In 1994, 58% of them got a job within six months of the end of their training, while another 14% went on to full-time education or training, and about half of all trainees gained a qualification or credit (*Labour Market Quarterly Report, February 1996*).

Guidance is recognised as a vital part of the process which must be explained to young people by the end of Key Stage 3 (age 13/14) and credits issued by end of Key Stage 4 (statutory school-leaving age).

Modern Apprenticeships

In 1995 Modern Apprenticeships were introduced in England – actually an extension of the option for work-based training under Youth Credits. They have been developed by employers, Industry Training Organisations and TECs working together. Apprentices should generally be employed throughout the training. For 16- to 19-year-olds the apprenticeship takes about three years to complete; but the determining factor is when you have demonstrated competence rather than how much time you have served – unlike the traditional apprenticeship. To get an apprenticeship you need good general education – usually some GCSEs at grades C and above – but the spirit of the initiative encourages the use of aptitude tests and structured interviews rather than rigid academic criteria for entry.

Modern Apprenticeships draw on the prestige of the old traditional apprenticeships, but many industrial/occupational areas are included that did not use apprenticeships in the old days, e.g. Care, Information Technology, Retailing, and so on. There are apprenticeships in most occupational areas now.

Training under modern apprenticeships should lead to NVQ level 3 or above. In some cases, they may also open the way to university higher education.

Separate comparable schemes exist for other areas in the UK.

Further information

The Institute of Careers Guidance, National Association of Careers Education and Guidance Teachers, National Council for Vocational Qualifications, School Curriculum and Assessment Authority, Scottish Consultative Council on the Curriculum, Training and Enterprise Councils, Local Enterprise Companies, Department for Education and Employment.

Contents

The Job Search

Job search organisations

There are a number of organisations concerned with job search. These include the local careers services; university or college careers services; Jobcentres; private employment agencies; recruitment consultants; and the appointments services of appropriate professional institutions or organisations.

Careers services

Careers services cater for particular clientele. Local careers services (previously part of the LEA but now operating under a variety of names and working for different employers) specialise in school-leavers, but many of them also provide help for adults and graduates. Help for adults may also be channelled through educational guidance services agencies, through Jobcentres, or through local Training and Enterprise Council (TEC) or Local Enterprise Council (LEC in Scotland) initiatives. It is important to get up-to-date information; TEC/LEC initiatives and programmes vary considerably from year to year and region to region and the same scheme may also appear under different names!

Graduate careers services primarily help their own graduates both during their course and for the first few years after graduation. However, under an informal reciprocal Mutual Aid Scheme, universities and colleges usually allow graduates to use the careers service nearest to them, although the extent of help given will vary considerably. There is also a national telephone advisory service based at the universities of Bristol and Glasgow for graduates during their first three years after graduation. Graduates who have been away from study for longer periods may be able to get help through TEC/LEC initiatives.

JobCentres

JobCentres usually only display jobs and training places for the local area, but they also have access to the largest computer-based vacancy system in the country, containing national and international job vacancies. They will have information on government-sponsored schemes for job seekers such as Training for Work, Youth Training, Build Your Own Business, Graduate Gateway programme, etc. Information on schemes is also obtainable from TECs and LECs.

Private employment agencies

Private agencies charge employers for filling vacancies (17–20% of the annual starting salary) and are more likely to be used by employers to fill vacancies for experienced personnel. Apart from those specialising in providing office staff, they are unlikely to be much use for school-leavers. However, occasionally they can be useful for newly qualified graduates without work experience, or for temporary work in catering, clerical or building jobs. Although there are usually no introduction fees for the job applicant, there may be a charge for careers advice.

There are estimated to be about 15,000 organisations in this country running recruitment services. Many of them specialise in particular types of jobs.

Around 3,500 agencies are members of the Federation of Recruitment and Employment Services which produces a Yearbook listing their members and the types of job each covers. A new edition is due out end 1996. Between them their members cover all types of jobs – from nannies and au pairs through to accountants and lawyers. They may have titles which indicate their specialist field – *RMS Leisure* and *Leisureforce* are specialist sports and leisure job agencies.

The Federation of Recruitment and Employment Services
36–38 Mortimer Street
London W1N 7RB
Tel: 0171-323 4300 Fax: 0171-255 2879

Consult the *Yearbook of Recruitment and Employment Services* for other names and addresses.

Recruitment consultants

Recruitment consultants look for candidates to fill specific jobs at technician, professional, executive or director level. Some high level positions are filled by 'head-hunting' but recruitment consultants may also advertise these vacancies both to fill the specific vacancy and to build up their own bank of qualified candidates for the future. Many of these agencies specialise in particular types of jobs; computing, electronics, medical personnel, etc.

Professional institutions and organisations

Professional institutions and organisations sometimes provide job search services for their members. These can range from help with writing curricula vitae (CVs) to advertising relevant vacancies in their professional journals. For example, the Institute of Physics advertises job vacancies for physicists in *Physics World*. The British Veterinary Nursing Association runs an employment register to put prospective students and qualified personnel in touch with employers. The Library Association has a specialist recruitment agency, INFOmatch, the Institute of Field Archaeologists runs a jobs information service, and ILAM (the Institute of Leisure and Amenity Management) has an appointments service. The Operational Research Society, Society of Chiropodists and Podiatrists, the Royal Statistical Society, and the British Dietetic Association have newsletters which contain vacancy information. Occasionally practitioners who do not belong to a professional body may buy the society or association's newsletter.

How jobs are advertised

There are a variety of advertising methods used by employers to fill job vacancies. They may:

- notify the recruitment bodies (*see above*);
- advertise in the national and/or local papers, or in specialist professional journals;
- use other media such as internal bulletins or local advertising;
- advertise in specialist careers publications available through schools, colleges and universities;
- attend job or recruitment fairs;
- take advantage of advances in information technology to advertise on the Internet.

National newspapers and journals

Job advertisements appear in most daily and weekly newspapers and in a wide range of specialist journals and periodicals. Where possible, employers tend to target those publications which specialise in their particular employment field and which have the 'right' readership. The job advert may appear only once so job-seekers need to become familiar with the most likely outlets for their particular type of vacancies.

The national newspapers are surprisingly unforthcoming about what job advertisements they carry on which days in case their competitors get to know their advertising policy! Advertising policy also seems to change periodically. However, this appears to be the current pattern in 1996.

Daily Express

Tuesday: retail, hotel and catering, sales and general appointments.
Thursday: engineering, technical, sales and general appointments.

Daily Mail

Thursday: all jobs in a careers feature.

Daily Mirror

Thursday: sales, clerical, security, drivers/HGV, retail, catering, building, engineering (particularly domestic heating), construction. Overseas employment advertisements are mainly in construction and business.

The Daily Telegraph

Tuesday: accountancy, engineering and general appointments.
Thursday: general vacancies - all included in Appointments Section Supplement.
The Daily Telegraph appears to carry a very high proportion of professional engineering vacancies.

Financial Times

Wednesday: accountancy, financial vacancies within the square mile of the City, senior general management, IT recruitment in the City plus some senior IT throughout industry.
Thursday: accountancy, financial.
Friday: International Edition (which you can't buy in the UK) has all vacancies lumped together.
Special features include a *Career Choice* magazine for first job graduates in October and occasional specialist supplements covering a particular job area. The Wednesday edition may cover aspects like job market trends, recruitment, etc.

The Guardian

Monday: creative, media, sales, marketing and secretarial.
Tuesday: education.
Wednesday: public sector organisations, environment, health, charities.
Thursday: sciences, technical and computing.
Saturday: repeats from Monday and Thursday in the *Careers Guardian* plus some job adverts from the other days.
The Guardian is probably the overall market leader for job advertisements.

The Independent

Monday: IT including telecommunications and computing.
Tuesday: media, marketing and sales.
Wednesday: finance, accountancy and legal.
Thursday: education, public sector and graduates.

The Independent on Sunday

General appointments particularly for young, well qualified professionals.

The Observer
No recruitment advertisements.

Sunday Telegraph
General vacancies.

The Times
Monday: secretarial.
Tuesday: legal.
Wednesday: mainly secretarial, IT supplement, media, marketing.
Thursday: general appointments, sales, engineering, graduate opportunities, public appointments, public finance.
Friday: education.
The Times has occasional features on particular types of employment.

The Sunday Times
Senior appointments – chief executive posts, public appointments, education, universities. Carries additional vacancies and is not purely a reprint of *The Times* appointments.

The Scotsman
Friday: general vacancies.
Wednesday: teaching and education.

Evening News (Scotland)
Thursday: general vacancies.

Scotland on Sunday
General vacancies.

The ***Daily Record*** and the ***Herald*** (both published in Glasgow) carry job vacancies.

Local newspapers and free newspapers

These are usually a good source of local vacancies. Occasionally they carry national vacancies if employers feel that people living in a particular area are likely to have the appropriate skills.

Weekly magazines available nationally

Weekly magazines such as *New Scientist*, *Nature*, *The Times Higher Education Supplement*, and *The Times Educational Supplement*, carry appropriate job vacancies. *The Lady* carries nanny and au pair vacancies.

Professional and trade journals

These can be an important source of vacancies. Some of these will be available in public reference libraries. Others are available by postal subscription. Many will not be on sale in the local newsagents. Some are published by the appropriate professional body – addresses in Appendix 1. Even if the journals are published independently the professional body should be able to supply details of availability.

A publication called *Executive Post* used to be published by the Professional and Executive Registry for job changers and redundant executives but this has now been discontinued and there are no signs of a replacement.

Consult the *BRAD Directory* or *Benn's Media Directory* for a list of specialist publications available at public reference or business libraries.

Although it is by no means comprehensive, here are some examples listed by CLCI category :

C: Administration, business, clerical and management
Health Service management/administrative jobs: *Health Service Journal*
Local government jobs: *Opportunities, Public Service, Local Government Appointments*
Chartered secretary*: Administrator (published ICSA)*
Computing*: Computer Weekly, Computing, Data Processing, Electronics Weekly*
Personnel officer: *Personnel Management*, *PM Plus*
Organisation and Methods: *Management Services* (published IMS)

E: Art and design
Fine art: *Artists Newsletter*
Photography: *British Journal of Photography, UK Press Gazette*

F: Teaching and cultural activities
Archaeologist: *Museums Journal*, usually *The Guardian* and *The Independent*
Conservator: *Museums Journal*, *Conservation News*, *Paper Conservation News*
Information scientist: *New Scientist*
Journalist: *UK Press Gazette*, *Media Week*
Librarians: *Library Association Record*
Museum and art gallery work: *Museums Journal* (published Museums Association)
Religious: *Church Times*, *Catholic Herald*, *The Tablet*
Teacher: *Times Educational Supplement*, *Scottish Educational Journal*, *The Teacher*
Teacher (HE): *Times Higher Educational Supplement*
Teacher (English overseas): *EFL Gazette*
Training officer: *Training and Development*, *The Training Officer*

G: Entertainment and leisure
Actors, dancers, etc. plus temporary 'resting' jobs: *The Stage and Television Today*
Music teacher: *Music Teacher*, *Music Journal*
Orchestral player and singers*: Church Music Quarterly, Classical Music, Melody Maker, Music Journal, The Stage and Television Today*, usually *The Daily Telegraph*
Sports coaching and instructor: *Times Educational Supplement*

Sport and leisure: *Times Educational Supplement*, *Leisure Opportunities* and *Leisure Management* (monthly), *The Guardian*, *Opportunities* (weekly) (for jobs in the local government), *Harper Sports and Leisure and Sports Retailing Index* (for sports retailing), *Groundsman*, *Diver*, *Golf Club Management*
Health and fitness instructor: *Health and Fitness*, *Leisure Week*
Broadcasting: *The Guardian*, *Broadcast*, *Screen International*, *The Stage and Television Today*. Note that BBC external vacancies are advertised on Ceefax.
Travel industry: *Overseas Jobs Express*, *Travel Trade Gazette*, *Travel Weekly*
Publishing: *Bookseller*, *Media Week*

I: Catering and other services

Hotel work: *Caterer and Hotelkeeper*
Embalmer: *The Embalmer* (British Institute of Embalmers)

J: Health and medical

Dentistry: *British Dental Journal*, *Dental Technician*
Dietitians: *Health Service Journal*
Nurse/health visitor/midwife: *Nursing Times*, *Midwifery*, *Health Visitor and Community Nurse*
Medicine: *British Medical Journal*, *General Practitioner*, *Lancet*, *Nature*
Ophthalmic work: *Optician*
Pharmacist: *New Scientist*, *Pharmaceutical Journal*
Physiotherapist: *Physiotherapy* (Chartered Society of Physiotherapy)

K: Social and related services

Psychologists: *British Psychological Society Appointment Memorandum*
Social workers: *Community Care*, *The Voice*, *The Independent* and *The Guardian*
Youth work: *Times Educational Supplement*

L: Law and related work

Lawyers: *Law Society Gazette*, *Lawyer*, *Local Government Chronicle* (*see also* PROSPECTS Legal *below*)
Legal executive: *Legal Executive Journal*

M: Security and protective services

Fire: *Fire*

N: Finance and related work

Accounting: *Accounting Technician*
Accountancy: *Accountant*, *Accountancy Age*, *Management Accounting*, *Certified Accountant*, *Health Service*, *Public Finance*, *Local Government Chronicle*
Actuaries: *Money Management*
Banking: *Banking World*
Building societies: *Mortgage Finance Gazette*
Pensions management: *Pensions Management*

O: Buying, selling and related services

Sales, marketing, buying, etc. mainly for the food industry: *The Grocer*
Marketing: *Marketing*, *Marketing Weekly*, *Campaign*
Market research: *Marketing*, *Marketing Week*
Booksellers: *Bookseller*
Floristry: *The Florist Trade Magazine*, *Complete Florist*
Public relations: *Campaign*, *Public Relations Consultancy*, *PR Week*

Q: Science, mathematics and related work

Science: *Laboratory News*, *Nature*, *New Scientist*
Chemistry: *Chemistry in Britain*, *Chemistry Industry*
Physicist: *Physics World* (Institute of Physics)
Biomedical: *The Institute of Biomedical Science Gazette*
Microbiologist: *British Medical Journal*, *Nature*, *Pharmaceutical Journal*
Economist: *The Economist*

R & S: Engineering

Engineering and Manufacturing: *Chemical Engineer*, *Chemistry in Britain*, *Control and Instrumentation*, *Electronics Weekly*, *Marine Engineers Review*, *Naval Architect*, *Off-shore Engineer*, *Opportunities*, *Plastics and Rubber Weekly*, *Process Engineering*, *Energy World*, *Textile Month*, *Fashion Weekly*, *Manufacturing Clothier*, *Drapers Record*
Food and drink: *Food Manufacture*, *Food Processing*

U: Construction and land services

Architecture: *Building Design*, *Architects' Journal*, *RIBA Journal*, *Building*, *New Builder*, *Planning*
Building: *Construction News*
Housing Manager: *Opportunities*, *Inside Housing*, *Housing Associations Weekly*
Landscape architecture: *Landscape Design*, *Landscape Design Extra*, *Building Design*, *Architects' Journal*
Surveying: *Building*, *Chartered Surveyor Weekly*, *Estates Gazette*, *Estates Times*, *Land and Mineral Surveying*, *The Building Surveyor*

W: Animals, plants and nature

Farming and agriculture: *Farmers Weekly*, *Fish Farmer*, *Fish Farming International*
Horticulture: *Grower*, *Horticulture Week*
Groundsmanship: *The Groundsman*, *Horticulture Week*
Forestry: *Quarterly Journal of Forestry*, *Forestry*, *British Timber*, *Timber Grower*, *Scottish Forestry*
Veterinary nurse: *Veterinary Record*, *Veterinary Nursing*
Veterinary surgeon: *Veterinary Record*, *Nature*, *Farmers Weekly*
Horses: *Horse and Hound*, *Pony*, *Riding*
Zoos and wildlife: *International Zoo News*, *Cage and Aviary Birds*

Y: Transport

Airline pilot: *Flight International*
Passenger services staff: *Flight International*
Yachting: *Yachting World*

Other media

Large organisations and companies such as local authorities often produce internal newsletters advertising job vacancies. Although these are designed to be filled internally it can be worth trying to get hold of a copy if you want to work for a specific employer.

Clerical, factory jobs and work for private individuals like gardening, helping with housework, looking after children, etc. are often advertised through cards in newsagents' windows or cards on factory gates. Some shops advertise their own jobs by a notice on their shop window or in their shop.

Specialist careers publications

School-leavers are not particularly well-served by job vacancy bulletins and their needs are more likely to be covered by job vacancy noticeboards in Careers Offices and JobCentres. Magazines for sixth form students such as *Springboard* and *Careerscope* carry some recruitment advertising.

Graduates have a number of vacancy sources available in Higher Education Careers Services and sometimes in public reference libraries:

Graduate employer information

PROSPECTS (formerly *ROGET*). This is a comprehensive list of employers published by the universities Central Services Unit. If you are unable to obtain this from your university or college contact CSU, Armstrong House, Oxford Road, Manchester M1 7ED. Telephone 0161-236 9816.

PROSPECTS Scotland. A guide to graduate recruiters and postgraduate study in Scotland. Published by CSU.

PROSPECTS Legal. A guide to training contracts with solicitors in England and Wales. Published by CSU.

Note that all PROSPECTS information is also available on computer program in Higher Education Careers Services.

Directory of Employers of Graduates in Ireland. Covers Northern and Southern Ireland.

GET (Graduate Employment and Training). Published by Hobsons Publishing plc. GET is also available on CD-ROM.

Trade directories are available in public reference libraries, such as *Kompass Register, Kelly's Manufacturers, Key British Enterprises.*

Most Higher Education Careers Services have comprehensive employer files.

Graduate job vacancy information

PROSPECTS Today (formerly *Current Vacancies*). Fortnightly bulletin of graduate vacancies published by CSU, who estimate that around 60% of nationally advertised vacancies for new graduates and diplomates are carried in *PROSPECTS Today.*

PROSPECTS for the Finalist (formerly *Future Vacancies*). Highlights vacancies for those expecting to graduate in the following summer. Published by CSU.

(PROSPECTS Postgrad covers vacancies for postgraduate courses).

Many Higher Education Careers Services also publish their own job bulletins.

Job or recruitment fairs and employer visits

Local Careers Services sometimes hold careers conventions for school-leavers which include employers offering job vacancies. However, most of these events are designed to provide careers information and careers advice.

Graduate Fairs are specifically designed for newly qualified graduates and job-changers. They usually take place in the autumn.

Summer Fairs are organised by individual universities but are usually open to graduates of any institution.

Postgraduate Fairs often concentrate on a particular subject area, for example Law or Master of Business Administration.

The 'milk-round'. Employers also visit many higher education institutions on the 'milk-round' to conduct preliminary job selection interviews. Individual employers visit only a selection of universities each year and their individual preferences vary considerably. Each Higher Education Careers Service will have a list of visits planned for the academic year. Most take place in the Spring Term. These are primarily aimed at undergraduates in their final year but may also be suitable for graduates.

The Internet and other media

Jobs are increasingly being advertised on the Internet either nationally or through local initiatives. They may go through a certain amount of teething troubles but in the long term they are a very exciting development which may revolutionise job hunting.

National initiatives

YouthNet was launched in November 1995 to enable young people to find out about all kinds of careers, adventure challenges, training for business and industry at all levels, vocational training, further and higher education, gap-year challenges, opportunities abroad, summer vacation jobs, working holidays, volunteering and expeditions. It will also cover job vacancies and information about setting up your own business. It should become fully operational in autumn 1996 and by then *YouthNet* will have a site on the Internet with thousands of entries. They say the information should be 'user-friendly'.

Essentially what happens is you ring the web site number and once connected *YouthNet* acts as a gateway to other providers of information. The entry under 'Work' will cover job vacancies, training, CVs, and interviews. One of the provider organisations will scan all regional and national newspapers daily for job vacancies, and information on these will remain available on the Internet for a week.

Contact details are available from *YouthNet.* Telephone 0171-823 3333.

GO-Web for graduates was launched in January 1996. The *Go-Web* site contains details of more than 3,000 UK companies and their employment requirements, and final-year students can search the information by business type, career field, location, degree required and size of company. It should also provide access to 5,000 major pan-European companies with graduate opportunities.

The *GO-Web* site is at http:/www.go.reedinfo.co.uk. home.html or it can be accessed through the Reed Information Services home page at www.reedinfo.co.uk.

Local initiatives

Individual organisations may make use of the Internet to advertise vacancies for a particular group of people. For example, Loughborough University Student Union uses the Internet to run an employment exchange for in-house vacation jobs. Academic departments post their job requirements on the university Info Gateway Web pages, the Student Union collates applications and sends details of suitable candidates.

The creative job search

Some jobs are not advertised, because the employer gets so many unsolicited applications. For example, media companies, recording studios and publishers rarely advertise jobs but vacancies for new entrants do crop up occasionally. Although it requires a lot of effort, a creative approach to job-searching is worthwhile.

It is sometimes worth writing 'on spec.', i.e. sending a speculative letter, to firms where you would like to work to see if they have any vacancies. Whatever the level of job, your application and curriculum vitae need to be carefully prepared to interest the employer, and each application should be tailored to the individual employer. Sending out a standard photocopied CV or application form does not usually get results for professional-level jobs.

Telephone canvassing and cold-calling, i.e. turning up in person to ask if there are any job vacancies are other methods which sometimes get results, but they can be very time-consuming and sometimes counter-productive.

'Networking' is a key job-seeking method. It is well worth getting in touch with individuals working in a career area in which you are interested. Initial contact can be made through a letter to a firm or professional organisation asking for information on the job area. Alternatively, use relatives, friends, work colleagues, etc. to get useful information about their work.

Whatever job-search strategy you use you will need to target your application and assess carefully what you have to offer an employer. There are numerous books on writing CVs, job applications, interviews, etc. written for school-leavers, graduates and career-changers. Look in the public library or careers service for the following:

- *Applications and Interviews* (AGCAS) Written for graduates;
- *Job seeking after graduation* (AGCAS) Written for graduates;
- *Getting into Job Opportunities* (Trotman 1995) Written for school-leavers, graduates and adults;
- *Preparing your own CV* (Trotman);
- *Excel at Interviews* by Patricia McBride (Hobsons 1995) written primarily for students and school-leavers;
- *CVs and Applications* by Patricia McBride (Hobsons 1996) written for school-leavers;
- *How to write a CV that works* by Paul McGee (How To books);
- *Super Job Search* by Peter Studner (1996);
- *Successful CVs in a week* by Steve Morris and Graham Willcocks (Institute of Management 1996);
- *Successful Career Planning in a week* by Wendy Hirsh and Charles Jackson (Institute of Management);
- *Succeeding at interviews in a week* by Alison Straw and Mo Shapiro (Institute of Management);
- *Where to find that Job* by Alan Bartlett (Hobsons 1994);
- *Where to look for Job Vacancies* (Joseph Clarke 1994).

Consult *The 1996 What Color is your Parachute?* by R. Bolles, published by Ten Speed Press for ideas about creative job search. This is a practical manual for job-hunters and career-changers.

Contents

Changing Your Career

Background

It is likely that constant change will be a continuing feature of our lives. We are living in such a fast-moving world, with such rapid product development cycles, sophisticated communications networks, computer technology and increased competition in almost every industry, that we need to be constantly moving to stay ahead of the field.

Only 62% of Britain's workers (the working-age population) are now in full-time employment. This figure is set to decrease to 57% by the year 2001 (Labour Market Trends 1995/96) and reflects the growing trend for companies to employ more part-time staff to replace full-time staff. The number of people in part-time jobs is likely to increase to 28% of the working-age population by the year 2001.

These figures illustrate the fact that the way we work is changing. This has implications for all of us – for those considering a career for the first time and for those already established in a career and considering a change.

Why our working lives are changing

There are three main reasons for the fact that our working world is continually changing. Firstly, much of the change is as a result of the progress of technology, which has touched all our lives. The implications of the power of the computer combined with the attractiveness of television and the availability of telephone lines are far-reaching, particularly as we move towards the creation of information 'super-highways'.

This new technology has changed both the nature and content of work. Its introduction often means the use of fewer workers and the de-skilling of others. For example, supermarkets have electronic points of sale and till-scanning systems which update stock automatically. There is therefore no longer any need for staff to price products manually or do labour-intensive stocktakes. Computers are able to carry out many low-level, routine jobs previously done by human beings. New technology therefore inevitably means change: change in the way work is performed, in the skills now required and in the way the workplace is organised.

Secondly, economic recessions and increased international and national competition have meant that companies must become more cost-efficient in order to compete. By reducing the core functions within the organisation they are able to decrease their overheads.

More and more organisations are deciding to retain a small permanent core of staff with increasing numbers of part-time staff. They then contract out the peripheral, less important aspects of the job, thereby reducing their workforce considerably. The advantage to the employer of this way of working is that contract and part-time staff can be more flexible than their full-time colleagues and may be cheaper for the employer.

Thirdly, major international and national events, such as the ending of the Cold War, the establishment of the Peace Dividend and the Northern Ireland Peace Treaty, have meant that the countries involved no longer need large armies to defend territories. In Britain, this has meant a reduction in military spending and large-scale redundancies within the Armed Forces.

This subject is explored more fully in THE WORLD OF WORK.

Interrupted career pattern

Traditional patterns of work are changing (*see* THE CHANGING PATTERN OF WORK *in* THE WORLD OF WORK). It is generally accepted that most people will now experience a more interrupted career, with at least one period of unemployment and/or part-time employment and/or self-employment during their working-age life. Many people will undertake at least two to three major occupational changes of career within their working lives. The reality is that rather than being employed by one company for a lifetime, it is becoming increasingly common to start one's working life in one career, finish in another, and experience other careers in between. Some of us may be faced with a career as a series of projects rather than jobs.

However, changing jobs is no longer regarded by employers as a sign of instability. Varied experience can be seen as a distinct advantage. People bringing skills from other industries and knowledge from other fields of study are often respected by employers for their experience and resourcefulness.

Reasons for changing career

Unfortunately, many people are forced into a career change through a variety of reasons, such as redundancy, ill-health or early retirement. Corporate restructuring, new company initiatives and mergers often mean that employers have to make some workers redundant. In the past, redundancy was rooted in manufacturing industries. Nowadays executive and professional people are much more vulnerable, especially older workers, who tend to be made redundant first.

The trend towards the decentralisation of organisational functions and flatter hierarchies means that highly trained and experienced professional staff may become victims of 'downsizing' or 'delayering' and therefore are made redundant. The risk of losing their jobs, which most blue-collar workers have always lived with, is now likely to apply also to white-collar workers and to professionals. Increasing numbers of people will have to change not only their jobs but the type of organisation for which they work, and the basis of their employment – which will not necessarily be full-time.

Companies which have reduced in size need less space for fewer staff and may therefore relocate. Some staff may be unwilling or unable to move and therefore have to leave the company.

Career change is also becoming a big issue for executives in their early to mid-forties, partly because the traditional and anticipated steps in hierarchical promotion no longer exist. Those who have not been made redundant, but who have remained employed in organisations, now question more seriously whether or not to commit themselves to corporate life or to do something different with perhaps less stress and pressure. Although a change of career can happen to anyone at any age or at any stage of their working life, executives in their mid-forties to fifties may experience more difficulty changing careers than younger people, as many employers continue to adopt an ageist recruitment policy, preferring young people.

Many people voluntarily consider changing their career for a variety of reasons. They may be unsatisfied or unfulfilled in their current job, their job may have changed due to reorganisation, or they may have always wanted to do a particular kind of job and feel that the time is now right to try it out. Other people may simply recognize that a number of job and career changes are necessary to give them the job satisfaction they need.

Skills required for career change

All kinds of career changes are possible. Some people are still able to move upwards from job to job, gaining more responsibility or better pay. However, for many people, career development now consists of a number of horizontal career changes – moving sideways rather than upwards (different company, same job; different job, same status, same company). Other people may have to take a downwards move, accepting a less demanding job and possibly less pay. Whatever the direction of the change, a different job may provide the variety and stimulus needed.

It is important to remember that with any career change, the work experience and skills previously acquired will never be wasted, as they may be immediately transferable to a new career, or it may be possible to build on existing knowledge, skills and experience.

If organisations are to be as flexible as the economic market suggests they need to be, it follows that people must be flexible too. An organisation needs to have access to its human resources at short notice and to use them in whatever way it chooses. As has been stated above, a large number of jobs are becoming more project-oriented, and the option of people working for an organisation on a flexible basis is becoming much more common. This often means in practice that organisations using more part-time, contract and temporary workers are likely to recruit people who have a broad base of skills. The core skills (generic skills, abilities and characteristics) are common requirements: literacy, numeracy, team-work and a knowledge of information technology.

Individuals need therefore to acquire skills and an openness of mind (adaptability) that can be taken away with them and reapplied elsewhere. This flexibility means that individuals are now responsible for managing their own career development.

How to effect a positive change of career

A career change can be a negative or a positive experience, depending on how it is viewed. Although redundancy can be a devastating and depressing experience, it can also be considered an opportunity as individuals are forced to review their careers and the direction in which they wish to go. Redundancy could therefore turn out to be a springboard to another, perhaps more fulfilling, career.

Individuals considering a career change need to consider various factors, such as what they want from a career, the level of their current skills and experience and where the opportunities are. Some computer-aided guidance programs or career change publications (available from careers services, adult guidance services or public libraries) may help with self-assessment and in defining relevant kinds of work. Talking it over with someone else may also help. Some careers service and private guidance companies offer adults guidance interviews, which help individuals explore their options.

It may be a good idea for individuals who are unhappy in their current job to try to analyse the cause of job dissatisfaction to identify what changes to make. A new career may or may not be the answer. By talking to senior management, some changes may be effected, such as increased responsibility, more contact with workmates or improved working conditions. These may be enough to give some people a new stimulus to their career. Other people may find satisfaction through developing themselves rather than the job, by having new interests or developing their personal rather than their job-related skills.

It may be possible to build on some skills in order to change direction within the existing occupation or career area. Opportunities for training, retraining or for gaining more qualifications could be considered. There may be in-company courses and training programmes, or part-time, day-release or evening courses at local colleges. Distance-learning is another option. Obviously funding may be a problem for many individuals if their employer is reluctant to pay or if they are between jobs. A Career Development Loan (CDL) may be an answer for some people. A CDL is a deferred repayment bank loan which provides certain individuals with initial help to pay for vocational education or training. Careers Services or JobCentres have information on CDLs and who is eligible to receive them.

For those individuals who want to change companies and/or career, it is important to research in advance what opportunities exist for their particular skills and experience in the job market. Information about the local labour market can be obtained from a variety of sources, such as careers offices, JobCentres, local and national newspapers, trade publications (available from the library), friends and professional bodies.

Conclusion

Graduates are changing direction in greater numbers than ever before. The career decisions made when students start university may change drastically once they enter the workforce. Students are advised to keep their minds open about which direction their careers might take. Employers today are looking for employees who are flexible, adaptable and experienced, and who have a variety of skills. Students should therefore try to ensure they acquire a broad base of transferable skills.

In this uncertain and changing world, people must be willing to recognise that their careers also should be responsive to change. Staff career development is no longer a priority for employers but has become the responsibility of individuals, who have to make career decisions and choices, based on their own self-knowledge. The overwhelming message is that the career ideal of the future is to be lifetime employable – by as many companies and with as many different careers as it takes.

Further information

Training and Enterprise Councils (for labour market information); Grants and Awards section of Local Education Authority; further education colleges; adult guidance services; careers service companies; private careers guidance companies; ECCTIS 2000 (computer database with details of all UK courses); TAP database (for details of local training courses); Career Development Loans; computer-aided guidance programs.

Contents

Education and Qualifications

Qualifications and initiatives 14–16

Despite the changes, both already underway and planned, for the education system over the coming years, the subject and course choices students make at school will continue to be crucial for their futures. Whatever the long-term effects of developments in training and vocational qualifications, the subjects studied at school, and examination results, are still going to be used in selection by recruiters, and inevitably by admissions tutors for degree and other higher-level courses.

Certainly, from the age of 14, pupils (and their parents) are faced with a series of complex and difficult decisions, all of which must be based on accurate and very up-to-date information, because prospects and the consequences of these decisions are changing all the time. Difficult as it may be, schools, with the help of careers advisers, have to keep pace with the changes, and the effects they have on pupils' choices. Time has to be spent ensuring that pupils and their parents understand the importance and significance of their choices.

The choices, and decisions, that pupils must make at various stages in their school lives should be part of the process of careers education, preparation and counselling. Pupils must have all the necessary information. They need to know, for example: what choices the school offers; how their choice of school, and subjects for school examinations will affect, even limit, any choice of subject for study after school or particular occupations; which subjects will give them the greatest choices; what the advantages are of the various 'programmes' being offered.

The choices that young people have to make at 13-plus, on what they will study from 14 to 16, have always been difficult ones. Theoretically, the range of post-16 options and greater opportunities to go on from vocational qualifications to more advanced academic or other study should make these choices less critical in the future. In practice, this is probably still some time away. Entry to many training schemes, professions and courses can still be a minefield, and is likely to remain so for some years. Sciences, particularly physics and chemistry, are hard to catch up on if not studied from 14 to 16, and are often unexpectedly crucial for some career starts. It is not so difficult to start a second language later on.

National Curriculum

Until 1987, LEA-maintained schools in England and Wales had considerable freedom in what to teach and how, but this has changed with the introduction of the revised National Curriculum which formed part of the 1988 Education Reform Act.

Scotland does not have a national curriculum. The Scottish Consultative Council on the Curriculum (SCCC) is the principal advisory body of the Secretary of State for Scotland on school curriculum and issues guidelines, but the responsibility rests with regional authorities in each region and with school managers, who decide what is taught. The regional authorities and school managers pay close regard to the Circulars from the Scottish Education department, the Guide-lines of SCCC and the Guide-lines for teachers on 5–14 programmes, and this ensures a large measure of consistency across the country as a whole.

The National Curriculum consists of ten subjects, which are mandatory up to the age of 14, including three 'core' foundation subjects (English, mathematics and science) and seven foundation subjects (design and technology/IT, history, geography, a modern foreign language, art, music and physical education). Religious Education is also compulsory but not part of the National Curriculum. In Wales, Welsh is taught as a 'core' foundation subject where Welsh is the usual language of instruction.

At age 14 the number of subjects to be covered is reduced to allow schools greater opportunity to respond to the particular needs/talents of their pupils. From 14 to 16 all pupils carry on with English, maths, science, design and technology/IT, a modern foreign language and PE. The amount of science studied from 14 to 16 will vary. Most pupils will continue to do 'double science' leading to a double GCSE award, but 'single science' is the only statutory requirement. Schools may also offer GCSEs in the three separate sciences of biology, chemistry and physics.

The recent review of the National Curriculum by Sir Ron Dearing resulted in a reduction of the mandatory requirement at Key Stage 4 (14–16) to about 60% of the curriculum time. To fill the timetable, pupils can choose from a range of other subject options at GCSE or start on a 'vocational pathway' and gain credit within the General National Vocational Qualification framework (*see below*).

The National Curriculum became effective in state secondary schools in 1994 in England and Wales and was fully implemented by September 1996. Independent schools are expected to follow the curriculum principles as one of the conditions of registration. The 'city technology colleges' are also required to keep to the 'substance' of the curriculum.

General Certificate of Secondary Education (GCSE)

GCSE courses began in September 1986 with the first examinations in 1988. There are four Examination Boards for England, one for Wales and one for Northern Ireland. They provide a variety of courses for each subject, usually lasting two years. In 1995 City & Guilds and the Royal Society of Arts (RSA) could also award GCSEs, in Technology and related subjects.

The subject range of GCSE examinations is similar to the old General Certificate of Education O-level and Certificate of Secondary Education (CSE), but GCSE differs from O-level and CSE in that there are published criteria which provide a nationally agreed framework. Results are given on a scale of A to G grades with A being the highest. Employers and course entry requirements often specify GCSEs to be passed at grades A–C. Candidates who do not reach the required standards are ungraded. From 1994 there has been an additional grade of A starred to reflect A-level of performance above grade A. GCSE differs from previous national examinations in that the emphasis is on positive achievement, and candidates can demonstrate what they know and can do. It also includes a coursework element.

A range of other courses may be studied alongside GCSE, including GNVQ Part One, examinations or certificates awarded by the Royal Society of Arts, or City & Guilds foundation programmes.

GNVQ Part One

Initially, GNVQs were introduced as part of the 16–19 qualifications framework but Sir Ron Dearing's review of the National Curriculum proposed that general vocational qualifications should be brought into Key Stage 4 and provide a vocational option for students of all abilities. The intention was to broaden the curriculum and provide an understanding of the world of work for students who subsequently progress to GCE A-levels, as well as for those who will progress through GNVQs or take NVQs, or a combination of academic and vocational qualifications. GNVQ Part One is also a recognised qualification in its own right.

The Part One GNVQ is designed to be followed over two years and take up about 20% of curriculum time. It is made up of three vocational units plus three core skills units in communication, application of number, and information technology. It is available at two levels. The Intermediate Part One is broadly equivalent to two GCSEs at grades A–C while the Foundation qualification is broadly equivalent to two GCSEs at grades D–G.

Pilot Part One GNVQs in Business, Health & Social Care and Manufacturing began in 1995. In England, Wales and Northern Ireland, 159 schools were involved. This pilot was expanded in September 1996 to include more schools and deliver Part One GNVQs in Art & Design, Information Technology and Leisure & Tourism. Part One qualifications are likely to become more widely available from September 1998.

The examination system for England and Wales and Northern Ireland is different to the examination system in Scotland, so these are dealt with separately. Secondary school courses in Scotland start at the age of twelve (see next page).

Academic qualifications and initiatives 16–18

GCE Advanced level/Advanced Supplementary level

There are eight Examination Boards for England and Wales which award A levels. Northern Ireland has its own Examinations Council. Not all Boards offer the same subjects.

A-level examinations in two or three subjects (some students occasionally take four) are taken after an intensive two-year course at 17 or 18. There are five levels of pass grades, A–E, with A being the highest. A grade N is used to indicate a narrow failure, and grade U is 'unclassified', i.e. a definite fail.

Advanced Supplementary level (AS-levels) were introduced in 1987 to broaden the curriculum for A-level students. At present they contain about half the content of an A-level subject but are at the same standard. They are graded A–E.

The Dearing Report (1996) proposed that AS-levels should be renamed Advanced Subsidiary and provide an interim accreditation for those who do not wish to complete the full A-level course. This means that AS-level would become an intermediate level between GCSE and A-levels rather than the unpopular and difficult vertical half of an A-level. If implemented, the new AS-level is likely to bring a breadth of study for many post-16 students, and studying four or five subjects over two years may become commonplace.

Dearing also proposes rehabilitating S(special)-level for gifted students to stretch them further and test their intellectual grasp of a subject. S papers are currently taken in conjunction with, and at the same time as, the A-level examination in the same subject. They are not available in all subjects and at present are not taken by many candidates.

All GCE A-level and AS syllabuses must be approved by the School Curriculum and Assessment Authority (SCAA). OFSTED (the Office for Standards in Education) are responsible for the quality and standards of education in schools including the delivery of A/AS-levels.

From 1996 all examination boards award modular A-level and AS-levels as well as the more traditional examinations. Modular courses offer choice and flexibility for both students and teachers, and enable candidates to select a specified number of modules from the range offered.

A/AS-level choice narrows future career options so students must have clear information on what their choices will mean. They should be clearly advised on the consequences of choosing to drop particular subjects, and helped to keep their options open as wide as possible.

The Scottish system

The Scottish Examination Board currently sets examinations leading to the Scottish Certificate of Education (SCE) at standard grade (S level) at age 16 and at higher grade (H level) at 17-plus.

Standard grade awards are made in terms of a seven-point numerical scale 1–7 where 1 is the highest. The attainment levels for grades 1–6 are specified by Grade Related Criteria. At Higher grade, awards are given in one of four bands, A–D, with A being the highest. Each band corresponds to a range of scaled marks: A = 70–100, B = 60–69, C = 50–59 and D = 40–49. The C/D interface represents the pass/fail boundary.

SCE awards equate to those in the rest of the UK as follows: S grade 3 or better is equivalent to GCSE grade C or better; SCE H grade A or B pass is equivalent to a pass at GCE Advanced level; three SCE H grade passes is equivalent to two passes at A-level; and four SCE H grade passes is equivalent to three passes at A-level. A-level is usually regarded as the higher standard while H grades cover a broader range of subjects.

Some students move straight to a higher education course after 'Scottish Highers', but many take the Certificate of Sixth Year Studies (CSYS). The CSYS may be taken by a pupil who already possesses a Higher grade pass in a subject. However, CSYS is likely to be phased out with the introduction of the new development programme called Higher Still.

From 1998/99 a new system of courses and qualifications will be introduced in schools and further education colleges in Scotland for everyone studying beyond Standard grade. The current Highers will be revised and additional courses provided at levels between S grade and H grade. There are likely to be five levels of courses, and provisionally they are being called Foundation, General, Credit, Higher and Advanced Higher. The aim is to provide opportunity for all to continue their studies after S grade at the appropriate level. Subjects currently taught through SCOTVEC (Scottish Vocational Education Council) modules which may be studied alongside SCE will be brought under the same umbrella.

Higher Still will provide assessment and certification in core skills. These are likely to include communication, numeracy, problem-solving, personal and interpersonal skills, and information technology.

Baccalaureates

A small number of schools and colleges offer the International Baccalaureate (IB) or the European Baccalaureate (EB). These offer a broader-based curriculum than the specialised A-level syllabus and are increasingly being recognised for entry to higher education.

The Technological Baccalaureate (TechBac) (Advanced) was introduced in 1991 by City & Guilds and piloted for three years. It became generally available from September 1995. It is a level 3 qualification designed to bridge academic and vocational routes and encourage a breadth of studies. It enhances A-levels and GNVQ (*see below*) by giving a further qualification, but it can also be an alternative to a full GNVQ, by offering technological studies together with the study of A-levels.

A student can achieve a TechBac (Advanced) with a minimum of two A-levels (or equivalent AS levels), or an Advanced GNVQ plus the Technological Studies component.

Vocational qualifications

In the past, qualifications and awards have been introduced as needed, mainly to meet a particular demand. The result has always been a maze of qualifications of Byzantine complexity. Attempts at rationalisation have been made several times, but change has become endemic, with reorganised examining bodies being overtaken by events and having to react to unexpected developments. The overwhelming problem, of course, is to provide sets of qualifications flexible enough to cope with rapidly changing conditions and needs, to raise standards, and to give people qualifications on which they can base further 'progression'.

Constant attempts were made to impose some kind of 'order'. Successive reorganisations tried to create a coherent and stable structure of awards, as well as firm and clearly recognisable identities, for broad levels of skills – craft-, technician-, and professional-level. But the effect was to produce increasingly rigid divisions, or chasms, between the career levels, making progression from one to another virtually impossible.

During the 1980s and early 1990s in England and Wales a whole series of pre-vocational educational initiatives were introduced aimed at young people - Technical and Vocational Education Initiative (TVEI), Certificate of Pre-Vocational Education (CPVE), BTEC (Business and Technology Education Council) First diploma, and City & Guilds Diploma of Vocational Education (DOVE). Most of these have disappeared or are being phased out and replaced by General National Vocational Qualifications (GNVQs) (*see below and chapter on GNVQ/GSVQs*).

In 1986 the National Council for Vocational Qualifications (NCVQ) was asked to sort out the qualifications jungle and develop a framework of national vocational qualifications for England, Wales and Northern Ireland. They came up with National Vocational Qualifications (NVQs) (*see chapter on* NVQS AND SVQS for details) which demonstrate competence in the workplace. General National Vocational Qualifications (GNVQs) were a later development for pupils at school and further education college (*see chapter on* GNVQS AND GSVQS).

Scotland too went through a major review of vocational education in the mid-1980s, and the Scottish Vocational and Education Council (SCOTVEC) implemented an Action Plan which replaced all existing non-advanced vocational courses with a system of modules. This has been very successful, and SCOTVEC later introduced 'national awards' for specified groups of modules to form the basis of General Scottish National Vocational Qualifications (GSVQs) (*see chapter on* GNVQS AND GSVQS). SCOTVEC also developed Scottish Vocational Qualifications (SVQs) which are very similar to NVQs.

General National Vocational Qualification (GNVQ)/General Scottish Vocational Qualification (GSVQ)

GNVQ/GSVQs are qualifications aimed primarily at 16–19-year-olds. They are designed as a stepping-stone to a wide range of employment opportunities, and to further and higher education. These new qualifications focus on the skills, knowledge and understanding which underpin a broad occupational area and offer a vocational alternative to academic qualifications like A-levels and Scottish Highers. They are being taken by an increasing number of pupils both in schools and colleges either as a qualification in their own right or in combination with academic or national vocational qualifications. The take-up in Scotland has been significantly less than in the rest of the UK probably because of the uncertainty caused by the Higher Still development programme, and by October 1995 there were only 11,200 who had either achieved or were working towards GSVQ qualifications. However, under the Higher Still development programme all GSVQs will be included in the new framework of courses, so numbers should increase.

The Dearing Report 27 March 1996

Sir Ron Dearing's report reflects his concern regarding meeting the proposed national targets, and his conclusions point the way forward. However, the education system cannot be revolutionised overnight, and it will take time to implement some of his proposals. The National Targets for Education and Training for the year 2000 are:

- By age 19, 85% of young people to achieve five GCSEs at grade C or above, an Intermediate GNVQ or a full NVQ level 2.
- 75% of young people to achieve level 2 competence in communication, numeracy and information technology (the core skills of GNVQ/GSVQ) by age 19; and 35% to achieve level 3 competence in these skills by age 21.
- By age 21, 60% of young people to achieve 2 A-levels, an Advanced GNVQ or a full NVQ level 3.

By 1995, only 63% had reached the first target, and only 44% the third one.

There are 200 proposals in the 700-page report. The central proposal is that there should be a single qualifications structure which will allow easy comparison between A-levels, GNVQs and NVQs. However, since there is little common ground between existing syllabuses, the three pathways will continue to remain separate, although a merger between the School Curriculum and Assessment Authority from the academic qualifications side and NCVQ from the vocational side may help to create modules that serve more than one route. The government has (1996) accepted there is a strong case for a merger.

The three main pathways will be at four levels: Advanced, Intermediate, Foundation and Entry. They should be known as National Levels (although of course these proposals will not apply to Scotland).

- *Advanced* covering AS- and A-level; Advanced GNVQ; or NVQ level 3 (obtained primarily through a Modern Apprenticeship or Employment).
- *Intermediate* covering GCSE grades A–C; Intermediate GNVQ; or NVQ level 2 (obtained primarily through Youth Training or Employment).
- *Foundation* covering GCSE grades D–G; Foundation GNVQ; or NVQ level 1 (primarily through Youth Training or Employment).
- *Entry level* – common to all pathways: three grades A/B/C.

Dearing uses the name Applied A-level and proposes that:

- a full GNVQ of twelve units, plus the three core units equals Applied A-level (double award);
- six units plus the three core units equals one Applied A-level;
- detailed consideration should be given to the creation of a three-unit award at advanced level to be known as the Applied AS – three prescribed mandatory units would then equal an Applied AS level;
- consideration should be given as to whether GNVQs at Intermediate and Foundation levels and Part One GNVQ should be renamed;
- additional units should be developed to extend the choice of units available to GNVQ students so that they and others can direct their studies more closely to particular NVQs and build up the required knowledge and understanding underpinning them.

Dearing also proposes establishing two new overarching awards, a National Certificate at intermediate and advanced level to recognise achievement of the national targets and a National Advanced Diploma to recognise achievement in studies both in depth and in breadth and achievement of the three key skills of communication, and applications of number and information technology. The government welcomed these proposals and has said that detailed proposals should be made by SCAA and NCVQ for new certificates from 1997.

How far the new certificates and diplomas will be feasible remains to be seen. There has been considerable criticism of the diploma, as to achieve this, successful candidates would have to pass A-levels, AS-levels or their equivalents in the arts; maths or science; a modern language; and a civics-based subject such as law. They must also demonstrate ability in the three key skills of numeracy, communication and information technology. This looks like the English equivalent to a Baccalaureate qualification, but whether the combination will be acceptable to students, and whether UCAS will give added tariff points (for present UCAS tariff points *see under* 'The changing face of higher education' later in this chapter) as an incentive for entry to higher education, is open to question.

Examining bodies

Examining bodies today are, in effect, operating in a tough and competitive market and have to be almost entrepreneurial themselves. There are no longer any 'gentlemen's agreements' to stay out of each other's territory. They have to react, as quickly as anyone else, to fast-moving changes, to be ready to develop a new scheme, a new 'package', or curriculum, whenever a need is identified.

Sometimes this means that essentially the same qualifications will have different awarding bodies. For example, GNVQs may be awarded by City & Guilds, BTEC or RSA, but the mandatory units for the same title, at each level, will be identical. However, there will probably be some variation in the optional and additional units. Each examining body decides what to cover in their optional and additional units although they have to operate within guidelines laid down by NCVQ. Schools are more likely to offer City & Guilds GNVQ; FE colleges are more likely to offer BTEC GNVQ; but employers and HE institutions are unlikely to worry about the awarding body unless they want particular optional or additional units.

The City & Guilds of London Institute

City & Guilds is the UK's leading assessment and awarding body. The City & Guilds 'Group' comprises City & Guilds, City & Guilds International, Pitman Qualifications, NEBS Management, and City & Guilds Training & Consultancy. Through City & Guilds International, the organisation offers qualifications in over 85 countries worldwide, promoting both City & Guilds and Pitman Qualifications awards.

City & Guilds specialises in developing qualifications and assessments suitable for work-related and leisure occupations and for general education. It awards nationally recognised certificates in over 500 subjects, many of which are National Vocational Qualifications (NVQs). Its progressive structure of awards spans seven levels, from basic skills to the highest level of professional achievement. Working closely with lead bodies, employers and training organisations, City & Guilds has developed a range of services to meet their needs.

City & Guilds is an independent body. The regulations and syllabuses for its schemes are drawn up by specialist committees, whose members come from industry, education and government departments.

Qualifications are available across all areas of industry and commerce and include agriculture, horticulture and animal care; business and commercial services; computing and information technology; construction and construction services; creative arts; education, training and development; electrical and electronic engineering; hairdressing and beauty services; health and social care; hospitality and catering; leisure and tourism; media and communication; process industries; production and mechanical engineering; retailing, warehousing and sales; science and technology; sport and recreation; textiles, clothing and leather goods; vehicle and transport engineering.

City & Guilds has developed schemes for use in schools, which include a range of GCSEs, as well as a variety of other certificates.

City & Guilds schemes are designed to provide a combination of practical experience and theoretical knowledge. Courses leading to City & Guilds qualifications are run in approved centres, which include schools, colleges of further education, training organisations, companies and adult education institutes. It is possible to study full-time, part-time, as part of a training scheme, in the evenings, or, where appropriate, through distance-learning. There are currently over 10,000 centres approved to offer City & Guilds qualifications, although centres do not offer every award. The pattern and duration of courses vary. City & Guilds does not stipulate minimum course lengths and this will vary according to type of qualification and the way in which individual centres operate.

National Vocational Qualifications (NVQs) are based on national standards developed by lead bodies. These standards define the skills or competencies needed by people working in particular occupations. City & Guilds, as an awarding body, works with lead bodies to develop qualifications based on their standards, which meet the requirements of industry and are approved as NVQs. These are available at levels 1–5.

City & Guilds offers the largest number of NVQs of any awarding body and they are available in most occupational areas. Up to 30 September 1995, over half of all NVQs issued were awarded by the City & Guilds Group (Annual Review 1994–95).

City & Guilds offers a range of Scottish Vocational Qualifications – the Scottish equivalent of NVQs. Areas available include administration; agriculture and horticulture; care; catering and hospitality; customer service; electronic engineering, hairdressing, health, information technology; motor vehicles.

General National Vocational Qualifications (GNVQs) are programmes developed primarily for young people aged 16–19 and are available at three levels: Foundation, Intermediate and Advanced. They are the vocational alternative to GCSEs and A-levels and are currently available in 13 occupational areas.

City & Guilds offers GNVQs in Art and Design; Business; Health and Social Care; Leisure and Tourism; Hospitality and Catering; Science; Manufacturing; Construction and the Built Environment; Retail and Distributive Services; Engineering; Information Technology; Media Communication and Production; Management Studies.

City & Guilds schemes are assessed in a variety of ways. For NVQs and some other vocational qualifications, the most commonly used method is workplace observation. Candidates are assessed on their ability to perform everyday activities in their place of work or in a realistic work environment. The assessment is carried out by appropriate supervisors/managers, who have experience of the work they are required to assess and are skilled in the assessment process. Workplace observation may also be supplemented by any of the assessment methods outlined below.

GNVQs, general education and leisure schemes are assessed by written papers, multiple choice questions, assignments, oral questioning, projects, or any combination of these. There are more than 1,200 separate tests.

City & Guilds Senior Awards recognise significant achievements made by individuals in their area of work. They offer a progressive employment-based, rather than academic, route to professional qualifications. The senior awards are the Licentiateship (LCGI), for combined achievement in education, training and employment; the Graduateship (GCGI), for project and work-based competence at Master's degree level; Membership (MCGI); and Fellowship (FCGI), for the highest professional achievement. For general information about City & Guilds, contact the Customer Services Enquiries Unit on 0171-294 2800/1/2/4/5.

The Business and Technology Education Council

BTEC provides a range of vocational further and higher education courses and examinations related to employment, covering a wide range of subject areas and levels. In future, it will also be involved in academic provision – BTEC and the University of London Examinations and Assessment Council merged in 1996. The new body is currently unique in offering a coherent range of qualifications – both academic and vocational – for students from 14 years old to adults in work.

BTEC First qualifications are on a level with GCSEs, Intermediate GNVQs and NVQ level 2. They are designed to provide an initial vocational qualification for those who, at or after 16, have already chosen the area of work/employment for which they are being prepared, and who may 'realistically' expect to go on to technician- or equivalent-level studies at a later date. In 1994, around 23,000 students completed BTEC First Diplomas in Art & Design, Caring, Construction, Engineering, Land-based Industries, Leisure & Tourism, Science and Technology. Of a sample of 7,000 students who completed a BTEC First Diploma, 75% went on to other further education. BTEC First qualifications may be phased out and replaced by Intermediate GNVQ.

BTEC National Certificates and Diplomas are the equivalent of A-levels, Advanced GNVQs and NVQ level 3. They have no formal entry requirements but may expect students to have a BTEC First, or four good GCSEs, or NVQ level 2, or Intermediate GNVQ, or relevant work experience. Courses usually take two years to complete – the Certificate by part-time study and the Diploma by full-time study. BTEC National awards are designed for entry into junior management in commerce, industry and technology. In 1994, around 63,000 students completed a BTEC Diploma course. Over 50% of a sample of 15,380 students moved on to further or higher education.

BTEC Higher National Certificates (HNCs) and Diplomas (HNDs) are generally seen as being on a level with a pass degree. There are no formal entry requirements but this qualification usually requires prior completion of a BTEC National, or at least one A-level, or an NVQ level 3 or and Advanced GNVQ, or relevant work experience. HNCs and HNDs usually take two years to complete – the Certificate by part-time study and the Diploma by full-time study. In 1994, approximately 22,306 students completed an HND. Students with an HND often move on to the second or third year of a related degree course. The percentage embarking on first-degree courses in 1993–94 was 52.2%. BTEC HNC/HND are nationally recognised qualifications for higher technician, managerial and supervisory posts.

BTEC Continuing Education courses are designed for adults who want to extend and develop previous education and experience. The courses are very flexible and can last from a few days to several months.

BTEC also offer GNVQs in all subjects (*see* GNVQS AND GSVQS *chapter*) and a wide range of NVQs covering most jobs.

The Scottish Vocational Educational Council (SCOTVEC)

SCOTVEC is the national body in Scotland with responsibility for developing, awarding and accrediting vocational qualifications. Increasingly these operate alongside traditional subjects in Scottish schools.

SCOTVEC is responsible for National Certificate Modules, Advanced Courses at HNC and HND and workplace assessed units (SVQs). SCOTVEC has a similar role to both NCVQ and BTEC and has mutual recognition agreements with these bodies covering SVQ/NVQs and Higher National Certificates and Higher National Diplomas.

SCOTVEC's qualifications are based on a system of free-standing units which can be taken individually or built up into group awards such as National Certificate 'Clusters', National Certificate Group Awards such as GSVQs, Higher

National Certificates and Diplomas. For those not already involved in mainstream education and training, SCOTVEC has introduced National Certificate (Skillstart) awards.

There are over 3,000 National Certificate Modules covering everything from languages to livestock and childcare to computer graphics. Each unit achieved is separately listed on the candidate's Record of Education and Training (RET), and candidates also receive a special group award certificate when appropriate.

National Certificate Modules provide a very flexible framework; they may be grouped into 'clusters' of three modules. National Certificates, sometimes called GSVQs, can be made up from either 12 or 18 modules and can be taken at three levels of difficulty.

SVQs are a special group of nationally recognised awards based on national standards set by industry itself, and assessed in the workplace. By October 1995, there were 65,300 people who had either achieved or were working towards SVQ qualifications.

There are more than 1,000 HNC/HNDs on offer at Scotland's colleges, and some universities. Both are built up from Higher National Units – 12 for an HNC and 30 for an HND. They can be studied full-time, part-time or on an open-learning basis.

SCOTVEC also offers professional development awards that are specially designed to help people further their careers. They are suitable for people (usually at postgraduate or post-experience level) who want to advance their career or make a career change.

Further information

National Council for Vocational Qualifications, Scottish Vocational Education Council (SCOTVEC), City & Guilds of London Institute, and the Business and Technology Education Council (BTEC).

Further education

Further and higher education provide, between them, for most of the educational, and many of the vocational-preparation, needs of young people, and adults. Together they form a sometimes-overlapping spectrum of provision, stretching from increasing involvement in and with the schools, in many instances from 16 and even 14 for FE, through to high-level postgraduate training and research at universities.

Further education has always been hard to describe. Traditionally FE was quite different to both school and higher education. While schools and higher education provided set courses and expected students to choose between them, further education did the opposite – trying to tailor the courses offered to the needs of their 'customers', and to respond and adapt to the many and often conflicting demands made upon them. The result was a pyramid of colleges – of further education, technical colleges, colleges of technology, and specialist colleges, of agriculture, art, dance, drama, building, etc.

The number and status of FE colleges change regularly in response to government policy and local and even national need. The changing needs of the 14/16 to 18 age group has also meant growing convergence between school- and college-based provision with academic and vocational courses being offered in both sectors. In the Further and Higher Education Bill 1992, FE and sixth-form colleges were removed from the LEAs and placed under the control of the Further Education Funding Council (FEFC). Scotland has a separate Further Education Funding Council. The FEFCs have a duty 'to secure the provision for the population of their area of suitable facilities' for both full- and part-time students. In addition, the FE sector has a number of independent FE institutions (not funded by the FEFCs) which are accredited by the British Accreditation Council for Independent Further and Higher Education (BAC).

FE colleges put on a constantly changing and very complex structure of overlapping courses, operating as a series of interconnecting ladders, with 'bridges' to fill in the gaps between one set and another, creating various routes to similar educational goals, generally shorter and straighter for the conventionally qualified, and longer and more tortuous for others. Increasingly some FE colleges are forming links with higher education and act as 'feeder' institutions for university degree courses, or they may be franchised to offer the foundation or first year of a degree course.

The FE sector continued to expand during the 1990s. In 1995 colleges in the FE sector in England alone provided courses for 2.4 million people. Of the students on FEFC courses in 1995–96, 5% were GNVQ precursors, 5% were studying for GNVQs, 9% for NVQs, 10% for GCSEs, 22% for A/AS-levels, 2% for NVQ/GNVQ additional units. The remaining students were predominantly studying for vocational qualifications other than NVQs and GNVQs. 30% of students on FEFC courses were aged 16–18, and 78% were studying full-time. Of the 69% adults (i.e. over 18), only 17% were studying full-time (FEFC Statistics 1996).

The changing face of higher education

Higher education is the generic term used as a convenient label to describe universities; Scottish central institutions and colleges of education; and other colleges and institutes of higher education offering degree-level courses.

For a decade or so, starting in the early 1960s, all sectors of higher education expanded, under the impetus of the Robbins Committee's recommendation that higher education should be available to all who qualify, and the sharply rising numbers of 18-year-olds. New universities and colleges of education were founded, older ones grew out of all recognition. Between 1969 and 1973, 30 polytechnics were formed – mainly by amalgamation of colleges of technology, commerce, art and design in metropolitan areas. All had a tradition of vocational teaching with special relevance to employers, and new types of courses were developed in new subject areas, some of which subsequently spread into the university sector.

In the 1980s, the economic and political situation resulted in retrenchment and cuts in funding while student numbers continued to expand. The role of higher education came under increased scrutiny and long-accepted traditions were questioned. In 1992, the government abolished the binary divide between the university and polytechnic/colleges sector and created a unified funding structure with separate funding councils for England, Scotland and Wales. All the former polytechnics and a number of colleges of HE opted to become 'new universities'. By 1996, there were around 270 institutions in the Universities and Colleges Admissions Service (UCAS) which acts as a clearing house for HE applications.

The new unified HE system is more diverse than the one which preceded it. It offers university degrees to a wider range of people studying a wider range of subjects, and a wider variety of sub-degree courses to many more full- and part-time students. New subjects, skills and disciplines have been brought within the definition of a university education and new opportunities have been opened up.

However, in 1996, Sir Ron Dearing has been asked to undertake a thorough review of higher education and 'make recommendations on how the shape, structure, size and funding of higher education, including support for students, should develop to meet the needs of the UK over the next 20 years. The committee should have regard, within the constraints of affordability and the government's overall spending priorities, to the following principles:

- there should be maximum participation in initial higher education by young and mature students, and lifetime learning by adults, insofar as this can be shown to be consistent with the needs of the nation and the future labour market;
- students should be able to choose between a range of courses, institutions, modes and locations of study;
- standards of degree and other higher education qualifications should be maintained and assured;
- the quality and relevance to employment needs of teaching and learning and higher education's contribution to basic, strategic and applied research should be enhanced to match international standards of excellence;
- arrangements for student support should be equitable and not distort students' choices inappropriately. The committee should report by summer 1997.

One of the central issues for the Dearing HE inquiry is 'whether expansion has gone too far' (Gillian Shephard, Secretary of State for Education and Employment in February 1996). 'You have got to ask yourself whether the continued wholesale expansion of the kind we have seen over the past 15 years will continue to result in improved economic effort. Can we maintain quality, and is the quality of what we have as good as we would like?'

The total numbers of HE enrolments at English institutions in 1995/96 was 1.63 million, an increase of 6% between 1994/95 and 1995/96. Postgraduate enrolments rose by 4%, first degree enrolments increased by 4%, and other undergraduate enrolments increased by 16%. 11 million (68%) of all enrolments are full-time; 51% of students are female in 1995/96 (HESA Statistics April 1996).

In the 1960s, 1 in 17 went on to HE. Today it is 1 in 3. In 1995 there were 184,000 new graduates, nearly three times as many as in 1975, and 86,700 postgraduates completed higher degrees. There are now more than a million full-time higher education students in the UK and half a million part-time students. By 2001, the number of graduates in the workforce is likely to be well over 3 million, twice as high as in 1981. Applications to UCAS by 15 December 1995 were 341,842.

Changes have taken place as a result of increased enrolments and rising student–staff ratios: larger numbers in lectures, fewer tutorials, etc.; more flexibility and experiments with the length and nature of degree courses; changes in how the content of a course is delivered to students; changes in the application procedures; and radical changes to sources of funding for students. *See* STUDENT FINANCIAL SUPPORT. Some of these topics are discussed in more detail below but for more information see the range of books available on higher education listed in the 'Bibliography' in Appendix 2.

The structure of higher education

Higher education courses post-18 fall into three levels:

- first-degree courses;
- postgraduate courses (entry to which is normally confined to graduates regardless of the academic standard of the course), which are dealt with later in this chapter;
- sub-degree HE courses which include HNC/HND and Diplomas of Higher Education; courses leading to a variety of professional qualifications; individual institutions' certificate and diploma courses and some courses of degree-equivalent standard. HNC/HND qualifications have already been covered above under BTEC and SCOTVEC.

First-degree courses

Most first degrees in the UK have the title of Bachelor – usually Bachelor of Science (BSc) or Bachelor of Arts (BA). However, there are others such as Bachelor of Laws (LLB), Bachelor of Education (BEd), Bachelor of Engineering (BEng) and Bachelor of Music (BMus), etc. Most subjects fall automatically into one category, but some subjects such as psychology and geography, may lead to either a BA or BSc; and at Oxford and Cambridge degrees in Science and Engineering are BA rather than BSc. In engineering and physics some 'special' first degrees may lead to Master of

Science (MSci) or Master of Engineering (MEng). In Scotland, because of the different pattern of education, most arts courses lead to a master's degree (MA).

Traditionally most first-degree courses take three years full-time, but there are variations and this is likely to diversify further. Some courses take longer to complete. Language courses, with an extra year spent abroad, may take four years (five years in Scotland). Some institutions offer four-year engineering courses leading to an MEng, while in Physics four-year courses lead to an MSci, an MPhys or a BPhys. Honours degree courses in Scotland are four years, although Scottish universities also run a three-year ordinary or general degree, whose aim is to confer breadth of learning. Some four-year courses are 'sandwich' rather than full-time with industrial training providing work experience as an integral part of the course. Some courses are five years minimum: medicine, veterinary science and dentistry.

On the one hand, courses in some subjects like engineering and physics are becoming longer than the average, while on the other, some institutions have experimented with two-year degree courses. The private University of Buckingham has been offering two-year courses in a selected range of subjects for many years, but a few degree courses, primarily aimed at mature students, are two-year fast-track degrees.

Transferring from one course to another has now become easier. Under the credit accumulation and transfer scheme (CATS) students gain maximum possible credit for any qualifications they already have and learning they have done, including 'experiential' learning.

Universities

Universities have existed in the UK for nearly 900 years, the oldest being Oxford and Cambridge, followed by St Andrews, Glasgow, Aberdeen and Edinburgh. Expansion resumed in the nineteenth century with more universities being established in industrial cities and in Wales, and more civic universities were founded in the early twentieth century (including Birmingham, Leeds, Sheffield and Bristol), followed by Reading, Nottingham, Hull, Exeter and Leicester.

With the expansion of HE in the 1960s, new universities were created, either from pre-existing colleges of advanced technology (Salford, Brunel, etc.), or as new 'green-field' campus sites like Lancaster, York and Sussex. Three universities founded at this time were untypical: the Open University, which teaches by distance-learning; the University of Buckingham, which is private; and the University of Ulster, which has separate funding from the Northern Ireland Office. Further expansion occurred in the 1990s when the new 'new universities' were formed from polytechnics and some of the larger colleges of higher education.

Some universities have a collegiate structure where students are enrolled as members of colleges of the university, i.e. Oxford, Cambridge, Durham, Kent, York and Lancaster. There are two federal universities in the UK – London and Wales; each consists of separate largely independent institutions but the degrees awarded are from London or Wales.

Most universities at present combine teaching and research and offer both undergraduate and postgraduate qualifications. However, traditional universities (as distinct from the 'new universities') have a greater share of postgraduate work and do very little sub-degree work.

The whole ethos of university education is still academic excellence, training in intellectual, and especially analytical skills, to a very high level indeed. Traditionally, university study is concentrated on the 'single honours' course, in which students study in considerable depth a single subject, with only subsidiary and supporting studies outside their main field. However, many universities now offer joint, general and combined and modular degree courses which enable students to make a much more flexible choice between various levels of specialisation. Additionally, many courses now offer a European dimension, and under the SOCRATES programme, students in many disciplines can spend a year abroad at a foreign university or institution, or even have a work-experience placement abroad.

Colleges/institutes of higher education in England and Wales

Colleges and institutes of HE emerged from the reorganisation of HE in the 1970s. Some had origins in teacher-training colleges; others were amalgamations of existing HE and FE institutions. They are located throughout England and Wales and vary considerably in size. They are usually campus-based. Some of the colleges are religious foundations, but they now welcome students of any cultural background.

Most colleges provide a range of academic and professional subjects at different levels, and no two colleges are alike. Many still retain their links with teacher training. A few are specialist institutions which concentrate on agriculture, art and design, or drama. The bias at many of these colleges is towards liberal arts, and comparatively few offer specialist degree courses in physical sciences or engineering.

Scottish colleges

There are nine colleges in Scotland (in addition to the 13 universities): Edinburgh College of Art, Glasgow School of Art, Moray House Institute of Education, Northern College of Education, Queen Margaret College, Royal Scottish Academy of Music and Drama, St Andrew's College, The Scottish Agricultural College and the Scottish College of Textiles. Two of the colleges (Queen Margaret College and the Royal Scottish Academy of Music and Drama) can award their own degrees while the other colleges have their courses validated by a university or degree-awarding body. All institutions offer postgraduate facilities.

Degree and diploma subjects

The number of degree and diploma subjects has proliferated in recent years. Here is a list of some of the possibilities.

Accountancy, acoustics, actuarial science, administration, advertising, aeronautical engineering, agriculture, American studies, antique restoration and management, archaeology, architecture, art and design, arts administration, astronomy, astronautics, auctioneering, audio-visual communications, banking, biochemistry, biological sciences, biotechnology, building studies, business studies, calligraphy, catering, ceramics, chemistry, Chinese, civil engineering, classical civilisation, classics, community studies, computers, conservation, counselling, craft, cybernetics, dance, dentistry, dietetics, drama, dress, earth studies, ecological studies, economics, education, electrical/electronic engineering, engineering, English, environmental health, environmental studies, equine studies, ergonomics, estate management, European business studies, European nursing, exhibition and museum design, expressive arts, field biology, film/television, finance, fine art, fishery studies, food science and nutrition, food technology, forestry, French, fuel and energy, furniture, general science, genetics, geography, geology, German, glass, global relationships, golf studies, graphic design, guidance and counselling, health studies, history, history of art, home and community studies, home economics, horse studies, horticulture, hotel management, humanities, human movement studies, illustration, industrial design, infant school education, information studies, information technology, insurance. integrated arts, interior design, international tourism, Italian, jewellery, land administration, landscape architecture, language studies, Latin/Greek and journalism, law, leather technology, leisure studies, library studies, linguistics, marine engineering, maritime leisure management, maritime studies, marketing, mathematics, mechanical engineering, media studies, medicine, metallurgy, microbiology, minerals, mining studies, modern languages, motor vehicle engineering, multi-cultural studies, music, music technology, natural science, nautical studies, naval architecture, needlecraft, nursing, occupational health, operational research, ophthalmic optics, organisation studies, outdoor pursuits, pathology, performing arts, personnel administration, pharmacy and pharmacology, philosophy, photography, physical education, physical sciences, physics, physiology, physiotherapy, podiatrics, politics, polymer science, printing, product design, production engineering, psychology, public administration, public relations, purchasing, quantity surveying, quarrying, radiography, recreation studies, religion, retail management, rural science, science, secretarial studies, social sciences, social work, sociology, Spanish, speech pathology, sport, stage management, statistics, surveying, systems technology, teacher training, telecommunications, textile technology, theatre arts, theology, timber technology, tourism, town planning, transportation, urban studies, valuing and auctioneering, veterinary science, Victorian studies, voice studies, Welsh, wildlife management, youth studies.

Entry requirements

A university has a general requirement and a course requirement. The general requirement sets out the minimum qualifications expected. These days, universities are more flexible in their approach and accept A-levels, AS-levels, GCSE, SCE, Advanced GNVQ/GSVQ, BTEC, SCOTVEC, IB and EB qualifications. However, not all courses will accept all the alternative entry qualifications and anyone offering these should check with the prospectus. (*See* GNVQS AND GSVQS *chapter.*)

University and college entrance offers are often made on the basis of points scored in examinations, where at A-level, grade A=10, B=8, C=6, D=4, and E=2, while at AS-level, A=5, B=4, C=3, D=2, and E=1. For SCE Highers, A=6 points, B=4 points and C=2 points. At present there is no points grading system for GNVQ/GSVQ, but this is currently under discussion. The maximum number of points possible is 30. The minimum offer for a degree is 4 points (for an HND, 2 points). Actual requirements are likely to be much higher.

The ratio of applications to acceptances by subject group for home applicants in 1994 within the UCAS system was as follows:

	Applications	Applications per place
Medicine and dentistry	73,271	13.3
Subjects allied to medicine	163,122	12.5
Biological sciences	146,446	9.0
Agriculture and related subjects	27,555	6.8
Physical sciences	115,856	7.4
Mathematical sciences	134,176	6.5
Engineering & Technology	182,850	7.0
Architecture, building and planning	53,488	7.4
Social sciences	332,675	9.2
Business & Administration	332,941	8.8
Mass communication and documentation	77,368	11.2
Languages and related studies	148,651	8.3
Humanities	85,907	7.8
Creative Arts	105,484	11.7
Education	240,422	11.3

There is no precise equivalence between SCE Higher grades and GCE A-level grades but, in general terms, applicants who have achieved high grades (A and B) in SCE Higher grade exams may be regarded as comparable in general ability and intellectual potential to candidates who have done well at GCE. A candidate with four good quality Higher passes would be likely to receive an offer of a place on most courses at Scottish universities, with the exception of heavily over-subscribed courses such as medicine and veterinary medicine where five Highers are normally demanded, with most or all at grade A. CSYS may be required for some subjects at

English universities but this qualification is being phased out.

There are also course requirements to meet for many degree subjects, and these reflect the policy of the subject department at the various universities. *University and College Entrance: The Official Guide* is the best source to establish what these are.

Applications procedures

UCAS now (1996) handles applications for most degree (and HND) subjects including teaching and art and design. From 1997 it will also handle applications for nursing. Candidates can list up to six courses on the UCAS application form, which is then photocopied by UCAS and sent simultaneously to all six institutions. Experiments are underway with electronic transmission of data.

The system for art and design is slightly different and candidates have a choice of whether to follow normal UCAS procedures or to follow what was the old Art and Design Registry route for studio-based courses. Scottish art schools accept individual applications.

Consult the *UCAS Handbook* and the *Entrance Guide to Higher Education in Scotland*.

Further information

Committee of Vice-Chancellors and Principals of the universities (CVCP), UCAS, Committee of Scottish Higher Education Principals (COSHEP).

Degrees, vocational preparation and careers

Formal entry to the majority of professional-level careers is now, with few exceptions, a degree. Organisations of all kinds believe that to operate in today's conditions, young and highly intelligent, trained minds – graduates – are essential in almost every 'function'. This extends from the largest multinationals through to some of the smallest companies, especially those which are innovating, moving over from older to new technologies, and/or adopting the latest managerial/ production techniques. Although most organisations are holding down hard the total numbers they employ, in general they expect to maintain or even increase the proportion of graduate recruits.

But graduates, like everyone else searching for a career, will still have to be more open-minded about the kind of work they will accept. The movement of graduates into new areas of employment is a continuous process which has been going on for as long as the supply of graduates has been growing. New opportunities will continue to be in areas of employment which may not have recruited graduates before, and in totally new areas of work. The employment sectors, and the jobs, requiring graduates will be changing, often swiftly and fundamentally. Graduates will almost certainly have to be as flexible, adaptable and innovative as the rest of the workforce.

Most degree courses are not intended to have direct, practical vocational value. There are advantages, however, in following a degree course as it provides a better base for the career changes which face even the highly qualified in the future. A degree gives considerably wider career choice than lower-level qualifications, and generally shortens the time needed to complete professional qualifications. It also lets young people put off final decisions about what occupation to start with in working life until graduation or after, which means they are likely to know themselves better and be more mature, be better informed about the possibilities and be able to take account of the most recent changes in the labour market.

For most graduates the major problem is coping with the dramatic switch from being 'driven' above all else to try for the highest-possible level of intellectual and academic excellence, to the ever-tightening drive for cost-benefit and meeting performance targets and schedules out in the real world. A degree is an advantage, but even a good degree will not automatically ensure graduates a good job, rapid promotion, managerial status, or a high salary.

Graduates, like everyone else, have to prepare, plan, plot, research, and use all their skills and intelligence to compete effectively in the job market. It makes sense for students to think about life post-university and use the services provided by the careers advisory service at their institution. Without going to extremes, it is worth mapping out a broad general personal strategy, starting to look at the broader possibilities, and finding out about employers' demands of graduates sometime during the first year.

By the middle of their final year, well-prepared students should have done a lot of research. They will know a great deal about the graduate job market in general and about particular career opportunities and employers, as well as having a fair idea of what they want and what they have to offer employers. They will know what skills, academic and other, are needed for specific openings, and have some idea of what jobs involve. They will know something about firms or organisations in the areas that interest them, their successes and problems, facts and figures on them. They may have spent time adding to the skills and experience learnt on their courses.

Well-prepared students have a plan which either keeps their options as wide open as possible, or allows for alternatives, since they will know that it is very unrealistic to be too single-minded. They have taken the trouble to learn how to sell themselves to employers, how to fill in application forms to the best advantage, and how to handle an interview.

All this takes time, and cannot be done in a rush in the few short weeks at the start of the final year. The process ought nowadays to begin much earlier, especially for the very many students who have little idea of what they want to do. The alternative, which is increasingly popular with many students, is to leave career-searching until they have completed their final examinations. This may be safe to do when demand for graduates is healthy but can cause real problems in times of recession when there are fewer vacancies.

Employers generally take a reasonable academic record for granted. They will also tend to assume that university will have taught all graduates to think logically, to search out relevant information, marshal facts and arguments systematically and analyse them properly, be able to see what information is important in a given situation, and have the basic skills needed for problem-solving, whatever subject they may have studied.

They also want qualities and skills not necessarily taught on a degree course. They expect graduates they recruit to be capable of developing organisational, supervisory, planning and administrative skills. They want graduates who can learn quickly, apply their intelligence and contribute early. They want their graduate recruits to fit in; to be able to work with people at all levels, as part of a team; to be able to communicate easily and clearly, both in talking and listening to people and making verbal reports, and on paper; to be 'self-starters', and to adapt quickly to the 'real' world where solutions inevitably involve compromises.

It is also useful for students to have some kind of real work experience at least once between 16 and 21, if only to convince employers they can do it. The more responsible the job, the more 'relevant' it can be. Sandwich courses of course have an advantage here.

Many employers also like graduates to show they have taken on some kind of real responsibility – and most universities are ideal places to gain this in real situations, where mistakes can be made without major consequences. It is possible to edit a student newspaper – and so learning to coordinate a team of voluntary journalists and meet tight set schedules, to organise printing the paper within budgets set by a management committee, to see that advertising space is sold, and often sell the paper itself too. Here students can learn fast that meeting deadlines is difficult, that printers charge a lot for overtime if copy is late or has to be re-edited, that journalists have to be able to count words if a story is to fit into the space allocated to it, that even in a creative business careful planning is needed, and that being organised is important, as is communicating well with staff.

Alternatively, it is possible to gain 'work experience' on a voluntary or full-time basis in the student union, organising student entertainments or welfare, managing student facilities such as bars, shops and cafeterias. Being secretary of a departmental society, organising student social/community work effort, putting on plays, or running sports programmes all give the right kind of experience. Getting involved in student activities, voluntary work, etc. can help students to see that there are skills other than those learnt on a formal course, and these are just as important for their careers as their academic abilities.

Universities are also good places to improve on numeracy, and experiment with IT systems and computers – recruiters would like their graduate recruits to have some business-related IT training on both the user and 'computer professional' sides. For most engineers and scientists this usually all comes as part of the course package. Arts students may also have a free choice of some kind of subsidiary study, which could be in maths or statistics, and the computer centre generally puts on spare-time IT/computer appreciation and/or elementary programming courses for anyone who wants them.

University language centres/labs mostly give undergraduates the chance to keep up their languages, or start them from scratch, in their spare time – and these too are useful 'add-on' skills, with the new European dimension to consider.

Students aiming to prepare themselves properly will use their careers advisory service. Careers advisers will help graduates to come to an informed decision, and organise their thinking about themselves and their futures, and help them assess themselves realistically. Higher education careers services collect a wide range of literature and information about all kinds of careers, statistics, directories, data on areas of employment and individual employers. Careers advisers both sell graduate skills and try to stay ahead of developments in graduate employment. Careers services put on talks and seminars, and courses, like short introductions to aspects of management – a week spent playing business games with people from industry, commerce and public service; give practice interview sessions, and help with filling in forms and making up a curriculum vitae. They run recruitment fairs and operate the 'milk round' of employers. *See also* THE JOB SEARCH.

Degree subject and careers

In some subject areas a degree combines the educational base required for particular careers – for example, medicine, dentistry and architecture – but for these the practical training is integrated into the degree course, lengthening it appropriately to some five or more years. The need for engineering graduates with greater understanding of industry's needs is also lengthening a considerable proportion of engineering courses, to four (and even more) years. Courses in some other subjects provide a large measure of the educational requirements and specialist knowledge needed for entry to particular professions – for example, law, and some sciences (including, for instance, pharmacy) – but practical training or professional courses are needed before the graduate is considered fully 'professional'. Sandwich courses, in which a student spends some part of his or her degree course gaining relevant work experience, go some way towards meeting the need for a practical component for some degrees, but again the period of study has to be lengthened to allow for this, to four or five years.

As an approximate guide, therefore, a graduate with a degree in a subject which is relevant to a profession or function should expect to spend two years in addition to the three for the degree in completing vocational training. The graduate who has read a subject which has no direct vocational value, or who enters a career unrelated to his or her degree subject must usually be prepared to spend rather longer training, although this depends to some extent on the occupation or function. There are, of course, exceptions. Teaching, for example, where the study of the subject(s) to be taught is considered far more important than learning teaching skills, still offers only one year's formal training on top of a degree.

School-leavers can, of course, choose to read subjects at university which are more specifically vocation-orientated. Demand for such courses has been rising sharply but there are possible pitfalls. Very narrow vocational specialisation makes it difficult to move into a different career if the choice proves wrong for the individual – or the job vanishes as a result of competition or technological change. Law is an example of a subject which has both direct vocational value in a legal career, but is also appreciated by employers in many other sectors, so its vocational 'value' has held up remarkably well. Accountancy, as a degree subject, may not have such currency because it tends to be rather narrow. Neither the legal nor the accountancy profession restricts entry to graduates with relevant degrees – because they would rather recruit from amongst the best graduates than from people with degrees in appropriate subjects but poor results. One of the best routes to management consultancy in industry is via an engineering degree, a professional accountancy qualification, and an MBA – not a route often recommended to candidates.

The answer is to encourage candidates to study the subject – or subjects – that really interest them, and interest them most. A good degree is almost essential, and gaining a good degree means enjoying the subject. There are plenty of ways of improving career prospects which are better than choosing a subject which can easily prove boring in pursuit of what may be an illusory career three or four years hence.

Graduate employment

In general, graduate employment tends to go in cycles as the employment market is so volatile lurching from too few graduates of the right calibre to fill the plentiful supply of vacancies through to too many graduates chasing too few jobs. The broad trend of graduate recruitment in any one year, however, may not always correspond to the demand and supply of graduates in particular disciplines. Many employers too, despite the recession in the 1990s, still in 1995 mention some difficulty in recruitment of graduates with the personal skills they are looking for, i.e. 'basic', 'personal transferable' or 'core' skills in business awareness and communication. Other skills in short supply include ability to work as a team, leadership, and problem-solving.

It is highly unlikely that there will ever be a return to the situation prevailing in the late 1980s when companies could not recruit enough graduates. Graduates are inevitably affected by recession and cutbacks in recruitment, but they are in a better position to take advantage of current employment opportunities than most other groups in the population. More graduates too are staying on in higher education to do postgraduate courses leading to a higher degree or diploma and in most years this figure is around 25%.

In 1995 the supply of vacancies for graduates rose by 10% (AGR). However, an independent survey by the Industrial Relations Services (IRS) in 1995 says students graduating in 1996 are likely to find it more difficult to get a degree-entry job. Their survey of nearly 200 employers, representing a total workforce of more than 1 million, found that while graduate output is expected to increase by 14% in 1996, graduate vacancies are projected to rise by only 2.4%. Over 25% of employers in the survey said they expected to cut their graduate intake in 1996, with the big recruiters being most likely to forecast lower vacancy levels. The IRS survey also claimed to have found evidence of an unofficial 'two-tier' quality threshold among graduate recruiters, with an in-built prejudice against the former polytechnics.

Targeting of specific universities by 'milk-round' employers was also identified in a report by Cranfield School of Management in 1996 – 'universities were targeted because they were considered of high quality, because of their close research links with the company, or had graduates with degrees in specialist subjects'. These findings are disputed by the higher education Careers Services Unit (CSU) and Association of Graduate Careers Advisory Services (AGCAS). 'The job market is coping remarkably well with the increase in graduate numbers. The whole of the higher education sector, including the new universities, has recorded a big rise in the percentage of degree holders finding jobs and a drop in unemployment' (President of AGCAS, April 1996). So the picture is confusing!

Graduates are recruited for particular, and a widening range, of 'functions' by firms and other organisations in almost all sectors of employment now. Most organisations recruiting graduates expect the majority to develop as future managers, some to become the senior managers.

Graduates are being encouraged to think of working for small firms, and to set up businesses of their own. The Association of Graduate Recruiters in their book *Skills for Graduates in the 21st Century* say 'Smaller businesses are the most likely growth employment sector for the future. Between 1989 and 1991, businesses employing fewer than 20 people created over a million extra jobs, twice as many as large firms.'

In most occupations/functions/professions it is usual to have special entry arrangements for graduates, with either exemptions from parts of the professional examination according to the relevance of their degree, or shorter, more intensive, and specially designed training courses. Many major firms and other organisations have formal graduate development programmes lasting up to 24 months, but the number taken on each year varies considerably according to the economic climate. However, after induction and initial training few companies have formal career development for graduates, and graduates are now expected to manage their own careers. 'Graduates can no longer expect the promise of a guaranteed career from employers, but the offer of a development opportunity instead' (Cranfield report 1996).

Graduates are also increasingly employed into 'real' jobs, and expected to perform well from day one. The competition for places on graduate training schemes in popular occupations, e.g. the media, is likely to go on being stiff, since the number of actual places per year is very small.

The AGR have identified a number of areas where graduate roles are changing:

- smaller proportion of graduates in traditional graduate jobs;
- vanishing career ladder;
- more graduates filling 'non-graduate' jobs in large organisations;
- more graduates in small and medium-sized businesses;
- more graduates becoming self-employed;
- many graduates needing to cope with unemployment;
- many graduates underemployed.

First-destination figures do not, obviously, reflect the very latest trends, since they are inevitably somewhat out of date. However, the latest available (for 1993–94, published July 1995) are at least some indication of trends. The university statistics for home first-degree graduates with known destination in permanent home employment 1993–94 analysed by employer category and subject group is as follows:

		Percentage of total				
Subject group	Total	Public service	Education	Industry	Commerce	Miscellaneous
Engineering and technology	4,707	7.2	2.4	69.7	16.7	3.9
Medicine and dentistry	3,995	90.0	0.1	–	0.1	9.8
Social sciences	4,077	17.6	4.9	12.6	50.8	14.2
Business and finance	2,449	8.0	1.8	21.1	61.2	7.8
Physical sciences	2,269	14.0	6.0	33.5	37.3	9.1
Mathematics	2,658	6.0	4.0	22.7	61.2	6.1
Languages	3,008	8.5	8.0	13.1	53.1	17.3
Biological sciences	2,260	20.2	12.6	21.0	31.9	14.2
Humanities	2,212	14.3	8.2	9.5	48.1	29.9
Allied to medicine	1,843	53.9	2.2	6.8	25.8	11.3
Education	1,060	6.8	82.6	1.1	4.4	5.0
Veterinary science, agriculture, etc.	593	5.6	6.2	35.8	9.3	43.2
Architecture, etc.	616	12.7	2.8	71.9	8.6	4.1
Creative arts	487	7.2	13.1	5.5	27.1	47.0
Multidisciplinary	3,842	12.3	5.9	16.5	51.5	13.7

Postgraduate qualifications

There are three types of postgraduate qualification: a master's degree (MA/MSc or MBA); a doctorate (Doctor of Philosophy styled PhD/DPhil); or a postgraduate Certificate or Diploma.

These qualifications may be obtained by instruction or by research.

Master's degrees

Some masters courses are wholly taught and involve little or no original research. Others are research-based. Most courses last one or two years.

Taught courses are available in almost every subject, and for a number of quite different purposes. Some allow students to study a topic from their first-degree subject in considerable depth. Some are designed to give students high-level training in an applied area of their original degree subject, e.g. medical biochemistry. Some are designed as 'conversion' courses, e.g. to train physics graduates as electronics specialists, chemists as chemical engineers or in control and instrumentation, mathematicians as engineers. Extra awards may be available to increase the number of specialists in crucial subjects e.g., biotechnology and information technology. Some courses, e.g. an MBA (Master of Business Administration), are mainly designed for graduates who have worked for some time.

Doctorates

Doctorates are awarded for original research which makes a real contribution to knowledge, and both arts and science students are awarded the degree of Doctor of Philosophy. Research is normally done in the HE institutions, but it is possible to do a research degree elsewhere if the arrangements for supervision are suitable.

In theory it is possible to do research in almost any subject. In practice the problem is one of funding, and this is much easier to find to do research which has practical value for industry. Some awards are tied to work at particular universities, either because the research/training being done there is approved by the grant-awarding body and/or, in social sciences, because they are successful at getting students to complete their theses to time. *See* STUDENT FINANCIAL SUPPORT.

Certificates and Diplomas

Other one-year courses can lead to professional qualifications. Even for graduates, full-time training is normally essential for some occupations, e.g. archive work, law, librarianship, museum work, planning, clinical and educational psychology, and social work. For some other occupations it may be an advantages to have completed a course before looking for vacancies. Examples are arts administration, journalism, personnel and secretarial. Some courses are 'taught' higher degrees (*as above*); others are certificate or diploma courses at university, or other colleges: yet others lead to the exams of professional bodies. Competition for some places, at e.g. law schools, can be considerable.

Career prospects for people with postgraduate qualifications vary, although the percentage of postgraduates who are still unemployed six months after completion of their studies has always been very low.

The University Statistics for 1993–94 show that there were 44,223 home higher-degree graduates (double the number of 1983–84) and, of those with a known destination, just under three-quarters found permanent employment in the UK; a further 15% went on to further study in the UK. The destinations varied according to subject group. Education continued to have the highest proportion of home graduates entering employment (91%).

The destinations of home higher-degree graduates in permanent employment in the UK were: 29.4% into education, 25.4% into public service, 21.4% into industry and 13.5% into commerce. About 39% of postgraduates were female. A high proportion of postgraduates are overseas students returning home.

Contents

General National Vocational Qualifications (GNVQs) and General Scottish Vocational Qualifications (GSVQs)

GNVQ/GSVQs are comparatively new vocational qualifications which have been designed as a stepping-stone to a wide range of employment opportunities, and to further and higher education. GNVQs and GSVQs have developed from a different base so are considered separately although the qualifications are broadly comparable.

In England, Wales and Northern Ireland the National Council for Vocational Qualifications (NCVQ) developed GNVQs and now ensure that standards are maintained. The individual examining or awarding bodies are Business and Technology Education Council (BTEC); Royal Society of Arts (RSA); City & Guilds of London Institute.

In Scotland GSVQs fit into the framework of established qualifications administered and awarded by the Scottish Vocational Education Council (SCOTVEC).

GNVQ/GSVQs are aimed primarily at 16–19 year olds but are also suitable for adult returners. Those aged 14–16 can build up credits in England, Wales and Northern Ireland on a Part One GNVQ (*see* EDUCATION AND QUALIFICATIONS) but cannot get the full qualification. In 1995, 44,781 students completed a GNVQ course.

GNVQs

Structure

GNVQs offer a learning programme which spells out exactly what is required rather than covering a knowledge-based traditional syllabus. Students are encouraged to take responsibility for their own learning and teachers use a wide range of teaching and learning strategies including projects, assignments and other activities which are carried out individually or in groups.

GNVQs are available at three levels:

- Foundation or level 1
- Intermediate or level 2
- Advanced or level 3

A Higher GNVQ at level 4, equivalent to a first degree, may be a future possibility.

Advanced GNVQs have sometimes been referred to as 'vocational A-levels', but the Dearing Report (1996) proposes renaming them as Applied A-levels.

At present GNVQ is broadly equivalent at Foundation level to four GCSEs grades D–G, at Intermediate level to four GCSEs grades A–C, and at Advanced level to two A-levels. There is, however, no cut-and-dried definition of equivalence, and to a certain extent the value of a GNVQ is in the eye of the beholder – it depends on the organisation, institution or individual! One of Dearing's central proposals is a single qualifications structure which will allow easy comparison between A-levels, GNVQs and NVQs. If this is implemented:

- a full Advanced GNVQ of twelve units, plus the three core units will be equivalent to an Applied A-level (double award), i.e. two A-levels;
- six Advanced GNVQ units plus the three core units will be equivalent to an Applied A-level, i.e. one A-level;
- three mandatory Advanced GNVQ units will be equivalent to an Applied AS-level.

Note that the last recommendation presupposes the creation of a new three-unit award at Advanced level to be known as the Applied AS. Dearing proposed that the Advanced Supplementary examination should be renamed Advanced Subsidiary and be reformulated as an interim qualification for those who do not wish to complete the full A-level. The new AS would still count for half the UCAS tariff points of an A-level for university entrance (*see in* EDUCATION AND QUALIFICATIONS for an explanation of the UCAS system).

Advanced GNVQ is designed to take two years full-time. A typical Intermediate GNVQ and Foundation programmes are designed to take one full year. However, many students taking Advanced and Intermediate GNVQs need longer to complete.

GNVQs are very different from traditional academic qualifications. The backbone of any GNVQ programme is broken down into chunks, called 'units'. At present, the different levels consist of:

Advanced GNVQ

- 8 mandatory vocational units

- 4 optional units from a range of about 8
- 3 core skills units at levels 3 or above

Intermediate GNVQ
- 4 mandatory vocational units in the chosen vocational area
- 2 optional vocational units in the same area
- 3 core skills units at level 2 or above

Foundation GNVQ
- 3 mandatory units in the chosen vocational area
- 3 optional units
- 3 core skills units at level 1 or above.

Unlike Intermediate and Advanced GNVQs, optional units for Foundation GNVQs may be chosen from several vocational areas.

Additional units may also be studied.

All GNVQs at present have three mandatory core skills units in: Communication, i.e. communicating with people; Application of Number, i.e. using numbers in the GNVQ subject matter; Information Technology, i.e. using computers. There are also optional core skill units in personal skills.

Each unit is subdivided into *elements* which specify what skills, knowledge and understanding must be achieved in a particular area. These elements are then further broken down into over 100 specific *performance criteria* or the essential things that need to be done. All performance criteria operate within a *range* or area of knowledge. The range outlines the information to cover and provides depth. For example, in GNVQ Business, the range might cover different types of business: franchise, partnership, sole trader, etc. The performance criteria and the range produce materials, known as *evidence*, which is gathered together in one place: the *portfolio*. The portfolio of evidence is examined by continual assessment according to the unit specifications.

The evidence may be collected by carrying out a wide range of activities such as reading, writing, measuring, questioning, calculating, interviewing, designing, etc. The evidence can include written reports, letters, sets of notes, tapes, videos, photographs, and other artefacts. If a portfolio contains sufficient evidence and it is all fully indexed and fully tracked, the student is awarded a GNVQ.

There are multiple-choice tests (which have to be passed) but there are no traditional written examinations. GNVQs are assessed and graded on the basis of the evidence in the portfolio. There are three grades: pass, merit and distinction. To get merit and distinction you have to satisfy the grading criteria. Units are not graded separately. Universities may ask for merit or distinction grades for Advanced GNVQ.

Entry requirements

There are no set entry requirements. However, many schools and colleges consider the minimum entry for Advanced level GNVQ is four GCSEs at grades C; the average Intermediate student has between one and two GCSEs.

Progress is possible up through the levels, but while a student with an Intermediate GNVQ with merit may achieve a reasonable Advanced GNVQ, a student who has only just passed their Intermediate GNVQ will probably find Advanced GNVQ difficult.

GNVQ Subjects

GNVQs provide the background knowledge and skills required for a broad occupational area, rather than specific skills which may only be suitable for a very narrow range of jobs. They usually contain work experience (but not always) and subjects are related to local companies and other organisations outside school and college.

GNVQs are currently available in Art and Design, Business, Construction and the Built Environment, Engineering, Health and Social Care, Hospitality and Catering, Information Technology, Leisure and Tourism, Management Studies (Advanced only and pilot extended 1996-97), Manufacturing, Media: Communication and Production, Retail and Distributive Services, and Science (at Intermediate and Advanced levels).

Art and Design develops creative skills, and a knowledge and understanding of the art and design industry. Courses cover painting, drawing, modelling, working with textiles and using computers. Students investigate art and design businesses, and gain practical experience of working to briefs and evaluating and presenting their work.

Business develops the understanding, knowledge and skills needed in the business world today. During the course students investigate a wide range of areas and learn about accounts and handling finance, how to promote and sell products and how to provide good customer care. Students visit companies and organisations to find out more about working in business.

Construction and the Built Environment increases understanding of the built environment, and helps to develop the knowledge and skills needed to work in the construction industry. During the course students investigate materials and their uses and the technology of houses, towers, bridges and airports. Students also develop practical skills in drawing, CAD, laboratory work, surveying and measurement.

Engineering increases the understanding of engineering, and develops the knowledge and skills needed to work in the engineering industry. During the course students investigate engineering systems and processes, produce engineered products, produce design briefs and design solutions, and apply mathematics and scientific laws and principles to engineering activities.

Health and Social Care helps to develop an understanding of health and care, and teaches some of the skills and knowledge needed to work in the health and social care services. During the course students look at physical, psychological and social aspects of health and care, and how services meet people's needs. The course develops practical skills like communicating with people and how to provide emotional support. Students usually spend time working with, and talking to, people in a health and social care environment.

Hospitality and Catering increases understanding of hospitality and catering and develops the knowledge and skills needed to work in the industry. During the course students investigate employment opportunities in the industry, and develop practical customer care skills in preparing and serving food and drink, reception, and other hospitality and catering functions. Students usually spend time visiting local businesses to see hospitality and catering in action.

Information Technology increases understanding and knowledge of information technology and develops the skills needed to work in IT. During the course students explore information technology in action, find out about tools and techniques for working with information, analyse information needs in different contexts and produce effective solutions.

Leisure and Tourism helps students to understand the leisure and tourism industry in the UK, and develop the skills needed to work in leisure and tourism. During the course students learn how different businesses operate, how to organise an event and make sure it runs smoothly, how to market leisure activities and tourist facilities and how to provide good customer service. To gain a better understanding of the leisure and tourism industry, many students visit different facilities to evaluate their performance and report on aspects of health, safety and security.

Management Studies focuses on the roles and responsibilities of management. It covers services and products, customer relations, communication skills, employment and recruitment, handling budgets and handling information.

Manufacturing increases understanding of how products are made, and develops some of the skills and knowledge involved in manufacturing today. During the course students gain technical knowledge and experience of the processes involved, design and present specifications for products and plan and carry out production processes. Students also investigate environmental issues. As well as carrying out practical work students usually visit local businesses to see manufacturing in action.

Manufacturing is not specifically an engineering qualification, but it can embrace varying amounts of engineering.

Media: Communication and Production develops knowledge, skills and understanding of media items and products. During the course students plan and produce an audiovisual product and a print and graphic product, investigate local, regional and national media, and carry out media marketing and audience research.

Retail and Distributive Services develops the understanding, knowledge and skills needed for the distribution and retail industries. During the course students cover distribution, warehousing and retail operations, learn about selling and how to provide good customer service, and develop the skills needed for marketing, purchasing, finance and administration.

Science helps students to understand the work of scientists, and to develop the skills and knowledge needed to work in science. During the course students develop skills across the biological, chemical and physical sciences, find out more about materials and their uses, learn how to make new chemicals, explore scientific areas such as sports science, forensic science and ecology, and learn about food production, nutrition and healthcare.

Two new GNVQs are being piloted at Foundation, Intermediate and Advanced levels starting 1996–97.

Performing Arts and Entertainment Industries covers music, dance and drama with their stagecraft and prepares students for a variety of employment areas, including arts administration and production management, as well as performance. The qualification can be delivered in the art form preferred. Optional and additional units will be available.

The Land and Environment GNVQ is a qualification for anyone interested in working with plants and/or animals, working outside, with their hands, and with nature. It prepares students for a variety of vocational areas, including: agriculture, horticulture (amenity and commercial), forestry, animal care, environmental conservation/management, and extractive industries. Students will have the opportunity to focus on their particular interests. These may be animal-related (e.g. pig farming), plant-related (e.g. forestry), or land related (e.g. nature reserves).

Additional subjects

GNVQs were designed so that they could be taken in combination with other qualifications, or units of qualifications. With Advanced GNVQ you could take: one or two GCSEs, one or two A-levels, AS-levels, extra units from your GNVQ subject or other GNVQs, extra units from NVQs, BTEC National modules. With Intermediate you could take three additional GNVQ units, NVQ units, one or two GCSEs, BTEC modules or an AS-level.

GSVQs

Scotland has a vocational education system based on individual units of study: National Certificate Modules, Higher National Units, and Workplace Assessed Units. Each vocational unit covers a particular topic and can be free-standing; or the units can be put together to form one of the following group awards:

- National Certificates (including GSVQs);
- SVQs;
- Higher National Certificate/Diploma
- Professional Development Awards

GSVQs are broadly comparable to GNVQs so:

- GSVQ level I = GNVQ level 1
- GSVQ level II = GNVQ level 2
- GSVQ level III = GNVQ level 3

Most GSVQs are available at levels II and III

At present there are no GSVQ level IV or V. Level IV qualifications are likely to be based on existing Higher National Certificates (HNCs) and Higher National Diplomas (HNDs). HNCs and HNDs are widely recognised qualifications at higher technician/junior management level. They are made up of a fixed number of Higher National Units; twelve for an HNC and 30 for an HND. They are offered by colleges on a full-time, part-time or open-learning basis.

Structure

All GSVQs include mandatory and optional modules and a range of core skills covering communication, numeracy, information technology, problem-solving and interpersonal skills. Most modules should take about 40 hours of study to complete.

Some advanced course programmes, e.g. Technology, may have additional specialist modules which should help students progress to HNC/HND and possibly to degree courses as well.

Students and trainees taking GSVQs at levels II and III can obtain 'merit' grading which indicates significant achievement in the GSVQ programme as a whole. Individual National Certificate Modules making up the programme will not, however, be graded.

GSVQ National Certificate level I consists of twelve module credits. Six of these credits may be common to Skillstart 2 (*see below*). Level I is broadly based and flexible. It is not linked to any particular vocational area. It normally takes one year to complete.

GSVQ National Certificate level II consists of 13 credits and normally takes one year to complete.

GSVQ National Certificate level III consists of 20 module credits and normally takes two years to complete.

National Certificate Clusters are made up of three units from a single vocational area.

Skillstart awards are less demanding courses designed for slower learners and those with mild to moderate learning difficulties.

Subjects

GSVQs are available in 13 broad occupational areas: business administration, hospitality, leisure and tourism, care, technology, arts and social sciences, design, information technology, land-based industries, science, construction, engineering, and communication and media.

GSVQ programmes can be combined with other courses including additional National Certificate Modules or Highers.

Numbers taking GSVQ are much smaller than for GNVQ. GSVQ uptake for 1994–95 for all levels was only 3,437. This is because centres are holding back from introducing GSVQs until they know what will happen under *Higher Still*. Moreover, the further education colleges already have National Certificate programmes of their own which link with their HNC/HND programmes. The most popular courses are care and hospitality as this is the area where further education colleges wanted to update their courses.

Higher education

GNVQ

Of the 22,500 Advanced GNVQ students approximately 9,555 GNVQ students applied through UCAS to HE in 1995, almost 90% of whom achieved at least one offer of a place on a degree or diploma course. This represents a slight increase on the offer rate for 1994 applicants. Applicants to HND courses were more likely to receive an offer than those to degree programmes.

All applicants for HE were taking additional studies as well as their Advanced GNVQ. An increasing proportion of those receiving offers supplemented their GNVQ with additional GNVQ units rather than other types of qualification: 1,667 offered one GCE A-level, while 294 students offered two A-levels. The additional A-levels were more likely to be in related subjects, i.e. Art, Design, or Photography with Advanced GNVQ Art and Design, or Accounts, Business Studies, Economics, General Studies, Law or Sociology with Advanced GNVQ Business. HE admissions tutors have mixed views on the value of combining A-levels with Advanced GNVQ. Some find it reassuring that students can cope with three-hour unseen examinations and/or essay-writing, while others are concerned at the apparent duplication and lack of breadth of the sixth-form studies.

Most GNVQ applicants had studied Art and Design, Leisure and Tourism or Health and Social Care. Applicants from subject areas such as Business, or Leisure and Tourism were significantly more likely to receive offers than those taking Art and Design or Health and Social Care. Most Advanced GNVQ applicants selected courses closely related to the title of their GNVQ programme area. NCVQ is investigating the Advanced GNVQ in Health and Social Care to clarify whether HE selectors are looking for more science in a student's background for entry onto courses in subjects allied to medicine.

Applicants from the newer GNVQ titles – Science, Hospitality and Catering, and Construction and the Built Environment – were very successful in gaining offers.

GNVQ applicants to 'post-1992 universities' (i.e. former polytechnics and some colleges of higher education), or to colleges of higher education, were more likely to receive an offer than those who applied to the more traditional Higher Education Institutions (HEIs).

For numerate degree courses selectors were often concerned about Advanced GNVQ students' abilities to cope with the mathematics content. The core skill of Application of Number at level 3 was not necessarily seen as an alternative to GCSE grade C in mathematics. Students without GCSE mathematics were also at a disadvantage for HND courses with this requirement.

UCAS had 393,000 applicants for 1995 entry so the number of Advanced GNVQ applicants through UCAS is still very small. ADAR identified 1,180 Advanced GNVQ Art and Design applicants for 1995 entry, some of whom were jointly registered with UCAS.

Most applicants were taking Advanced GNVQs in college and were accredited by BTEC. However, there is apparently no particular bias in favour of a particular accrediting body.

GSVQ

There are no up-to-date statistics on what happens to GSVQ students applying to HE. UCAS/GATE do not keep separate statistics because numbers are very small. However a SCOTVEC survey of GSVQ students showed that:

- 5% were probably aiming for a degree
- 18% were aiming for an HND
- 37% were aiming for an HNC
- 12% were aiming for a professional qualification
- 22% were aiming for a higher level GSVQ
- 6% were aiming for standard grades or higher grades

A very high percentage of Scottish students go on to an HNC/D linked to a degree course.

Employment

There are no statistics at present to show how successful the GNVQ/GSVQ route is into employment. A high proportion of Intermediate students progress to Advanced GNVQ/GSVQ and from Advanced level most students looked to HE rather than employment.

With any new qualification it can take a long time before employers become familiar with it, but recognition of its potential is growing:

- most employers are aware of work-related NVQ/SVQs and some students combine units of these with their GNVQ/GSVQ to increase their employability;
- some employers provide work experience as part of GNVQ/GSVQ;
- some employers, such as the Hairdressing Employers Association, have set up GNVQ compacts which either facilitate entry into their industry or at least guarantee a job interview;
- some employers are involved in the 'GNVQ scholarship scheme'.

Under the GNVQ Scholarship Scheme, major national companies have agreed to support students in a variety of ways. Some companies offer work placements or part-time employment opportunities to GNVQ students as part of their course; others provide information, assignments or other learning materials. Scholarships may also include financial rewards or benefits in kind for certain categories of student, or employment opportunities for GNVQ graduates.

The first schemes began January 1995 and included employers such as Peugeot, Vidal Sassoon, American Express, Laing, Hilton International and Sainsbury's. With the latest scholarships announced, BUPA Dental will be providing opportunities for Health and Social Care students to investigate customer service in the health industry; and World Wide Fund for Nature, and Tioxide plc, will encourage Advanced GNVQ students to look primarily at the role of science in environmental management. There are currently (1996) around 15 national scholarships, and 125 local scholarships up and running

Local scholarship awards encourage employers and schools and colleges to work together to increase the vocational relevance of GNVQ programmes.

Further Information

NCVQ, SCOTVEC and awarding bodies.

Contents

National Vocational Qualifications (NVQs) and Scottish Vocational Qualifications (SVQs)

Background, evaluation and future developments

The *Review of Vocational Qualifications* in 1986 set up the National Council for Vocational Qualifications (NCVQ) to sort out the qualifications jungle and establish a simpler, clearer and better-linked system, a 'national vocational qualifications framework' to meet the employment needs of industry, commerce and the professions. NCVQ is a 'quality assurance body' covering England, Wales and Northern Ireland and is not in itself an examining or validating body.

The 1986 review also set the criteria for NVQs, and NCVQ worked with other interested bodies to define the 'competence' requirements: skills, knowledge, understanding and ability.

The development of SVQs in Scotland started from a different basis. SCOTVEC had been created in 1984, and the whole of Scottish non-advanced further education was already competence-based. SCOTVEC now introduced 'national awards', i.e. SVQs, for specified groups of modules which matched industry-specified standards. SVQs therefore developed in parallel to NVQs and are very similar. However, unlike NCVQ, SCOTVEC is an examining and validating body and this has had certain advantages with rationalising qualifications. Despite the different structures, the two bodies, NCVQ and SCOTVEC, work reasonably closely together and in 1995 they issued joint guidelines *Criteria and Guidance*.

One of the major problems for NCVQ is that it is not the awarding body. This means that there are still an enormous range of awarding bodies in England, Wales and Northern Ireland (118 at the beginning of 1994) who offer NVQs and thus the content, scope and breadth of qualification at any one level can differ markedly for the different occupational areas. These awarding bodies encompass:

- examining bodies such as BTEC, RSA and City & Guilds;
- professional bodies, e.g. the Institute of Bankers;
- individual companies, e.g. British Steel;
- industry lead bodies, e.g. Sea Fish Industry Authority;
- training organisations, e.g. Security Industry Training Organisation;
- trade associations, e.g. Chemical Industries Association.

Some specialised NVQs are offered by only one awarding body, but in other areas there may be up to 14 different awarding bodies all of which compete with each other for clients. No wonder people find NVQ/SVQs confusing!

The CBI, with support from the trade unions and the government, announced in July 1991 their new national targets for the attainment of vocational qualifications. These were that by:

- 1996, all employees should be taking part in training or development activities as a matter of course;
- 1997, 80% of 16–18-year-olds should reach NVQ level 2 or equivalent;
- 2000, 50% of the age group should achieve NVQ level 3 or equivalent.

We are still a long way off achieving a national skilled and trained workforce. Initial take-up of NVQs has been low but is now increasing. Certification figures show an average of 50% increase year-on-year to date. In 1990, 47,403 certificates were awarded, and this rose to 239,780 in 1994. As of September 1995, a total of one million NVQs had been awarded. However, there are many areas where take-up is well below what had been expected, and there is some indication (1995) that the rate of expansion is declining. The take-up in Scotland of SVQs has also been significantly lower than the take-up of NVQs in the UK.

In December 1995 the Beaumont Report *Review of 100 NVQs and SVQs* was published. It outlined a number of benefits mentioned by employers:

- improved employee performance;
- enhanced ability to do the job;
- improved employee motivation;
- readiness for future demands of the job;
- improved quality of goods and services;
- more cost-effective training;
- increased flexibility in working practices.

The report says there is widespread support for the NVQ/SVQ concept but the early implementation of NVQ/SVQs was rushed and this, together with a fundamental shift from existing practice, has resulted in mistakes in implementation and bad practice. The report has a number of criticisms and recommendations

- There are still too many qualifications. These need to be rationalised to avoid overlap and duplication of qualifications.
- More active employer participation is needed to ensure that the qualifications meet their needs.
- There are still barriers to progression and the structure of levels 3–5 needs to be reviewed; not all levels are used; the step between levels 2 and 3 is said to be too great; and it is difficult to develop through the technical route as levels 3–5 contain a significant supervisory/management component.
- Simulation of the workplace can only be a limited solution. It is the work-based element that appeals to employers, so more part-time, work-based training, for the unemployed, work returners, and pupils from age 14, must be developed.
- Excessive bureaucracy should be eliminated.
- All NVQ/SVQs should be reviewed by April 1998 and improvements should be in place by the end of 1998.

The Beaumont Report's overall conclusion was that despite a number of problems NVQ/SVQs appear to be working reasonably well although there is scope for improvement. They should not need a further major review until the year 2000!

The findings of the Beaumont Report were referred to in the Dearing Report of March 1996. Dearing recommended a national framework giving equal status to academic, applied and vocational qualifications. The report recommended that the number of bodies awarding NVQs should be rationalised but it left reform of NVQs in the hands of the Confederation of British Industry and NCVQ. *See also* EDUCATION AND QUALIFICATIONS.

Therefore NVQ/SVQs will continue to be part of the qualifications scene and probably increase in importance both in the UK and overseas. There is great interest from overseas, particularly in some countries, e.g. Malaysia, Spain, Japan, and for some occupations, e.g. road haulage, and beauty therapy. NCVQ is developing a European database of qualifications. NVQ/SVQs have the potential to lead the world in competence-based training and become truly international.

A simple guide to NVQ/SVQs

This section is intended to be a straightforward guide to NVQ/SVQs for potential users.

- NVQ/SVQs are qualifications about work. They prove to an employer that their employee measures up to national standards, and can understand and actually do the job, not just talk or write about it.
- NVQ/SVQs define what people will be competent to do when they are trained (whether on or off the job, or in an educational environment). They are not training programmes, although they may involve some training, and they are not courses.
- NVQ/SVQs are related to the 'real world'. They analyse work roles and emphasise the skills and knowledge needed to perform a particular job. Experts from the boat-building industry, for example, have drawn up a list of what is needed for someone to work well as a boat-builder or boat repairer.
- There are no entry requirements and, unlike traditional qualifications, they do not rely on conventional, written examinations.
- They are not just for young people and are suitable for people of any age.
- NVQ/SVQs are available at five levels. Level 1 is the lowest; level 5 the highest. At level 1 the emphasis is more on 'doing', but as you work your way through the levels the emphasis is more on 'knowing'. To put it another way, the emphasis at level 1 is more on practical abilities, while at level 5 the emphasis is more on knowledge, understanding and diagnosis.

The five levels range from the most basic occupations at level 1 to the higher professions at level 5. The levels are described by NCVQ as follows:

- *Level 1* shows competence in the performance of a range of varied work activities which are primarily routine and predictable, and provides a broad foundation for progression.
- *Level 2* is appropriate for many routine jobs and occupations of a predictable character in a variety of contexts. Some of the activities are complex or non-routine allowing an individual to demonstrate a degree of flexibility in adapting to new situations. Level 2 involves greater autonomy and individual responsibility than Level 1.

  Level 2 is generally accepted as equivalent to several GCSEs. City & Guilds and other craft-level qualifications equate to level 2.
- *Level 3* is suitable for many non-routine skilled jobs and occupations, denoting a broad range of work-related activities, including many that are complex and difficult, and showing the ability to sustain regular output to set standards. Awards at this level indicate capability for supervisory and junior management roles, or progression into advanced further education and learning.

  Generally accepted as equivalent to A-level. BTEC National Certificates and Diplomas equate to level 3.
- *Level 4* is appropriate for specialist, supervisory or professional occupations requiring adaptability to major job role changes, while maintaining full accountability and responsibility for outputs. Awards indicate ability to perform a range of complex, technical, specialised

and professional work activities usually carrying a substantial degree of personal accountability. This level will normally require taking responsibility for the work of others and allocation of resources.

BTEC Higher National Certificates and Diplomas or pass degrees equate to level 4.

- *Level 5* recognises competence which involves the application of a significant range of fundamental principles and complex techniques across a wide variety of contexts. Requires substantial personal autonomy and accountability for analysis and diagnosis, design, planning, execution and evaluation.

At present most qualifications are at levels 2 and 3. There are only a few qualifications at level 5, e.g. in Management.

The levels relate to attainment of competence, irrespective of the time it takes to do so.

- An NVQ/SVQ qualification can be built up piece by piece. Each NVQ/SVQ is made up of individual units which can be collected over a period of time. The number of units to complete varies with each NVQ depending on the requirements of the occupational area for which it is designed. You can choose what you want to learn and follow your own interests, or you can pursue a particular career path. You can follow one unit at a time or take a combination of units and train and qualify at a pace that suits you and your employer. This approach makes it easier to update, change or widen your skills.
- NVQ/SVQs are very flexible. There are no rules about the time taken, or how or where you learned the skills to perform competently. You work at your own pace, full- or part-time. You may take an NVQ in a college, in a training organisation, in the workplace, or any combination of these, whichever is the most appropriate. There are different methods of assessment depending on the situation;
- NVQ/SVQs cover thousands of jobs in most trades and occupations. There are currently about 800 NVQ/SVQs available in eleven occupational areas: tending animals, plants and land; extracting and providing natural resources; constructing; engineering; manufacturing; transporting; providing goods and services; providing health, social care and protective services; providing business services; communicating; developing and extending knowledge and skill. Examples include accounting, aircraft maintenance, animal care, aquatics, beauty therapy, boat-building, book-editing, broadcast and film, craft baking, design, dry cleaning, erecting and maintaining wood pole overhead lines, floristry, footwear repair, housing management, insurance, landfill operations, physiological measurement (neurophysiology), post-natal care, press photography, racehorse care, sea fishing, shopfitting, software production, sports coaching, sports turf maintenance, steeplejacking, travel-guiding, etc.

NVQ/SVQs are as relevant for managers and administrators as they are for trades and crafts.

- NVQ/SVQs do not bestow professional membership of an Institute, etc., but professional bodies can and increasingly do accept them as evidence that part of their requirements have been met.
- Wherever possible, NVQ/SVQs are earned on the job because they are about performance in the job. But it is possible to get one in a college if you can show the necessary practical know-how in a simulated work environment. For example, if a college offers an NVQ qualification in building, it must be able to offer all the skills and experience which you would get if you were working on a real building site.
- Although NVQ/SVQs are designed to test what you can do in a particular job and industry, you cannot be guaranteed a job using that particular NVQ/SVQ. There is no formal entry route into employment from specific NVQ/SVQs. It all depends on the employment market locally.

NVQ/SVQ units can be achieved in combination with other qualifications, e.g. GNVQ/GSVQs.

- if you already have the necessary abilities and can prove you can do the job, then you can be assessed for an NVQ/SVQ without doing any further training.

In a recent survey of major companies with over 500 employees, 44% were using NVQ/SVQs. This means, therefore, if you work for a large company you have a good chance of working towards an NVQ/SVQ qualification. Many small employers are still ignorant or confused about national vocational qualifications. If you go to work for a small company with fewer than 50 employees, you are less likely to work for an NVQ/SVQ. At present only about one in sixteen people in small companies work towards an NVQ/SVQ.

Further information

NCVQ, SCOTVEC and awarding bodies.

Student Financial Support

Contents

Background

A system of grants to finance students through their undergraduate studies was set up in 1960 'to ensure that those qualified to take advantage of these costly facilities (i.e. higher education) are not deterred from doing so' (Cmnd 1051). During the 1960s and 1970s further measures were introduced to help students and encourage participation in higher education, for example the payment of tuition fees for all students receiving mandatory awards.

However, the principle of state support for students began to be eroded in the 1980s. The maintenance grant was allowed to decline in real value during the late 1980s, and in 1990 the government split the responsibility for financing students between itself, parents, and (for the first time) the students themselves. Mandatory grant levels were frozen and a government student loan system was introduced to 'top up' awards.

Undergraduate funding is currently based on three main areas of financial support: mandatory grants; government student loans; and self-support through earnings/or from parents.

In 1993 the government announced that the mandatory grant was to be cut progressively by 10% each year over three years until 1996/97 while the loan system would be increased to compensate. In financial terms this meant that in 1993/94 a student attending a university outside London was eligible for a maintenance award of £2,040 and a loan of £1,150 whereas in 1996/97 they would only be eligible for a maintenance award of £1,710 but could apply for a loan of £1,645. Maintenance awards and loans are now relatively equal.

During the last ten years these progressive measures have undermined student financial support to the point where in 1996 the system may well be nearing collapse. It is no longer possible to survive entirely on the maintenance grant and 'the maximum maintenance grant doesn't even cover the cost of some university hall fees!' (National Union of Students). Student debt has risen dramatically in the last few years. The most recent figure available, Barclays Bank 1996 Debt Survey, says the average student now owes £1,982. The Committee of Vice Chancellors and Principals (CVCP) in their report published 1995 estimated that students embarking on a three-year degree course in 1995 will owe £4,943 in loans, plus interest, when they graduate in 1998. Those completing a four-year degree course in 1999 will owe £7,142. The National Audit Office investigation of the Student Loans Company in 1995 revealed that up to £142 million of loans may never be repaid due to continuous deferment, default or death.

New measures are now needed and various proposals affecting student finance are currently under consideration:

- a new privately backed scheme, the Private Finance Initiative (PFI), running alongside the existing public student loans scheme, may be introduced by the government (although the private financial sector is not enthusiastic);
- universities, hard-hit by 40% cuts in capital support, have proposed a tuition levy;
- introduction of a graduate tax which is paid throughout a person's earnings lifecycle and which is unrelated to the real cost of the education received;
- a loan scheme covering some portion of the real cost of the education which is repaid with interest through taxation;
- an employer user charge for employers recruiting graduates.

A committee under Sir Ron Dearing has been asked (February 1996) by the government to undertake a thorough review of higher education and to make recommendations on how the shape, structure, size and funding of higher education, *including support for students,* should develop to meet the needs of the UK over the next 20 years. In its review the committee should have regard to the principle that 'arrangements for student support should be equitable and not distort students' choices inappropriately'. The committee should report by summer 1997, but until new initiatives emerge the current situation is as outlined below. Whatever the outcome of the HE review, it is probably unrealistic to expect a return to the idyllic days when higher education was 'free' for all.

A practical guide to undergraduate awards and loans

Mandatory and discretionary awards

Mandatory awards are available for students doing a first degree, HND, NVQ level 4 (where this is awarded along with a first degree, DipHE or HND), or a course on the list drawn up by the government. Awards for other courses are discretionary, and there are no national rules. It depends on where you live.

A mandatory award is not automatic:

- if you have already had a grant before for a similar course;
- if you started another course and dropped out after 20 weeks of that course;
- if you have not lived in the UK for the last three years.

Mandatory awards cover maintenance and tuition fees. Most fees are paid in full directly to the institution but there are some exceptions. For example, fees for courses at a private college or university (such as the University of Buckingham, or the Royal Agricultural College) may only be funded up to a certain limit and you will have to pay the rest.

The amount of the maintenance grant depends on your parents' residual income. For example, if their residual income (after certain expenses have been deducted) is below £16,050 then you will get the full grant. Above this a sliding scale operates. Students own income may also be taken into account: if you receive more than £3,865 from sponsorship or scholarships your grant will be reduced; however, earnings from a part-time job during the course or vacation will not affect the mandatory grant.

In England and Wales mandatory awards come from the Local Education Authority (LEA). Awards for courses in orthoptics, occupational therapy, physiotherapy, radiography, and dental hygiene/therapy are obtained from the Department of Health.

In Scotland the Student Awards Agency Scotland (SAAS) covers degrees, HNDs, and also the professions allied to medicine, e.g. speech therapy, occupational therapy, physiotherapy, radiography, chiropody and dental hygiene.

In Northern Ireland the local Education and Library Board covers degrees and HNDs in the UK and Republic of Ireland. For information on dental technology, dental hygiene and nursing 'Project 2000' courses telephone the Management Executive on 01232 520500.

Student loans

These are funded by the government and administered by the Student Loans Company. They are intended to meet student living costs but they are not compulsory and they are not means-tested. They are usually available for courses for which mandatory grants are payable.

There are various personal criteria for eligibility: you will

- be aged under 50;
- have a bank/building society account;
- agree to inform the Student Loans Company promptly and in writing if the course is abandoned before completion, or completed earlier than anticipated;
- not be in breach of any agreement for a loan;
- be a 'home student'.

Interest on the loan is linked to the rate of inflation when the loan is taken out. For example, the rate up to 31 August 1996 is 3.5% (based on the annual inflation rate measured in March 1995). Although they are not interest-free student loans are cheaper than a bank loan.

Repayments start the April after finishing or leaving a course through a fixed number of monthly instalments. At present, most borrowers will pay 60 instalments over five years. Anyone unemployed or on a 'low income' may defer repayment.

Mandatory awards and loans are not available for certain courses such as:

- nursing courses under 'Project 2000';
- access courses;
- part-time courses (except some initial teacher-training courses);
- correspondence courses.

Other sources of funding

Banks and building societies

Most banks allow a free overdraft of up to about £750.

Access funds

Colleges receive Access Funds so that they can provide selective help to students in serious financial difficulties. The size of the Funds is limited. In 1996/97 the total amount available for eligible students in England and Wales was about £23 million. This also covers postgraduates. They are not repayable.

Career development loans

Career development loans of between £200 and £8,000 may be available for vocational courses lasting up to 24 months. The loan does not need to be repaid until up to six months after completing the course. Applications must be 'endorsed' by the local TEC or LEC (Scotland). Further information is available from the DfEE on 0800 585 505.

Guide to postgraduate awards (English and Welsh students)

Grants for postgraduate study are not automatic except for teacher training. There are a number of bodies who make awards, but in almost every case only one body is appropriate to that area of postgraduate work and if that body refuses finance, then you cannot apply to another funding body. Some postgraduate courses such as the Master of Business Administration (MBA) are not government-funded at all.

Awards are rarely given by LEAs for full-time postgraduate masters or doctorates.

The research councils and the Humanities Research Board of the British Academy fund PhD and MPhil research students and those on taught MA/MSc courses. The MRes (a masters degree by research) has been introduced in some science areas as a prerequisite for a PhD but it is not compulsory because of funding implications. It is anticipated (1996) that the MRes will continue for at least another four years but note that research council attitudes vary on funding. For example, EPSRC supports chemists for an MRes but not physicists (although they will support courses that physicists can do, such as mechatronics). PPARC does not fund the MRes at all because the MSci in Physics (a four-year undergraduate qualification) is considered to be a suitable alternative.

Postgraduate awards cover fees and maintenance. The usual minimum requirement is a 2:1 (upper second-class honours degree) for a PhD or a 2:2 (lower second-class honours degree) for other advanced courses. Competition for funding is fierce, and even a first-class honours degree does not guarantee funding, particularly in the social sciences. The research council awards are not means-tested. The awards are tax-free and there may be additional allowances for study-related travel, dependants and students with disabilities. A very high proportion of postgraduate students are self-financing, particularly for taught masters. The problem is particularly acute for humanities and social sciences.

The amount of the postgraduate maintenance grant usually depends on the subject discipline and geographical area, and for some subject areas like teacher training, on whether the student is living in the parental home (these may also include means-tested dependants' allowances). In 1995/96 maintenance rates varied between about £5,200 and £8,500 from the research councils and Humanities Research Board, and between £1,530 and £3,375 for DfEE bursaries in teaching and social work. For shortage subjects for PGCE teacher training an additional bursary of £1,000 may be available.

The main funding bodies are:

- *Biotechnology and Biological Sciences Research Council (BBSRC)*, Polaris House, North Star Avenue, Swindon SN2 1UH. 01793 413200.

  This was formed in 1994 from the former Agricultural and Food Research Council and the biotechnology and biological sciences programmes of the former Science and Engineering Research Council. It covers agriculture, food, pharmaceuticals, chemical and health-care industries, biological sciences, biotechnology and some related areas of physics and engineering.

  Awards cover research studentships, cooperative studentships with industry (CASE studentships) and advanced course studentships. Closing date 31 July. Open to all UK students. No direct applications accepted from students.
- *Engineering and Physical Sciences Research Council (EPSRC)*, Polaris House, North Star Avenue, Swindon SN2 1ET. 01793 444000.

  Covers physical sciences, manufacturing technology, mathematical sciences, operational research and engineering. Most physics courses come under EPSRC except for particle physics and astronomy.

  Awards cover research studentships, cooperative studentships with industry and advanced course studentship.
- *Particle Physics and Astronomy Research Council (PPARC)*, Polaris House, North Star Avenue, Swindon SN2 1ET. 01793 442000.

  Covers particle physics, astronomy, astrophysics and solar system science.

  Awards cover research studentship and advanced course studentship.
- *Economic and Social Research Council (ESRC)*, Polaris House, North Star Avenue, Swindon SN2 1UJ. 01793 413000.

  Covers accountancy, computing, economics, education (except for teacher training), ethnology, human geography, international relations, management and industrial relations, planning, political science, psychology, social anthropology, sociology and social administration.

  Most closing dates 1 May.
- *Medical Research Council (MRC)*, 20 Park Crescent, London W1N 4AL. 0171-636 5422.

  Covers medicine, dentistry and biomedical sciences

  Awards cover advanced course studentships, research studentships and collaborative studentships. Closing date 31 July.
- *Natural Environment Research Council (NERC)*, Polaris House, North Star Avenue, Swindon SN2 1EU. 01793 411500.

  Covers life sciences and geological sciences.

  Closing date 31 July.
- *British Academy (BA) Humanities Research Board*, Studentship Office, Block 1, Spur 15, Government Buildings, Honeypot Lane, Stanmore, Middlesex HA7 1AZ. 0181-951 5188.

  Covers archaeology, art history, architecture, classics, English history, law, linguistics, modern languages, music, philosophy and theology. Some subjects overlap with other funding bodies.

  Awards cover one-year studentships and major state studentships. Closing date 1 May. In 1995 the British Academy gave 500 studentships for masters degrees and 472 studentships for PhDs. Students in Scotland should apply to the Scottish Education Department.
- *Ministry of Agriculture, Fisheries and Food (MAFF)*, Nobel House, 17 Smith Square, London SW1 3JR. 0171-238 5598

  Covers agricultural science, animal and crop production, horticulture, farm management, agricultural economics, agricultural statistics, agricultural marketing, agricultural engineering, rural estate management.

Awards cover CASE awards, advanced course awards and research awards. Northern Ireland students should apply to their own Department of Agriculture.

The number of postgraduate awards given by the different bodies varies from year to year but as a rough guide in 1994/95 the number of awards were:

EPSRC	4,868
ESRC	1,137
BBSRC	727
NERC	617
MRC	449
PPARC	162
British Academy	980
Total	8,940

The science research councils operate a quota system under which they allocate a quota of awards to departments. The emphasis for funding scientific research has recently moved strongly towards 'wealth creation', and this may have implications for student funding. The departments themselves decide which students to nominate for the awards. The closing date for applications is usually 31 July.

Scientists and engineers may also qualify for CASE awards which are jointly sponsored by industry and the government and administered by the research councils. These awards are aimed at commercially oriented research and are usually funded at a higher rate than other awards.

Some courses may also have a quota of European Social Fund awards.

The British Academy awards are allocated by national competition, i.e. you compete with other applicants who have been put forward by other departments. The closing date is usually 1 May.

The ESRC seems to fluctuate between operating a quota system like the science research councils or a national competition like the humanities.

Other awarding bodies are:

- *Department for Education and Employment (DfEE)*, Mowden Hall, Staindrop Road, Darlington, Co Durham DL3 9BG. 01235 460155.

  Covers some taught courses of a vocational or professional nature, i.e. library and information science, art and design, archive administration, archaeology, drama, language interpretation, film and TV studies and other similar courses. Not every course in these subjects is included in the bursary scheme. The institution decides who receives the bursaries. Closing dates vary from 1 May to 1 August depending on the subject. Open only to residents of England and Wales. Students in Scotland and Northern Ireland should apply to their education authorities.

  There is also a competitive studentship and fellowship scheme for advanced study offered by the DfEE for librarianship and information science. Details of this are given in a separate publication produced by the DfEE.
- *Central Council for Education and Training in Social Work (CCETSW)*, Derbyshire House, St Chad's Street, London WC1H 8AD. 0171-278 2455.

  Provides a limited number of quota awards for social work courses.
- *LEAs*

  PGCE teacher-training courses attract a mandatory award. Other vocational courses such as law, journalism, music, secretarial work, youth work and computing are discretionary and LEA attitudes and policy on funding varys. Most students are unlikely to be funded.

Guide to postgraduate awards (other UK students)

Scottish students can apply for awards from most of the funding bodies covered above, but not those from the British Academy, DfEE or LEAs. Scottish students may also obtain funding from the Student Awards Agency for Scotland under the Scottish Studentship Scheme (SSS) or Postgraduate Students Allowances Scheme (PSAS). SSS gives awards for advanced study in arts and humanities. Closing date 1 June. PSAS primarily funds vocational diploma courses on a quota basis. Closing date 1 May.

Postgraduate students in Northern Ireland can apply for funding from the BA, BBSRC, ESRC, EPSRC, MRC, NERC and PPARC. Other funding is through the Department of Education for Northern Ireland (DENI) or the Department of Agriculture for Northern Ireland (DANI). Closing dates vary.

Other sources of postgraduate funding

There are a number of possibilities:

- Industrial scholarships may be provided by some companies for their employees. These are more likely to be for science masters or PhDs or for MBA courses.
- University scholarships. Many institutions fund a limited number of studentships, usually in the form of scholarships. They usually fall into two main categories: three years for outstanding candidates; or one-year studentships for those wishing to do extra research or for those who have not completed their PhD in three years.
- European Social Fund training allowances. Subjects and funds allocated vary on a calendar year basis. This may cause problems if the funding criteria change part way through a course and funding is withdrawn.
- Research assistantships are salaried posts in academic departments which may offer a chance to do a higher related degree. These are most common in science and engineering.

- Educational charities and trusts. These are rarely worth more than about £500. Consult *The Grants Register* (Macmillan); *Directory of Grant Making Trusts* (Charities Aid Foundation); *Charities Digest* (Family Welfare Association); *Study Abroad* (UNESCO); or *Scholarship Guide for Commonwealth Postgraduates* (Association of Commonwealth Universities).
- Government-funded scheme for the unemployed. This is currently (1996) the Training for Work scheme. You usually need to have been unemployed for six months. Apply for details to TECs and LECs.
- Career Development loans (*see above.*).
- Access funds. Most institutions combine the allocations for undergraduates and postgraduates and allocate on the basis of need (*see above*).

Note that postgraduate students are *not* eligible for student loans unless they are doing a teacher-training course.

Further information

DfEE, Student Awards Agency for Scotland, Department of Education for Northern Ireland, Welsh Office Education Department, Student Loans Company, Research Councils and other bodies listed above.

The Armed Forces

(CLCI: B-BAZ)

Background

Britain's Armed Forces operate under the terms of three overlapping roles of defence policy. Role One: ensure the protection and security of the United Kingdom and its Dependent Territories, even when there is no major threat. Role Two: insure against a major external threat to the United Kingdom and its allies. Role Three: to contribute to promoting the United Kingdom's wider security interests through the maintenance of international peace and stability.

Contemporary defence policy is based on a deliberate decision to maintain a relatively small, but highly skilled and trained, flexible military force which is capable of using to maximum efficiency the extremely sophisticated and complex equipment with which modern warfare, nuclear or not, is fought.

The technological demands made on the Forces, and the cost- and productivity-consciousness needed to keep within the budget, mean defence has to use modern managerial methods in strenuous attempts to achieve maximum efficiency. 'Efficiency' is the watchword in defence, both nationally and in NATO. It means near-continuous rationalisation in defence generally, as well as the Armed Forces.

The estimated outturn for the defence budget in 1994/95 is £22.32 billion. Defence expenditure planned for 1995/96 at £21.720 billion is about the same as 1990/91 levels. This is expected to rise to £21.92 billion in 1996/97, and to £22.32 billion by 1997/98. Britain's per capita defence expenditure, at $585, puts the UK fourth behind the US ($1,088), Norway ($791), and France ($764). The division of expenditure in 1995/96 is: Equipment 40%, Service Personnel 28%, Works and Miscellaneous Services 20%, and Civilian Personnel 12%.

Improving 'management' of defence has, for some years, involved the Ministry of Defence in its own battle to restructure for efficiency. In the 1990s, the Services have been the subject of a number of studies. *Options for Change* reviewed and recommended restructuring measures for the British Armed Forces in the light of the new strategic environment post-Cold War. In 1994 'Front Line First' was the policy which concentrated resources to the support and maintenance of British front-line forces.

The thrust of policy is a steady move towards a common defence effort rather than three semi-independent services. In the Forces themselves, senior officers increasingly work, and are trained, together. Achieving good management practice, particularly in procurement of defence equipment continues to be of central importance to the MOD. *See also in* CENTRAL GOVERNMENT.

Despite the enormous changes in Europe, the unification of Germany, the collapse of the Warsaw Pact and the demise of the Soviet Union, many uncertainties and instabilities remain. Whilst still maintaining a capability to act as a single sovereign force, Britain pursues its three defence roles through a number of multinational structured defence alliances.

NATO has formed the centrepiece of European defence for the last 40 years, and the major role of Britain's forces will remain within NATO. Britain still provides the only strategic nuclear force committed to NATO. All but a few ships and all Royal Marine units, wherever they are deployed, are earmarked for assignment to NATO in an emergency. The Army and Air Force units stationed in Germany are treated as components of NATO in Central Europe, backed up by combat units of both the Army and the Air Force in Britain. The UK's main contribution to NATO forces is to the Allied Command Europe Rapid Reaction Corps (ARRC), which is commanded by a British general. Britain contributes some 55,000 regular soldiers to the Corps, together with a substantial number of Individual Reservists and TA units. The Royal Navy provides around 70% of NATO forces in the Eastern Atlantic and Channel. The Air Force supplies appropriate support.

Other partnerships are being developed: the Western European Union (WEU) acts as the defence component of the European Union, designed to enable the European Allies to take greater responsibility for their common security.

The Partnership for Peace (PfP) programme seeks to deepen political and military ties between NATO and (to date) 25 Central and East European states. The PfP offers close cooperation in fields such as the preparation of forces for use in peacekeeping and humanitarian operations.

The United Nations' role in the maintenance of international stability has been greatly enhanced since the end of the Cold War. Britain's Armed Forces, when called upon, respond to a wide range of UN operations around the world.

Through these structures Britain carries out multinational joint military operations and exercises, performs training missions and supplies international observers.

Apart from these responsibilities, Britain has garrisons in Hong Kong, Gibraltar, Brunei, Cyprus, Belize and the Falkland Islands. The garrison in Hong Kong will close when the territory reverts to China in 1997. Royal Navy ships are on station in the Caribbean and the Gulf area. Units of all three services deploy from time to time to a variety of locations worldwide for training, exercises and where necessary to carry out military operations in support of British interests – the most recent major example being the Gulf conflict in 1991. The Armed Forces also act from time to time in support of the Overseas Development Administration to provide humanitarian relief in the wake of disasters overseas.

Apart from the Forces currently stationed in Germany, Hong Kong, etc., regular foreign postings are few and continue to decrease as overseas commitments are reduced. Instead, the Forces train and exercise regularly overseas - in the snow and ice of Norway, or the plains of Germany, for example.

The Forces, mainly the Army, are also called upon to support the civil power in upholding law and order, as in Northern Ireland. They have, then, to accept all kinds of anti-guerrilla/anti-terrorist style activity as a normal part of their duties. The Forces also consider they have a role to play in the community at large, at least as far as feasible, as in air–sea rescue, flood relief, building temporary bridges, etc. Maritime forces, both at sea and in the air, protect fisheries and the offshore oil and gas installations.

The Armed Forces

The Forces have changed very considerably since the end of the Second World War, especially in terms of the expertise demanded of everyone, officers and non-commissioned ranks alike. However, traditions remain, and anyone joining can expect to find themselves in an organisation which retains many traditional ceremonies, values and attitudes, which help bind them together as an efficient and close-knit unit. Certainly tradition is maintained to a degree less common in civilian life. By the very nature of the Forces, discipline remains central to efficiency, as does clear organisational structure and, where necessary, a formal relationship between the various ranks. It is still also a team business, with lives at stake if personnel of all ranks are not welded into an efficient unit. It involves living almost all of the time at close quarters with others, and living in communities sometimes separated from those of civilians.

Today, trained people are the main asset of the Armed Forces. Within the inevitable restrictions imposed by budgets and other operational and administrative constraints the Forces have a very strong commitment to the welfare of servicemen and women; indeed their efficiency depends upon it.

Many of the routine tasks on which people in the ranks traditionally spent much time when not in combat no longer exist; the role and work of the Armed Forces of the 1990s is very different to that of the past. Life in the Forces is geared to intensive preparation for something which everyone hopes and trusts will never happen, and this must inevitably bring its own challenges and the need to maintain professionalism. Because of this, it is hardly surprising that some Army authorities have welcomed the action in Northern Ireland, the Falklands, and more recently the Gulf, as opportunities to sharpen capabilities and skills in 'real' situations. These situations allow them to try out systems never before tested in real life, to find out, inevitably with some tragic results, the power of modern weaponry and the weakness of some defensive systems.

Since the Forces now have to count very carefully the considerable investment they have put into their men and women, from the ranks up, conditions of service have been improved. Standards of living are higher than they used to be; officer training and selection has been sharpened and is geared to the kind of officer–rank relationships needed by combat and operational teams which must work so closely together. Life in the Armed Forces can still be demanding. Discipline remains important, work can be hard at times. However, the way in which people work can vary considerably depending on their job and the tasking of their unit. Some have an almost nine-to-five existence, whilst others' work involves twelve-hour days, round-the-clock watches at sea, night exercises – sometimes in appalling conditions – and very strenuous training. And war, with death and injury, does still happen. However, for many the Forces offer a challenging and varied life. A career in the services offers many opportunities, the respect of society, and payment, and a standard of living which compares well with most civilian jobs.

Working in the Armed Forces

Britain attempts to support its defence policy as efficiently and cost-effectively as possible. The consequence of *Options for Change* announced by the Defence Secretary in July 1990, and subsequent policies, mean that the number of Armed Forces personnel will, by April 1996, have fallen from around 332,500 (1986) to about 231,500.

In recent years there have been significant developments in the career opportunities available to women in the Armed Forces. In 1989 the RAF opened employment as aircrew in non-combat roles to women and extended this in 1991 to combat roles. In 1990 the Navy decided that women should serve at sea in surface ships, including those with a combat role, and all naval aircrew roles are now open to women. Women are not yet allowed to serve in submarines, as existing accommodation facilities do not afford men or women a sufficient degree of privacy to allow mixed-manning.

The demise of the Women's Royal Army corps on 1 April 1992 saw the integration of females into their employing corps. The amalgamation of the men and women of the Ulster Defence Regiment with the Royal Irish Rangers, to form the Royal Irish Regiment, has seen the first example of women serving in the infantry. Very few roles now remain closed to women, and the Armed Forces' policy is that in future they will normally only be excluded from those posts where their presence would impair operational effectiveness. This currently includes some infantry, Royal Marine and Armoured Corps roles.

To make sure their needs are properly covered, the Armed Forces recruit at as many levels as possible, from amongst school-leavers at 16- and 18-plus, through to graduates and trained personnel. They are also increasing and improving the training and education for personnel at all levels: via both their own educational establishments and scholarship/cadetship schemes for entrants to study at universities, colleges, etc.

Almost anyone recruited to the Forces must expect to become involved in combat if war happens, but the Forces aim to have teams of highly trained specialists, and to some extent the combat personnel are now a separate breed from the men and women who provide the elaborate support services built up to aid them. For combat teams, the emphasis is on specialist training in one aspect of the art, or rather the science and technology, of warfare. Both officers and non-commissioned ranks become highly skilled as, for example, seamen, or gunnery (which includes guided missiles) experts, or in tank warfare. The support services require engineers and mechanics, technicians and craftsmen/women, medical and dental officers, psychologists and nurses, educationalists, accountants, lawyers, purchasing and supply staff, etc.

Because many people who go into the Forces must have second careers, the Forces are trying, as far as possible, to integrate their own training with the national structure. Specialist officers take broad-based engineering degrees, and trades- and craftsmen/women are entered for City & Guilds examinations (several training centres have their schemes validated by BTEC). Some National Vocational Qualifications (NVQs) have been introduced with more being developed. Wherever possible, trades have trade-union recognition, so people can transfer to related civilian work.

Manpower planning within the Forces is a difficult task. On the one hand, the Forces not unnaturally wish to keep personnel, on whom considerable time and money have been spent, for as long as possible. On the other, it is recognised that it is at times necessary to shed people; that some cannot be usefully employed throughout their working lives; and that not everyone wants to make the Forces a lifelong career. Many of the roles undertaken are more appropriate to younger people, and it is not easy to tell how many of them will develop the right skills for 'management', or be suitable to move into other jobs. New technological equipment, new strategic methods demand different skills to the old.

To give themselves and the men and women they employ a reasonable degree of flexibility, therefore, a range of different-length engagements is offered. It is possible to stay in the Forces for a full career to the age of 55, but in practice most engagements range from three to 22 years, with intermediate terms which vary according to service.

The government commissioned a study into Service careers and manpower structures which reported in 1995 and is currently under consideration. Under the chairmanship of Mr Michael Bett, the report *Managing People in Tomorrow's Armed Forces* contains some 150 recommendations, including: a review of rank structure; rationalisation of trade structures; new and more flexible pay structures; improvements to family stability, welfare and other conditions of service; closer alignment of Service rental charges with civilian norms, and a more taughtly focused allowances package, with equivalence of treatment between married and single personnel. The work is to be taken forward in conjunction with the Armed Forces Pay Review Body; however, the government envisage 'a substantial study and development period before final decisions are taken'.

In the meantime, there is recognition that it may be better to restrict length of engagement rather than expect members of the Forces to accept a ceiling on their promotion opportunities. Therefore, only those accepted for permanent, as opposed to special, regular commissions in the Army can try for possible promotion to major and above, and on a special regular commission it is possible to retire after 16 years instead of continuing on to age 55. Restrictions on changing the length of service under which the entrant signed have been eased, particularly for those recruited under the age of 18. However, it is still not possible to leave the services on terms comparable with those in general operation in civilian life, by simply giving a week's or month's notice.

As a general rule, the Forces expect men and women to stay long enough to give a reasonable return on the educational and training investment made in them. This generally means a minimum of three years, and four to seven years for those whose training was an extended one. Thereafter, whatever term of engagement was actually signed, it is possible in given circumstances to leave following a period of notice, ranging from seven months to two to three years, depending on service and branch or trade. When Service personnel under 18 years of age enlist they are committed to serve for 28 days. They have the statutory right to leave, if they wish to do so, at any time after this period and before six months have elapsed. There is no forfeiture of a week's pay on leaving the service for recruits under the age of 17 years 6 months.

The Forces management recognise their responsibility to help people leaving the Forces transfer to the civilian world. This is obviously easier for those with training in skills widely used in civilian employment than for those who are trained as combat specialists and so must rely on less tangible assets, such as managerial skills, to get them into a new career, although specialist retraining is arranged. However, there is evidence to suggest that the problem is not simply one of acquiring the right skills for a new career. It may well be that the problems of adjusting not only to a new job in a strange setting, but also to a completely new way of life, are far more important, especially for those who enjoyed Service life. The very qualities of life in the Forces – security, provision of basic needs, the structured society, and so on – are in direct contrast to the life of the average civilian today.

Women in the RAF and Army retain the right to leave on marriage, but new recruits to the Royal Navy now have to give the normal period of notice to leave. Until 1990, women in the Armed Forces were required to leave on pregnancy. This policy was changed in August 1990 and women could choose whether to leave or to take a period of unpaid leave and return to work after the birth of their children. In December 1991, improvements were made to the maternity leave policy, including the introduction of up to 14 weeks' leave with full pay.

Recruitment and entry

All entrants must be British citizens, born of British or Commonwealth parents, and have been resident in the UK for at least five years immediately prior to making an application. No boy or girl can be enlisted before completing the school term during which he or she reaches the school-leaving age.

While the Forces encourage boys and girls to gain school-leaving qualifications (and for certain levels of entry these are mandatory), there is no formal bar to entry without them, although intelligence and aptitude tests are required at all levels. Pupils studying for recognised educational qualifications are encouraged to stay at school until they have taken the examination, provided they will not exceed the upper age limit for the particular type of entry. Such qualifications can usually be gained within the Forces anyway.

Young entrants are accepted for both commissioned and non-commissioned entry, although higher educational potential is needed to qualify for officer training. In general, types of entry are classified by very specific age requirements linked to educational and/or skill qualifications. Broadly speaking, the upper age limit is 29 or 30. Entrants over 25 or 26 must, in most cases, have qualifications which are of use to the particular arm of the Forces. Entrants must pass a medical and, for some types of entry, conform to particular physical measurements.

The Army

The Army is traditionally the most labour-intensive of the three Forces and, until relatively recently, less scientifically/technologically orientated, compared to the Navy and Air Force. Now, says the Army, 'the day of the simple soldier is past. These days almost everyone is an expert of some kind'. At 1 April 1991, there were 147,200 serving personnel in the Army, 16,700 of whom were officers; 1996 estimates suggest a strength of about 117,000, which includes 8,645 officers.

Major restructuring of the Army since 1990 has seen a number of regimental/corps amalgamations and disbandments. Despite this, the list of regiments and corps of the British Army still makes impressive reading.

The regiments and corps are organised into: the Combat Arms, the Supporting Arms, and the Services. The Combat Arms and Supporting Arms are made up of highly mobile units, ready to respond to any emerging crisis anywhere in the world. The Services provide essential administrative and logistic support.

The Combat Arms

The Combat Arms pack the most powerful punch at the head of any battle.

- *The Household Cavalry* provide an Armoured Reconnaissance Regiment (and also the Mounted Regiment in London, which is well known for its ceremonial duties).
- *The Royal Armoured Corps* operate as either Armoured or Armoured Reconnaissance Regiments; they are equipped with either main battle tanks or fast armoured reconnaissance vehicles.
- *The Infantry* accounts for about a quarter of the Army. The infantry soldier's job is to close with the enemy and defeat him. Fit, alert, tough and resourceful, soldiers in the infantry are highly skilled individuals, schooled in the art of infantry warfare.
- *The Special Air Service Regiment* are the combat elite of the British Army with a formidable worldwide reputation for professional soldiering. Entry is highly selective (most fail) and only open to those who are already serving elsewhere in the Army.
- *The Army Air Corps* flies and operates all the Army's helicopters. Their primary role is to launch missile attacks on enemy armour. They also transport men and equipment around the battlefield at short notice, carry out reconnaissance missions, and act as an airborne command post for certain operations.

The Supporting Arms

The Supporting Arms work alongside the Combat Arms. They may be deployed in any area of the battlefield: at the front or in deeper positions in rear areas.

- *The Royal Regiment of Artillery Gunners* provide ground fire support and air defence for the Army. Weapons include surface-to-surface missiles, shoulder-controlled missile systems, and longer-range Rapier missiles.
- *The Royal Engineers* help the Army to live, move and fight whilst preventing the enemy from doing the same. Soldiers in sapper units are multi-skilled tradesmen. Together, they are capable of almost any construction or demolition task, as well as bomb disposal, underwater survey and repair tasks, and land survey work.

- *The Royal Corps of Signals* the Army's communication experts, use the latest information technology systems to provide modern field communications. They also provide satellite communications, operate electronic warfare systems, and provide linguistic services.
- *The Intelligence Corps* collect, collate and analyse information to answer the questions: 'What is the enemy going to do; when, where, how and in what strength.' They are also responsible for security and other intelligence, and are as likely to be found on the battlefield as in an office.

The Services

Whilst always prepared for combat, the Services provide essential administrative and logistical support.

- *The Royal Army Chaplain's Department*. Chaplains of various denominations look after the spiritual and moral needs of soldiers and their families in a worldwide ministry.
- *The Royal Logistic Corps* sustains the Army in peace and war. The Corps is responsible for storing and distributing all stores and equipment used by the Army; for the movement of personnel, and equipment by rail, road, sea and air; for all catering and food supplies; and for providing postal and courier facilities for all three services. The Corps also provides the Bomb Disposal Service.
- *The Royal Army Medical Corps* the RAMC, together with the *Royal Army Dental Corps* and *Queen Alexandra's Royal Army Nursing Corps*, offer a complete medical service to Army personnel, and overseas, to their families. Qualified doctors, dentists and nurses are assisted by trained clinicians of a range of disciplines, from radiographers to physiotherapists. The service extends from the GP type of practice in units and garrisons, to that based in hospitals with a full range of consultant and other medical facilities.
- *The Royal Electrical and Mechanical Engineers* keep operational and, if necessary, repair the Army's immense range of technical equipment. Soldiers trained as skilled technicians look after tanks, vehicles of every kind, guns, guided weapons, radar, radio, and aircraft – all in large numbers and of many different types.
- *The Adjutant General's Corps* consists of four branches. The largest is the Staff and Personnel Support (SPS). This branch is responsible for all personnel administration. The Provost branch are the Army's police force. They operate on similar lines to the civilian police, with their own equivalent of the CID. Educational and Training Services (ETS) are responsible for education in all its forms, including development of training systems and the provision of resettlement advice and training for those leaving the Army. Finally, the Army Legal Services provide legal advice to all, and prepare and prosecute proceedings before Courts Martial.
- *The Royal Army Veterinary Corps* provides, cares for and trains the Army's animals – mainly horses and dogs. Qualified veterinary surgeons are supported by veterinary technicians, dog and horse trainers and farriers.
- *The Corps of Army Music*. Between them, the Army's 30 bands employ more than 1,100 Army-trained, male and female professional musicians. The Bands present the public face of the Army. In war, musicians act as medical orderlies or Large Goods Vehicle drivers.

Every regiment and corps has its own specific job to do, and so has specific requirements in terms of particular skills, in both officers and non-officers. Officers and men in the armoured regiments, for example, mostly specialise in 'working' tanks, armoured cars, and anti-tank guided missiles. The Royal Artillery employs mainly gunnery experts but also needs people trained in the use of radar and other electronic devices to locate air or ground targets and to guide homing weapons.

All entrants have to opt for a particular regiment or corps before enlisting. If then accepted, they are enlisted into that regiment or corps. Some regiments continue to recruit in the counties where they were first raised. But in general the Army aims to provide everyone with a wide-ranging introduction to all the opportunities open to them, depending on the type of entry, so that they can make an informed choice.

Choice of regiment or corps usually dictates what job most officers and soldiers get – especially in the 'combat' regiments.

Officers

Officers are expected to be managers and organisers, but principally leaders, as soon as they finish their training. Even the most junior officers are expected to take responsibility for up to 30 soldiers, organising their training and instruction themselves, as well as making sure that food, welfare facilities and leisure activities are organised. Young officers can also be put in charge of equipment worth several million pounds. While they have to learn a great deal about the systems they are deploying (and in technical corps like REME, must have engineering degrees), they are not technicians – the skilled soldiers under their command do much of the practical work. Officers though, have to be able to understand and operate the equipment if need be.

In September 1992 a new common Commissioning Course of 44 weeks replaced the three previous courses. Training takes place at the Royal Military Academy Sandhurst (RMAS). Men and women, graduates and non-graduates alike, train together to common objectives. All are commissioned as Second Lieutenants and then complete their Young Officer training with their particular Arm or Service to fit them for their first appointment in the regiment of their choice.

After the first two-year 'tour' of regimental duty, career officers are given varied experience of both regimental/corps and 'staff' – administrative and, later, managerial – work, both within their units and elsewhere. The Army claims that no two tours are ever the same. Throughout their service, officers are trained for the next stage of responsibility and promotion.

Officers who are doing well can expect promotion to captain at 26. Career officers at this stage complete an intensive Junior Command and Staff Course carried out at Sandhurst, and the Royal Military College of Science at Shrivenham. (The promotion exam to major takes place at the end of this course.) This is normally followed by at least another two years' regimental duty as an adjutant or junior staff officer. Promotion to major can happen at age 32–34, after first passing a promotion exam covering military, academic and current affairs subjects. There is a further exam, the passing of which qualifies officers for selection to attend the one-year Staff College course (with RN and RAF officers), which is preceded by another three to twelve months at Shrivenham. Those who do well can expect promotion to lieutenant colonel in their late thirties, and could spend much of their time on staff work management, policy-making and working with the other Forces and police.

There are two main types of commission available: Regular Commission and Short Service Commission. Candidates for a Regular Commission usually intend to make the Army a career and may serve up to the normal retiring age of 55. They may, however, opt to leave after a minimum period of service of three years. Officers on Short Service Commission serve initially for three years, but can extend their service to a maximum of eight. There is also an option to convert to a Regular Commission.

In addition to the above there is also the Short Service Limited Commission (SSLC) for those with a firm place at university. This GAP year commission lasts for a minimum of four, maximum of 18 months with no further commitment to the Army.

Recruitment and entry

In 1991/92 officer recruiting targets were 800, in 1992/93 611, and have been set around the 700–750 mark since.

The Army has a number of different ways to become an officer. All assume that applicants have, or are capable of gaining, at least five GCSEs at grade C or above, or their equivalent. For a Regular Commission entrants must have a minimum of two A-levels and three supporting GCSEs at grade C or above, or their equivalent. Subjects should include English language and mathematics; a science or a foreign language may be required. Currently, around 75% of officer candidates hold a first degree. Entrants for Regular or Short Service commissions should be over the age of 17 years 9 months but normally under 25. Graduate entrants for some of the engineering and technical corps may be admitted under the age of 27.

Educational sponsorship schemes

Scholarship. Sixth-form Army scholarships are available for 16-year-olds (upper limit 16 years 6 months) studying for A-levels. At February 1996 the award, paid termly, was worth £1,050 p.a.

Welbeck College. Welbeck College is the Army's own sixth-form technical college offering a two-year A-level course. Mathematics is compulsory and physics strongly encouraged. The College caters for both girls and boys, who should be between the ages of 15 years 9 months and 17 years on entry and should have appropriate GCSEs. Most Welbexians apply for commissions in one of the technical corps, but some go into Royal Armoured Corps, Royal Artillery, Royal Logistic Corps and the infantry. Most can go on to a degree course at the Royal Military College of Science at Shrivenham, or a civilian university, after commissioning.

Scholars and Welbeck students who gain their A-levels are exempt selection at the Regular Commission Board and are effectively guaranteed a place at Sandhurst.

University cadetship/bursary. Cadets are commissioned and paid whilst at university and, like all graduates, receive antedated seniority on completion of initial training. Thirty cadetships are available each year, with the majority reserved for those studying engineering subjects. Cadets are commissioned as Second Lieutenants, and receive a special rate of pay, (£7,657–£10,771 per annum at April 1995). They must serve for five years after training. Bursary holders are paid an annual sum (currently £1,500) and remain civilians until they graduate; they must serve for at least three years after training.

Commissions from the ranks

Serving soldiers can apply for a commission up to age 25 and must be able to show they have reached the educational standard needed to do the Sandhurst course. Currently about 25% of Army officers are promoted from the ranks.

Professionally qualified officer

Doctors, dentists, vets, lawyers and chaplains also serve on Regular or Short Service Commissions, but undergo a much shorter training period at Sandhurst. Medical and dental officers may join once qualified but have the alternative of cadetship or pre-registration entry. The remainder join after qualifying.

Non-commissioned soldiers

A comparatively small modern army is heavily dependent on complex technological equipment, speed, flexibility, and intelligent use of resources. Its soldiers, as well as its officers, then, have to be more intelligent, more highly trained for the strategy to work. Most personnel have to be capable of operating intelligently, that complex – and very expensive – equipment. Many now learn to do more than one, often several, jobs: every member of a tank crew, for example, can do everyone else's job if necessary. This does not, though, obviate the need for strength and fitness, and 'roughing it' is still inevitable. But while it is common to think of the troops 'yomping', as they sometimes still must, even the infantry divisions are heavily mechanised, and troops are moved by carrier rather than on foot wherever possible. Teamwork is the other ingredient of army life which is heavily stressed.

All soldiers are taught first and foremost to fight and handle weapons, as infantrymen, for example. But even infantrymen can also learn a second, 'follow-on' trade, and the range of technical jobs for which training is given is widening steadily. All can add to their skills, and also gain academic qualifications, such as GCSE and A-levels, which may be needed for further training. The Army also offers generous financial support for those undertaking Open University degree studies.

Trades

Every regiment and corps employs different skills, so choice of trade can, of course, limit choice of unit. Almost all regiments and corps are mechanised, and so employ soldier-drivers, but only the Household Cavalry has mounted dutymen: now, men in the Cavalry may spend one tour on horseback in ceremonial dress, and the next as drivers of 54-ton tanks. Some skills are unique to the Army: assault pioneer, gunner, parachutist, mortar man, bomb disposal engineer. A wide range of army trades would be useful in civilian life: radio technician, construction materials technician, data telegraphist, crane operator, recovery mechanic, building craftsman, chef, design draughtsman/woman, electrician, operating theatre technician, radiographer, fitter, and so on.

Technician and craft opportunities are mainly in the specialist corps – REME trains electronics technicians (specialising in telecommunications, control equipment, or avionics), aircraft, and instrument technicians. Craft skills include those of vehicle mechanics and electricians, armourers and gun fitters, and metalsmiths.

The Royal Engineers employs, and trains, design technicians (specialising in construction materials, surveyor engineering), design draughtsmen/women or electrical and mechanical draughtsmen/women, survey technicians (specialising in field or air survey, or survey cartography, photography or print), and electricians. Craft trades include bricklayer, concretor, carpenter, joiner, electrician. fitter, metalworker, painter, decorator, plumber/pipefitter.

The Signals Corps also employs and trains electronics technicians (specialising in radio, radio relay, or terminal equipment). Telegraphy trades include radio and special telegraphists, and electronic warfare operators who have to be good at languages.

Other corps employ and train their own specialists; for example Adjutant General's Corps accountants learn to use computers in handling pay, allowances and records, and the Royal Logistic Corps supply controllers for stock control, and train chefs and cooks. The Royal Army Medical Corps trains radiographers and lab technicians.

In the 'frontline' regiments, some of the jobs are just as technical and skilled – operating the Royal Artillery's computer-controlled missiles for example. The Artillery also employs surveyors, intelligence operators, and meteorologists.

Army musician. Army-trained musicians are extremely versatile performers. They play in large, versatile symphonic wind bands, and in smaller combinations as the occasion demands. Army musicians are of course necessarily also soldiers: they have to be fit, trained and kept up to date in basic military skills. They are trained for their mobilisation roles in case of national emergency or war – most often as medical orderlies, or sometimes as signallers or Large Goods Vehicle (LGV) drivers.

Promotion from the rank of private – via lance-corporal, corporal, sergeant, staff sergeant and warrant officer – depends on experience, educational and technical qualifications, and the ability to handle personnel. While there are minimum periods to be served in each rank in most cases, accelerated schemes exist and extensive use is made of incentives. The Army encourages non-commissioned soldiers to work towards a commission.

Accelerated schemes and continuous assessment of ability make it hard to generalise about promotion, but in general it is clear that those who qualify as technicians gain promotion faster than those in the other trade groups, with automatic rises to lance-corporal and corporal in two years after completing training, and promotion to sergeant after five. Time promotion, however, applies only up to the rank of sergeant; thereafter promotion is by selection to fill particular vacancies, except in certain supervisory appointments. Anyone who reaches junior NCO rank in certain trades is eligible for special training as a supervisory technician in, for example, the Royal Engineers, which has posts for clerks of works and military plant foremen, and in REME, which has supervisory artificers (who are encouraged to take HNC examinations).

Terms of service; all entrants are offered a full 22-year Open engagement with the option to give 12 months' notice to leave after serving two years – hence three years minimum. However, time bars are in force for those who complete lengthy training – length of time bar depends on the training received.

Recruitment and entry

From 1 April 1995 increased recruiting targets mean that the Army is aiming to recruit around 15,000 new entrants. Most of these will join as adults (over 17 years 6 months). The scrapping of the Junior Army (Junior Soldier, Junior Leader, Junior Bandsman, Junior Musician) robbed the Army of a valuable recruiting source and contributed to the Army's manpower difficulties. This is now recognised at senior levels within the Army, and the re-establishment of the Junior Army is now under consideration. However, the Army still offers Apprentice Training for young people between 16 and 17½ years old.

For adult entrants, unskilled entry is possible up to the age of 26, with choice of training in up to 150 trades, depending on aptitude. Applicants aged 23–30 who have the equivalent of a BTEC National and have managerial/supervisory experience may be recruited for artificer trainer.

Qualifications and training

All new entrants start with a period of training at one of five Army Training Regiments located around the country. Here they undergo the Common Military Syllabus, which lasts for ten weeks. Following this period soldiers go on for 'special-to-arm' training.

Apprentices and technicians are given both skilled and basic military training, as well as continuing their general education. Courses for technicians last up to three years and lead mainly to BTEC National awards initially. Apprentice training involves a Foundation Course followed by trade training at a specialist Army School, together with on-the-job training, and further courses. All Apprentice training results in the award of BTEC, City & Guilds, or NVQ qualifications.

Queen Alexandra's Royal Army Nursing Corps (QARANC) offers unique opportunities for nurses; it combines a full nursing and Army career. Apart from in the Falkland Islands, and Germany, the Army no longer has its own military hospitals. The officers and servicemen and women of the Corps now work in 'Services wings' of NHS hospitals. However, they still train to extend their nursing roles in preparation for a wartime situation, e.g. the Gulf conflict, and opportunities to travel abroad remain, although these are becoming fewer.

Officers must be qualified RGNs with at least one year's post-registered experience. All new officers are commissioned on a Short Service Commission for a minimum of two years, plus six years on the Regular Reserve. The commission may be extended up to eight years with a corresponding decrease in the Reserve liability. At any time after one year's service they may apply to transfer to a Regular Commission and serve up to the age of 55.

Servicemen and women are recruited with the following qualifications: RMN, EN(G), EN(M). They serve a minimum of three years but have the option to a full service career of 22 years. RGNs are recruited on special enlistments for two years' service, and this period is used for assessment towards possible commissioning.

The Corps train Health Care Assistants to work under the supervision of the qualified nurses. No formal academic qualifications are required for entry into this career group, they serve a minimum of three years and also have the option of a full 22 years' service. *See also* SUPPLEMENTARY HEALTH PROFESSIONS.

The Royal Air Force

By comparison with the Army the Air Force is far smaller. In line with *Options for Change* the number of personnel is being significantly reduced in recent years; from around 87,000 in 1992, to 55,500 by April 1997, and 52,200 by April 1999.

It is also organisationally far less complex, with fewer units. It is an 'integrated service', with women doing largely the same job, as men, particularly now that women can fill all flying categories including pilot and navigator.

The cost of keeping the RAF supplied with the latest generation combat and other aircraft rises greatly each year, but the operations in the Gulf clearly demonstrated just how effective it can be. Compromises, both between strategic needs and capital costs in terms of new aircraft, and on the use of aircraft for training, must constantly be found. Currently, the mainstay of the RAF's offensive capability is provided by the strike/attack and reconnaissance versions of the Tornado, ably abetted by the ubiquitous Jaguar and the latest and more capable version of the Harrier 'jump-jet'. It is expected that from the end of the decade the European Fighter Aircraft (EFA) will be introduced into service, providing a powerful reinforcement to the RAF's capabilities. New support and attack helicopters are on order, and the tanker/transport force has been updated with the Tristar. The Nimrod looks after maritime patrol, while the airborne early warning task is undertaken by the E-3D Sentry.

Flying

Flying is the *raison d'être* of the RAF, and careers are firmly divided between flying and 'other', generally termed 'ground', specialisations, all of them geared to support for aircrews. Except in such aircraft as the Nimrod and Sentry, the day of very large aircrews is over, and most British combat aircraft now carry only pilot and navigator (the Nimrod has two pilots, an engineer, two navigators and six air electronics operators).

Contemporary combat aircraft are flying electronic laboratories and, with their phenomenally high speeds, require men and women of considerable skill and aptitude to fly and navigate them. Accordingly, all pilots and navigators in the RAF are officers. Not every pilot or navigator, however, flies 'strike' aircraft. Other opportunities to fly include the transport, maritime reconnaissance, airborne early warning, and helicopter operations roles.

Obviously aircrew officers do not spend their entire careers on flying duties, although in the early stages they are employed almost exclusively in the air. Subsequently, a great proportion of their time is spent in ground appointments, related to flying operations and planning. In peacetime, it is not uncommon for a pilot's 'flying week' to total six to ten hours in the air. The close and detailed preparation for each sortie, though, can well take longer than the flight itself. A great deal of time, even for trained crews, is spent in simulators, and more hours in analysing the work done in the air; for example, fighter pilots develop tactics by studying the photographs and video recordings of their own interception training flights, strike and attack crews go over bombing and rocket exercises, and so on. In addition, most aircrew officers have 'secondary duties' which may be anything from having an appointment on the Officers' Mess Committee to officer in charge of a sporting activity, and most junior officers must also take 24-hour spells as orderly or duty officers, acting as the Station Commander's representative in the quiet hours.

Ground support

While flying is obviously one of the major attractions of a career in the RAF, this does not mean that careers on the ground need be any less demanding. In many respects these may have more to offer. Aircrew are, of course, totally dependent on people like engineers and flight controllers. Both aircrew and ground support personnel must, in fact, be welded into a tight and efficient unit if a combat team is to operate effectively. Ground specialisations include air traffic and fighter control, intelligence, engineering, supply, administration, catering, and ground defence, plus the educational and medical tasks.

On air traffic and fighter control, the RAF likes to quote the old adage, 'the watcher sees most of the game', and applies this to supersonic aircraft approaching each other at closing speeds of 10 miles/minute along computer-predicted flight paths, in support of its claim of its key importance. Fighter control employs the most advanced long-range radar and radio, and computer-aided tactical planning to direct the airborne fighter aircraft and the ground-to-air missiles.

The introduction into active service of the Sentry Airborne Early Warning aircraft in 1991–92, and the progressive introduction of advanced ground-based command, control and communications systems, have greatly enhanced the RAF's ability to monitor and control activity in UK airspace. Fighter controllers keep a 24-hour vigil all the year round in various permanent stations both in the UK and abroad, and even in mobile air control centres. Stations not only direct combat aircraft, but also, for example, keep track of satellites and spacecraft, using computer-plotted radar (for instance, at Fylingdales) to distinguish possible re-entry vehicles from space junk, and in vectoring a combat aircraft onto a tanker for air-to-air refuelling. Air traffic control performs a function very similar to that of the civilian control tower (*see also* THE TRANSPORT INDUSTRY). The gathering of intelligence includes analysing air-reconnaissance photographs to extract intelligence information.

RAF engineers not only do maintenance work, although this in itself is very exacting because of the highly sophisticated nature of the electronic and flight equipment in use today, and because all installations must be kept in constant operational readiness. Engineers also help to formulate the RAF's requirements in terms of new aircraft and defence and control systems, in shaping their development, translating them into a complete programme, and helping to introduce the end-product into service. Engineering officers specialise, initially at least, in either aerosystems (the aircraft themselves, their weapons and air-to-ground communication systems) or communications/electronics dealing with ground-based radio, including satellite, systems, radar and electronic systems for air defence, and command and control communications.

The RAF also has its own ground defence, the RAF Regiment, a highly mobile force trained as infantry, gunners and parachutists all in one. It also supplies fire-control services and missile protection to airfields. The supply branch is responsible for moving aircraft, personnel and equipment around the world, combining purchasing, forwarding and stock control with a kind of travel agency. It must be just as efficient at moving a complete aircraft as at ensuring the supply of parts required for maintenance (down to the smallest split-pin), and this can mean many millions of items to be made available on a worldwide basis.

The RAF also needs a considerable amount of administration, and has its own personnel, catering, physical fitness, medical and dental, legal and training branches. Stations have a high degree of autonomy, handling their own accounts, budgets, etc.

Royal Air Force musician

This is one of the ground trades of the RAF. Bands and orchestras are established to provide musical support for RAF, joint service and national occasions. Musicians are recruited as woodwind, brass, percussion and string players. Entry is open to airmen and airwomen. They are employed exclusively on musical duties, playing a wide range of music to a very high standard.

There are two levels of entry. The qualified entry is for musicians who have a performer's diploma or play at the equivalent standard. They may well have professional experience. The unqualified entry is for musicians who perform to a good standard. Though formal qualifications are not necessary, the normal standard expected is equivalent to Grade VIII of the Associated Board of the Royal Schools of Music.

Candidates selected for entry as qualified musicians will normally be given the rank of senior aircraftman/woman or junior technician and, after seven weeks' basic training, will undergo a period of familiarisation training at the RAF School of Music before being appointed to one of the RAF bands. Promotion is possible through corporal, sergeant, chief technician and flight sergeant to warrant officer, subject to ability and successful completion of the appropriate courses.

Officers

Officers (men and women) are commissioned on a single list, but recruited for specific branches. Terms of engagement can vary slightly between branches.

The main branches are: general duties (flying); operations support (flight operations); air traffic and fighter controls; intelligence and RAF Regiment; engineer; administrative (personnel, training, physical education, provost and catering); supply. Permanent (PC) and short service (SSC) commissions are available in most branches. The initial PC commitment is to age 38, or for 16 years from 21, whichever is the later. A full career to 55 depends on promotion and/or availability of posts, and is competitive.

Graduates have 'built-in' promotion through the junior ranks. They join as pilot officers, and with a first- or second-class honours gain 21 months' seniority; with a third or an ordinary pass 15 months; and for four-year courses qualify for an extra twelve months. Promotion to flying officer then, can come in six months, flight lieutenant within a year (for pilots or navigators) or two and a half years (for ground officers).

Promotion from pilot to flying officer is normally (non-graduate entry) after two years and from flying officer to flight lieutenant after four years. Thereafter promotion to squadron leader (normally in the early thirties), wing commander (average age for aircrew is 39), group captain, air commodore, air vice-marshal, air marshal, and air chief marshal, is entirely on merit. The large majority of the most senior officers, however, come from general duties (flying) branch. Anyone not selected, or who does not wish to enter the career structure above squadron leader, can retire at 38, or for aircrew officers, follow a 'specialist' stream if they want to go on flying. All officers can choose to go back to civilian life at a 'marketable' age.

Short Service Commissions are initially six years for ground officers, twelve (with the option to leave after eight) for aircrew.

The RAF divides officers' careers into 'tours of duty', each lasting two to three years, at the end of which officers move on to a new appointment. In many cases this may mean promotion or widening experience, and may also provide a chance to serve overseas. Additional training often forms part of the third and/or fourth tour.

Recruitment and entry

Officer entry to most branches is at a minimum of 17 for both men and women, and a maximum of 29 (24 for aircrew, which means applying by 23 at the latest). Age and qualification requirements vary for the different branches; however, candidates must have at least two A-levels/Highers or equivalent, together with five GCSEs at grade C/3 or above, to include Maths and English language. About 75% of candidates hold degrees. Selection for aircrew is carried out at the Officers and Aircrew Selection Centre (OASC), RAF Cranwell. Here, potential pilots and navigators spend four days undergoing a demanding series of aptitude tests, exercises, a medical, and interviews (two and a half days for ground duties). Those who do not make the grade for flying duties are counselled and may be considered for other duties in the RAF.

For some specialisations, e.g. engineering, training or medicine, a relevant degree is needed. Graduate entry is also encouraged, with the award of cadetships and bursaries for students attending university, full sponsorship is available for sandwich courses in air transport engineering at City University, and in electronic and electrical engineering at Salford University. Scholarships are available for A-level study, and there are also Flying Scholarships to be won. Competition for places is considerable.

Qualifications and training

All officer recruits start with 24 weeks' training at the RAF College, Cranwell. Following this, officers undertake professional training in their chosen specialisation, then go on to an appointment at a unit.

Aircrew officers are trained as either pilots or navigators, but for combat aircraft the emphasis is now all on welding the crew of two into a single unit – the latest aircraft, especially the Tornado, are largely computer-controlled, and the pilot cannot fly in combat without a highly skilled navigator. Student pilots with little flying experience receive 62 hours' basic training in Fireflys. This is followed by 120 hours on Tucanos, with a thorough introduction to the mechanics of flight, meteorology, navigation, weaponry and electronics. Fast-jet pilots then go on to RAF Valley for another 33 weeks' high-performance flying with the Hawk.

Once a pilot has earned their 'wings', they go on to train on the aircraft they will fly in their squadron. This could be a on single-seater such as the Harrier, or as part of the pilot/navigator team on the Tornado. Helicopter or multi-engined pilots are trained to fly aircraft such as the Chinook or the Hercules, learning how to operate as part of a crew.

Navigators begin with about a year on the Basic and Advanced Air Navigation Courses at RAF Cranwell and RAF Topcliffe. Navigators are sent up in the Dominie to learn the principles of navigation, from flying without instruments to complicated avionics. There are sorties in the Tucano, where they learn to fly 'low-level' and real and simulated exercises with Air Traffic Control, there is also a considerable amount of deskwork. Navigators are then selected either for two-man fast jets (going on to attend the Tactical Navigators Course) or for multi-engined aircraft. Depending on their specialist training, navigators join a Tornado, Hercules, Nimrod, VC10 or E-3D Sentry squadron.

Ground branch officers go on to their own specialist training, which varies in length. For instance, air traffic control officers do four months plus six to nine months' practical experience before certification. Fighter control officers train for six weeks. Engineers start with an orientation course, and then 20–25 weeks' training in their specialist field. Further training is given later for work in, for example, R&D, procurement, and introducing new equipment. Supply officers have four months' basic training which includes computer familiarisation. Advanced training in, for example, movements (air and surface), fuels, explosives or data-processing can lead on to higher qualifications in management and/or transportation studies.

Non-commissioned airmen/women

Non-commissioned airmen/women number around 52,500, down about 2,500 on 1995/96 figures, and almost 19,500 less than the 1991/92 figure. Women are excluded from only one of the RAF trades, namely RAF Regiment gunner.

Airmen/women aircrew comprise air engineers, air electronics operators and air loadmasters/mistresses.

- *Air engineers* fly the larger, multi-engined non-combat aircraft. They make the pre-flight checks, handle throttles during take-off, and monitor all the aircraft's systems (hydraulics, electrics, etc.), make fuel checks and redistribute the fuel, cope with in-flight refuelling, diagnose and where possible solve any engineering problems.
- *Air electronics operators* operate avionic equipment, e.g. communications, radar, underwater detection systems, all used in locating, identifying and tracking ships and submarines, surveilling oil and gas rigs, and in search and rescue operations.
- *Air loadmasters/mistresses* despatch troops by parachute and other air drops, supervise loading and check weight control/positioning for balance, and supervise cabin service in passenger aircraft.
  Loadmasters/mistresses could also act as crewmen/women on support helicopters, do some servicing, and act as winchmen/women on search and rescue helicopters.

Ground trades. The range of ground trades includes: aircraft engineering; airframe, propulsion, and weapons technicians.

- Electrical and electronic engineering: flight systems, telecommunications, air communications technicians and air radar specialists.
- General engineering: electrical technicians (looking after maintenance equipment, ground radar power supplies and vehicle electrical systems), ground-support equipment technicians and workshop technicians.
- Airwatch teams include aerospace system operators (controlling satellite systems), air photography processors, assistant photographic interpreters, and assistant air traffic controllers.
- Security and safety police (including dog-handling, counter-intelligence and special investigations, preventing and detecting crime), survival equipment fitters, gunners, and firemen.
- Communications: aerial erectors, special telegraphists, voice radio operators, and telecommunications operators.
- Support: chefs and cooks, stewards, supply staff (locating equipment in stores on computers, packing, storing, handling and transport loading), drivers (of anything from high-powered aircraft-towing vehicles, mobile cranes and refuellers, to staff cars), and administrative clerks.
- The full range of paramedical, medical lab professions are also employed.

Men and women serve on nine-year 'notice' engagements, and so can leave full-time service on giving 18 months' notice, although they must serve at least three years (from age 18 or end of training, whichever is later). They must still do six years in the reserve, but liability for reserve service ends on pregnancy or 'acquisition of dependent children'. Promotion is competitive, depending partly on experience, training and qualifications.

Recruitment and entry

The RAF recruited some 4,100 airmen and women in 1991. Numbers fluctuate from year to year, and targets for 1995/96 are about 2,800 but will rise to about 4,500 by 1999. For entry to most trades the minimum age limit is currently 16 years, with an upper limit of under 24 at the time of entering the Service. Educational qualifications required vary with the trade selected. For example some engineering trades require three GCSEs grade C/3 including English language, maths and an approved science or language subject. For paramedical work, the school-leaving qualifications appropriate to the profession or, in some cases, the appropriate professional qualifications are required. Many of the other trades on offer require no formal academic qualifications.

Qualifications and training

All entrants begin with basic training: seven weeks (eight weeks from November 1996) at RAF Halton, or RAF Catterick, depending on which branch of the RAF they join. Trade training follows (three weeks to three years depending on the trade chosen). In the engineering trades candidates are streamed into technician or mechanic careers. Once trade training is complete individuals are posted to an RAF establishment in this country or overseas, and begin work under supervision. Most trade training now attracts NVQ accreditation.

Further education/training is given as needed, with facilities and encouragement to qualify for promotion.

Selection for aircrew: All NCO Aircrew candidates must pass a demanding selection process. This is carried out at the Officers and Aircrew Selection Centre (OASC), RAF Cranwell. Here, potential NCO Aircrew; Air Engineers, Air Electronics Operators, and Air Loadmasters undergo four days of demanding aptitude tests, exercises, a medical, and interviews. Successful candidates go on to the Aircrew Initial Training Course which lasts for twelve weeks, followed by further specialist training depending on the specialism.

Princess Mary's Royal Air Force Nursing Service (PMRAFNS).

PMRAFNS operates on similar lines to the Army's QARANC. Nurses work in RAF hospitals and station medical centres, both at home and abroad. They provide nursing support when the sick and injured are flown to hospital, etc. For entry into the PMRAFNS candidates are required to hold the appropriate professional qualifications. *See also* SUPPLEMENTARY HEALTH PROFESSIONS.

The Royal Marines

Traditionally known as the Royal Navy's soldiers, the Marines are, in fact, actually part of the Royal Navy. Their contemporary role, however, is primarily as commandos and amphibious specialists, with less emphasis on the detachments which serve in HM ships. The corps is relatively small, numbering (1995) about 7,000 officers and men.

The three commando units are each about 700-strong. Each unit has its own mortars and anti-tank weapons and is in many ways similar to the infantry. They are trained in mountain, Arctic, urban, jungle and desert warfare. They also serve in Northern Ireland.

As amphibious specialists they are trained to make full-scale landings, as front-line assault troops even in major invasions. They use fast light craft as well as troop-carrying and heavy-duty tank and vehicle carriers. The Special Boat Service (SBS) is made up of highly skilled frogmen, canoeists and parachutists, who carry out reconnaissance raids 'clandestine operations', sabotage and demolition. Marine detachments serving as shipborne infantrymen on board ship go wherever needed: to deal with emergencies, carry out search operations, help in disasters such as hurricanes. Detachments serve as integral parts of ships' companies and their officers are encouraged to qualify for a bridge watch-keeping certificate.

Although part of the Navy, the Marines are a military corps. However, they pride themselves on their versatility, and on their extremely tough reputation. Officers and men alike go through extremely gruelling physical training. Both officers and men change jobs every two years.

Officers

Officers number (1995) around 700. Once trained (*see below*), they get a new posting every two or three years. All can specialise; for example, in signals and communications, or as helicopter pilots. They can become, for example, troop officers in charge of new recruits, intelligence officers, mountain leaders, or landing-craft or special boat officers. Administrative, 'staff' posts start around age 26.

Most officers join on a 'full career' commission (*see* NAVY *below*), but short-service commissions of five years, extendible to eight, are possible. Full-career officers serve as lieutenants for seven years, and are then automatically promoted to captain, usually before the age of 30. It is possible to become a major at 35 and a lieutenant-colonel by the early 40s.

Recruitment and entry

Around 50 officers a year are recruited, of whom about half are graduates. Entry to a 'full career' is between the ages of 17½ and 22, with a minimum of two A-level passes and three GCSEs at grade C or above, or their equivalent, with English and mathematics; but direct graduate entry has an upper age limit of 25. Scholarships with reserved places are available for boys with five GCSEs grade C or above or their equivalent (including English and mathematics) to study for A levels, and cadetships for university students.

Short-career entry is between ages 17½ and 23, or 25 for graduates. Minimum entry requirements are two A-levels and three GCSEs grade C or above (including English and mathematics), or their equivalent.

Qualifications and training

All candidates for the Royal Marines must attend a Potential Officer, or Potential Recruit course, and pass rigorous selection procedures including aptitude tests, physical fitness tests and interviews. Both officers and men undergo the longest infantry training programme of any NATO combat troops. Officers spend their first 15 months at the Commando Training Centre at Lympstone, Devon. A further nine months is practical, with a commando unit in charge of a 30-man rifle troop. For full-career officers this is followed by a further year of academic studies at Dartmouth, plus a series of advanced and refresher courses at military and marine establishments. Staff training can start at 26.

Non-commissioned

There are around 6,100 men serving in the Royal Marines in 1996. Some marines serve in the General Duties branch, where they can specialise in assault and weaponry (anti-tank missiles, assault engineer, heavy or platoon weapons, sniper), or in crewing landing-craft. Other specialisms include the Marines' two Special Forces Units; as parachutist, swimmer-canoeist operating in an SBS unit, or as a Mountain Leader in mountain and Arctic warfare (including cliff-climbing and skiing). After promotion it is possible to compete for jobs as drill or physical training instructor, and helicopter or light aircraft pilot or observer. The technical branch includes armourers, drivers and motorcyclists, telecommunications technicians and vehicle mechanics. There are also jobs for clerks, signallers and chefs.

Recruitment and entry

Junior entry (including musicians and buglers) is between 16 and 17½, adult entry from 17½ to 28. No formal educational requirements, but candidates are tested for reasoning, English language, numeracy and mechanical comprehension.

Qualifications and training

Training lasts 30 weeks, which consists of an initial phase of 15 weeks of individual skills teaching (weapons, husbandry, seamanship, drill and elementary tactics), physical training and character development followed by a second phase of nine weeks of team skills including advanced tactics, weapons, physical training and drill leading, to,wards the commando tests and the Kings Squad passout, all undertaken in the last six weeks. Marines are then assigned to a unit, but can continue with further training later.

Royal Marines Band Service

Musicians and buglers serve in the Royal Marines Band Service, which provides musical support for the Royal Navy and the Royal Marines on every type of occasion. Today's Band Service is a unique musical blend of versatility, talent and tradition, on top of which it has a key military role as part of a fighting force. The Band Service has a total complement of around 350 personnel. Bands vary in size and structure. Musicians and buglers usually spend about two years with a band, but can also be detached to other RM bands as required.

Qualifications and training

Entry to the Royal Marines School of Music at Portsmouth, usually between 16 and 28, follows an interview, medical, audition and further interview. New entrants undergo eight weeks of military training. Subsequent training is predominantly musical. Total training period is two years and eight months for musicians or one year eight months for the buglers' branch.

After initial training and experience promotion is possible, e.g. to band corporal, band sergeant, through to bandmaster. Beyond that lies the opportunity to take a commission – all officers in the Band Service are promoted from the ranks. Since May 1992 females have been admitted for training for the RMBS.

Marines serve on an open engagement which provides for a full career of 22 years' service over the age of 18, or the date of entry if later. Service before the age of 18 will not count for engagement or pension purposes. If service is terminated on notice before the 22-year point, there may be a requirement to serve in the Royal Fleet Reserve (RFR) for the balance of 22 years, or for a period of three years, whichever is less. Promotion is based on ability and length of service.

The Royal Navy

Political and strategic policy dictates a Fleet with fewer and smaller ships, a Fleet with no battleships or full-scale aircraft carriers, and a sharply reduced force of men and women. Figures for RN and RM numbers stand at around 41,000 in 1996 including around 7,500 officers. Since the disbandment of the Women's Royal Naval Service (WRNS) in 1992, the Navy is now an integrated service, and women serve at sea. With the exception of submarine service and some minor war vessels, women serve in all types of ships.

The Royal Navy has 16 submarines, four of which carry Britain's nuclear deterrent; and one of these is on patrol at all times. Three through-deck cruisers act as command ships for air operations and anti-submarine warfare, carrying Sea Harriers, Sea King helicopters and missile systems. The Royal Navy also has twelve destroyers and 23 frigates. These deploy a range of weapons for the conduct of maritime warfare. They can control aircraft or provide air defence for other ships, are equipped for anti-submarine operations and contribute to surface maritime warfare with surface-to-surface missiles.

The surface fleet also contains amphibious assault and landing ships, mine counter-measure vessels, patrol craft and survey ships. The Royal Fleet Auxiliary Service, which replenishes warships at sea, has 21 ships.

The RN Fleet Air Arm operates more than 200 fixed-wing aircraft, including Harrier, Hawk and Jetstream aircraft, and Sea King, Lynx, and Gazelle helicopters.

Modern warships, both large and small, surface and submarine, are built to highly advanced technological specifications, and are armed, propelled, guided, and search with sophisticated, automated electronic equipment, etc. Warships at sea are self-contained communities, and officers and ratings have to be skilled people to manage, operate and maintain them.

The Navy divides its employments by branch: Warfare Branch, Engineering Branch, Supply Branch, Medical Branch, and Fleet Air Arm. Warfare Branch includes those trained as operator/mechanics specialising in electronic warfare, radar, missile, sonar, sonar (submarines), radio and communications. These are the people directly responsible for 'working' and 'fighting' the ships and submarines.

Linked closely is the Engineering Branch; and artificers (technicians) and mechanics who specialise in marine, weapon, electrical or air engineering.

Providing support for the Navy is the Supply Branch, which comprises the 'writers' (administrators), cooks, caterers, stewards, and stores accountants who ensure the smooth running of any naval base or ship.

Medical Branch is staffed with medical assistants and technicians.

The Fleet Air Arm provides the aircraft – helicopters and fixed-wing aircraft – operated by pilots and observers, and supported by naval airmen – aircraft handlers, survival equipment specialists, meteorologists and oceanographers.

The ships are supported by the shore establishments, mostly air stations or training bases, some of which have sophisticated communications stations. The Navy also uses specialist divers, and has its own training managers, medical and dental staff, lawyers, and chaplains.

Officers

There are around 7,500 serving officers in 1996, who are trained for specific categories.

Warfare officers 'work' and 'fight' their ships. They are trained in all the ways and power of the sea, to handle and navigate ships and boats in all weather conditions, as well as how to use them as weapons of war and make the most effective use of their armament, detection equipment and, if carried, aircraft. All warfare officers must qualify for bridge watch-keeping and ocean navigating certificates. Ships' commanding officers all come from amongst warfare officers.

Within the warship specialisation, it is possible to sub-specialise, for example, in submarines, aircraft control, aviation (flying), mine warfare and clearance diving, or hydrographic surveying.

Engineer officers specialise in marine, mechanical, aeronautical, electrical or electronic engineering. They all sub-specialise in one of:

- weapon systems (surface ships) including the ship's sensors and weapon communications systems, e.g. sonar, radar, computers, satellite, gun, torpedo and missile;

- weapon systems (submarines): as surface ships (but including Trident if the submarine is equipped with them), plus control room watch-keeping; marine engineering (surface ships): controlling, monitoring, maintaining and repairing the hull and general structure, engines and machinery, generators and electrical distribution, air-conditioning, ventilating, heating, fuel and water, refrigeration, etc.;
- marine engineering (submarines): as surface ships but also nuclear reactors and specialised hull equipment;
- air engineering (mechanical and electrical): keeping naval aircraft fully operational and safe, 'managing' maintenance and repair of all systems, and aircraft flight-control radar and weapon systems, electrical/electronic systems; may involve serving at sea or on an air station.

Supply officers look after pay and cash, naval stores, catering, etc. The captain's secretary handles official correspondence, and deals with a range of administrative, welfare and personnel work on ship or shore establishment. A ship's supply officer feeds and pays the crew, is in charge of stores and spares – 40,000 items on a frigate – and usually has an 'operational' job as well, e.g. as flight-deck officer.

Training Management officers help officers and ratings gain the underpinning knowledge they need to use complex equipment, and to apply that knowledge in difficult conditions, such as on board a moving ship in heavy seas. As well as passing on expertise in science and engineering, training management officers may also carry out other kinds of naval teaching, from basic maths and English to postgraduate studies.

Only limited numbers of pilots and observers are needed, mainly for helicopters. Warfare officers may choose to fly, but the best opportunities are via short-career commission flying-duties direct entry. A small number of pilots are selected to fly the Sea Harrier.

Commissions and lists

Types of commission vary depending on chosen area of specialisation, but essentially officers choose full-career commissions; with the opportunity to serve until 50, or medium- or short-career commissions with a minimum return of service ranging from three to seven years depending on specialism. It is intended that the current commission structure will change. A single 'Initial Commission' (IC) will replace the current range of commissions and associated lists. The IC will be for a period of twelve years for the RN and eight years for the RM. This will allow all officer entrants, regardless of their entry route, an equal opportunity to demonstrate their future potential in productive employment, and aid selection for longer commissions. From about two to three years after completion of initial training, selections for further commissions will commence.

Medical/dental officers sign on initially for six and five years respectively, but can apply for the opportunity to transfer to a pensionable commission.

All officers change posts every two or three years. Even young officers in their twenties are given command for small craft, such as minesweepers or patrol vessels, with complete responsibility for their efficiency and up to 40 personnel. On a full-career commission promotion from midshipman (aged 17–26) to sub-lieutenant (between 19 and 26), lieutenant (between 22 and 34), and lieutenant commander (between 30 and 36), is automatic. Promotion to commander and above is by selection.

Recruitment and entry

Numbers recruited have dropped to a small fraction of the 620 recruited in 1990/91. Full-career naval college entry is between 17 and 23 with five GCSEs at grade C or above plus two A-level passes (subjects to include maths and English, with maths and physics at A-level for engineering). Scholarships to study for A-levels are limited to warfare, aircrew and engineering entrants. University cadetships are awarded for all branches except Training Manager. Short-career commissions naval college entry at age 17–26 require two A-levels and three GCSEs, or equivalent, including English and maths for most. Engineers, however, still need at least A-level maths and physics or a BTEC equivalent.

Direct graduate entry to both full-career and short/medium service has an upper age limit of 26. Training Managers must have a degree or equivalent (professional) qualification, with an upper age limit of 34. Medical officers can join in their pre-registration year if under 33. Qualified medical entrants must be under 44 and must be a fully registered medical practitioner. Dental direct entrants must be under 32.

Qualifications and training

All Naval officers prepare for Naval service with two terms of training at the Britannia Royal Naval College Dartmouth. The first term is spent at the college. In the second term they 'go operational' in a ship of the Fleet, which is also the Dartmouth Training Ship. Next follows a period of ten to 20 months as an Officer Under Training in the Fleet (OUT). This is followed by a Fleet Board – an oral examination to ensure individuals possess the basic skills required of a Naval officer. Following this is specialist training in the Fleet. This can vary from a term for engineering specialists who were qualified on entry, to a year for Naval College entry officers. Training begins with basic 'action-centred' leadership training, but also 'seamanship and naval knowledge'. (Flying-duty direct-entry officers go on to air training for 16 months.)

Thereafter, training varies according to specialisation and type of commission. Full-career engineer officers who have not already graduated, for example, go to the University of Southampton to read for an engineering degree; warfare and supply officers take a series of professional courses.

Ratings

There were around 33,600 ratings in 1995 (against 41,000 in 1991), who are recruited to particular categories.

The seamen group 'work' ships, attending to ropes and wires, anchors and cables, help in refuelling and restocking at sea, act as lookout, steer, lower and crew boats, and also specialise as operators/mechanics in one of the following:

- electronic warfare, working equipment in the operations rooms to intercept 'enemy' transmissions radar, working on warning radar, and plotting positions of ships and aircraft; missiles, controlling and operating ships' weapons systems;
- sonar, operating equipment to detect and hunt submarines, either in surface ships or submarines; diving, mainly on mine disposal and clearance, but also experimental;
- mine warfare, working in minesweepers and hunters, survey recording, helping to collect navigational and oceanographic data for admiralty charts, working on special computer-assisted survey ships; tactical systems on submarines, involved in navigation, 'enemy' detection by radar and sonar, and computer-assisted plotting.

Operator/mechanics in the communications group specialise in one of the following:

- general/tactical operating, combining all types of long- and short-range radio equipment, signal traffic with message-handling systems and communications procedures in the tactical movement and working of ships;
- submarine radio operating, in conventional and nuclear submarines.

In the engineering branch, artificers (technicians) and mechanics specialise in similar areas, although the artificer is more highly skilled (having completed a four year apprenticeship). The specialisations are:

- marine engineering artificer: operating and mechanical maintenance of ships' propulsion machinery (gas turbine, diesel, nuclear powered) and associated plant; maintaining and repairing ships structure, fitting, and boats, and power generation, etc.; associated electrical/electronic, including control systems;
- weapon engineering artificer: (action data) – surveillance radar and displays computer, and action information systems, computer peripherals, digital processing, sonars, software applications, radio navigation aids; or (communications and electronic warfare) – radio communication, cryptographic, satellite equipment, digital processing, etc.; or (weapon data) – weapon control and guidance, navigational aids, tracking radars, etc.; or (ordnance control) – gun mountings/turrets, rocket and missile launchers, torpedo systems, bomb lifts explosives and ordnance;
- air engineering artificer: (mechanical) – airframe structures, engines, hydraulic and pneumatic systems, aircraft propulsion and transmission systems and other mechanical components; or (radio) – communications, navigation, sonar and radar systems of aircraft; or (weapons electrical) – power generation and distribution, flight control systems, flight instruments and weapons systems.

Mechanics work mainly on: mechanical systems – boilers, turbines and so on, and auxiliary machinery – the ship's structure, fittings and boats; electrical systems – propulsion machinery, semi-skilled electrical maintenance, e.g. generators, switchgear, lighting, telephones; weapons – either radio (radar, wireless and TV equipment, automatic plotting and data-handling systems and sonars) or ordnance (navigation systems, internal communications, gun mountings. missile launchers, explosers and control of weapon and missile systems); air engineering – mechanical (systems, airframe, hydraulic systems), radio (e.g. navigation, radar and sonar), weapons (electrical power supply and distribution, flight instruments, weapons and their control, and release systems).

Naval airmen (Fleet Air Arm), 'ground crew', work on flight decks and airfields, in hangars and in aircraft control positions and towers, controlling aircraft movements. Training also includes fire-fighting and rescue techniques, and it is possible to specialise in this or become heavy goods vehicle drivers.

Writers are the Navy's administrative and accounting staff who serve at sea, and work in shore establishments at home and abroad, and in RN air stations. Their duties include general administration, secretarial practice, personnel records, personnel movements, technical records, security, cash accounting, foreign exchange, financial counselling, naval law and discipline, typing and word processing, computer programming and computer management, office machinery operation and maintenance.

Stores accountants help to keep their ship running and ready for action. They are responsible for the reception, custody, control, issuing and accounting for the large range of stores, and for ensuring that faulty items are returned for repair and replacement items ordered.

Chefs and catering managers, whether serving ashore or at sea, are expected to provide food of the highest standard to meet the daily needs of Royal Navy personnel. They also prepare banquets, cocktail parties, and lunch and dinner parties for VIP visitors.

Stewards are trained in hotel service and management and use their skills to look after officers' and ratings' accommodation ashore and afloat.

Medical assistants work alongside medical and dental officers, medical technicians and the Queen Alexandra's Royal Naval Nursing Service. Their work includes providing advanced first aid and life-saving measures, nursing duties, health education, medical administration and dispensing. Medical assistants may work in hospitals or serve at sea, either assisting the medical team on larger ships or providing all medical services on smaller ships.

Ratings enter on 'open' engagements of 22 years from age 18 or date of entry (if later). They must actually serve at least four years from completion of training, and can give notice to do so 18 months before that. They may have to forfeit the right to give notice for an agreed period in return for any higher training. Entrants under 17½ become junior ratings, with automatic advancement to ordinary rate at 17½. According to category, and subject to tests, ordinary seamen are advanced to able rate after six to 15 months in the ordinary rate. Thereafter the average age of advancement to leading rate is 22 to 23, to petty officer 26 to 28, to chief petty officer (which is decided by seniority, recommendation and qualification) early to mid-30s. A warrant officer, the highest rating, is described as a manager and is expected to plan, allocate and control work, but is also expected to serve at least 27 years.

There are opportunities for promotion to the Officer Corps.

Recruitment and entry

Current recruiting targets are 2,800. Ratings can join between 16 and 33 (but a large percentage start before they are 20), and need only to pass a selection test (reasoning, English language, numeracy and mechanical comprehension). The exceptions are:

- Artificers join between 16 and 28, with GCSE/SCE grades C/3 in English, mathematics, and physics, or other appropriate science-based subject, or appropriate BTEC National or City & Guilds part II.
- Medical technicians join between 16 and 33, with qualifications appropriate to planned specialisation, but a limited number of places are available, subject to educational qualifications, to train in certain specialisations.

Qualifications and training

All Naval ratings begin their career with eight weeks (14 weeks for Artificers), New Entry training at HMS Raleigh, Torpoint (shore base). Following this they move to different locations to complete specialist trade-training before being posted to a ship or shore base. Naval ratings enter as either a Junior or Ordinary Rating, and undertake promotion and trade-training tests to advance through the promotion structure. Artificers spend 14 weeks at HMS Raleigh, then proceed to either HMS Sultan, or HMS Collingwood for technician training, which lasts up to four years. During this time they can qualify for a BTEC National Certificate in engineering.

For other work at sea, *see in* THE TRANSPORT INDUSTRY and FISHING *in* LAND USE INDUSTRIES.

Queen Alexandra's Royal Naval Nursing Service (QARNNS)

QARNNS looks after Royal Naval, and Royal Marine personnel, and families of those serving overseas in hospitals, sick bays and other medical centres. QARNNS nurses do not serve at sea in peacetime, but nurse in hospital ships when there is a war.

Officers are all RGN-qualified ward or theatre sisters or more senior staff. All nursing officers sign on initially for a five-year short-career commission, with no return of service requirement. They can opt to extend to eight years, and have the right to apply for a medium- then a full-career commission.

Non-commissioned nurses enter on 'open' engagements of 22 years. They must actually serve at least four years from completion of training and can give notice of their intention to leave 18 months before that. They may have to forfeit the right to give notice for an agreed period in return for any higher training. New entrants can leave at 14 days notice within the first three months.

Recruitment and entry

Divides between officers and ratings. Officers: male and females are recruited as fully qualified RGN nurses with at least two years' post-registration general experience, and age under 34. Ratings: Direct entry or student nurses. RGNs can join the QARNNS directly on completion of training, alternatively the QARNNS can train their own RGNs. Those interested must have at least five academic GCSEs or equivalents (four at one sitting) including English language. *See also* SUPPLEMENTARY HEALTH PROFESSIONS.

Further information

Contact the local Armed Forces Careers Office (listed in local directories under Army, Naval Establishments, or Royal Air Force). *See also* EDUCATION AND TEACHING for teaching in the Armed Forces.

Central Government

Contents

(CLCI: CAB)

Background

Civil servants are defined (in *Finding Your Way Round Whitehall and Beyond*, Cabinet Office, 1995) as employees of all the central government departments and agencies who conduct government business in the 1990s on behalf of and in support of government ministers.

There are essentially two types of civil servant: those who form the policy-making core of the Civil Service and the 95% of government employees who are concerned with the delivery of services.

The core role of the Civil Service is to give ministers advice and information on which to base policy-making; to look at the possible effects of a suggested change of government policy; to offer professional advice (e.g. legal) on specific issues; and to implement new policies or legislation. Civil servants must give their ministers totally impartial information and advice, and carry out instructions equally impartially, regardless of their own political views. Unlike some other countries, where civil servants work only for a particular political administration or term of office, in the UK most of these jobs are not dependent on which political party is in power.

The largest part of the Civil Service's work, though, is managing major public services. This means collecting taxes of all kinds (personal, company, and VAT for example); paying benefits; inspecting factories; dealing with customs and excise; administering the courts and prisons; giving advice to farmers, and services for industry and commerce; managing trading services, like National Savings, the Royal Mint; export credit guarantees; and passports.

Civil Service reforms

The division between policy-makers and the rest of the Civil Service has been accentuated by recent Civil Service reforms, notably the 'Next Steps Initiative', launched in 1988. The initiative, designed to improve management in government and to deliver a better quality of public services, has been described as 'the most important Civil Service reform this century'.

Next Steps involves delegation of the executive functions of government, such as payment of benefits, to separate units, known as Executive Agencies. Each agency is managed by a Chief Executive, who has considerable decision-making powers, for instance over staff pay and recruitment. The theory is that once ministers have set clear targets for the task to be done and the results to be achieved, and the necessary resources are made available, then there should be an 'arm's length' relationship between department and agency. The agency's Chief Executive should be left to get on with day-to-day management, unhindered by ministerial or departmental interference.

By September 1995, 109 Executive Agencies had been set up, and there were a further 59 candidates for agency status. About two-thirds of all civil servants were employed in Executive Agencies. Agencies cover an enormous range of activities – from the Benefits Agency and the Employment Service to the Royal Mint, the Queen Elizabeth II Conference Centre, the Coastguard and the Army Base Repair Organisation.

Further reforms were initiated by the White Paper *Competing for Quality* in 1991. The White Paper set out the government's commitment to concentrate on essentials, and to improve value for money in public services through competition and private sector involvement. Government activities were to be subject to rigorous questioning, which could lead to their abolition, privatisation, contracting out to the private sector or 'market testing' (inviting existing employees to compete with the private sector).

The Competing for Quality programme reviewed government activities worth about £2.6 billion between April 1992 and March 1995, and covered 69,000 civil servants, 20,000 of whom left the Civil Service. Not surprisingly, it led to enormous criticism, and to considerable anxiety and job insecurity amongst civil servants.

Nevertheless, reforms have continued, notably with the publication of two further White Papers, *The Civil Service: Continuity and Change* and *The Civil Service: Taking Forward Continuity and Change*. These have been characterised by some commentators as 'continuity for the mandarins, change for the rest'. The White Papers do signal a commitment to the continuation of a politically impartial Civil Service, recruited on merit, but also seek yet further improvements in value for money and a drop in overall numbers to 'significantly below' 500,000.

Numbers

There were in 1995 about 30% fewer civil servants than in 1979. About half of the reduction in numbers is the result of efficiency gains; the rest the result of transfer of functions and privatisation. However, the size of some departments, such as Social Security and the Home Office, has recently increased – Social Security because of unemployment, and the Home Office to cope with new prisons.

According to *Civil Service Statistics 1995*, the total number of permanent civil servants was 516,893 on 1 April 1995. There were also 18,244 casual staff. Over the previous 12 months the number of permanent staff had fallen by 4%.

Recruitment

Despite the cutbacks, recruitment does continue – just under 20,000 people entered the Civil Service in 1994/95. An increasing proportion (64% in 1994/95) of these recruits are aged 25 or over. Experience outside the Civil Service is therefore becoming more important, and it is expected that in future there will be more movement in and out of the Civil Service, at all levels.

An important change in the Civil Service is that the majority of recruitment is now carried out by individual departments and agencies. For many years, anyone applying to join any government department would contact the Civil Service Commissioners at Alençon Link, Basingstoke. No longer. For most posts, applicants should contact departments and agencies direct. Advertisements are placed in the national, local and/or specialist press when vacancies arise. Careers service and JobCentres may sometimes hold details of relevant schemes. Factsheets giving information about specialist posts (for instance accountants, lawyers and surveyors) are available from University Careers Advisory Services or the Graduate and Schools Liaison Branch of the Cabinet Office.

It is only applications and brochures about fast-stream entry (aimed at the most able graduates) that are available from Alençon Link, Basingstoke (Recruitment and Assessment Services).

Equal opportunities

The government is committed to providing equality of opportunity for all its staff. In support of this, three programmes for action have been introduced: for women, people of ethnic minority origin, and disabled people.

Women in 1995 represented 51% of the non-industrial Civil Service. At the junior grades of Administrative Officer and Administrative Assistant, 69% of employees were women. They are still under-represented at the most senior levels, but over the last few years there have been increases in the proportion of women at management grades (from Executive Officer up to Grade 5). The growth in the number and seniority of female staff is probably partly due to flexible working hours and conditions and a 'Career Break' scheme, enabling staff to take up to five years off and return to the Service at their old grade. Maternity leave is generous, and some departments both in London and the provinces are starting to provide nurseries and creches. There are increasing opportunities for part-time work – nearly 20% of all women non-industrial staff work part-time. 1.6% of civil servants are registered as disabled, which compares well with other employers. There are also about 1.2% non-registered disabled staff in the rest of the workforce. Special facilities, e.g. hearing loops, Braille documents and wheelchair ramps, can normally be provided for those who need them.

Ethnic minorities make up about 5.4% of non-industrial civil servants. This compares with 4.8% in the working population, although they are not heavily represented at senior level. There is an ethnic monitoring policy for applicants and, during recruitment campaigns, posts are normally advertised in the ethnic minority press.

Nationality rules

All government departments and agencies are subject to certain rules as to the origin of the people whom they employ. However, most appointments are open to British or Commonwealth citizens, or citizens of the Republic of Ireland. Many are also open to all European Economic Area nationals. For some departments such as the MOD, GCHQ and the Foreign and Commonwealth Office (*see under* GOVERNMENT DEPARTMENTS *below*), there are additional requirements, e.g. about parentage. And for some posts and departments, positive vetting, i.e. security clearance, is necessary. In most departments there is usually room for some flexibility in the interpretation of these rules, providing the candidate has all the other qualities necessary to fill a particular post. A full set of the nationality rules is obtainable from individual departments and agencies.

Government departments

Most applications to join the Civil Service are now made directly to departments or agencies (with the exception of fast-stream applications). The choice is considerable, although obviously there is greater competition for some departments and agencies, particularly the more glamorous ones. Many people stay for most of their careers within one department or agency, although there is increasing flexibility on this, and transfers are possible, for professional/career development or for domestic reasons, e.g. if someone needs to move to another part of the country.

Contrary to popular belief, a relatively small proportion of civil servants, only one in five, works in London, let alone the Whitehall part of the city. Relocation of many departments means that nearly two-thirds of all civil servants work in offices outside the South-East, with an increasing share of jobs going to Yorkshire and Humberside, East Anglia, the North, the Midlands, the South-West and the North-West.

Government departments are not static organisations. New policies and political decisions; widening, or contracting, scope of government activity in particular fields; changing conditions; constant attempts to rationalise, streamline, and improve efficiency: all have their effect. As a result no description of the shape of departments is ever accurate for very long. Some departments, such as HM Customs and Excise, have existed for over 200 years, some have been closed within a few years of being formed, others merged or reduced in size, and new ones, such as the Department of National Heritage, created. While the Civil Service itself has to remain politically impartial, the following descriptions of the work which departments do reflect a certain political 'tone' and current political strategy

Not all government offices are listed here. The main departments are all described and some of the other smaller organisations are also detailed to give an idea of the range of work. Brief information about some of the main Executive Agencies is also given, under departmental headings (for instance, information on the Public Record Office is given under the heading 'Lord Chancellor's Department').

The Ministry of Agriculture, Fisheries and Food (MAFF)

This department looks after government policy on agriculture, horticulture and fisheries in England and policies relating to the safety and quality of food throughout the UK. It negotiates (with the other UK Agriculture Departments and the Intervention Board), on EU common agriculture, food and fisheries policy. Increasingly the Ministry is involved in protecting both the marine and rural environments. It provides technical advice (via the Agricultural Development and Advisory Service (ADAS)) and carries out and commissions relevant research and development. It administers schemes to control animal, fish and plant diseases, and acts as a licensing/registration authority for veterinary medicines and pesticides. MAFF also provides advice and services to the farming and horticultural industries.

The Ministry and its Executive Agencies have a total staff (1995) of about 10,000 (unchanged from 1991), of whom 40% are employed in six Executive Agencies. These are: the Agricultural Development and Advisory Service (ADAS), which employs 1,800; the Pesticides Safety Directorate; the Veterinary Laboratories Agency; the Central Science Laboratory; the Veterinary Medicines Directorate and the Meat Hygiene Service. About a third of MAFF staff are London-based. Outside the capital, ADAS has relocated its headquarters to Oxford, the Pesticides Safety Directorate is now based in York, and the Veterinary Laboratories Agency is located near Addlestone, Surrey. There are also offices, laboratories and other centres around the country.

MAFF is one of the government departments most closely connected with work in the EU and has been one of the leaders in placing staff in Europe. In-house language training is available as necessary.

See also AGRICULTURE; HORTICULTURE; *and* FISHING; *in* LAND USE INDUSTRIES.

The Cabinet Office

The Cabinet Office, which includes the Office of Public Service, is one of the two main central departments of the Civil Service (the other is the Treasury). Although the Cabinet Office employs only just over 1,000 staff, it has a pivotal role in government. Its principal objectives are to support the Cabinet and Cabinet committees and to develop, encourage and support improvement in management, efficiency and effectiveness throughout the Civil Service.

The Cabinet Secretariat helps to coordinate policy, serves ministers collectively, and administers Cabinet business – arranging meetings, preparing and circulating papers, and keeping records and minutes. The Cabinet Secretariat reflects the structure of the Cabinet's Standing Committees – covering defence and foreign affairs, economic and domestic affairs, and legislation. There is also a European Secretariat to coordinate the work of departments on European Union issues.

The Office of Public Services (OPS) promotes improved standards in public services and greater efficiency and effectiveness throughout the Civil Service – for example through the Citizen's Charter initiative and the Next Steps programme. It also works on the use of information systems in government, recruitment, training and development, senior and public appointments. Its Deregulation Unit is responsible for competitiveness and deregulation; the Competitiveness Division aims to ensure that government departments promote national competitiveness.

The OPS includes four Executive Agencies: the Civil Service College, the Occupational Health and Safety Agency, Recruitment and Assessment Services and the Chessington Computer Centre.

The Central Statistical Office/Office for National Statistics

The Central Statistical Office (just over 1,200 staff) prepares and analyses the statistics used in economic policy and management including the national accounts, balance of payments, financial statistics and measures of production and output. It also produces a number of regular statistical publications. The Central Statistical Office merged on 1 April 1996 with the Office of Population Censuses and Surveys (OPCS) to form the Office for National Statistics.

The Charity Commission

The Charity Commissioners are appointed under the Charities Act 1993 principally to further the work of charities by giving advice and information and checking abuses. They maintain a computerised public register of charities; investigate misconduct and the abuse of charitable assets and take or recommend remedial action; give advice to charity trustees to make the administration of their charities more effective; and make schemes and orders to modernise the purposes and administrative machinery of charities and to give trustees additional powers. The Commission employs over 500 people in its three offices in London, Liverpool and Taunton.

The Crown Prosecution Service

The Crown Prosecution Service was established in 1986. It now has more than 6,000 staff throughout the country. As the name implies, it prosecutes offenders on behalf of the police. Lawyers working for the department have to decide whether it is in the public interest to bring a case to court and whether there is sufficient evidence to proceed. The CPS also advises and liaises with other government departments, police forces and justice departments on criminal matters. Less than half of the workforce are lawyers (prosecutors can be either solicitors or barristers) and they are aided by teams of support staff who complete administrative work, manage cases as these go through the courts system, instruct prosecuting counsel and do casework, preparing briefs.

See also Lawyers *under* WORKING IN THE CIVIL SERVICE: SPECIALIST AND OTHER GRADES *below*; THE LEGAL SYSTEM; *and* THE POLICE *in* SECURITY AND PROTECTIVE SERVICES.

HM Customs and Excise

HM Customs and Excise is the sixth largest government department and also one of the oldest. Traditionally it administers and collects indirect taxes, including VAT (which comprises 40% of the department) and taxes on tobacco, petrol, beer, wines and spirits. The department also investigates tax frauds, sees that any duty and tax is paid on imported goods and collects duty on goods exported from bonded warehouses. For tax collection, Customs and Excise is heavily computerised, and relies less and less on older physical methods of checking and control. The department is accountable to the Chancellor of the Exchequer and also has to liaise with many other branches of the Civil Service, e.g. MAFF and the Home Office.

Customs and Excise not only collects taxes. Customs staff at sea- and airports, freight depots, etc. see that import and export restrictions are observed (e.g. health and trade control), prevent smuggling, and control movements of passengers and crews of ships and aircraft. Again, customs officers do 'agency work' on behalf of other government departments such as licensing of goods like firearms and antiques for the DTI and compiling overseas trade statistics. It is impossible to go directly into this type of work, and most customs officers begin their careers on the administrative and clerical side.

Following the Next Steps initiative, Customs and Excise now has regional headquarters in London, Southend, Liverpool and Manchester, and 30 executive units at these headquarters and elsewhere. It also has 900 local offices throughout the country.

Customs and Excise employs some 24,000 staff. Less than 3% of staff are customs officers or investigators. Most are office-based, although their work will often bring them into contact with the public. Customs staff at the ports have been cut back.

The Ministry of Defence (MOD)

The Ministry of Defence has always been a massive department, the largest in the Civil Service, and in April 1995 still employed over 116,000 staff throughout the UK. But it is getting smaller – in 1991 it employed over 140,000 – and many staff are relocating to the south-west of England.

The Ministry helps to formulate, and implements, defence policy, and also controls, administers and supports the Armed Forces. MOD agencies are run on increasingly commercial lines and sell their services to outside bodies. The Ministry's main role is the provisioning of all the facilities and services needed by the three armed forces.

Management is heavily emphasised in Ministry recruiting literature, since managing a huge defence budget has its own special problems. Computers – for management information systems, organisation and methods, and so on – are used extensively.

On policy, administrative civil servants and military personnel, some on secondment from the Forces, usually work together, contributing both military expertise and financial and political knowledge, to joint reports, assessments, and advice to ministers.

The Procurement Executive develops weapons and other equipment for the Forces, and looks after all aspects of purchase and supply. This includes administering the massive research and development budget, commissioning work both elsewhere and in its own establishments (aircraft at Farnborough and signals and radar at Bracknell, for example). Central procurement establishes policy and deals with industry links, and provides quality assurance oversight for all Ministry of Defence contracts and work, and technical costing.

The MOD has a number of Executive Agencies including the Defence Evaluation and Research Agency (DERA) and the Meteorological Office. *See also* Engineers *and* Scientists *under* WORKING IN THE CIVIL SERVICE: SPECIALIST AND OTHER GRADES *below*.

The Department for Education and Employment (DfEE)

The Department for Education and Employment (DfEE) was formed in July 1995 by the merger of the Department for Education and parts of the Employment Department. The new Department is responsible for developing policies on education and training for all age groups, for analysis of what is happening in the labour market, and for measures and services to help people find jobs.

As part of the reorganisation, some matters previously dealt with by the Employment Department were transferred to other departments. Policy on industrial relations and on some individual employment rights is now with the Department of Trade and Industry, while policy on health and safety at work, and liaison with the Health and Safety Commission and Executive, is with the Department of the Environment. Responsibility for the preparation and publication of labour market statistics has been transferred to the Central Statistical Office.

The aim of DfEE is to support economic growth and improve the nation's competitiveness and quality of life, by raising standards of educational achievement and skill and by promoting an efficient and flexible labour market. The merger of the former Education and Employment Departments is intended to help the development of more coherent policies and programmes across the field of education, training and employment as a whole. Particular areas of interest are policies for the 14–19 age group and the development of lifetime learning.

The organisation of the department was reviewed following the merger, and grouped into eight directorates: Schools; Further and Higher Education and Youth Training; Employment and Lifetime Learning; the Employment Service; Strategy, International and Analytical Services; Operations; Finance; and Personnel and Support Services. The main offices of the Department are in London, Sheffield, Runcorn and Darlington.

The DfEE includes the Employment Service, an Executive Agency which operates through a network of about 1,600 JobCentres. A number of statutory and non-statutory bodies also have close links with the Department, including the Office for Standards in Education (OFSTED), the Funding Agency for Schools, the Further Education Funding Council, the Higher Education Funding Council, the National Council for Vocational Qualifications, the School Curriculum and Assessment Authority, and Training and Enterprise Councils throughout England and Wales.

See also EDUCATION AND TEACHING.

The Department of the Environment (DoE)

The DOE has a wide range of responsibilities for the manmade and natural environment. These include environmental protection, housing, town and country planning, policy on waste disposal, maintenance of public buildings and regeneration of the inner cities. It is also responsible for the organisation, structure and finance of local government and for analysing trends in the property market.

Through the Inspectorate of Pollution it controls emission of pollutants to air, water and land.

The DoE employs over 7,000 staff, mainly in London, and has five agencies: the Planning Inspectorate, the Building Research Establishment, the Security Facilities Executive, the Buying Agency and the Queen Elizabeth II Conference Centre. The Ordnance Survey, which is a separate government department and an Executive Agency, reports directly to DoE ministers, as does PSA Services (formerly the Property Services Agency).

The DoE has recently taken over responsibility for the Health and Safety Commission/Executive, which is made up of a central executive, and the inspectorates (which are independent of each other): Factory, Agriculture, Off-shore Safety, Railways, Mines and Quarries, and Nuclear Installations – plus the technical, scientific and medical group and the Employment Medical Advisory Service (*see also* THE MEDICAL AND DENTAL PROFESSIONS). Working through a network of 20 area offices, HSE inspectors visit and review working situations, monitoring and enforcing standards via enforcement notices and prosecution, giving expert advice and guidance. They try to see that statutory requirements are met, and to ensure that there are as few accidents as possible, that safety is inbuilt rather than an afterthought. They also work with designers, manufacturers, importers and suppliers of equipment, plant, etc. used in industry, commerce, or any area of employment where safety is at stake. A substantial amount of research and lab work is done, and the Commission runs an information and advisory service. Senior staff work on policy development, and new legislation and safety measures – crucial as science and technology develop new processes and products.

The Commission had over 4,200 staff in 1995, an increase since 1991. Its headquarters staff are based in London, and in Bootle on Merseyside.

The Export Credits Guarantee Department (ECGD)

The Export Credits Guarantee Department insures exporters against the risks of not being paid by overseas customers (for whatever reason), and gives guarantees to banks so that exporters can finance their overseas business. It is, then, a business organisation.

Most staff spend their time assessing the risks of particular export markets and overseas buyers, underwriting business, handling claims, or providing support services. Following the sale of its short-term credit insurance operation in 1991, staff numbers have reduced dramatically. ECGD now employs less than 500 staff. It has moved out of central London to the Docklands area, and also maintains a small office in Cardiff.

The Office of Fair Trading

The Office of Fair Trading watches over commercial activities in the UK, to protect the consumer and encourage competition, and divides its work accordingly. It reviews the effects of trading practices on consumers, and attempts to change unfair practices by legislation and voluntary agreement. It administers the Consumer Credit and Estate Agents Acts, registers restrictive trading agreements, monitors mergers and monopolies, and collects and organises relevant economic information.

The staff is small, just under 400 people, and all work in London. Numbers and location should remain stable in the foreseeable future.

The Foreign and Commonwealth Office

The Foreign and Commonwealth Office (FCO) looks after British interests abroad. Its main job is to see that Britain and its government are properly represented on every relevant topic. It is also the London headquarters of the Diplomatic Service.

In London, the FCO gathers information and views from its overseas posts, as the basis of reports and analyses for ministers and their advisers. The departments are divided both into regions (i.e. gathering information on a wide range of subjects on the countries within the region) and functionally (dealing on a worldwide basis with particular subjects, such as defence). These 'political' departments are supported by research departments and legal advisers, professional economists and other specialist staff.

The FCO also helps to formulate and implement financial and technical assistance to developing countries. This is largely done through the Overseas Development Administration (ODA), which has approximately 1,400 staff in London and Scotland. There are also regional offices in Africa, the Pacific Islands, the Caribbean, India and Bangladesh and south-east Asia. The help provided centres around education, technology, health and the environment and includes grants, interest-free loans, technical expertise and equipment, training, and support for research and advisory services. Staff have a high possibility of working abroad.

It has an in-house scientific unit, the Natural Resources Institute, with headquarters at Chatham in Kent, working on the sustainable development of renewable natural resources in the tropics. There are three main areas of work: resource assessment and farming systems; integrated pest management; and food science and crop utilisation. The work covers applied research, surveys, technology transfer and advisory and consultancy programmes. Scientists employed usually have degrees in biochemistry, chemistry, engineering, food technology and nutrition, or land use disciplines such as agriculture, surveying, etc.

The Diplomatic Service is the link between the British government and the governments of other countries, and international organisations. Diplomatic work stretches widely, from conventional political dealings and explaining British policies, to delegations representing Britain in, for example, the UN, the EC and NATO, on topics from outer space to the seabed. It negotiates commercial treaties and financial agreements, helps and promotes exports, administers remaining dependent territories, runs 140 overseas embassies and about 75 consulates, missions and trade offices for British subjects abroad, and issues visas for people wishing to visit or emigrate to Britain.

An average-sized 'mission', e.g. an embassy, would have the following sections:

1 The chancery looks after political matters, producing reports on political developments in the country and telling the country's government about British policy, as well as dealing with any negotiations. Chancery also coordinates the work of the entire mission.
2 The commercial and economic section's main job is to help British industry sell in the country, by notifying London of new developments in local industry and commerce, the economy, legislation, etc. which affect exporters. It also advises UK companies and negotiates any commercial/trade treaties and agreements.
3 The consular section provides a service for people – to British residents in the country or British travellers and also to locals of the host country. It issues passports and visas, and handles any formalities when British ships arrive in port. Information sections primarily promote a positive image for Britain, via the media, and any other available contacts. They also help the commercial section, trade and tourism in Britain. Some missions also have scientific sections.
4 The Management Section administers the running of the mission, e.g. engaging local staff, ensuring smooth day-to-day running of the embassy as a whole.

Fast stream officers spend half of their time overseas. Main stream officers spend two-thirds of their time overseas. Languages are important at all levels and, where necessary, personnel are given intensive in-house language training before they go abroad. Some officers are selected to study a 'hard' language, e.g. Chinese or Russian.

The FCO has a total UK-based staff of around 6,000. Approximately one-third are in the Diplomatic Service, the other two-thirds are 'home-based' and will never travel abroad.

See also WORKING OVERSEAS.

The Forestry Commission

The Forestry Commission is based in Edinburgh and employs about 6,000 people to administer and oversee the development of forests throughout the country for environmental, commercial and tourism purposes. The main patterns for recruitment will be for graduates of forestry and related subjects as Forest Officers.

Government Communications Headquarters (GCHQ)

GCHQ provides the British government with defence and foreign intelligence, by studying telecommunications and other electronic signals. It also ensures the security of the nation's official and military communications networks and advises government and industry on communications and computer security.

GCHQ is an important centre for computer technology (both hardware and software) and develops satellite and other high-technology communications techniques.

Another important aspect of GCHQ's work is linguistic. It employs language graduates to translate, transcribe and analyse information in a range of languages. Required languages vary from year to year, and candidates should apply to the GCHQ Recruitment Office for current language requirements. GCHQ also houses the Joint Technical

Language Service (JTLS), which is administered by the Foreign and Commonwealth Office. JTLS translates technical or specialist material for government departments.

Most staff spend their careers at GCHQ's two Cheltenham sites, but there are occasional opportunities for postings elsewhere in the UK or abroad. There were in 1995 around 6,000 people employed at GCHQ.

The Department of Health

The Department of Health is responsible for the development and review of healthcare policy and its implementation in the NHS, the social services and public health bodies. The Department employs nearly 4,500 staff, based mainly in London and Leeds.

The Home Office

Numbers employed by the Home Office, including the Prison Service, grew by about a third between 1988 and 1993 to around 51,000; this figure has remained static, making it the fourth largest government department. As well as the Prison Service, its agencies include the UK Passport Agency, the Forensic Science Agency and the Fire Service College Agency. The Criminal Injuries Compensation Board also falls within its remit.

The Home Office's main responsibilities are: criminal policy and justice, the police and prison services, probation and aftercare of offenders, and magistrates' courts. It controls and administers immigration (including refugees and asylum seekers), equal opportunities, race and community relations, and voluntary social services.

In addition, it deals with the use, control and licensing of drugs, explosives and firearms; public safety; betting and gaming; the awarding of honours; and births, marriages and deaths. It also oversees animal welfare, opening hours for shops and licensed premises, the fire service and some issues related to broadcasting.

There are offices in London, north-west England and Scotland, computer centres at Hendon and Bootle, and the Immigration and Nationality Department, which has headquarters in Croydon.

The Prison Service, which employs almost 39,000 staff, has been expanding, and this trend is likely to continue, although some privatisation may be involved. Its headquarters is expected to relocate to Derby.

Inland Revenue

Inland Revenue administers and collects direct taxes (mainly income, corporation, capital gains, and inheritance tax), and advises Treasury ministers on policy issues, such as their effect on social and industrial policy, and what happens when taxes are changed. It also values land and property for, e.g. taxation purposes. There are specialist departments dealing with, e.g. Foreign Dividends and Superannuation.

Inland Revenue has a very large staff – 59,000 in 1995 (a drop of 7,000 since 1991). Further cutbacks seem likely. Most staff work in one of the 600-plus offices, which can be quite large, spread throughout towns up and down the country. Main centres are London, Worthing, Nottingham and Edinburgh.

Management is once again strongly stressed in the work of the department – looking after the organisation and staffing of all the offices. Computers are increasingly a major part of the operation, and there is a massive centralised system. The local tax offices take in income tax returns, work out what is owed by individuals or companies, and ensure that the tax is paid on time. Staff are known as revenue assistants, revenue officers and revenue executives. These broadly equate to the Administrative Assistant (AA), Administrative Officer (AO) and Executive Officer (EO) grades common to most other government departments. There are also tax inspectors, who investigate the taxes of self-employed individuals and companies and deal with any complex problems which may arise, e.g. international taxation.

The Department's Valuation Office is an Executive Agency which provides advice on valuation policy. It is also responsible for valuing property for tax purposes and (in England and Wales) for local rating purposes.

See also WORKING IN THE CIVIL SERVICE: ADMINISTRATION *below*.

The Lord Chancellor's Department

The Lord Chancellor's primary task is to ensure the efficient administration of justice in England and Wales. The Lord Chancellor appoints, or recommends for appointment, judges, judicial officers, magistrates and Queen's Counsel. Other responsibilities include Legal Aid, the Law Commission, reform of the civil law, the development of the legal profession and legal services. The Lord Chancellor's Department is the sponsoring department for the following Executive Agencies.

The Court Service is responsible for the administration of approximately 400 Crown and County Courts.

The Land Registry records ownership of land, houses and other property. Some staff examine and record documents of title (with a plan of the property), others prepare and keep maps and plans up to date. The work ranges from straightforward copying to preparing complicated plans at various scales. The work is largely computerised. The Registry had in 1995 some 8,500 staff.

The Public Record Office cares for documents created by law courts and departments of state since the Norman Conquest, including the Domesday Book. Records to be kept are regularly transferred from departments, and Public Record Office staff help select and preserve the records and make them available to the public. The Public Record Office had in 1995 a staff of just under 450. It is based in a modern complex at Kew.

The Public Trust Office acts as executor for wills, administrator of estates, or as a trustee. The Public Trustee can manage funds of pension schemes, friendly societies, disaster appeals and individuals' funds.

As well as legal staff, the Lord Chancellor's Department recruits graduates from all disciplines to Executive Officer and Administration Trainee posts, although an intake is not guaranteed every year.

See also Lawyers *under* WORKING FOR THE CIVIL SERVICE: SPECIALIST AND OTHER GRADES *below*; *and* THE LEGAL SYSTEM.

Department of National Heritage

This is a new department (formed April 1992). It is responsible for the arts, museums and galleries, libraries, the national heritage (e.g. the historic environment, listing of buildings), film, sport, tourism, broadcasting, the press and the National Lottery.

The department employs over 1,000 staff, mainly in London. A high proportion of their work is of a policy nature.

Two Executive Agencies – the Historic Royal Palaces Agency and the Royal Parks Agency – fall within the remit of the National Heritage Department. Its role also includes sponsorship of non-departmental government bodies such as the British Film Institute.

The Department for National Savings

The Department for National Savings administers a wide variety of savings securities, to all age and income groups.

It makes extensive use of computers, and so employs systems analysts, programmers, etc., as well as a large administrative staff dealing with finance, advertising, planning and policy, relations with the Post Office and banks, etc. Total staff was in 1995 about 5,400. The administration offices are based in Blackpool, Glasgow and Durham, with a headquarters office in London.

The Northern Ireland Office

The Northern Ireland Office was set up in 1973 to oversee the running of the province and has a staff of around 200, based in London and Belfast. Some of the Whitehall staff are home civil servants, others are on secondment from Belfast. The office covers security and international relations, constitutional and political matters, and human rights. There is close liaison with Northern Ireland departments and other government departments, such as the Foreign and Commonwealth Office and the MOD (*see above*).

The Office of Population Censuses and Surveys/Office for National Statistics

The Office of Population Censuses and Surveys administers centrally the law on civil marriages and the registration of births, marriages and deaths, keeps central records, and controls the network of local registrars and superintendent registrars. The central office provides copies of certificates, and an advisory service on the law on registration, marriage, legitimacy and adoption; it also prepares statistics of population, migration, fertility, births, marriages, deaths and diseases, and carries out regular population censuses every 10 years. The Department's social survey division does survey research for other departments on social and economic problems. The data which is collected is used to make and monitor policies, on e.g. health and medical care, education, etc., in line with demographic trends. It employs interviewers throughout the country to assist with social surveys and, at census times, over 100,000 temporary enumerators

In 1995 it had about 1,700 staff (a decrease of over 400 since 1991). Although it has headquarters in London, and another department in Southport, the main office, with its computers, is in Hampshire.

The Office of Population Censuses and Surveys (OPCS) merged on 1 April 1996 with the Central Statistical Office to form the Office for National Statistics.

See also ARCHIVE WORK *in* HISTORICAL AND RELATED WORK.

The Scottish Office

The Scottish Office is the largest of the offices covering the non-English countries of the UK. Its size reflects the different legal, education, demographic and employment situations in Scotland. It consists of five departments: Agriculture, Environment and Fisheries; Development; Education and Industry; Home; and Health. These work in close cooperation with other UK government departments, the EU, Scottish local authorities and other organisations. The headquarters of the Scottish Office are in Edinburgh, but its civil servants work from around 100 locations throughout Scotland. A small number are based at the Scottish Office's liaison office in Whitehall.

There are nine Executive Agencies in Scotland. Six – Historic Scotland, Scottish Fisheries Protection Agency, Scottish Agricultural Science Agency, Scottish Prison Service, Scottish Office Pensions Agency and Student Awards Scotland – are agencies of the Scottish Office. A further three – Registers of Scotland, Scottish Record Office and Scottish Courts Service – are separate departments.

Staff numbers (1995) for the Scottish Office were around 5,500 with a further 5,600 employed by Executive Agencies.

The Department of Social Security (DSS)

The DSS is one of the largest and most diverse of all government departments. It plays a vital role in shaping society, with policies and operations affecting everyone in Britain. The DSS is responsible for the administration of welfare benefits, collection of contributions and implementing government policy. It employs almost 90,000 staff nationwide.

The Department comprises a central headquarters and (1995) six agencies which are responsible for its executive operations.

Headquarters staff deal with a wide range of functions which include the development and review of policy matters, planning and finance, personnel, administration and operational management. Most headquarters staff are based in London, but there are also opportunities in other areas.

The *Benefits Agency* is the largest government Executive Agency and is responsible for the administration of more than 20 social security benefits through a network of district offices and directorates in Newcastle upon Tyne and Fylde. Since 1992 its headquarters has been located at Quarry House, Leeds.

The *Contributions Agency* administers the National Insurance Scheme through a combination of field and central operations.

The *Child Support Agency* administers arrangements for child maintenance though a combination of assessment centres and field offices.

The *Resettlement Agency* operates resettlement units (hostels) which provide temporary board and lodging to single homeless people without a settled way of life. The agency also works with local authorities and voluntary organisations to plan and make grants for alternative hostel facilities. The agency will cease to exist in 1996 and its residual funding responsibilities will return to the main body of the DSS.

The *War Pensions Agency* administers the payment of war pensions and provides welfare services and support to war disablement pensioners, war widows, their dependants and carers.

The *Information Technology Services Agency* provides information technology and telecommunications services to the DSS, its agencies and other customers in government.

The Department of Trade and Industry (DTI)

The DTI is a major government department, responsible for creating the framework and conditions in which UK business can compete successfully at home and abroad.

After the 1992 General Election it took over the responsibilities of the former Department of Energy. Other reorganisations have brought parts of the Cabinet Office and the former Employment Department to the DTI.

Most areas of British business are affected in some way by the work of the Department, in spheres as varied as business expansion, overseas trade, science and technology, consumer protection, regional policy/industrial assistance and industrial and commercial legislation.

On trade, it looks after international policy, including UK interests in the EU and other international organisations, and works for trade liberalisation worldwide. It highlights UK exports and gives practical help, information and advice to exporters. There is some scope for DTI staff to travel abroad, mainly for short periods, and for secondment to European organisations.

The Department deals with government general industrial policy, identifying the needs of industry and commerce, promoting competitiveness and fostering the creation of small and medium-sized businesses. The Department also promotes the development of UK energy resources and ensures that the nation's energy needs are met cost-effectively.

It regulates business to ensure a level playing field for companies and to protect the consumer. It deals with measures on science and technology, research and development, standards and designs, and support for innovation, promoting information technology.

The Department has research laboratories which include the maintenance of the National Measurement system. They also undertake important innovation programmes and work on environmental issues, the analysis of foods, drugs and agricultural materials, etc. These laboratories are all Executive Agencies and the DTI's other agencies include the Insolvency Service, the Patent Office and the Radio Communications Agency.

The Department staff was in 1995 down to about 10,250 (a drop of over 1,000 since 1991). About 60% of staff are located in central London, others throughout the country, with a particular concentration in South Wales, including the Companies' Registration Office in Cardiff.

The Department of Transport (DoT)

The Department of Transport has responsibilities in the areas of shipping, aviation, railways and road transport. The policy core of the Department is based at the headquarters in central London and assists Ministers in the formulation of policy on all aspects of domestic transport, as well as negotiating on Britain's behalf with other nations and within the European Union on international aspects of transport regulation. Headquarters staff also liaise with local authorities about developments in, and the funding of, local transport.

The rest of the Department's staff work for DoT Executive Agencies, putting policy into practice: building trunk roads; supervising vehicle certification, inspection, and licensing; licensing drivers and operators; and monitoring marine safety (including running the Coastguard). Nine regional offices cover local transport matters, and the Traffic Director for London is responsible for traffic-planning for the capital.

See also TRANSPORT.

HM Treasury

The Treasury is one of the smaller government departments, with a staff of about 1,100, but it has a wide range of responsibilities covering all other government departments and institutions.

It helps ministers to formulate and implement economic policy and control public expenditure (including that of local authorities). It also deals with international finance, including trade and foreign aid, and represents UK interests in the EU. Taxes and revenues from the Inland Revenue and Customs and Excise come within its remit, as do procurement policy, competitive tendering and purchasing.

The Treasury Solicitor's Department provides legal advice, litigation and conveyancing services for many government departments. The domestic economy section oversees monetary and fiscal policy, including taxation, banking and other financial institutions, and government lending. The preparation of computer-based economic models and economic forecasts is undertaken by the Chief Economic Adviser's office. Other responsibilities include non-tax aspects of charities, privatisation and share ownership, value for money in public services, export credit and public-sector pay.

The Welsh Office

The Welsh Office looks after many aspects of Welsh life, including agriculture and fisheries, financial help for industry, tourism, roads and transport, housing, education, language and culture, local government, water and sewerage, environmental protection, sport, land use, conservation, new towns, ancient monuments, the careers service, urban programmes and redevelopment programmes, health and personal services, and financial aspects of all these including the council tax. It oversees economic affairs and regional planning too. Based in Cardiff, it had in 1995 a staff of some 2,200, about the same as in 1991.

Civil Service structure: general

Since 1 April 1996 all departments and agencies take responsibility for the grading structure and pay of their staff (with the exception of staff in the new Senior Civil Service, formerly at grades 1–5). With the delegation of pay and grading to departments and agencies, the old Civil Service grade structure will probably become less important. However, grades still generally conform to the following format:

- Top Management: Grade 1 – Permanent Secretary, Grade 1A – Second Permanent Secretary, Grade 2 – Deputy Secretary, Grade 3 – Under Secretary. The Executive Agencies are headed at a level appropriate to their size and responsibility.
- Senior Management: Grade 4 – senior professional civil servants, Grade 5 – Assistant Secretary, Grade 6 – Senior Principal, Grade 7 – Principal
- Fast Stream: Higher Executive Officer Development, Administration Trainee. Fast Stream entry is for selected graduates or those civil servants with two years' service chosen for the scheme.
- Middle Management: Senior Executive Officer, Higher Executive Officer.
- Junior Management: Executive Officer.
- Support Staff: Administrative Officer, Administrative Assistant.

There are also openings for secretaries and other kinds of support staff – including catering personnel, messengers, reprographics and security staff.

The majority of recruitment is now carried out by individual departments and agencies, and for most posts, applicants should contact departments and agencies direct. *See* Recruitment *under* BACKGROUND *above*.

Graduates

The Civil Service is among the largest recruiters of graduates in the country. The majority enter the Civil Service through departmental and agency recruitment schemes. They may enter specialist grades – e.g. for lawyers or engineers – or join at the same levels as non-graduates. Small numbers are recruited through the fast stream.

Fast-stream recruitment is specifically aimed at graduates with exceptional ability and the potential to progress quickly. The fast stream covers a number of different career areas, and includes an option for those wishing to follow a career in one of the European Union Institutions. There are specific fast-stream schemes for administration, the Diplomatic Service, scientists, engineers, Inland Revenue, statisticians, economists and management trainees at Government Communications Headquarters (GCHQ).

The main entry requirement is a good honours degree (in practice, usually an upper second or first) in any subject. A relevant discipline is required for science, engineering, economist and statistician schemes. (For details of the economist and statistician schemes, initial enquiries should be sent to the Government Economic Service or Government Statistical Service – not Recruitment and Assessment Services.)

Non-graduates

Entry to departmental and agency recruitment schemes is open to candidates with GCSEs, A-levels, HNDs, HNCs or equivalent including GNVQ/GSVQs. For some posts, formal qualifications may not be required – skills gained through work experience may be equally valuable.

Qualifications and Training

The Civil Service has a long track record of training for all its staff, from high-flying graduate administrative trainees and diplomats through to school-leavers, frequently with the opportunity to gain formal qualifications, relevant to the job, e.g. accountancy, personnel or legal work. Young people under 18 may be given day release for further study and adults may be given assistance with, e.g., evening classes, open-learning, etc. New graduates are given the practical experience and training they require to gain membership of professional bodies, and some departments are developing their own management training schemes.

Some departments, most notably the Ministry of Defence, offer sponsorships to degree level, mainly sandwich courses, usually in science and engineering; and technician-level training is given, again mainly by the Ministry of Defence, but also by other departments requiring specialist technical and scientific staff, e.g. GCHQ. Trainee librarians are also offered placements in a range of departments. A booklet about sponsorships and another about sandwich course placements across a wide range of departments and specialisms is available from the Graduate and Schools Liaison Branch of the Cabinet Office.

Working in the Civil Service: administration

Civil Service careers still divide fairly easily into administrative and specialist.

By definition, a very large proportion of civil servants are administrators, working on policy, and planning, managing, and implementing policy. The administration group consisted of about 185,000 people in 1995 (down from 220,000 in 1991).

Their functions range from coordinating government machinery and managing departments at higher levels, to clerical duties in the departments in the lower grades.

Most administrative staff are recruited at the following four grades:

Administrative Assistants

Administrative Assistants are the 'junior clerks' of the Civil Service, doing work similar to their counterparts in any other organisation: dealing with incoming mail, keeping records, doing simple figure work (perhaps using a calculator), some straightforward letter-writing, and dealing with telephone calls, other enquiries from the public and so on. It is all fairly routine. They numbered in 1995 around 23,000, compared with nearly 51,000 in 1991 working in departments and agencies throughout the Civil Service and in all parts of the country. Promotion is to administrative officer.

Administrative Officer

Administrative Officers are generally more closely involved in the function of the particular department, although most posts still involve routine deskwork. They work alongside administrative assistants, but usually have more responsibility. They handle incoming correspondence, write or draft letters, give the public advice, information and help across counters (e.g. in benefit offices), check accounts and keep statistics and other records.

They numbered in 1995 almost 81,000 (a small drop since 1991) working across the country, in most departments and agencies. Most gain promotion to executive officer.

Recruitment and entry

Recruitment is on a local basis. GCSE/SCE grades or equivalent may be required for entry to administrative assistant or administrative officer posts. Alternatively, it may be possible to take a written test, or show evidence of skills gained through previous work experience. Administrative assistants may be promoted to administrative officer on merit or by examination.

See also ADMINISTRATION, BUSINESS MANAGEMENT AND OFFICE WORK.

Executive Officers

Executive Officers are the Civil Service equivalent of junior managers. They may organise and supervise the day-to-day work of a branch or section made up of a number of administrative officers and assistants within a department. They may be an assistant to a senior civil servant, arranging meetings, collecting and collating information, and generally getting the spadework done on any policy development. They may go out on the Department's work to factories, offices, or into people's homes, dealing with casework. They may deal with day-to-day administration such as finance, office records, communication systems, or personnel. They may be trained to do specialised work, e.g. in accountancy, or computing.

Examples of executive officers' work are: giving advice in a JobCentre; computer programming for the Ministry of Defence, in a branch looking after the personal records of Army officers; examining in the Department of Trade's insolvency branch; personnel work and general administration in a county court; being a VAT field officer visiting firms (from small shopkeepers to large companies) to check their accounts.

Executive officers number, as of 1995, over 48,000, a decrease of about 4,000 since 1991, working in all departments across the country. All executive officers are given training for their jobs – for some it may be for work which is only done in the Civil Service (e.g. taxation work), but for others it may be in a skill useful elsewhere, e.g. computer programming. All executive officers should become at least higher executive officers; many will become senior executive officers, and may go higher.

Recruitment and entry

Direct entry to the executive officer grade is usually with at least five GCSE (A–C) passes or equivalent including two at A-level or equivalent. Some departments which recruit at this level may require specific academic qualifications. For main-stream entry to the Diplomatic Service, for example (similar to Executive Officer grade), the emphasis is on previous work experience.

Traditionally the entry point for sixth-form school-leavers, graduate entry to the grade has increased steadily.

Promotion to executive officer is fairly common for administrative officers, and a high proportion of executive posts are, in fact, filled from amongst them.

Administration Trainees/Higher Executive Officers (Development)

Administration Trainees and Higher Executive Officers (Development) – shortened to AT/HEODs – about 100 of whom are recruited annually to the fast stream, i.e. accelerated promotion group, work only in the major departments, and are groomed and trained specifically for higher management/policy-making posts – developing an expertise in getting to the root of complex problems quickly and devising solutions. Entry is highly competitive – in 1994/95 over 7,000 applicants competed for some 115 vacancies. The pre-entry test eliminates 85–90% of all those who apply.

They work on one or more of: research and analysis of policy options; consultation and negotiation with other organisations; development and management of major projects; delivery of services within limited resources; supporting Ministers in their accountability to Parliament; and management of departments. Formal training, including courses at the Civil Service College, is provided.

Most AT/HEODs are based initially in London, although there are opportunities to work in some other locations such as the Scottish Office in Edinburgh, the Welsh Office in Cardiff and the Department of Social Security in Leeds. Even those whose early postings are in London should expect to spend part of their careers in other places.

AT/HEODs can expect promotion within 3–5 years of joining the Civil Service (earlier promotion is possible for exceptionally able and experienced candidates). The first substantial promotion is to grade 7, where responsibilities might include, for example, managing executive operations or working on legislation and other parliamentary business in support of Ministers.

Recruitment and entry

Direct entry to the AT/HEOD scheme requires a first or second class honours degree: most candidates have at least an upper second, and the criteria for selection are very high – vacancies are left unfilled rather than lowering standards.

Final year undergraduates account for around one-third of applicants. There is no upper age limit for the Home Civil Service Fast Stream, but most successful candidates have graduated within the previous 10 years.

The qualities sought are 'a high level of intellectual ability, the capacity to work effectively with others and the determination to get results'. Applicants do not need a detailed knowledge of the workings of government, but they are expected to show an intelligent interest in current issues and how they affect the choices to be made in government.

In 1994/95 successful candidates had studied a range of arts, sciences and social science subjects and had attended 32 different universities.

Working in the Civil Service: specialist and other grades

The Civil Service employs a great many other people in specialist roles. Some groups are employed in many departments and so come into general categories. Some are employed only on work within a single department. In alphabetical order, the Civil Service has work for:

Accountants

The Government Accountancy Service (GAS) employed around 1,000 qualified accountants and 600 trainees in 1995. They work in over 40 departments and their agencies.

Mounting pressure for efficient management of public resources over the past 15 years has led to greater stress within the Civil Service on financial accountability and operational efficiency, thus emphasising the role of professional accountants.

The work of government accountants is described under ACCOUNTANCY in FINANCIAL CAREERS.

Training for professional accountancy qualifications (mainly the Chartered Institute of Management Accountants, but also other professional accountancy bodies) is provided.

Recruitment and entry

Executive Officer: entrants must have at least five GCSE (A–C) passes or equivalent including two at A-level or equivalent. Maths and English are required at GCSE level. Graduates are also accepted. Those who enter at this grade serve a probationary period of at least one year before being considered for professional accountancy training.

Administration Trainee/Higher Executive Officer (Development): entrants need at least a second class honours degree or equivalent, or a postgraduate degree of equivalent value. The degree should be in a relevant subject; alternatively, candidates must demonstrate evidence of numeracy.

Actuaries

Actuaries work on, for instance, projections and analyses needed to guide policy on state benefits and pensions. In the Civil Service they work mainly in the Government Actuary's Department, which provides a consultancy service to other government departments and to outside organisations. Candidates for trainee actuarial posts should have a second class honours degree and if this is not in a mathematical subject, should possess Maths at A-level.

See also ACTUARIAL *under* FINANCIAL CAREERS.

Communications

The Government Communications Headquarters (GCHQ) employs a range of specialist staff including:

Mathematicians, who work on the analysis of complex signals, techniques for code-breaking and code construction. They need a strong grounding in pure mathematics, plus some knowledge of probability theory and statistics. An aptitude for computer programming is also required, because many of GCHQ's mathematicians are concerned with the development and support of highly efficient algorithms on supercomputers. Most mathematicians are expected to have the potential to take on management responsibility, although there are a few posts for those who wish to become technical experts. Mathematicians are expected to become involved in practical assignments as soon as they join GCHQ. During the first two years they usually take refresher courses in relevant areas of mathematics.

Computer scientists and *electronic engineers*, who work on the research and development of communications systems – from signal processing to satellite systems, supercomputers and high-speed networks. In electronic and communications engineering, typical tasks include: writing a technical study paper on a satellite system; designing a modification to an advanced signal demodulator; or helping with the systems engineering for the installation of a new supercomputer. In computing, projects may include, for example: undertaking a feasibility study for a new electronic messaging system; customising an off-the-shelf package; or linking a communications network to a local area network. Staff also provide customer support across the whole area of IT, communications and electronic engineering. A continuing personal development programme is provided for staff working in technology; it involves assigning each individual to a mentor who assists with long-term career development.

Linguists, who translate, transcribe and analyse information both for GCHQ departments and outside organisations. As well as translating, they need to be able to judge the value of the information translated, so a good understanding of relevant world affairs is important. Linguists may be asked to learn new languages.

Management trainees: GCHQ runs a small graduate management training scheme (four to six trainees are recruited each year). As future senior managers, trainees follow a fast-track training programme providing experience across a wide range of core work carried out at GCHQ, spending periods of several months in different departments. The emphasis is on high intellectual ability, team-work, effective communications skills and an appreciation of a fast-changing technological environment.

Intelligence analysts and *administrators*. Analysts are directly concerned with intelligence work. Work may be of a long-term nature: taking a subject, analysing different sources of information, looking for patterns and building up a picture that will be useful to others; or it could be more short-term: evaluating traffic that has been intercepted to see if it contains intelligence and producing a report if it does. A number of analysts may move into administration for a few years in order to broaden their experience, obtaining professional qualifications as required. Posts are in areas such as purchasing, contracts, personnel, security and general service. Some choose to specialise in these areas, whilst others return to operational work.

Recruitment and entry

The main requirement is for graduates in mathematics, IT, electronic engineering and languages. Graduates in any discipline may apply for the graduate management trainee scheme, but there is intense competition for the handful of vacancies available each year.

Although many people enter GCHQ straight from higher education, applications are welcomed from older applicants with relevant degrees and appropriate experience in other organisations.

Non-graduates are recruited from time to time to fill a variety of posts from clerical support officer/assistant to security officer. A good standard of education is needed, plus work experience in some cases.

The specialist and secret nature of GCHQ's work means that successful applicants must adhere to strict nationality rules and undergo a vetting procedure (which can take some time) before being formally appointed.

Computing staff

Computing staff of all kinds are employed extensively throughout the Civil Service. The Civil Service is the largest user of computers in the UK, and future plans include the provision that most staff will work from their own individual terminals. Both Inland Revenue and the DSS have introduced massive nationwide systems. Work ranges from systems analysis and programming to operating machines, and data preparation. Programming, etc. is done mainly by people recruited as executive officers (who can return to or go into administrative work if they wish) and assistant scientific officers. Administrative officers handle input and output, but one special group, data processors, operate computers. No official figures for Civil Service computing staff exist, but it is an expanding field for staff at all levels.

Recruitment and entry

Data processors do not need any particular qualifications. Other people recruited for computing work need the same qualifications as other executive or assistant scientific officers. An aptitude test is normally set, but it is possible to join without any background in computing and be trained and promoted to a fairly high level.

See also INFORMATION TECHNOLOGY AND COMPUTER WORK.

Customs and Excise Officers

See under GOVERNMENT DEPARTMENTS *above*.

The Diplomatic Service

The Diplomatic Service has its own grade structure.

Diplomats' work ranges from high-level negotiations on high-level affairs (including defence, energy, science policy) down to the everyday practicalities of looking after UK citizens abroad and promoting British exports. (*See also* Foreign and Commonwealth Office *under* GOVERNMENT DEPARTMENTS *above*.)

About 70% of the 2,000-odd members of the Diplomatic Service are 'generalists', so-called career diplomatic staff, ranging from clerical people to ambassadors and permanent under-secretaries. The other 30% are 'specialists' – legal advisers, research officers, etc. Just over half, mostly 'generalists', are based overseas at any one time. Another 4,000-plus people are members of the 'home' civil service who work for the Foreign and Commonwealth Office, and very few work abroad. Other staff are people engaged and employed locally overseas.

Diplomatic staff, says the Foreign and Commonwealth Office, have to produce high-quality work in conditions that may be unpleasant or even dangerous. Responsibility for financial and personnel management, at home and overseas, is now assumed relatively early. 'Career' diplomatic staff of all grades spend about half to two-thirds of their working lives overseas, in 'tours' of two to four years, interspersed with periods in London. Staff do not, normally, stay with one country or even one region, and may move each time to a quite different continent. Part of their time in London, then, may have to be spent learning a language. The career structure more or less matches that of administration.

Fast Stream graduates, of whom 21 were taken on in 1995, start at grade 8 or even grade 7, working from the start on policy, including subjects such as financial relations or defence, as well as looking after political relations with individual countries. They go overseas after about 18 months in London. Promotion is accelerated in the early years. Most will reach grade 4 – Counsellor – and some the Senior grade.

Main-Stream officers start at grade 9. They do a range of work, including consular, accounts and administration as well as some 'political', but it can be routine. They usually spend three years in London. Most are capable – age permitting – of reaching grade 5; a few may progress further.

Executive Assistant Branch (EAB): an amalgamation of the former grade 10 and the secretarial grade. EAB officers provide essential support within the FCO in London and diplomatic missions abroad. They are involved with many aspects of Diplomatic Service business, from running communications to managing overseas embassy accounts and filing official papers. Their main areas of work are: Registry – filing and retrieving paperwork; communications – using electronic equipment to maintain links between London and FCO posts overseas; clerical and secretarial; management – e.g. of accommodation and transport; accounts; immigration. Applicants for EAB posts need a good mix of abilities, including IT and keyboard skills. They can expect to change jobs regularly. Although EAB officers are full members of the Diplomatic Service, they are not eligible for promotion within the service into the Main Stream. Entry to the Main Stream is via the open competition only.

Everyone has to accept a very peripatetic life, with regular changes of country and job. However, career planning is expertly done (personnel is managed by diplomatic staff themselves, on London posting). Everyone is taught languages as and when needed and also gets training in, e.g., economics, marketing and information work. Overseas benefits include free accommodation and education allowances for officers' children.

Recruitment and entry

Diplomatic staff need to be physically and mentally tough and highly adaptable, as well as intelligent and quick witted. Literacy, ability to communicate, numeracy and ability to master complex economic and technical issues are all wanted. Candidates are tested for aptitude to learn languages, but pre-entry language qualifications are not insisted on. Those who do best in the aptitude tests, though, are most likely to be sent to countries whose language is difficult to learn, e.g. Japan, China or Russia.

Fast Stream (grades 8/7D) candidates must have at least a second class honours degree. Competition is tough.

Main Stream entry: there are no minimum educational requirements. Instead, there is emphasis on previous work experience.

Executive Assistant branch: no minimum educational requirements, but a minimum typing speed of 30 wpm, at least two years' office experience and prior knowledge of IT are required.

The preferred age range for all office recruitment is 21–55.

Economists

The Government Economic Service (GES) is the largest employer of economists in the UK, with staff in all major government departments. The majority of the 500 government economists work in London, but there are also opportunities in Sheffield, Birmingham, Edinburgh, Glasgow and Leeds.

Applicants for Assistant Economist posts should have a first or second class honours degree in economics or an economics-related subject, or a postgraduate degree in economics. It is also possible for economists to join the European Fast Stream, in order to prepare for entry to European Union institutions.

See also under ECONOMICS *in* MATHEMATICS, STATISTICS AND ECONOMICS.

Engineers

The largest employer of engineers is the Defence Engineering and Science Group (DESG), with about 16,500 engineers, technologists and scientists. Engineers in the DESG work in all areas of the mainstream Ministry of Defence and in its agency, DERA (Defence Evaluation and Research Agency). DERA, which deals with advanced defence research and technological development, has four divisions:

- Defence Test and Evaluation Organisation – chiefly concerned with conducting weapons and equipment trials.
- Defence Research Agency – provides science and technology expertise to support the MOD, and is concerned with transfer of technology to business and industry.
- Chemical and Biological Defence Establishment – primarily responsible for ensuring that UK armed forces are protected against nuclear, chemical or biological attack.
- Centre for Defence Analysis – carries out studies into areas such as military capabilities, resource allocation, procurement of equipment and tactics.

DERA's main sites are at Portsmouth, Farnborough, Malvern, Dorchester, Sevenoaks, Chertsey, Boscombe Down and Porton Down. There are smaller sites elsewhere.

In the mainstream MOD, engineers mainly provide technical expertise at the post-research and evaluation stages of the MOD equipment programme. They are involved in areas such as procurement, maintenance and modernisation, technical and operational support. They work at sites in North Bristol, London and a number of other establishments around the country.

The other main departments and agencies employing engineers are GCHQ, the Department of Transport and the DTI. There may also be some openings with other departments, including the Ministry of Agriculture, Fisheries and Food; the Foreign and Commonwealth Office; the Department of Health; the Patent Office; the Home Office; and the Scottish Office. For further information, contact individual departments directly.

Recruitment and entry

A small number of engineers (with at least a 2:1) are recruited via the Science and Engineering Fast Stream. In 1995/96, there were ten Fast-Stream vacancies in the MOD and four in the DTI. Details from Recruitment and Assessment Services.

There are, however, many more vacancies in individual departments; for example, in 1995/96 DESG was looking to recruit 100 graduates in electrical/electronics, software or communications engineering (with at least a 2:2) for its Graduate Engineer Training Scheme; and DERA had approximately 300 vacancies for graduates in scientific, engineering and numerate disciplines. (Details from DESG and DERA Recruitment Offices, which can also supply information on sandwich course placements, sponsorship and vacation work.) Details of engineering sandwich course placements in other departments are available from the Graduate and Schools Liaison Branch at the Cabinet Office.

Health and Safety Inspectors

Health and Safety Inspectors are employed mainly by the Factory Inspectorate of the Health and Safety Executive, of which it is the largest single division. Agricultural inspectors are also employed to cover issues relating to farming, horticulture and forestry. Inspectors visit workplaces – ranging from hospitals and research labs to factories, building sites and fairgrounds – to identify health and safety problems. They give advice, and where necessary issue enforcement notices for breaches of the law on health and safety, and often have to prosecute.

For particular problems inspectors may call on the advice of the Health and Safety Executive's medical and technical specialists, who provide sophisticated research, investigation and analysis. For example, after the fire at King's Cross Station, a specialist forensic laboratory produced a scale model of the escalator to show how the fire had spread.

Training consists of a two-year programme leading to a health and safety postgraduate qualification from Aston University. The programme covers legal, managerial and technical skills and consists of formal courses (some of them residential), distance-learning and on-the-job training.

Recruitment and entry

To apply for a position as HM Inspector of Health and Safety, candidates should have a degree with honours, HND or equivalent combined with experience at management level and a full driving licence. They must also have GCSE maths (A–C) or equivalent.

Immigration Service

See Home Office *under* GOVERNMENT DEPARTMENTS *above*.

Information Officers

Information Officers are members of the Government Information Service (GIS). They are the equivalent of press and public relations officers elsewhere, promoting government policy, keeping the press and public informed on all aspects of government activity, and advising ministers and senior civil servants on public relations. Almost all departments, agencies and government bodies have information officers.

Information officers numbered 830 in 1995, a slight drop since 1991.

Recruitment and entry

For entry as an Assistant Information Officer, candidates usually have a degree or relevant qualification and a clearly identifiable leaning towards information work. The same requirements apply to Information Officer posts, but in addition candidates should have at least two years' experience of media work. Most entrants are at Information Officer grade.

Recruitment is only through advertisements in the media pages of *The Guardian* and advertisements in the trade press.

Inland Revenue

Inland Revenue is a career on its own within the Civil Service, since specialist training is needed, but the jobs and the career structures are designed to run in parallel with administrative careers. The work involves assessing what is owed in taxation, and collecting. Assessing is rather more technically demanding.

Tax inspectors make tax assessments for businesses of all kinds, from the high-street shop to the multinational chemical company. To become a tax inspector takes three years' training (in book-keeping, accountancy, law and the expertise needed to check the credibility of taxpayers' accounts) combined with practical experience on the job. Trainees start on case work very early, are expected to make their own decisions, and take responsibility for them. After exams have been passed, a year is spent in junior management, a year on more complex casework, with promotion to higher grade and responsibility for a tax district in six years.

There is also valuation work in the Valuation Office Agency.

See under GOVERNMENT DEPARTMENTS *above*.

Recruitment and entry

Direct entry to inspection needs a first or second class honours degree although it is also possible to come up from higher tax officer.

Lawyers

Lawyers are employed throughout the Civil Service in some numbers. In 1995 1,100 worked for the Government Legal Service (GLS) in 24 government departments and other public bodies, over 2,000 were employed by the Crown Prosecution Service, and there are also opportunities for lawyers in other government departments and public bodies.

The Government Legal Service offers solicitors and barristers an alternative to private practice, in which the prime motivation is the ideal of public service, rather than the need to make a profit. Working in the public interest, GLS lawyers make an important contribution to the safety and quality of life of large numbers of people.

GLS lawyers carry out every type of legal work found in private practice, as well as other tasks which are unique to government, such as parliamentary work. This involves preparing instructions from which Bills are drafted by Parliamentary Counsel, advising ministers and policy advisers during the progress of a Bill, and drafting subordinate legislation.

In many government departments GLS lawyers have an important advisory role, and they are also concerned with a wide range of civil and criminal litigation. Additionally, they are closely concerned with developments in European law, which impinges on almost every aspect of GLS work.

The main departments employing GLS lawyers are:

The *Treasury Solicitor's Department.* The Department works for the Treasury and provides legal services to other government departments. As such, it is one of the largest legal organisations in the United Kingdom. Its legal advisory work ranges across areas such as education, defence, employment, transport, government administration and European law. Its litigation department offers the whole range of work found in private legal practice – from personal injury to commercial disputes – as well as work unique to the public sector, such as acting for the government before the European Court of Human Rights. The Department's Executive Agency, Government Property Lawyers, is the principal legal office for central government land transactions.

Land Registry. Lawyers work on a variety of problems arising from dealings with registered land. Most of the 130-odd lawyers employed in the Land Registry are located in 19 district land registries throughout the country.

Lord Chancellor's Department offers a variety of legal work. At headquarters, some staff have close contacts with the Lord Chancellor, and may advise on policy, legislative matters and judicial appointments. They also deal with parliamentary questions and draft speeches.

The Crown Prosecution Service, headed by the Director of Public Prosecutions. Each of the 13 areas is headed by a chief crown prosecutor, and each area has a number of branch and sub-branch offices. Head office, and all the other offices, employ teams of lawyers, with the emphasis on delegating as far as possible, although headquarters lawyers deal with some specialised types of casework. All cases are reviewed by crown prosecutors first to decide whether or not to take them to court. If the case proceeds, the crown prosecutor will normally conduct the prosecution case in the magistrate's court. If it is committed to a higher court, the crown prosecutor instructs counsel, and monitors progress.

Crown Office and *Procurator Fiscal Service:* in Scotland, the crown has always been responsible for all criminal prosecutions. Each of the 49 sheriff court districts has a procurator fiscal (plus legal staff), not only responsible for prosecutions but also able to direct police investigations.

Legal staff are also employed in the criminal appeal office (dealing directly with cases for the court), the Official Solicitor's department (effectively acting as solicitors or barristers for the people the Official Solicitor represents), the Law Commission (working on schemes for reforming the law, including academic-style research, examining policy and formulating proposals), and in the Public Trust Office (dealing with the management of assets and estates).

Recruitment and entry

CPS: The CPS recruits both trainee and qualified lawyers. Trainee solicitors and pupil barristers are normally recruited two years in advance of commencing their training contract or pupillage.

Government Legal Service: most staff join after qualifying, and all posts are open to both solicitors and barristers. Additionally, a small number of trainees are taken on each year for training contracts or pupillage. As with the CPS, they are recruited two years in advance.

See also THE LEGAL PROFESSION *in* THE LEGAL SYSTEM.

Librarians

Librarians work in most departments and agencies, providing a library and information service which enables staff to research work-related issues, and sometimes for the public too. For example, the DTI has library facilities which can be used by business people, students, etc. Librarians may become involved in a variety of work, including assisting ministers or working in very specialist environments, e.g. the DTI, or the Solicitor's Department. Most library services are now heavily computerised. Librarians numbered just over 400 in 1995, a similar figure to 1991. Candidates for these posts need professional library qualifications and some relevant experience.

See also LIBRARY AND INFORMATION WORK.

Linguists, Translators and Interpreters

Linguists, Translators and Interpreters work in a number of departments, mainly in the (small) Joint Technical Language Service at GCHQ (Cheltenham) and GCHQ itself, the Ministry of Defence, the Home Office, the Immigration Service and, increasingly, those departments involved in work with the EU. A few departments also employ translators, mainly of material from European languages into English. They may also do research work on foreign publications.

Recruitment and entry

A degree, or equivalent qualification, in at least one modern foreign language is usually needed. Most posts would expect people to have more than one Western European language, and there is greatest demand for people with Slavonic or oriental languages.

See also TRANSLATING *in* LANGUAGES.

Medical Officers

Medical Officers are employed in such areas as the prison medical service, the Department of Health and the Medical Research Council.

See also THE MEDICAL AND DENTAL PROFESSIONS.

Museum staff

See in HISTORICAL AND RELATED WORK.

Patent examiners

See in THE LEGAL SYSTEM.

Photographers

The Civil Service employs just over 200 photographers. The main employers are the Ministry of Defence and the Department of the Environment. However, opportunities are very limited. Increasingly, photographic work is contracted out to the private sector.

See also PHOTOGRAPHY *in* ART, CRAFT AND DESIGN.

Prison staff

Prison staff are technically Home Office employees. *See* THE PRISON SERVICE *in* SECURITY AND PROTECTIVE SERVICES.

Psychologists

There are openings for psychologists in the Department for Education and Employment, the Prison Service, the Home Office, the Ministry of Defence and the Defence Evaluation and Research Agency. Their main activities are casework and research. Numbers have been increasing – to 300 in 1995 (compared with 200 in 1991).

Applicants must have a first or second class honours degree that is acceptable for registration with the British Psychological Society. A postgraduate qualification is desirable, and relevant experience useful.

Research Officers

Research Officers in the Civil Service are not normally scientists. They gather, analyse and evaluate information, much of it economic, geographic or sociological, studying the impact of government policies and providing the information on which to base future policy. They have to explain their findings to non-professionals.

In some cases research officers carry out work in-house; in others, they manage research contracts, where the research is carried out by external organisations.

The work varies considerably in different departments. In the DSS, for instance, it includes studying the operation of the benefits system and assessing the effectiveness of service delivery, whereas in the MOD research is concerned with defence issues.

The other major departments employing research officers are the Department of the Environment, the Foreign and Commonwealth Office, the Home Office and the Welsh Office.

Recruitment and entry

A first or second class honours, or postgraduate, degree in an appropriate subject is needed.

Scientists

Scientists are employed in quite large numbers (about 9,000 in 1995, a drop of 5,000 since 1990) in a wide variety of both civil and defence work. Government scientists do and/or supervise fundamental and applied research, are involved in design and development (of, e.g., navigational aids and weapons systems), work in advisory and inspection services, in working out how to measure things even more accurately and in setting standards of all kinds. They may be problem-solving in the building or agricultural fields, for example.

Much of the work may be very similar to work they might have done in university or industry and they cooperate closely with these bodies and with the armed services. A substantial proportion are managers or administrators – directing research, or overseeing contracts placed outside the Civil Service. This move towards scientists acquiring and using managerial skills is being accentuated as departments move towards agency status. This should help career scientists compete for the most senior managerial posts in the Civil Service.

The Service employs not only professional scientists. As elsewhere, lab technicians are employed in practical and supporting roles; for example, in applying established scientific principles or supervising more routine scientific work.

Examples of scientific work include:

- looking for evidence in the Forensic Science Laboratories;
- measuring and analysing stresses in road bridges;
- ensuring that chemicals and equipment produced by industry to clean up oil spills actually work;
- investigating the use of meteor scatter as a medium for air-to-ground radio communication, and ironing out problems;
- automating the analysis of the nutritional properties of different foods.

The largest groups of scientists work in the following:

The *Ministry of Defence* (MOD) employs scientists in the Defence Engineering and Science Group (DESG), which includes the Defence Evaluation and Research Agency (DERA), responsible for much of the MOD's research and development. (For information on DERA, *see under* Engineers *above*.) Another MOD Executive Agency is the Meteorological Office, which provides meteorological services to central and local government, aviation, industry, the media and the general public, as well as undertaking research in meteorology and geophysics. *See also* METEOROLOGY *in* EARTH AND SPACE SCIENCE.

The *Department of Trade and Industry* employs scientists in managerial posts and research scientists in the Laboratory of the Government Chemist, the Patent Office (investigating scientific innovations), the National Physical Laboratory (which works mainly on accurate measurement) (privatised 1996), the Radiocommunications Agency, and the National Engineering Lab (which employs multidisciplinary teams in mechanical engineering R&D, feasibility and design studies, testing, calibration, etc.) (privatised 1996).

The *Department of the Environment* employs scientists in the Building Research Establishment (with work on, e.g. geotechnics, energy conservation, fire prevention and detection, timber, soil testing), and in HM Inspectorate of Pollution.

GCHQ (*see* Communications *above*), the *Natural Resources Institute* (which investigates the development of renewable natural resources in the tropics on behalf of the Foreign and Commonwealth Office), and the *Medicines Control Agency* (Department of Health) are other examples of government departments which employ scientists.

Scientists also work for the *Home Office*, the *Health and Safety Executive*, the *Scottish Office* and for *MAFF*. MAFF's Executive Agencies include the Agricultural Development and Advisory Service, which gives technical advice, scientific services and undertakes research and development into farming and rural issues. Examples of this are pest control and plant health. MAFFs other agencies are the Pesticides Safety Directorate, the Veterinary Laboratories Agency, the Central Science Laboratory, the Veterinary Medicines Directorate and the Meat Hygiene Service. Horticulture Research International, a non-departmental public body sponsored by MAFF, employs graduates in biological sciences and other scientific disciplines such as veterinary and food science.

The majority of science posts are now in the physical and mathematical sciences, and 'new technology' disciplines. There are growing opportunities to move into administration and management, into areas such as project and contract management, and into policy advisory work.

There are opportunities for both permanent and fixed term appointments.

Recruitment and entry

Fast-stream scientists and engineers: the scheme is intended for candidates who wish to make use of their scientific/technical knowledge and receive in-depth management training. Recruitment is very limited – in 1995/96 only two departments, the MOD (with up to ten vacancies) and the DTI (up to four vacancies) participated. Candidates should have, or expect to gain, at least an upper second class honours degree in a relevant discipline. Details from Recruitment and Assessment Services.

Other recruitment is organised on a departmental basis. The greatest number of vacancies is likely to be with the Ministry of Defence (including DERA, the Defence Evaluation and Research Agency). DERA had around 300 vacancies for graduates in scientific, engineering and numerate disciplines in 1995/96. The mainstream MOD's Defence Engineering and Science Group runs a Graduate Science Training Scheme, likely to have about 20 vacancies in 1995/96. Applicants for the latter should have a 2:1 (exceptionally, a 2:2 may be accepted) in a relevant discipline. There are also some vacancies at Higher Scientific Officer and Senior Scientific Officer grades for those with relevant postgraduate experience.

The MOD provides opportunities for scientists to take postgraduate degrees and to join relevant professional organisations. There is also the possibility of secondment to industry or other government organisations.

Contact individual departments and agencies for details of other scientific vacancies. The Cabinet Office Graduate and Schools Liaison Branch produces a series of factsheets listing government departments and agencies which recruit graduates in specific degree disciplines (e.g. biology, physical sciences, metallurgy and materials technology).

Secretaries and typists

The number of secretaries and typists in the Civil Service has been falling, because more and more staff are able to use their own computers for typing. The secretarial group consisted of 13,500 staff in 1995 – down from 19,400 in 1991. Contact individual departments and agencies for details of vacancies.

See also SECRETARIAL, OFFICE AND CLERICAL WORK *in* ADMINISTRATION, BUSINESS MANAGEMENT AND OFFICE WORK.

Statisticians

Statisticians, working in the Government Statistical Service, which serves over 20 departments and agencies, numbered about 600 in 1995. They collect, analyse and interpret data on behalf of most government departments, usually specialising in economic or social statistics. There is an increasing need for statisticians to have good computing skills. Assistant statisticians must hold first or second class honours degrees which involve a minimum of 25% formal training in statistics.

See also MATHEMATICS AND STATISTICS *in* MATHEMATICS, STATISTICS AND ECONOMICS.

Surveyors and architects

The Valuation Office (an Executive Agency of the Inland Revenue) employs general practice, building, quantity and mineral surveyors. The Ministry of Defence employs general and rural practice surveyors. ADAS (an Executive Agency of the Ministry of Agriculture, Fisheries and Food) employs rural practice surveyors.

There are very limited opportunities for architects – contact the Ministry of Agriculture, Fisheries and Food or the Scottish Office for further information.

Recruitment and entry

Surveyors must have passed or gained exemption from the written examinations leading to qualifications with the Royal Institution of Chartered Surveyors or the Society of Valuers and Auctioneers.

Architects must hold a recognised diploma in architecture.

See also SURVEYING *in* LAND USE PROFESSIONS.

The Civil Service and Europe

Some government departments have more contact with their counterparts in the EU than others – e.g. MAFF and the DTI – but there are also opportunities to work directly for the EU institutions themselves, notably the European Commission, at its bases in Brussels and Luxembourg. The Commission is not the only EU institution – there are others such as the Court of Justice, but it is the largest, employing 15,000 officials, including 3,600 in administrative policy grades, drawn from all the EU member states.

The Commission advises on legislation and policy, e.g. the abolition of customs controls, action on acid rain, EU aid to the third world.

Staff are divided into 4 grades:

grade A are policy-makers and administrators;
grade B are executive staff who would normally hold 2 A-levels or equivalent;
grade C comprises secretarial and administrative officer staff at roughly 5 GCSE (A–C) or equivalent level;
grade D is made up of other support staff such as reprographics technicians or catering personnel.

All vacancies are advertised throughout the EU, which means that British applicants will be in competition with candidates from, e.g. Portugal and Greece. Apart from recent graduates, all staff should have at least two years' work experience. To encourage British applicants, a scheme called the *European Fast Stream* recruits up to 30 British graduates each year into the UK Civil Service, where they are given special training to prepare for recruitment to one of the EU institutions. The scheme is open to potential administrators (who may be graduates in any subject), lawyers, legal trainees or economists. It is also possible for external candidates to apply directly to EU institutions.

The application process is fairly lengthy, consisting of a written exam, which varies according to the level of work, but typically consists of multichoice papers, followed by an interview in Brussels for successful candidates. It is at this stage that a candidate's language skills are tested. All applicants must have a working knowledge of at least one EU language other than their mother tongue. Obviously, the level of skill will vary according to the job – a messenger would need less linguistic ability than an administrator.

If a suitable job is not immediately available, successful candidates are placed on a reserve list until one arises, and the majority of applicants obtain work in this way. Temporary staff are also engaged on annual contracts and are eligible to apply for permanent posts.

See WORKING FOR THE EUROPEAN COMMUNITY *in* WORKING OVERSEAS.

More British staff are needed within the Commission, and further information is available from the European Staffing Unit within the Cabinet Office or from branches of the European Commission in London and the other UK capitals.

Further information on the Civil Service

For information on fast-stream recruitment of generalists, scientists and engineers, economists, statisticians and lawyers contact the Recruitment and Assessment Services.

Factsheets and brochures on other opportunities in the Civil Service are available from the Graduate and Schools Liaison Branch of the Cabinet Office.

Additional information is available directly from Government Departments and Agencies – see addresses in *Appendix 1*.

Contents

Local Government

(CLCI: CAG, COP)

Background

Local authorities provide services for their communities. Traditionally, this means the most practical and essential, like collecting rubbish, cleaning streets and looking after sewers. Over the years, though, they have taken on many other, and wide-ranging, roles and responsibilities. The full list of these 'functions' covers (as of spring 1996): architecture, building and design; economic development; education – from schools at all levels to further education colleges and adult education institutes; planning, traditionally called town and country planning, which involves everything from making plans for the area, and controlling development, to checking regulations; social services; health education; housing; transport – from planning to managing services (buses, tubes, even airports) although many services are now operated by private companies, looking after highways and lighting; police and fire services; libraries, museums and the arts, which can include theatres, art galleries, and orchestras; recreational facilities – like swimming pools and sports centres, parks and open spaces and tourism; environmental health – including collecting and getting rid of refuse, street-cleaning, food hygiene and controlling diseases, clean-air regulations; consumer protection; markets, smallholdings and allotments; cemeteries and crematoria; licensing and registration – births, deaths, marriages, licensing hours.

The pattern of local government was radically simplified into a two-tier structure of county and district, and the number of authorities cut by about a third, in 1974. A further change was made in 1986 when the six metropolitan counties created in 1974 were abolished. This means that in England and Wales there are now some 447 authorities: 47 counties which are further divided into 331 districts; 68 authorities which are not divided into districts; 36 metropolitan districts and 32 London boroughs, both known as unitary authorities because they provide their communities with all services; plus the City of London Corporation. Scotland's nine regions are divided into 53 districts, with both regional and district councils. Orkney, Shetland and the Western Isles have their own, almost all-purpose, authorities.

In England, there are two kinds of local authority. First, the metropolitan authorities, which look after the special needs of these heavily populated and urbanised areas. They range in terms of population from 155,300 to 477,000 people. Second, the counties, which have populations ranging from 124,800 to 1.59 million (excluding the very smallest, the Scilly Isles with a total population of 2,100) and districts/cities (between 24,300 and 397,600 people each). In Wales, counties range in size from 119,900 to 544,300. In Scotland, authorities range in size from a region with a population of 2.5 million down to a district with a rural population of under 10,000.

The London boroughs have populations ranging from 145,500 to 323,200. The City of London has only 3,900 residents, but copes with a daytime population of over 400,000.

This present pattern in England and Wales is currently undergoing a new restructuring which is being completed in stages, the last of which is due to be completed by April 1997. More unitary authorities will be created and some counties will disappear. By December 1995 the Local Government Commission had recommended that in England there should be 34 counties divided into 248 districts plus the 36 metropolitan authorities and present London boroughs. In Wales recommendations were made not by a Commission but by the Secretary of State, who recommended that Wales was simply to have 22 unitary authorities. At the time of writing, legal challenges by one English county council mean that the final outcome could be slightly different.

Just as there are enormous variations in population between authorities, so of course their areas vary: from several hundred square miles, to the City of London's one. They vary in character, from those which are completely rural, to others with both dense inner-city centres as well as industrial estates, and residential suburbs, while others are entirely urban. It follows that every authority has a different mix of problems to manage and solve: cliff-falls or inner-city decay, potential flooding or collapsing sewers, poor housing to replace or massive unemployment to solve.

Counties and districts divide services between them. In general, larger counties tend to run services which benefit from economies of scale, such as education, social services, transport, structure planning, police and fire services. Districts run the more everyday services: street cleaning, housing, local planning, building regulations, cemeteries and crematoria, and allotments. Museums, libraries, and recreational facilities, amongst other services, may be run by counties or districts. The London boroughs and district councils have taken over the responsibilities of the GLC and the metropolitan counties, although some services are run jointly. Uniquely, the Metropolitan Police are the responsibility not of any London council, but of the Home Office. The division of responsibilities is not permanently fixed, and can and does change.

Local authorities can decide, within certain legal limits, on their own organisational and managerial structures, and many seized the chance to change their managerial structures following the reorganisation in 1974.

Traditionally, the full, elected council delegates day-to-day policy-making for individual services to special committees – for education, housing, social services, and so on. Each committee has its own department of paid staff answerable to them, and not to any higher level of management within the council's staff. This means that the committee of elected members inevitably has a major influence on what happens within a service, and therefore on the daily lives of the paid staff who work within it. Individual services – housing, education, etc. – can be run in watertight compartments without much reference to what is going on in what may be a related service, and individual departments may have a high degree of autonomy. There may also be lack of cohesion and unity in running the authority.

Since 1974, however, most authorities have been looking for ways to improve their management methods, and in particular to introduce corporate management, in other words to create structures which allow councillors and senior, or chief, officers to watch over what is happening in the authority as a whole, across all the individual services. Typically, authorities have, for instance, added policy and resource committees to the functional ones. The very autonomous departmental structures have been replaced in many authorities by a series of directorates which coordinate the work of groups of related departments. This creates another management 'tier' – for example, libraries, museums, sports centres, entertainment, swimming pools and squash courts may now be the responsibility of a director for leisure and recreation. These directors form a top managerial team of officials led by a chief executive. As part of this modernisation, old titles like 'town clerk' have been dropped in favour of terms used in other organisations. The organisation of local authorities is now much more concerned with the management of resources, and in order to achieve this, some have introduced the best management practices, comparable with those in commercial organisations.

Working in local authorities

Most local authorities are large organisations. However, tight financial control and some contracting of services to commercial firms have steadily reduced the numbers employed. As of January 1996, local authorities (in England, Wales and Scotland) employed 2.38 million people (full- and part-time), against 2.46 million in 1990 and 2.71 million in 1986. The reduction in numbers can be in part accounted for by the removal of some functions from local authority control. For example, all the polytechnics formerly run by local authorities have become universities; 97,000 further education lecturers are now employed directly by their colleges which left local authority control in 1994; and some airports are no longer local-authority-owned. Another reason for the reduction is the introduction of compulsory competitive tendering (*see below*).

Even with the abolition of the huge metropolitan counties, many local authorities are very large. One major county has an annual budget of some £800 million and over 50,000 full- and part-time employees. Even rural district councils with relatively small populations (but often spreading over a sizeable area) could have budgets of around £1 million.

Traditionally, local government was a lifelong career. Its unique conditions led to professions or branches of professions set up especially for local government service – for example municipal engineering and accountancy – always with the accent on 'professionalism'. It has always been professionals who have filled the top posts. This exclusiveness is being steadily diluted, with increasing cross-fertilisation, mainly stemming from local government's need to bring in more and more professionals from outside the service, for example architects, and people with qualifications in the whole range of management services, such as organisation and methods, operational research, computer programming and systems analysis. It is now far more common than previously for staff to move between local government and the private sector during their careers.

The work and career structures of local authority staff are changing in many ways. Having larger and fewer authorities has obviously changed life in local government. These are a public-sector equivalent of very large businesses, spending a great deal of money; costs have risen very sharply, and greater expertise and efficiency are needed to control expenditure. Local authorities are now obliged by law to apply competitive tendering to certain services. Contracts may be awarded either to private sector companies or to a department or section of the authority itself. Staff have to submit bids in the same way as external contractors, and contracts are given to the bidder offering the best value for money.

While the number of posts at the top of the local-government tree is comparatively small, the number of posts with intermediate responsibility has probably increased, and the kind of responsibility they carry is considerable. These increased responsibilities require people of higher calibre at both top and intermediate level, particularly for general management – with commensurate salaries. A favourite example quoted in the press in the late 1980s was that the chief executive of one county council in the South-East earned more than the prime minister.

This suggests a new kind of career structure within local government, and increasing recruitment of, for example, graduates directly to careers in administration and management. While it is probable that more managerial posts will go to specially recruited graduate administrators, it is still more usual to go up through the ranks of one of the departments as a professional. Here, promotion begins with administering one service, may go on to managing several, and for a very few, will lead to a chief officer or executive's job. Some professional careers in local government are more closely related to running the authority as an organisation, and not with just one of its services. It is still more usual for the chief executive and immediate deputy staff to come from these departments (often legal or accountancy) – it is still virtually unknown for a chief librarian or education officer to reach the top administrative post.

Local authorities employ people in a great many different jobs, and at most levels. They are major employers of many professional staff, such as accountants, architects, computer/management services experts, engineers, lawyers, librarians, personnel managers, surveyors, some (relatively few) scientists, and (effectively) teachers. They are almost the only employers of, e.g., consumer protection officers, environmental health officers, social workers and town planners. Most employees work in a specialist area of local government (*as below*).

Technicians are employed mainly in engineering and construction, for planners and architects, etc., with a comparatively small number of (scientific) lab technicians. Office technician-level work includes accounting.

Local authorities obviously employ, in all departments, secretarial and clerical staff, computer operators and data preparation staff, receptionists, telephonists, etc.

Craft and manual workers are employed in the building trades, gardening and groundsmanship, catering, in the maintenance of vehicles and other equipment, in road works, refuse collecting, as traffic wardens, drivers, recreation and (swimming) baths attendants, caretakers and cleaners, etc.

Administration, legal and finance

These are at the heart of local government, backed up by, for example, management services. Although local authorities may appear to be huge bureaucracies, in fact relatively few of their very large staffs are actually just administrators or managers.

The central administration

This has general oversight of the authority's work and improving its organisation, but is also responsible for advice on policy formation, management services, committee and secretarial work for Council committees (such as making up agendas, taking minutes, drafting reports and so on), preparing and keeping up to date electoral rolls and arranging council elections, public relations and information services. Many local authorities also have centralised purchasing and supplies; some also purchase cooperatively. Staff administration (including training) is still the responsibility of central administration. Many councils have training departments – also personnel, although there is a move in some to reduce the numbers of staff in central personnel departments and move them to individual departments (e.g. social services, education).

Legal departments

Legal departments are important in all local authorities. All authorities have legal functions and responsibilities. They must be able to interpret government legislation (of which there has been a considerable amount in recent years) where it affects them. Legal departments look after the authority's transactions involving land and property, advise both elected members and professional officers on the interpretation and implementation of legislation such as the Children's Acts or laws concerning mental health, debt recovery, consumer protection, etc. and handle employment matters affecting the council's own staff. Their solicitors also represent the authority in court, for example in conducting prosecutions on behalf of trading standards, environmental health officers, planners, etc. The size of a legal department depends on the size and type of the local authority and also on the amount of work that the authority contracts out with consequent requirement for legal advice.

Authorities' legal staff qualify via the usual routes (*see* THE LEGAL SYSTEM).

Financial management

Financial management was traditionally done by what used to be called the treasurer's department, more often now 'finance'. Whatever the title, finance officers are responsible, under the finance committee, for controlling income (from government grants, from the community charge, business rates, rents, interest, various entry fees and so on) and expenditure, and for raising loans, advising the Council on the financial implications of policy decisions, preparing budgets and financial forecasts, collecting rates/community charge, carrying out accounting procedures and generally ensuring that the authority gets value for money. Authorities normally have audit sections, responsible for ensuring that individual departments are spending carefully what is after all public money (even so, councils' accounts are also subject to external audit).

Most finance officers are or become qualified accountants. Although most gain the qualifications designed especially for accountants working for public bodies, others may hold management, certified or chartered accountancy qualifications. Ratings officers are also normally specially trained.

See also ACCOUNTANCY AND FINANCIAL MANAGEMENT *in* FINANCIAL CAREERS.

The service departments

Each of these looks after a particular 'function', service, or responsibility of the authority. Depending on the function, each department employs a range of professionally qualified staff, sometimes technicians, some supporting administrative, clerical staff, and sometimes manual staff too. Land, buildings, and the related support services are a major concern of many local authorities.

Planning departments

Planning departments carry out the local authority's legal responsibilities, and also prepare detailed schemes. Most professional planners work for local authorities, with the support of technical staff. Planning departments employed about 17,750 staff in 1996. *See also* LAND USE PROFESSIONS.

Transport departments

Transport departments manage road systems, and design and build roads. Some authorities also operate transport systems, but these are generally separately managed, and can now be operated by commercial companies. *See* THE TRANSPORT INDUSTRY.

Engineers' department

Engineers' departments provide drainage systems, sewers, sewage treatment and disposal, land drainage and flood prevention, refuse collection or disposal, and street-cleaning services. Some also supervise authority construction sites, using direct labour.

Engineers' departments employ qualified engineers (mostly civil and some mechanical, most of whom become qualified municipal engineers whatever their original specialisation), surveyors, building inspectors and building control officers. *See also* THE CONSTRUCTION INDUSTRY; *and* SURVEYING *in* LAND USE PROFESSIONS.

Architects' department

Architects' departments in local councils design and oversee the building of public buildings such as colleges, schools, community centres, libraries, and youth and leisure centres.

Local-authority architects qualify in the usual way – *see* ARCHITECTURE *in* LAND USE PROFESSIONS.

Surveyors and valuers are also employed in all aspects of work concerned with the authority's land and building interests, including valuation, maintenance and management, although housing management itself is usually a separate department and a separate career. *See* HOUSING MANAGEMENT *in* LAND USE PROFESSIONS.

Any major local authority projects involve all these departments, and the various professionals and experts work as members of a team or act as consultants, depending on the project, particularly on large-scale developments. Even building a sports centre involves cooperation between planners, valuers, architects, structural and municipal engineers, mechanical and electrical engineers, technicians, draughtsmen, landscape architects and heating and ventilating engineers, many of whom will be local government employees, some from the private sector.

Environmental health departments

Environmental health departments administer legislation and other government regulations designed to maintain and improve standards of health and hygiene.

Mostly this involves inspecting food shops, restaurants, slaughterhouses and warehouses to see that food is being stored and handled properly and cleanly, that it is bacteria-free, and that staff, their clothing and equipment are frequently and properly cleaned. Department staff have to check, for instance, for any kind of vermin. They also trace the source of any outbreak of food-poisoning. They look into unhygienic housing conditions and approve schemes for improving them. They are responsible for disease-control at ports and airports, and administer all anti-pollution legislation (including noise as well as smoke, chemicals, etc.). They see that working conditions in shops and offices are reasonable: sanitation, ventilation, lighting, hours of work for young people, opening and closing times, and so on.

More time is spent out of the office than in, although obviously there is plenty of report writing, etc.

Departments employ mainly environmental health officers – for whom there are some 6,000 posts (which are not always filled) – but also some other experts, such as chemists and public analysts, as well as support staff. In all, some 24,100 (1996) work in environmental health, down from 30,000 in 1992.

Environmental health qualifications and training

Environmental health officers are graduates. They may qualify either by taking an approved first-degree course in environmental health/science or by taking a two-year postgraduate MSc course following a first degree in science. Approved first degrees, a list of which may be obtained from the professional bodies, are offered by twelve universities and colleges. A stipulated amount of practical training must also be completed. Most students do this as part of a four-year sandwich degree course, but it is possible to complete it by gaining two years' work experience with a local authority after graduating from a three-year (approved) course. Usual entry requirements to degree courses are A-levels/Highers/GNVQ or GSVQ advanced awards in science subjects. The professional bodies are the Chartered Institution of Environmental Health Officers and the Royal Environmental Health Institute of Scotland.

Consumer protection departments

Consumer protection departments developed from weights and measures, and still take care of all kinds of trading standards. They make sure, for example, that cash registers of all kinds, petrol pumps and pub measures are all working accurately. They now also implement consumer protection legislation, investigating all kinds of complaints from customers, about substandard goods or services. Some authorities also run consumer advice centres. It is a job which involves spending a lot of time out of the office, and often means trying to persuade traders to cooperate. Local authorities employ about 2,300 trading standards officers.

Trading standards qualifications and training

This is only via a diploma in trading standards, administered by the Local Government Management Board. Trainees, employed by local authorities, must complete a three-year course combining release for study with practical training. Study is done on a block-release basis as only three colleges run the course. An alternative method of qualifying is to take a degree course in Consumer Protection followed by a period of practical training in a trading standards department. Trainees must have at least five GCSEs at A C or S grades at 1–3 including two at A-level or three H grades (subjects must include English, maths, and physics), but most authorities now also recruit graduates – and the exams do need academic ability. The professional body is the Institute of Trading Standards Administration (ITSA).

The ITSA's Diploma in Consumer Affairs is for other staff employed in consumer protection departments. Evening and day-release courses are available in certain parts of the country. It is also possible to study for the diploma through distance-learning.

Social service departments

Social service departments, which have some statutory duties – for children and under the Mental Health Acts – are largely staffed by qualified social workers, as described *in* SOCIAL AND RELATED SERVICES.

Social services employed, in all, over 420,000 people in 1996, up from 339,000 in 1990.

Educational services

Educational services are still a major responsibility of larger local authorities, primarily counties, which *must* provide full-scale education for children from the age of five through to 18-plus (and *may* do so from age three or four), and further/higher education thereafter. However, many education departments' responsibilities have decreased since schools assumed responsibility for their own management and financial affairs under the Local Management of Schools system (LMS), or chose to opt out of local authority control altogether and receive funding direct from central government. To date 1100 schools have done so and a further 25 have been approved to do so. The number of posts for administrators in central departments is bound to decrease with time.

Duties still include planning the services, possibly designing and building new schools and providing support services such as educational psychology and careers advice (although other organisations may now tender to run careers services, and many have been successful) and school meals – which may be contracted out.

People directly employed by the local authority are educational administrators, some advisers/inspectors – not the ones who conduct official inspections on behalf of the Department for Education and Employment (many of whom will have had teaching experience first) – some welfare and careers officers, school librarians, etc. Teachers come under a separate structure but are still counted amongst local authority employees.

In all, local authorities employed over 557,600 teachers and lecturers as of early 1996 (down from some 616,000 in 1990, but many who had previously been employed by local authorities are still in employment, now working as direct employees of schools and colleges). Education also employs a large number of support staff (in the school meals service, as caretakers, cleaners, etc.) as well as administrators and specialists (*as above*). A total of 605,800 non-teaching staff were employed by local authorities in 1996.

See also SOCIAL AND RELATED SERVICES *and* EDUCATION AND TEACHING.

Library, museum and arts services

There are around 3,000 museums in the UK, most of which are managed by local authorities. They may be administered as part of educational services, but some authorities group them with cultural or even recreational activities.

At present, all county authorities are required to maintain free library systems, and the qualified librarians who run them generally specialise in *public* library work, although their qualifications are largely the same as those of other librarians. *See* LIBRARY AND INFORMATION WORK.

About 28,000 people were working in libraries in 1996, of whom just over 7,000 were professionally qualified librarians.

Some authorities also have their own museum and art galleries. *See* MUSEUM WORK *in* HISTORICAL AND RELATED WORK.

Larger, urban authorities also run concert halls and some have theatres. *See* ARTS ADMINISTRATION *in* THE PERFORMING ARTS.

Recreational and leisure facilities

Managing recreational and leisure facilities, ranging from games and sports facilities, swimming pools, country parks and adventure playgrounds through to arts festivals, is a major area of activity for most local authorities. They employ and subcontract to a range of specialist staff in designing, building, managing and maintaining open spaces and centres, and also in organising leisure activities, as e.g. recreation managers or sports officers. (This is an area where the introduction of compulsory competitive tendering has had a major impact. Many leisure centres are run by private companies on behalf of local authorities.)

Over 152,600 staff worked in recreation, parks and baths in 1996, some directly employed by local authorities, others by private companies.

See PROFESSIONAL SPORT AND THE RECREATION AND LEISURE INDUSTRIES.

Police and Fire Services

These are fully described *in* SECURITY AND PROTECTIVE SERVICES.

Recruitment and entry

There are different methods of training for careers in local government, depending on the career area chosen. Specialist professional staff, e.g. architects, engineers, planners or lawyers, must gain the qualifications awarded by their own professional bodies (sometimes as employees of local authorities through sponsorship or sandwich courses).

See the appropriate chapters for details of training in those professions not covered earlier in this chapter.

Technician-level staff are also expected to gain qualifications from the appropriate body, but in their case this is nearly always done while employed in local government, the majority being recruited at the age of 16 or 18 and given day-release to local colleges, e.g. planning, architectural, laboratory or engineering technicians, and legal executives.

At craft level, some 16–17-year-olds may be recruited for training in, e.g., gardening and other craft-level work in parks, playing fields, etc., and in building trades. GCSE/SCE S grade passes are an advantage, but not essential.

Clerical and administrative staff may enter at any of the following levels.

16-plus entry

Councils recruit some school-leavers at 16-plus, normally with four or five GCSE/SCE S grade passes at A–C/1–3 or equivalent qualifications, for clerical posts and as computer/machine operators, or data preparation staff.

YT

Local authorities run schemes, and may require 16–17-year-olds to start in the above via YT. (YT is the umbrella term, but youth training schemes are marketed under different brand names by different TECs.)

18-plus entry

With at least two A-levels or a GNVQ/GSVQ advanced level award in business studies or public administration.

Graduate entry

Some, mainly the larger authorities, run formal graduate entry schemes to train graduates in general management. (The term 'administration' is going out of favour in some authorities, with the equating of councils with commercial companies.) The Local Government Student Sponsorship scheme, designed to attract high calibre undergraduates, sponsors a small number of students through the final year of a degree or diploma course after satisfactory completion of a period of vacation work experience. Not all authorities take part in this. Information may be obtained from the LGMB or METRA (*see* FURTHER INFORMATION *below*).

Qualifications and training

Local government has long emphasised qualifications, for all grades of staff. Authorities make fairly extensive provision for entrants to be trained by a variety of methods: in-service training leading to NVQs, and/or paid leave of absence to attend full-time, sandwich, or day-release courses, in professions employed by the authority.

Where necessary, i.e. if a suitable 'outside' qualification did not exist, the authorities have developed their own, via the Local Government Management Board, but few are now offered except in one or two specialist areas.

The Management Board has a wide-ranging role. Much of its work is geared to developing in-service training within authorities, which is closely linked to its advisory work. The Board is also responsible for identifying jobs and their training needs, making training recommendations, and helping to arrange courses.

BTEC now sets the main qualifications in public administration, which are closely linked with business studies schemes. This allows local-government employees in clerical and administrative work to study alongside people working in commerce, or training for administrative/clerical work in other organisations, and so gain broadly based business qualifications which make it easier for them to change employers. (Other relevant schemes include those in caring, leisure studies, and engineering and other construction skills.)

BTEC Intermediate GNVQ awards in business/finance, etc., while not specifically designed for local-authority employees, do cover the skills, etc. needed, since many are common to both public and private sectors. Entry is as for all BTEC Intermediate awards.

BTEC GNVQ Advanced awards in public administration are largely common with business and finance, and distribution. The required core includes units in public administration, taken with finance, people in organisations, and the organisation in its environment. Option units include housing studies, practical administration, library and information work, social services and the developing social structure of modern Britain, although local government employees can also take options in, e.g., secretarial and keyboarding skills, tourism, etc. Entry is as for all BTEC advanced awards.

BTEC Higher awards in public administration include some core studies in common with business, etc. These are work organisations, the external environment, and operational techniques and procedures. The rest of the core studies cover public sector organisations, structures and processes, and resource management in the public sector.

Option units which are locally designed cover a wide range. Entry is as for all BTEC Higher awards.

Degree courses

A number of universities offer degree courses in public (and/or social) administration, which are policy-oriented.

Professional qualifications

The main professional body is The Institute of Chartered Company Secretaries and Administrators (ICSA). About 25% of ICSA members work in local government. ICSA's examinations have a special stream in local government administration. Entrants with A-levels or GNVQ Advanced awards take both parts; candidates with relevant degrees or HND can gain subject-for-subject exemptions.

The Institutes of Administrative Management, and of Management Services, provide useful alternatives.

Further information

The Local Government Management Board (LGMB), the relevant professional bodies, individual local authorities, and METRA, the Metropolitan Authorities Recruitment Agency, which provides a careers advisory and information service on behalf of a consortium of local authorities.

Managing the Health Service

Contents

(CLCI: CAL)

Background

Managing an organisation as large and complex as the Health Service is a difficult and highly skilled business and so far it has proved hard just to get the organisational structure right. There are special problems in providing healthcare to everyone in the country, in inner cities as well as remote rural areas, to the very ill and those with minor ailments, for people who are sick for a short period and for those with long-term problems, for the very young and the very old.

Management of the NHS has, until quite recently, been handled rather differently than in most other organisations. The uppermost tier of management is (still) outside the NHS altogether – in the hands of health ministers and the Department of Health. Political factors also have to be taken into account. Inside the NHS, management was a collective responsibility, shared mostly between the professional medical staff – mainly doctors, but also nurses and other groups – and professional administrators, with other groups, such as representatives of local communities and health-service unions, also involved. The problems are further complicated by the numbers of so many different professional groups, with varying degrees of autonomy, each with long-established and complex lines of responsibility, both within their own professional groups and to others as, for instance, the ward sister is responsible to each consultant for the day-to-day care of the consultant's patients, but to the nursing officers for the administration of the ward.

In 1984, the decision was made to 'strengthen', and introduce 'more dynamic' management into the health authorities. Since then management structures as used in other organisations have been replacing the distinctive NHS collective style. The main career effect has been the appointment of 'general managers' who carry greater personal responsibility and are accountable for seeing that decisions are made, actions taken, to make the organisation more efficient and effective with the available resources.

General management and administration

General managers – finance – personnel management – purchasing and supply – medical records – secretarial staff

Hospitals were traditionally 'managed' by medical staff – 'superintendents'. They then employed administrative staff simply as assistants, but the job expanded and developed as they took over functions from the medical staff. However, they did not gain the kind of responsibility that managers in other organisations have. The growth of the service meant the administrative problems grew also, but given the background, and on the evidence of continuing major difficulties, the authority and skills of the managers and administrators did not develop as fast as perhaps were needed. Although hospital administrators have been developing their skills ever since the Health Service was formed, the difficulties of running an integrated, regionalised organisation without full responsibility were very different and came at a time when costs were rising sharply as resources became harder to find.

Up to the early 1980s, the problems were dealt with by increasing the numbers employed, nearly fivefold between 1949 and 1977, and by 54% between 1971 and 1981; by 1993 over 20,000 general and senior managers were working in England alone. Some of the increase was attributed to the 1974 re-organisation which, it is generally agreed, created too many layers of administration. However, as the 1979 Royal Commission pointed out, more administrative staff were needed, because doctors and other professionals had to be relieved of clerical and secretarial paperwork, because communications needed improving, and because the Health Service must have people with modern managerial expertise, in e.g. management services, and personnel (including industrial relations).

Health Service administration has constantly to take account of the fact that any decision, large or small, may affect patients' health. Health service planning, within tightening government-set budgetary limits, and given the costs involved (of labour, and of scientific and technological equipment particularly) always presents considerable problems. Public demand for better healthcare is growing faster than the available resources.

Despite the special factors, Health Service management and administration has always had a great deal in common with the management of other large-scale commercial, industrial, and state organisations, and the latest developments (*see below*) are a deliberate attempt to bring in the most up-to-date 'commercial'-style managerial methods.

Following reforms initiated in 1991, the District Health Authorities and Family Health Service Authorities are expected to merge in 1996, when Regional Health Authorities will become Regional offices of the NHS Executive.

General managers

They take charge of operations in each of the regions, districts, hospitals and other units. At regional and district level, hospital general managers are planners, coordinators, setting objectives, working to achieve set targets within agreed budgets; and the top managers are now on 'rolling' three-year contracts and their pay is performance-related.

District general managers are responsible for planning, implementing and controlling the full range of healthcare services across the area.

Within the district, most 'unit' general managers are responsible for several hospitals, although a few large hospitals have their own managers. Some manage a particular service or group of services, including community care for, e.g., people with mental handicaps.

The work is extremely diverse, ranging through planning major changes (e.g. turning surgical wards into long-stay accommodation for old people); seeing through practical changes to improve services/budgeting (e.g. going over to cook-chill methods so meals can be prepared ahead more cheaply); negotiating (sorting out problems between theatre staff and porters or trying to improve the admissions system); troubleshooting (industrial relations, dissatisfied patients, dealing with the consequences of breakdowns); interviewing new staff; discussing budgets and preparing financial reports; etc.

Some administrators specialise, in a 'function', but with promotion routes through each function to more general management.

Finance

These posts range from, for instance, salaries and wages officer for a single hospital; through management accounting in a district (which may involve developing and operating a 'functional' budgeting system, estimating annual allocations, monitoring expenditure against budget, and analysing in detail any variance with monthly and yearly statements); and district finance officer, or regional management accountant, who provides and assesses costing data across the region as just one part of the exercise of allocating resources; to regional treasurer.

Most professional finance staff are, or become, qualified public-sector accountants (*see in* FINANCIAL CAREERS).

Personnel management

The NHS is putting greater stress on professional personnel management, especially in recruitment and training for management.

Purchasing and supply

The NHS buys in great quantities. It buys high-cost capital equipment like high-technology kidney dialysis machines, whole-body scanners and radiotherapy cyclotron units, as well as the never-ending daily supplies of bedpans and surgical dressings, face masks and surgical gloves, syringes and thermometers, sheets and pillowcases, prescription pads, etc. Purchasing officers also buy supplies for the people who maintain the hospital buildings, and replacement parts for the very many machines hospitals have (many of which cannot be allowed to break down). Firms supplying the Health Service, or NHS staff themselves, develop or ask for new equipment, or better designs of existing equipment, or suggest that something can usefully be made disposable, or more cheaply. All the possibilities have to be studied with the professional staff concerned, for practicality and cost-effectiveness: will a new type of bedpan really cut out cross-infection, take less time and effort to sterilise, be easier for patients to use, and therefore justify and partly save the extra price?

Like purchasing and supply officers in all organisations (*see* BUYING, PURCHASING AND SUPPLY *in* BUYING, SELLING AND RELATED SERVICES), the NHS staff have to be expert at all the techniques which bring down costs, such as balancing the benefit of buying in bulk to hold down prices, against the cost and problems of storage. Some people specialise in managing central sterile supply departments; the NHS also employs hundreds of storekeepers.

Some posts, though, are unique to the Health Service, for instance, the dental estimates board and prescription pricing authority.

Medical records

Medical Records, sometimes called 'patient services', is another aspect unique to the Health Service. Medical records officers organise and supervise the system and the staff who give patients appointments, for admission to hospital or for an out-patient clinic; maintain waiting lists; actually admit patients; book transport or ambulances; keep patients' records, and see that case notes and items like x-rays are added and logged; record, maintain, and analyse statistics; and organise the medical secretarial service.

At district level, the medical records officer also supervises systems for the family health services. MROs set up and manage computer-based systems to handle, for example, appointments, waiting lists, registrations, scheduling, and statistics – but there are still problems in putting patients' actual records onto computer files because they must be kept confidential.

Accurate information systems in the Health Service are crucial, and there are also senior posts for health intelligence or information officers. They keep numerical and statistical records and analyse and report on them, and are involved in statistical aspects of areas like who gets what diseases. In some areas, the MROs also help with medical research work.

Secretarial staff

The NHS also employed (1993) the full-time equivalent of some 13,269 administrative and clerical staff including secretaries. They work in hospitals, in administration and for general practitioners. It is possible to specialise in medical secretarial work.

Recruitment and entry

The NHS recruits for administrative work at all levels from school-leavers with at least four GCSE or equivalent passes (it may be possible to start in clerical work with fewer), although long-term career prospects are probably rather better with (two) A-levels or a degree.

The vast majority of administrative staff start in the lower grades, and then apply for promotion when they have appropriate experience and/or qualifications. The exceptions are:

General management training scheme: designed as a 'fast-stream' entry for the next generation of most senior general managers, with about 65 places yearly. Entry is with a first degree or a suitable professional qualification, but NHS staff who are over 21, have been in the NHS for at least a year, and have either two A-levels or the intermediate exam for a suitable professional qualification (i.e. they can be pharmacists, nurses, physiotherapists, doctors, etc.), are eligible.

Finance training scheme: special entry for graduates.

Qualifications and training

The NHS trains extensively at all levels of administration.

General management training: trainees are normally employed by a region. The formal scheme lasts 22 months, including 12 months' practical working experience in a junior management post, followed by a more senior post. Formal courses throughout training give opportunities to study management at different levels in the NHS and other organisations. GMT trainees are expected to study for a relevant professional qualification (*see below*) during training, and promotion is conditional on gaining it.

Finance: staff are generally trained and qualify as accountants, via CIPFA, or accounting technicians, depending on basic qualifications. *See* ACCOUNTANCY AND FINANCIAL MANAGEMENT *in* FINANCIAL CAREERS.

Other general administrative staff: release and help is normally given for school-leavers to qualify, starting with BTEC National (16-plus entry) or Higher National (A-level entry) awards in public administration.

Purchasing and supply, and *personnel* staff are expected to gain appropriate professional qualifications for promotion.

Professional qualifications

The main qualifying body is the Institute of Health Services Management (1996 membership 8,000 including 1,000 students). Most members work in the NHS, only 2–3% in the private health sector. The main qualifications available are the following:

Diploma in Health Services Management examination (for full membership) – a three-part exam (four papers each) at degree standard, normally taken over three years. Minimum entry requirements are at least five GCSE passes with two at A-level (or an equivalent, subjects to include English and a maths-based subject). In practice, most of those registering to take the exams are now graduates.

The *Certificate in Managing Health Services* is an open-learning programme of some 440 hours of study designed for health-services staff who already have a relevant professional qualification in nursing, medicine, scientific work, ambulance work, etc. It can lead to NVQ/SVQ level.

The *Certificate in Health Management Studies* is designed mainly for young administrative and clerical staff, and is awarded to anyone gaining a BTEC Higher award in public administration with health service option modules.

Other relevant qualifications:

The Institute of Health Record Information and Management sets exams for a certificate (GCSE equivalent passes at 16-plus in English and maths) and a diploma (five GCSE equivalent passes at 16-plus) which is normally needed for promotion as a medical records officer.

The Association of Medical Secretaries, Practice Administrators and Receptionists has since 1995 collaborated with the Royal Society of Arts to award joint certificates and diplomas at NVQ level 2 for Health Service receptionists and level 3 for medical secretaries. Qualifications at MCI standard 1 are currently (1996) available and AMSPAR is preparing an advanced diploma in practice management at MCI standard 2. The aim is to get accreditation at level 4 for NVQ administration. The FE colleges offer part-time courses to prepare NHS and GP employees for these exams; some provide one-year full-time courses for Health Service receptionists for which an entry standard of two to four GCSE/SCE passes may be required.

Further information

The professional bodies quoted above, and from the personnel department of any regional health authority or hospital.

Support and auxiliary services

Catering services – domestic services – 'helpers' – laundry services – works staff – other support and auxiliary staff

Thousands of people provide essential support and auxiliary services for the NHS.

Each service has its own specialist managers and other staff. The services are controlled and coordinated by district managers who, in each case, supervise the service throughout the district; advise senior managers on future developments; liaise with supplies on purchasing, e.g. food and kitchen equipment; and look for ways of improving and economising on the service on a district and hospital basis, perhaps by concentrating laundry services in one hospital in the district, by 'contracting out' some or all of the service, or by more standardisation of items being used. They also monitor budgets, and look after staffing and training within their service.

Catering services

The Catering Services provide meals for both patients and staff in hospitals, and in NHS offices' staff canteens, in numbers ranging from 250 to 3,000. Numbers of catering staff have been falling: centralised kitchens, advanced preparation of meals, contracting-out and economies have continued to cut staff numbers.

Most of the catering is fairly straightforward, although obviously special diets must be provided for some patients and a careful watch has to be kept on the nutritional value of meals. It is the sheer numbers (several thousand meals at a time), timing and problems of getting hot meals to wards, and so on that create the headaches.

The hospital catering officer is responsible for the entire department and organises and controls the work, under the district catering manager, planning menus (with the dietitian), seeing that supplies are delivered, supervising food preparation and cooking, advising wards on servicing meals, and managing staff dining-rooms. In large hospitals there is normally a deputy catering officer; assistant catering officers and catering supervisors are the grades below this. Skilled workers are also employed: kitchen superintendents; head, assistant head and assistant cooks and dining-room supervisors, and in some hospitals, experienced butchers and bakers.

Domestic services

Domestic Services have to see that every part of every hospital is kept as scrupulously clean, and therefore germ-free, as possible, and uses the most advanced cleaning equipment available. Fewer hospitals, increasing efficiency, and some contracting-out have all reduced numbers since the peak year of 1979.

Under the district domestic managers, services within each hospital are managed by a domestic superintendent, who is responsible for the care, maintenance and cleaning of the inside of the hospital, its furniture and fittings, for services to the wards, reception areas and clinics, and for intensive care units, theatres and maternity wards. The hospital is generally split into smaller units, each managed by an assistant. The senior housekeeper normally looks after the domestic services of about 120 beds, while a domestic supervisor sees to day-to-day cleaning of an area of the hospital.

'Helpers'

Helpers support professional staff in a number of hospital departments. They are trained to do specific routines.

On the wards, they are NURSING auxiliaries and assistants (*see in* SUPPLEMENTARY HEALTH PROFESSIONS), who help patients bath, dress, eat, etc. English hospitals employed nearly 4,000 in 1993.

In occupational therapy departments (*see section in* SUPPLEMENTARY HEALTH PROFESSIONS) (where nearly 2,000 work) they help patients to learn to do things again, under instruction from the therapist. RADIOGRAPHERS had over 750 helpers. PHYSIOTHERAPISTS' helpers (of whom there are some 2,150) meet patients and help them to change (if necessary) or with some forms of treatment (e.g. applying ice packs), check equipment, and help keep the department neat and tidy.

Laundry services

Laundry Services deal with millions of items a week, and have to maintain a constant supply of sheets, towels, blankets, staff jackets and overalls, all of which must be sterilised and are likely to be more difficult to clean than the normal laundry's throughput. Amalgamating laundry services for part or all of a district, increasing use of disposable materials, installing more modern, labour-saving equipment, and contracting-out, have steadily reduced the numbers of people needed to handle NHS laundry.

Works staff

Works staff design, build, manage and maintain NHS buildings: hospitals, offices, laundries, training and recreational centres, and so on. New and rebuilt hospitals incorporate the latest in automation, mechanical-handling, communication, sterilisation and labour-saving equipment, with energy-saving environmental control systems. The NHS employs some 16,000 full-time equivalent staff, most of whom work full-time (1994), against some 24,000 in 1974.

Amongst the staff are the regionally based architects, engineers (building services, civil, mechanical, electrical), and surveyors (building and quantity); *see* LAND USE PROFESSIONS; *and* GENERAL ENGINEERING. Works staff also include building officers, the equivalent of clerks of works. Maintenance employs technician engineers (who supervise the operation and maintenance of mechanical and electrical plant, mainly central heating, air-conditioning and ventilating and electrical systems), electricians, plumbers, and operatives who mend windows, maintain heating, lighting and air-conditioning plant, etc.

Other support and auxiliary staff

Other support and auxiliary staff, including porters (who take patients from wards to operating theatre or physiotherapy department, and back again, and take supplies to departments), drivers, cleaners, gardeners, etc. totalled 72,800 in 1994.

Recruitment and entry

Managers (catering, domestic service, laundry, etc.), professionals (e.g. architects), and skilled staff (e.g. cooks), are normally recruited from amongst people who have completed appropriate professional qualifications, e.g. degrees or higher diplomas in institutional management (*see in* HOTELS AND CATERING, CATERING SERVICES, HOME ECONOMICS AND RELATED CONSUMER SCIENCES), ARCHITECTURE (*see* LAND USE PROFESSIONS), *or* engineering (*see* GENERAL ENGINEERING) or, for skilled workers, City & Guilds NVQ/SVQ qualifications in e.g. cooking. However, the NHS does recruit people to train either as managers or in some other skills. For long-term career prospects, it is generally necessary to meet the educational entry requirements for the profession or skill in question. The NHS now usually asks for two or three GCSE equivalent passes for jobs like 'helping'. Experience, for work like cleaning and in the kitchen, is useful.

Qualifications and training

Induction training is given to entrants with appropriate qualifications. Anyone joining in the basic grades of support and other services is given on-the-job training, and those who prove suitable may be given full-time or day-release to study for appropriate exams. Some groups (e.g. medical secretaries, and ambulance staff) have their own organisations which award special qualifications. See also the relevant sections above on individual professions, skills, etc.

Further information

Institute of Health Services Management, National Health Service Training Authority, Health Service Careers.

Contents

Administration, Business Management and Office Work

(CLCI: C; CAM – CAT)

Background

All kinds of organisations have to be managed and administered, not just commercial and industrial firms. The National Health Service, charities, theatres, police forces, trade unions and local authorities, all need expert management and administration.

The Institute of Management defines management as 'the achievement of objectives through other people', i.e. it involves getting others to do the necessary tasks rather than doing everything oneself.

The word 'management' overlaps several other words including 'supervision', 'organisation', 'administration' and 'leadership' and there are distinctions between them. Technically, for example, 'administration' is supposed to be the function responsible for seeing that any organisation runs smoothly on a day-to-day basis, while 'management' concentrates on decision-making, planning, innovating, and preparing for change. However, these distinctions are often blurred and the terms used are often interchangeable.

Management is not really a career in its own right, rather a long-term career aim. It has always been open to anyone to try working their way up the ladder to take increasing responsibility for the work of others, and as a result doing less of whatever it is – selling, auditing, teaching, policing – oneself.

Managerial status was traditionally a reward for a relatively long period of service – stressing time-serving and promotion on an age and seniority basis, often without any real assessment of managerial potential or aptitude. For many people, and in many occupations and areas of employment, this traditional pattern continues, with the result that people can be, and still are, promoted to a management level which they cannot handle.

Responding to changing economic conditions, coping with the immense problems in financial management, knowing when and how to invest and innovate, how to take advantage of and adjust to rapid technological and scientific development, and how to compete in tough world markets, are all factors making it more difficult to be profitable or even just cost-effective. Many companies and organisations are now finding it tough just to stay alive. They need expert, 'professional' managers who can understand and analyse what is happening in their business, who can look ahead, plot and plan efficiently for an uncertain future. The manager in the 1990s must be flexible and able to respond rapidly to changing conditions.

Management is fundamentally the same in whatever field it is carried out. It is a skill in its own right, and good managers are not confined to managing work which they can carry out themselves. Managers, of all kinds of companies, now need to be people of the highest potential. They need skills which may well be different from those needed in 'primary' careers or functions, or for administration. They must have planned training and experience to prepare them for management.

Managers prepare forward plans which may cover the next year or the next five to ten years. They make the decisions on how to implement these plans and see that the resources needed in terms of money, materials, equipment and people are made available and organised efficiently, and that delivery of their service or product satisfies their customers. They plan and organise communication and information systems which monitor and keep managers fully informed of what is happening throughout the organisation and ensure that decision-making is soundly based. Today, they must be up to date with computers and other aspects of information technology to help to analyse data and statistics, and trends. Above all, managers must take responsibility for their staff – for motivating, developing and appraising, maintaining discipline, and for selecting or dispensing with an individual's services.

There are two basic routes into management: through experience and promotion or through academic qualification followed by accelerated training.

The majority of potential managers start in one of the main 'functions', although there some schemes designed to giving new entrants a chance to sample several functions before making a choice. In a specialist organisation like a bank or a retail store, this will be the main business of the firm (sometimes called 'line' management), in these examples, branch banking or selling. In manufacturing firms and some other organisations there is generally more choice, although the main route to management is most usually via the main interest of the firm – electronics specialists in the electronics industry, chemists and chemical engineers in the chemical industry, and so on. The main choice of functions is between production, research and development, management services, finance, marketing/sales, general administration, purchasing and supply, and personnel.

Once potential managers have qualified in and gained reasonable experience of a function, and demonstrated the expected management potential, which usually means going through a fairly stiff weeding-out process, promotion may come fairly fast. This takes them through a series of increasingly demanding and responsible jobs, perhaps with experience of different types of work, as well as training in managerial skills, leading first to a junior management or 'supervisory' post, and then perhaps continuing through further levels of middle and senior management.

For example, a junior manager or 'supervisor', may be responsible for a small group of people who are all usually doing the same work, or for a single production line. At middle management level they take on wider responsibility, for a group of junior managers, and their staff, perhaps in regional sales management, as a branch manager, or in charge of a group of production lines. At senior management level they may be responsible for entire departments, such as marketing, finance, production, personnel, purchasing.

This route into management depends upon establishing a good track record, establishing good relationships and seizing opportunities for promotion when they occur.

With the second route, some organisations have schemes designed to recruit potential managers directly from full-time education, usually at degree level, and give them intensive training aimed at immediate entry into management. These schemes should not be confused with graduate recruitment in general because employers do not see graduates as automatically qualified for management, and graduates will be expected to prove that they have management potential and ability.

Only a few people reach the top levels of management, and the majority of those originally recruited for management training find their upper limit somewhere in middle management. It is rarely straightforward or easy to reach senior managerial positions. Some organisations, like the major manufacturers of consumer goods, the clearing banks and the larger retail and supermarket chains, expect to keep their management trainees for life, and so usually give reasonably varied, planned career experience and regular promotion. In most industrial and commercial firms, though, while such prospects may be there, it is usual to have to use the drive, initiative and self-confidence demanded of management material to gain essential experience and promotion at the right times. It may be necessary to change firms to gain sufficiently broad experience and/or promotion.

It is a very demanding, competitive life. Managers, or rather potential managers, are expected to be ready to change jobs whenever asked, and often to move around the country or go overseas.

Prior to the recession, the proportion and number of managerial staff had increased steadily, and an increasing number of employees began to see themselves as being of managerial status, whatever terms their employers may have used. However, the recession led to tougher and changing trading conditions, and together with new technology, this led to major organisational change. Firms have cut, often drastically, the numbers of workers to be managed. This restructuring has resulted in job losses in management. More than 70% of employers have experienced the loss of at least one tier of management. Senior and departmental managers can now increasingly gain access to sophisticated information directly and rapidly from computer-based systems without any need to go through middle/junior managers. Therefore, firms are thinning out the managerial communication lines, particularly in non-productive areas, resulting in a flatter structure. Slightly fewer job losses are predicted for future restructuring exercises, with one in ten employers forecasting an increase in jobs. However, the cut in management layers is set to continue, with almost six in ten firms anticipating further reductions. There is a noticeable shift in the composition of cuts, however, with only 8% of employers predicting the loss of more than one layer of management, compared to 28% in 1994. One in five managers expressed extreme insecurity over their job permanence in the Institute of Management's recent joint report with Manpower PLC *Survival of the Fittest*. *See also the* WORLD OF WORK *and* CHANGING YOUR CAREER *chapters.*

Senior management has not been exempt either. One of the effects of the 1990s recession has been large-scale redundancies and/or 'early retirement' (either voluntary or compulsory) for many in senior management. One of the spin-offs of this has been the increase in ex-managers setting up their own businesses or consultancies.

Recruitment and entry

Most firms, large, medium-sized and even quite small, as well as other organisations, look quite deliberately for their next generation of middle managers and the senior managers of twenty years hence from amongst the most able young people available to them. For a growing proportion of firms and other organisations, including the Civil Service, these 'fast streams' are recruited from amongst graduates. Because so many of the best of the age group go on straight from school to university, many firms ceased recruiting managerial trainees with A levels or their equivalent some time ago, let alone with GCSE or equivalent passes. The main exceptions are clearing banks, insurance companies, retailing generally, and areas of employment with a relatively large number of middle-management and administrative posts.

Anyone determined to go as far in management as they are capable is clearly, therefore, going to start out with the highest possible educational qualifications. Except in areas like those quoted above, working up from lower entry levels is generally getting more difficult all the time.

While firms and other organisations recruit their future senior managers, and even administrators, from amongst graduates, a degree or higher national qualification, even a very good one, is not enough. Graduate recruiters take academic ability for granted. Often they are not even concerned about the subject studied. Obviously in some sectors firms need a proportion of managerial recruits with particular degrees – electronics for the electronics industry, and so on. They also want their management trainees to be numerate. A subject which demonstrates this and some understanding of the 'real' world, e.g. marketing, maths or statistics, economics, finance, or business studies, is increasingly useful, but some graduate recruiters still prefer the rigour of history, classics, etc., even for marketing consumer products. There are virtually no degree subjects that preclude a graduate from entry to an accelerated management training scheme, although those who have followed a vocational course such as architecture or medicine may have to explain why they are looking for a change of direction.

Graduate recruiters are just as, if not more, concerned about personal qualities. They expect that most graduates will have learnt certain skills as part of their courses – to think logically and clearly, to analyse accurately, to be able to research facts, and to be able to assess what information is important in a given situation. They want them to be able to absorb, assess the importance and see the implications of, a great deal of very detailed and often highly technical, statistical, information, and to learn how to forecast the consequences of known and possible future events. For their future managers they are also looking for people with organising ability, who can work with anyone at any level and get the best out of them, create and keep up working relationships, and sum up people accurately. Ability to work as part of a team is, then, essential. 'Communicating' skills are paramount – the ability to explain and discuss clearly verbally, to write concise and clear reports and so on. Self-confidence, and the signs of a sound business sense are important.

Qualifications and training

'Academic' courses – degree and postgraduate – in business/management studies have been fully established for many years now, and some universities had 'commerce' degrees well before that. Yet it is still not essential to study this subject in order to begin a career in business and management.

The problems faced by firms of all kinds, the increasing complexity of the business world, the rapid changes, the intensified competition, and so on appear to demand more expert and sophisticated business and managerial skills on the commercial and financial side of business as well as in design and production. However, some still think the necessary skills, particularly for management, are best taught 'on the job' with integrated, preferably short, training courses.

Some firms still prefer to recruit their future managers from amongst graduates who have gone through the most rigorous intellectual training possible at university, consider this is best done through traditional and conventional courses in subjects like history, English, and classics, and are not fully convinced that business studies courses are, for this purpose, sufficiently academically rigorous. Firms recruiting graduates for non-technical management training make certain assumptions about graduates' intellectual ability and achievement and tend to be more concerned with their personal qualities than with the subject they have read. They look for graduates who are well motivated, can work with other people and are potential leaders, who can think and act independently, solve problems, take on responsibility quickly and so on. To be acceptable to prospective employers, graduates in business studies need these qualities too.

Nevertheless, a significant proportion of employers do see a business studies degree as an advantage – enough to ensure that business studies graduates have fewer problems in finding a first job than graduates in many other subjects. Such employers recognise that graduates in business studies have already tested their motivation to work in industry or commerce. What a degree in business studies may lack in high academic content should be counterbalanced by a realistic knowledge of what happens, and how, in the business world. Business studies graduates will normally understand the language of business before they start work, will know how to apply statistical and other management techniques, what kinds of problems may be met, how to work with other people, and so on. They are less likely to be against profit as a motive. Many business studies graduates will have had lengthy work experience as part of their sandwich-based courses.

Degree courses in business studies

First-degree courses in business studies generally give a broader base than can be gained by studying for a single professional qualification. They provide a foundation in the principles and techniques of modern business and management and the directions in which they are developing; training in one or more specialised aspects of business studies or management; contact with the business world; and training in the sources and uses of information and methods of investigation.

Courses mostly start with a firm basis of economic principles; the human and behavioural sciences such as sociology and psychology, generally emphasising the 'organisational' aspects relevant to industry and commerce; mathematics and statistics to an appropriate level; computing; and relevant aspects of law. Most also put some emphasis on finance and/or accounting, but to varying levels. The first year may also include the opportunity to spend some time on a subject outside the business field, or to add a useful skill like languages.

Courses generally continue with training in the core skills needed to run any business: deciding on and achieving set objectives, policy- and decision-making, developing systems and analysing information. They generally also cover the setting in which business has to operate. Some continue the broad approach, teaching everyone functional skills like accounting, marketing, manpower and personnel management. Some give students the chance to specialise in some depth in one of these, or in the management service skills like operational research. On other courses, students can choose a middle route and study to a fairly advanced level two subjects – accounting and systems analysis, or marketing and personnel.

First destinations in business studies (1994)	
total graduating	*2383*
destination unknown	152
overseas students	388
research, etc.	161
teacher training/other non-degree courses	110
believed unemployed, Dec. 31	118
temporary work	112
permanent UK work	1159
not available for employment	119
employers	
accountancy	136
banking/insurance/finance	197
other commerce	299
Civil Service	34
local government	51
public utilities and transport	68
oil & chemicals	38
engineering	98
other manufacturing	79
higher/further education	23
armed forces	9
entertainment, leisure	14
functions	
financial work	327
marketing, etc.	286
admin./operational management	270
management services	74
personnel, social, etc.	60

As the table shows, a high proportion of graduates went into financial, marketing and administrative work.

Sandwich courses are usually the more directly vocational. Nearly all the four-year courses outside Scotland include 12 months' practical training as an integral part. The practical training occupies either the whole of the third year – a 'thick' sandwich, or two or more periods of six months in different years – a 'thin' sandwich. Many higher education institutions can now arrange for placements to be spent working abroad and provide language tuition for students before they depart. Students taking sandwich courses may be either employer-based or college-based. A few firms sponsor students for business studies courses.

Higher national diploma courses in business studies are offered by many universities and colleges of technology/higher education. Topics studied are very similar to those on the sandwich type of degree course and allow students to specialise in one or more aspects of management, for example, marketing, personnel or finance, in the later part of the course.

Business studies are not taught just by conventional lectures and seminars. They usually also involve extensive project-based work, case studies, problem solving, business games and other simulations of the real business world.

Postgraduate study

A wide range of courses of all kinds are offered by universities and colleges. The academic nature of some are under constant scrutiny, and not all employers consider lengthy full-time courses worthwhile. Business schools of all kinds, including university schools, are becoming more and more entrepreneurial, tailoring their programmes to the perceived needs of their market.

The major qualifications available are:

Master of Business Administration (MBA or MBA-type). The MBA is a postgraduate, post-experience qualification. It is designed as a pathway from middle into senior management. In the UK, full-time courses usually span one to two years. Part-time courses last one to three years and are often held in the evenings or at weekends. There are various types of MBA course:

- Distance Learning/Open Learning courses are offered by a limited number of organisations, including the Open Business School (Open University), Durham, Heriot-Watt, Nottingham and Oxford Brookes Universities, together with Henley Management College.
- Modular MBAs are similar to sandwich courses and involve college-based study together with practical work in the workplace. Courses generally last from 18 months to two years and students are usually sponsored.
- Executive MBAs last 2–3 years and are for high-fliers. Study is usually at weekends and students must be sponsored. Consortium MBAs are designed by a group of 3–6 companies specifically to meet the needs of those companies.
- In-Company MBAs are tailored to an individual company's needs.

MBA programmes emphasise an analytical approach to managerial problem-solving, and much of the teaching is by case study. While covering the main core managerial disciplines such as economics, accounting and statistics, business finance, quantitative methods, human resource management, behavioural studies, information technology and marketing, MBA programmes now give students increasing choice as to whether or not to specialise, and to put together their own 'package' of options or electives.

For most MBA programmes, schools prefer students to have gained some working experience first, although they do accept new graduates. Graduates in unrelated disciplines, or with lower than a second-class honours degree, people with professional qualifications only and candidates with extensive business experience but no formal academic or professional qualification, may be accepted, but may have to take a two-, instead of a one-year course .

Tuition fees for a full-time course can be between £5,000 and £10,000, and for a part-time course between £2,500 and £6,000. Most students are self-financing, but employers sometimes assist with funding. Some institutions offer scholarships and bursaries, so consult prospectuses. AMBA (Association of Masters in Business Administration) offer a low-interest bank loan, as does the government's Career Development Loan scheme.

Diploma in Management Studies (DMS). This is a post-experience postgraduate diploma mainly intended for the practising manager. Most people take it part-time over two years, but there are full-time courses of around 25 weeks. The DMS is a general introduction to management and the industrial/commercial background, introducing management processes, tools and techniques. The courses include quantitative methods, finance, etc., behavioural studies, new technology and management, decision-making and problem-solving, the main business functions, including marketing, industrial relations and law, and policy-making. Most courses give students a choice of specialist options, and these may be geared to the needs of local firms. The course is normally in two parts and transfer between colleges is possible.

Entry is with a first degree or equivalent, HNC, or an appropriate professional qualification.

The DMS is offered by numerous universities and colleges. Some of them run it within a flexible postgraduate management course which gives the award of a DMS after two years' part-time study and completion of an MBA after four.

Professional courses. Since managerial training generally starts in a particular function – sales, marketing, purchasing, production, personnel, finance, company secretaryship, etc., the trainee will be expected to study for an appropriate professional qualification such as accountancy, or marketing. Engineers and scientists with appropriate degrees usually have to complete a period of practical training and experience before gaining their professional qualification, but this can be done largely 'on the job'.

There are various qualifications that can be valuable in developing a management career, often after work experience:

- NEBSM (National Examination Board in Supervisory Management) Certificate and Diploma. These are regarded as qualifications for supervisors and first-line managers.
- NVQ/SVQs (National/Scottish Vocational Qualifications) in Management are offered at Levels 3, 4 and 5. NVQ/SVQ Level 3 is regarded as a qualification for supervisors and first-line managers. Levels 4 and 5 are for those with correspondingly greater experience and responsibility. The lead body responsible for these qualifications is the Management Charter Initiative (MCI). Level 5 covers all the specifications of the Management Charter Initiative, is assessed through a series of work-based projects and assignments and includes topics such as managing people, resources, operations and information.
- NVQs in Management are awarded by a number of bodies including the Institute of Management, BTEC and NEBSM.
- BTEC Certificate in Management Studies. Each module takes 60–90 hours. Participants must be aged at least 21 with A levels or equivalent.

See also FINANCIAL CAREERS; THE LEGAL SYSTEM; MANAGING THE HEALTH SERVICE; CENTRAL GOVERNMENT; LOCAL GOVERNMENT; INFORMATION TECHNOLOGY AND COMPUTER WORK; WORKING FOR CHARITIES *section in* SOCIAL AND RELATED SERVICES; *and* LOGISTICS MANAGEMENT *in* BUYING, SELLING AND RELATED SERVICES.

Further information

Institute of Management. For MBA courses, Association of Business Schools (ABS), 344/354 Gray's Inn Road, London, WC1X 8BP and Association of Masters in Business Administration (AMBA), 15 Duncan Terrace, London, N1 8BZ, Telephone 0171-837 3375 *(produce useful course/school guides).*

Office or administrative management

Office administration is not usually perceived as a high-profile job. Administration managers (or admin managers for short) are often viewed as just another overhead, a necessary evil to keep the office machinery going. They are stereotyped as reliable, consistent, stolid, dull people who keep the wheels turning by monitoring performance, recording, measuring and doing those jobs that do not fall into anyone else's brief. This implies that administrative managers do not make any creative contribution to the business. The truth is that a professional administration manager has as much effect on a company's actual performance as do any of the so-called productive personnel such as sales, marketing and manufacturing.

Administrative managers are the core of a successful business, underpinning all other functions. Professionalism in this role is paramount. Professional administrative managers are the organisers who can efficiently and systematically get things done. A professional manager in any discipline must learn certain skills that enable him or her to delegate authority, eliminate time wasted in meaningless tasks, organise a workload efficiently, keep customers (internal and external) happy, and contribute towards the profitability of an organisation. The necessity for these skills applies to administrative managers as well.

The best administrative managers do keep the business running smoothly, not by just doing the drudge work that others don't want to be bothered with, but by recognising key issues and problems, reading long-term trends and setting up strategic plans to deal with them, spotting opportunities in the organisation that can be developed, and recognising potential threats and weak spots.

The Institute of Administrative Management (IAM) is the only professional management body concerned exclusively with the management of administration and office systems. In 1995, the IAM celebrated its 80th anniversary of promoting best practice in administrative management. The majority of IAM's members are concerned with the management of information through people; information is the life-blood of all organisations in the business public sectors. Effective managers of information must bring to the task a creative blend of information systems know-how and people skills.

In 1990, the IAM set up the prestigious Administering Total Quality Award (ATQ) that recognises the achievement of organisations in the application of Total Quality principles in an administrative context.

Administrative management is a wide-ranging area of management, and the Institute's members are to be found in a wide range of jobs and sectors – from Administration Director to Commanding Officer, from Office Manager to Personnel Manager, from Sales Administration Manager to Production Controller. Managers of small businesses are also in membership. Senior Civil Servants and officers of HM Forces are also enthusiastic members of the Institute.

The IAM has a unique Continuing Professional Development Scheme (CPD). This is a Registration Scheme (persons enrolled are designated IAM Registered Manager) and the IAM will provide certified copies of an individual's CPD achievements to third parties – when authorised by the Registered Member.

Qualifications and training

The Institute of Administrative Management offers internationally recognised Certificate and Diploma courses focusing on the practical application of skills, knowledge and understanding of concepts and techniques used in the workplace to facilitate the handling and flow of information.

Courses are offered in a flexible, modular form, as taught courses in FE and HE, as distance-learning programmes and at Catterick Resettlement Centre. The Certificate is also accessible to RAF Admin (Sec) Officers.

Courses are offered in flexible modular formats in all types of providers – universities, colleges, training consultancies and HM Forces establishments – and holders of the Advanced Diploma may take the distance learning based BA(Hons) final year course.

To study for the Diploma, it is necessary to register as a student of the Institute (qualifications required are one A level and four GCSEs or equivalent, or a minimum age of 23 with three years' relevant employment experience). The course requires a minimum of 180 hours of study. On completion of the course, students may apply for Associate membership of the Institute, which confers the use of the designatory letters AInstAM and the title Certified Administrator. Individual module certificates are issued.

The Advanced Diploma requires 360 hours of study. This leads to Corporate membership (MInstAM (Dip)) and the title Incorporated Administrator.

The IAM plans to launch an NVQ Level 4 in Administration in 1996.

Further Information

Institute of Administrative Management.

The Post Office

The Post Office is one of the UK's largest employers and in recent years has changed out of all recognition. It employs a total staff of about 180,000. It comprises three main businesses: Royal Mail, Post Office Counters Ltd and Parcelforce and Subscription Services Ltd (a wholly owned subsidiary of the Post Office). There is also a small Group centre which has a strategic role as befits an organisation in which there is a maximum delegation to the businesses.

The *Royal Mail* delivers some 63 million letters every working day through a highly complex distribution network, using advanced new technology. Investment in people as well as technology aims to ensure that Royal Mail is acknowledged as the best organisation in the world distributing text and packages. By far the largest of the three Post Office businesses, the current structure of Royal Mail comprises a small strategic headquarters and 18 business units. Nine divisions are responsible for the day-to-day running of Royal Mail, four strategic business units focus on developing products (bulk mail, national, international and cash carrying). The remaining four business units are run as internal business centres (catering, property, consultancy and engineering).

Royal Mail recruits graduates via its Management Access Programme. This programme provides an introduction to operations, customers, products and processes of Royal Mail before placing graduates in jobs in their chosen function.

Post Office Counters is Britain's largest retail network, with 20,000 outlets – more than all the major banks and building societies combined. Over 28 million customers per week take advantage of 160 different transactions. Post Office Counters is continuously looking to improve client and customer services through electronic machine vending, flexible staffing, increased automation programmes, etc. Post Office Counters recruits graduates into its Management Trainee Scheme, which provides training in core management skills, commercial business and retail concepts.

Parcelforce is the largest parcels carrier in the UK, with a unique commitment to deliver to every one of the nation's 24.5 million addresses. Its international network covers 98.9% of the inhabited world. Parcelforce provides the widest range of delivery services at home and overseas, employing the latest computer tracking and tracing systems to monitor the 160 million parcels travelling through its network each year.

Group Headquarters is concerned with Post Office strategy and performance and acts as an active catalyst for key activities.

Government policy and government intervention, for example the proposed possible closure of many sub-post offices, together with more efficient mail processing and automation and increased competition, may lead to a reduction in services and further staff cutbacks. Competition from private delivery services who specialise in guaranteed sameday, overnight or secure delivery of certain letters, documents and packages is increasing, but there is considerable resistance by the general public to complete privatisation of postal services and to closure of post offices.

Recruitment and entry

The Post Office recruits at several levels: see below for details.

Qualifications and training

Graduates

Graduates are employed in each of the businesses and in the corporate centre at various locations throughout the UK. Although many new vacancies are advertised in the summer months to attract newly qualified graduates, Royal Mail also advertises and recruits several times a year for experienced graduate job changers. Graduate jobs are always advertised in the *Prospects* series.

The Post Office aims to provide challenge and variety, backed up by appropriate training and support to prepare graduates for senior management positions. As a large organisation, the Post Office is able to provide highly professional staff-training facilities, with encouragement given to graduates to study for relevant professional qualifications. The Corporate Accountancy Training Scheme (CATS) provides graduates with the training and experience to become qualified accountants with any of the English professional bodies and won the prestigious CIMA Training Award in 1991.

Many jobs are open to a wide range of disciplines, although numerate or business/finance-related degrees are preferred in some job areas. All require a good honours degree, and a relevant postgraduate qualification may be an advantage. Key selection criteria include intellectual ability, interpersonal skills, achievement motivation and long-term managerial potential. Relevant work experience is also taken into consideration.

School-leavers and others

School-leavers are recruited mainly for work behind the counter, but also for some administrative jobs. There are no set formal qualifications for entry to counter staff (basic), counter staff (higher) or retail assistant grades, but some GCSE/SCEs or their equivalent are an advantage. An aptitude for figure work is the main requirement. Selection is by aptitude test and interview.

Postmen and postwomen

There are no formal entry requirements for entry as a postal cadet, as a postman or postwoman with Royal Mail, or as a parcel handler and sorter with Parcelforce. Selection is by aptitude test and interview. Entrants at 16 or 17 join the Postal Cadet training programme.

GNVQs are an acceptable entry qualification for basic-level vacancies. A number of NVQs are now also in place with the corporation. These are (Generic): Management, Customer Service (Retail Post Office Counters Ltd) and Road Haulage; and (Specific): NVQ for Postmen/women.

Further information

The Post Office.

Company secretary and administrative work

The company secretary has a formal, legal role, but is normally also a senior, more general, administrator with much wider responsibilities. People qualified as chartered secretaries are employed in a very wide range of other kinds of organisations, including public bodies, not just companies.

Company secretaries ensure that the company and its directors and managers comply with the Companies Acts and other relevant legislation. They service and advise the board of directors and ensure that the board's decisions and instructions are carried out in a timely manner.

Company secretaries of public limited companies (generally, those quoted on the Stock Exchange) are normally required to hold a professional qualification as a chartered secretary, lawyer or accountant. The regulations which apply to public companies are far more complex and exacting, and in addition to the more normal duties relating to meetings, company secretaries of public companies will also be responsible for complying with Stock Exchange regulations, dealing with acquisitions and disposals and increasingly be responsible for foreign subsidiaries and compliance with foreign regulatory requirements.

Company secretaries are responsible for convening meetings – of the board of a company, a local authority committee, or the governing body of a college (for example), where policy is generally decided. They make up the agenda for such meetings, and see that the committee or board have all the legal, financial, statistical and technical information they need for their discussions; and write papers for them on the implication of any suggested plans, in accurate but concise and easy-to-digest form. They take and draft the minutes of these meetings, and see that board or committee decisions are carried out. They maintain the register of members and other statutory books, and make any statutory returns. In companies, they also pay dividends and debenture interest and deal with capital issues. They are often involved with policy-making, play a major role in the development of an organisation, and take part in board or committee discussions. A high proportion of company secretaries eventually join the board.

In smaller companies, the company secretarial role is normally combined with another function such as finance or the administration of pensions and insurance. The role of secretary also exists in local authorities and many other public bodies. In all these cases the secretary is employed in a quasi-legal capacity to ensure that the body complies with internal and external regulations and will normally be responsible to the board, council or governing body.

The Institute of Chartered Secretaries and Administrators (ICSA) list a range of organisations in which chartered secretaries hold senior secretarial, administrative or financial appointments right up to and including top management and board level. ICSA qualifications are fully recognised for local government administrators. Other organisations include building societies, charities, the Civil Service, cooperative societies, docks and harbour boards, the National Health Service, nationalised industries, universities and colleges, professional societies, research associations, stock exchanges and trade associations. About half of all ICSA members work in private and public companies in all areas of industry and commerce, and only 20% of ICSA members actually are company secretaries.

Recruitment and entry

Most people start out in administrative work as trainee administrators within a firm or other organisation. The range of possible organisations is so wide that there are no hard and fast rules about entry, although it is probably still possible to get onto a career ladder as a school-leaver with A levels or equivalent.

Broadly, potential company secretaries/administrators ideally need to be organisation-minded and good at organising, reasonably numerate, methodical, orderly, careful and meticulous, prepared to give great attention to detail, tactful, diplomatic and very discreet. They need to be good communicators both verbally and on paper, able to think and work logically, able to analyse, summarise and write clear reports.

Qualifications and training

Training arrangements vary between different kinds and size of organisation, and can range from formal schemes to very ad hoc arrangements. Much of the training tends to be on the job, combined with part-time study, for the examinations of the Institute of Chartered Secretaries and Administrators, which has a total worldwide membership of over 46,000 together with around 25,000 registered students, and aims to provide a broadly based, multi-purpose qualification in administration.

The Chartered Institute is recognised under the EU Mutual Recognition Directive.

The Institute's professional qualification is divided into three stages: the Foundation, Pre-Professional and Professional programmes.

The Foundation programme, which consists of five modules, and the Pre-Professional programme (four modules) are broad-based business courses giving a sound knowledge of accounting, business law, management and administration. These knowledge-based studies underpin the more practical and applied studies in later modules.

The Professional programme is a programme of study and assessment at postgraduate level. All eight modules embrace the themes of statutory and regulatory compliance, finance, governance, administration, and management. The Professional programme is separated into two stages: Stage 1: Professional Administration, Management Practice, Corporate Law, Financial Accounting; Stage 2: Administration of Corporate Affairs, Company Secretarial Practice, Corporate Finance, Regulation and Taxation, Management Accounting.

Applicants must be 17 years of age or over. The Institute has an Open Access policy for entry to its Foundation programme and a range of access points for holders of particular qualifications. The full ICSA qualification is recognised by the DfEE as equivalent to a first class UK honours degree.

Holders of NVQ/SVQ in Administration at Level 4 are eligible for exemption from the Foundation and Pre-Professional programmes. Holders of BTEC HNC/HND gain credit from the Foundation programme, whilst holders of UK degrees gain credit from the Foundation and Pre-Professional programmes. In both cases additional exemptions are available for courses which have been developed in collaboration with the Institute. Exemptions are also available for a variety of professional qualifications.

Further information

Education Help Desk, The Institute of Chartered Secretaries and Administrators.

Management consultancy

Management consultants give objective, professional, expert and sophisticated advice to all kinds and sizes of organisations. They deal with change, whether technological, organisational or behavioural, and with the inevitable conflicts change causes. They pinpoint the need for change, and provide the expertise needed to plan and implement changes.

Management consultants can provide greater, or different, expertise than is available within an organisation. Firms which slimmed down sharply during recession now 'contract out' more work instead of employing their own experts, increasing demand for consultants. Consultants make outside, and therefore more objective, appraisals, and may be able to see the broader picture and identify longer-term needs. They can also provide additional support when the load on management is temporarily increased. They make reports on an existing system or method, propose changes, or design completely new systems. Mostly they work for commercial and industrial firms, but government, local government and health services are now major customers as they search for value for money and greater efficiency, and museums and charities, and even religious organisations use them.

Services are constantly developing in range and technique to meet changing needs, in particular to the demand for more specialised services and to new technologies. Changes in financial services (especially in the City), have created a major new market for consultancies. Management consultants earn their UK fees mainly in the following fields:

- Information technology, ranging from developing IT strategies for organisations, through planning systems, integrating computing and telecommunications systems, giving advice on packaged software, to market research and product strategy for the IT industry, and developing management information systems (defining information needs, doing feasibility studies, systems analysis and design, providing the computer systems and software).
- Finance and administration, for instance, planning and installing budgetary control systems, or planning the reorganisation of office administration.
- Personnel management and training, advising on personnel policy and manpower planning, job evaluation and selection, finding people to fit particular posts.
- Corporate strategy and organisation development, long-range planning, reorganising a company's structure, rationalising services or production, and making general appraisals.
- Manufacturing management and technology, developing new strategies for manufacturing with the emphasis on new technology and its implications for the company as a whole, planning and installing advanced manufacturing systems, improving organisation and plant layout, etc.
- Marketing sales and distribution, for instance, organising and training a sales force for a new product, examining sales forecasting methods, surveying the potential market for a range of new financial services.
- Some consultancies have their own R&D labs, developing new manufacturing systems, assessing computer systems, for instance.
- Economic and environmental studies, urban and regional development planning, cost–benefit and social-analysis studies.

Every project is different. Each project involves a different 'mix' of specialists, depending on the nature of the project; and how long they spend on it depends on its complexity and scope – it may be a few days, it may be months.

MCA (Management Consultancies Association) members earn about 50% of the management consultancy fee income in the United Kingdom.

Management consultants from 21 countries are now linked up via the International Council of Management Consultancy Institute (ICMCI) worldwide web site on the Internet (http://www.mcninet/icmci.com). Most of the larger management consultancies operate internationally. It is common for them to assemble project teams comprising consultants from various countries in order to service the needs of multinational clients effectively. Some of the larger firms now manage their European operations as one business entity, with Europe-wide recruitment.

Recruitment and entry

It is unusual to go directly into management consultancy from school or university, except for graduates with special skills. It is effectively a second career with most starting in their late twenties or early thirties.

Management consultancies want people who have had extensive industrial and/or commercial experience, preferably in 'line' management, and who are well qualified, ideally with a very good first degree (preferably in a technology, computing, or economics), topped up with a professional qualification in, e.g., accounting, and even a higher degree. Language skills are increasingly important.

Management consultants' staff must be able to work as part of a team, to absorb and assess new and often complex information, to analyse and think logically, to see what is important, and to understand organisational problems. Consultants criticise, assess and advise from the outside, inevitably creating tensions by the mere fact of their arrival, so they have to be able to work easily in new situations, to put clients' staff at their ease and work with them.

Qualifications and training

Training is largely on the job, with an initial period of some months' induction, largely spent learning diagnostic skills, report-writing, etc. The Institute of Management Consultants is in the early stages of developing an NVQ in Consulting Skills under the auspices of the Management Charter Initiative. It is anticipated that this will take approximately two years to develop. In Europe, the International Council of Management Consultancy Institutes (ICMCI) is developing a strategy for the promotion of Certified Management Consultant status.

Further information

The Management Consultancies Association, which is the organisation for management consultancy firms, and the Institute of Management Consultants, which is the professional body for individual consultants.

Personnel management

Personnel management specialises in making the most of the people – 'human resources' is the jargon phrase – working for an organisation. Organisations of all kinds, not just industrial firms – banks, the NHS, local authorities, department stores, airlines, all employ personnel staff.

The development – and image – of personnel work has been hampered by its origins in industrial welfare work, by the early paternalistic attitudes of so many companies, and a reputation for merely being a way of keeping workers both quiescent and productive.

However, personnel management is now fairly well established as a fully-fledged management function, although it has still not developed its full executive potential in some organisations – relatively seldom (although increasingly) personnel directors are on the board of directors. Although in many companies personnel is still only an advisory function with little executive responsibility for decision- and policy-making, more posts are now at strategic levels as some of the more obvious personnel functions have devolved to line managers. Some firms are now also 'contracting-out' some areas of personnel work, to, e.g., management consultants, and this may bring some changes to the employment patterns of personnel staff.

There can be no doubt about the importance of really efficient and sophisticated personnel management, but personnel managers often have to fight quite hard to show that their expertise is needed as part of strategic planning, and is not just advisory or peripheral.

Not many employing organisations are increasing staff numbers any more. Most have contracted sharply, a trend accelerated by the 1991/92 recession, but complexity and pace of change for almost all organisations have, if anything, made expert personnel management still more, rather than less, important. Organisations need to recruit staff with up-to-date, often very different, skills; crucial skills and abilities are in short supply, and personnel may have to find ways to retrain existing staff to cope. Management wants more sophisticated information from the personnel department for future planning, etc. Reorganisation, automation in the factory, computerisation of the office, involve personnel in assessing, retraining, regrading, staff, and perhaps planning and pushing through redundancies. The legal framework of industrial relations has brought a different dimension to negotiations. Personnel must develop programmes for YT trainees. Organisations are generally expected to be more responsible towards employees – although current cost-conscious policies have brought back some tougher attitudes.

The range of activities which make up personnel management is now extremely wide and varied. At its most advanced levels it involves both problem-analysis and problem-solving, to help implement properly and efficiently overall organisational policy changes, to improve efficiency, and make manpower planning a part of the organisation's general strategic forecasting. This also involves complex statistical and other research studies of, for instance, trends in training, skill requirements and availability, job specifications (grading and appraisal) and pay policies.

On a more day-to-day level, the personnel management department must match recruitment to manpower needs, both in terms of the number of general trainees recruited at various levels of intake (school-leaver, graduate, and so on), and for specific posts. To do this it must liaise closely both with its own departments, to quantify their present and future needs and to make sure the right kinds of staff are recruited, and with the sources of staff such as careers offices, schools, university careers advisory services, and recruitment agencies. The ability to manage a flexible workforce is vital.

Personnel managers may also be responsible for day-to-day recruitment: carrying out detailed job analyses, preparing job specifications, dealing with advertisements for vacancies, the resulting applications, interviews and tests, and everything that goes to make up efficient selection. In some organisations, however, departments for whom staff are intended may also be involved in some or all of these processes; in others they may take full responsibility, and close consultation is necessary between personnel and departments. Personnel managers must now also be able to manage the contracting out of services such as catering, cleaning and IT/Communications. In addition, they should be able to develop business concepts.

Personnel management is, of course, closely involved with the whole field of employee–employer relationships – so-called 'industrial' relations. This normally means negotiating with employees' representatives (and, in more serious disputes, with outside union officials too) on salaries and pay, redundancies, hours, working conditions – in fact any area where company policy may be changing, and problems or disagreement arise. Radical restructuring and major upheavals in working practices may have to be negotiated. Employee relations is a rapidly changing field, and personnel managers working in it have had to develop new expertise – on legislation, for example – to add to the growing range of highly specialist techniques and procedures which make up arbitration, conciliation, and consultation. For example, EU legislation is having an effect on European organisations with bases in the UK, who are already introducing Employee Working Councils. Demand for employee relations experts has risen quite sharply.

Education and training are generally the responsibility of personnel management. Organising education and training involves both setting up and running training schemes within the firm and arranging for employees at all levels to go on courses at educational institutions on both a short- and long-term basis, on day- or block-release, or on sandwich courses. Schemes may have to be designed for craft and technician trainees, sales staff, new graduates, and for management development. Personnel must deal with retraining, both for immediate and longer-term needs, as well as managing, e.g., YT programmes.

Finally, personnel management also carries responsibility for all kinds of employee services. These include canteen, lunch and tea/coffee break facilities, industrial health and safety, sickness and pensions schemes, and transport, which may also mean allocating company cars. In some firms, personnel organises day nurseries for staff children; some personnel departments also organise sports and other recreational facilities and activities.

Personnel departments also maintain extensive records, now mostly computerised.

The range of personnel work is so extensive that it is only in the smallest organisations that the personnel manager can cope with the entire field. In most, and especially those employing more than 1,000, personnel work is likely to be divided between teams of specialists whose leaders will probably be titled according to the functions they carry out, for example, industrial relations manager, staff manager, education and training officer, recruitment officer, and so on, and it is possible each area of specialisation will become increasingly independent in the future.

Recruitment and entry

Personnel work needs at least some maturity and experience, and so it has never been a career to start straight from school. Generally, entry is either via some other experience, normally in industry or commerce, or via a degree or BTEC Higher award. Graduates and others are accepted as trainees by some organisations, but it is possible to take a full-time course first.

Over 500 graduates went into personnel work in 1988 but the picture now is not so rosy. The number of new graduates into personnel over the last four years is very low. Most of the graduate trainee schemes were reduced or stopped in the early 1990s. Those that are still available tend to offer a general management trainee scheme, which is still useful. There is much competition for jobs. Although many Human Resource degrees have appeared over the last 5 years, most would not be recognised by the Institute of Personnel and Development (IPD). As undergraduates, students should be advised to gain useful work experience and hold positions of authority in university societies.

Personnel work can absorb a range of different backgrounds, qualifications and personalities. Collective bargaining takes one set of abilities, qualifications and experience, recruitment another, so it is difficult to be specific about the qualities needed. Most personnel staff spend more time in deskwork – writing up reports and recommendations, making up statistics and records, writing letters, etc. – than is generally appreciated.

However, everyone in personnel has to be able to get on with other people, to communicate easily and well with everyone and anyone in an organisation, from top management to the shop floor. Much personnel work involves the patient creation of or improvement in working relationships, so it takes a realistic, unemotional approach, the ability to stay calm and make cool judgements. Personnel managers must be able to listen and persuade, know how to discover the root causes of and resolve conflict, and have plenty of tact and patience. Anyone wanting to reach director level will need plenty of drive and persuasiveness, since personnel is not always accepted as a direct route to the upper echelons of management. Organising ability, and numeracy (to deal with statistics) are essential.

Qualifications and training

Professional qualifications (IPD) are not mandatory, nor indeed essential, but they are strongly encouraged by many major employers of graduates. Personnel management is an option in many business studies degrees and BTEC/SCOTVEC Higher National Diplomas.

Training, for most people, is largely on-the-job, with part-time study for IPD qualifications. For those who are unable to take day-release or evening classes, the IPD has a flexible learning programme for home-based study. There is also a correspondence course (International Correspondence Schools Ltd, in Glasgow) and the Open University Business School offers some appropriate modules.

The IPD's membership has been rising steadily over the past few years. The IPD (Institute of Personnel and Development) was formed as a result of the IPM (Institute of Personnel Management) and the ITD (Institute of Training and Development) joining forces on 1 July 1994, resulting in a membership of 76,000. Its entry qualifications and examinations are now in line with those of similar bodies, partly reflecting a real need for broader training and examinations as for other management functions (including economics, for example), partly to demonstrate more formally personnel management's claim to professional status. It is also clearly necessary to provide a sound educational and professional base from which personnel staff can try for senior managerial positions.

The IPD's new Professional Qualification Scheme (PQS) is a demanding qualification with an 85 CATS (credit accumulation) point rating. The PQS comprises three parts: core management, core personnel and development, and electives in specialist areas (four modules from a choice of 22). Successful completion of any one part gives Licentiate membership (LicIPD) and successful completion of all three areas gives Graduate member status. So people can follow a generalist personnel and development route, but the new standards also cater for those in training or who wish to specialise in a particular area. Colleges will be offering the new courses from September 1996.

Some relevant first degrees or management qualifications can be accredited for Licentiate membership through an approved prior credited learning (APCL) route. Details of the APCL route can be obtained from the IPD. First and second degrees previously granting full accreditation towards IPM's Professional Education Scheme are currently being considered by the IPD for accreditation against the new standards. Therefore it is necessary to check with the IPD about the status of any particular course. There are also some full-time courses at colleges/universities throughout the country, which normally run over one academic year, and are predominantly aimed at students who have already achieved a degree level qualification. Again, it is necessary to check the status of such courses with the IPD. IPD professional membership is open to those with an *approved* qualification, and all the approved centres are listed in the IPD's *Qualification Routes* booklet. It is not essential to be IPD-qualified to work in personnel management, but employers often regard it as desirable.

IPD Graduates who are deemed to have 'appropriate personnel practitioner experience' may progress to the Institute's full professional qualification, MIPD.

The minimum entry requirements for PQS student membership of the IPD are five GCSE grades A–C in different subjects, two of which must be at A-level (or five SCE grades including three Highers and two S grades 1–3). Advanced GNVQ is regarded as equivalent to A-level. Students may also offer BTEC/SCOTVEC National qualifications. However, those who do not have these qualifications can take the Certificate in Personnel Practice, a part-time or in-house course. This is mainly designed for those in personnel-related jobs (line managers, personal assistants, clerical staff, etc.) to acquire a range of relevant practical personnel skills. Successful completion grants Associate membership (AssocIPD) of the IPD and may enable them to proceed on the Professional Qualification Scheme.

NVQ/SVQ Level 4 and 5 in Management grant Licentiate membership of the IPD. NVQ/SVQ Levels 3 and 4 in Training and Development are recognised by the IPD for Associate membership and Licentiate membership respectively. NVQ/SVQ Level 5 in Training and Development is still under review by the NCVQ. NVQ/SVQ Levels 3, 4 and 5 in Personnel are expected to be available by Autumn 1996. Contact IPD for information about membership in relation to NVQ/SVQs in Personnel.

Further information

The Institute of Personnel and Development.

Secretarial, office and clerical work

Working in an office – secretarial work as a route to other careers – recruitment and entry – qualifications and training – further information

An estimated four million people, a sixth of the workforce, are clerical workers – the junior staff, the clerks, the receptionists, telephonists, typists and secretaries who provide the support services for administration and management in organisations of all kinds and sizes. Many work for organisations such as industrial and commercial firms, the Civil Service, local government and health service, but university departments and their professors, legal and medical practices, theatrical agents and architects' offices all need office and secretarial staff.

Almost a quarter of school-leavers, it is estimated, have traditionally gone into office work of some kind.

Secretarial and office work has changed with office automation. All the indications are that, after a slow start, the pace of automation in UK offices is speeding up, with most organisations now using PCs, and many office procedures are now computer-based.

For clerical staff, automation means the computer, or a terminal to it, which gives visual and keyboard access to, for example, customer accounts in insurance or mail order companies; booking systems in airlines and travel agencies; financial or other information systems and databases. It means the compact telephone switchboard, the sophisticated photocopier, fax machines and electronic mail.

The term 'typist' is now often replaced by 'word processor operator' and for secretarial/typing staff word processing is the norm. The document – letter, report, etc. – is printed out when the operator is satisfied it is correct – s/he can edit, correct, revise the text and print it by simply pressing another key.

Like all expensive machinery, systems have to be used to maximum efficiency to pay for themselves. For example, it becomes difficult to justify one secretary to one executive, if the secretary deals mainly with letters. The massive typing pool may be a less efficient way of organising typing than assigning a word-processor and operator/typist to a group of executives.

Automation in the office is likely to reduce, or at very least hold down, the number of jobs, especially for the unskilled. It could increase demand for technical experts, administrative staff, and could create some office jobs, simply because the machinery makes possible new activities for some people and organisations. For instance, with laser printers and desktop publishing software, secretaries can produce reports, etc. themselves at a standard which was only possible using conventional typesetting.

For young people going into secretarial or office jobs, the future will mean many, and frequent, changes. The route up for the poorly qualified school-leaver has already become much more restricted. Secretarial work may no longer be easy to return to after a career break without skills updating. Above all, the new entrant must gain as much training and experience on new machinery as possible and try to stay abreast of technology thereafter. *See* INFORMATION TECHNOLOGY AND COMPUTER WORK.

Working in an office

Clerical work – secretarial work, typing and word processing – personal or private secretaries – specialist secretaries – personal assistants

The tasks involved in office and secretarial work vary greatly, and the distinctions between 'secretary', 'private' secretary, 'executive' secretary, 'personal' secretary or assistant, shorthand typist, audio typist, clerk, etc. are often unclear. Work and responsibility varies from employer to employer. Work which is treated as clerical in some organisations becomes secretarial in others. In some organisations the work is entirely desk-, or workstation-, based. In others, there may be plenty of contact with other people, variety of tasks, opportunities to move around. The degree and level of personal responsibility, scope for initiative and decision making varies considerably.

Size can dictate the nature of the job. In a small organisation a single secretary may be able to cope with all the different tasks done separately by many office workers in a larger one. In a small firm it is possible to gain all-round experience, while there is a greater chance of specialising in the larger one, and it may be necessary to move around to gain different kinds of experience.

New technology has removed the worst drudgery from office work, e.g. tasks such as photocopying and calculations have become much quicker to perform, computer-based filing systems are less tiring to use and more efficient, the post room has been mechanised, etc.

Clerical work

Clerical work is mostly assumed (there are few hard-and-fast definitions) to involve a considerable amount of record- and account-keeping (which links up with financial work, book-keeping and accountancy, *see* FINANCIAL CAREERS), filing, photocopying and dealing with letters and telephone calls.

Clerical workers can begin as office juniors (and some will start as YT trainees), learning how work is organised through a series of minor but nevertheless crucial jobs which need little or no experience. They may collect, sort and distribute incoming mail, and collect and dispatch outgoing letters, learning about an organisation (what departments there are, what the organisation does, and who works where) at the same time. They may photocopy, do simple typing and filing, and generally help more senior staff, doing whatever jobs come up. In very large organisations, where something like the mail occupies an entire department, planned moves can help them to gain more rounded experience.

With experience, and training (in general office studies, in book-keeping, and/or in keyboarding, for example: see below), young office staff are usually given a job of their own, dealing with one task or possibly a series or group of related tasks. The work varies from organisation to organisation and from department to department. For example:

- in sales departments, each administrator deals with a group of accounts and sales records;
- in personnel, administrators look after staff records, list applicants for interviews, sort out job applications, deal with letters;
- 'figure work' may include calculating costs;
- transport clerks in public services work out timetables, rates and charges, and chart and record the journeys;
- transport and haulage administrators keep vehicle and driver records, seeing that vehicles are tested, sending out new licences as required, organising insurance, making out accident reports, etc.;
- shipping and export administrators become highly expert in customs, currency and other export regulations and may need languages.

Examples like this can be quoted from a wide range of occupations and employers, such as banking, insurance, educational institutions (including schools), trade unions, local government and the Civil Service, TV and film companies or building contractors.

Some administrators become telephonists and/or receptionists, or counter staff, for example, in travel agencies, hospitals, local council offices, firms of all kinds. Here they deal all the time with the public.

Some administrators specialise in, for example, filing – to store all kinds of paper records such as letters and invoices, personnel data, technical reports, drawings and blueprints, technical information, photographs.

In industry, administrators can become progress-chasers, combining office work with visits to the factory floor. Progress-chasing involves working out delivery dates for goods being made and finding out what needs to be done to meet them. (For example, when capacity is available on the factory floor to produce the goods, what components and raw materials are needed and what needs to be ordered.) Pricing jobs may be involved. This kind of work requires an interest in, and some knowledge of, technical detail, but this can be learnt from experience and observation. Progress-chasing, however, is one of the first jobs to go when a factory is fully automated.

Administrative work in more and more areas is being computerised – invoicing, making up pay, keeping records and accounts, calculating costs, figure work of all kinds, address lists, even filing. In such cases, the administrator becomes a computer, or VDU operator, using computer terminals to call up, input and extract data as needed from the computer file, keeping accounts and records up to date, revising address lists, abstracting information like production costs, or a list of overdue accounts. The administrator answering the phone may also use a screen to find out what to tell customers about the latest position on their order, the exact amount owing, or what theatre seats are available, for instance.

Most modern office technology is quick and easy for anyone to use. Some equipment may require special training, e.g. organisations that have their own printing/reprographic departments, where administrators may also be trained in, e.g., microfilming, which uses special cameras to record documents on film at a fraction of their original size.

Administrators have often learnt to type. Today, everyone in the office has to be able to use a keyboard, to access computer-based systems.

Secretarial work, typing and word processing

While there is no clear distinction between a clerk and a typist, or between a typist and a secretary, at the very least copy, shorthand and audio typists, and secretaries, should be trained to do accurate work at speed. Anyone who is a competent typist or secretary should be able to type at 50 words a minute, take shorthand at 90–100 words per minute, and/or transcribe directly from a dictating machine.

In some larger organisations, all the typists work together in one or more special sections, forming central, or sectional word processing services, producing work for whoever has work to be done, whether it is a tape or taking dictation, or documents to be retyped.

In other organisations, they may work in an office alongside other staff, or in an office of their own. Copy typists – or more usually word processor operators – also work on more complex documents such as invoices or other forms, and sheets of statistical data which may involve, for instance, taking figures from rough drafts, as well as handwritten manuscripts.

Shorthand typists take dictation in one of the accepted shorthand languages, such as Pitmans, and transcribe it; much of the work is inevitably letters, reports and memos. However, this does not always take up all their time, and so shorthand typists may also do other work, some of which may be secretarial (see below). Typing/secretarial staff often do their own filing.

Audio typing is when an administrator transcribes directly, eliminating the shorthand stage. The system not only saves typists' time in taking down the letters, but also makes it possible to arrange their work more efficiently, since anyone can type from a given tape, where shorthand typists generally transcribe only their own shorthand. Sales and other staff away from the office can also dictate into these machines over the phone or other communication links. Audio typists generally need better English (including spelling) and grammar than copy and shorthand typists, since they work from a verbal, not written, draft.

Shorthand typists and other secretarial staff can go on to become personal or private secretaries, but can also become administration supervisors, and office managers.

Personal or private secretaries

Personal or private secretaries must also be able to take dictation, type and word process extremely well, but they generally have other work to do. In fact, it is difficult to define exactly the role of the secretary, since most employers and individual secretaries have their own, usually fairly firm, views on what it should be.

Secretaries may work all the time for one, two, three or even more people. They generally do rather more than dictation and typing – indeed all but confidential material may be done by someone more junior. A properly employed secretary is, or should be, an assistant, who organises the employer's personal office and tries to see that it runs as smoothly as possible, takes at least some responsibility for day-to-day affairs, relieving the employer of the more mundane and time-consuming minutiae of working life.

Mostly secretaries deal with correspondence, draft the simpler replies, see that appointments are made (and do not clash) and travel arrangements organised, keep the diary up to date, make sure that filing is dealt with. A secretary acts as a buffer, takes phone calls and messages, and generally tries to solve as many problems as possible without bothering the 'boss'. Good employers let experienced secretaries take straightforward decisions on their behalf (although too many do not delegate at all, however well qualified, mature and experienced the secretary may be).

Specialist secretaries

Some secretaries specialise in the type of work they do.

Demand for secretary-linguists, fluent in at least one other language, is increasing. Their work generally includes reading and translating letters and orders both into and from their other language(s); coping with telephone calls in the language(s) they know; interpreting when people from overseas visit and sometimes going with staff to other countries to interpret for them there; reading, translating, and summarising reports, memos and newspaper or other articles. Secretary-linguists work for firms involved in importing and/or exporting either in the UK or overseas, multinationals, or inter- and supranational organisations. The role of the secretary-linguist is likely to increase in importance, with the European Single Market and the opening up of Eastern Europe.

Legal, farm, and medical secretaries specialise in working within one particular field, where secretaries have to understand and be able to use the specialised terminology and understand something of the nature of their employer's work – the legal framework, agricultural and EU regulations, or Health Service organisation, for example. Legal secretaries work for legal practices, the courts, and in legal departments; in addition to the usual secretarial work they prepare the more straightforward legal documents. Farm secretaries work for agencies, and travel between farms, spending one day a week dealing with all the paperwork for the farmer. Medical secretaries work for general practices, private consultants, and in hospitals.

Personal assistants

Personal assistants may have a fair amount of responsibility to use their own initiative and delegate routine secretarial work such as typing to others. They may draft letters, reports, memos, etc., collect and collate information, take minutes, greet and help entertain business contacts, organise meetings and conferences, etc. and possibly supervise other staff. Genuine PA posts are normally only with very senior executives. Elsewhere there is no guarantee that the title means any more than secretary.

Secretarial work as a route to other careers

Many school-leavers and graduates believe that they can use secretarial training and work as a stepping-stone into other work, especially in some of the more competitive areas. There are no hard-and-fast rules about this, except that it is usually much, much tougher than most anticipate, even where it is possible, and the competition is likely to be just as great. Initiative, drive, persistence, being ready and able to step in for an emergency, are all essential.

In many organisations in industry and professional practices, there are no recognised routes through to management or professional work. This can be because set qualifications are needed. Legal secretaries, for example, however well qualified and experienced, cannot become lawyers without going through the full training required. Secretary-linguists in export/import, on the other hand, can and do move on into sales and marketing.

Some industrial/commercial functions are open to secretarial staff who are capable of the work, although it may be difficult to get through to more senior positions without formal qualifications. Personnel, sales/marketing, public relations are possibilities.

Publishing recruits graduates first into secretarial work, to test motivation, aptitude and ability. The experience can act as a springboard into production, promotional/PR, contract-administration and, occasionally, editorial.

In broadcasting and films, the secretarial route can be a way into other careers, although the competition for production/creative jobs is just as intense as it is by the more formal routes. Experienced secretaries who show initiative and practical and creative skills compete for the formal training as production assistant some companies give, and in others work hard for a foot on the production ladder. Getting secretarial work in a non-production department – legal, personnel, engineering, publicity, etc. – may be necessary, to be on the spot when secretarial posts in drama, current affairs, and news fall vacant.

Journalism, generally, is not easy to break into in this way.

Recruitment and entry

Organisations of all kinds recruit clerical and secretarial staff direct from the education system, although most increasingly want trained, experienced and mature people, of whom there is a significant shortage. The trend is also to recruit more part-timers. There are fewer jobs for the unqualified, although some organisations still take on young people as trainees.

Modern, sophisticated office equipment and competitive conditions require better-educated workers. Learning how to use new technology takes intelligence – although once learnt it can be rather boring to operate. Some organisations do take on people offering the best available qualifications, even degrees, whether or not needed to cope with the job,

While formal educational qualifications may not be stipulated, in practice it makes sense to have the best possible general educational qualifications, and preferably as many appropriate skills as possible to stand the chance of a good career start.

For clerical-level work, the minimum should be around three or four GCSE/SCEs (grades A–C/1–3), or a GNVQ/GSVQ at Foundation or Intermediate level or NVQ Level 2 in Administration.

For secretarial training, at least one or two A-levels or equivalent in AS levels, with a numerate background (e.g. maths at GCSE) or an Administration/Information Technology NVQ/SVQ. There are also FE college secretarial courses for those with GCSEs or equivalent (*see below*). There is no real advantage to studying for an HND or degree just to become a secretary, but a postgraduate, or post-HND secretarial course may provide a route to a prestigious PA job.

Office and secretarial staff are personal assistants to the people for whom they work and so a temperament that accepts a supporting role is helpful.

A secretary is expected to be able and prepared to follow instructions and yet be capable of showing initiative; to be a good organiser, and to stay cool-headed and resourceful, particularly in a crisis; to be loyal, tactful and discreet, able to protect an employer from trivia, and capable of adapting to the employer's (reasonable) needs. Secretaries are expected to be unfailingly discreet, polite and good communicators. Additional qualities, particularly intelligence, confidence and business sense, will be needed by anyone aiming for promotion.

Qualifications and training

The advice is to gain as many business and secretarial skills as possible, which suggests a full-time course or training scheme. Very few organisations now give full-scale initial basic training, though some might, as part of a YT programme. It does not really matter how or where the essential skills are gained, but they now need to be as broadly based, and as up to date, as possible. They should include understanding how the office works, how to process information, organisational skills and word processing and audio typing as well as shorthand. Additional skills, such as one or more languages, are always useful.

Around 3,000 educational establishments offer secretarial training of some kind, including schools, and technical, commercial and further education colleges. Private colleges account for less than 5% of the total. Intensive courses at private schools offer a time advantage but may be expensive. It is essential to check that students are taught on modern office equipment, and that the training is in current office practices.

The type and length of course will depend on the qualifications and intentions of the students, but it is probably better now to spend a year gaining a full spread of business/secretarial skills than simply to learn shorthand typing in the shortest possible time. Most further education full-time courses last one or two years, depending on entry qualifications, and are generally 'integrated' courses covering the full range of office and secretarial skills backed by English, mathematics and other more general, useful, subjects such as economics, finance, basic law and languages. Some include the 'basics' of a function – advertising, marketing and personnel management.

FE colleges also put on 'specialist' courses, for legal secretaries (Association of Legal Secretaries exams, LCCIEB), medical secretaries (Association of Medical Secretaries, Practice Administrators and Receptionists exams), and farm secretaries (BTEC/SCOTVEC agricultural- or business-based award, or college award). Most courses are post-GCSE (A–C) or equivalent.

The variety of choice even within one college is often considerable, catering for all levels of qualifications and abilities from 16-plus school-leavers (normally now with at least some GCSE or equivalent qualifications) through to intensive courses for graduates aiming to become personal assistants. The courses now have a great variety of titles (e.g. Office Technology, Administration, Information Technology) to reflect the wide range of skills involved.

The major examining bodies, BTEC, LCCIEB, Pitman Qualifications, RSA and City & Guilds, provide tests in typing, shorthand, shorthand typing, audio typing, word processing, clerical duties, office procedures and secretarial duties. All offer NVQs in Administration and Information Technology, and many colleges now offer NVQ Level 3 and in some cases NVQ Level 4 courses. BTEC, City and Guilds and RSA have also developed GNVQs in Business at Foundation, Intermediate and Advanced level. It is often possible to select certain units which help students to specialise in their chosen career path, e.g. Administrative Operations.

Courses can include a European dimension, such as 'Living and Working in Europe', or a European language can be studied as part of the BTEC GNVQ. For those aiming to work as a secretary/administrator with foreign languages, several courses are offered by LCCIEB, RSA and the Institute of Linguists, e.g. The LCCIEB Commercial Language Assistant Certificate, the European Executive Assistant Certificate and the Diploma in European Business Administration. These Euroqualifications are bilingual awards at three levels designed for native speakers of English, French, Spanish and German. The LCCIEB also offer language units at Levels 1, 2 and 3 in French, German, Spanish, Italian and English, which can be take with an Administration NVQ.

Personal secretaries have to reach typing speeds of about 50 words a minute, and shorthand at up to 120 words a minute (although 80 words is acceptable). Audio typists are generally expected to type a 350-word tape in half an hour. Many colleges provide GCSE, A-level or equivalent courses as part of a secretarial training if students need them. Languages are increasingly useful, particularly those used commercially in Europe, and students should improve on their school-leaving skills if possible.

GNVQs (General National Vocational Qualifications), which are awarded by City & Guilds, BTEC and the RSA Examinations Board are now widely available in FE colleges and in school sixth forms. Business and IT courses are offered at Foundation and Intermediate levels (one year) and at Advanced level (two years) and prepare young people for employment in the business sector and (at Advanced level) provide access to higher education.

Further information

Examination syllabuses, etc. from the Business and Technology Education Council, the RSA Examinations Board, the London Chamber of Commerce and Industry Examinations Board, Pitman Qualifications, City & Guilds and the Associations mentioned above.

Contents

Information Technology and Computer Work

(CLCI: CAV, RAL)

Background

What is Information Technology? It includes the specification, design, development, testing, use and support of computer systems as well as the activities of maintenance and quality assurance (does it do what it was supposed to do, how well and what are the required standards?). The term 'information systems' is preferred by some to 'information technology' nowadays, because the computer, although still a central component, is increasingly part of a wider integration of communication networks and media. In any case solutions to the sort of problems involved need more than simply the writing of computer programs (software) – and more than computer science is needed to solve them. Many activities may be seen as a branch of engineering, particularly where the computers control highly technical equipment or machines. The British Computer Society has also chosen to describe the activities of its members as 'engineering' in a broader sense, because of the analogy between the process of design and construction of an information system and similar processes in engineering itself. But many applications have more to do with the analysis of business methods and organisations, or the science of information management, than with technology as such.

At least one in four people in the UK workforce now makes direct use of information technology in their jobs and by the year 2000 it is suggested this may double. To create and design the Information Technology systems they need and to support, maintain and develop these in use require technical knowledge and expertise, social and communication skills and an increasingly in-depth awareness of the nature of the business to which the information system applies.

One computer professional will be designing complex electronic circuits – this is a branch of electronic engineering. Another will be working with database systems, deciding the data to be held and how each item relates to the others. Another will be in charge of a HELP desk – ready to sort out queries coming in from a wide range of people using a particular computer system or software package. Then there are programs (software) to be designed and written and communication networks to be organised so that people in many parts of the world can work together. Documentation has to be written and 'end-users' trained to make the best use of the technology available.

There is a broad division between those jobs that require specialist technical knowledge – there is an overlap with the work of electrical and electronic engineers – and those that need the ability to take a logical and analytical view of the way people and organisations do things, in order to develop computer programs to support or replace human activity.

Some people specialise in one aspect of IT, for example, networking (getting a number of computers in different places to work together). Others work in a particular area of industry or business where computers are used – banking and financial systems, manufacturing, retailing, libraries and other information-providing services, hotel systems, local government and many more. Here they may use a range of skills and knowledge to provide support, advice and problem-solving for the less knowledgeable users of the systems. Some people, as they progress in their careers, start with a knowledge of IT and add experience in their chosen application area. Others may begin with experience of a business or industry and gravitate towards acquiring expertise in computing to apply to it.

The scope of IT is so wide that there cannot be a single profession called information technologist. As already described, more and more people spend more of their working time handling information and using IT systems, working at a computer terminal or a PC connected to a network of computers without being formally employed in information technology – or computing – as such. Jobs are being transformed by IT as well as new jobs being created and others lost. However, this does not mean everyone has to become an IT or computer expert – in fact much of the industry is now deliberately intent on making its systems as easy to use with as little training and computer expertise as possible, with growing success. Design engineers, architects, financial managers and business people of all types work with data as their raw material, using information systems to give them the required support. Journalists, printers, secretaries and doctors are just a few more examples of people using information systems to help them in their work.

However, even though users are becoming more involved in developing systems for themselves, this will not do away with the need for IT 'experts'. What it does mean is that new pathways into the profession have opened up. Some companies are now recruiting IT trainees from among internal staff already experienced in the business.

Future developments

Almost by definition, the information technology skills required for the future are going to be even more difficult to predict than in other occupational areas. IT itself is at the forefront of change, but is also no longer such a young industry as it was and is increasingly likely to follow the trade cycles in the rest of the economy. Interestingly, the National Computing Centre reports that in their 1995 survey of salaries and staff in IT, 'the five year forecast was abandoned as so many were unwilling or unable to predict their long-term staff requirements'. More even than in many other occupations, those working in IT will have to accept that the ability and willingness to retrain regularly are going to be vital to the survival of their careers. According to the Institute for the Management of Information Systems (IDPM) 'the half life of most IT skills is now only three years and is falling. Current training and experience provide only a toe-hold in the job market. Most skills content will be obsolete inside five to six years, leaving only the basic discipline.' The following comments must be read in the light of this.

The key developments to the year 2000 are likely to come from the linking of computer technology with a new generation of information and communication media – telephones, TVs and video – to provide what is referred to by some experts as 'social computing': on-line information services (call up the information on your own computer via a network from some other organisation or outside source, don't collect or store it yourself), video conferencing (don't waste time travelling to meet people, simply put them all in visual, audio and computer contact with one another at once and let them talk) and multimedia (linking text to sound and static or moving pictures, controlled by a computer, thus greatly improving the impact of marketing or the speed of learning depending on your purpose). The telecommunications and cable TV companies will be big players and developers in the new world of IT but in close cooperation with hardware manufacturers and software providers.

The developing use of such communications networks, whether internal to an organisation, connecting it to external collaborators, customers or competitors, or international as in the case of the Internet, the worldwide 'network of networks' has implications for future careers. However, despite the massive increase in access to information produced by the uses of the Internet, it has so far had little direct impact on job structures in professional Information Technology work. What is clear is that those who work on the creation, installation, management and maintenance of networks are likely to be in considerable demand. This is where the main shortage of skills is likely to exist. Such networks are just as likely to be in-house or between organisations as international.

Networks, because, *ipso facto*, they increase the insecurity of the system, are also likely to lead to a rise in jobs associated with security of data, from specialists dealing with anti-virus defences and treatments to those concerned with patent and copyright law, or the confidentiality and protection of data against unauthorised access.

One possible negative implication of worldwide networks, however, is that to work with others, you no longer need be in the same room, the same building or even the same country. In this way someone with IT skills can work in several countries at once. By the same token, any other IT professional in the world could be his or her direct competitor for that work. Software needed in Europe might easily be written by a programmer in the Far East who can be in regular touch with the software house or user s/he works for via international communication networks. This aspect of global competition is, of course, likely to affect many occupations in the future, but IT is often in the vanguard of such developments, and its professionals have often made them possible.

After the electronic communications business, retailing and distribution (including hotels and catering) is one of the areas of fastest growth at the time of writing. 'Electronic retailing' (with all kinds of retail businesses offering information to customers via pages on the Internet and so on) is one reason. Many people see a clear potential for developments here, with multimedia and networking playing a big part. Increasingly automated checkouts and stock control systems linked to suppliers are other developments in this area. Other major areas of growth will be in finance and business services (one of the areas of highest financial reward for IT staff), utilities (energy and water supply for example) and transport.

Multimedia, though an exciting development, is not expected to have great impact on career progressions, although it clearly opens up new options for the delivery of training of all kinds, and will mean a demand for professional IT skills in improving the interface between human users and the computer systems.

IT employment in the past has tended to follow a cyclical pattern, according to a survey in 1995 by the Institute for the Management of Information Systems (IDPM) and 'Computer Weekly'. After a static period in the early 1990s, skill shortages are emerging again in the latter part of the decade, but may peak around the year 2000. Demand is likely for electronics design and software engineers, and others working with information systems. New operating systems currently being introduced and the products linked with them will also mean work to be done on converting old systems and implementing the new over the next few years. Those whose job it is to provide support to the less knowledgeable users of IT are also likely to have good prospects in the future.

There has been an increase in 'outsourcing' of some kinds of IT work, according to the survey, with companies taking a hard look at how much they need in-house technical skills, and how far these can be contracted out or bought in when wanted. Like many other professionals, the IT specialist's traditional career opportunities in a large company with an IT department may be replaced with work in smaller central units, outside consultants, or specialist firms contracted to deliver IT services or manage projects for a range of companies. By the same token, companies will need managers whose knowledge of the business and of IT enables them to monitor the progress of such contracts and liaise with such external suppliers to ensure quality of service.

Programming, particularly applications programming, perhaps the most obvious of the IT occupations, is likely to do less well. Employment for programmers dropped considerably in the first half of the 1990s. This may be in part because there was a drop in recruitment of new staff in Information Technology due to the recession, and trainee programmer is a common entry point to the profession for many, particularly at graduate level. A more durable trend, on the other hand, is that development of new programs is becoming more and more subservient to ability to analyse the needs of user organisations. This may be one reason why, along with network skills, demand for support staff for the end-users of computer and information systems is likely to experience the most rapid growth in the next few years, along with (but more than) that for systems analysts and analyst/programmers. New types of skills required include (according to the National Computing Centre's 1996 survey) 'a number of technologies associated with the development of client-server applications (e.g. UNIX, relational database management systems, and GUI development packages and languages.' (GUI = graphical user interface – i.e. the form the computer uses to convey its information to the user, and how that user enters his or her requests and controls what happens.)

Surprisingly, perhaps, as personal desktop computers, often networked, replaced the use of mainframes, operators were still in demand in 1995. As the IDPM report comments '. . .even decentralised and networked client-server systems still need someone to monitor performance, change the paper and take the back-ups!'. However, the overall employment trend is gently downwards.

Working in Information Technology

The professional/technical functions

Just as other workers are learning how to use the technology, people whose main skills are in IT have had to become acquainted with the application area in which they work. An organisation needs to integrate its information systems, which include the human resources implementing and running them, with its business goals. Thus the people in the IT department must be aware of the overall business strategy and relate to the organisation rather than just to the world of IT.

Technology changes are almost continuous. As a result, organisations change the way in which they work and, in turn, the jobs and type of work within IT also change. There used to be a fairly obvious division between those working in software development (the majority) and those designing, manufacturing, installing and maintaining the physical equipment – the hardware. As with the division between computing and application, the division between hardware and software has also become blurred. For example, organisations working in the telecommunications and networking areas require people with experience in both software and engineering or else people willing to learn and train in those disciplines.

Information systems and technology is a frequent agent of change in working practices in other occupational areas, causing some jobs to disappear, others to become less skilled or important, and requiring others again to master new areas of knowledge and competence. It is not surprising that working in IT means dealing with similar changes in the nature of one's own work role.

Job specifications are thus changing all the time and the boundaries between, for example, what a 'programmer' does and what a 'systems analyst' does have become much less clear. A large amount of programming having been absorbed into systems analysis and design, IT staff need to be more people-orientated. The solitary programmer sitting absorbed at a terminal is now a rarity. Job titles such as 'analyst/programmer' are a product of this development, and can offer particularly satisfying work for those who enjoy a balance between working in a team and solving problems on their own.

In part this may be to do with the general tendency in all forms of industry towards working in teams with all members being responsible to some extent for the end product, as opposed to the older divisions of labour with strict demarcations. However some basic types of work in information systems and technology have remained relatively stable, though who actually does them and what they are called may be decided more by the needs of a particular organisation than by any unique qualities of the occupation.

Equal opportunities in IT

The ratio of women to men in professional IT work roles is still in men's favour but this is changing. The Women into Information Technology Foundation (WIT) was created at the end of 1989 with the objective of raising the number and proportion of girls and women entering and sustaining IT careers at all levels. Due to lack of funding, the organisation died in October 1995. Percentages of women in different occupations vary, but probably average between 25% and 35% in most cases (1995 data). Competence and qualifications in IT may have particular advantages for men or women who need to combine looking after children at home with a career, because of the relative ease of working at home, connected by network to various other centres of the organisation.

More important in many ways is the continuing bias against older workers. The percentage aged under 30 was down from 37% in 1993 to 29% in 1995 according to the IDPM report, but there is still discrimination against those over 40 entering the profession. The fact that the sharp fall in recruitment of new staff during the recession of the early 90s has meant the average age of existing staff has risen, and it is possible that this may have a longer-term effect in softening attitudes to older employees as the industry itself becomes more established if not more stable.

The main occupations

Systems analyst – business analyst – systems designers – software engineer – programmer – computer operators – computer operations management – research and development work – information centre work – computer sales support – maintenance – consultancy – selling – training staff – managing in IT – communications/ network management – database management or administration – project management – security

Because the rate of change in information technology is relatively high, it is difficult to keep track of the specific job titles used, many of which overlap and merge into one another. The traditional names of operator programmer, systems analyst and manager are still a helpful starting point, though not sufficiently flexible or comprehensive. Programming can be divided into applications programming, which is less technically demanding than systems programming, and the title is combined as analyst/ programmer to indicate someone who performs functions drawn from both programming and systems analysis, perhaps before moving on to the latter job. Software engineer is a similar title to systems programmer and may indicate someone particularly involved in developing software to control equipment or machines rather than commercial or business activities. Other job titles may include database administrator, computer sales support, consultant, project manager, and so on.

The National Computing Centre's survey of staff salaries uses seven broad occupational headings which provide an alternative way of defining the functions involved as opposed to occupations – management, systems analysis, analyst/ programmers, end-user support, technical support, network staff and operations.

Systems analyst

It is impossible to say what is a typical systems analysis task since such a very wide range of activities are covered. Some may take no more than a morning. Some may take years. Some may be carried out by a single analyst. Others may require the efforts of a large team. The person concerned will probably have some experience already in another role such as programming before becoming an analyst.

The first part of a systems analyst's job is usually to prepare a 'feasibility study' to decide if, for example, a problem could be solved or a new idea for the development of the business could be feasibly supported by the use or development of IT. The feasibility study identifies the users' objectives, investigates the way the business is carried out and establishes an outline solution together with costs and the benefits it will bring. The analysts carrying out this study identify information bottlenecks and also idiosyncratic activities tolerated in a human environment but not by a computer demanding predictability and precision.

If, after the feasibility study, it is decided to proceed with the project, the analyst carries out a more detailed requirements study. This involves looking at how data, documents and reports are used and organised, observing how things are done, interviewing the staff and collecting details of the volume of work carried out – how many orders are received in a day, how many during the peak period, what is the average (and maximum) number of items on an order? The aim is to define exactly all the data items and their relationships, all the relevant procedures, output requirements and performance objectives. These are written up as a specification from which the system designer will work. (With smaller projects or systems, the same person may carry out both roles.)

One of the most important aspects of working as an analyst is to win the cooperation of the people being interviewed, the people who will be the actual users of the new system. Staff are often initially mistrustful of analysts whom they see as a threat to long-established and familiar work practices. Fear of the technology may no longer be so prevalent but fear of losing their jobs is still there. A good analyst tries to overcome this mistrust by keeping staff fully informed of the purpose and progress of the analysis, listening carefully to their suggestions and assuring them that wherever possible they will have a say in the design of the new system, will be fully trained and that its implementation will lead to improvements in their job.

Systems analysis and design needs people who can think themselves into the potential user's position, to see what they and their organisations do, and why, and what they want a computing system to do for them. They have to be able to explain technicalities in non-technical terms, know how to get people to explain their work, and be tactful.

Business analyst

There is no clear demarcation line between business and systems analysts and designers, but, as people progress in their career, they tend to specialise in different areas.

Business analysts investigate user requirements and interpret them to IT staff. This involves looking at the way data enters, flows round an organisation and the form in which it is sent out. Business analysts have a detailed knowledge of, and experience in, the particular business area and also sufficient knowledge of IT to be able to see the work closely with IT specialists to work out the best solution. In many cases, the role of business and systems analyst may be combined in the same person.

Systems designers

The result of systems analysis is the specification of requirements. The next step is to decide how these will be met. If the system is a completely new one, the hardware for it will have to be selected. If the user organisation already has other systems running, this will probably determine what hardware is used and the database system may have been selected for earlier applications. Even so, it will be necessary to decide what extra resources are required. These may be central ones such as extra processor power or data storage as well as the local workstations and printers.

Data analyses have to be carried out so that decisions can be made as to how the data items are to be stored in the database. Screen and report layouts must be designed. The system is divided into a number of programs; some of these will run on-line giving users access to the data from their terminals as and when they need it. Others will be batch programs which, once started, run to completion. One example is the printing of customer statements. Since this program has to access details of invoices to produce a summary of all those outstanding for each customer, it cannot run at the same time as new invoices are being created or payments of existing ones being entered.

There are various techniques for specifying what programs are to do. Some are very formal, perhaps using mathematical notations but, whatever the method, the user has to agree that the specification is correct and therefore needs to be able to understand it. The specification also needs to be rigorous so that there are no arguments at a later stage as to whether or not the finished product meets requirements. While specifications are being produced, test data needs to be assembled. Some of this test data will come from the analyst/programmers but data for acceptance tests should be provided by the users.

Systems designers will probably tend to have a more technical qualification or background, and may come to this job from software engineering. But the job may also be combined with analysis if the project or the system is a small one.

Software engineer

The term software engineering is used in a variety of ways. In the strict sense it has the same relationship to programming and system development as structural engineering has to building a bridge. It includes the work involved in deciding exactly how a particular IT task is to be carried out. Concerned with high technology, it requires knowledge of the hardware as well as the software. Many of the projects carried out by software engineers are ones which have to respond in real time, often in safety critical situations, exciting to do but requiring in-depth and wide-ranging knowledge of IT. They may involve the programming of technological equipment rather than business activities. However, 'software engineer' is a term sometimes used almost interchangeably with that of systems designer/analyst and which term is used may have more to do the nature of the organisation than that of the job carried out.

Programmer

It is the programmers' job to translate the specifications (e.g. from the system designer) into a computer program and fully test it using, firstly, test data they have devised, and then that provided by the users.

A computer program is a step-by-step list of instructions that conveys the logic of the program in a form which the computer can use. Programs for the earliest computers had to be in the binary code (on/off pulses) in which computers work. The first improvement was to low-level 'languages', easier to write but each one still specific to a particular type of computer. Higher-level languages evolved with some standardisation between different computers. These were usually designed for particular types of work: FORTRAN (mathematical and scientific work) and COBOL (business applications). Source code, written by the programmer, is translated into the object code (which the computer understands) by the computer itself.

The use of fourth generation languages (4GLs) has led to the division between analyst and programmer becoming more blurred, which is perhaps shown by the now common term 'analyst/programmer'. Using a 4GL, a simple personnel or stock recording system can be developed in a day. At the other extreme are complex problems involving hundreds of man-years and corresponding large budgets. The building of the pyramids took hundreds of man-years of effort but was relatively simple. Designing and making a watch in the sixteenth century was complex but could be carried out by one man. It is the mixture of size and complexity that makes the development of many systems, particularly if they are real-time systems, such a problem.

4GLs, which tend to be linked with the use of a database management system, allow the person writing the programme to specify what is to be done without specifying how it is to be done. 4GLs can make it easier to build a prototype, a simplified version of all or a part of the proposed system. This can be tried out by users prior to full development. This can help users discover the best way of carrying out certain procedures before it is too late to change the specification and also test out some of the assumptions made by the designers.

The use of modern database systems allows tailored programs to be built up from blocks with the programmer just specifying a number of parameters such as the name of an item to be displayed on the screen, how many characters must be allowed for it, whether they can be letters as well as figures, and what checking must be carried out if an item is being entered.

A very simple example of how programming has become much more streamlined and, to an extent, deskilled, in the last few years is the entering of a date. At one time, a programmer would include in a program using dates a routine to check, for example, that 29th February was entered only in a leap year. Each time the program came to the point where a date was to be entered, there was an instruction to call this routine. Now, having specified that a particular input item is a date, the software system 'knows' what checking is to be carried out, what error messages are to be produced and how the figures entered are to be stored.

Routines such as this are stored in 'libraries' available to the programmer who needs to know nothing about them except that they are there. It is partly because of advances like this that applications programming, in particular, is being absorbed into the work of the analyst/programmer.

While hardware costs have been falling, staff costs have been rising, so that there has been the spur to develop still easier ways of programming and thus reduce the time required for it. Two other reasons for the introduction of fourth generation languages are: an emphasis on end-user facilities; and the need for modern programs to be flexible so that they can be modified and enhancements added.

With 4GLs data structures and how data items are manipulated are the starting point for coding. With object-oriented languages, one type of fifth generation language, the data structures and the processes which manipulate them are combined into one unit – the object. Objects respond to messages from other objects and are triggered into performing a particular action depending on the form of the message and its source. The idea behind the organisation of this type of language is that it mimics the real world, for example a company with a number of departments, each carrying out particular functions depending on the messages it receives from other departments

Programmers have to be methodical, accurate, very painstaking and able to concentrate for fairly long periods. To go on to more complex programming, into systems analysis or design, needs, in addition, the ability to analyse complex situations and processes, reduce them to basic essentials and produce practical, sensible solutions in clear, easily understood instructions.

Many people enter IT at this level. The traditional progression is from trainee programmer to analyst/designer or analyst/programmer and then team/section/project leader. How much responsibility and managerial work team leaders carry varies from job to job and the size of teams. Most continue to do a considerable amount of technical work but also decide how to divide the work between the team and supervise and co-ordinate it. They may also have to cost the projects on which they are working and deal with budgets. They may be involved in planning the work of the department and in assessing new products.

Applications programming

Application programs, the instructions which carry out specific tasks required by the users, can be written specially for a particular user; this is bespoke or tailor-made software. This can obviously be an expensive way of acquiring software and, where there are numbers of users requiring the same type of processing, a service company may write a package which divides the development costs between all the users. Payroll and accounting are obvious examples but packages are available in practically all application areas. Programs that enable you to carry out word processing on your computer or use a spreadsheet (e.g. LOTUS) are also applications software packages. (So are computer games, and the sort of software used in careers education and guidance to provide self-assessment and matching to jobs.)

Systems programming

The systems programmer's job is to write and develop systems software. This is the software which 'internally manages' the functioning of the hardware. The major part of it is the operating system and even the smallest computer needs at least a simple one to organise the writing of data to disc and keep track of the instruction sequence. As systems become multi-user and distributed over wide areas, operating systems become more and more complex.

Systems programming is more technical than writing applications programs and requires a higher degree of technical knowledge or background. Systems programmers also monitor and tune the operating systems to improve performance, for example reducing the time taken for a terminal to respond to a request from the user. Sometimes, if a fault develops, a systems programmer, working for either the supplier or the user organisation, may write a 'fix' which bypasses the problem until new software can be produced. When changes are made or new software installed, it has to be fully tested before the applications go 'live'. To do this, it may be necessary to set up and maintain a complete set of test data and programs specifically for this purpose.

Computer operators

When the system is up and running, there is the everyday work of looking after the computers and their associated peripherals. In a small company, this job is generally the responsibility of one or two of the senior end-users. It mainly consists of ensuring suitable procedures for the day-to-day running are set up and adhered to, maintenance and servicing are carried out as required, consumables available and newcomers trained to use the system. Those organisations with a larger system require some specialised staff. Distributed systems – decentralised use of the computer – both changed the work content and reduced the number of people required so that the demand for operators is falling. Output which used to be produced in the computer centre and distributed to users is now generally printed at local sites so that servicing and care of printers and terminals become the responsibility of the user departments. However, they are likely to come to the computer operations department if any problems occur or when upgrades are required.

In some installations, operators have to keep the systems working round the clock on a shift basis with routine maintenance and enhancements being carried out at the less busy times – weekend and overnight. Much of the work is routine, monitoring that the system is running properly, making backup files, keeping records but ready to spring into action if anything goes wrong. This may mean running diagnostic routines and sending for the appropriate expert – systems programmer, maintenance engineer, etc.

As an operator you need to be methodical and able to work under pressure. You need to be able to learn and understand the various commands which have to be entered into the computer, to remember how to reply to responses given by the computer and have to become familiar with the various operating systems used. You are likely to be working as part of a close-knit team, perhaps on shift work so that you must be able to develop good personal relationships with your colleagues.

Computer operations management

This is primarily concerned with keeping the installation, usually with a network of distributed terminals, working as efficiently as possible. It involves seeing to staffing levels, scheduling and organising maintenance, repair and enhancement to keep 'down-time' to a minimum. With workstations in departments, there has to be a facility to rapidly respond to problems encountered by end-users. In a large IT department running for a large part of the 24 hours, there will be a team of shift managers/supervisors.

Research and development work

Much of the fundamental research and development in IT is carried out in universities. Manufacturers and larger service companies also have R&D departments. People in IT R&D departments may be working at the 'frontiers' of research in materials science, physics, electronics and computer science.

Information centre work

The old-fashioned Data Processing Department has now changed into an Information Centre concentrating more on helping users than doing the data processing for them. This means assisting them to manage their own information needs, perhaps providing the internal equivalent of a full consultancy or, alternatively, helping them choose a service supplier with the required expertise. Designing a local area network for their PCs, assessing software packages for use in departments and training users on new software, equipment etc. may all be part of the job provided that the skills are available in-house. But the computer system must still be kept running so there is still the need for some operators. The centre may also provide expensive equipment which departments can share, for example graphic plotters.

The HELP desk facility comes within the province of the Information Centre, but a similar 'hotline' is sometimes provided by hardware and software suppliers. By dialling in, the user can get advice on a particular problem and it may be possible to connect the user's machine to a terminal in the supplier's office so that the problem can be diagnosed remotely without an on-site visit.

Computer sales support

Such a person usually works for a computer hardware or equipment manufacturer and will give technical advice to customers in support of the sales force, about the systems that are proposed or available. It may involve demonstrating products, or writing technical proposals, etc.

Maintenance

The installation and servicing of computer systems are carried out by field service technicians and engineers. They perform diagnostic tests to identify the source of failure or the need for preventative maintenance and work mainly at the customer's site. Those concerned with the hardware tend to have qualifications in electronics but knowledge of the software is needed for many maintenance tasks. Specialist training is given by the service companies with progression from simpler to more complex systems and more responsibility for the work carried out. Further promotion can be to troubleshooting where the technician cannot solve the problem, supervisory work and management of maintenance services.

Consultancy

A carefully thought out IT strategy can help companies open up new opportunities, achieve higher productivity and gain a competitive edge. This requires a full study of the organisation's philosophy and management style and the identification of current business needs and opportunities for new and enhanced IT systems. Production of such a strategy can often be helped by the expertise of outside consultants.

Each consultant tends to specialise in a particular area but they can be used to produce requirement specifications, design computer systems and help select specialist suppliers. They work with, and draw on, the expertise of other IT professionals. They must be able to communicate with customers at every level in the organisation and involve them in the decisions being made.

A consultant starts by gathering the facts, finding out exactly what the position is now and what is required. This sounds simpler than it often is. It can be that traditional practices should be changed or that management attitudes need to be modified – hence the need for tact and careful presentation of the findings. Sometimes it is advisable to put forward a number of options, leaving the final decision to the customer.

Selling

This ranges from the highly technical business of selling sophisticated and expensive systems to commercial, industrial and other organisations to the rather more straightforward job of selling small personal computers in High Street shops. The latter is learnt, mostly on-the-job, in the same way as learning to sell other electronic goods, such as videos. Microcomputers for smaller businesses are sold by specialist computer/systems shops and here some experience both in computing and in running a business is needed.

Sales teams selling more sophisticated machines generally specialise in a particular kind of computer or system and/or selling to a particular market, for example insurance companies or banks. These sales men and women need plenty of experience of the company's products; this is normally gained in sales support – answering simpler queries from potential customers, organising training for new users' staff and so on. Some sales staff come through the analyst/programmer route and, in some companies, the line between systems analysis/engineering and sales is very ill defined. Promotion is to sales management and marketing although it is possible to go over to IT management.

Training staff

Manufacturers, software and systems houses and larger users employ their own training staff and there is a growing number of independent training establishments as well as opportunities to work in schools, further and higher education. Training ranges from teaching the simplest keyboarding to trainees on a training for work or youth credits programme through to giving seminars on the latest 'state-of-the-art' product to already highly qualified professionals.

Training is usually a 'second career' for people who have extensive experience in the relevant area of the technology. But this is not enough. Also essential are the abilities to communicate, to establish a positive relationship with 'students', whether school children, operators of a newly commissioned computer system or managing directors, and to structure a learning program to suit the intended audience.

Managing in IT

Without IT staff who understand the business and line managers who are computer-literate, solving the problems of responsibility, strategy planning and priorities is difficult.

To whom an IT manager reports and whether or not they have a seat on the board are indicators of status, and board membership is becoming more common. This improving status has considerable implications for IT experts' career structures. Their skills are crucial in the management of the rapid change with which many organisations now have to cope. They have to assess projects carefully, set realistic limits to what can be done with available resources, look for more effective ways of achieving what is needed – in other words positively 'manage' demand.

An IT manager running a small department will deal personally with most functions. Within larger departments, the growing range of managerial and administrative responsibilities may be divided and, in some areas, a team of staff may be needed. Planning, tackling the thorny problems of future hardware and software needs, responsibility for efficient services (despite machine and software failures, problems with input etc.), recruitment and training are all part of the managerial job. Not least is managing a group of people with different skills and experience.

Choosing to take on a management role means realising that staff (often an interdisciplinary team) will know more about their own speciality than does the manager, but the manager's responsibility is to give them the support and create the conditions in which they can work most productively.

Communications/network management

The goal is to integrate all communication systems – fax, telephone and computer text, data and graphics – and telecommunications managers are currently in great demand with comparatively few people having the right technological background. They have to be able to keep up with the fast-moving technology, to assess what is on offer and how important new products are, assess company needs, know what to buy, work out what will 'talk' to what, spot the problems and troubleshoot.

Database management or administration

Responsible for the development, control, maintenance, security and administration of the database system, the database administrator plays an important role in an organisation. It includes setting up procedures to ensure that the data cannot be corrupted and setting up and enforcing standards for its use including those necessary to comply with external regulations such as the Data Protection Act. There must be forward planning – monitoring what users want in future and how this is to be met – as well as the day-to-day tasks of seeing that new and revised information is loaded to schedule and accurately. This also involves organising staff, making sure that programs and equipment are maintained and updated, that users' problems are solved, etc.

The introduction of a systems encyclopedia may require significant changes to the whole organisation since it should become the pivot around which all system development and maintenance revolve. Database administrators should be senior enough to be party to corporate policies and politics and have sufficient authority to ensure that the systems encyclopedia strategies are implemented. Whether or not they come from the IT or business side of the organisation depends on the career paths within the organisation, the management structure and the availability of the 'right person at the right time'.

Project management

If a project is to be successful, it must be well managed. The more complex the project, the more important this task becomes compared with the technical tasks. External events, maybe outside the control of the organisation developing the system, can have an effect on the progress, quality, cost and viability of the project. These influences may be political, organisational, legal, technical or financial. Thus project managers of large IT systems have a great deal of responsibility; they may come originally from either the IT or business side but, in both cases, they need an overall knowledge of both the problem area and the proposed solutions.

Security

One specialist area into which a career in IT might develop is security. This term has a special meaning in relation to computer and information technology, where particular problems of protecting sensitive data and systems from unauthorised access often combine with a need to allow wide public access to information over relatively open networks. The issues may include such matters as developing protective and curative solutions for problems caused by computer viruses or business and industrial espionage, to legal matters relating to copyright, intellectual property, and the Data Protection Act. Some larger organisations will employ an information security officer

Employment prospects

Users – hardware manufacturers and equipment suppliers – service companies and organisations offering special support to users – bureaux – facilities management – software services – systems houses – value added resellers – maintenance – self-employment or freelance contracting – consultancy – other areas

IT is a tool enabling a wide range of activities to be carried out more efficiently. IT systems are used in all sectors – financial institutions and business services (banks, the City, insurance, etc.), the Civil Service and local government, the Armed Forces, transport, manufacturing of all kinds, the Health Service, the media (broadcasting, newspapers, etc.), retailing, education. Their use is spreading fast within smaller businesses and also through the professions – accountants, general practitioners, lawyers, architects, surveyors.

Thus practically all employing organisations are using IT in some form. But this does not mean that all do now, or will in the future, employ IT professionals. In many cases it is the architects and engineers, clerks and accountants who are using IT to help them in their work. The packages now widely available – word processors, spreadsheets and application packages – make it possible for many organisations to manage their internal information systems efficiently and effectively without the need for specialist internal staff. Even with sophisticated and complex systems, it is often more efficient to use outside resources (service companies) for the technical work and to provide training, than to have an internal IT department.

Employment patterns are changing. The particular form in which information is required changes as strategies and market conditions change and obtaining it is increasingly being carried out by end-users themselves. In large organisations these people will be working to a ground plan devised by an IT services division or department or information centre which will also provide support. However, this trend cannot go too far; not many lawyers and doctors want to spend large proportions of their time developing computer systems instead of dealing with clients or treating patients.

The size of the UK IT industry has been estimated at around 400,000 people, though because it includes functions and activities carried out right across UK industry as a whole the definition is a little vague. Users (as opposed to hardware manufacturers, software houses and so on) are currently estimated to employ some 75% of specialist computer staff but developments such as facilities management (where a company's computer department is run by another, specialist IT service organisation) make this also a difficult statistic to assess.

Of the seven main occupational areas surveyed by the National Computing Centre in 1995, the largest numbers of current employees were Analyst/Programmers (68% of respondents employ them and expect to increase this number significantly), Managers (obviously enough nearly all organisations have these), Systems Analysts, End-user Support staff and Operations. In each of these last three categories around half the firms surveyed employ such people.

Users

In terms of sectors, computing departments are the largest recruiters of IT specialists – any sizeable organisation has such a department and about half to two-thirds of the IT professionals in the UK work in such departments.

However, as more companies contract out their IT work, the proportion of total staff employed directly by users may fall. For example, if a large user company hands over the work of its IT department to an outside service organisation, hundreds of people can move from being employed by a user to being employed by a service company. One reason for the move to 'facilities management' (as it is called) is the difficulty users find in obtaining specialist skilled staff – for example, those with experience of setting up a complex network of computers. A site may only need such a specialist for a short time, whereas a service company can move 'experts' to different users as necessity demands. Not only does the user get a better service but the specialist does not become bored by working in an environment which is much less exciting once the system has been implemented.

Many of the departments are small with ten or less people. The extent to which specialist IT staff is employed depends largely on:

1 the size and range of the organisation and its IT/computing systems
2 how much use they make of 'outside' specialist companies and staff and this can range from hardly any to the 'contracting out' of all IT work
3 how far IT responsibilities are 'integrated' into other people's work.

For example, most small businesses and professional practices go to outside specialists when installing or upgrading their systems, buy 'off-the-shelf' software and train their own staff in its use and operation. In larger organisations, use of IT can expand to the point where a director or partner 'becomes' a specialist IT manager and some IT staff are employed. Note, however, the 'becomes': at the management level, it is perhaps more likely that someone within the business gains IT experience than that an IT expert comes in and learns the business. Sometimes the move may be in the opposite direction. An in-house systems analyst may develop and install an IT system for a department or small business working with the manager in charge of the department and gaining a great deal of experience in the procedures carried out. If the manager leaves, or is promoted, the systems analyst may be the person selected as the replacement.

As is to be expected, it is the larger organisations which employ the most specialist IT staff and some of these departments may employ a few hundred people.

IT departments/divisions in larger organisations may be semi-independent 'profit centres', working on 'contract' to other such separate units within the organisation, possibly competing with outside contractors and even, in some instances, working as an outside contractor for other organisations. This forces these departments to work to tighter budgets and schedules, perhaps with their own financial managers, and means that some IT staff effectively become consultants within their own employing organisation. Some larger organisations have major research facilities working on the development of IT systems; others are looking at advanced applications, for example a major chemical company developing expert systems for use both in-house and by customers.

Major user groups include the energy companies (one example being the use of computer control systems for oil and gas platforms), manufacturing industry (as well as administrative purposes and management information the use of IT here may include production control and automation), banking and financial services, retailing and distribution, the public sector including education, local and central government and, of course, the armed forces.

Hardware manufacturers and equipment suppliers

A number of large, mostly international, companies dominate the market, developing, making and selling computers and systems of all shapes and sizes. Some make components, peripheral and ancillary equipment (printers, terminals, modems or scanners, for example) or network and communication systems, etc. In such a fast-moving business they have to make fine judgements about how long to go on making products. Some specialise in particular markets, for example retailing (with its needs for point-of-sale terminals), manufacturing or financial services.

Computer manufacturers produce software as well as hardware, not only systems software but also applications programs to run on their equipment and machines. In addition to selling, leasing and renting computers, ancillary equipment and software packages, they may also provide many of the services associated with a service industry. Maintenance may be carried out by the manufacturer although it is often done by specialist firms. Manufacturers also provide hardware to other IT suppliers for incorporation into systems being developed for single customers or into products for general sale. They also carry out research and development, often in collaboration with universities and other research organisations and often covering software as well as hardware.

Configuring (working out which components are needed for a customer's system) and installing computers or IT systems may be carried out by the manufacturer or by a service company. Running-in and testing larger systems can still be quite a lengthy business, and may need a team of systems experts and engineers.

Employment in this sector may draw on the more technical skills and backgrounds. A background in materials science, chemistry, or mechanical or electrical engineering may be as useful as computer science or software engineering. Roles will probably include the management of materials, production planning, and supervising, testing and quality assurance of products. Maintenance engineering is also a part of this area.

There will be vacancies in design and development work, implementing ideas generated by a much smaller number of research staff. Network design and management will be an opportunity where the company is involved in telecommunications.

There are major world competitors for the UK hardware and equipment suppliers particularly from the Far East.

Service companies and organisations offering special support to users

The UK software and services industry has grown rapidly since its inception but, as described above, this growth slowed by the recession of the early 1990s. It is now picking up again rapidly.

Service companies are given various names – software/systems houses, bureaux, consultancies, value added resellers (VARs) being just a few. It is easier to list the types of work carried out than describe the companies themselves since some specialise in one type of service, others provide many different types. All service companies are geared to constant change, to developing in parallel with what is happening in the IT business and to meeting – and anticipating if possible – demand from customers.

Bureaux

Even if a company has its own computer, there can be circumstances in which it needs an outside processing ability. Bureaux provide this with companies able to rent time or have their work carried out on a regular or irregular basis with, if necessary, telecommunications links between the customer and bureau machines. Until the advent of the microcomputer and off-the-shelf packages, sales and purchase ledger processing were the major bureaux applications, but this work is now nearly all carried out in-house. But a large minority of UK companies may use a bureau for payroll because continual changes in legislation pose an unacceptable burden on in-house systems.

Bureaux also provide network services – for example, organisations can locally attach their computers and terminals to managed voice and data networks set up to provide extensive coverage. There is now a strong trend to international value added data services (VADs) with an increasing number of organisations turning to VAD providers because of the prohibitive cost and large amount of managerial effort required to support a private network.

If, for whatever reason, an organisation loses its computing power, reverting to manual procedures is often impossible. Thus an effective contingency plan needs to have been set up. Setting up a backup computer system in a different location is very expensive and mutual backup agreements between two companies are rarely practical. Thus disaster recovery is another service available from third parties.

Facilities management

Bureaux provide facilities off the customer's site; facilities management (FM), which we have already mentioned, is the provision and management of a customer's complete on-site data processing needs. It can include the hardware, software and computer staff or the customer's own resources can be used.

Software services

These include the provision of:

- application software packages providing pre-written business solutions;
- custom software development, a design and programming service to provide tailored software solutions;
- application-enabling software which assists in the development of applications, for example computer-aided systems engineering and database management;
- the provision, modification and installation of systems software.

Packages can sometimes be customised so that they meet a customer's special needs. Another way in which the cost of bespoke software can be reduced, particularly if the service company specialises in a particular application area, is by building modules which can be assembled in various ways with amendments to certain parameters.

Systems houses

These provide a complete service for customers, starting with feasibility studies and systems analysis, going on to designing the system, programming and testing it, followed by implementation, training and maintenance. Some, as part of this service, also buy the hardware. This may mean putting together a special package of components from different manufacturers as well as providing the software and training the staff – this is called a 'turnkey' service. Some select and recruit staff, some manage and run the computer system for customers – thus providing an FM service.

The assembly of different computer software products and hardware to form a complete system is called system integration. It is undertaken by a prime contractor with the necessary skills and financial responsibility. Many of these projects are costly and complex so that risk analysis is carried out at the tendering stage and a risk management plan will be part of the contract.

The customers of a systems house look upon the people advising them as professionals who can provide them with convincing solutions to involved and sometimes highly technical problems. Thus the ability to communicate and build good working relationships with customers is important.

Value added resellers

The reduced cost yet increasing power of minicomputers and microcomputers has opened new markets for manufacturers. Where little specialist expertise is required, products can be sold direct to end-users through catalogues, mail-order and high street outlets. Where a combination of products, application software, technical skills and services are required, the solution is VARs. Resellers have significant expertise in specialist markets and take full responsibility for the systems they supply.

Maintenance

Some service companies provide hardware and software maintenance independent of manufacturers and suppliers. This means that one company is responsible for all the maintenance on the site regardless of the number of suppliers from which it has come. These companies may also wire up buildings for the use of computer terminals and workstations – a cabling service.

Self-employment or freelance contracting

Self-employment has been common in the business for a long time but only for people who have worked as an employee for a number of years. Skilled and experienced programmers used to find it comparatively easy to make a living as a 'contractor' but, except for those with specialised and sought after skills, this is becoming much more difficult. You would need at least two or three years of employment in the IT industry before considering contract work. However, the general tendency towards 'outsourcing', i.e. not employing your own staff to do a particular task but buying in the skills as needed, means there is likely to be work of this kind for those have unusual or particularly sought after combinations of skill and experience in a particular aspect of the industry.

Consultancy

The term can include quite a range of organisations of differing size and purpose. The best-known are often associated with accountancy or financial services and some provide more general management consultancy as well as advice on information technology. The category includes the National Computing Centre, as well as companies such as Exxel Consultants, Price Waterhouse or Andersen Consulting. Advice will be on how to use information technology to improve business efficiency and effectiveness as much as on technical problems. In addition to the large consultancy firms, there are small companies or individuals providing specialised services.

Security is one particular area where consultancy is called upon. While hackers and viruses get the publicity, an NCC survey showed fire and equipment damage, feared by 46%, to be practically as much as a worry as unauthorised access (47%) and deliberate corruption (46%).

Other areas

Education and training

Staff development courses and training for both IT staff and end-users is another service provided by outside companies. Public courses and seminars are one method but many large organisations commission tailor-made courses to suit their particular needs. This may involve designing the content and structure of the course (which may last from one day to three months), producing the materials required (overheads, slides, exercises to run on the computer) and then giving the course which may be on the customer's premises.

A training service may include the production of operations and end-user documentation, on-line training and 'help' screens. More ambitious still are computer-based learning packages using a mixture of computer-aided learning, videos and written documents.

IT education also includes 'awareness' courses for people who will use or at least come into contact with IT in the course of their lives and will therefore need to be able to assess its impact. This now means everybody!

There are also companies which provide specialist recruitment services and contract staff for short term hire to work on the customer's premises or elsewhere.

There is a large area of employment for teachers of information technology and computer studies in schools and colleges where this is now part of the National Curriculum. This will involve training either as a secondary school teacher or working in a further education college or in higher education. Beyond secondary level, experience of working in the industry will be of increasing value and higher qualifications at postgraduate level become important. You need to be as interested in educating others as in the development of your own IT knowledge and skills.

Information providers including journalism and publishing

These include trade and professional magazines and periodicals, and publishing houses. The IT trade press is the biggest of any industrial sector with items of every aspect of computing, networking, and communications.

Information is also provided for particular markets by specialist organisations sometimes called 'hosts' or 'networks'. Hard copy publishing in all its forms – reference books, scientific and other journals, newspapers and magazines – has been the main way of delivering information until now. However, there are large databases of information, the marketing and exploitation of which can be a profitable business in its own right. This may be linked in the future to the simultaneous provision of information services over the Internet.

Many services are market-led so that information providers are competing with each other. Marketing, often closely linked to training users, is quite different from selling books.

Librarians and information scientists today are heavily involved in the use of computers to support their research and management of information, and the issues involved in making it accessible to other people. See LIBRARY AND INFORMATION WORK.

A background in journalism, publishing, information science or librarianship will be value in some of these contexts. Technical writing is a related skill.

Of course, as IT users, major publishing and media companies can be quite big employers of IT staff. Reuters, for example, has its own technical training scheme for those with technically orientated degrees and another scheme to recruit software engineers. It uses electronic networks to provide information and news across the world

Recruitment and entry

New technology is changing the industry but there will still be the need for people with specialist skills – or the ability to learn them. One broad issue to consider is how far your interest in IT is a technical one, with a desire to be involved in an 'engineering' approach to the analysis and solution of problems or whether you see your main interest as the application of IT to areas where the complexity of the problem is more to do with understanding people and organisations than the technical possibilities, problems or nature of the hardware and software. The answer to this question may indicate a different route to qualification and entry and a different role within the team. In a few cases it may suggest different types of employer as well. 'Software engineering and design' may involve developing complex software for technologically complex equipment instead of business or commercial applications and the required training or qualification will involve software engineering, electronics, or a specialist computer science course with this emphasis, and be less accessible for example to the non-specialist graduate who will fit better into systems analysis and design in a business or commercial context.

Research needs specific pre-entry qualifications. Maintenance, servicing and installation also need an appropriate technical background.

Very rapid growth and constantly changing demands have meant that getting qualified is a much more flexible business than in many other professions, with opportunities for those who have not followed a 'traditional' route. The industry itself has change built in to it, but to this must be added the impact of the National Vocational Qualifications framework (see below), which means basically that the exact route to acquiring competence (full-time or part-time, degree or diploma, this subject or that, this professional body or that) will be less important in future than the possession of the competencies themselves.

Communication is vital, so good basic English, both written and spoken, is essential. Increasingly, employers are looking for people with broader, more cross-disciplinary skills and training, all-round abilities – adaptable, intelligent problem solvers. Demand is declining for straightforward programming and most lower-level aptitudes and skills.

While it is still possible to get into skilled computing work by a variety of routes, pre-entry qualifications are useful and important in many of the specialist job areas in IT. There are few firm rules or guidelines to follow and few clearly defined sets of qualifications. However, some courses are more suitable for some areas of work than others and employers have become more discriminating in recent years. It is crucial, therefore, to analyse and assess very carefully what pre-entry courses have to offer – they vary greatly, and change frequently, so up-to-date information is essential.

Qualifications and training

Unless you are interested in research, systems programming, etc. a degree course in science- or electronics-oriented computer science is not necessarily the best preparation because they do not normally cover the applications side. Courses do, though, vary greatly and more schemes now provide a basis for a business-orientated career. Essential elements include some business studies, computing which includes both theoretical and applications-based practical project work and preferably a year of industry- or commerce-based training. However, as mentioned above, the subjects studied in higher education are not always important when looking to work in IT; in fact, it may only be after you have gained your degree that you decide to consider a career in IT.

Sandwich courses give the opportunity to practise IT while also learning about it and there are various courses which combine business studies or accounting with computing. Some universities offer interdisciplinary courses with a wider range of subjects.

While postgraduate training is not essential, it is possible to take special IT or computing conversion courses.

Graduates

Graduates are recruited, as elsewhere, for their intellectual training and potential, so a degree has advantages. Degrees in computer science, or another numerate or scientific discipline (e.g. maths, electronics, physics) are a good idea if you intend to move into the more specialist or technical areas such as software engineering, systems design and development, systems programming, or research work. In some cases, especially research, a specialist degree such as Computer Engineering or Information Technology, science-oriented Computer Science (biased to, or combined with, electronics, for hard/software design) is increasingly essential. Mathematics or physics with a substantial computing content or option is an alternative. Most relevant courses need maths and physics A levels or the equivalent.

Otherwise your degree could be in any discipline and arts graduates often have equal success. If you want to study a foreign language, for example, this could be a good choice: not only might it be useful with the UK looking to Europe but some studies have shown a better correlation between aptitude for foreign languages and success in IT than between a mathematical ability and IT success. Business awareness and some 'hands-on' computing are useful and can be gained via work experience or vacation jobs. Many degree courses also now use computers as a tool. Some employers are wary of people with computer science degrees and positively encourage arts graduates to apply, preferring to train from scratch rather than take on science-based graduates with preconceived notions of computing that may not fit the organisation.

Employers are generally interested in people who have a broader understanding of the world of work in which the computer systems will operate. A joint degree in computing with another subject such as business studies, management or languages may add to your attractions. If your career aims are towards the technical side of the work, consider combined degrees in computing and electronics or similar.

Computer science

Computer science is an academic discipline which studies all aspects of computing from abstract theory through to practical applications. Hardware used to be considered electronic engineering and software computer science but the design of systems is now an integrated discipline and computer scientists often work in teams with other experts. They may be working in R&D departments researching into the design and application of computer systems in industry, commerce and administration or in government establishments.

However, if you take a computer science degree it could be important to check that it is accredited with the British Computer Society. This will mean that the course takes an integrated approach – all course units are linked by an overall conception – and the course covers certain professional issues such as design (of systems or software), engineering principles, a study of the industrial, managerial, organisational and economic context of computing, supervised work experience, practical work and projects. The accreditation committee will also have looked at the resources available and their accessibility to students. Such a course will exempt from Part I of the BCS examinations and usually from Part II as well. Some students may be able to get an employer to sponsor them for their first degree, or may get sponsorship for the final year after going on a sandwich placement in industry as part of their course. This may or may not involve a guarantee of employment when you graduate, but it will certainly help.

Conversion courses

If you did not take a degree or diploma that leads to such accreditation, postgraduate programmes and 'conversion courses' are available. The BCS can provide a list of those accredited for Parts I and/or II of their examinations. Some Masters-level courses may be designed for advanced or specialist training for those who already have experience and prior qualifications. There is also the possibility of degrees by research.

The alternative route in is via a formal training scheme, which usually means starting as a trainee (applications) programmer, but in most organisations with graduate-entry schemes, time spent actually programming is getting shorter all the while – organisations want much more out of graduates. You may also join a company in some other function and develop an interest in the application of information technology and computing to your area of work.

Non-graduates

Some employers like to recruit at 18-plus instead. A-level entrants (or, more recently, those with GNVQ levels 2 and 3 – see below) may be recruited as trainee programmers or computer operators but, as we have seen, these two areas are diminishing in importance and you may be expected to be able to move on to the next stage fairly soon. For long-term career prospects, particularly if you want to end up in a management position, qualifications will be important and it probably makes more sense to gain a higher qualification first.

It is possible to move into IT after starting in something else and gaining experience of a particular application area, especially if it includes using IT/computer systems. Organisations are sometimes prepared to train – or send on training courses – experienced staff who show an aptitude for IT.

Many organisations use aptitude tests to discover to what extent a person looks at problems logically. Working through such a test is not like doing an examination, its objective being to discover how you approach a task rather than find out how much you know about a particular topic. Personality/interest tests are also sometimes used.

National Vocational Qualifications (NVQ/SVQs)

Like other industries IT now has its own 'lead body' – the Information Technology Industry Training Organisation (ITITO) – whose key task is to work with employers to set agreed standards of competence for all IT staff to work towards. The map of competencies laid down by the ITITO has four broad headings – Systems Development, Service Provision, User Support and Use. The last of these is applicable to anyone using IT in their work and not specific to the IT professional but the others clearly outline different areas of competence at four NVQ/SVQ levels. Systems Development includes Systems Analysis, Design, Creation and Delivery (including such traditional tasks as programming, writing design requirements, and producing support documentation for the end-users). Service Provision includes Installation, Acquisition (selecting and buying the system needed) and/or Support for multi-user, networked or stand-alone computer systems. User Support includes operating the system, whether as an operator, supervisor or manager in a central computer services department for example, or as manager, supervisor or operator of a networked system.

The accreditation and award of a NVQ/SVQ in these areas is available from eight different awarding bodies – the British Computer Society, the Business and Technology Education Council, the City & Guilds of London Institute, the London Chamber of Commerce and Industry, the National Computing Centre, Pitmans Examinations Board, the Royal Society of Arts, and SCOTVEC (the Scottish Vocational Education Council).

The NVQ/SVQ framework has many advantages, among them the definition of clear progression routes for acquiring, demonstrating and assessing competence, step by incremental step, within a work-based context. It will be important to check the availability of work-based assessment for NVQ/SVQs when applying for IT-related jobs. The employer should have either become an 'Approved Centre' with its own internal assessors and verifiers for NVQ/SVQs, or have registered with an Approved Centre for this purpose. Such an employer may be able to offer the possibility of on-the-job training and assessment of competence (or a combination of this with off-the-job or distance learning) leading to the trainee's being able to get qualifications that otherwise would only have been possible via a full-time course. More experienced staff who have not got themselves qualified on paper, may now have opportunities also to get their experience accredited, by providing the necessary portfolio of evidence.

One important development is that of the Modern Apprenticeship. Apprentices will get a supervised training and development programme in IT (specialising in one strand of three: Use of IT, Service Provision/User Support, or Systems Development) and core skills. Such an apprenticeship, unlike the old-fashioned variety, is not time-limited but depends on your own rate of progress and the opportunities to demonstrate competence provided by the employer. Modern Apprentices will be encouraged to pick up and demonstrate interpersonal and business skills as well as technical competence. The final outcome is intended to be a qualification at NVQ/SVQ level 3 (equivalent to A-level in academic terms but also at a supervisory level in career and occupational prospects).

At the time of writing (1996) there is still some way to go before the 'professional' NVQs (as opposed to those for 'users') are fully accepted. Most analysts and others working at this level in the industry have degrees and would not necessarily regard an NVQ as adding much to their qualification (this is a similar situation in other industries). NVQs have so far been developed at the lower levels first but developments at graduate and degree standards of competence are continuing and take-up will probably increase even at these levels in future as the advantages of work-based assessment of competence become more obvious.

Such assessment can be particularly relevant to older entrants or staff with experience which can be accredited for higher levels of qualification.

NVQ/SVQs are awarded by: British Computer Society (BCS); National Computing Centre (NCC); Business and Technology Education Council (BTEC); Scottish Vocational Education Council (SCOTVEC); City and Guilds of London Institute (C&G); Royal Society of Arts (RSA); Pitmans Examinations Institute (PEI); London Chamber of Commerce and industry (LCCI)

In-service training

Training is difficult for the large number of small user sites. It used to be the manufacturers and service companies which did the majority of training but when the recession of the early 1990s hit the supply side, numbers recruited and trained fell. In addition, the rate at which products, techniques and tools are introduced means that retraining is a continual need.

Professional bodies

Professional qualifications are usually added to other qualifications to help gain promotion and show one's status in the industry. The main bodies are:

The British Computer Society

The Society sets educational, training, professional, ethical and technical standards for IT and has 33,000 members worldwide. It is a Chartered Engineering Institution, so Members of the BCS who have the right qualifications can register as chartered engineers and Associate Members can similarly become incorporated engineers. Over 6,000 Members of the society are registered in this way as chartered engineers.

It is an awarding body for National Vocational Qualifications (NVQs – *see above*).

The BCS has also established the Professional Development Scheme (PDS) which can lead to professional qualifications. It is a framework by which you can progress within the industry in a structured, logical and validated way and has been designed to work within employers' existing arrangements for training and career development. Cycles of experience are validated by recognised professionals and recorded in a Log Book which belongs to you. To participate in PDS you need to be working for an organisation which is registered with the BCS as a PDS Employer.

The shortest route to membership is based on an accredited Honours degree or Parts I and II of the Society's Examinations. The Examinations are held annually and courses to prepare for these are available at some 50 centres within the UK and abroad.

The Institute for the Management of Information Systems

The aims of the IDPM are to advance the interests of the profession and its members, to set standards for the profession and confer recognition upon those practitioners who meet the standards. It has a rather more business than engineering orientation. There are five courses from Foundation to Honours Degree Level with no prerequisites for the Foundation Course.

Foundation Course. This consists of 12 modules, each designed to take some 60 hours of study leading to an examination of 2.5 hours. Completion of the six core modules leads to the Foundation Certificate with the completion of four more giving the Foundation Diploma.

Diploma. Entry requirements for the next lowest level are at least four GCSE or equivalent passes or completion of the Foundation Diploma or, for those over 21, two years relevant experience in computing or a related field. Again there are six modules. Successful completion of these leads to the Diploma. This gives access to the Higher Diploma.

Higher Diploma. Alternative entry requirements are a BTEC National Certificate or Diploma in Computing or a related subject, GCSEs at grades A–C in five subject and two A level passes (or two AS levels and one A-level) with one in computing, similar Scottish Standard and Higher Grade passes, or for those over 21 four years relevant work experience.

Graduate Diploma. Finally there is the Graduate Diploma at Honours Degree Level in the management of Information Systems (developed with City University), which can be taken up by those with the Higher Diploma or BCS part I, or BTEC HND/C in Computer Studies or a UK degree in any discipline plus one year's relevant work experience in business computing.

Various grades of membership are available depending on the length of appropriate experience or approved qualifications.

The National Computing Centre

Though a consultancy rather than a professional body, NCC offers a full range of education services to user organisations who are members and runs a large number of accredited training centres internationally with courses ranging from computer literacy for 14–16 year-olds to postgraduate certificates for computing professionals. Qualifications include the International Diploma in Computer Studies and an honours degree programme in Business Information Technology. The NCC has several varieties of membership from Enterprise Membership for the small user to Partner Membership for larger ones. It is also an awarding body for NVQs – *see above*.

Other relevant bodies include The Institution of Electrical Engineers and The Worshipful Company of Information Technologists.

Private/commercial courses

These can be very expensive and instead it should normally be possible to find appropriate training with an employer, or at a higher or further education institution. If it is necessary to choose a commercial school, it is crucial to check that the course leads to a recognised qualification, that teachers are properly qualified and have the necessary equipment available for student use and to ask for details of the kind of jobs gained by previous students. No school can claim to guarantee a job.

Further information

British Computer Society (BCS); Computing Services and Software Association (CSSA); Institute for the Management of Information Systems (IDPM); Information Technology Industry Training Organisation; Institution of Electrical Engineers; The National Computing Centre.

Contents

Politics

(CLCI: COB)

Working in politics

For most people, politics is a voluntary interest, something quite separate from their daily work, and must stay so right up to and including membership of a local authority as an elected councillor. At this level it is rare to be able to earn a living from being a politician, although the leaders and people chairing the major committees of larger authorities are paid expenses which allow them to work full-time there. For some, like the Lord Mayor of London, it actually means having enough money to pay the expenses of a year in office.

Members of Parliament and Members of the European Parliament

Members of Parliament (MPs) and Members of the European Parliament (MEPs) are the only people who can really be called 'career' politicians, in the sense that they are paid a salary to represent their constituents at Westminster or Strasbourg. At present there are seats for only 648 members in the UK Parliament and 81 for British members of the European Parliament. It is one of the most insecure of careers, since it can be ended so easily and abruptly by the whim of the electorate.

The prospective Member of Parliament, or candidate, has first to be adopted as such by a constituency party. To reach this point, the aspiring MP has to prove capability, political acumen, suitability, drive, and devotion to his or her party. Traditionally this is demonstrated by working hard and long within the (local) party, usually at constituency level. Most often this means serving as a councillor on a local council at some stage. However, younger MPs are increasingly coming straight into national politics via other political, or semi-political, activist organisations (e.g. trade unions, student politics). Some constituencies prefer candidates who have made a name for themselves already, even in an area totally unrelated to politics, if this makes them immediately recognisable to local electors. Some constituencies have other preferences: for married candidates, for local or younger candidates, or for mature candidates, and so on. Of course it means waiting until a candidacy falls vacant, and the competition for a 'safe' seat can be considerable. Constituency parties have a high degree of local autonomy in choosing their candidates, but the central party offices are becoming more interventionist. Central party offices offer constituencies lists of 'vetted' candidates, and may try to help some prospective candidates to gain experience of elections first in constituencies where they are unlikely to be elected.

All politicians have second, or perhaps they should be called first, careers, both to support them during the time before they achieve their ambition, and to fall back on in the event of a permanent or temporary decline in their political fortunes. While it is probable that MPs have come from almost every area of employment, some careers fit in with politics better than others, these being careers which can be followed without working a full day or week, including, for example, the law and journalism.

While all Members are constitutionally entitled to choose for themselves how they will vote in Parliament, in practice they must also take into account the demands of the parliamentary party and the views of their own constituency, which can on occasion cause conflict, especially when the Member develops a strong personal line on something. This is just one way in which an MP's career can be put at risk. While a local party can withdraw its support from its MP, it cannot remove him or her from Parliament except by waiting until the next general election (unless the Member resigns by 'applying for the Chiltern Hundreds') and even then the Member may still stand as an independent candidate against the new official party nominee.

Most Members of Parliament spend weekdays (or at least Monday to Thursday) in London when the House is in session. At least one day a week is spent in the constituency, seeking to solve social and other problems for individual constituents. Members are also expected to be available to their constituents while at Westminster. This means an MP's day is a long one, since the House generally sits well into the evening, while the mornings may be taken up with correspondence and visitors, and a growing number committee meetings too.

Most MPs have full lists of engagements outside their strictly parliamentary work, with speeches, conferences, radio and television appearances. Since most MPs also expect to specialise in a particular subject (education, health, housing, and so on), this means a lot of background research and reading, so an MP's life can be extremely busy and full. It can also be very peripatetic, especially for the MP whose constituency is a long way from Westminster, and for the MEP.

Becoming a minister, a member of an opposition party's front-bench 'shadow' team, or chairing a 'backbenchers' committee, is obviously promotion, but this does not exempt any Member from losing his or her seat at the next election.

Members of the European Parliament are elected on the same party lines as British MPs, but they represent much larger constituencies.

Full-time official in a political party

Becoming a full-time official in a political party is the other main career in politics. In today's political parties this means becoming either a regional or a constituency political agent or working in the central office.

Constituency agents or organisers are the paid officials of the local or national party. They act as secretary to the constituency party, and are responsible for organising the local party so that it is ready and able to contest any election (and the agent is likely to be involved in local as well as national polls) with maximum efficiency. They organise their members, look after records and publicity, and also act as communication links, particularly with the candidate or MP, and try to ensure electoral rolls are kept up to date. Increasingly they have to be marketing experts, 'targeting' potential supporters, and use computer-based systems. To do the job, they are trained in the latest techniques, and are expected to have a really thorough knowledge of electoral law and practice.

No party can afford full-time agents in all constituencies these days, and regional offices handle much of the work, providing agents and organisers as and when needed. Numbers employed fluctuate, depending on how close a general and/or local election is, the state of party finances, etc. All three of the major political parties have training schemes for agents. The Conservatives' is full-time, those for the Labour Party and Liberal Democrats are by correspondence courses and study weekends.

The Conservative Party trains people over 18 as agents and demands a minimum of four GCSEs (A–C) or equivalent, including Maths and English. Of course, as in all the other political parties, personality is also important. Applicants do a preliminary exam, involving a day-long written test, followed by a one-day panel. If successful, they have a further two-day induction, followed by several months in a constituency prior to the final exams. All appointments to posts in the Conservative Party are made at constituency level, while the Labour Party recruits organisers nationally, where they are appointed directly by head office and cover a number of constituencies. In addition, Labour has a small number of locally funded posts covering one or two constituencies.

All agents generally have long voluntary experience within the particular party before becoming an agent, and it goes without saying that the job demands intense dedication to the party cause. Promotion, for the Labour or Conservative agent, is to larger, more key constituencies, and for some to posts at area and regional level, or to central office.

The Labour and Conservative central offices both have large permanent staffs, while the Liberal Democrats' is rather smaller.

Many of the jobs in central party offices are administrative and organisational, but there are also departments responsible for providing the background work on party policy, monitoring current developments, and gathering information, and these employ specialist research staff. Central-office staff also prepare material for speeches, service policy committees, deal with press and other publicity, do market research, prepare campaigns, fundraise, and provide information about the party and its policies, for politicians, press and the general public. Central offices all use sophisticated computer systems, and employ staff to program and operate them. However, much of the work on sophisticated 'marketing' and advertising/PR strategy is done either by professional agencies, or by professionals who are party supporters.

Staff may also be provided for the parliamentary party and MPs working at Westminster, but some of these are unpaid researchers on study leave from colleges (which gives useful experience for a later political career).

Organisational posts in both central office and area offices are generally filled from amongst party agents and organisers. Most research posts need a good economic/social studies and political background, and particular areas of research may need additional qualifications.

Further information

From the central, regional, or local offices of the appropriate political party.

Politics, political science and public administration

None of these subjects are intended to train people to take part in politics or to be a civil servant or local government officer, although many students on these courses do go on to follow these types of careers. Political science makes objective studies of politics, politicians, government and political life. It studies the function of government, how it operates, what influences it, the causes of political changes, and theories on which political systems and life are based. Each subject can be taken as a separate degree or diploma, but they are all interlinked and any study of one will inevitably cover some aspect of the other topics; e.g. a politics degree will include some content on public administration, local government and international relations.

Political scientists observe, analyse and assess what happens and how people behave in political life. They do not (normally) suggest what should happen in politics or government, although politicians frequently take account of and use studies made by political scientists, e.g. their analysis of voters' reactions to particular policies.

British government and the British political system are an obvious central interest for political scientists. They study in detail the way the machinery of central government works, how it changes and evolves, its problems, and particularly the way in which policy and decisions are made, as well as the policies and decisions themselves. They examine the complex tensions between elected members of government and permanent civil servants, and the influences on policy- and decision-making of all the many interests and pressure groups – farmers and fishermen, employers, industries, trade unions, people for and against a particular reform. They also look at the role of factors such as social status, personal links, and class loyalty, and study the effect of external factors, such as EU decisions, on policy-making.

They also study the electoral system and how it works, analysing problems such as the way 'third' parties fail to gain the number of parliamentary seats in line with voters' support. They analyse political parties and movements, and the voters and how they behave, as both individuals and groups (e.g. by age, class, ethnic origins, social mobility). This is called political sociology. Political change is a theme running through much research: how people change their voting behaviour with changing circumstances, for example.

Local government (e.g. borough councils, town hall and civic centre departments and policy-makers) and public administration and their relations with central government, form another major area of study.

The political systems of other countries are all studied, both because they are interesting in their own right, and because they can form part of comparative studies so that political scientists can try to make generalisations good for all political systems.

International relations studies not only relations between different states (this started as diplomatic history) but also international bodies like the European Commission and United Nations. Strategic studies of war – and peace – are related.

But political science does not only study the practicalities of political systems. A central theme is the theory and philosophy – of political thinkers and philosophers, from Plato and Aristotle through to Marx and John Stuart Mill, and beyond. This analyses key issues such as power and authority and what rules are used to control those who hold them; freedom, democracy, and the rule of law; the rights and obligations of the government and the governed; how the governed give their consent to be ruled and how they withdraw it, and so on. Political science also studies the language of politics: what exactly is meant by democracy, totalitarianism, or participation?

Much of the raw material of political science comes from written papers: the reports and minutes of not only government and parliamentary assemblies, but all kinds of bodies and organisations. In some areas, though, political scientists also work on data acquired through surveys, for instance, in studying the attitudes and behaviour of voters.

Opportunities for political scientists/public administrators

There are very few areas of work or opportunities for further study which are directly related to the courses mentioned above. Most people who do manage to follow a career in political science combine research with university teaching. Some also write popular books on political affairs, and/or provide expert commentary for the press, television or radio, although this is usually only a part-time possibility.

A look at recent destination statistics shows that only a very small percentage of politics graduates 'use' their degree in the accepted sense of the term in e.g. Civil Service traineeships, parliamentary advisory work, or union or political work. Many others will use the skills which they learnt on politics courses – such as analysis or dealing with complex and fluctuating data – less directly. The great majority of graduates in political science have to treat their degree subject as completely non-vocational.

Graduates in public administration are at least part prepared for careers in central or local government, or related organisations, but as recruiters are also looking at personal qualities, they do not necessarily have an advantage over others.

Studying political science

Politics is generally available only as a first, or higher, degree subject, although relevant aspects may be covered in some vocational courses. Vocational courses in public administration, i.e. the study of institutions such as parliament, the Civil Service and local government, are available at all levels from BTEC National upwards.

First-degree courses

Government, politics, public administration, and political studies or science are available at many universities. Depending on the institution, these courses can be taken as a single-subject honours course, or as a joint honours subject, or as a major option within a social science degree, such as sociology or the combined or modular courses now offered by many universities. Some institutions offer more than one degree covering these subjects, so care should be taken when choosing a course, particularly as course numbers tend to be small, and applicants far outweigh the number of places available.

Politics or government degrees are taught at a large number of universities and colleges. Many start with a period spent studying politics along with other social sciences, usually for one year. Some courses offer the opportunity for work placements in Parliament (as a research assistant), local government, quangos or voluntary organisations.

Public administration and related subjects such as public sector studies, public sector management or public policy are taught at: Aston, Birmingham, Bradford and Ilkley Community College, Brighton, Central England in Birmingham, De Montfort, Glamorgan, Glasgow Caledonian, Kent, Leeds Metropolitan, Liverpool John Moores, Luton, Manchester Metropolitan, Newcastle upon Tyne, Robert Gordon, Royal Holloway, Sheffield Hallam, Southampton, Staffordshire, Teesside.

Entry qualifications for the above courses: no specific A-level subjects are normally needed. A good level of maths is necessary to cope with the statistics included in most courses, and a foreign language is often helpful. Admissions tutors look for applicants who are sufficiently articulate and well-informed to give reasons for their choice of course and to discuss politics and current affairs at interview. Actual political persuasion is irrelevant, but the ability to analyse all factors and to make a case for a particular point of view is vital.

Postgraduate courses

Postgraduate courses in politics are mostly quite specialised, with a choice from a wide spectrum of topics, from the study of foreign governments and political systems to specialist study of, e.g., political behaviour or theory, social theory and public policy, or modern political analysis. Courses in public administration are also available.

Other courses

Currently, 14 BTEC centres run HND courses in Public Administration. In all instances, courses share some core studies, core themes and skills, with other business schemes.

Higher National courses – Diploma (two years full-time or three years sandwich-based) and Certificate (two years part-time) – include core studies on work organisations, external environment, and operational techniques and procedures, as other business studies, plus public-sector organisations, structures and processes, and resource management in the public sector. Option units are designed by the centres. Entry is as for all BTEC Higher awards.

National courses – Diploma (two years full-time or three years sandwich-based) and Certificate (two years part-time) – include core studies in business-related skills, people in organisations, the organisation and the environment, and finance, as other business studies, with one core unit on public administration. Public administration option units include housing studies, introductory practical administration, and the developing social structure of modern Britain, but students can take other appropriate options in, e.g., commerce or finance. Courses are available at a large number of colleges. Entry is as for all BTEC National awards.

Contents

Management Services

(CLCI: COD, COF)

Background

The methods and techniques available for both decision-making (in commerce, industry and public service) and research (in disciplines as widely spread as archaeology and sociology as well as the sciences and technology) have been getting increasingly exact, and numerically based, for many years now. In particular, scientific methods of observation and analysis, quantification of data, mathematical and statistical analysis, and mathematical model-making, are now used by more and more organisations and not only by academics and research workers.

The use of scientific and mathematical tools and techniques would, of course, have been impossible without the massive advances in computers and computer technology. These, in turn, made possible the development of more techniques designed to improve decision-making, such as operational research, organisation and methods, and work study.

In many occupations this means that both training and work content have become much more mathematically orientated, as shown by the fact that numeracy is now almost universally demanded for entry to most careers.

While work in these fields obviously demands a reasonable degree of numeracy and the ability to work with, and an interest in, figures, it does not necessarily require graduate-level training in mathematics. Just as crucial are logical thinking, communication skills, and an interest in problem-solving.

The demands, and therefore the satisfactions of these careers, are mostly intellectual, although they also need people who are exact and meticulous.

While the careers described below are those which are most closely involved with scientifically based management and research services, they are not the only ones. MATHEMATICS *and* STATISTICS (both in MATHEMATICS, STATISTICS AND ECONOMICS) are obvious examples, and ACCOUNTANCY AND FINANCIAL MANAGEMENT (*see in* FINANCIAL CAREERS) also apply techniques like these. *See also* INFORMATION TECHNOLOGY AND COMPUTER WORK *and* ADMINISTRATION, BUSINESS MANAGEMENT AND OFFICE WORK.

Operational research

This uses scientific principles to define and solve the more complex and difficult organisational, policy, and technical problems met in industry and commerce, local and central government, transport organisations, health and education service, defence, etc.

Most of the problems dealt with by operational research experts are by definition difficult because the 'system' involved is a complicated one. Any problems or any attempt to make changes will therefore inevitably bring more problems and disruption. The 'system' itself is probably extremely difficult to describe and analyse in the first place. A problem is given to operational research (OR) experts to solve just because so many factors have to be taken into account, and because some of the factors may involve chance, risk, and uncertainties, all of which must be treated as variables, variables which can interact with each other to give a great many different possible outcomes. It may be very difficult to identify all the factors involved. There may be a great many different possible solutions to a single problem, and it may be very difficult to decide which is the 'best' in any given circumstances. 'Best' itself may depend on a great many variables, and objectives themselves may change when the possible solutions are identified. OR experts often find that the problem they are working on is a symptom of another problem.

Operational research may, of course, be used to set up a new system from scratch, or it may be used just to assess and measure the effectiveness of an existing system, or to look forward to try to estimate future developments.

The OR expert – it may be one person, or it may be a team of people – has first to decide what the problem is and define the objective. To do this, the team has next to understand how the system involved works, what factors make it operate and what creates problems. They collect all the information they can about the system and watch and listen to the people who operate it.

Next, using the acquired data, they attempt to find one 'best' or several 'good' solutions. These may be tested through simulation, by for example, constructing a mathematical model (expressing the factors involved in numerical terms so that they can be analysed mathematically), or by using a visually interactive model (VIM) in which animated diagrams show, for instance, components moving through a factory on a computer screen. The OR team is able to assess the effects of different actions, perhaps speeding up a particular machine or installing a standby one to provide breakdown cover, and looking at the behaviour on the screen of the modified model. Much use is made of computers, but some OR techniques are less mathematical than others. (The use of non-mathematical techniques, often leading to a pictorial description of the problem, is known as 'soft OR'.) The VIM technique is particularly useful in letting managers explore alternatives.

Finally, the possible solutions are assessed in relation to the objectives, and a report written analysing the whole exercise which may be presented verbally to managers and directors during a meeting.

Operational research itself is not particularly new (it goes back to before the First World War), but it uses newer and newer techniques all the time. Its use in the Second World War – when it was first used as a way of consulting more than one kind of specialist, by creating teams from different disciplines, and success in, for example, analysing why air and sea forces were not sinking German U boats and then producing a more successful plan – gave it firmer standing. Experts returning to peacetime employment tried their techniques on non-military problems. Today, most organisations of any size have their own OR groups or use independent consultants. The OR Society estimates that about 10,000 people either work as OR experts or do something similar.

OR at its most sophisticated today is used extensively by, for instance, the oil industry. Oil companies have to decide how to plan their long- and medium term futures, given both that oil reserves are known to be finite, and that it is not clear how long they will last, given changing patterns of demand. Linked to this is the increasing unpredictability of oil price structures, which makes it difficult for oil companies to plan, for example, their investment policies in new oilfields and their own pricing arrangements. Oil companies import, and bring into the UK from the North Sea, around 100 different types of crude oil, by ship and by pipeline. Each type has to be delivered to the appropriate refinery, which at any one time may be making up to 100 basic products. These must be further treated and blended to produce 200 finished products, which must be what the market is currently demanding, without wasting a single drop of crude, so that it is often necessary to change the proportions of both basic and finished products made. The refined and blended oils, petrols, feedstock for chemicals and plastics, etc, must be distributed to plants and depots all over the UK and Europe, going by ship, rail, pipeline, and road.

Oil-company OR experts must build and keep up to date with new factors and changes, a model of the whole oil industry, the company, and the production system. This they monitor to see that it constantly operates as efficiently (i.e. profitably and economically) as possible. The system may have to be examined because, for example, more crude is coming into the country by pipeline from the North Sea, and so less is arriving by tanker. Is the whole tanker fleet still needed, then? Analysis shows that it might be, because more refined petrol or chemical feedstock may be going to European plants. Are the refineries still in the right place if, in five years' time, double the present proportion of crude comes from the North Sea, or half? Which depots and filling stations are still economic, and what is the optimum number of deliveries of how much petrol per month? And so on...

Operational research staff in electricity companies study the *Radio Times* and *TV Times* in working out how best to meet peak demands for electricity economically, which means having as little as possible of very expensive generating capacity on 'standby', given that the entire nation switches on the kettle when *Match of the Day* ends; what effect does breakfast TV have on demand for electricity at 6.30, 7.30 and 8.30 a.m.? Simpler, perhaps, is trying to find the most efficient way of getting newspapers from printer to newsagents in different parts of the country. Many OR exercises deal with planning – for companies and government – with stock control, with scheduling, with financial forecasting or manpower planning, with shift planning (e.g. for airline pilots or train drivers), optimum ship sizes for given routes and cargoes, and rerouting bus services.

Working in OR can be very varied. It is not as heavily mathematical as is often thought. Time is spent out of the office, observing, and finding out; time is spent discussing, working on solutions, preparing and writing reports, putting forward and explaining suggestions. Working with other people is in fact a major part of the job. OR experts spend twice as much time in communicating (listening, explaining, giving presentations, writing reports) as they do in modelling.

It is usual to change jobs fairly regularly. Prospects seem to be reasonable, and promotion into general management not unusual.

Recruitment and entry

It is possible either to start as a trainee, or to train before looking for a job. It is common to go into OR after experience in another occupation.

Most entrants have degrees (good honours generally), in mathematics, statistics, engineering, economics, business studies, computer science, physics or psychology, provided A-levels/Highers include maths, a science or statistics. Most employers these days demand a master's degree.

Operational research does require numeracy, to about A-level equivalent. People considering OR as a career also need to be well-organised, capable of thinking logically, and with analytical minds, an interest in complex problem-solving – and 'creative intelligence'. OR experts need to be happy to work as part of what can be a very closely knit team. They have to be good communicators, able to explain complex matters simply and clearly, and to write well-argued and clearly presented reports.

Qualifications and training

There are some first degree courses which include OR. Most entrants, however (depending on the content of their degree course), go on to do a one-year full-time master's course, either before starting work in OR (the commonest route) or after one or two years' experience in employment. Some employers with large OR departments have good graduate training programmes which may offer the opportunity to study for a master's degree or postgraduate diploma part-time.

Further information

The Operational Research Society.

Work study, and organisation and methods

These are closely related and overlapping techniques used to ensure that working methods are as efficient as they can be, and that employees are being used as effectively as possible. *Work study* originated in the factory, *organisation and methods* in the office, but they use more or less the same principles and methods, so they joined forces to become a single profession.

This is an advisory (rather than a 'line') 'function'. Work study/O&M staff advise management how to achieve set targets with as few resources (manpower, materials and capital equipment) as possible, and how best to coordinate their use. The techniques are not only used in industry and commerce, but also in, for instance, farming, the Armed Forces and the public services.

There are two main aspects to modern work study/O&M, and work study officers are usually expected to be able to do both.

Method study examines and analyses critically and closely the way particular jobs, or series of related jobs, such as assembling a car, cleaning a hospital, delivering mail, organising a filing system, estimating or ordering, sales forecasting, keeping statistical records or running internal communications, are being done. Its techniques are then used to see if there are any ways to improve the existing method or system, both for greater efficiency and if possible to make the work easier – perhaps using robots on an assembly line or microcomputers for word processing or for computerising systems that have previously been operated manually. They may have to plan changes to a system, e.g. when a food manufacturer decides to make several versions of a breakfast cereal instead of just one in bulk and so has to batch produce.

To do this, the job or system is broken down into all its stages, and the stages are laid out in the form of a flow chart, so that it becomes possible to see where there is a better route through them, whether one or more can be eliminated, or whether some tasks should be split in order to make them easier to do. A method study expert will look to see if there is any equipment which will speed the process, reduce manpower and other costs, and perhaps make the work easier to do. Method study may be used to solve a problem, such as a bottleneck in a production line or in supplies. It may be used to try to improve efficiency, or in planning and designing a new system. Since many new office and industrial systems involve computers, this will usually mean working closely with computer experts, normally systems analysts (*see in* INFORMATION TECHNOLOGY AND COMPUTER WORK).

Work measurement, the other half of the function, does what it says. Work measurement experts measure the time it takes someone to do a job or part of a job. Again, the job must be analysed, by breaking it down into all the individual actions and then timing and observing these actions over and over again, using a number of different people, to find a mean time for the operation. Work measurement is used to provide standards against which output can be measured and is usually the basis for pay calculations and costing, but is also used in evaluating working methods, particularly new ones on a trial basis before they are adopted.

There are four broad working grades. At the most junior level, the practitioner is generally sufficiently trained to be able to make measurements of most straightforward activities for method study. The main working grade is that of engineer or officer, normally able to do any work measurement or method study project, while senior positions include senior, or section team leader, and manager or consultant, who organise and coordinate mixed teams of management specialists. Experienced work study practitioners are expected to be able to detect a need for a change in the system, decide on the form it should take, organise and collect the necessary information, analyse it, and helping to carry out the new procedures.

The work is painstaking, with days spent in careful observing and timing. It involves deskwork, time spent in other departments and, possibly, visits to other company sites. It may involve some overseas travel.

The work is technological, mathematical and psychological, involving at various times accounting, communications, computers, costing, economics, ERGONOMICS (*see below*), industrial relations, layout and design, management and organisation, network analysis, OR, payment and incentives, production planning, psychology, quality control, social science, statistics, systems analysis and value analysis. Demand for work study experts is steady. There are plenty of opportunities for promotion and for career development in, e.g., production or personnel management, data-processing, and eventually general management. Some go into MANAGEMENT CONSULTANCY (*see in* ADMINISTRATION, BUSINESS MANAGEMENT AND OFFICE WORK).

Recruitment and entry

It is not usual to start training in work study/O&M without some experience in industry or commerce, and before one's mid-twenties. Even graduates are advised to spend a year or two working in an industrial or commercial environment first.

Although people start work in work study with a variety of educational backgrounds, for the best long-term prospects above-average intelligence is needed, and it is worth extending academic studies as far as possible, to at least BTEC Higher award standard, and a degree is increasingly useful.

Work study takes maturity and tact, with the ability to work with people – who may feel threatened by work study processes. A reasonable level of numeracy is needed, as are the abilities to think logically and analytically, to be methodical and to have organisational skills. Many work study/O&M applications do not, however, require more than basic mathematical skills.

Qualifications and training

Training is normally and mostly on the job, with part-time study for professional qualifications.

The Institute of Management Services (1996 membership about 9,000) now asks for A-levels, Highers or a GNVQ/GSVQ Advanced or equivalent for entry to the certificate examinations, for which the course lasts a year part-time. There is no longer any direct entry to diploma examinations. A wide range of qualifications give subject-for-subject exemptions at the diploma level.

The Institute of Administrative Management also sets examinations which are useful for O&M staff.

Further information

The Institute of Management Services and the Operational Research Society.

Ergonomics

Ergonomics studies and applies scientific and technological principles to the relationship between worker and machine, and between people and their environment. Its origins were military, used in the Second World War, as aircraft manufacturers began to design fighter planes around their pilots so that they 'interacted' with maximum efficiency. It became a technique for relating worker and working environment more closely to each other's needs, and now is applied wherever fitting people more comfortably and efficiently into what can be very complex environments has beneficial results, and where designs can be practically improved.

Ergonomics is now used in all kinds of situations: in the design of factory and office layout, in matching machine or computer/word-processor to operator, and even in the detailed planning of kitchens for safety, convenience and efficiency. It is used in designing planes and ships, schools and hospitals. It can help solve problems for disabled people. It is used in systems design by, for example, suggesting which processes are best done by people and which by machine, and by tailoring work to human skills rather than making people adapt themselves to the machine. It can also be used in preventing accidents and promoting safety, in particular the rise in repetitive strain injuries and work-related upper-limb disorders.

Increasing use of automation and much more sophisticated machinery add to the possible applications of ergonomics. In a healthy economy the employment prospects for ergonomists are good, especially in view of new legislations and directives which are being introduced in the European Union, and of which more may be expected before the turn of the century, with the increasing emphasis from our European partners on a healthy and efficient labour force.

Ergonomics is a very advanced field of study, and as such generally requires a high level of education and training. It does not have any formal educational or careers structure. It is multidisciplinary study and most people come to it having started out in one of the related disciplines.

Where ergonomics experts work depends a great deal on their previous experience and expertise. Previous experience may have been gained in design work on buildings, factories, machines or consumer goods, in analytical research and advisory work in personnel and industrial relations as well as industrial training.

It is common practice now for larger businesses to carry out ergonomic audits of offices and factory layouts to improve comfort and efficiency of employees. There is some research going on for example into the ergonomics of complex switchboards and control systems, into the contribution of experimental psychology to technological systems and into finding new applications of ergonomics.

Qualifications and training

Studying ergonomics combines a range of basic sciences, including human biology (especially anatomy and physiology), psychology, physics (including experimental design and instrumentation), together with mathematics, statistics, and technological and social studies.

It is taught as a first-degree subject separately from related areas only at Loughborough University. Postgraduate courses are available at the Universities of Aberdeen, Birmingham, Loughborough, Surrey and London (Birkbeck, Royal Free and University College).

The most useful first degrees that would prepare a student for postgraduate study in ergonomics are physiology, psychology, engineering and architecture.

Further Information

A list of approved courses is available from the Ergonomics Society.

Art, Craft and Design

(CLCI: E – Ez)

Background

These three terms art, craft and design seem to sit easily together to many people. They seem to refer to areas of related activity that can be considered as a group. But beware. To people engaged in these three activities each term can seem exclusive, and they may feel that there are key philosophical differences between them and that one of these activities is superior to the other two. So each one needs a separate introduction.

Art

A simple definition of an artist might be: someone who makes pictures or images. Immediately there is a problem here created by the fact that technology – in the form of computers, instamatic cameras and video recorders, for instance – allows everyone these days to make pictures with very little skill or imagination. Consequently a term is commonly used to refer to a kind of image- or picture-making which has some measure of cultural status. The term is 'fine art'. It refers to the art of the museum and gallery and more specifically to the media of painting, drawing, sculpture and print-making. Although these four media are the most common, many fine artists have extended their working practice into other media too. Some artists use photography or video to make their own images. Some use themselves or others to perform works of art, perhaps as 'living sculptures'. Others will create whole environments or installations through which people can move and experience sights, sounds and even touch and smell.

There are a number of reasons for these experiments. One is to use new media that are more compelling to a modern audience and relate more closely to the modern experience of living in the late twentieth century. Implicit is a turning away from established media that carry a weight of cultural baggage with them. They may be seen as reactionary, safe, elitist, male or ethnocentric. When looking through the prospectuses for practical or studio-based courses in art, you will most frequently see the term 'fine art'. And this term refers to courses which want to define themselves along traditional lines of painting or sculpture and those which encourage students to experiment across a variety of media.

Just as fine art differentiates itself from popular or commercial art, so too it keeps itself at a distance from its utilitarian cousins craft and design.

Design

Design refers to an activity that has to do with products and objects that are used to fulfil practical functions. It is impossible to dissociate the term design from the term manufacture. A design is a plan to make something and if we look around for evidence of the work of designers we can hardly miss them.

And yet the contribution of 'industrial' designers is not as widely recognised as it might be. There are a number of reasons for this. One of them is that most people who design the largest parts of the environments we live in and use are not called designers. They are called things like engineers and architects. Engineering and architecture are fundamentally design-based activities, but they encompass such a wide range of other skills, interest and knowledge that they are usually considered as completely separate career areas. The Chartered Society of Designers occasionally considers whether engineering designers should be allowed to become members – and thus far has always said no (although 'product' designers are accepted). However, the Design Council has always regarded engineering design as part of its legitimate realm of concern.

Again, if you go to the prospectuses of colleges and universities offering design courses you will see that design is divided up into a number of separate areas: 'graphic design', 'fashion and textile design' and 'three-dimensional design'.

Graphic design started as design for the printing industry – books, posters and magazines – but has grown and expanded into other media, so that it is now considered to include photography, film and video, scientific and technical illustration, the production of educational and industrial training materials, multimedia/audio-visual production, information graphics and general illustration.

Fashion and textiles is more self-explanatory, linking clearly to particular manufacturing industries.

Three-dimensional design covers a wide area of activities including interior, exhibition, furniture, packaging, industrial, theatre and product design plus model-making. It overlaps with a number of areas also referred to as 'crafts', such as jewellery, silversmithing, glass and ceramics.

Craft

Craft, too, normally denotes an activity related to products with practical functions. However, it is often seen as a different kind of activity to designing. It carries with it notions of manual skill and dexterity. Craft objects are not by any means all 'handmade', but the technology that is used tends to be simple, and 'traditional' in the sense it dates from pre-industrial cultures. Examples would be the potter's wheel and kiln, wheel-driven lathes or foot-operated looms, hammers, saws, chisels and all kinds of hand tools. Because of this association with past technology, and its implied irrelevance to modern life, some have chosen to avoid the word craftworker in favour of other terms such as designer/maker. The latter term points to a widely accepted view of the difference between craft and design, and that is that craftspeople actually manufacture the objects they design. They manipulate the material they are using, be it wood, metal, glass, yarn, clay or whatever. They develop an intimate knowledge of, even an emotional attachment to, their material. Many of them will say that their design ideas are suggested to them by the material itself as they handle and use it.

There has always been a problem about discussing the intellectual content of craft work which has made it difficult to fit into the framework of art and design education. In fact, many art and design students in further and higher education are working in craft as earlier defined, but they are doing them on courses designated as 'design' courses.

The term craft has a number of related references which rather confuse the issue. For instance, the term craft is used in British industry when referring to someone with highly developed manipulative skills in occupations such as machine sewing, bricklaying, mechanical fitting or catering. Such people often have paper qualifications for their skills, and the body most noted for certificating such craft skills is the City & Guilds of London Institute.

But those kinds of craft skills are not taught on the designer/maker courses in Britain's art colleges and universities. Here the emphasis is on visual design and the creative use of the material. Some students on such courses lament the relatively sketchy training in 'hand' skills, clearly because they place the acquisition of skills at a higher priority than do their colleges.

The Crafts Council, whose brief it is to promote the crafts in Britain is more concerned with the area of work that is creative in its approach. But it too is engaged in the debate about the relative importance of traditional, technical and manual skills, and innovation in design and materials.

Finally the word craft has become associated with nick-nackery sold in tourist shops often with a folklorist theme, whether it be corn-dollies or love spoons. You will occasionally see the words 'Fine Crafts' used to denote a craft removed from the world of more skilled manual labour, or worse, the manufacture of souvenirs.

It is important to separate the three threads of the chapter, art, craft and design, if for no other reason than that many people find that their aspirations can only be met in one of these sectors. But other people could feel at home in two or all three because they are inextricably linked. Most artists develop and use manual skills and technical know-how in their work. Designers and craftspeople often regard themselves as artists working in different media. Designers often do actually make things, handle materials and develop prodigious craft skills. Craftspeople often choose craft because they would like to be artists, but see it as an 'impractical' career choice, and opt for something that allows them to be creative but has a more vocational relevance.

Recruitment and entry

The commonest reaction to the idea of pursuing a career in art, craft and design is: is there a career to pursue? Is there any work out there for any more than the favoured few, those talented and lucky enough to fall on their feet?

Public perception would be that to choose a career in art, craft and design is a foolhardy action. They perceive that JobCentre vacancy boards and newspaper 'situations vacant' columns do not show openings in the fields of art and design. Perfectly true, but neither do they show vacancies for solicitors or dentists. There are magazines that advertise openings for artists and designers, but these are specialist papers only bought and read by the 'trade'.

But what are these openings? It might be easier to say what they are not. They are not regular 9–5, 35-hours-a-week, 4-weeks-holiday-a-year type situations. Such things do exist, but they are the exception, and far more common in design than in art and craft.

Most artists realistically do not expect to make a living solely through sales of their creative work. They either 'buy' time to do their own work by working casually at other jobs (a sculptor might for example work on a freelance basis for a model-making business; a painter for an animation studio) or else they fashion a career out of art-related activities such as teaching, doing residencies in schools, youth projects, hospitals or factories, competing for commissions often in the field of public art works funded by local authorities, industry or charitable trusts. Some artists manage to cross over to work in design-related areas – illustration, theatre design, or computer graphics.

Craftspeople often approach their career-building in this same piecemeal way. However, for some of them the option of setting up a small business is a real possibility. They design and make functional products for which there may be a market. The craft fair where makers sell their own work can put craftspeople in touch with the general public, specialist craft buyers for retail, and trade buyers like architects and interior designers, who commission pieces to use in their buildings. A range of financial assistance schemes is available through TECs, LECs, the Crafts Council, the National Arts

Councils (Scotland, Wales and Northern Ireland) and the regional arts boards (England) to help people set up in business.

For designers the picture is more complicated because the work patterns vary from industry to industry. The 1980s saw the growth in the UK of the 'design consultancy' the largest of them employing in excess of 100 designers. Some experimented with becoming public companies quoted on the stockmarket with decidedly mixed results. Advertising expanded enormously both in print and broadcast media and, through direct marketing, by post to people's homes, and this created a boom in jobs for a whole range of specialists – art directors, illustrators, typographers, animators, photographers, model-makers, etc.

But even when there is a lot of work around, there may not be a lot of employment in that traditional sense. One of the features of many creative businesses is their freelance structure. People are brought in to do some work on an hourly rate or a fee per job. The freelance can earn much more than the staff designer but there is no security, and the freelance needs to be able to develop and maintain a healthy list of contacts who can provide a constant flow of work. So social skills, reliability and consistency are important. Most designers have rueful tales to tell of colleagues who trained with them who were stars at art school, but who simply did not have the personality to go out and get work, and so fell by the wayside.

The portfolio

All artists and designers need a portfolio to get work. There is no mystique about a portfolio. It is simply a collection of an artist's previous work. In the case of fine artists, slides are often used as a portable record of achievement. Craftspeople, too, commonly use slides when approaching galleries, shops or buyers, but they often like to present physical samples too. For designers, drawings are essential, sometimes it is 'concept' drawings that are required, sometimes finished artwork, sometimes both. The portfolio that is taken to an employer or buyer, then, should be a representative selection of pieces, demonstrating the type of work done. Every selection made should be different, and tailored to meet the particular situation. If artists are in any doubt about what to include, then they should check with the prospective viewer what would be appropriate.

But the message for anyone considering this work is that from day one of their training they should get into the habit of documenting, recording or keeping their work.

In addition to professional skills, those who would earn their living through art and design need a whole extra panoply of survival strategies. They need to find work – often through networks of professional and personal contacts. They will probably have to supplement their income with non-relevant work at barren times. They will have to be happy with a succession of short-term contracts and commissions, certainly in their early career and quite possibly through the whole of it. They will probably be self-employed, which does have some distinct advantages but some corresponding disadvantages like ineligibility for unemployment benefit.

The job market

If the job market for artists and designers is full of short-term freelance opportunities, got through contacts or the showing of an excellent portfolio, how do you make a start into this kind of world? As with so many other professions and occupations, the route by which a young person could leave school, start as a junior and end up as top dog has, if not disappeared, then dwindled to a confusing series of narrow, overgrown, seldom-visited tracks, many of them leading to dead ends. Even in industries like design and video which still employ runners and messengers, people who start in this way straight from school frequently find that in order to progress they need to leave their firm and return to full-time education to develop skills and abilities that they cannot acquire in a casual manner in between running errands.

How many people earn their living in art, craft and design? The answer to this question is a complex one because of the preponderance of freelance and similar types of working. However, it is worth looking at a number of indicators.

In the 1991 census, the latest for which figures were available at the time of writing – 1996, 45,200 people in the UK described their main occupation as artist, commercial artist or graphic designer.

In November 1993 the Crafts Council conducted a major survey into how many people in Great Britain were operating as craftspeople. The total was 25,000 people. Of this total, 54% were working full-time (defined as spending at least 31 hours a week in their own production and no more than ten in teaching), 29% were working part-time – 11–30 hours a week, and the remaining 17% were classed as semi-professional or spending less than ten hours a week on their own work. The survey revealed an interesting shift in the proportion working full-time. The last survey, conducted in 1981, had revealed only 35% working in this way. The largest number of craftspeople (27%) are engaged in producing textiles, followed by ceramics (22%), wood (14%) and metal/jewellery (13%). Glass, toys and musical instruments, graphic craft, leather and miscellaneous accounted for proportions varying from 7% to 3%.

A recent book on the fashion industry estimated that in an industry employing 200,000 people, only about 2,000 were designers. More disturbingly, it was mentioned that designers in the fashion industry may have only a limited shelf-life, before younger designers with fresh ideas came up to replace them.

The Chartered Society of Designers, the professional body representing designers of all disciplines, had a membership at the beginning of 1996 of 7,000, and their own estimate was that they represented a third of all designers. Membership is particularly strong among 3-dimensional designers (3,600) with graphics also well represented at 2,200. Fashion and textiles is the least well represented at under 500.

However loosely we interpret the figures it seems that even after the designer decade of the 1980s, the number of people seriously gaining a living from design could comfortably be accommodated in Wembley stadium. It is worth saying that the Crafts Council survey and the CSD figures refer to individuals with considerable training in craft and design. Other surveys on how many people were working in craft and design businesses would produce a much bigger number: there would be a whole army of personnel involved in activities such as silk-screen printing, desktop publishing, print planning, assisting in potteries, fashion sample rooms, design studios, and photographic labs, who are doing art- and design-related work although they would not describe themselves as artists and designers.

Qualifications and training

The UK has an extraordinarily comprehensive range of art and design education, much more extensive than our colleagues in the European Union, and for this reason many foreign students come to UK colleges to do their higher education in art and design. Conversely, British graduates, particularly in fashion, textile and product design find that their qualification opens doors for them right across the world.

Work-related further education

A cohesive system of education and training in art, craft and design has been established. There are hundreds of art and design courses on offer in colleges all around the country, many in both full- and part-time modes. These programmes can take a student from the early phase of vaguely thinking about a career in something 'arty' to a high level of skilled competence in a specialist area of design.

At the lower end of professional development most colleges of further education offer preparatory diplomas in art and design usually validated by BTEC or SCOTVEC, although City & Guilds is also active in this area with Intermediate GNVQs, *plus* first certificates/diplomas (which have not been phased out in this area and are to stay for the foreseeable future). There is also a large network of national diplomas, also BTEC/SCOTVEC validated (and like the first-level awards, to stay for the time being) that lead to entry to higher education or in some cases to design or production assistant positions in industry.

National diplomas/certificates and advanced GNVQ/GSVQ programmes

Programmes in general art and design provide an introduction to the principal areas of art and design – fine art, graphics, fashion textiles and 3-D studies. In most cases students of these courses will use the course as a diagnostic experience and as an alternative to a foundation course (*see below*) to choose an area of specialisation at BA or HND level. Typically, the second year of the two year programme would concentrate on one area of specialisation so that the student can prepare a portfolio for acceptance on a degree or HND course

Courses in design also offer a diagnostic experience in a range of design areas but not in fine art.

Specialist courses also exist at this level, in areas such as communications, 3-D design, fashion, graphic design, etc. Unlike the general programmes, these are intended for students who are able to commit themselves firmly to one career area at this stage and do not include diagnostic work. They lead naturally to HND and degree courses in the same field or into related employment.

Three-dimensional design is one such area. There are over 30 colleges offering programmes which typically would introduce students to working in a variety of materials – wood, plastics, plaster, clay and metal. Then, different colleges offer different courses of more vocational specialisation such as jewellery, ceramics or model-making.

Audio-visual design is offered at 13 centres and covers the full range of techniques associated with visual aids – photography, video, film and animation, scripting, storyboarding, producing and editing.

The Diploma in Communications run at 14 centres, tends to have less technical content than audio-visual design and a greater stress on writing and journalistic aspects.

There are diplomas in design crafts in which a number of options are offered. Alternatively, they may be concerned with one area only, such as ceramics, jewellery, textiles, bookbinding or footwear.

A whole range of other design disciplines are offered. Fashion design is offered at over 40 colleges, graphic design at over 90, photography at 40, interior and spatial design at 13. Smaller numbers of colleges offer display, exhibition, surface pattern, industrial, model-making, technical illustration, paper and print conservation.

All of these courses feed into related higher education courses, either HNDs or BA degrees.

Numbers on BTEC courses

Since BTEC is by far the largest provider of art and design programmes a glance at their enrolment figures can be interesting. In 1995, nearly 24,000 students registered on BTEC design courses. Of these 13,000 registered for the national diploma, and 5,000 for the higher national diploma. First diplomas accounted for 4,500 registrations. Only about 700 students registered for the part time options for these courses (which lead to certificates rather than diplomas), which reflects the general reluctance of employers in the art and design fields to sponsor students on day release.

In 1994 nearly 2,000 students were awarded GNVQs at intermediate level; 500 at advanced.

Foundation courses – the route to a degree

Much longer established than the vocational diploma courses are the 'Foundation' courses. These are one-year diagnostic courses in art and design leading to application to an advanced course in a specialist area such as fine art, graphics, fashion/textiles or 3-D design. Although officially students can enter these courses at 17 with 5 GCSEs (grade C and above) these have become very much courses for the two-A-level entrant.

These courses have been seen as equivalent to the first year of a degree course, but with the disadvantage of not attracting a major award for grant purposes. Scottish art schools have an advantage here in that their art and design courses last four years, of which the first acts as a foundation, but because it is an integral part of the degree it does attract a major award. One or two similar programmes have now been established in England. Students take the first or foundation year at a school or college of art which feeds students into degree courses at linked universities and art schools. To date such students have been successful in receiving grants for all years of study.

Some students with A-levels apply directly to degree courses in art and design. Such an approach is more likely to be successful with the handful of courses in fine art in the 'older' universities, which have a tradition of accepting students on A-level or equivalent grades plus a good portfolio. A very small percentage of students succeed in gaining admittance to a degree or diploma course in free-standing art schools and the newer universities (which have absorbed many of the former art schools) without having taken a foundation course.

For students who have no A-levels, then, a diploma at national or advanced level is an increasingly acceptable alternative. But for mature students, people in their mid twenties and older, an 'Access' course in art and design taken part-time for 12 months might be sufficient to get them onto a higher education course. They may have to demonstrate their own commitment to the subject by talking about their own involvement in art and design, but the lack of formal paper qualifications may not be a bar.

Higher education

There are degree course in a wide range of art and design disciplines which are validated by universities – either by the parent university or, in the case of art colleges, by a link university. BTEC also has a role in validating higher education courses. The BTEC higher national diploma course are mainly two-year programmes in applied design areas.

One developing feature of these two separate systems is their moves towards mutual compatibility. A number of institutions are offering a programme of study that can be concluded after two years with an HND or extended into a third year for a BA. This is an important development, since previously a number of HND students who wished to complete a degree had to take an extra two years. Now that grants are slowly being replaced by a loan system, there may be a large number of students who would wish to conclude their studies as soon as possible leaving open the option of returning at a later stage.

The skill levels achieved by students on BTEC HND and BA programmes are very similar, though some degree students complain of insufficient drilling in skills, while BTEC students have been known to feel that two years was not quite sufficient to consolidate the design methods to which they had been introduced.

Application procedures

Application for the majority of degree and HND courses is made through UCAS. (A small number of Scottish art schools accept individual applications). The UCAS form looks unnecessarily complicated for an art and design applicant, but the reasons for this are historical! Prior to 1996 there were two parallel if unequal systems. UCAS covered a small number of degree courses in universities. Originally these were mainly in fine art. Most other degree courses and all the HNDs, collectively known as 'studio-based' courses, were the province of another applications system, the Art and Design Admissions Registry (ADAR). Gradually some institutions began to choose to use UCAS, particularly if as a new university (former polytechnic) they were using UCAS for all their other applications. It therefore became less easy for applicants to distinguish between types of course and furthermore they had to decide whether to use one or both systems. In theory this confusion was eased in 1996 when the two systems merged, ADAR effectively disappearing. However, the distinction between 'studio-based' and other courses still exists – and applicants require careful advice from (usually foundation course) tutors when applying for HND or degree courses.

Art and design applications may be made in two ways on the UCAS form. Route A follows the normal UCAS timetable. Applicants make up to six choices of course in alphabetical as opposed to preference order and send in their forms by 15 December. Forms are photocopied and sent simultaneously to all the named institutions. If they wish, they may make less than six and reserve the remainder for Route B, indicating this decision on the form. UCAS then sends them a supplementary application form which must be returned by 31 March. This is for application to (mainly) former ADAR members. These institutions must be listed in preference order since they will interview candidates or inspect their portfolios in strict sequential order. In other words, should an applicant be successful at institution one, the application form is not sent to the others. The existence of the two routes is due to the fact that some ADAR institutions, brought whether they liked it or not into the UCAS system, insisted on keeping their previous method of application and selection. Applicants not wishing to make any Route A applications may request the supplementary form straight away.

No one gets a place on a studio-based course without a face-to-face interview and the inspection of a portfolio of work.

Applicants need advice either from tutors or from the colleges they are interested in, on several crucial topics:

1 Have they got a portfolio suitable for the course to which they are applying?
2 Does this course get such a large number of applicants that it is advisable for only the strongest applicants to go for it?
3 Does this course get such a large number of applicants that it is very unlikely to be worth putting it as a second choice?

4 Is it worth making a double application for BA and HND in the same subject to maximise chances of success?

ADAR used to publish statistics on applications to courses in the system. Its last figures published in 1995 showed that 19,766 candidates applied to art and design degree courses. Of that number, 10,782, just over half, were offered places. For BTEC higher national diplomas, applications totalled 5,904. A higher proportion, 4,394 in total, were accepted.

Very few people apply direct from school. One trend that seems to be happening is the increase in the numbers of people applying to art and design education who are not attached to a school or college. They are described as 'external' in the statistics. They include people who have taken a year or two out from foundation or BTEC courses, as well as people who apply under their own steam possibly without any guidance. The important factor about this group is that they come up in the statistics as the group least likely to be accepted onto courses. It is possible that this group just happens to contain more weak applicants. However, a more likely reason is that without some sophisticated understanding of the application system, it is possible that these external applicants are concentrating on applying to colleges they have heard of without any thought of their chances of success in that particular institution. Anecdotal evidence would suggest that they go for colleges with a 'name', a reputation either in the creative field generally or in a particular specialism. Unfortunately, these 'names' do tend to attract the heaviest applications and are frequently the toughest places to get into. A visit to the college a student wishes to apply to is advisable in every case. Most colleges will accept visits from interested students. Some offer a weekly time slot for applicants to look round. Most have an 'open week' each spring where they welcome potential applicants.

ADAR 1995 statistics – the last to be compiled on acceptances onto higher education courses, showed that the following number of places were available on 'studio-based' courses:

BA courses	
Fine Art	2,332
Graphic Design and Visual Communication	2,447
3-D Design	2,308
Fashion/Textiles	1,919
HND courses	
Graphic Design/Film/Video	3,998
Photography	377
3-D Design	1,000
Fashion /Textiles	802

Overall, fewer than 10% of successful applicants had come through the 'direct entry' route, i.e. had not taken either a foundation or appropriate BTEC course.

Analysis of a sample of applications to fine art courses in traditional UCAS universities shows that the ratio of applications to acceptances was as follows: Newcastle University 24:1, Aberystwyth 11:1, Edinburgh 21:1, Oxford 11:1 and Leeds 44:1. Reading University's typography and graphic communication course had a ratio of six applications to one acceptance.

Postgraduate courses

Although there are an increasing number of postgraduate courses in art and design, postgraduate study is bedevilled by a lack of finance. MA centres usually have a handful of bursaries to give out but never enough for the students who require them. Many students survive on bank loans; others may work between the BA and MA courses in order to save and finance the second course. There is a certain amount of industrial sponsorship at this level, but the lion's share of it is taken by students at the prestigious Royal College of Art, a purely postgraduate institution. Consequently a lot of new courses are offered on a part-time basis only, allowing students to use part of the week getting the finance necessary to continue their work. These part-time courses serve to initiate students into the difficulties of surviving as a practitioner.

NVQs/SVQs

NVQ/SVQs have been accredited at levels 1–4 in the following areas of design: ceramics, constructed textiles, exhibition, fashion, furniture, graphic, interior, product and surface pattern textiles.

Destinations of students leaving courses

Surveys of students leaving art and design courses suggest that they have more difficulty in getting established than other disciplines, but that over a longer period their success rate in employment is comparable to other specialisms. Figures from the university careers advisory services on the destinations of 1994 graduates indicate that those in art and design had an unemployment rate of 15% six months after graduating. This was higher than figures for other humanities/social science subjects, comparing with 10.7% for English, 10.8% for history and 13.4% for social studies. However, the survey points out that 'a significant percentage find course-related work' – which is not true of the other disciplines.

Further information

Arts Council of Great Britain, Design Council, Crafts Council, BTEC.

Design

For most people a career in art and design is really a career in design.

In design it is a question of applying creative and artistic skills and talents to a practical end. Designers work to a brief set by someone else. It may seem obvious to say, but there is a view around that designers are in some way a law unto themselves, creative people who must be left to develop their own genius. Nothing could be further from the truth.

They work under commercial pressure and to schedules which in some industries can be very tight – in advertising for instance overnight working is by no means uncommon. The design must stay within any technical, manufacturing or budgetary limits. Also, the design must 'work'. It must do the job intended for it.

The profession of design has come a long way in the last ten years or so. It has more public recognition both as an area of our economic and cultural life and the design 'business', or 'design industry', has expanded in terms of the employment opportunities it offers. It is still, however, not a particularly easy area in which to establish a career.

Graphic design

Marketing – technical considerations – designing with computer – employment in graphic design – advertising – publicity and promotion – direct mail – packaging – corporate design – design for the moving image – film and TV animation – illustration – technical and medical illustration – photography – courses in graphics

Graphic design is really the design of communication, and has developed considerably from the days when it was known as commercial art.

Graphic designers work with print, pictures and patterns on flat surfaces. They 'lay out' words and pictures on pages for books and magazines, in advertisements, posters, sales brochures, product packaging, TV programme title sequences, and the sides of company vans.

Marketing

The aim of graphic design is to make all these kinds of communication as understandable and as clear as possible. But clarity is not the only consideration. The design has to attract and engage the viewer in an appropriate way. A record cover has to communicate with the kind of people who might like the particular musician concerned. A company's annual report needs to communicate with the kind of people who might have shares in that particular company. The reason designers are used very often is for the purpose of marketing; a powerful cover, for instance, can vastly increase the sales of a book. You can't judge a book by looking at the cover of course, but that is precisely how many people decided whether to buy a book or not.

Technical considerations

The work is as much technical as creative. Designers have to understand the technicalities of printing processes, photography, colour reproduction type with all its varied fonts, sizes and weights. These areas have a vocabulary to themselves little understood by outsiders, but designers need to talk to the technical specialists to make clear what they are trying to achieve with a design. They also need to understand what is technically possible and what is not. And finally they need to have an awareness of the cost implications of what they specify. Designers also need an awareness of psychology, particularly the psychology of perception. How can the elements of a page, a poster or a piece of food packaging be combined to be clear, interesting, informative and aesthetically pleasing? How can a graphic signing system help people find their way around a hospital or a hotel?

Designing with computer

More and more of the everyday work of the graphic designer is done on computer systems. Typesetting, making sure that text fits into the space allocated to it in the design (often called a layout), a process called copy fitting, used to be a very delicate job for a highly skilled paste-up artist, but now individual letters and the spaces between them can be manipulated at the push of a button. It is not that it has become 'easy', because you have to know exactly what you are doing, but the need for manual dexterity is just not there. *See also* INFORMATION TECHNOLOGY AND COMPUTER WORK.

Employment in graphic design

The range of possible work for graphic designers is extensive. Over half of all designers working in industry and commerce are working in graphics. Many of them will specialise in working in one particular field such as advertising, publishing, packaging or corporate identity.

Advertising

The high-profile side of advertising is the advertising agency which creates the kind of advertising seen on TV, in newspapers and magazines, on poster sites. This kind of advertising is conceived in agencies by people who carry the general job title of 'creatives'. Normally such people work in teams of two, an art director and a copy-writer. Art directors' skill is in originating ideas which promote products in imaginative and exciting ways. However, they usually do not execute the ideas themselves. That is normally left to other specialists whose skills are in drawing and design. Art directors do not necessarily have to be excellent artists. Some of them are, but it is not an essential skill for the job.

The other specialists mentioned are people called visualisers, whose skill is in their ability to paint up a rough sketch into detailed colour drawing or 'visual'. The visual can be a single drawing, but more often it is a whole series showing the development of an ad. These are called storyboards. Visuals and storyboards, and simple animated sequences called animatics, are produced in order to show the client and get approval for the campaign to go into production. Often many different versions of ads are shown before agreement is reached. Rarely does a client say 'fine, it's just what I wanted', so 'creatives' often have to fight for their ideas against opposition from the client and possibly from their own colleagues in the agency.

Publicity and promotion

Another and less well known side of the advertising industry concerns so-called 'below the line' work. This includes brochures which describe products to potential customers (an enormous slice of the market), or a whole variety of giveaway material carrying the company name, logo and slogan.

Direct mail

Direct mail concerns the design of leaflets mailed through the post to people who are known to be potential buyers of the product or service in question.

Packaging

Although packaging makes heavy use of graphic techniques, it is really a form of product design. *See* 3-D DESIGN *below*.

Corporate design

Although much of design is used in the marketing process in order to 'sell', many designers resist a too-close identification with advertising, as they see their job as giving visual expression to a company's values, aims and traditions, to give its own staff and those that do business with the company a sense of the company's identity. Much of their work in fact goes under the title of corporate identity. This may include the company logo, the company colours, the typefaces to be used in company publications, the letterheads and the livery on company vehicles.

Designers of a corporate identity will look at all aspects of the way a company is perceived in order to produce a coherent image. They have for example redesigned the telephone book so that it used less paper and became easier to read and to use, and have designed new graphics that were to be painted onto the side of rail goods wagons to indicate the kinds of goods being carried, but also to give a sense of an efficient unified national service. A recent design brief that received some national publicity was to design a corporate logo for the government Department for Education and Employment, formed from a merger between the former Departments of Employment and Education.

Design for the moving image

In the age of the rented video, the multiple TV channel, the satellite broadcasting, the all-day and all-night broadcasting, the sales conference video, the training video, the interactive video, the video game, the video holiday brochure, university prospectus, etc., it is clear that a lot of information is communicated through electronic pictures. Graphic designers are used to produce storyboards in the development of ideas for films. It is necessary to produce storyboards in order to give everyone a clear idea of what the film will look like before the whole expensive production process gets under way. In television, each programme that goes out needs a title and credit sequence for programmes and the designer's job, like that for a book cover or record sleeve, is to entice a viewer to sample what is inside the 'package'.

Film and TV animation

Film and TV animation is another area that has expanded in the 'traditional' sense, where teams of artists and designers draw and paint hundreds and hundreds of drawings which, put together in sequence, create the illusion of movement. But in addition, this field of work is being increased by the spread of more and more sophisticated computer animation systems. The principles of animation are the same, but new technology allows a designer to put together sequences of movement much more rapidly. This speed has encouraged the use of animation in advertising as well as TV, and has meant that it can be used in non-broadcast material such as training films.

Illustration

Illustration is a specialist area of graphic design that concerns the drawing and painting of images that will appear alongside text in a book, poster or magazine. An illustrator will be briefed by a designer or editor on the kind of style required and the subject matter. In practice, illustrators get a reputation for a particular style and are commissioned on the basis of work that has been seen before. This is actually the main reason that it is hard for illustrators to get started; they have personally to visit art editors in magazines and art directors in advertising agencies showing their work and presenting a good professional image. A reputation needs to be built not just on quality of work, but on reliability too.

Technical and medical illustration

There are specialist branches of illustration that are closely allied to the fields of education and training. Illustrations can show the internal workings of a turbine or a human kidney. Illustration by selecting detail can demonstrate what is happening in things impenetrable to the eye or even the camera. There are specialist courses in technical and medical illustration at degree and higher national diploma level in colleges and universities.

Photography

Photography will be dealt with later in this chapter, but it is as well to realise that photography is just as much a part of graphic design as illustration. It is simply another way of producing pictures, and freelance photographers who want to work in publishing or advertising build their career in exactly the same way as illustrators.

Courses in graphics

There are numerous BTEC national diploma courses covering basic training in graphics.

In higher education, many universities and colleges offer BAs including the study of graphics, or visual communication, including typography and book illustration.

The slightly confusing aspect is that many courses describe themselves as 'graphic design' or 'visual communication', and you need to study course details carefully to check whether they offer the specialism you require such as illustration, animation or computer graphics.

Fashion and textiles

These two are frequently linked together mainly because the fashion designer must know a great deal about the fabrics used in clothing, and the fabric designer needs to have a feel for the fabric used.

Textile design

Textile design is concerned with all sorts of fabrics: those used for clothes, curtains, furniture coverings, bed linens, towels, carpets and lace – even for things like car and train seating. Fabrics are made of many different fibres which are mixed together to make a yarn that is appropriate for a particular use. Natural fibres like cotton and wool are mixed with all kinds of synthetics, and many designers experiment with mixes to develop new qualities in textiles. Some textile designers see their role not just in terms of cloths, but also across a whole range of products that can carry a printed and repeated pattern on their surface – wallpaper, wrapping paper, linoleum, formica. Sometimes these designers will call themselves surface pattern designers, and this is a term that some college courses use.

Because the design has to take into account the way the fabrics are produced, textile designers usually specialise. Normally this is either in woven (or 'constructed' as it is sometimes called) fabrics or printed fabrics. In 'weave' the design is woven in, and depends greatly on yarn quality and colour and the technology used in the manufacture of the cloth. So the designer must know about and understand fully yarn-making, dyeing and weaving processes to make the most out of them. Designing printed fabrics is more like graphic design and needs an understanding of print and in particular screen-print or serigraphic processes.

Textile design in Britain today often means reproducing traditional patterns – pin stripes for suits, tweeds and paisleys, tartans and polka dots. Many patterns are based on flowers and foliage. The designer is strictly ruled by the market, and many designers get involved in redrawing and adjusting traditional designs and painting them up using a variety of new colour combinations or 'colourways'. The designs need to be economical to produce since each new colour used is going to need a separate screen to print and therefore an extra stage in printing. There are always new fibre mixes being developed, some by designers themselves but more often by the textile technologists, and new way of manufacturing textiles that have repercussions on ways that design can be incorporated.

Large manufacturers have their own staff designers, and some independent commercial studios will design textiles for a number of companies. However, there have never been enough jobs to go round for textile designers leaving college. Consequently designers have had to be quite broad-ranging in the kinds of jobs they looked for after qualifying. One fruitful area has been the retail industry, particularly in the areas of buying and to a lesser extent style and fashion forecasting. Others have had to operate freelance selling their collections of designs either direct to manufacturers or through agents. The difficulty here is that the manufacturing industry is largely based abroad, and so designers have to travel to the USA and the Far East to make sales.

Fashion design

Fashion design is an extremely volatile area of employment. London in particular has made a name for itself as a centre of bright innovative designers. However, it is noticeable that many of them are shooting stars who have a brief period of prominence before running into financial difficulty.

The majority of jobs for fashion designers are in wholesale garment firms and mass production companies supplying the well known retailing names like Marks and Spencer. The fashion trends or fashion 'stories' as they are called are picked up by designers and specialists called fashion forecasters who work for major chains or for specialist forecasting consultants. These stories derive from a whole range of factors. A popular film featuring a naval setting was picked up by one chain while still in production. They guessed its likely impact and successfully brought out clothes with naval inspiration. Another blockbuster set in Africa gave rise to a successful 'safari' theme using khaki and sand colours. Ideas about ecology, business, fitness, and whatever is having an impact on people's lives will influence in some way the kinds of clothes people are interested in buying. Designers then have the job of creating a range of garments influenced by these themes that can be made and sold at prices that are affordable by the target market.

Designers and their assistants generally make working drawings, cut sample garments and patterns using as little fabric as possible, keeping the number of operations needed to make the garments to a minimum, and calculating work schedules. Students will often start off in their first job as a pattern cutter. At any stage design staff must be prepared to modify their design if the costs are wrong or it is too complicated to make. All this demands a mixture of technical know-how and a good business sense.

Many designers specialise in one area of the market such as children's wear, bridal wear, theatre costume or leisure wear or they may go into slightly more specialist and 'accessory' fields like lingerie and corsetry (sometimes called 'contour'), bags, belts, shoes and hats.

Some fashion and textile courses have links with the international world of fashion and have work placements in Milan, Paris, New York and other major cities. Others build business studies into their programme to assist students to set up small businesses, in order to create their own niche.

Qualifications and training

Further education

There are numerous BTEC national diploma courses in fashion design as well as courses designated as 'clothing' which are more production-oriented but carry some design training.

Higher education

Many universities and colleges run fashion, textiles or fashion and textiles courses. Several have textile and clothing degrees that are combined with management or technological training. The majority of courses are in the UCAS system, with the exception of some Scottish colleges to which you apply direct. Some courses offer specialist opportunities to study areas like sports and leisure wear, 'contour' (corsetry and lingerie), millinery, footwear, embroidery or theatrical costume.

3-D design

This category of design is the broadest one. It encompasses a wide range of materials and a wide range of industries. It is concerned with products, objects, things. But the most significant divide within 3-D design is in the way of working: on the one hand there is craft or studio-based design, and on the other there is industrial design. Some courses are exclusively one or the other, but on many courses students are given projects involving individual one-off, small-batch and larger-scale production.

Craft-based design

Craft-based design covers ceramics, china, pottery, silver and jewellery, furniture, glass, all things which were once made by skilled craftspeople using hand techniques.

Such small-scale manufacture is seen to be 'uneconomic' in an age of mass manufacture, and so the designers in these areas tend to look for a market that will pay a premium for individually designed and made products. Such a market does exist, though it is small, and may not offer a steady income. Another possibility is to go into small-scale batch production – quite common with potters and jewellers – to create products that have a wider appeal and a more competitive pricing. Others have made a living by offering a service to the film and advertising industry making anything that is required for the purpose of creating a special effect. However that may be, getting a steady living is very tricky, and such designers have often moved for the traditional fall-back of teaching, and particularly the teaching of design technology, which has grown in importance over recent years and for which subject there has been a long-standing teacher shortage.

In addition to being visually creative, craft designers must have a feel for the functional properties of the material they are working with and the functional requirements of the object they are making: teapots must be heat resistant and must pour well, pieces of jewellery must not disintegrate if the wearer of them is running for a bus.

Craft designers have to be their own technologist, production manager, marketing and sales expert, book-keeper and buyer.

Qualifications and training

Further education

There are over 30 colleges offering BTEC national diploma programmes in 3-D design.

Higher education

The choice of BA and HND course in this sector is very wide, including specialisms in wood, metal, ceramics, jewellery, furniture and murals. These areas can be studied either singly or in combination.

Industrial design, engineering design, product design

In some senses, all design is industrial design. Although many think that the excellent network of art and design courses in this country is a mark of our interest in promoting fine art, this is in fact not the case. Most of Britain's art colleges, now mainly subsumed into universities, were instituted in Victorian times in order to improve the 'design for manufactures' that were perceived then to be relatively poor and to be threatening our preeminence as the leading industrial nation, which was beginning to be challenged, notably by Germany. Most of those courses relate mainly to the craft design activities already discussed. But a growing group of courses is available to service the needs of more modern industries of transport, electronic communications and domestic technology.

In manufacturing industry, traditionally, the engineer who designed the working parts of a carpet sweeper or a food mixer also designed its exterior and without any art-based training, did so rather haphazardly, more or less according to the shape and size of the product's parts and the demands of the manufacturing process.

Rapid growth in consumer spending and growing competition for sales led manufacturers to see the possibility of designing products which not only look good and can be sold on appearance, but can also be more efficient and convenient to use.

Qualifications and training

Further education

There are about 10 BTEC national diploma level courses offered in the UK specialising in industrial design or in model-making (a specialist, more craft skill based on part of the industrial design process).

Higher education

A number of design and technology degree and HND courses include specialisms in transport, design representation (sometimes called simply model-making, packaging and industrial as opposed to craft-based ceramics).

Spatial design

Interior design and decoration – theatrical and set design – exhibition and retail display – packaging – model-making

These areas have as much to do with other professions such as ARCHITECTURE and PLANNING (*see in* LAND USE PROFFESSIONS). These designers tend to work in teams which include technical experts (lighting and electrical people for example) and craftspeople capable of turning sketches, detailed drawings and models into reality, although all too often the designer has to do some of the practical work.

Designers in these fields need to know a lot about and be skilled in using colour, materials, texture and style of decoration. They must be able to visualise spatially and keep ahead of new ideas.

Interior design and decoration

Interior design and decoration are used not just to make the inside of a building attractive, but also to see that it is functional, practical, comfortable for the people using it, and easy and cost effective to run and maintain. The interior designer has to work closely with architects and building service engineers (who design heating, electrical, lift and air-conditioning systems) as well as the client. Architects are technically only responsible for the shell of the building. However, architects normally think in terms of designing a building as a whole, and some prefer to be their own interior designer or to have an interior designer as part of their own team.

Interior designers plan colour schemes and materials for walls, floors and ceilings; furniture and fitments (such as built-in cupboards, bedheads and bathroom suites) right down to the detail of light fittings and even doorknobs and house plants. In both appearance and practicality, the designs for a disco or a fashion store, a hotel, a public house and a set of offices will be very different from each other. Choice of materials, for example, must take account of the kind of wear they must withstand as well as creating the right kind of image and atmosphere. Limits on cost, time and space must be met – and the space must be used efficiently. Safety may well be an important factor.

Interior designers work mainly for commercial, and some industrial organisations. Work on individual homes is less common. Some very large organisations, e.g. multiple retail stores and hotel chains which redesign their outlets quite frequently and want to create an instantly recognisable, nationwide image, employ their own design teams. Most organisations, though, put the work out to tender, and freelance designers or design consultancies submit sketches, ideas and estimates. Sometimes the work comes via an architect, and indeed some interior designers work permanently for architectural practices. A high proportion of interior designers' work is not on new buildings at all but on the refurbishing of things like restaurants, banks, shops and clubs, where there is very heavy wear, and a restyled interior is part of the business of staying competitive.

Interior designers prepare the sketches and ideas for quotation. If the contract is won, they must then prepare detailed specifications and working drawings and get approval for them. They put the contract for the actual physical work on the site out to tender, and then supervise it, and see that what is put up is in fact what was designed and planned.

Interior decorators tend to work on a smaller scale and often install the designs they create. They normally confine themselves to the choice of colour scheme, furnishing and lighting, though some of them also train in the application of decorative surfaces such as marbling and rag rolling. Some work with specialist bedroom or bathroom companies providing design advice, and drawings done either by hand or on a CAD (computer aided design) system.

Theatrical and set design

Theatrical and set design covers not only the conventional stage, but also stages and sets for film and TV. Designers work to the director's plan for the whole production. This may be a realistic setting, a spectacular design for a musical or a background for a current affairs TV programme. The design must take account of the limitations of the theatre or TV or film studio, the complexities of scene changing, and camera angles and positions. It may mean searching for locations that suit the script, and finding or making appropriate props. In filmwork, the main designer is often called the art director, whose job it is to brief the carpenters, lighting people and set dressers and decorators.

The number of openings for theatrical designers is very limited. However, many of the people qualified in theatre design get freelance work as craftspeople working on lighting, costumes and props. Work is mainly freelance, even increasingly with an organisation like the BBC, which has employed many set designers.

Exhibition and retail display

Exhibition and retail display ranges from planning entire exhibition sites to designing individual stands. It merges with graphic design at this point, with either exhibition or graphic designers preparing display panels which are used both in shop and other displays, and which do not need any construction work or complicated decoration.

Exhibition work is done for trade or public exhibitions which bring together for a short time many different exhibitors – firms making or selling cars or office stationery, computers or cartoon books, textiles or alternative lifestyles. There is also a small area of work involved in designing museum exhibitions, which try to excite, inform and entertain the public about some scientific, technological or historical matter. General and trade exhibitions work to an overall plan and usually have a theme – 'Ideal Homes' or 'Camping and Caravanning'. The designers have to give the show an image within the exhibition itself and the publicity material (a corporate identity – *see* GRAPHIC DESIGN *above*) while at the same time allowing individual exhibitors to put their own images on their stands. Apart from the graphic look of the exhibition, the layout of stands and services, public concourses, etc., the designer needs to have a sense of the ergonomics of the available space so that people can circulate safely and comfortably and can find their way around the exhibition.

Retail display includes the simple arraying of goods in a shop window – take a look at a typical shoe shop which simply shows a sample of as many of the styles available as possible. But it can involve the developing of visual themes that possibly relate to a special marketing drive; many shops for instance have a special Christmas display. Fashion shops have spring, summer, autumn and winter displays to signal the changing of the stock available. It is up to the skill of the individual designer to come up with new ways of presenting perennial topics like the changing of the seasons. Other shops have abandoned the notion of a window in favour of wide open entrances enticing customers in. In these cases the whole store is seen as the display, and designers try to create an exciting environment – whether it be hi-tech with chrome, steel and glass, or repro with lots of uses of wood and warm fabrics. A particular trend over recent years has been the theatre of shopping with atriums and glass-walled lifts to make people visually aware of all the other shoppers thronging the store. When the shop becomes a complete design concept then the appropriate term for it is retail design.

Packaging

The design of packaging has developed into a specialism of its own, with some companies offering a service exclusively within this area. Even advertising agencies do not carry out this work usually these days, though some employ a packaging design group on their own premises to offer a wider service to clients and to ensure that the packaging works together with the advertising campaign.

The packaging designer needs strong graphic skills in order to design packets, etc. which can contain suitable descriptions and instructions in confined space, but they must also be aware of the properties and uses of materials as diverse as paper, cardboard, wood, metal, plastic and glass. The UK is a European leader in the provision of higher education courses in packaging design. Six institutions offer degree courses; five, HNDs. On some courses it may be combined with packaging technology.

Model-making

The making of three-dimensional models is part and parcel of the design process. Architects, interior and product designers, and theatre designers use models in order to refine their ideas and to present them to laypeople who cannot 'read' technical drawings. Yet because models have come to be constructed by separate departments, even separate companies, it has developed into a specialism in its own right with HND courses and even one degree course in model-making and its more academic title, design representation.

Specialist model-making companies tend to specialise in one of two main areas:

1 Architecture and civil engineering. Here companies would construct scale models of large new developments – an office block, an oil refinery, a marina. They may have to make a model of not only the new project, but also the existing buildings that surround the site so that people can assess how it will impact on what is already there.
2 The other field for models is the field of film and advertising in particular. This is often to create special effects on film. It may be a matter of building a model ship that will be filmed in a tank where a simulated storm can be staged.

Qualifications and training

Further education

National diplomas: there are over 40 courses in spatial design areas in the UK. They may be in interior, retail, display, spatial, theatre or exhibition design.

Higher education

Degree or HND courses are available in spatial design and in the specialisms of interior, theatre, film and TV set, exhibition and retail design.

Further information

Chartered Society of Designers.

Fine art

Fine art is often thought to refer to four 'traditional' media: drawing, painting, print-making (sometimes confusingly referred to as graphic art), and sculpture. However, many artists extend their work into other media. It would be hard to categorise all the forms that art has taken. Frequently, artists choose media that consciously challenge or subvert the public notion of what art should be. More often these non-traditional artists are trying to explore the aesthetic qualities of new media like photography and video, computers, photocopiers or lasers.

No one entering fine art as a career should really have any illusions about it. Few people are going to make any money from it, still fewer a good living. Nevertheless, artworks in new and traditional media continue to be made and shown by artists who spend a considerable proportion of their working week in the making of art. In London and other major cities organisations exist which run large usually derelict industrial premises for the benefit of artists. Artists have often taken advantage of grants to help people set up in business in order to keep going until they can generate some cash through sales of work or commissions.

Because of the realities of the economics of fine art, it is not really an area that anyone could be 'advised' to enter.

Rather it is an area that you enter despite advice. People enter it because in some sense they have to. What is very interesting about fine art courses generally is that the students tend to be older. Many of them have had a 'proper' career – many have been extremely successful at their career, but have given it up because it has been essential to develop that part of themselves that wishes to make artworks.

Qualifications and training

Further education

GNVQ/GSVQ advanced diplomas in general art and design and foundation courses offer preparation in the areas of fine art.

Higher education

There are over 60 degree courses in fine art – but no HND courses. Most courses introduce students to all four disciplines, but at a small number it is possible to take dedicated degrees in sculpture or print-making. There is one HND course in print-making and one in sculpture.

Photography

Advertising and editorial photography – fashion photography – press photography – industrial, scientific, medical and other technical photography – photographic technicians – digital photography

Frequently just as creative, just as demanding on artistic talent, aesthetic judgement and technical skill as the more traditional art forms, photography can be used in many different kinds of context. An advertisement may need a photograph to be a highly composed piece of work, where the lighting, the grain of the film, the work done in the laboratory in printing and perhaps retouching certain parts of the image to emphasise particular points of detail are calculated in most meticulous detail. A set of wedding photos, however, will have different priorities. The photographer is making a record of an important event that will never be repeated. Apart from romantic shots of bride and groom, there is a whole etiquette to be observed of the grouping together of relatives. The shots must be good first time as there will not be a second chance, and the photographer only has a limited time to get all the pictures required – and it might be raining hard enough to rule out the possibility of particular shots that had been planned. Unlike the advertising situation where many specialists and professionals have a piece of the whole action, the general practitioner who does the wedding photographs will probably take the film back to his/her own darkroom to develop and print.

Advertising and editorial photography

These areas are generally considered to be the glamorous part of the industry, offering the chance to travel. In fact, the photographers working in these areas are just as likely to work in cramped studios as to do location work. They are also the most difficult areas in which to find openings.

What they have in common is that they are usually self-employed and are commissioned to work by art directors and art editors from advertising agencies, magazines or design groups. This means that they are paid a fee for a job, and do not get paid if they are not commissioned. It also means that they spend a lot of time in the search for jobs and in running their own business – billing clients, booking jobs in, showing their portfolio.

Advertising photography destined for advertising purposes can be of just about any subject, but it is often categorised into the following specialist areas: still life, cars, food, portraiture, landscape. An advertising photographer is likely to build a reputation for excellence in one of these areas and will often be commissioned on the strength of work in past campaigns. Some photographers, however, do manage not to become typecast and can do a wide variety of work.

Editorial photography is work which is commissioned for magazines. The budgets in this area tend to be lower than in advertising, so often new photographers start off by doing editorial work. However, the subject matter may be exactly the same as for an advertising or fashion shoot.

Fashion photography

Fashion photography is basically the advertising of clothes. Specialists in this field develop a style or feel to their work which is appropriate to the requirements of one section of the marketplace. For example, a photographer used for a teenage magazine is not likely to be used for *Vogue*. Often the photographer attempts to capture an atmosphere at the expense of detail in the clothes themselves. Garments often sell because they are associated with a certain age group or style. A fashion photographer will attempt to reinforce this. Fashion photography is probably the most overcrowded and competitive area of work and is therefore the most difficult to break into.

Press photography

Photographers working for the press are providing illustrations for news events. Some of the work is fairly humdrum, recording perhaps a mayor opening a swimming pool, or a crossroads that is going to have a flyover built on it. However, press photographers can be involved in dangerous situations, in riots, in disasters such as fires, floods and major transport crashes. Some specialise in sports work. Others, perhaps more dubiously, become what are known as 'paparazzi', whose role is to provide fodder for gossip or society columns. The common factor, though, is that apart from all the technical knowledge about photography they work closely with journalists and have to have a journalist's sense of the newsworthy image. Most press photographers who are not freelance work for one of approximately 90 national and local newspapers or 1,500 weeklies. See JOURNALISM *in* MEDIA CAREERS.

Industrial, scientific, medical and other technical photography

In industry, the staff of a photographic unit may work for the public relations department, photographing new products, new machinery or new plants for research and development and quality control. Public relations work may be more like advertising, and the best industrial photographers can produce shots of chemical plants or cranes which are as original as any other.

In research and development or quality control the work is similar to photographic work in a university or research establishment. Here special fluorescent ultraviolet and other techniques are used to photograph, for example, plant sections, crystals, fractures in metals and fibres under microscopes which can magnify many times the normal size to illustrate details which would be otherwise invisible. Scientific research also uses high-speed cine and time-lapse photography to examine processes and activities which happen either too fast or too slowly for the human eye to record the exact sequence of events. Photography is also used extensively in areas like astronomy, space research and meteorology.

Some areas of scientific photography are becoming very specialised

Medical photography

Medical photography is one example where a wide range of both straightforward and highly advanced techniques and equipment are used to record the progress of a disease and/or treatment; to photograph slides of, for instance, tissue cultures and sections and under-skin photographs; and even to photograph inside the body. The work is exacting and highly technical – for example, colour accuracy is crucial, and depends on using exactly the right staining medium to prepare a tissue section and on the right use of film.

Forensic photography

Forensic photography is another example of highly technical work. Here photographers must make very accurate records of the scene of a crime or of an accident; produce enlargements of evidence such as finger- or shoe-prints, tyre and skid marks or signs of forced entry, and use infrared and ultraviolet photography to reveal microscopic detail, of cloth fibres or blood stains for example, or evidence that has been covered up. For all these areas a genuine interest in science is required.

Photographic technicians

There is an area of employment in photography that does provide regular paid employment. This is with the army of highly competent technicians who, for instance, process and retouch 'professional' film, that is film used in advertising, publishing, etc. as opposed to personal snaps which are processed in a high-volume or highly automated process. Professional laboratories on the other hand offer a bespoke service to professional photographers. The photographer can specify exactly the kind of look or feel required. Conversely, the printer can spot problem areas on the plate and suggest ways to remedy them. Uneven lighting can cause problems, for instance, and the printer has techniques that can alleviate this. This 'hand printing' can bring out the true quality of a shot, and can minimise the effects of mistakes made by the photographer.

Digital photography

Advances in computer technology have meant that photographic images can be taken and then manipulated electronically. There are numerous scientific uses for such computer-generated photographs, notably in medical and forensic work. However, the techniques are beginning to have commercial application in areas like holography, where 3-D images can be created. The most common commercial usage, however, is the retouching of photographic images that have been generated on photochemically sensitive film. What happens is that the film image is scanned into the computer (the technical term is digitised); then changes in the image can be made electronically. To give an example, say you had a picture of a man's face and an elephant's trunk. It would be possible to combine the two images so that the man appeared to have an elephant's trunk instead of a nose. Such manipulation has been done for years by skilled retouchers of photographs. The difference now is that such trickery can be achieved much quicker on computer. Photography is no longer, if it ever truly was, a mere recorder of external reality.

Qualifications and training

For work in all scientific and technical areas a genuine interest in science is required.

For photographic technician work in professional labs it is still possible to start off as a general dogsbody and learn the necessary skills on the job with perhaps day release to college to get City & Guilds qualifications.

For people interested in becoming professional photographers, a full-time college course is often advisable. This is not because it is always necessary – it isn't. Photography is one of the careers in which entry at all levels is still possible. In general photographic and in industrial studios, and in fashion and editorial work it may be possible to find a job as a photographer's assistant and study part-time for qualifications. However, the availability of such openings and the likelihood of their appearing at the right time make a course the chosen route for most people.

Courses exist at all levels, from City & Guilds, BTEC and SCOTVEC diplomas to higher national diplomas and degrees. A well-respected alternative to the higher-level courses is the Professional Qualifying Examination (PQE) of the British Institute of Professional Photography. Courses leading to this qualification are currently offered at five institutions, but due to the difficulty experienced by students in obtaining discretionary awards, some of them have started to include study for the PQE in their degree and HND courses.

Given the different slants – artistic or scientific – of the various courses, prospective students need to seek careful advice before making applications.

Press photography has an established training route. People who have five passes at GCSE A–C/SCE 1–3, including English or equivalent, may apply for places on one of two training schemes run under the auspices of the National Council for the Training of Journalists (NCTJ): on-the-job training supplemented by block release to Sheffield College, or a one year full-time course at the same college. (It is not necessary to have an NCTJ-approved qualification for freelance work.)

Medical photography too has a prescribed training route. There are some full-time courses. Alternatively, traineeships are available in some hospitals. Applicants must have a minimum of four GCSEs A–C or equivalent, including English, maths and science, and are expected to study for the Medical Photography Examination of the BIPP (an essential qualification for work in the NHS).

NVQ/SVQs have been accredited at levels 1–4 in photography and at levels 1–3 in photographic technician work.

Other opportunities

Art galleries and museums – conservation and restoration – arts administration – art teaching – art therapy – picture research.

Art galleries and museums

Those maintaining large collections of paintings, sculptures and other works of art employ people with degrees in art and design or art history. The work may include administering the day-to-day running of the gallery, cataloguing the collections, planning and selecting new exhibitions and organising publicity. Some galleries and museums are central- or local-government run and offer pay and conditions similar to that of other public sector workers. Others may get public subsidies but have to run very much on a shoestring.

It may be advantageous to follow an art-based degree with a Diploma in Museum Studies. There are about 2,000 museums in the country. *See also* MUSEUM WORK *in* HISTORICAL AND RELATED WORK.

Conservation and restoration

There are a small number of opportunities that occur in conservation and restoration of artworks. Usually conservators specialise in one material – books, pots, furniture, oil paintings, prints, stone carvings, gilding. There are some courses available around the country ranging from national diploma to postgraduate level. Some specialise in gilding and carvings; others in the conservation of oil paintings. Many people specialising in the conservation and restoration of paintings have normally taken a postgraduate course. See also CONSERVATION AND RESTORATION *in* HISTORICAL AND RELATED WORK.

Further information

The Association of British Picture Restorers.

Arts administration

People running galleries and museums would probably describe themselves as being in ARTS ADMINISTRATION (*see in* THE PERFORMING ARTS), a category which also includes running small theatre or dance companies, film cooperatives, arts magazine publishing, or running a complex of craft workshops. Although many people seem to feel that to move into such an organisation is a natural step after an 'arts' degree, in fact such companies tend to need people with a wide range of very practical skills. An administrator may find that he/she needs to be a book-keeper, painter and decorator, publicity officer, ticket seller and electrician all rolled into one. It is for this reason that people intent on arts administration should use their college days to get involved in running student arts events which have the same flimsy financial backing.

Art teaching

Further and higher education

In general, teachers in this area of art and design education start by doing part-time teaching while carrying on their own professional practice. You would need a postgraduate qualification and a track record of success in your own field – whether that be commercial success, or artistic success, such as a number of exhibitions or shows that had attracted attention.

In addition there are four courses in Britain that specialise in training people to teach at further education colleges: Bolton Institute of Higher Education; University of Greenwich; University of Huddersfield; and University of Wolverhampton.

Adult education

Again teachers in this sector tend to work part-time to gain extra income. It is a useful way of seeing if teaching is something you enjoy because you can start off by taking a group one evening a week as a way of dipping your toe in the water.

Teaching in secondary schools

This is the largest sector of teaching in terms of opportunities. The usual route is to take a one-year postgraduate course offered at 23 colleges across Britain. People sure that they want to teach art could do a four-year degree in education with an art specialism, which is a way of studying art to degree level and training to teach concurrently. However, this route into secondary teaching is fast disappearing.

Design technology, sometimes known as technology, may sound as though it is too technical for art specialists, but many art and design graduates go into teaching this subject. They say it features a very strong base of creative problem-solving and understanding of materials which is very close to the way of working on design courses. In addition, this subject has been experiencing a shortage of teachers for some time, and there are a number of ways in which it has been made easier to train to become a teacher in this area. There are special two-year courses for people who do not have a degree but have a higher national diploma. Also some local authorities offer people jobs where you can train while you are employed by them as an 'articled' or 'indentured' teacher. It is a scheme particularly useful to those not wishing to spend the further year in college that they would otherwise need.

About 550 places are available each year for art and design students to train as secondary teachers. *See also* EDUCATION AND TEACHING TEACHING.

Art therapy

Art therapy is a form of treatment for people with emotional or psychological problems. Art therapists work in hospitals with psychiatrists and occupational therapists, but also in other treatment centres like child guidance clinics or prisons and remand centres. Training is offered at the following centres: Hertfordshire College of Art and Design, Sheffield University, and Goldsmiths' College, London. These courses are open to art and design graduates, but also to trained social workers and psychiatric nurses who wish to extend the range of their therapeutic skills. *See also in* SUPPLEMENTARY HEALTH PROFESSIONS.

Picture research

Picture researchers locate and select pictures to illustrate books and articles. When they have established with the author and editor just what type of illustration is required they set about tracking down something appropriate. It may be a picture held in a library, press agency, museum or picture library, and the researcher needs considerable detective ability – and contacts – if it is not listed in any catalogues or standard sources. When they find something suitable they then have to negotiate its loan fee and any copyright fee together with transportation and possible insurance costs. Travel is often involved – to inspect possible material, and this may be overseas. Training is by means of short courses. Book House Training Centre in West London, for instance, offers two-day courses covering the skills of picture selection, finding pictures, copyright and negotiating. Most picture researchers are freelance.

Contents

Education and Teaching

(CLCI: F – FAB, FAP)

Background

Education is a major industry, and a large employer. It includes not only the schools – primary and secondary, state maintained (whether local authority, grant maintained or voluntary-aided status) or independent – but also universities, colleges of higher education, further education and specialist schools and colleges (teaching, e.g., students with special needs, *and see in* ART, CRAFT AND DESIGN; MUSIC AND DANCING *and* ACTING AND DRAMA *in* THE PERFORMING ARTS; *and* HOME ECONOMICS *in* HOTELS AND CATERING). It still employs about 1.5 million people, a high proportion of whom teach, plus administrators (in, e.g., local education authorities), other professions (*see* LIBRARY AND INFORMATION WORK; CAREERS ADVISORY WORK *in* SOCIAL AND RELATED SERVICES); educational and child psychologists, medical staff, laboratory technicians, catering managers and domestic staff.

Other organisations have their own educational facilities (although they are usually restricted in scale and normally have a fairly narrow educational aim), for example the educational/training facilities of the larger employers (e.g. the banks and government departments), managing agents for training schemes, training centres run by professional and other bodies, and other major organisations. THE ARMY (*see in* THE ARMED FORCES) has its own education corps (*see below under* OTHER WORK IN EDUCATION). Many other organisations provide education/training for specific purposes, from learning to swim or play golf to private business schools.

The education 'industry' supports parts of a number of other sectors, for example, educational PUBLISHING *and* BROADCASTING (*see in* MEDIA CAREERS) and professional bodies.

The education system

For years a steadily expanding state-provided educational system has been virtually taken for granted in the UK, with compulsory schooling for all between the ages of 5 and 16, and expanding opportunities for those under 5 and over 16. From the start of the coordinated national education system in 1902 to the mid-1970s, education was a growth industry. For example, state expenditure on education rose by 154% between 1946 and 1970. In 1994–95 total expenditure by central and local government was £35 billion – a real-terms increase of 31% since 1984–85, representing over 5% of GDP.

Education, expanding or contracting, is always changing, often radically, with all kinds of political, social and economic forces exerting pressure – for expansion, for reform of one kind or another, for improved standards or greater vocational input – and this is never likely to stop. Indeed, political 'initiatives' in the education sector have in the 1990s become almost endemic, with often unforeseeable results, especially for those who must teach or administer in education. Argument and debate about education is endless: what it should be and do, how it should be done, how far it should be 'relevant' to the needs of employers, etc.

From the late 1970s to the mid-1980s, the climate was rather different. Expenditure on education fell in real terms. The whole education system had to come to terms with both less state financial support and fewer pupils/students. Overall the result was largely fewer opportunities and jobs in an education system widely regarded as under-resourced.

The 1990s so far, however, have witnessed wide and far-reaching changes in the way education is structured and delivered in the UK. Some of these include the introduction of the National Curriculum; the setting up of new examinations and testing procedures in school; the establishment of local management of schools; the increase in involvement of parents and local businesses in school management, especially through governing bodies; the restructuring of the higher education sector; the independence of further education colleges from local government control; the provision of new types of secondary education such as grant maintained schools ('opted out') and City Technology Colleges; major changes in the system of teacher-training.

Change is likely to continue to gather pace in the future as Britain's needs for a highly skilled workforce change and develop. Numbers of pupils in education are increasing and higher education is set for further expansion in the late 1990s. The impact of the European Union is significant on the education system as a whole. This includes a range of

European educational and exchange programmes in schools, the recognised importance of modern languages as a subject area and established links between higher education institutions across Europe as well as training and work experience exchanges in further education.

The introduction of new qualifications such as NVQs (National Vocational Qualifications) giving competence-based evaluation of work activities across a very wide range of occupations has meant that retraining and updating of skills (often linked into local FE colleges) is now part of many people's working lives. This is a pattern that is likely to continue to increase.

In the past, direct central-government intervention in what happens inside educational institutions has supposedly been minimal, but now everyone working in the educational field has to live with not only the indirect, but also centrally directed change, and under much greater scrutiny and debate on educational issues and methods.

Schools and school teaching

Working as a teacher – pre-school and nursery teaching – primary school teaching – secondary school teaching – sixth-form and tertiary colleges – special-needs teaching

The total number of schools in the UK is now (1995) about 34,000 (down nearly 7% since the mid-1980s). About 93% are state schools. The number of nursery schools has increased by 18% since 1985, while primary schools have dropped by 6% over the same period. Secondary schools again have declined in number by 15% and special schools down also by 12%. Independent schools number about 2,500 (a 5% decrease since 1985). A total of 9.5 million pupils attend all schools, of which about 590,000 are in the independent sector. The number of those attending independent schools has risen slightly in the last ten years. Pupil numbers at nursery and primary levels have been rising for several years. Pupil numbers of under-5s have been rising – an increase of 46% since ten years before. In the same period, the participation rate of 16–18-year-olds in education has risen by about 14%. Numbers in secondary schools have also risen after a major decline in the late 1980s, but still remain 14% less than in 1985.

Schools have traditionally been run by local education authorities (LEAs). However, this situation has changed with Local Management of Schools (LMS), which now gives school governing bodies the responsibility for employing staff, financial management and control, maintenance of school property as well as formulating a school development plan. (Independent schools are usually managed by trusts or governors.) In practice, the role of the Senior Management Team on the school staff, including the Head and Deputy Heads, has become critical in advising governors' committees. The power of parents has also been enhanced, with more information about schools made available, including examination results and more choice possible by individual parents. Schools are also allowed to obtain 'grant maintained status' (7% of pupils in 1994 were taught in grant maintained schools) by opting out of LEA control altogether, receiving central government grants under the Department for Education and Employment. In addition, 'City Technology Colleges' (CTCs or 'technology academies' in Scotland) have been set up with funding from both central government and industry. Fifteen CTCs have been established by 1995, having an emphasis on science and technology and a wider post-16 curriculum.

The individual teacher has traditionally been master or mistress in his or her own classroom, deciding how and to some extent (i.e. as limited by, for example, examination syllabuses) even what to teach. The introduction of the National Curriculum has altered this greatly in both primary and secondary schools. In addition to curriculum changes, standard assessment procedures are also required. Nevertheless, schools are still run by a kind of consensus. The senior management team has to gain the agreement of the teaching staff for particular plans or changes and is required to consult governors especially. As a rule, schools continue to attract and appoint teachers who broadly agree with the school's approach and ethos. Running a school is a team business.

This is still first and foremost a 'scholarly' and academic occupation, whatever the type of school. But it also involves communicating, making relationships, working with and getting on with people (of all ages), and also organising both people and resources. Managerial skills are fast becoming very important for senior teachers' work. The higher the staff grade, the more time is spent outside the classroom itself on administration and organisation.

Schools try to achieve a balance between educating the whole child; helping them to develop their potential; teaching them how to learn, to find out and think for themselves; passing on subject knowledge; teaching them specific skills; and enabling them to pass examinations; and schools are increasingly expected to prepare them for options after school, including employment.

The total number of teachers was 544,000 in 1984/85, now standing at 542,000 in 1995, of whom 59,000 work in the independent sector (a 20% rise since 1985). Teacher numbers in primary schools have increased by 12% to 231,000 in the same period, while those in nursery schools have increased by 13% and special schools have fallen slightly by 3%. Secondary school teachers have fallen by 14% to 230,000 reflecting the reduction in pupil numbers in recent years. Pupil–teacher ratios have for all schools have remained roughly the same for the last ten years. The average size of a primary class is just under 22, and secondary classes are just below 16 – similar to a decade ago.

Future demand for primary and secondary teachers is subject also to government policy; between 1994 and 1997 there will be a 24% reduction in primary teacher training places with a preference towards candidates with science, maths and technology qualifications. There will be a corresponding increase in the number of teacher training places across all subjects at secondary level over the same period. Nearly all new recruits are now graduates (about

98%); 17,000 teachers entered secondary teaching in 1995 compared to just over 12,000 for primary. The demand for secondary teachers will increase with the rise in the school population in the late 1990s. Shortage subjects, especially in science, maths, modern languages and technology, will continue to exist. The Priority Subject Recruitment Scheme beginning in September 1996 aims to help meet the demand for trained teachers in shortage subjects.

Working as a teacher

The time teachers spend in the classroom is only part of their working day, week, and year. While it might seem that teachers' working days are short by comparison with most other jobs and the working year is 195 days, in fact the teaching day and term are only too often the proverbial tip of the iceberg. Teachers are required to work 'the additional hours needed to carry out effectively their professional duties' – a survey in 1991 showed that the average classroom teacher worked 54.4 hours a week. A maximum of 25 hours each week are spent in the classroom itself, the rest of the time being taken up with preparation and administration. Deputy heads average about 58 hours per week.

Not only must teachers mark pupils' work done in school and at home (even five minutes per pupil per week may mean several evenings' work), but teaching today demands far more pre-lesson preparation than traditional 'chalk-and-talk', and teachers must prepare for new and different exam syllabuses. The year's work has to be planned well in advance, and annual reports need to be written. Many teachers make all kinds of teaching aids for themselves. For many teachers computing skills are also an increasingly important teaching tool to use.

Teachers are also expected to spend time on extra-curricular activities, often after school hours, ranging from sports, drama and music, through fundraising, home–school links and parent–teachers' associations, to school journeys, outward bound courses and community social work. Teachers must also spend time keeping up with new developments, and where possible attending courses. In addition other administrative duties need to be carried out, e.g. completing attendance registers, collecting dinner money, etc. This can all add up to a working year at least no shorter than the national average.

Teaching is, for most people, a very demanding job, mentally, emotionally and physically requiring considerable commitment. Factors affecting the job now include: more demanding teaching methods; and children and young people who are more independently minded, less passive and amenable to traditional discipline. All combine to ask much more of today's teacher. Many schools now have a large proportion of pupils from ethnic and religious minorities, thus requiring sensitivity to different cultures and new approaches in matters such as the teaching of religion.

Promotion in secondary schools is mainly via the subject route, with senior teachers often going on to more academically demanding teaching, for instance for A-levels, and then on to departmental head – headteachers usually come through this way in state maintained schools. Alternatively, it is possible to move up via the pastoral system, to head of year or house, or head of upper or lower school – in boarding schools especially, this is more often a route to a headship. To gain promotion, in state and/or independent schools (teachers are not in any way restricted either, except by choice or availability of posts), it is often necessary to change schools. The number of senior teaching posts is finite, and falling, particularly in state schools. Intermediate posts in large schools give scope for considerable responsibility. Smaller, and independent schools have fewer posts of middle responsibility Geographical mobility, a willingness to take on added responsibility and in-service training can all enhance prospects for promotion. Some move out of teaching altogether into, e.g. educational administration, or inspectors as a form of promotion.

Although schoolteaching is generally considered as a single profession, it is now almost essential to decide whom, what and where to teach before training. Different qualifications, and different personal characteristics too, are needed to teach, for example, a lively single group of seven-year-olds all day compared with teaching physics to a succession of different classes of teenagers of different ages and abilities.

Pre-school and nursery teaching

While the legal age at which children start school is still five, it is generally recognised that children under that age can benefit from a stimulating environment of 'creative learning', organised by trained staff. Provision is also made for children with special needs. Traditionally this has been non-statutory and funded at the discretion of Local Education Authorities. Hence the demand for places, whether full- or part-time, has usually been higher than places available. Currently (1995) voucher schemes are being piloted for parents to buy places at either a state or private school. The automatic right to nursery education is likely to continue to be a subject of strong political debate in the future.

Teaching the under-5s is either in state nursery schools, special schools or classes in primary schools, or in private play and part-time 'nurseries'. About 728,000 under-5s in 1994 attended nursery classes in primary schools, about 62,000 the 1,300 separate nursery schools employing 2,700 teachers throughout the UK. They may be helped by one or two trained nursery 'nurse' assistants. Nursery classes, of about 20 children, are not 'taught' in the conventional sense. Free play, which is physically and creatively stimulating, is mixed with activities which help children to learn skills like painting, printing, making masks, acting, storytelling, singing and making music generally. They work with sand, water, climbing equipment, 'wendy' houses, pets, etc.

The very many private nursery groups (about 154,000) as well as a small number of council-run groups give 3- to 4-year olds similar opportunities of a few hours' 'structured' play. All LEA nursery schools and groups require qualified staff, whereas the picture in the private sector is much more varied. Most state nursery schools are in the larger towns and cities. Church-controlled primary schools are common, and may require staff to be members of a particular religion.

Primary school teaching

Five- to 11-year-olds (sometimes 5- to 13-year-olds) are taught in primary schools in the maintained sector. Independent preparatory schools traditionally teach from 7 or 8 through to 13, but many now take younger children, certainly down to 3, in kindergartens or 'pre-prep departments', which are growing in number.

Maintained primary schools normally 'stand alone', separate from secondary schools. They are all day schools, usually small, and mixed, all but 25% have fewer than 300 pupils with only 10% having more than 400. The 'average' school has about 250 children, six full-time teachers, one or two part-time, and a head. In 1984–85, primary schools numbered 25,000 with 4.5 million pupils. Presently the number of schools is about 24,000 with 231,000 teachers and a total school population of 5 million. Pupil numbers increased particularly during 1986-90 but proportionately less than teacher numbers up to the present time, hence the improvement in primary pupil–teacher ratios.

Independent preparatory schools range from the junior departments of public schools through to cathedral choir schools. Some, apparently quite separate, in fact prepare children for entry to specific public schools. Over 600 schools are members of appropriate associations which apply set conditions of entry regarding educational standards and staff employment. Nearly 50% are coeducational, but many still teach boys only.

In primary school, teachers in 1996 have a single class throughout the day, for the whole academic year, teaching the same children all the time, whatever and however they are being taught. However, trends may suggest a return to many traditional methods in primary teaching with a much greater emphasis on reading schemes to improve literacy. Whole-class teaching is being favoured, with less time on 'project work'. The introduction of the National Curriculum into primary schools provides teachers with a framework for primary education with assessment and evaluation at the ages of 7 and 11, aimed at monitoring pupils' development. Primary teachers are also encouraged to take responsibility for a specific subject or to coordinate an area of the curriculum.

Primary teachers try to build up relationships and establish trust with their pupils. In particular, children are helped to develop their ability to use their language skills and to handle numbers and mathematical ideas; to gain knowledge of science and technology, as well as of the world we live in, its history and people; and to gain moral awareness and sensitivity as well as aesthetic awareness through creative work. Teachers also play an active part in developing the school's links with the local community. Classes, on average, have about 22 children, mostly all of the same age and with all kinds of different abilities and aptitudes, although streaming or setting may become a more commonplace feature of primary teaching in the future. Some schools, though, use different methods, for example 'team' teaching, which involves two or three teachers working together with a rather larger group of children.

Teaching in independent 'prep' schools may be similar to maintained primaries, especially for younger children. Even so, most independent schools are in business to get pupils through common entrance exams for public school, at 13, and so formal subject teaching starts by age 8 or soon after, with English, maths, and French lessons from 9, sciences and Latin (now optional) from 10. Days and classes have to be more 'structured', and people able to teach specific subjects as well as generalists are needed.

Teachers in state primary schools as well as in preparatory schools all have a great deal of preparation to do for classwork; they have to research projects, dig out books and materials, arrange outings, organise plays and concerts, look over children's work and keep a check on their progress, write reports, and cope with emergencies and problems. In boarding prep schools, teachers also have to spend time with the children in the evenings and at weekends, organising and helping with hobbies and other activities; many boarding-school teachers have to live in.

Secondary school teaching

Most state maintained secondary schools teach pupils from 11 through to 16 and usually on to 17 and 18. For example, some education authorities teach 9- to 13-year-olds in 'middle' schools, and some the 16–18/19 age group separately in sixth-form colleges. Independent schools generally teach from 13, sometimes 11, and a higher proportion of pupils tend to stay on at school until they are 18.

Maintained state secondary schools are still mainly 'comprehensive', teaching all the young people, of whatever ability, who choose to attend the school. All but about 100 are day schools, many are coeducational but some are single-sex. They are not all the same – they vary just as much as other types of school and Local Management of Schools has meant that they are much more diversified than before. They vary greatly in size, but only 140 or so have 1,500 or more pupils and under 33% have more than 1,000 pupils.

The number of maintained secondary schools has been falling for many years, first as smaller schools merged to form comprehensives, and then as pupil numbers fell. By 1995, numbers were down to well under 4,000, against over 6,600 30 years earlier. They now teach under 3.65 million pupils, against 4.2 million in 1985. However, the reduction in pupil numbers is likely to continue to reverse during the rest of the 1990s. The number of teachers at secondary level stands as 230,000 and will be likely to correspond to any further increase in the school population during this decade. Both pupil and staff numbers in independent secondary schools have increased since 1985.

Independent schools are generally smaller than maintained secondary schools. Few have more than 800 pupils. A high proportion are still single-sex, although many boys' schools now take girls into their upper forms. Quite a few are boarding schools, although day schools are expanding most. About 1,350 independent schools are accredited by the Independent Schools Joint Council. Each independent school selects its own pupils from those who apply. Some are highly selective academically, although they do teach children from a wide range of different abilities, and some 'progressive' independent schools have liberal teaching policies, put less emphasis on public exams and have fewer rules, etc.

Secondary schools teach a wide range of subjects, which vary to some degree with the school. The complete range of subjects taught in state schools often depends on the level of funding available. Independent schools teach what is called a 'common core' – English, maths, sciences, geography, history, French, and some form of religious studies. In the state sector, school subjects are prescribed by the National Curriculum (although CTCs are allowed to vary this with a technological bias).

The National Curriculum consists of ten 'foundation' subjects which children must study at school – English, mathematics, technology, science, history, geography, a modern language, music, art and physical education (this varies to some degree in Northern Ireland, Scotland and Wales). Religious Education is also taught. Each child's school career from the age of 5 to 16 is divided into four 'Key Stages' where he or she follows set programmes of study to help reach so-called attainment targets in each subject. Assessments are made in each Key Stage to help measure progress. Many schools teach social sciences, such as economics and sociology. State schools which have sixth forms also usually teach vocational courses as well as 'advanced' general courses such as A- and AS-levels. An independent school with a high academic reputation will teach only at the highest levels, i.e. to GCSE standard, and much of the emphasis will be on working for public examinations, which are sometimes taken earlier than in maintained schools. Some comprehensives and most of the major independent schools also teach languages other than French and German, such as Latin. State and some independent schools also teach commercial subjects, technical skills, etc. The introduction of GNVQs (General National Vocational Qualifications) gives opportunities to teach vocation-related subjects.

Most teachers at secondary level usually specialise in teaching one subject, but an increasing number teach a second. In contrast to primary school, each teacher takes different groups of children in the same subject, throughout the school year. Classes may stay together for all their school work, or they may break up into ability groups for different subjects. Independent schools tend to set or stream more tightly than maintained schools, and test progress more frequently. In larger schools teaching is organised in departments, each with their own team of teachers and a 'head of department'. Teachers may both specialise in a subject, and also teach just part of the age range. A maths teacher in one large school may teach 11- and 12-year-olds in all-ability groups, or specialise in teaching for GCSE and/or A-level. Another department, even in the same school, may 'band' or 'set' pupils into ability groups from the first year.

Secondary school teachers must prepare both their lessons and teaching material, organise classroom and other displays; and set, mark and check pupils' work, out of class time, although they may have some 'free' periods in which to do some of this. Exams and other tests have to be prepared, supervised and marked; reports on individual pupils must be written. For GCSE and some other exams, some amount of coursework has to be assessed. Departmental and full staff meetings and parent–teacher meetings are regular events too.

Superimposed on the teaching structure is a 'pastoral' framework, designed to make sure every pupil has the right kind of support. Every teacher is generally also a form, or class, teacher, but may not actually teach the pupils in their form. Looking after the class includes basics like seeing who is away and why, and supervising their progress and behaviour, looking out for problems, acting as mediator when problems crop up and being both disciplinarian and counsellor. At various stages, form teachers must ensure that pupils make decisions on what they will study in the next phase of their schooling, and perhaps what public exams they will take. This has to be discussed with pupil, parents and other staff. A form teacher is everyone's point of contact for all the pupils in the class, from head to parent, from English teacher to Careers Adviser and Education Welfare Officer. For pupils, a form teacher is someone to go to with problems and to get practical help and advice. The form teacher is usually supported by 'house' and/or 'year' heads or tutors, who may have a lighter teaching load to allow them to deal with the many and varied problems their group of forms throw up. Teachers are often involved in arranging work experience through local contacts in industry and commerce. Many schools have also introduced Records of Achievement for pupils which teachers are involved in preparing.

Most teachers also help organise other activities, such as drama groups, chess clubs, musical activities, sports fixtures, camping and climbing expeditions, and holidays abroad. In independent boarding schools, teachers spend time with pupils on out-of-school activities, and teaching times may be different.

Sixth-form and tertiary colleges

Traditionally, a mark of a school with a strong academic record has been a sixth form capable of getting pupils through A-level exams and into university. Teaching intelligent and well-motivated sixth formers is often considered as a form of bonus, or promotion, for many teachers. In many areas, local education authorities have established separate sixth-form colleges to teach the 16- to 19-year-old age group rather than continue with the traditional school sixth form. Over 160 such colleges exist at the present time, including 55 tertiary colleges. Tertiary colleges have a wide range of courses and subjects on offer, including both vocational and academic ones in a college-style environment for 16- to 19-

year-olds plus part-time courses for both adults as well as young people.

Special-needs teaching

The other main area of teaching is in special schools for children who are considered to have 'special educational needs': either physical, mental or emotional/behavioural factors which can affect learning. It has been estimated that 1 in 6 of all children have special needs at some point during their school years, but that at most 2% may require completely special provision. A small proportion of children are allocated places in special schools with appropriate facilities and trained staff. Education policy has for some time favoured the integration of children with special needs into the mainstream school system wherever appropriate.

Numbers of special schools have been falling. This is partly due to the fewer numbers of children as a whole and also as a result of integrating special needs pupils into mainstream schooling. The number of teachers has also declined slightly to 19,000 since 1985 – a drop of 3%.

More children with special needs are being taught in mainstream schools than before, either in the classroom itself with extra support or in a special unit with the school.

More special-needs children are being taught by the school's ordinary staff. But the schools still also need teachers trained to cope with children's special needs and learning difficulties. Experienced and qualified teachers are required to take specialist training to move into some kinds of Special Needs work. As a result of the Children's Act, Specialist Special Needs Co-ordinators are required in all schools. Demand is also there for teachers with special expertise to train other teachers, to be advisory and 'peripatetic', who travel extensively seeing children in many different units and schools.

Recruitment and entry

Schools within the state sector as well as reputable independent schools only recruit those with 'qualified teacher status' (QTS). The government aims to match the output of qualified teachers with the level of demand.

The planned intake (England and Wales) was for primary teachers: to 13,000 (1994), 12,000 (1995), 11,000 (1996); and for secondary teachers: to 16,000 (1994), 17,000 (1995), 18,000 (1996).

The government has said that there will be a possible extra 5,000 (full-time equivalent) teaching posts created to match the increasing pupil numbers for 1996/97. However, colleges find it difficult to meet their exact intake targets: in 1995 they over-recruited in primary teaching and under-recruited for secondary.

The actual employment prospects for teachers varies according to the subject(s) they can offer and the part of the country they are applying to. There is a fluctuating demand for supply teachers to fill the posts of absent staff due to ill health, training courses or other reasons.

The Teacher Training Agency (TTA) was established in 1994 to take responsibility for all aspects of teacher training and education. It is responsible for funding initial teacher training, for providing information on routes into teaching, for raising standards of teacher training and for promoting teaching as a profession.

Qualifications and training

Teachers in state schools require teacher training leading to Qualified Teacher Status (QTS). In England and Wales, training is usually for a specific age range, but this means being eligible to teach any age, although switching may well be difficult. However, in Scotland it is necessary to be specifically qualified for the age range taught.

Teaching is now a graduate-only profession for new entrants and so requires a Higher Education degree. This is normally either a BEd (Bachelor of Education) or a subject degree followed by a postgraduate teaching qualification (PGCE). For school and college leavers, entry to a degree needs two A-levels or equivalents and GCSE grades A–C in English and maths. Advanced GNVQs instead of A-levels may be equivalent sometimes with additional studies. For primary teacher training after 1 September 1998 (for those born on or after 1 September 1979), a GCSE grade C in science is also needed. Access courses for adults without academic qualifications provide a route into a degree course.

The main routes to qualification

The BEd (or sometimes BA/BSc with QTS) combines a degree with a teacher training qualification. Courses usually last three or four years at HE colleges and universities. It involves studying one or more academic subjects as well as the practice and theory of teaching itself. This route tends normally to be regarded as particularly suitable for the younger age range. A shortened two-year BEd is available for those with appropriate prior learning or experience.

The other main route is a degree followed by a postgraduate course lasting one year full-time. Some two-year PGCE courses exist, and the Open University offers a part-time distance-learning PGCE lasting 18 months. Some two-year PGCE conversion courses are offered for training in a shortage subject which is not necessarily connected with the main degree subject. The degree itself normally, however, needs to be appropriate to the school curriculum. This route is usually considered to be more appropriate to teaching to exam level in secondary schools.

Certain degree courses treat education as a subject of purely academic study, often referred to as Educational Studies. These courses do not offer QTS and have a more theoretical and analytical content than teacher training courses.

Other routes into teaching

The Licensed Teachers Scheme allows unqualified people to gain their training on the job in school itself over two years. However, those eligible are often graduates (with a minimum of two years' study at higher education level) aged 24 or over. English and maths GCSEs at grades A–C are still required. The overall number of those taking this route and gaining QTS is still relatively small.

School-Centred Initial Teacher Training courses (SCITT) are recently available through school consortia and CTCs, offering 600 places in 1995. This is a school-based postgraduate entry scheme leading to QTS. Students are offered a flat-rate, non-means tested bursary rather than the usual grants and loans. Graduates, particularly from the local area, are often asked for. Some courses also offer a PGCE qualification if closely linked with an HE institution.

Special Teachers Assistants (STAs) is a recent qualification offering a part-time one-year course for those working in primary schools helping qualified teachers. The main focus is on supporting the teaching of reading, writing and maths at Key Stages 1 and 2. Some formal qualifications may be needed. Nearly 1,000 classroom assistants gained an STA qualification in 1994/95.

Trained teachers from the EU may be granted QTS to teach in the UK. However, overseas teachers generally may have access to additional training funds through their school to ensure any equivalence of qualification.

Teaching training in Scotland

To get employment as a teacher in Scotland in a local authority school, it is necessary to be registered with the General Teaching Council in Scotland (GTC). To be eligible for this, a teaching qualification awarded by a Scottish teacher education institution or equivalent recognised by the GTC is needed. The teaching qualification (Primary Education) entitles the holder to teach across the curriculum in primary schools. It can be obtained via a four-year BEd in a teacher education institution or a university degree followed by a PGCE. The teaching qualification (Secondary Education) entitles the holder to teach particular subjects. It is obtained via a four-year BEd for music, PE or technological education, or a combined or concurrent degree (combining subject study, study of education and school experience), or alternatively via a university degree followed by a PGCE. Application for PGCE course places are made through the TEACH system. Degree course applications are made in the usual way through UCAS.

Entry requirements for a primary education course include an SCE Standard Grade award (grades 1–3) in mathematics and a SCE Higher Grade award in English. A SCE Higher Grade pass in English is also needed as part of the entry requirements to secondary education teaching courses.

Further information

Department for Education and Employment; the Scottish Office Industry and Education Department; local education authorities; Teacher Training Agency.

Further and higher education

Education after school has traditionally been divided between further and higher education, although the boundary between them is not rigid and they overlap considerably. Some colleges straddle the two and teach in both areas. Major changes have occurred in the further and higher education sectors under recent legislation, aimed at ending the division between vocational and academic study.

The further education sector

This includes colleges of further education, colleges of technology, community colleges, and so on. A few colleges specialise – in building or agriculture, for example – but most provide a spread of courses. All these colleges are self-governing, receiving grants from the Further Education Funding Council and other sources. There are also a number of private further education colleges. They provide almost any kind of course or off-the-job training, full- or part-time, for which there is a need and sufficient demand in the area, for people ranging from 16-year-olds through to mature students.

No two colleges teach exactly the same subjects. In some areas, colleges teach both 'advanced' (i.e. HND, degree and diploma level) and 'non-advanced' (craft, technician, etc.); in others the two may be split between different colleges themselves. The possible range of studies is from the most practical to the most academic. A typical large college may have up to ten departments, of engineering, construction, science, business studies, hotel and catering, art and design, general education, etc. Courses can range from GCSE, GNVQ and A-levels, or pre-vocational studies to day- or block-release courses for people from a wide range of different jobs and training schemes. They put on short and evening courses to teach people how, for instance, to use word processors or learn languages. While most courses are for younger people trying to gain their main qualification they cater for adults needing to retrain and upgrade their qualifications.

Unlike at school or university, only a proportion of students study at college full-time, from September to June. Each college has a constantly changing student population, although teaching goes on from early morning to mid-evening. Some students come in only one or two days a week, but may stay on into the evening. Some arrive once or twice a year for six-week bursts of study.

There are some 450 FE colleges. They vary greatly in size, and full-time staff may also vary in numbers from 50 to 500. Further education colleges are often loose federations of fairly independent units (which may even be in different places) each specialising in a particular set of skills. Often they provide a balanced and comprehensive mixture of academic and vocational courses, while some tend to specialise in areas such as art and design or hotel and catering. The teaching staff are generally specialists and professionals in their field, often with extensive experience in practising their profession. Some courses are of a highly practical nature and require the teaching staff to demonstrate specific skills, supervise in the workshop, etc., while 'advanced' further education courses largely involve preparing students for higher education.

Most lecturers work up to 40 hours a week, but the actual teaching time is not usually more than 20–22 hours for lecturers, 13–16 for senior lecturers. However, the hours may include evening work. There is always a great deal of preparation and administration. Courses must be revised frequently to meet changing industrial and commercial demand, and teaching staff have to spend time talking to colleagues in industry and commerce – finding out what needs to be taught, selling their services, discussing trainees and their training in detail with their firms. They must develop new courses and programmes. Some FE staff are also involved in developing new ways, including 'distance-learning' and 'flexible learning', for people to add to their qualifications and to retrain.

Some 61,000 people (1995) teach full-time in further education in Britain. Opportunities vary locally, but part-time teaching in particular is still widely available. Currently about 143,000 staff are employed in total on a part-time basis by FE colleges. FE student numbers have increased since the mid-1980s and have seen a further 3% increase between 1993/94 and 1994/95 to 3,819,000, of whom 3.1 million are part-time.

Recruitment and entry

Teaching in FE is often a second career. In general, relevant work experience is essential for posts in vocational courses, while appropriate teaching experience and a teaching qualification is preferred for more academic subjects. Otherwise non-academic education awards, e.g. the City & Guilds Further and Adult Education Teachers Certificate, can be taken. For instance, to teach electronics will normally require an appropriate degree, a professional engineering qualification, and extensive industrial experience. There is, however, no statutory requirement for a teaching qualification.

Employment prospects are difficult to predict in the next few years, particularly with colleges keeping tight reins on their budgets, despite increases in student numbers. However, off-the-job training for young people and unemployed adults offers opportunities, as do the teaching of basic skills, pre-vocational courses, English as a Second Language (ESOL) and general studies.

Qualifications and training

About 50% of all teachers in FE are now graduates. A teaching qualification is not legally required, but is usually expected and increasingly required: at least 50% of FE teachers have some form of professional teaching qualification. Training leading to the Certificate in Education (Further Education) can be taken as a full-time one-year course – about 500 people take this each year. This covers both the subject itself as well as the study of teaching theory and methods in addition to eleven weeks' teaching practice. Alternatively, part-time and day-release courses are available for those already working in a college.

The higher education sector

At the present time, there are two groups of HE institutions in the UK: universities, and colleges (or institutes) of higher education. Both teach higher education courses and some have a range of research opportunities.

Higher education has seen rapid changes over the last 25 years. In particular the recent 'New Framework' introduced in 1992 resulted in 42 HE institutions (mainly former polytechnics) being awarded university status, having responsibility for maintaining academic standards and awarding their own degrees.

The expansion of overall student numbers from 943,000 in 1988/89 to 1.53 million in 1994/95 is projected to continue until the year 2000 and probably beyond. The participation rate in HE for the under-21s is likely to increase as well as the actual size of this age group itself. However, the continued expansion in HE will be influenced partly by any future funding arrangements for students, whether part- or full-time.

Employing institutions

These include 90 universities (several have collegiate and federal structures) and 68 colleges of higher education. The HE sector produces about 90% of all graduates in the UK. Although most higher education courses are full-time, a range of short, part-time, 'sandwich' and flexible courses are also available. All HE institutions are much larger than any school. They vary greatly in size and may have up to 1,000 full- and part-time staff.

Universities combine teaching and research and offer postgraduate masters degrees and doctorates (PhDs) as well as first degrees, HNDs and DipHEs. Some institutions are more orientated towards science and technology while others concentrate on arts and social sciences. Universities are still the only institutions where it is possible to study medicine, dentistry and veterinary science.

Colleges (and institutes) of higher education, like universities, offer a variety of courses to degree level, and professional courses. Most of these colleges offer a broad range of academic and professional subjects. Some tend to specialise in a single area of study, e.g. education, since many of them began life as teacher-training colleges. Tending to be smaller in size than the universities, the colleges have an ethos which encourages close contact between students and tutors.

Academic staff in higher education may not only teach. They can also be engaged in research, mostly in the universities. The proportion of time devoted to teaching and to research varies between disciplines, departments and institutions. The balance between the two may change during a career, with more time on research and active teaching in the earlier years and more on administration, committee work, etc. for older and more senior staff.

Lecturers do not only work in term time (usually between eight and ten weeks at present although some universities have changed to a semester system). Term-time is normally spent mainly on teaching and so research has to be done in vacations or at evenings or weekends. Since universities are under considerable pressure to achieve excellence in research, staff have problems in finding enough time to pursue their research interests, publish papers, attend conferences, sit on national and college committees, obtain research funding, and supervise postgraduate students, as well as teaching undergraduates and coping with the vastly increased amount of paperwork and administration. To meet commitments, staff will often end up working well over 60 hours a week, particularly in science or research-orientated disciplines.

Academic lecturers in higher education aim to develop analytical and logical skills in their students, to teach them to think clearly, to present ideas and facts in the best order, to be able to decide what information is important and what is not in any given situation, to be able to analyse and criticise, to assess and weigh evidence, to be objective, and argue logically. Many institutions are adapting teaching methods to help students take more responsibility for their own learning. Lecturers work with students to devise particular programmes of study and enable them to develop useful skills, e.g. research and writing skills.

Degree-teaching combines formal lectures for large classes of 25–100, with 'small-group' teaching in seminars (for 6–12 students) and tutorials (for one or two). Staff also supervise students in both undergraduate final-year project work and graduate research or study. 'Small-group' teaching can be very demanding. Scientists teach experimental work in labs; engineers conduct experimental and design work; mathematicians take 'examples' classes. Creative subjects like art and design are taught differently again.

Academic staff in most universities and HE colleges are based on their departments, so they spend most of their time with people teaching the same subject. Academic staff in higher education expect students to learn to organise their own work and their own time, and do not usually tell them what they should be doing when, so the staff stay more in the background than in schools. Most lecturers, though, act as personal tutors to a group of students, giving them any support they may need on academic or personal problems. In some universities and colleges, students may build their courses by taking 'units' or modules from several different departments and so some academic staff are course coordinators, helping to see that students make sensible choices.

Research has traditionally been carried out in the universities, which have received funds on the basis of student numbers. In practice the bulk of this work was carried out in only 20 or so universities with large research facilities. A system is available where any institution of higher education has to apply to the Research Councils and to central government for specific grants. Besides original research, universities and colleges of HE have also turned to industry for funds to carry out applied research work.

Researchers work to strict rules. The problem being researched has to be defined exactly, facts must be carefully collected, and observations made with great objectivity. Research workers may set up possible explanations, or 'hypotheses'. They then test these theories – through experiments, or against other evidence. Research can involve working in a laboratory, in a library, at a desk, or out in the 'field', depending on the subject.

Research also means 'presenting' and publishing results: as a paper in the appropriate journal or at the relevant conference, or in a book. There are rules about this too. Researchers do not work in isolation. Argument and discussion (often quite acrimonious), and dissecting each other's work in print is an integral part of the system of setting up – and knocking down or modifying – hypotheses. It can be a highly competitive business, and what promotion prospects there are may depend on a the 'right' research track record, on the quality of original and even imaginative thinking (and rather less on teaching skills). The successful researcher knows which problems to choose to research – problems to which the answers matter and which can be solved, either using existing techniques or where techniques for which the basic technology already exists, and which are practical propositions.

Not all lecturers go on researching throughout their working lives. Some think it is a young man/woman's game, and some give up full-time research when they have clearly reached their promotion ceiling. They may then give more time to, for instance, student counselling, being a warden of a residential hall, external examining, popularising their subject through books or the media, or being a consultant to other organisations, e.g. in industry.

The number of full- and part-time lecturers in HE fell considerably from 75,000 in the mid-1980s to 50,000 in 1991, and now stands at 60,000. This coincides with the expansion of HE student numbers over this period. Less than 10% of academic staff in HE are part-time. In theory the HE system has become more efficient, teaching more students with fewer staff. In practice the system is considerably overstretched, with too few resources and too many demands on staff time.

Recruitment and entry

Generally, for academic posts, extremely high academic qualifications, and research, teaching and/or other appropriate experience are needed. This applies as much to any new posts which may result from financial 'pump-priming' of disciplines as to any 'normal' recruitment there may be. In the late 1990s, many academic staff are due to retire. During the 1980s and early 1990s few young academics have been recruited, although some schemes for appointing 'new-blood' posts have been funded. There is an increasing trend for appointing short-term research workers rather than permanent members of staff.

Academics are recruited mainly on their academic, scholarly and intellectual capabilities. This is generally based on the evidence of a very good initial degree (i.e. a first, or at least an upper second), plus a higher degree (so it is rare to get a first real job before the age of 24). Most scientists are now expected to have completed at least several years postdoctoral research work, often abroad. The degrees and research have to be in the right subject. Departments usually want to recruit someone whose research and teaching interests and recent experience 'fit in' with what the department is doing and/or fill in a gap. This, of course, reduces the number of opportunities still further. In education, lecturers are expected to have had several years' teaching experience, as well as showing evidence of further study and possibly research too. Where relevant working experience is wanted, departments are unlikely to recruit anyone under 28.

Qualifications and training

Apart from the academic qualifications and any experience as above, little formal training in teaching is given (a higher degree is designed to train in research). Any training for higher education lecturers is normally given by the employing institution.

Other teaching opportunities

Custodial institutions – creative and vocational subjects – the Armed Forces

Custodial institutions

Education and training is provided in community homes run by local authorities for young people under care orders, young offenders' institutions, and prisons. With young people, the work is obviously similar to teaching in the schools, while for older people it gets closer to further and adult educational work, with some emphasis at both levels on basic skills teaching.

Most children and young people in care go to local schools, but residential teaching is provided for a proportion by the local education authority. Only a very small proportion of the staff working in community homes are teachers or instructors. They are expected to work as members of a team with other care staff, and the teaching needed depends on the needs of pupils living in the homes at any one time.

Since the competitive tendering of prison education services in 1992, the process of funding and supplying the education service within establishments has been radically altered. Contracts for such services have been awarded to contractors for a five-year period – these include further education colleges, local education authorities and private companies. The governor of each establishment issues an order for the classes and courses required.

In every establishment, whether prison, young offender institution or remand centre, there is an education coordinator assisted by a panel of part-time teachers. At young offender institutions, inmates under the school-leaving age have at least 15 hours education per week, and at both junior and senior centres an hour of physical education. Education is compulsory for those under school-leaving age and encouraged, but optional, for those aged between 16 and 21. There is a high proportion of basic skills teaching and trade training. Only 10% of the prison population take public examinations, but the range varies from NVQ/SVQs through to A-levels and Open University degrees. Teaching conditions are rarely ideal and must fit in with the prison routine. Resources are tight, and shortages of prison officers mean that prisoners do not always get to classes. Educational programmes mostly operate in the evenings and overall generate some 8 million student hours annually.

Creative and vocational subjects

Art, music, drama, ballet, accountancy, law, librarianship and the craft subjects are generally taught post-school by people who have trained in and practised their profession or skill first (but to teach art, music, drama, dance, etc. in school a full teaching qualification is required). They are taught in state schools and FE colleges, but some are also taught in private colleges and schools and others by correspondence colleges, adult education institutes or by private tuition.

The Armed Forces

The Royal Navy, the Army and the Royal Air Force are all committed to providing a professional educational and training service for all personnel. The increasing complexity of both the political world and the technology of modern warfare means that the requirement for education or training remains, despite reviews and economies.

Teaching in the Forces encompasses a wide range of subjects at all levels but is consciously targeted at providing service personnel with the military, technical and managerial skills needed to perform their roles effectively. The work varies from traditional classroom teaching, often leading to external examinations such as GCSE, City & Guilds, BTEC, and degrees, through laboratory and workshop training and military skills training. Much teaching is very practical with a strong emphasis on vocational skills, e.g. the training of linguists, bandsmen/women, craftsmen/women and technicians in mechanical and electrical engineering, electronics, avionics, aircraft and vehicle maintenance, as well as the maintenance of weapons systems.

All young entrants in the Army for technical employment categories receive education and training at specialised training establishments, where they may also have the opportunity to undergo further higher-level training later in their careers. The Army runs its own sixth-form college at Welbeck for prospective officers of the technical corps. All three services have their own education centres and training schools/colleges. However, much training and instruction of personnel is carried out on site.

To obtain promotion at key points during their careers, service personnel are required to achieve prescribed educational standards, which are achieved by means of taught courses and examinations.

Officers too undergo lengthy initial training, which combines formal academic study with the learning and practising of specific military skills. All officers go to staff colleges at set points in their careers, and promotion above certain ranks is dependent on passing exams covering academic and current affairs as well as military subjects. To qualify for promotion to the highest ranks requires lengthy attendance at staff college studying managerial and strategic subjects.

While the Army maintains its own separate education corps, both the RAF and Navy do not. The Navy carries out the necessary training of its personnel through the use of existing servicemen/women acting as instructors in their own field. It does not recruit qualified teachers to do so. The RAF similarly does not require qualified teachers; instead there is a training specialisation for RAF officers. This specialisation is not one where they act as instructors themselves, rather it is a managerial and supervisory role having responsibility for all aspects of service personnel training.

In the Army Educational Corps, the recruitment and entry standards are the same as for other officer entrants – *see in* THE ARMED FORCES. The main requirement is for graduates: in engineering, other technological or scientific subjects, languages, education and some arts subjects. Education and instructor officers undergo the same initial training as all other officer entrants. They may attend staff colleges, and undertake postgraduate and other higher-level training. Opportunities exist for promotion to senior ranks.

Other work in education

Administration – local authorities – the Department for Education and Employment – individual educational institutions – educational broadcasting, publishing and related opportunities – educational research and curriculum development – health and welfare services – inspectors of schools – librarians and information officers – training officers and advisers

The rest of the people working in education run what are generally called 'support' services. Over 110,000 such people work within schools in Britain.

Administration

Professional educational administrators are employed by local education authorities and by larger educational institutions such as HE institutions. Civil servants in the Department for Education and Employment and the Education and Industry Department at the Scottish Office are also involved in educational administration. There are also countless smaller organisations and administrative bodies like the Universities and Colleges Admissions Service (UCAS), the Further Education Development Association (FEDA) and the Teacher Training Agency (TTA). Staff are employed in organisations like the Committee of Vice-Chancellors and Principals of universities in the UK (CVCP). Teachers' and lecturers' professional unions also have relatively large staffs.

Local authorities

Education is at present still one of their major responsibilities, absorbing a large proportion of their resources and employing a significant number of people. However, in the near future this may be reduced to only those statutory services that LEAs are required to provide, e.g. the School Psychological Service.

For the full-time officials in the education department, this is a career which means working within the framework of LOCAL GOVERNMENT, with all the associated committee work, etc. However, recent legislation has given the schools themselves more responsibility for day-to-day management and the option to leave local authority control altogether, if parents and governors wish. As a result the number of administrative posts with LEAs has significantly decreased and is likely to continue to do so.

For clerical/administrative staff the work involves some of the day-to-day routines of liaising with schools, keeping records, organising supplies and equipment, paying teachers and other staff, advertising posts, etc. 'Middle managers' may be in charge of one type of school (e.g. primary), or one age group (e.g. 16–19), or all the schools in one area of the authority, or they may be in charge of any building programmes, or overseeing allocation of children between schools. Advisory teachers may be employed to assist schools in a particular subject area or curriculum issue.

At the most senior levels (chief education officer or director of education), the work is forward planning and budgeting, advising schools on the introduction of new legal requirements, LEA policy and educational developments. They liaise and consult with, e.g., other departments within the authority, with central government and with the inspectors.

Recruitment and entry

Clerical and administrative staff usually join education departments from school, college or from other employment. For a high proportion of more senior posts, though, this is a second career, requiring a teaching qualification and extensive teaching experience first.

The Department for Education and Employment

DfEE staff deal with education on a national scale, with future policy and forward planning, collecting statistics, conducting research and administering other funds under the control of the Secretary of State. They also settle disputes between parents and LEA, or between LEA and school managers, and allocate funds to grant maintained schools. DfEE staff are mostly career civil servants, with a few specialists. *See also in* CENTRAL GOVERNMENT.

Individual educational institutions

Some, mostly the largest and/or residential, employ full-time, career administrators.

Mainly these are universities and other colleges in the higher and further education sectors. HE institutions are run by committees of academic staff (with representatives of other staff and students), and the administrators provide the information on which these committees can make decisions and then carry out the decisions, 'managing' the institution on a day-to-day basis. They produce budgets and look after the finances. They maintain records, organise examinations, run complex admissions systems, produce student prospectuses and provide public relations, and generally see that the academic life of the institution runs as smoothly as possible.

Most HE institutions are like small towns, with a great many buildings, complicated engineering plant, boilers, sewers, lifts, labs, telephone systems, student residences, grounds and even streets to be maintained and cleaned. All this, and the large number of people – students and staff – means that running such an institution is a complex business. Higher education administration is a career in its own right, with most career administrators starting as graduates in junior posts.

Although many schools have secretarial staff, only the largest state and independent schools (where they may be called 'bursars') traditionally had full-time administrators who are not qualified/practising teachers. A greater number of these posts is becoming available in the state sector in the grant maintained schools.

Educational broadcasting, publishing and related opportunities

Both the BBC and independent companies devote a substantial proportion of daytime output to education, both conventional schools programmes and adult education. Radio and television also put out a variety of other educational programmes, both vocational and non-vocational for adults. *See* MEDIA CAREERS.

Most institutions of higher education have their own closed-circuit television systems which can be used in a variety of ways for both live and recorded lectures, demonstrations and so on. These systems all employ both technically trained people and teachers to script, present and direct the educational programmes.

Few educationalists find full-time careers in educational PUBLISHING (*see in* MEDIA CAREERS). Most of the people employed are professional publishers rather than teachers. Professional teachers do, however, find second or spare-time careers writing textbooks, and preparing other types of educational material. They may also work as salespersons 'promoting' the publisher's educational catalogue in schools. Some opportunities for education officers also exist in museums, charities, trade unions, etc. Other teachers find outlets through teaching abroad, especially those with language skills, including teaching English as a Foreign Language either overseas or to foreign students in Britain. There are also openings in HM Forces schools and in company-run and British schools abroad.

Educational research and curriculum development

Research is supported by the DfEE, directly through its own research programmes and indirectly through other bodies (e.g. the Economic and Social Research Council), by LEAs, by charitable bodies, by HE institutions and by teachers' organisations.

Most research is done in the higher education sector, mainly in departments, schools and institutes of education, and to a lesser extent in departments of sociology, psychology, etc.

Outside higher education, the main research organisation is the autonomous National Foundation for Educational Research, whose programme covers most aspects of primary, secondary, and further education. It also provides test, statistical and information services. Some research, much of it published, is also carried out by the School Curriculum and Assessment Authority (SCAA), which is responsible in England and Wales for developing the National Curriculum and its assessment.

Health and welfare services

In education, these include the school health service, which provides medical and dental examinations and some treatment services and is now part of the National Health Service (*see in* THE MEDICAL AND DENTAL PROFESSIONS).

Child guidance centres and clinics are provided by LEAs, by the NHS and by some voluntary organisations. Intended to assist children, whether they have learning difficulties or emotional/behavioural problems, the clinics are staffed by teams of qualified educational psychologists and psychiatric social workers under the clinical supervision of a medically qualified psychiatrist.

Educational psychologists, who try to diagnose the nature of the difficulties and to provide treatments for them, are also employed in the school psychological service. Some large schools have full-time educational psychologists (who may be called counsellors) on their staff and may organise programmes of teaching and support within the school, often with the help of trained voluntary social workers. The number of training places for educational psychologists has remained stable for the last few years and currently (1996) there is a shortage of candidates. *See also* PSYCHOLOGY *and elsewhere in* SOCIAL AND RELATED SERVICES.

LEAs also employ teams of education welfare officers (or Education Social Workers). They are involved in a range of duties working with other professionals both inside and outside school to support individual young people and their families.

Universities and some HE colleges are large enough to need full-scale health services on the campus for students and staff. An HE institution with 3,000 or more students can easily support what is, effectively, a National Health practice, although the kind of medicine practised differs from that of the usual general practice, since students and the staff have different medical problems – accidents (especially from sports activities), preventive medicine (e.g. for students going on expeditions), and psychiatric services are generally more important than in the family general practice. Campus health services are staffed by full- and part-time state registered nurses and some have a full-time medical practitioner. The traditional support given to students by the personal tutor in university is often supplemented by full-time professional counsellors, employed by the university and/or the student union. Practical welfare problems, like where to live, are generally dealt with by administrative staff.

Inspectors of schools

The academic year 1993/94 saw the start of a new system of school inspection in England and Wales. Under arrangements created by the Education (Schools) Act 1992, independent teams of inspectors authorised by and under contract to Her Majesty's Chief Inspector are inspecting and reporting on schools, regularly, on a four-year cycle.

The allocation of schools (wholly or partly state maintained) is done by competitive tender with OFSTED (Office for Standards in Education) awarding contracts. Organisations who have won such contracts include local education authorities, specialist companies and educational trusts. OFSTED is responsible for monitoring the whole inspection system and the performance of individual inspectors to ensure quality and consistency is maintained within the framework of nationally agreed guidelines.

In addition to independent inspection teams, Her Majesty's Inspectors (HMIs) from OFSTED also inspect independent schools and teacher-training institutions and report on particular issues or aspects of education in general.

Only inspectors who have successfully completed OFSTED's training and assessment programme can participate in inspection. The background of inspectors is usually that of an experienced teacher or other academic, normally at least 35 years of age.

Librarians and information officers

They are employed extensively throughout the education system, not only in universities but also in colleges of further and higher education, as well as in schools, particularly larger schools. Librarians are also sometimes employed in careers services, largely in higher education. *See* LIBRARY AND INFORMATION WORK.

Training officers and advisers

Although training instructors still play an important role and are employed throughout commerce and industry, the concept of training has changed dramatically over the years and is now recognised as an important and integral part of the working environment. It is essential that organisations have the correct skills, flexibility and adaptability to cope with the ever-increasing changes in the business environment. Training and development is the key to this and has to be a planned activity within the organisation.

Before a training plan can be implemented, all the requirements of an organisation need to be taken into account. A forecast of training needs is made, and methods of training are considered and the results evaluated.

Trainers usually possess very good communication skills and are able to interact with their trainees effectively. Good organisational and diagnostic skills are also important aspects of the work. Although they are seldom recruited as graduates, trainers usually have a degree, and it is getting more common to find them in the late twenties and early thirties. Trainers are no longer seen as instructors but assist management in problem-solving, performance appraisal and developing a corporate training plan. Many work as consultants with organisations who buy-in specific training programmes.

Training is normally a second career which develops after gaining experience and qualifications in other areas of work. An understanding of the needs of business and knowledge of vocational education is very important.

Some organisations have their own training department, while others have a training section within the personnel department. Estimates of the number of training officers vary, with a top figure of about 25,000 altogether. Once established, trainers' promotional prospects and salaries increase considerably.

For those interested in training as a career, a professional qualification is advisable. The Institute of Training and Development offers a Certificate in Training Practice on a part-time or distance-learning basis.

Further information

Details of centres authorised to run courses from the Institute of Personnel and Development.

Related work

Other employment opportunities in the educational system include CAREERS ADVISORY WORK (*see in* SOCIAL AND RELATED SERVICES), and that of laboratory and workshop technicians, a small number of media resources staff, school meals staff and caretakers.

Further information

The Department for Education and Employment; the Scottish Office Education and Industry Department; local education authorities; Local Government Management Board; the Institute of Careers Guidance, the National Association of Careers and Guidance Teachers and the Institution of Personnel and Development.

Media Careers

Contents

(CLCI: FAC – FAD, GAL, GAN)

Background

Media describes what are, for the present at least, several separate industries using quite different technical methods – printing, radio and television, broadcasting, multimedia and film – to put over ideas, information and entertainment, to large, mass audiences, through television, books, newspapers, magazines, and the cinema.

But technology, as part of the electronic and computer-based revolution in communications, has broken down the divisions between the different media as they are today, to make quite major changes in the way ideas, information and entertainment are delivered.

Of course there is a great deal of interchange between them. There is already as much film as live broadcasts on television. The 'book of the programme' is on the bookstall next morning, just as books have long been turned into a film or television series. Films can be bought on video cassettes and shown on a television screen. Films, television and books can go on a video disc, so they can all be projected on screen. Newspapers, too, are taking advantage of new means of communications, and since 1995 *The Times* can now be read on the Internet.

The television screen is also used to play games, and teletext systems like Ceefax give printed rather than spoken information via the television set. Soon it may be possible to call up television programmes or films from computer banks on demand, and not have to watch or record them when companies schedule them. Already 'television' programmes showing races are being beamed directly into betting shops, via Satcom, the business television network, and not coming onto other sets at all.

The advent of better compression systems means that the telephone lines will probably be the main source of interactive and video on demand and will be used for facilities such as home shopping in the future. It already connects us with the World Wide Web, a slow but interesting tool.

With the exception of the BBC, media companies are all commercial firms, in business to make a profit for their investors and shareholders, and so are no different in this to firms making and selling, say, soap powder or pizzas. The same problems of competition for business, and hard trading conditions give the London-based publisher or newspaper owner problems very similar to those faced by the Midlands car manufacturer. New media products must pay their way, and questions have to be asked on just how much media expansion the buying public wants. It is no use doubling the choice of entertainment available through the TV set if the viewing audience is all out of the house, running in marathons – which might make it more profitable to invest in making running shoes and Walkmans.

The only prediction it is possible to make is that there will continue to be change. People have decided that they are prepared to pay for even more choice of television programmes and for all the information and other services that cable systems can bring. The structural and technological changes that have taken place in the industry have created a series of significant redundancies in areas of permanent employment and a massive growth of the casual or freelance, workforce. Approximately 60% (1996) of the workforce is now freelance and that figure is likely to grow.

At present (1996) there is very high unemployment in the industry. Media industries are also having to cope with all the other effects of the converging new technologies. For example, computer-based information and retrieval systems are already starting to erode some of the most profitable areas of publishing: lawyers can now have computer screens on their desks which give them instant access to up-to-date case law and precedent, so that legal reference books are becoming redundant. Only by becoming database companies can these publishers stay in business.

The business and commercial aspects of the media industries are often rather forgotten by people attracted to careers in them. Obviously the work is often creative, challenging, interesting, rewarding and satisfying, and can fully extend anyone's talents. The printed word is hallowed by time, giving it some kind of mystique based on centuries of philosophical discussion and political argument on the nature, liberty, privilege and power of the press, and by implication and extension, of broadcasting too.

All this sometimes makes it difficult to get people who want to work for the media to appreciate that these industries demand just as sound and practical managing and business sense as do supermarkets or hotels. If anything, the routine and pressures of the commercial world tend to be more obvious just because it can be difficult to reconcile creative demands with criteria on which a business must be operated to survive.

The media are, of course, perceived as glamorous. It is exciting to be at the apparent centre of events, to rub shoulders with public figures, to see a book into print, or a programme onto the screen. Press, publishers and broadcasters can be influential, and do have a tradition of being the guardians of liberty and free speech. But it is still necessary to get over just how tough the business is to work in; that there is never enough time, money or resources to do a job full justice; that the strain of working continuously in the public gaze and the stress of producing high-quality papers, books or programmes every day of the week (when they may only be read or seen once) is considerable; that the hours are long and irregular – and that there is always someone ready to take on the job should the present occupant flag. Employers can, and often do, demand total dedication to the job, which means a reasonable private life is very difficult in many media posts.

Working for the media

There are four different kinds of work in media industries:

First are the people who write the books, the scripts, the plays, the news stories; the people who appear on screen, or are heard over the air. These are the actors and musicians, the journalists and disc-jockeys, the presenters and commentators, and other entertainers. Few of them work full-time for one employer. Mostly they are employed for the length of a contract, to write a book or script, or to appear in a certain number of programmes, for whichever publishing or broadcasting company or theatrical or film management has work for them at the time.

Second are the policy-makers, the editorial staff and, in broadcasting and the theatre, the people who make programmes, and put on plays. These are the producers and directors and their staff. Some of these are permanent posts, and they form the career structures in the media, but increasingly production jobs are on contract, and this is increasing as publishing tries to cut costs, and broadcasting companies aim to increase the number of independent productions.

Third are the technical people who make publishing or broadcasting possible: the printers who produce books and newspapers; the radio and TV technicians, and the broadcasting engineers who see that programmes reach the listener and viewer.

Finally, efficient administration and management are just as important to media organisations of all kinds as to any other firm or organisation, and so all but the very smallest employ quite a few people to keep them operating as smoothly as possible. This means accountants, personnel managers, librarians, computer experts and operators, public relations staff, marketing staff, secretaries, telephonists, and so on. People have to take down news copy (in both newspapers and broadcasting) on the phone (although new technology is making inroads here), or operate machines which record and transcribe reporters' dispatches.

Newspaper, periodical and some book publishers, and the independent television and radio companies, also employ quite large numbers of people to sell advertising, on which profitability is largely based. Specialist jobs include looking after contributors' (authors', actors', scriptwriters', etc.) contracts, and other rights (such as film rights to books, or the publishing rights to television programmes). Television companies also have quite large departments to negotiate the sale and purchase of films and programmes abroad. Some broadcasting companies publish their own books and the weekly programme and other magazines, so employing editors, journalists, production staff, etc.

Broadcasting

According to Skillset, the industry training organisation for broadcast, film and video, the past decade has witnessed unprecedented change across the industry. Technological developments, increased competition, a freeing of established monopolies and a major upheaval of working practices have changed the atmosphere of the industry for everyone involved. This has created new job opportunities for many people but at the expense of the secure existence previously experienced by many full-time staff.

Ninety-nine per cent of the UK population watch television, a video recorder is available in most households and the cinema is attracting larger audiences than it has for a decade. It is not surprising, therefore, that very large numbers of people express an interest in working within the industry. However, only a small proportion find jobs and develop careers in their chosen field, by offering a combination of relevant skills, personality and considerable persistence.

Takeovers within the ITV sector have begun to concentrate and increase the power of some media organisations, and it is likely that ownership and shareholding of companies will continue to change in the next few years. Channel 5 will launch in 1997. Satellite and cable are now part of everyday life, with the number of subscriptions steadily rising. Technological developments such as digitalisation continue to force change in all areas, creating more channels and genuine possibilities for, say, interactive television in the near future. The multimedia sector is already established and is providing work for some individuals whose careers started in more traditional areas.

The role of the trade unions has also changed and, although most professionals within the industry are members of the appropriate body, membership is no longer essential for employment. Multiskilled individuals will often work on a cross-sector basis, performing tasks that, in the past, would be handled by several different people. And most people who work in the industry will not be employed by any one company. Self-employed freelances will be found in almost any team.

The technological revolution

A primary reason for change has been the increased sophistication and availability of technology. In some cases, machines now do the job that used to require people. More commonly, the effect has been to reduce the need for highly skilled and qualified operators in some areas. The engineering profession has probably been hardest hit, but the effects have been evident in every work area. For example, during post-production, a graphic designer may now be employed as a 'consultant' for a few days only to produce an initial concept and design theme. These ideas can be realised by a less highly skilled operator, using a powerful but expensive computer.

In other cases, one person may be employed to operate a range of equipment, in response to the needs of the production. This 'multiskilling' is one of the most significant changes to occur within the industry. It has many advantages: in financial terms, and also personal, as individuals often have much more varied jobs. However, there are well-founded worries that this trend may lower overall quality. The development of the Skillset NVQs/SVQs has established standards (*see* Recruitment and entry *below*).

The employers (television)

BBC

The BBC runs two national television networks, BBC1 and BBC2. It is divided into six regions – three national: BBC Scotland, BBC Wales and BBC Northern Ireland; and three English: BBC North, BBC Midlands and BBC South. All are involved in making TV programmes for local consumption and the UK network channels, and also for commissioning and purchasing programmes from outside the Corporation. Since 1993, 25% of all non-news and current-affairs material shown on the BBC network must come from independent producers. The BBC is the largest single employer in its field, providing work for about 20,000 people across the industry spectrum, but with an increasing tendency to offer fixed-term contracts.

Having financial skills is very important. No production decision is made now without considering every aspect of cost and possible return. This is affecting the style, and many would say the quality, of broadcast television. The BBC initiative, Producer Choice, gives each producer greater responsibility for every aspect of the production, providing the opportunity to use external facilities and staff in preference to an in-house 'business unit' if they appear to offer better value.

The independent television companies (ITV)

ITV consists of 15 regional franchise areas, each with its own specific licence commitments. The licences are held by eleven independent companies which work together, through the ITV Network centre, to deliver a coordinated nationwide network throughout the UK. Each company is responsible for transmitting ITV programmes to a particular geographic region. Some of these companies (e.g. Granada and Scottish Television) will continue to be both broadcasters and programme-makers. The relative newcomers (e.g. Carlton Television and Meridian Broadcasting are 'publisher/contractors'. They commission independent producers to make programmes for them to show, and as a result, need to employ almost no programme production staff. The traditional ITV companies have shed large numbers of staff since the mid-1980s and now regularly employ freelance, creative and technical staff on longer-term contracts. At least 25% of programmes shown on ITV come from independent producers.

Channel 4

Channel 4 was launched in 1982, with a remit to innovate and experiment with imaginative new ideas, often with appeal to minority groups and interest areas seldom catered for by the other broadcasters. It serves all the UK except Wales. Since January 1993, it has been funded solely from the advertising revenue it generates.

Channel 4 does not make programmes in-house, but commissions them from independent producers and ITV companies or buys direct from other organisations, often outside the UK.

Channel 5

The fifth terrestrial licence has been awarded to Channel 5 Broadcasting Ltd, a specially formed company, backed by a consortium of leading cross-media organisations. From the start it will be self-financing, with no support from other ITV companies. And before any household can receive its programmes, all domestic TV and video equipment will have to be retuned. Channel 5 is due to transmit in 1997.

Sianel Pedwar Cymru (S4C)

The Welsh fourth channel provides a service in Welsh and English. The Welsh programmes are provided by HTV, the BBC and independent producers. The small staff of S4C are mainly administrative and engineering specialists.

Independent Television News (ITN)

ITN is the organisation currently 'nominated' by the Independent Television Commission (ITC) to provide a high-quality national and international news service to Channel 3. ITN also supplies news programmes to Channel 4, and NBC Super Channel, and since October 1992, ITN has supplied news to Independent Radio News (IRN).

Cable and satellite companies

There are numerous companies providing material for use on cable and satellite services. Much is 'ready-made' but there is evidence that new programming is increasing, especially in the locally based cable companies. Most of these companies are small, BSkyB being an exception. Staff at BSkyB are chiefly administrative, with some technical and engineering professionals.

Independent production companies

Independent producers are responsible for making programmes and other broadcast products, but not for transmitting them. Most companies are very small, employing few permanent staff. The growth of the independent sector has encouraged the development of about 50 production houses into larger organisations, employing between 50 and 100 people. Most companies specialise in a particular type of product (e.g. 'real life' documentaries, quiz shows, etc.). Information on the output of different companies can be found in the PACT (Producers Alliance for Cinema and Television) directory.

However, even the larger independent production companies are unlikely to employ more than ten permanent staff. People working in the independent sector need to be commercial and 'customer-focused' as they will be involved in marketing and producing work to satisfy an often demanding client.

Full-time staff are usually producers, administrators and marketing, with additional professional staff hired for individual productions. These companies provide the first job for many people wishing to enter the industry, usually at a junior level.

The employers (radio)

The BBC has five networks – Radios 1, 2, 3, 4 and 5 Live – and the World Service, which offers a 24-hour English channel and also broadcasts in 40 other languages to a huge international audience. The BBC also has three regional broadcasting centres in Scotland, Wales and Northern Ireland. There are also 38 local radio stations in England and national services in Scotland, Wales and Northern Ireland. Commercial radio has expanded steadily since it became legal in 1973. At the time of writing there are three national stations: Classic FM, Virgin 1215 and Talk Radio, and approximately 150 local stations.

Almost 90% of the adult population listen regularly to radio. As a result, radio in the 1990s is big business, attracting a significant proportion of the national advertising 'spend' and communicating with an enviable percentage of the target markets. The ratings battle is in full swing. Until recently, that battle has been waged on a local level, but the advent of national independent stations has dented the listening figures recorded by the BBC networks.

The increasing importance of ratings means that the output is more 'managed' than in the past. Producers in both commercial radio and the BBC are more 'customer- i.e. listener-focused' which means there is less opportunity for risk-taking or innovation than previously. However, the radio industry will be an area of continuing growth and it is likely to provide interesting and rewarding careers.

The job opportunities

Announcers

Announcers work to detailed and carefully timed scripts, communicating information to the viewer from a soundproof 'behind the scenes' office. They sometimes write or adapt their own material. They need to be able to work independently for long periods, communicate clearly, possess a calm and friendly manner, and be attentive to detail. They come from a variety of backgrounds but drama, teaching or TV administration are particularly useful.

Art and design

The art and design function is to create a visual effect to meet the needs of the production, creating manual or computer-generated graphics. People in this field need the ability to interpret a brief and keep within a tight budget and time constraints. They also need to be excellent communicators. Specialised art college training and experience outside the industry in a commercial environment is a useful background.

Costume/wardrobe

The wardrobe department interpret the production requirements in terms of costumes and accessories to ensure historical accuracy and an accurate portrayal of the style and ethos of the period. Those working in this area need the ability to design, make, adapt or hire costumes, communicate effectively with artists whilst dressing them, and to service all customer requirements. Good planning, administrative and organisation skills are necessary as is the ability to work within tight budgets. A background in textiles, a degree in fashion or theatre design, or experience with a touring theatre company are all useful.

Direction

The director is responsible for achieving the creative and visual effect of a production. He or she needs the ability to coordinate effectively the skills and personalities of performers, designers and technical specialists. Audience and financial awareness is necessary as is a high tolerance of stress. A high level of academic ability, practical experience of television, film or theatre, plus the ability to work with a wide range of people is essential.

Distribution

The distribution of programmes and the exploitation of other programme rights is an important side of the business. It contributes major revenues and reflects the importance of co-production, pre-sales and overseas financing for programming.

Engineering

Engineers provide a design, maintenance and installation service to the production site and equipment. Research specialists are usually employed by the equipment manufacturers or design consultancies. They need to be good at problem-solving and work quickly and neatly. Good interpersonal skills and high safety awareness is necessary. Engineers usually have a qualification in electronic, electrical sound or mechanical engineering plus work experience with equipment manufacturers.

Graphic design
Graphic designers, using film and the latest video and computer technology, produce opening titles, credits and programme information sequences that embrace a variety of visual styles. The designer also helps to brand the Channel through animated station 'idents' and on-screen promotion of programmes. Designers need to be able to think imaginatively and logically to combine image with sound and keep pace with changing technology and coordinate a wide range of production resources. They also need to be able to work well in a team. A background which includes a degree in art and design, some understanding of typography and experience with computer design systems is useful.

Journalism
Journalists generate and report on local, national or international stories, and research relevant background information. Bi-media (radio and TV) contracts are increasing. Some journalists present their own work. They need the flexibility of approach to reflect the needs of different audiences, clear communication skills, and the ability to work to deadlines and be calm and tenacious. Training and experience in newspapers or periodical journalism is a useful background. (*See* Newspaper Publishing *and* Periodical Publishing *under* WRITING FOR A LIVING *below*)

Lighting
Lighting specialists ensure that the stage or set is correctly lit to meet the needs of the production. They need the ability to design layouts, organise lighting effects and operate the lighting system to meet the requirements of the indoor or outdoor production. Computer literacy, physical agility and a good head for heights are necessary. Most people working in this field have specialist college or industry-based training plus theatre experience.

Make-up and hairdressing
Make-up and hairdressing professionals interpret the requirements of the production and research to ensure accurate representation of the historical or design concept. They maintain a continuity of approach throughout the production in studio or on location. They need the ability to translate abstract ideas into practical applications quickly, be inventive and think laterally. They also need to be calm and reassuring and have good communication skills. Relevant training and experience outside the industry is required. History and art qualifications are useful.

Management
The management direct and coordinate the different elements of the industry to ensure their efficient function – ranging from commissioning a production to negotiating international rights. It is essential to have specialist knowledge of the chosen function area (e.g. personnel, finance) plus the ability to communicate with the creative team. Strong financial awareness, planning and organisational skills are necessary. A high level of academic training plus a relevant professional qualification and experience outside the industry is considered useful.

Producers
Producers perform a variety of management and operational roles to bring together the many elements of a production either in the studio or on location. They are often responsible for both the initial concept and raising the essential finance. They are the team leaders and need to think creatively and have excellent communication, planning and negotiating skills. They need to be able to motivate others and have strong financial awareness.

Production assistants
Production assistants provide high-quality administrative and secretarial support to the producer and director at every stage of production. During filming/recording they sit with the director cueing-in cameras and sound and recording a log of timecode numbers which are invaluable in the edit stage for finding specific takes on videotape. Production assistants need excellent secretarial and administrative skills and to be able to communicate effectively. They must be cheerful and unflappable, and good at solving problems and at mental arithmetic.

Production management
Production managers organise all essential support facilities for the team: accommodation, catering, transport, etc. They also roster crews and arrange payments. They need to have good 'people'-management skills, and to be organised, calm and practical. They also require sound administrative, financial and problem-solving skills. A background as a crew member or floor manager plus stage management training is useful.

Recording still and moving images (camerawork)
Workers in this area operate and assist with still, film and video cameras to record images, as directed using different techniques. They require creative flair, general technical skills, the ability to accept direction plus a good visual sense. A technical qualification and relevant work experience plus a background of amateur photography or fine art is useful.

Researching
The researcher supports the producer, helping to turn ideas into reality – providing and following up ideas, contacting and interviewing people, and acquiring relevant factual material. They write briefings for presenters. They need to be very well organised, be able to take initiative and work unsupervised and have excellent interpersonal skills. Experience in newspaper or magazine journalism (*see* Journalism *under* WRITING FOR A LIVING *below*) or TV administration is useful.

Stage/floor management
Stage/floor managers coordinate and manage everything that happens on the studio location or rehearsal room 'floor', from cueing actors to organising props. When there is a

studio audience, the floor manager will be in charge. There is close liaison with the director. They need to be well organised, practical. unflappable, with a broad range of TV skills and knowledge. Excellent communication skills and the ability to command instant respect are essential. Stage/floor managers usually have experience in theatre, especially on tour, plus several years' experience as an assistant.

Sound

Sound craftspeople interpret requirements of a production in terms of sound collection. During post-production they may be involved in recording, editing and dubbing using a range of sophisticated equipment. They require general technical ability and perfect hearing plus being calm and quick to respond. A technical qualification and work experience is a useful background.

Recruitment and entry

Skillset, the industry training organisation for broadcast, film and video, is a small professional organisation solely concerned with the promotion and development of training within the industry. It aims to establish and maintain a full range of high-quality training pathways and qualifications in response to the needs of this creative and highly diversified industry. From 1995 a range of NVQ/SVQs are being introduced which will enable individuals to develop and gain credit for competency in their chosen employment area(s). It is expected that over 30 industry-based NVQs/SVQs will be in operation in 1996. These unique qualifications have been developed by respected industry practitioners and will be assessed by others who currently work in the specific area of interest. The advent of these qualifications has been welcomed by leading figures throughout the broadcasting world, who are convinced that this form of skills development and assessment will revolutionise career pathways for both employed and freelance people.

Some jobs, however, will continue to require formal qualifications or proven evidence of relevant skills, especially in technical areas like engineering, but the consistent theme that runs through the person-specification for different jobs is the need for real interest in, and commitment to, the business, and, of course, genuine talent. Those who are successful in gaining jobs in the industry are likely to: watch a lot of film and television; listen regularly to the radio; be critical and knowledgeable about their viewing/listening; notice the input of different professionals; and have real opinions about what they like, and why.

Media degree courses are seen by many in the industry as being a disadvantage. There were 35,000 students on media courses in 1995 and only 28,000 jobs in the industry, so competition is more than fierce.

People who work in the industry often 'live and breathe' it. To be surrounded by others of similar commitment and interests, in a creative atmosphere is still one of the major benefits of working in this business. The money is often not great, the hours are very long, the work is often physically demanding, but for those who love the business, it is often worthwhile.

The freelance factor

In 1993/94 Skillset undertook a major study of working practices within the industry. They identified that, because of the structural and technological changes taking place within the industry, there had been a shift from permanent employment to freelance. At the time of the survey, there were approximately 15,000 freelances in the industry. This represents approximately 60% of the industry's workforce. Although 63% of freelances are male, there is wide variation between the different skill groups. In the traditional technical areas (camera, sound and lighting) there are very few women; however, women predominate in wardrobe, make-up and production support. Most freelances are white, with only 3% of respondents to the survey coming from ethnic minority backgrounds; and most are young. Approximately 65% of freelances are based in Greater London and the south-east of England.

The industry now has Positive Action programmes which aim to recruit and train into shortage areas. For example, a woman choosing a technical craft area may find more opportunities for entry than choosing a career in a more traditional female employment area.

In order to be a successful (i.e. employed) freelance, it is essential to have specific skills: personal marketing – it is up to the individual to 'market' themselves to potential employers and this means making direct approaches; administrative ability – successful freelances are well organised, keeping records of established and potential contacts, information about what is going on in the industry, and who is involved; the most-employed freelances are talented, reliable individuals who provide a 'cost-effective' service; team skills – when a freelance crew comes together, it is expected to function effectively in a very short time; the ability to 'get on' and work with a wide range of people is an essential attribute; financial awareness – freelances are self-employed and responsible for their own tax and national insurance contributions. Freelances need to manage their money effectively. Something to fall back on – most freelances periodically need to earn money outside the industry. People do lots of different jobs from lecturing in media studies to waitressing.

It is a tough business. People work very hard and often spend long hours getting a job finished in uncomfortable surroundings. Employers are concerned about any individual's ability to 'fit in' to the team. Most of the opportunities available to new entrants in the 1990s are going to be within the independent sector – and in small teams everyone has to mix well, and contribute several skills.

Getting an entry-level job

Most jobs that become vacant throughout the industry are never advertised to the general public. Many organisations have a policy of 'promoting from within' if suitable talent is available. This means that most entry-level jobs are very junior and generally low-paid. Most vacancies occur in the following areas: airtime sales, administrative and secretarial, camera/sound/other technical assistant, trainee film editor, assistant floor manager. The majority of new entrants will start their careers in small independent companies as 'runners' as a result of direct, speculative application, or through contacts.

Increasingly infrequent training schemes in television companies offer chances to a few highly motivated individuals to enter production and journalistic areas. Enthusiasm and demonstrable commitment to the industry are key qualities which are looked for. Those who are successful generally have relevant experience and are confident that they understand the fundamentals of the work as a result of practical involvement. Many have considerable general work experience and are in their mid-twenties when they enter the training schemes.

Entry-level jobs, when advertised, often specify quite modest essential qualifications and experience, but shortlisted candidates will often exhibit well above the minimum requirements.

Training schemes

BBC

The BBC, which used to be the most reliable source of many trainee vacancies, has dramatically reduced its intake over the past few years, and any trainee vacancies will be closely related to programme-making operational needs. Vacancies, when they do occur, either in television or radio, are advertised in the national press and on CEEFAX page 696.

ITV

Some ITV companies are already recruiting and training small numbers of multiskilled operatives to become familiar with a wide range of equipment, thereby providing a core of flexible talent. Very occasionally more specialised trainee positions are advertised in the larger organisations. These may be in creative, craft, engineering, journalistic or management areas. When trainee schemes are operating they will be publicised. ITV companies often have strong links with colleges in their franchise area and frequently recruit trainees from the graduating student body.

Channel 4

C4 does not make its own programmes but either commissions them from independent producers or buys direct from other organisations. The Channel therefore relies on a trained pool of experienced and talented people to make the quality and standard of programming required for its schedule. C4 funds a production scheme 'FOURFIT' every two years. The scheme is specifically targeted at people from an ethnic background, given the shortage of such people within the broadcasting industry. The two-year training is broad-based and consists of both college-based formal training and placements with independent production companies. The training will provide the necessary grounding for a potential career in the freelance and independent sectors in areas such as camera, editing, production assisting and sound. The training scheme is advertised in the national and ethnic press, and the next intake will be August 1997.

Schemes within the independent production sector

Further details on all of the following training courses can be obtained from Skillset.

ft2 – Film and Television Freelance Training. ft2 is a national new-entrant technical training scheme, funded by the industry and supported by the European Social Fund, to train talented individuals for the freelance labour market. Similar to an apprenticeship, the trainees are attached to a variety of productions over a two-year period and are paid a monthly grant. Practical experience is supplemented by specially commissioned intensive short courses.

CYFLE. CYFLE is aimed at fulfilling the needs of the Welsh film and television industry. Training is offered on a full-time one- or two-year course for six to eight people per year. Following a three-month introductory period, most of the training is location-based. Ability to speak the Welsh language is essential.

Gaelic Television Training Trust. This is a two-year training programme, supported by a range of organisations that are committed to the provision of high-quality television programming for the Gaelic-speaking community. Trainees experience both college- and industry-based training

Scottish Broadcast and Film Training Ltd (SBFT). Scottish Broadcast and Film Training act as a training coordinator and provider of broadcast and film training in Scotland. The SBFT involves all of the major broadcast and independent employers and trade unions on its Board. Courses meet specific short-term needs and also provide new entrants with training in selected skill areas, working locally and nationally to ensure that all training is to a professional standard and available to a wide range of people.

Intermedia Film and Video. Intermedia is a media development agency, which works in partnership with the film and broadcasting industries and key public agencies including Skillset. It offers a range of courses for newcomers to the industry and for people hoping to enter the industry. Its 'Head Start' programme lasts 42 weeks and covers single-camera video, multi-camera studio, 16mm film and digital production. In 1996, Intermedia plans to develop extended production attachments which offer NVQ assessment.

First Film Foundation. A charity set up to develop the talents of first-time film-makers in feature film, TV drama and documentary production. First Film Foundation offers apprenticeship-style training to new writers, producers and directors with assistance in script-editing, budgeting and scheduling, packaging and fundraising, as well as office facilities and related services in kind

The National Film and Television School. Through funding from the European Social Fund, the NFTS runs two courses each year (funding permitting) for people who have recently entered, or are new to the industry.

Further information

Skillset, the BBC, the ITC, the Radio Authority, the ITV Network Centre, the Association of Independent Radio Companies, NTL, PACT (independent producers), and BECTU (Broadcasting, Entertainment, Cinematograph and Theatre Union).

Particular thanks must go to Skillset, the industry training organisation for broadcast, film and video, who have kindly provided the bulk of the information for this section on 'Broadcasting'. Skillset are shortly to produce (1996) a highly detailed pack of information, covering all areas of the broadcasting industry,

Film and video

Traditionally, film and video have been categorised as separate industries with film-making being seen as the production of full-length feature films for presentation on the big screen and, as such, not comparable to smaller-scale video production. However, developments over the past decade have brought the two closer together, as both have been through considerable structural change and technological transformation, which of course have implications for employment opportunities, routes in, education and training in general.

The British film industry continues to face financial problems. The cost of making films is astronomical, film-makers have to think not only about their production overheads but also the cost of promoting and marketing their films. Feature films are as successful as their audiences say they are, that is they are financed by the number of people who pay money to watch them. Box office revenue must pay for production, promotion and profit! As such, many British films are stilll backed by US money.

The film industry has received a mini-boost from a couple of its major competitors, TV and video, particularly TV as a result of the 1990 Broadcasting Act. This Act paved the way for the advance of the independent film and video production sector. These small production companies have no part whatsoever in the transmission of films or programmes, rather, they sell completed programmes to TV broadcasting companies. Historically, they had found it tough to break into the BBC and ITV markets, experiencing difficulty selling their productions. The Act ensured that 25% of all new programmes must be supplied by independent producers. Now, for example, Channel 4 commission a large amount of their output from independents. Deregulation of the BBC, and the growth in the number of channels, have created extra outlets for British film and video. In addition, technological changes have brought cable and satellite into our homes.

The cost of equipment has fallen over time, and this has made film- and video-making far more accessible. Video has come into its own here, proving itself a useful and flexible medium. With lower overheads and TV broadcasting companies tending to buy in more programmes and films, this sector has grown. Small independent video companies mainly produce pop videos, promotional and publicity materials for corporate firms, health authorities, etc. Companies have set up, offering studio space, hiring out specialist equipment, and offering to build sets and scenery and provide specialist post-production facilities such as video editing, mixing and dubbing.

Working in the industry

The developments outlined above have resulted in considerable changes to the structure of the industry and hence employment opportunities. The majority of independent production companies have few full-time staff and hire in freelance workers to work on aspects of pre-production (e.g. scriptwriting), production (e.g. lighting, sound, make-up) and post-production (e.g. editing). Larger independents have their own premises and post-production facilities and thus employ more permanent production staff. However, most employ 'skeleton' staff and buy in services as and when required. The same is true for small feature-film production companies.

Broadcast TV companies, for example the BBC, no longer maintain a stranglehold on film- and TV programme-making. As many programmes are now bought in, those who work in the film/programme-making side of the BBC are employed on short-term contracts for one assignment at a time. Staff are employed in all aspects of production. Satellite companies buy-in films and programmes. Some produce their own news bulletins, for which they hire freelance staff. Most full-time staff are employed in marketing departments selling subscriptions and advertising space as opposed to making films and programmes. Just as some companies have emerged which provide specialist video/film-making services, so have in-house production units. For example, these can be found in some large industrial/commercial companies, where skilled technicians are hired to produce corporate videos in-house. Similarly, training companies and universities can also have their own units and look for staff to run these. Multiskilled technicians are preferred for this area.

Essentially, film and video is a volatile and unpredictable area of employment, although there are some growth areas in the video industry. Short-term contracts punctuated by periods of unemployment are a typical career pattern. With fewer opportunities in TV available, many employers have turned to video and film, and 'freelancing' is the name of the game. Independent production companies take on few staff and those who are employed on a permanent basis are expected to be 'multiskilled', i.e. a jack of all trades.

So, while there has been considerable change and upheaval, employment opportunities have not necessarily expanded. These industries have become more accessible –

particularly video, which is a useful training ground for anyone considering a career in film or TV.

Film producers

Film producers are the entrepreneurs and managers of the industry, although there is nothing to prevent producers directing their own films, and many do. It is the producer who looks for a commercially viable idea, novel or story for a feature film, and has it turned in to a 'treatment', with suggestions for the stars to appear in it, on which to raise the finance from investors to make the film. Alternatively, for example, the producer may go to a Channel 4 commissioning editor with a synopsis for a programme, or a series of programmes, or be commissioned by the television company, or another organisation, e.g. a training board, to make a film for them. When the finance is arranged, or the programme or film commissioned, the producer sets up the production, deciding personally on the director, scriptwriter, production manager and members of the crew. Only on small-scale productions would the producer have a hands-on role. Video can provide a useful training ground for feature film producers, and many started out in video companies. Video producers are highly likely to enjoy a hands-on as opposed to a purely organisational role due to the smaller size of their teams. They are also able to have greater creative input.

Film-makers

The director is responsible for the creative hands-on role. S/he takes the script and guides the actors and technicians through it having the final say in the end-product. Theatrical backgrounds are common amongst film directors as creativity is essential. In turn, the director can be assisted by first, second and third directors who take on administrative and organisational tasks in order to help the director out. They ensure that all runs smoothly, working closely with the production manager, who is in effect the producer's deputy. The latter produces a budget, manages the schedule and organises the location: again tasks involving greater organisational as opposed to creative input. S/he has a good all-round knowledge of the business, financial and legal side and is likely to have been in the business for a while.

The director will appoint a director of photography who supervises the lighting and camerawork in order to achieve the desired visual mood of the film. S/he, in discussion with the director, draws up a camera script for the film which is then followed by the camera crew, under the direction and supervision of the director of photography.

This is a brief outline of the key figures in the film-making process. Obviously, the number of staff employed will depend largely on the size of the production. In video particularly, the producer and director may well take on additional roles and production managers are often a luxury.

Making a film involves a large number of other people. A casting director may well be employed to find actors for the film. An art director and a team of staff will be responsible for designing sets and costumes. Make-up artists, hairdressers and wardrobe staff prepare the actors. The camera crew, who will work with the director of photography, are made up of an operator, with assistants to help with focusing, loading film and moving the camera. A sound crew will also be required to ensure the best possible sound to create the director's chosen atmosphere.

Once the film is processed, it has to be edited and the soundtrack completed. Editing is just as creative a role as shooting the film: deciding which are the best shots to use, making transitions from one shot to another, etc. The editor works closely with the director at all stages.

A growing area is special effects, which traditionally have involved hiring specialist freelances. These effects can range from computer graphics to physical special effects such as explosions or special set designs. Recently this area has been revolutionised by computer graphics. Video effects companies have established themselves and produce effects which are incorporated into pop videos, TV programmes, etc. There is no specialised entry route, though technical expertise, creativity and ingenuity are essential. A passion for computers and a flair for design can help. The industry is crying out for special effects artists.

Animation is highly costly as it is so labour-intensive. The animator breaks down the action of the proposed cartoon character into very small movements drawn on pieces of paper. When photographed and shown one after the other, the characters appear alive and moving. Animation companies exist and a key animator leads a team of animators through any particular project, mostly commercial, for TV or pop videos. This area will remain labour-intensive until computer graphics are able to reproduce what the human hand can draw. Art skills are essential in this field. A start can be made by obtaining an art school education. Skills in rapid drawing and sketching are a must. See details below for specialised courses available in this field.

Recruitment and entry

First jobs usually mean starting right at the bottom, even for those who have been to film school. The 'gopher'/runner-type jobs provide an excellent opportunity to see all aspects of film and video production and can lead to other things. Actually securing these roles can be down to contacts, knowing people in the business or sheer determination and persistence on your part.

Qualifications and training

The gap in skills training for those working in the film, video and TV industries has been recognised by the establishment of Skillset, the Industry Training Organisation for Broadcast Film and Video, in 1991. With the growth in freelancing, access to independent training has become vital, and Skillset have been developing standards leading to National Vocational Qualifications which it is hoped will provide training for new entrants in the industry and ongoing retraining for those already in employment.

Thirteen NVQs are now available in the areas of Camera Assistance, Camera Operation, Camera Direction, Sound Assistance, Sound Operation, Sound Direction, Lighting Provision, Lighting Direction, Production, Production Research and Broadcast Journalism. The following are awaiting accreditation: Make-Up/Costume Design, Post Production/Graphics/Animation, Studio Operations, Set Crafts, Film Processing and Projection. Contact Skillset for further information. Further developments will be taking place on qualifications in Special Effects, Props/Set Dressing and Multimedia.

Courses are available at institutes of further and higher education in various fields, and at various levels. When considering courses, the practical component should be noted. Also note that new courses are springing up all the time and those given below are only a sample.

Various BTEC two-year HND courses exist with components in video and film, normally under the guise of media studies. Check prospectuses for details.

The National Film and TV School run a three-year full-time film-making course where students get the option to specialise in art direction, animation direction, fiction direction, cinematography, screenwriting, editing, music composition, producing and sound.

At undergraduate level the following universities offer courses: Bournemouth University, BA (Hons) Scriptwriting for Film and TV, BA (Hons) Media Production, BA (Hons) Computer Visualization and Animation; Canterbury Christ College of Higher Education, BA Radio, Film and Television; Central Saint Martin's College of Art and Design, BA (Hons) Fine Art, Film and Video; University of Derby, BA (Hons) Photographic Studies (Film and Video); Edinburgh College of Art, BA (Hons) Design (Animation), BA (Hons) Design (Film and Video); Liverpool John Moores University, BA Fine Art (Film, Video and Animation); London College of Printing, BA (Hons) Film and Video; Napier University, BA (Hons) Photography, Film and TV; Sheffield Hallam University, BA (Hons) Film Studies; Staffordshire University, BA (Hons) Film, TV and Radio Studies; University of Westminster, BA (Hons) Film, Video and Photographic Arts; Surrey College of Art and Design, BA (Hons) Film and Video, BA (Hons) Animation.

At postgraduate level, Bournemouth and Poole College of Art and Design run a one-year full-time Advanced Diploma in Media Production (Film and TV), an intensive production-based course in film and TV. Bournemouth University offer a postgraduate Diploma in Film and Television; Bristol University, a postgraduate Diploma in Film and Television; Duncan of Jordanstone College of Art, MSc Film and TV Production; London College of Printing, MA in Independent Film and Video, MA in Screenwriting and Screen Research; London International Film School, a two-year Diploma in Film Making; Middlesex University, MA in Video.

The above lists represent a sample of opportunities to acquire academic qualifications in this area. Most of the above courses will contain practical elements which will be welcomed by employers.

Training schemes

The BBC still runs training schemes for graduates, but intakes have decreased. Competition is fierce for entry on their Production Training Scheme, which can provide good training for launching into a career in film or video. Carlton TV and Channel 4 now also run similar schemes.

ft2, who were previously JOBFIT (Joint Board for Film Industry Training) run a two-year training course specifically for technical and production grades (i.e. not producers, directors or writers): art department assistant, camera assistant/clapper loader, production/continuity assistant, sound assistant, grips, make-up and hair. There is nothing to prevent anyone who has done the scheme trying to work their way up. The number of places varies from year to year, depending on funding. There are no formal entry requirements, but commitment and enthusiasm, communication skills, strong visual sense and all-round literacy are stipulated. Training is specifically for the freelance labour market, age at least 18 years.

Further Information

Skillset, the organisations/schools cited above, BBC, Channel 4, ft2, Scottish Film Training Trust, CYFLE for Welsh-speakers

Writing for a living

There is a world of difference between being able to write, even to write extremely well, and being able to make a living from writing.

The central problem for writers is that publishers, newspapers, theatrical producers, in fact anyone who is likely to employ and pay them, are in business to make a profit. Many books, plays, poems, etc. that authors really want to write never will sell enough copies, or attract large enough audiences, to make anyone any money. Yet for most authors there is very little point to their literary efforts if their books or poems are not published somewhere, or if their plays are unseen.

Anyone with genuine literary or dramatic talent should eventually see their work produced if they persist (although it gets more difficult all the time). But the only way to write and survive is to begin, at least, by treating writing as a non-profitmaking activity, and to earn a living at something else. Writing is often improved by maturity (which does not necessarily equate with age, since many of the most creative writers have achieved this remarkably young) and with as much experience of the real world as possible. It is also at least possible to write at any time and virtually anywhere.

For a lucky few, their talents may coincide with commercial success, which may bring them enough money to live on. Usually, though, this means getting several books into print first, and even then the largest part of the income may well come from selling 'rights' to paperback publishers or film makers, or adapting the book for television, serialisation, and even royalties for foreign-language editions. Public lending rights (fees for library loans) have very marginally improved some writers' incomes. However, the maximum allowance to any one author in a year is £6,000, and most writers get under £100 a year.

A small number of competitions, prizes, etc. help to create opportunities for younger/newer writers to see their work in print.

For many people, the only way to write for a living is to accept that they must write to a commission, from publishers, magazines, theatrical producers, or broadcasting companies, or become a journalist or advertising copywriter. There is, of course, nothing wrong in writing for someone who is prepared to pay: Shakespeare and Dickens produced some great literature under extreme commercial pressure.

Usually if a piece of work is worth publishing then a publisher will publish it. However, some writers whose work is not accepted by a publisher have been tempted to have their book or article published by a vanity publisher, i.e. one who charges the writer for publishing and advertising their book. This can lead to exorbitant costs for the writer and so would-be authors are strongly advised not to take this route. If a writer cannot find a publisher and is determined to see their work in print they could consider publishing their work themselves, something that has been done in the past by a number of authors including Beatrix Potter, James Barrie, Mark Twain, D. H. Lawrence and William Blake. The *Writers' and Artists' Yearbook* contains very helpful information on both vanity and self-publishing.

Most people who write for a living do not restrict themselves to one medium. They have often previously been in full-time jobs which have given them contacts in the media world; it is generally much easier to get a first book accepted if you already have a track record elsewhere, or to get a play put on if you have worked in the theatre or for a television company.

Competition is enormous for all the writing outlets, and some of the fees are pitifully small. These can include magazine short stories; talks, plays, and short stories for radio; one-off plays (although television uses fewer original, 'one-off', plays today, preferring to put on series of plays with a single theme which have to be commissioned); and scripts for serials and series on both radio and television. Film companies don't employ resident writers now, and the film scriptwriter freelances with the rest, with more film scripts going to established novelists and dramatists. It is probably impossible to live on any one of these by itself, with the possible exception of regular scriptwriting for long-running serials. Most writing for radio and television documentaries goes to established journalists, although it is possible to get into radio, particularly by starting as an occasional contributor and having expert knowledge to offer in addition to writing skills.

To make a reasonable income from writing books and/or plays (and this applies particularly to TV drama), a good agent may be necessary. Agents are better able to negotiate contracts, with all the complexities of rights and royalties, than writers can, and because of their contacts in the media, they keep writers informed of publishers' and broadcasting companies' future plans, and suggest 'their' authors for particular projects. Agents usually only take on writers they consider have some chance of success. They play little or no part in journalists' careers (unless, of course, they also write books or plays) and there are many successful writers, particularly specialists such as educational and technical writers, who do not use an agent.

Most writers expect to spend a high proportion of their time doing research. Few novelists, even, can produce books without first delving deeply into the background of the book's subject material, whether it is a spy thriller, a story set in an earlier period, or even a novel about contemporary life. Alternatively, they must have extensive experience, which amounts to the same thing. Readers today expect books to be factually accurate and authentic, however imaginative they may be. People who write for television and radio documentaries, series, etc., can expect to have paid research assistance. Authors of even the most solidly factual reference book are expected to provide their own, and this can be very expensive.

Writing is both creative art and craft. Writing demands both creativity and craft skills, skills which must be learnt. Evidence suggests that the discipline of writing to a brief can be a valuable training. One of today's major novelists was first a successful advertising copywriter. Not everyone who has writing ability is necessarily capable of being successful in every form, though. While many young reporters and advertising copywriters may dream of writing a best-selling novel, it could be that they are already making best use of their talents. For some dramatists the novel is an impossible form, while few poets write novels or plays. However, those who can are obviously at a great advantage: many journalists produce books of one kind or another. One recent poet laureate worked in publishing and wrote detective stories, and a public relations expert writes best-selling novels on the train to and from the office.

Learning one's craft, gaining experience and then recognition are the major problems facing the apprentice writer, whatever type of writing they choose. Learning and experience go hand in hand in writing. Only journalists have formal training schemes (*see below*), although there are a number of writing schools and centres such as the Avon Foundation and Swanwick; creative writing courses at the Universities of East Anglia and Leicester; and courses like the Robert McKee screenwriting seminars. However, for many writers it is mostly a matter of sitting at the feet of the experienced, by working either with or alongside an older writer, possibly as a research assistant, or metaphorically, by extensive critical reading. Most forms of writing involve learning special techniques, as for drama, for example; and of course the techniques differ between theatre, television, radio and film (most broadcasting companies produce booklets on writing for the media, covering technical points, and some also discuss writing dialogue). Most writers need a broad background of experience, and this can be gained by working in almost any other job.

Writing is, in the last analysis, a lonely business. Even in a crowded newspaper office, reporters work alone on their copy. It is also very difficult. Few writers find it easy to write creatively (although those with the skills and techniques at their fingertips sometimes find it less agonising), and a great deal depends on self-discipline and the ability to concentrate.

Newspaper publishing

The British newspaper industry is big business. According to the Newspaper Society approximately 1,500 newspapers are published in Britain of which only 20 are national. The remainder are morning titles, evening titles, Sunday newspapers, paid weeklies or – the largest number – free weeklies.

But the economics of the newspaper business are not easy to manage. One major difference between book and newspaper publishers is that the newspaper industry, because papers must be produced at such speed, mostly owns and operates its own presses, although some now 'contract out'. The costs are huge, even with the tightest financial management. Publishers have bitten the bullet of new technology, and almost all are now going over to computer-based setting and printing methods. Because this needs new plant and modern accommodation, the nationals took the opportunity to move out of their valuable Fleet Street sites, mostly going to redeveloped docklands.

Newspaper editors are under continual pressure to sell more copies, not because extra sales will bring in more money, but because higher sales attract more advertising, and advertising produces up to 80% of a regional newspaper's income and 48% of a national newspaper's income. The competition can be cutthroat, and dominate policy. Competition for both readership and advertising, between different types of publication and between different publications of the same type, is a dominant factor in the economics of most sections of the press. Methods used to attract clients include presentation and content of the newspaper, size, speed of production, and publicity, ranging from direct advertising to sponsoring competitions and exhibitions. Advertisers are attracted by the number and type of clients, the price of advertising space, services offered and publicity.

Employment in the newspaper industry

Traditionally, only about a fifth of a newspaper's total staff were editorial, but as papers go over to computer-based production, this is rising sharply. Not generally because more journalists are employed per paper, but because far fewer production staff are needed.

Responsibility for the paper's content is the editor's, helped by the deputy and an assistant. Under the editor, senior editors look after different 'sections' of the paper – domestic and foreign news, City (finance), features, literary, sports, travel, etc., – with new ideas (sections on 'living', 'work', science, etc.) and new ways to develop older sections (for women, etc.) always being tried. Art editors (running their own art departments) look after the photos and drawings. All the other editorial staff count as journalists (*see* Journalism *below*). The journalists are backed up by librarians (*see* LIBRARY AND INFORMATION WORK).

Managers and top newspaper executives are not always ex-editors or journalists. They are just as likely to be accountants or specialists in other areas, but there is nothing to prevent a journalist or editor moving into senior management. They administer newspaper production, revenue and expenditure. Newspaper sales and advertising are important departments in the industry: newspapers have their own publicity people, and employ people in all the functions normally needed by any commercial organisation, from accountants to clerks and personnel.

Traditionally, up to half of a newspaper's staff were in production, but this is often no longer the case. Almost all newspapers have rapidly gone over to computer typesetting, which means journalists, and advertising people, input their own copy into a computer terminal, from where it is 'set' into film. Even page make-up can be done on-screen by editorial staff. Modern, high-speed presses need fewer people to operate them, and papers are packaged by machine. *See also* PRINTING *in* MANUFACTURING INDUSTRIES.

The three major news agencies are a crucial part of the newspaper industry. They collect news at home and overseas for subscribers (mostly newspapers and the broadcasting news services at home and abroad). One, Reuters, provides sophisticated business, stockmarket and other financial information services delivered on-screen to subscribers' offices in nearly 160 countries.

Other agencies collect and supply photographs to the press and publishers. The news and other press agencies employ large numbers of journalists and sub-editors at home, and correspondents overseas, as well as managerial staff and computer, telex and teleprinter operators (*see under* SECRETARIAL, OFFICE AND CLERICAL WORK *in* ADMINISTRATION, BUSINESS MANAGEMENT AND OFFICE WORK).

Recruitment and entry

For editorial work and production, entry is normally via an employer-recognised training scheme.

Qualifications and training

Training for the newspaper industry is generally by function rather than on a newspaper-by-newspaper basis. Training for journalists, for example, comes under a national council, although some newspaper groups do make their own arrangements. *See* Journalism *below*.

Periodical publishing

In 1996 almost 6,500 magazines are published in the UK. They are commonly divided into consumer, business, trade, technical and professional, with an expanding range of 'alternative' publications, and a rather smaller (but no longer declining) group of several hundred house magazines produced by employers mainly for their own employees, although some do go out as part of companies' PR effort.

About a third of the output is consumer magazines and specialist publications. They include magazines for women; interior decorating and do-it-yourself magazines; publications for particular leisure and sporting activities, such as gardening, angling, athletics, rock music, computers, etc. At present, this is the boom area, with new titles catering for new interests appearing constantly.

The business and scientific press – over 4,000 publications in all – cover the business and specialist interests of people working in particular industries, trades, etc., keeping them up to date on new technological and business developments in, say, the chemical industry, computers or the grocery trade. Included in this figure are magazines published for people working in, amongst other things, law, accountancy, medicine, nursing, or librarianship.

Some magazines appear weekly, others fortnightly, monthly, or on a quarterly basis. Some publishers or institutions produce only a single journal, others manage a 'stable' of periodicals, some in a single area or type of publication, others in several. It is an increasingly volatile area of publishing, with new publications starting up to cater for a new or developing readership, while others which may have done well for a while, close down (e.g. in home computing), or merge with each other.

Working in periodical publishing

Although there are a great many magazines (2,164 consumer titles and 4,377 business titles in 1995), figures suggest only some 400 firms publish commercially, and at most 150 are of any size. Of these, four employ over 1,000 people and a number employ between 500 and 1,000. Many publishers have under fifteen staff. Total numbers are probably no more than 35,000.

All commercially run periodicals have their own editorial staff of sub-editors and writers, but on the smaller magazines journalists are expected to both write and edit. Staff requirements vary according to magazine type. For example, on technical publications editors and journalists are expected to have some subject expertise; consumer magazines are likely to seek features writers as opposed to news journalists. Many magazines use outside contributors, freelance writers or experts in particular fields who are commissioned or invited to write articles on their specialised or preferred subjects. Some academic journals exist purely on the contributions made by academics publishing theses or reports, and thus their staff consist solely of editors. 'Alternative' publications are often put together by voluntary staff: where people are employed, numbers are small.

The range of jobs taken on by editors will vary according to the size of the firm and the publication. So in a large firm, sub-editors will carry out many of the practical duties, allowing the editor more time to concentrate on managerial and policy issues in liaison with senior managers. Sub-editors will do much of the checking of copy and manipulation of copy into a more consumer-oriented form by adding headlines.

Free magazines rely solely on advertising space for their revenue. As such these positions are vital, and in some firms the ad sales department will be the largest. Through the use of market research and statistical surveys they aim to attract new advertisers. This can be done either by telephone, as in the case of small classifieds, or through more proactive research methods and face-to-face contact, as for display ads. Advertising sales is often considered a good starting-point for those considering careers in magazine publishing.

Graphic designers are employed in art departments to produce the look/image of magazines. They must be able to work to the brief provided by the art director, who will decide this in liaison with senior managers. Illustration is often 'farmed out' to freelance illustrators, so drawing skills are not necessarily required.

Finally, the marketing department will promote the magazine. Roles here include sending mailshots, sales promotions, advertising, special events and offers in order to ensure that the magazine sells and establishes its place in the market. This is an increasingly important role as magazine sales become more and more competitive.

Recruitment and entry

The number of trainee journalist places is far fewer than in newspapers, but a number of publishers do have (graduate) training schemes, for example IPC Magazines.

Art department staff are normally expected to have a graphic design degree or technician qualification. It is possible to start in production as an assistant or junior, and train on the job, but experience is often wanted. The easiest route into the commercial side is advertisement sales.

Qualifications and training

There are various vocational course in periodical journalism and the following ones have been monitored and accredited by the Periodicals Training Council (PTC): College of Cardiff, postgraduate diploma; Graduate Centre for Journalism, diploma; Highbury College, one-year course in Magazine Journalism, open to A-level students and graduates; the London College of Fashion, BA degree in Fashion Promotion (Journalism and PR); PMA Training, postgraduate course; School of Communications, diploma for ethnic minority graduates; the London College of Printing (part of London Institute), graduate diploma or pre-entry certificate; and the Journalism Training Centre, offering training for magazine journalism.

The Periodicals Training Council has developed NVQs in Periodical Journalism and also offers a range of training courses in Editorial, Advertising Sales, Circulation, Subscription and Multimedia for the magazine industry.

Further information

The Periodicals Training Council.

Copywriting

This is a skill used only in the ADVERTISING industry. *See in* BUYING, SELLING AND RELATED CAREERS.

Journalism

Journalists combine writing with news-gathering and interpretation.

Numbers being recruited into the industry fluctuate in proportion to the economic climate. For instance, the number of trainee journalists registered with the National Council for the Training of Journalists (NCTJ) was around 450 in the twelve months ending in June 1995.

Journalists work on national and local newspapers, for news agencies, on periodicals, in radio and television, and on a freelance basis. The number of newspapers has been rising (each national employs up to 200), and broadcasting is also expanding. New technology affecting the rest of the industry's employees is now starting to make inroads into journalists' jobs. While the recent growth rate is unlikely to continue, the NUJ expects numbers to at least stay at their present level.

While the journalist's work obviously varies from newspaper to newspaper, and from magazine to magazine, all journalists are as much researchers as they are writers. They don't only write their own news or feature stories, but must find and research them first; however, a great many stories hunt the journalist, who must reject many of them. Only a relatively small proportion of news comes from the unexpected, since most people who supply stories are aware that newspapers want advance warning to give good coverage to anything. The real 'scoop' is a very rare event. Every newsdesk and every journalist gets vast shoals of paper every day, plus endless telephone calls on items that people want to get into the newspaper or magazine.

Much of what actually goes into local and even national papers is routine, and on anticipated events, such as court cases, debates in parliament or the local council, weddings, royal occasions, company reports, or the month's unemployment figures. Much of the rest of the news is given to journalists through press releases, press conferences, and unofficial briefings, or either can be anticipated, or is planned (e.g. a commissioned public opinion poll), or is a running theme of the moment.

The journalist's job is to give the story an individual slant, to get a better quote on the story than the next paper, to dig deeper behind the official line, or to find the crucial question to ask that will improve on the story. All of this often means doing a lot of background work first, and being able to think on one's feet. Obviously every journalist is also looking out all the time for a story that no other journalist has found, but this is fairly unusual. They normally come not 'out of the blue', but from a journalist's well-nursed contacts, or because s/he has the hard-won expertise to see a story in an apparently trivial piece of information.

Journalists have to work fast, to meet deadlines that do not wait for events. Their stories must be checked, and they must be newsworthy. They must put their stories together at speed, in crowded offices with a lot of phones all going at once, in a bar or at the back of a conference hall, in the street, or on a train. They must phone it in if necessary. Stories should be accurate, short, pointed, and interesting. Superb prose comes a long way behind these, but a journalist whose writing is lively, imaginative, sharp and very readable too has a strong advantage. Journalists move around for much of their time – going to press conferences, meetings, events, and so on – have to be on the telephone a great deal, and work long and irregular hours, under pressure.

Most journalists begin as general reporters, on local newspapers working under a news editor. The general reporter spends many days covering very routine, and often quite boring, assignments, and may go for some time with nothing out of the ordinary happening. However, they learn a very great deal through doing the basic stories: about sources of information; how to cope with people and with the less pleasant side of life; interviewing techniques (including how to listen); the use of simple, straightforward English and an economical style of writing; how to turn a basically ordinary story into an interesting piece of copy; how to write for a particular audience; and so on. They must also develop or acquire an instinct for news, an insatiable curiosity (especially about people and what motivates them), the ability to meet deadlines come what may, astuteness, and endless adaptability.

Although traditionally reporters cover any story, and many still do, competition from television and radio means that many journalists are assigned to look after particular subjects: politics, finance, education, defence, local government, the environment, industry, farming, fashion, sport, travel, science, motoring. Mostly journalists specialise only on national papers, television and national radio, but on many regional papers journalists combine general reporting with in-depth coverage of one area, for instance, education. Journalists who specialise do not just report on the latest news in their specialist subject, but deal with it in depth, commenting on events, pointing out trends, reporting on future developments, explaining causes and effects, etc. These journalists build close contacts in their subject areas, and get to know and talk to experts on their own level, but they must still write stories in non-technical language which the average newspaper reader can understand. Established specialist journalists have a more independent position than general reporters, and work directly under the editor.

With fast and fairly efficient travel more or less worldwide now, fewer foreign correspondents are based permanently abroad, and those that are cover larger areas. Even so, some still become established residents of one country, specialising in all types of news and comment on that country, but having to do whatever the editor wants, frequently at short notice. Other foreign specialists are based on the newspaper, or freelance, flying off to wherever a story breaks.

Some journalists specialise in writing in-depth articles or longer features, or interviewing; but with the growth of specialist journalism, demand for feature writers as such is down, and most journalists get the chance to write in depth now. Some journalists combine reporting with photography, as photo-journalists (*see* PHOTOGRAPHY *in* ART, CRAFT AND DESIGN). Some work on the so-called gossip columns, others write humorous pieces, others become political columnists.

Leaders put over the newspaper's own views and policy on current affairs. Traditionally written (anonymously) by the editor, larger regional and national papers usually have small teams of specialist leader-writers.

Editing mostly means giving up reporting and writing, at least on daily papers, although some people do move between the two. Some do combine editing with some writing, particularly on weeklies.

Editing is desk- and teamwork. A larger paper may have up to 25 sub-editors (agencies even more) all working as a team under a chief sub-editor, and senior editorial staff, the copy-tasters. They decide how important each story is at it comes in, and then pass them to the chief sub-editor, who decides what should go where on which page, how long it should be, etc.

The 'subs' then 'work over' the copy to get it the right length; tighten up the language, grammar, style, etc.; check its accuracy and rewrite it if necessary; deal with running stories which may be coming in from different places, a bit at a time; and write headlines which must be apt, concise, informative and perhaps amusing or ambiguous, but must always fit into the space allowed. This may have to be done all over again between editions if a story develops further, or is overtaken, or a major new story breaks somewhere in the world. Some subs specialise in particular subjects, e.g. sports, and also lay out the pages. Subs work at very high speed and under considerable pressure. They need good memories and to be able to spot any links between apparently unconnected stories. Stamina and unflappability are crucial.

On large newspapers, or periodicals, editors are in charge of each section: home news, overseas news, features, sports, City pages. The news editor manages a team of reporters, decides which stories to cover, assigns reporters, and supervises progress. Features editors look out for ideas, commission articles from staff and other journalists, and so on. Editorial decisions, on policy, on the balance of the paper, on disagreements on which stories to print, or any major problems, are made at editorial conferences – throughout the day and night if need be. Editors are policy-makers and organisers, and although this is a recognised promotion route, not all journalists want to take it because it may mean no actual writing or research at all. Top managers are rarely journalists.

On a large national paper there may also be a deputy and several assistant editors, and the editor becomes more remote. Weekly papers have fewer editors. News agencies generally have at least three editors, one of whom is editor-in-chief, since the post must be manned round the clock.

A high proportion of journalists work for regional and local papers all their lives, sometimes acting as a 'stringer' for a national paper, radio or TV. On national and specialist periodicals there may be a little more time to work on a story and more careful planning and thinking, but less immediacy. Life is different again in the news agencies.

The BBC is one of the largest employers of journalists for its radio and TV news services, with ITN close behind. On local radio stations, with news programmes throughout the day, life is probably even more hectic than on a daily paper. Like the BBC, the major independent TV contractors all have at least one current affairs programme for which journalists work, normally on contract for a set number of programmes. *See also* BROADCASTING *above*.

Some journalists work on a freelance basis, but not usually as general reporters. Most freelance journalists build up considerable expertise in a subject and so have a specialist knowledge to sell, perhaps in something that is too technical for papers to cover, or have access to particular sources. Mostly freelance journalists either have worked as full-time journalists first, and so have the contacts to whom they can sell their output (or who will commission them), or have been experts at something and find there is a market for their ability to explain what is going on in that field. Some people combine freelance journalism with technical writing (*see below*).

Recruitment and entry

Entry to newspaper and news-broadcasting journalism is by a variety of routes, and demand for places always exceeds supply by a considerable degree. For instance, there are a variety of newspaper training schemes, from those accredited by the NCTJ to the independent in-company schemes such as those operated by East Midlands Allied Press, Trinity International, The Training Centre.

Within the NCTJ approach there are pre-entry courses (full-time on leaving school, college or university) and direct-entry courses for those gaining employment with a newspaper and receiving training at that stage.

The minimum entry qualifications for direct entry courses are five GCSE/SCEs (A–C/1–3) including English or equivalent. However, most entrants have at least two A-levels/H-grades or equivalent. Pre-entry journalism courses require two A-levels/H-grades or equivalent including English at GCSE/SCE or A-level/H-grade.

Graduate entry has been rising steadily, with over 50% of successful applicants having completed graduate-level courses, and the NCTJ now advises any potential journalist who can, to gain a degree. Evidence suggests that a degree in, e.g. politics, economics or a science, is more useful than, for example, English or history. The number of trainees is approximately 450 on average, and there is probably an average of five applications for every vacancy, with many more for the more popular papers and the BBC news traineeships.

Periodicals take on about 400–500 new entrants a year. This figure has been stable for the last few years. There is no formal scheme, but the larger publishers give training. Periodicals probably take a higher proportion of graduates, especially professional, scientific and technological publications, than newspapers.

Journalism takes real curiosity, the ability to work up an interest in anything and everything, to absorb new subjects and ideas easily, to be good at simply finding out and always wanting to know, and a sense of what is important for the moment. Journalists need to be very observant and patient. They need the kind of scepticism that questions anything they are told. Potential journalists ought to show the ability to write clearly, crisply, concisely and simply, and should be able to work fast and very accurately. They need to be able to handle people of all types and from all backgrounds, and to be good at listening and putting people at their ease, but persuasive and persistent too. Journalism demands physical and emotional stamina, and the ability to cope with both moving around a lot and waiting through long and often boring events.

Editors also expect successful applicants to have shown determination and persistence in trying to get in. They also expect any applicant who has had the opportunity to gain relevant experience (in student journalism, for instance) to have done so, or to have done something in their spare time and/or holidays which demonstrates interest in the media, the ability to hold down any job, and to have had some kind of responsibility.

Qualifications and training

The NCTJ accredits a number of universities and colleges around the UK to teach the syllabus leading to attainment of its national certificate. Some institutions additionally offer awards to HND or degree standard, while others offer access courses.

In general, course applicants are pre-entry candidates – they have not yet obtained a job in the industry.

The accredited colleges and universities are: Bell College of Technology (HND), Bournemouth University (degree), Calderdale College (day-release), City of Liverpool Community College (day-release, degree, postgraduate), City University (postgraduate), Cornwall College (pre-entry, postgraduate), Darlington College of Technology (block-release, pre-entry), Gloucester College of Arts and Technology (pre-entry), Gwent Tertiary College (pre-entry), Harlow College (block-release, pre-entry, HND), Highbury College (block-release, pre-entry), Lambeth College (pre-entry for ethnic minorities only), Napier University (block-release), Sheffield College (block-release, pre-entry), Strathclyde University (postgraduate), Surrey Institute of Art and Design (HND), University of Central Lancashire (pre-entry, degree, postgraduate), University of Wales College of Cardiff (postgraduate), and Yale College (day-release). In addition, the London College of Printing and Distributive Trades run the following courses: BTEC HND in journalism; BA (Hons) in journalism; certificate in periodical journalism for graduates; and postgraduate diplomas in European journalism, radio journalism and photojournalism.

Journalism degrees and HNDs are viewed with a certain amount of suspicion within the industry. In looking at any journalism courses it is very important to look for accreditation from the NCTJ. Courses vary in quality considerably, and it is therefore vital to go and see the course and also find out what technology is available. Prospective candidates should also ask admissions tutors what sorts of jobs previous students have gone on to.

Formal trainee schemes last three years for non-graduates and two for graduates after a six-month probationary period. Most newspapers taking trainees have reasonably well organised systems of on-the-job training in basic journalistic skills, supplemented by block-release and distance-learning courses covering subjects such as law, public affairs, shorthand and practical journalism. Because computer-based production systems mean that journalists input their own copy and edit on VDU screens, most courses include typing to a high level of accuracy. Graduates take an intensive version. The National Certificate carries cash benefits and is increasingly required for appointments and promotion. It is well worth while ensuring that the training provided by any employer is as stated, and it is questionable whether it is any use taking a first post which does not provide full and proper training.

Successful completion of appropriate courses and sufficient workplace experience leads to a recognised industry qualification such as the NCTJ's National Certificate or equivalent. It is likely that more competence-based assessment will be introduced in the future leading to a level-4 NVQ.

Periodical publishers now generally give new entrants practical, on-the-job training, and many are also likely to provide competence-based assessment leading to an NVQ/SVQ.

Further information

The National Union of Journalists, National Council for the Training of Journalists, Periodical Training Council, Newspaper Society.

Technical, scientific and other specialist writing

This is probably an expanding area of employment, although it is hard to prove. The work ranges from writing, compiling and editing text- and reference books on specialist subjects through to preparing user, service and maintenance manuals and leaflets, abstracts and information bulletins. It can shade over into creative writing (e.g. biographical), into teaching (many textbooks are prepared by teachers and university staff), technical journalism, editing house journals, and information science.

Many people in this field work on a freelance basis once they have become established; others are employed by the technical press or by larger industrial and commercial companies. Publishers who produce a significant number of reference works, particularly encyclopedias and dictionaries, may also have professional editors on the staff, some with small teams of researchers and editorial assistants.

Recruitment and entry

Generally a second career. Most people normally gain relevant expertise and experience first, although graduates are recruited by some industrial firms on manual writing, etc., and it is possible to go straight into technical journalism. Teachers, for instance, may have written, e.g., textbooks in their spare time before switching to it full-time for an income.

Technical writing takes considerable expertise in a subject area, plus the ability to write clearly and concisely about the subject in a language which can be understood by those for whom it is intended, and which takes account of the needs of the particular public. While a user's manual must obviously explain even to the densest reader, it is no use writing at too elementary a level in an information bulletin on research designed for research scientists. For some technical work, particularly on illustrated textbooks and manuals, a good background knowledge of technical illustration and layout, notation, etc. is needed. Languages are increasingly useful.

Qualifications and training

No formal training schemes.

Literary and media agents

Many people in the media business work on contract or a freelance basis, and because they want to use their creative skills, as writers or performers, and not spend time marketing themselves, they use an agent. The media agent acts as their links with the firms and organisations that employ and use their services.

An agent works for the client, not the media company, to 'sell' their actors or actresses to producers, and writers to publishers or radio or television companies. An efficient agent does not only find a publisher, say, for an author's new manuscript. An agent stays closely in touch with the client's potential market, and finds out, for example, what plays are coming into production and when, and who will be the director. A literary agent talks regularly to publishers, and knows what their future plans are, or whether a projected television play series will have room for an author's new idea.

Agents negotiate the terms of contracts, and are expert at getting the best possible deal – not only in terms of royalties (for authors), but also rights, repeat fees, and so on. They try to make sure that standard contracts do not take away rights, that they are appropriate for the particular project, and that fees are keeping pace with those offered by other publishers, or companies.

Agents act as both buffers and links between the individual writers or performers and the companies they are at present working for. They ensure that their clients get publicity. They make sure their clients actually get paid.

Agents make their income by charging their clients a percentage of the money earned from contracts successfully negotiated. A successful author or actor/actress is therefore more profitable than a new and unknown one, and it is to an agent's advantage to find work for clients. While agents must constantly look for new talent, they must also have a balance of established and potentially successful clients, and clearly cannot afford to have too many people on their books who are not earning very much. New authors or actors are a form of investment. Getting onto the books of a successful agent is crucial for actors and actresses, and can be quite difficult. It is not so essential, although still useful, for a writer.

Literary agents need a blend of aesthetic judgement and skills. While the agent's interests are always with the client, they have to try to bridge the gap between the writer and the commercial realities of the marketplace. Agents may have to be at one and the same time wet-nurse, business and legal adviser, and devil's advocate: the relationship can be a close, if difficult, one.

Being a literary or theatrical agent is usually a second career, since to be of any use to clients, agents must have extensive experience and contacts, and will therefore usually have spent some time working in publishing, broadcasting, or the theatre. It is, though, possible to work up from the bottom, learning on the job, or to start as a secretary. There are not all that many jobs. Few agencies have more than 50 staff, and most only a dozen.

Publishing

Publishing, according to the Publishers Association, 'is a difficult trade, a compound of art, craft and business'. The art is that indefinable but essential quality, 'flair', the craft, the design and presentation of the author's work in the best possible form for the clients, and the business the source of finance.

Publishers have to earn their living in a small, overcrowded and highly competitive market where one of the major forces, public taste, can change quite unpredictably at any moment. It is easy to lose money on books, and even the most experienced publishers do it. Sound commercial judgement is therefore essential. Lack of it in a publishing firm has always led to early insolvency.

Publishing books is a commercial operation. Publishers are in business to make a profit from selling books, just as food manufacturers expect to make a profit from breakfast cereal. Publishers have books 'manufactured' (by printers) and distribute them (although through book shops or by mail order) just as do food firms. Making a profit from books is, though, probably more difficult than from breakfast foods. The market is smaller, and it is hard to find out ahead (through marketing), what will and will not sell. Books are amongst the first products to suffer when there is a recession. Book publishers do not control their own manufacturing plant, and production and distribution costs are relatively high.

It is not so much the ability to discover a literary success that is important in publishing, as the skill to find the books that will sell the most copies. High-level management skills (especially in finance, marketing and production, and in 'human resources') are crucial, and the industry is using modern marketing methods to increase domestic sales.

Publishing is under great pressure, and has just been through some bad years, with many firms slimming, and merging. Libraries have always been one of the largest customers, but their expenditure has been cut and borrowings are down. Novels make up only one in eleven of all new books published. A third of turnover comes from paperback books, which is what the general reading public buys.

Although some 80,000 new titles were produced in 1995, publishing is a small industry. While 10,500 organisations produced at least one title in 1995, estimates by the Book

House Training Centre (BHTC) suggest only about 3,500 firms are full-time publishers. The 180 member-companies (450 imprints) of the Publishers' Association produce two-thirds of the industry's 1995 £3 billion retail sales, and under 100 companies publish more than 100 titles each a year. Some 50% comes from the eight largest.

Employment in the industry is estimated (by BHTC) to be about 20,000 (against estimates of 13,800 for 1982 and 13,200 for 1978). The largest group employs 1,500 in the UK, and BHTC suggests 500 is the average for the other top ten, with the vast majority of small firms employing ten or less.

Large publishers produce several hundred titles a year in a wide variety of different subjects. Some quite large publishing houses specialise – in law, medicine, art, education, academic and technical books – but the trend is to multi-imprint large firms. Some small publishers, without the high overheads of larger firms, make a reasonable income by exploiting particular markets. Packagers are an innovative feature of publishing. They do all the work in finding, creating and producing a book – usually one with a likely mass readership – but sell (in advance) the edition complete to a conventional publisher, who then puts it on their list.

Book publishing

New developments in the industry which are worthy of a mention are those involving the expansion in the production of non-book products and new forms of publishing, for example multimedia, interactive CD, CD ROM and electronic publishing on the Internet. Many publishing firms see these as the main form of publishing in the future years. Interactive CD and video are a combination of text and moving-screen images operating within a data processing system. Users are able to control what is heard, seen and printed out by responding to questions and interacting with the content of the CD or video. These are particularly useful in training and educational roles. CD ROMs are produced alongside written encyclopedias and are useful reference tools, replacing microfiches as a means of storing reference material. As these are still relatively new developments it is difficult to say how more traditional forms of publishing have been affected. As yet, no research has been produced. So far, most of the concern has centered around copyright management, particularly with regard to the Internet. Book House Training Centre, the industry training organisation, have developed short courses to cater for these new developments and now run a 'Multimedia Publishing Workshop' which looks at the design, production, costing and marketing of multimedia products and 'Publishing and the Internet' which provides participants with practical experience of using the net.

Working in publishing

There are three main areas of work in publishing: editorial; production with design; and marketing, which combines sales, promotion and publicity. In the larger houses these are separate departments, and in the largest there may be several editorial departments, each with a specialised list, e.g. educational titles, reference books (e.g. dictionaries), novels, or art books. In the smallest firms, individual members of staff may combine several jobs. Publishers are, increasingly, putting out work, using packagers, and freelances for almost all functions, to save in-house costs.

Publishing policy comes from the top of the editorial tree. In the larger firms this means an editorial director or senior directors, and may be decided more by what the marketing people say will sell, or what is wanted by overseas customers, than by what the authors want to write – particularly in non-fiction. Only a very small percentage of unsolicited manuscripts are published. What to publish is often decided between editors, marketing staff, literary agents and professional writers, and may be a compromise between the original ideas of both sides. A few books, mostly large reference works like encyclopedias, are put together 'in-house' by a team of editorial staff, but the great majority are written or edited by people working on contract or freelance. Publishers build their own computer databases from which information can be 'sold' directly, or from which information can be extracted automatically for reference books, such as dictionaries.

Editorial

The editorial departments probably employ no more than 20% of a publisher's staff, and are increasingly outnumbered and outgunned by marketing managers. Some commissioning editors are more managers than editors. Some now spend more time in sales conferences than at their desks or with authors.

Commissioning editors are responsible for finding, developing and matching marketable ideas with good authors, and for new editions. The commissioning editor is the main contact between author and publisher and it is their job to build up a 'list' of books. In consumer book publishing, editors may cover adult fiction and non-fiction. Alternatively, they may specialise in an area such as children's books or science fiction. In an educational publishing house, the editor might focus on a number of subjects covering a variety of academic levels and markets. Commissioning editors work to a brief, but the style and identity of each list are primarily the result of each editor's attitudes and effort.

A publisher relies on commissioning editors to provide a regular flow of publishable manuscripts in order to keep its projected level of activity. Commissioning editors are assessed on how much profit is brought in by their books.

Copy editors may sometimes be the only people other than the author who read the book prior to publication. Their job is to make sure that the text and illustrations are clear and factually correct. The copy editor may also look out for any text which could be libellous. The copy editor must first ensure that they have received all the manuscript items and that they are clearly labelled and numbered by the author.

Once in receipt of all the manuscript items, the copy editor's job is to check the author's spelling, hyphenation, use of capitals, verbs, quotation marks, etc. The editor must also look out for the accuracy and relationship of some parts of the text to others. In addition, the editor will point out to the designer/typesetter any parts of the text that would benefit from special typographic treatment such as italicising.

Increasingly, copy editors employ freelance and specialist *proof-readers* to check manuscripts and text. Proofs are the first printed copy which must be examined before mass production, to ensure that no spelling, grammar or punctuation mistakes have been made. All facts must be checked. Freelance work in this field can be sporadic and not particularly well paid. In order to establish yourself on a freelance basis it is best to have acquired some form of training or trained experience in editorial work within a publishing company. Book House Training Centre offer short courses in this area, and further advice on obtaining experience can be obtained from the Society of Freelance Editors and Proofreaders.

The compilation of indexes, technical or otherwise, is also increasingly 'farmed' out to freelance workers. *Indexers* compile indexes for books, journals and encyclopedias. It is precise, time-consuming work, again sporadic and not particularly well paid. It would be unlikely that anyone would be able to survive solely on this source of income. Again, training is provided at BHTC, and further information can be obtained from the Society of Indexers.

Growing numbers of writers use word processors, and deliver their books on computer disks, not manuscript – which reduces some of the work of the editor. Manuscript from a word processor, whether on paper or disk, is generally 'cleaner' than when typed. Linked to publishers' drive for lower costs, all this is slowly cutting into the editorial time spent in-house, on books.

Picture research is a growing and expanding industry. The current membership of the Society of Picture Researchers and Editors is over 250, the majority of whom work freelance. They are responsible for finding the right pictures and illustrations for books, which involves considerable liaison with editorial staff. Pictures used are from a variety of different places, hence a good researcher must have their ear to the ground. Potential sources are museums, art galleries, freelance photographers, corporate press offices, picture libraries and government departments. Picture researchers must be skilled communicators and detectives, being aware of all available sources when choosing the picture to fit their brief. Routes in can be tough: gaining experience in picture agencies/libraries, or even in an administrative capacity in a publishing firm.

Production

The production department takes the manuscript from editorial, and turns it into a printed book.

Designers (who may be on the staff if the publisher is large or produces many illustrated books, or who may be freelance) specify what the book will look like, decide on the book jacket or cover, and commission any illustrations. They work to a brief from the editor, and within set budgets.

Production decides firms to set it into type (more often than not on film today), and to print and bind it to an agreed schedule and within a tight budget, and according to the designer's specifications.

Production takes careful planning and organisation. All the parts of a book, including illustrations and artwork, have to come together at the right moment. The paper must get to the printer just when needed, and the jacket must be printed as soon as the printer confirms the estimated thickness of the book, and so on. Production staff have to know a great deal about the print business: how to cost accurately, where to buy paper, what paper is best for a particular job; and keep pace with very rapid technological changes in printing, and be able to assess their usefulness.

Production staff must work closely with editorial staff, with designers, and with printers, and liaise between them, keeping them all to a tight and complicated schedule. They have to be very good organisers, and methodical, able to work under pressure.

Promotion and publicity

Promotion and publicity staff have to gain attention for their books when some 80,000 other titles are also clamouring to be bought. Routines are set up for each book: to see that it goes into the right lists and catalogues; that it is advertised to the trade; that librarians are told about it; that it gets reviewed if possible; and that publicity material is designed and printed for it. The book must be in all the right book fairs, exhibitions, and conferences. And because books often sell best through free publicity, the publicity staff must use ingenuity and sophisticated marketing techniques to get their books onto radio and television, and into the press.

Distribution and sales

Books are distributed through warehouses, but most of the large publishers sell through teams of sales representatives (they may be employed full-time, or freelance), who visit bookshops, multiple stores, libraries, education authorities, schools, etc. Sales staff provide the publisher with critical information from the marketplace. The actual number of sales representatives is usually quite small, but with the sales manager and office staff may make up a third of a publisher's staff. Smaller publishers contract their distribution and sales to larger publishers or distributors, agencies or freelancers.

Administration

A significant proportion (probably at least 20%) of the jobs with most larger publishers are administrative. Like all commercial firms, publishers employ financial staff (*see* FINANCIAL CAREERS), personnel managers and secretaries (*see* ADMINISTRATION, BUSINESS MANAGEMENT AND OFFICE WORK), etc. But some aspects of publishing are more specialised, e.g. contracts, rights, etc., and legal work (*see* THE LEGAL SYSTEM).

Recruitment and entry

Vacancies are generally few, and competition for them great, with no structured entry route. Only a small number of larger houses have (very small) graduate recruitment schemes. It may be slightly easier to get into marketing, sales or production than editorial, initially. A good class of degree (by itself not enough), evidence of wide interests and reading, and a demonstrable and very realistic understanding of publishing as a business are basic requirements. Some kind of previous experience, in bookselling, or sales and promotion generally, may help, or a pre-entry course (*see below*). People do get into editorial work by starting as secretaries, and it is possible to get into production by training in the print industry. Persistence, endless letter-writing, and extensive use of any contacts are all needed to gain a toehold.

Book design and illustration – *see* GRAPHIC DESIGN *in* ART, CRAFT AND DESIGN.

Qualifications and training

A number of courses have recently been added to the longer-established ones, but their record in getting students into publishing should be checked.

Graduate and postgraduate courses in publishing are available at: West Hertfordshire College, London College of Printing, Stirling University, Loughborough University, Napier University, Middlesex University, Thames Valley University, Oxford Brookes University, Robert Gordon University, Swansea Institute of Higher Education. Training is otherwise mainly on the job.

The Book House Training Centre is the industry's recognised training organisation, and runs a wide range of courses in all aspects of publishing (2,300 people already in the industry attended one or more of their 70 courses in 1995). In-house training, at least in larger firms, seems to be improving.

NVQs (but not SVQs) are now available at levels 1, 2, 3 and 4 in editing, production, commissioning, design, publishing contracts, publicity and promotion, publishing rights, journals production and journals management.

All editors have to gain a wide and sound knowledge of all aspects of publishing as a business, plus modern production and printing techniques (including computer typesetting).

The importance of word-processing skills should also be noted, especially for those considering working freelance.

Further information

The Book House Training Centre.

Historical and Related Work

(CLCI: FAE, FAG, FAH, UX)

History

Very few people who read history can, or even want to, become professional historians, and although openings for teaching history in higher education are likely to increase in the late 1990s, entry into the profession is highly competitive. Successful applicants will normally have done a postgraduate course leading to a PhD after their first degree. History, though, is generally seen as a reasonable basis for many non-academic careers.

Working as a historian

Professional historians never expect to discover the whole 'truth' about any aspect of the past, and are never really satisfied that the last word has been said. A training in history is designed to impose a sceptical mind, a refusal to be indoctrinated. They can usually work on any aspect of the past that interests them, such as European trade in the later Middle Ages, the English working classes, modern Sino-Japanese relations, early Islamic history – all examples of topics being researched by individual historians. They may try to find answers to questions other historians failed to answer, or reexamine the answers given by others in the light of new evidence, make new analyses of older evidence, or just try to show greater insight. History, though concerned with the past, is always changing, as highlighted by the greater use of computing for the analysis of evidence.

Historians work on factual evidence, and first try to discover as nearly as possible what actually happened. But they are just as, if not more, interested in causes, effects, and trends. They not only chart political events, wars, kings and governments and their struggles for power, but also how people of all kinds lived, worked and thought; they are interested in social structures, e.g. the feudal system – in fact the whole complex interplay of cultural, political, economic, social, technological and religious development over the centuries, to analyse, for instance, the many strands which caused the industrial revolution to happen when it did.

Historians work where possible from original and other documentary sources, such as the state papers of kings and their chancellors; government records, and parliamentary papers and reports; church records (e.g. parish registers and the reports of mediaeval inquisitors on heretical villages); Norse sagas and medieval chronicles; memoirs and papers of individuals; the output of contemporary biographers and diarists; political and other pamphlets and records of speeches; even the work of playwrights, novelists and poets. The records of trade, agricultural and industrial output, of employers and trade unions; statistics of all kinds, from how many people were born and died to migration figures and so on; popular literature and broadsheets; are all used in historical evidence.

Documentary evidence is, however, often incomplete, and not only in the distant past: the telephone has created great gaps in the written evidence of the twentieth century. Documentary evidence and oral testimony can often be one-sided or actually biased: people who could write rarely put down anything about the majority who could not; many of the people who wrote official records documented their own views (so historians usually treat this kind of evidence as opinion not fact). Records may only be made years after the event when memories have faded, and so on.

Historians must, then, look elsewhere for other evidence, or evidence to prove or disprove doubtful records: from archaeology; or from philology (which, by analysing the language of English place names can chart the spread of Danes and Norsemen through Britain). Historians take into account the work of scholars in other disciplines, e.g. economists (on, say, early nineteenth century industry and working conditions), and anthropologists. Like other scholars, historians use statistical techniques and the computer, to analyse evidence on, for instance, the age at which women first marry, in studies of population changes.

While historians make up their own minds on topics they are researching – and at least one contemporary historian admits relying on intuition as much as on documentary research – they usually test their own findings against those of other historians, and deliberately look for flaws in the arguments. Historians spend a lot of time in libraries and archives; read many books, articles, reports, opinions, discussions, and get involved in debates, disagreements and controversy about past events.

Most professional historians combine historical research with teaching in higher education, and since communication is an important part of history, it is generally a happy combination. Just a few historians can make a living editing books or journals. Most historians specialise in teaching a particular period of history.

Studying history

History is taught at first-degree level at most universities, and is a major option in some liberal arts degrees in colleges of higher education. History is often offered as part of a modular degree. Almost all courses are based on European and British history (because it is easier to teach methods and analysis through material that is familiar and dealing with a culture which is easily understandable). Even so, it is normally possible to specialise in ancient, mediaeval or modern history. Some courses include options in non-European history.

'First destination' figures* (1994) are:

total graduating	*4125*
research/further study	460
teacher training	270
law and Bar exams	206
other training	209
believed unemployed 31 Dec	356
overseas employment	131
short-term UK employment	276
permanent UK employment	1749
employers	
commerce (excluding finance)	478
accountancy	106
banking/insurance	140
industry (chemical/building/transport, etc.)	143
local government	102
Civil Service	54
higher/further education	67
entertainment/leisure	61
schools	38
functions	
financial work	217
administration/operations management	193
marketing, etc.	217
management services	26
library and information work	93
teaching	38
personnel/social/medical	127
creative and entertainment	74

* These figures are for History and do not include Economic & Social History figures, which are collated separately. It is interesting to note that the highest numbers of graduates went into financial work.

Most candidates have history at A-level, but in fact many universities do not actually require it. Many do want students to have language qualifications to at least 16-plus and preferably A-level. There are an increasing number of mature students. An Advanced GNVQ may be acceptable, usually at Distinction. UCAS statistics show that 4,325 students were accepted for history in 1994.

Heritage management and interpretation

Heritage management is concerned with promoting the understanding and enjoyment of historic properties and monuments, sites and landscapes, historical theme parks, nature reserves and museums, while ensuring their safety and preservation. Some of these topics, such as museums and galleries, are dealt with further on in this article. Some are covered in other chapters – *see* CAREERS IN CONSERVATION AND THE ENVIRONMENT.

Heritage interpretation is concerned with promoting understanding and appreciation. This can take various forms: reenacting civil war battles, audiovisual programmes, wearing the appropriate costumes, etc. Managing and interpreting aspects of national heritage to the public has expanded enormously in the 1990s, and heritage interpretation now covers almost any kind of visitor attraction. In recent years approximately 60 heritage interpretation centres have opened, with emphasis on reconstruction and presentation to the public of the evolution of the local community. These organisations often include *marketing* and *design* posts as well as managers, historians or archaeologists.

The main national organisations in Britain concerned with heritage management, archaeology and history are English Heritage, which is part of the Department of National Heritage established in 1992, Historic Scotland, and Cadw (Wales). Other major employers include the National Trust, local authorities, tourist boards, amenity societies such as the Victorian Society, projects like the Jorvik Viking Centre and private historic houses.

English Heritage

The DNH was formed in 1992 from parts of six other government departments and is split into four groups. One of these is the Heritage and Tourism Group.

English Heritage employs around 1,500 people including seasonal and part-time workers. Many are administrative and professional. They include custodians or 'housekeepers' who have developed skills and sensitivity in caring for monuments/buildings; sales and marketing teams who promote English Heritage activities and monuments, carry out market research into what visitors want and set up cooperative sales promotion schemes; and education officers who organise a range of programmes and activities. Other administrative/professional staff are involved in a wide range of activities such as dealing with applications for grants and scheduling, planning and administering improvement schemes, setting up management agreements with owners of sites, collecting information on other sources of grants, and developing systems for local authorities to monitor listed buildings. Not all are qualified specialists – some area managers have worked their way up.

Specialist staff include those concerned with the conservation of finds, illustration and publication, and those who provide specialised scientific services including dating and site prospecting through the *Ancient Monuments Laboratory*.

The *Central Archaeology Service* in Portsmouth is a branch of English Heritage employing 25 full-time archaeologists plus a backup team which includes a graphics artist. Their role is to advise on archaeological activities funded by English Heritage, and form a mobile field team carrying out surveys, evaluations, watching briefs and excavations. *See also* CAREERS IN CONSERVATION AND THE ENVIRONMENT.

Historic Scotland

Historic Scotland is responsible to the Secretary of State for Scotland and has executive agency status under the Scottish Office. Its remit is to preserve and present historic buildings of archaeological interest and is very similar to English Heritage and the National Trust (*see below*). Under its umbrella are the *Scottish Conservation Bureau*, which is also based at the same address, responsible for the internal conservation of buildings, e.g. the restoration of an Adam fireplace or the paintings on a ceiling. It has a works and professional services division staffed largely by architects. It works in close partnership with the Scottish Civic Trust in the field of preservation. It employs approximately 600 staff, more than half of whom are located at historic sites throughout Scotland. In addition to custodians, shop assistants, and masons to repair the stonework, Historic Scotland also employs historians to write the guidebooks and the display boards, archaeologists, architects and managers.

The *Inspectorate of Ancient Monuments* forms part of the Heritage Policy Group of Historic Scotland. The *Inspectors of Ancient Monuments* deal with the preservation and protection of sites and monuments, monitor fieldwork projects and recommend grant aid. Inspectors usually work within a large region, and this generally involves much travelling. Much of the work is taken up with writing reports and giving advice. *Historic Building Inspectors* have a similar role in relation to buildings and must have a detailed knowledge of art history or architecture as well as a degree in archaeology. Inspectors are assisted by a range of specialists including architects, conservators, illustrators, photographers, research assistants and draughtspersons.

Cadw Wales

Cadw Welsh Historic Monuments operates similarly to English Heritage and Historic Scotland.

The Royal Commissions on Historic Monuments for England, Scotland and Wales (but not Northern Ireland)

The main aim of these organisations is to compile and make available surveys of ancient monuments, standing buildings and other field remains of all periods, details of which are collated into the National Monuments Record. An important aspect of this is the curation of a major collection of aerial photographs. The Commissions employ *air survey officers* to identify and interpret archaeological features from aerial photographs; *field recorders* to carry out site investigation; and *archival recorders* to input and plot new data into the records and maps. A knowledge of surveying is essential.

The National Trust

This organisation, founded in 1895, exists to promote the permanent preservation for the nation of land with outstanding natural features and animal and plant life, and buildings of beauty or historic interest. There are estimated to be more than 40,000 sites of archaeological interest in the ownership of the National Trust, about 6% of the national total.

The NT employs around 34 archaeological staff, who advise, research, record, survey, manage and occasionally excavate sites in its care when the archaeological deposits are likely to be disturbed. Many of these archaeologists are based in regions or on specific estates, such as Stourhead, Petworth or Kingston Lacy.

Archaeological work is interpreted broadly and the Trust's archaeologists are interested in every aspect from the archaeology of the coastal zone and marine archaeology, to the archaeology of gardens and woodlands, to historic buildings and industrial landscapes. The Trust is also compiling national computerised *Sites and Monuments Records* of all their historic sites and buildings.

The National Trust employs about three thousand staff plus thousands of voluntary workers. The equivalent body in Scotland is the National Trust for Scotland. *See also* CAREERS IN CONSERVATION AND THE ENVIRONMENT.

Qualifications and training

There are various postgraduate courses in heritage management including an MA/Diploma in Heritage Management at Birmingham University and Ironbridge Institute, and an MPhil in Tourism and Heritage Sciences at Bournemouth University. *See also courses under* MUSEUM WORK *below*.

Archaeology

Archaeology is the study of the human past through material remains. By using evidence ranging from buried cities to microscopic organisms, backed by an increasingly scientific array of techniques, archaeologists seek to reconstruct the historic environment, and the dynamics of past cultures, societies, economies, technologies and beliefs. The multidisciplinary approach of archaeology provides the only way of finding out about the greater part of the development of our species. Such milestones as the beginnings of agriculture, urbanisation and metallurgy can only be understood through the examination of physical evidence.

Archaeology studies the recent past as well as more remote times. One current project involves a national listing of all Second World War defensive structures in Britain.

The popular image of archaeologists as simply people who dig holes is far from accurate. They can be found in the Civil Service, local authorities, museums, trusts and research units, carrying out a wide range of activities from conserving finds to drawing up legislation to protect ancient monuments. The use of computers in archaeology is now widespread.

Archaeology can be an exciting and absorbing occupation, although at the present time jobs are difficult to find. Anyone considering joining the profession should be aware that in many cases it is neither secure nor well paid. There is no clear career structure unless the archaeologist is employed in a Civil-Service type organisation or museum. In order to gain promotion it would be expected that a person would have to move around.

Jobs in archaeology are advertised in *The Guardian* and *Independent* newspapers. Journals concerned with museums (*Museums Bulletin*) architecture, planning and local authorities also advertise vacancies. Jobs are sometimes advertised in the local press.

In a workshop on women in archaeology (1994), Deirdre O'Sullivan says there appear to be equal numbers of women and male applicants to study archaeology at university but 'as a profession it slides depressingly close to others in its pattern of male dominance'. It may well be the case too that 'field archaeology is mostly dominated by men, for example, and artefact research by women'. However, the Institute of Field Archaeologists is addressing equity issues.

Archaeologists can be found in all the organisations and institutions which are covered below.

National agencies

The main archaeological organisations in Britain are English Heritage, Historic Scotland, and Cadw (Welsh Historic Monuments) and the Department of the Environment for Northern Ireland. *See the section above.*

The *National Parks* also employ archaeologists to look after archaeological sites in their area. Their job involves recording, surveying and sometimes excavating sites. *See also* CAREERS IN CONSERVATION AND THE ENVIRONMENT.

British Gas, the *Forestry Commission* and *Thames Water* employ field archaeologists, as do a number of civil engineering, architectural and planning practices. They consider it necessary to have expert knowledge available on their staff.

There are several other organisations, such as the *Council for British Archaeology* and *Council for Scottish Archaeology* which employ small staffs. These bodies provide a bridge between amateur and professional archaeology, acting as pressure groups to promote the subject, with special emphasis on publication, education, conservation and information.

Local and regional authorities and independent Trusts

Archaeologists in Britain are employed by county and district councils in England and the new single-tier districts in Scotland. Wales is divided between independent regional trusts.

In some areas, fieldwork is carried out by independent units, run as trusts or registered charities. These often operate in cities of particular historic importance, or have interests in particular geographical areas. The freedom that developers now have to choose who carries out archaeological work on their sites has meant that some of these organisations now work outside their home region.

The numbers of jobs within each county unit vary a good deal from a handful to twenty or more. Units usually consist of a core of permanent staff with others employed on temporary contracts to work on excavations and policy projects. The unit is managed by a senior archaeologist who is also responsible for securing and allocating funding, staff organisation and matters of policy, especially the implications of planning.

Sites and Monuments Officer

All counties and most Scottish regions have a Sites and Monuments Officer, and usually a small staff, responsible for the Sites and Monuments Record (SMR), a database of all reported archaeological landscapes, sites and finds in the area. As well as looking after this major archive of information, the SMR officer also monitors the archaeological implications of planning applications. The role of SMRs has become increasingly important as the emphasis of national policy is now on the preservation of archaeological evidence where this is possible. This recent trend has had a direct impact on the number of excavation-type jobs.

Field officers

Field officers coordinate and supervise fieldwork. This includes field 'evaluations' (small excavations and surveys to assess the quality and nature of archaeological deposits prior to a proposed development), fieldwalking (the systematic collection and plotting of pottery and other material brought to the surface by cultivation); and the surveying of earthworks, landscapes and monuments. Geophysical survey of sites is increasingly important in field archaeology. Study of the sediment deposits on the site, caused by the decay of buildings or development of the soil and vegetation, can build up a picture of the site's history.

The archaeological recording and study of buildings forms an increasingly important part of the unit's work. Some units have their own specialists in this area.

Larger excavations are carried out where archaeological deposits must be removed in advance of development and sometimes for the purposes of research. An example of this was the excavation of a site in the centre of Winchester prior to building the new Brooks shopping and parking complex. All these activities must be reported on before the work can be regarded as complete.

Other work

Most work on site is undertaken by *excavators*. Their job can range from heavy manual work to the recovery of delicate and fragile objects. Excavators often work to tight deadlines enduring all weather conditions, experiencing relatively tedious periods interspersed with moments of great excitement. They are expected to have some basic surveying experience and be able to draw, describe and record the archaeological features found. Other 'on-site' personnel include *photographers*, who record archaeological deposits and finds, and *site finds assistants*, who clean, catalogue and carry out the necessary conservation.

The study, analysis and interpretation of what is found are an essential continuation and completion of the archaeological process. The catch-all term for these aspects is post-excavation. The post-excavation stages of a project will vary in scale, and usually take much longer than the excavation itself.

Find researchers clean, catalogue and study objects for the information they reveal about the way of life of people in the past. They will then write a detailed report either for the project archive – the body of records of the project which is permanently maintained for future access and consultation, and possibly publication. These people are often specialists in particular materials such as pottery, glass and certain types of metalwork.

Other remains, such as environmental materials like plants and seeds, are often sent to other experts outside the unit who work in museums, government departments, or universities or who are self-employed (*see* Archaeological consultants *below*).

Likewise, there are *archaeozoologists* (for animal bones), *palaeoanthropologists* and *palaeopathologists* (for human remains), and other kinds of environmental specialists.

Conservators are employed in many units as well as in museums. (*See also* CONSERVATION *under* MUSEUM WORK *below*.) Their job is the long-term preservation of finds.

Draughtsmen/women draw excavation plans and finds for publication and some units have their own *editor* responsible for the preparation and publication of the final report.

Archaeological consultants

There are also a growing number of self-employed archaeological consultants, or freelance specialists. They have to be a leading authority in their chosen field and are usually graduates with further research degrees. They will normally have had wide experience in a variety of archaeological activities. They work on a contract basis, for employers such as archaeological units and museums, and competition for contracts may be fierce, both on grounds of quality and of price charged.

Museums and heritage centres

Some units are based on museums. Within museums archaeologists tend to hold positions as *Curators* or *Assistant Curators* of Archaeology. The nature of their job largely depends on the type of museum they work in: national, regional or local. Some are directly involved in fieldwork but are usually responsible for the curation of artefacts and related tasks of interpretation and research. Most finds from various types of fieldwork are destined for the museum store. Only a minority of the objects held by a museum are actually displayed: the bulk of material is put in store for reference, research or future consultation. It must be remembered that objects which seem to have no intrinsic value to the non-archaeologist, may represent a vital piece of evidence to some researchers. An important part of the job of the museum archaeologist is to deal with enquiries from the public, often identifying finds that they have brought in. There are also opportunities for *conservators* in museums. *See* CONSERVATION AND RESTORATION *below*.

Archaeology in education

Universities offer careers as lecturers or technicians. Competition for lecturers' posts is fierce, and is not usually to be considered without a doctorate, or an equivalent level of achievement. Universities are centres of archaeological research, and some of the most interesting and progressive projects are based on them. A number of universities also foster specialised aspects of the discipline: for example, maritime, aerial or industrial archaeology.

Some schools and sixth-form colleges also offer archaeology as an examination subject, though these are rare: approximately 40 centres in the UK. Some aspects of archaeology can be found in National Curriculum subjects such as history, geography, technology and science. National bodies, archaeology units and trusts employ *Education Officers*, though these are more usually found in museums. There is great demand for public courses in archaeology run as day schools or evening classes which offer temporary employment opportunities for teaching in university and continuing education departments.

Qualifications and training

Degree courses

Currently (1996) most career archaeologists are expected to have a degree which includes archaeology, though some have equivalent qualifications in other subjects. In higher education, archaeology is found in combination with a wide range of other subjects. There are now 37 universities offering archaeology and over 70 undergraduate courses to choose from.

'First destination' figures (1994) are:

total graduating	*517*
research/further study	102
teacher training	17
law and Bar exams	17
other training	29
believed unemployed 31 Dec	79
short-term employment	47
permanent employment	147
employers	
local government	20
commerce (including banking/accountancy)	30
industry	19

Civil Service	25
university	17
cultural/leisure, etc.	1
functions	
information and library work	59
administration/operational management	18
personnel/social work	14
marketing, etc.	9
financial work	7
management services	2

It is interesting to note the high numbers of graduates going into librarianship and information work.

Entrance requirements for university and other higher education courses vary considerably although it is usual to have at least five GCSE/SCEs (grades A–C/1–3) in a range of subjects. English, maths, history, geography, and a foreign language at GCSE/SCE are generally useful for a BA in archaeology. Most BSc courses ask for physics or chemistry, especially those including conservation. A growing number of institutions offer GCSE archaeology, which gives a potential archaeologist a useful guide as to what the subject involves, but universities do not expect applicants to have taken this subject.

The growing popularity of archaeology as a degree course has meant that 3 A-levels or three to four H-grades, or A/S equivalents, often at high grades, are needed. At A-level there are few universities which have specific subject requirements although some prefer a modern language. For BSc courses, two science A-levels or equivalent are required. An Advanced GNVQ may be acceptable, usually at Distinction grade and sometimes with additional A/AS-levels specified. However, as entrance requirements vary considerably, applicants must consult the appropriate handbooks and prospectuses and, if necessary, contact the admissions tutor and archaeology department concerned.

For a post in a museum a relevant degree is usually preferred, and the institution may also require the Diploma of the Museums Association; this is an in-service, postgraduate qualification based on experience and training. Some universities offer a one-year postgraduate certificate in museum studies which counts towards this diploma, and completion of a postgraduate course can often help in gaining a museum post. *See* MUSEUM WORK *below*.

Certificate and diploma courses

A two-year HND in Practical Archaeology is available at Bournemouth University in conjunction with Yeovil College. Entrance requirements are an A-level or two H grades, preferably in archaeology, history, geography, physical sciences or classical civilisation, together with GCSE/S grades in English and maths or a physical science. Equivalent qualifications may be acceptable. Relevant work experience is expected. On completion of the course most students transfer to a degree in archaeology.

Various certificates and diploma courses are offered by university continuing-education departments on a part-time basis.

Postgraduate courses

There are a number of postgraduate courses for those who want to become archaeologists after taking other degrees; indeed there are opportunities in archaeology for those wishing to change careers. Postgraduate specialisation may cover archaeological science, aerial photography, conservation, heritage management and museum studies.

Vocational qualifications

National Vocational Qualifications (NVQs) and their Scottish equivalent (SVQs) at levels 2, 3 and 4 for all aspects of archaeology are in preparation. Photographers, illustrators and people in similar jobs often follow vocational training courses .

Professional bodies

The Institute of Field Archaeologists monitor archaeological practice in most aspects of professional archaeology.

Further information

Council for British Archaeology, Institute of Field Archaeologists.

Archive work

Archives are stores, of the records of the past. In this context, the 'past' stretches from Anglo-Saxon times, right through Tudor and Victorian eras, to the present time. Archives store any records which have historical interest or value, but which are no longer in day-to-day use.

Pre mid-nineteenth century, records are mostly handwritten and printed documents, such as ledgers, loose papers, parchments, maps, plans and drawings. Material going into archives now may also be in the form of printed and typed papers, film, photographs, tape-recordings, and even computer tape or disks.

Archives range from large national collections to small local ones. National archives include:

- the Public Record Office at Kew (there are equivalents in Scotland, Wales and Northern Ireland), where state and government papers (including court records) go back to, and include, the Domesday Book;
- the National Libraries in Edinburgh and Aberystwyth and the British Library;
- smaller national repositories such as the House of Lords Record Office, and the National Maritime Museum.

County, municipal and other local record offices house archives of their particular area, and may go back to the records of mediaeval manorial systems. All official administrative documents (for example, minutes of council meetings, court proceedings, market records, and planning papers) are automatically deposited there. They also acquire other material about the region, for instance poor law and parish relief records, records of local trusts and charities, family papers, maps, charts, and deeds, in fact anything which documents any aspect of the life of the community.

The size of office may vary considerably, but few exceed a total staff of twenty, but this number includes a group of professional staff supported by technicians (conservationists, reprographic assistants), modern records clerks, secretarial, clerical and manual staff. Some offices have a person responsible for liaison with schools and colleges.

The churches also have their own repositories, at Canterbury, York, Westminster, and other diocesan centres. These hold all kinds of ecclesiastical records, ranging from sets of parish registers to original monastic documents going back beyond the sixteenth century.

A few universities may employ archivists to manage their own current and semi-current records, control collections of former members of staff, care for special subjects, e.g. papers of politicians, and occasionally ecclesiastical archives.

A growing number of larger industrial and commercial companies or public institution now have their own archives, documenting the history of the company or professional body, and employ professional archivists, often called record managers. Medical/health records also employ archivists. Some charities, local antiquarian societies are large and rich enough to employ archive staff.

Working as an archivist

Archivists look after these collections. The work obviously varies from archive to archive, depending on the type of collection. They all look after the physical well-being of the records, to see that, for example, any parchments, frail paper and film is treated, handled and stored – which may have to be in special conditions – so they will not decay or get damaged. They also index and catalogue the records, so they can be found when wanted, and so that it is possible to find out what the collection houses on particular topics. For earlier documents, particularly, this means being able to decipher and read handwriting and scripts which are very different from those of today, sometimes to identify and date documents.

Archivists also help and advise anyone with a genuine reason for using the collections. They can be eminent scholars or young students, people who are trying to complete their family tree, or school pupils doing serious project work. They also answer specific questions, do research for other people, edit records for publications, produce documentary histories – for example, of industry in an area, or on the changing pattern of landholding and use on a particular manor house during the three centuries after Domesday. Archives can produce evidence, for example, for insurance companies trying to decide what caused subsidence on a housing estate (such as a long-forgotten mine), by producing records on previous use.

Archivists help to decide what should and should not be added to an archive collection, what is worth keeping and what is not, or whether material should be kept only on microfilm. They may go out to survey and assess material being offered to an archive.

It is often perceived as a very academic-style research-oriented career working mostly at a desk with books and documents but it can be very physically demanding. Hospital and business records can be large, heavy, dirty and measured in tons, and they have to be physically moved, usually by the archivist. Very few archivists these days spend time poring over mediaeval manuscripts.

Archive conservation

Conservation of archives is a specialist field and will necessitate having an understanding of basic chemistry and physics, paper chemistry, the composition of inks and pigments, the structure of leather, the mechanics of books, and photographic and printing processes. *See* CONSERVATION AND RESTORATION *below*.

For archive conservation the Society of Archivists recommends at least five GCSE or equivalent qualifications including English, mathematics and chemistry, and any of the following: physics, biology, technology, art, history or geography. The only full-time course is at Camberwell School of Arts and Crafts (part of the London Institute). See below for other conservation courses.

The Institute of Paper Conservation is the only organisation devoted solely to the conservation of paper and related materials with members who are practising conservators, picture restorers, librarians, archivists, bookbinders, picture framers, papermakers, and paper scientists.

Archives is a small profession – the Society of Archivists has (1996) a membership of around 1,300 – but numbers are growing, if slowly, with the main growth in work for industrial/commercial firms (national and local-authority archives are vulnerable to expenditure cuts). Because there are so few posts (the Society estimates 30–40 vacancies a year, only) it may be difficult to find work in particular areas of the country and/or in particular types of archive.

Recruitment and entry

An all-graduate profession. A good degree plus a knowledge of Latin is most usual. Traditionally the degree has been in history, but this is increasingly less true, and other disciplines, e.g., languages, or geography, are becoming common. Latin is necessary only for work with older archives, but a reading knowledge of Latin is likely to be required by the universities. A professional qualification is normally essential.

Archivists must have a very strong interest in history, particularly the kind of original source material stored in archives, and the very fine detail of daily life. It means being very keen on academic work and study. Archivists need to be intelligent, careful, meticulous, and prepared to do detailed work, e.g. deciphering handwritten documents. Ability to judge and assess the importance of documents, and enough practical ability and scientific sense to cope with the physical care of records, are also needed.

Qualifications and training

Training is normally via a postgraduate course leading to an MA or diploma at Aberystwyth, Bangor, Liverpool, or University College London. Courses combine archive studies, practical training (e.g. physical properties of the materials from ancient parchment through to modern film, the conditions under which they must be stored to preserve them, what methods to use to prevent deterioration and how to repair them) with palaeography (the study of handwriting and scripts in the historical sense), which is one of the skills needed by archivists dealing with older documents. East Anglia University offers a course in film archiving.

Further information

The Society of Archivists.

Museum work

Archive and museum work careers are not necessarily directly creative, but they do preserve, care for and display the results of centuries of human creativity. For many years archives and museums were far more concerned with the 'preservation' to the near-exclusion of the promotion and display of the objects in their care, and so careers in this field inevitable suffered from this rather dusty image. Now, however, most museums see preservation as only one part of their role, and see positive presentation of their collections, as well as the development of services around them, as equally important and totally justifiable. Many museums have become places where the past is brought to life through creative displays and activities. These are, nevertheless, careers which demand fairly stiff academic qualifications. However, promotional and administrations skills are also needed. Staff must also have as great an interest in helping people who visit and use archives and museums as in collections themselves.

Britain has probably between 1,700 and 2,000 museums and art galleries, with more being opened all the time, such as the Royal Armouries Museum in Leeds in March 1996. Museums fall into four groups.

There are 19 *national* museums including the British Museum, the Victoria and Albert, and the Tate Gallery in London, and the National Museums of Scotland, Wales and Ulster plus about 11 other museums and galleries with historic national collections, e.g. the London Museum.

There are about 700 or so *local-authority* museums, including about twenty large city and civic museums in places like Aberdeen, Leeds, Leicester, Manchester, Norwich and York.

The growing number of smaller *independent* museums include those which remember famous people, like the Brontë Museum in Yorkshire, and the Ironbridge Gorge Museum. The independents are run by boards of trustees and they rely heavily on volunteers for staffing.

Many *universities* have major museums including the Ashmolean at Oxford and the Fitzwilliam at Cambridge although most are departmental collections built up for teaching purposes and staffed by university lecturers or laboratory technicians who combine their museum work with teaching duties and other work.

National and most LEA museums have collections which spread widely over many artistic, archaeological, historic and other interests. Others specialise, e.g. the Maritime Museum in Exeter, the York Railway Museum, or the Museum of Army Transport at Beverley. Smaller museums concentrate on toys, prams, windmills, or local industry. There are museums of war, for individual regiments, and for the Roman legions. Castles, ships and historic houses have also been turned into museums.

Most museums today are more lively and imaginative places than they used to be. They put on permanent and 'special' exhibitions designed to bring alive for visitors part of the past, or an aspect of science, or another part of the world. They do this by recreating scenes or themes, such as the Vikings or Pompeii, an Anglo-Saxon village, or dinosaurs, with natural settings. This is in great contrast to the dusty, traditional room upon room full of glass cases packed with flints, coins, bronzes, weapons, Egyptian mummies, etc., which were really the exotic storehouses of nineteenth-century travellers, overwhelming the casual visitor.

Museums are much more selective now. They still try to build collections which illustrate as many aspects as possible of particular periods, types of objects, or themes; but if only for practical reasons, even national museums have to set strict limits on what they collect now. Most new museums specialise, often collecting objects which may not seem museum material, such as a potato museum, an industrial hamlet (originally an iron works) in Sheffield, and a woodland museum of historic buildings saved from development schemes. New maritime museums seem extremely popular.

The public is generally much more interested in museums: the fascination of the past, fuelled by the media (especially TV), foreign holidays, etc. Schools encourage families to use museums and galleries. Interest is not limited to the more glamorous exhibits of the distant past: museums and galleries of all kinds report a growth in attendances.

Museums, of course, face considerable problems in becoming more outward-going, and it is difficult for them – and their staff – to get the balance right between all the demands made on them. Few, like the Victoria and Albert, were actually started to foster public taste and improve aesthetic standards. Most were founded entirely as repositories and therefore were not built, organised or financed to act as educational or creative institutions. They have endless financial difficulties, and must cope in monumental buildings often ill-suited and difficult to adapt to modern ways of showing exhibits.

Yet they try to serve the widest possible public, experimenting with interesting and attractive displays and exhibitions. They must also collect and care for historic objects, not just for today, but for generations to come. Some collections, then, are clearly of the twentieth century – the Beaulieu motor museum has Minis, Metros and Maestros as well as a 1926 Silver Cloud. Museums must still try to make their collections comprehensive enough to provide the material needed by research workers making detailed studies of the past, and things suitable for use by schools and children in project work.

Many national and larger regional museums provide full-scale educational services. They make space for lectures, film shows and holiday-time activities; put on concerts, sometimes using historic instruments; help researchers with information, pictures, etc., for books, films and TV programmes.

Employment in museums

Although the number of museums is increasing, the growth is mainly amongst smaller, specialist and local museums. Figures for the total number of staff employed in museums, galleries, and heritage centres throughout the country give estimates of between 30,000 and 40,000, of whom up to half could be security staff/warders. This figure includes staff working in museums and galleries run or funded by local authorities, and those owned by universities and colleges, societies, hospitals, industrial and commercial firms, and a range of foundations. Only some 200 are large enough to employ more than a handful of professional people each.

The major employers are the 20 or so national museums, led by the British Museum, which employs around 1,000 staff. The Natural History Museum and the Victoria and Albert Museum are also major employers. Although the national museums are nominally independent of government, their staff are largely treated as civil servants. Many are highly specialised and tend to make their careers in one museum.

Most small museums, existing without government aid, employ only a few people. Some of the staff will be full-time, others part-time, and some will be working on a voluntary basis. Jobs are increasingly hard to get due to cutbacks and the use of external contractors rather than museum staff for such work as display, conservation, cleaning, catering, maintenance and even security. There is also a trend towards short-term contracts.

A recent survey shows the ratio of men to women is approximately 50:50, but ethnic minorities are still under-represented, and positive efforts are being made to redress this.

Museum curators and art gallery keepers

Professional museum staff are usually called curators or keepers but may be called museum assistants or officers, or even project officers depending on their level and job content. The term registrar is sometimes used for someone responsible for organising the storage, documentation and movement of collections. Art galleries usually call their staff keepers.

The core of the job is work with the collections: acquiring objects, researching, cataloguing, storing, displaying and explaining them. Although curators and keepers are still expected to be scholars, the emphasis is now usually more on administrative efficiency. Management of museums is increasingly seen as a job distinct from curatorship and requiring different skills and abilities (*see below*). The more imaginative, and often interactive, approach to displaying collection means curators spend a great deal of time on the creative aspects of running a museum, such as designing exhibitions and preparing attractive, illustrated catalogues.

The way the work is divided depends to a considerable extent on the size of the museum, and how specialised it is. A typical national or large local museum is generally divided into departments, each specialising in, for example, a historical period (Anglo-Saxon, or Tudor), or a group of like objects, such as computers or swords. Each department is generally staffed by a curator, a number of assistant curators and possibly also research and museum assistants, all of whom are experts in a subject relevant to the collection they look after. The smallest museums, at the other end of the scale, may have just one, possibly retired, person to look after them. They may well live on the premises, and look after the building as well as the collection.

In larger museums, curators generally have considerable responsibility for, and freedom in, they way they run their departments, within overall museum policy and a tight budget. The curator supervises the collection and its care; plans and controls its development, looking for ways to improve it where possible – for example, watching out for items which fill gaps and which the museum can afford – and takes policy decisions on, for example, better ways of exhibiting. Departments may put on special exhibitions, which usually means borrowing major items from other museums or private collectors, involving staff in extensive negotiations, or they may provide space for a major travelling exhibition. Curators and keepers have to see that items are properly identified, classified and recorded in catalogues, usually now using a computer, and cleaned and stored correctly. They also supervise research, publish books and articles and give lectures, demonstrations, and sometimes lecture tours.

Administrative duties range from dealing with letters to planning new layouts for exhibition rooms; or from deciding on new settings for particular objects, to supervising design, conservation and other staff (e.g. security attendants, guides, carpenters who make stands, model-makers, and even taxidermists).

Curators and keepers now spend considerable time with people who come into the museum, or write or phone for help, advice and information. They may bring in objects to be identified and/or dated, for example. Other people may want help with source material for their research; children may want help with school projects; a film or TV researcher may want detailed information for a period production.

Curators and keepers spend what time is left on research, books or articles for publication. Many senior museum staff are acknowledged experts in their own fields. In some museums staff are both curators and archaeologists.

The work of art gallery keepers is very similar to that of curators, but in private galleries particularly they will also be responsible for selling art work to the public.

Recruitment and entry

Competition for posts has always been considerable, and has been made worse by sharp reductions in recruitment, with posts left vacant. There never have been more than two or three vacancies a year for curators in the national museums. No recent figures for recruitment in local and regional museums have been collected, but reports suggest they are very small.

Intellectual ability and other skills are needed for museum work. Curators need at least a good honours degree in a relevant subject and increasingly a postgraduate qualification. The Museums Association says it is in the candidate's interest to gain the highest possible relevant academic qualification, in a subject which will make a good basis on which to build a detailed, expert subject knowledge of all or part of a museum's collection, for example, anthropology, archaeology, art history, history, classics or science. English or modern languages are less useful normally, although the ability to read and write fluently in one or two languages is an obvious advantage and essential for some posts.

Scientific and technological/industrial museums usually want degrees in science, engineering or technology; art galleries/museums are likely to prefer a degree in art and/or design. The implication is that anyone thinking of a museum career has to decide on their area of interest when choosing a degree subject.

Administrative potential (as shown by, for example, being able to run a school or university society efficiently) is important. Museum work needs a kind of artistic sense which can appreciate objects both for what they are and for their significance in human history or the natural world. It also prefers people who have a strong interest in what museums are trying to do, and not only in a subject like railways – although enthusiastic, interested, longstanding and detailed knowledge of this sort can be very useful. Museum staff have to be able to get on with people of all kinds, from the very scholarly to school-children, collectors, designers, packers and carpenters.

Work or voluntary experience, via a holiday job in a museum, working on an archaeological excavation, helping to restore old buildings, buses or industrial experience, for example, can help when applying for posts.

Qualifications and training

Museum training is changing and developing rapidly, with many new specialist courses and a new system of professional qualifications being developed by the Museum Training Institute (MTI).

MTI says that new curators need three sorts of training either before or immediately after they start their first curatorial job. These are academic study, museological training (i.e. the special museum skills involved in caring for collections and in welcoming visitors and interpreting the collections to them), and management.

Postgraduate courses

A number of universities and colleges offer postgraduate training courses in museum studies and related subjects. Courses vary considerably in approach and emphasis. These include:

- *Leicester University*: MA/MSc or postgraduate diploma in Museum Studies, one year full-time or two years part-time. Courses are run on a modular basis. Students take modules on museum provision and professionalism, museum management, material culture, communication, education and collection management. Students may specialise in one of the following: management; documentation and information technology; archaeology; art; history; or science and natural science;
- *Manchester University*: Art Gallery and Museum Studies diploma (one year full-time) – emphasises art gallery work, concentrating on gallery administration and techniques and including a choice of special subjects within the decorative arts;
- *City University, London*: MA in Museums and Gallery Management;
- *London Institute of Education*: MA in Museums and Galleries in Education;
- *St Andrews*: MPhil/Diploma National Trust for Scotland Studies.

The DfEE has a few bursaries for postgraduate courses.

Other relevant courses include Christies' Fine Arts course and Sotheby's Works of Art course.

Degree courses

Some universities offer museum or art gallery studies options or experience at undergraduate level. These offer valuable insights into the profession but are not a qualification in themselves. Courses include History of Art (Courtauld Institute), Heritage Conservation (Bournemouth University), Heritage Management (Cumbria College of Art and Design) History of Art and Design (De Montfort University), History of the Fine and Decorative Arts (Leeds University).

NVQ/SVQs

MTI is developing NVQ/SVQs at levels 2–5, and all areas of museum work will be covered. Other organisations are also developing NVQ/SVQs relevant to the work of a museum, e.g. in photography, book publishing and archaeology.

Museums Association Diploma

MTI also administers the Museums Association Diploma (AMA) which is currently the professional qualification for curators. The diploma is an in-service qualification with the minimum requirement of two years' full-time (or equivalent part-time) employment. Only graduates who have completed museum studies postgraduate courses at London, Leicester, Manchester or St Andrews universities are now eligible to enrol for the examinations. Although NVQ/SVQs will become increasingly recognised in all areas of museum work, the AMA will remain a mark of professional achievement.

Museum managers and directors

The work of managing museums is increasingly seen as a separate job distinct from curatorship. Some large museums have appointed directors from outside but most senior managers have curatorial experience. The management skills required for running museums are similar to those for other management areas, but museum managers should also have a special feeling for museum collections and their development.

Museum managers usually require a postgraduate qualification, either in museum studies or in generic management, e.g. an MBA, together with experience of running a small museum or department. Leicester University runs an MBA course specifically in Museum Management.

NVQ/SVQs in management are useful. MTI will also be including management units when its courses are operational.

Documentation officer

Managing the information on the museum collection is becoming another separate area of work. Documentation officers need computer literacy and keyboard skills combined with an understanding of museum collections or an in-depth knowledge of a particular field. Some documentation officers are curators with a particular interest in information management.

The Museum Documentation Association currently provides short courses, and a complete training package, covering all aspects of documentation and computer applications in this field, is in the pipeline.

Design department

Museum designers design exhibitions and permanent displays. Graphic designers produce catalogues and other publications, posters and publicity material generally. Many museums use independent design companies specialising in museum work and heritage interpretation rather than employ their own designers.

Designers are usually expected to have a degree in art and design specialising in 3-D or graphics. A degree in museum design is available at the University of Humberside. *See* ART, CRAFT AND DESIGN.

Some large museums have their own photographers to photograph exhibits, copy historic photographs, record the progress on excavation sites, and prepare publicity and display photographs. A qualification in photography and relevant work experience in a photographic studio are helpful. A few model-makers are employed.

Taxidermists

Taxidermists reconstruct animals, birds and fish using the creatures' own skin and, where appropriate, the skull also, to make them look as natural as possible. They prepare the skin, make a manikin over which the skin is fitted and add glass or acrylic eyes.

There are limited positions in Museum/Area Museum Services employment. The commercial market includes work for museums, schools and colleges, commercial photography, TV, film work and private commissions.

Taxidermy training is largely on-the-job in a museum or commercial workshop, and can take quite a long time, since very detailed knowledge has to be built up. The number of traineeships is very small. Taxidermists need manual dexterity, artistic flair/ability, an eye for detail, and craft skills plus a love for wildlife. For senior posts, professional membership of the Guild of Taxidermists is an advantage if not in some cases essential.

Preparators and laboratory technicians

Preparators preserve and prepare whole and dissected material, mainly human. Laboratory technicians prepare slides, skeletons and mounted and dissected animals for teaching and display. These posts are found only in the large natural history museums and in a handful of university and medical museums.

For posts as junior preparators GCSEs or equivalent qualifications are an advantage but manual and artistic dexterity are more important; for senior posts BTEC and membership of the British Institute of Embalmers. (*See* EMBALMING *in* PERSONAL SERVICES.)

Laboratory technicians should usually have GCSE/SCEs or equivalent for junior posts, including English language, maths and a relevant science. For senior posts a BTEC qualification at least, if not a degree, is essential.

Other work in museums

Some museums have their own libraries, run by qualified librarians not museum staff, and their own publishing departments employing editors, etc. Sales and publications staff usually need relevant work experience. An NVQ/SVQ in Customer Services is available.

The larger museums also have their own public-relations and marketing staff. Fundraising is an increasingly important task. A degree or relevant experience is desirable.

Security staff are essential to the running of all larger museums to guard the collections. In smaller museums they may also do a variety of administrative, technical, sales and cleaning duties. The job title varies but is usually called *security officer, attendant or warder*. Sometimes they are called *museum assistants*. There are no specific educational qualifications or pre-entry courses. A background in another security service or the police can be valuable. A few in-service training courses are now available in larger museums. NVQ/SVQs are available at levels 2 and 3 in Warding and Visitor Services. Visitor services cover a variety of other staff: reception, guides, cloakroom attendants, etc.

Further information

The Museums Association, Museum Training Institute, UK Institute for Conservation, Museum Documentation Association, Guild of Taxidermists, and individual museums.

Conservation and restoration

Conservators and restorers examine, clean, repair and maintain anything collected by museums or private individuals. These may be archaeological artefacts, sculpture, mediaeval textiles, early industrial machines, animal remains, or geologically significant rocks. Conservation work also covers ceramics, paper, metalwork, stone, paintings (particularly oils), traditional crafts and folk items, textiles, furniture and woodwork, ethnography, watercolours and prints. Conservators and restorers are expert on understanding the processes of deterioration and in giving objects a new lease of life. They advise on how to store or display objects to prevent further decay and how to avoid the damage which large numbers of visitors can inadvertently cause.

Conservation is scientific work and often involves three stages: an initial examination to assess the properties of the object, its condition and causes of deterioration; preservation to arrest deterioration and ensure long-term stability; and restoration to ensure the object's physical and aesthetic integrity.

Conservators give scientific judgements on origins, dates, and material composition of objects and other works such as paintings or sculptures, but they do not 'authenticate' objects. This is expressly prohibited by the Code of Professional Ethics of the International Council of Museums (ICOM). Some conservators specialise in certain types of objects, or in things made from one or more particular materials.

Conservators and repairers can work in the conservation departments of museums, or work for the ten area museums councils which provide local museums with more specialist services. Some of the national museums with large conservation departments have sections for different kinds of material: ceramics, metals, prints and drawings, etc. However, in small museums, one or two conservators might have to deal with a wide range of materials and artefacts.

Conservators also work for English Heritage, some in the Ancient Monuments Laboratory in London, Historic Scotland and Cadw. Some cathedrals now have specialist studios to care for their wall paintings, stained glass and libraries.

Most major museums have their own laboratories, and employ qualified scientists and technicians to help conservators. They may, for instance, analyse the composition of eighteenth-century paint, or textile fragments from an Egyptian tomb, so helping to work out how to preserve or restore them. Labs also do tests; for example, to date objects.

By far the largest number work privately as self-employed conservators undertaking work for private collectors, antique dealers, auction houses, the National Trust or commercial organisations specialising in restoration and repair of historic and other valuable objects. Private conservators usually specialise by material or type of object: textiles, furniture, paintings, etc.

Conservation has become increasingly sophisticated and diverse with different ideas, techniques and training. Some specialisms have professional associations. For example, picture restoration entails preserving and reinforcing the support of a painting, whether on canvas, metal or wood; the removal of dirt, varnish and discoloration; and retouching and varnishing. The *picture restorer* uses his or her judgement to choose the most appropriate method and material to carry out the work.

Recruitment and entry

While it is still theoretically possible to start straight from school (with two A-levels including chemistry), most major museums prefer either a degree, normally in conservation, chemistry, physics or materials science or a related subject, or an appropriate restoration/conservation certificate or diploma. Technical skills, manual dexterity, good colour vision, and the ability to work with one's hands, patience and care (given the value and uniqueness of many objects) are all needed. Aesthetic judgement, and a good background knowledge of appropriate areas of art history and technology are very useful, as are appropriate voluntary experience and/or relevant expertise.

School-leavers may be recruited as trainee technical assistants, but these posts are currently very difficult to find. There are a few apprenticeships, e.g. tapestry or upholstery conservation at the Textile Conservation Centre. Entry to picture restoration is by either becoming an apprentice in the studio of a competent restorer or following an appropriate course in the UK (*see below*), in Europe or the United States. According to the professional association, the Association of British Picture Restorers, there are one or two training places a year with picture restoration studios.

Qualifications and training

Conservation is taught in a wide range of institutions at various levels from first-degree and postgraduate level to certificate and diplomas. Commitment to continuing professional development is considered essential by codes of conduct and rules of practice. Some specialisms, such as furniture conservation, are widely taught at several levels, while others, such as the conservation of fine metalwork, are only available at higher level. Courses include:

Degree courses

BSc Restoration and Conservation at London Guildhall University and Lincolnshire College of Art. BA Paper Conservation, Camberwell College of Art (part of London Institute); BSc Archaeological conservation at Cardiff and London: Institute of Archaeology. *See also* ARCHAEOLOGY *above* for other science-based courses.

Postgraduate courses/qualifications

- Picture Restoration. Courtauld Institute, London: Postgraduate diplomas in Conservation of Easel Paintings or Conservation of Wall Paintings (three years, 4–5 places a year) or MA/MSc (one year);
- Hamilton Kerr Institute, Cambridge: (1 place a year for postgraduate certificate and diploma in Conservation of Easel Paintings);
- University of Northumbria at Newcastle: MA in Conservation of Easel Paintings or Works of Art on Paper (two years, 5 places a year).
  Entry requirements for the above courses are a degree in fine art, history of art or a science such as chemistry or physics.
- Textile Conservation at Hampton Court Palace leading to a postgraduate diploma of Courtauld Institute, London.
- MA in Conservation of Historic Objects (Archaeology), Durham University (two years, A-level Chemistry required plus a degree in any subject).
- MA in Conservation (Decorative Arts) at the Royal College of Art, in conjunction with the V&A Museum (three years).

Higher National Diploma courses

Architectural stained glass: HND, Swansea Institute of Higher Education; Restoration sculpture: HND, Carmarthenshire College of Technology; Historic Decorative Crafts: HND, Lincolnshire College of Art; Furniture Restoration: HND, Rycotewood College.

Craft level

Craft courses available in, e.g., repairing antiques, furniture, musical instruments, ceramics, clocks, book-binding/repairing, embroidery, architectural stonework, etc. Some of these courses are at specialist private colleges, e.g. City & Guilds of London Art School and West Dean College.

Professional bodies

United Kingdom Institute for Conservation (UKIC) is the main national body representing professional conservators and restorers.

The Museums and Galleries Commission Conservation Unit was established as the national forum for information, advice, planning and support relating to conservation of the cultural heritage. It maintains a register of firms and individuals in conservation work and awards grants. Some of their work is paralleled in Scotland by the Scottish Conservation Bureau, which comes under Historic Scotland and operates from the same address.

The Museum Training Institute is developing NVQ/SVQs for conservators.

Further information

United Kingdom Institute for Conservation (UKIC).

Genealogy and heraldry

The main careers in these fields are as an archive researcher or an artist craftsperson.

Genealogy

Professional genealogists and record agents carry out research into family history and trace lines of descent for clients. It is meticulous and detailed research work. In theory, the genealogist acts as the consultant, sorting out lines of enquiry and initiating the work, while the record agent searches records in libraries and record offices for particular pieces of information. In practice, however, the genealogist will often carry out both types of work. A few genealogists or record agents specialise in a particular type of record, subject or area of the country.

Interest in genealogy and family history has grown considerably in recent years, but there are only occasionally vacancies, and fewer than 30 full-time professionals working in this field with bodies such as the College of Arms or firms of genealogists. Most genealogists work part-time and are self-employed freelancers. Their range of possible employers covers charitable trusts, research organisations, the legal or medical professions (for cases involving intestacy or hereditary disease) and private individuals.

There are no formal qualifications, but genealogical work requires a good basic education as well as a sound knowledge of social and local history sources. A knowledge of palaeography, and some Latin, are essential. Most professional genealogists are likely to have A-levels/Highers or equivalent, and many will have a degree. History and Latin are the most useful subjects.

Short courses in genealogy are run by the Society of Genealogists, and details are advertised in its quarterly magazine. The Institute of Heraldic and Genealogical Studies also runs short full-time, part-time, residential and correspondence courses. The Centre for Extra-Mural Studies of London University runs a two/three-year certificate/diploma course in Genealogy and the History of the Family.

The corporate bodies are the Association of Genealogists and Record Agents (for England and Wales) and the Association of Scottish Genealogists and Record Agents. Membership is open to well-qualified professional researchers who have been working as genealogists or record agents for a number of years. The Society of Genealogists promotes and encourages the study of genealogy and heraldry. It has a membership of approximately 13,000, mainly amateur genealogists.

Heraldry

Heraldry involves painting coats of arms and requires a very high standard of craftsmanship. Sometimes heralds combine scrivening (charting genealogy) with painting. Opportunities are very limited. A few become heralds or pursuivants at the College of Arms or the Court of the Lord Lyon in Scotland. Heraldic art is taught with design at some art colleges and at the Institute of Heraldic and Genealogical Studies.

Further Information

Institute of Heraldic and Genealogical Studies, Association of Genealogists and Record Agents.

Contents

Library and Information Work

(CLCI: FAF)

Background

Librarians and information officers, also known as information officers and information managers, are the expert professionals who manage and exploit information, and it is they who have been at the sharp end in devising and exploiting new technology to manage the explosion in information and knowledge of the last forty years which is one basis of the need for information technology.

Information technology has been an integral part of library and information services for some years now. It began mostly with computer-based systems for cataloguing, recording library loans and other routine administrative work. Back issues of periodicals, newspapers, government papers, etc., have long been kept on microfilm. All academic and many specialist libraries are connected to the Internet and use on-line information services. *See also* INFORMATION TECHNOLOGY AND COMPUTER WORK. Schools also have increasing access to the Internet and public libraries are now seeking connection to the Internet for public use. Most libraries of all kinds provide CD-ROM databases for end-user access and virtually all provide on-line public access catalogues (OPACs) and use computerised library management systems. These systems manipulate and utilise data to greater advantage and can for instance cut down long manual searches through reference books and journals. Libraries therefore do not have to keep so much material on paper, and can provide a faster, better information service. Some libraries now justifiably call themselves 'multimedia resource centres'.

Libraries and information centres may look and be very different places in the twenty-first century. For the 500 years since print was invented, individual libraries have collected as much material as they considered they needed and could afford. Now the traditions of centuries are being revolutionised as digital information systems develop and are widely used. The image of a library as a place full of books, periodicals, and so on, is changing as information technology spreads everywhere. Information is now frequently accessible as text and data held on computers or CD-ROM in-house, or on remote computers. While it may be printed out or downloaded on disk for the end-user, the skills librarians/information officers bring to identifying, finding and bringing information to the end-user, are largely the same as when they handled only print material, but simply adapted to new media.

The skills of librarians/information officers as navigators and pathfinders in the information web are unparalleled. Librarians/information officers need computer skills to handle and apply the technology, people skills to understand and work with their clients, and their traditional information skills to utilise the information that is out there in cyberspace, or on CD-ROM and in-house databases, to best advantage. In particular CD-ROM is a medium which is beginning to replace certain types of printed material, e.g. dictionaries, encyclopedias and other reference books, plus newspapers, abstracts and reference indexes, and journals. Libraries have for many years cooperated with each other over what each should stock to save unnecessary duplication; and they operate an extensive inter-library loan system. The British Library Document Supply Centre also supplies books or articles as needed within twenty-four hours to customers through their library service. With computerised information systems, from which one can (for a charge) download on to disk or print out abstracts and even full articles, the need to stock long runs of journals or even some books is obviated.

Libraries and information centres

Public libraries – academic libraries – school libraries – 'special' libraries and information centres

There are many different kinds of library and information services, each providing a service for a different group of clients.

Public libraries

Public libraries and information services make up the largest single sector, and are the most familiar even though only one person in three uses them. They are supported and controlled by the local authorities, and the organisation of public libraries and career structures within them are as in LOCAL GOVERNMENT generally. These libraries have to be provided by law. Since 1976 the local authorities' financial position has made expansion almost impossible, and many authorities have cut budgets and services – book funds have fallen significantly in real terms since the 1980s as book prices rose steeply, at the same time as an explosion in the number of titles published, and an increase in the variety of publishing media, to include CD-ROM, on-line services, etc. According to the *Library and Information Statistics Tables for the United Kingdom 1993-94* produced by the Library and Information Statistics Unit (LISU) at Loughborough University, there has been a marked reduction in the United Kingdom in the numbers of public library service points open 45 hours a week or more, from 906 in 1988/89 to 749 in 1993/94.

Local authorities are the largest group of employers of qualified librarians and information officers. Local government reorganisation and internal restructurings are causing a trend resulting in an overall reduction of posts. Some 6,659 members of The Library Association worked in 167 public library systems (LISU statistics), some 27% of the membership. Public libraries also employ a range of support staff including library and information assistants, computing professionals, secretarial staff and maintenance stewards.

Public libraries range from the large city-centre library offering a full range of lending and reference services, through smaller branch libraries with less extensive facilities, to mobile libraries, which serve remoter areas with specially fitted vans taking the service to urban estates and to villages and outlying places. Public libraries mainly provide services for local people – books, CD-ROMs, software, CDs and videos to borrow; reference collections to answer questions on anything and everything from entertainment to employment, consumer affairs, social benefits, and commercial and technical problems. Public libraries also provide resources for independent adult learners engaged in open-learning courses by distance-learning. Most public libraries have special services for children. Services offered, though, vary according to the area. The large city-centre library, for example, may provide a sophisticated information service for the business community, with CD-ROM and on-line information services. Some libraries, again in inner city areas, provide services designed to give all kinds of support to disadvantaged and ethnic minority groups, and give backup help for people who are unemployed.

Public libraries try to keep up a broadly based, balanced collection of materials across many subjects, but some also build collections in particular subjects – Shakespeare at Birmingham, for example, or music at Westminster – so that one library somewhere has specialist materials if wanted. One library in a local authority may provide technical information services for local industry, perhaps in cooperation with a local university library.

Most public library systems are large, with a number of libraries of varying sizes spread throughout a borough or county. The structure is hierarchical, and staff work up from junior positions through, for example, the branch or reference library structures, or from small children's library to group and borough children's librarian. Or they gain promotion through competing for more senior posts in other local-authority libraries or in other employment sectors.

Academic libraries

Academic libraries are mainly to be found in universities and higher education colleges. Some 2,900 (just over 11.5%) of Library Association members were working in academic libraries in 1993/94. Academic libraries like public libraries also employ a similar range of support staff. Academic libraries, too, are having to adapt services to sharply falling resources and are increasing reliance on electronic media as opposed to expensive print media.

Universities have libraries ranging from the million or more book collections dating back to the Middle Ages at Oxford and Cambridge, through to the libraries started by the newer universities, with rather smaller collections. University libraries are usually large enough to be split into large subject divisions, each staffed by teams of professional librarians who specialise in the subject field (to the extent that some also teach), and each division may deal with everything from buying their own books and journals to special reader services. They have to cope with the very differing needs of university staff doing advanced research and the students who all have to read the same chapters of books and articles for project work at the same time. New university libraries (whose universities incorporated in 1992) also provide services for an even broader range of users including people studying for technician-level qualifications.

All academic libraries provide services for full- and part-time students and academic staff. Many also serve distance-learning students. Academic libraries have to build collections in the subjects taught, and some are therefore specialised, such as the art colleges, where libraries may have more slides and CD-ROMs than books. Academic libraries use on-line bibliographic and other information services. Use of non-book multimedia material is extensive everywhere.

School libraries

School library services help pupils learn how to use information gained from CD-ROMs and the Internet, and provide material for study and project work, and a quiet place to study. Not every secondary school has a proper library or qualified or full-time librarian: some school libraries are run by teachers with some (or no) library training. Some schools sometimes buy in library services run centrally by the local education authority. About 1,228 members of the Library Association were working in school libraries in 1993/94.

'Special libraries' and information centres

'Special libraries', so called because they specialise, are, with information centres, the most diverse group. They include national libraries, the libraries and/or information centres of industrial and commercial firms, government departments, public corporations, learned societies and professional bodies, research associations, and others. In 1993/94 3,755 (15%) of Library Association members worked in special libraries. Most special libraries are now staffed by qualified librarians/information officers.

National libraries, with some exceptions, serve mostly people doing academic or other research work. Most important is The British Library, a huge system based in London and Yorkshire. It has three main public-service divisions: Humanities and Social Sciences, Science Reference and Information Service, and its Document Supply Centre (inter-library loans and photocopies). In addition it covers special collections of manuscripts, sound recordings, etc. Scotland and Wales have their own national libraries. Others are the Public Record Office Library, and the libraries of the Houses of Parliament, working for MPs and the Lords.

Although many of these libraries, as well as those of the learned societies, are traditionally highly conservationist, conforming more closely than most others to the traditional image of the library as an academic retreat, they have introduced electronic information retrieval for their users. In particular The British Library markets a range of its own on-line information services. Staff of these libraries are usually a combination of subject experts and professionally qualified information specialists.

Industrial organisations in all sectors – oil and chemicals, drugs, electronics, coal, gas, steel, electricity, etc. – have their libraries and/or information centres. Most of these libraries/information centres have been built around their companies' research and development programmes, and so have traditionally been heavily biased to particular areas of science and technology. They have to provide a steady flow of the latest technical and scientific information for the research staff, to keep them up to date on what is going on elsewhere in their particular field, give answers to highly technical questions, etc. Industrial and commercial firms also use sophisticated commercial information, including current on-line information and statistics, and surveys on potential new markets, government policies, the economy, industrial relations policy, financial markets and so on. Some companies have very large and sophisticated combined libraries and information services, while others are very much smaller and can be fairly basic. Most professional firms of solicitors, accountants, architects, engineers, etc. employ professional librarians/information officers to manage the firm's library and information services. The most professional are using on-line services, etc. extensively,

Most professional bodies, particularly the larger ones, such as the British Medical Association, and the Institutes of Bankers, Personnel and Development, and Mechanical Engineers, have libraries for their members which now form some of the most important collections in that particular field. Some of these also provide on-line access for their members to their OPAC and CD-ROM databases.

The 'Whitehall' group of libraries include those at the Foreign Office and the Treasury, which also have historical collections. While these, like those of the Ministry of Defence, the Home Office, and the Ministry of Agriculture, Fisheries and Food, and so on, are primarily sophisticated working libraries for civil servants, many like the Department for Education and Employment, and the Statistics and Market Intelligence Library of the Department of Trade and Industry, can be used by the public. Many government libraries now provide on-line information services on the Internet and a telephone enquiry service for the public. Government libraries also exist in government research institutions.

The services provided by special libraries obviously vary greatly, from the large and very sophisticated – producing high-level information analysis abstracting and/or indexing services, providing access to a range of databases, etc. and maintaining a large collection of printed and other material – through to the fairly rudimentary.

Working as a librarian, information officer, information scientist or information manager

There is no real difference between a qualified librarian and an information officer/scientist. In practice, and wherever they are employed, they do broadly similar work; the difference is one of emphasis and degree rather than fundamental. Both are information providers, skilled at collecting, organising, and using whatever source material is needed. Information technology is likely to make the librarian more, rather than less, like an information officer. But while librarians use computer-based systems extensively, the main uses at present in many public and academic libraries are still for library management – acquisitions, cataloguing material, keeping track of loans, etc. – and on-line bibliographic searching. Financial constraints are the main reasons for this. Other remote on-line services in public/academic libraries are often available but the user is charged.

At one end of the spectrum, librarians build broad, comprehensive collections for their clients, to meet as many of their possible needs as can be afforded, of books, newspapers, journals, maps, pamphlets, CDs, cassettes, micro and video film, tapes and so on. At the other end, the specialist librarian or information officer concentrates on acquiring up-to-date information needed by the staff of the organisation, and keeping them informed about it. This is most likely to mean working with on-line databases, CD-ROMs, journals, abstracts, published and unpublished reports (technical, scientific, government, marketing, etc.), patents and so on. It means a greater mass of paper rather than shelves of books, and heavy use of and reliance on, on-line databases. In between, many people combine traditional librarians' work with information science in varying proportions. Both chartered librarians and information officers run information services.

Both librarians and information officers have to acquire – mostly buy – books and other materials. This can be a complex business, both in finding out what is available and in matching budgets to purchases. There have to be policy guidelines, checks on what clients want (and sometimes why), on likely future needs, on how far to be selective on new books or journals in a specialist field, and what and whose judgements to use on what is worth acquiring.

Both librarians and information officers must organise their material in some kind of order, so that particular items can be found easily, and related material is kept together. A library's books are usually somewhat easier to group in a meaningful subject order, easier and more straightforward to index, than is the more complex paperwork of all kinds that an information service stores, and where indexing may have to be much more detailed. Both libraries and information centres store and sort their catalogues and indexes on on-line public access catalogues (OPACs) using computers. On-line information services are beginning to reduce the amount of indexing, etc., that libraries/information centres have to do for themselves because the work has already been done by the database provider.

Both librarians and information officers expect to help their clients find out almost anything they need or want to know, whether it is to look up a straightforward address or ferret out all the data available on an obscure chemical. The same questions may be asked of the staff of a city public reference library and the information bureau of a chemical company, but the information officers in a chemical company will spend more of their time on in-depth searching through specialised scientific and technical literature mostly at an advanced level. The city librarians will never know what subject will come up next as they deal with the whole spectrum of knowledge, or how simple or complex the question will be. The prevalence of on-line information services in academic and special libraries means that all staff now need to be expert in the best ways to search and exploit databases and host networks, and the fastest ways to retrieve information from them.

Both public and academic librarians and special librarians or information officers aim to keep their clients informed. Librarians, though, are more likely to compile straightforward reading lists – on new books, or on specific subjects such as personal computers, for example. Information scientists and specialist librarians, on the other hand, have to know in detail what research their readers' are doing; they often do much of the clients' preliminary reading for them by scanning a wide range of publications and preparing weekly current awareness bulletins, or making summaries of papers in the scientific press, translating them if necessary. Sometimes they help with the writing of technical reports.

In most larger libraries and information centres, professional staff specialise in specific tasks or subject areas. The different tasks can include cataloguing and classifying, database design, indexing, book purchasing (acquisitions and processing), reference work, work with children in public libraries (which includes organising story readings and many other lively activities as well as more conventional library duties), advisory work with clients, training clients in suitable information retrieval systems and their use, running services for the housebound, or specialising in a subject area – music or medicine, for example. A small number teach library/information science in universities.

While professional librarians and information officers do switch from one kind of library and information service to another, this can be quite difficult particularly after having amassed significant experience in just one sector of professional practice. They may also change the type of work they do, although in public libraries for example, it is common to stay on the lending side (progressing through branch to central library, from a smaller library system to a larger one, possibly up to senior and chief librarian) or in reference work which has a similar structure. Information officers/scientists often start in an area related to previous subject expertise. Career progression in all sectors of the profession is often by changing organisation.

There are increasing opportunities for experienced information officers to be self-employed. The information broker or consultant will undertake work for any client with an information-related problem. This may involve, for example, designing a tailor-made information system to handle a company's records, or providing information for a market survey for a proposed new product.

Most librarians/information officers spend just as much of their time with people and on the telephone as with books, journals and computers, etc. These they use as tools to provide a service, and do not just look after them. A few places employ librarians specifically to manage specialist historic collections, but for most library/information staff the job is mainly about helping people solve the problems of what to read or how to find out. Librarians/information officers, though, cannot choose their own research topics. They are always doing just part of someone else's project, which can be frustrating. Working hours are irregular in the public and academic sector, as many libraries open in the evenings and on Saturdays.

Libraries try not to waste expensive professional staff on more routine work – for example on lending-library counters or putting books away on shelves. Most libraries employ paraprofessional assistants for this and for general day-to-day administration.

Libraries take a lot of administrating. Just to get staff timetables right for a large library system is a major headache. Like all other managers, senior librarians and information officers have to cope with budgets, planning, deciding on priorities, and so on. All have to be capable of managing change as nothing remains static in the information world. Librarians/information officers aiming for the most senior positions, particularly in public and academic libraries, have to accept that they will spend most of their time administrating and managing, and little time in direct library/information work. There are, however, many posts of intermediate responsibility which combine professional work with administration/management, and a growing role in assessing and managing the total information needs of organisations.

Prospects for professional staff are difficult to predict. There are problems for public-sector librarians, as local-authority expenditure is cut, and the same is true for academic librarians as education goes through a period of great change. Continued expansion in the number of jobs in special, and particularly industrial/commercial, libraries and information centres depends to some extent on how far information staff become involved in the wider provision of expert information via new technology. Computerised library management systems – for recording loans and sending out reminders – are reducing demand for support staff, but there is still a demand for paraprofessional staff, particularly in the public/academic sectors in order to enable extended opening hours to be maintained.

Recruitment and entry

In order to become a professional librarian or information officer it is necessary to have a degree or postgraduate qualification or equivalent in information studies which is accredited by the Library Association or the Institute of Information Scientists. It is not generally possible to find professional work without appropriate accredited graduate-level qualifications. It can be more difficult to move on to more senior posts, beyond first professional posts, without becoming a Chartered Member of the Library Association and/or a Corporate Member of the Institute of Information Scientists.

The characteristics needed for professional library and information work depend to some extent on the type of work. Children's librarianship makes quite different demands from work with scientists and engineers, for example. The level of academic/intellectual achievement and depth of subject knowledge needed varies greatly. Broad rather than narrow in-depth interests are most useful, except for a few very specialist posts. It is useful to have the kind of mind that must have an answer once a question has been asked, that has detective-like persistence, that likes to keep up with new ideas, can absorb and understand subjects and ideas easily, and is resourceful. It is essential to be logical, tidy-minded, and methodical. A good memory is helpful. Management skills (especially staff management, handling committees and extracting resources, and making the best of budgets) are needed for professional posts. At all levels good interpersonal and communication skills are essential.

Being 'keen on books and/or reading' is not in itself a good enough basis for wanting to be a librarian or information officer, although an intelligent interest in books and reading is needed. Few libraries are places for people who want to retire from the world. In fact the reverse is more likely the case, and the reader is as important as the source material. Most librarians and information staff need the patience and ability to draw out of people what it is they really want to know, to be able to interpret vague and badly expressed questions.

Library and information assistants are recruited directly by libraries of all kinds from amongst school-leavers or older non-graduates. There are no formal entry requirements as such, but normally four GCSE/SCEs grades A–C/1–3 are needed. Usually there are possibilities to study by day-release or distance-learning for a vocational qualification such as City & Guilds, BTEC or SCOTVEC. NVQ/SVQs levels 2–4 in Information and Library Services are also available. Level 5 is expected to become available during 1996.

Qualifications and training

There are two routes to professional qualification. One is via a first degree in library and information studies (the course titles vary). The alternative is to read for a degree in any subject or subjects – again, science, technology, law, business studies, economics or modern languages would be useful – and then to take a one-year postgraduate diploma or masters degree in information studies. A year's relevant work experience is usually required to obtain a place on a postgraduate course.

Appropriate degree and postgraduate courses are available at – Aberdeen: Robert Gordon University; Aberystwyth: University of Wales; Belfast: Queen's University; Birmingham: University of Central England; Brighton: University of Brighton; Bristol: University of Bristol; Edinburgh: Queen Margaret College; Glasgow: University of Strathclyde; Leeds: Leeds Metropolitan University; Liverpool: John Moores University; London: City University, Thames Valley University, University College London, University of North London; Loughborough: Loughborough University; Manchester: Manchester Metropolitan University; Newcastle: University of Northumbria; Sheffield: University of Sheffield.

Professional bodies

The *Library Association* (1995 membership over 25,000). Chartered membership is essential for all professional posts in the public library system. It is increasingly required or at least preferred by academic, government and other specialist libraries, and useful elsewhere. A period of professional training and experience is required for chartered membership – this is shortest (one year) following a formal, workplace-based approved training programme, but can be longer without a formal training programme (two years). Candidates then can apply for admission to the professional Register of Chartered Members in the grade of Associate on the basis of evidence of their professional development. The forms of submission are either by writing a report, compiling and drawing together a portfolio, or by completing a proforma questionnaire followed by a professional interview.

The Library Association has broadened its membership to include professionals and paraprofessionals in the information field. The Association is also marketing the professional skills of its members as crucial to managing information generally.

The *Institute of Information Scientists* (membership around 2,700, of whom about a third are also Library Association members) requires (for Corporate Membership) a degree and either a qualification in information studies/information science plus two to four years' approved information work experience, or five years' information work experience.

ASLIB (the Association for Information Management) covers specialised library and information services and represents the corporate sector rather than individuals.

Further information

The Library Association and the Institute of Information Scientists.

Languages

Contents

(CLCI: FAL)

Background

Language skills on their own do not, and cannot, make a 'career'. To make them marketable, it is normally necessary to graft onto them (or graft language skills onto) another set of skills and/or knowledge to be of practical use to any employer. This can mean being a qualified lawyer who is fluent in French, both as a colloquial and a legal language, together with a detailed knowledge of French law; or a scientist or technologist who is fluent in German as a technical language and who can translate technical material (*see* PATENT WORK *in* THE LEGAL SYSTEM) or computer programs; or having business or secretarial training and being able to work in at least one language as well. *See* OTHER OPPORTUNITIES WORKING WITH LANGUAGES *below*.

Secondly, for the very small number of openings for which language skills are the most important qualification it is rarely possible to reach the level of fluency and skill needed just by taking a course. For these posts, it is essential to be able to 'use' the main language (and more than one is usually needed) with the same fluency, freedom, ease and understanding that would be normal in the 'mother' tongue of someone who is both intelligent and well educated. This takes long years of practice (for most people from childhood), and a great deal of time spent living and preferably working in a country where the language is generally spoken. GCSE/SCE or A-level/H grades in languages, even a degree, however good the result, are never enough.

There are only two occupations for which languages are the most important skills, namely interpreting and translating. Both demand exceptional skill with languages and a strong background knowledge of a broad subject field, such as science or technology.

The number of posts in interpreting is extremely limited; there is considerably more work for translators. However, competition both for such full-time posts as exist and in the freelance field is extremely intense, and the level of linguistic competence demanded is very high.

Interpreting and translating take quite different skills and abilities, even personalities – yet it is often only possible for an interpreter to make a living by working as both translator and interpreter.

Interpreting

A full-time career is only possible in conference interpreting, and then for only very few people, although numbers creep up year by year. The Association Internationale des Interprètes de Conférence has just over 2,000 members worldwide (including 120 in Britain), and admits only 50–60 members each year (on the basis of proven competence to practise professionally and having practised as an interpreter for at least 200 days).

In Britain, most interpreters work on a freelance basis, and frequently do some translating as well to live. Outside conference interpreting, only a dozen or so organisations in Britain are known to employ full-time interpreters, and then only in ones and twos. Other organisations, such as transport firms, usually have people on the staff in other 'functions', whose language skills are good enough to cope with situations or problems when and as they happen. If not, the firm can always hire a freelance interpreter.

Interpreters are employed for all international 'set-piece' occasions, such as disarmament conferences, UN debates, foreign ministers' conferences, state occasions, and banquets, when foreign delegations or visitors are present. There are many less glamorous events too: international conferences, seminars, working sessions between experts on, for instance, methods to improve third-world agriculture or irrigation, in the medical field, or in economic cooperation.

Interpreters don't make mechanical, word-by-word translations of speeches or discussions. They attempt to get over the real sense of what is being said, to use expressions and phrases that will sound right to people listening in the language of the translation, to make it as alive and spontaneous as the original. They use one of two methods. In simultaneous interpreting, the speech is translated as it is given, normally by interpreters sitting in soundproof booths with windows, through which they can see the speaker, hear the speech through earphones and transmit the translations to their audience through a radio or telephone link. The alternative method is consecutive interpreting, where the interpreter takes notes while the speaker is speaking and then, after each statement, conveys the message in full in the other language. Simultaneous interpreting is obviously suitable for large conferences where a number of languages are in use, whilst consecutive interpreting is more adapted to smaller bi- or trilingual meetings (e.g. negotiations).

Conference interpreting is generally limited to a relatively small number of languages: English, French, Spanish, Russian, Chinese and Arabic at international level, and the languages of the member countries of the EU in Europe. There is comparatively little demand for interpreters trained in non-European languages in the West, with the exception of Japanese, for which there is a considerable demand. There is also a growing need for Russian. Interpreters normally translate into their mother tongue (in simultaneous interpreting); in consecutive interpreting many work into a second language.

The only full-time jobs for conference interpreters are with international organisations such as the UN, the EC, NATO, the FAO and OECD. In all, the total number in full-time work is less than 1,000, of whom 400 work for the EC conference interpreting service. There is no real career structure, and therefore no promotion, in interpreting, except for some dozen semi-administrative posts for those who head the interpreters' divisions of international organisations.

Freelance interpreters have a greater variety of work, more travel, but much less security. Many have second occupations to fall back on – which may be translating and/or teaching languages, or something quite different. In season, there is work for interpreter-guides, but they have to know enough about a tourist centre like London, Edinburgh or Stratford to be accredited and accepted by travel agencies and tour operators.

There is some work for those who provide interpreting services in the courts, hospitals and local government, for people living in the UK whose command of English is insufficient to allow full access to public services. A qualification for this, the Diploma in Public Service Interpreting, is awarded by the Institute of Linguists.

It is, of course, possible to make an income from translating, and interpret as a sideline.

Recruitment and entry

Competition for the estimated 50–60 permanent posts per year is intensive. An estimated 10,000–15,000 students are at interpreters' schools in Europe alone, and for some the success rate, as measured in terms of posts, is said to be one in every 200 students.

For freelance private-sector conference work membership of the AIIC is useful, since it is known to denote quality and professionalism. New conference interpreters can become candidate members of AIIC as soon as they begin to work, and as such will benefit from the help and advice of the Association and its members. They can then apply for full membership after completing at least 200 conference-days.

An interpreter needs the ability to talk clearly and fluently in their mother tongue, plus complete and 'colloquial' mastery of at least two other languages, which must be those in demand for conference work. Many interpreters offer three foreign languages in addition to their mother tongue, and the European Commission is now actively seeking to recruit only those interpreters who can offer three or more additional languages, especially if their mother tongue is English.

Wide and varied knowledge of as many subject areas as possible is needed: a degree is useful here, but it need not be in languages – law, economics, politics, international affairs, a science, or a technological subject are all useful.

Interpreters need also to be able to think analytically, to think and react, and so interpret, very quickly indeed, and be adaptable – to different speakers, subjects, and situations. Interpreters must be able to concentrate for relatively long periods, take in ideas easily (and not need telling anything twice), and have a good memory, and sharp intelligence. Physical stamina is needed, and it helps to be completely unflappable.

Qualifications and training

There is no single route.

A degree is useful, and some language courses do train in interpreting (and usually also translating) skills, and students also study a useful subject (or subjects) in depth – *see* LANGUAGE COURSES *below*.

Other ways of gaining the necessary skills include, for example:

Bath University: one-year postgraduate diploma specially geared to preparing candidates for the entry tests of the international organisations;

London, Westminster: two-term diploma course in conference interpretation techniques (AIIC-recognised);

Salford University: MA/Diploma in Translating and Interpreting.

The European Commission runs a six-month course in conference interpreting, for graduates under 30. At the end of the course, if they pass the Commission's professional examination, they must agree to work for the Commission for at least two years.

NVQ/SVQs in interpreting and translating, at levels 4 and 5, have been developed. Accreditation is expected in 1996.

Continental Europe has a large number of interpreters' schools, but their success rate is very variable, and expert advice should be sought before applying to any of them.

Translating

This combines language expertise with the ability to write clearly and well. A translation should read as smoothly as though it were written originally in the language of the translation, make complete sense, and not be 'awkward' in any way.

There is, though, a considerable difference between on the one hand translating scientific, technical, business, and legal material, and on the other hand the literary side of translating. In scientific and business work, complete accuracy is needed, to get over exactly what the original says, using the correct technical terms and phrases, in language the reader will expect and understand. In literary translation, there is a creative element, and the translation should somehow get over the style and 'flavour' of the original. The best literary translations have an originality all of their own, while not departing from the author's original intentions.

While there is more work for translators than for interpreters, it is mainly scientific, technical, business, legal, and so on, with very little demand for literary translators working into English, translating novels, biographies, or academic studies.

Translators work in a slightly wider range of languages than do interpreters, but demand for non-European languages, with the exception of Arabic, Chinese and Japanese, is still quite small, although increasing. Professional translators rarely, unless they are really bilingual, translate out of their mother tongues.

Most translators who have full-time posts work for international organisations, for example, the United Nations and its agencies, and the European Commission, for the larger government departments and the joint technical languages service at GCHQ at Cheltenham (*see in* CENTRAL GOVERNMENT), for major firms, especially those operating internationally and/or who are major exporters to the non-English-speaking world, for research organisations, and for the larger translating agencies. The number of translators employed in any one organisation is generally small, and few teams number more than a dozen. Translators who work full-time, while mainly employed for scientific and technical work – translating from, for instance, journals, research papers or patent documents – are usually expected to deal with any other paperwork, such as letters, reports, sometimes contracts, instructions on packaging, and maintenance manuals.

Many translators, though, work on a freelance basis, working mainly for and through agencies, who have on their books people who can translate anything from a particular language. They do not, however, guarantee a regular income. Many people who translate on a freelance basis do other work as well, for instance some interpreting and/or teaching. Freelance translators need to operate as a small business: they should be able to sell their services, keep up to date with changes in the marketplace and use a range of modern office equipment. IT skills are increasingly important, as translations are frequently commissioned on disk, or by fax or modem.

Few make a full-time living out of literary translation, and as a possible career it is comparable with trying to make an income out of creative writing. Many literary translators do so as part of an academic career in university teaching/research, or they make part of their income from other forms of writing. A few work for publishers, either on contract for particular works or authors, or even on the staff, but most produce their translations on a royalty basis, as do other writers. Unlike technical translators, who are always trying to improve their records to avoid unnecessary duplication of existing translations, literary translators quite often try to improve on earlier translators, or to present the original writer in a new light via a new translation. In contemporary literature, writer and translator may achieve a fairly close relationship.

Translating is mainly desk and library work, and tends to be more isolated than interpreting, involving more time and thought. Theoretically, the pace should be slower than interpreting, with time allowed to 'polish' prose, but in practice most clients want their translation quickly.

Recruitment and entry

There are probably more openings than for interpreting, but not that many. There is also a shortage of people able to combine a strong subject background in the scientific and technological field, with the linguistic expertise to translate well. Freelance work usually needs some years of experience and some well-established contacts.

Qualifications needed include technical mastery of at least one, and preferably more, languages, to a level far greater than is needed to pass an A-level or even a degree. This has to be linked to 'in-depth' knowledge of a subject area, most usefully science, technology or business. Translators need to be intelligent, quick to grasp a point, adaptable, accurate, and intuitive, with ability to write clearly, simply and understandably.

Qualifications and training

The most common entry route is via a modern languages degree plus a postgraduate course in translation (which may be combined with interpreting). In addition to the courses listed under INTERPRETING *above*, Kent, Manchester (UMIST), Surrey and Warwick Universities train in translating, and Hull has a Diploma/MA in Applied Languages and New Technologies.

A limited number of first-degree courses provide the necessary type and level of language training (*see below*). Alternatively, students may take a degree in a subject useful to potential employers, for example in science, technology or business studies, especially if it also includes one or more languages geared to day-to-day use in translating.

The Institute of Linguists offers its own postgraduate-level qualification, the Diploma in Translation, for those who wish to prepare for a career in translation. A correspondence course leading to the Diploma is offered by the National Extension College.

Further information

The Institute of Linguists, and the Institute of Translation and Interpreting.

Teaching languages

The range of languages taught in secondary schools is increasing. The government wants to break away from the predominance of French as the first foreign language, and is encouraging schools to offer a greater variety of languages. Under the National Curriculum, all secondary pupils have to study a foreign language, and more are to be encouraged to continue with their language in the sixth form. In some areas there are shortages of modern-language teachers, and increasing numbers of students intending to teach languages are being recruited to initial teacher-training courses. There is a particular demand for Spanish, and also a need for Italian and German.

There are also some opportunities to teach languages in colleges of further education, and a few openings in higher education institutions. Most languages are taught somewhere in higher education, but the number of jobs teaching non-European languages is very small. Most intending teachers and academics read for a degree in modern languages, normally studying at least two. *See also in* EDUCATION AND TEACHING.

Private teaching, mainly in commercial schools, provides employment for some, but the opportunities are generally better overseas, teaching English. There are training courses for this.

Other opportunities working with languages

Some years ago it was predicted that Britain's membership of the European Union would greatly increase the demand for foreign language skills in all sections of industry and commerce. It was also expected that the growing economic importance of the former Communist-bloc countries, and the countries of the Pacific Rim, would increase demand for the languages spoken in those areas.

However, these predictions have proved only partially correct. The 'globalisation' of business has led to increased international contacts, but at the same time use of English as the international language of business has increased enormously. So, from the point of view of English native-speakers, the problem is not so much one of learning their overseas counterparts' language, as of understanding the thinking behind many and varied forms of English, spoken as a second language. It is almost impossible to do this unless one has had the experience of learning a foreign language – and of spending a period of time in a foreign country – oneself. Language awareness – an understanding of how people in different cultures have very different attitudes and approaches, and how this can affect communication – is therefore extremely important. But in the English-speaking world it would be misleading to draw hard-and-fast conclusions about how the study of a particular language will relate directly to job opportunities in a specific industry.

In the world of international business, those who have been fortunate enough to be brought up in a multilingual environment – perhaps by attending an international school in Switzerland or another European country – have a head start. A person with an international background is well placed to operate with relative ease in more than one country, and to learn new languages. The experience of learning one foreign language successfully – ideally, in childhood – gives an individual the confidence to tackle other languages later on.

However, even without the advantages of an international upbringing, anyone with an aptitude for languages should be encouraged to develop their potential, as it can be useful in many careers, as a secondary skill grafted on to another qualification.

Organisations, or firms, do not want people who are language experts first. They want people who are, where possible, complete 'hybrids', who are trained professionals in a 'function' like marketing, law or accountancy, and who can also speak and write at least one language fluently and have in-depth, practical knowledge of their field (accountancy, law, marketing, purchasing, insurance, trade, finance, etc.) in the country or countries concerned.

In industry and commerce, it is particularly important for salesmen and women dealing with non-English-speaking countries to speak the customer's language – this can provide a competitive edge, even when the buyer speaks some English.

Particular developments may increase demand for foreign-language speakers – the development of aircraft cooperatively, between firms from several countries, needs managers and production people capable of conversing idiomatically and able to use technical language.

Sales and development engineers, particularly in chemical plant manufacture and indeed in any field where plant and equipment is sold on an international basis, may need languages – German, Russian, Chinese, Arabic.

Any commercial or industrial company with strong links abroad is likely to give preference to specialists or other professional staff who are able to converse fluently and have some skill with technical vocabulary. Travel and transport firms – airlines, travel agents, freight forwarders and hotels – expect many of their staff to learn to speak other languages as a matter of course.

In Law, universities are now training people in English, French, German, and Spanish law, as well as teaching them to use the language colloquially and in legal situations. They spend time at European universities, and graduate able to practise in Britain and another country or be useful to firms with a considerable amount of commercial and legal (including contract) work in Europe. In accountancy a similar range of opportunities is expanding.

There is a steady demand for secretaries with one or more foreign languages, both with British and European firms. There are also posts in international organisations like the European Commission. They want high-level, 'normal' secretarial skills, plus one or more languages in which the secretary can read and translate correspondence, deal with phone calls, look after visitors, write some letters, type in other languages at more or less full speed, and use the different keyboards easily. *See also* SECRETARIAL, OFFICE AND CLERICAL WORK *in* ADMINISTRATION, BUSINESS MANAGEMENT AND OFFICE WORK.

The Diplomatic Service recruits people first and foremost who will make good diplomats, but also looks for those able to learn languages easily. Although English is widely used in the diplomatic community, diplomats generally expect to learn the language of the country where they have been posted. Since postings rarely last more than three or four years (usually interspersed with periods in London), most diplomats have to learn several languages during their working lives.

It is possible to prepare for a career in the European Commission and other EC Institutions via the UK Civil Service's European Fast Stream. *See also in* CENTRAL GOVERNMENT.

In BROADCASTING (*see in* MEDIA CAREERS), the BBC's monitoring services employ small teams of people listening to broadcasts from overseas stations, round-the-clock, seven days a week, noting and translating important material and making transcriptions for the news service. The BBC's World Service also employs people who speak and write another language fluently, but the total number of posts is very small, and native speakers may be preferred to those whose first language is English.

Other occupations where languages are useful include journalism (*see in* MEDIA CAREERS); LIBRARY AND INFORMATION WORK; and PATENT WORK (*see in* THE LEGAL SYSTEM).

Recruitment and entry

Recruitment is unlikely to be on the basis of language skills, although these may be useful for a range of posts. First and foremost, selection will be on suitability, and possibly qualifications, for the particular function or sector of employment.

Qualifications and training

While a growing number of teaching institutions in both private and public sectors are providing linguistic training for people already working, it probably makes sense for more people to gain the necessary skills pre-entry.

First-degree courses specifically designed to prepare for international business careers are now widely available in a variety of different forms, combining a range of business studies with one, two or more languages, usually European.

BTEC National and Higher National awards can also include language options. A number of languages are available, including French, German, Italian, Russian and Spanish. A few centres offer an HND for bilingual secretaries.

See ADMINISTRATION, BUSINESS MANAGEMENT AND OFFICE WORK.

NVQ/SVQs in languages, at levels 1–5, can be taken either as additional qualifications within other NVQ/SVQs or GNVQ/GSVQs, or as free-standing qualifications in their own right.

Secretary-linguist training – with at least A-levels/H-grades, but also for language graduates, and leading to, e.g., Royal Society of Arts awards – is available at a number of colleges and higher education institutions.

Some institutions specialise in practical language teaching at several levels:

Kent University, for instance, has a diploma in vocational techniques for career linguists which includes applications in industry or international organisations; Westminster has a long tradition of teaching over 20 languages, in various 'packages'; other universities have language-for-business teaching facilities.

Institute of Linguists examinations, in many languages, and at levels from beginner through to degree-equivalent, and with a vocational bias, can be studied for at some universities and FE colleges, and the National Extension College.

Language courses

Language courses after school range across the spectrum from purely academic to completely practical.

Degree courses in modern foreign languages

There are two different kinds of degree courses in languages. The first group consists of traditional-style courses which concentrate on literature and literary language; the second group is made up of courses which teach the kind of language used in everyday working life, and links this to subjects other than literature which could form the basis of a career using the language(s) learnt.

Generally the standard of 'practical' language teaching on degree courses, training graduates to communicate with people who use the language all the time, has been rising steadily. Most universities now have language laboratories, and on most courses students are expected to (or can) spend a year in the country (or countries) where the language(s) they are studying are spoken.

Traditional-style courses are, though, not designed to provide the level of linguistic competence needed to work in the language and so are still rarely enough (and standards of fluency that students reach vary considerably from department to department) without additional training and experience. Further, a career which uses languages demands a second set of skills and knowledge of use to an employer, and courses that concentrate on literature do not and cannot provide this. The exceptions are teaching, and possibly literary translation – although this demands other skills too, and the number of openings is infinitesimal.

Traditional academic-style modern-language degree courses involve studying one or two languages and their literature, or one language and its literature combined with another subject. These courses inevitably concentrate largely on teaching the language of literature: the language of the playwright, the novelist, and the poet, and more often than not the language of the very best writers, who will usually have written not only in a literary style but in an earlier century. This language is always very different from that used by today's business-men and -women, lawyers, accountants, industrialists, journalists, economists, scientists and engineers. While these courses can obviously bring the graduate to a reasonable level of competence in one or more languages, they cannot be more than a useful backup skill.

In contrast, a lot of universities are now running more practical courses, usually involving the study of two or three modern languages, with an emphasis on oral fluency. Some of these courses concentrate almost entirely on the skills needed by a professional translator or interpreter, teaching at least two languages and appropriate background studies. Some courses integrate languages with business studies. Some combine linguistic training either with a subject such as law, which is studied with reference to Western Europe as a whole, or with the technological background to particular industries.

Since Britain joined the EU, courses have also been developed which integrate a professional subject with a language, and which in some instances provide training in the professional subject which allows the graduate to practise in two countries. Law is a major example of this, offering pre-professional training in English and French (or German, Italian or Spanish) law with the language to the level of practical competence, but it does mean reading law with a language rather than the other way round.

Graduates who have taken such a 'practical' language course usually have no problems in finding relevant work, and their skills are generally in considerable demand, not least among Europe-based companies. However, these courses are not soft options. Learning techniques like interpreting and translating, or studying the law of England and another country in sufficient depth to practise in them as well as learning the language, can be very hard work, and requires high-level aptitude for languages.

Between the two extremes are a range of language courses where there is a greater emphasis than is traditional on achieving real competence in the day-to-day use of languages, but which do not train in interpreting and translating techniques; some of these still concentrate on literary or social studies, but others have broader syllabuses, particularly in the less-commonly taught languages, such as Russian.

Most major languages can be studied on a first-degree course. Obviously many students prefer the languages they know best, and in the context of life in the EU French and/or German are likely to be of increasing value for the foreseeable future. But there are other languages which can usefully be studied. Holland, for example, is also a member of the EU, yet few people study Dutch (which is taught at only six universities). Russian, Chinese and Japanese are languages now in demand from employers; African languages in contemporary use are rarely considered. Demand for language teachers in schools is growing.

There is no disadvantage in beginning a new language at university. Anyone showing real aptitude for language study at A-level/H-grades should not find it too tough. Where languages are not normally taught at school, most universities have specially designed and intensive first-year courses for beginners. Otherwise, candidates are normally expected to have A-level/H-grade passes in the language(s) they plan to study, GCSE/SCEs (grades A–C/1–3 or above) in English, and sometimes GCSE/SCE maths or science.

Most universities teach some languages, more usually French, and German, but quite a few Italian and Spanish too. There is a significant number of Russian courses. A growing number of universities let students combine another vocationally useful subject, such as engineering, a science, economics, with one or more languages; for these combined courses, an A-level/H-grade in the language may not be necessary.

'First destination' figures, for all graduates in languages and related studies, are (1994):

total graduating	*10,123*
research/further study	926
teacher training	1,049
Law Society and Bar exams	193
other training	744
believed unemployed 31 December	790
overseas employment	828
short-term UK employment	594
permanent UK employment	3,039
employers	
commerce (excluding finance)	1,147
industry	399
banking/insurance/finance	310
accountancy	158
Civil Service	96
local government	138
university/FE	175
(school) teaching	69
functions	
financial work	383
marketing, etc.	549
administration/operational management	483
personnel/social work	204
information/library work	173
management services	72
creative/entertainment	260
teaching/lecturing	124

Degree courses in classics

Although a purely academic subject – with teaching, academic or museum work, or perhaps archaeology, offering only a few openings which are directly relevant – much has always been claimed for a classical education as a preparation for high-level careers. Classics has been one of the traditional entry routes to a career in government administration, and the computer industry considers a degree in classics evidence of the right kind of intellectual ability for programming, systems analysis, etc. A classics degree does not lead to jobs working with languages although it indicates an aptitude with languages which may be helpful in applying for jobs where new languages may have to be acquired, e.g. the diplomatic service (*see in* CENTRAL GOVERNMENT).

Classics (Greek and/or Latin in varying proportions but usually both) can be studied at about 25 universities, but the number of courses is falling and the numbers of students graduating have fallen considerably as can be seen in the destination figures below. Academics have radically reformed degree-course syllabuses to bring them closer to the modern courses being taught in schools. Many universities teaching Classics now also offer courses for complete novices, since so many schools no longer teach Greek or Latin. They also provide courses on classical civilisation and literature which can be taken by those who do not wish to study the languages in any depth.

'First destination' figures (1994) are:

total graduating	*510*
research/further study	48
teacher training	131
Law Society and Bar exams	18
other training	86
believed unemployed 31 December	69
short-term UK employment	32
permanent UK employment	172
employers	
commerce (excluding finance)	120
accountancy	17
banking/insurance/finance	25
industry	39
Civil Service	2
local government	7
entertainment/leisure, etc.	11
universities/FE	10
functions	
financial work	37
administration/operational management	35
marketing, etc.	24
personnel/social work	15
management services	3
creative/entertainment	10
teaching/lecturing	8

Entry: most departments have flexible entry requirements. It is usually possible to start Greek as a complete beginner, and some offer the opportunity to start Latin from scratch.

Regional or area studies

There was great enthusiasm in the 1960s for developing courses which allowed students to make integrated studies of coherent areas of the world, although the University of London has had two schools specialising in studies of particular areas – the School of Oriental and African Studies, and the School of Slavonic and East European Studies – since the early 1900s. Most courses introduced in the 1960s continue, but it is no longer an expanding area of study.

The vocational value of these degrees is probably no greater than that of traditional modern-language courses, but in some areas the number of graduates is so small that some should be able to find posts related to their degree subject if they so wish, especially if one or more languages are studied to complete fluency.

Examples of these courses are European studies, African studies, Hispanic studies, Latin American studies, Scandinavian studies, South East Asian studies, and Middle East Studies.

Other courses

Most other courses concentrate on teaching the hard practicalities of using – speaking, writing, and working in – one or more languages. While there are many useful ad hoc courses concentrating on just one language, in both public-sector and private colleges, some of which lead to formal examination and qualification, the most valuable in career terms combine language training with other skills, usually some form of business training, which may be linked to information technology.

Qualifications for courses which are widely available include the following:

The *Institute of Linguists'* set examinations in a wide range of languages at five different levels from preliminary (beginner/learning for pleasure) through to the diploma in languages for international communication, which is at degree-level but with a practical/vocational bias. Courses put on by FE colleges throughout the country and by the National Extension College.

Students on *BTEC/SCOTVEC* National and Higher National courses have the option of studying a foreign language at many colleges.

The *Royal Society of Arts/London Chamber of Commerce* set examinations for secretary-linguists and other office staff, and award NVQs in languages.

See also INTERPRETING *and* TRANSLATING *above.*

Further Information

Institute of Linguists.

Religious Organisations and Services

(CLCI: FAM)

Background

Religious organisations in Britain today are mostly Christian, despite increasing interest in other religions, and with the exception of the Jewish, Muslim and other faiths practised by ethnic groups living in Britain. Careers within all religious organisations, whatever the faith, demand a vocation, a conviction, based on a firm belief in the faith in question, that the entrant is called to carry out the will of the deity. Acceptance of such a calling generally implies being prepared to devote one's entire life to the service of God, to members of the religious organisation, and also the disadvantaged. It implies a rejection of materialistic values, and being ready to go without many material comforts. In most instances the training is long and fairly arduous, as well as intellectually and emotionally demanding.

The Christian Churches

Baptist Union of Great Britain – Catholic Church – Church of England – Church of Scotland – Elim Pentecostal Church – Methodist Church – Salvation Army – United Reform Church

For the most part, the Churches are looking for people with a specific calling to the ministry, or priesthood.

Many Churches are experiencing considerable theological and practical problems as modern society increasingly questions fundamental issues of doctrine and faith. Some denominations can be viewed to be in disagreement within themselves on a wide range of contemporary issues. Those entering the ministry will need to be aware of such issues and the challenges to their personal convictions in an age largely indifferent to religion. There is, however, for those responding to such a call, a real sense of vocation, in encouraging individuals to a deeper and more personal experience of God's love for them.

The majority of ministers or priests are attached to a community church (the parish for Anglicans and Catholics), conducting corporate worship, preaching, teaching, and doing pastoral work within the church's parish. The pattern of ministry is changing in response to changing society. In most churches the clergy have the freedom to search for and implement new pastoral ideas and creative approaches, geared more to the needs of the present day. A good example of this is the increasing value placed upon using, and often training members of the church in areas of Lay Ministry, where individuals and groups are encouraged to take more responsibility within the parish community.

While the traditional ordained organisation of the local church remains generally the same, with an incumbent assisted by one or more assistant curates (who may be priests or deacons), so again churches are trying different approaches, e.g. the team ministry, where a group of priests work as equals, sharing responsibility for effective pastoral care and service in a specific area or community, such as within an industrial setting.

Despite their commitment to the propagation of the faith, clergy are also expected to help build a better world, and to make such criticisms as may be necessary. This is not so much exclusively from the pulpit, but increasingly and particularly after some years of experience working alongside people or groups through chaplaincies and other special pastoral ministries.

In EDUCATION AND TEACHING, for example, most universities have teams of chaplains, normally including one from each of the major churches and faiths. Many colleges, Church-aided educational establishments and public schools employ chaplains.

Most chaplaincies now concentrate on pastoral care for the community and on conducting services, etc. To combine this with teaching (as was traditional) now requires a degree and a teaching qualification.

All three ARMED FORCES have chaplains from the major churches. They usually enter on short-service commissions initially but can (with permission), stay in on a permanent commission, and may be promoted. Service chaplains care for any community to which they may be sent. Often this will be very like a parish, as the families of service personnel under their care may live on or close to the station, but like other officers, chaplains rarely spend longer than three years on the same station. Chaplains can be expected to go on active service where this may be required. Normally fairly young, they usually will have had three to five years' experience in a local church before joining.

The Prison Service (*see* SECURITY AND PROTECTIVE SERVICES) employs chaplains. The accent is supposed to be on rehabilitation, and chaplains works with other prison staff here, although they also conduct services and provide conventional pastoral care for the prison's community. Full-time chaplains are normally appointed for seven years, although this can be extended to twelve. For the first year, priests normally serve as assistant chaplain. Entrants to the Prison Service should usually be mature men with several years' parish experience. Most prison chaplains are, however, part-time, working from churches in the area.

The HEALTH SERVICE employs some 200 full-time chaplains. Hospital chaplains provide an essential link between parish and health setting, providing spiritual and practical welfare for individuals, their families as well as hospital staff. Other hospitals have part-time chaplains, usually working in the local parish.

Broadcasting companies (*see* MEDIA CAREERS) have a few chaplains on the staff to work on religious programmes, although in most cases this will be on a part-time contractual basis.

Since clerical life is a vocation more than a career, it seems inappropriate to discuss promotion, but nevertheless, not all clerics spend their lives in the service of a local church or in other special ministries (*see below*). Of course, in the non-hierarchical churches (the so-called free churches and the Church of Scotland) there is no other role to be filled – the moderator of the assembly of the Church of Scotland, for example, is elected annually.

Within the hierarchical Churches certain ministries are filled by those who are considered to have the appropriate qualities for leadership. In the Church of England and the Catholic Church the hierarchical structure of parish, deanery, archdeaconry, diocese, archdiocese or province remains. The cathedrals of both Churches also have their own clergy, who generally hold senior status. In the Catholic Church the hierarchy goes higher, to cardinal and pope; however, the papal seat has not been occupied by a priest from the British Isles for several centuries. The proportion of priests who are promoted to senior positions within either Church is clearly quite small.

Both the Catholic Church and the Church of England have religious orders for men who do not want to be parish priests (or priests at all), and for women. There are several different kinds of orders, the most commonly known being monks or nuns where, for instance, a large proportion of time is spent in prayer and contemplation; others devote most of their collective energies to active work, such as training ordinands, doing missionary or community work, teaching or nursing, or caring for children. Individuals take solemn vows of poverty, chastity and obedience, after a period of novitiate or training, and prayer, which usually lasts between three and nine years after entry to the order. The life, which is lived in a closed or semi-open community, is often one of extreme self-sacrifice, although some orders have relaxed the more stringent rules and modernised their dress.

Traditionally, the churches take candidates for the ministry from among university graduates or school-leavers. However, this has been changing, both because the number of suitable candidates coming forward has fallen, and because the Churches have seen a need for clerics who come from a wider background and from among those who have had some experience of living as an ordinary member of society. Increasingly candidates are coming forward in their 30s and 40s. For entry to both the ministry and religious orders, vocation and personal qualities are the most crucial qualifications.

Baptist Union of Great Britain

This is an association of some 2,000 churches, with a total membership of about 150,000. Full-time service in the ministry is open to both men and women and all colleges accept women ministerial students.

All candidates for the ministry must first be recommended by the applicant's own church. The applicant is next interviewed by the General Superintendent of the area and then by the Ministerial Committee of the appropriate county Association. The final step is a college interview and probably an entrance examination. During this process, prospective entrants are expected to take every opportunity to practise preaching and lead congregations in worship.

Candidates are normally expected to have the intellectual ability shown by five GCSE or equivalent passes and one A-level pass, or professional qualification. However, candidates may be accepted without, if they have 'marked compensating strength of personality and character'.

Training is normally via a three- or four-year full-time course at a Baptist theological college, but for those who cannot attend a college other courses of preparation are possible.

Seven colleges prepare those qualified for a university theological degree or a diploma: Bangor: N Wales; Bristol; Cardiff: S Wales; Glasgow: Scottish; London: Spurgeon's; Manchester: Northern; Oxford: Regent's Park.

Further information

The Baptist Union of Great Britain.

Catholic Church

Britain has about 9,000,000 members (including those no longer active in the Church) spread through some 4,000 parishes. Despite its traditional international hierarchical structure, the Church selects its priests on a diocesan basis in the British Isles. The 22 dioceses are divided between five provinces in England, Scotland and Wales, and four dioceses in Northern Ireland. The Church has, at present, some 12,000 priests in Britain.

A candidate for the priesthood, who must be male, is normally expected to have discussed his vocation with a priest, preferably one known to him. He is then put in touch with the diocesan director of vocations, since the first stage is to gain the acceptance of a bishop. Training does not normally begin before 18, and very often at a later date.

The Church prefers candidates to show the sincerity of their vocation by working for whatever educational qualifications they can; for example, if a student can qualify for university, then he would be expected to work for this. However, the Church does not consider such qualifications essential, and treats personal qualities, experience or professional status as more than compensating for lack of academic qualifications in appropriate cases.

Qualifications and training

Catholic seminaries are going through a period of transition and change. The rising number of mature candidates for the priesthood, and of candidates capable of reading for a degree or similar qualification, has led to some changes, while the demands of the modern priesthood have brought revisions in the syllabus of the training courses. For example, the normal seminary course is six or seven years, but for mature candidates courses have been adapted and last only four years. In all seminaries the emphasis is on pastorally orientated courses.

There are five colleges in the UK, five on the continent which accept English-speaking students. Some students may undergo formation in Ireland. The courses differ to some extent from college to college.

In England and Wales, the seminaries are – Durham: Ushaw College; London: Allen Hall; Sutton Coldfield: St Mary's, Oscott College; Wonersh: St John's; late vocations – Osterley: Campion House.

Overseas – Rome: Venerable English College, Pontifical Beda College (which specialises in training men who have already qualified or worked in something else), Pontifical Scots College; Spain: English College, Royal Scots College in Salamanca.

Further information

Diocesan Vocations Service.

Church of England

The Established Church has some 1.6 million confirmed members, in about 13,000 parishes. The Church has about 11,000 priests and is at present ordaining about 350 men and women each year.

The Church has a centralised recruitment selection procedure, but expects candidates to discuss their vocation first with a priest, and then the diocesan director of ordinands, who will decide if and when the candidates should be sponsored for a three-day selection conference. All candidates for the ministry must attend a selection conference arranged for the diocesan bishops by the Advisory Board of Ministry (ABM). The selection board consists of six selectors who are a representative group of clergy and lay men and women. Each candidate is individually and informally interviewed. Talks and discussions are designed to help candidates consider, with the selectors, where their vocations lie.

The normal entry requirement for candidates under 25 is as for university entry (i.e. five GCSE grade A–C passes, including English language, and at least two A-levels) or the equivalent. Candidates under 25 without these passes are required to enter the Aston Training Scheme. Over 25, no academic standard is set in terms of particular qualifications, and each candidate is considered and assessed individually.

Qualifications and training

Graduates in theology aged under 30 normally do a two-year course at a theological college. Other candidates under 30 do a three-year full-time course at a theological college, sometimes including a degree. Over 30, the training course is normally two years full-time or three years part-time. Some candidates under 35 may also have to do the Aston Scheme or the Simon of Cyrene Theological Institute course prior to entry to training.

The Aston Training scheme is a non-residential, pre-theological course. It is intended for candidates who have not had the chance to develop their potential to the point where they can reasonably be expected to begin direct theological study, but who have shown evidence of this potential since leaving school, and for candidates whose education and experience have trained them in ways of study and thought which make theological thinking difficult without preliminary training. Candidates who follow the scheme stay in full-time employment, under the care and direction of a tutor chosen by the course principal, in consultation with the diocese. The academic work is based on the Open University degree programme under an Open University tutor; four residential weekends and a two-week summer school are an integral part of the course.

The Simon of Cyrene Theological Institute also provides a pre-theological course, with particular reference to the experience of black church members. Further details from ABM, or the Principal.

Most theological colleges are linked in some way to a university (some are an integral part), and their awards are generally those of the university. Most have a strong link with one of the 'movements' within the Church (evangelical or anglo-catholic, for example), and the academic and religious environment differs quite considerably from one to the other.

Colleges with full-time courses are – Birmingham, Queen's: the first fully ecumenical college; Bristol, Trinity: evangelical tradition; Cambridge Federation (Ridley Hall, Westcott House, Methodist Wesley House and United Reformed Westminster): possible to read for Cambridge degree, strong practical emphasis; Cuddesdon (Oxford), Ripon: broadly catholic tradition, Oxford University awards; Durham, St John's/Cranmer Hall: evangelical tradition, constituent college of Durham University; Edinburgh: Scottish Episcopal, Edinburgh BD; Llandaff (Cardiff) St Michael's: part of Cardiff University College; London, Oak Hill: evangelical tradition; Mirfield, College of the Resurrection: closely linked to religious order, Leeds University awards; Nottingham, St John's: evangelical, with a strong missionary tradition, Nottingham University awards; Oxford, St Stephen's House: catholic outlook, mainly graduates, Oxford University awards. Wycliffe Hall: evangelical, Oxford University awards.

There are part-time schemes at twelve centres.

Further information
The Advisory Board of Ministry.

Church of Scotland

The Church has an adult membership estimated at over 750,000. All ministers of the Church are of equal status, and every church is governed by the local kirk session. Men and women are accepted as candidates for the ministry.

The Church also employs some 1,200 people in its eventide homes, homes for children and young people, and handicapped people, and in rehabilitation work. Young men and women are also employed as field workers, in parishes, hospitals, prisons, in isolated communities, etc.

Anyone seeking recognition as a candidate must be accepted by the Committee on Education for the Ministry, and must be nominated by his or her presbytery. Candidates under 23 must have the SCE passes needed for admission to university in Scotland. Mature candidates must have qualifications acceptable for university entrance. Applicants must normally have been members of the Church of Scotland for at least three years and be not more than 45 years of age.

Training for the ministry normally takes not less than six years' full-time study. Candidates may take either the regular or the alternative course; there is also a special course for mature students.

The regular course consists of a first degree, which may be in any subject, followed by at least three years' study for a BD or LTh at a university.

The alternative consists of four years' study leading to a BD as a first degree at a university, followed by a further two years' study.

Further information
The Church of Scotland Department of Education.

Elim Pentecostal Church

Founded in 1915, the Church has some 450 churches in Great Britain, with a membership of approximately 40,000.

Many facets of full-time Christian ministry are open to both men and women who have the appropriate training for the particular vocation they seek to enter. Applicants to full-time ministry are assessed by the Ministerial Selection and Training Board with regards to their course of training, evidence of call, and suitability for the ministry.

Minimum vocational training in theology is generally two years, though mature students may be able to enter the ministry with less formal theological training, but with longer supervised field training.

The denomination's theological institution is Elim Bible College, in Nantwich, Cheshire. It offers the Cert HE (one year) in Theology and Christian Ministry which is validated by the University of Manchester. Also available are the internally validated one-year Certificate and the two-year Diploma courses in Theology. Validation by the University of Manchester for the MA and MTh in Applied Theology is pending.

Further information
The Ministerial Training and Selection Board.

Methodist Church

The Church is based on a 1932 union of most separate Methodist churches and has some 450,000 full adult members. There are still a number of independent Methodists, and some in the Wesleyan Reform Union.

Candidates have to be admitted as fully-accredited local preachers, and must have passed the local preachers' exams at grade A, B or C, or completed the Faith and Worship training course. GCSE A-C grade passes in English language and three other subjects are also needed. Candidates must be nominated by the members of the circuit meeting. After nomination, the candidate must submit two essays on theological and pastoral subjects, pass two three-hour written examinations (one on the Bible and the other a general paper), conduct trial services (with sermons), and be interviewed by various committees, plus a psychologist.

The Methodist Church uses six residential theological colleges, where courses normally last three years full-time for those under 30, two for those over 30. There are also a number of non-residential, part-time courses used in appropriate circumstances.

Training requirements are decided for candidates individually, but those qualified to do so normally read for a degree in theology. Including the course, candidates under 29 are 'on probation' for five years, over 30 for four. Between one and three years must be spent on a circuit appointment under a superintendent, academic studies are continued, further training continued, and tests given.

Further information
The Methodist Church Division of Ministries.

Salvation Army

The Army has some 50,000 active members in Britain, working from more than 800 centres of worship. The total community strength is estimated at about 250,000. They also run centres which give help to people in need. Both men and women are accepted for training for full-time service as officers in the Salvation Army and as accredited ministers of the gospel.

Candidates should normally be between 18 and 35, have been recommended by local Salvation Army officials, and have completed a pre-residential distance learning course. The Army requires at least basic educational attainment in English and Maths, but beyond that expects a strong educational commitment. Candidates would normally have satisfactory work experience and give evidence of personal development.

In addition to service as officers (ministers) in the Army, there are opportunities for service as employees, often in social centres and sometimes in administrative posts. Requirements would be according to the position and would often include appropriate professional qualifications or the willingness to undertake training.

Training takes two years full-time at the William Booth Training College in London. On completing the course there is a continuing education programme during the early years of service.

Further information

Salvation Army Territorial Headquarters.

United Reform Church

The Church was formed in 1972 by the merging of the Congregational Church in England and Wales and the Presbyterian Church of England. The Reformed Association of Churches of Christ joined in 1981. The URC now has 1768 churches and some 102,582 members. The Church accepts both men and women for the ministry.

Candidates must be recommended by the local church and the minister, and have the approval of the district council. Selection is by a national assessment conference followed by a Provincial Synod ministerial committee. Educational entry requirements vary from college to college, but the basic requirements are usually five GCSE A-C grade passes, and two A levels or their equivalent.

Qualifications and training

Training is at one of four institutions – Cambridge: Westminster College; Manchester: Northern College; Oxford: Mansfield College; Birmingham: Queen's: ecumenical (*see* CHURCH OF ENGLAND, *above*).

Training follows a four-year Basic Course of full-time training which can be reduced in the light of age, experience and previous qualifications, or a four-year Alternative Course, part non-residential, part residential or a Community Based Programme of four years (Northern College, Manchester, only). Courses can be studied to degree or certificate level according to needs and ability.

Further information

The United Reformed Church.

Christian missionary work overseas

Churches are still sending some missionaries overseas, although increasingly partners from overseas are supporting particularly the more evangelical churches in the UK. Churches overseas have their own programmes, projects, leaders and workers. They do, however, occasionally ask Christians from other countries to join them in full-time service. Missionaries or Mission Partners go only where they have been invited, and accept the direction of the church in that country.

There is a wide variety of agencies sending missionaries and mission partners overseas, often for a minimum of three years. Sometimes this is an ecumenical activity supported by member bodies of the Churches Commission on Mission of the Council of Churches for Britain and Ireland.

In general, direct service through a church is not only for clergy, but also for people with professional or technical skills – teachers, doctors, nurses, agriculturalists, accountants, carpenters, etc. Some Christians go overseas through secular organisations with government, commercial, or non-governmental organisations. *See also* WORKING OVERSEAS.

Further information

Christian Overseas Information Service/UK Christian Handbook

Jewry

The Jewish community in Britain totals some 300,000 people, including both Sephardi (who come from Spain and Portugal) and Ashkenazi (from Germany and Eastern Europe). There are two main religious schools of thought: the Orthodox, to which about 60% of practising Jews belong, and the Reform, or Liberal Jewish Movement. There are about 450 congregations. The Chief Rabbi is head of the Ashkenazi group within Orthodox Jewry, the Haham is head of the Sephardi group.

Training for intending rabbis is basically similar, however, for both schools and groups. It involves a period of intensive study which lasts, on average, five to eight years, although it can be longer. Part of the time is spent in studying secular subjects and part at a recognised institution of higher Jewish learning.

Orthodox training is mainly via a three-year degree course at Jews' College (London) followed by a further three to five years' intensive study of rabbinics, and an MA course in Jewish studies. It is also possible to complete the Rabbinics segment at a Talmudical College, either in Israel or in the United Kingdom over a period of three to four years.

Reform/liberal training is via any degree followed by a five-year rabbinical training course at London: Leo Baeck College, including an MA in Hebrew and Jewish Studies, in addition to undertaking a vocational training programme. One year of the course is normally undertaken in Israel.

Leo Baeck College through the Centre for Jewish Education (CJE) offers a Master's Degree in Religious Education jointly with the Institute of Education of London University.

Further information

Jews' College and the Leo Baeck College.

Other religious faiths

Islam, Hinduism, Buddhism and Sikhism are other important faiths followed by ethnic minority groups living in Britain. In addition, a range of Pentecostal and other Christian churches, that are not affiliated to the more established Christian church organisations described above, are supported by members from within the Afro-Caribbean community. For most adherents, these religions represent not just a way of faith, but a complete way of life, inextricably bound up with culture and identity.

Religious leaders are often also leaders of their community in a wider sense, chosen not just for their religious knowledge and religious commitment, but also for their leadership qualities, and for the status that they command within (and without) the community. Formal religious training, although that may be important, is often not as important as other factors, such as family standing, age, a comprehensive body of knowledge (both cultural and religious), and the extent to which the leader may be seen to enhance the community which they represent.

As ethnic communities become increasingly established within the UK, there is more possibility of communities being able to support full-time religious leaders, as many Sikh and Islamic communities now do, and many of these may return to their country of origin to study at the great religious centres, such as Amritsar (Sikhs), Varanesi (Hindus), and Mecca (Muslims). Where communities are smaller, or there is no tradition of a paid clergy in the Western sense, religious leaders may be part time, or unpaid, while holding other jobs. Entry to such positions may be more in the gift of the community than something open to career choice in the accepted sense, and in the case of Hindus, is in any case only open to members of the Brahmin caste. The majority of religious leaders are men.

Religious studies and philosophy

Religious studies (including Biblical studies, theology and divinity)

Many universities and colleges in the UK offer degree courses in theology and religious studies. There has in recent years been a considerable increase in the number of courses including specialist, joint or combined course options, where the subject forms a major or minor part of study.

For anyone seeking particularly ordination to the Christian ministry, theology forms a vocational training. However, theology and the wider discipline of religious studies also have a great deal to offer, to those who are interested, in terms of a deeper understanding of particular cultural traditions.

Until relatively recently studies at undergraduate level were restricted to Christianity and the theology associated with it, but in the 1970s the boundaries of the discipline were expanded to take in other major religions too. However, the influence of Christianity has been so all-pervasive for so long that the major part of almost all courses is devoted to its study, but in more general religious studies degrees it is set into historical and comparative perspective. Joint honours courses frequently link the two subjects studied. For example at Leeds, students taking Arabic specialise in Islam in the religious studies for half of their course.

There are degree courses, for those training for particular ministries, at specialist colleges (Bristol: Trinity, London Bible, Oak Hill, Oxford: Westminster, Spurgeon's), and in Jewish studies at Jews' College (London).

Many HE institutions include religious studies in their BEd and liberal arts degree courses which have developed from courses provided for teachers in training.

All graduates gain some exemption from the training requirements of their particular churches according to the subject read. Most theological colleges are affiliated to a nearby university, and their qualifications are university awards. Where feasible, theological colleges make use of the facilities of their 'parent' universities, and students can usually study right through to a higher degree.

'First employment' figures are (1994):

total graduating	*796*
research/further study	55
teacher training	23
other training (e.g. for the ministry)	80
believed unemployed at 31 Dec	40
overseas employment	21
permanent UK employment	257
employers	
commerce	64
civil service	19
local government	12
education	22
industry	93
functions	
pastoral/social work, etc.	114
admin/ops management	28
marketing, etc.	20
financial work	11

Institutions do not normally set particular A-level subjects, but a classical language, preferably Greek, is the most useful. Membership of a particular church, or indeed any church, is not normally needed, although some college courses are based on the teachings of one of them. The average A-level 'score' for universities and colleges was 15 pts in 1996.

Philosophy

As taught in British universities, philosophy does not just study the work of individual philosophers and schools of philosophy, it also aims to train students to think for themselves, and to examine critically the ideas used outside philosophy, either in everyday life or in specialist fields. Although philosophy has no direct value in career preparation, like other arts subjects, it is supposed to train in independent thinking, critical analysis and logical thought. As such it should allow graduates to offer a trained mind, developed communication skills and the ability to marshal thoughts on paper.

Philosophy is taught for first degrees in a majority of universities, either as a single honours subject or combined with another, which can (for instance) be a science, so teaching how to apply philosophical techniques to scientific thinking.

'First employment' figures are (1994):	
total graduating	*661*
research/further study	97
teacher training	128
other training (e.g. law)	14
believed unemployed 31 Dec	40
overseas employment	14
short-term UK employment	42
permanent UK employment	174
employers	
commerce/industry	66
local government	12
accountancy	4
Civil Service	5
education	18
culture/leisure	16
functions	
financial work	11
personnel/social work	17
marketing	23
creative/entertainment	13
admin/ops management	20
management services	8
research/information	7

No school subjects prepare for a degree course in philosophy and so there are rarely any specific course requirements, although a language (and possibly logic) can be useful. Some reading of the works of the leading philosophers is recommended prior to applying for these courses. The average A-level 'score' for universities was 18 in 1996.

The Performing Arts

Contents

(CLCI: GAB – GAF, GAT, GAV)

Background

Acting, dancing, being a musician, and singing demand exceptional talent, trained to a very high level. Talent and training though must be matched by the kind of personality which can go out and perform before an audience. Such intensely competitive fields demand extreme dedication and hard work, and the emotional and physical stamina which can cope with the stresses and the long and irregular hours. The knack of being in the right place at the right time plus a great deal of luck are also essential factors.

The dedication and the hard work needed mean that for most people in these careers their whole lives are affected by the demands of their work, which, for success, has to come first at all times, regardless of how they feel. Personality factors must include the ability to press on against all odds – the kind of self-confidence which is not dented by rejection at audition after audition and can still go on to the next audition expecting to succeed.

When and how to begin serious training is a major problem for young people interested in music and dance, and by implication therefore their parents and teachers. It is generally accepted that training for performing careers where physical skills are involved should start in the very early teens, while the body or essential parts of it (the violinist's hands and fingers, for example) are still developing. Yet the odds against a successful career for those showing even the greatest talent at this age are enormous; and as students mature, talent may fade, they may not develop the right kind of personality, or they may simply not want to go into a career which makes such heavy demands or dictates such a restricted lifestyle. It should always be remembered that music, dancing, acting and so on make very satisfying spare time activities, and that some people with even the greatest talents are happier as amateurs, earning their living at something else.

This problem should not really affect people thinking of acting as a career, since there is no need, or even necessarily any advantage, in starting young.

Starting training so very early, with the inevitable hours and hours of daily practice, almost inevitably reduces the chances of preparing for many other careers, because without great care it means curtailing general education too early. All this means planning very carefully and taking precautions. First, parents and pupils must have the very best possible advice, and independent assessment of a child's potential, which should be reassessed regularly. Second, parents and teachers must watch very carefully that the student continues to enjoy, and is still interested in, the very time-consuming and hard work involved in reaching the standards needed, in spending so much of their free time on these activities, and always has (age-for-age) a reasonable understanding of what a professional career involves. Finally, and most crucially, the student's 'normal' academic and other education must be continued as broadly and to as high a level as possible. For pupils in the ability range, this ought to mean at least four GCSE/SCEs, or equivalent passes, and more if possible.

A few schools have developed ways to see that talented children have both the specialist training they need and a good general education, but they are few and far between. Some maintained schools do this, but a high proportion are privately run, and finance has to be found. Some education authorities may be prepared to pay for a child to go to a reputable school in another area, although cuts in educational expenditure may affect this. Some local education authorities have schemes which give talented pupils specialist tuition out of school hours – on Saturdays and during the holidays, for example. Musicians are generally reasonably well catered for; acting and dancing not so well.

In 1991 the British Record Industry Trust and Department for Education and Employment founded the BRIT School for Performing Arts and Technology in Croydon. Here approximately 700 students aged between 14 and 18 gain a grounding in performing arts, technological skills and business management. Students under 16 study the core subjects of the National Curriculum together with a choice of major and minor option. Students over 16 follow a strand in dance (higher education and performance or performance routes); media (TV, film and video, or broadcast journalism routes); music (higher education and performance, music technology, or performance routes); design or production; or drama (musical theatre, or theatre). Students also study for appropriate qualifications such as the BTEC ND in Performing Arts or Media, Advanced

GNVQ in Performing Arts, or A-levels in Film Studies, Media Studies, Performing Arts or Theatre Studies.

Any special scheme, private or state-supported, should be very carefully checked to see that it is suitable for the particular child – what is ideal for one child may not be the answer for another. Some commercial ballet, dance and theatrical schools claim to provide general teaching right through to A-level/Higher grades, in addition to specialist training; but in practice, however good the general teaching, the child has to be highly motivated and positively encouraged by the school (and parents) to continue with general education in a non-academic atmosphere, and this does not always happen. Parents should, therefore, check very carefully on academic results as well as professional achievements.

Formal courses devoted to the academic study of dance, drama, music, and the related areas like media studies, are a relatively recent phenomenon. Training for careers in these arts has, traditionally, been given in colleges and schools specialising in them, but now thc trend is to bring them into the 'mainstream' of higher and further education. Courses in the performing arts range from the purely theoretical and critical to the most practical, with every permutation in between. While most courses specialise – in music, dance or drama, etc. – there are some which combine and integrate the study of more than one, in varying weights and combinations. Options and specialisation may also include subjects like film, history and theory of art, arts administration, and writing scripts.

The vocational value of these courses is difficult to assess in terms of careers, and it is probably safer to treat them as interesting and worthwhile, but with not much more vocational value than more conventional arts degrees, particularly those that are more historical, analytical and theoretical than practical. Moreover, the occupations for which even the most practical are apparently a preparation are extremely overcrowded, and a degree is not necessarily going to carry any advantage. Even with a degree, it is still necessary to have exceptional performing talent, well above average drive, and the knack of being in the right place at the right time, although a degree can help if it becomes necessary to find an alternative career.

Employment in the performance arts is very competitive, and new entrants are likely to have problems both getting in and getting on. In 1995 Equity enrolled 2,124 new members. These included 69 West End theatre; 743 provincial theatre; 84 films; 177 television; 59 ballet and opera; 755 clubs and circuses; 15 directors and choreographers; 3 ice skaters; 35 concert, session and recording singers; 45 professional broadcasters; and 10 designers.

National Vocational Qualifications

The Arts and Entertainment Training Council (AETC) are developing NVQs in Arts Development and Teaching, Circus, Dance, Mime, Music, Production and Programming, Puppetry, Stage Management and Visual Arts. AETC anticipate that the Standards for Visual Arts and Music will be submitted in 1996. *See below* for NVQs in Arts Administration. There are no plans to develop NVQs for Drama.

The Arts and Entertainment Technical Training Initiative (AETTI) have developed a range of NVQs for technical jobs in stagecraft. AETC and AETTI are merging in 1996. *See* Theatrical administration and production *below*.

Acting and drama

Actors and actresses are communicators and interpreters. They interpret (usually) someone else's creative writing. They have to achieve a difficult balance between getting over the script as faithfully as they can and becoming as far as possible the character that the dramatist created, yet adding to the part an original spark of their own. They must also work within the director's (or producer's) personal plan for that particular production, and absorb his/her interpretation of the part too.

Obviously some plays ask more of the performers than others, but in general television and cinema have made audiences far more critical, demanding far higher standards and far more 'believable' and realistic performance, whether it is Shakespeare or a TV soap opera, from all actors and actresses. Today, actors and actresses also have to be very versatile, and be able to adapt to the very different technical demands of stage, film, television and radio. Very few in the profession can now afford to restrict their careers to stage or film. Being a 'specialist' actor or actress (e.g. 'Shakespearean') is virtually a thing of the past. Being 'typecast' is to risk very long periods of unemployment in a profession where some 80% are unemployed at any one time.

Prospects for young actors and actresses, however talented, however well trained, however tough and determined, go from bad to much worse. The theatre has been declining for more than 40 years and suffers badly in times of economic recession. Even theatre for schools, and local authority support for theatres are affected by cuts in public expenditure. Few films are produced in Britain: films are made with money raised internationally, on an international basis, and in locations where costs are lowest, which means there is no protected filmwork for British actors and actresses. Television and radio drama can in no way make up for the quite enormous loss of work in the theatre and films, especially as TV and radio plays and series tend to have relatively small casts.

Overcrowding and chronic unemployment in the profession are not new. Equity, the acting union, has about 42,000 members (1995), about half of whom are actors and actresses (the rest are dancers, and other entertainers). Estimates of numbers of acting members unemployed at any one time vary, but are rarely less than 75%, with an average employment of 17 weeks a year for men, and 12 for women. This, of course, hides the fact that the most successful work most of the time – sometimes doing a film or TV production while also appearing in the theatre – and the least successful very rarely, perhaps only at Christmas. At best, and when the theatre is showing more life than during the recession, Equity has estimated there is only enough regular work (and therefore an income on which it is possible to live) for at most 6,500 actors and actresses. Making television and film commercials cushions life for some, but not beginners. Educational and training films, 'voice over' commentary for radio and TV documentaries, readings of serials and poetry for radio, TV and radio quiz and panel shows are all quasi-dramatic ways of improving income – but again generally only for established actors and actresses who will automatically attract an audience by their presence on a show, or who have a recognisable voice for commentary, etc.

Very few of the 300 or so theatres used professionally have full-time, resident companies. Only a very small proportion of actors and actresses have, then, long-term contracts. Most work only for the period of a production, whether a one-off show or a longer season, and for many there are long gaps in between. Income has to be found from other work, or money saved to live on, but any work must allow time to go to auditions. Most actors and actresses are dependent on, and must pay a percentage of earnings to theatrical agents to provide the link with theatrical managements or television or film companies, to get them engagements, to put their names forward for parts, to tell them when new productions are coming, and to help them plan and promote themselves. A good agent is important, but the best agents can pick and choose the actresses and actors they will have on their books – and they usually choose people already showing some success. Getting on to the books of a 'top' agent can be a major step in itself.

Efforts are continuously being made to cut the size of the profession and regulate entry to the profession, but so far success seems to have been limited to slowing down the increase in numbers. Equity Casting Agreements with the main employers now mean that normally only artists with previous professional experience may be considered for parts in the London West End theatre, the major subsidised companies, major pantomimes and tours, feature films, independent television productions, TV commercials, BBC television and radio productions. Membership of Equity is deemed to be proof of such experience. (*See* Recruitment and entry *below* for engagements which can be offered to beginners, i.e. those without professional experience.)

Most people starting out in the professions do so in the provinces, in 'theatre-in-education', children's or rep companies, 'small-scale' or fringe companies. Even for people with real potential and full training there can be ten years of such work. The main aim is to gain as much experience as possible in a wide variety of different kinds of work, in theatre, film and TV (even on a local network), and to learn the different techniques and problems of each thoroughly through practise. There are always difficult decisions to make, such as whether or not to turn down a certain small part on the vague promise of something better, or whether to risk the kind of typecasting associated with taking on a part in a long-running TV serial. However despondent, actors and actresses must always appear regularly in accepted theatrical haunts. Actors and actresses increasingly look for financing for themselves for both theatre and films.

It is a peripatetic life even for the successful, with much of the early years spent in lodgings. Nowadays films and television plays are more often than not 'shot' on location rather than in studios, and radio plays produced outside London. Working conditions are rarely comfortable, and rehearsals take place in any available space, often draughty church halls or empty warehouses. The working hours and frequent travelling throw actors and actresses into each other's company a great deal, and make long-term personal relationships difficult, especially with anyone outside the profession.

Recruitment and entry

As has been already mentioned, Casting Agreements between Equity and the main employers seek to regulate entry to the profession, while allowing newcomers to be engaged in certain areas. These agreements generally give preference to artists with previous professional experience, with membership of Equity deemed to be proof of such experience. Provisional membership of Equity depends on a current Equity contract, and full membership on having done at least 30 weeks' work as a provisional member. The main way of doing this is via an engagement with an employer who has a casting agreement with Equity which allows them to employ artists without any professional experience.

The main categories for actors are as performer or assistant stage manager, in a repertory, theatre-in-education, commercial children's, or small-scale theatre company. Quotas are set for the number of artists without professional experience, except for 'Registered Graduates' (who have completed drama school courses accredited by the National Council for Drama Training, where no quota applies), that any of these companies may take. It is also possible to work as a concert or session singer, as an Assistant Stage Manager (ASM) in some other companies, as an opera singer or ballet dancer, as a director or assistant director, professional broadcaster, or dancer with an overseas dance troupe, and to try for Equity membership on the basis of an appropriate contract for any of these. A contract for extra or walk-on work in TV, or as background or crowd artists or as doubles or stand-ins in films and commercials is not accepted as qualification for membership. Equity enrolled 2,061 members in 1994, and 2,124 new members in 1995.

Although some actors/actresses who have not been through drama-school training do have very successful careers, they are the exceptions, and surveys show that graduates from the reputable drama schools do have the best chances of success. Directors say the level of technical training always shows at audition, and it can take ten years on stage to learn what the schools can teach in two or three.

Acting takes intelligence, imagination, sensitivity, and the ability to observe and listen to people accurately and analyse their behaviour. Actors and actresses need to be well coordinated physically and able to control their bodies well even before training. They need to be able to submerge their own identity, and to work under and learn from constantly critical direction and teaching, to have a positive personality, and a good memory. Acting also demands self-confidence, determination, dedication, initiative, guile, and courage, all far above the average. Physical attractiveness is not necessary for acting, but can help in getting related work.

There are also arguments for not starting on stage training straight from school. Today's acting 'styles' depend on intelligence and maturity, on knowing a great deal about people of all kinds to bring intelligent observation and characterisation to parts. Regular experience in good amateur drama can also be useful. A significant number of today's most successful actors and actresses came into the profession comparatively late, and say they benefited from their experience of working in other jobs.

Qualifications and training

The National Council for Drama Training is responsible for accrediting courses. The Council is made up of equal numbers of members from British Actors Equity, the drama schools, and employers (including the BBC, ITV companies, the Theatrical Management Association, and the Society of West End Theatre).

NCDT accredited courses

In 1996 there were accredited courses in acting at the:

Academy of Live and Recorded Arts; Arts Educational Schools; Birmingham School of Speech Training and Drama; Bristol Old Vic Theatre School; Central School for Speech and Drama; Drama Centre London; Drama Studio London; Guildford School of Acting; Guildhall School of Music and Drama; LAMDA; Manchester Metropolitan University School of Theatre; Mountview Theatre School; Oxford School of Drama: Queen Margaret College, Edinburgh; Rose Bruford College of Speech and Drama; Royal Academy of Dramatic Art; Royal Scottish Academy of Music and Drama; Webber Douglas Academy of Dramatic Art; Welsh College of Music and Drama.

Note that accreditation applies to specific courses only, not the drama schools as a whole. Contact individual drama schools for further information.

Schools aim to give students complete control over voice and movement, to instil creativity and flexibility, and teach detailed acting craft skills. Each school has a different approach and theories, and its own 'method'. Most courses combine these in a syllabus which generally covers voice production, improvisation, play analysis, mime, sight reading, history of the theatre, practical training in fencing and stage fighting, movement and dance, music and singing, and the different techniques for film, radio and TV, costume and make-up. Courses include acting and rehearsal classes and frequent productions. Courses usually last three years, and most courses do not attract mandatory grants. A few courses lasting one year are run for graduates and mature students. Intake to these courses is usually a maximum 45 a year, with ratios of applications to places of 25 to 1.

Other courses

A range of schools not members of the Conference of Drama also teach acting. They include some 'straight' acting schools, some schools of speech and drama, and some teaching drama as an extension, or replacement, of work in training schoolteachers in drama. A number of university drama departments teach some practical skills including acting. See below for degree courses in drama. Graduates from non-accredited courses may have more difficulty in obtaining an Equity card.

An Equity survey conducted in 1987/88 showed that 73% of Equity members had received some form of formal training, including 51% at drama or dance schools. There are no recent figures.

Drama schools look for potential rather than achievement at audition, for good movement and coordination, the ability to improvise, imagination, a trainable voice and good ear, for example. They are not likely to be impressed by a career, however apparently brilliant, in school drama or even as a child actor or actress.

Entry to drama school is generally by audition. Although academic qualifications are not the most important criteria, most schools now expect entrants to have a good general educational background as shown by, for example, a reasonable number of GCSE/SCE or equivalent passes at 16-plus, and some ask for A-levels/Higher grade passes as well. There are various courses which may help prepare for auditions:

- the BTEC National Diploma in Performing Arts provides practical experience in drama, music, dance and stagecraft, through workshops and performance;
- pilot Intermediate and Advanced GNVQ courses in Performing Arts started in 1996;
- the BRIT Performing Arts and Technology School in Croydon runs a full-time two-year course in theatre or musical theatre.

The Arts and Entertainment Training Council say there are no plans to develop NVQs for Drama as both Equity and NCDT felt that NVQs are inappropriate as a benchmark qualification for drama.

Drama degree courses

Purely academic study of drama generally happens within literary degree courses – in e.g. English, French or German – where the emphasis is usually on textual studies (style, structure, theme) and their relation to the literary and cultural life of the day, some also examining the theatrical setting, but not including any practical drama. On these courses drama is only one theme in the study of literature.

Specialist drama departments, in universities, polytechnics and colleges of higher education, treat all aspects of drama, ranging from purely theoretical and historical study of texts right through, in many cases, to practical involvement in play-making: acting, directing, technical aspects, backstage crafts, and writing for the stage. Courses vary considerably, though, in the proportion of time they give to performing plays, and some university courses offer little or no practical theatre.

However great the proportion of training in theatrical skills, though, most drama courses are still not intended to give a full vocational training, and particularly not in acting. Nevertheless, a significant proportion of graduates from some departments do go into directing, production management and theatrical administration generally, and broadcast drama/film.

'First employment' figures for 1994 were:

total graduating	*352*
research/further study	15
teacher training	13
law and bar exams	2
other training	31
believed unemployed 31 December	33
short-term UK employment	41
permanent UK employment	133
employers	
entertainment, cultural, etc.	57
education	15
commerce/industry	28
central and local government	10
functions	
creative, etc.	52

Most universities prefer English literature and language at A-level; some advise history and languages.

Further information

The British Actors Equity Association and the National Council for Drama Training.

Theatrical administration and production

Actors and actresses are only part of the team that put a play on the stage. Plays have to be organised, and theatres managed to make the entertainment possible.

Most theatres are owned by commercial companies, a few are owned nationally, some by trusts, and some by local authorities. Some, like the National Theatre or Stratford, have permanent companies, others are 'let' to producers for the length of time that a play runs, with a company (director, actors and actresses, stage manager, etc.) put together for that production. The owners employ administrators to look after the building itself, letting it out, etc.

Producer

The producer, in any theatrical production, play or musical, is the impresario or presenter. Producers have to combine the talents for putting together a production which is both artistically worthwhile and commercially viable, so that, while they are essentially organisers, they must have sound artistic and critical judgement and a really good knowledge of the theatrical world. The term producer is usually associated with the commercial theatre while in publicly funded companies they are referred to as administrators.

The producer organises a production, and may have to finance it. In the commercial theatre, the producer is in business both to provide entertainment, to stage a creative work, and to make money personally and for the people who invest in the production. The administrator of a subsidised, permanent company like the Royal National Theatre may not actually have to find investors for productions, but must work within a set budget based on known income.

Producers look for productions to stage in, say, London. They may bring over a New York success (or vice versa), but plays are also brought and sent to them, by the authors, and by their agents, by directors who want to direct a particular play, by an actor (or his agent) who wants to perform in a play he has found. A producer in the commercial theatre wants a commercial success, and has to be able to judge dramatic merit and entertainment value. In a permanent company, the producer works to an agreed policy on the plays to be staged – which may only be Shakespeare, or only new writing, etc.

Getting a play into production in the commercial theatre is a balancing act which is not always successful. The producer has to find people to invest in the play, find a suitable theatre at a reasonable price, a director willing and able to direct the play, and perhaps a 'star' too. Investors may only be convinced by the whole package, yet director and star may only commit themselves when the money is 'up front'. Even permanent companies may have to wait for directors and actors to become available.

Commercial producers are as much businesspeople and managers as theatrical. They must have a good financial background, and entrepreneurial instincts to meet contractual requirements. There are very few of them, and they need initiative and contacts rather than formal training to get there. Some young producers are graduates, and may have worked in student and then professional theatre. Some producers have been actors or directors, others have worked up through a producer's office.

Director

Directors are the orchestral conductors of the theatre. The director's personal interpretation of the play guides the particular production. The director must get highly individualistic actors, actresses, possibly dancers and singers, as well as designers and technicians, to work together in a single team. Some directors have a completely free hand, others may have to work within constraints set by the producer – for example, to work with a particular playwright, or accept a particular star to ensure a commercial success. They generally decide on the cast together, at auditions.

The director studies and gets to know the play (which is rarely changed in the way a film script is rewritten), and decides how to interpret and stage it. Sets, costumes, and so on are designed to support this. The director works hardest during rehearsals, working with the cast and technicians to make the play believable, to bring it to performance pitch. The director helps individual actors and actresses to interpret their parts effectively, to get their movements, the pauses and build up of tension right, and to find the 'rhythm' of the play.

Directing a stage production is very different from directing a film or television play, although some directors do all three.

Although some directors work regularly for particular companies such as the Royal Shakespeare Company the majority work freelance.

Most directors have had no formal training for their role, although they have often worked previously as actors or stage managers and usually have had plenty of experience in the theatre. The Gulbenkian 1989 report *A Better Direction* was critical of the fact that 54% of working directors have had no formal training in any branch of the profession and recommended the setting up of a Directors' Training Council. Some directors are graduates, and a degree course in drama can be useful. Some directors come to the theatre from broadcasting or film.

Directors can become members of Equity.

Courses are available at the Central School of Speech and Drama, Drama Studio, East Anglia University (MA), East 15 Acting School, Mountview Theatre School, Rose Bruford College (BA Directing), the Welsh College of Music and Drama. The Scottish Arts Council offers a few trainee directors' bursaries at theatres in Scotland.

Stage management

Stage managers are the directors' assistants. They have to see that everybody and everything is in the right place at the right time, that everyone involved in a production, from star down to scene shifter, knows what to do and when. They keep records of decisions as they are made, on everything from props to lighting, from costumes to sets, sound effects, even the moves actors and actresses are to make. They make sure that scenes and sets are made, props bought or made, that scene changes are realistically timed, that lighting is organised, that curtains rise and fall on cue, and that the cast is ready when needed.

Stage management is a career in its own right, but some people use it as a stepping stone to, for example, directing. A stage manager usually has several assistants known as ASMs and in small companies ASMs sometimes play small parts or understudy.

In a large theatre, the stage manager will be in charge of very sophisticated equipment with an intercom system that allows the stage manager to talk to the technical staff, musical director and colleagues.

Stage managers need to be well organised and very practical, able to deal with people from the most temperamental of stars to the scene-changers, to cope with emergencies, and be extremely resourceful. They have to care about the work they are doing, and not constantly pine for the acting job they cannot get.

Full-time courses at drama schools are broadly based, training in a full range of skills needed in the theatre including, on most, the technical skills such as lighting, sound, photography, scenery construction, etc.

NCDT accredited courses

Bristol Old Vic Theatre School (two-year HND Stage Management and Technical); Central School for Speech and Drama; The Guildford School of Acting; Guildhall School of Music and Drama (three-year BA Stage Management and Technical Theatre); LAMDA; Mountview Theatre School; Rose Bruford College of Speech and Drama; RADA; Royal Scottish Academy of Music and Drama (two-year HND in Production and Technical Stage Management); The Welsh College of Music and Drama (three-year BA Theatre Studies: Stage Management option). Most courses are two years.

There are also non-accredited stage management courses.

Stage managers can become members of Equity.

Other backstage work

The stage manager's team often includes *technicians operating lighting, sound and other equipment*; *wardrobe staff*; *model-makers*; *props staff*; *scene-shifters*; etc.

Many technicians are qualified electricians, dealing nowadays with very sophisticated, computer-controlled equipment. The theatre technician may be in sole charge of lighting or, in larger theatres, have a team of assistants. A lighting plan is prepared for each production, and in modern theatres this is fed into the computer to activate memorised cues. The lighting team sort out all the technical problems, set up the lights and operate them during the performance.

The sound technician or designer provides and plays the required sound-effects on cue at the appropriate time during the performance.

Model-makers make set models on a 1:25 scale so that the painters, propmakers, carpenters and metalworkers can work from them.

Stage carpenters make and paint scenery and sets, and stage hands move them around.

Wardrobe staff hire, buy, dye and print, fit and make costumes and look after them for the length of the production. Some of the larger theatres have built up large stocks of costumes. Wardrobe staff may specialise in particular aspects, such as wigmaking or cutting period costumes.

In the larger companies specific people will be employed to make props and maintain and run the props store. Further specialism may be possible. For example, at the Royal Opera House, the *armourer* is responsible for the making, repairing and supplying of 800 swords, pikes and other edged weapons plus 300 muskets.

Technical courses are available at:

- City of Westminster College (Film and Television Lighting; Entertainment and Theatre Electricians; Sound Engineers; TV and Video Studies);

- Middlesex University (BA Technical Theatre Arts);
- Oldham College (BTEC HND Electrical Engineering (Theatre));
- Rose Bruford College (BA Lighting Design);
- RADA (Stage Carpentry, Scene Painting, Stage Electrics and Prop-making);
- Wimbledon School of Art (Dip HE and BA (Hons) Theatre Design, Technical Arts).

Wardrobe and make-up courses are available at:

- Bristol Old Vic Theatre School (Wardrobe);
- London Institute (London College of Fashion) (HND Theatre Studies (wardrobe, specialist make-up option));
- Oldham College (BTEC ND Costume Design);
- Rose Bruford (BA Costume Design and Wardrobe);
- Wimbledon School of Art (Dip HE and BA Costume Design or Costume Interpretation).

The Arts and Entertainment Technical Training Initiative (AETTI) have developed NVQs at level 1 in Stagecraft (Costume Running) (i.e. wardrobe); at level 2 in Stagecraft (Lighting); Stagecraft (Flying) (i.e. moving scenery in and out of the stage and aerial flying of people on wires for Peter Pan, etc.); Stagecraft (Scenic) (i.e. props); and Stagecraft (Scenic fabrication) (i.e. making sets). There is also a level 3 in Stagecraft (Scenic fabrication). AETTI are developing NVQs at level 3 in lighting and costume-making, and a level-4 Technical (which is aimed at production management, i.e. drawing the whole performance together technically). They are also planning an NVQ in sound for a later date.

AETC and AETTI are jointly developing the Standards for Stage Management. The two bodies are merging in 1996.

There are some modern apprenticeships in stagecraft.

For stage design *see in* ART, CRAFT AND DESIGN.

Dancing

There are many types of dancing, but they fall into two main categories: social dance, including ballroom dancing, disco, etc., which people do to entertain themselves; and theatre dance, including ballet, modern dance, etc., where the dancing entertains others.

Dancing is also an art form. It uses the human body like a musical instrument, and it has to be tuned and played as finely as a violin. The dance movements are usually directed by a choreographer, but the dancer uses their personality and emotions to convey and interpret the meaning artistically.

Dancing can become a career for only a very small proportion of the many thousands who dream of becoming a dancer. It is rare for dancers to be employed professionally without full training, and it has been estimated that even of those who are fully trained, only one in ten become full-time professional dancers. Even an accident which would be a small problem to someone else – a damaged foot, for example – can end a promising career.

A dancer's body has to be the correct shape, proportion and size. A strong back, well-formed feet (the bone structure is crucial), and good muscle coordination are essential. Neck and set of head are important for the ballet, and girls must stay slight and small boned. Lack of height for male dancers can be a problem in partnering, but some short male dancers have been very successful, even in ballet, and get good character roles. For ballet, women should be from 1.52 m to 1.65 m and men 1.6 m to 1.78 m.

Before any child is allowed to start on the long and rigorous regime which is necessary for a career in dancing, parents should ensure that their potential is thoroughly and expertly assessed, preferably by an independent, leading teacher or dancer and not by a local school. This should include tests to predict growth rate, and medical checks to make sure there are, for example, no joint weaknesses. Some LEAs use the Council for Dance Education and Training (UK) (CDET) testing before awarding places, grants, etc.

All dancers have to be naturally well poised and graceful, and not 'gawky'. Modern dancers can be, and often are, much taller than ballet dancers, and they should have long legs. Every dancer has to be very healthy indeed, and strong enough to stand up to the long hours of exhausting practice and exercise. Dancers need to be reasonably intelligent, to have a strong musical sense, of rhythm and timing, plus some acting potential, especially imagination and intuition. It is useful to be able to play the piano.

More women than men apply to dance schools, so men have more chance of training and later working as a dancer.

Performing

Classical ballet makes the greatest demands on the dancer and on their body, and a ballet dancer's life has to be totally dedicated to and disciplined by those demands. A ballet dancer should not ride a bicycle or a horse, because this develops the wrong muscles. The female ballet dancer in particular will, from an early age, have to spend progressively more and more time of every single day, without exception, in practice and exercise, to reach levels of physical fitness and agility greater than is needed by most Olympic athletes.

Performing on stage is only the tip of the iceberg for a ballet dancer. Most of their days are spent in spartan practice rooms, and they must go on taking classes even when technically on holiday or when there are no performances.

Ballet is a highly competitive area. Most ballet dancers are generally employed full-time by a ballet company, but probably no more than 250 ballet dancers have full-time jobs in Britain, and only a tiny proportion of these become principals or soloists. Most ballet dancers will remain in the 'corps de ballet'. Jobs with the Royal Ballet and the Birmingham Royal Ballet normally go to former students of the Royal Ballet Upper School. Not all students are chosen by the companies. There are opportunities with the English National Ballet and Northern Ballet Theatre and a handful of other smaller ballet companies in the UK. Ballet dancers may find work abroad, particularly in Europe.

Contemporary or modern dance is usually less formal and more experimental, covering a range of styles including tap. Disco-dancing is a more recent development. It is an expanding area, but job prospects with established companies are limited and competition intense. Dance schools encourage students with initiative to set up their own dance company. Start-up grants from the Arts Council or Regional Arts Boards may be available.

Modern dancers work throughout the entertainment business: on stage, in musicals and pantomime, on television in light entertainment programmes, on promotional videos and in cabaret and clubs. Large film musicals are no longer commercially viable, and although there is probably more work than there used to be, it is generally for individuals or much smaller groups.

Most of the opportunities are part-time or on short-term contracts, but a few permanent troupes and some small groups still work together regularly. More time is spent in auditions, and in rehearsing and building routines in draughty church halls than on the stage itself. The training, and physical and artistic demands, are not so great as for the ballet.

Although early professional training is useful, it is possible to start rather later than for ballet, and the enthusiastic disco-dancer who has kept up with lessons may be able to start as late as age 18. Competition for work is very intense. Again, the British-trained dancer can find work overseas, but it is sensible not to do so without experience in this country first, and Equity should be consulted before accepting any engagement abroad.

Opportunities in social dance, such as disco, ballroom and folk-dancing are mainly in teaching.

South Asian and African dance are becoming more important in the UK. Non-Western dance can be very demanding, requiring years to learn the wide range of formalised movements. Employment is mainly in dance groups although there may be opportunities for solo performers.

An active performing career usually comes to an end by the age of 35 or 40 for women, possibly later for men; and almost all dancers have to find a second career normally by their mid-thirties. For a few there is choreography: creating and composing dances.

Recruitment and entry

There are no minimum educational requirements for most performance courses in dance although some require specific passes in dance examinations. Auditions, requiring participation in one or more classes and sometimes performing a solo piece, are usually required. Some colleges give aural tests. A medical examination is usually necessary.

A background in ballet is useful for all dancers, although it is not essential for contemporary dance.

For entry to degree courses in dance or performance arts, normal university entrance requirements apply. The BTEC/SCOTVEC ND in Performing Arts or Advanced GNVQ/GSVQ (piloted 1996) may be acceptable. *See also* Dance teaching *under* OTHER CAREERS WITH DANCE *below*.

Qualifications and training

Training is essential for any dance teacher or performer.

Female ballet students must start serious, near-professional-level training by the age of eleven or twelve because ballet has different teaching methods to other dance forms and the body needs longer to adapt to that technique. Training is extremely demanding and must start when the body is still developing and the bones and joints are still flexible, even before it is clear whether the body will in fact grow to be the required height and shape.

Male dancers can, and sometimes do, start training a lot later – Rudolf Nureyev, for example, did not start training until he was 17, but it is probably better to have started training by 14.

Where possible training should start at a professional residential school where training is combined with a good general education; for example the Royal Ballet Lower School accepts pupils from around the age of 11, but the number of places is very limited. Standards between schools vary, and it is advisable to check first with the Council for Dance Education and Training (UK), the Stage Dance Council International or the British Council of Ballroom Dancing.

The alternative is to study part-time with a well-qualified teacher who prepares pupils for one of the officially recognised grade examinations of, for example, the Royal Academy of Dancing (RAD), the Imperial Society of Teachers of Dancing (ISTD), the International Dance Teachers Association (IDTA), or the British Ballet Organisation (BBO). The acceptability of any school or course should be checked with a relevant organisation.

Modern dancers are generally advised to start full-time training by age 16. Many study ballet up to intermediate level, although there are no hard-and-fast rules. Many then complete the full ballet course, but they can do modern stage dancing. Most good ballet schools teach not only classical ballet and modern stage dancing, but also national and Greek dancing, mime, notation and musical appreciation. Practical work includes point work, pas de deux, character dance and choreography.

It is possible to train part-time, but given the level of competition it is more sensible to gain as much training as possible.

A number of dance courses (post-16) have now been accredited by the Council for Dance Education and Training. Course content varies but may include ballet, modern theatre dance, jazz and contemporary dance, tap, choreography, or dance forms from Africa, India, Spain or Greece. These are intensive vocational courses, although they obviously cannot guarantee future employment in dancing. CDET accreditation also covers degree courses in dance at Laban Centre for Movement and Dance (BA Dance Theatre), London College of Dance (BA Dance) and

London Contemporary Dance School (BA Contemporary Dance).

There are numerous other degree courses in dance, human movement, creative arts or performing arts in various combinations at universities and colleges of higher education. These do not offer intensive vocational training and are not usually intended for performers. There are a few postgraduate courses.

Other careers with dance

Choreography and notation

Choreography is a comparatively small and difficult field to enter, and traditionally most choreographers have been performers. Some performers now successfully combine choreography with performance, and they may lead their own small touring group. Choreographers need years of experience, a good musical training, and sense, imagination and creativity.

There are two main systems of notation, Benesh and Labanotation, which use different series of symbols to represent the detailed position of the body at any moment and record the movements of a dance on a musical stave so that the dance can be recreated and performed by other dancers. These systems can be studied as part of a full-time performers' course or can be studied separately by full-time or correspondence courses. Choreologists, or notators, are usually employed by dance companies.

Dance or movement therapy

Dance therapy is a comparatively new career in the UK. Dance therapists seek to provide a physical means of expressing emotions and feelings through dance and movement. They work in the healthcare professions or treatment centres for the emotionally disturbed, the elderly or physically and mentally disadvantaged.

Dance and mime animateur

Dance animateurs work in the community or education to encourage activity and participation in dance – tap, belly dancing, jazz exercise, flamenco, classical Indian dance, mime and movement, contemporary dance, etc. Their job title may be community dance worker, dance development officer or dance adviser rather than animateur. They organise workshops for groups of children, adults, or those with special needs, depending on the needs of the community. As part of their work animateurs may teach dancing or do the choreography for local productions and youth groups, but their primary role is administration and marketing. There are an increasing number of relevant courses on dance in the community such as the degree in Dance in Society course at Surrey University.

Dance critic

A few dance critics write for specialist dance publications and daily newspapers but will normally combine this role with other dance activities and experience.

Dance teaching

Teaching dance is the main career area for dancers. Some teachers go on to have a career as a teacher after a career as a performer while others choose to teach from the outset either full-time or part-time. Teachers can specialise in one area of dance or teach a variety of dance forms.

Applicants for teaching posts of virtually any subject in all state primary and secondary maintained or direct grant schools must hold Qualified Teacher Status (QTS). This requires either an approved Education degree (usually a BEd) or a Postgraduate Certificate of Education (PGCE). Normal entry requirements for teaching any subject apply. *See* EDUCATION AND TEACHING.

Dance teachers can also teach privately, in small dance schools or studios, in further and adult education establishments, and on higher education courses. People who have the resources can start their own schools or classes.

There are two major types of dance teaching in the private sector; one is for theatre dance (ballet, tap, modern dance) and the other in social dance (ballroom, disco, Latin, etc.). Although academic qualifications are not required, many teaching courses for the private sector look for two A-levels or three Higher grade passes. An Advanced GNVQ/GSVQ in Performance Arts may be helpful (pilot course started 1996 at selected schools and colleges). Applicants are expected to have achieved a high standard of performance and passed graded examinations or, for social dance, medals up to the third gold bar.

Most of the leading examining bodies for dance teaching have registration schemes and are members of the Council for Dance Education and Training, Stage Dance Council or the British Council of Ballroom Dancing. It is unlikely that anyone would be able to find a teaching post in the private sector unless they are registered. Only registered teachers, for example, are allowed to enter candidates for the Royal Academy of Dancing, the Imperial Society of Teachers in Dancing, the British Ballet Organisation examinations, and the International Dance Teachers' Association.

There is usually plenty of work for dance teachers, and it is also possible to find teaching posts abroad. According to the British Council of Ballroom Dancing (latest statistics available 1991) there were 2,500 'schools' of dancing entering candidates for medals of various dancing bodies and there are 350,000 such tests in social dance every year, with the bulk distributed between traditional ballroom dancing, Latin dance and freestyle (rock 'n' roll, disco, etc.).The Council estimates that there are 8–9,000 teachers of ballroom dancing. The International Dance Teachers Association says (1995) it sets over 200,000 examinations and tests a year in ballroom,

Latin, sequence (old-time), ballet, stage, tap and modern dance, disco, gymnastic dance and rhythmic fitness.

For teaching dance classes more related to keep-fit or movement-to-music, information can also be obtained from the Sports Council or Keep Fit Association.

For Dance Administration, *see* ARTS ADMINISTRATION *below*.

Further information

The Council for Dance Education and Training (UK), Imperial Society of Teachers of Dancing, International Dance Teachers' Association, Stage Dance Council International, British Ballet Organisation, British Council for Ballroom Dancing, Royal Academy of Dancing, and British Actors Equity Association.

Light entertainment

This, the world of comedian/ennes and variety artists, singers, etc., is a career which depends almost entirely on the ability to capture an audience, and on personality. While the majority of old-style variety playhouses are long gone, there is steady demand for such performers, mainly from clubs and cabarets, and particularly the new-style night clubs of the industrial areas of Britain, cruise ships, holiday camps, and for the best, radio and television.

A career as a popular entertainer is never easy, and even the most successful can suffer long periods of semi-obscurity. It demands a high degree of intelligence and intuition about the business to be able to stay abreast of trends in public taste and not to go on with a particular act until it has been overused. One problem faced by the modern entertainer is the insatiable demand for new acts and new scripts because so many people hear or see them on the media. In the past, radio and television entertainers could live for many years on the same act, but today they must constantly change their performances.

In the past, entertainers have generally come into the business via a family connection, but this is traditionally a field for the able amateur to break into, who has built up an act and gained audience approval on, e.g., a local pub circuit. Formal training, however, e.g. a drama course followed by a period with a repertory company, is useful, and can improve entertainers' chances of success. Of course contacts, a good agent, and some luck come into it too.

Music and performance

Background

Music of some kind, classical, modern and avant-garde, 'rock' and 'pop', dance, soul, indie, reggae, heavy metal, light music and jazz, is listened to by most people in Britain at some time and at some level. Pop and dance music is a major part of teenage culture, and inevitably a lot of people want to work in the music business.

The economics of the music business changes frequently depending partly on the fluctuating popularity of different types of music and the technology behind it.

People may listen to more music than ever before, but it is played by fewer and fewer musicians. The number of live performances of music continues to fall. Radio, and technically high-quality, relatively cheap music systems have accustomed the listening public to hear the very best performers in the comfort of their own homes – and therefore the audience for all but world-class orchestras and performers has largely vanished. The disco revolution decimated the dance band leaving mainly the club and pub circuits (many of which employ mainly semi-professionals), and much slimmer gig circuits for the rock groups. Many young people prefer to go to clubs to dance rather than attend live gigs. Now the computer-based synthesiser, which can simulate several instruments at once, is also replacing human musicians – largely at present in theatre orchestra pits, and in 'session' work, providing backing for groups and solo artists in the recording studio.

On the technology side, the CD revolution has heralded the 1990s breakthrough in multimedia formats such as CD-Rom, CD-Plus and CDi, while digital delivery of music via the Internet could become an adjunct to the retail sales of sound carriers.

The total numbers actually employed in music are debatable – the Musicians' Union for example has some 50,000 members, but probably only a small proportion have regular full-time employment. The most recent survey, by the British Phonographic Industry (1992, but they say the figures are still valid in 1996) covering employment in the UK Record Industry, breaks down the total of 48,600 people into: 14,500 in retailing; 8,000 professional musicians; 7,900 in record companies (4,100 manufacturing and distribution, 3,800 record company administration and marketing); 3,800 in service and support industries; 2,500 in journalism and publishing; 2,500 composers and songwriters; 2,000 in recording studios; 2,000 in music publishing; 2,000 in broadcasting and video production; 1,900 managing entertainment venues; 1,500 in recording equipment manufacture.

Life for most professional musicians is very tough and insecure, whether they play serious/classical, pop/rock, jazz or any other kind of music, sing, or are composers or conductors. However talented and well trained, it may take some years to get established. Except for the full-time posts, it is usually necessary to take on all kinds of work to live – even otherwise 'serious' musicians will take on session work playing pop music. It may mean extensive travelling, and rehearsals in difficult and uncomfortable conditions. Fame and fortune, to match the talent and hard work of the majority of professional musicians, happens to very few. Even the smallest accident to a pianist's or violinist's hands, or to teeth for a wind player, can mean the end of a career.

Musicians, as individuals or as members of orchestras or groups, depend for a living on a delicate balance between live performances, broadcasting and recording. Britain spends far less on serious music than other European countries, and rising costs are cutting into the profitability of orchestras and opera companies.

Instrumental playing

In classical music there is full-time work for about 1,600 instrumental players in the major British symphony, string and operatic orchestras. This figure also includes freelance musicians who fill in for full-time players, and about 200 who work for the London theatres, but of course the two groups may overlap.

There are two types of orchestra: contract orchestras with permanent staff and ad hoc orchestras which operate with freelance musicians. Some instrumental players have permanent contracts with a particular orchestra, e.g. Bournemouth Symphony Orchestra, or City of Birmingham Symphony Orchestra (CBSO), while others prefer to work freelance. The size of orchestras vary but most of the major orchestras employ between 85 and 120 players. There are five BBC orchestras, two in London and one each in Scotland, Wales and Manchester, employing around 400.

Many musicians, including both people who normally play serious music as well as those who play light and pop music, make some of their income from freelance session work. Few full-time bands now play popular music or play for ballroom dancing. Many pop musicians spend a considerable amount of time making records, tapes, compact discs or promotional videos in a recording studio.

Opportunities for work vary with the instrument. Prospects are probably best for string players, particularly violinists, since they form the largest section of most orchestras, and there has been a worldwide shortage of string players, particularly good ones, for some time. There is probably some demand for the more unusual and difficult instruments, like the bassoon. In between, there is intensive competition to play popular instruments, like the flute, where orchestras need only two or three each, and to gain an income as a concert pianist, for whom there is no place at all in any orchestra. Violin players, though, may have to work and wait for many years to move up to the front desks, while the flautist, once a member of an orchestra, can get solo work much sooner.

Orchestral life combines concerts, recording sessions, and regular rehearsals with quite a lot of travelling. Most orchestras are fully booked for long periods ahead; and they have to take on as much work as possible to make a reasonable living for their members, who have to pay for their instruments, dress clothes, and so on. Orchestral players work unusual hours, which can be long, but players can decide not to play for a particular concert – as long as they can find a good enough replacement.

Many instrumental players want to become solo performers, but this demands much greater talent even than is needed to play in an orchestra. This is not just virtuoso-standard musical talent, but also the personality and stamina to match. Some players aim for a solo career from the moment they leave music school, while others go on playing with an orchestra while trying to establish themselves as soloists. Solo work involves far more and harder practice than is normally needed by orchestral players (most young soloists expect to study and practise for at least six hours a day), because the music is generally artistically, technically, and physically much more demanding, and a substantial repertoire of solo parts has to be built up.

Probably around 200 attempt to make a living as pianists, but only a few can fill a major concert hall. As an alternative to solo work, pianists are employed as accompanists, repetiteurs or coaches for singers and choirs, and for rehearsals, but few posts are full-time. Concert and recital organ playing can support very few organists. Organ-playing is loosely linked with choir-training, since the majority of church organists are also choirmasters. Only cathedrals and the largest other church centres have full-time organists; fewer and fewer can afford to pay their organists-cum-choirmasters more than minimal expenses. Crematoria employ organists on a sessional basis. Although interest in older keyboard instruments, such as the harpsichord, has grown, it is difficult to make a living playing, so most musicians therefore play more than one such instrument.

Getting work, gaining experience, becoming known to promoters and audiences and established is the major problem for every instrumental player, orchestral or solo. This can take a long time and a great deal of luck. Once established there is a wide range of opportunities ranging from broadcasts down to concerts in village halls.

Orchestral places, for which players audition, are few and far between, and plenty of experience is normally asked for, so posts rarely go to people just out of music school. Most young musicians take whatever work is offered. Of six French-horn players graduating from music school in any one year, one may, through a chance contact, be given an evening's work, play very well, and find that s/he is in increasing demand, while the other five go on waiting for their first engagement. The traditional recital, for which the young musician pays and invites critics and impresarios to listen, is not now used so much, except by some hopeful soloists. For many soloists, though, and particularly pianists and violinists, much more depends now on competing in, and winning, international musical competitions.

Music schools, concert promoters, and one or two trusts, try to make opportunities for young players to be heard. Busy players will be able to get an agent to manage their career. The chance to make a record is a major step forward. Occasionally, a group of instrumentalists manages to start an ensemble of their own while still at college, and to make a reasonable living from it afterwards, but it is rare, despite the increased number of ensembles in regular work.

Freelance musicians, young or older, have very varied working lives. They may fill in for a member of one orchestra (who may be sick, resting or have a conflicting solo engagement) one day, and play in a quartet another. Another day they may 'augment' another orchestra playing a very large-scale work. Versatility is needed to take advantage of session playing – backing for records, television commercials, films, radio and TV plays, and documentaries. They may also play regularly with a group of friends from musical school in an ensemble which produces some income, and they may play in festivals where they have got to know the organisers. At the other end of the scale are summer shows, and a few musicians 'busk'. Many musicians teach privately, and for some, teaching is their main business (*see below*). Some take part in a wide range of musical activities for children, for instance running LEA holiday orchestras.

Singing

Singers interpret vocal music using their knowledge of voice production, phrasing, melody, and harmony. They are classified according to the type of music they sing and the range of their voice, i.e. soprano, mezzo-soprano, contralto, tenor, baritone, or bass. They may sing character parts or perform in their own individual styles.

There are no figures to show how many singers can make a full-time career in opera, oratorio, recitals or concert work, but since there are only a few opera companies in Britain, and fewer live performances of oratorio and other serious choral or solo concerts for voices every year, the number has to be very small. The largest opera chorus in Britain, at the Royal Opera House Covent Garden, employs only 60 singers. A singer would be unlikely to be employed at Covent Garden, or any professional opera company, under about 23.

Operatic soloists sing internationally. They may be contracted to sing for a season or for a number of performances all over Europe, in Britain, America and Australia, with recording sessions and sometimes concert tours in between. They have to be able to sing roles in several languages, and have a repertoire (mostly learnt in their own time) large enough to give them enough engagements to provide an income, yet not too heavy to keep in practice. Solo singers have especial problems of getting known and gaining experience, because their voices must be allowed to mature only slowly, and they may not sing the most powerful roles until they reach their thirties.

Young singers usually start work in an opera chorus and can gain early experience with a few small companies such as English Touring Opera, Pavilion and City of Birmingham Touring Opera. Only the most exceptional singers make the change from chorus to solo work. The National Federation of Music Societies runs a scheme to promote young soloists.

The opportunity to sing professionally in a choir is very limited, except in a few cathedrals and very large churches. There is some session work, and still some light music for stage musicals, pantomime, radio and television, but this generally also involves some acting and dancing.

Conducting

Conducting offers full-time work for very few people indeed. Although young conductors are generally more acceptable to orchestras and audiences today, in serious music youth is still something of a disadvantage. Conducting a full orchestra demands a great deal of experience. A conductor has technical skills to learn, must know a great deal about all the instruments in the orchestra, and their capabilities. Orchestral music is extremely complex, and the conductor must know each work well. It takes maturity and in-depth knowledge to be able to interpret it properly. Plenty of experience of working with musicians and maturity is also needed to handle players, gain their confidence, and perhaps persuade them to perform works in particular ways. In a sense, an orchestra or choir is the conductor's instrument, and he or she must be able to persuade it to play for them as if it were one.

Conductors usually train on an instrument (particularly keyboard) and many work for a while as *répétiteurs*, only specialising in conducting later. As a *répétiteur* (rehearsal pianist) is the traditional continental way for conductors to train, but there are opportunities now also in the UK.

Aspiring conductors need to take every possible opportunity to work with groups of musicians whether amateur or professional. Since orchestras today have very heavy schedules, there are occasionally opportunities to stand in for a conductor at rehearsal, or to perform the occasional concert.

There are some postgraduate courses at music conservatoires, and there are summer schools, seminars and short courses, all offering valuable experience and training.

Pop/rock music

Making an income in pop/rock music depends not so much on conventional talent on an instrument or in singing as on the ability to find and create a 'sound' and an image which will sell, to create a 'buzz', and to stay ahead of what must be near-unpredictable trends, perhaps singing and playing alone, but more usually as part of a group.

It is a fast-changing business. Record companies make several thousand singles a year, trusting that a proportion will make an impact and a profit. Only a handful of groups make it to the top 50, and only a handful survive more than three or four years, re-forming with different names and different musicians to try to keep pace.

There is no formal training. Most groups start in a small way, playing together as friends and then trying for gigs in local pubs, wine bars, theatre foyers and clubs. If a group regularly starts attracting 150–200 people to a gig, then an A and R scout (employed by the Artists and Repertoire Department of a record company) will attend and, if they think the group has potential to make successful albums, they may 'discover' the group, and it may lead to a recording contract. A new group might make their own 'demo' tape, which is now often also needed to get onto the bigger gig circuits. An independent label may turn this tape into a disc if it has any commercial chance at all, or the group could even set up its own record label.

The great majority of groups only ever manage to become semi-professional, and life on the gig circuits for groups trying to make the grade can be very uncomfortable. Increasing success brings increasing expenses, including the cost of a manager, public relations, sound and lighting technicians, pluggers, equipment, and 'roadies'.

The manager will look after the band's interests and will promote and represent the band to record companies, publishers and the music press, enabling a band to concentrate on their musical development. A booking agent will organise performances and tours by selling an act to a promoter. The music promoter is an organiser and financier of music performances and will usually book the band and the venue, organise the public address and lighting systems, and arrange the publicity.

Jobs like 'manager', 'booking agent' and 'promoter' have their counterparts in the classical music world. *See also* THE RECORD INDUSTRY *below*.

Jazz

Jazz has become more popular in recent years and there is a flourishing circuit of clubs (mainly in London) and festivals. Most jazz musicians supplement their earnings with session work.

Military and brass band music

All three armed forces employ and train musicians of both sexes – and it's not just brass band players they want or those who are only interested in brass band music – they train woodwind, percussion and string players too, and some Scottish regiments have drum and pipe bands. Military musicians play all types of music. The army say (1996) they are currently looking to recruit up to 120 per year.

The armed forces are looking for good musicians who have achieved at least a grade 5 pass on an instrument and preferably grade 8. This does not necessarily have to be a brass instrument. They offer a good training in music, but musicians must be interested in the forces generally and their way of life. An interest in music alone is not enough. Training can start at 16. Anyone who shows exceptional promise is given advanced tuition on full-time courses, and there are also courses for potential bandmasters, although the number on the bandmaster courses averages only about five or six a year. Most musicians will get the opportunity to travel abroad.

An annual bursary of up to £1,500 is available from the Ministry of Defence for those students attending a performance-based music course at university, conservatoire or music college, and who may wish to consider a musical career in the armed forces. Certain criteria will have to be met, but interested students can obtain further information on 0345 300123 (calls charged at local rate) or from an Armed Forces Careers Office or local JobCentre. *See also* THE ARMED FORCES.

The police also have professional bands.

Most other brass bands are amateur, but there may be some career opportunities, particularly for conductors.

Electronic music

There is increasing demand for musicians specialising in electro-acoustic music, particularly with film, television and theatre companies, although electronic instruments are being used more frequently in contemporary classical music. Most music colleges and universities have studio facilities. Kingston and York Universities offer degrees in Music and Technology.

Recruitment and entry

It is possible to find work as a musician, notably in pop/rock, without training first, but opportunities in an extremely competitive field are greatly improved for anyone who has gained technical skills.

Exceptional talent for playing at least one, and normally two instruments, is essential. Orchestral and ensemble players need faultless technique, must be able to read music efficiently, have a good sense of musical style, and enjoy playing with others. Musicians need to have physical stamina and very good health – wind and brass players, for example, need strong lungs and teeth, and it takes real strength to play some instruments. Musicians have to be the kind of people who can get off a train or plane and go straight into a rehearsal or even a concert and play as well as ever.

With the level of competition, musicians need to have a certain amount of pushiness, initiative, and talent for being in the right place at the right time and making the best of every opportunity. It also helps to be rather more hard-headed about the music business than many musicians are now.

Qualifications and training

Musicians develop at their own pace. Most show early talent but this in itself is not enough. There has to be commitment over a long 'gestation' period. This can be at school, home, specialist school or, occasionally, even later, at college.

All maintained schools provide music teaching from the age of 5 to 16 as part of the National Curriculum and children are given the opportunity to learn a musical instrument. Despite the cuts, most LEAs give (or pay for) instrumental teaching to advanced levels, have their own youth orchestras, organise Saturday music schools and holiday courses for their pupils who have musical ability and interest.

There are also a few specialist schools, including choir schools for boys, where children's musical talents are trained to professional level without affecting their academic work.

The normal route from school into performing is via a specialist music school (preferably at 18 with one or more A-levels or equivalent; sometimes at 16), although some very successful musicians have only studied privately with leading performers and/or teachers of their instruments.

Classical music training for performance

Music conservatoires

Most specialist music conservatoires or colleges offer three- or four-year music courses leading to a:

- Performers' Diploma, with limited academic content. Those interested in a career as a performer should have reached an advanced level of performance, at least grade 8 with distinction in the principal instrument and grade 6 on a second instrument, before leaving school. Ability to play a keyboard instrument is useful, as are passes in theory examinations or an A-level/Higher grade pass in Music.
- Graduate Diploma, equivalent to a degree, which may still lead to work as a performer. Entry as above but additionally two A-levels or three Higher grades usually including music are required.
- Degree. Normal university entrance requirements usually including Music at A/H-level.

All courses use auditions and interviews as part of the selection process.

The Conservatoires are: Birmingham Conservatoire; Guildhall School of Music and Drama; London College of Music; Royal Academy of Music; Royal College of Music; Royal Northern College of Music; Royal Scottish Academy of Music and Drama; Trinity College of Music; Welsh College of Music and Drama.

Some music conservatoires are reluctant to take instrumentalists over 21, while singers are preferred between the ages of 20 and 24. The voice takes time to develop and settle down, so training starts later and may be spread over some ten years including postgraduate training.

Gaining entry to a music school, competitive as it is, is no guarantee of a successful career. It is estimated that at most one in ten of those who graduate become full-time musicians.

Degree courses

Music is taught as a first degree subject by many universities and several other colleges. It is also an integral part of some performing arts and liberal arts degrees. Most university degree courses are academic.

Music is taught as though it were a language, and students are expected to be able to read, understand and write music as well as they do English before they are accepted for most degree courses. Music at A-level or equivalent is normally essential for entry to a degree course, and some departments also want a language. Most departments now want candidates to be able to play at least one and preferably two instruments (including a keyboard), one to Associated Board grade 8 (distinction may be assumed).

Subjects studied include history of music, musicology, methods of composition, musical analysis, etc. The degree may lead to a BMus or a BA, and although there is no difference in the status of the degree, the syllabuses may differ.

Over the last 20 years many university music departments have widened the scope of their courses, and in particular most have increased very substantially the amount of instrumental teaching and training that they do, and also spend more departmental time on performing – in orchestras, groups of all kinds, and choirs. Composition, as a creative skill and not just a formal academic exercise, and conducting, are also taught now. There are also some unusual courses, including Tonmeister studies at Surrey which teaches electronics and recording engineering as well as more conventional music subjects, and at City University, London, which also combines traditional with scientific aspects.

Although all degree courses offer some opportunities for performance, few give intensive enough instrumental training for a professional performing career. It is, however, possible to progress from an academic music degree to a specialist conservatoire to train for performance.

'First employment' figures for 1994 were:

total graduating	*816*
research/further study	104
teacher training	175
other training, including law	81
believed unemployed 31 December	25
short-term UK employment	42
permanent UK employment	225
employers	
education	15
commerce/industry	77
cultural, etc.	19
local government	6
Civil Service	6
functions	
creative, etc.	47
teaching, lecturing, etc.	41
administration/operational management	27
personnel/social work	20
financial work	14
marketing, etc.	14
library and information work	2

Postgraduate courses

Most intending professional musicians expect to go on studying after their first course at music school. Instrumental players can go, for example, to the national orchestral centre (The Orchestra for Europe) to do a one-year postgraduate course, or to train for chamber orchestra work at the Royal Northern College of Music. The Guildhall School of Music and Drama offers a one-year course for orchestral string section leaders in conjunction with the LSO. Some go to conservatoire abroad, and/or to study with particular musicians or teachers.

The National Opera Studio and most of the music colleges offer specialist postgraduate courses in opera and lieder. The course at the National Opera Studio has an intake of around 12–13 singers and three *répétiteurs* (rehearsal pianists) and covers stage movement, languages, etc. The average age for students on this course is the late 20s.

It is anticipated that the Standards for accreditation of NVQs for Music will be submitted in 1996 by the Arts and Entertainment Training Council.

Popular music training

Most performance courses are in classical music, but a few universities and colleges offer jazz or other types of music degrees: the City of Leeds College of Music (Jazz Studies); Middlesex University (Jazz and Popular Music); Barnsley College (Band Studies); Bretton Hall (Popular Music Studies); Liverpool University (Music/Popular Music); Salford University (Band Musicianship or Popular Music and Recording); Thames Valley University (Popular Music Performance – Guitar, Bass Guitar, Drums); Wolverhampton University (Music – Popular).

There are a range of BTEC/SCOTVEC HNC/HND courses in popular music including those at Newcastle College and Perth College.

There are several colleges of bagpipe music. See also the BRIT Performing Arts and Technology School for courses 14–18.

The record industry

Sales of music are closely linked to the economic health of the nation, and it is not surprising that the industry went through a bad time in the early 1990s. However, by 1994 sales were back at a record level of £917.5 million. It is difficult to assess the number of record labels because these range from small Indies (operating from a bedroom) up to the multinational major companies such as EMI, CBS-Sony or Polygram.

Working for a major record company

Staff may be employed in the following departments:

A & R (Artist and Repertoire). Staff deal with the finding, signing and developing of acts. This is probably one of the most difficult departments to enter. This is partly because vacancies are rarely, if ever, advertised and also because it is one of the most popular. It is a case of building up contacts – going to lots of gigs, not of major, signed artists, but of small, up-and-coming bands who are starting to get a good following, getting to know other A & R people; getting to know bands and managers. A person would start as a 'scout', either freelance or employed by the record company, and move on from there. A scout is expected to go to five or six gigs a night and report back on them to the A & R manager the next day.

Marketing, which can be subdivided into departments like Video, Creative, Product, Marketing Services, Press, and Promotion. The job of Video, Creative and Product departments is to come up with a package which will, they hope, bring the band to the attention of the press and the public. The result will include a video, record sleeve and promotional items such as T-shirts and posters. Marketing Services have to ensure that enough of the product is produced to supply demand. Press and Promotion departments bring the finished product to the attention of both the media and the public. Press is through newspapers and magazines and Promotion through radio and TV. A press officer would be expected to have good English and relevant journalistic experience.

The record labels use *pluggers* (their own staff or self-employed) to promote new releases to producers and presenters on radio stations, such as BBC Radio 1, Capital, and local radio.

Sales and distribution is sometimes split into three: Classical Sales, Album Sales and Pop Sales (often called Strikeforce). A strikeforce representative would preferably have had sales experience in a record shop, a clean driving licence and be aged between 20 and 25. Sales reps for Classical and Album sales tend to be older.

Legal and Business Affairs department are concerned with the artists' contracts and with the day-to-day running of the company's legal and business affairs.

Finance and Administration are also concerned with the day-to-day running of the company, taking decisions on how much to advance an artist or how much to spend on a video.

Some of the larger record companies will also be involved with production and manufacturing: EMI, for example, have the Abbey Road recording studio in London and a CD production factory at Swindon. They will also have an international department to identify the right territory for a particular product and negotiate for its release.

Record company staff and the people who supply supporting services and contacts within the music world may be trained musicians or those who have a real interest in the music business. They may have business, management or marketing qualifications. Buckinghamshire College offers a degree course in Music Industry Management.

Music retail shops

At the end of 1994 there were 4,245 shops selling records, tapes, CDs, and music videos. Many of these are specialist chains like HMV and Our Price, or multiple chains like W H Smith and Menzies, but there are still over 1,000 independent specialists.

Some music retail shops also sell hi-fi, musical instruments, music books, scores and printed music, while others specialise in one of these aspects.

Advanced music qualifications are not usually required, although they are an added advantage, particularly for areas like sheet music and classical CDs, etc., where a knowledge of composers, their works, conductors and musical terminology is helpful. As in most sales careers, a knowledge of the product and selling techniques are both important.

For specialist hi-fi or selling electronic instruments a knowledge of electronics is useful. It can help to be able to play and demonstrate to a customer the differences between for example a traditional keyboard instrument and a digital piano.

The recording studio

As well as the sound or recording engineers who record live concerts for radio or television, many work in studios recording and mixing music to produce a master tape to use for producing records, cassettes and compact discs.

Intensive competition makes survival very difficult for all studios from the one-man operation up to large recording studios such as EMI's at Abbey Road.

Abbey Road employs about 70 staff, of whom about 14 are sound engineers working on recording sessions. The other staff are secretarial, administrative, technical, and engineers, who are trained in post-production, doing remastering and disc-cutting. Since Abbey Road is strong in classical music, their classical sound engineers would be expected to have a degree in music and then receive training in digital editing and digital remastering before working in the studio as an engineer. Recording or sound engineers at the BBC would also be expected to have a degree in music before being recruited as trainee studio managers.

The more traditional way into recording studios is with GCSE/SCE or equivalent qualifications, preferably including English, mathematics and physics, and working your way up. Competition is fierce and they may only have one vacancy a year.

Courses in sound engineering and music technology are increasingly available, from BTEC to degree level. They include:

- Degrees in Popular Music and Recording at Salford University; Tonmeister course in Applied Physics and Recording Techniques at the University of Surrey; Music and Technology at Kingston University; and Audio and Music Technology at Anglia Polytechnic University.
- Several BTEC ND courses in recording technology at Salford and a recording technology option at the BRIT Performing Arts and Technology School in Croydon.

Other opportunities with music

Performance is the most obvious way of working with music but creating music involves a great variety of jobs and processes:

- Composers, songwriters and lyricists create original music for artists, session musicians, ensembles and orchestras to play.
- This may be recorded by a record company with the aid of music producers and recording engineers, or by a publisher as sheet music.
- The master tape is used to produce CDs or tapes, and the product is packaged, advertised, distributed and sold in retail shops and ends up in homes, in libraries, and being played by the media.
- Jobs in broadcasting include working as a DJ, music presenter, producer or studio manager.
- The performer has usually been taught how to play an instrument or sing by a music teacher.
- The musical instruments will need to be built and maintained.
- A successful performer may need an agent and manager to look after their interests.
- The record company needs staff to find artists to record and then promote them.
- Journalists may write about performers and performances.
- Music therapists use music to help those with emotional and behavioural problems or learning difficulties to communicate.

The opportunities for people who are musically talented or have musical interests are extensive but almost as competitive as the opportunities for performance. Some of these areas have already been dealt with: others are covered below.

Broadcasting

A high proportion of radio output is music – an estimated 80%. Disc-jockeys are broadcasters who have popular appeal and who know a lot about pop music. The music policy for any radio station is usually handled by the station's production team.

The BBC has three predominantly music networks – Radio 1, Radio 2 and Radio 3. Most of the programme material for these three networks comes from in-house BBC programme departments, based in either London or one of the BBC's six regional centres. The producers who are responsible for the programmes assess standards of musical performance, keep in touch with artistes and orchestras (including the BBC's five in-house orchestras) stay abreast of trends and developments in music-making from local to international level, and contribute generally to keeping up high standards. Performing ability is not needed, but producers are likely to have a mixture of good professional qualifications, sound musical and critical judgement, wide knowledge of repertory artists, the ability to plan, the ability to manage resources, tact, and an imaginative approach to music broadcasting.

The three London departments responsible for music production – Radio 1 Production Department, Radio 2 Music Department and Radio 3 Music Department – employ about 150 producers and broadcasting assistants. There are only a few vacancies every year. Light and popular music and gramophone programmes are the responsibility of separate Departments.

Outside London, each National Region and Network Production Centre has a Head of Music or Senior Producer with one or more producers, who are responsible for music output for network within their area.

BBC Television has a small number of Music Producers in its Music and Arts Department. Applicants not only need the musical background of other music producers but also a visual imagination and some knowledge, and preferably experience, of cameras and film-making.

There are five BBC orchestras, two in London and one each in Scotland, Wales and Manchester. Orchestral management staff assist with general routine and correspondence. They need to know how orchestras and chorus work and are made up, need to be able to read a score, know how to organise players for performance, have a wide knowledge of appropriate repertoire, and be able to work with musicians of all ages. *See also* ARTS ADMINISTRATION (*below*) *and* MEDIA CAREERS.

Composing

The Composers' Guild of Great Britain has over 500 members, who write predominantly for the serious genres such as concert, opera, and liturgical music. Many composers in the Guild also write music for theatre, dance, film and television and many are involved in education. Others supplement their income from composing with arranging and orchestration.

Although there are a significant number of premières of classical works, many of which are commissioned, few receive a second performance, and even fewer are accepted by a publisher for printing and distribution.

With the advent of desktop publishing and advanced score writing software, many composers are choosing to print and market their own works. They are also using the Internet to promote recordings of their works, often produced by DAT from a home studio. The Composers' Guild produces information about how to become a composer-publisher.

It is difficult for a composer to earn a living purely from composition, unless he or she has attained a measure of success in either the concert or the media world. However, most composers write for more than one genre, thus providing themselves with a variety of income-generating opportunities.

The Composers' Guild publishes *Composer News* three times a year, a *Members' Handbook*, and *First Performances* annually. *See also* Publishing *below*.

An HND in Music Composition is available at Coventry University.

Journalism

Music journalism has expanded quite sharply in recent years. In the classical field new titles such as the BBC *Music Magazine, Classic CD, CD Review, The Great Composers* and *The Classical Collection* have joined the long established *Gramophone*. The main pop magazines *Smash Hits, Q, New Musical Express, Melody Maker* and *The Face* have been joined by new music-oriented consumer magazines such as *Mojo*. *Music Week* is the record industry trade magazine.

All kinds of newspapers and magazines now require journalism skills combined with a broad and solid musical background; but although opportunities for music journalists have expanded, only a handful of newspapers and magazines employ 'serious' music critics, and many journalists are freelancers. Technical knowledge can be important for rock, CD and hi-fi magazines. See also *in* MEDIA CAREERS.

Librarianship

National libraries and certain specialist libraries such as music publishers and record producers, broadcasting organisations (notably the BBC), and university and other college libraries where music is taught, employ music librarians to build and manage collections of books, scores, CDs, records, tapes, etc. Most music libraries of any importance employ only qualified librarians, but a musical background, and preferably a first degree, are obviously an asset. Most orchestras also employ a professional librarian to look after their scores. Graduates in disciplines other than information studies (including music graduates) take postgraduate information studies qualifications accredited by The Library Association (Diploma/Master's degree) but none include options specific to music. *See also* LIBRARY AND INFORMATION WORK.

Further information

The Library Association, and the UK Branch of the International Association of Music Libraries.

Musical instrument technology

The demand for musical instruments supports a number of manufacturers and craftsmen/women in both building instruments and maintaining, repairing and restoring them. Musical instrument technicians specialise in a particular type or group, such as keyboard, strings or fretted, woodwind, brass or electronic instruments. It is highly skilled work and each instrument has its own set of challenges. A background in technical subjects involving woodwork, electronics and metalwork is useful. Academic qualifications are not always essential, although some courses may ask for three or four GCSE/SCEs or an A-level or equivalent. Training is usually via a course rather than on-the-job.

Piano tuners or technicians adjust the piano strings to the proper pitch using a tuning fork and tuning hammer. *Piano repairers* diagnose problems and realign, replace or rebuild the thousands of parts which affect the performance of the piano. It is crucial to have a good ear for tuning, although it is not essential to be able to play an instrument. Most piano technicians are self-employed but some work for piano dealers or piano factories.

Pipe-organ repairers tune the flue or reed pipes, and repair and install organs.

Stringed instrument makers cut, shape, assemble and varnish the wood and fit the strings. The *repairer* replaces damaged panels or strings, seals cracks and scratches, cleans and varnishes the wood, and restrings the instrument. The work is extremely detailed and difficult, and major restoration work can take up to two years. The main world musical repair centres are London, New York, Chicago and Vienna.

Wind instrument repairers work on small intricate mechanisms such as keys and levers.

There are several piano-tuning courses, including one for the visually impaired at the Royal National College for the Blind in Hereford. Courses last for up to three years and include chipping up, rough tuning, fine tuning and toning, piano construction, history of the piano and acoustics.

There are courses for other instruments, including electronic musical instruments, at a few colleges or universities including London Guildhall University (courses lead to a certificate, BTEC ND, BTEC HND or degree), West Dean College, Merton College, Morley College and Newark Technical College. The Institute of Musical Instrument Technology awards a diploma.

Further information

Pianoforte Tuners' Association.

Music therapy

Music therapy is a growing profession, and music therapists work with people of all ages and abilities. They are employed by the NHS and education services, and in private practice, trusts and voluntary organisations.

The predominant client groups are people with learning disabilities, people with mental health problems, the elderly and people with conditions such as autism or speech and language impairment.

Music therapists aim to help people communicate emotional or psychological difficulties by using improvised music. A strong relationship between therapist and client develops, which promotes trust and helps the client to express sometimes difficult thoughts and emotions.

There are currently five postgraduate courses available, at: the Guildhall School of Music and Drama; Roehampton Institute of Higher Education; Nordoff-Robbins Music Therapy Centre; Department for Continuing Education, Bristol University (part-time course); and Anglia Polytechnic University, Cambridge. Courses are planned for Wales and Scotland.

The Association of Music Therapists estimates that there are around 290 practising music therapists in the UK. The Association is the organisation for qualified music therapists. There is also a British Society for Music Therapy open to anyone interested in music therapy.

Further information

Association of Professional Music Therapists.

Publishing

The music publishing industry is based on the exploitation of copyrights and the collection and distribution of royalties from performance and sales of the copyright. It is also concerned with the production and sale of printed music, music books, and the development and promotion of living composers.

A large publishing house might have departments covering copyright, royalty administration, editorial, production, composer promotion, hire, sales and marketing.

Music publishers employ relatively small numbers of people with technical music skills, as editorial assistants, copyists, and arrangers, mainly in a freelance capacity. Editorial assistants liaise between composers and printers and ensure proofs are read. Copyists are employed doing the copying of instrumental parts for orchestras and groups. Book publishers do employ a very small number of people with music degrees if they regularly publish books on music. *See also* PUBLISHING *in* MEDIA CAREERS.

The Performing Right Society (PRS) is the organisation which licenses music users, and which collects and distributes to its composer, author and music-publisher members, any royalties for the public performance and broadcasting of their copyright musical works. PRS has over 28,000 members, who write or publish all types of music. The majority of writer-members of the Society (68%) receive less than £250 per annum from PRS, whilst only about 4% receive more than £10,000.

Further Information

Music Publishers Association.

Teaching

Teaching requires commitment and enthusiasm. It should not be treated as a financial safety net. Music teachers work in a wide variety of settings.

Private teaching

About 90% of musicians do some private teaching on a one-to-one basis, and many private teachers arrange their timetables to combine teaching an instrument with performing or composing. They work with people of all ages and abilities. Instrumental teachers are concerned with developing performing skills on individual instruments to a high level.

To be a private teacher needs communication skills, patience, perseverance and resourcefulness. Good musical qualifications are essential, and since private music teachers are usually self-employed it helps to have business skills as well.

There is a Diploma course in Teaching in Private Practice run by the University of Reading in collaboration with the Incorporated Society of Musicians.

School teaching

Music is one of the foundation subjects of the National Curriculum in England and Wales, and the Northern Ireland Curriculum, and is part of the Expressive Arts curriculum in Scotland. Throughout the UK, music is compulsory for all pupils from 5 to 14.

Secondary schools usually have specialist music teachers on the staff supplemented by visiting instrumental and singing teachers. They teach composing, performing and appraising as part of the curriculum, for GCSE/SCE, A-levels or Higher examinations. The peripatetic music service has been cut back and in some areas of the country there is a move away from one-to-one tuition in favour of group tuition.

Music teachers organise the musical life of the school. A well-equipped school should have access to modern instruments such as electronic keyboards, synthesisers and electric guitars. Music teachers will usually have responsibility for organising bands, orchestras, choirs, and concerts, although some LEAs employ music organisers to coordinate musical activity in a group of schools and manage any special provision, e.g. youth orchestras, and teaching for able pupils.

In primary schools, class teachers are expected to cover all subjects, but usually the school has one teacher who has some musical knowledge, or will be able to get classroom support from a primary music consultant serving several schools.

Full-time school teaching requires a professional qualification leading to Qualified Teacher Status (QTS). In Scotland, it is necessary to gain a recognised teaching qualification (QT) and complete two years' satisfactory probation for registration with the General Teaching Council.

Music teachers usually qualify either through a three- or four-year graduate diploma, or a degree in music at a school of music or institution of higher education followed by a postgraduate certificate in education; or through completing a four-year Bachelor of Education (BEd) or a BA course with Qualified Teacher Status. The latter route is generally seen as more suitable for primary school teaching. There are only two institutions offering secondary school teacher training with music: the Welsh College of Music and Drama, and a consortium of colleges in Scotland. A few new experimental courses combine two years' study at a conservatoire with two years at a university leading to a combined BEd and a diploma in music. *See also* EDUCATION AND TEACHING.

Other teaching posts

Universities, colleges of higher education, and music conservatoires employ lecturers, and instrumental teachers, but the number of new posts is very limited, and high academic and/or musical qualifications are needed.

Arts administration

This is a rather amorphous area of employment, never clearly defined, with no set career structure, and not simple to describe. It overlaps considerably with leisure/recreation administration/management, and some argue that they are indistinguishable. Arts administration is commonly taken to mean the non-performing, non-technical functions in any organisation which provides facilities to watch, or take part in, 'artistic' activities. In other words, the emphasis is on administration rather than the arts part of the title. Some sectors which might be considered 'arts', however, are administered and managed by people qualified in that field – museums and libraries are two examples (*see in* HISTORICAL AND RELATED WORK *and in* LIBRARY AND INFORMATION WORK).

As in all other sectors, arts administration/management is a mix of the work needed to plan, finance, organise and run any organisation, with the specialist skills needed to solve the particular problems faced by organisations trying to provide facilities for performing, watching or taking part in arts-based activities. Money for the arts is restricted, so administrators have to make the best use of the money available, and this may influence artistic policy. It is not, though, a single 'profession'. While arts administration, if interpreted fairly widely, can offer quite a few actual jobs, the number of longer-term career opportunities is never likely to be large. Vacancy lists and advertisements try to stretch the field almost beyond credibility: to media, advertising, selling, and administration of a musicians' benevolent fund, for example.

National organisations

The Arts Council of England

The Arts Funding Structure was restructured in 1991 and the Arts Council of England now employs 180 staff whose administrative staff supervise projects, investigate proposals for grants and supervise them, and do general promotional and liaison work. The Council is divided into nine art form departments: Combined Arts; Dance; Drama; Film, Video and Broadcasting; Literature; Music; Touring; Visual Arts; and Education and Training. Other departments include: Business, Assessment and Planning; National Lottery; Policy, Research and Planning; and Finance and Information. Most of the staff are specialists in one of the departments.

There are also Arts Councils for Northern Ireland, Wales and Scotland, which have similar functions, as well as regional arts boards (*see below*).

The British Council

The British Council has specialist services in drama and dance, music, the visual arts, literature and films, television and video. In promoting British arts overseas the Council demonstrates their diversity and quality and also fosters collaborative relationships. Nine per cent of the Council's budget is spent on the arts, of which more than £3 million is used to subsidise overseas tours of British events. Staff working overseas are expected to take an interest in the cultural life of the country in which they work and to promote two-way cultural understanding. *See also* WORKING OVERSEAS *and* TEACHING AND EDUCATION.

The British Film Institute

The British Film Institute (BFI) helps to fund and gives technical help to film-makers; funds film and video workshops (with Channel 4); administers the National Film Theatre and the National Film and Television Archive; has research, information and education divisions (not careers advice); produces a number of publications (including a monthly journal); promotes and helps to fund some 40 regional film theatres; and helps set up film and TV centres in several larger cities.

Regional organisations

The ten regional arts boards are funded by local authorities, the Arts Councils, BFI, the Crafts Council and private funds. They support and promote the arts in their areas, by providing grants and subsidies, promoting particular events, putting out publicity material, helping to plan and coordinate activities, giving advice generally and supporting research. Their staff, some of whom specialise in e.g. drama, music, visual arts, community arts, or who administer finance, range from only six up to about 20.

Most of the larger authorities have some involvement in the arts aside from their museums, libraries and art galleries. Some have their own theatres, many put on arts events such as concerts of all kinds and art exhibitions, and some provide arts centres, etc. Mostly administration of these facilities and services is part of their leisure and recreation management structure (*see in* PROFESSIONAL SPORT AND THE RECREATION AND LEISURE INDUSTRIES).

Individual arts organisations

The range of possible employers here is quite wide, although the numbers employed by them individually are mostly small, however large the centre or theatre. Smaller organisations may only be able to employ people on a part-time basis, or have to rely on volunteers.

Arts centres

These vary in what they do, where they are based and in their size. Some are purpose-built, some are in converted premises, some are based on universities or schools. For most, numbers employed are very small, but centres like the Barbican Centre in London employ about 200 staff covering Administration, Arts, Marketing, Conference and Exhibitions, Engineering and Finance Divisions. Another major employer is the South Bank Centre.

The professional theatre

Administering and managing in the theatre may mean managing just a 'facility' including the building (which is often quite technically complex and may have, e.g., catering facilities too); managing a building and a resident company; or managing just a theatrical company which does not have a permanent home. Managing a concert hall or a cinema is in many ways similar to managing a theatre without a resident company.

Administrators control finance (including cashiers, etc., organise the programme of events and/or bookings for the facility, liaise and work closely with the theatre's artistic director(s) or performing-company administrators, deal with publicity and marketing, and supervise services, stage management, maintenance, etc. Although certain areas have expanded, such as cinemas, jobs in technical fields like film projectionist have not necessarily increased, as with new technology one projectionist can control eight screens.

Music administration

Music administration often employs people with musical backgrounds and qualifications.

Every professional orchestra, ballet and opera company and music festival needs administrators, to organise finance, concerts or performances; arrange contracts and travel; look after players, the music, etc. Staffing numbers are comparatively small. A single orchestral contractor may manage a small orchestra, assembling the players only as and when it is booked. Only the largest festivals can maintain full-time administrators year round, and the main opportunities are on fixed contracts for the period of the festival itself with a run-up period.

Music promoters can be local authorities, orchestras, concert agents and musical venues, e.g. the Barbican, as well as independent promoters such as festivals. Few staff are usually employed. The main function of a venue is to organise bookings and run the box office, provide front-of-house staff, produce diaries and other publicity material and promote their own events.

A concert agency's main job is to represent and promote the artist in negotiations with promoters. The work is demanding and requires good interpersonal skills and some knowledge of law to handle contracts.

Some universities have their own directors of music to organise a full programme of concerts, etc.

Community arts

Community associations of all kinds – some specialising in arts, some organised by specific groups, e.g. a local Afro-Caribbean or Asian community wanting to organise their own arts activities – can afford to employ full-time administrators, organisers, coordinators, development workers, etc. Some community workshops also employ administrators.

Working in arts administration

The work involved ranges from being responsible for raising, allocating, distributing and accounting for many thousands, even millions of pounds, through to marketing and publicity, organising exhibitions, collecting money at the box office or selling programmes in the auditorium. Some work involves subject expertise, especially where decisions have to be made on funding for specific arts, e.g. music, or where events such as art exhibitions have to be arranged. Some administrative posts in large arts centres such as the Royal Opera House Covent Garden, or in theatre companies or orchestras overlap/shade over into education (*see* EDUCATION AND TEACHING); not necessarily teaching or instruction, but developing and running educational and 'outreach' programmes such as actors' workshops, dance classes and post-performance discussions.

Since most arts organisations these days have to live within tight budgets, the number of administrative staff any one employs is usually kept as low as possible. Even in the largest organisation managers and administrators will take on a range of different functions and tasks, and team cooperation is essential. A large theatre, however, must employ managers/administrators to ensure that all front-of-house and box office operations run smoothly. Most large box offices are now computerised but may still employ up to 18 full-time staff, plus casual staff at peak booking times. Box office staff may have to work shifts over seven days. Staff turnover is usually high.

Working in arts administration has many special aspects. Efficient financial management to make the best use of income is obviously essential. It may also extend to looking for alternative sources of finance, hunting and applying for grants, etc. Finance may link closely to the growing need for expert marketing, not only to customers but, e.g., to potential sponsors, and in some organisations this is full-time work. Publicity and public relations are also essential functions. Few organisations are large enough to have full-scale personnel management departments, or even full-time personnel/staff managers, and so many managers must have this expertise.

Arts administrators must be good organisers and have good communication skills. They need dedication, as they will have to work long hours, and pay can be low. Arts administrators must be versatile, because they cannot follow a predetermined career path, and to get on and develop their careers they move from one organisation to another, often doing completely different types of work.

Recruitment and entry

There is no straightforward career structure, so no simple way in. Many posts take special expertise (and previous experience), not just for direct administration of arts funding or events, but also for publicity and accounting.

For any post which provides a start to a career, a degree in a suitable subject is probably essential. For example, art/history for organising galleries or exhibitions, or music for organising orchestras or concerts. A teaching qualification may also be useful. Onto this must be grafted all-round basic administrative skills: typing and word processing for managing mailing lists, book-keeping ability to keep accounts and use computer spreadsheets. Competition is fierce and organisations are able to be very selective.

Essential work experience is probably best gained through doing voluntary administration for student societies or a community or experimental arts group which cannot afford to pay. The organisers of arts festivals often need temporary staff to help with administration and publicity. After this it should be relatively easy to get into either low-level jobs in larger organisations, or general administration for smaller, poorer ones. Traditionally the box office route is an easy way into arts administration, but there are no guarantees of progress beyond this. Arts administrators need flexibility and initiative and should be prepared to take on almost anything to get in.

Qualifications and training

Pre-entry training specifically for arts administration has been rare, and most arts administrators have an arts degree supplemented by short courses. However, the number of courses available has recently increased:

- There are degrees or options in arts management (various slants) at Dartington College of Arts, and De Montfort, East London and North London Universities.
- Anglia Polytechnic University, and City, Durham, Northumbria and Warwick Universities run postgraduate courses.
- Roehampton Institute and De Montfort University offer short courses.
- There are specialist HND courses at New College, Durham (Music Industry Management) and at Fife CT, and an HNC Business Studies (Music Management) at West Lothian.

The Arts Council of England has set up a Regional Training Network with four centres around England and which coordinates Arts Management Training. These are the Arts Training Programme in Leicester, the Centre for Arts Management in Liverpool, Arts Training South at the University of Sussex, and Arts Training South West in Somerset.

The Arts and Entertainment Training Council (AETC) has accredited two NVQs in Cultural Venue Operations levels 2 and 3. Level 2 is aimed at administrative staff such as box office (including the sale of tickets and lettings/room hires), front-of-house (covering the control and direction of patrons) and promotional support. Level 3 is designed for a wide range of complex work with responsibility for overseeing all aspects of venue administration and front-of-house management. Two more have been submitted for accreditation in 1996: Administering Cultural Products level 3 and Developing and Delivering Cultural Products level 4. These are all connected to Arts Administration, covering Front of House, Box Office, Production and Programming.

There are a few modern apprenticeships in Front of House.

Further information

The British Actors Equity Association, the Incorporated Society of Musicians, the Arts and Entertainment Training Council, the Arts and Entertainment Technical Training Initiative (AETTI).

Contents

Professional Sport and the Recreation and Leisure Industries

(CLCI: GAG, GAJ, GAK, GAN)

Background

Consumer spending on leisure is running at £102.9 billion, made up as follows: alcohol, £25 billion; eating out, £18.7 billion; overseas holidays, £13 billion; home entertainment, £9.7 billion; house and garden, £8 billion; UK holidays, £6.2 billion; hobbies and pastimes; £6 billion; reading £5.4 billion; sport £4.3 billion; gambling, £3.2 billion; local entertainment, £2.7 billion; and sightseeing, £0.7 billion.

During the last ten years there has been a consequent expansion in job opportunities in sport, recreation and leisure. It is estimated that over 402,200 people are currently employed in 1996 in these areas (including jobs in theatres, libraries, museums, galleries, and sports and leisure services). Of these, over 320,000 work in sport and recreation.

Sport is firmly part of the entertainment industry. Even the language of the entertainment industry is widely used in professional sport – top professional sports men and women are called 'stars'; the income, for a few, can be astronomic, and they have all the glamour and media-interest the entertainment industry expects.

Professional sports men and women are expected to entertain their audiences, to be 'personalities', as well as to play at ever higher standards, and so to ensure an income and a profit for all the huge sub-structure of interests which have developed around sport.

These interests range from the firms making and selling to the general public sports gear and equipment which are replicas of those used by the professional, through newspapers which sell more copies if their sports coverage is good, to the bookmakers. In some sports, e.g. boxing and snooker, players may be the earners for a management 'team'. Direct and indirect sponsorship of sport by business and commerce is also part and parcel of many sports, although the scale of investment fluctuates with the economic climate. The Central Council of Physical Recreation estimated in 1995 that over 1,350 commercial companies in the UK between them subscribed over £270 million each year in various sponsorship schemes. This massive investment of money into sports sponsorship has brought with it increased opportunities in the field of sports promotion and sports marketing.

The effect of all this is an increasingly commercial attitude to sport itself, and of course greater demands on the players. Play may have to be geared to both crowd-attracting and winning, which are not always the same thing. Players live under enormous psychological pressures, both within their sport – since winning takes psychological as well as physical stamina and training – and from outside, the media and the fans. Conditions of employment are still not as good as they should be, and it is still only the smallest handful of men and women who make the kind of money that gets headlines.

The rate at which the more popular entertainment sports burn up players is increasing, and the success-rate of young entrants falling. The increasing demand for new talent (with no greater chances of success, however) only serves to strengthen the popular image of professional sport as a highly glamorous occupation, especially as the off-field activities of professional sports men and women are paraded across the newspapers and TV screens.

Nevertheless, the attractions of professional sport, with all the fun of doing something really interesting well, and being paid for it, and the added bonus of outdoor life, potential public acclaim, opportunities for travel, and the fact that professional sport can take people into new social leagues – boxing was traditionally the bright working boy's route up the social ladder – must be balanced against the disadvantages.

The competition, throughout a sports careers and not just to get started, is always intense. There is always the pressure of someone else trying to beat you for your position in the game. Then, professional sports men and women do not always enjoy the social life the newspapers suggest – to achieve what is demanded of them most have to be totally dedicated to their sport and must stay in top condition. Even travelling can become unpleasant when it means going straight from one tournament to the next without any time to relax and enjoy the scenery. The physical conditions in which sports are played are not always comfortable, and players often have the pain and discomfort of minor injury to live with.

However, the main disadvantage is that careers in sport are almost all extremely short. All professional sportsmen and sportswomen must expect to find themselves a second career. If they are very lucky indeed they may be able to go on playing until they are 30 or 35, which leaves another 30 or 35 working years. A high proportion are forced to end their playing careers much earlier than that, and many barely get started at all. Partly this is a natural hazard: people are bound to lose form, or to suffer injuries which make it impossible to continue. However, with players being pushed into playing to far higher standards at ever younger ages, and into playing more often, the odds on players simply burning out, or suffering disabling injury, are inevitably increased.

For every ten people playing there are thirty or more who can no longer do so. There is only non-playing work – training, managing, coaching, umpiring, administering, etc. – within their sports for a very small proportion of retired players, and some sports can still find people to do some of this part-time or on a voluntary basis. The other, rather obvious, areas of possible work, such as sports journalism, are also overcrowded, and demand skills which sports men and women do not necessarily have. Some professionals make use of the commercial and business contacts they may have made during their playing careers – with sponsoring firms or the sportswear business, for example. The problems they meet are those of anyone going into business without the appropriate training and/or experience in the techniques needed to make a profit, and again they may not have the necessary aptitudes. Investing money earned during a sporting career in order to turn it into an income for life is as hazardous as investment is generally.

Most worthwhile, interesting and reasonably paid work these days requires some kind of preparation and training, and this is just as true for work started in middle life as for any other. Training for a high proportion of careers just cannot be started as late as the thirties. The incomes paid to players (and their contracts) take little or no account of this problem, and it is made worse because few players manage to stay at peak income throughout their playing lives – which means that towards the end they may not have the financial resources to prepare for something new. Provision for players to prepare for second careers is still, generally, very inadequate.

Young sports men and women must, then, take this problem very seriously before starting out on the route to a professional career. It is no use just assuming that 'something will turn up'. The pressure can be extremely strong to begin professional-level training, with all the time and effort that this involves, in the early to mid teens, without worrying about the apparently distant future.

It is sensible to plan and prepare for every eventuality. This means, first, carrying on with as broadly based a general education for as long as possible and to as high a level as possible. All prospective professional players of any sport have to continue their general education to 16 anyway, and they should take as many GCSE/SCE examinations as they can. The arguments are strong for going further along the education route (*see below*). Even if, after careful consideration, a young player decides to go into full-time training at 16-plus, they should by then have some idea of what alternative careers interest them, and be firm about spending time regularly on some kind of preparation for this. This can be a part-time course (there are, for example, professional footballers doing degree courses part-time at their local universities or colleges), taken throughout the year, or some form of intensive study/training during the out-of-season period.

Recruitment and entry

There are generally two ways of becoming a professional sports man or woman. One is straight from school, normally via a kind of apprenticeship, the other is to become a top-level amateur first and then switch to a professional career. The prevailing school of thought considers that any sport ought to be started as early as possible, with professional-level training beginning in early or mid-teens at the very latest. It is, however, very difficult to reconcile this with the need to make certain every entrant has the educational background to ensure that he or she can begin a second career in the mid-30s.

This implies that the amateur route may well be in the long-term interests of many potential professionals. Many higher education institutions have unrivalled facilities, including training, for most sports, some specialise (e.g. Loughborough), and some Universities (Bath, Stirling and University College Swansea) have a few sports scholarships to offer. (These vary in the amount of assistance provided. At Bath for example, students are funded for one additional year to complete their studies. The time may be used for several short blocks – or an entire year of intensive preparation for the Olympics). First division footballers, for example, have taken degrees and did not begin their professional careers until after graduation. A degree in the area of sport and/or physical education can also provide the basis of an alternative career, e.g. in the recreation and leisure industries.

Some sports managers object to the educationalists' argument, because they think that the idea of safeguarding against the possibility of failure creates a negative attitude among young players which in turn could result in their not succeeding. Parents and pupils should, however, be properly informed of both sides of the argument, whatever decision they may make.

All potential professional sports men and women must obviously be absolutely physically fit, and be the right shape, size, etc. for the sport in question. Most players spend a high proportion of their time keeping their bodies in peak condition, with continuous and often very strenuous exercise and rigorous training routines which must be combined with a life of considerable self-discipline.

A very real aptitude and ability for the sport in question are also, equally obviously, an absolute necessity. Every sport requires different physical and mental skills, although some sportsmen do combine sports. Many organisations recruiting young sports men and women complain that today's comparatively good living conditions produce youngsters who lack the 'killer' instinct that many sports require to play the game in a particular way. A professional player, today, is usually also an intelligent player, capable of understanding and exploiting tactical and psychological techniques, which in turn makes a better educational background useful. Emphasis is increasing on the ability to concentrate, determination and the ability to come back after a defeat, and on being able to cope with the psychological and emotional stresses of high-level competition.

The sports

Athletics – basketball – billiards and snooker – boxing – cricket – cycling – darts – football – golf – horse racing – ice skating – motor-cycle sport – motor racing – rugby – tennis – wrestling

It is not possible to earn a living at all sports.

Athletics

Athletics is dominated by the Olympics, for which amateur status is required, so there can be no professional careers as such. However, the demands of international competition mean that most top athletes must still spend most of their time training and competing, and find it difficult to earn a living. They therefore have to accept financial assistance wherever they can find it, and trusts are now set up to allow them to benefit from, e.g. sponsorship, advertising, etc., without jeopardising their amateur status.

Basketball

The sport is governed in Great Britain by the four independent Associations for England, Scotland, Ireland and Wales. Basketball is growing in popularity and the English Basket Ball Association says numbers of players are increasing rapidly, with 26,369 registered club players in England (1995). There are approximately 100,000 participants in English schools and around 9 million followers. The sport has a number of leagues and competitions but most players support themselves by other jobs.

Billiards and snooker

Billiards and snooker have been played professionally for many years, but it is only in the last 15 years, built on better organisation of tournaments, heavy television exposure, a sharp rise in players' skills, 'packaging and personalities', and sponsorships, that it has been able to support players in any number.

The right to play in professional tournaments is strictly controlled by the World Professional Billiards and Snooker Association. A high proportion of professional players make most of their incomes from exhibition matches and straightforward personal appearances, on top of any prize money. Some run their own clubs, etc.

Most potential snooker players show ability in their early teens – and should be playing for a club, county or regional team, and winning regularly. Learning good technique early is crucial. The best younger players are now signed up by professional managers.

Boxing

Boxing is one of the most physically demanding of professional sports. While contests are the pinnacle towards which a boxer works, most of his time is spent following a particularly severe training programme, aimed at building up and maintaining physical stamina, endurance, and muscle, and developing and improving boxing skills and techniques. Training becomes really punishing in the weeks before a fight, when the boxer moves into a strict, training-camp regime away from home. But in between fights boxers have to stay very fit and control their weight, with exercise, gym-, ring- and road-work.

Most professional boxers are contracted to a boxing manager who arranges contests and negotiates terms for each fight. He provides gymnasium and training facilities, training and contest staff, and arranges publicity, etc. In return the manager takes an agreed percentage of the boxer's earnings.

Boxing matches usually take place in the evenings or weekends and last over a prescribed number of two- or three-minute rounds, or until one contestant is knocked out, or until the referee judges that one has reached the limits of physical endurance.

All boxers, managers, trainers, promoters and anyone else connected with professional contests must have a British Boxing Board of Control licence. The Board is the main regulatory body together with the recognised international governing bodies.

Cricket

Cricket, supported by sponsors, TV coverage, 'super-stars', and one-day competitions, keeps up its popularity. However, only 18 'first-class' counties compete for the Championship and cups with, between them, fewer than 320 players on contract.

Most cricketers are in full employment only during the season from mid-April to mid-September, during which time they play 20 to 30 three/four-day matches, beginning on Tuesdays and Saturdays, one-day knock-out competitions, and a one-day league, played on Sunday. Test matches with overseas teams intervene for those selected to play for England, and most counties also play any tourists. Top players tour overseas for the other half of the year, but the rest must find something else to do during the autumn and winter. Some play or coach overseas, or play a winter sport, like football.

Cricketers can play for almost any county but many still play for their 'home' county, all the same. (NB anyone wishing to play for Yorkshire must have been born there!) Clubs can also register one overseas player on contract. There is no transfer system between the clubs, so players normally stay with one club throughout their playing careers. Most players can expect to get into the first XI by the age of 25 if they are going to be good enough, and many go on playing until around 40 or over, although others give up before then to get into a second career. Many find employment in the game as coaches, club officials, umpires or scorers.

Most umpires are former first-class cricketers and they are appointed by the Test and County Cricket Board.

Most potential first-class cricketers have been spotted by their county club during their school-days and if they have not, the school is generally the first to inform them. Most boy cricketers with potential will have played for county schoolboy sides, in any case. Some boys play in local league cricket to gain attention. The chances for a boy who has not been spotted by the time he is ready to leave school are therefore very slim. County clubs see hundreds of boys at trials; only a very few are offered engagement and the failure rate among these is very high. Young players spend their first years playing for club and second-XI sides.

Cycling

Cycling has revived to some extent in Britain, but is still extremely popular in continental Europe. There are approximately 30 foreign-based British professional riders. Almost all began as amateurs and are members of sponsored teams (not necessarily by cycle manufacturers). It is difficult to make a living from cycling, but some British cyclists do find regular work on the continent. There is now no distinction between amateur and professional as the sport became 'open' at the beginning of 1996.

Darts

Darts has become a popular professional spectator sport, with about 12 people now earning a living from it, and about four or five classed as 'super stars'. Professionals now compete in a dozen or more major national and international tournaments, and in between travel the counties taking on local amateur teams and giving exhibitions. The difference between a professional and the 30,000 or so top amateurs is said to be showmanship, the ability to keep the psychological advantage, and knowing the fastest and easiest combination of shots to give a specific number of points.

Football

Football is probably the world's most popular participatory and spectator sport. It is supported by and supports quite a large commercial industry giving real problems when the game loses popularity. Fewer people – about 22 million in 1996 against 40 million in 1950 – go to matches now. (That however, is an improvement on the 20 million of 1991.) The industry is being squeezed between rising costs and falling income, with failure to solve deep-seated problems going back over many years adding to the difficulties.

Although many thousands of clubs are affiliated to one of the three Football Associations (England, Wales and Scotland), only 130 employ professional footballers. Ninety-two clubs compete in the two league championships. The top 20 clubs are in the FA premier league which was formed in 1992, 72 compete in the Football league which is divided into three divisions. Thirty-eight clubs compete in the three Scottish league divisions. Between them they employ (1996) around 2,250 footballers. Given the present problems, clubs could go out of business or merge, and the number of full-time players is likely to be cut further.

The more prominent and successful the club, the larger the number of footballers on its books. A club's success depends not only on its footballers and their manager and trainers. Skilful business management is also crucial: every club has a board of directors, generally made up of local businessmen and/or personalities who can either invest in the club themselves or have access to funds. Without this players may find (and have been) themselves sold to another club, not because their play is poor, but because the club has to realise the investment they represent.

The football season is now so long that, taking into account overseas tours played in the summer months, few footballers now have more than a six-week break, so do not have to find other work out of season. Modern pressures do, in fact, result in many players finding that the number of matches they must play, with mid-week and Sunday matches, is a considerable strain, injury rates are up, and younger footballers are gaining places in first teams possibly too early for their proper development. Only the exceptional player manages to survive in a first-division first XI throughout his playing career (which probably lasts an average of about eight years). Most are transferred from club to club, either upwards as their talents develop or downwards as they decline, with changes in income and status to match.

The Professional Footballers' Association works continuously to improve conditions for professional footballers. Players are employed on contract, the terms depending on the player's status, skill and bargaining ability, and the financial standing of the club itself. Contracts are for one or more years, with the club retaining an option on the player for a period after that. Players whose services are not retained by a club for any reason, or who wish to move, are placed on transfer; for those with future potential the club may ask for a fee appropriate to the player's standing and abilities, the player receiving 15% of this if the transfer is initiated by the club (none if it is at the player's own request). A good season generally produces bonuses.

Training and travelling take up a large part of a professional footballer's time. Training combines exercise routines with ball practice designed to improve dexterity, balance and skill in play. Football demands tight team work, so practice at this and strategy also form part of a day's activity. Travelling, and therefore periods away from family and friends, means a great deal of idle time on trains and planes and in hotels. The close relationship between players in a club has its advantages but also produces strains and tensions which can affect team performance on the field; temperament in players is not, therefore, very popular with management or fellow footballers.

Only a few players are able to stay with professional football when they retire, as coaches, trainers, managers or club secretaries. The Professional Footballers' Association, which has about 2,500 members, estimates that under 3% of its members find permanent careers in management when they stop playing. The Football Association organises a wide range of certificate courses in training, coaching, ground maintenance, club administration, care of injuries, and refereeing. The Professional Footballers' Association provides advice, information and counselling, and the Footballers' Further Educational and Vocational Training Society, financed jointly by the Football League and the PFA, also helps. The FA also has a scheme which helps match candidates to club vacancies.

Recruitment and entry

Potential professional footballers are usually 'spotted' by talent scouts while they are still at school, and it is rare for them to miss talented boys, although there is nothing to prevent a boy writing to a club for a trial.

Despite the inevitable tensions between school and clubs, clubs are allowed to register 'associated schoolboys', under strict regulations, from 13 on, but only for coaching and training, and only with the consent of school and parents. Associated schoolboys may not play for the club, except against other schoolboys, until the season after their 15th birthday. Clubs have options on associated schoolboys' services when they leave school. Boys must tell the club when they are leaving school three months' before, and the club has to tell the boy within 14 days whether or not they wish to sign him as a full-time apprentice. If not, the boy is free to sign for another club. If the club makes an offer which does not seem good enough, a boy may sign for another club, but that club must compensate the registering club. The Professional Footballers' Association suggests it is not in boys' best interests to sign as associated schoolboys, but to keep their independence until they are ready to leave school.

Apprenticeships have now been replaced by a YT scheme, with clubs taking some 600 boys a year, not just for football training and formal coaching, but also all-round work experience, and day-release to study at a local college. Boys may be accepted as professional from 17 onwards. The PFA suggests it is still better to stay on at school, or go on to further or higher education. A growing number of boys are joining professional clubs after they have taken a post-school course, or have completed training in something else, and again the PFA recommends this.

Of those who join clubs at 16-plus, at least half are not offered contracts at 18, and a further 25% have left by the age of 21. It is therefore essential to prepare for an alternative career. Release to study is built in to the YT contract, and anyone signing on with a club should have further time for study/training written in to their contract. Some professionals go as far as taking part-time degree courses at local universities or colleges.

Golf

Golf is the major leisure occupation of a great many people for whom it provides both exercise and a hobby. The constant effort to improve their playing takes help from professional coaches, although equipment manufacturers are also making the game easier by improving clubs and balls.

The Professional Golfers' Association has over 5,500 members. Of these, over 2,000 are Class A professionals who operate their own golf clubs and approximately 1,000 are trainees. Membership of the PGA European Tour, which manages the major tournaments (for over £22 million in prize money in 1995), is restricted to 250 professionals (of those who want to compete, that is). But estimates suggest only 120 or so players make a reasonable living out of tournaments The 40th placed professional earned over £43,000 in 1995. Travelling expenses alone can be £1000 a week with competitions held in 14 different countries. Sponsorship is important and this depends on winning.

While a large part of the club professional's day is spent on the course teaching or playing, as much or even more of their time is spent running the golf shop and repairing and maintaining golf equipment. The pro's income is therefore made up of a very small retainer paid by the club, and the rest from fees for teaching and repairs and from sales in the shop. Time off to play in tournaments has to be agreed with the club. Tournament play takes a very high level of ability indeed, with the right temperament, and golfers have to be able to play well despite crowds and television cameras. Like other sports men and women, golfers must practise continually and stay at peak fitness.

Golf has one advantage over other sports, however, in that it is possible to go on being a professional, although probably not a tournament player, right through working life. While many tournament players turn to teaching after their playing days are over, this is now also becoming a young player's occupation, and a number of schools and centres employ, and train, full-time golf teachers.

Recruitment and entry

Separate for club and teaching work, and tournament playing.

For club professionals, the normal method of entry is employment and training as an assistant with an established club professional. In return for a very low starting wage, assistants are taught workshop practice and helped to improve their game. They also have to help in the workshop and the shop, to clean equipment and do many chores. Training normally lasts about three years, and during that time the assistant gains increasing responsibility for teaching and playing in addition to other duties. All assistants register with the PGA and become provisional members after a trial year. Full membership normally requires three years in employment. The PGA runs an annual course for assistant professionals, emphasising the non-playing aspects of the work.

Many young assistants of course hope to become leading tournament players, and working as an assistant does give plenty of time to practise. However, other entrants prefer to play as amateurs until they can show they have reached championship standard.

For tournament players, membership of the PGA European Tour is via an annual qualifying competition and a challenge tour. The leading 120 qualify automatically as do the top 15 from the Challenge Tour. About 450 players (from all countries) compete in a six-round tournament qualifying school (in Spain) for the other places. The top 40, plus any players who tie, go through. Players will usually have gone taken part in a pre-qualifying school in the UK or Spain. Amateurs turning professional have to be officially scratch handicap to attend the school.

Horse racing

Horse racing is a largely spectator sport, with the main interest very often in betting on the results, rather than in the performance of horse and rider. However, the administration of horse-racing, the management and maintenance of race-courses, the breeding, training and riding of horses and the various services provided by these, employ about 25,000 people in Great Britain, of whom about 5,000 are in racing stables.

Horse racing is a very competitive industry and the success of trainers, and hence their stables, is judged on the number of winners he or she achieves in a season. This, plus the current recession, means that many stables are in grave financial difficulties caused by owners taking away or selling their horses.

A racing stable boss is the trainer and under him or her there may be a staff of Assistant Trainer, Head Lad, Travelling Head Lad and stable staff. Staff may also include jockeys, apprentices, conditional jockeys and amateur riders.

Professional jockeys normally ride in either flat or national hunt (over jumps) races, although a few do both. There are about 140 flat race jockeys, and 450 national hunt. A jockey's time is divided between riding at race meetings, helping to training horses, and travelling from one race meeting to another or to a trainer's stables. Out of season many jockeys ride abroad. It is a very strenuous life, for both male and female jockeys, with some danger of serious injury, especially for national hunt jockeys.

The Jockey Club licenses all riders. Jockeys may not own racehorses or bet, and there are strict Jockey Club rules against selling information or accepting money to ride in any way other than to win.

Recruitment and entry

The normal way to become a jockey, if you already have experience in looking after horses and can ride quite well, is first to be apprenticed to a trainer as a stable 'lad' (the term applies to both sexes). The addresses of trainers can be found in a book called *Horses in Training* or you can write to the National Trainers Federation. Entry is a matter of persuading a trainer of your potential as a jockey, or getting a place at one of the Racing Schools (see below), or obtaining a YT scheme. Around 500 apprentices are in training in any one year, with about 60 boys and girls at most taken on annually. There is no guarantee that, at the end of the five- to seven-year period of indentures, you will qualify as a jockey. Very few in fact make the grade from a stable lad and progress to become a fully fledged jockey. However, there are positions of increasing responsibility to move on to after gaining experience in a racing stable – as a travelling head lad, assistant head lad, head lad, assistant trainer or even trainer.

An apprentice jockey ceases to be an apprentice when he or she has ridden 75 winners or is 24, whichever is the earlier. Without 75 winners before the age of 24 a career as a jockey is most unlikely.

Flat-race jockeys have to be light, and must weigh no more than 9 stone (57 kg), which normally means weighing no more than 7–8 stone (44–51 kg) at 16. Despite this, a jockey must be physically strong, strong enough to control a very strong and high-spirited animal through all the vicissitudes of a race, to win, if possible. Ability to approach (without unsettling) and handle horses, and to ride, good hands and wrists should go without saying, and most top jockeys have a certain 'flair' for winning. National hunt jockeys need similar qualities, but they can be heavier – about 10 stone (63 kg). At 16 they would normally expect to weigh around 8–9 stone (51–57 kg). National hunt jockeys must be able to race over jumps.

Qualifications and training

Most apprentices go to either the British Racing School at Newmarket or the Northern Racing College in Doncaster where they are taught to handle racehorses, racing techniques and trained for work in a racing yard. The primary aim of these two schools is to train stable staff and not jockeys, although lads who ride exceptionally well may become apprentice/conditional jockeys. Trainees are expected to get up early in the morning to look after their horses but they also have practical instruction in riding and stable management together with lectures on horse care, veterinary practice, taking horses to the races, etc. Trainers who want to send apprentices they have already taken on get priority for places, but it is possible to apply direct. The British Racing School trains about 100 students on five nine-week residential courses each year and all students who complete the course satisfactorily are ensured employment with trainers. The Northern Racing School provides 12-week courses for up to 100 young people a year. Courses at both schools lead to National Vocational Qualifications in Racehorse Care and Management at Level 2. There is also an NVQ Level 3 which may be taken in employment. (Racing yards may apply to have a senior member of staff – usually the head lad – trained as a workplace assessor).

Normally a licence is given to those showing real aptitude for riding between the ages of 16 and 20. They are then called 'Apprentice' jockeys on the flat and 'Conditional' jockeys in jump racing. Apprentice and Conditional jockeys have a weight allowance when riding in races to compensate for lack of experience. Once a jockey's licence is obtained this allowance can no longer be claimed and the new young jockey must take their chance in a very competitive world.

The failure rate is high, mostly because apprentices grow unexpectedly. However, apprentices who are good riders but too heavy for the flat can change to national hunt racing. Only about 340 apprentices are licensed to ride (and usually not until they have been apprentices for at least two years).

Apprentices work very hard. Work starts very early and ends late, with afternoons and one day a fortnight free. Apprentices are taught how to care for horses, to groom and exercise them, to care for and use riding tackle, and also, of course, how to ride. Once an apprentice shows promise, he or she is entered for apprentices' races, of which there are about 100 every year. Apprentices go with horses to race meetings to care for them both in transit and at the meeting.

Other possible jobs in horse racing are working on a stud farm where racehorses are bred and reared, or in the administration office of a yard.

See also WORK WITH ANIMALS.

Further information

The National Trainers' Federation, the British Horseracing Board.

Ice skating

In the 1980s more skating rinks were built as part of multiplex leisure complexes to meet the increased demand, but popularity now seems to have peaked and further expansion is unlikely. Most of the country's rinks have instructors, although they are usually self-employed. A very few skaters manage to turn professional, mostly to work in the entertainment industry.

Motor-cycle sport

The Auto-Cycle Union is the governing body for motor cycle sport and oversees the four different disciplines within it. Grasstrack and Speedway is the biggest section with the most money to be made. There are 19 clubs which each race teams of seven full-time professionals. This means that there are approximately 133 full-time, professional speedway riders. Permits are issued by the Speedway Control Board. The remaining three disciplines are: Road Racing, Trials and Enduro and Moto Cross. Each one supports about 50 full-time riders.

Most riders start as amateurs, either scrambling or in grass-tracking (speedway on grass). Some speedway tracks give novices a chance to use their own machines, but competition for entry to the tracks' teams and training squads (who have coaching schemes) is fierce and requires contacts and/or proven ability on the grass track.

Motor sport

Motor sport has two main elements: motor racing (the various formulas in circuit racing) and rally driving.

Motor racing supports about 24 professional Formula One drivers of all nationalities. It is a very expensive sport and, unless the driver has an independent income, requires sponsorship or support of some kind from motor or component manufacturers, or other commercial interests.

Rally driving accounts for 70% of organised motor sport events. It is anticipated that there will be an increase in interest since the British driver Colin McCrae became the 1995–6 World Rally Champion. Rally driving is not as expensive to make a start in as motor racing since drivers can initially use their own cars.

All British drivers have to be licensed by the RAC Motor Sports Association (RAC MSA), which requires evidence of ability. Most drivers begin as amateurs and demonstrate their skills at race school, through rally driving and events, or by renting a racing car.

There are about 750 registered motor clubs and about 30,000 individuals hold Competition Licences. Motor sport employs around 100,000 people in Britain – as truck drivers, mechanics, engineers, tyre fitters, electricians, salespeople, secretaries, and in public relations, administration and planning. It has a total turnover of £1.3 billion.

Rugby

Rugby Union football went professional in August 1995. This step has not, however, affected the prospects of players as much as those who play rugby league (*see below*). According to the Rugby Football Union, only ten of the first division clubs have many professional players, and of those only the top 1% of players, who also play for England, make a full-time living from the game. The remaining players continue to hold day jobs and play in their spare time. The Association thinks that in due course sponsorship will be introduced and then more clubs will be able to pay professional players.

Rugby League saw enormous changes in 1996. The British game's 32 clubs are divided into three divisions – Super League, Division One and Division Two. A team from Paris also competes in the Super League which was launched in March 1996. The playing season has been switched from winter to late March – September.

The introduction of the Super League has attracted a television contract of £87 million. Sponsorship deals have increased with the result that clubs are generally more wealthy and able to pay players more. The result is that nearly all players are now professionals. This is important since more demanding and structured training makes it virtually impossible to pursue full-time employment.

Tennis

Tennis is an 'open' sport, with no distinction between amateur and professional status, and played equally by male and female, so any player can compete for prize money. Only a limited number of full-time professionals can make a living, and to stay in the game demands a punishing schedule of matches throughout the world, some played indoors. British tennis players, with a few notable exceptions, have not done very well on the international circuits, but that is no reason why any talented youngster should not attempt it.

To become a professional means starting to play seriously by the age of seven or eight. Reaching international standard is, however, extremely hard work and requires expert tuition as well as the resources to live while training. Young players can try for first county, regional, then national training schemes in Great Britain, but these, and the key junior tournaments, are by invitation. There are also private training schemes. Training abroad, for example, in the USA, may be necessary, and some young players gain scholarships to study and train there.

Wrestling

Wrestling is primarily an amateur sport, but there is a professional circuit of 'all-in' wrestlers, most of whom began as amateurs and are prepared to combine a flair for showmanship with wrestling skills.

Further information

The Sports Councils and the governing bodies of individual sport.

Ground maintenance/groundsmanship

Some 100,000 or so professional groundsmen/women (plus a further 50,000 or so casual workers), according to the Institute of Groundsmanship, care for over 300,000 acres of sports grounds provided by local authorities, professional and other sports clubs, universities and other educational institutions, and commercial/industrial firms.

Grounds staff make and maintain, for example, cricket squares, tennis courts, football and rugby pitches, golf courses and bowling greens. Sports grounds of all kinds are being used more and more intensively and players and spectators alike demand pitches of peak perfection. To achieve this ground staff have to combine traditional skills with modern scientific techniques, and know how best to use the sophisticated machinery and horticultural products.

In large organisations the grounds staff may just look after the pitches, but in some they may also look after surrounding gardens, help organise events, or run pavilion facilities as well. In a broader sense groundsmanship is a specialist branch of amenity HORTICULTURE (*see in* LAND USE INDUSTRIES). Some posts provide work for husband-and-wife teams and housing is available. The main employers are private sports clubs, horticultural contractors, local authority parks and recreation and leisure departments, schools and colleges.

There are opportunities for promotion, particularly with qualifications of the Institute of Groundsmanship, but these are likely to be in the more general area of managing leisure facilities.

Qualifications and training

Professional courses

While most training is 'on-the-job', the Institute of Groundsmanship sets a series of professional examinations, with a national practical certificate, a national technical certificate, an intermediate and a national diploma in the science and practice of turf culture and sports-ground management. There are no formal entry requirements.

BTEC/SCOTVEC and other courses

There are also a BTEC National Diploma in Horticulture (specialising in turf science and sports ground management of amenity horticulture, and a National Certificate in Horticulture (options in groundsmanship, greenkeeping and sportsground management) awarded by the National Examinations Board for Agriculture, Horticulture and Allied industries.

There are also six HNDs in Golf Course Studies and Greenkeeping.

SCOTVEC National Certificates include modules in greenkeeping and groundsmanship.

National Vocational Qualifications

NVQ/SVQs in Amenity Horticulture (Greenkeeping, Sports Turf, Sports Ground Maintenance) are in place at Level 2.

Further information

The Institute of Groundsmanship.

Coaching, instructing, leading, teaching

These have offered only slender career prospects in the past, with the great majority of coaches working on a voluntary basis, but official promotion of sport for all, and expansion in the number of multi-purpose and specialist sports centres have led to a steady increase in the number of posts for trained and qualified coaches and instructors. Of course in the major professional sports, such as football, cricket, and golf, every club has always had full-time coaches (see sections on individual sports above), and in sports where there has always been a strong commercial interest, instructors are generally employed – particularly in skating, in ski-ing in Scotland, and in horse riding. Coaches instruct at all levels from beginners to top competitors but in professional coaching the coach tends to be judged by results.

The national governing bodies of sport usually employ coaches on fixed salaries and contracts but the amount will vary depending on the popularity of a sport, its media coverage, and how well a team or individual is performing.

National and regional sports centres employ their own full-time instructors and coaches and some centres employ part-time coaches for those who use the facilities in their leisure time. The larger multi-purpose sports centres may have a complement of between 15 and 20 full-time coaches, and 24 or more part-time staff. The 'mix' of coaches employed will obviously depend on the facilities offered by a centre, but it seems prospects are improving, especially for those able to instruct and coach in swimming, squash, tennis, golf, water sports of all kinds, table tennis, badminton, and the martial arts. However, financial cutbacks may limit the ability of a centre to continue to offer sports with high equipment replacement costs, i.e. trampolining.

Coaches may also be employed in holiday camps and private hotels, with some sports goods manufacturers, and in outdoor pursuit centres.

Instructors in outdoor activities, like climbing, canoeing, sub-aqua, ski-ing, and yachting, are also employed by Outward Bound schools and outdoor pursuits centres (such as the National Centre for Mountain Activities at Plas Y Brenin and the National Watersports Centre at Plas Menai), but in fairly small numbers. However, there has been an upsurge in private holiday companies selling outdoor sporting and adventure holidays, like river rafting, ballooning, hang gliding, canoeing, mountaineering, skiing, sub-aqua, etc. and this plus the opening of a new market which uses outdoor centres for specialist management training, has meant an increase in demand for suitably qualified instructors and leaders. Many of these opportunities are likely to be seasonal.

Outdoor pursuits have no clearly defined career structure, although recently the Outward Bound Schools have started to initiate career progression schemes to remedy this. However, progress is still largely through personal interest and endeavour and practical experience to develop professional expertise. The British Mountaineering Council and the Mountain Leader Training Board, for example, run courses in mountaineering and mountain leadership, as do many of the other governing bodies in outdoor pursuits. A recognised practical skills qualification is important and can provide a stepping stone into employment in outdoor pursuits, but often the employers will look for a positive interest in education as well. Teachers who have qualified in outdoor pursuits on teacher training courses may have some advantage.

There are approximately 30,000 Physical Education teachers in schools and colleges in England according to the DfEE. It is important to understand, however, that physical education is not the same as sport although clearly there is an inter-relationship between them. A good physical education programme provides the base line from which sporting activities can flourish and excellence emerge.

The National Curriculum concentrates on laying a foundation of skills in a range of physical activities that will help pupils to specialise later. Teachers have to be prepared to teach one other subject in secondary schools and in primary schools the full range of subjects have to be taught. *See also* EDUCATION AND TEACHING.

Recruitment and entry

Coaches, instructors and leaders will normally require training and qualifications appropriate to the sport(s) concerned. Coaches and instructors are usually also expected to be extremely good at their sport and it is, of course, one way of financing a career as a sports competitor, particularly working part-time. All qualified sports coaches become members of their professional body – the British Institute of Sports Coaches.

A recognised teaching qualification is normally required for teaching in schools.

Qualifications and training

Professional bodies

Education and training for teachers, and coaches and instructors for some sports and employers, have been well established for some years. Efforts to improve training standards throughout sport are now being made, and a National Coaching Foundation established. The Foundation runs a series of study and training programmes for all coaches, whatever their sport or level of experience.

Every sport has its regulating body, and these set the appropriate training requirements and examinations for instructors and coaches.

The CCPR (Central Council of Physical Recreation) Sports Leaders Award is a non-professional course intended for voluntary helpers of sports clubs and youth clubs. It is a structured training scheme supported by the governing bodies of sport, who form an integral part of the award. Although it has no direct job opportunities, sports leaders have been able to find employment in some sports centres.

There are specific degree courses in Sports Coaching at Liverpool John Moore's and at Nottingham Trent Universities plus an HND at Nottingham Trent and an HND in Sports Science (Outdoor Activities) at the University of Glamorgan.

National Vocational Qualifications

The governing bodies of sport and the Central Council of Physical Recreation intend that all coaching/instructing schemes and leadership awards will become National Vocational Qualifications or Scottish Vocational Qualifications. To date the following are established: Sport and Recreation, Level 1; Sport and Recreation Coaching (separate awards for coaching adults, children and participants with disabilities), Level 3; Sport and Recreation Coaching and Activity Delivery (separate awards for coaching adults and children); Sport and Recreation Coaching, Level 4 and Sport and Recreation, Outdoor Education, Level 3.

Degree and postgraduate level courses

There are a range of Physical Education, Human Movement Studies and Sports Science BEd, BA, BSc, Diploma and Postgraduate courses for intending teachers and those interested in studying sport. For these and other courses in the field of sport and recreation, including related courses such as Sports Podiatry and Sports Physiotherapy, the best source is probably a booklet published by the Sports Council called *Careers in Sport* and a series of leaflets called 'Careers in Sport' from the Scottish Sports Council.

Further information

The Sports Council, National Coaching Foundation, British Institute of Sports Coaches, National Association for Outdoor Education.

Other sports-related careers

The prison service – the armed services – health and fitness – sports medicine and therapy – research and consultancy – sales and sponsorship – journalism

The prison service

The prison service looks for officers who have an active interest in sport and physical recreation although no particular qualifications in these are specified.

Officers who complete all stages of initial professional training can join the physical education staff at an establishment. *See* THE PRISON SERVICE *in* SECURITY AND PROTECTIVE SERVICES.

The Armed Forces

The Royal Air Force recruits at two levels. Physical Education Officers (PEdO), are recruited with a BEd or related degree with Physical Education as its main component, or with a postgraduate certificate in Education (PGCE).

Physical Training Instructors (PTI) are recruited to follow an intensive 26-week course at the RAF School of Physical Training, RAF Cosford. This course prepares them for a non-commissioned officer (NCO) post managing physical education activities on RAF stations.

The Royal Navy takes volunteers between 18–25 from other branches of the Royal Navy to become Physical Trainers. After a six-month training course a physical trainer can expect to instruct, promote, organise and control physical training, sport, recreation and Outward Bound type of activities at sea and on land.

The Army runs a School of Physical Training at Aldershot. Training lasts for one year and then Instructors work as physical fitness and adventure training advisers throughout the Army. They may also work in hospitals and rehabilitation units.

After leaving the forces instructors often find employment as coaches.

See also THE ARMED FORCES.

Health and fitness

For many years specialist centres combining health and beauty have existed but during the 1980s there has been an increasing emphasis on health and the need to be physically fit. In 1996 the most frequently practised sports were mainly those generally associated with a healthy lifestyle – athletics/jogging, gymnastics/indoor athletics and walking, while swimming became the most popular indoor sport.

Many local authorities provide a good range of gym equipment and facilities and have encouraged aerobics and weight training, while in the private sector, health and fitness clubs or studios have increased rapidly, particularly in the hotel industry, where the provision of health and fitness facilities – a gym and pool – have greatly improved the weekend trade. In the Barbican complex in the City of London an American company has set up a large prestigious health and fitness studio. Fitness is now big business.

The health and fitness industry is becoming increasingly professional with well qualified instructors and often a commitment to further training for its staff.

One of the market leaders in providing health and fitness is a company called Fitness For Industry (FFI) which started in 1981 in the corporate sector to provide health and fitness facilities in companies and the House of Commons. It linked up with the hotel group Forte and now has numerous corporate clubs and clubs in hotels.

Health clubs and fitness centres may look for degrees or BTEC/SCOTVEC and other qualifications such as the RSA/Sports Council Validated Basic Certificate in the Teaching of Exercise-to-Music, the British Amateur Weight Lifters' Association Instructors Certificate or the Royal Life Savers Society Pool and Lifeguard Bronze Medallion. Qualifications in more traditional types of exercise are offered by organisations like the Keep Fit Association. A certificate in Exercise and Health Studies is offered by the Physical Education Association and the YMCA offers a variety of modular courses in aerobics, exercise and fitness.

Sports medicine and therapy

The NHS has various sports injury clinics and there are also private clinics, hydros and clubs. Doctors and consultants must qualify as doctors first before secondment to a NHS sports injury clinic. *See* MEDICAL AND DENTAL PROFESSIONS. There are a few postgraduate courses which can lead to a diploma in sports medicine.

Qualified PHYSIOTHERAPISTS (*see in* SUPPLEMENTARY HEALTH PROFESSIONS) may work in clubs, particularly professional football clubs, on a full-time or part-time basis, or practise privately. There are increasing opportunities to work sessions in both private sector and local authority owned gyms and health clubs.

Sports therapy is a growing field whose main concerns are to prevent injury and to improve and maintain physical performance. Sports therapists need a good grounding in anatomy and physiology, a range of techniques such as relaxation and massage, and they need to know how to plan and put together an exercise programme.

Until recently there has been no specific training and qualifications for sports therapy and individuals have come from a variety of backgrounds, e.g. physiotherapy, success in the field of sport, or through an interest in health and beauty. However, Vocational Awards International, which incorporates the Institute of Sports Therapy, specifically covers sports therapy. Their qualifications include various modular courses leading to:

- International Health and Sports Diploma
- International Master's Diploma in Sports Therapy
- First Aid and Sports Massage Certificates and the Finnish Sauna Diploma

The International Therapy Examination Council (ITEC) schools and colleges run courses leading to a Sports Therapy Certificate or Diploma.

Further information

Vocational Training Charitable Trust, International Institute of Sports Therapy and International Therapy Examination Council.

See also BEAUTY *in* PERSONAL SERVICES.

Research and consultancy

Graduates in sports science may be able to research into human performance and capability, into equipment manufacture, or acting as a consultant in a sports club.

Sales and sponsorship

Many manufacturers and retailers of sports goods employ people with an interest in sport. Some companies specialise in sports promotion or sponsorship and here an interest in sport plus business qualifications and experience is useful.

Journalism

A sports journalist usually trains as a journalist before specialising in writing for the sports page. Entry may be more flexible for periodical journalism.

Recreation and leisure industries

Background – administering and managing for leisure and recreation – recruitment and entry – qualifications and training – further information

Background

It is virtually impossible to define leisure and recreation. Any attempt to do so founders on what any one individual sees as recreational. While to one man or woman DIY or digging the garden may be a terrible chore, to another it is a welcome change of activity and a pleasurable way to spend time. People relax with books, music, films on video, at the theatre, watching sport, playing golf, going to a museum, walking a nature trail, taking photos, visiting a historic house or ancient monument, staying at a hotel for a weekend, camping, having a meal at a restaurant. Many of the other careers in this book, then, contribute to leisure and recreational services – the media, museums, libraries, hotels and catering, professional sport, forestry and tourism play their part in the leisure industries too.

The leisure industry is very volatile – the history of the cinema is a case in point For example, in the 1950s, cinema admissions were on average twenty-six million people a week whereas by 1984 they were down to just over one million a week. This period of steady decline meant the industry reacted to falling attendances by closing cinemas. However, during the last few years the video revolution has led to renewed demand for watching films on the 'big-screen' so surviving cinemas have been converted to multiple screens and new 'multiplex' entertainment centres with eight–ten screen cinemas are now (1996) springing up all over the country. Another major mass leisure activity in the 1950s was spectating at professional football matches, but now three times as many people watch football on television regularly as go to 'live' football. Leisure demand may expand very quickly, providing rapid growth for a company supplying that market, but the risk is always there that the demand will disappear just as quickly. New technology can create a new leisure demand, for instance microelectronics and computer games, but it is difficult to predict which will continue to survive.

A wide range of recreation and leisure activities and facilities are almost taken for granted, even though some of the major providers, dependent on public funding, cannot now spend at the levels of previous years. That recreation is 'one of the community's everyday needs', that people have more time for leisure activities (for whatever reason), and that the leisure industries can provide more jobs are not questioned. Evidence suggests people want to spend more time doing something active, less sitting and, say, watching television. Many people too are more interested in improving their health, with official encouragement. But they want their healthy activities to be interesting, and something that can be done with friends and/or families. What interests them changes all the time and the changes in the age profile of the population, with more retired people, will also affect developments.

Local authorities have in the past made the largest capital investment in purpose-built facilities for recreation, especially for sport and other outdoor activities, and many are responsible too for so-called 'resource-based' activities, activities which need parks and other open spaces, sea and rivers, etc. Despite financial restrictions, most expect to continue to find ways to expand and improve their facilities and services. Local authority recreation departments mainly respond to what the community wants, but also see such expenditure as a way of attracting income – firms, tourists, etc. – to the area, particularly where job losses have been severe.

However, the Government's Compulsory Competitive Tendering (CCT) legislation was extended to the management of local authority sport and leisure facilities under the 1988 Local Government Act in October 1989. This means that in some areas, although the local authority still owns these facilities, they are now run by private contractors rather than local government employees. Where recreation facilities are run by private companies, the emphasis may change, e.g. expanding profit-making facilities and cutting back on the less profitable. Local authorities may well be restricted too or unable to make investment in recreation facilities because of controls on local authority capital expenditure.

The private sector is the other major provider and the list of activities is a long one. It includes leisure and amusement parks, bowling alleys, casinos, bingo halls (4.5 million people play bingo), night-clubs, zoos, country clubs, billiard halls, golf courses, horse riding, ice rinks, discothèques, squash courts, public houses, and a host more.

It tends to be dominated by a few large groups. For example, in August 1995 the Rank Organisation opened its sixth multi-leisure centre, Leisure World, in Hemel Hempstead – the largest leisure and entertainment complex of its kind in Europe. The organisation also acquired night-clubs in Stockton and Bradford, and opened new clubs in Huddersfield and Walsall. New bingo clubs were opened in Leeds, Huddersfield, St Helens, Oldbury and Glasgow. They are currently developing holiday villages and a 'virtual world' entertainment centre at the Trocadero in London. In 1995 Rank employed 37,252 people in total in the UK, Europe, and North America and had a profit before tax of £407 million. (This was broken down as £82 million, cinemas, studios, videos; £50 million, gaming and bingo; £69 million cafes, and discos; £63 million, holidays.)

Other large groups may be primarily associating with brewing or hotels – Bass Leisure or Grand Metropolitan – or a particular sector of the industry – Ladbrokes (betting), Granada (broadcasting) – but most big leisure companies have diversified their interests. A high proportion of private-sector leisure organisations, however, are small companies, trusts and owner-proprietors, only some of them – an estimated 4,000 – with managerial and other help. They include, for instance, over 300 owners of historic homes and gardens who open them to the public.

Holiday organisations cater for the active and particularly children, with sports (including coaching 'schools' for e.g. tennis), pony-trekking, walking, canoeing, etc. All these organisations clearly see profits to be made from the leisure and recreation industry, but have to be constantly on the watch for changing public interest, effects of new technology, etc.

Between local authorities and commercial firms come a range of other providers and provision. While great numbers of voluntary clubs, societies, etc. organise all kinds of activities, those which employ staff are concentrated mainly in sports like bowls, squash, golf, sailing. Universities and colleges of higher education all provide sports facilities, with staff to run them, and some have professionally managed arts centres also. Most larger industrial and commercial firms provide sports and other recreational facilities for their staff. Other organisations either wholly, or partly, concerned with leisure and recreational activities include outdoor pursuits and adventure centres, the Youth Hostels Association, FORESTRY (*see in* LAND USE INDUSTRIES) and THE WATER INDUSTRY (*see in* CAREERS IN CONSERVATION AND THE ENVIRONMENT), British Waterways Board (developing canals for leisure as well as commercial use and hiring out its own fleet of narrow boats), and many of the organisations whose primary interest is in conservation.

Finally, administration of recreation and leisure facilities also includes the quasi-independent bodies which channel government funds, attempt co-ordination, forward planning, etc. and act as focal points for all kinds of pressure both upwards and outwards to improve, develop, and rationalise facilities, etc. These include the four sports councils, the organisations listed under ARTS ADMINISTRATION in the PERFORMING ARTS chapter, and the governing bodies of individual sports and other leisure/recreational activities.

Sports facilities expanded rapidly during the 1980s, and development continues, if at a slower rate. Ten national sports centres (six in England, two in Scotland, one in Wales and one in Northern Ireland) have now been built (1996). In 1994 there were 1,500 public indoor sports centres in the UK and 1,300 public indoor pools. Community use of school facilities has also increased. In 1994 there were 3,182 swimming pools in schools in England.

A number of national sports 'arenas' are now being planned involving government, local authorities and commercial developers. Local sports centres range from the very large and purpose-built such as Ponds Forge in Sheffield down to school sports facilities which can be used by the public. Centres include those at Crystal Palace in south London (a national athletics and swimming centre providing for a range of indoor sports), the Picketts Lock complex stretching 23 miles from Ware in Hertfordshire to the Thames – over 10,000 acres – with facilities for almost every kind of land and water sport), the Holme Pierrepoint National Water Sports Centre built from worked-out gravel pits near Nottingham (with a 2,000-metre rowing and canoeing course, a 2.2m 'white-water' canoe slalom course, water-ski-ing lagoon, facilities for power boating, angling and model boating), the National Sports Centre for Wales in Cardiff, and three mountaineering centres (one in Wales, one in Scotland and one in Northern Ireland).

Arts facilities, including the growing number of arts centres, are also part of the leisure and recreation scene. They range from the huge modern Barbican Centre in the City of London (which houses a resident orchestra, a theatrical company, library, art gallery, exhibition areas and a music/drama school), and the older South Bank complex, to adapted Victorian premises (formerly a teacher training college) in a small northern city. Most are local authority owned and administered, and have developed from the tradition of municipal theatres, on which many such centres are based. In some local authorities the emphasis has been changing, from providing facilities where the public can only watch, see or listen to, professional performers, to creating conditions for the community itself to take part in a range of activities. Many authorities also put on programmes of popular and classical music, carnivals, street entertainments, events for public holidays, special programmes, and so on.

Commercial facilities for leisure, sports and the arts are not usually so large or multi-purpose, concentrating on specific activities – cinemas, bingo halls, health clubs, gymnasiums, skating rinks, golf courses, marinas, etc. Sometimes they occupy large multiplex sites but each leisure facility is usually run as a separate business.

A 'day out' has become increasingly important and a major comparative recent development has been the creation of 'theme' parks. They may have evolved from zoos or safari parks, fun fairs, amusement arcades, or country estates, and themes may include historical, the wild west or be based on Disney characters. All of these give access to a great variety of rides and facilities.

Since 1992 European operators like Center Parcs (self-catering holiday accommodation in 'villages' in scenic areas) and Accor Hotels have invested in the UK.

Administering and managing for leisure and recreation

Comprehensive leisure and recreational facilities of the kind which have been developing since the 1960s need professional administration and management. Resources have to be high standard, and such finance as is available used to maximum effect. Sports centres, etc. are costly to build and have increasingly expensive and sophisticated technical equipment. Some facilities have been under-used, suggesting poor planning and/or marketing. Running costs have been too high, and need more efficient and tighter control. One of the aims of Compulsory Competitive Tendering is to make local authorities more commercially oriented with quality management and customer service which (hopefully) will provide a well balanced innovative programme providing the needs of the local community as well as expanding commercial opportunities. Natural facilities – rocks for climbing, paths for walking, picnic sites, etc. in conservation areas – are easily damaged by wrong or over use, and must be as efficiently managed as more apparently expensive centres. Ensuring the safety of participants and spectators also requires effective management.

Professional administration and management have been slow to develop though, with some resistance to more formal methods. This has been largely overcome, and all kinds of organisation are developing better management methods. The Sport Council is, for example, committed to improving the quality of recreation management. It has monitored the usage, income, cost and energy efficiency of sports halls, having developed a design and construction package for a high-standard 'off the peg' sports hall.

The great variety in leisure/recreation providers (i.e. employers) and services makes a single, one-structure recreation-management function almost impossible, and people in it are still coming to terms with the resulting problems in hammering out a professional 'profile'. It has to be multi-structured and multi-disciplinary. Recreation management in any one organisation may involve a single activity (e.g. swimming, golf, bird-watching), several activities in one area (e.g. sport), or activities across a range of different types of activity. Providing leisure activity may be the primary purpose of the organisation, it may be one of several which are equally important, or it may be subsidiary to the main activity of e.g. a water authority, and may then involve constant problems of reconciling conflicting interests as in, for instance, the national parks.

Recreation managers have to work within established organisational structures. Currently many live within the framework of local authorities (*see* LOCAL GOVERNMENT), working for the community; others work for firms – or themselves – where achieving a profit is the dominant purpose, yet others for organisations where conservation is the over-riding aim, so leisure facilities have to be controlled and the public educated in their use.

Recreation managers, then, are not just people who see that the grass is cut, the pool water purified. They are not land agents or landscapers, although land management and advising on aspects of landscaping may be part of the job. Some local authorities include amenity horticulture within recreational management, and this can extend to, e.g. improving cemeteries. They have to cope with a great variety of tasks. Planning, finance, marketing and advertising, personnel management, negotiating, organising, leading may be involved. They may have to administer catering services and bars, shops, and coaching as well as the actual recreational facilities. Employers put great emphasis on skills common to any area of management – the ability to select and handle staff, financial skills – budgeting and accounting – and general business skills, including marketing and promotion, both for the public and private sector. Even the Sports Council talks of 'corporate' planning. Recreation managers are expected to understand and use modern management techniques – OR, O&M, 'critical path analysis', statistical research methods, etc. – just like managers in any other sector.

In local authorities, swimming pools, squash courts, parks and playing fields, climbing walls, ice rinks, even libraries and cemeteries, are administered by single, large recreation and leisure departments. They can have several hundred staff, organised as a single directorate, but divided by service, with recreation as one of several sections. Many people administering 'multidisciplinary' recreation departments in local authorities probably still see themselves as librarians or entertainments officers although some are career administrators, and people are now coming up to the top who began their careers in broader sports/leisure centre administration.

The range of jobs in recreation/leisure is enormous, often with little in common between them. It is only really possible to give some general pointers. The main opportunities are in individual centres, or the relevant central department, which looks after overall planning, budgeting and policy, and may also manage some facilities and services, e.g. playing fields and bowling greens, or festivals.

Even the largest multi-purpose sports/leisure centre has a full-time, permanent staff of less than 100, probably a third of whom are administrators and full-time coaches (the rest include attendants, groundsmen, catering staff) –

although more, including coaches, will be employed part-time.

The general manager implements policy, deals with accounts and budgets and has overall supervision. They will also be responsible for ensuring that health and safety regulations are adhered to and equipment checked regularly. They must have an eye to commercial ventures = hiring the halls and car parks out for weddings, birthdays or special events like karaoke, concerts, craft fairs, conferences, and quiz shows, and, where possible, negotiate for sponsorship of events. They will also be responsible for promoting their centre through talks to schools, colleges and clubs.

'Middle managers' look after the general administration (e.g. bookings, reception, sports shop), catering, or buildings and grounds. A team (three or four) of assistant managers or recreation officers promote resources, monitor demand, supervise coaching, or may look after a group of activities/sports, planning programmes and events, liaising with promoters, local clubs, etc., seeing that equipment is available and maintained, etc.

'Recreation assistants' deal directly with the public, supervise activities (e.g. a swimming pool or squash courts), coping with problems and emergencies on the ground, etc.

In smaller centres, commercial units, university or college sports departments, etc., fewer managers/administrators take on several functions, and this often means combining administration with, e.g., coaching.

Leisure/sports facilities are, by definition, used at times when people are not working, so staff running facilities have to expect 'unsocial' hours and shift work.

There are a lot of bodies concerned with administration and advice in the sports fields. Some of these may be fairly major employers such as the Sports Council, with a staff in 1996 of 450 people. However, many of them will only have a small secretariat of administrators.

Recruitment and entry

With the wide variety of opportunities there is no single, straightforward route into leisure administration and management. Recruitment has, in the past, not normally been directly from the education system, and a high proportion of people are recruited on the basis of a training and/or specialist skills relevant to the organisation – PE teaching, swimming-pool administration, or horticulture for local authorities for instance, rather than business training. Backgrounds in professional sport, landscape architecture, hotel management, tourism, prison work or the armed forces, have been common.

The pattern of recruitment is changing, though, with more people taken on straight from school and higher/further education. Probably most professional leaders/managers will in future come from among people who have completed post A-level higher/further education, but it is possible to start at the bottom at 16/17 with some GCSE/SCE passes, to train on-the-job and gain relevant qualifications. This would mean starting in a 'basic' job on a trainee grade, e.g. trainee gardener, trainee chef, trainee recreation assistant, etc., LOCAL GOVERNMENT administrative trainee, or going through a relevant YT scheme.

Some larger commercial firms and local authorities recruit graduates as trainee managers (starting in smaller units), whatever their degree subject/background. First jobs in smaller, poorer organisations are another way in. However, relevant training, and background (as a participant and/or e.g. unpaid experience running a club or society, or as a play-group leader), is a great advantage, and for some posts essential. A business/management qualification would also be useful.

Qualifications and training

Major efforts are being made by the Institute of Leisure and Amenity Management (ILAM) to develop comprehensive education and training for the leisure business. The aim is to develop training and courses for a single, multidisciplinary leisure and recreation profession, with encouragement for proper training 'pathways' for management, and training for related specialist professions (e.g. PE, community education, tourism, hospitality management, arts, libraries, museums) that includes a distinct element of general leisure and recreation training.
The following courses are provided:

School leavers

For school leavers of 16+ with few qualifications –

City & Guilds Recreation & Leisure Studies
City & Guilds Management of Tourist Attractions
City & Guilds Visitor Attraction Operations (for those working in box offices, shops, historic houses, theme parks, etc.).
BTEC First Courses in Leisure Studies, Intermediate GNVQ/GSVQ in Leisure and Tourism.

For school leavers with some qualifications –

GNVQ/GSVQ Advanced Diplomas in Leisure Studies, Countryside Recreation, Exhibition and Museum Design, Performing Arts, or Business and Finance.
SCOTVEC National Certificates include modules in recreation and leisure.

For school leavers with at least one A-level (or equivalent) –

There are numerous Higher National Diplomas and Higher National Certificates in Leisure Studies, some of which have specialised options. Examples include: arts and entertainment, travel and tourism and recreation and sport, or an HND in Science and Management of Health and Fitness (Farnborough College), Leisure Studies (Waterbased Recreation at Southampton Institute), Recreation Leadership (Leeds Metropolitan University), Sports and Recreation Management (Exeter College). The slant of some courses is recognisable from their title – but there is an increasing number of courses simply called Leisure or Recreation Studies. The emphasis of the course can vary from sport to tourism to hospitality management. It cannot, therefore, be too strongly stressed that it is important to check thoroughly the content of any course before making an application.

Degree level courses

Here again there is a vast range of courses in Recreation, Leisure Studies, Ecology, Recreation and Tourism Management, etc. The same remarks apply regarding careful choice of syllabus.

A 'Directory of Higher Education Courses in Leisure Management' is available from ILAM.

Postgraduate level courses

An increasing number of courses in Leisure Management, Recreation Management are now available. They are often taken by graduates with non-relevant first degrees to improve their employment prospects.

For those over 21 there are various open and distance learning courses. There are BTEC Post Experience Courses including the BTEC Continuing Education Certificate in Leisure Management, which has been purpose built by BTEC and ILAM to provide exemption for the professional examinations, and the Certificate in Management Studies.

National Vocational Qualifications

These are now in place as follows: Sport and Recreation Development, Level 3; Sport and Recreation Facility Operations, Level 2; Sport and Recreation Supervision, Level 3; Sport and Recreation Management (Facility or Development), Level 4; Sports Administration, Levels 3 and 4.

See also under THE SPORTS, *above.*

Professional qualifications

The Institute of Leisure and Amenity Management (ILAM) (membership in 1996 about 6,800) has four different qualifications for leisure managers.

A *First Award* is aimed at new entrants to the industry or for people who hold junior positions within leisure organisations. Entry requirements are: appropriate NVQ/SVQs at Level 2, GNVQ/GSVQ Intermediate awards in Leisure and Tourism, First Certificates/Diplomas in Leisure Studies, four GCSE Passes at C and above/S-grades 1–3/General Band 4 or equivalent qualifications.

The *Certificate in Leisure Operations* is for people with a basic understanding of the industry or who hold junior supervisory positions. Entry requirements are: appropriate NVQ/SVQs at Level 3, GNVQ/GSVQ Advanced Diplomas in Leisure and Tourism, National Certificates/Diplomas in Leisure Studies, two A-Levels/three Highers – or one of several equivalent qualifications.

The *Certificate in Leisure Management* is available to holders of HND/C Leisure and/or Recreation awards, business studies graduates and holders of degrees and to holders of HNDs in subjects such as Horticulture, Leisure, Tourism, Events Management *from specified universities and colleges only.* (A list is available from ILAM.)

The *Diploma in Leisure Management* is available to holders of specified degrees from certain institutions. Again a list of approved courses is available from the same source.

All the above qualifications require the completion of a work-based project.

ILAMs latest booklet of guidance to students should be consulted. The Institute also puts on short courses, seminars, and training programmes.

The Institute of Baths and Recreation Management (IBRM) has various technical training schemes.

The National Examination Board for Supervisory Management has a certificate with leisure specialism for supervisors and junior managers.

First-degree courses (as considered relevant within the profession).

See also ARTS ADMINISTRATION *in* THE PERFORMING ARTS; COACHING, INSTRUCTING, LEADING AND TEACHING *above* (for PE courses); HOTELS AND CATERING; *and* THE TRAVEL INDUSTRY.

Further information

The Institute of Leisure and Amenity Management, Institute of Baths and Recreation Management and the Sports Councils.

The Travel Industry

Contents

(CLCI: GAX)

Tourism

Tourism has been one of the fastest growing areas of employment over the last ten years. In the UK, it employs some 1.5 million people (1996). In 1995 tourism to the UK was up by 4%. By the year 2000, tourism is expected to be the largest employer in the world. Travel and tourism are major earners for the country.

Although tourism has become a separate career area, it contains components of other careers, gaining only part of their income from tourists, e.g. CATERING SERVICES. Disneyland in Paris, for example, employs many people in catering jobs such as housekeeping, bartending, etc. as well as having the more obvious tourism jobs.

Tourist boards and other promoters

The British and four national tourist boards, the network of regional organisations (twelve in England, three in Wales) and many local authorities (*see* LOCAL GOVERNMENT), promote holidays in this country, to both British and overseas visitors. Some local authorities have special departments to develop their area's tourist potential and to boost the economy and local jobs market. This has led to posts as Tourist Development Officers in many authorities.

Tourist Boards market an area by using promotional campaigns, advertising, and compiling brochures and also try to have facilities (such as hotels and transport) improved, perhaps also encouraging new attractions in an area.

Tourist Boards also provide a network of Tourist Information Centres (known as TICs), some full-time and others seasonal. Boards have funds to help encourage firms to fill in gaps in services and help develop new ideas to attract visitors. For example, an old industrial site such as a mine might be developed to become a heritage site so people can trace the history of the area. In some of these new developments, former industrial workers such as miners have gained new employment as guides.

The tourist and local authorities involved employ people in MARKETING, PUBLIC RELATIONS, promotion, finance, development work, and as information centre staff. They employ full-time, seasonal and part-time staff.

Recruitment and entry

A high proportion of staff will probably have experience (and qualifications) from elsewhere in tourism, or RECREATION AND LEISURE INDUSTRIES, or in MARKETING or PUBLIC RELATIONS. Tourist Information Centre and administrative staff may be recruited with a reasonable educational background, of three or four GCSEs or equivalent. Senior staff often have a relevant degree or postgraduate qualification.

City & Guilds offer a Certificate of Tourist Information Centre Competence.

Further information

Regional tourist boards or local authorities.

Tourist guides

Tourist guides take tourists around towns, show them the sights or historic buildings and tell them interesting facts about the place. They may escort groups on coach tours, take smaller parties out by car or minibus, or specialise in an area or building that can be covered on foot. Some guides offer specialist theme tours such as Ghost walks or tours for special groups such as young people or children.

Most tourist guides are self-employed, although some tour operators and other organisations hire guides full-time for the tourist season. Some work for organisations owning historic or other places on the tourist routes. Demand for guides fluctuates with the number of tourists, which often depends on currency changes or other political and economic events, and so is unpredictable. It is not easy to get work between November and March or April, which means either earning enough in the summer to cover the winter months, or having a second, winter occupation. Some guides work on a purely voluntary basis.

Recruitment and entry

Entry is very competitive, and means building contacts, and proving reliable, interesting and helpful to tourists. It may be useful to gain experience first with a tour operator. It is essential to have an in-depth, detailed knowledge of several subject areas, a good, clear speaking voice, be relaxed about speaking in public, to be imaginative and humorous, be patient, and good at shepherding groups of people without upsetting them. Fluent languages, especially the less usual ones (e.g. Arabic, Chinese, Japanese), are an advantage.

Qualifications and training

Tourist Board Registered Guides are awarded a 'blue badge'. This is given to those who can pass a written and practical examination showing knowledge of their chosen area. Courses are run by the tourist board or at a local college.

The London Tourist Board and Convention Bureau gives a six-month training for a 'blue badge' that allows holders to work in London. Entry requirements are ability to pass a test on current affairs, history and the Greater London area, previous experience of public speaking and a language.

NVQ/SVQs in Travel Services (guiding services) are available at level 2 and in Travel Services (guiding) at level 4.

Further information

London Tourist Board and Convention Bureau, British Tourist Authority and English Tourist Board or regional tourist boards.

See also CONSERVATION, HOTELS AND CATERING, RECREATION AND LEISURE, MUSEUM WORK, TRANSPORT AND TRAVEL.

The travel industry

The majority of people seeking a holiday will use a travel agent rather than making their own travel arrangements. A travel agent can provide them with attractive packages that are matched to what they can afford, taking advantage of the tour operators' bulk buying. The travel trade is a highly volatile and fiercely competitive business. Predicting travel and holiday business at least a year ahead is difficult and sometimes results in tour operators becoming involved in price wars. Computerised booking systems, allowing travel agencies to deal directly with tour operators and airlines, have increased efficiency and reduced staffing levels.

Travel agents

Travel agents are the retailers, the shop windows of the travel and transport business. They sell tickets for road, rail, coaches and air travel over the counter. Some also issue travellers' cheques and foreign currency. They sell several million package holidays a year, mainly to British people going on holiday abroad. They may make travel arrangements for business people going on perhaps a sales trip or conference. Business travel is often dealt with separately by a Business Travel House. They sell holiday lettings in villas, and other self-catering accommodation. They arrange more complicated tours and other travel arrangements for people either travelling independently or in a group. They work out travel arrangements so that people can spend as much or as little time as they wish in particular places, check all the connections, arrange hotels and sightseeing trips, etc.

The number of travel agencies has been growing steadily since the 1980s, and is now estimated at 7,000 (1996) (up from 6,300 in 1992).

The organisation of the work depends on the size of the agency – in larger agencies it is often divided, while a few people may do everything in a smaller outlet. Most jobs in travel agencies are for clerical and counter staff. Most start as a junior doing clerical work, checking availability of flights on the computer, making simple bookings, keeping records, dealing with documentation, checking timetables, and ordering currency. They usually move quite quickly to more complex bookings and into counter work. This can be on simpler services, like arranging a flight to Glasgow, or finding brochures for people. More experienced staff help people choose holidays and arrange more complicated itineraries. Counter staff have to deal with payments, visas, currency and be able to advise on vaccinations, insurance, etc. Some agencies specialise in travel arrangements for companies and are known as business travel houses. All staff must have the ability to communicate effectively in order to sell their products.

Trained and experienced counter staff have fair chances of going on to supervisory and managerial work in the office or branch. Managing a travel agency outlet is very like RETAIL MANAGEMENT – meeting budgets, deciding which products, i.e. holiday packages, will sell in the area and marketing them, being aware of what is on offer (e.g. the latest TV advertising campaign) and preparing to deal with demand, coping with staffing, accounts, problems with computer links and telephones, etc. Promotion, for a few, may be to head office of a travel agency chain, in for example MARKETING, but specialist qualifications are needed for functions such as FINANCE.

Recruitment and entry

Most people enter as juniors at 16 or 17 years on a Training Programme organised by the Travel Training Company (TTC) formerly the ABTA National Training Board. There are no prescribed entry requirements but personality, enthusiasm and a good grasp of maths and English are important. You will be dealing with the public both on the telephone and face to face. The ability to cope with detail and accuracy is important. It is worthwhile starting with an ABTA (Association of British Travel Agents) member who is committed to providing training.

The Travel Training Company operates a nationwide 24-month Travel Training Programme (about 1,000 places on 40 courses). Recruitment is via travel agents, and some of the larger groups are taking on trainees only via the Travel Training Programme. Some 98% of trainees gain full-time employment in the industry.

Larger travel agencies and tour operators may recruit a very small number of graduate and other trainees for, e.g.

MARKETING or ACCOUNTANCY, and people with relevant professional qualifications are recruited for specific vacancies.

Qualifications and training

Training is largely on the job and often the trainee is allowed study time while in the office to work through self-study packs especially written by the TTC. Larger companies may provide in-house training themselves. Other study may be by distance learning or part-time release to college. Some agencies offer study trips abroad for their trainees.

Qualifications (some leading to membership of the Institute of Travel and Tourism) include –

NVQ/SVQs in Travel Services:
- Level 1, 2 and 3 specialising in Leisure, Business, Tour Operations, Resort Representatives and Guiding and Interpreting.
- Level 3 and 4 Supervisory and Management are also available covering all areas above

ABTAC:
- At Primary and Advanced level this is designed as a stand-alone qualification and to underpin the NVQ/SVQs. A written examination offered at FE colleges.

There are some additional qualifications available for more specialised areas in the industry. They are all offered through the CGLI:

- Introduction to Tourism in the UK
- Certificate in Tourist Information Centre Competence
- Certificate in Visitor Attraction Operations
- Certificate in Farm Tourism

School and FE college courses

- Foundation GNVQ/GSVQ Leisure and Tourism (level 1)
- Intermediate GNVQ/GSVQ in Leisure and Tourism (level 2)
- 'Advanced' GNVQ/GSVQ in Leisure and Tourism (level 3)

The last is a full-time, two-year course for 16–18 year olds with a minimum of four GCSEs or equivalent. It may include ABTA and NVQ units. There may be travel options on GNVQ/GSVQ Advanced Diplomas in Business.

- BTEC/SCOTVEC Higher National Diploma in Travel and Tourism

There are a number of these courses available around the country, or the BTEC/SCOTVEC HND in Business and Finance may include travel options.

Degree courses

Universities: Abertay Dundee, Brighton, Bournemouth, Glasgow Caledonian, Hertfordshire, Humberside, Leeds, Luton, North London, Oxford Brookes, Northumbria, Plymouth, South Bank, Thames Valley, Wolverhampton.

Institutes of HE: Bangor Normal, Birmingham College of Food, Tourism and Creative Studies Cardiff, Canterbury Christ Church, Cumbria College of Art and Design (Heritage Management), Durham New College.

In addition to those listed, there are courses that combine tourism with related subjects such as Hotel Management, Leisure, Recreation or Business Studies.

Postgraduate

There are some full-time postgraduate courses as well as postgraduate level 5 qualifications offered by the main professional bodies such as the HCIMA, CIT and ILAM

Further information

Travel Training Company and the Institute of Travel and Tourism.

Tour companies and operators

Tour companies and operators put together package holidays and tours mainly for mass travel markets, although some make a business of high-value tours with a specialist slant (e.g. to archaeological sites led by an expert), or by specialising in a particular part of the world or country. Some specialise in winter skiing holidays, or school trips. Some large holiday companies have their own travel agencies. The competition verges on cut-throat.

The work of a tour company divides between designing, planning and negotiating packages, promoting and marketing them, and ensuring that the package holiday is delivered.

A package holiday includes transport to the resort, transfer from point of arrival to resort and accommodation. Plans have to be made well over a year in advance, on market research estimates of what the public want and might pay. A limited number of staff visit new resorts and check out their suitability for inclusion in their brochure. Detailed and complex costings have to be agreed. Negotiating the discounts with hoteliers and airlines is a tough business and drawing up contracts involves legal input (*see* THE LEGAL SYSTEM).

MARKETING and promoting holidays range from producing brochures (which employs writers, photographers, designers, print production staff, etc.), through ADVERTISING campaigns to SALES staff going out to travel agencies to see that the company's products are being promoted properly.

A considerable proportion of the work is clerical, sending out brochures, confirming bookings, invoicing and preparing travel documents, compiling costings, making up passenger lists and aircraft seat plans, collating and filing information on resorts and their facilities. Much of the routine work is computerised.

Travel is linked to the country's economy as a whole and so the number of people travelling, either for business or pleasure, will be affected by recession or political conflict. At present, more visits are made abroad by UK residents than by overseas visitors to the UK. In 1994 there were 2.1 million visitors to the UK (up from 1.7 million in 1991) whereas in 1994 3.9 million UK residents travelled overseas (compared to 1.1 million in 1975).

Tour companies of course employ people in FINANCE AND ACCOUNTING, MARKETING, and also COMPUTING. Statutory rules apply in the industry, so LEGAL STAFF are also needed.

Couriers, and resort representatives are also employed by tour organisations, to look after tourists. They may travel with them over part or all of their route or meet them at their destination. They have to cope with all the practical problems of customs, difficulties over food or rooms, lost property and medical emergencies. They may also take tourists on excursions and sight-seeing trips. Some tour operators employ NURSERY NURSES for the resorts. Winter sports companies also employ chalet staff and ski guides.

Recruitment and entry

School leavers need a good basic education and a few large firms recruit people with A levels (or equivalent) and graduates, potentially for professional and managerial work. Couriers and resort representatives will need to be fluent in at least one European language, and are normally recruited only in their twenties. Representatives need some kind of experience of a public contact job. Work is often seasonal and on a short-term contract.

Qualifications and training

For tour operators there are the NVQ/SVQs in Travel Services (Tour Directing) available at level 4.

For travel reps or couriers there are the NVQ/SVQs in Travel Services (Field Operations) level 2 and 3 and also in Travel Services (guiding) at level 4.

Further information

Travel Training Company and the Institute of Travel and Tourism.

Contents

Hotels and Catering, Catering Services, Home Economics and Related Consumer Sciences

(CLCI: IB – ID)

The hotel and catering, and catering services industry

Almost one in ten of the UK workforce are now employed in the hotel and catering industry, in the huge variety of jobs involved in the provision of food, drink, and/or accommodation. The commercial sector of the industry includes not just hotels and restaurants, but also holiday camps and leisure centres, pubs, cafes, wine bars, motorway services, roadside restaurants, fish and chip shops, takeaway burger and pizza restaurants, and entertainment clubs; and contract catering in a huge variety of establishments and settings from livery halls in the City of London, to burger bars and self-service restaurants at sports stadiums.

Over half – 66% – of the industry's workforce of 2.03 million (1994) are employed in the commercial sector. The balance provide catering services in other sectors for which catering is not the primary function. The old-fashioned term 'institutional management' (covering catering services in institutions such as prisons, schools and hospitals) is no longer used and has been replaced by 'hospitality management'. The catering services sectors, as they are known, cover rail, airline and cruise catering, and the catering and accommodation services at all types of institutions such as schools, colleges and universities, nursing homes, hospitals, residential hostels and other establishments for the elderly, ill, and others unable to provide for themselves. They also include catering in the armed services: the Army, Navy and Air Force. Total employment in the catering services sectors declined by 8% from 1992 to 1994 (HCTC).

Improvements in productivity led to a fall in employment in the industry in 1994. However, jobs are expected to increase in hotels and catering by 21% (300,000) from now to the year 2001.

The Hotel and Catering Training Company (HCTC) forecasts employment growth of 8.6% in the commercial sector over the five years 1995–2000, and just over 3% in the catering services sector. By the year 2000 the number of jobs will have risen from 2.39 million (1992) to 2.62 million.

As in the 1980s, the most dynamic sectors in terms of employment are likely to be hotels, restaurants and contract catering. The proportion of jobs in restaurants is expected to rise to over 28% in 1999, making it the largest sector. Pubs and hotels will show steady but slow employment growth. Overall, employment in the commercial sector will increase by 122,000 between 1994 and 1999, with a faster expansion of 165,000 between 1999 and 2004. Catering services will provide an increase of 23,000 jobs to the year 2004 (excluding domestics and housekeepers who come within this category). The fact that this increase is smaller than in the commercial sector is mainly due to the shift towards contract catering, and job cuts in education, medical and public administration catering, etc.

The hotel and catering industry, like many other industries, experienced a series of company takeovers and rationalisation programmes during the late 1980s and early 1990s. The twin pressures of high interest rates and reduced spending wiped out a number of companies which had tried to grow too fast, and exposed others to takeover.

However, UK-owned companies are now major operators on the world scene, with Forte, Bass and Ladbroke focusing on developing their business outside the UK, particularly in Europe. European operators who are starting to break into the UK market include the French companies Novotel, Ibis and Campanile.

The growth of contract catering is to a large extent the result of privatisation and compulsory competitive tendering in local authorities: directly, when for example a local authority places its meals-on-wheels service in the hands of a private contractor, and indirectly, as in the privatisation of nationalised industries, such as British Telecom. BT later put its entire catering operation out to tender – the largest single catering contract to be placed in the UK.

All sectors constantly look for new areas of business and for ways of improving managerial methods and reducing costs. Conferences and exhibitions, for instance, not only mean hotels can 'sell' their space, but also bring in people who will usually spend money on food and drink. Universities and colleges 'sell' conference facilities in the vacations to make their rooms profitable while students are away. All this implies highly sophisticated modern management methods, particularly in finance and marketing, and hoteliers are going out and selling their services hard.

Technology, too, plays a part; it makes possible meals mass-produced in large central, or contractors, 'production' kitchens, to be frozen or chilled for delivery to restaurants or canteens, airlines and hotel chains for heating in microwave ovens. The computer industry offers hotels sophisticated integrated systems for day-to-day running and management. These look after everything, from reservations and accounts, through issuing room 'keys' (which are in fact plastic cards unlocking a microprocessor-controlled lock), to systems which log guests' use of the telephone and drinks consumed in their rooms. The door 'key' will, amongst other things, automatically turn lights on and off and the heating up and down as a guest enters or leaves a room, so saving expensive energy.

The Food Safety Act 1990 and subsequent hygiene regulations threaten caterers with unlimited fines and jail sentences of up to two years. The public's concern with food safety continues to grow as a result of the widespread publicity given to the dangers of BSE, listeria, and the use of plastic cling-film.

Quality is an ever-present issue facing the hotel and catering industry, and one which needs to be continually in the forefront of the successful organisation. Most major companies are working towards total quality culture.

There was a slight increase in the levels of training provided by the catering and hospitality industry and licensed retailing sector between 1992 and 1994. However, winners of the prestigious National Training Award have included many hotel and catering firms. In 1996 HCTC was presented with the award for the best Modern Apprenticeship framework.

Hotels and guest houses

There are around 52,000 hotels and guesthouses in the UK (HCTC, 1994). The majority are located in the south-east of England. Most are small: in 1991, 87% employed between one and ten staff and only 6% over 25 staff (HCTC). Hotel employment accounts for 26% of the commercial sector workforce. Although opportunities are provided in the domestic sector via special deals on out-of-season, weekend breaks, conference packages and so forth, the principal growth potential lies with foreign visitors. Here the industry is vulnerable to high exchange rates, fears of terrorism, and the economic well-being of key countries such as the USA, Australia and Japan.

Restaurants

There are around 100,000 restaurants, cafes and snackbars in the UK (HCTC, 1994). The majority (92%) employed fewer than ten employees in 1991. Generally, the move has been away from high-spend gastronomic restaurants, towards mid-price bistros and fast-food outlets, as consumers aimed to cut down on their restaurant bills during the recession. These include anything from tapas bars, themed restaurants and brasseries, to ethnic restaurants representing most of the countries and cultures of the world. Vegetarian dishes have established their place on menus, as has mineral water and a variety of low- and non-alcohol drinks. The fast-food market continues to expand, with a growing number of takeaways and fast-food restaurants.

Catering contractors

The 1996 UK contract catering survey published by the British Hospitality Association (the hospitality industry's main trade body), states that this sector is perhaps the most dynamic sector of the British hospitality industry, providing well over a billion meals a year in over 15,000 outlets: twice as many as in 1990. In the same period, UK turnover in the industry has doubled. Business and industry continues to be a core sector (number of outlets up by 7% since 1990), although much of the recent expansion in the industry has been in emerging sectors such as education, healthcare and commercial catering (catering for the public). The latter, which represents one of the industry's potentially biggest and most profitable markets, has only emerged in the last five years, but now poses competition to the traditional restaurant chains. State education grew marginally in 1995, and contractors increased their penetration of National Health Service and Trust hospitals.

Public houses

According to the British Institute of Innkeeping (1995) some 70,000 public houses employ around half a million people, the majority of whom work part-time. The brewers own and operate about 20% of the pubs, the rest are run as free houses or brewers' tenancies. The image of the quiet 'local' with 'old codgers' sitting in a corner sipping a pint of mild is largely a thing of the past. These days pubs market themselves extensively; food is increasingly important and many pubs are now licensed restaurants in all but name. Another 156,000 people work in some 33,600 night- and other licensed clubs, but only 20% of them have full-time jobs.

Catering service sectors

Employment in education, which accounts for 24% of the sector, is forecast to increase to 104,000 in 1999, according to HCTC. This reflects the expansion in student numbers in further and higher education. Moderate growth is also forecast for the medical sector, up from 40,000 in 1990 to 78,000 in 1999. This is mainly as a result of the rise in numbers in residential homes, and the growth in meals-on-wheels and day-centre provision.

Employment in industrial and office catering, which accounted for 24% of the sector in 1990, is likely to decrease from 89,000 in 1990 to 73,000 in 1999. This reflects the trend towards using contract caterers (*see above*). The numbers of catering staff employed in public administration are expected to remain steady at around 26,000, or even decline if contracting-out continues apace.

The retail distribution sector, which includes both staff and customer catering facilities, is likely to be relatively buoyant in terms of employment: up by 5,000 from 1990 to

49,000 in 1999. This reflects the steady consumer spending growth and a continuing trend towards shopping centres and superstores. Another buoyant sector is RECREATION AND LEISURE and cultural, employing 39,000 by 1999, compared to 32,000 in 1990. Rising real incomes, increased leisure time and the widening preoccupation with health and fitness are all pointing to greater investment and participation in this sector in the longer term, and consequently increasing demand for catering services.

Travel sector catering jobs declined in the 1980s as provision, especially on the rail network, was taken over by commercial catering companies. HCTC forecasts marginal growth in the 1990s, with around 20,000 jobs. Of these, two-thirds are associated with air travel, a particularly vulnerable sector, as the impact of wars or trouble-torn countries on international business travel and tourism proved.

Working in the industry

The hotel and catering industry is all about people. The impact of staff and management on the success of what is basically a hospitality business is immense. A visit to a pub, or a snack in a roadside restaurant, can be greatly enhanced by the knowledge, skills and attitudes of the people that customers meet, or by the actions of those working behind the scenes.

The industry needs staff with a friendly, outgoing personality. The first impressions customers get is usually their lasting impression. Staff with a pleasant manner, smart appearance and enthusiasm are great assets. Teamwork is important too: staff must be able to get on with their work colleagues. Staff need to be able to use their initiative, think quickly, and remain flexible, friendly and courteous whatever the difficulties.

Although the industry's track record as an employer has not, in the past, generally been very good, larger employers in particular have greatly improved career structures, training, and working conditions. It can be a very stressful occupation, with long and irregular hours, and all the problems of keeping customers happy, day-in and day-out. 'Despite obvious employment disadvantages, the hotel and catering industry, offers much to employees that other industries do not; for example, many employees do not appear dissatisfied with their remuneration, few complain of boredom ... and the opportunities ... for variety of work, personal expression and for the development of individual skills compare favourably with other kinds of manual work. Moreover, at managerial level the autonomy of individual establishments offers comparatively high rewards for most young men and women and the opportunity of independent command at a relatively early stage in life.' (NEDC Report)

Variety of jobs

The variety of jobs in the industry is reflected in the vast range of job opportunities it offers. They include front-line staff meeting customers, such as receptionists or restaurant waiting staff, to roles behind the scenes, e.g. chefs or maintenance staff. As well as the backup services, those who help keep the organisation or business running smoothly include accountants, secretaries, personnel staff, and those who help attract more business: sales and marketing staff.

The same job title can cover very different roles. Being responsible for preparing and cooking all the dishes on the menu of a small country pub is not the same as being part of a large kitchen team, responsible for preparing certain aspects of a banquet for a thousand people. Working in a hotel with its own swimming pool, jacuzzi and gym is quite different from being part of a team operating the city's main leisure centre.

Small businesses, of which there are many thousands in hotel and catering, can offer the opportunity of being involved in all aspects of the operation. So receptionists may help in the restaurant and bar as part of their normal duties, while housekeeping staff may have the opportunity to earn extra money by serving meals in the evening.

In the industry generally, and particularly in the larger companies, moving from one area of work to another is straightforward. With the expansion of UK companies into Europe and vice versa, company training programmes encourage staff to work in different countries and learn other languages. A number of college programmes also build in the opportunity to work and study abroad. Work is well under way on establishing the comparability of the various hotel and catering qualifications.

Around 12% of the industry's work force are in managerial jobs, 25% in food preparation and cooking positions, according to HCTC. Food and drink service jobs (bar and waiting staff) account for 13%, and reception and portering jobs nearly 30%. In 1994, the majority of employees (65%) worked part-time, with females dominating the industry, accounting for 73% of its workforce in 1994. The proportion of females was much higher in the catering services sectors: 86% as opposed to 63% in the commercial sectors (HCTC).

Administration and management

General hotel managers

Managerial careers within the industry have largely come into line with management in other areas of commerce, especially in the larger hotel and catering groups. What do supervisors and managers need to be able to do to perform their job effectively?

For supervisors the most important areas are people-related. People-management and team leadership are rated very positively. Customer relations and training are also seen as important.

For middle managers budgeting is very important, followed closely by training, delegation, marketing and commercial awareness. Manpower planning and decision-making also plays a leading role.

For senior managers the financial emphasis is even stronger. Financial decision-making is paramount, closely linked with team leadership and time management. Corporate planning, marketing, public speaking and people-management are also an integral part of the work.

In smaller establishments, with a single management tier, the individual manager/proprietor needs to combine all of the above with a sound knowledge of employment legislation, and food hygiene laws, and often an ability to manage equipment, buildings and other resources.

Good managers are particularly concerned about improving staff relations, and managerial support for front-of-house and service staff in their relations with the customers, ending the traditional gulf between management and staff which was largely the cause of high staff turnover and over-subservience to the customer. Managers in the catering services sector are just as much concerned with coping with change, and financial planning, decision-making, organising, staff supervision, and problem-solving as in the commercial sector.

General hotel managers run individual hotels. This can mean being the working proprietor of a small hotel with a small staff, doing all the managerial jobs, from supervising the kitchen (and even cooking in crises), the housekeeper, and the front office, to doing the stock control, the financial paperwork, and 'marketing' and personnel too.

At the other end of the spectrum, it can mean being the manager of a large hotel, perhaps as part of a chain, with several hundred bedrooms, conference and banqueting facilities, and a leisure centre fitted with the latest equipment. Here the staff will be much larger – up to 1,000 perhaps – and depending on its size, there may be a single assistant manager, or a number of middle managers, each with their own area of responsibility: food and drink, finance, accommodation, personnel and training, perhaps marketing, and so on. If the hotel is large enough, there may be assistant middle managers, who may be trainees, and supervisory managers in charge of specific departments: the chef, the housekeeper, head porter, and so on.

The larger the hotel, the less involved is the manager in day-to-day routine, and the more responsibility is carried by the middle managers. Here the general manager is primarily a coordinator, planner and troubleshooter, making decisions on, for instance, maintenance and repairs, discussing designs for redecorating, new marketing plans, checking sales returns and preparing forecasts, reporting to head office. In the smaller hotel the manager may have to do some of the day-to-day work of supervision too.

Catering and restaurant managers

Here the work is very similar, whether the manager is in charge of a university's student meals service, a 'top' restaurant, a fast-food franchise, or meals for a hotel's guests. There are some differences of course. In the catering services section, the manager knows how many people he or she is feeding and when – university students, hospital patients and staff – all need balanced and varied meals at set times, and so menu planning is a major function. Restaurant managers, on the other hand, usually offer a greater choice of food and wines, and have all the planning problems of never being quite sure how many customers to expect, and when.

Some catering managers, of airlines or local authority departments for example, may not be directly in charge of food preparation at all. Their job may consist of liaising with the contractors who prepare the meals in bulk at central production units, chill or freeze them, then deliver whatever is required under very strict conditions of temperature and time, so that the food is safe to eat. Catering and restaurant managers are expected to give value for money and customer satisfaction within tight budgets and, where the operation is a commercial one, have to meet profit targets. Even where planning and ordering are done centrally, managers are normally given a fairly free hand to 'manage'. They are usually quite closely involved with day-to-day problems.

Efficient catering managers have to be personnel officers, and be good at choosing and supervising catering and service staff, and scheduling work. They have to be good at finance, able to budget, forecast, keep books and records, know how to keep stocks at the right levels, control portion size, and minimise waste. They need at least some culinary skills – to be able to plan menus, control quality. They need marketing and promotional skills, and know how to create the right atmosphere and deal appropriately with customers. They need to understand and take advantage of any new technology.

Catering services managers

Catering services managers look after the 'catering and domestic' organisation of places like hospitals; colleges, boarding schools and universities; residential homes for old people, children or the handicapped; day centres, and so on. At one end of the scale, this may be as demanding a job with responsibilities similar to, and with many of the problems of, hotel management, at the other – and for people in junior management – it may be closer to housekeeping.

It may involve not just the general management of a home or student halls, overseeing everything from maintenance to cleaning and catering, but also the marketing of conference facilities and holiday accommodation in the vacations. Managers may have to provide domestic services for an ever-changing population, as in a hospital or conference centre; the population may be semi-permanent, like students, or permanent, for instance elderly people. The manager may have little to do with the 'residents', as in hospitals, or part of their work may involve day-to-day contact with them, as in old people's homes.

Public house, or licensed premises management

Managing a public house is a seven-days-a-week, all-the-year-round job, closely tied to set (and long) hours, and often means living on the premises, as manager or tenant of a 'tied' (to a brewery) 'house', or managing or owning a so-called 'free' house. It is often seen as a career for married couples, and is more than just a job, rather a way of life.

Although the publican is popularly seen as a 'host', serving drinks, the work is just as much managerial/administrative. An increasingly competitive business, licensees and managers must work hard and imaginatively in order to find ways of improving sales and profitability using proven as well as new ways to attract custom (food and games, music, for example), to control cash and stock efficiently, and to manage staff (recruit, train and organise) well.

The bar manager must have the right social skills and outgoing personality needed for life behind a bar, and be able to understand the licensing laws and to keep control in sometimes difficult situations; stay abreast of popular trends in drinking and pub games and entertainment, and know how to keep both regular and new clientele happy.

Related jobs include managing bars and cellars in larger hotels, clubs, and so on. Some bar staff, particularly in large establishments and hotels, may have a degree of independence in running their own bars. There are also openings in the off-licence retail trade.

Craft and supervisory work

The industry employs large numbers of craft and supervisory staff. It is common to start at the bottom of the ladder, train in different departments and types of work, then move up to supervisory posts. Some decide from an early stage in their career that they eventually want to have their own businesses. Not all succeed: the recession at the start of the 1990s saw many business failures.

Food preparation and cookery

Cookery books written for catering students and professional chefs were once organised according to the traditional, multi-course menu. They started with hors d'oeuvres and soups, then moved through the meal with egg, farinaceous and fish dishes, various types of meats and poultry, to the sweet or dessert course, ending up with savouries. The emphasis was on following recipes.

The approach changed in the late 1980s, with the view that a more thorough understanding came from knowing how each of the cooking processes – boiling, roasting, grilling, deep and shallow frying, microwaving and so forth – worked and could be applied to different food commodities. With this grounding in the basic principles, any variety of dishes could be cooked, from the traditional haute cuisine of France, to putting the finishing touches to a dish which had been bought in ready prepared – chilled, frozen or vacuum packed (the sous vide process).

The choice of work for the fully trained chef/cook ranges from the kitchens of a large hotel, where there may be a strict hierarchy of chefs, each with their own special area of work (cold larder, vegetables, pastry, fish, meat, poultry) and each with assistants and trainees, to the small operation where two or three share all the cooking. Many trained cooks work in staff canteens, hospitals, universities, schools or for catering contractors. Some work on a freelance basis, for directors' dining rooms, for banquets and parties, or preparing business lunches.

In some kitchens the chef may do his/her own planning, budgeting, buying, and food ordering, in some it may be done by, or with, a food and 'beverage' manager or the general manager (who may also be the working proprietor). Some food may be prepared in advance, but food also has to be cooked when ordered, sometimes in front of the customer. Healthy eating is more important everywhere, and chefs may be involved in preparing special diets. At the most senior levels, the chef's job can be increasingly supervisory.

Cooking is, at its best, a highly developed creative art and skill, with satisfactions of its own. Despite increasing mechanisation, including the latest in food preparation and dishwashing equipment, life in the kitchen is still physically hard, often unavoidably uncomfortable (hot, steamy and often noisy), with a great deal of standing, lifting, difficult hours and periods of great rush, when it takes a lot to stay calm and produce good food.

Food service

This is the modern term for waiting. The major career opportunities (as opposed to short-term jobs) in food service are in the larger hotels and more expensive restaurants, especially those which still practice 'haute cuisine' cooking or provide 'silver' or table service. Waiters and waitresses are the main point of contact with the customer, and must always be welcoming and patient, take the orders (and get them right), serve food efficiently, cleanly and unobtrusively, sometimes cook at the table, and follow the formal rules of the kitchen. They may have to help keep the restaurant clean, vacuuming, etc., as well as laying tables.

Wine waiters and waitresses must be well versed in their 'mystique': which wine should accompany what food, and how to serve and store wines properly. All waiters and waitresses must be able to work with, meet and get to know people of all kinds. Promotion is to head waiter/waitress, and higher supervisory positions.

The work is physically hard. Waiters and waitresses must be able to meet all kinds of situations and stay calm, however tired they may be. Social skills, a neat and tidy appearance, physical stamina, a pleasant personality and a good memory are considered essential.

Front office and reception

This is the industry term for the people who welcome guests into hotels, larger restaurants, conference and leisure centres, private hospitals and so forth. They make the bookings, allocate rooms, do the billing, keep account of the 'extras' (such as room service and drinks) and prepare the accounts. In small hotels all this may be handled by one receptionist, but in most, and especially in the larger ones, there is an entire team, under a reception manager.

Reception staff keep detailed records of rooms and guests, tell the housekeepers who is arriving (or leaving) when, and about special problems. The front office itself may have a cashier and a receptionist, or a receptionist-cum-cashier. A clerk may look after reservations.

The cashier's office is where bills are paid, travellers' cheques and currency changed, and valuables cared for. In small hotels the front office and the manager normally deal with accounts, but in larger hotels there is often a separate control manager or accountant with a sizeable staff who deal with accounts, wages and national insurance, tax, and so on. The majority of hotels have computerised systems to keep most of the records, and these can also show which rooms are occupied and which vacant, supply 'keys', keep track of room service and telephone calls, and so on. Receptionists and cashiers spend a lot of time with customers. The job also involves being able to keep records, telephone work, and so on.

Housekeepers

They look after the accommodation services in hotels, hospitals, residential homes, student halls. They actually organise and supervise cleaning and general care of bedrooms, bathrooms, corridors, lounges and other 'public rooms' and offices; they see that linen and curtains are changed, bedding and furnishings cleaned and mended as needed. In large places the housekeeper will have several assistants (a 1,000-bed hospital may need five assistant managers, 20 supervisors and 300 domestics), in smaller ones the housekeeper may work alone and be in charge of the whole operation. Reporting to the housekeeper will be the cleaning staff, and depending on the size of the establishment, linen room and laundry staff, valets and house porters. Special problems include avoiding cross-infections in hospital cleaning. The housekeeper must keep an eye open for problems, and report quickly where maintenance or repairs are needed. The housekeeper works closely with the front office and reception staff. The old-fashioned term 'bursar' used to be associated with housekeeping functions, but now only refers to someone who works in an educational establishment, dealing with the finances.

Toastmasters

There are only some 20 toastmasters, who announce toasts at royal and state banquets, civic and government occasions. Training courses are run privately by the Guild of Professional Toastmasters.

Uniformed staff

These are the porters, night porters, doorkeepers, lift operators, cloakroom attendants and page 'boys'. Mostly they work for hotels and larger restaurants. The hall porter and staff look after guests' personal comfort. Senior porters and doorkeepers count as 'front-of-house' staff, greeting guests, showing them to reception, calling porters, taking messages, suggesting places to see, or how to get from one place to another, sending for cars, booking tickets. Night porters may serve refreshments and act as night security. There is a considerable amount of fetching and carrying for junior staff. Hall porters and their staff are traditionally expected to be able to anticipate guests' needs and solve unexpected problems. Discretion and experience are needed.

Butlers/personal assistants

Although the demand for professional domestic staff such as butlers, valets and housekeepers is extremely limited, British trained staff can find some openings elsewhere – the USA, Saudi Arabia and the Far East being favourite destinations. In some American and international hotels, the valet is the car park attendant. In large hotels, valets may do other jobs such as work on the door, night porter, porter, etc. Training for butlers is by private course only. The Ivor Spencer International School for Butler Administrators/Personal Assistants runs five-week intensive courses that attract students from all around the world. Students are expected to have a 'fair standard of education', and a knowledge of a second language is considered useful. Field trips include lunch at Claridges or other top-class hotels and tea at the Savoy.

Fees in 1996 were £3,155 per course, rising to £3,255 in 1997. The school also runs its own agency, which is the only one in the UK that places butler administrators trained at the school. Although it has been successful in placing butlers in the royal households, with heads of state and embassies, etc., it makes no guarantee to find employment in this extremely specialist and limited area. Further information from Ivor Spencer School for Butler Administrators/Personal Assistants.

Other staff

Hotels are often large, and hotel chains have a number of buildings to look after. Most employ their own maintenance staff, and the large ones property/building managers, surveyors, etc.

Recruitment and entry

People have made very successful careers in the hotel and catering industry from all types of background and experience. Many top managers have worked their way up from the bottom. Some planned it that way; some simply found their niche and were swept upwards by the quality of their work and the suitability of their personality. Others have come to hotels and catering from the retail or manufacturing industries. Others have found that they could practise their profession as an accountant, architect, or administrator with greater satisfaction and considerable success by specialising in hotels and catering. Yet others have switched after obtaining a first degree in the arts or the sciences.

On the one hand there is no doubt that the considerable success of people who have joined the industry with appropriate qualifications has raised the level of expectation that aspiring craftspeople, supervisors and managers in the future must themselves have such a qualification – be it a basic cookery certificate, an NVQ or SVQ, or a degree, BTEC or SCOTVEC Higher in hotel and catering management.

On the other hand there is a huge imbalance between the industry's demand for qualified staff, and the output from college and industry training schemes. HCTC estimates that college output provides less than 28% of the annual replacement needs of skilled personnel in the industry. The shortfall is most severe at management level, where the college output is less than 7% of the replacement needs. So for the foreseeable future it is certain that jobs in the industry – at all levels – will be taken up by people whose only relevant qualification is that they have the right personality for the job, are willing to work hard, and demonstrate a real interest in making a success of the kind of personal service from which the industry makes its profits. It is these people that will most benefit from NVQs and SVQs in catering and hospitality.

Entry routes in the industry fall into four basic categories:

- by obtaining via a full-time college course, a qualification appropriate to the level of job (*see* Qualifications and training *below*);
- by joining a company training scheme which offers experience in different departments and types of work, and increasing levels of responsibility as well as on- and off-the-job training. The latter may take the form of release to attend a part-time or block-release college course, or, increasingly, the provision of distance-learning material. Generally, the objective will be to obtain the appropriate qualifications, such as an NVQ or SVQ, HCIMA (Hotel, Catering and International Management) Professional Certificate and/or Diploma, DMS, MBA or postgraduate diploma. Many company training schemes are designed for those who already hold a qualification – a hotel and catering degree, a BTEC or SCOTVEC Higher, or HCIMA Professional Diploma, or, more rarely, a BTEC National or SCOTVEC Certificate. These schemes concentrate on providing experience in different parts of the company's operation, and are designed to lead to a senior position;
- by obtaining work experience and NVQ/SVQs to at least level 2 or on a Youth or Employment Training scheme run by the HCTC or other large employer. Of those leaving youth training programmes in catering and hospitality in 1993/94, 52% went into employment. However, 25% of youth trainees were unemployed on leaving (HCTC);
- by finding a job – getting a foot in the door, as it were. This might mean starting in quite a humble position, on low wages. At most times, in most parts of the UK, JobCentres and local newspapers carry advertisements for chefs and cooks, waiting, bar and housekeeping staff. Those following this route are advised by the HCTC to go first for the jobs where on-the-job training will be provided, and where proven ability in the workplace is likely to be rewarded by greater responsibility, a chance of promotion, and a place on a company training scheme. Avoid employers who exploit their staff – the hotel and catering industry, like any other, has its rogue employers.

Qualifications and training

The hotel and catering industry has been the frontrunner in developing National Vocational Qualifications and Scottish Vocational Qualifications (NVQ/SVQs). The new system covers all activities carried out by the industry, from cooking and serving food and drink, to managing a large hotel, and all jobs from luggage porter to reception manager, room attendant to housekeeper.

The lead body for the industry is the Hotel and Catering Training Company. In England and Wales and Northern Ireland, the Hotel, Catering and International Management Association (HCIMA) and City & Guilds is a joint awarding body for NVQs at level 4. HCIMA also endorses City & Guilds NVQs at levels 1–3. In Scotland HCIMA and SCOTVEC are joint certificators, with HCTC and the British Institute of Innkeeping at levels 3 and 4.

NVQs and SVQs are available for six occupational areas, with some specialisms. The award titles at levels 1 to 4 include the following:

- Food Preparation and Cooking – with specialisms at level 1 only: General and Quick Service;
- Serving Food and Drink – with four specialisms at level 1: Bar, Table/Tray, Counter and Take-Away; two at level 2: Restaurant and Bar; four at level 3: Table, Counter, Drinks and Wine Service; and two at level 4: Food and Drinks;
- Reception – known as Reception and Portering at level 1; two award titles at level 2: Reception, and Reception and Serving Food and Drink; three specialisms at level 3: General, Functions and Portering; and two at level 4: General and Functions;
- Housekeeping (levels 1–4, with no specialisms);
- Guest service (level 1 only) known as Serving Food and Drink/Housekeeping;
- Catering and Hospitality is offered at level 3 only in Patisserie and Confectionery, Kitchen and Larder Work.

These qualifications all carry the main title Catering and Hospitality (levels 1 and 2), Catering and Hospitality Supervisory Management (level 3) and Catering and Hospitality Management (level 4).

Separately, there are also two qualifications for the licensed trade – at level 3, On-Licensed Premises Supervisor; and at level 4, On-Licensed Premises Management – jointly administered with the BII.

GNVQs are available in Hospitality and Catering and can lead to a range of jobs or prepare students for NVQs in Catering and Hospitality which they can work towards when they obtain a job. Advanced GNVQs can lead to degrees and diplomas in hotel management.

Degree level

The provision of supervisory and management qualifications in hotels and catering has been widely developed over the last three decades. This expansion has probably been greatest at degree and postgraduate level.

The full list of degrees can be found in the UCAS *Handbook*. Titles vary from Food Management, Hotel and Catering Management to Hospitality Management, with some institutions offering International Hotel or Catering Management. The majority of degree programmes include the study of one or more modern languages, and so do many Higher National Diplomas. Some include work experience and/or study abroad, in Europe, North America and as far afield as Australia.

The modular structure of many programmes means that individuals have a greater choice of subjects and award combinations. For example, sometimes catering management can be combined with retail management, and cartographic design and communication is one of the huge choice of subjects that can be studied for a joint tourism degree. A modular structure can also make it easier for students to change to another degree should the original choice prove unsuitable to them. Often the Diploma of Higher Education is available to those who want a shorter programme, or who, two-thirds through the degree course, decide they cannot continue at college for some reason.

It is becoming easier for mature students without the required academic qualifications to gain entry to management programmes on the basis of their experience. Exemption from certain parts of programmes is given more readily, including from the industrial experience element. Transfer from a Higher National Diploma to a degree programme is usually straightforward, with full credit given to HND studies.

The organisation of some degree programmes reflects the American approach, with two semesters per year rather than three terms. Although most hotel and catering degrees are still four years in length, usually with a year's industrial experience, shorter programmes are likely to be more readily available, and a two-year degree is a possibility before the end of the 1990s.

A number of private establishments offer hotel and catering qualifications at various levels from cookery school and Cordon Bleu diplomas, to American university degrees (as at Schiller and the United States International universities). The degree course at the University of Buckingham (Britain's only chartered independent university) includes a year in Europe.

Postgraduate level

Many of the postgraduate programmes are conversion courses, designed for those with a first degree in a non-hotel and catering subject. Others, as at Surrey and Strathclyde, are intended to explore a first-degree subject in greater depth. The following institutions offer courses, leading to Postgraduate Diplomas, MSc, MPhil or PhD qualifications: Birmingham College of Food, Tourism and Creative Studies; Bournemouth University; University of Buckingham; Glasgow Caledonian University; Huddersfield University; King's College London; Leeds Metropolitan University; Manchester Metropolitan University; Napier University; Oxford Brookes University; Portsmouth University; Queen Margaret College; Sheffield Hallam University; South Bank University; Strathclyde University; Surrey University; Thames Valley University; and Ulster Jordanstown University.

Professional courses

The Food Safety Act 1990, with its provision for the compulsory hygiene training of all food-handling staff, focused the attention of the industry on the well-established range of qualifications offered by the Royal Society of Hygiene, Royal Institute of Public Health and Hygiene, Royal Environmental Health Institute of Scotland, and the Institution of Environmental Health Officers. Some of these can be run as in-company courses. Some are available on a distance-learning basis (through the Open College, for example). Some are available as short courses run by environmental health officers, colleges, HCTC, the award-making bodies themselves and a wide range of consultants and training organisations.

The Wine and Spirit Education Trust and the Academy of Wine Service offer courses, support material and qualifications in wine knowledge and wine service.

The HCTC offers a wide range of courses from craft to management, supported by training videos, books, and self-study material, in line with NVQ/SVQ standards, leading to HCTC certificates.

Professional bodies

The Hotel and Catering International Management Association (HCIMA), 1995 membership 23,000, is the professional body for the hospitality industry. HCIMA offers its own two-stage programmes of study leading to professional membership.

The professional certificate is for those aspiring to or working at supervisory level, and the professional diploma for those holding jobs of management responsibility. Flexible and modular study packs allow those at work to enrol for single areas of study or a complete programme. Study may be by day-release, block-release or, by using distance-learning material, in the person's own time. One-year full-time courses are available to those with appropriate prior work experience. The Association accredits many qualifications such as degrees and higher national diplomas. Accredited programmes enable students to gain exemption from HCIMA programmes in addition to gaining student membership of the Association. Ultimately, full corporate membership is available on completion of a recognised qualification and additional work experience.

The British Institute of Innkeeping (BII) is the professional body for the licensed trade; formed in 1981, membership stood at over 12,500 in 1995. Various grades of membership are open to those with a mixture of qualifications, and experience in the day-to-day supervision of public houses. The BII provides a framework for its own qualifications, as well as being the joint awarding body with the HCTC for NVQ levels 3 and 4 in On-Licensed Premises Supervisory and Management.

Further information

The Hotel and Catering Training Company Careers Information Service, the Hotel and Catering International Management Association, the British Hospitality Association, and the British Institute of Innkeeping.

Home economics and related consumer sciences

Home economics is officially defined as 'the study of the interrelationship between the provision of food, clothing, shelter and related services and people's physical, economic, social and aesthetic needs in the context of the home and the environment'. It has evolved a long way from its origins in domestic-science teaching.

Home economists (other job titles are 'consumer scientists', 'consumer services managers', or 'home economics advisers') have become, according to their Institute, 'professional advisers on food, clothing, home management and design, household services and research related to home and community, acting as a link between producers and consumers of goods and services...' They are professional advisers both to consumers and to the organisations who supply them with goods and services. Home economists do, of course, continue to teach.

Qualifications in home economics appear to be taking people into a number of different types of work. The work of many home economists at entry level and skilled level is physically demanding, often requiring long periods of standing and talking, so stamina and good health are required. At graduate/professional level (skilled and experienced), the work is likely to be more managerial with a reduction in the physical demands balanced by greater intellectual demands.

Working in home economics

Industry

The main sectors employing home economists are domestic appliance manufacturers, the Food industry (*see in* MANUFACTURING INDUSTRIES) and THE ENERGY INDUSTRIES (*see in* THE MINING AND ENERGY INDUSTRIES).

Home economists are employed in research and development on testing and evaluating new and improved products. Many work in the food industry in marketing and/or in the research and development of new products to supply retailers. Their counterparts in retailing are the home economists who, as buyers/selectors, choose the products to be stocked. Home economists are similarly employed in the domestic appliance manufacturing industry and with those retailers. There have been considerable changes in the utility industry employment patterns and numbers.

In market research home economists test new products on consumers and do surveys to see if there is a gap in the product range to be filled – both involve fieldwork. In marketing/sales and public relations they may help prepare publicity material (for photographs of new food products, copy for leaflets) or instruction booklets for domestic cookers, etc.; or demonstrate products on promotional stands at exhibitions, in stores, at WI meetings, press conferences, etc. The work is not always directly sales-oriented: home economists may advise consumers on how to save on fuel, or make best use of a particular appliance.

Consumer advisory services

Home economists work either directly for a manufacturer or supplier (*see above*) or in local-authority or independently run centres. Here they are expertly assessing and evaluating products and services for the customer. Closely related are journalism, publishing and consumer-advisory work for the media – radio, TV, newspapers and magazines – either writing and/or presenting consumer-oriented material, or testing, evaluating, and preparing material for the columnist or presenter. Advertising, public relations and market-research agencies may also employ home economists if they have contracts with, e.g., food manufacturers, or consumer goods

Community services

Social service departments employ home economists to help solve the problems of families in difficulty, show them how to budget, and teach economic and nutritious healthy cooking, family care, etc. They also work in home help services, residential care, and other rehabilitation units. Home economists are qualified to train as NHS domestic services managers.

Retailing

Large groups employ home economists in developing and evaluating new products, buying/selecting, liaison with customers, demonstration and promotional work, and staff training. Home economics is an accepted qualification for trainee management.

Recruitment and entry

On-the-job training is rare, and most employers now look for qualified applicants.

Most new entrants take full-time courses ranging from City & Guilds through BTEC/SCOTVEC National to HNDs and BA, BSc (Ordinary and Honours) degrees requiring up to three A-levels. Many degrees and HNDs require at least GCSE (A–C) or equivalent in one or more sciences. The introduction of NVQs and GNVQs has increased the range of acceptable qualifications.

Home economists care about people and the quality of life and need therefore to have an interest in the quality, performance and safety of goods and services related to the people who use these products. The products are those used principally by the homemaker, and understanding consumer choice and family resource management are thus major areas of interest and concern. Much of the work involves communicating with the general public on the one hand and specialists on the other. Thus home economists must be confident and have the ability to express themselves in both oral and written work. Good self-management and good interpersonal skills are needed.

Qualifications and training

The study of home economics is now broad and wide-ranging. It begins with basic sciences and social studies; goes on to specialist areas like nutrition, food science, practical studies of the home, equipment evaluation, and management, including planning a family budget and menus, budgeting and caring for clothes and therefore studying textiles and their composition. Courses also extend into the whole field of consumer affairs, the position of women in society, the problems of the family, and the wider field of community studies.

Degree and postgraduate courses

Degree courses may be entitled Home Economics or related subjects such as Food, Textiles and Consumer Studies; Home Economics and Resource Management; Applied Consumer Science; or BEd Home Economics/CDT Home Economics, etc. Titles give an indication of the emphasis of different courses. Home Economics is also offered in combination with other subjects such as media/management with Food and Health studies at Trinity and All Saints College, Leeds, and modular courses are available. Most degree courses include some work-based learning – usually a placement.

BEd degrees prepare students for teaching CDT home economics/food technology/textile technology/home economics, design and technology. *See* EDUCATION AND TEACHING.

No specific A-level or equivalent subjects are required, but maths, English language and a science are usually required at GCSE/SCE level. Mature-student entry and non-standard entry is encouraged, but details should be obtained from universities and colleges. Entry may be possible for those with previous achievements and learning/experience. Those with advanced standing may be able to join part way through the course.

Postgraduate courses are available in teaching and for specific areas. Examples include MA(Ed) Technology and Consumer Science option at Roehampton Institute, MPhil Consumer Science/Home Economics at Cardiff and Roehampton Institutes, and MSc Product Management (part-time course) at South Bank University.

BTEC/SCOTVEC courses

Most BTEC courses include four main areas of study: food studies; technical studies of consumer products such as household equipment and detergents; behavioural studies such as the consumer and sociology; plus business and management studies such as marketing and communications. These are studied in more depth at HND level. With the introduction of modular (unit-based) courses, some optional subjects may be studied. Courses include work placements. In Scotland, colleges offer a modular programme that can be tailored to home economics.

NVQs

NVQ/SVQs at levels 1 and 2 in Food Preparation and Food Service are available.

Other courses

The City & Guilds Certificate for Family and Community Care, a two-year FE college course, offers the chance to train for practical caring or housekeeping jobs in residential homes, day centres, special schools, etc. GNVQs in Food Manufacture or City & Guilds courses in Food Preparation and Food Service may also be suitable preparatory courses.

Professional body

The Institute of Home Economics (2,000 members in 1996) requires a degree for full membership. Those with HNDs and other qualifications are eligible with appropriate work experience.

Further information

The Institute of Home Economics.

Contents

Personal Services

(CLCI: IG – IZ)

Beauty

Background

Beauty specialists provide professional personal beauty care services for customers to improve their condition and appearance and make them feel better. They perform body treatments including manicure, pedicure and massage, facial treatments, and advise clients on skin care, which cosmetic products to buy, and how to use them to get the best results.

Job titles in the beauty industry can be very confusing but generally they fall into one of two main categories. They either cover beauty treatment (beauty therapists, aestheticiennes, beauticians, cosmetologists, massage therapists, epilationists, electrolysists, etc.), or they promote and sell cosmetics and toiletries (beauty consultants). In the UK, the title beauty therapist is often used for those who provide an extensive range of beauty treatments and that of beautician for those with more limited skills and training who concentrate on the face and hands. Beauty work may be combined with hairdressing in some countries (cosmetology) but in the UK they are usually separate. Some job titles reflect a specialist area of work, e.g. a massage therapist is a person specialising in massage treatment for relaxation, stress and the general well-being of the client.

Make-up for the stage, film and television is a specialist area. Make-up artists apply corrective make-up before appearing on stage or in front of the camera, alter features for character parts, simulate scars, injuries and wounds, and create period hair-styles. *See* Make-up Artist *in* MEDIA CAREERS *and below under* HAIRDRESSING.

Image Consultants are another small specialist area related to the beauty and fashion industries. 'Colour Me Beautiful' have trained over 1,000 image consultants throughout Europe.

Beauty treatment staff

Beauty treatment may cover the whole or parts of the body and can include:

- facial treatments such as deep cleansing, skin toning, eyelash/eyebrow tinting, applying face packs, or make-up including cosmetic camouflage to cover skin blemishes or make-up for photographic sessions or special occasions;
- face or body massage using hands, mechanical or electrical equipment to stimulate blood circulation, tone muscles, assist lymph drainage or break down fatty tissue;
- using specialised oils and creams and/or aromatherapy in conjunction with massage;
- pedicure (the care of the toenails and feet) or manicure (the filing and polishing of customers' nails and trimming the cuticles);
- advising on skin care, cosmetics, diet and exercise;
- using warm wax, electrical epilation (electrolysis) or chemicals to remove unwanted hair from the face and body, or electrical treatment to soften wrinkles;
- supervising clients using saunas, steam cabinets, infra-red and ultra-violet equipment, or hydrotherapy.

All jobs in beauty involve very close personal contact with customers and beauty specialists must not feel embarrassed or uncomfortable about physical contact. Most beauty treatment staff and their clients are women so beauty salons can claim exemption from the Sex Discrimination Act.

Beauty treatment staff usually work in attractive and comfortable private beauty salons or a salon of a department store, in health and fitness clubs, hotels or on health farms. A few may work on cruise ships.

It is also possible to work from home, either with a room set aside for beauty treatment, or by providing a service to people in their own homes.

Beauty consultancy

Beauty consultants advise and sell customers beauty products such as make-up, creams, perfume, lotions and toiletries. They find out what cosmetics customers use, what skin problems they have, answer any queries, and then recommend products.

Beauty consultants must have a thorough knowledge of all their products. Their primary role is selling and beauty consultants may be under contract to a particular cosmetics manufacturer. The work can be very competitive and in order to boost sales, beauty consultants may introduce special offers and carry out make-up demonstrations for individuals and groups. If they reach specified sales targets then they will receive commission on top of their basic salary.

Most beauty consultants are also responsible for bookkeeping operations, ordering and maintaining stock, and arranging attractive displays.

Beauty consultants generally work in department stores or in large high street chemists. They may be employed by cosmetic houses such as Elizabeth Arden or Estée Lauder or directly by the department store to sell a wider range of products. There are also opportunities in the duty free shops at airports and on cruise ships, in hotels, and occasionally at health farms. Temporary work may be a possibility during the Christmas period and there are a number of specialist beauty agencies who supply staff and provide a few days basic training.

Recruitment and entry

All beauty specialists should be able to relate to a wide range of clients and enjoy working with them. Personality is very important and staff need patience and tact. Anyone working in the beauty business must be well groomed, clean, neat and tidy and prepared to wear a uniform or overall when required. Most jobs in beauty require a great deal of standing so physical fitness and stamina are necessary. Working with beauty preparations can cause skin irritations.

Beauty treatment staff

There are a few training schemes for young people combining work experience in a beauty salon with off-the-job training but the trend is towards full-time courses at FE colleges and some independent beauty schools.

Educational requirements vary but many courses prefer a minimum standard equivalent to three or four GCSEs (A-C) including English and a science. Traditionally, courses have had a minimum age of 17/18 for entry but this is now less likely.

Beauty consultants

Although there are no set entry requirements most stores and cosmetic companies prefer trainee beauty consultants to have passed examinations and have qualifications in beauty. Maturity is an asset and beauty consultants are usually expected to be at least 21, with good communication skills and previous experience of selling. Cosmetic manufacturers provide training in their own products.

Qualifications and training

Qualifications and training are changing rapidly in the beauty business. The most usual method now of training for beauty work is by following a course at a further education college and around 90% of students qualify through this route. All training is unisex. Many of the FE courses are full-time, but since colleges of further education now have a considerable degree of autonomy over course provision, they are increasingly competing successfully with the private sector by running specialist weekend and short courses at lower costs than the private colleges. Private colleges still offer a range of courses but the private sector is shrinking rapidly and is now very small with schools, in for example aromatherapy, closing down.

There are a number of professional and examining bodies in the field and it is important to distinguish between them in terms of size and responsibilities. It is extremely complicated. The majority of small bodies providing examinations have chosen to stay outside the NVQ/SVQ framework.

NVQ/SVQs were established in 1992 in the beauty business and are gradually superseding many of the previous diploma and certificate courses. NVQ/SVQs encourage a variety of learning methods, with the possibility of open learning and part-time tuition, together with mixing units from different levels. The UK is leading the field in the development of vocational beauty therapy qualifications for Europe. It is anticipated that over the next few years a pan-European qualification will be developed based on British NVQs. For anyone wanting to work in Europe, NVQ/SVQs are increasingly likely to be the best route. Other qualifications may be acceptable abroad but it is up to each individual country to decide, and some countries may require further qualifications or licensing.

Ten years ago the beauty industry was dominated by two organisations – City & Guilds and the International Health and Beauty Council (IHBC). They still provide the majority of beauty therapy qualifications in the UK.

City & Guilds offer a range of full- and part-time courses lasting one or two years in beauty therapy, electrical epilation, cosmetic make-up, manicure and salon management as well as NVQs at levels 1, 2 and 3.

IHBC has now split into Vocational Training Charitable Trust (VTCT) which is only responsible for examining NVQ awards and Vocational Awards International (VAI). VAI issues awards itself and has three subsidiary awarding bodies – International Health and Beauty Council, International Institute of Health and Holistic Therapies (IIHHT) (*see also* ALTERNATIVE MEDICINE chapter) and International Institute of Sports Therapies (IIST).

VAI offers awards in anatomy and physiology, nutrition, first aid, counselling etc.

IHBC offers awards including manicure, ear piercing, wax depilation, make-up, remedial camouflage, red vein treatment, body massage, beauty therapy, advanced nail techniques, colour consultancy, beauty consultancy, electrology, theatrical and media make-up.

IIST offers a range of sports massage and health and fitness certificates and diplomas. (*See* SPORTS THERAPY *in* PROFESSIONAL SPORT chapter).

VTCT offers NVQs in Beauty Therapy at levels 1, 2 and 3 and NVQs in Epilation or Aromatherapy at level 3 (*See* AROMATHERAPY *in* ALTERNATIVE MEDICINE).

SCOTVEC is responsible for awarding SVQs in Scotland. These are identical to NVQs as the standards have been laid down by the Health and Beauty Therapy Training Board (*see below*).

NVQ/SVQ level 1 is an introductory taster course to assist generally within the salon and specifically to assist with reception duties and help the therapist with cosmetic application, nail treatment and wax depilation treatments.

NVQ/SVQ level 2 includes reception duties, make-up, facial massage and skin care, nail care, wax depilation, and lash and brow treatments. Additional units cover ear piercing, marketing cosmetics, artificial nails and stock control. Level 2 does not cover electrical and mechanical work on the face.

NVQ/SVQ level 3 covers all beauty therapy corrective treatments – massage, dietary control and individual exercise, plus mechanical and electrical treatments for the face and body. Options are available in remedial camouflage, sunbed tanning and heat and bath treatments.

NVQ level 3 Electrical Epilation covers diathermy needle epilation in addition to the beauty therapy core units. An additional unit covering galvanic/high frequency 'blend' epilation is available.

NVQ level 3 Aromatherapy Massage has two skill units covering selecting and blending oils and providing aromatherapy massage, in addition to the level 3 core units.

At present there are no substantial chains of salons in the beauty business, but when these arrive an NVQ at level 4 in management may be developed.

Other courses and bodies

BTEC National Diploma courses normally last two years full-time and are available at a number of colleges of FE. They may combine hairdressing and beauty therapy.

The BTEC/SCOTVEC Higher National Diploma in Beauty Therapy is only offered at a few colleges in England and Scotland. It concentrates on business and science and students may emerge lacking some of the basic beauty skills. More HND graduates go into teaching than into the physical hands-on side of the beauty business. HND students should normally have a biological science at least at GCSE (A-C) or equivalent.

BTEC is also accrediting NVQs at levels 1, 2 and 3.

The International Therapy Examination Council (ITEC) is getting smaller and their courses are now only offered in a few colleges of FE. Most of their income is from overseas students.

The Confederation of International Beauty Therapy and Cosmetology (CIBTAC is the examining arm of the British Association of Beauty Therapists and Cosmetologists (BABTAC). BABTAC is the professional body. CIBTAC offers NVQs but it is the smallest of the NVQ providers. CIBTAC also runs a number of non-NVQ diplomas in body therapy, beautician, electrolysist, aestheticienne, and anatomy and physiology, sugaring, reflexology, remedial epilation and aromatherapy certificates.

The Comité International d'Esthétique et de Cosmétologie (CIDESCO) is a continental organisation. It examines mostly in private schools in a number of European countries including the UK. Their exams have no connection with national standard qualifications in beauty work.

The Institute of Electrolysis is a small body training about 100 epilationists a year. This compares with about 2,000 epilationists who qualify through City & Guilds and IHBC each year.

The Federation of Holistic Therapists is the professional body representing a number of specialist bodies such as the Finnish Sauna Society and the Health and Beauty Employers' Federation.

Health and Beauty Therapy Training Board

The lead body for the industry (and future Industry Training Organisation) is the Health and Beauty Therapy Training Board. As an ITO they will be responsible for strategic planning for the whole of the industry including other qualifications as well as NVQ/SVQs.

Further information

Careers information is available from BABTAC and the Federation of Holistic Therapies. Information on examinations is available from the bodies listed above (addresses *in* Appendix 1 *under* BEAUTY).

Hairdressing

A great many women go to the hairdressers fairly regularly and many men have become much more fashion-conscious about their hair – 'styling' has taken over from straightforward 'barbering'. Hairdressing has become a '2 billion pound international growth industry' according to the Hairdressing Training Board. There are now around 36,000 salons operating throughout Britain employing approximately 170,000 hairdressers. While the industry is still largely (around 75%) made up of owner-managers working from 1 or 2 salons, the 1980s and 1990s have seen a growth in large hairdressing chains and franchising operations. The largest 30 or so run salons overseas, put on fashion shows and have their own international training schools. Essanelle for example has (1995) 450 salons across the UK, Germany and Switzerland. Although the numbers employed in hairdressing declined during the recession this trend appears to have halted.

Hairdressers cater for a very wide range of people, from older women who prefer traditional styles through to the more natural and livelier styles of the younger generation, for which hairdressers have had to develop new and greater expertise, particularly in cutting, upon which so much depends in modern styling. African-Caribbean hairdressing is a specialist area. It requires careful analysis, along with extensive chemical knowledge and includes Relaxing, Pressing, Weave-on, Braiding and Plaiting.

The qualified stylist (a trained hairdresser) has to be able to cut, set, colour and perm hair and most stylists are expected to undertake all types of hairdressing work. In some of the larger salons, stylists may specialise as colouring/perming/cutting technicians. Some of the more routine tasks such as washing hair may be undertaken by juniors or apprentices.

Hairdressing involves both art and craft – the art of creating a hair style for a client which is both in fashion and suits her (or his) appearance, and the craft of knowing how to produce the best result, and the materials and techniques to use. Most hairdressers need to learn to deal with the practical side of running a salon.

Most qualified hairdressers work in medium-sized, high-street salons, but there are opportunities in larger salons in town centres, in beauty salons, in department-store salons, in residential beauty and health clinics, in hotels and clubs, at sea on passenger liners, etc. The African-Caribbean hairdressing sector is rapidly expanding and there are now approximately 2,000 salons in the UK. Some hairdressers provide a home service – for people who cannot get to a salon, or who want their hair done just before they go to an event. Some freelance hairdressers provide a service to nursing homes and hospitals. It is possible to work abroad, especially in European resorts popular with English-speaking tourists. The armed services run hairdressing salons on military bases both in the UK and abroad. Hairdressers also work in prisons and a recent innovation has been for hairdressers to train inmates to NVQ/SVQ level 2 as hairdressers before they are released. The Home Office sets stringent criteria for all hairdressers working in prisons.

Film and television work offers a very limited number of openings for skilled hairdressers, and they must usually also know how to set hair in historical styles.

Manufacturers employ technicians to work as trainers in their tuition centres or as field representatives, responsible for in-salon training and product/equipment testing.

While many young men and women want to own their own salons eventually, the trend is to larger firms running 'chains', and the investment involved is substantial. Hairdressing is a business like any other, and so owner-managers, or managers for multiples need management skills, an ability to handle staff, and business knowledge. The administration will include accounts, book-keeping, PAYE, banking and stock control. A knowledge of health and safety regulations is also required.

Teaching hairdressing at a college of further education or private hairdressing school is another possible employment area for experienced hairdressers. A further qualification in further education teaching may be required.

Trichology

Some skilled hairdressers who have 4 GCSE/SCEs can progress to other fields such as trichology. Trichology is the study of the hair and the scalp and trichologists specialise in the treatment of disorders and diseases such as baldness and thinning hair. Their work involves diagnosis, massage, heat and electrical treatments, lotions and ointments, and advice on diet and hair care. Trichologists usually run their own private clinics or private practices and their clients include those referred on from hairdressing salons. Some trichologists work in scientific research or as consultants in pharmaceutical or cosmetic firms. Most trichologists qualify through distance learning courses.

Recruitment and entry

Entry is via a YT programme, a 3-year apprenticeship, a 2-year full-time course at an FE college, or a short intensive course at a private college. There are no fixed entry requirements. A 'good' educational background, with some GCSE (or SCE) subjects, including a science, at reasonable grades, is usually needed. The normal entry age is between 16 and 18. Adults may enter via government adult training routes or a full-time course.

For working in the film and television industry candidates must have 5 GCSE/SCEs (English Literature, Drama and History are preferred), preferably 2 A-levels or equivalent, have completed a full-time course in hairdressing, beauty therapy or make-up, have achieved NVQ/SVQ to level 2 and preferably to level 3, and be at least 21. Training consists of 6 months learning the basic skills of TV make-up, period hairdressing, wigmaking, etc., followed by 6 months on secondment to a make-up department before becoming a full member working under supervision. *See* BEAUTY *above and* Television Make-up *in* MEDIA CAREERS.

Hairdressers need artistic and creative ability, manual dexterity, and should be friendly people, who enjoy working with customers. Conventional employers generally expect entrants to be well groomed, to look neat and be tidy, but some popular styles clash with this – and hairdressers promoting them like their staff to 'advertise' the newest styles – so it is a matter of judging what a particular employer may want. Adaptability and the kind of intelligence which can keep pace with fashion changes are a considerable advantage. Business skills are also useful.

Physical stamina is essential – most salons are very busy places, with long hours of standing, and usually at least some evening work. Salons will not normally accept entrants with major skin problems.

Qualifications and training

Whatever their training route, new entrants usually undertake qualifications developed by the Hairdressing Training Board (HTB) in conjunction with City & Guilds and the main qualification, which covers the essential practical skills, is at NVQ level 2. The skills include: shampooing, conditioning hair and scalp, cutting, setting, blow-drying, perms, colouring processes and dealing with clients. Afro-Caribbean styling is also covered. The HTB has also developed an NVQ/SVQ level 3 qualification which includes specialist techniques, training and supervisory skills, and organising promotion activities for the salon. HTB is working on NVQ/SVQ level 4 which will incorporate salon administration and business management rather than additional hairdressing skills.

Those who enter via Youth Training or Training Credits gain work experience in a hairdressing salon and attend a training course on day-release. The training lasts up to 2 years and trainees are expected to work towards NVQ/SVQ level 2, as described above.

Apprenticeships last 3 years. Apprentices work alongside and assist qualified hairdressers, receive practical training and attend college on day-release. Most apprenticeships now incorporate YT and NVQ/SVQs and YT trainees go on to the third year of an apprenticeship on completion of their YT programme.

Some salons do their own training, outside NVQ/SVQs – this may well be of good quality but trainees may be at a disadvantage if their certificates are not nationally recognised.

FE college courses last 2 years and students study for NVQ/SVQ level 2, as described above. They may also take the National Diploma of Hairdressing which is awarded by the Guild of Hairdressers. After the course, most students start work as an improver and take a final year's training, similar to the third year of an apprenticeship.

A recent development (1995) is the Modern Apprenticeships initiative which combines the best of traditional apprenticeships with modern training systems. The main outcome is NVQ level 3. Contact your local TEC or Careers Office for more information.

Some private hairdressing colleges offer courses which are approved by the HTB and lead to NVQ level 2, but prospective students should check this out before spending what can be a considerable sum on tuition fees.

Hairdressers with an NVQ/SVQ at level 2 may apply to the Hairdressing Council to become state-registered hairdressers.

Further information

Hairdressing Training Board. Institute of Trichologists.

Laundries and dry cleaners

The laundries and dry cleaning industry has changed significantly in its structure and operations. In the 1960s, the typical domestic laundry business provided a service to households throughout the country. However, launderettes combined with the widespread ownership of washing machines led to its rapid decline and today (1996) no more than 100 laundries provide domestic services compared to 3,000–4,000 35 years ago. In recent years small firms and retail shops offering ironing services for shirts and other items have appeared.

As domestic laundry dwindled, so textile rental began its spectacular rise. The typical services are linen hire to hotels and restaurants, workwear rental to industry and commerce, and cabinet towel rental to all types of outlet. The significant difference between textile rental and conventional laundry is that in the former, the articles are owned, processed, repaired and eventually replaced by the supplier company.

The industry is dominated by the larger firms whose operations are done in large factories, with collection and delivery carried out through van routes. Only the few remaining domestic laundries operate door-step deliveries.

The structure of the retail dry cleaning industry has also changed dramatically. Originally, all dry cleaning was carried out in central processing plants, with items for cleaning being collected via receiving shops or van rounds. The advent of smaller, more efficient machines made possible the growth of the unit shop carrying out dry cleaning on site. Currently, there are approximately 5,000 unit shops, about a third of which belong to groups. The rest are owned and run independently. These shops may offer a range of specialist services – retexturing, dyeing, flame-proofing, repairs and alterations, etc.

A high proportion of the people working in the industry are semi-skilled. The most skilled tasks in the laundering and cleaning processes themselves are in, for example, hand-pressing, care of specialist materials or garments (e.g. leather) and removal of difficult stains. It is here that there has been the greatest fall in employment. There are, however, career opportunities, even if the actual number of openings is relatively small, in laundry and dry-cleaning technology and engineering, and in supervisory and managerial work.

Engineers and technologists develop new equipment and techniques, both to improve the service offered and to cope with new materials. Efficient management is crucial in an industry constantly fighting to maintain its position.

Recruitment and entry

There are no formal qualifications required for entry to the laundry and dry cleaning business as such – unless you count those who enter as engineers and technologists. However, some GCSE/SCEs may be an advantage and some firms may set entrance tests for numeracy and literacy.

Qualifications and training

The industry's needs for senior staff in England, Wales and Northern Ireland are met by in-company training and courses run by the Industry Training Organisation, the Fabric Care Research Association (FCRA), the Guild of Cleaners and Launderers (GCL) and City & Guilds. In Scotland the awarding body consists of FCRA, GCL and SCOTVEC. The industry has developed occupational standards for all sectors within the NVQ/SVQ framework. Levels 1 and 2 are in place and level 3 is in preparation. FCRA runs courses for supervisors and managers which provide the knowledge and skills for the technical resource management required. The trade associations are the Textile Services Association and the National Association of the Launderette Industry.

Further information

The Textile Services Association the Fabric Care Research Association.

Funeral services

Unlike other industries which depend on the economic climate for their survival, the turnover of the funeral service remains, inevitably, fairly steady from year to year. 17,000 people work in the funeral service nationally. There has been some increase in the number of larger firms with several branches, mainly in the major cities (the Co-operative Funeral Service is particularly prominent) but many funeral businesses are family firms.

It need hardly be said that the work of a funeral director, or undertaker, incorporates a great deal that is unpleasant, difficult and distressing. However, the tasks are more varied than is commonly supposed and those who take part derive satisfaction from the support and sympathy they are able to give the bereaved.

Funeral directors prepare the deceased for burial or cremation and arrange and supervise funerals. They visit relatives or friends of the deceased and arrange to collect the remains; they make administrative arrangements – dealing with enquiries, arranging for obituary notices, receiving charity donations, organising transport, ordering flowers, printing service sheets. They make financial and legal arrangements and obtain the necessary paperwork. On the practical side, they are responsible for preparing the body – washing, setting hair, shaving, inserting pads under the eyelids, suturing the mouth to stop the jaw opening, and applying make-up discreetly to the face if required. Preparation may also include embalming (*see below*). It is not a legal requirement for bodies to be embalmed but it is an increasing trend. Some funeral directors employ their own embalmers, others call in a trained embalmer when necessary. On the day of the funeral the funeral director arranges the cortège, attends, and maybe leads the ceremony and provides some moral support to the mourners.

Funeral services are offered to the public 24 hours a day, 7 days a week. Administration can be done during normal office hours but staff must be prepared to deal with the laying out or the removal of bodies at any time requested by the next of kin, especially in cases of sudden death.

Recruitment and entry

There are many family firms in the funeral business, which may be intentionally kept small in order not to lose the personal touch. Consequently, funeral directing can be difficult to get into unless there is a family connection. In a small town or village, the local undertaker may, in any case, only operate part-time. Opportunities for school-leavers are not numerous and at 16/17 years they may lack the necessary maturity.

A new entrant could start as a funeral service operative. This would mean dealing with the more routine side of the business including driving and maintaining vehicles, finishing the coffins (which are normally bought in from specialist manufacturers), and acting as a bearer at funerals. The funeral service operative would gradually be introduced to the full range of tasks.

Larger organisations sometimes take on prospective managers. Alternatively, individuals might consider setting up on their own (provided they have sufficient capital for vehicles and premises), but they would need to have learned the trade from an established funeral director.

No formal educational requirements are laid down but the National Association of Funeral Directors (NAFD) asks for a 'reasonable grade' at GCSE or SCE. A full driving licence is usually required.

Personal qualities are crucial. Above all, funeral directors must be good communicators who can deal tactfully and sympathetically with people who may be very distressed. They should be able to adopt a serious, dignified and mature approach to their work. They need to be good managers and organisers. Attention to detail is important. It's helpful if they have some familiarity with religious rituals so that they can understand the needs of their clients.

Qualifications and training

Training is usually on-the-job. NAFD-approved tutors run part-time courses leading to the Diploma in Funeral Directing, the recognised professional qualification. It is helpful but not compulsory if students are already in employment. The course is of a modular type with a foundation module which all students are required to take.

Courses can take up to one year and are run from tutorial schools in all parts of the UK. Correspondence and open learning methods are also used. Students register with the NAFD and the British Institute of Funeral Directors (BIFD) and with an approved tutor.

The syllabus for the Diploma includes: the Last Offices (preparing the body), an insight into embalming, law, funeral arrangements and different forms of religious funeral observances. Students have to carry out 25 funerals under supervision and on their own, work in the industry for a minimum period as well as taking theoretical and practical examinations.

Larger companies may run their own training schemes.

Embalming

The embalming process disinfects and preserves the body until it is ready for burial or cremation. The body is washed with germicidal soap and injected with sterilising fluid, wax and other materials to restore as normal an appearance as possible. Many funeral directors train as embalmers but embalming is also a specialist profession and self-employed embalmers may work for a number of local funeral directors.

Embalmers work in a clinically clean environment with the temperature slightly lower than normal room temperature. Most work in funeral homes but a few work in hospitals and medical schools preparing bodies for autopsies and dissection classes, or assisting hospital pathologists during autopsies.

It goes without saying that a career in embalming is not for the squeamish! An interest in science, particularly anatomy and chemistry, is essential. Other important qualities are cleanliness, attention to detail and manual dexterity for handling surgical instruments.

The British Institute of Embalmers (BIE) has an international membership of around 1,400 in 1996. Vacancies are advertised in their publication *The Embalmer*.

There are no formal entry requirements to become an embalmer. Trainees don't have to be in full-time employment – the BIE provides a list of private colleges who offer full-time courses. There are also part-time and correspondence courses. The examinations are set by the National Examinations Board of Embalmers.

Students must be at least 17 and have to pass a Foundation Test based on elementary knowledge of anatomy and the history of embalming. The part-time course is based on a modular system and includes anatomy, physiology, bacteriology and chemistry.

Further information

The National Association of Funeral Directors, British Institute of Funeral Directors and the British Institute of Embalmers.

Contents

The Health Service

(CLCI: J)

Background

Caring for the nation's health is very expensive – not only financially, but also in terms of other resources and the numbers of people employed. Demand for health services has been growing ever since the NHS was formed in 1948, and with it the number of people employed.

It is very difficult to reduce the number of healthworkers without adversely affecting the service. Mechanisation and automation can have only a marginal effect in primary care, although they are used in support services like cleaning and catering. Robots cannot yet replace surgeons, nurses, or physiotherapists – though a robot has been used in 1995 to perform certain prostate operations.

Problems with financing mean that the health service cannot employ as many people as it would like and according to reports of a 1995 survey by Incomes Data Services, nine out of ten NHS organisations experienced shortages of skilled employees, particularly physiotherapists, occupational therapists and psychologists.

Jobs and careers within the health services change and develop all the time. Many of the changes are a direct result of scientific and technological developments and improvements in diagnosis and treatment. Their effect is to bring much greater specialisation into many jobs, and to make the work more technical. Recently new attitudes have moved towards 'humanising' health services, and treating patients as whole people and not just their symptoms and illnesses, in isolation from the rest of the person and their environment. More thought is being given as well to the psychological and social effects of illness.

Experiments go on all the time. For example, in some general practices qualified (RGN) nurses have been trained, on an 'apprenticeship' basis, to become what is called a 'nurse practitioner'. They have learnt to take case histories and basic diagnostic techniques and so can deal with some patients instead of the GP, but under supervision. They do not prescribe, have learnt which problems must be passed on to a doctor, and must discuss any referrals they want to make with the supervising GP. The idea is not so much to ease the GP's caseload, but to give patients the choice of someone they may feel is more approachable and easier to talk to about some symptoms or problems than a GP.

In 1987, the government published a White Paper, *Promoting Better Health*, a major theme of which was to shift the emphasis in primary care from the treatment of illness to the promotion of health and the prevention of disease.

Working in health care increasingly means working more and more closely with other healthworkers, as part of a team. It is work which combines a concern for people who have health problems with a high scientific and technical content: there are more and more machines, more and more technical equipment, more scientific tests, more computers. Most of the work combines doing, observing, and talking, but paperwork generally (except for administrators) comes second, although obviously records are crucial.

It is a way of life which can swing from extreme to extreme, from the humdrum to the harrowing, from the ultra-clean to conditions of appalling mess, from periods of tedium and waiting to days or hours of continuous rush and great stress. The hours are inevitably long and irregular, and have not improved very much lately, although following a review of Junior Doctors' working hours they have been significantly reduced in 1995.

For most there is shiftwork. Not everyone cares directly for patients, but those who do have to deal sympathetically, patiently and reassuringly with both patients and relatives, and must accept that patients are now less willing to accept paternalistic and authoritarian attitudes in healthworkers, and want to be treated as intelligent people.

All healthworkers must have the same aims and the same standards. Everyone has to take the same care, and cleanliness and sterile conditions are as important for the laundry worker as for the surgeon 'scrubbing up'.

Caring for patients directly involves situations ranging from the relief of seeing a new baby howl or a child recovering from a serious illness, and joking with patients to help their morale, to coping through long nights with patients made bad-tempered by pain or continuous discomfort, and the inevitable reality of incurable illness and death.

Staff who are in closest day-to-day touch with patients often find themselves being counsellors, listening to and helping to ease problems such as loneliness and anxiety. Patients may also tell them about factors which may help to solve medical problems.

Recruitment and entry

Most professional healthworkers must train and qualify before they are recruited. Direct entry is only to lower-level occupations, and to traineeships.

All careers in the medical and health spheres are extremely demanding, on mind, body and emotion. Concern and compassion for suffering has to be combined with the ability to learn to understand and use scientific and technological equipment, tools and techniques. Professionals in the health service have to learn keen and careful observation, to make skilled analyses of situations and sound judgements; they need emotional and physical stamina, and the ability to remain calm and reassuring in crises. They have to accept responsibility for patients' lives.

Qualifications and training

Most health professions have their qualifications (and so effectively their training also), laid down by law, and by law many professionals must be 'state registered' before they can practise. Generally, training standards (and therefore educational requirements too), have been rising, and now involve three or more years' full-time study. Stated minimum entry requirements for courses may not always be enough, and so it is important to check the actual requirement with the schools. Patterns of training have been changing too: more degree courses for paramedicals, and some schools have become attached to universities and colleges, so that training is less isolated.

The National Health Service

The (state run) NHS looks after most of the nation's health and medical needs and is Europe's largest single employer. Not surprisingly, its size, importance and cost mean it is extremely difficult to make the NHS both efficient and effective. Demand for more and better services, which keep pace with increasingly expensive medical and technological advances, grows and grows, and the problems of an ageing population almost cancel out improvements elsewhere in health care.

Despite the criticisms and the problems, the NHS provides a service which compares reasonably on most criteria with those of other countries. However, the managerial and organisational problems have been endemic for all of its 48 years, despite regular attempts to solve them.

The innovations following the *'Working for Patients'* initiative in 1989 include major restructuring within general practices and hospitals. General practitioners may now become 'budget holders', responsible for buying healthcare from the hospitals they choose, whether self-governing, directly managed or privately run. Many hospitals are now 'self-governing', reorganising their structure and services to include the concepts of profitability and accountability.

The eight regional health authorities are responsible for regional strategy. The emphasis is on improving management and management systems. *See* MANAGING THE HEALTH SERVICE.

The 104 district health authorities (DHAs) are responsible for the health of those living within their boundaries. On average, each DHA has around half a million residents. From 1 April 1996, the DHAs merged with their corresponding Family Health Services Authorities (FHSAs), of which there are about 100.

The DHAs commission care and treatment for their residents, as required, from the providers of healthcare services. Hospital services are also purchased by GP Fundholders.

The main providers of hospital services are the NHS Trusts who are funded by the NHS but are free to raise additional funds independently. There are a total of 439 NHS Trusts, of which around 407 provide hospital services. Figures for 1994/95 show that 97% of in-patient treatment was provided by Trust hospitals. An Audit Commission report in 1995 indicated that up to 10% of hospital budgets may go on employing senior managers, and that management costs have generally risen by 35% since the NHS reforms were implemented. In 1995 managers made up 2.5% of the total NHS workforce.

Community care includes not only GPs but also health visitors, district nurses, social workers and home helps. In the community services, the main feature has been the steady development of group practices and health centres, bringing together general practitioners, dentists, etc. under one roof, with other members of the community services, such as health visitors and home nurses, attached to each. A government review in 1986 suggested a number of changes in community services and increasing emphasis has subsequently been placed on building effective, well-trained community health teams.

In 1994, there were 940,000 people employed in the NHS hospital and community health services in England, of whom about 7% were medical and dental and 58% non-medical direct care staff, and 35% other non-medical staff.

In 1994/95 the total cost of the NHS was £32 billion, of which more than two-thirds (£21.6 billion) was spent on hospital and community health services.

The private health sector

This consists mainly of an increasing number of registered private hospitals, nursing homes and clinics. Some private practices are staffed by medical and dental practitioners and other professionals qualified to work in the NHS, but who choose to work outside it, and by practitioners not normally employed by the NHS, such as osteopaths and chiropractors. Professional people working for the NHS can also practise privately at the same time. Many private hospitals belong to health insurance companies, and are run by professional managers.

Private hospitals, clinics and nursing homes are regulated by the Registered Homes Act 1984. At the end of the financial year 1994/95 there were 344 hospitals/clinics and 5,332 nursing homes registered under Section 23 of this Act. Most of the homes care permanently for older people, and some look after the mentally ill.

Private hospitals provide beds for short-term, 'acute' surgical/medical care. More private hospitals now provide 'high-tech' surgical treatment, and have radiotherapy and advanced diagnostic facilities, sharing some of them with the NHS. Hospitals and centres provide a range of other services, including health screening and diagnostic testing, and are trying out-patient, psychiatric and alcohol-abuse care. More private hospitals are still being built, but too many patients are still chasing too few beds.

There has been little growth in private general practice and only a small number of individual doctors practise only privately.

Occupational health services

The Employment Medical Advisory Service gives a broad, nationwide service of advice on all medical aspects of employment problems, to employers, employees, trade unions, family doctors, doctors working for firms, and so on. The service also has some legal responsibilities: to carry out medical examinations which may be required by law. The service should have a staff of some 60 medical advisers, plus ancillary staff. It is based on the main industrial centres.

Many larger employers, particularly industrial firms, have their own medical services for employees over and above those legally required. Here doctors and nurses provide a service which gives emergency and rapid medical treatment for anyone taken ill at work, or hurt in an accident. They arrange regular checks for people at risk, for example in labs where radioactive materials or dangerous chemicals are used. They may also deal with minor illness and accidents, may give immunisation or vaccination, for instance against a particular form of flu, so that staff do not have to take time off work. The medical service may also deal with other preventive measures, especially on safety. Most organisations employ local GPs on a sessional basis, but services are now being offered on a contract basis by some private companies. Only the largest firms have full-time medical staff. Many, however, employ full-time nurses.

The Armed Forces each have their own extensive medical services which specialise in the occupational hazards of the Army, the Navy and the Air Force, with their own hospitals. They treat soldiers, sailors and airforce personnel casualties in war and deal with the peacetime effects too: even training and simulating war can result in some extremely serious accidents. The Forces' medical services do a fair amount of research and development work into treatment for wounds caused by modern weapons. As the Falklands war showed, they have made considerable advances in, for example, treating burns, and the Navy has made extensive studies of the physiological and other problems of diving and other underwater work. The Gulf War threw up particular psychiatric problems. The Forces also provide a general-practitioner service for both serving men and women and their immediate families. They employ qualified doctors, nursing staff, and technicians. Aviation medicine is an interesting speciality.

Universities, colleges with resident students, and some boarding schools, also provide medical services. University and college health services combine occupational health services – for staff – with a general-practitioner-style service tailored to the needs of students, whose age generally makes them healthier than the patients in a conventional practice, but who are prone to, for instance, accidents on the sports field or in the lab, and to stress and psychological problems linked to their studies. Few employ full-time doctors or dentists, using local GPs on a sessional basis, but most have a small team of nurses working full- and/or part-time.

Medical staff in the Prison Service both care for inmates' physical and mental health, and also help in any rehabilitation, by diagnosing and treating where possible any physical, mental or psychological problems. Every prison has its own hospital accommodation, although where necessary outside medical services are used. The service carries out its own research into ways of treating and otherwise aiding offenders. Medical staff have to be at least 28, and postgraduate experience and/or training in psychiatry is useful. *See also* THE PRISON SERVICE *in* SECURITY AND PROTECTIVE SERVICES.

Other organisations employing medical and paramedical professions and supporting health staff include the POLICE (*see in* SECURITY AND PROTECTIVE SERVICES), Missionary Medical Services and the Merchant Navy (*see in* THE TRANSPORT INDUSTRY).

Contents

The Medical and Dental Professions

(CLCI: JAB, JAF)

Background

Although they still make up less than 10% of all NHS employees, and probably even fewer in other health sectors, doctors and dentists are the key personnel in health service provision. Numbers have been rising steadily – 1992 numbers for Great Britain show nearly 100,000 employed in four main fields: hospitals, general practice, and community and public health. The latest figures for England alone (1994) are 63,320. As the Royal Commission points out, most people expect that a doctor will diagnose what is wrong with them and prescribe the treatment: they initiate most health service expenditure, and play a major part in both financial and general management.

Worldwide, there is a shortage of medically and dentally qualified staff, particularly in underdeveloped areas which find it difficult to afford qualified doctors. In 1994 there were 14,000 overseas doctors working in the UK (including those from EU countries).

Medicine

Hospital doctors – general practitioners – community medicine

Medicine is not just one career. While it is common to think only of becoming 'a' doctor, there are, in fact, many different kinds of doctors. Certainly, most doctors spend most of their time doing what is generally considered to be a doctor's job: diagnosing (trying to discover what a patient's health problem is) and treating illness. However, they may also (for example) do research, look for ways to prevent disease, become medical advisers, or indeed not practise as doctors at all. Doctors also have a wide choice of different specialisations and settings in which to practise medicine.

The BMA lists 24 main areas of work for medically qualified men and women: Accident and Emergency Medicine, Cardiology, Dermatology, Endocrinology, General (Internal) Medicine, Geriatric Medicine, Neurology, Paediatrics, Renal Medicine (Nephrology), Respiratory Medicine, Radiology, Radiotherapy and Oncology, Rheumatology and Rehabilitation, and Occupational Medicine (on all of which further information is available from the Royal College of Physicians); Anaesthetics, General Practice, Ophthalmology, Obstetrics and Gynaecology, Pathology, Psychiatry, Radiology, and Surgery (which all have their own Royal Colleges); Medical Research, Public Health Medicine and Sports Medicine. Between 1984 and 1994, consultant numbers grew fastest in accident and emergency, paediatrics and radiology. Geriatrics and Anaesthetics are the least popular specialisms.

As the 1979 Royal Commission pointed out, the role of the doctor is not defined, and varies according to individual inclinations and circumstance. The doctor's role has also changed in response to developments in medicine, and as a result of changes in attitudes and aspiration, not only amongst doctors themselves, but in changing aspirations and roles amongst healthworkers as well, and in the demands of the public. The Commission noted that few detailed studies have been made of medical work in the UK, and suggested this is an important area for future research. More information is now required from medical services: figures relating to numbers of patients treated, the proportion immunised or screened for diseases such as cancer, and the length of waiting lists, are all now submitted for scrutiny. GPs are now subject to annual audit.

Authorities are in total disagreement, it would appear, on how many doctors will be needed in the future. The last two official predictions were based on very inaccurate estimates of, for instance, the birth-rate. The Royal Commission suggested that current output of the medical schools was about right, and that there was unlikely to be any medical unemployment up to the end of the century, but did say, quite sharply, that 'doctors will not have the choice of specialty and place of practice they have at present…' There are, however, some fears of unemployment, despite the fact that there is a shortage of some specialities and many doctors work very long hours.

The main choice is still between becoming a family doctor in general practice, or working in the hospital service. The 1992 figures for Great Britain show nearly 100,000 medically qualified in the four main fields as follows: hospitals 60,400, general practice 33,800, community service 3,100 and public health 1,100. As an example of notable trends the numbers entering medical schools for pre-clinical training rose from 2,478 in 1965/66 to 4,270 in 1992/93; numbers obtaining the first registerable qualification rose from 1,939 to 3,494. The proportion of women rose in the same 27 years from 20.8% entering training to 52.4% and from 24.8% of those qualifying to 47.1%.

Younger doctors have, in the past, been able to spend a few years in the hospital service, and then switch to general practice, possibly with a part-time hospital appointment. The compulsory three-year vocational training for GPs means that this is not so easy now. It has always been more difficult to transfer from general practice to hospital service. Hospital work and general practice are, of course, very different. The doctor in general practice needs a broadly based knowledge of medicine and must expect to deal with the more common ailments of the community (but still be able to detect the less usual), while the hospital doctor or surgeon goes on to specialise in depth in one aspect of medicine or surgery, and treats mainly patients with more serious conditions.

Fewer than one in ten of all doctors teach in medical school and/or do research full-time. Even fewer work in the community service, in occupational medical service, or are members of the Armed Forces, Civil Service, prison service, etc.

Hospital doctors

Hospital doctors usually specialise in a fairly narrow branch of medicine or surgery and, according to the Royal Commission, the specialities are likely to become narrower with advances in scientific knowledge and technology.

The Commission reported that numbers of general physicians and general surgeons have been declining as new specialist skills develop in particular areas – heart surgery, for example, is a relatively new speciality. Change in the range of specialities is almost continuous within the hospital service. Some diseases have been virtually eliminated, reducing the need for doctors who specialise in treating them, while other areas have become more important: treating the victims of road accidents is now a major specialisation, for instance, simply because there are more serious road accidents.

However, the decline in demand in some areas of medicine does not always result in fewer specialists. The fall in the birth-rate theoretically should have reduced the number of obstetricians, but in fact it has been counterbalanced by having virtually all babies born in hospital. Medical advance means more lives are saved, so there is more demand for specialists able to deal with the problems of those who survive with some form of handicap, from babies with spina bifida to the very old. Some diseases are on the increase simply because people live longer and more stressful lives, which means more cancer and more people with heart conditions.

The Royal Commission also thought that increasing specialisation, and the rigidity in staff roles which tends to go with it, was likely to lead to higher staffing levels, as were patient expectations and influences. The number of posts depends upon government funding decisions.

Other developments could bring more changes. For example, doctors in the acute specialities, the Commission suggested, may see their role as being predominantly physically orientated and dependent on the findings of biomedical research and development in technology. In other specialities, e.g. those dealing with people whose behaviour is disturbed, the emphasis will be on developing better relationships between doctor and patient.

Young doctors planning to make a career within the hospital service have to choose their specialisation by the time they qualify. Since it is policy to treat as many people as possible at home, by choosing hospital work any doctor is choosing to work with the most seriously ill, with people who need surgery, or with groups where hospitalisation is believed to mean a better service, for instance in delivering babies. Medical students can use the clinical years at medical school to gain insight into the work of the various specialities; many medical schools now let students choose between a series of 'elective' studies of the various specialities. Not all specialities involve directly treating patients: pathologists and anaesthetists, for example, administer services for other doctors and surgeons, only coming into contact with patients at certain points in their treatment.

The Royal Commission urged that students should be encouraged to work in the specialities where more staff are needed. The evidence is that the main shortage specialities are mental illness and handicap, geriatrics, radiology, anaesthetics, and the pathological specialities.

Although most hospital staff specialise, in England 4,802 (1993) still worked in general medicine (4,124 in 1983). Anaesthetists – 5,009 in 1993 (3,987 in 1983) – made up the next largest group. General surgeons were still a large group, but a declining proportion: 3,619 (1993) up from 3,481 in 1983. Obstetrics and gynaecology was still also a large group, over 3,094 (1993) up from 2,575 in 1983.

Numbers working in mental illness, handicap and related areas had risen from 3,500 in 1983 to 3,833 in 1993.

Within the specialist surgeries, the largest groups were accident and emergency (2,094 doctors in 1993; 1,594 in 1983) and traumatic and orthopaedic (2,504 doctors in 1993; 1,850 in 1983).

Largest of the medical specialities was still (just) paediatrics (children's medicine), with 2,804 staff in 1993 (1,767 in 1983). But fastest-growing was geriatrics, with 1,996 staff (1,894 in 1983). Ophthalmology had just 1,328 staff (1,020 in 1983). Other medical specialities – rheumatology and rehabilitation, infectious diseases, chest diseases, dermatology (skin), cardiology, and genito-urinary – had far smaller numbers: 1,183 against 831 in 1983.

Doctors specialising in 'scientific' aspects of medicine form quite small groups from a few general pathologists to rising numbers of chemical pathologists, haematologists, histopathologists, immunopathologists, medical micro-biologists, and clinical pharmacologists. These specialists administer and work in medical laboratories and are almost entirely backroom men and women. Numbers rose from 2,200 in 1983 to 2,337 in 1993.

For newly qualified doctors, already aged 24, there is still a long way to go, and much hard work, to reach a senior position in a speciality. The young doctor joins a team of doctors, traditionally called a 'firm', within his or her chosen speciality, for several more years of training. The firm is led by a consultant, a fully qualified and experienced specialist, who takes responsibility for diagnosing what is wrong with and treating patients referred to the hospital by a GP. The consultant physician or surgeon holds out-patient clinics, visits and examines patients on the wards, and decides on treatment, and in surgical fields, may operate. However, most consultants delegate much of the day-to-day work with and for patients to the members of the team, most of whom are still training, learning mainly on the job under supervision from the doctor in the next grade up. They normally also try out – pioneer – new methods of diagnosis, testing, treatment and/or surgery, and write up, give and publish papers on these, or write up observations on unusual cases, all of which is essential for promotion.

The newly qualified doctor currently spends about three years as a house officer, a job which involves admitting new patients, taking their case histories, making the first examination, organising and in some cases carrying out tests, recording findings, perhaps starting on treatment, and then keeping up-to-the-minute checks on patients' conditions, reporting all the time to the firm's registrar. House officers usually live in the hospital and must often work long hours in the day-to-day care of very ill patients.

After the house posts, hospital doctors work their way up through a series of, usually, two-year short-term contracts (which means everyone except the consultants change jobs and move from hospital to hospital quite often), first as registrar, then as senior registrar. Each step up usually involves taking increasing responsibility for patients' treatment or for more difficult surgery, but these are still junior, training posts. It is also usually necessary to pass further, highly specialised, tough, examinations. For some specialities it can also be useful to spend a period gaining lab experience. The total time spent as a registrar depends on both the popularity of the speciality – competition in some fields is intense – and the expertise needed: it can be as short as four years or as long as ten, but on average anyone who is going to become a consultant does so by the age of 37 or 38, and rarely after the age of 40. Becoming a consultant involves a combination of hard work, ability, and some luck, and it is crucial to gain the best and widest possible experience and training: younger doctors compete to train under the best consultants in their field.

Specialist training has recently been reviewed, and from 1996 various changes will be implemented. The grades of registrar and senior registrar will be combined into one title, specialist registrar. The period spent as a senior house officer will last about two years while specialist registrars will spend four years in their grade. This means that the time taken to reach a consultancy will reduce from the present average of twelve years to seven years to tie in with the rest of Europe.

The latest available (1994) figures (for England only) show 15,640 consultants out of 44,640 hospital doctors. Career prospects for junior hospital doctors are improving. It has been policy to increase the number of consultants faster than junior grades for twenty years now; the more consultant posts there are available, the more likely the junior staff are to progress. However, there have been criticisms of 'too many chiefs and not enough Indians', so a balance has to be found. The ratio of junior doctors to consultants has reduced from 1.60:1 in 1984 to 1.51:1 in 1994. In 1994 women formed 18% of consultants.

The 1979 Royal Commission suggested a revised hospital career structure, but conflict of interest between senior and junior doctors has made agreement on how to change the system difficult. There are just too many doctors in the training grades below senior registrar for the present number of consultant posts: most senior registrars can be sure of a consultancy in due course, although the wait can be a long one, given that many consultants spend over 30 years in the grade. The number of registrars and SHOs together outnumber consultants. Hospital doctors also complain that they do not gain true clinical responsibility (which they often carry in all but name) early enough, and that the training aspects of the lower grades are neglected at the expense of using registrars simply as 'pairs of medical hands' to maintain the service.

Consultants work increasingly closely together, and surgeons, in particular, are especially dependent on teams of specialists. Some consultants work full-time in the Health Service, but about half work part-time, combining Health Service work with private practice and/or clinical teaching in medical school. The hours consultants work are rarely shorter than those of junior doctors. A full-time consultant is now estimated to be on duty for some 35 hours a week, not counting emergencies which happen out of hours, being on call, time spent keeping abreast of new developments, teaching, or doing administrative or committee work.

General practitioners

General practitioners look after the day-to-day health problems of a list of up to 1,200 people, who have chosen, and been accepted by, them as their GPs. Although there are no rigid catchment areas for doctors' practices, normally most of their patients live within reasonable reach of the surgery, and so the kind of practice may vary with the locality. Since GPs mostly live close to their surgeries, this often means being a member of the same relatively small community, at least in rural areas. Some practices may be mostly residential estates, perhaps with a high proportion of young families, which means plenty of work with children and their mothers; it may be in a country or seaside town with a high and rising proportion of older people; it may be an industrial centre which means that working conditions may be particularly hard on people's chests or feet; in rural areas, farmworkers, living in isolated spots, may predominate.

GPs treat 90% of all illness, physical and mental, and so expect to meet and treat almost any kind of ailment the community can produce. In most practices, GPs spend most of their time treating a wide range of different illnesses, most of them very ordinary, such as childhood ailments, influenza, stomach upsets, traumas and small accidents, the daily problems of ageing and anxiety. Normally they will see only a few people with very serious conditions, although they must always be on the watch for the unsuspected, for the threatening coronary, for example. There may be unusual symptoms to diagnose, patients with chronic or recurring disease to care for, and only too often, patients who are fatally ill.

A general practitioner tries to find out what is wrong with a patient quickly, and to catch all illnesses in their early stages if possible. They care completely for most of their patients, from deciphering the first symptoms through to final outcome, whatever it may be: full recovery, the problems of long-term care, or helping relatives through a patient's death. Modern drugs and the use of vaccines (for example) have cut the length of time people (and particularly children) actually spend being ill, but as people live longer there are more diseases of old age to be treated, more patients who have conditions caused by, for instance, smoking, and more stress and anxiety problems to deal with.

General practitioners have a good deal of independence. They are self-employed and work on contract to the NHS. In 1991, a new contract came into force, laying out revised terms and conditions of service. The GP is now, for instance, required to reach certain targets for childhood immunisation in order to get higher remuneration. GPs are required to offer all patients over 75 years old annual check-ups.

The General Practice service now comes under the auspices of the Family Health Service Authority (FHSA). Currently, practices of over 7,000 patients can opt to become budgetholders. This means that they become purchasers of services for all the patients' needs, and gives them scope to make savings which may be ploughed back into the practice or used to purchase further services for their patients. These changes mean that practices are becoming small businesses and often employ full-time accountants to manage them. GPs must also keep to certain professional standards which are monitored by the General Medical Council. But it is entirely up to the GP to decide how to treat each patient, and if and when to call in a consultant or send the patient to hospital. GPs are encouraged to treat the 'whole' patient, not just the present illness or symptoms, taking into account also the more general effects on patients and their families. The Royal College of General Practitioners has explicitly proposed a comprehensive approach to the physical, psychological and social aspects of patients' illness. Not every GP, though, accepts that it is part of the job to help solve non-medical family crises.

General practitioners can and do practise on their own, but increasingly they work in partnerships:

	1983	1994
Singlehand	2,952	2,824
2 doctors	3,912	3,644
3 doctors	5,084	4,218
4 doctors	4,316	4,700
5 doctors	3,410	4,275
6 doctors	3,580	6,906

Group practices make possible more regular working times, better emergency and night-service arrangements, better chances to take time off for further training, and generally improved working conditions. It may be possible to specialise: most group practices run their own child surveillance and maternity clinics, and some GPs specialise in mental illness. Many practices share purpose-built accommodation provided by the NHS as local health centres, which may also house, for example, dentists, chiropodists, opticians, district nurses and health visitors, family planning, and medical social services. This makes it easier to develop 'primary care' teams, where nurses, for example, can take over, e.g. dressings and injections. More recently, GPs have been able to build their own surgeries under the 'cost rent' scheme.

A GP's day is based on morning and early evening surgeries, which can take up to four or five hours, increasingly seeing patients on an appointment system rather than first-come, first-served. Home visits, checking on lab or consultants' reports, signing prescriptions, writing letters, discussing cases with colleagues, and so on, are fitted round surgeries. Most GPs now run special clinics, some work part-time in hospitals, or for a local university or college, or a firm's health service. Some find time to do research or report-writing. Allowances are now paid to GPs who reach various government-set 'targets' in terms of numbers seen in well-person clinics, child surveillance, cytology screening or immunisation. Clinics have been set up specifically to educate and encourage the public in healthy ways of living.

Of course patients are never ill to order, so that working days can be long and difficult. However, most group practices now have rotas for evening/night and weekend duty, so GPs can have more 'normal' working hours/lives – even though they are still personally responsible for 24-hour care for the patients on their lists.

All GPs must now complete a three-year vocational training scheme, comprising two years in designated hospital posts and one year as a trainee in a training general practice.

Once settled into a practice, GPs tend to stay put – life is relatively uncompetitive, since promotion to senior partner normally comes naturally with age. Most practices have room for doctors who want to work only part-time. Women made up 26% of GP principals in 1993.

It is possible to start a new practice (literally 'put up a plate' on a door or gate and wait for patients to arrive) rather than join an existing one, although plenty of experience is needed first. But this is only allowed in areas which the NHS considers are 'under-doctored' – and they tend to be predictably unpopular places. Most doctors work for the NHS, some also practise privately, but relatively few have only private practices.

Community medicine

Community medicine divides into work done by the community medicine staff and work done by the clinical medical officers.

The community medicine staff, who include regional medical officers, district community physicians and other specialists in community medicine, are 'doctors who try to measure and predict the health care needs of the populations, who plan and administer services to meet those needs, and who teach and research in this field'.

Community medicine is a relatively new speciality. The main functions are medical administration, environmental health and preventative medicine in the community, and epidemiology. This means they help plan healthcare for each region and district, as well as tracking down the reasons for particular epidemics, and dealing with the problems and consequences of trying to find people who may be carrying a dangerous disease (e.g. typhoid), investigate outbreaks of food-poisoning, or work on the manifold problems of 'new' diseases, like AIDS. They deal with all environmental health problems, with preventing disease where possible, and with health education. They do research into the patterns of illness in different areas, trying to discover why (for example) more people suffer from heart disease in one place than in another, and so help the NHS to plan the distribution of resources, what should be given priority, and whether or not prevention is feasible. Some community physicians do research in these areas in university rather than the NHS. Around 3,100 qualified medical staff work in this branch of community medicine in the NHS. At least until recently there was a shortage of quality recruits for the service.

Clinical medical staff in community health service run the school health service, giving regular health checks for children in state schools, mother-and-baby clinics, family-planning services, immunisation programmes, and so on. Of over 5,000 doctors employed most work part-time – they may be women doctors working part-time or combine community health work with other part-time doctoring – and quite a few doctors do occasional sessions. The Royal Commission suggested that they have been somewhat isolated from the GP and hospital service, and should be properly integrated into whatever pattern of child health services ultimately emerges.

Linked to community medicine is the national *Public Health Laboratory Service* which has a countrywide network of ten regional and 54 area bacteriological and virological laboratories which do research and help with the diagnosis, prevention and control of epidemic diseases, study the way in which microbial diseases are spread, and look for new methods of controlling them. It is usual to enter the service as a newly qualified medical graduate after two six-month house appointments, since the postgraduate training lasts five years. *See also* CENTRAL GOVERNMENT.

Other opportunities

Research – teaching – other possibilities

Medicine is so much the vocational degree subject that it is rare to consider it as a purely scientific discipline in its own right as well, with career potential outside the strictly medical field. Yet the form and content of medical education are solidly scientific enough (and at most medical schools it is possible to complete a science as well as a medical degree with only an extra year) to be the basis of a number of scientific or other careers. Six years is a long time, and a medical training is very tough. It is unrealistic, therefore, to expect that every 18-year-old who begins a course in medicine will still want to practise medicine when he or she graduates at 24.

Research

Probably the closest alternative to a career as a medical practitioner is in research, either clinical or in medical sciences, which usually means working in the laboratory. Other scientists (*see* e.g. *in* BIOLOGICAL SCIENCES), have always played a major part in medical research, but medically qualified people are also needed, both because of the multidisciplinary nature of their 'pre-clinical' training (*see below*), which matches the generally interdisciplinary nature of the research, and because their clinical training gives the necessary practical slant.

Medical qualifications are on a par with other scientific degrees as a basis for a career in research, and qualified medical people are recruited for fundamental general or clinical research, where often they work as members of a team. Some make a lifelong career in research, others spend only part of their working lives in this. Postgraduate training, under Medical Research Council fellowships and scholarships, in medical research methods and clinical trial techniques, is available.

Medical research takes two main forms: work on solving specific problems, and developing new techniques and instrumentation, with a great deal of overlap between them. Since medical research is multidisciplinary, medically qualified researchers work alongside and/or in teams with other scientists. Research workers are employed either in hospitals (where the employer may be the NHS, the teaching university/medical school, the Medical Research Council, or even all three), or in research units in universities or government-sponsored laboratories or those of pharmaceutical companies.

The Medical Research Council currently has some 40 units spread throughout the UK and employs (1995) 190 medically qualified staff (and 900 other scientists) and 1,200 research support staff, who are mostly employed through universities.

Although all its work is medically oriented, MRC also supports fundamental research, believing that it will provide important leads – the Council has been deeply involved in promoting research in molecular biology, for example. MRC units either do long-term, multidisciplinary research on problems of public concern (e.g. AIDS), or build up research potential in subjects before they become fully established in universities. A molecular neurobiology unit has been set up to concentrate on the molecular processes responsible for normal and abnormal behaviour of nerve transmitters and receptors, using the latest methods, including DNA cloning, to study the brain and nervous system at genetic, molecular and cellular level. This research could be the basis for the design of new drugs and strategies to prevent and treat mental illness. Other examples of MRC research include working out the structure of the influenza virus, developing gene probes to diagnose inherited diseases, and a possible vaccine against malaria, and studying the junction between nerve and muscle to learn more about auto-immune responses.

Teaching

Some 8,500 people with medical qualifications do not practise as doctors at all, but work in medical schools (which are generally part of universities) as teachers (although they may combine this with some clinical work) and do research too, or they may be involved entirely in research, in a university department or other research unit.

To teach any medically related subject in medical school or university (e.g. psychiatry), a medical degree is also needed.

Other possibilities

Doctors also work in OCCUPATIONAL HEALTH SERVICES (*see in* THE HEALTH SERVICE); THE ARMED FORCES; *and* THE PRISON SERVICE (*see in* SECURITY AND PROTECTIVE SERVICES).

Medical qualifications, and preferably some experience as a GP, are a basis for work in advisory services, such as those run by local authorities, and the public health services (*see in* LOCAL GOVERNMENT *and* THE HEALTH SERVICE). *See also* BIOMEDICAL ENGINEERING *in* PROCESS ENGINEERING, BIOMEDICAL ENGINEERING AND MATERIALS SCIENCE.

Beyond the strictly medical field, medically qualified staff are employed by, e.g., pharmaceutical firms in research or advisory and consultancy work.

A degree in medicine can be treated purely and simply as any other science degree, and graduates can consider jobs open to graduates of any discipline. Medical graduates may have to be flexible if employment prospects for doctors deteriorate. There are well-known examples of doctors who work as MPs, writers, journalists, playwrights and TV presenters.

Recruitment and entry

Prospective doctors need to be highly intelligent, and scientifically minded, just to get into medical school and through the course. They must also be able to work hard, often for long and irregular hours, and this means having physical stamina, energy, and really good physical health. Being a doctor involves carrying considerable responsibility and being very conscientious. It needs the ability to concentrate, to be resourceful, patient, and good at listening. Doctors must be able to deal sympathetically with people of all kinds, and be able to get them to talk about themselves. Doctors need to be practical, hard-headed and realistic, concerned for people and their health problems. Doctors should not be easily upset by the unpleasant symptoms of disease or accident; they need to be psychologically and emotionally stable, and must be able to live with the more brutal facts of life and death.

Qualifications and training

No doctor may practise in the UK without obtaining the necessary university degrees or professional qualifications to be registered by the General Medical Council. It is extremely difficult for anyone over the age of 30 to embark upon a medical training, not least for financial reasons if the applicant has already had a grant or loan for another degree course. Entry is very competitive, and most entrants will have taken three A-levels or equivalent in chemistry, physics and biology; typical grades expected for entry in 1996 ranged from AAA for Oxford and Cambridge, AAB for Edinburgh, Glasgow and Queen's Belfast to BBB at the London schools with ABB elsewhere. The course itself lasts five years with an extra year for those universities offering a science degree as well as the MB.

The pattern and content of medical courses have changed quite considerably over the past twenty years, although they still start with a firm grounding of relevant sciences. At least three kinds of change have affected medical teaching.

First, all the many developments in medical research mean that there is so much more to learn, and since many of the advances in understanding disease and in treatment are science-based, the emphasis is on understanding the scientific basis of medicine and on scientific method.

Second, most medical schools teach students more about the people they are treating – the 'whole person' and their family and community – and do not just concentrate on the body, how it works, what goes wrong with it and how to treat it.

Third, some schools no longer divide the basic scientific studies (called 'pre-clinical') quite so rigidly from the vocational, clinical stage, which means introducing students to the patients and the wards rather earlier than is traditional. In the traditional course, healthy lungs are studied and dissected in the first year (for example), and lung diseases (and patients with them) are not met until (say) the fourth. In the modern, more 'integrated' course, the chest and lungs in health and disease are studied at the same time.

Schools have also introduced a range of 'elective' studies as part of medical degree courses, giving students some opportunity to broaden or deepen their studies in ways that interest them individually. Intending medical students should, then, study syllabuses carefully, since the range and depth of such options varies between schools.

Whichever way the course is organised, studying medicine involves some solid science: physiology, biochemistry, anatomy, and so on, usually with some behavioural/social sciences. There is some variation in the balance between these: not all schools insist on so much dissection, for example. As we have seen, some schools introduce medical techniques and clinical work fairly early, others still do not start clinical studies until the third year. While the teaching of medical techniques is more integrated than it used to be, via a system of team teaching, the traditional clerkship – short periods attached to specialist teams in particular areas of medical and surgical practice – is still usual. However, more time is now given to work in, for example, community medicine and general practice, geriatrics and psychiatry, with chances to specialise in some. One now common, and popular, 'elective' allows students to spend some weeks on a relevant 'project' almost anywhere in the world.

Training does not, however, stop on graduation day, despite the five or six years already spent studying and training. New graduates in medicine are 'provisionally registered' once they have completed their final examinations, and are considered qualified doctors, but full registration requires satisfactory completion of a preregistration year, involving two six-month appointments as house officer (houseman) at specially approved hospitals. Each six-month appointment must be spent in a different branch, i.e. in two from medicine, surgery and obstetrics.

Hospital doctors then go through a further series of training grades, and must usually also study for postgraduate qualifications if they want to be promoted. As mentioned earlier, all doctors going into general practice must complete vocational training.

Postgraduate study

A second qualification is generally needed for advanced and specialised work in particular branches of medicine and surgery, and for research. This may be via (university) higher degrees and diplomas following further medical-school training, and/or via membership and fellowship of one of the Royal Colleges (e.g. General Practitioners, Obstetricians and Gynaecologists, Pathologists, or Physicians of Edinburgh and London; Physicians and Surgeons of Glasgow; Surgeons of Edinburgh or England; and Psychiatrists), or the Faculty of Radiologists. In most cases these qualifications require candidates to have practised in the appropriate branch for a set period and to pass an examination. Some candidates do take courses to prepare for these, but formal study is not required. A great many other diplomas in specialist areas of medicine are awarded by universities, the Royal Colleges, etc., and for most of these, full- or part-time courses of instruction are required.

See also THE HEALTH SERVICE.

Further information

British Medical Association.

Dentistry

Most dentists today spend more time treating the results of gum disease and bacterial attack on teeth, stressing continuous care and conservation; less time has to be spent on treating emergencies like sudden toothache, or extracting teeth, but dentists still see their main role as repairing the effects of dental disease – which means drilling and filling, scaling, putting crowns and caps on damaged teeth – rather than preventing it.

Dentists also design and fit (but have made by technicians) replacement teeth, from bridgework to full dentures. Some dentists, but mainly those who work in hospitals or as specialists, also treat children's teeth which are growing in the wrong directions (orthodontics). Others help to mend jaw fractures and are members of the teams (including plastic surgeons), which deal with all kinds of facial injury, mostly in general hospitals and accident repair units.

Dentistry has gained greatly from modern technology, including the use of lasers and highly sophisticated equipment: the ultra-high-speed air turbines for drilling, cutting and slicing; modern materials for filling and coating; laboratory equipment for making prostheses, plus modern anaesthetics and improved radiological techniques. A recently developed vaccine offers the prospect of preventing dental decay altogether.

Dental 'fitness' in adults, and even more in children, has improved dramatically over the last 25 years, with levels of decay down by as much as half. In theory, there is still a shortage of dentists, despite the fact there are now twice as many dentists as there were 30 years ago, which could mean the breakdown of the service if everyone who needed and is entitled to treatment actually asked for it. However, in practice, the combined effects of rapidly improving dental health and rising charges for dental treatment has actually cut demand, so fewer are now being trained.

Registered dentists number (1995) about 27,000, of whom 18,000 work as general practitioners. They have total independence, working on a form of contract to the NHS and, if they wish, also treating patients privately. An increasing number are reducing their NHS work, to treat more privately. Dentists don't have set lists of patients: they give each patient who comes to them a course of treatment, and the patient can then choose to go to another dentist the next time, although in fact many stay with the same one. Dentists can decide for themselves where to practise, what hours to work, and what treatment to give. Many work on lists of patients who register for regular dental check-ups and treatments.

Although some dentists employ assistants, it is now so easy to set up in practice with loans against future earnings that there are very few assistants. Some dentists practise in health centres and community clinics, and a scheme encourages dentists to work in areas of social deprivation. Some areas are very short of dentists. There is a retainer system to help women dentists keep in touch with their profession while bringing up children.

Nine hundred dentists work for the hospital service, some combining this with part-time general practice. Most hospital dental staff specialise – mainly in oral surgery, orthodontics, and restorative dentistry, doing more difficult repair and replacement work. There are some opportunities for research (e.g. into the causes and cure of dental decay, the causes and repair of malformation), and some full-time teaching posts.

The community health service employs the full-time equivalent of about 1,700 dentists. They inspect and treat the teeth of children, mothers-to-be and mothers with children under a year old. Mostly the work is general, but the service does employ some part-time consultant orthodontists.

The role of the Community Dental Services has been redefined since 1989 to incorporate more preventive work through dental health education and monitoring national improvements in dental health by epidemiological surveys. The community service also provides dental treatment for certain members of the population such as homeless and travelling people, patients who may require general anaesthetics or sedation during treatment, the mentally ill and handicapped, housebound and elderly, and patients identified as HIV positive or suffering from hepatitis B.

A small number of industrial dentists are employed by large companies to provide dental treatment for employees at their place of work. The work is very similar to general practice. Fewer than 100 are (1995) working in Europe where problems of language and sometimes of licensure are limiting.

THE ARMED FORCES have some 300 dentists on short service and permanent commissions. They also offer cadetships, sponsoring students through university. Dental surgeons in the Forces both specialise in treating and repairing the kind of oral and facial damage which happens in modern warfare, and also provide a general service for members of the Forces and their families.

Research work is normally combined with teaching in university dental schools and offers the opportunity to pursue special interests in greater detail. The range of topics is very broad, from oral medicine and cell biochemistry to dental materials and the physiology of saliva. The route through the academic field to university professor is via higher degrees and clinical qualifications. Five hundred dentists are teaching in university dental schools (1995).

Recruitment and entry

All dentists have to qualify through five years of study and training at dental school before they can practise and be registered with the General Dental Council.

Prospective dentists need to be intelligent and should have A-levels in chemistry, physics and biology to gain entry to dental school and get through a difficult course. Dental schools tend to put academic ability well above the generally quoted need for manual dexterity (they claim this can be taught), but clearly anyone considering dentistry is going to like working with their hands and inside the mouth, using fine instruments. Dentists have to treat their patients as whole people, not just as mouths or inanimate objects. Dentists have to recognise that many people find dental treatment intolerable, and so must be able to put them at their ease as far as possible, and try to gain their cooperation.

Although dentists normally have DENTAL TECHNICIANS (*see* SUPPLEMENTARY HEALTH PROFESSIONS) to do most of the day-to-day technical work, they must be interested in the technical aspects. Dentists also need some aesthetic skill to be able to recreate the foundation of bone and teeth which give each face its own character. Dentists need good health, physical stamina and good eyesight.

Qualifications and training

At every dental school, academic education is combined with theoretical and practical training in all branches of dentistry. Subjects include anatomy, physiology, biochemistry, pathology and dental materials science. Clinical training equips the student to provide most of the treatment required by patients in general practice.

Dentists have a responsibility to update their professional knowledge throughout their career, so postgraduate training is ongoing.

Universities offering a dental course are: Birmingham; Bristol; Leeds; Liverpool; London: United Medical and Dental Schools of Guy's and St Thomas's Hospitals, King's College School of Medicine and Dentistry, the London Hospital Medical College Dental School; Manchester; Newcastle; Sheffield; Cardiff; Belfast; Dundee; Glasgow.

New graduates are required to complete a salaried one-year vocational training scheme to ease their transition from dental school to general practice.

Further information

The British Dental Association, General Dental Council.

Supplementary Health Professions

(CLCI: JAD, JAF, JAL–JAT, JOZ)

Contents

Background

There are a whole range of professions supporting and supplementary to dentistry and medicine. 'Supporting' and 'supplementary' professions these may be, but potential demand for their services is very high and they are crucial to the health needs of many people.

The expertise of each profession is increasing, whether they treat specific parts of the body (opticians for eyes, chiropodists for feet), or specialise in particular diagnostic or remedial techniques. Highly skilled as it is, the work involved does, for many, have its own satisfactions. However, it is generally recognised that at their present levels of expertise and skills, these professionals are not yet gaining the independent responsibility to match, and promotion and careers structures are still rather limited. Partly this is because decision-making and clinical management have always been in the hands of the medical and dental professions, but it is also because training has in the past been too narrow.

The professions themselves are keenly aware of this, and hope for more senior posts at both clinical and administrative levels. The nursing profession is, in fact, having some success in achieving senior status in administrative roles, but so far lacks similar opportunities in clinical work. Members of all these professions are frequently included in multidisciplinary clinical teams, but the medical profession can be reluctant to allow other medical workers to take some of their responsibility.

While each profession has its own, traditional, area of specialisation, they do share a common role. Because they all spend so much time in close contact with individual patients – talking to them as they treat them – they are most naturally the people to whom the patient turns for information or advice, or to talk about a problem, anxiety, or straight loneliness. By simply accepting that many patients need just to talk, or by helping to solve problems, or by discovering (just because they tend to be rather more 'approachable' than some doctors) a crucial new factor about a patient's condition, these professionals can contribute even more than is apparent from their formal skills to patients' recovery. It is, however, an aspect of the work which tends to be forgotten, especially when describing the work of paramedicals to young people.

Recruitment and entry

The paramedical professions which have, to date, largely been staffed by women, appear to face some severe recruitment problems. They have, in the past, absorbed a high proportion of qualified female school-leavers. The decline in their numbers in the 1980s and 1990s, plus the increasing competition from other occupations for them, is already a serious problem.

For all these occupations, a combination of intelligence and personal qualities is needed. The academic achievement needed to start out in these careers has been rising steadily, and with some exceptions is generally now roughly equivalent to that needed to gain two or three GCE A-level passes with reasonable grades, and for some, the ability to go on to a degree course. For most of these professions, entrants also need to be scientifically minded. Partly this is because the amount of theory and scientific and medical background, taught on the training courses is being increased all the time, which takes a higher-level educational background to master. Partly it is because the work itself demands a greater understanding of relevant sciences, of medicine, and of the psychological background to dealing with patients, and the ability to cope intelligently with the increasingly sophisticated equipment and machinery which they must use. For a variety of reasons, EC regulations relating to parity of qualifications are also increasing the pressure for higher qualifications.

Personal qualities, though, are still extremely important. Almost all the people in these professions spend most of their working days with patients, who will come from all kinds of backgrounds. Many of them will be upset, worried, and tense. To help them successfully means being the kind of person who makes friends easily with anyone, who can put people with problems at their ease, gain and give them confidence, listen and chat to them easily, explain what is going on clearly and simply, reassure, and get them to accept what may be painful or unpleasant tests or treatment. It is no use being put off by patients whose reactions to stress, illness, pain, depression and so on are extreme. While they must obviously find it easy to be sympathetic and understanding, they must also be realistic and practically minded, and help patients, and their relatives, to accept the inevitable however bad. They may have to be firm and even tough to put patients back on the road to independence. Tact, patience, perseverance and the ability to stay calm in any situation, are all essential qualities. Paramedicals need to be responsible, reliable and conscientious, level-headed and sensible. A sense of humour helps.

Finally, these are all professions which make considerable physical and emotional demands. It is essential to be really healthy, to have plenty of energy and physical (and emotional) stamina, and be able to take long hours and time spent 'on one's feet'.

Qualifications and training

Full-time, three-year training courses are required for entry to most of these professions.

At present, entrants to these professions are mostly trained separately. Courses are broadening, and more basic biological, physical, medical and behavioural/social sciences – useful in the medical world if these professionals are to develop wider and greater responsibilities – are being taught. However, they still tend to concentrate largely on the skills needed for the particular profession, and often in isolation not only from other future paramedicals, but also from young people studying for other qualifications and different careers.

While it seems most unlikely that 'generic' training will develop across the range of these fairly diverse professions, most developments in education and training are in the direction of broader-based studies, and more links with the 'mainstream' education system and other professions, as has happened with nursing. The seven professions governed by the statutory Council for Professions Supplementary to Medicine and State Registered are, in 1995, anticipating legislative changes to the 1960 Act by which they are regulated. They are also in discussion with NCVQ on alternatives to A-level for entry to degree courses.

The so-called remedial professions (occupational therapy, physiotherapy and remedial gymnastics) do, however, appear to be moving (if slowly) towards more common training. Physiotherapy and remedial gymnastics have effectively merged altogether. People in the professions have been generally in favour of proposals for broader, more generic initial courses covering a wide range of clinical practice, possibly with specialisation delayed, possibly with introductory paramedical courses which would allow them to delay their choice of profession without lengthening the basic course. Suggestions have also included common teaching programmes, particularly for an expanded academic content (which, in addition to basic subjects, e.g. anatomy and biology, could include comprehensive coverage of the types of problems met and services needed in the community, and of the roles of the professions in community care).

A small number of degree courses increase the academic content of training for a proportion of those coming into these professions and may include 'integrated' generic health sciences degree courses specialising in physiotherapy, occupational therapy, diagnostic or therapeutic radiography, orthoptics, or medical photography.

It is also possible to add to training after qualifying – for example, via a part-time degree course for people already qualified and working in one of the remedial professions. For nurses, there is a range of postgraduate courses ranging from an advanced diploma to research studentships, as well as the second qualifications in, e.g., district nursing.

It is important to recognise that rapid changes are taking place in the entry and training for many of these professions. Responsibility for training is moving away from the NHS to the universities and colleges while more health service professions are aspiring to State Registration in the interest of public protection and higher standards of performance. The CPSM in 1995 registered 92,000 qualified members of seven professions: chiropodists, dietitians, medical laboratory scientists, occupational therapists, orthoptists, physiotherapists and radiographers. Arts therapists and orthotists and prosthetists are expected to join shortly. The impact of the NCVQ is growing as it tackles level-5 qualifications for professions and encourages young people to offer GNVQs as alternatives to A-level for entry to degree courses. Amendments to the 1960 PSM Act or new legislation may herald changes which reinforce the advice to young people to enquire of the chosen professional body and study the University Entrance publications to see whether universities are offering new courses which may lead to registration and a licence to practise. The CPSM is actively reviewing the arrangements for mutual recognition of qualifications within the European Union.

Note: for entry requirements in health professions please note that the Scottish Health Office use the English details plus 'or equivalent'.

Chiropodists/podiatrists

These care for and treat feet. Many of the problems they deal with are caused by neglect, by fashionable but wrongly shaped shoes for example. They are, however, primarily trained to diagnose and treat the more serious conditions and diseases, and not just minor discomforts or superficial problems. This gives them considerable clinical responsibility, and they only call in a doctor for the most serious problems, for example, when surgery may be needed.

Chiropodists/podiatrists care for people's feet when they have had surgery or after an accident, and help to get them back into the best possible condition. They try to correct the effects of any bone or muscular weakness. They deal with the day-to-day foot problems caused by other diseases (e.g. heart conditions and diabetes), the effects of ageing, the pressures of, for example, standing all day – or pregnancy – on the feet, as well as common problems with corns and nails. They treat sprains, rheumatism, and some skin lesions.

Where possible they try to keep healthy feet healthy, to prevent minor problems getting worse, and to teach people how to look after their feet, to walk and stand properly, and wear shoes which help in avoiding problems. They prescribe special shoes or adaptations for patients who need them. They make plaster casts, and can adapt shoes or make appliances themselves where necessary. Chiropodists inevitably work more with older people (especially in community clinics where the elderly take up most of their time), and they may be treated at home. Although a significant number of children are treated, they take up only a minority of chiropodists' time. In hospitals, chiropody is available only as a specialist service for patients already receiving some other form of treatment, and much of the work is post-operative care.

State-registered chiropodists numbered 7,400 in 1995 (an increase of over 2,200 since 1983), but many work part-time. Many are self-employed, over half working mainly in private practice or commercially run clinics, with some employed by firms to treat employees. However, an increasing number work for the NHS, working mostly in community health clinics but also in hospitals. Demand for treatment rises steadily, and NHS staffing levels are generally considered inadequate, despite the increase in numbers qualifying for registration.

Most chiropodists in private practice expect to work fairly long and/or irregular hours (including evenings), since many patients are themselves working during the day. Chiropodists do visit some patients at home, but normally they see patients in a surgery, which can be in their own homes, although increasingly chiropodists have offices in the same buildings as, for example, dentists, or in community health clinics which house general medical practices. Nevertheless, they still work alone most of the time, and do their own administrative work.

The Royal Commission suggested that there is a need for an auxiliary grade of foot hygienist to take over simpler tasks from the chiropodist.

Recruitment and entry

Normally entry is via a recognised training course and state registration. While it is possible to set up privately to treat feet without gaining officially recognised qualifications, unrecognised courses do not give essential training, and without state registration it is not possible to work for the NHS.

Chiropodists need the same kind of intelligence and personal qualities as other paramedicals (*see* BACKGROUND *above*). Treating feet and using special tools also needs the ability to work easily with the hands, a sure and steady touch, and not being clumsy, and good eyesight.

Qualifications and training

All recognised training courses are full-time and last three years, and are deliberately designed to train chiropodists not only to diagnose and treat a wide range of foot disorders, but also to be able to detect conditions that need medical help. Two-thirds of the time is spent on practical work (including appliance-making), and the rest on scientific/medical studies of the structure and function of the human foot, and their relation to the rest of the body, foot abnormalities, and diagnosis and treatment, and so on, involving anatomy, physiology, bacteriology and pathology, chemistry, physics and biology, as they relate to chiropody. State registration and membership of the Society of Chiropodists (almost 7,500 members in 1995) depend on successfully passing the final exams. The profession is in the process of changing its title and the Society of Chiropodists will be renamed when it obtains Privy Council approval.

Entry requirements have risen steadily. While the minimum is GCSE/GCE (or equivalent) passes in at least five subjects, including two at A-level (subjects to include English language and a science subject or mathematics) schools can and do ask for more. Some want a third A-level or reasonable grades, and at least one requires two science A-levels, including chemistry. About 5% of entrants are graduates, and the Society reports that more and more members are adding degrees to their initial qualification. Traditional diplomas are being replaced by degrees in podiatric medicine, and in future only graduates will be eligible for state registration and for membership of the Society of Chiropodists. All courses will be inspected by the Board of Chiropodists of the Council for Professions Supplementary to Medicine, which in 1995 expressed some doubts about acceptance of NVQ/GNVQs as alternatives to A-levels.

Further information

The Society of Chiropodists, Council for Professions Supplementary to Medicine.

Dental hygienists

They clean and scale teeth, put on preventive preparations (such as fluoride and fissure sealants), do any preparation needed for mouth surgery and care for patients afterwards, but do not give any other kinds of treatment or fillings. They look after both adults and children and must work under the supervision of a dental surgeon.

One of their main tasks is dental health education, helping patients to achieve good oral hygiene to counter tooth decay and diseases of the gums. They explain the importance of plaque control and demonstrate effective methods of brushing teeth and using floss to clean between teeth. They may undertake dental health education with groups of children to point out the consequences of excessive sweet-eating and inefficient tooth-cleaning. Some hygienists specialise and can take a certificate in oral health education.

Most hygienists work for dental surgeons in private practice, community service clinics and hospitals; some work in the Armed Forces, which provide training comparable to the two-year course in dental hospitals. There is a special need for hygienists to work in hospitals for the mentally and physically handicapped; some work with dentists in mobile clinics as well as community service clinics treating children and the elderly.

Recruitment and entry

Normally via an approved training course.

Hygienists need intelligence and personal qualities similar to those of other paramedicals (*see* BACKGROUND *above*), as well as the dentist's dexterity, carefulness, etc.

Entry requirements are at least five GCSE passes at Grade C or equivalent. Some schools ask for one or more subjects to be studied at A-level, although not necessarily passed. The minimum entry age is 17, but most schools want students to be older (the average age of entry is 21), and to have had some previous experience as dental nurses (preference is given to people with the National Certificate, or an equivalent).

Qualifications and training

Full-time training lasts for two years, starting with pre-clinical studies of anatomy, histology, physiology, bacteriology and pathology and tooth morphology, followed by practical clinical training.

Further information

The British Dental Hygienists' Association.

Dental surgery assistants/nurses

Surgery assistants, usually now called dental nurses, do whatever the dental surgeon they work for asks of them. In some, usually smaller, practices the assistant both helps at the chairside and has to be receptionist-cum-secretary as well. In larger practices or in a dental hospital, the assistant may only do chairside work. Chairside assistants look after the patient before and after treatment, both putting them at their ease first and helping them to recover from, e.g., an anaesthetic, afterwards. They look after the instruments and other equipment, keeping them clean and sterilised. They help to mix materials for fillings and with taking mouth impressions, and tidy up after each patient; they see that patients' records are kept up to date. They may also process X-ray films.

Most dental nurses are employed by general dental practitioners, but there are also some opportunities in hospitals and the community dental service. Small numbers work in the Armed Forces and in large firms which provide dental checkups and treatment for their employees.

Recruitment and entry

Some dentists prefer to train their own assistants, and probably many start this way direct from school. It is possible though to train on a full-time course first, and this is normally needed for work in a dental hospital or community health clinic.

Trainees are normally expected to have had a good general education to GCSE standard, and schools and practices will normally want at least two GCSE passes or their equivalent, normally including English. It is possible to start at 16, but some schools and practices prefer 17- or 18-year-olds. Assistants are generally expected to be neat and tidy, and be sympathetic, tactful and caring in dealing with patients facing treatment. The technical side of the work needs meticulous care and attention to detail, and some manual dexterity and good physical health. A calm and friendly manner, willingness to work long hours if the dentist provides evening surgeries, and the capacity to cope with emergencies, such as a patient collapsing, are helpful.

Qualifications and training

Most assistants train on-the-job with a dental surgeon in general practice, at the same time studying for national certificate exams in part-time day or evening classes.

Full-time training facilities are increasing. It is possible either to do a one-year full-time course at an FE college, and follow this with another year of part-time study for the National Certificate (two years' practical experience are needed for this) or to do a more practical one- or two-year course at a dental hospital. Studies include practical surgery work, and associated theory, e.g. anatomy and physiology, dental and surgical instruments and their use, X-ray developing, oral hygiene, mixing dental fillings, bacteriology and sterilisation, plus some coverage of receptionist's work, including clerical work and typing.

Training for dental nurses is also given by THE ARMED FORCES.

Further information (including up-to-date details on courses)

The Examining Board for Dental Nurses, the British Association of Dental Nurses.

Dental technicians

They make and repair dentures, gold or other, plates, bridges and inlays, 'caps' and crowns for individual teeth, splints and braces for straightening teeth or post-surgical treatment. They work with a very wide range of materials, from precious metals, through steel, chrome, cobalt and porcelain, to the very latest in plastics and use an equally wide range of metal- and plastic-working techniques, including spot-welding, electro-plating and deposition, moulding, curing. It is not just a technical or craft job, since the technician plays a considerable part in making the patient's mouth comfortable and keeping their appearance as natural (and attractive) as possible. This means no two jobs are the same, and replacements for lost teeth do not come off a production line, but have to be crafted for each individual, normally using a cast.

Dental surgeons in general practice all used to employ their own technicians, but today they use commercial laboratories, which can afford to employ a wider range of staff, can buy the latest (and usually very expensive), increasingly sophisticated equipment, and do the work more economically. Some practices have set up joint labs, and some technicians have formed their own groups. Some technicians work for clinics and in hospitals. Technicians today often specialise – in orthodontic work, in making dentures or crowns and bridges, or in making appliances for patients who have had operations, or accidents, which have affected their teeth and jaws, for instance, wiring for a broken jaw. Larger laboratories obviously provide the main opportunities for promotion.

There are some 7,000 dental technicians in all, a fifth of whom work for dental practitioners within the NHS.

Recruitment and entry

This is still via either an apprenticeship, or a full-time course. Entry requirements vary with the route chosen, but the minimum is four GCSE passes at Grade C or above, or their equivalent, including physics and chemistry, or a BTEC certificate in science.

Technicians need to be scientifically and technically minded, to be skilled with their hands, able to do fine work and having a patient temperament.

Qualifications and training

This is via one of the following:

- an apprenticeship with a commercial lab or in private practice, lasting five years for 16-year-olds but which may be shortened to three for older entrants, combined with day-release; or
- a training scheme, lasting four years and leading to a BTEC/SCOTVEC diploma in dental technology. Students combine on-the-job training in a hospital, dental school or community dental clinic, with coursework at college, either on a day-release or sandwich basis. After passing the diploma exams, students must complete a further year of full-time practical training; or
- dental-hospital-based training by sandwich course or day-release for four years.
- Some colleges offer a three-year full-time course in dental technology.

It is also possible to train as a member of THE ARMED FORCES.

After initial training it is possible to go on to more advanced studies in a specialist area of technicians' work, including research and instructing in a dental school.

Further information

The Dental Technicians Education and Training Advisory Board.

Dental therapists

There are limited opportunities for dental therapists, mainly working with children under twelve. Dental therapists do simple forms of treatment, e.g. simple fillings, extracting first teeth, cleaning, scaling and polishing, after the patient has been examined by a dental surgeon and under written instruction. They also go to schools and give talks on looking after teeth.

Introduced experimentally in 1960, dental therapy gained acceptance in the late 1970s. The few hundred dental therapists working for the NHS are mainly in community health services, although some work in hospitals. Dental therapists may not work in general practice.

Qualifications and training

One two-year course (entry eight a year), at the Dental Auxiliary School, London, survives, training students as dental therapists and hygienists.

Entry qualifications are at least five GCSE equivalent passes with English language and/or a science subject preferred. Age at least 18.

Further information

The Dental Auxiliary School, London.

Health education officers

Health Education Officers are concerned with promoting and managing good health and increasing awareness and understanding of the issues involved in e.g. disability, drug addiction, etc. Most are employed by district health authorities but there are increasing opportunities in local authorities and in the voluntary sector. Health Education

Officers give talks, write leaflets, organise courses, and promote exhibitions and displays.

Members of the Society of Health Education Promotion Specialists (HEPS) work within the public and private health services and voluntary organisations, NHS Trusts, local authorities and community agencies to coordinate the provision of materials, conferences and training sessions for health educators. Some people undertake health education promotion as part of, or developing from, their initial training and career; they may be medical staff, teachers, social workers or other professionals who are in contact with members of the public who can benefit from help in understanding ways to improve their health and fitness.

Qualifications and training

Various courses are available including a Diploma in Health Education. Choice of course or method of training may depend upon applicants' previous qualification and experience within a teaching, health or social science setting, e.g. nurses, midwives, doctors, dentists, dietitians, environmental health officers, dental hygienists, occupational therapists, pharmacists, health visitors or podiatrists.

Full and part-time courses in health education are available at a number of universities and colleges, leading to a master's degree or postgraduate diploma recognised by the Society. A few colleges offer distance-learning programmes. Enquiry to the Society is advisable to obtain current lists of training opportunities. Courses apparently vary but aim to cover the basic core of communication skills, psychology and behavioural science.

Further information

Health Education Authority, Society of Health Education and Health Promotion.

Health visitors

They go out into the community, helping generally to solve family problems but specialising in child health. The formal definition of the health visitor's work gives five main areas: preventing mental, physical and emotional ill health or alleviating the consequences; detecting ill health early, and monitoring high-risk groups; recognising and identifying need and mobilising appropriate resources where necessary; health teaching; and providing care where needed (including support during periods of stress and advice and guidance in cases of illness as well as in the care and management of children).

Health visitors are links between patient and hospital, between mother and postnatal clinic, between a teenager and a drug-dependency unit. Health visitors listen, talk, counsel, watch out for health problems, and try to find out what – if anything – is wrong. They give support to mothers with new babies and help with any problems through the early years. Health visitors help families to adjust – to the shock of a handicapped baby; to the loss of a parent. They encourage families to try to anticipate or prevent problems, for instance getting the elderly to have regular health checks.

Formally, they are part of the community health service, which employs the equivalent of over 10,000 full-time health visitors in England.

Recruitment and entry

All health visitors have to be registered nurses, and also have approved midwifery or other obstetric qualifications. They must also (then) qualify as health visitors.

Health visitors need the same intelligence and personal qualities as other paramedicals (*see* BACKGROUND *above*). They also need considerable maturity, as well as a solid grounding in nursing.

Qualifications and training

There are several possible routes:

- via registered general nurse and then a post-registration one-year course in health visiting;
- via an 'integrated' degree or nurse/health-visitor course starting at 18, so gaining all the appropriate qualifications together – entry requirements are at least five GCSE passes including two at A-level;
- registered general nurses may take a degree course in relevant studies which includes a health visiting option, leading to registration as a health visitor.

Graduates of relevant disciplines may take modified courses.

Post-registration courses are available at a number of colleges of further education and universities.

Courses are designed to train in observation, in developing relationships, in teaching both individuals and groups, and in organisation and planning; to sharpen students' capacity to see early deviation from the normal, to provide practice in working out a programme of help for the individual where needed, to show the student how to choose the most appropriate method of health education in given circumstances, and to introduce the principles of learning and teaching.

Further information

See NURSING *below*.

Midwifery

This is a separate career although some midwives still take the general three-year course for registration, usually specialising in the adult branch and then after a little experience embark upon the 18-month course leading to qualification as a midwife. A number of three-year courses are now available for entrants at 18 who know they want to be midwives. Trained midwives can take further advanced courses to specialise in, e.g., family planning or to join a team of physicians, obstetricians and social workers engaged upon research programmes related to fertility, childbirth and prenatal care.

The modern tendency for most mothers to have their babies in hospital has changed this career somewhat in that midwives are more likely to be working in a team in a maternity ward or hospital with access to modern technology if the birth is not straightforward whereas previous generations spent more time delivering babies at home. Midwives need special qualities of caring and interest in the parents' approach to their new role, giving advice and support during the pregnancy and confidence to cope with an unexpected emergency during labour.

Although there are still very few male midwives, there is no bar to men training and practising in midwifery.

Nursing

Psychiatric, mental health/ handicap nursing – promotion – the community health service – occupational health services

'It is difficult to overestimate the importance of nursing services in the NHS' wrote the Royal Commission on the Health Service. 'Nurses', they continued, 'are the most numerous and most costly group of health workers, but more important is the close relationship they have with patients.' The Report concluded that 'The role of the nurse is varied and is being further extended and expanded by, for example, research into the caring function of the nurse, and development of specialisation.'

Expanding on this, the Report said, 'Within nursing there are many levels of skill and different roles. Nursing in the NHS may involve providing unskilled but devoted care which might otherwise be given by relatives and friends. It is carried out by nursing assistants and auxiliaries, with the minimum of in-service training, under the supervision of trained nurses, and it forms a substantial part of the care given to patients. Skilled professional nursing care is provided by trained nurses or those in training...

'Nursing is an immensely varied profession. In hospitals, nurses work in acute, long-stay, children's, psychiatric, maternity and other specialised units. But growing numbers work outside hospitals – as health visitors, district nurses, midwives, community psychiatric nurses, and nurses working in clinics and in general practice as part of a "primary health" team. Nurses also work in administration in the NHS and health departments, in education and research, the Armed Forces, voluntary organisations, occupational health (company, school or university health centres) and international agencies.' Nurses also work for private hospitals, and agencies – which includes nursing people in their own homes; and some nurses care for children.

Most nurses, though, are still hospital nurses, caring for patients in the wards, the intensive care units, the casualty and accident departments. They care for them round-the-clock, hour in, hour out.

The NHS alone needs to employ the equivalent of some 622,000 nurses. Eight out of ten work in hospitals, about 9% in the community health services (as health visitors, district nurses, school nurses, etc.), 6% as midwives, and the rest in administration, blood transfusion services, etc.

The profession has been going through a difficult period. It has suffered major structural changes following the recommendations of various reports, and has been affected by management changes. Nurses themselves are putting their professional role under the microscope, and are surer of the positive contribution they have to make to patient care, and of their own ability to determine this. They are consequently even more critical of the career structures which mean that promotion is limited to administrative positions and give them no clinical ladders to climb.

As well as the traditional areas of nursing specialisation, nurses take on other 'extended' roles – in renal dialysis, care of spinal injuries, and special-care baby units, for example. Advances in medical science often need parallel advances in nursing care, and nurses working closely with doctors are pioneering new roles – in keeping very small babies alive, in heart-transplant units, etc.

Modern nursing practice means caring for the whole patient, not just a condition, and building a working relationship between patient and nurse without any of the traditional 'nannying' overtones. Nurses now have more responsibility for treating and caring for patients, as discussed earlier. The profession believes the role of the nurse should be extended, enabling them to undertake tasks traditionally the province of the medical staff, for instance in some long-stay care areas, they could take the lead. Nurses should be enabled and encouraged to prescribe nursing care programmes, including the mobilisation of other services such as physiotherapy and occupational therapy. It is increasingly recognised that the major health need of groups such as the chronic and long-term sick, and the elderly, is for nursing care. Nor should the tasks of other groups be given as a matter of course to nurses simply because they are always there; and staff shortages, whether of domestic or other professional staff, should not be an excuse for persistent misuse of nurses.

Nurses do not, however, want to lose their role as the medical team's closest link with the patient, and will keep the bedpan and bed-making routine to this end, even though it makes it more difficult to achieve the new kind of relationship they have been trying to create with the medical profession.

But new roles for nurses – acting as consultant in nursing practice, developing new ideas and teaching – have emerged in only a few places. The management role leaves little time for clinical involvement, because training has emphasised management, because the medical profession has traditionally consulted the ward sister and has not been prepared to change, and because there is a real difficulty in grades above ward sister acting as consultants and advisers if they do not take responsibility for the care of individual patients.

The profession has recently been assessing the future of nursing, mainly as part of 'Project 2000', which puts forward a radical new plan for training (*see below*). Project 2000 proposed that nursing should become more concerned with health, rather than being illness-oriented, promoting healthy living and teaching people self-care.

Nurses have a widening choice of different jobs and places to work, although the great majority are still hospital-based.

In medical/surgical hospitals, wards and departments are run on tight routines, staffed and managed by nurses. Nurses are in contact with their patients round the clock, observing, monitoring – reassuring, comforting and listening if they can. The wards are staffed mainly by auxiliaries and assistants, by nursing pupils and students, with a relatively small number of qualified, registered nurses, ward and charge nurses.

In general hospitals, the ward may have a mixed group of medical or surgical patients, or all the patients may have bone and joint problems, or they may all be mothers and new-born babies, children, old people, or neurological cases. Caring for patients is now described as an integrated 'nursing process', which includes planning, monitoring, assessing for each patient individually, as well as doing the necessary tasks. Each nurse takes total care of, and 'manages' the needs of a group of patients – how many depending on how sick they are – instead of just doing set tasks, e.g. taking temperatures, etc., or responding to any patient on the ward.

The nurse's working day is not an easy one. For some it is not even a 'day', but a night, since there must be shifts. The more practical, 'domestic', and less skilled routines, of waking and washing patients, giving out meals, bedpans and bed-making are usually done by students, juniors and auxiliaries, as may be some of the simpler medical routines like taking temperatures and pulses. But this does not mean these routines are not important: they are, both for the patients' comfort and improvement, and also because through these apparently ordinary, daily contacts, young nurses learn to observe their patients, to watch out for danger signs, to reassure and comfort patients who are in pain or distress, listen to problems, and ease any tensions.

Even trained nurses do their share of routine, as part of the job of keeping a watch on patients. But they also do the expert work, which ranges from planning the skilled nursing care needed for each patient individually, to measuring and administering drugs and injections; dealing with dressings and post-operative care; monitoring the complex machinery, drips and drainage to which patients may be attached; and watching for sudden crises, assessing the significance of changes, either coping themselves or calling for medical help.

Trained nurses are also the ward managers and organisers, who see that work is done within the tight routines (designed to ensure that as little goes wrong as possible), who check and recheck everything because patients' lives and health are at stake. They must create an atmosphere in which it is possible for the patient to recover without anxiety. They are the point of contact with doctors, to whom they report on patients' progress. They not only look after their patients, but also cope as sympathetically as possible with anxious relatives (including mothers who come into hospital with their children), and supervise, teach and support junior staff. The organisation of the ward, of each patient's day (for instance, ensuring they have drugs at the correct times, go to physiotherapy or surgery and are got ready for this, or see social workers), and of meals and ward supplies; checking cleaning; and keeping patients' records up-to-date, make a demanding administrative job for staff nurses, charge nurses and ward sisters, on top of direct patient care.

Life on the wards is changing all the time, with all the new medical ideas and modern technologies. Advances in treatment mean that most patients get better faster than they used to, are out of bed sooner, and go home earlier. More of the people on the ward are more acutely ill, then, than used to be. Many time-consuming and dirtier routines have, however, been cut down, by new medical and surgical techniques, and by disposable equipment and materials.

Modern electronics, modern drug therapies, life-support systems, new surgical techniques like neuro- and microsurgery (so severed nerves and muscles can now be joined), more implants and transplants, new diagnostic techniques (such as the tiny electronic eye which can inspect more and more of the body from the inside), and modern treatments like kidney dialysis, make the nurses' job steadily more technical. Nurses themselves are also involved in improving methods of nursing care, and doing research on the way individual patients react to illness.

Psychiatric, mental health/handicap nursing

There are considerable differences between nursing people with physical illnesses or traumas, and those who have psychiatric problems or are permanently mentally handicapped. In psychiatric hospitals and residential homes for the mentally handicapped, routine is less tight, and nurses become more closely involved, first in helping to discover why patients have suffered a breakdown and trying to understand their problems and background, and then in helping to solve the problem. As members of the treatment team (in which all staff work even more closely together than in general hospitals), with psychiatrists, doctors, psychologists, and occupational therapists, they contribute equally to the diagnosis of and treatment plans for their patients. Where patients are permanently handicapped, nurses try to help them lead as active and normal a life as possible. While the psychiatrists and other therapists see psychiatric and handicapped patients only at intervals, nurses are with the patients all the time. They develop a close relationship with them, take part in all kinds of activities with them (games, shopping expeditions, outings), teach them new skills, or just listen and talk to them.

Psychiatric and mental health/handicap nursing is, however, changing. Fewer and fewer patients are now spending long periods in hospital. Instead, they are being encouraged, and helped, to live lives as normal as possible, either in their own homes or in small residences which are as home-like as possible. Nurses will, therefore, increasingly work in the community, visiting people at home, seeing them in a 'surgery', and/or caring for some in sheltered accommodation or day hospitals. Some community psychiatric nurses are still NHS/hospital-based; some health authorities have already set up their own community mental health units; and in some areas the service is run from the local authority social service department.

Promotion

The profession still has a tight hierarchical structure. Within the hospital, promotion past ward sister has been into purely administrative posts, such as nursing sister/charge nurse (in charge of up to six wards, a theatre unit, or intensive care unit), or senior nursing officer (formerly matron). It was, and still is, very difficult to gain promotion and still have direct involvement in caring for and treating patients. Clinical responsibility stops with the ward sister who reports to the consultant on patients and to the nursing officer only on ward administration. It was intended that senior posts would give responsibility for 'patient care of a high order, for seeing that the requirements for nurse education are met and that the unit is efficiently managed'; that nursing officers' functions, for example, would include keeping abreast of clinical developments, advising unit nursing staff on nursing practice and helping to solve problems in patient care. Attempts are being made to transfer to senior nurses some responsibilities traditionally held by doctors, e.g. deciding on the kind of care needed by older people or long-term sick, but progress is slow.

Apart, therefore, from administrative posts – which give responsibility for all nursing services within a region, particular sectors, districts, or hospital (over 5,000 posts) – moving away from the ward is mainly still sideways.

Within the hospital, the opportunities to specialise include theatre work, the intensive care unit, out-patients, children, or special kinds of nursing – orthopaedics or midwifery (there are full-time equivalent posts for over 15,000 midwives in hospitals), for example. Nurses can also train to become tutors and/or teach in nursing schools.

The community health service

Nurses can also move out of hospitals as either a district nurse, a midwife, a family planning nurse, a school nurse, a health visitor or a community psychiatric nurse.

Nurses in the community have a considerable degree of independence, but this can mean some isolation too. Here again, the role of the nurse is being extended, to running some kinds of clinics, taking blood, making 'first assessment' visits instead of a doctor, and being trained in the use of more sophisticated equipment and drugs for patients at home. Proposals are being discussed to extend this further, to include the right to prescribe, e.g. dressings, and some forms of treatment, and to be able to control drug treatments for, e.g. the terminally ill.

Home, or district, nurses provide skilled support for families who are caring for patients at home. They give injections, change dressings or administer any special treatment; provide support for people on kidney dialysis at home; help give baths, and generally give support and advice. They liaise between the family and the GP or hospital, or with other services if needed. Increasing numbers of GPs employ practice nurses who run the treatment room within the practice.

Family planning nurses work in clinics which supply contraception, advice on family planning, infertility and sexual health, as well as smear-testing and counselling.

School nurses are concerned with the health of children and adolescents in schools, monitoring their development and teaching them about health issues.

In all, more than 41,000 nurses (including health visitors and midwives) work in the community.

Occupational health services

These are the centres that firms run for their staff, and that universities and schools have for their staff and students. Few of these have full-time medical staff, so the nurse carries the day-to-day responsibility, dealing with any emergencies, minor accidents, or ailments; giving injections; changing dressings; perhaps running a sick bay; keeping medical records; dealing with health education.

See also THE ARMED FORCES, each of which has its own nursing service.

Recruitment and entry

Nursing absorbs some 40,000 students, a high proportion of the qualified age group. The profession is suffering from a shortage of trained nurses, and this is getting much worse as numbers of 18-year-olds fall. Fifteen per cent of entrants are male, many of whom will aspire to senior management positions.

There are a number of routes in, but all nurses have to gain registration after approved training. Entry requirements depend on the level of entry and the route (*see* Qualifications and training *below*).

Nursing requires considerable personal commitment. It is not an easy career. Personal qualities are most important, but intelligence is needed too (both as described in the BACKGROUND above). Nurses are probably in constant contact with unpleasant physical conditions, severe suffering, and death, more than other paramedicals, and young entrants need to be aware of this.

Qualifications and training

Qualifications and training for nurses are going through a very lengthy period of change – it is now over 20 years since the Briggs Committee (1972) started the process and 17 since the Nurse's Act of 1979 – and the profession estimates it will take some time to complete the process.

The process of change started in 1983. The UK Central Council for Nursing (called UKCC), and four national boards replaced the old statutory bodies. They are specifically required to 'improve standards of training and professional conduct for nurses, midwives and health visitors'.

The 1.25 million qualified nurses, midwives and health visitors are now (1996) registered by the UKCC as first-level nurses, previously state registered, and second-level nurses, previously termed enrolled nurses. The parts of the register indicate the level of qualification and area of expertise of nurses:

Part 1 First-level general nurses;
Part 2 Second-level general nurses (England and Wales);
Part 3 First-level nurses of the mentally ill;
Part 4 Second-level nurses of the mentally ill (England and Wales);
Part 5 First-level nurses trained to nurse the mentally handicapped;
Part 6 Second-level nurses trained to nurse the mentally handicapped (England and Wales);
Part 7 Second-level nurses (Scotland and Northern Ireland);
Part 8 Sick children's nurses;
Part 9 Fever nurses (no more registrations);
Part 10 Midwives;
Part 11 Health visitors;
Part 12 First-level nurses trained to nurse adults;
Part 13 First-level nurses trained in mental health nursing;
Part 14 First-level nurses trained in mental handicap nursing;
Part 15 First-level nurses trained in children's nursing.

Parts 12–15 represent nurses whose pre-registration qualification is the DipHE – Nursing (Project 2000 Programmes).

UKCC put forward the profession's plans for reforming training for nurses in a document, called *Project 2000* (1986), which looks forward to the next century. Two main themes are a stress on health, and positively promoting it (so nursing is no longer just concerned with people when they are ill), and on extending 'primary' care into the community. UKCC suggest that future goals should be to make services local, accessible and appropriate, to encourage further the move towards supporting people in their own homes and in the community, redressing the balance so that healthcare is not so centred on high-tech hospitals. UKCC sees an even greater trend towards shorter stays in hospitals, rapid turnover, more day-cases, five-day wards, and investigation units. The strategy for training, then, they say should be to make initial preparation more community-oriented, breaking with the hospitals as the basis for so much training, with new thinking on placements and practical experience, to be developed over the whole range of care settings.

The strategy also suggests initial training must be designed to cope with uncertainty, i.e. make nurses flexible, with the confidence and readiness to deal with change, to have problem-solving skills, and to be able to think 'creatively'. They must also be better informed, on e.g. planning processes, information systems, and able to debate policy, to evaluate their own practice and argue for necessary services.

UKCC wants to end the system of once-for-all, 'encyclopedic' training, cut off from other sectors and closely tied to practical work. First-level nurses, says UKCC, should in future be competent to make nursing assessments of patients' needs; to plan, implement and review nursing care; to teach, and advise on the promotion of health, and to recognise situations which adversely affect health. The emphasis should be on teamwork, on managing the care of groups of patients, and organising appropriate support. But while nurses should assess need, providing, monitoring and evaluating care, combining thinking with analytical skills, they will still give care, and not just supervise.

UKCC proposed a broadly based 'common foundation' programme, lasting two full academic years. This is health- not illness-based, teaching self-care, promoting 'independent living', and covering social and behavioural sciences – 'normal' living, reactions to stress, coping and support, etc. – as well as nursing theory and practice. Part of the time is spent in a range of placements, not just hospitals and community health services, but also workplaces, residential homes etc., and with other care groups.

The final year provides the necessary training for the main areas of nursing (adult, mental, handicap, children's, midwifery), again with placements both in hospitals and in the community. Health visitors, and occupational health, school, district, and community psychiatric nurses, clinical specialists, and 'team leaders' (managers and teachers) are trained, after full registration.

Since 1989, colleges of nursing began to implement new education programmes, whereby students are enrolled on diploma or degree courses and not regarded as NHS employees.

First-level training (mainstream route)

This continues to be via a three-year period of training, combining theory with practice. In England and Wales, most training courses lead to specific qualifications in general, mental or mental handicap nursing, although at some schools it is possible to combine general with mental or mental handicap nursing in a slightly extended course (up to four years), and all general courses include some training/experience of mental/mental handicap nursing, obstetrics, etc. Children's nursing is normally taken with, or after, a general nursing course, as one of the branches after the common foundation programme.

RGN training (in England and Wales) covers nursing, the individual, and the nature and cause of illness with its prevention and cure – social, biological and psychological sciences are integrated into all three sections. All aspects of nursing are dealt with comprehensively. While keeping a very strong practical element, courses do include a substantial proportion of classroom time on theoretical and scientific studies. All courses include some training in community, mental-handicap and mental, maternity, and children's nursing, and care and welfare of the elderly.

RMN training divides into nursing, organisational and management skills, professional skills and the knowledge-base with experience in a wide range of different types of care and psychiatric problems.

RNMH training covers the nature and causes of mental handicap, development of individuals in and outside the family, and the process of learning; plus practical experience with a range of people with different handicaps, and in social, adult educational, occupational and recreational training.

Project 2000 nurse education

Project 2000 nurse education takes place in a college of nursing which has links with a college of higher education. The first 18 months are spent on the Common Foundation Programme, which provides a general introduction to nursing. After successful completion, students specialise in one of four Branch Programmes – general nursing of adults, mental health nursing, nursing people with a mental handicap, or children's nursing. The training is patient/client-based, giving practical experience in a variety of settings under the supervision of qualified nurses.

Minimum entry requirements are five GCSE or equivalent passes at 16-plus. Some colleges prefer entrants with A-levels, BTEC National or Higher (but not General or First certificates) and for courses combining midwifery training passes in English and an approved science in GCSE are required. The UKCC still (1995) sets an educational test known as DC for candidates, many of whom may be mature entrants, who lack the normal GCSE/GCE passes.

Under an agreed point system, the requirement can be made up of a range of exam passes (with at least five points in at least three different subjects). A GCSE equivalent pass equals one point, an A-level pass 2.5 points. Individual schools may ask for specific subjects (most often English and maths or a science), some may want all five passes at one sitting, and a few want one, or two, A-levels. It makes sense to take the most appropriate subjects – e.g. sciences, sociology, economics, or languages.

Whilst the UKCC accepts Advanced GNVQ/GSVQ as equivalent to two A-levels, at present (1995) they do not accept Intermediate GNVQ/GSVQ as equivalent to five GCSE/SCEs, which is the minimum legislative requirement for entry to programmes of nursing and midwifery. Neither do they accept Intermediate GNVQ/GSVQ plus one GCSE/SCE as meeting the statutory requirements.

While the formal lower age limit is 17½, in practice most people do not start training before 18.

Entry to courses in England is via the Nurses' and Midwives' Central Clearing House; in Scotland, via the Scottish Health Service Centre; in Wales via the Welsh Office; and in Northern Ireland, via the National Board for Nursing, Midwifery and Health Visiting for Northern Ireland. For 1998 entry UCAS will handle applications for nursing and midwifery diploma courses.

Degree-level courses

Nursing is not likely to become a fully graduate profession, but graduate entry is expected to rise.

There are two kinds of degree course. Most integrate nursing studies with theoretical/academic studies and lead to degrees in nursing. The second type grafts training for state registration onto a conventional degree course, normally in life or social sciences, and some combine a degree with midwifery qualifications. There are also some offering DipHE for intending midwives. There are obvious advantages to the integrated degrees, although it is quite difficult to combine the roles of undergraduate and student nurse.

Entry requirements are as for any degree course, but usually with specific subjects required at A-level (e.g. a biological subject).

Pre-entry training

Since training cannot start before the age of 17½, and more usually 18, there are good arguments for staying on at school or going to a college of further education to add more GCSEs, one or two A-levels, or Advanced GNVQ in Health and Social Care. Alternatively, a job with people, and/or voluntary work (especially in hospital or the community), is useful preparation.

Post-registration

After registration and some experience, there is an increasingly wide range of further training possibilities for nurses. They can go on to train as district or occupational nurses, midwives or health visitors, take advanced nursing diplomas or specialist clinical nursing courses, read for a degree or higher degree, train to teach or do research, or take courses for nursing management.

Those with appropriate language skills may apply for posts within the EU. Some nurses choose work in mission hospitals or with overseas aid organisations. An interesting development is for qualified nurses to add a legal training and specialise in medical liability cases or just using their communication skills in law firms generally. The Nurses in Law Association had 60 members in 1995.

Further information

The English National Board Careers Section, or the other National Boards.

Occupational therapists

They help patients to get back to active life after an illness or an accident, or help them to adapt to any disability resulting from either. They try also to keep long-stay patients in hospital in touch with 'normal' life, and stop them becoming institutionalised. They work with patients in psychiatric hospitals, building up relationships with them, trying to get them to learn new skills and to join in everyday activities with others. They work with older people, helping them to keep their joints flexible and mobile, their circulation moving, and their minds alert.

Occupational therapists help people to settle back into their homes after they have been in hospital, and as part of their work may organise any necessary adaptations. These can range from simple handrails beside steps to installing a lift, or having a ground-floor bathroom built. By giving people practical, independent skills again, occupational therapists help them to regain their self-confidence, to feel that they can be useful, and plan for the future.

There is probably no limit to the kinds of activity occupational therapists try in treating their patients. Once it was mainly crafts, but today they use mainly the practical, familiar tasks of ordinary life, and attempt to find activities that may help individuals or groups over a difficult problem. The modern occupational unit uses foot- and hand-powered lathes and drills, engineering machinery, forging and welding equipment, carpenters' tools and printing presses, and typewriters. It has a kitchen adapted for all kinds of disability and usually a laundry as well. All these make possible activities which can strengthen muscles, improve coordination, help people to relearn or practise their old skills, find ways to do things with fingers deformed by arthritis, weakened muscles, or a stiffened limb. Occupational therapists design ingenious gadgets to help patients hold pens or spoons, to dress or wash themselves. They make special splints for bent fingers, and get patients in the workshops to make or adapt equipment.

In homes for the elderly, occupational therapists may, for example, start a knitting circle, to keep fingers working and, by chatting and listening to the knitters, keep their minds active too. They may also organise gardening or picnics for patients who can get around, run drama groups, dance and art classes, and craftwork. They find things to do for patients confined to bed.

Occupational therapists also work with handicapped children. They look for ways for them to 'explore' the world as naturally as other children, e.g. special sandpits, water trays, and air-filled mattresses. They use toys which can be handled easily, and use them to teach the children as many ordinary activities as they can.

Most occupational therapists work in hospitals. There they may treat a frequently changing population of patients with all kinds of different problems, or work with long-stay patients (e.g. the physically handicapped). Some areas of work, particularly with, for instance, children with congenital handicaps, are very specialised and need special training, but otherwise occupational therapists can change the type of patient and kind of work they do. A growing number work for local authorities, in day centres or residential homes, or planning and arranging home adaptations for disabled people. There are also some advisory and some teaching jobs.

In most units, occupational therapists spend most of their time with patients, gaining their confidence, trying to find out what their problems are and what activities might best help to solve them, and what they will most enjoy doing. No two patients react to illness or disability in the same way, and the emphasis in occupational therapy is now on making the right response to individual patients.

The occupational therapist's job is to assess what their patients might be able to do, plan and work out a programme of activity for them, perhaps trying to find something that will help solve both the physical and the psychological difficulties, but within the available resources, often limited by cost, and therefore needing ingenuity and imagination. They may have to be very skilled, to persuade, for instance, frightened or withdrawn patients to join in, and they cannot always be successful.

Occupational therapists plan and organise, write reports and attend case conferences, supervise patients – assistants and technicians in workshops do most of the actual teaching and help the patients when they need it – and liaise with other specialists, such as physiotherapists to see, for example, that a patient is getting all the help needed.

Numbers of occupational therapists have doubled in ten years. In 1995 there were 15,300 on the state register.

It is also possible to work as an occupational therapist helper or technical instructor.

Recruitment and entry

Occupational therapists are recruited only after full-time training. They need the same level of intelligence and personal qualities as other paramedicals (*see* BACKGROUND *above*). Resourcefulness, ingenuity and imagination, with some practical skills, are also useful.

Occupational therapists have to learn to be good managers and negotiators, and to work closely with fellow professionals and assistants.

Qualifications and training

The conventional route is now via a three-year full-time degree course in occupational therapy. These courses are jointly validated and monitored by the College of Occupational Therapists and the Council for Professions Supplementary to Medicine. Successful completion confers the right to state registration as a qualified occupational therapist and to membership of the British Association of Occupational Therapists, and the World Federation of Occupational Therapy.

Courses cover subjects such as anatomy, physiology, psychology, psychiatry, medicine and surgery, and orthopaedics, plus the techniques and skills used in occupational therapy, organisation and management of occupational therapy departments or units, and providing aids and appliances for patients.

In 1996 there were 28 approved courses, 13 of them traditional degree programmes; but other full- and part-time courses offer a variety of training methods by which students can achieve the necessary degree qualification for state registration.

The schools (attached to hospitals or other educational institutions) are at: Canterbury, Cleveland, Coventry, Derby, Exeter, Lancaster, Liverpool, London, Newcastle, Northampton, Norwich, Oxford, Salford, Sheffield, York, Cardiff, Aberdeen, Edinburgh, Glasgow, Ulster.

The College of Occupational Therapists' Clearing House Service has ended and applications are through UCAS or direct to individual schools.

Minimum entry requirements are five GCSE passes including two at A-level or equivalent, which should include 'suitable' subjects – each school has its own requirements, but English, a science subject (biology is most useful) and/or mathematics are most usual. Minimum age 18. Schools may accept alternative qualifications; one of the most usual is a BTEC National Diploma in, for example, Science or Health Studies at level 3. Appropriate GNVQs are acceptable. There is a four-year part-time conversion course for occupational therapy support workers at South Bank University; this course does not require the same level of academic achievement, but applicants have to be currently employed as a helper or technical instructor and to have worked for at least a year. Older applicants are welcomed at all schools, and considered even if they do not have the stated academic entry requirements.

Graduates from other disciplines may take two-year courses for the qualifying diploma at Eastbourne, Essex and the London Hospital Medical College.

Further information

The British Association of Occupational Therapists, College of Occupational Therapists, Council for Professions Supplementary to Medicine.

Opticians and orthoptists

These are two of the three professions looking after eyes and sight. There is some overlap in the work done by the various specialists. Medically qualified ophthalmologists diagnose and treat eye diseases and damage, and/or specialise in eye surgery. They work normally in hospitals and eye clinics and may, as part of any treatment, prescribe spectacles for patients. Their careers are along the same lines as other professionals in MEDICINE (*see in* THE MEDICAL AND DENTAL PROFESSIONS).

Opticians

They have a two-tier profession: ophthalmic (now called optometrists) and dispensing. Optometrists are trained to do all aspects of the work, ranging from testing, through prescribing to dispensing spectacles. Dispensing opticians are mostly restricted to supplying and fitting spectacles, as prescribed by an optometrist or an ophthalmologist, although they may also supply other aids, such as artificial eyes, and some are trained to fit contact lenses. While optometrists may have more technically demanding work, dispensing opticians do just as well in gaining promotion to executive and managerial posts.

Optometrists examine and test eyes, look for and measure the kinds of defects which produce (for example) short or long sight, or any kind of inability to see properly. They then decide what kind of lenses will help the patient to see most clearly. They can also do orthoptic work (*below*). Optometrists use sophisticated instruments to measure accurately the errors in refraction which cause blurred vision, and also examine thoroughly the interior of patients' eyes to make sure there is no disease, or evidence of side-effects of other diseases which can affect the eyes. Optometrists refer any disease to doctors, but 'treat' or correct defects in vision themselves.

Many optometrists do their own 'dispensing', i.e. have the lenses made, help the 'patient' decide between different kinds of frames, work out with them the frames which fit best and look well, and check that the lenses – which are made by technicians working either for the optician or for a lens-making firm – are accurate.

This is the part of the work done by dispensing opticians, who are not qualified to examine or test eyes, or decide on the lenses needed. They must work to prescriptions supplied by ophthalmologists or optometrists. They may fit contact lenses, if trained to do so, but any aftercare has to be done by the optometrist. They also supply and fit aids specially designed for older people to use for reading, and deal with optical instruments of all kinds – such as the equipment used by ophthalmologists and optometrists, labs, and so on.

The technical side of this work is changing considerably. The lengthy and time-consuming business of measuring exactly visual refraction errors will be cut to seconds with microprocessor-based automatic refractors which will also print out the measurements automatically. A computer-based system is being developed to test the accuracy of new lenses automatically, and three-dimensional holography will make it much easier to measure the cornea more accurately for contact lenses. Laser-based equipment is being introduced.

Most opticians work in private practices, either as employees or, when they have had experience, setting up in business alone or with partners. Only a small proportion of spectacles are now provided by the NHS, but 7.41 million NHS sight tests were carried out in Great Britain in 1994–95. A significant proportion of these opticians' gross profits come from selling optical instruments (e.g. microscopes), sunglasses, etc. There is an increasing trend to fewer, larger, practices. They may also work for commercial firms making lenses, frames and instruments, either in management or, mostly for optometrists, in research and development on, for instance, improvements to lenses or developing new optical instruments.

There are a few teaching jobs for optometrists in universities which also give the opportunity to do research.

Recruitment and entry

Optometrists must train full-time before they can start work, but some dispensing opticians are recruited as trainees and can qualify via part-time study.

Opticians of both types need to be scientifically minded, and to have the kind of mathematical understanding which can cope with complex and intricate measurements. This means a reasonable level of academic ability, higher for optometrists than dispensing opticians. All opticians need to be able to work with their hands. They need to be meticulous, accurate and patient. They must get on easily with clients, be able to help them relax, and cope with their anxieties. Owning or managing a practice requires organising, administrative and selling skills.

Qualifications and training

These are different for optometrists and dispensing opticians. Optometrists are trained on full-time degree courses in order to meet statutory education/training requirements (there are also exams to be taken for registration with the General Optical Council, but most degrees are exempt from these).

Degree-level courses

Degree courses in ophthalmic optics are designed to give optometrists a sound scientific training and provide a basis for research in the optical field. Research on ophthalmic optics itself is mainly clinical and in developing diagnostic techniques and new, computer-based equipment. In physics, though, there is also optical research in such areas as lens theory and design, optical instrumentation (including fibre optics), lasers and coherent optical techniques including holography and optical data-processing, and electron optics and optical design, which also means developing new techniques using computers. Graduates are also employed by, for example, glass and lens manufacturers in both production and research.

First-degree courses in ophthalmic optics begin with physical and biological sciences, and some anatomy and physiology, since opticians must understand fully the structure and function of the eyes, nerves and muscles and how they work, in detail, and how they can go wrong. Optical principles are also introduced early, and courses go on to apply these; then how to test eyes (including how to deal with patients), and how to recognise abnormalities which indicate injury or disease and which must be referred to a doctor.

Courses cover the complex instruments (e.g. ophthalmoscopes and retinoscopes) and how to use them. They teach how to work out what lenses are needed to correct vision using trial lenses, how to fit contact lenses, and how to make them, how to advise on colour vision. There may be work on industrial needs, on problems of lighting and illumination, and safety in industry. More than half the time is spent in practical work, in labs and workshops, making lenses and frames and examining and testing 'real' patients.

Only seven first-degree courses in ophthalmic optics exist, at: Universities: Aston, Bradford, Cardiff (UWIST), City, Manchester (UMIST), Glasgow Caledonian, and Ulster at Coleraine. The number of places is about 270.

Entry requirements vary, but A-level subjects should include physics, biology or zoology, and another science or mathematics; for university schools at least 11 points are needed. Advanced GNVQ in Health and Social Care is unlikely to satisfy the university admissions tutors, although Advanced GNVQ in Science may be considered.

Postgraduate courses which can be taken after a degree in a related subject, but which train for research rather than professional practice, are available at City, London (Imperial), and Reading.

Professional qualification for optometrists

All optometrists must register with the General Optical Council. To do so, they must have an approved degree, pass examinations set by the College of Optometrists and complete a year's experience under supervision; 7,215 optometrists are registered (1995).

Courses for dispensing opticians

Dispensing opticians can at present train either full- or part-time. The full-time route involves a two-year course followed by a year's practical experience. Part-time involves three years' practical, on-the-job training combined with day-release or evening study, and it is also possible to study by correspondence course. The qualifications are awarded by the Association of British Dispensing Opticians which has (1995) 6,500 members.

Courses approved by the General Optical Council are at: Anglia C, Bradford/Ilkley CC, Glasgow CT, London (City), E London CFE.

Entry requirements are at least five GCSE or equivalent passes, to include English, mathematics or physics and another science-based subject (e.g. general science, biology, human anatomy, chemistry or zoology).

Dispensing opticians can go on to take specialist courses and examinations (set by the Association) in e.g. contact lens fitting.

Further information

From the professional bodies quoted above and the British College of Optometrists.

Orthoptists

They mostly work as aides to medically qualified ophthalmologists, although the work may also be done by optometrists (*see above*) if they qualify to do so. Many eye problems, for example squints or 'lazy' eyes, are caused by difficulties in coordinating eye movements, or because eye muscles do not work properly. Orthoptists do the detailed testing needed (which means using very complex equipment), to find out what the causes really are, and to make sure that there is not a more serious problem (some ophthalmologists also delegate other diagnosis and non-surgical treatment to them). The ophthalmologist may decide to operate – in which case the orthoptist measures the exact angles, and does tests before and after the operation – or to prescribe spectacles. More often, though, the ophthalmologist tries more than one approach. This generally involves the orthoptist in trying to correct the defect using exercises to 're-educate' the eye muscles, including teaching the patient exercises to do at home.

Some other consultants also use orthoptists, for instance to test handicapped children, in neurological diagnosis, and to screen children in schools. Most patients are children.

The NHS employs most of the 1,100 registered orthoptists. Most work in ophthalmic hospitals, or hospitals with ophthalmic departments, a few in the school health service, and a few with ophthalmic surgeons in private practice (orthoptists may only treat patients referred by a medically qualified practitioner). It is possible to work on a part-time, sessional basis, and so combine hospital with private practice or work in other clinics.

Qualifications and training

Orthoptists are only recruited once trained and state registered. Orthoptists need the same kind of qualities as opticians, plus teaching skills.

The full-time training takes three years in all. All courses lead to a degree. The course starts with a three-month introductory study of general anatomy and physiology, and normal child development; the main part of the course covers the eye, the use of diagnostic and measuring equipment, and treatment of eye abnormalities. Practical placements are integrated with theory to give students clinical experience. There are courses at Liverpool, Sheffield and Glasgow.

Minimum entry requirements are five GCSE passes or equivalent, including at least two at A-level. The subjects must include English language, mathematics and at least one science subject, but some schools have additional requirements, e.g. biology or zoology. Alternative educational qualifications, including BTEC, will be considered.

Further information

The British Orthoptic Council.

Physiotherapists

They work on the physical damage resulting from injury (a motor cycle or football accident) or disease (a stroke or virus), trying to restore or improve function. They try to prevent the effects of disease or injury from getting worse, help some people to get over operations (e.g. hip joint replacement), and gain confidence again, and teach others how to live with any permanent damage.

They use a wide range of scientifically designed exercises, some 'manipulation' (of arms, legs and bodies), and games and other recreational activities, and also (increasingly) use heat treatment and electrotherapy. They work with people whose fractured legs have been in plaster and/or traction, to get their muscles strong and supple again; they exercise bed-bound patients; they do all they can to help disabled children become as physically active as possible, trying to prevent their growing bodies becoming deformed. They teach patients how, for example, to walk on crutches, how to get from a wheelchair to a bed or bath and back again. They run exercise classes for the many people with back problems. They try to ease the worst effects of arthritis.

Physiotherapists decide what kind of appliances patients need, from wheelchairs to leg supports. They are also involved in assessing a patient's level of, perhaps permanent, physical disability, and work with OCCUPATIONAL THERAPISTS (*see above*) and SOCIAL WORKERS (*see below*) in helping them back to as much normality as possible. Some physiotherapists specialise in, for example, orthopaedics (diseases and injuries of bones and joints), rheumatology, working with children or old people, or with people suffering from diseases which affect the nervous system.

In 1995 there were almost 26,100 physiotherapists on the register. Most work in hospitals, and most of their days are spent in hospital gymnasia and exercise rooms, on the wards with bedridden patients and patients just learning to walk again, and, in some hospitals, in heated hydrotherapy pools, where patients are exercised in water. Physiotherapists have also acquired along the way the job of keeping patients' chests clear after operations and helping to avoid thrombosis, and so are also often members of the intensive care team.

A small number of physiotherapists work for the community health service, particularly in rural areas where it may be easier for the physiotherapist to visit some patients at home, although most work for day clinics. Some physiotherapists work full-time in residential homes, maternity clinics and schools, although they may travel around, doing three-hour 'sessions' in different centres.

Professional sports clubs mostly employ their own physiotherapists, as do some large firms, to help employees recover from injuries at work, and teach them how to avoid back injuries by lifting and carrying correctly, for example. Some university and college health services have a physiotherapist on the staff too.

The work is fairly strenuous, since most of the day is spent in some form of physical activity. Physiotherapists not only teach people how to exercise; they also physically help to exercise limbs and so on, when muscles are weak or nerves damaged. They have to support, lift and move people around, for instance from wheelchair to exercise bed, when they are often 'dead' weight. Many of the techniques they use are based on theories which require them to be fairly tough on many of their patients, and they have to be firm as well as sympathetic if they are to help patients gain independence again.

While most physiotherapists work a 'normal' nine-to-five, five-day, week, in most hospitals physiotherapists have to be on call some evenings and weekends, and they may have to work out of normal hours if needed to help with seriously ill patients.

Physiotherapists are steadily gaining more responsibility for planning patients' treatment, although they can still only treat patients when they have been referred to them by medically qualified people. The career structure, however, does not give them any real managerial opportunities, and there are not nearly enough senior or responsible posts for the rising proportion of well-educated and intelligent people in the job. As a result, physiotherapists tend to move from post to post regularly, to gain variety.

Over a thousand qualified physiotherapists work in private practice.

Generally, there is a shortage of physiotherapists, and although Health Service expenditure cuts may be leaving some posts vacant, there are no problems in finding a post. The Chartered Society of Physiotherapy has an active membership of around 25,000 in 1995.

Physiotherapy departments also employ helpers who are trained on the job. About 3,000 full-time equivalent helpers work in the NHS.

Recruitment and entry

Physiotherapists are recruited by the NHS only after training and state registration.

Potential physiotherapists need the same level of intelligence and personal qualities as other paramedicals (*see* BACKGROUND *above*). Physical fitness is emphasised. They should enjoy spending most of their time in physical, sports-type activities. Applications are welcomed from mature students.

Qualifications and training

Physiotherapists now undertake a degree course which lasts three or four years full-time at a university or college. Other graduates take the Graduate Diploma in Physiotherapy. These courses lead to state registration and membership of the Chartered Society of Physiotherapy. Degree and diploma courses are available at many universities. Glasgow Caledonian has just started (1996) the first accelerated postgraduate course in physiotherapy and offers a two-year MSc in Rehabilitation Sciences for those with appropriate first degrees such as Sports Science, Physiology or Microbiology.

Courses cover anatomy, physiology, physics, pathology, movement and behavioural sciences and the theory and practice of the treatment skills of physiotherapy. Theoretical study and clinical placements are integrated throughout the course and practice placements are organised to enable the student to acquire a variety of experience.

Minimum entry requirements are five GCSE passes or equivalent, including two at A-level or three Highers; the subjects should include English language or literature, two sciences and two other academic subjects, and physics, chemistry and physical education should have been studied. Some schools, however, ask for higher qualifications, and most entrants in fact have three A-levels; it is rare for students who offer the bare minimum to be accepted. Normal minimum entry age is 18 years. Competition for almost 1,000 places a year via UCAS is very high.

Further information

The Chartered Society of Physiotherapy, Council for Professions Supplementary to Medicine.

Psychology, psychotherapy and analysis, and arts therapies

Psychology, psychotherapy and analysis

Psychologists, psychotherapists and analysts generally work by trying to gain their patients' trust to help them put into words, or 'talk through', their thoughts, feelings and problems, which the therapist/analyst then helps them to explore, examine in depth, and understand – which may take weeks or, sometimes, years. With children particularly, psychologists may use forms of play, and get them to express their problems through, for instance, drawings. The exact form of the therapy used varies according to the 'school of thought' that the therapist/analyst accepts, if any, which may be analytic, or may be behavioural. Psychotherapy and analysis are often used interchangeably, but analysis is always on a one-to-one basis (psychotherapists sometimes work with groups), and is more 'in-depth', i.e. the analyst generally works on the assumption that the problems lie deep in the patient's unconscious, and sometimes that they stem from prenatal and early experiences.

Clinical psychologists work within the NHS in various hospital and community settings, with the mentally handicapped, young children and other clients. They may also combine this with a private practice. Some have just private work. Sessions may be in a group situation or on an individual basis. Each normally lasts for around an hour, with an average of six to ten sessions in all. Some clients, however, may need therapy for several months or even years. Of the 1993–94 psychology graduates entering employment, 35% entered health or social services.

Qualifications and training

University psychology departments have increased their output of graduates (by 17% in 1994) and this subject has become the fifth most popular among applicants to university. In 1993–94 27% of psychology graduates took further academic study or training in a specialist branch of psychology. Three years' postgraduate training and experience is normally demanded for admission to the register of the British Psychology Society (BPS) and for designation as a chartered psychologist. For clinical psychology posts in the NHS this requirement can be met by master's degrees or a qualifying examination. Competition is extremely keen, and in recent years only 18% of graduates applying for clinical training have been accepted for this training. *See also* Clinical Psychologist *in* SOCIAL AND RELATED SERVICES.

The BPS has recently established a diploma in counselling psychology, and another specialism on health psychology working with patients recovering form various injuries or diseases by devising regimes to help them to cope with changes in their lifestyle. (*See also* psychiatric nursing *and* HEALTH EDUCATION OFFICER *above*)

Psychoanalysis and psychotherapy involve treatment by talking and listening within a supportive setting. Both require four years of training after initial qualification in medicine or psychology; for psychoanalysis a period of continuous personal analysis, and for therapy experience of work with people suffering emotional disturbance, are also required.

Child psychotherapists work in hospitals, special schools, clinics and social services helping children of all ages to achieve normal standards of behaviour and communication using discussion, games and other activities.

Further information

The British Psychological Society, Association of Child Psychotherapists, British Association of Psychotherapists, British Psycho-Analytical Society, British Association for Counselling.

Arts therapies

Art therapy – dance and movement therapy – drama therapy – hearing therapy – horticultural therapy – music therapy

The growing recognition of the contribution that the creative arts can make to the progress towards health and contentment of patients suffering from many types of physical and mental illness or handicap has enabled practitioners of these small professions to look forward eventually to general acceptance and ultimately state registration. Graduates or equivalently qualified people from courses in art and design, dance, drama and music need a profound interest in people with health problems as well as teaching or instructional abilities. They should ideally have several years' experience in education, social work or volunteer work in hospital before taking a postgraduate course combining the use of skills previously developed in an undergraduate course with theoretical study or psychology and psychiatry in order to work in a therapeutic setting. Good communication skills are essential together with patience, as results are often slow to appear; also confidence, experience of people management, an emotionally stable personality, and sufficient early scientific schooling to cope with the anatomy, physiology and psychology in the course.

Art therapy

Art therapy concentrates on helping people whose problems are too deep or confused to be handled in speech. Therapy normally begins with a psychotherapy session, listening and sharing problems or fears, leading on to an expression of them through an image on paper. Sessions may last for weeks, months or, occasionally, a couple of years, with the ultimate aim of helping the patient to come to terms with their problems and control their distress. *See also in* ART, CRAFT AND DESIGN.

Some art students are especially attracted to the idea of using their art training to work in hospitals helping patients to come to terms with physical or mental illness by drawing, painting, sculpture, collages, etc. After a degree in art and design and some practical experience such as adult education instructing, artists can apply for a full- or part-time course of one or two years at Hertfordshire College of Art and Design, St Albans; Goldsmiths College of London University; or the Royal Hallamshire Hospital, Sheffield. This course combines psychological and psychiatric theory with practical training helping patients to overcome frustration or communicate ideas and feeling through the medium of art. Doctors increasingly accept the efficacy of art therapy in the healing process of mentally ill patients since the first experiments were made in the 1950s; it is thought that the comparatively rare vacancies for art therapists in the NHS will increase.

Recruitment and entry

Requirements vary, but candidates are usually selected for training by interview. Candidates should have a degree in art or psychology, or a social-science-related subject, with proof of art competence.

Further information

The British Association of Art Therapists.

Dance and movement therapy

Movement classes in psychiatric hospitals can help patients to overcome some inhibitions, and express themselves confidently in imaginative activities which also contribute to calming frayed nerves and general tension. Dance and movement combine relaxing physical activity with the soothing effect of background music to improve patients' psychological stability.

Courses for dance and movement therapists are also available at the Hertfordshire College of Art and Design and Goldsmiths' College as well as the Roehampton Institute. They may be taken on a full- or part-time basis.

Drama therapy

Drama therapists can work in prisons or mental hospitals encouraging their clients to act out some of their problems or come to terms with distressing past experiences by simulating real or imagined events; this is intended to reduce tension and combat emotional frustration, withdrawal or self-consciousness.

A basic drama qualification should be followed by full- or part-time training leading to a recognised diploma in dramatherapy offered by Hertfordshire College of Art and Design; South Devon College of Arts and Technology, Torquay; University College of Ripon and York St John, York; Central School of Speech and Drama, London; and Roehampton Institute, Surrey. An interest in psychology is as important as the practical skills of drama production and improvisation together with the capacity to persuade sometimes reluctant patients to work in a group towards a common goal.

An increase in employment opportunities within the NHS following acceptance of drama therapists within the career structure of the hospital service has given them hope of incorporation in the future within the Council for Professions Supplementary to Medicine as a state registered speciality.

Hearing therapy

Helping hearing-impaired adults to communicate for social, family and employment purposes involves giving advice on the use of hearing aids, lessons in lip-reading and general encouragement to inspire deaf patients with the will to enter the hearing world and the confidence to accept its challenges.

A one-year course is available at City Lit in London and leads to the Certificate in Hearing Therapy or the RSA Certificate for Lip Reading Teachers. Interested applicants for training should be graduates or otherwise qualified and mature, preferably with some experience of the problems of the hearing impaired; an interest in people and sensitivity to their problems is obviously paramount.

Horticultural therapy

Horticultural therapists work in hospital grounds and greenhouses, planning and designing gardens to be tended by patients who may be suffering from psychiatric illnesses, physical handicap (such as deafness or blindness) or the mentally handicapped. Patients derive enormous satisfaction from the physical activity of gardening, with its non-competitive timescale where their developing skills match the tangible evidence of their efforts in the fruit, vegetables and flowers they produce. A horticultural qualification and experience or some time spent in other health occupations is normally followed by a one-year part-time course at Coventry University. Apart from posts in the NHS, there are a few opportunities to work with disadvantaged or slow-learning young people in community centres where plants are grown for sale under the supervision of a horticultural therapist.

Further information

Horticultural Therapy, Goulds Ground, Frome.

Music therapy

Musical training and talent can be used by music therapists with patients hospitalised for a wide variety of conditions, when their physicians consider they may be helped to communicate or cope with their emotional or psychological difficulties by making music on their own or in a group.

After obtaining a degree or diploma in music, intending therapists should apply for a one-year postgraduate course at the Guildhall School of Music and Drama, London; the Roehampton Institute, Surrey; or the Nordoff-Robbins Music Therapy Centre in London; alternatively there is a two-year part-time course offered by the University of Bristol.

Therapists need a capacity for improvisation as well as conventional teaching skills and must be willing to accept low standards of performance in the interest of patients' progress towards mental and physical health.

Further information

British Society of Music Therapy.

Radiographers

They specialise either in diagnostic work (taking X-rays) or in giving radiation treatment. They work under medically qualified radiologists. They usually have considerable responsibility and independence, although the radiologist decides what treatment should be given, and/or interprets what the X-ray films show.

Most radiographers work for the National Health Service. Membership of the (qualifying) Society of Radiographers – most of whose members work for the NHS – was nearly 17,500 in 1995.

All types of radiation are dangerous, and radiographers have to protect themselves and their patients from over-exposure, although all diagnostic and radiotherapy departments have to be properly equipped and monitored to prevent any accidents.

There is usually a shortage of radiographers, especially for diagnostic work. There are senior and superintendent posts for radiographers, but no promotion or responsibility beyond that, except for teaching. UK qualifications are recognised overseas, but it may be necessary to learn a language to work in particular countries.

Diagnostic radiography

The majority of radiographers do diagnostic work. In most hospitals this is done in central diagnostic departments (although mobile equipment is used where patients cannot be moved). Here the familiar X-ray films are taken to show where and how bones are broken, spines or skulls damaged, or how far they have mended; to show the state of teeth or lungs, or how and where to continue a surgical operation. For stomach or other soft-tissue X-rays, the patient takes (or is injected with) something opaque to X-rays. Diagnostic departments are also responsible for operating the newer machines which explore the body internally, for example ultrasonic scanning, imaging, and gamma photography (to check on progress in bone-fracture repairs).

Doctors who want X-ray films or scans of their patients simply tell the radiographers what it is they want to see. The radiographer works out the technicalities – for example, which machine to use (there are, for example, special units for skull X-rays); the angle at which the patient should sit, stand, or lie; how many different frames to take; whether or not the machine should be adjusted, and how; and what film and exposure to use. X-ray machines become more technologically sophisticated all the time, and although they have more automatic controls, the radiographer has to understand how they work to get the best results. The radiographer must also take great care of the patient, and may have to find ways to take X-rays so that they do not cause pain, or make an injury worse.

In more complex work – on casualties where speed must be combined with care for the seriously injured, for example – the radiographer works as a member of a team which will include the medically qualified radiologist, and when screening techniques are used, as assistant to the radiologist.

Diagnostic departments keep patients only as long as it is necessary to take the film or scan, but radiographers must nevertheless reassure them and try to ease any anxiety or stress. In some departments, or out of normal working hours, the radiographer may have to develop the X-rays as well, although in most hospitals they have darkroom technicians to do this.

Therapeutic radiography

Therapeutic radiographers directly administer radiotherapy to patients with malignant and non-malignant conditions. Treatment of all forms of cancer is changing rapidly and continuously, and results are improving. New treatments link radio- and chemo- (drug) therapy, and the doctors administering these programmes (which have to measure dosages so exactly that computers must be used to work them out) have to work closely with the radiographer. Teamwork is essential, and therefore the therapeutic radiographer has less independence than the diagnostic radiographer.

The radiographer has to see that the sophisticated and very delicate machinery, with its battery of instruments and controls, is accurately angled, and the patient positioned for the radiation to home in on one small area. The radiographer operates and monitors the controls and, although these have to be outside the actual treatment room (for safety), must watch the patient (through a glass panel), and reassure them over a microphone. The radiographer may also have to prepare the patient, and help treat any side-effects. The radiographer also helps the radiotherapist to administer treatment with radium and other radioactive isotopes, and makes devices to apply them.

Patients who are given radiotherapy usually have a course of treatment, and so over weeks or months the radiographer must help to keep up their confidence and create and keep a friendly relationship under very difficult circumstances. The radiographer must also keep accurate records of the treatment, and can never afford to make a single mistake, because radiation treatment cannot be reversed.

Recruitment and entry

Radiographers are recruited only when trained and state registered.

Radiographers need the same level of intelligence and personal qualities as other paramedicals (*see* BACKGROUND *above*). They must be meticulous, accurate, and careful people.

Qualifications and training

Training for both diagnostic and therapeutic radiographers lasts three years. There are various ways of training – either at a hospital training school, or on a group scheme, where students from a number of hospitals are given collective theoretical training (sometimes with a local technical college) and gain their practical experience in hospitals within the group.

Training is available in most areas, but there are more places for diagnostic than for therapeutic radiographers.

The first part of the Society of Radiographers' Diploma examinations, required for state registration, is common to both branches, and covers physics, hospital practice, patient care, anatomy and physiology. Part 2 in diagnostic radiography covers equipment, radiographic photography and technique; for therapeutic radiography, the subjects are radiotherapy physics and equipment, and radiotherapy technique. Some schools of radiography offer honours degree courses. In 1995–96 these were available at East Anglia, Kingston, and Teesside Universities; and at Queen Margaret College, Edinburgh.

Minimum entry requirements are five subjects at GCSE including two at A-level, or equivalent. Subjects must include English, maths or physics, and another science subject. The Society encourages universities and colleges to accept appropriate Advanced GNVQ/GSVQs.

Further information

The Society of Radiographers.

Social workers

They are not now employed by the National Health Service. Medical social workers, who help patients with personal and social problems resulting from illness or disablement, are employed by local authorities, although individual social workers may be based in hospitals. *See* SOCIAL WORK *in* SOCIAL AND RELATED SERVICES.

Speech and language therapists

They assess and treat speech defects, mostly in children but also in adults. Speech defect is more than just talking badly – putting that right is a job for schools. Speech therapists deal with the kind of problems which result from, for example, a cleft palate or loss of larynx (removed possibly because of a growth), or brain damage after a stroke or an accident. The problem may be emotional and/or psychological, and cause someone to stammer, or it may be the result of a congenital disease. They may also treat children or adults who find talking, reading and writing difficult because their language skills have not developed 'normally'. Their aim is to help people to communicate as effectively as possible.

At present, speech therapists work mainly with children, and most work in NHS clinics. Few speech therapists work in hospital full-time, most dividing their time between the community service clinic and the hospital. Some work in special schools or units for the mentally and physically handicapped. A small proportion work with deeply deaf patients, for whom speaking clearly is a major problem.

There is a great deal of work to be done with adults, but services are expanding only very slowly. The Royal College of Speech Therapists has over 6,000 qualified members, of whom most work for the NHS, the rest working for charities or in education, or privately. There is generally a considerable shortage of speech therapists, although posts may be left unfilled for financial reasons.

Speech therapists are trained to assess and evaluate problems, and not only to correct them. A speech therapist begins by trying to establish the cause of the defect (if it is not already obvious or has not been diagnosed by someone else), before assessing and evaluating the case, and deciding what to recommend. No two patients are ever the same, however similar the symptoms may be, so each has to be assessed and their treatment planned individually. Assessing and evaluating involves finding out a great deal about the patient, with time spent observing and talking to them, getting to know them, perhaps talking to parents and teachers as well as other therapists, and possibly having tests done – for deafness, for instance. They may decide speech therapy as such is not the best way to treat a problem, and recommend, for example, some form of counselling or psychotherapy.

Mostly speech therapists work on a one-to-one basis, but they also organise play groups, so children can learn to talk naturally to each other; and they may have group sessions for some patients. They may see patients once or twice a week, or more often if the treatment is intensive. Much of the treatment involves ear-training and breath control, 'structured' language programmes, remedial voice work and exercises, practice in relaxation, conversation practice. Where problems have psychological and/or emotional causes, treatment is designed to help solve these as well as to control the symptoms. Where possible, therapists treat children through play, to gain their confidence and interest, and to create a relaxed atmosphere. Speech therapists also counsel parents and train them to help with the child's treatment, and work closely with schools and anyone else involved in a case.

Although most speech therapists work alone, they do come in contact with other people besides their patients, and where cases have complex causes, they may work as part of a team. Speech therapists attend case conferences, keep case notes and prepare reports for hospitals, schools, GPs, etc.

Recruitment and entry

Speech therapists are recruited by the NHS only when trained and state registered.

Speech therapists need the same level of intelligence and personal qualities as other paramedicals (*see* BACKGROUND *above*). Good hearing, with the ability to analyse sound accurately (a musician's 'ear'), and clear, accurate speech are essential, and a real interest in sound and language very useful.

Qualifications and training

Entry to the profession at 18-plus is only via officially approved degree courses. Not all degree courses that look appropriate are in fact approved speech therapy qualifications, so it is important to check. It is also possible to qualify via a postgraduate training course after a degree in another subject.

Degree courses lasting three or four years are offered in 1995 at the following universities: Central England, De Montfort, Leeds Metropolitan, Manchester Metropolitan, Strathclyde, City, Manchester, Newcastle, Reading, Sheffield, UCL, Ulster, and at: the College of St Mark and St John, Queen Margaret College Edinburgh, Central School of Speech and Drama, and Cardiff Institute of Higher Education.

Two-year postgraduate courses are available at City, UCL, Newcastle, Reading and Sheffield universities for graduates from other disciplines aiming to qualify as speech and language therapists.

Syllabuses and entry qualifications vary, but all require the minimum five GCSEs or equivalent, including English language and some sciences. Some institutions accept Advanced GNVQs.

Further information

The Royal College of Speech Therapists.

Alternative Medicine – the Natural, Complementary Therapies

(CLCI: JOD, KEK)

Contents

Background

'Complementary' or 'alternative' forms of treatment and therapy mostly see health, disease and treatment in terms of the 'whole' person, and are in many ways a reaction against the very scientific and technological approach of conventional medicine today. Anyone who is not a member of the established medical or other paramedical professions can have problems in practising these therapies, often because they are misunderstood, and because the increasingly scientific trend of the medical sciences has led the profession to discount forms of treatment which are not based on proven scientific methods. Outside Britain and Western Europe, older methods of treating illness have continued to develop, and over the past few years interest in these therapies has grown enormously. Surveys in 1990 confirmed that 75% of respondents wished to see complementary medicine available on the same terms as NHS treatments.

Since these occupations are not officially recognised, the chances of employment, except in private practice, are very limited, at least at present, and because they have not gained state registration, treatment cannot be provided under the National Health Service. The Institute of Complementary Medicine estimates that several thousand people are qualified in natural therapies, although the numbers remain small in each.

The Institute of Complementary Medicine (formed 1981) is attempting to bring together the numerous therapies (it estimates some 20 are in general use and another ten not so commonly used), and (amongst other aims) to establish standards of training. ICM has set up an independent coordinating body able to assess and define standards in any of the therapies, and has begun an assessment of professional training standards. This is the first 'outside' body providing moderation of standards and examinations. They have also begun the British Register of Complementary Practitioners, the only national register in existence.

In 1995 this had 16 divisions: Aromatherapy, Chinese medicine, Chromo therapy, Counselling, Energy medicine, Healing counselling, Homoeopathy, Hypnotherapy, Indian medicine, Japanese medicine, Massage, Nutrition, Osteopathy, Reflexology, Remedial massage and a general division. There are other identifiable occupations such as Alexander technique teachers, Kinesiologists (working on muscle disorders), Bates practitioners (helping people with eyesight problems) and the creative arts therapists. *See also* BEAUTY in PERSONAL SERVICES.

According to the ICM 'Complementary Medicine "complements" the needs of the patient at the level of Body, Mind and Spirit' and its mission statement as a charity reads: 'The Institute is a focal point of learning and healing for those concerned with the future of humanity, the future of health care and the way in which people are educated in personal development. It is a meeting point for those wishing to share in the deeper understanding of the philosophies of life and living. Complementary Medicine is Holism in practice.' The difficulty for people seeking careers advice on complementary medicine lies in the diffuse nature of the various skills, techniques and practices involved. However sceptically the medical profession may traditionally have regarded complementary medicine the fact that people have for years paid for treatment by various exponents shows that they believed in their efficacy. The ICM's aim of a statutory system of registration following training in approved institutions would protect the public and provide doctors with access to qualified practitioners to whom they could refer their patients.

ICM says that to make a career in the natural therapies, it is essential to make sure the professional training is right, and that trainees can become members of a reputable association which has a strict code of ethics and furthers the professional development of its members. ICM suggests training should be college-based, rather than by apprenticeship. This will usually mean a course lasting three or four years, and ICM specifically warns against short courses lasting only two or three weekends. The course should cover basics such as anatomy, physiology and differential diagnosis; thorough training in the particular skill or system of treatment, including practical demonstration and supervised practice as well as classroom teaching; general studies ranging through ethics, relationships with patients and colleagues, business management, etc. ICM considers that reputable courses will ask entrants for at least two A-levels, or equivalent, preferably in sciences.

ICM suggests that professional therapists will, in future, look to practise in a specially designed clinic or health centre (even a 'health farm'), sharing accommodation with other therapists, which makes it possible to employ receptionists and secretarial staff, and ensures legal requirements, etc. are met. This is certainly likely to attract more patients.

ICM has identified 30 therapies, but suggests there are identifiable types: structural (e.g. osteopathy, chiropractic), nutrition (e.g. macrobiotics, naturopathy), psychological, physical, emotional and spiritual development (e.g. acupuncture, homoeopathy, herbal medicine).

The main career opportunities appear to be in the areas detailed below.

Acupuncture

This is widely practised in China and other parts of the Far East as part of established medical practice. Acupuncture tries to treat a wide range of conditions, but particularly 'functional' disorders, and to anaesthetise, by penetrating the skin very accurately at predetermined points (acupuncture theory states) to correct imbalances in the dual energy flows which acupuncturists believe are within the body, and which are considered to cause the disorder in the first place. The practice of acupuncture is at least 3,000 years old, but it is still developing. For instance, electroacupuncture helps practitioners locate the acupoints on the skin.

An estimated 7,000 acupuncturists practice in Europe. It is used officially in some hospitals in France and Germany and can be provided under their national health schemes. In Britain, there are about 600 acupuncturists.

The Acupuncture Association aims to persuade the government to legislate for adequate training and registration, but in the meantime sets its own standards. The Association, with the Acupuncture Research Association, runs a training college, but trains only postgraduates. All entrants must already have a degree or other recognised qualification in medicine, naturopathy, osteopathy, physiotherapy, nursing, or homoeopathy, and they must first have completed appropriate full-time training in one of these. The first-year diploma course involves some 140 hours' attendance at the college plus 400 hours of directed individual study; a further year's study leads to a licentiate, and a thesis prepared over another year's study leads to a bachelorship; the doctorate requires a further two years' work in the preparation of another thesis.

The Council for Acupuncture can provide details of other recognised courses.

Further information

The International College of Oriental Medicine, the Acupuncture Association, the Council for Acupuncture.

Alexander technique

This is named after its inventor, an actor who developed a method of retraining himself in the right use of his body and voice after experiencing a number of professional disappointments which he attributed to learned habits of faulty posture. Pupils testify to the emotional and psychological benefits which they feel they have derived from the improved use of their bodies. The emphasis throughout is on the correction of individual detailed faults in breathing, speech and movement.

A-level or equivalent education is normally the minimum to train as an Alexander teacher. Trainees should have experience of the technique. Many people who take up the subject have already completed a medical or artistic education (including actors, musicians and dancers). Teachers develop their practice through the Society of Teachers of the Alexander Technique (STAT) founded in 1958 as a professional forum. There were around 500 teaching members in 1995 in the UK out of 1,200 members worldwide.

Courses are generally arranged over three years of three 12-week terms, during which 20 hours a week are classwork. This fits the Department for Education and Employment definition of a full-time course.

Further information

The Society of Teachers of the Alexander Technique.

Anthroposophical medicine

Anthroposophical medicine is a system of thought based on the ideas of the German mystic Rudolf Steiner. As well as strictly medical work, there are opportunities to train in art therapy, eurythmy and speech therapy within the anthroposophical system.

Only doctors are admitted as anthroposophical doctors. Candidates are usually selected for training by interview. The holistic approach is exemplified by the use of herbal medicines, diet, massage, counselling, arts therapies, etc. to help patients spiritually as well as physically.

There are several ways for non-medically qualified persons to implement anthroposophical principles in therapeutic work, e.g. Plymouth University validates courses at Rolle College for teachers in Steiner schools, and Emerson College at Forest Row offers a variety of courses for adults based upon 'Education, Ecology and Social Renewal'. Other forms of caring include work in communities for adolescents and adults with problems of mental illness or handicap or adjustment to normal social life. Eurythmy can be studied at Stourbridge as well as in Switzerland.

Further information

The Anthroposophical Society.

Aromatherapy

Aromatherapy may be practised at different levels of skill and knowledge. Properly, it is an attempt to improve the patient's state by very precisely using any combination of a range of 40 or more aromatic essences to stimulate the receptor cells of the body. These cells then send messages via the deepest levels of the brain to instruct the whole person how to get better. The biochemistry underlying the subject is not fully understood, although France, where the practice is most highly developed, produces the most comprehensive information about it.

It is based upon the skill of massage with knowledge of the properties of certain oils. Its practitioners claim to ease skin and digestive complaints and the psychological problems arising from, e.g., chronic insomnia or migraine besides assisting the general well-being of many seriously ill patients. It exemplifies the combination of physiological and psychological healing which underpins holistic medicine.

The qualities required are a caring attitude and genuine interest in people and holistic healing, good health, stamina and business sense to run a private practice, as aromatherapists are not employed in the NHS, though some may work in health clubs, private hospitals, clinics and hospices.

Training takes place in London. There are no specified entry qualifications for the nine-month full-time or two-year part-time courses, the latter designed to enable students to learn this new skill at weekend courses while remaining in their original occupation. Most students are over 21 and finance their own training.

The diploma of the Tisserand Institute is accredited by the Register of Qualified Aromatherapists, belongs to the British Complementary Medicine Association and is working towards NVQs in aromatherapy (1995). The course comprises academic study of healing philosophy and the relationships between complementary and conventional medicine, the chemistry of oils and their safe application, pharmacology, anatomy and physiology besides the practical skill of massage and recognition of conditions requiring referral to a doctor or hospital. An aromatherapy massage NVQ/SVQ at Level 3 has been approved by the Health and Beauty Therapy Training Board. *See* BEAUTY *in* PERSONAL SERVICES.

Job opportunities are expected to increase as the public becomes more aware of various forms of complementary medicine.

Further information

The Association of Tisserand Aromatherapists.

Arts therapy

See under PSYCHOLOGY, PSYCHOTHERAPY AND ANALYSIS *and* ARTS THERAPIES *in* SUPPLEMENTARY HEALTH PROFESSIONS; *and* ART, CRAFT AND DESIGN.

Chiropractic

Chiropractic practitioners relieve back pain and other ills by specific spinal adjustments. This is one of the range of therapies which depend upon the manual skills of the practitioner. Chiropractic is used widely as a way of relieving back pain, without the use of drugs or surgery.

School-leavers need at least two science A-levels or their equivalent. Mature entrants may be admissible with other relevant experience.

The Chiropractors Act of 1994 established chiropractic as a profession whose members are now registered by the General Chiropractic Council and recognised by the medical profession. The specialism was established in the USA in 1895, but training was not available in Europe until 1965, when the Anglo-European College of Chiropractic was established. Situated in Bournemouth, its students, half of whom come from overseas, study for four years for a BSc (Hons) in Human Sciences (Chiropractic) of the University of Portsmouth; a further year of clinical practice leads to the final diploma and registration. Appropriate science A-levels are expected. The first two years of the course are similar to medical courses, anatomy, physiology and biomedical science, followed by two years concentrated study of spinal construction and movement, radiography, diagnosis of back pain and tension, orthopaedic conditions and spinal degeneration, while developing the practical skills of manipulation, adjustment and support.

Registration is confidently expected to lead to a marked increase in demand for chiropractors; in 1995 there were 900 practising in the UK, twice the number in 1990 and forecast to double by the year 2000.

Pilots are being set up (1996) to test the possible inclusion of osteopathy and chiropractic in the GP fundholding scheme.

Further Information

British Chiropractic Association and Anglo-European College of Chiropractic.

Colour therapy

Colour therapy has developed as a result of noticing that people are affected by the colours that surround them and that they express a great deal about themselves and their emotions by their choice of colour. There are now not only consultants who advise on choice of colour in make-up and clothing, but also those who advise individuals, firms and institutions on suitable colours for buildings and furniture.

This involves taking into account the effect of colour on health and welfare as well as aesthetic considerations. Trials have shown that it is possible to make considerable physical differences by the effect of light alone – in lowering blood pressure, for example, or relieving Seasonal Affective Disease (SAD).

Most training courses are part-time and give a framework of information about light and colour. The Tobias School of Art offers a course at the Peredur Centre in East Grinstead for people seeking training on Steiner methods.

Further information

The British Register of Complementary Medicine (Colour Therapy Section) at the ICM.

Counselling

Counselling has been described as the art of listening constructively. Most counsellors do not aim to influence their clients in a particular direction, but to help them explore the options open to them. Counselling is used within many of the other disciplines of complementary medicine, as well as in the main stream of the Health Service – by doctors, psychologists, social workers and therapists, for instance.

Most people embarking on training already have a degree, but more important is the ability to digest and learn from life experience.

There are many courses available for people who want to counsel as a profession, through universities, colleges, private training courses and groups. They usually last about two years, leading to a diploma, or one year for a certificate. Short courses in counselling skills are also available from many of the same sources. They are not a qualification to practise, but are a useful introduction to the skills involved.

Further information

The British Association for Counselling.

Dance therapy and Drama therapy

See under PSYCHOLOGY, PSYCHOTHERAPY AND ANALYSIS *and* ARTS THERAPIES *in* SUPPLEMENTARY HEALTH PROFESSIONS.

Herbal medicine

Western pharmacists have always been interested in naturally occurring therapeutic substances but tend to believe that it is necessary to extract single active ingredients and then, if possible, synthesise them artificially to produce a standard product and work out dosages. Medical herbalists, however, believe that plant materials offer a naturally balanced combination of chemicals which interact with each other and reduce the instances of damaging side-effects. Interest in plant remedies is worldwide: long-running programmes of testing and evaluation exist in Eastern Europe, Pakistan and other Asian countries. China has long had a tradition of herbal medicine. Western Europe is comparatively slow to develop its potential.

A good general education is necessary, with a biological science bias. Two A-levels or their equivalent in biology-related subjects are preferred. The use of plants for therapeutic purposes is sometimes known as Phytotherapy.

Training takes four years. The course includes basic human sciences, the study of human disease and diagnostic skills, as well as subjects specifically relating to the recognition and use of herbs in medicine. A four-year degree in Herbal Medicine is available at Middlesex University.

Doctors can take a one-year course at the School of Herbal Medicine, concentrating on those aspects of the syllabus which they have not already covered.

Further information

The National Institute of Medical Herbalists and the National School of Phytotherapy or Herbal Medicine.

Homoeopathic medicine

Homoeopathic medicine, in which small quantities of substances are used to stimulate the body to produce its own defence to disease, is, despite its rather unorthodox nature, practised by qualified doctors and is available under the NHS. It works on the premise that a minute dilution of a substance which will normally cause a particular illness will actually cure it. This is cross-referenced with a description of different constitutional types, so the same illness in different people will not necessarily be treated by the same medicine – rather by one appropriate to the person.

Specialist homoeopaths who have no previous medical training undertake a full-time course which combines homoeopathic studies, human sciences and diagnosis. This lasts for three or four years. Two A-levels or their equivalent are desirable. They should be in scientific subjects, one of them being biology. Homoeopaths who are not medically qualified work as private consultants.

Further information

British Homoeopathic Association.

Hypnotherapy

Hypnotherapy is used to help patients overcome all kinds of problems – they can be helped to fulfil their potential without wasting time and effort or, at the other extreme, they may be helped to give up smoking or overeating. Some patients even use hypnotherapy instead of anaesthesia during operations.

Further information

National College of Hypnotherapy and Psychotherapy.

Kinesiology

Kinesiology uses muscle responses to test, diagnose and treat health problems. In the past it has been used mainly by chiropractors, but is now developing into a specialty on its own.

Further information

International College of Applied Kinesiology.

Naturopathy

Naturopathy is based on the belief that the living body, in health, is a self-regulating, self-maintaining organism and, provided internal and external environments are favourable, broadly speaking, a self-repairing organism. Natural therapeutics are therefore primarily aimed at correcting body chemistry by such methods as fasting and eliminative routines (partial fasts, restricted diets, hydrotherapy, and so on). It is closely linked to osteopathy (*see below*) and most naturopaths are also osteopaths, although the reverse is not necessarily true.

The British Naturopathic and Osteopathic Association, which is the most generally accepted representative body in the field, has some 250 members, all of whom work in full-time practice as naturopaths. Full-time training (lasting four years) in naturopathy and osteopathy is given by the British College of Naturopathy and Osteopathy.

Entrants must have studied to GCE A-level standard, including A-level chemistry and physics, and/or biology or zoology with chemistry and GCSE or equivalent physics; GCSE or equivalent English is also required.

Further Information

British College of Naturopathy and Osteopathy

Osteopathy

Osteopathy is mainly a manipulative therapy, aimed at correcting disorders of muscles and joints, and relieving pain and disability from a wide variety of conditions, based on the theory that the body is a vital organism whose structure and function are coordinate, and that disease is a perversion of either. The value of manipulative therapy is increasingly accepted by established medical authorities, but they disagree on how it should be applied, how long is needed to acquire the skills and, above all, the range of conditions in which it can be of value. As a result, relations between osteopaths and qualified medical practitioners vary considerably, some remaining hostile whilst others refer patients to osteopaths; the passing of the Osteopaths Act 1993 should improve cooperation, with the establishment of the General Osteopathic Council.

Osteopathy is currently only available under the NHS if the osteopath is also a qualified medical practitioner or physiotherapist. However, pilots are being set up (1996) to test the possible inclusion of osteopathy and chiropractic in the GP fundholding scheme. Osteopathy is increasingly accepted by patients, and prospects are good for those with recognised training and the capacity to run a private practice.

The General Council and Register of Osteopaths confined registration to those who have completed an approved training course, leading to an Open University BSc in many cases.

Recognised schools are the British School of Osteopathy, the British College of Naturopathy and Osteopathy, the European School of Osteopathy and the London College of Osteopathy (which takes only registered medical practitioners). Non-graduates enter the four-year course with A-level or equivalent (over half, in fact, have three or more A-levels), with preference given to A-level passes in chemistry and either biology or zoology.

Qualified physiotherapists are exempted from the basic science course, and anyone who has studied medicine can be exempted from others. The four-year, full-time course, taking about 80 students a year, begins with basic science and practical anatomy, with extensive practical training in the school's clinic during the clinical years of study.

Osteopathy has always been part of the nature-cure practitioner's work, and it can also be studied as part of the training in naturopathy.

Further information

The Institute of Complementary Medicine, the General Council and Register of Osteopaths, the British Naturopathic and Osteopathic Association, and from the schools.

Reflexology

Reflexology is based on using the pressure points on the feet and the corresponding ones on the hands to diagnose and relieve problems, both medical and psychological. Each zone on the feet refers to a different point in the body. In its most basic form, reflexology is practised throughout the country, often in beauty salons. The more complex *Reflex zone therapy of the feet* is practised only by qualified nurses or medical practitioners who have undertaken more in-depth training.

Training in Reflex zone therapy is open to registered doctors, nurses, midwives, physiotherapists and occupational therapists and to trained practitioners of osteopathy, naturopathy and acupuncture. It takes the form of a series of short courses held in London and Lancashire to inculcate the particular skills of hand treatment of the feet to alleviate pain and stimulate patients' healing processes. It is hoped in future to obtain validation of this training from South Bank University.

Further information

The British School of Reflex Zone Therapy of the Feet.

Scientists and Technicians in the Health Service

(CLCI: JAG, JAV–JOC, JOL, JOZ)

Contents

Background

Science and technology have been helping the health services make gigantic strides in diagnosis and testing, patient monitoring, surgery and treatment ever since the NHS was formed, over 40 years ago. Heart pacemakers, life-support systems, radiation therapy, artificial hips, kidney dialysis and scanning machines, are only a few examples of sophisticated developments now taken for granted.

No less important are the vastly improved backroom lab equipment and other machines – for recording, measuring, sampling and analysing – which have improved substantially the techniques for analysing blood, tissues, etc. and therefore accurate diagnosis of all kinds of conditions. New developments appear all the time – ultrasonic scanning (of the brain, for example) – and most of the lab equipment is now almost completely automated.

The equipment, the machines and the scientific techniques are not necessarily actually developed in NHS labs, although these do take some part in fundamental research and development work, especially trials. University departments and research centres, firms which manufacture medical and surgical equipment, and chemical and pharmaceutical companies are also involved.

However, the wide range of the science-based techniques and equipment in use mean the Health Service has to employ a comparatively large scientific staff, as well as a large number of technicians. The figures spell out the effect of science and technology. The number of professional and technical staff (excluding doctors and dentists) working in the NHS rose by 300% between 1949 and 1975, by 55% in the decade 1971–81, and by 30% between 1979 and 1989, and by 1993 was 91,130 compared with 68,690 in 1983.

NHS labs, and other science-based diagnostic/treatment services, employ multidisciplinary teams of scientific staff, with some units also employing technicians. While labs need people with varying levels of skills, ranging from PhDs through to young staff (trainees) with just GCSEs, automation and other technological advances have cut the most low-level and routine tasks considerably. Together with some strong 'marketing' by the professional body, this has given almost everyone working in the science-based NHS labs the status of 'scientist', if they are professionally qualified, but not necessarily graduates – although they may still be colloquially called 'technicians' within the hospital. Differentiating between the work of one kind of NHS scientist and another has become quite difficult as a result.

The NHS grading distinguishes between 'scientific' staff, i.e. biologists, biochemists, physicists, etc., 'medical laboratory scientific officers' (MLSOs) and medical laboratory assistants (MLAs), so it seems safest to describe the work under these headings. Biologists, biochemists, and chemists (particularly) may, and do, though, go for MLSO posts, probably because there are more of them than there are within their own disciplines.

Scientists working within their own disciplines probably do some of the most specialist work, and have more opportunities to do research, while the youngest and least-qualified MLAs do the most routine. In addition to the work of the lab or department, staff have to monitor equipment, and often work on developing new equipment and techniques, as well as trying to improve on present methods. They may also work with doctors on clinical trials of new equipment, materials, machines, prosthesis, and drugs.

Scientific and related services in the NHS grew in a very haphazard way. For many years, scientists in particular disciplines were recruited to work alongside individual medical staff for specific jobs, as and when needed, to provide expertise doctors did not have. Labs grew and expanded in individual hospitals as and when the hospital saw a need and could finance development. Attempts to rationalise and integrate services have been going on for 30 years and are now coming to fruition.

Medical physics and pharmaceutical services are now mostly organised on a regional or district basis, and many medical labs are now attached to the larger district hospitals, providing a single service both for smaller local hospitals and to the family doctors. Laboratory services are increasingly organised regionally, many smaller labs have been merged, and so some scientific staff now work in teams of up to 100. Managerial changes in the NHS have changed the way labs are organised and managed: many have MLSOs, or other scientists, managing and organising the data-producing service, although clinical responsibility stays with medically qualified consultants.

In large hospitals laboratories are divided into sections: haematology, dealing with blood analysis; clinical chemistry, biochemistry, and chemical pathology, where body fluids, tissue and excreta are analysed; medical microbiology and bacteriology, where bacteria and viruses are isolated and identified; and histopathology, where tissue samples taken during surgery or a post-mortem are preserved and studied.

In the NHS, most scientists are doing work which is directly related to the discipline of their academic studies, although there are some working in multidisciplinary teams.

Note: for entry requirements in health careers the Scottish Health Office use either the English details plus 'or equivalent'.

Audiological scientists

Traditionally most of the work involved in measuring hearing has been done by TECHNICIANS (*see below*). This is unlikely to change very much. However, more sophisticated techniques for difficult cases mean some posts for qualified scientists, who deal mainly with the tougher problems involved in assessing and measuring hearing loss and speech defects, using electronics to make more efficient instruments to test more accurately (e.g. a device for a cot which can help detect whether a small baby is responding to sound), and developing new forms of hearing aids. The number of jobs is small – in the NHS, and doing research, in universities and research units.

Audiological scientists are recruited from people with a relevant science degree (e.g. biology, physics, physiology, psychology) topped by a postgraduate degree in audiology, and a one-year in-service training course for a certificate in audiological competence.

Clinical biochemists

The number of clinical biochemists working within the NHS in England grew from barely 700 in 1974 to 1,860 in 1983 and dropped to 1,610 in 1993. Several hundred others do clinically related research, mainly in universities.

In the NHS, mainly in hospitals, clinical biochemists work in teams alongside medically qualified pathologists and MLSOs in laboratories analysing blood samples, making microscopic sections of skin and tissue, and examining them for signs of disease, using highly complex chromatographic, spectrophotometric, radioactive and other techniques. The routine laboratory work is highly automated and is done mainly by MLSOs and MLAs.

Biochemists are the supervisors, who check the accuracy of results, make expert assessments of test results, and look for ways of improving methods (such as computer-based and automated systems) and efficiency. They may do some tests themselves, especially where the problems are unusual or particularly critical, or in an emergency. They report non-routine tests, or unexpected results to routine tests, to the clinician responsible. They take part in case conferences and discussion of particular forms of diagnosis and treatment or cases with clinical staff where needed. Biochemists may also do some research, for instance on the biochemical causes of particular diseases, and if they work in teaching hospitals, may teach clinical biochemistry to student doctors, dentists and nurses. Some specialise in endocrinology or toxicology.

Training is normally in-service, but with study leave for short courses. On this basis it takes about five years to work for Master of Clinical Biochemistry examinations, set jointly by the Royal Institute of Chemistry, the Royal College of Physicians and the Association of Clinical Biochemists. Alternatively, postgraduate degrees can be taken at about half-a-dozen universities. A number of first-degree courses include some specialisation in clinical biochemistry. *See also* Biochemist *in* BIOLOGICAL SCIENCES.

Further information

Biochemical Society.

Biologists

The biologists employed are mainly microbiologists and a few zoologists and physiologists. Most work for the Public Health Laboratory Service and the blood transfusion service. They screen and test for bacteria and viruses, and combine this with research into the spread and control of microbial diseases.

Dietitians

Nutrition experts and dietitians measure people's food intake, promote healthy eating and balanced diets, plan menus for specific groups (e.g. patients in hospitals or children in school), and advise on special diets, for the overweight or diabetic.

Nutrition experts generally make scientific studies such as the effects of food processing, or practical ways to improve nutrition in elderly people. Dietitians translate scientists' findings and doctors' recommendations into actual diets, taking into account all the factors – psychological, economic, etc. – which affect people's choice of food. They assess the nutritional value of particular foods, and teach cooks and patients how to prepare and present them. They help people to solve what can be very difficult nutritional and dietetic problems, explain the reasons for a diet, and help them put it into practice, bearing in mind the shopping, cooking and budgeting problems most families have, as well as their food fads and fancies. They advise not only people with medical problems, but groups such as the elderly, or immigrants who must follow strict religious dietary rules, but cannot get or afford in Britain the food they are used to.

Over 3,800 dietitians are state registered; many work for the NHS, largely in the hospitals, where they plan and advise on diets. In some hospitals they may be employed as catering officers. For other work as a dietitian and in nutrition *see* FOOD AND DRINK SCIENTISTS AND MANUFACTURING *in* MANUFACTURING INDUSTRIES.

Further information

The British Dietetic Association; Council for Professions Supplementary to Medicine.

Geneticists

Geneticists are employed in NHS medical genetics advisory services (each region has one), but work only in the labs (for counselling, a medical qualification is needed). The work in the labs is mainly, for clinical cytogeneticists, identifying chromosomes using tissue culture and blood or bone marrow to identify foetal abnormalities or reasons for infertility. (They also do enzyme analyses but more usually employ biochemists and/or microbiologists for this.) Some research into genetic aspects of medicine is done, and some molecular geneticists work on DNA analysis to determine possible genetic disorders. *See* genetics, molecular biology *in* BIOLOGICAL SCIENCES.

Medical laboratory scientific officers

They make up the largest group of scientific staff – numbers rose from 14,700 in 1983 to 15,140 in 1993. Mostly they work in hospital-based services, staffing the pathology departments. They are the familiar 'technicians' who take blood samples on the wards and in out-patients, and the 'backroom' scientists who do the actual examining, testing and analysing: of samples of blood and urine, etc. sent in both by GPs and from hospital wards and clinics; and of the scraps of tissue, spinal fluid and other samples surgeons send for analysis during and after operations to find out what is wrong with a patient, to monitor the progress of treatment, or to try to isolate bacteria or viruses. For a few, in some hospitals, promotion can be to supervisory work, and even lab management.

While much of the routine testing has been automated away, and graduates (degree and HND/C) recruited, most of the work is still very practical and may not always 'stretch' highly qualified people. On the other hand, promotional prospects are probably generally better with a higher-level qualification.

The techniques and equipment are mostly very similar to those used in any scientific laboratory but adapted to, or specially developed, for medical work. It is fairly common in larger labs for qualified MLSOs to specialise in, e.g.

- *clinical chemistry* – analysing blood and other specimens to diagnose disease or identify toxic substances, monitor body metabolism, etc.;
- *blood transfusion* – identifying blood groups, checking on compatibility, and preparing blood products for use;
- *haematology* – doing blood-cell counts in, e.g., leukaemia or anaemia, and investigating clotting defects;
- *cellular pathology, cytology and histopathology* – preparing and studying tissue samples from patients, or for post mortems;
- *medical microbiology*, including *bacteriology* and *virology* – culturing organisms taken from patients, food, water, etc., and identifying them;
- *immunology* – work related to allergic reactions, infectious diseases, organ transplants, immune deficiencies, etc..

Automation may have reduced the routine substantially, but diagnostic tests and other investigations have to be given priority, and be done with great care and accuracy, yet as fast as possible, especially when there is an emergency, or when a surgeon needs information while operating. The work ranges from fairly basic but absolutely crucial work of booking-in specimens, loading tests into machines, and recording results, through operating some very complex computer-based equipment and carrying out more difficult non-routine tests, to some more advanced scientific work which may include being involved in research.

Labs are largely under the clinical direction of, e.g., medically qualified pathologists. However, principal/senior MLSOs may be the actual laboratory 'managers', with 'line' responsibility for organising the data-producing service itself within agreed budgets, in charge of other MLSOs and other lab staff. Promotion, though, is generally into administrative rather than more advanced scientific work, and cannot give any clinical responsibility. Experience of two or three areas of MLSO work is normally needed.

MLSOs may also work in, for example, the 'special' services. These include the following:

The *Public Health Laboratory Service* is where MLSOs run the emergency service; it tries to find causes of epidemics – often in a great hurry – and also continuously monitors and controls potential sources of disease, which may be water-, air-, or food-borne.

The *Blood Transfusion Service* is where MLSOs analyse blood to decide its exact group, do a range of other tests on blood cells and sera, prepare plasma and blood for transfusion, and test donors' fitness to give blood.

Clinically-related research in Medical Research Council units and in university, government and industrial labs also employs some MLSOs.

Other employers include pharmaceutical firms, veterinary services, forensic labs, private diagnostic lab services, government departments, universities, and the Armed Forces.

Recruitment and entry

For routine lab work the minimum is four GCSE or equivalent passes including mathematics and a subject with a major proportion of chemistry, or a relevant BTEC National, and it is still possible to gain entry at this level, especially if individual labs are short of recruits. Career prospects are limited since MLSO registration requires an appropriate honours degree followed by specific training. Degrees in biomedical sciences are most relevant, but in 1995 only 50 of these graduates were recruited, the remaining 850 having to add a special IBMS examination before applying for state registration.

The work takes people with a range of scientific skills. Further, some MLSOs do come into contact with patients, for example taking blood samples. This means that they have to be able to put patients at their ease, and deal with their worries.

Qualifications and training

The NHS trains and gives release to study for professional examinations, essential for state registration, upgrading to the basic MLSO grade, and further promotion. All MLSOs have a period of training on the job, and so courses are normally closely linked to training in the laboratory. The Medical Laboratory Technicians' (State Registration) Board keeps a register of approved laboratories which includes most large hospitals, public health authorities, blood transfusion centres, and some industrial and research laboratories. On-the-job instruction is generally linked to lectures and individual tuition from senior staff.

School-leaver level

School-leavers with GCSEs would normally take BTEC National in (appropriate) sciences, either for a Diploma (full-time pre-entry) or a Certificate (part-time on release from work with training).

School-leavers with A-levels/Higher grades would normally take BTEC/SCOTVEC HNC/HND in medical laboratory sciences; or a four-year degree course in medical laboratory sciences at a university. Part-time degrees in biomedical sciences are replacing HNC courses at many institutions.

Graduates, with a degree in preferably biochemistry, chemistry, microbiology, or animal physiology/zoology, and people with BTEC/SCOTVEC Higher awards, can become student members of the Institute of Biomedical Science (1995 membership 21,000 including 900 students), and can apply for state registration (and associate membership of the Institute) after a year's professional experience. For promotion, it is usually necessary to take the 'special' examinations (with the alternative of a thesis), for IBS fellowship, for which a further year's experience/study is needed. IBS also sets exams for a diploma in medical laboratory management.

Further information

The Institute of Biomedical Science, Council for Professions Supplementary to Medicine.

Medical physicists

About 750 full-time equivalent physicists worked for the NHS in England in 1993 against 660 in 1983; a further 250 worked in the rest of the UK. Most district hospitals have medical physics departments providing a wide range of services including new ways to use ultrasound, microwaves, radiation, lasers and electronics.

They deal with the clinical use of radiation. Here they work in treatment planning – to see that required doses are kept as far as possible to the part of the body being treated – and also supervise safety and protection for both patients and staff. They must be involved in planning and designing any department where radioactive materials are to be used, and they must monitor the control on hazards.

They work with both doctors and engineers on development and use of the growing range of equipment and techniques using radiation in both radiotherapy and diagnosis and on the various ways in which radioactive material is used to provide information on physical conditions; in developing the uses of ultrasonics, NMR imaging, computerised 'whole-body' tomography, etc.; and on the physics and electronics of new equipment to monitor patients. Increasing amounts of data are being collected from patients with these newer systems and physicists work on improving both the equipment and its use.

Physicists also work in audiology (*see above*).

Physicists work closely with clinical or biomedical engineers (*see in* PROCESS ENGINEERING, BIOMEDICAL ENGINEERING AND MATERIALS SCIENCE) on the growing range of implants and other electronically operated prosthetic aids.

Medical physicists work in respiratory physiology (e.g. on the properties of bronchial secretions), urology, and pathology. A degree in science or engineering may provide suitable background for work in teams of surgeons and engineers helping patients to achieve mobility and independence with the aid of prosthetic or electronic aids. Some may work in rehabilitation units with patients who have suffered strokes; others concentrate upon the design and construction of equipment.

They also teach at all levels – lecturing, for instance, on radiation hazards – and can do research, particularly in medical schools.

While it is possible to find a post in medical physics on graduating, the NHS prefers higher degrees and/or relevant industrial experience. Some physicists now start as technicians but transfer to a professional post can be difficult.

See also PHYSICS *in* SCIENCE CAREERS AND THE PHYSICAL SCIENCES.

Further information

Hospital Physicists Association, Institute of Physics.

Orthotists and prosthetists

Orthotists fit and supply surgical appliances such as cervical collars, surgical footwear, plaster casts, leg supports, finger splints, etc. Most orthotists work for the manufacturers who are contracted to supply the particular appliance for the Health Service. And so while the orthotist does not actually work for the NHS, a large part of his or her time is spent in NHS hospitals and clinics, working closely with medical and other professional staff. The specialist decides on the appliance needed, and mostly these must be made specially to fit the individual. The orthotist measures the patient, or takes a cast, and writes out the specification for the technician who will make the appliance. The orthotist tries the appliance on the patient, checking that it fits, is comfortable, is doing the job needed, etc., and shows the patient how it works, how to get it on and off, how to adjust it, etc. They may have to help the patient come to terms with the appliance, and will check at intervals to see it is still satisfactory. Qualified orthotists number about 500.

Prosthetists measure and fit amputees of all ages, shapes and sizes, etc. for artificial limbs – mostly legs. Even if the limb fits, and works properly when first made, it usually has to be checked, adjusted and repaired frequently, and they eventually wear out – and children grow out of them – and they have to be replaced. Like orthotists, prosthetists are employed by the firms making limbs on contract to the DSS, but at present they work from DSS artificial limb and appliance centres throughout the country. In Scotland, they are employed by Health Boards. The limb service and these centres are being re-organised, so where – and for whom – they work may change, but the job itself will remain essential, and essentially the same. If, as hoped, the service is improved, demand for prosthetists will probably increase.

Recruitment and entry

Because training includes a large 'practical' element, entrants have to be taken on as a trainee by an approved organisation (one of eight orthotic firms and two hospitals; and four limb companies). Minimum entry requirements are as needed for entry to a BTEC Higher course, i.e. at least four GCSE passes or equivalent, with at least one at A-level (subjects to include English and sciences/technological subjects) or an equivalent, e.g. a BTEC National.

Orthotists and prosthetists have to be intelligent enough to understand both the medical/anatomical basis of what they are doing and the (rising) technological basis of the appliances they provide. They have to be practical and accurate, and be prepared to take time and care. They must work sympathetically and helpfully with people whose quality of life depends to some extent on their efforts.

Qualifications and training

Both orthotists and prosthetists must go through statutory required training.

This now involves a new four-year degree course at the Universities of Salford and Strathclyde. Students will join in a 'shared learning' programme which has been designed to bring them together with the different groups of students studying respectively in physiotherapy, occupational therapy, chiropody, radiography, nursing and social work. The degree programme comprises three interlinked elements: academic studies, practical training in the fabrication and forming of prosthetic and orthotic devices, and clinical experience in the assessment and fitting of patients. These three elements are developed, in a coordinated way, through the first three years of the course. The fourth year is then a 'pre-registration' year, spent working in clinical practice in the Health Service or with a commercial orthotic or prosthetic manufacturing company.

The academic element of the course includes biological sciences, engineering and materials sciences, mechanics and biomechanics, clinical studies, principles of prosthetics and orthotics, mathematics, professional studies and research methods. The practical programme is linked closely with the academic studies and follows their course. All students may also join an optional language training programme.

Further information

British Association of Prosthetists and Orthotists.

Pathologists

Pathology is the study of disease. A great deal of medical research is in pathology – for example in preventing transplanted organs from being rejected, measuring hormone levels to ensure that test-tube babies are successfully implanted, and identifying and typing cells in diseases such as leukaemia. Pathology is becoming increasingly specialised; pathologists can specialise within the areas of histopathology/cytology, haematology, clinical chemistry or microbiology. Clinical microbiologists are more directly concerned with patient treatment than some other scientists because they may be employed in diagnostic labs working on sources of infection or the study of parasites, fungi and bacteria to help physicians devise appropriate treatment. They also contribute to epidemiological research.

Some pathologists have medical degrees, following a post-qualification year on hospital wards with a four to six year training in pathology to become a consultant pathologist. Pathologists who are medically qualified examine dead bodies and perform autopsies to establish the causes of sudden unexpected death, or to study the effects of medical treatment. Science graduates can join pathology laboratories to become medical scientists or medical laboratory scientific officers (MLSOs), taking appropriate postgraduate training.

The Royal College of Pathologists admits to membership non-medically qualified graduates who have specialised in genetics, immunogenetics, histopathology, etc. in labs attached to hospitals undertaking operations for patients with diseased kidneys or needing life-saving organ transplants. Some graduates with particular interest in molecular biology apply for the few training places in labs specialising in problems of organ compatibility in, for example, cases needing bone marrow transplants. Molecular biologists may be attracted to the comparatively new specialism of clinical immunology developing new ways of studying patients' immune systems with the aid of complex equipment and meticulous recording.

Pharmacologists and pharmacists

Pharmacology

Pharmacology is that branch of the medical sciences which studies the preparation, uses and effects of drugs, both the substances which affect the body so that they can be used to treat diseases and also their harmful effect on the body. A drug is a chemical, an active ingredient which affects the body and the way the organs function. A medicine is the form in which the drug is prepared so that it can be administered to a patient. Pharmacology involves chemistry, biochemistry and physiology, and is integral to the study of medicine, veterinary medicine and pharmacy. Some medicines are produced naturally and extracted from plants, such as caffeine from coffee, or penicillin from the fungus *Penicillium*, whereas others are produced synthetically like aspirin. Pharmacologists also study the effect of agricultural chemicals such as insecticides, food additives, environmental pollutants, and cosmetics on humans, and studying the harmful effects of these is toxicology.

Pharmacologists carry out research to discover and prepare new drugs using a whole range of techniques, then test them in laboratories and in clinical trials and then find ways of developing them. This process may take many years from discovery to commercial production. Pharmacologists also study the physiological systems of the body such as the respiratory system, the nervous system and the circulatory system and the relation between the chemical structure of drugs and the way they affect the human body both in beneficial ways and in producing undesirable side-effects. Drugs may be developed from many different sources. Some substances which occur naturally in common plants, such as digitalis from foxgloves, or the hallucinogenic drugs from certain species of mushrooms, have been known for centuries, in various cultures, whereas other drugs such as penicillin was discovered by careful observation. Yet others are found from chemicals manufactured for other purposes, for example such as sulphonamides from the dyestuff industry.

It is important in the treatment of disease to develop new drugs which have a completely new effect on the human metabolism, or which act more quickly, more reliably, for a longer time or with fewer unwanted side-effects than existing drugs. Very thorough and detailed laboratory work is carried out by pharmacologists who do exploratory tests on the effects of various chemicals and natural products on tissue cultures, and later on laboratory animals, usually rodents, and then in clinical trials on patients. Before this stage is reached, the adverse side-effects of the drug must have been investigated and eliminated as far as possible, and appropriate dosages must be recommended for various circumstances. Thousands of compounds are prepared in the UK every year in pharmaceutical laboratories, but only half a dozen or so of these become licensed, and most of these are then superseded by other more efficacious products.

Drugs grow steadily more complex and sophisticated, and pharmacology learns all the time from biochemists' and physiologists' work on cell, protein and genetic structures, making possible new ways of attacking disease. The action of drugs generally interferes in some way with the body cells' communication systems, which operate via chemical substances, so that the most effective drugs intervene chemically. As more is learnt about the body's chemical-messenger system, so new drugs to block or stimulate messenger substances can be developed. Equally, pharmaceutical research on the effects of particular substances can lead to the discovery of other biological pathways and control systems in the body. In the foreseeable future, pharmacologists predict, 40% of new, 'designer' drugs will be genetically engineered, and will be protein- and peptide-based rather than the simpler chemical substances which are in common use now.

There are still many diseases for which treatments and cures are needed such as AIDS, Creutzfeld Jacob's disease (CJD), cancer, cystic fibrosis and malaria.

Pharmacy

Pharmacy is the dispensing of drugs and other medical products, which may include the compounding or mixing of different substances, and their preparation in appropriate strengths as directed by a doctor or dentist. Pharmacists measure liquid medicines to be taken by mouth or injection, count out tablets and capsules, and prepare ointments. Pharmacists need to be able to recognise and identify a very large number of different products, be systematic in their storage and keep careful records. The supply of drugs is very strictly controlled in law, and they are grouped into classes according to the strength of the effect they have. The security of store cupboards and of premises is very important. Pharmacists generally pack and label these products and must be very accurate in dispensing prescriptions, as the information on the label gives the correct dosage and times when the prescription should be taken, and so mistakes could have very serious repercussions.

Pharmacists study the chemical structure and the properties of all the different substances which they deal with, and also the physiological systems of the human body and the way in which medicines affect these systems. They need to know the effect of different dosages, the side-effects of drugs, and what the combined effect of different medicines can be.

Opportunities for pharmacologists and pharmacists

To work as a pharmacist it is necessary to be registered with the Royal Pharmaceutical Society (RPS), for which candidates must have a degree in pharmacy. A degree in pharmacology does not qualify for RPS membership. Apart from working as pharmacists, pharmacology and pharmacy graduates are qualified to work in similar fields.

About 20,000 pharmacy graduates work in community or retail pharmacy, about 5,000 work in hospital pharmacy and 1,500 in industry.

Pharmacy work in both community and retail shops and hospitals mainly involves pharmacists in both preparing and supplying medicines and medical products from doctors' prescriptions. In practice, many drugs are now prepared and pre-packaged by pharmaceutical companies, so there is little compounding to do. This does not, however, reduce or remove pharmacists' responsibility for making sure that the correct drugs are dispensed in the correct dosage. Pharmacists in retail outlets also use their expertise to advise people on minor health problems.

Pharmacists working in the Health Service (rather than general retail practice, industry or the academic world) mostly deal with the supply and quality of drugs and other medical preparations used in the hospital, and compound and dispense them for both in- and out-patients. They also work with the medical and dental staff to see that medicines are used safely, effectively and economically, and are consulted by them on pharmaceutical problems – for example, drug interactions, whether or not there are contra-indications to using a drug in particular circumstances, and whether or not there may be side-effects, and if so what can be done to alleviate them. Pharmacists order drugs and other medicines for the whole hospital, and may also be involved in buying medical and surgical instruments and other equipment.

Most get the opportunity to do some physiological research, often with other researchers – developing new treatments, investigating pharmaceutical problems, and working on clinical trials of new drugs. The clinical trials of drugs and medicines are supervised by clinical pharmacologists who are medically qualified, and usually based in hospitals. They work with pharmacologists who are not medically qualified, but who undertake associated laboratory work.

In teaching hospitals, senior pharmacists lecture to both medical undergraduates and other student trainees.

Pharmaceutical companies employ the largest group of pharmacologists, but only 5% of pharmacists, to develop new and improved drugs and collaborate with other scientists in fundamental research. Some specialise in the effect of drugs and medicines on particular physiological systems; such are the neuropharmacologists who study the effects of drugs on the nervous system. They also do product coordination, monitor clinical trials, register drugs, and collate information. The full-scale production of drugs, may include developing new equipment, product support, controlling and supervising production and packaging, and quality assurance.

Marketing, sales and advertising (*see in* BUYING, SELLING AND RELATED SERVICES) are technical functions in pharmaceuticals, and so also employ pharmacists and pharmacologists, as well as other life scientists and people with medical qualifications. The pharmaceutical industry has problems in recruiting high-calibre pharmacy graduates, and probably needs more of them, especially as licensing legislation is tightening.

The government employs pharmacologists and a few pharmacists. Mostly they do research, working for example in the Chemical and Biological Defence Sector (part of the Defence Evaluation and Research Agency (DERA)), on compounds of high pharmacological activity, investigating synthetic routes and the relationship between chemical structure and biological activity. Pharmacists also work for the Department of Health, sometimes in an advisory capacity. Some pharmacologists work in forensic laboratories investigating suspicious deaths; others work for the Medical Research Council.

Some pharmacologists work for regulatory bodies to ensure the safety of substances before they become widely available, and check on the toxic effects of pesticides and other chemicals used in agriculture and horticulture, food additives, solvents, detergents and other household chemicals. Other pharmacologists work in medical information and medical publishing, others in drug registration and some in toxicology.

A few pharmacologists and pharmacists work in research and teaching in universities and colleges.

Studying pharmacology and pharmacy

Both pharmacology and pharmacy courses generally start with a year of pure sciences – chemistry, physiology and some biology or biochemistry are the most usual, although some give a choice. Some pharmacology courses introduce pharmacology in the first year, but many leave it to the second. Some pharmacy courses also leave pharmacology and/or basic pharmacy until the second year.

Pharmacology courses, after the first year, continue basic sciences in the second, but increasingly they are biased to aspects relevant to pharmacology such as the effect of drugs and chemicals on humans and animals and the development of new and more effective drugs with fewer side-effects. Much of the final year is usually spent on recent advances. Pharmacology can also be studied with another subject, e.g. biochemistry, cell biology, chemistry, immunology, physiology or psychology. Courses are for either three or four years. Four-year sandwich courses allow a period of time for industrial release so that students can obtain firsthand experience in a research environment.

First destinations of graduates in pharmacology were, in 1994:

total graduating	*261*
further study or training	128
permanent employment	66
employers	
public service (including hospitals)	10
teaching HE	7
chemical and pharmaceutical industries	23
other manufacturing	4
building, civil engineering and architecture	1
accountancy	5
banking and insurance	2
other commercial	11

Postgraduate courses are mainly intended to give advanced training to graduates in related disciplines.

In pharmacy, the main body of the course generally covers pharmacognosy (studying crude drugs of plant and animal origin), pharmaceutical chemistry (the chemistry and analysis of naturally occurring and synthetic substances used in medicine, including their structure and synthesis and the relation between chemical structure and biological action), pharmaceutics (how to formulate, prepare and test compounds for medical use) and chemotherapy. Basic sciences, like chemistry, continue. 'Professional practice' is taught, and options may prepare students for work in, e.g. research on new drugs, quality control, etc.

Courses in pharmacy are available at the following universities: Aston, Bath, Bradford, Brighton, Cardiff, de Montfort, Greenwich, Liverpool John Moores, London (School of Pharmacy), Manchester, Nottingham, Portsmouth, Queens Belfast, Robert Gordon, Strathclyde and Sunderland.

Entry requirements normally include A-level chemistry, and one or two other sciences; sciences not offered at A-level should normally have been passed at GCSE/SCE (grades A–C/1–3). Advanced GNVQ science may be acceptable, usually at distinction level, and A-level chemistry may be an additional requirement.

First destinations of pharmacy graduates were, in 1994:

total graduating	*771*
permanent employment	696
further study or training	6
employers	
public service (including hospitals)	225
chemical and pharmaceutical industries	62
other manufacturing and services	1
commerce (includes retail pharmacy)	401
private practice	2

Pharmacy graduates who wish to practise in either retail or hospital pharmacies must be registered pharmaceutical chemists and Members of the Pharmaceutical Society of Great Britain, which has over 30,000 members including pharmacists working in industry and academic institutions.

Pharmacists must also gain a year's experience pre-registration. At present half has to be in hospital or community/retail pharmacy, the other half may be in industry, in pharmacy school, or in agricultural, veterinary pharmacy. In practice, over 54% spend the full year in retail or community pharmacy, about half of these in the major retail chains; and almost 40% in hospital pharmacy. Changes to the pre-registration year, proposed by the Nuffield Foundation Report, are being discussed.

Postgraduate courses are mainly intended to give advanced training to graduates in related disciplines.

Technician-level qualification is now via BTEC National and Higher National Certificates in Science (pharmaceutical). Entry qualifications should include appropriate sciences.

At present no formal route through from technician to professional qualification exists.

Further information

The Association of the British Pharmaceutical Industry, the National Pharmaceutical Association, the Pharmaceutical Society of Great Britain, and the British Pharmacological Society, all produce careers information.

Photographers and medical illustrators

Medical photographers specialise in providing records to the physicians and surgeons to illustrate patients' progress or deterioration, identifying pathological specimens, etc. They often also produce slides and illustrations for audio-visual presentations in medical and dental schools, books and articles and any other purpose requiring accurate visual representations of disease or conditions and sometimes film and video records of patients' mobility. In cases where photography is inappropriate, illustrators may produce line drawings or paintings for similar purposes.

Medical photographers are employed by a number of hospitals, although the photographic department itself may be very small. The NHS employs some 300 full-time equivalent medical photographers. *See* PHOTOGRAPHY *in* ART, CRAFT AND DESIGN.

Statisticians

Statisticians are employed in government departments concerned with health and social services, in the Office for National Statistics, and in certain other organisations in the health field; in particular they may be engaged upon research with epidemiologists to calculate the spread of infections and diseases. They are important members of teams of doctors and scientists conducting randomised controlled trials (RCTs) when new drugs are being developed and it may be necessary to give the drugs to large numbers of people. In this way their usefulness can be tested since people react differently and statistically small samples may not assess the validity of particular treatments. Examples of such collaboration include the development of streptomycin in the treatment of tuberculosis, the links between smoking and lung cancer, and megatrials using placebos to evaluate different treatments for conditions such as heart attacks or depression.

They do medical investigations – statistical analyses of drug trials; or the relation between social conditions and ill health; or the incidence of particular diseases in particular parts of the country – as the basis for a better understanding of the spread and control of disease, or discovering the causes of certain conditions.

They may do surveys, e.g. a detailed study of the use of hospital out-patient departments. Statisticians are also used in administrative work on, e.g., manpower forecasts, budgeting, planning problems, statistical analysis of patient waiting times, or trends in births and deaths.

In medical schools they also teach and do personal research. Highly sophisticated techniques, including computer analysis and modelling, are used, and graduate statisticians are usually involved in developing these.

See also STATISTICS *in* MATHEMATICS, STATISTICS AND ECONOMICS; *and* COMPUTER SCIENTIST *in* INFORMATION TECHNOLOGY AND COMPUTER WORK.

Further information

Royal Statistical Society.

Other scientists and engineers

The NHS also employs other scientists and professional engineers (*see in* GENERAL ENGINEERING), and computer scientists (*see in* INFORMATION TECHNOLOGY AND COMPUTER WORK), but in quite small numbers. *See also* physiology, toxicology *in* BIOLOGICAL SCIENCES.

Recruitment and entry

Recruitment is directly for specific vacancies in the NHS or for organisations like the Medical Research Council, for those holding appropriate qualifications.

Qualifications and training

Entry is normally via a conventional first degree in the science concerned, i.e. physics, biochemistry, biology, electronics, maths, statistics, computer science, followed by postgraduate training. Some degree courses in these subjects include options in the medical applications.

Higher degrees specialising in medical applications are available in most sciences, and on-the-job training linked to some form of release to study for appropriate qualifications may be provided.

Technicians

The NHS, and other firms/organisations in the medical field, have technician-level work for a number of groups. There is no coherent, 'technician' grade or career structure. Each group specialises in a particular type of work, and as each group works for professional/medically qualified seniors, and also in small numbers in any one hospital, there are few senior posts. The NHS employed in England 14,300 technicians in 1983; 22,300 in 1993.

Medical physics technicians

About half work in hospitals, and half in research departments and medical schools.

Some work under physicists on radiation therapy: technicians prepare and carry out tests which use isotopes; prepare sterile radiopharmaceuticals; help to design, construct, set up and operate the equipment used in radiotherapy; do checks to see that staff have not been over-exposed to radiation; check and monitor leak-detection systems, and generally make sure that radiation exposure is kept to a minimum and proper protective measures used.

These technicians perform vital functions in hospitals which have the most modern equipment as they have to monitor its performance and undertake regular maintenance and servicing to ensure accuracy and safety for patient and operator. They may be required to construct sophisticated equipment for special purposes and techniques designed by doctors, scientists and engineers. They must be familiar with electrical and electronic measuring devices, and computer-controlled machines and be sensitive to patients' possible discomfort when constructing or adapting equipment and to the demands of safety within the ward. Some technicians work especially in the X-ray department or as part of a radiotherapy team working directly with patients. They may be expected to test radioactive and nuclear materials, and generally to maintain equipment for the disabled, renal dialysis machines (this work may involve home visits), lasers in ophthalmology departments, and gynaecology units where ultrasound imaging is now commonplace.

Qualities required are a conscientious and responsible character, concentration and accuracy of recording, mechanical skills and acute powers of observation. Good physical health and eyesight may be as important for success as the academic qualifications of four GCSEs or equivalent, BTEC National in electronics, or A-levels in sciences. Training is provided in a hospital combined with day- or block-release to college for the appropriate BTEC/ SCOTVEC examinations.

Operating department assistants

Operating department assistants help to keep theatres running smoothly and relieve medical and nursing staff of some routine tasks. They help the anaesthetist (checking they have the right patient, checking the anaesthetic equipment is working, preparing the trolley, getting the patient into the theatre, monitoring equipment), check the patient's notes and X-rays are available and correct, see that equipment and materials are there and ready, prepare plasters, move lights and equipment. They help clean up and check stores and equipment between operating sessions; they keep control of supplies and care for patients before and after their operations. Sensitivity to the needs of nervous and vulnerable people will contribute to their ultimate recovery and willingness to undergo future surgical operations.

Training is given for two years within the hospital and may include day or block release for theoretical study leading to the award of an NVQ level 3.

Pharmacy technicians

Working under supervision of hospital pharmacists they dispense prescribed medicines for use with individual patients or for general supplies to wards. These may be tablets, medicines, phials, creams, or sterile products, and will be subject to detailed control of quality, composition and quantity. The normal two years' training may include computerised record-keeping and stock control; day- or block-release to college is provided for courses leading to BTEC/SCOTVEC National Certificates in Pharmaceutical Sciences.

Physiological measurement technicians

Physiological measurement technicians cover various specialisms in measuring and recording physical characteristics, usually with the aid of machines and equipment which may have been especially designed and constructed. An interest in people and capacity to put them at ease is as essential as the skill to manipulate sophisticated apparatus.

Audiology technicians

They do the tests used to assess hearing, of adults, the elderly, children and even the very young. They mostly use highly complex and advanced equipment like speech audiometers and psycho-acoustic apparatus, cooperating with medical staff on problems of balance, tinnitus, etc. Some audiology technicians fit and issue hearing aids, make specially moulded ear inserts for them, and train patients to use them. They make any adjustments and do some repairs. Audiology technicians work with the patients as well as on equipment, and need the personal qualities to do this.

Cardiology technicians and cardiographers

Cardiology technicians set up and operate the increasingly sophisticated equipment used in diagnosing and treating heart conditions. They sterilise and prepare apparatus for cardiac tests and examinations; attach electrodes to the patient; operate and monitor equipment used to measure and record, for example, a patient's heart rhythm; monitor heart readings during surgical operations. They do respiratory function tests; record heart sounds photographically; analyse the level of oxygen in the blood and measure its circulation; help monitor patients' conditions after surgery; and look after monitoring and recording equipment in cardiac units.

Cardiographers do routine electro-cardiology and minor maintenance.

Cardiology technicians and cardiographers work with patients who have been given pacemakers.

Gastroenterology technicians

They help to investigate disorders in the acidity level or pressure changes in the alimentary canal by inserting tubes containing measuring devices into the stomach or rectum.

Neurophysiology or EEG technicians

They set up and operate equipment which records the brain's electrical activity and also measure, for instance, heart and breathing rates as they affect, or are affected by, brain activity. They have to know which technique to use, where to place electrodes, what level of stimuli to give, see patients have any necessary drugs, operate the equipment, and generally look after patients during the recordings. They work in surgical units, under neurologists, or in psychiatric hospitals. Some technicians also test nerve and muscle reactions to electrical stimuli and record their findings with meticulous accuracy in order to assist the doctors in determining the causes of peculiar patterns of brain activity which may be caused by a stroke, trauma or infection.

Respiratory physiological technicians

They measure the patient's breathing function during operations or while in hospital awaiting diagnosis of suspected lung disease or malfunction.

Other technician groups

Other technicians employed in small numbers by the NHS include:

- *cervical cytology screeners;*
- *darkroom technicians*, who work mainly in radiography departments;
- *electronics technicians* maintaining equipment;
- *medical laboratory assistants and phlebotomists*, taking blood samples from patients;
- *perfusionists,* who work in the team of surgeons, anaesthetists and nurses at heart operations. They operate heart–lung machines to keep the patient supplied with blood and oxygen during bypass operations. They may have to use machines to prevent lung failure or maintain correct blood pressure when the patient's natural organs are failing. Training is given within the hospital and can lead to a BTEC HNC or for graduates a Diploma in Clinical Perfusion Sciences;
- *post-mortem room technicians/pathology technicians, etc.* These team members work in the post-mortem room helping the pathologist to discover the cause of death if this has occurred in suspicious or criminal circumstances, for insurance claims, negligence cases or as part of ongoing research into the progress or distribution of particular diseases or conditions.

Technicians work on parts of the body itself and on the equipment used for pathological investigation, and in cases of normal death in hospital they contribute to the efficient running of the mortuary. They may be required to deal with the police and doctors as well as relatives and should be responsible, practical, tactful and careful to avoid infection. They can train for the Royal Institute of Public Health and Hygiene Certificate in Pathology Technology and higher qualifications.

Recruitment and entry

The NHS does not have a single entry to technician work; recruitment and entry levels vary from group to group.

For most groups of technicians, at least four GCSE-level or equivalent passes at A–C are needed to take the appropriate qualifications.

The work needs the same kinds of abilities as scientific laboratory work, but some groups of technicians do come into contact with patients. For example, when operating equipment which measures hearing, the heart, or brain activity. This means that they have to be able to put patients at their ease, deal with their worries, etc.

Qualifications and training

These vary from group to group, but promotion within the NHS depends on passing appropriate examinations. All technicians are trained on the job, and so courses are normally closely linked to training. On-the-job instruction is generally linked to lectures and individual tuition from senior staff.

Technicians in these groups study for BTEC awards which are variants on the medical laboratory schemes. For example, the BTEC Certificate in sciences can be taken with elective physics and physiological measurement, and the HNC in medical laboratory sciences has special options in physiological measurement and radiation technology. Entry requirements to BTEC Certificate and Higher Certificate are the same as for medical lab technicians. *See also* DENTAL TECHNICIANS *in* SUPPLEMENTARY HEALTH PROFESSIONS.

Further information

National Health Service Careers, Medical Research Council.

Ambulance services

Patient-transport staff must get sick and injured patients to hospital as fast as possible and at the same time try to see that their condition does not deteriorate. They work during the day mainly on non-urgent cases.

Ambulance technicians deal with accidents and emergencies and have to work shifts round the clock. They are expected to be not only physically fit, but of a calm temperament and able to find their way to the scene of an incident often with vague directions from a distressed relative or bystander. They are given training for a year to 18 months, depending upon their previous experience in related or volunteer work or as care assistants in patient-transport sections.

The most highly skilled paramedics are recruited by internal promotion from the ranks of technicians and are given special training to enable them to operate sophisticated equipment such as defibrillators and other life-saving techniques until the patients can be seen by a doctor or admitted to hospital.

Promotion is to work in the office, allocating work, and manning the radio controls. Health authorities in England employed 17,500 ambulance staff in 1993 (down from 18,400 in 1983), including maintenance staff.

Recruitment and entry

A full, current driving licence is normally required. Age limits vary but are normally between 21 and 45. For technician entry GCSE passes may be required in English and mathematics. Some authorities recruit cadets between 16 and 18 and train them in first aid, etc.

Further information

Area chief ambulance officers.

Social and Related Services

(CLCI: K–KEZ)

Background

The social sciences study people, and how they behave: as individuals, to each other, and in groups. Social 'scientists' study how people live alongside and 'interact' with each other, as members of families, communities and other organisations; how they earn a living and decide how to spend the money they earn; what rules they use to govern their communities; how and why societies and communities change. They try to describe as accurately as possible what happens inside communities and the complicated network of relationships between the people who make up those communities. They also attempt to draw conclusions from their findings.

The social sciences are relatively new disciplines, and still somewhat controversial. Some people still think that the scientific study of something so unpredictable as human behaviour and forms of social organisation is impossible. Yet people from the ancient Greeks onwards have thought and written about human behaviour and ways of organising societies.

More systematic studies of income and wealth – the beginnings of economics – started in the eighteenth century, as did the statistical study of populations, without which it is impossible to study any other aspects of society. The foundations of political science, psychology, and sociology were laid in the nineteenth century. However, it was not until the Second World War that psychologists, economists, and sociologists were able to show that their studies were accurate and could be useful – in providing, for instance, the basis on which to decide how to distribute scarce food and clothing through rationing; and how to test recruits to the Armed Forces to see which jobs suited their capabilities best; to find ways of keeping up morale; and to devise propaganda and counter-propaganda techniques.

The social sciences attribute their academic 'respectability' partly to this, partly to the importance of understanding more about large modern industrialised societies as they grow more complex and have more difficult social problems to solve, and partly to the fact that social scientists have adopted rigorous methods of observation and analysis from the natural sciences. They follow the same strict rules as scientists in collecting data and applying highly sophisticated and refined statistical and mathematical methods to analysing it, and building mathematical models to test theories. Obviously, though, social scientists can only go so far in using the scientist's controlled experiments: it just is not possible to dissect human society on the laboratory bench. Instead, social scientists use techniques not available to 'pure' scientists: they interview and survey their human subjects, and so claim an advantage over the scientist, who can hardly expect atoms or molecules to answer questionnaires. Social scientists also use comparative techniques comparing aspects of two, or several, societies to see if there is any similarity or difference and, by isolating the points of comparison, testing possible generalisations against different sets of evidence.

Even so, there are still many arguments about the validity of the social sciences: whether society is a living organism like a microbe, and can be studied in the same way; whether it is possible for social scientists to establish 'laws' about the behaviour of society in the same way that physicists can establish 'laws' of behaviour for the physical world; whether it is possible to measure accurately the information based on what people say to interviewers, and whether they even tell the truth.

Although it is common to refer to them as social scientists, in fact people working in this field are generally economists, psychologists, sociologists and political scientists. These subjects developed more or less independently, and are not branches of a tree called social science. Indeed, it is only quite recently that this umbrella term has been in general use, although it is commonly accepted that it is impossible to study society as, say, a sociologist, without being familiar with the work being done in psychology, economics, or politics.

The social sciences developed and expanded at an almost explosive rate up to the mid-1970s. Although expansion has more or less ended, a large and significant range of disciplines and courses exists.

The social sciences have taken proportionately heavier cuts in government expenditure on research (and on teaching in higher education) than sciences, except where it is of 'practical' value, and so the number of openings for research and teaching has also fallen substantially.

The Economic and Social Research Council (ESRC) is the UK's leading research and training agency addressing economic and social concerns. It is an independent organisation, established by Royal Charter in 1965, and funded mainly by government. With a budget in 1996–97 of £63 million, it aims to provide high-quality research on issues of importance to business, the public sector and government. The issues considered include economic competitiveness, the effectiveness of public services and policy, and our quality of life.

For the first time (1996), the strategic framework is provided by a set of nine priority themes which have been identified by academics and users and by the Technology Foresight Exercise, as covering the UK's most pressing social and economic concerns.

People with degrees in some disciplines, (psychology and economics for example), may be recruited for their specific academic skills by other employers, but in general people with social science degrees will not normally find work related to their disciplines.

There is some strength in the argument that a social science degree may provide some insight into the workings of society and the real world which is possibly a better preparation for some areas of employment than (say) an arts degree – trainee journalists, it has been suggested, are better off with a degree in economics or politics than history or English. Social scientists are, theoretically at least, rather more numerate than arts graduates, but social science degrees generally have to be treated as an intellectual training, not a strictly vocational preparation.

Social sciences

The social sciences are mainly studied at university, in colleges of higher education or as 'background' studies in further education, although some are also taught in many schools.

The range and variety of social science degree courses is quite considerable, and students have a very flexible choice of subjects and of the depth to which they can be studied. It is possible to combine social science subjects with many others, including more vocationally oriented professional studies (such as computer science or business studies) which may help them in preparing for careers in these areas.

Most universities and colleges recognise that many students starting social science degrees do not know very much about the subject or subjects they are going to study. Therefore, whatever subject or subjects students eventually choose for specialisation, the first year, or even two, of many courses is devoted to a broad general introduction to the social sciences in all their variety, emphasising common principles and methods, and demonstrating the overlapping territory between the individual disciplines. Courses of this type give students more time to discover which of the social sciences interest them most, and so make it possible to make a better choice of the one (or two) in which to specialise, based on a sounder understanding of what each social science involves.

Degree schemes which begin with a common first year (unless otherwise stated) in sociology are offered at the following universities or colleges/institutes of higher education: Bath CHE, Birmingham, Bradford, Bristol, Brunel, Cambridge, Central England, Cheltenham and Gloucester CHE (two terms), City University, Coventry, Durham, East Anglia, Essex, Glasgow Caledonian, Keele (six months), LSU Southampton (one term), Leeds, Leicester, Liverpool, Liverpool IHE, Manchester, Manchester Metropolitan, Middlesex (one term), Newcastle, Plymouth, Reading, Sheffield (two terms), Sheffield Hallam, Southampton, South Bank, Strathclyde, Surrey, Teesside, Ulster, Wales (Bangor, Cardiff, Swansea), West of England.

First destinations in social sciences were, in 1994:

total graduating	*14,606*
destination unknown	1,640
research, etc.	1,586
teacher training	335
law exams	2,563
other training	544
believed unemployed December 31	929
temporary work	659
permanent UK work	4,147
employers	
accountancy	529
local government	475
banking/insurance	615
Civil Service	173
engineering	105
other manufacturing	133
oil and chemicals	68
higher/further education	203
Armed Forces	72
construction	25
public utilities, transport	165
other commerce	979
functions	
financial work	1,107
administration/operations management	539
personnel/social, etc.	617
marketing, etc.	504
management services	157
research/information	111
legal work	94
teaching, etc.	96
creative	115

Entry requirements

Universities very rarely require social sciences at GCSE or A-level for entry to social science degree courses. In fact, some admission tutors prefer candidates to have a solid grounding in subjects such as mathematics, history and English rather than any inevitably simple introduction to social sciences. However, A-level social science can be quite useful for students who plan to go directly into vocational training, since they can provide a basis for the theoretical parts of further training.

Applied social sciences (including social administration)

While many students who read social sciences, particularly sociology, at university, intend to work somewhere in the field of the social services, their degree courses do not give the necessary training. However, one group of courses does deal more directly with social administration than, for example, courses in sociology. Since they take a very broad view of the social services and the disciplines used in developing them, they can prepare graduates for such careers, while still giving a broad enough education to allow them to opt for something different.

Social administration studies the human problems which can be dealt with by social work agencies. It examines the methods of solving such problems, and tries to analyse the causes, relating the problems to their wider social setting. This usually involves studying the disciplines which are designed to explain society and its mechanisms, as they impinge upon social problems. This type of course also gives a much wider view of social problems and their solution than would be the case otherwise – for example, through comparative studies of social service systems in other countries, and through the study of social policy, which relates the social services to the political and economic theories and practices on which they are based.

While graduates in social administration may still have to take further training and practical experience to become social workers (*see* SOCIAL WORK *below*), these courses are also a preparation for research and training, more general administrative work, careers in local and central government, and personnel work in industry and commerce.

Degree and postgraduate courses

First-degree courses in social administration or applied social studies at the following universities or colleges/institutes of higher education: Anglia, Bath, Birmingham, Bradford, Bradford and Ilkley Community C, Brighton, Bristol, Central England, Central Lancashire, Cardiff IHE, Coventry, Dundee IT, Durham, East Anglia, East London, Edge Hill CHE, Edinburgh, Essex, Exeter, Glasgow, Hertfordshire, Hull, Humberside, Keele, Kent, Kingston, Lancaster, Leeds, Leeds Metropolitan, London (Goldsmiths, LSE, Royal Holloway), London Guildhall, Loughborough, Luton, Manchester, Manchester Metropolitan, Middlesex, Newcastle, Northumbria, Nottingham, North London, Paisley, Plymouth, Portsmouth, Reading, Ripon and York St John C, Robert Gordon, Roehampton, Salford UC, Sheffield, Sheffield Hallam, Southampton, Southampton IHE, Staffordshire, Strathclyde, Stirling, Sunderland, Sussex, Teesside, Ulster, Wales (Bangor, Cardiff, Swansea), West of England, Wolverhampton, York.

Postgraduate courses include diploma courses intended to provide a professional qualification in social work (*see below*), and postgraduate, post-experience advanced courses such as that in methods in applied social research at Edinburgh University. In between is a range of courses aimed at providing higher degrees in social administration for graduates in other, but normally related, disciplines. Some of these are also recognised professional qualifications, but many are intended primarily as preparation for research or social policy administration.

Anthropology

Anthropologists study human cultural, social and biological development and adaptation from the earliest times up to today. Anthropology grew from an eighteenth-century interest in human origins and the differences between ethnic groups, first noticed by European explorers. After Darwin, it developed as the study of human social, psychological and physical evolution, but in a rather fossilised way. Social, or cultural anthropology emerged in the 1920s, studying non-Western small-scale societies as living and growing societies, not just as accidental survivors of prehistoric times.

Archaeology and linguistics have since developed as studies in their own right (although they still have very close links, and anthropologists are again making a major contribution to archaeological research). This leaves social anthropology, physical anthropology (which still studies human origins and evolution, heredity, the relation between primates and humans, and the differences between ethnic groups), and the study of how human tool-making and technology developed. Some anthropologists include ecology, studying the relationship between people and their environment, and how they exploit it. Some scholars even treat social anthropology as a branch of sociology, teaching the two together.

Anthropologists do study modern industrial societies – for example, recent researchers have examined national responses to the accident at the Chernobyl nuclear power plant and the role of anthropology in understanding AIDS. Most, though, study societies which are very different from modern, industrialised ones: Pacific Island tribes, peasant societies in remoter parts of Europe and around the Mediterranean, Eskimos, Amerindians and South East Asian civilisations.

Anthropologists do not just study, for instance, the meaning of myths or witchcraft, but also why and how they are important to the tribe involved, and this may throw light on attitudes in other societies, e.g. a study of Tibetan polyandry also involved examining concepts of fatherhood.

Anthropologists draw conclusions from their findings, especially as they compile more detailed, statistical records, and make comparisons between different communities and cultures.

A major area of study is change, and the social and economic problems of adapting to the modern world, particularly for less industrialised communities: what happens to tribes when major highways are driven through the forests of South America, or to nomadic peoples when they have to settle in one place.

Anthropology is largely an academic career, combining research with teaching. Studying non-industrialised societies normally means spending long periods, possibly years, living among the people being studied, learning the language, and gaining their trust and friendship, since this is usually the only way to find out about their customs, etc. Once home, anthropologists write up their findings, and analyse them. Some government and international bodies employ anthropologists as advisers, but more usually they hire anthropologists working in universities as consultants, or contribute to their research funds. Some anthropologists seem able to produce both very scholarly works on their research and popular books on their lives amongst unusual peoples. It is a very small profession, and very dependent on public funds.

Degree and postgraduate courses

Anthropology is studied mainly on first-degree courses, and for higher degrees. There are no restrictions on adult entry to the profession.

Undergraduate courses, mostly concentrating on social and cultural aspects, are taught for a first degree at the following universities: Belfast, Brunel, Cambridge, Durham, East London, Edinburgh, Hull, Kent, London (Goldsmiths, LSE, SOAS, UCL), Manchester, Oxford, Oxford Brookes, St Andrews, Sussex, and Wales (Swansea).

Postgraduate courses are provided at all of these except Brunel, East London and Oxford Brookes, and also at Keele and Newcastle Universities.

Further information

The Royal Anthropological Institute of Great Britain and Ireland.

Psychology

Psychology is both a subject for academic study and a professional career. It is a very large field, and so is generally divided in various ways. The divisions can be confusing, because inevitably the interests of the various groups overlap. A further complication is that the divisions of the academic subjects are not necessarily the same as the career divisions.

Psychology is officially defined as the scientific study of human and animal behaviour. Psychologists explore the way individuals act, behave, and think. They try to work out, describe and explain how people learn to speak, to read, to find their way about, to become skilled at work, and even to walk. They want to know how people come to understand and apply mathematics, to appreciate art or poetry, and why they want to play or watch football or tennis, drink alcohol or smoke. They investigate what memory is, and how and why people remember, and forget. They try to understand what makes people feel different emotions, why and how they make choices, what affects their relationships with other people – as friends, in families, at school and work. They study the way human and animal brains process and interpret information fed into them by external senses – eyes, ears, nose – and the messages sent by other parts of the body, about pain and hunger, cold and stress. They question the reasons why humans and animals react as they do to particular circumstances. They study people and animals awake and asleep (and dreaming), happy and depressed, calm and aggressive, working and playing, as child and as adult.

Psychology is rather more scientific than maybe are the disciplines of politics or sociology, because science's experimental methods can be used to some extent on people, but rather more on animals, and the methods of measuring, analysing, and assessing results can be much more exact. It is also closely linked to BIOLOGICAL SCIENCES, since mind and body are inextricable from each other.

Psychology does, however, study people in their social settings, so it is also a social science. Psychology has many controversial aspects; and the division between those who, to put it crudely, see all human behaviour in terms of scientific formulae, and those who stress the human personality, feelings and emotions – which cannot be expressed in scientific or mathematical terms – is only one example.

Although there is a very long way to go to anything approaching full understanding, psychologists know enough about human behaviour to be able to apply what they know in everyday life – to try to improve job satisfaction or productivity, to help find ways to teach particular skills, to design equipment that is easier to use, and to help people through crises in their lives.

Psychology should not be confused with psychiatry or psychoanalysis, although of course they have much in common. Psychiatry (which requires a medical qualification), and psychoanalysis specialise in diagnosing, explaining and trying to treat mental illness and behavioural problems, while psychology, although it does study so-called 'abnormal' behaviour, deals with behaviour of all kinds, and spends more time on normal rather than abnormal patterns.

Psychology as a discipline is divided into a number of clearly defined areas of study. First-degree courses generally provide a broad introduction to all of them, while professional psychologists usually specialise in a particular area.

Developmental psychology

Developmental psychology studies how behaviour, skills and abilities, such as perception, learning, remembering, problem-solving and motivation, are passed on from generation to generation, and how they develop within individuals. It probes into, for example, which characteristics are inherited and what is the balance between heredity and the 'environment' (the family, the school, the estate, the town, and the country in which people have grown up), in determining whether, for instance, people are more or less 'intelligent'.

Developmental psychologists try to decide what 'intelligence' is, and how it is best measured. They study the processes of learning – whether, for instance, babies have to reach a certain level of 'readiness' before they can be toilet-trained, and whether or not the same applies to learning to read or ride a bicycle. They investigate the value of play in a child's development, the effect of separating child and mother, and the way childhood experiences influence adult attitudes, behaviour and relationships with other people. They also study, and help to solve, actual behavioural problems caused by failures in social training.

Experimental psychology

Experimental psychology is a label used to describe any research which can use scientific, experimental methods, often in the laboratory, but also data-collecting and statistical analysis. It specialises in finding better ways of doing controlled research in psychology, and then carrying it out, but experimental psychologists more usually develop and refine their techniques as part of their research rather than in isolation from it. Examples of experimental work range from studying the psychological aspects of car sickness, through working on ways in which the blind can use sound to detect obstacles, or methods to improve the layout of an instrument panel of, say, an aircraft.

Cognitive psychology

Cognitive psychology is an important area within experimental psychology, involving the study of thought processes, memory and communication, particularly language.

Physiological psychology

Physiological psychology studies the relation between behaviour/emotion and the body, to discover the physical basis of behaviour. Specifically, it investigates how the body transmits information and substances to the brain, what the brain does with them, and how the brain triggers a reaction, and what the reactions might be. It involves investigating how the brain, as one of the most sophisticated processors of information there is, and the nervous system, work in detail. It is an area where the work is largely experimental (*see above*), and involves psychologists in working closely with, for example, biochemists, pharmacologists, and physiologists (*see in* SCIENTISTS AND TECHNICIANS IN THE HEALTH SERVICE *and in* BIOLOGICAL SCIENCES).

Social psychology

Social psychology studies the way behaviour of individuals is affected by groups – families, school, the firm, the community in general – and how individuals in turn influence the behaviour of the groups, how they interact with the other people in them, and the impact of social conditions (such as poor housing, or lack of transport) on individuals and groups.

Social psychologists study accepted social patterns of behaviour expected of, for example English boys or German girls, and the way parents influence their children – to become tennis stars or doctors, perhaps, but in more subtle ways too. They also study practical social problems, drug addiction, the effect of television on children, and the relations between ethnic minorities and the community at large, or the police.

Social psychology has much in common with sociology and social anthropology, but the viewpoint is different: it deals with the relationship between individual personalities and behaviour, and the social rules within which people live.

Psychometrics

Psychometrics or the psychology of Individual Differences studies and tries to measure the differences between one person and another in terms of temperament, intelligence, behaviour patterns, and personality structure.

Abnormal psychology

Abnormal psychology is concerned with the study of behaviour which deviates from the norm, particularly where this behaviour is seen as mental illness.

Comparative psychology

Comparative psychology specifically observes and studies animal behaviour partly because it is interesting in its own right, but mainly because such studies can illuminate some patterns of human behaviour. In the laboratory, animal psychologists study animals under controlled experimental conditions, to clarify learning processes (for instance, how rats find their way through a maze) or to discover how conditional reflexes work (the famed Pavlovian dog). Animals are also studied in their natural settings: the efficient division of labour amongst insect communities, for example, or the 'pecking order' amongst hens.

Degree and postgraduate courses

First-degree courses may be found in faculties of science or arts and social science. Courses in science faculties may be biased to biological aspects, others to behavioural aspects, but all courses listed provide an introduction to all the main branches of psychology listed above; and all teach psychology as a science. Entry requirements, and supporting subjects, are often the main difference. There are over 130 first-degree psychology courses at many universities and colleges throughout the UK. University admissions tutors tend to be flexible about which A-levels or Scottish Highers are necessary for entry to a psychology degree. However, undergraduate students need to be able to handle scientific concepts, to be numerate and to develop writing skills. The following Highers, A- or AS-level subjects are therefore considered useful: Biology or Human Biology; Mathematics; and English, History, Economics or similar Arts or Social Science subjects to which psychological factors are relevant.

Competition for places is very strong (1995) and this has resulted in fairly high grades being required. GNVQs are not accepted at the following institutions: Birmingham, Bristol, Cambridge, Edinburgh, Glasgow, Huddersfield, Lancaster, Liverpool, Loughborough, Manchester, Oxford, Surrey, Wales (Swansea). Where they are accepted at other institutions, admissions tutors may request a GNVQ distinction or an A-level as well.

In Scotland, most students enter university with a broader, less specialised background than in the rest of the UK, so the first year is often similar in function to a foundation course. Well-qualified students may be able to gain exemption from this first year for some courses at the older Scottish universities.

First destination figures for psychology were, in 1994:

total graduating	*2,649*
destination unknown	280
research, etc.	354
teacher training*	155
other training	123
believed unemployed 31 December	204
temporary work	171
permanent UK work	1,033
employers	
local government	240
commerce (excluding finance)	253
industry	72
accountancy	34
banking/insurance	53
Civil Service	27
higher/further education	156
functions	
personnel/social, etc.	381
marketing, etc.	91
financial work	65
administration/operations management	85
research/information work	33
management services	36
teaching/lecturing	61
scientific research	54
creative	21

* needed for entry to educational psychology

Postgraduate courses include advanced study and training courses in the following psychology specialisms: educational (for which teaching experience is normally required), clinical, counselling, forensic, health, legal, occupational, criminological, abnormal, social, applied, industrial, organisational, psychopathology, psychology of mental handicap and child computer applications in psychology. Competition for places on 'vocational' postgraduate courses is as intensive as for the more academic, and an upper second class honours degree is almost essential.

Professional qualification

The British Psychological Society (BPS) requires an approved honours degree in psychology to award the Graduate Basis for Registration as a Chartered Psychologist. It is possible for holders of degrees in other subjects to take a conversion course lasting one year full-time (two years part-time) to meet BPS requirements. Chartered Psychologist status is rapidly becoming an essential qualification for professional posts in psychology. BPS approves postgraduate professional training courses, and awards the Doctorate in Clinical Psychology, Diploma in Counselling Psychology and the Postgraduate Certificate in Occupational Psychology achieved through approved in-service training.

Psychology as a career

Research psychologists – educational psychologists – clinical psychologists – occupational psychologists – psychologists in the prison service – counselling psychology – health psychology – sports psychology – other psychology-related work

The British Psychological Society has (1995) about 22,000 members (including students). Not every psychologist belongs, but membership of the Society has been growing as a result of the growing significance of Chartered status. Only a small percentage of those who study psychology at degree level go on to become professional psychologists. First-degree output of graduates in psychology has reached the point where there are neither enough professional posts nor training places for everyone who wants to be a psychologist. A higher proportion of psychology graduates will, therefore, have to find other careers in future. Work abroad may be a possibility for some graduates, particularly in the fields of research and teaching posts. However, the direct transfer of qualifications abroad is still exceptional, and access to employment varies according to local conditions and legal requirements. Most psychologists specialise after graduation, normally as one of the following:

Research psychologists

Most psychologists do at least some research as part of their work. Opportunities to do research full-time are limited and psychologists able to do this usually hold a doctoral-level degree in psychology. There are a few research units which employ full-time research scientists, but most research appointments are for a fixed-term contract and it is difficult to develop a career based only on research work. Even in higher education, most have to combine research with teaching. About 1,500 psychologists work in higher education (1996).

The research may be the kind of studies described earlier; and so a research psychologist may be called a social or developmental psychologist, if that is his or her area of research. It may have practical applications: looking at the reliability of identification evidence in courts, working on the language problems of immigrant children in schools, or fundamental problems in the nature of learning and memory. The impact of unemployment is now an important area of research. Research psychologists also work on problems of new technology, in areas ranging from, for instance, designing 'user-friendly' computers and other machinery, to looking at ways of getting information technology accepted in the workplace and in the community.

Some government departments employ research psychologists – Ministry of Defence establishments, for instance, for work on the design of military equipment, to take account of psychological factors in, for example, the layout of submarine or tank interiors. Research stations may need psychological input in road research, for example, on psychological aspects of preventing road accidents via experiments on, for instance, drivers' reaction times.

A small number of independent centres exist, but they rarely employ more than one or two research psychologists. Industry and commerce offer a few research opportunities, for example on training and recruitment issues, in larger companies and trade unions.

Educational psychologists

Educational psychologists work mostly with children and teenagers who have problems in learning, whose behaviour is causing concern, or who have emotional problems. They try to discover what has gone wrong, using established tests, looking into the child's background, and talking to parents, teachers and the child.

They may treat a child or teenager themselves, largely through personal counselling, and/or advise the parents and teachers on how to help, and say whether or not some form of remedial teaching is needed. Psychologists also work with handicapped children. They advise schools on organisational problems, or help design programmes for particular groups of pupils. They also give talks or group counselling for teenagers.

Educational psychologists in England and Wales work mostly for local authorities, either in child guidance clinics, or in the school psychological service (*see* EDUCATION AND TEACHING), with a few posts in specialist assessment units, e.g. community schools, hospital paediatric units, or university or medical school research units. The 1993 Education Act increased the pressure for individual and institutional accountability which has led to a closer examination of how educational psychologists may best use their skills to service children, families, schools and communities within a complex local education authority structure. There is also some opportunity for freelance work, with independent schools and voluntary organisations, but this is limited. Some educational psychologists may also work in the National Health Service and a few may find posts in private practice.

Although the number of educational psychologist posts has continued to rise, it is likely that the increase will be at a slower rate in the future. In Scotland, they mostly work for child guidance services which deal with both school assessment and clinical treatment. About 1,500 educational psychologists work for local education authorities in England and Wales, 300 in Scotland and 60 in Northern Ireland (1995). Fears that changes in LEA financial management and, in particular, schools opting out of LEA control, would affect the educational psychology service, have not so far been realised. In Northern Ireland educational psychologists are employed by the province's five education and library boards.

Qualifications and training

To become an educational psychologist first requires qualifications in both psychology and teaching, followed by at least two years' teaching experience. The average age of entry to the profession has risen and is now probably the late thirties (1996). It is possible to start with either a teaching qualification or a psychology degree (at least to second class honours standard), but the latter route is two or three years shorter, since the Postgraduate Certificate in Education (PGCE) takes only one year. A postgraduate training course in educational psychology (at one of 17 universities) lasts at least one year full-time, two part-time, leading to a master's degree; trainees must then complete a probationary year under supervision. Competition for training places can be considerable. There are approximately 80 fully funded places on master's training courses (1996) for several hundred applicants.

In Scotland, psychology graduates wishing to train as chartered educational psychologists are not required to undertake any teacher training or other relevant pre-training experience. However, the educational psychology training courses in Scotland last two years and after completion, trainees are required to complete a further year's practice under supervision before becoming eligible to register as a chartered educational psychologist. It is important to note that educational psychologists trained in Scotland will need teaching experience if they wish to find employment south of the border.

Clinical psychologists

Clinical psychologists, of whom there are at least 2,400 (1996), work alongside psychiatric and other medical staff mainly in the National Health Service, and form the largest professional group of psychologists. There appears to be a continual shortage of qualified clinical psychologists.

Clinical psychologists may work in general, mental handicap or psychiatric hospitals and clinics, or with patients in the community, and increasingly in other settings, such as elderly people's homes, children's homes and hostels. They usually work within multidisciplinary teams of healthcare professionals, and there is often no clear dividing line between their work and that of psychiatrists. Much of their work involves one-to-one therapy for people who may, for example, be addicted to gambling, or have a fear of open spaces, or who are severely depressed. They help patients who have been in hospital a long time to prepare to live in the community again. They use their detailed understanding of how people learn, develop and can change their patterns of behaviour, in helping to overcome, for instance, compulsive shoplifting. They work with patients' relatives, and teach them to understand and cope with the problems.

They still do diagnostic work, and test intelligence, skills and aptitudes, or for possible brain damage. They work on new methods of assessment and treatment, and may have the opportunity to do some research. They also train and advise other healthcare staff. Senior staff are generally also involved in planning and administering psychology services, but there are no purely administrative senior posts. Work with the mentally handicapped and older people are the main growth areas.

Qualifications and training

To become a clinical psychologist requires either a full-time three-year postgraduate course for a higher degree at a university, usually in association with a teaching hospital, or a three-year 'in-service' training course, as a 'probationer' which leads to a doctorate examination set by the British Psychological Society. Both routes should carry equal status. After qualifying, at least two years are spent in the 'basic' grade working under experienced supervision. There is currently (1995) a very substantial demand for training places with many applicants for every place. Successful trainees typically have at least an upper second class honours degree and relevant experience before or since graduation.

See also PSYCHOLOGY, PSYCHOTHERAPY AND ANALYSIS, AND ARTS THERAPIES *in* SUPPLEMENTARY HEALTH PROFESSIONS.

Occupational psychologists

Occupational psychology is a growing field. Occupational psychologists investigate how people perform in work and training, how they behave at work and how organisations (a business or a work group) function. Occupational psychologists may work in organisational consultancy, assessment and training, or ergonomics, health and safety. They have to work as advisers, in teaching or research, and possibly administration. There are 520 people (1995) working as occupational psychologists: 80 are employed by the government in the Employment Service, the Ministry of Defence and the Defence Research Agency; approximately 140 work in universities and 300 are employed in the commercial world.

Occupational psychologists give expert help and advice to people who need assessment and guidance in finding work to suit their aptitudes, abilities and interests. Such services are usually only publicly provided for people who have some form of disability which makes finding work difficult, or who have been made redundant, or who may be leaving the Armed Forces for civilian life, for example. Rehabilitation and assessment work in the Employment Services Agency is carried out by area Placement, Advisory and Counselling Teams, which each include a psychologist. Related research programmes are carried out by staff at the Employment Services Headquarters, which employs about 35 occupational psychologists. There is also a careers advisory work research unit, and within each region of the Employment Services Agency is a regional psychologist who supports local management in a largely advisory role. There are some commercially run vocational guidance units.

Occupational psychologists also work in personnel selection, training, and career development programmes for staff. They design and evaluate tests and interview techniques for choosing people to match particular job requirements, or reassess the job to make it fit the type of people available in the employment market. Closely linked is work on developing and improving training programmes, based on the results of research on how people learn skills. Here again, they are employed within the Civil Service, in the Ministry of Defence, the Recruitment and Assessment Services Agency, and the Employment Services Agency, by larger employers, and by private consultants. The Ministry of Defence employs psychologists on defining and assessing the abilities, skills and personal qualities needed for service jobs; experimental studies of operational or training performance; surveys of motivation and morale; or personnel selection and allocation; and with physiologists and designers on designing and evaluating equipment, basic work on performance criteria, numeracy tests, incentives and job satisfaction.

Fitting work to people, the other aspect of occupational psychology, overlaps with work study and ergonomics (*see in* MANAGEMENT SERVICES). Here psychologists look at office or factory layouts and the design of equipment and machinery, to see that they take into account psychological factors, and are therefore designed for maximum efficiency. This can mean finding ways to reduce stress factors, improve safety (ensuring that guards are so designed that people will use them), etc., and so increase productivity.

Occupational psychologists are involved when new technology is introduced – for instance, helping to redesign office jobs around computers. They also help to improve working methods, and advise on ways of organising a firm to make communication between, say, the shop floor and senior management more efficient.

Qualifications and training

In the past it was possible to become an occupational psychologist without any formal training. This is no longer possible. There are now only two training routes available:

1 Graduates in psychology may go on to a British Psychology Society-accredited training course (usually lasting one year) in occupational psychology, followed by two years' practice as an occupational psychologist under the supervision of a Chartered Psychologist. The practice must be accredited by the Society's Division of Occupational Psychology (DOP).

2 Postgraduate Certificate in Occupational Psychology for anyone who has not undertaken one of the British Psychology Society approved training courses in occupational psychology, followed by at least three years' approved supervised experience.

Psychologists in the prison service

The prison service employs about 130 psychologists: occupational psychologists, forensic psychologists and about 30 assistant psychologists. Psychologists work with individual inmates, particularly younger people and disturbed and aggressive prisoners, counselling and giving therapy, running group sessions and training in social skills, etc. Some do psychological testing and assessment for the courts, and with probation officers, and in turn evaluate the tests and court reporting system. They help design, develop and evaluate the regimes/systems under which prisoners live, advise on security and control methods, and test the effects of, for example, industrial prisons on reconviction rates. The role of occupational psychologists in the prison service lies mainly in helping to ensure good communication systems within prisons, selecting and training staff, in the problems of dealing with prisoners, and in advisory services. Forensic psychologists apply psychological theories, research and techniques to the criminological and legal system related to offenders and criminal behaviour. The British Psychological Society has about 300 members (1996) in its criminological division.

Qualifications and training

The most common training route for forensic psychologists is through the Prison Service. Graduates (with a good honours degree and possibly relevant experience) are recruited annually to basic-grade posts and follow an in-service training which may include secondment to a forensic psychology training course. Competition for training places is quite high, with more than twice as many applicants as places.

Counselling psychology

Counselling psychology is a relatively new but rapidly expanding area. There is a similarity between the work of counselling psychologists and that of counsellors or psychotherapists. The difference is in the specific background training in psychology which counselling psychologists have undertaken. They apply systematic research-based approaches to help themselves and others understand problems and develop possible solutions. They may deal with people who have life-threatening diseases, who have been made redundant, or who have other crises in their lives. Counselling psychologists may work in private practice, in primary healthcare organisations (in General Practices) and in counselling centres. Some may carry out research and teaching within academic institutions; others may work in business organisations.

Graduates must undertake the British Psychological Society's Diploma in Counselling Psychology (DCoP) which is the equivalent of three years' full-time postgraduate training. However, graduates who have completed a Society-accredited training course (details from the BPS) may be exempt from part or all of the DCoP.

Health psychology

Health psychology is the application of psychological methods to the study of behaviour relevant to health, illness and healthcare. It is gradually gaining recognition but is still currently an academic discipline rather than a profession in the UK. It does not as yet provide a route to registration as a Chartered Psychologist. The majority of health psychologists will be either research workers in universities, or qualified clinical psychologists, or perhaps occupational psychologists concerned with the general issues of promoting mental health and developing healthy lifestyles.

There are currently no professional training courses in health psychology, although there are some master's degree programmes in the UK.

Sports psychology

Sports psychologists apply psychological methods to help improve sporting performance. Although this is a growing field, there are currently no particular training programmes or courses in sports psychology which are recognised as providing an approved route to qualification as a Chartered Psychologist.

Most of the Chartered Psychologists with the expertise to offer a service in sports psychology have postgraduate research degrees or training in another area of applied psychology.

Other psychology-related work

Psychology graduates can go on to train to be psychotherapists, or analysts (*see in* SUPPLEMENTARY HEALTH PROFESSIONS) and/or counsellors (*see in* ALTERNATIVE MEDICINE) or psychiatric social workers (*see below*).

A degree/qualification in psychology is a useful basis for MARKET RESEARCH (*see in* BUYING, SELLING AND RELATED SERVICES); MANAGEMENT CONSULTANCY AND PERSONNEL MANAGEMENT (*see in* ADMINISTRATION, BUSINESS MANAGEMENT AND OFFICE WORK); OPERATIONAL RESEARCH (*see in* MANAGEMENT SERVICES); EDUCATION AND TEACHING; *and* SOCIAL WORK, CAREERS ADVISORY WORK (*see below*); etc.

Further information

The British Psychological Society.

Sociology

This is the broadest of the social sciences, studying the whole of human society in all its many and varied aspects. Sociology and psychology obviously overlap, since they both deal with people and society, human behaviour and relationships. Psychology, though, focuses mainly on the behaviour of individuals, and is concerned with society only in relation to them. Sociology focuses mainly on society and the pattern and behaviour of people in and as groups.

Sociologists examine the behavioural norms or rules – called social 'institutions' – which society sets (consciously or unconsciously) so people can live close to each other. They study the characteristics of social groups – the family, social classes, religious groups, women, adolescents – and not individual personalities or intelligence as does psychology. They study social 'systems', or groups of related activities, such as education, and the established social 'structures' – everything which relates to economic activity goes to form a country's economic structure, for example, which means sociologists also make their own critical studies of the work of economists or educationalists. Sociologists examine the relations between social groups, between long-established citizens and recently arrived minorities, between workers and employers, and between doctors and patients. They study the forms of communication society uses, such as newspapers, and broadcasting, and their effects on young people, or on the political system.

Sociologists study ideas, such as power and inequality. They study conflict and change in society today, class divisions, how and why people change their position in society, what happens in society to produce people who do well and people who are disadvantaged. They compare aspects of one society with another (e.g. training systems in England, Japan and Germany), study the role of trade unions in different industries and countries, or of international companies in developing countries.

Whatever sociologists study, they never isolate their research from its complex and ever-changing social setting. There are no watertight compartments in society and so, in studying racial prejudice (for example), the sociologist has to take account of the effects of religious and political beliefs and behaviour, of social class, of educational background, of family attitudes, environment, and so on.

All sociological research, whether on the finer points of the British police constable's subculture, or the grand sweep of the social role of religion in India, is producing evidence for sociologists who specialise in building up a body of sociological theory. Here they may be trying to make generalisations about society, and test these against factual evidence. What is significant, for instance, about the fact that the family, in some form, appears to be common to all known societies?

Sociology is often confused with social work. Social workers are there to help people who have problems which can be described as 'social': sociologists may study the causes of such problems, or make analytical studies of the personal social services operated by local authorities, but as professional sociologists they do not work at the 'sharp end' with individuals.

People argue a great deal about the value and validity of sociology. Although it studies real, ordinary everyday situations and problems, it cannot provide easy answers to complicated issues. Some sociologists think they should just observe, analyse and report their findings, while others are prepared to make recommendations, and yet others want to take action themselves; but most sociologists probably want their work to make some contribution to improving the quality of life. There are even sociologists whose work can be described as 'interventionist' with teenage girls, for instance, to see if it is possible to change the image they have of themselves and their interests, mainly to allow them to develop their full potential, academically and in their careers.

Sociological research, although about people, is increasingly based on statistical analysis. Whatever the problems, the sociologist studies it against the background of a 'working model' of the society – of the people who live in, for example, Britain: how many are young, how many are old, how many are women, how many belong to trade unions and churches, how many own houses and videos, what people read, and how they vote, and spend their leisure time. Sociologists may use statistics on crime rates, on the levels of substandard housing, on the distribution of wealth. The statistics may pose questions – why, for example, has the birth-rate been falling so dramatically in Western industrialised countries?

Sociologists work largely through interviews and surveys, carefully designed to give the right 'mix' of people, and perhaps repeated with the same group over a period – for instance, a long-term investigation of how children are brought up interviewed the mothers of 700 Nottingham children on their first, fourth, seventh, eleventh and sixteenth birthdays. Using statistical analysis, such a study gives an account of what parents typically say and do in relation to seven-year-olds, and also charts the variations in views which differ (for example) according to social circumstances. Such a study involves, perhaps, two to four sociologists, two research assistants, and five interviewers.

Most professional sociologists do research, and combine this with teaching in higher or further education. Here they may choose their own studies, or work (as junior staff) on a senior colleague's project, or do research on contract to an organisation which wants information on which to base decisions or policy – such as government departments, political parties, religious bodies, or commercial firms.

There are few research posts outside the education system: in the Civil Service, in local authorities, in independent research organisations. In all these, research is usually directed at providing information for some kind of decision-making, and the sociologist is normally one of a team of experts.

Opportunities for a career in sociological research are limited. A very good first degree, plus a postgraduate qualification is needed, and even then there is no guarantee of a post – and a higher degree may not be an advantage in the open employment market.

Degree and postgraduate courses

First-degree courses in sociology are available at over 70 universities and colleges of higher education. It is often also included in other social science degrees, notably those in combined and applied social studies.

'First destination' figures were, in 1994:

total graduating	*1,029*
destination unknown	204
research, etc.	133
teacher training	43
other training	59
believed unemployed 31 December	105
temporary work	78
permanent UK work	321
employers	
local government	55
commerce	120
Civil Service	10
industry	31
higher/further education	30
Armed Forces	4
functions	
personnel/social	82
administrations/operations management	48
financial work	23
marketing, etc.	32
research/information	16
management services	5
teaching/lecturing	11
creative	13

Entry: specific A-level subjects are not normally needed.

Further information

The British Sociological Association.

Social work

There are many definitions of social work ranging from the most palliative to the most positive, the latter shading over into radical political activism, and it is probable that no two social workers would have exactly the same aims.

Social work is put regularly under a microscope and the need for paid workers questioned, but in evidence to the Barclay Committee, few suggested that it is either possible or desirable to do without them. Reportedly, much of the evidence pointed to widespread respect for them from, for example, their clients and other professionals who work with them, such as doctors.

Most social workers would probably agree that they are problem-solvers for the community. That they are there to help individuals – children, teenagers, adults – families, even whole communities as well as other groups, with problems which have become too great for them to cope with on their own. Beyond this, there is much disagreement. Disagreement on what 'problems' social workers should deal with: should they, for instance, try to help anyone who is socially 'inadequate' in any way, or should there be some limit, and if so what is it, and anyway, how do you define a 'problem'?

There is disagreement, too, on how far social workers should go in trying to 'solve' social problems. Should this be done regardless of how much it might 'cost' – in money, time, emotional stress, people, or any other resources – and how far should social workers help people to adjust to their situation: to mental or physical handicap, to ill health, bad housing, unemployment, or simple bad luck. Are social workers entitled to try to influence or change political decisions which they may consider have caused problems in the first place?

Recently, some of the dilemmas faced by social workers have been shown up in sharp focus. Creating support, and decision-making systems which can prevent damage to children without breaking up families unnecessarily has proved far more difficult than might seem.

Social work is still a relatively young profession, barely as old as the century. It developed from the charitable, voluntary pioneering research of the late nineteenth and early twentieth centuries, when the damage caused to many people by the post-industrial-revolution economic and social system was first recognised. Even then, and right up to the 1970s, the generic title 'social work' had little meaning, and there was no such person as a 'social worker'. Social work was a series of fragmented specialisations, with various bodies and authorities sponsoring specific services, and independent agencies dealing with specific types of problem and particular groups of clients.

Everyone specialised: there were child care officers, welfare officers, mental health officers, medical social workers (once almoners), welfare officers for the deaf, mental handicap officers, and so on. As more social problems were recognised, or ways of approaching problems suggested, so people were trained to deal with that specific area, and the conflicting and overlapping responsibilities grew more and more difficult to cope with. Cooperation was difficult. Each group had its own professional organisation; each group was trained separately on very specialised courses.

It meant that clients were all too often treated as a set of problems rather than as real people. A family with more than one problem member – a delinquent child, a physically handicapped father, a mentally-confused grandmother, and an exhausted mother – might be dealt with by several different people, as a series of unrelated problems treated in watertight compartments, which could mean solutions proposed for one person might conflict with the needs of others in the family.

The end of fragmentation came with the Seebohm Report (1968), which recommended unified social services. By the mid-1970s most of the social services were 'integrated' and 'turned round' to put people, not their problems, first, as the focal point of the service. This means that a problem family is helped by only one social worker, who sees the family's problems as a whole, is in a position to consider whether (for instance) the child's difficulties are a reflection of problems in the rest of the family, and can try to find solutions which will help everyone in the family as much as possible.

Most social workers, therefore, are now trained 'generically'. Seebohm was not, however, the last word on social work. Social work is still developing and changing, learning what it can and cannot do, how best to help, and how best to organise the help.

In practice, although trained to take on any job, or to tackle any problem, many social workers can and do choose the kind of people they would prefer to work with, or decide not to deal with particular kinds of problems. In choosing their first job, for instance in a hospital, they automatically decide to specialise to some extent. The difference is that they are not restricted in their choices, and they have a broader view of people's problems than before Seebohm. In fact, concern is increasing that the completely generalist approach is not satisfactory, because it looks as though some problems do need specialist handling. Within the broadly based social services, then, some social workers do take on special responsibilities for, for example, children at risk, and there may well be increasing return to a greater degree of specialisation. The Children Act 1989 has major implications for the work of social services departments and many are having to devote an increasing proportion of their resources to child protection.

Ideally, social workers have two aims. First, they try to help the client get over the immediate crisis or problem which has brought them to the social services in the first place: rescue. Second, the long-term aim is to look for ways to help clients to learn how to manage their lives better, to avoid crises, to gain or regain self-confidence, to make decisions, to be more independent, and so on. A social worker will try to work on and strengthen a client's own abilities to cope with their own lives and problems. Social workers do not tell their clients what they should, or should not, do; they aim to get them to understand their own difficulties, so that they can work out for themselves what to do. For instance, they will not tell a girl whether or not to keep her baby. Instead, they will try to help her see what the problems are and what may happen whichever course of action she takes. Social workers will support her, and give any practical help, whether or not they agree with her decision. The aim is always to see an end to the client's need of help from the social services, while avoiding quick solutions.

Where they can, social workers try to prevent crises, to identify problems and deal with them before they can become acute, for example, knowing which families are at risk and giving them support to prevent, for instance, the need to take children into care.

However, although social workers must aim high, and do the very best they can for all their clients, they must also be realists, and accept that there are limits to what they can do; that in many cases they may be only partly successful in their aims. They have to accept that people's problems do not fit into neat categories and that there are rarely any easy answers to them. They have to work with people for whom it is just too late to learn to cope; for many the realistic answers are often unacceptable, and some even find it too difficult to accept a social worker's help. People may have been apathetic, or accepted an unsatisfactory life for too long to change. Social workers also have to make many difficult decisions and know they will inevitably make mistakes – classically on whether or not to take a child at risk into care.

Often there is little anyone can do about the central problem in someone's life. The social worker is then left to find ways of helping a client to, for example, live with a physical disability (but with adaptation and aid), come to terms with fatal illness, or make the best of poor housing or long-term unemployment. On the other hand, for many just a sympathetic ear may in itself be enough.

Social workers' ability to help may be limited by lack of resources, such as people, time, and money. This means that rescue, or crisis management, tends to dominate and will go on doing so while finances are so heavily restricted. Prevention, and attempts to make positive improvements in social conditions, have to take second place.

Social work is neither woolly-minded humanitarianism, nor official interference – nor is the social worker a universal aunt. Social work has a strict, some would say scientific, methodology, which both researchers and practising social workers are always trying to improve and refine. They try, for example, to define the process of prevention, and to find ways not to lose the therapeutic value that a degree of conflict and learning to manage a crisis have for people in difficulties. Some social workers also consider they have a duty to act as a bridge between the disadvantaged and society, and to educate the appropriate authorities and the public on the human problems and social needs of their clients. There is an increasing emphasis on the development of a professional, businesslike approach, with high-level knowledge of subjects like welfare law and welfare rights.

Social workers generally deal with clients on an individual, one-to-one, person-to-person, 'casework' basis, although family-based casework is also used a great deal in some areas. Social workers treat the crises which bring people to the social services as the tip of an iceberg of likely problems. They set out to build firm, long-term relationships with their clients, individually or as families, to help them understand their problems, to make it possible for social worker and client(s) to work together to improve their whole situation longer-term.

In crisis situations, the social worker must often first negotiate with another authority – preventing an electricity board cutting off the supply from a family with a new baby, for example. Then, patiently and carefully, using all their training in interviewing, and listening, the social worker must discover how the crisis occurred. Practical help may be possible, such as checking that a family is receiving all the state benefits to which it is entitled. The social worker may be able to help the family organise their budget better, and get the family to discuss the priorities for the money that does come in, suggest cheaper recipes, help them look into cheaper forms of heating, and so on.

In helping their clients, social workers use a range of psychological and other techniques, their knowledge of how people behave, and their experience of similar situations. They give them positive encouragement, and advice if wanted, sometimes being firm, but staying detached and not getting emotionally involved – or disapproving.

Some clients are helped through group work, but it is less usual. Here the social worker can bring together people who have related problems: young mothers living in local high-rise flats, or people who feel isolated and lonely. They bring together 'helpers', like foster parents, again to discuss and 'talk through', the problems they all have together, in regular sessions, on the principle that some people find it easier, and more helpful, to talk about their problems with people who are going through the same or similar difficulties. Community work (*see below*) is a form of group work, since it deals with groups of people where they live.

Areas of social work

The employers – community social services – hospital social services – residential social work – community and youth work – non-professional social work

Employment prospects for newly qualified social workers remain good, for those with the right qualities and experience, as there continues to be a shortage of qualified social workers.

The employers

The great majority of social workers are employed as follows:

- In England and Wales: by local authority social services departments, which also employ social workers in the health service; local education authorities, which employ social workers in the education welfare service and in special schools; the probation service; and voluntary and private agencies.
- In Scotland: by local authority social work departments, whose responsibilities include social work with offenders and in the health service; and voluntary and private agencies.
- In Northern Ireland: by health and social services trusts/directly managed units; the Probation Board for Northern Ireland; education and library boards; and voluntary and private agencies.

Other employers include government departments and the armed services.

Local authorities

Local authorities (statutory social services) are by far the largest employer of social workers. Local authority social service departments in England alone employ, between them, some 237,800 people (full-time equivalents 1994), of whom about 32,000 are professional social workers or care managers, and about 69,000 work in residential homes; most of the rest are administrative and clerical staff (about 20,000), home helps (about 53,000 mostly part-time), and day-nursery staff (about 5,300).

They have large, multi-purpose social services departments, which provide a comprehensive service to virtually anyone living in the area who needs the kind of help they can offer. A high proportion of social work time goes to coping with children, young people and families under stress, but they expect to deal with problems posed by the elderly, the homeless, or people who are physically and mentally handicapped. Most of these services are organised on an area, community, basis and are orientated to the family. Other subdivisions of a social services department run residential and day-care facilities of various kinds (for the handicapped, or the elderly); another provides home helps, another 'meals on wheels'. Within central administration may be staff responsible for certain services, e.g. OCCUPATIONAL THERAPISTS (*see in* SUPPLEMENTARY HEALTH PROFESSIONS), who deal with home adaptations for the handicapped.

Local authorities organise social work services in hospitals, and manage child guidance clinics. Local authorities also have specific legal responsibilities which are delegated to social services – under the Mental Health Acts, and the Children Act 1989, for example. They also supervise adoptions and work with the juvenile courts. Some local authority social service departments have people to do research, and someone has to administer training.

Social services within each authority are centrally managed – there are about 8,800 senior directing, managing, professional and advisory posts – but most services are run on an area basis. There are some 29,900 social workers (including team leaders) running day-to-day services, with 2,500 care managers, over 4,000 welfare or social work assistants, about 1,700 community workers and over 1,500 occupational therapists. Promotion to senior posts in a social service department is now generally from amongst people who have come up through the area or other (e.g. medical social work) teams and have plenty of experience, although senior staff and directors are sometimes outside appointees. Promotion is largely at present into administrative/managerial work, with little opportunity to stay in field work.

Voluntary, independent agencies

Voluntary, independent agencies range from some which are quite small and based on a single locality, to some which are very large, national bodies. Most were formed for very specific purposes and to deal with the needs of fairly narrow groups, but have now mostly developed into more broadly based services. Examples include a society which was at first concerned only with unmarried mothers but has now expanded to provide help for all one-parent families, and societies founded to look after orphans which now work with all disadvantaged children. Other agencies provide services for the disabled and handicapped, both generally and for specific groups: the deaf, the blind, or people with multiple sclerosis, for example. The inspectors who work for the National Society for the Prevention of Cruelty to Children are social workers. Social workers cope with problems in a way similar to that of local authority social services, and sometimes supplement what the social services can do – especially where resources like residential homes are concerned.

Other employers

Other employers include various departments of the Civil Service (*see in* CENTRAL GOVERNMENT) and THE ARMED FORCES. The Department of Social Security employs experienced social workers in advisory and inspectoral posts. The Ministry of Defence employs social workers in military hospitals, and there are specialist organisations to provide social work help to members of the Armed Forces and their families.

Community social services

Each local authority area social service office is a semi-independent unit, responsible for casework within the area or neighbourhood, but working within policy and budgets set by the social services committee, and implemented by the authority's director of social services. Social workers within each area office work in teams, each social worker having a 'caseload' of between 20 and 40 'clients', who may be individuals or families, or both. Most social workers in the team will cope with most problems, but there may be some specialists, e.g. a psychiatric social worker.

A high proportion of a social worker's time is spent with clients, and a high proportion is spent out of the office visiting people. This may mean a daily check to see that someone who is living alone and is physically handicapped or elderly is all right, or going to see the mother of a child supposedly in care who has absconded from a community home, or seeing a doctor to talk about the problems of someone coming home from hospital. It may mean talking to the home-help supervisor to see if a home help is available, or looking for a place in a residential home. Many clients, though, visit their social workers in the office. They may be young parents who are desperate for better housing, a young girl who is pregnant and needs support, or a mother worried about a truanting son.

A considerable amount of time is spent telephoning – finding out about the availability of aids or home helps or residential places; talking to other social workers, to disabled resettlement officers about jobs for ex-psychiatric patients, to doctors, to the police, to hospital staff.

Every social worker has to spend part of the week being 'duty' officer, dealing with emergency calls and crises. Since it is a round-the-clock service, seven days a week, every social worker also has to be on call some nights and some weekends too.

Every area office has regular 'case' conferences, and there is generally also a regular weekly area team meeting to discuss problems, and allocate new cases. There are endless letters to write and answer, and reports to be written. It can never be a nine-to-five job, in fact hours are often long and irregular. The work is physically and psychologically tough and strenuous most of the time.

Hospital social services

Social workers who work in a healthcare setting may specialise in dealing with psychiatric patients but, in general, the trend towards generic social work has lessened the distinction that used to be made between work with different types of patient in the hospital service. There is an increasing trend towards employing only 'approved' social workers, i.e. those who have taken specialist in-service training, in the healthcare sector, especially for work with psychiatric patients.

Hospital-based social workers aim to see that patients have as few worries as possible, help them (and their families) to adapt to any consequences of their illness, and help to solve any practical problems, such as making sure that children are being looked after while their mother is in hospital. They may also look into any social/personal causes of or contributions to illness; they will explain the illness and what the treatment is or means to patients and their relatives. They may explain the long-term treatments of diseases like diabetes, or the after-effects of a duodenal ulcer or a heart condition. They help with problems over jobs and money. They give information on statutory benefits, addresses of helpful organisations and help with counselling. They help patients accept forms of treatment which may be, for instance, frightening, such as radiotherapy, and also help patients and their families come to terms with a fatal illness, or an amputation or other permanent disability. They start the process of organising any home adaptations, wheelchairs or other appliances, working with local social workers or occupational therapists.

Hospital-based social workers may be attached to specific departments or specialists, e.g. radiotherapy, general surgery, or paediatrics. Their jobs are more on a nine-to-five basis than in community social work, and they spend more of their time in their own office seeing patients and relatives there, although they obviously make many ward visits. They spend quite a significant part of their time in case conferences, and have to liaise with, for example, community social workers, occupational and physiotherapists, and chaplains.

Social work with psychiatric patients is similar, mainly in psychiatric hospitals or wards, but increasingly in the community service. It involves coping with the social consequences of emotional and psychological breakdown: patients in hospitals have problems – with their jobs, money, their families or home backgrounds. They may not need physical adaptations to their homes, but they may need considerable help in settling back into the community, especially if they have been in hospital for any length of time.

It is now policy to return psychiatric patients home as quickly as possible or to move them from institutional care into the community, perhaps in hostel or self-help group accommodation, and so social workers may also have to arrange support for them with their local community office.

In psychiatric hospitals, social workers often contribute to patients' diagnosis and treatment. They may, for example, try to discover if there are any social problems that may have contributed to a patient's breakdown, perhaps interviewing relatives, and at the same time helping them to understand the patient's problems. They may run group-therapy style sessions for some patients.

Community case workers also expect to cope with the social consequences of any illness, physical or psychological, and more and more work with people who have been in hospital is being done in local offices. Although hospital social workers are local-authority employees, once the patient goes home, the continuing social care is taken over by the local 'fieldwork' team which, because of the statutory requirements of the Mental Health Acts, usually includes approved social workers. Here they try to see that people with psychiatric problems have the support they need to live their lives as independently as possible.

Social workers may also work for child-guidance clinics, alongside therapists, on the social problems of disturbances in children, particularly within the family.

Residential social work

This involves working in a home or hostel. These may be for children, who may be 'in care' because they are disturbed or have been in some kind of trouble, or because their parents are ill, or have lost their home. There are homes for the physically or mentally handicapped, and for the elderly. Some homes are quite large, but the trend is for them to become much smaller, to be no larger than a large family. Generally the policy is to return as many people as possible to live in the community, even if it has to be with some form of supervision or support, in 'sheltered' housing. Numbers working in local authority residential homes in England stand at a total of about 72,000 full-time equivalent (1994). There has been a decrease of 9% in residential provision for adults compared to an increase of 35% in day care for adults over the period 1984 to 1994. These statistics confirm the trend from residential to community care provision. During the same period there has been a decrease of 33% in staffing for residential provision for children, reflecting the long-term decrease in the use of residential accommodation for children.

Residential social work is not necessarily social work in the same way as family or personal casework. In some homes – for the very old, and the disabled – the work is also part NURSING (*see in* SUPPLEMENTARY HEALTH PROFESSIONS), part institutional management, and can be part teaching (*see in* EDUCATION AND TEACHING).

Residential care work does not necessarily involve living in the home or hostel, though this may sometimes be required for senior care staff. Usually, it is required only to 'live in' on duty shifts. Residential care work can offer opportunities for a suitably qualified married couple to be given a joint appointment.

There are still fewer fully trained social workers in these homes than elsewhere. The social work content is strongest in homes caring for children under court 'care' orders, who are in some way disturbed; and in homes and hostels for the mentally handicapped. However, even the warden of a hostel for homeless people may have to spend time trying to deal with some of the social inadequacy of the people who stay there. In some homes the level of social-work-cum-psychiatric-skills needed might be quite high.

Much of the work in the homes is the strictly practical business of organising day-to-day life: meals, getting people out of bed and back in again, seeing they have baths and haircuts, dental treatment or exercise, that children go to school, and some adults to work. It also involves encouraging people to keep up some kind of activity, taking them out and about if possible, organising entertainments, or just talking. Poor residential care can do as much damage as the original situation, and 'institutionalisation' has to be avoided, which needs skilled staff.

In even a medium-sized home, housing perhaps 30 or 40 people, the staff will consist not only of wardens and care staff, but also several care assistants, cooks, domestics, and so on. Occupational and other therapists, teachers, psychologists and so on may visit. The hours are inevitably long, and involve more working time in evenings and at weekends than in most other occupations.

Community and youth work

This is part social work, and part education. It has been a developing area, and in many places the most radical in approach and effect. There is a great deal of overlap and lack of definition, and differences in concept and practical implementation from authority to authority, since local needs, real or perceived, vary so greatly.

The work evolved on the one hand from providing leisure activities for young people, mostly in inner-urban areas, and on the other from the work of organisations such as the traditional settlement association and rural community councils. Youth, community, or youth-and-community workers may be employed by the education, social service, or recreation and leisure departments of local authorities or by voluntary organisations.

Youth workers still organise and manage traditional-style clubs for young people living in a particular area. Clubs used to be based on fairly formal leisure (and sports) interests, but today they are more likely to be 'social centres' with informal activities often geared to the latest fashion, and catering for younger and younger children. Many young people visit and shop or decorate for old people, get involved in conservation, help in hospitals, adapt and repair accommodation for homeless people, etc. The youth worker frequently leads these activities. Youth workers also run adventure playgrounds. There may be involvement in projects for the care and counselling of young people at risk, e.g. drop-in crisis or advice centres for drug, alcohol and solvent abuse.

In many areas the job has broadened in scope. The youth worker may go out into the community, and try to make contact with young people who might not normally think of joining a club. Some youth workers may be completely 'detached' and work on a roving commission, for example, with young unemployed people, in pubs, cafes, bars and on the streets. In other areas, the youth club may be part of a community centre, set up to cope with needs of groups other than young people, where community workers are also active.

Community work is less easy to define than youth work and can include an even wider range of activities and groups of people – for mothers with young children living in gardenless (and perhaps high-rise) flats who need a playgroup; lunch club meetings for senior citizens; helping Asian wives to learn English; or sports for handicapped young people; all of which the community worker may help to organise as part of his or her role in trying to solve local group problems and difficulties.

A newly appointed youth and/or community worker may, for instance, find him or herself with a building, which may be expensive and purpose-built or a large house due for demolition in a few years' time, and the freedom to plan and put into operation something completely new; or s/he may deal with an existing fully established programme. Community, and youth, workers always have to keep in close touch with local needs, which can so quickly and easily change – with high unemployment for instance – and they have to be ready to persuade their local authority or management committee to do something different, such as organise a voluntary training scheme for unemployed school-leavers. They also train and encourage part-time voluntary help and work with members of clubs and groups to plan and develop activities for themselves. Youth and community workers 'lead from behind'. They arrange events, like sports fixtures. They have administrative work to do, such as accounts, and seeing that buildings are cleaned and maintained. Much of their time may be devoted to apparently routine things like driving the snooker or darts team to a match in the minibus, or mending the record player.

Like other social workers, youth and community workers try to build relationships with, and gain the trust of, the groups they are working with. Working day-by-day in the community, the community/youth worker gets to know families and individuals in the groups well, and is in a position to understand their problems, and to see crises coming. The community/youth worker is on-the-spot, to give information to people or to act as a counsellor when needed, through the daily contacts over a cup of coffee or tea, during a drive to a match or while mending equipment. The community/youth worker can help people through difficult patches, know when they have problems, listen to their worries, channel energies into non-destructive activities and be supportive and encouraging.

There has been an increasing trend in recent years towards specialisation, e.g. in liaising with local ethnic groups.

This is a very varied job, sometimes rather isolated from other professional social workers, and with very irregular hours, including working evenings and weekends.

There are comparatively few full-time youth workers, and the service depends heavily on part-time and voluntary workers. This can mean that a significant proportion of a professional youth worker's time is spent on planning, administration and coordinating the work of others.

Non-professional social work

A relatively small proportion of staff working in social services are actually qualified social workers. Within the social services there are also a range of other posts, such as:

Social work assistants or welfare assistants

They are general aides to teams of professionally qualified social workers, doing a range of tasks which do not demand the skills and training of the professional. It is normally treated as a job in its own right, rather than as a stepping stone to professional training. Some 4,200 people work (1994) as social work, or welfare, assistants in social service departments in England alone. In addition, there are 2,800 home help organisers in England.

Welfare officers

Welfare officers are employed by a wide range of organisations ranging from voluntary agencies, through to universities and colleges. These officers provide information, help, and sometimes services, e.g. finding accommodation for students.

Care assistants

Residential homes employ quite large numbers of care assistants (over 38,000 of them in local authority residential homes in England, 1994). They do many of the practical, day-to-day tasks of caring for residents.

Recruitment and entry

Social work agencies can recruit social workers without formal qualification, but formal qualifications are more often than not required for community work, and with tight finance (and therefore recruitment), agencies are likely to choose qualified people. In any case, career prospects probably depend on them.

Social work of any kind is extremely demanding physically, emotionally and intellectually. Maturity is essential, with a realistic view of what life is like for so many people, and a stable personality. It needs a genuine interest in making life easier for others, but it takes the ability to stay reasonably objective, not to be easily hurt by rejection, not to be paternalistic, not to be someone who always 'knows best', or who is over-protective. The work requires endless patience, the ability to listen and to encourage people to talk, to hear what is not said as well as what is. Social workers must be able to get on with people from all kinds of backgrounds, with all kinds of problems.

Florence Mitchell in *The Social Worker* wrote: 'People in trouble look for certain characteristics in the person from whom they seek help. They hope to find someone who will treat them seriously without being critical or shocked; who will respect their feelings and their confidence; who will assure them that help will be given without robbing them of their independence, and who will give them a feeling of security and worth. It goes without saying that workers must have a real concern for people, warmth, integrity, tolerance, imagination and a sense of humour.' It is not a career for those who are rigid in their outlook or views.

Qualifications and training

Whatever the formal position, the complex problems of social work are easier to cope with after training, however suitable a candidate's personal qualities. The pattern of education and training in social care is changing significantly as increasing use is made of NVQ criteria and accreditation for full-time and part-time courses and for employment-based assessed training. It should, in future, become much easier for staff working in social services to progress through different levels of work and training and to see a route for the care assistant without academic qualifications to work through to qualify as a professional social worker.

There is competition for places on training courses. In 1994, 11,145 applicants registered with the Social Work Admissions System (SWAS) which replaced CCETSWs own clearing-house for social work courses in 1992. Only 2,923 (26%) were successful in obtaining a place. SWAS now (1996) comes under the Universities and Colleges Admissions Service (UCAS).

There has been a continuing decrease in the number of trainees seconded to full-time courses (there were 234 in 1994 compared to 340 in 1990) but at the same time there were 2,133 (2.6% of the total) field social workers undertaking in-service professional training in 1994/95.

The Central Council for Education and Training in Social Work (CCETSW), which oversees social work training, offers the Diploma in Social Work (DipSW). The two previous main qualifications, the Certificate of Qualification in Social Work (CQSW) and the Certificate in Social Services (CSS), have been merged and replaced to create this single qualifying Diploma in Social Work (DipSW).

CCETSW does not set its own examinations or syllabuses, but approves courses run by individual educational institutions, and awards the nationally recognised certificate.

All training courses are now broadly based, preparing students to practise in a variety of services, in public and private agencies. Courses vary, though, in the extent to which they train for residential or day services. Some give extra attention to special aspects of social work, e.g. community work, or work with ethnic groups.

Which course to choose depends mainly on academic qualifications and age; the older the entrant, effectively the less academic qualifications may matter. No one can be awarded a professional qualification before the age of 22, and for many courses there is a preference for applicants who will be significantly older on qualification. Whatever route is chosen, some experience of social work (paid or voluntary), or in related work, is normally needed.

The Diploma in Social Work

The course of study entails a combination of theory and practice. Courses are widely offered at universities and colleges throughout the United Kingdom. There are three options available:

1 a two-year postgraduate route: master's degree in a related topic combined with the DipSW;
2 a three- to four-year undergraduate route: first-degree in a related topic combined with the Dip SW;
3 a two-year non-graduate route: Diploma in Higher Education (DipHE) combined with the DipSW.

Most of these courses are for candidates over 21.

In addition, there are part-time and open-learning routes available. To gain entry onto these courses, candidates need two A-levels (grades A–E), and five GCSEs (grades A–C). In Scotland, entry requirements are normally five passes for the Scottish Certificate in Education including three at the Higher level. An equivalent qualification such as an Advanced GNVQ/GSVQ, NVQ level 3, or completion of an appropriate access course will also be acceptable.

For candidates over 21 there are no formal academic requirements, although it is expected that evidence of the ability to study at a higher level is attained. All courses require evidence of pre-training relevant social work experience to display an aptitude for social work.

While fieldwork courses are now more and more broadly based, they vary in the extent to which they emphasise particular aspects of social work, and it is important to ensure that individual courses provide the kind of content needed for a career in a particular area. About half the time on a course is spent on practice placements with a social work agency, which can be chosen to fit in with particular career directions.

CCETSW produces an annual handbook, *How to Qualify for Social Work*, which lists courses and their entry qualifications with some detail of course content. DipSW programmes are designed jointly by educational institutions and social work agencies and can be very varied in delivery: modular, open- and distance-learning methods can be used. Programmes cater for graduates, non-graduates and undergraduates. CCETSW sets out the knowledge base, core skills and professional competence to be covered in a DipSW course. These include knowledge and understanding of human growth and behaviour; how to observe and assess; the administrative and legal framework of social work practice; clients' rights; and analytical, interpersonal and decision-making skills. Courses may be very different in emphasis and approach, and potential students should investigate each course carefully before deciding on applications.

Formerly probation-officer training was provided by a specialist option within the Diploma in Social Work. The Home Office has reviewed the arrangements for probation-officer training and has decided to withdraw it from current social work training. It is intended to be offered as an employment-based route by Probation Services leading to a specialist probation diploma. *See* THE PROBATION SERVICE *below*.

Post-qualifying training leads to the Post Qualifying Award in Social Work (PQSW) and the Advanced Award in Social Work (AASW) of CCETSW. These are available to provide continuing professional development in social work practice and opportunity for any additional (assessed) training that may be needed, e.g. to carry out statutory duties under the Mental Health Acts.

National/Scottish Vocational Qualifications (NVQ/SVQ).

These are work-based awards recognised throughout the UK and are available to people working in social work, social care, child care and education, health, and in the criminal justice services. The awards allow workers to have their work performance assessed and their skills recognised, and can assist in career progression. Assessment for an entire award may take from 6 to 24 months. Levels 2, 3 and 4 are awarded by CCETSW. An award at level 3 is equivalent to GCSE A-levels and provides a route into social work qualifying training for the Diploma in Social Work.

BTEC First Diploma in Care

This is a one-year course which covers basic skills and knowledge in human development, health, behavioural studies and caring skills. It can lead to: BTEC National Diploma in Social Care. This is a two-year course requiring four GCSEs at grade C or above for direct entry. Both BTEC courses involve a variety of work placements.

Youth and community work qualifications

These can be gained on courses endorsed by the Education and Training Standards team within the National Youth Agency or by the Scottish Community Education Council. There is a wide variety of approved courses and qualifications. Study can be full- or part-time and entry requirements also vary greatly although the most important requirements are maturity (the average age of students is 27) and proof of commitment. There are about 360 places available on special two-year full-time courses and a similar number on other approved courses, full- and part-time.

Further information

The Central Council for Education and Training in Social Work.

The probation service

The Criminal Justice Act of 1991 set out a number of changes to the Probation Service and placed it firmly within the Criminal Justice system. The service concentrates mainly on people who have broken the law, and so is separately organised from most other state-supported social services (it comes under the Home Office). Probation officers are employees of local area probation committees (not local authorities). There are 54 probation committees (April 1996) in England and Wales, employing 8,000 probation officers.

The purpose of the probation service is to serve the courts and the public by:

- supervising offenders under probation orders made by the courts, which allow them to stay at home instead of going to prison: this normally means a not-so-serious offence, a first offender (young people are now supervised by the local authority), and anyone a court thinks might benefit from such an order;
- working with offenders, so that they lead law-abiding lives, in a way which minimises risk to the public;
- safeguarding the welfare of children in family proceedings.

Probation officers provide the courts with advice and information on offenders to assist in sentencing decisions. In most cases, the first main task is to prepare a pre-sentence report for the court. The purpose of this is to advise the court about the offence that has been committed, the relevant circumstances of the offender and the probation officer's opinion of the most suitable sentence the court might decide to impose. This involves looking into an offender's background and circumstances, and talking to him or her and to the family, and anyone else who may be able to contribute. Courts take these reports into account before deciding on a sentence.

Community sentence work

Community sentences are for offenders whose offences are not so serious that only a term of imprisonment will suffice, but are nonetheless serious enough to justify such a sentence. Probation officers are responsible for ensuring that offenders comply with the terms of the sentences passed by the courts. They design, provide and promote effective programmes for supervising offenders safely in the community. They also provide an 'after-care' service for people newly released from prison; they try to help them find somewhere to live, see that they have clothes, and help them look for a job, and so on.

Work with prisoners

All prison welfare officers in THE PRISON SERVICE (*see in* SECURITY AND PROTECTIVE SERVICES) are seconded probation officers, who assist in the rehabilitation of offenders and help prepare them for their release.

Family court welfare work

In family disputes, separation or divorce proceedings, probation officers provide information to the courts on the best interests of any children involved.

Most probation officers work from local area offices. Like community social workers they each have their own 'case load' which can be up to 50 clients, who may be on probation, on parole, and so on. Clients are required to report regularly to the office, although most probation officers visit their homes sometimes, if only to get to know more about the client's background. Probation officers usually work along the same or similar 'casework' lines as community social workers.

They do not act as a kind of prison officer or just try to keep their clients out of more trouble. They look for any emotional, psychological or social causes for the kind of antisocial behaviour which has brought their client into conflict with the law, and try to sort out any other personal, emotional, social, educational or work problems, even anything that is physically wrong. They have to cope with clients' hostility and resentment, and being treated as a symbol of antagonistic 'authority'. It is often difficult to build the essential relationship, to gain trust, and to get probationers or parolees to accept help. Probation officers have to accept that there is not always much they can do for some people, and inevitably some will find themselves in court again.

Probably no more than half a probation officer's 'day' is spent behind a desk in the office. Since they must be available whenever a criminal court sits, most probation officers spend at least one day a week in court. The office also has to be staffed continuously in case of emergencies. Otherwise, probation officers often work on a 'flexitime' basis because many clients can only get in after work. Probation officers also have to make visits, go to a full complement of meetings, liaise with other social workers and other agencies (e.g. on hostel places, jobs, social security, etc.), write reports, and keep records.

Recruitment and entry

Individual probation areas receive a cash-limited budget (80% from the Home Office and 20% from local authorities). The area probation committees and local management decide how to spend the money in the most effective manner, including how many probation officers to recruit. A new scheme is to be introduced in Spring 1997 to allow probation committees to recruit trainees directly, following a regional selection procedure. Prospective probation officers will be recruited regionally as salaried trainees. A range of tests, exercises and interviews will be used to determine the suitability of applicants and to define training requirements. According to the Home Office, probation committees will be encouraged to draw upon a range of backgrounds, skills and disciplines in order to provide a well-balanced workforce. Probation officers must be between the ages of 22 and 65, and able to live and work legally in the United Kingdom.

Qualifications and training

The Probation (Amendment) Rules came into effect in December 1995 rescinding the requirement for probation officers to hold a social work qualification, or any other qualification. Once recruited, training will be mainly work-based and will be modular, recognising prior qualifications and experience (such as paid or voluntary work experience in care or closely related work). The Home Office anticipates that training will lead to Qualified Probation Officer Status (QPOS) and to an appropriate level NVQ. *See also* THE PRISON SERVICE *in* SECURITY AND PROTECTIVE SERVICES *and* LEGAL WORK *in* THE LEGAL SYSTEM.

Further information

The Probation Service Division of the Home Office.

Careers advisory work

Local careers services, the main employers of careers officers (or careers advisers as they are increasingly called) offer information and advice to young people and may also deal with adults. In some areas there are separate advisory services for adults, funded in a variety of ways. Some careers advisers work in higher education institutions, offering careers advice to students and graduates.

Wherever careers advisers work, and whichever age group they deal with, the job is similar. They give people help in coming to decisions about work, training, and any extra education they may need. They help to assess as realistically as possible their abilities, interests and potential, and provide the information – about occupations, trends in employment, courses, etc. – on which an informed decision can be based. They may also provide an employment service to help people find jobs, and employers to find the recruits they need.

Careers work for the under-18s is divided between the school and the careers service.

In schools

Careers education in schools is usually the responsibility of a careers coordinator, who may also be a subject teacher with, ideally, a reduced teaching timetable. It is rarely a full-time post although, according to the National Association of Careers Guidance Teachers, 66% of schools have between one and five members of staff timetabled for careers work. Careers education involves many staff through its inclusion in the PSE (Personal and Social Education) curriculum, work experience and education-industry links. Much careers advice is still given informally – by group tutors, form teachers, for example – particularly at the point when decisions are taken about subjects to be studied for school-leaving examinations; and by subject teachers, keen for their best pupils to go on to university, perhaps.

What careers teachers do varies from school to school. Some may simply provide information, others may also be involved in extensive programmes to prepare pupils for life and work. They advise, and talk to, pupils about their plans. Careers work can mean a great deal of organisation – of information which also has to be collected, exhibitions, visits and work experience; imaginative teaching on preparing, planning and deciding about the future, and on the world of work; counselling individual pupils; working with, e.g., the careers service.

Careers services

New arrangements for the operation of careers services came into force in April 1994, when responsibility for the provision of careers services was transferred from Local Education Authorities (LEAs) – Local Authorities (LAs) in Scotland – to the Secretary of State. Since that date, careers services have been run increasingly by both private and public organisations rather than LEAs/LAs. Many are managed jointly by LEAs/LAs and Training and Enterprise Councils (Local Enterprise Councils in Scotland). It is intended that eventually all careers services will become private companies, with responsibility for developing their own policies and making their own decisions. In Northern Ireland, however, careers advisers are civil servants.

Universities and colleges of higher education employ their own careers staff (*see* Higher education careers services *below*).

Most careers advisers (approximately 5,000 in 1995) work for either public or private careers service companies. They work both from their own offices, and within the schools, where the help they give has to be dovetailed into the way careers education and guidance is organised by the school, and colleges of further education. Careers services are asked to provide a wide range of services, which means that the work of a careers adviser is varied. There is increasing emphasis on educational and vocational guidance for young people, due to the strong upward trend in the staying-on-in-education rates, the increased competition between schools and colleges for 16-year-olds and the wider variety of post-16 educational routes available for different ability groups.

Work with individual schools and colleges involves knowing how each is organised, becoming familiar with the curriculum, developing a working relationship with the staff and planning with them a careers programme for the school, as well as getting to know the pupils.

Careers advisers spend much of their time interviewing and advising individuals, giving talks, providing up-to-date information, and giving careers teachers technical backup. Although they should be able to provide information and contacts for jobs or training/courses anywhere in the country, they try to get to know the local situation very well indeed. They have close contacts with individual employers, with whom they will probably keep up a fairly continuous two-way flow of information and discussion on changing educational and employment patterns, at all levels and for all kinds of work.

The careers adviser has to keep up to date on local training programmes to help the young unemployed, as well as advising school-leavers which training to try for, and helping trainees get into full-time employment.

Some careers advisers specialise – in working with particular age groups, or ability ranges, or special groups (e.g. teenagers with disabilities).

Careers advisers also supervise and organise administrative and clerical work in the office; see that any vacancies are recorded, processed and followed up, and that the careers library is kept up-to-date; ensure the appointments system is running smoothly, and that arrangements are made for visits or careers conventions, and that statistics are recorded. An increasing emphasis is being made on record-keeping, meeting targets (numbers of young people to be interviewed, employers to be visited) and developing action plans for clients. Most careers advisers use computers in their work, either for administrative purposes or for client use (computer-aided guidance – tests and interest guides).

Promotion within the service is to supervising an area or district, and from there to senior management, or to the inspectorate, or other advisory work. Some go on to work for central organisations like the Careers and Occupational Information Centre (Choice and Careers Division, Department for Education and Employment), which produces government-published careers literature, runs a monthly magazine and distributes careers literature.

Higher education careers services

Most universities and colleges of higher education in the United Kingdom employ their own specialist careers staff. In 1996 there are about 550 full- and part-time professional careers advisers who offer vocational guidance by means of individual counselling interviews, group discussions, self-assessment exercises and psychometric questionnaires supported by computer guidance systems. University and college careers services also provide a wide range of material on types of work, employers of graduates, self-employment, postgraduate courses, voluntary work, opportunities overseas and job-hunting techniques through their careers information rooms and specialised staff. Most of the services have a collection of videotapes on selected occupations and employers, as well as on application and interview techniques. Careers advisers also work closely with their academic colleagues in higher education to introduce programmes of careers education into the curriculum, through which students can identify and develop key career and life skills, increase their knowledge of the job market and make more reasoned career choices.

More than 130 higher education careers services, incorporating 800 individuals, are members of the Association of Graduate Careers Advisory Services (AGCAS) who, collectively and mainly through a number of sub-committees and working groups, collect and disseminate information and conduct surveys on a wide range of topics concerning graduate employment and training. Much of this information is contained in a series of information booklets and occupational profiles which are published by the highly professional Higher Education Central Services Unit (CSU). The higher education careers services work in partnership with the CSU to develop a comprehensive range of publications and services which also includes regular vacancy bulletins, directories, computer guidance systems and statistical information.

Recruitment and entry

A degree, or an equivalent, is normally needed to train as a careers adviser, although people aged 25 and over and with some five years' relevant experience may be considered without this level of qualification.

For work as a careers adviser in higher education, a degree and several years' work experience are normally needed. Some advisers hold the Diploma in Careers Guidance, but this is not essential. Other staff working in higher education careers services often hold professional qualifications related to their area of specialism – e.g. a librarianship qualification for information-based work.

Careers teaching has no formal entry system. The work is generally taken on by a teacher already employed in the school as an additional duty. It is therefore necessary to become a qualified teacher first (*see* EDUCATION AND TEACHING).

Careers advisers come from a variety of backgrounds, and although it is possible to begin training immediately after graduating, a high proportion have had experience in another occupation first – as teachers, or personnel officers, for example. Many careers advisers specialise, and so a specialised background may be relevant for a particular area of careers work.

Careers work combines counselling with gathering and passing on information. It needs a strong interest in young people, and in helping them to make the most of their abilities or to solve career problems. A great deal of time is spent in talking to people, particularly young people, from all kinds of background and of all types of ability and interest, and advisers have to be able to establish a relationship with them, and gain their confidence. It means developing sensitivity and shrewdness to gain the necessary insights into people's make-up and motivations to be able to advise them properly.

While some careers advisers begin their working lives as teachers, it is not a 'didactic' career. Careers advisers must also be interested in the world of work, and in gathering a great deal of very complex information on occupations, educational requirements, etc. They must also develop good working relationships with employers and be able to persuade them of the importance of, for example, education and training for young people.

Assessing young people and occupations and matching one to the other takes some maturity, so careers advisers need a great deal of tact and persuasiveness in coping with the conflicting views of schools, parents and the pupils themselves, in dealing with entrenched attitudes and opinions, in explaining the far-reaching effects on the careers and jobs of technological and social change, and solving difficult problems.

Qualifications and training

New careers advisers must normally hold the Diploma in Careers Guidance (DipCG) awarded by the Local Government Management Board, on appointment. The diploma is in two parts. Part 1 involves a one-year full-time or two-year part-time course; Part 2 a period of on-the-job training and development. There is also a two-year training programme which is employer-based with block-release to college and distance-learning modules. The courses are vocationally slanted and very intensive, covering principles and practice of careers guidance, study of employment and training, and education (including further education). Approximately 400 places are available annually. About 130 people received LGMB awards in 1994–95 for full- or part-time study.

Full-time courses are available at the following universities or colleges: Central England, College of Guidance Studies (Kent), East London, Glamorgan, Huddersfield, Manchester Metropolitan, Napier, Northumbria, Nottingham Trent, Paisley, Reading, South Bank, Strathclyde and West of England. Interested applicants should contact the individual institutions for details of their start dates, as not all courses start in September.

Part-time courses are offered at: Central England, College of Guidance Studies (Kent) (open-learning), East London, Huddersfield, Manchester Metropolitan, Napier, Paisley and West of England.

The first NVQs and SVQs in Advice and Guidance have been accredited. They are offered by four awarding bodies – City & Guilds, the Local Government Management Board/Institute of Careers Guidance, the Open University Validation Service and SCOTVEC – at levels 2, 3 and 4. Level 2 is appropriate for anyone who is the first point of contact for clients, and for all who work to support their organisation's service to clients. Levels 3 and 4 are for all advice and guidance practitioners.

For work in higher education, a degree and several years' work experience is needed. Some advisers hold the DipCG, but this is not essential. AGCAS offers its members an integrated Professional Development training programme. Through this, advisory and information staff can obtain the Certificate and/or Diploma in Careers Guidance in Higher Education. These post-experience qualifications are validated by the University of Reading.

For careers teachers, very little formal training exists. According to a survey by the National Association of Careers and Guidance Teachers (1992), only 4% of careers teachers had taken a one-year, full-time training course. However, careers teachers in 24% of schools had received between 5 and 20 days' in-service training in careers work. These figures are set to rise with the increased government funding for training for careers teachers. There are no pre-entry courses.

Further information

The Institute of Careers Guidance, Local Government Management Board, Association of Graduate Careers Advisory Services, National Association of Careers and Guidance Teachers.

Nursery nurses

These are not 'nurses' in the accepted sense of the word, in that they look after children who are not (normally anyway) sick. Mostly they work with children under the age of eight.

The falling birth-rate has been counterbalanced by the rising number of women with professional careers, who have kept up the demand for people prepared to look after young children – usually in the pre-school age group – in the home environment. This modern version of the 'nanny' role is rather different from the traditional one. Nannies (for want of a better title) do not nowadays work just for wealthier families. There are more opportunities with families where both parents are professional people who are out at work all day. Here, the nanny cares for children of pre-school age during the parents' working day, and younger schoolchildren after school and during the holidays. Such nannies have a more standard working week, with free weekends and evenings, but they are mostly on their own with the children for long periods. Some families share nannies, and some nannies organise local playgroups. In addition, some nannies work for agencies, as 'temps'.

Nursery nurses also work in nursery, infant or primary schools or classes run by local education authorities (*see* EDUCATION AND TEACHING), day and residential nurseries and family centres run by local authority social service departments, privately run nursery schools and playgroups, hospitals (*see also* THE HEALTH SERVICE) and special-needs settings. There are also numerous private nurseries or creches operating in holiday resorts in Britain and abroad, on ocean liners, or in commercial organisations as well as in more conventional urban and rural locations.

In recent years, opportunities in local-authority classes and nurseries have been severely reduced by cuts in public expenditure. However, new government initiatives mean that demand is likely to increase again. In these situations, a nursery nurse usually looks after a small group of babies or young children. The rules for local-authority nurseries state four or five children to each nursery nurse. The staff organise a wide range of play activities for them, as well as coping with feeding, washing and toileting, although the work varies between different organisations. It is a responsible and demanding career.

There are opportunities for progression, as with experience and/or further training it is possible to move on to jobs such as a nursery manager or a local authority 'under-eights adviser'. It is also possible to progress to higher education in related specialised subjects.

Recruitment and entry

A child care worker has a huge impact on a child's early experiences and plays a vital role in both a child's development and social education. It is therefore very important that potential workers in this field undergo thorough training and gain national recognition for their skills. It is possible to work without qualifications, but unqualified people may find it more difficult to get jobs and may not be given the same level of responsibility or pay as a qualified person.

The minimum age for starting a course is 16 years old, but this varies among further education colleges. There is no upper age limit. The Council for Awards in Children's Care and Education (CACHE) does not lay down any specific entry qualifications, but a good general education is an asset to candidates, and competition for training places means that some colleges will require all candidates to have three or more GCSE passes at grades A, B or C. Each college has its own selection procedures, and individual colleges should be contacted for further application details.

Anyone who works with children needs to possess certain qualities. First and foremost, potential child care workers must like children and enjoy being with them. In addition, they must be energetic and adaptable, tolerant and patient, imaginative and creative, cheerful, caring and committed. People working in families need to be able to get on with parents as well as children. Probably the most vital quality is a real belief in the individual worth of each child and a determination to ensure that children have the opportunity to develop their full potential. In order to do this effectively, the child care worker needs an understanding of, and a commitment to, the promotion of equality of opportunity.

Qualifications and training

At state-run further education colleges in England, Wales and Northern Ireland, students normally take a two-year full-time modular course leading to the CACHE Diploma in Nursery Nursing (DNN). It is also possible to complete the course on a part-time basis. There are over 250 state-run or private colleges offering the Diploma. In Scotland, the Scottish Nursery Nurses' Board issues certificates for training undertaken mainly through SCOTVEC national certificate courses. Private colleges offer residential courses which lead to the college's own diploma as well as the DNN.

All courses combine academic and practical studies, learning about children at different stages of their growth and development. The academic or theoretical content covers topics such as emotional and intellectual development, psychological and sociological perspectives on behaviour, nutrition, safety, play and equal opportunities. The practical work is carried out in work placements, which constitute about 40% of the time on the DNN. Assessment in each module is by national assignment. The DNN provides the basis for NVQ assessment in child care and education at level 3. The DNN can be used as a qualification in its own right or as a route to other qualifications such as the Advanced Diploma in Child Care and Education (ADCE). The ADCE is suitable for anyone who has been working with children for several years or who has just completed a child care and education training programme which meets the entry requirements. It can be taken as a one-year full-time course or on a part-time basis (up to five years). The Open University has awarded the ADCE 120 Credit Accumulation Transfer points (CATS) to this award, which means that candidates can gain remission in related subjects at higher education institutions.

There is also a one-year full-time modular course leading to the certificate in Child Care and Education (CCE) for those who want to begin working with children, but who may not feel ready to undertake the DNN. There are no entry requirements except that candidates must be aged 16 or over to register. The CCE modules cover the practice and theory of various areas of child care and education. Assessment is by assignment and a multiple choice question paper as well as assessment in practical placements. The CCE provides the basis for NVQ assessment in child care and education at level 2.

Playwork

Playwork is defined as work with children aged 5–15 to facilitate their development through play. NVQs are available at levels 2 and 3 in Playwork and at level 4 in Playwork Development. Level 2 is appropriate for an assistant playworker working under close supervision; level 3 is for a playworker working as part of a team, but able to work on their own initiative without close supervision; level 4 is appropriate for a play development officer who may not work directly with children but who has responsibility for the development of play provision in a particular area.

Further information

The Council for Awards in Children's Care and Education.

Working for charities

The world of charities has seen a decade of expansion and change. So often regarded as peripheral bodies for do-gooding amateurs, charities as a whole now play a much more central role in providing a range of services for the community at large. Many charities, for example, now work in partnership with local authorities to offer services for elderly people or children in need, or to protect the environment. There is a growing professionalism as Britain's 175,000-plus charities adapt to a new and increasingly competitive environment.

Working for a charity has thus become a real option for those starting out on their careers. It is no longer the sole preserve of those seeking a second career, or who have made their fortune elsewhere.

The range of opportunities

The variety of charitable work is often not appreciated. As well as major national and international bodies like NSPCC or Oxfam, the sector includes thousands of lesser-known charities, local organisations, educational establishments, hospitals, campaigning groups and welfare bodies. These cover an enormous range of activities, including medical research, nursing care, the environment, youth and community work, animal welfare, religion and the arts.

Many people are attracted to work for a charity simply because of their interest in the cause and are happy to undertake any type of work within the organisation. Others have more vague feelings of wanting to do a job which is worthwhile and of benefit to society.

The range of careers within charities is huge, reflecting the wide range of charitable activity. Like any employer, charities need managers, administrators, and clerical, accounts and computing staff. But they may also employ social workers, teachers, nurses, publicity officers, fundraisers, designers, environmentalists, researchers, and many other specialists.

There is a common misconception that charity work is an easy option away from the 'real world'. Nothing could be further from the truth. It is demanding and challenging; job security is not guaranteed either, since voluntary support, on which most charities depend, can easily fluctuate. Unsocial hours are another factor; it may often be necessary to attend meetings of volunteers or committees outside normal working hours.

The culture is an entrepreneurial one, with new ideas and projects always in the air. Versatility is important, especially in the smaller charity. You may be asked to help with all sorts of tasks, and those who seek rigid job descriptions and demarcation lines will not feel at home.

Everyone working for a charity must understand the need to work with volunteers. As trustees, committee members, policy-makers, collectors or general helpers, volunteers play a vital role in any charity. Paid employees must be sensitive to their views, and willing to cooperate with voluntary committees. Working with volunteers should be seen as helpful and stimulating, rather than a burden. Experience as a volunteer can be very helpful to those seeking their first charity job.

No one earns a fortune working for a charity, and most will expect to pay their staff at below commercial rates. But salaries are improving, and the demand for experienced people in certain areas (e.g. fundraising, and accounting) has led to increased salaries in those areas. The compensations are that the work can be very absorbing and varied, with excellent scope for taking initiatives and responsibility; above all, you are serving a worthwhile cause.

Fundraising

Fundraising is a job which is of special importance to charities and rarely found outside. The fundraiser's task is to organise and carry out a programme of approaches and initiatives which will provide the funds the charity needs. This may involve approaches to companies, grant-giving trusts or individuals; organising events or collections; working with members and supporter groups; or a combination of these and other techniques.

Fundraisers need good communication skills, and the drive and enthusiasm to succeed and motivate others. Charities are highly dependent on fundraising success, and the fundraiser must be able to cope with this pressure, and work to achieve a set target. The work can be very varied and carries plenty of scope for developing your own initiatives and new ideas. Success can bring great satisfaction in enabling new charitable projects to go ahead.

Qualifications and training

Because of the range of careers available, it is impossible to generalise about entry qualifications or training for work in the charity world. There are openings at all levels, and widely differing entry routes, depending on the career path chosen. Training would be that which is appropriate to the career in question; there are very few courses aimed specifically at the voluntary sector.

New entrants come from a wide range of backgrounds, but sales or marketing experience is useful. Training opportunities are limited, but the Institute of Charity Fundraising Managers (ICFM) offers fundraisers an opportunity to follow a structured training route via the Certificate in Fundraising Management. The Certificate is a programme of training which gives fundraisers comprehensive training from a basic introduction to fundraising (the Foundation Course) through to specialist courses for experienced fundraisers. In addition, the Open University Business School offers a six-month open-learning option for fundraisers called Winning Resources and Support, a programme developed with, and endorsed by, the ICFM.

The NCVQ is in the process (1996) of putting together a training body for the voluntary sector.

Overseas

A number of jobs in voluntary work are dependent on European funding. Voluntary work in Europe can be varied: it may be lobbying work, liaison with the European Union or project work (e.g. in Romania, or in any of the increasing number of countries becoming democracies). For work overseas, proficiency in a language other than English may be required.

Further information

Institute of Charity Fundraising Managers, National Council for Voluntary Organisations (please include a stamped addressed envelope).

Contents

The Legal System

(CLCI: L – LAZ)

Background

The legal system administers and enforces the 'Law of the land' – as laid down by Parliament in legislation, in the unwritten common law and law of equity, and in EC law which applies to Britain. The law is the country's rule book, which tries to set limits on the way people, organisations, and even the state should behave, and sets up systems which decide what should happen when the rules are broken or there is any disagreement.

Society is, however, extremely complex, and the activities and possible situations for which rules must be set are many and varied. Since the law and the legal system must mirror society, they are also very complex and, like society, the law and the legal system have grown haphazardly over many centuries. The law has many problems in trying to make rules to take into account any conceivable situation, and to keep a balance between the traditional and the modern.

The courts administer the law. Each branch of the law has its own courts but some courts deal with more than one branch. The two main types of court in England and Wales deal with civil and criminal law – the other branches are administrative, Admiralty and ecclesiastical law. Courts have other definitions – some are 'courts of record' (i.e. 'courts of which the acts and judicial proceedings prove themselves anywhere else and have power to fine and imprison for contempt of their authority') and some are not; some are lower courts, others higher.

Criminal law and the criminal courts deal with offences against the community or which contravene an individual citizen's rights. Civil law and the civil courts deal with disputes between individuals which affect only the disputing parties. Changes have been proposed which would rationalise and simplify the civil courts.

The 700 magistrates' courts in England and Wales form the lowest levels of both the civil and criminal courts, dealing with more minor cases or deciding whether or not a case should go on to a higher court. The 300 or so county courts are the main civil courts, but they try lesser cases.

The supreme court is divided into three. First, the high court which tries the most important cases in one of three divisions – Queen's Bench, Chancery and Family – each with quite different procedures based on complex rules and custom. Second, the crown court (which replaced the centuries-old assizes and quarter sessions) is a single court with over 100 different centres, dealing with criminal cases, and administratively divided into six 'Circuits'. Third, the court of appeal also has civil and criminal divisions. The supreme court of appeal is the House of Lords.

The legal system in Scotland is different. The Sheriff Courts exercise both civil and criminal jurisdiction. The High Court of the Justiciary is the supreme criminal court, and the Court of Session is the highest civil tribunal. Below the Sheriff Courts are the District courts.

Anyone coming into contact with the law, whatever the reason, normally finds it impossible to cope without expert help and guidance. This they get from the people who make a profession out of translating the law to lay men and women, and dealing with the legal processes on their behalf. The law also has to be administered, by legal experts such as judges who form the courts, and made by people, the government lawyers and, again, the judges. Lawyers now also decide on who should be prosecuted in the Crown Prosecution Service.

The legal profession

Although it is called a single legal profession, it is in fact two quite separate careers – as barrister or solicitor. They have to work very closely together, and their work even overlaps in some places, but the division of the legal profession into two quite distinct branches has a very long tradition.

A substantial number of solicitors are 'general practitioners', but an increasing number specialise and provide the first legal opinion; the barrister is the 'second opinion' who works in the higher courts. Since the Courts and Legal Services Act, solicitors who undertake further training are able to apply for the rights of audience in the Higher Courts and, subject to them passing certain tests, may then exercise those rights. However, fewer than 400 (1996) have any higher rights of audience.

The main formal differences between barrister and solicitor are that the former may only be briefed or consulted by a solicitor or members of other professional bodies granted the right of direct professional access, on behalf of the client, and barristers have automatic rights of audience in the Higher Courts on completion of pupillage.

The work of barristers, solicitors and judges has a common basis, though. They must all 'think' as lawyers, and be able to use all the complex sources of the law expertly and intelligently. The law is not rigidly fixed. Much legal time goes on deciding what the law on any point at issue actually is. Even the law passed by Parliament can be, and is, interpreted differently by different judges, and the way they interpret the law overrides whatever Parliament thought it said. Common law is not set down by Parliament at all, but refers simply to the decisions of judges. This is where 'test' cases come in, when the law as it stands is not clear enough, or a new, unexpected situation arises. Judges work on 'precedent', and theoretically only make new rules where none exist already. In practice, though, it is all too easy to get conflicting decisions, which have to be pronounced on in appeal courts, and even the House of Lords.

Facts are central to the lawyer's work, and a great deal of all legal time is spent on them. The law only exists in relation to facts, to what actually happened. Whatever they are dealing with, lawyers first dig out the facts, all the facts (however apparently unimportant, trivial, or irrelevant), check and re-check them for accuracy, analyse them and decide which are relevant to the case, examine them for inconsistencies and mistakes, and then put them into logical and understandable order. If any facts are in dispute in criminal cases, a jury must decide on the basis of the evidence presented (by both sides) what the facts really are, and verdicts are given on proven facts.

All lawyers also spend much of their working lives with documents. They search for the relevant law through the many pages of legal reference books – although this is now changing as case law, statutes, statutory instruments and legal texts (containing opinions) are being put into computerised legal reference systems, and can be recalled in seconds. Lawyers still have to deal with the documents of the case they are working on, though.

The law applies to people and their personal situations. Most solicitors and many barristers also spend as much of their time talking to, listening to, and arguing with people as they do in court or at their desks reading or drafting.

Lawyers are, after all, in business, and in business to make an income. The legal service they give widens steadily as the law moves into new areas – into consumer protection and industrial relations, for example. More people are buying their own homes, and contract and company law grows steadily more complex. Science and technology bring legal problems in the train of new inventions – personal protection from computer data files, copyright difficulties with video tapes and the many forms of electronic data transmission, or deciding on the responsibility for genetic damage to babies. The EC has also produced legal problems for UK lawyers, some of whom must take greater account of the law of continental countries and European Union law.

The computer-based files and indexes in lawyers' offices will result in other changes, as will any revision of legal aid. Lawyers find themselves in competition with other professionals – solicitors have already lost much of their traditional taxation work to accountants, and their monopoly of conveyancing. The decline in matrimonial work as divorce becomes steadily easier caused the Bar some problems. The trend to negotiate 'out of court' settlements is also reducing some legal incomes, and the ability to attract large-company business is increasingly important. Barristers are now broadening their work to include acting as arbitrators and conciliators.

There have been many changes in recent years within the legal profession. The government has gone ahead with plans to introduce the 'no-win, no-fee' agreements for lawyers, whereby lawyers' fees are conditional upon their success. If they lose a case under such an agreement, they will not get paid. Other major changes include the abolition in the Criminal Justice Act (1995) of the 'right to silence', and the change in the divorce laws, as mentioned above. Lawyers need to keep abreast of all changes in the law to ensure they can interpret it correctly on behalf of their clients.

Overseas

Many opportunities exist for those who are seeking careers in Europe, both in the European Union and in the larger Europe. English lawyers are in demand in institutions such as the European Commission, Council or Parliament, the European Court of Justice, the Court of Auditors, the Economic and Social Committee and also the Council of Europe, in particular with the European Commission of Human Rights. However, there is no established career path there. There are practical difficulties regarding training and the law and business practices of each country which have a bearing on the relevance of any qualification. Nevertheless, anyone qualified and proficient in at least one other language should stand a greater chance of securing a job abroad. There are numerous professional exchange schemes and training courses which can help anyone keen to pursue a European or international legal career. The Law Society has a booklet, *Careers in the International Legal Field*, which gives details. British firms of solicitors and accountants often have English-speaking offices world-wide and graduates may find fulfilling employment via this route. It is also reasonably easy to obtain recognition as a qualified lawyer in most of Australia and Canada (except Quebec).

Barristers and advocates

Barristers and the nearest equivalent in Scotland – advocates – are legal specialists, the expert advisers who work only for, or through, solicitors or members of other professional bodies who have applied for and obtained the right of direct professional access. They appear in court on behalf of clients when 'briefed' to do so, but more of their time is spent in giving expert advice than is generally realised. The only real difference between a barrister and an advocate is in the qualifications and training required (*see below*).

When members of these professional bodies consult barristers on a point of law, the barrister (or his/her pupil) may have to search through many years of legal cases to find court decisions with a bearing on the case, compare them, analyse what they mean in relation to the present case, and then give the solicitor or other professional intermediary a carefully considered, usually written, reply. This may involve much detailed research, much legal analysis of fact and precedent, and much unravelling of legal intricacies. The barrister may also be asked for an opinion on the likelihood of winning or losing a case on the basis of his/her experience and knowledge of the courts.

If a case does go to court, the professional intermediary gives the barrister he or she thinks most suitable a 'brief', or instructions, to act on the client's behalf in court. Much of the preparation of the case for court is done by the instructing intermediary, but when a barrister gets down to the documents, he or she must do an enormous amount of hard work, and get to know the case in all its complexity, and the client too. Barristers have to understand, learn and speak knowledgeably about many technical matters, and be able to cross examine witnesses about them. For example, evidence might be given by an expert witness on very complex aspects of nuclear physics where someone is claiming damages from a radiation leak.

Most barristers specialise. Their main choice is between common law, which is more widely practised, and chancery. If they choose common law, they do not usually deal with all branches, because there is too much to learn, but most barristers working at the common law bar do deal with a range of cases – crime, divorce, family and unspecialized civil work – although some chambers specialise entirely in one area, particularly in London. Out of London most practices are general. Individual barristers may specialise in more complex aspects, e.g. libel and slander, or patent and copyright work. Barristers specialising in commercial law or chancery may spend some of their time abroad, particularly in the Far East. Provided they remain available to offer legal services in England and Wales, there is no limit on the amount of time they may spend abroad.

The majority of chancery sets are in Lincoln's Inn in London, but there are established groups of chancery practitioners in sets of chambers in all the major provincial cities, particularly Manchester, Birmingham, Liverpool, Leeds and Bristol. Here barristers specialise in company law, trust, property and conveyancing, tax cases or estate administration.

How much time a barrister spends researching and drafting 'opinions', how much time advising, how much time in court and preparing cases, depends on which part of the law he or she chooses. Generally, much more time is spent in court in common law practices, very little in chancery – which is generally much more 'academic' and intellectually demanding, a back-room job drafting agreements as well as writing opinions. Barristers specialising in criminal law spend a very high proportion of their time in court, or preparing for it.

Appearing in court takes not only the ability to put over a case, but also to explain even the driest and most abstract evidence in (for example) a fraud trial, clearly and logically, so that a judge and an inexpert jury can understand it. Three-quarters of a barrister's success in court is usually based on the very painstaking preparation and the rest on practical experience. Barristers are experts on the laws of evidence, the rules of court procedure, the techniques of cross examination, and making legal submissions, and can 'manipulate' them to great advantage.

The Bar is a small profession: in 1995 there were 8,576 barristers in independent practice in England and Wales (362 practising members of the Bar in Scotland). About 1,000 a year take the vocational training stage but not all are called and go on to practise as barristers. At least 70% practise in London. Although there has been considerable modernisation of the rules of the Bar, the Bar fiercely guards its centuries-old ethos of independence. Young barristers, once through their pupillage, must find a 'seat' in barristers' chambers (offices), mostly sited near the senior courts in any town or city. They may set up practice with three years' experience with someone else if the other barrister has five years' experience.

Although barristers share chambers and the services of clerks, they are not partners – each is self-employed. Even when they find chambers there is no guaranteed income. Barristers are dependent on work coming in from solicitors and other professionals with direct access. Until they have established a reputation this can be slow to build up for young barristers, so they must rely on the barristers' clerk or practice manager to sell their services to professional clients and to pass on work from other barristers in chambers who have too much to do. They may also 'devil' (do work on an opinion for part of the fee), or undertake minor work in magistrates' or other lower courts. These 'minor' cases may be between landlord and tenant, hire purchase, road traffic and matrimonial disputes. In the crown court experience is gained in prosecuting or defending or making pleas in mitigation in a wide variety of criminal cases.

Around 15 years' experience at the Bar are needed before a barrister can apply to the Lord Chancellor to become a Queen's Counsel – called 'taking silk'. Once established, a QC wears a silk gown in court instead of the 'stuff' gowns worn by juniors. QCs are usually briefed to take the more difficult and complex cases. Not all 'juniors' decide to do this, although junior counsel of sufficient experience may (and frequently do) take up judicial office. A QC may take up judicial office as a circuit judge, stipendiary magistrate, chairman of a tribunal or possibly go on to become a High Court judge.

Recruitment and entry

All entrants to the bar are now graduates. They must complete required training before they can practise. There is no guarantee that fully-qualified barristers will be kept on by the chambers where they have trained.

Lawyers need to be reasonably intelligent (law exams are tough, and take memory and endurance), logical and very clear thinking. They need the kind of mind that can be trained to think analytically and factually, to be able to find facts and extract what is important from a mass of data. They must be able to absorb and understand all kinds of information easily (and equally to forget it again when the case is over). They have to be precise and accurate with words.

Most lawyers should be good at interviewing and 'handling' people (in an office or in court), in getting the necessary information from them, at assessing them and what they are saying, and able to make reasonable guesses at what is below the surface. High Court barristers must be self-confident and have the skills needed to perform well in court.

Qualifications and training

Prospective barristers must first be admitted as a student member of one of the Inns of Court (which originated as medieval 'colleges') – Lincoln's Inn, Inner Temple, Middle Temple or Gray's Inn – which are all in London.

The minimum entry requirement is a first degree in any subject with, at least, second-class honours (with very limited exceptions). Graduates in disciplines other than law must complete the academic-stage Common Professional Examination (CPE) via a full-time, one-year course common to both the Law Society and the Bar. The CPE is offered at an increasing number of higher education institutions.

There are some mixed law degree courses which do not include all the necessary core subjects. Students completing such courses may be required to take examinations in the subjects not studied before beginning the vocational stage. There are no NVQ/SVQs available or relevant. *See* STUDYING LAW *below*.

Only members of the Inns of Court can practise as barristers in England and Wales. To be 'called to the Bar' students should keep dining terms, i.e. attend 18 dinners in term, with a maximum of six per term. Students must also keep four further terms during pupillage.

The academic stage covers the 'core' subjects, i.e. law of contract and of tort, criminal and land law, constitutional and administrative law, equity and trusts. European law is incorporated throughout the other subjects. Human Rights Law is another professional and academic core subject which is being included within the curriculum.

At the vocational stage, those intending to practise at the Bar of England and Wales must undertake the skills-based vocational training course at the Inns of Court School of Law. Students take seven practical subjects on which they are continually assessed. Those not intending to practise at the Bar take an alternative course, offered at a variety of institutions, leading to the Bar finals examination.

There are approximately 1,100 places at the Inns of Court School of Law for the vocational course in 1995/96 and a similar number will be available in 1996/97. From September 1997 it is expected that the Bar Vocational Course (BVC) will be available at certain other validated institutions and, therefore, that the number of places available will increase. It is likely that the Bar Examination route for non-intending practitioners will eventually cease to exist. All people wishing to qualify as barristers will be required to take the BVC.

At present, individuals may be called to the Bar once they have passed the BVC. However, it is proposed that from 1997, students will have to have completed six months' pupillage before they can be called.

Once students have been called to the Bar, they must serve twelve months' pupillage, or apprenticeship, in chambers with an experienced barrister as pupil master. It is usual to split pupillage between two sets of chambers, specialising in different areas.

Pupil masters must be registered with their Inn. They monitor a check list system of tasks to be undertaken by the pupils. The pupil master must sign a certification form after the first six months to say the non-practising period has been satisfactorily completed. This form is lodged at the Bar Council who issue a 'provisional practising' certificate so that pupils may spend the next period 'standing on their feet' in court. The final certificate is issued after this stage to enable the pupil to enter independent practice as a tenant.

It is not easy for barristers to find a place in chambers for pupillage. The General Council of the Bar has approximately 750 places (1994/95), with the majority funded. The recommended Bar Council's minimum amount of funding is £3,000 per six months. In chambers with higher awards pupils may receive the same level of remuneration as articled clerks. There are also some unfunded places available. Barristers seeking pupillages must apply directly to every individual chambers. However, in 1996 the Bar Council is establishing a pupillage clearing house which should make life easier for potential pupils. Pupils can obtain information from the *Chambers, Pupillage and Awards Handbook*, published each year, which contains a list of all the chambers and their specialisations with details of pupils' awards.

Anyone wishing to qualify as a barrister should be sure that they have the necessary qualities and that the very individual lifestyle of a barrister would suit them. It is not uncommon, for example, for people to commence pupillage with debts of over £10,000.

Scotland

In Scotland, the Diploma in Legal Practice is the postgraduate course for intending solicitors and advocates after completion of the Law degree. About 72% (1995) of law graduates in Scotland go on to take the Diploma. Advocates must be admitted to the Faculty of Advocates and, in general, must undergo a period of 'devilling' or pupillage before being called to the Bar. Advocates do not practise from chambers as barristers do.

Further information

England/Wales: the General Council of the Bar, the Under-Treasurers of the individual Inns of Court. For Scotland: the Faculty of Advocates.

Solicitors

In an increasingly complex world solicitors are legal advisers for anyone who requires help with their affairs or problems, from the proverbial man or woman in the street through the small business to the major company. Mostly these will involve the law in some way, but once solicitor and client have established a working relationship, clients often use their solicitor's experience and trained objectivity as a source of general advice, counselling, and so on.

The majority of solicitors now specialise in a specific field such as: commercial property; residential property; family matters; business affairs; probate, wills etc.; personal injury; crime. Although the nature of work in private practice (a business partnership of solicitors) varies, many firms specialise and others dealing with the general range of legal work will have solicitors within the firm who are specialists.

The strictly legal work solicitors do is quite extensive. Some of it can be quite routine, some is more demanding. Until recently much of the work of the solicitor dealt with conveyancing property (houses, flats, offices, farms, factories) from seller to buyer, which meant they (or more accurately their trainee solicitors and other clerks who do most of the routine) made sure there was no problem with the title to the property, or that (for example) it was not likely to be bought or demolished by the local authority in five years' time, and draft the contract of sale, and so on. Now the range of work is more diverse and conveyancing represents a smaller proportion of work.

Solicitors draft wills, and act as executors and administrators to see that the terms of the will are carried out. They advise landlords on arrangements with tenants, and draft the lease or agreement, or advise tenants on their legal rights. They tell clients whether or not they may get compensation for faulty goods, or damages for injury in a road accident, or in an accident at work, and make claims on clients' behalf. They deal with divorce cases, especially where children's futures must be settled, property divided, and any maintenance agreed. They act for local businesses, collect debts through the courts, prepare partnership agreements, set up companies, and deal with contracts and agreements of all kinds, as well as carrying out international commercial work. Many companies rely on solicitors for advice about the conduct of their business.

Anyone faced with criminal charges, whether it is a road offence, burglary or even murder, must go to a solicitor if they are to be defended in court. Solicitors try to keep their clients out of court. They may ask for counsel's opinion just to show a client how risky, difficult, and expensive going to court may be. It is not, technically, a solicitor's role to tell a client whether or not to take action: the solicitor defines the client's position in legal terms, and explains the legal consequences of any action the client may, or may not, take. All the same, many clients will expect their solicitor to advise them. Some solicitors do a great deal of advocacy work in magistrates' and county courts.

When solicitors go to a barrister for advice, they choose someone who specialises in the particular area of the law, or who is known for defending a particular kind of case in court. Most solicitors have a working relationship with particular barristers, but may look out for a bright young barrister, who will be cheaper, for simpler cases. Whether it is a 'case for opinion' or an actual brief, it is the solicitor who must put together the relevant facts, make sure the main documents are in order, and summarise the rest. The solicitor is responsible (again, it is the trainee solicitors or paralegal assistants who normally do the work), for finding and interviewing witnesses, and collecting all the information needed by the barrister. During the case, the solicitor is the go-between between the client and counsel, and also 'wet-nurses' the client if necessary.

Outside the legal field, solicitors often advise clients on anything from whether or not it is a good time to move house, or what to do about a disagreement with an employer, to pension schemes, investment or business strategy generally. Solicitors must, though, always think of the possible legal consequences, immediate and long-term, of whatever their clients may want to do, and be prepared to advise on them.

Solicitors therefore spend quite a high proportion of their time talking to people – clients, other lawyers, officials – either in the office or on the telephone. They also have to write many letters, many of them in formal and legal terms, to clients, to other solicitors or other people against whom a client may have a claim, and to barristers. They draft a great many documents, and issue writs. They can conduct their own cases in magistrate and county courts, and usually go into other courts with counsel.

There are a great many more solicitors than barristers, almost 67,000 (1996) practising in England and Wales (an increase of 4% on the previous year), with 82% in private practice (1995). The remaining 18% are employed in commerce and industry, or in the public sector. Approximately 30% of practising solicitors are women (1995), an increase of 198% since 1985. This figure is set to increase still further as in 1994 54% of applicants for university first degree law courses were women. In Scotland there are 7,800 solicitors, of whom 5,883 are in private practice.

Solicitors' practices vary greatly in type and size. There is nothing to prevent solicitors setting up in practice on their own, but most go into partnership eventually (starting as assistants/employees in other practices). 46% of private practice firms are located in London and the South East. Rural practices are generally quite small, with at most five or six partners, but some large firms in the City of London, for example, have over 100 partners, many more practising solicitors, and a total staff of thousands. In small towns, in rural areas, practices generally accept any kind of work that clients bring in, although only a proportion of practices will deal with commercial work, while others specialise more in conveyancing, or road cases.

In larger centres, and especially in London, firms – and individual solicitors – increasingly specialise. In the City there are large firms most of whose clients are companies, and they may specialise in forming and re-forming companies, issuing stocks, drafting contracts, and so on. Other firms specialise in trust work, or in working for trusts, companies or families with large property holdings and who must have continuous access to legal assistance on estate duties, taxation, conveyancing. Some firms specialise in work for publishers, or writers and entertainers. In most practices of any size, individual partners and their assistants specialise – in litigation work, for example. Younger solicitors may have to move from firm to firm to gain experience, or for a chance to become a partner.

Work overseas

There are increasing opportunities for solicitors to work abroad or with organisations from other countries. For example in Brussels some firms of solicitors have offices so that they may provide a service to clients whose interests are affected directly by EC law. Solicitors from the UK are also employed by the United Nations in New York, the Commission of the European Community in Brussels and in Commonwealth countries where the English common law system is in use. There may be practical difficulties involved in working overseas where a UK legal qualification may not be relevant to the law and business practices of a country. However, anyone qualified and proficient in at least one other language should have more opportunity to secure a post abroad.

Recruitment and entry

See under BARRISTERS AND ADVOCATES *above*.

Qualifications and training

The professional bodies for solicitors are the Law Society of England and Wales, and the Law Society of Scotland.

Over 90% of new solicitors are now graduates and they must complete the required training before they can practise. There is no guarantee that fully qualified solicitors will be kept on by the practice where they have trained.

Non-graduates in England and Wales wishing to qualify as solicitors can do so only after qualifying as a Legal Executive (*see* LEGAL EXECUTIVES *below*), though this is sometimes waived in exceptional circumstances for those over 25 who can demonstrate considerable relevant experience or exceptional ability. Holders of the Justices' Clerks' Assistants Diploma may also go on to qualify as solicitors.

The Common Professional Examination

The 20% of solicitors who qualify after taking a degree in a subject other than law complete the Common Professional Examination (CPE). Law graduates who have not passed degree papers in any of the subjects set for the CPE must take the CPE equivalent. Full-time courses preparing for the CPE are given by the College of Law (in Guildford, London, York and Chester) and at many universities where students can study the subjects alongside law-degree students, on a full- or part-time basis.

The Legal Practice Course

This new course, which was introduced in 1993, replaced the old Law Society Finals Examinations and is more skills-based. The completion of the Common Professional Examination or a qualifying law degree is still the qualifying requirement.

See also STUDYING LAW *below*.

The training contract

Graduates must also complete an uninterrupted period of two years' service under a training contract (formerly articles of training). It is usual for training in private practice in larger firms to be split into 'four seats', with each spent in a different department giving experience of the possible areas of specialisation. Training contracts can also be served with other organisations including the Crown Prosecution Service, other central government departments and local authorities.

Information about firms and organisations offering training can be found in *PROSPECTS Legal* (incorporating ROSET/Register of Solicitors Employing Trainees) published by the CSU (Higher Education Careers Central Services Unit).

The professional skills course

This course is studied by all trainees during the practical stage of training (the training contract), or following the Legal Practice Course. The course lasts twenty days on a full-time basis, but it may be possible to study on a modular basis over a longer period.

Scotland

In Scotland, solicitors enter a traineeship on completion of the Diploma in Legal Practice which lasts two years, but only non-graduates have to pass the Law Society of Scotland's examinations; 97% (1995) of those who qualify do so by taking a law degree at a Scottish university or an arts degree followed by a law degree, then the Diploma in Legal Practice. This is the postgraduate course for intending solicitors and advocates. About 72% (1995) of law graduates in Scotland go on to take the Diploma.

Further information

England/Wales: the Law Society, and the Institute of Legal Executives. For Scotland: the Law Society of Scotland (Department of Legal Education).

Studying law

Law is both a vocational subject and a rigorous academic training, valuable as the basis for a wide range of legal and non-legal careers. It is not necessary to plan to be a lawyer to choose to read law at university – in fact the output of law graduates is now certainly too great for the profession to absorb.

However, the legal profession itself is now almost entirely graduate. Theoretically, it is not necessary to have a law degree, but in practice competition for training places, for both the Bar and in the larger solicitors' offices, is now so great that a law degree is a strong advantage.

Law is no longer practised, or studied, as a series of rules operated in isolation from life around it, but is examined in its social and economic setting, particularly in its relation to the business world on the one hand and to the community on the other. Law is now defined as a social phenomenon which both affects and is affected by society and what goes on within it, and is influenced by, and influences, political thinking. The law is influenced by thinking in, for example, psychology, sociology, and even criminology. The law is more complex than it ever was, and has greater problems to solve.

Funding for law studies

The Law Society is currently (1996) monitoring the situation regarding funding for law studies. Students may be eligible for local authority discretionary awards, Career Development Loans or even charities/grant-making trusts. There is a Law Society bursary scheme limited to awards for CPE, the Postgraduate Diploma in Law and the Legal Practice Course. The fund in total, however, is very limited and there are both competitive and hardship criteria which must be applied. A number of firms will sponsor students, mainly those applying for Legal Practice courses or those intending to take the CPE or Postgraduate Diploma in Law. Prospective students should contact university or college careers service for details of sponsorship.

Law degrees

Law is studied mainly on courses for first and higher degrees, although it is an element in most business-related courses at all levels. Most solicitors (64% in 1995) qualify by taking a law degree, which is the fastest way – six years – to become a solicitor.

A first degree in law is designed to be more than a straightforward vocational training, although the demands of the profession do mean that courses are mostly very specialised – at least in England and Wales. Law degrees in Scotland are usually more broadly based but do not train in English law. Law degrees study the law in its historical and social context and give a rigorous training in logical and analytical reasoning.

'Core' subjects on law degree courses are now (1995) known as 'the seven foundations of legal knowledge' and include European Union law and compulsory legal research as well as contract, tort, equity and trusts, criminal law, land law, and constitutional and administrative law. The core studies are needed for the pre-vocational stage of legal training – the Common Professional Examination (CPE). If any of the 'core' subjects are left out, a prospective lawyer would get exemptions for the ones passed and permission to study externally. All courses also cover the English, or Scottish, legal system (they have to differentiate between Scottish law and the law of England and Wales, since they are separate and quite different).

For the rest of the course, most law schools allow students a fairly wide choice of topics, but usually they are all legal. Some courses are still very traditional (at some institutions, for example, Roman law is still compulsory), and stay with more conventional subjects, like conflict of laws, equity and trust, family law, labour law, jurisprudence, legal history, procedure and evidence, revenue (tax) law, and succession. A high proportion, though, have moved into newer areas of legal concern – EC law, for example, and developing areas of legal practice, such as welfare law, consumer law, criminology, as well as socio-legal studies, and the law and medicine. Business and company law is another traditional area of study, and there are a few courses which offer the option to specialise.

The legal complexities of the European Community, and the need to have lawyers who can cope with French, German, Italian, or Spanish law and legal procedures, have resulted in a number of courses training graduates to work in English, EC, and French, German, Italian or Spanish law, teaching them also the language. African and Asian law can be studied at a small number of schools.

It is possible to study law with one or two other subjects at many institutions, although this does make it more difficult to qualify for the profession. Law may also be studied on several part-time courses.

Law schools

English/Welsh law: there are over 70 higher education institutions in England and Wales offering first degree full-time courses in law, and nearly 30 offering part-time degrees. The list of qualifying law degrees can be obtained from the Law Society.

Scottish law: Aberdeen; Dundee (includes English law); Dundee IT; Edinburgh (includes English law); Glasgow; Glasgow Caledonian; Napier; Robert Gordon; Stirling; Strathclyde (includes English law).

Northern Ireland legal system: Belfast, Dublin, Ulster.

Entry: no specific A-level/H grade subjects are named; however, three good passes (grade C or above) are required, as competition for places is intense. Science A-levels are as acceptable as arts subjects. A-level Law is rarely an advantage. An Advanced GNVQ in Business or Science may be acceptable, particularly if at Distinction.

'First destination' statistics for law graduates, 1994:

total graduating	*4,692*
destination unknown	342
overseas students	888
research, etc.	355
law exams	2,345
other training	85
believed unemployed 31 December	112
temporary work	90
permanent UK work	533
employers:	
accountancy	67
banking/insurance	54
other commerce	117
local government	35
industry	52
Civil Service	23
higher/further education	21
Armed Forces	12
functions:	
financial work	111
legal work	91
admin/operational management	67
personnel/social, etc.	58
marketing, etc.	43
management services	15
information	16
creative	19

Law graduates have a very low unemployment rate of under 5%.

Other opportunities for qualified lawyers

Although the great majority of qualified barristers and solicitors spend most of their working lives in private practice, there are alternatives:

Academic law

The academic lawyer is usually a rather different breed from the practising barrister or solicitor, and it is rare to combine the two. Academic lawyers usually combine teaching students with research and analytical and speculative writing about the law. They tend to live on a more theoretical and idealistic (about the law) plane than practitioners, although some do specialise in applications of the law. There has been a considerable increase in the number of institutions offering law courses and law is taught in over 70 institutions. *See also* EDUCATION AND TEACHING.

The Civil Service

The Civil Service employs about 2,000 lawyers in the CROWN PROSECUTION SERVICE (*see below*) and several hundreds in other departments. Work in the Civil Service involves a variety of responsibilities from advising ministers, implementing government decisions and drafting laws, as well as prosecuting those who have contravened regulations. *See also* CENTRAL GOVERNMENT.

Crown Prosecution Service

Since 1986 the Crown Prosecution Service (CPS) has been responsible for prosecuting cases in the Magistrates' Courts and briefing a barrister to present the cases referred to Crown Court. Crown Prosecutors are solicitors or barristers who work together in teams covering a geographical area.

There are 1.5 million cases received each year, and of those proceeded with in the Magistrates' Courts 97.5% result in a conviction. It is the police who make the decision to charge and it is the Crown Prosecutor's responsibility to decide whether or not to prosecute by reviewing the facts of the case against the relevant points of law to check if the case will stand. Crown Prosecutors usually spend up to four days a week in court and the rest of the time is spent in administration and the preparation of court papers.

The CPS is part of the Civil Service under the direction of the Director of Public Prosecutions. It is the biggest single employer of lawyers in England and Wales (1994) and employs over 1,600 solicitors, about 640 barristers and 4,000 administrative staff (1996).

To be appointed to the CPS an applicant must be a Commonwealth citizen, a British protected person or a citizen of the Republic of Ireland.

Qualifications and training

Trainee solicitors are offered a two-year training contract. The CPS training covers two topics required by the Law Society regulations: criminal litigation and magisterial law. In order to gain as broad an education as is reasonably practical, sabbatical periods of between six and twelve months are spent in the legal sections of other government departments, local authorities, private practice or industry. Pupil barristers spend their first six (non-practising) months in a set of chambers specialising in civil law. Their second six (practising) months are spent within the CPS supervised by an experienced advocate/pupil master. On completion of training or pupillage contract, qualified lawyers may be offered a post as a Crown Prosecutor.

Procurators Fiscal

Procurators Fiscal are responsible in Scotland for initiating criminal court proceedings. The police report details of alleged crimes to the local Fiscal who then uses discretion whether to prosecute, subject to the direction and control of the Lord Advocate and Crown Office. Although they have to be in court frequently, much of their time is also spent interviewing people and reviewing information gathered by the police during a criminal investigation. Procurators Fiscal are the representatives of the Lord Advocate and are the agents of the Crown Office. They are assisted by Procurator Fiscal Deputes (or legal assistants). They are civil servants and are usually solicitors.

Further information

Crown Prosecution Service. For Scotland: Crown Office.

Community legal services

Since the first law centre opened in 1976 until the mid-1980s over 55 were set up in large towns and cities. With funding problems many have now closed and others are under constant threat of closure. Funding sources include grants from the local authority, the Department of the Environment or the Lord Chancellor's Department.

They vary in their policies, but generally provide a free legal service in areas under-served by solicitors' practices and, therefore by definition, poorer places. Many give advice and assistance also on the blurred edges of the law: many cases deal with consumer problems, problems with landlords, employment and social security difficulties, youngsters who have clashed with the police, and queries on, for instance, a gas bill. Most law centres are run as workers' co-operatives, and all 'employees', including qualified barristers, solicitors and social workers, take turns at being, for instance, the receptionist, and take home the same pay.

The courts

All High Court judges, and recorders, were originally barristers (some continue to practise after appointment, to e.g. a Crown Court circuit, and so may be part-time), and have usually been QCs. Solicitors are eligible for the lower courts. Most judges work in one type of court and at present each court or division has a separate judiciary. In 1996 the judiciary consisted of the 12 Law Lords, 32 Lord Justices – Court of Appeal, 96 High Court judges, 518 Circuit judges and 8 official referees, 6 High Court Registrars, 11 Chancery and Taxing Masters and 19 Family Division District Judges (formerly known as Registrars). Over 1,200 recorders and assistant recorders sit on a part-time basis in the Crown and County Courts and 78 are in training.

Judges need appropriate experience – for example to qualify as a Lord Justice of Appeal or Lord Chief Justice, Master of the Rolls or President of the Family Division it is necessary either to be a High Court judge or to have had at least 15 years' experience at the bar. A High Court or Circuit judge must have been a barrister for at least ten years or a recorder for at least five, while recorders need the same length of service as a barrister or solicitor. However, there is no set pattern of promotion, and vacancies in the superior courts are filled more often from the bar than from judges in the lower courts.

The Supreme Court is administered by law officers, called masters and registrars. The masters of the Queen's bench division, for example, exercise the authority of judges in chambers, issue directions on points of practice, assess damages in certain cases, and supervise the court's central office, where the clerical work is done, the masters acting in turn as 'practice master'. The four masters of the chancery division make interlocutory orders and take accounts under the direction of judges, and are assisted by registrars. The family division has 19 District Judges who, for instance, exercise the authority and jurisdiction of the court in divorce, wardship of minors and so on. Qualifications for these posts vary, but they usually go to experienced barristers and solicitors.

The supreme court and the county courts are administered by a unified court service under the Lord Chancellor's department (*see* CENTRAL GOVERNMENT). The senior officer for each circuit is the circuit administrator, with court administrators for each sub-area. They arrange the business of the courts and see that the right number of judges and recorders are there when needed.

Bodies like the Criminal Injuries Board and the tribunals usually have chairmen/women and at least some other members with legal qualifications and experience.

In Scotland, each Sheriffdom has a Sheriff-Principal and a number of Sheriffs who act as judges. The Lord Justice-General and Lord Justice-Clerk, and the 25 Lords Commissioner of Justiciary (who are also judges of the civil Court of Session) are the judges in the High Court.

Other posts for which both barristers and solicitors qualify include 'stipendiary' magistrates who are mainly stationed in the Inner London magistrates' courts: they must have seven years' legal experience.

Magistrates' courts

There are 30,000 active lay justices in England and Wales. They normally sit in threes. The Lay magistracy is open to almost everyone in the age group between 27 and 60 years of age. The Lord Chancellor's policy is for each bench to reflect broadly the community it serves.

Justices' clerks

All other magistrates' courts are staffed by unpaid 'justices of the peace' who do not need legal qualifications, but have the support of a justices' clerk, who is a qualified barrister or solicitor with at least five years' experience. There are approximately 200 of them. Justices' clerks advise magistrates on points of law, see that proper procedure is followed, arrange court lists, and see that administrative work (e.g. preparing summonses and warrants, collecting fines, dealing with licences to sell alcoholic drinks) is done. Their offices employ between two and fifty assistants, who may be completing articles or are otherwise training.

Justices' chief executives

The administration of magistrates' courts is the responsibility of 'magistrates' courts committees' of unpaid magistrates. In each magistrates' courts committee area there is a justices' chief executive (JCE) who is the paid head of service for the area. JCEs have the same qualifications as justices' clerks and are responsible for acting as clerk to the committee and for carrying on the day-to-day administration of the magistrates' courts in the area. In some areas the JCE is also a justices' clerk.

Industry and commerce

The largest firms usually have their own legal departments staffed by qualified barristers and/or solicitors. These firms need instant 'on-the-spot' legal services, and lawyers who are closely involved in the company's affairs, understand the background and therefore do not need special briefing. The amount of UK and EC legislation affecting companies has increased sharply – contract law has been heavily affected by the EC, and companies have to cope with current legislation on, for instance, employment protection, sex and race discrimination, consumer protection and credit, health and safety, banking registration, food and drugs – all extremely complex.

Lawyers in business firms spend most of their time on advisory work, and on contracts. Barristers employed by a company may not also practise at the Bar. They have to balance their trained caution against the firm's need for fast and firm decisiveness. The number of lawyers employed in industry and commerce has been rising steadily, and they probably number several thousand, but few companies recruit young solicitors or barristers to serve articles or pupillage, most preferring experienced people.

Lawyers can and are promoted to management and/or become, e.g. company secretary. There were approximately 3,000 solicitors employed in industry and commerce in 1995.

Local government

Most of the services that local authorities provide for their communities are the result of government legislation – which either delegates services to local authorities (for instance education, planning and housing, social services, refuse collecting and library services) or expects them to see that other people do what the law says, on environmental health or consumer protection. Complex laws dictate how much money local authorities can spend, and how they must account for it, and ratepayers can challenge expenditure in the courts.

Local authorities can write their own by-laws. Local authorities must also work within the common law – on landlord and tenant, on contracts, and on employment protection or race or sex discrimination, for instance. Most laws which affect local government are complex, and are frequently amended.

Local authority lawyers must see that the council always acts within the law and translate the effects of new legislation for council members, so there is a great deal of advisory work. There is also plenty of court work – recovering payments, enforcing laws, defending a council against claims. Solicitors do all their council's conveyancing – on sales and purchases of land, leases (for e.g. shops), licences, and mortgages. Some local authority work is contracted out to private practice. Lawyers also advise on and help to draft minutes, council resolutions, orders, notices, and so on, making sure there are no legal loopholes.

Local authorities employ several thousand lawyers, most of whom are solicitors (2,600 in 1995), although a number of 'county solicitor' posts will be filled by barristers. A high proportion of senior administrative posts (e.g. chief executive) also go to solicitors. It is usual to follow solicitors' training contracts with a local authority.

See also LOCAL GOVERNMENT.

Other legal work

Legal executives – legal accountants – law costs draftsmen – barristers' clerks/practice managers – licensed conveyancers–court work

Barristers and solicitors are the experts of the legal world, and depend on a large army of support staff, many of whom also have considerable expertise. Legal executives and barristers' clerks, together with the courts' staff, actually make the cumbersome machinery of the law work. They are both administrators and experts in the day-to-day mechanics of the law. Contact between solicitors' offices and between solicitors and barristers is mostly via the clerks, who form a tight network of their own, and sort out many problems unofficially.

The policy of increasing competition for professional work is also increasing the range of quasi-legal work.

Legal executives

Legal executives are qualified lawyers who specialise in a particular area of law. There are over 22,000 legal executives and trainee legal executives (1996), who do most of the administrative and practical work in a solicitor's office in private practice and in legal departments in local government and the Civil Service.

Although the work varies from firm to firm, experienced legal executives can gain considerable responsibility. This is especially so for the great mass of practical, detailed and technical work – conveyancing, probate for wills, and preparing a case for court.

The legal executive, more often than not, actually issues writs, drafts statements, administers oaths, gathers together the material needed for an affidavit, collects documents, takes out summonses, checks titles to deeds, and so on. The day-to-day work is similar to that of many solicitors.

In all but the smallest practice or office, legal executives usually specialise – in wills and probate work, civil or criminal litigation, conveyancing, company formation or family law. They may manage the office or department of staff, including other legal executives and trainee solicitors, and deal with accounts. Legal executives can go on to become solicitors.

Qualifications and training

Legal executives take the examinations of the Institute of Legal Executives, which has the support of the Law Society. Minimum entry qualifications are either four GCSE/SCEs A–C/1–3, or equivalent qualifications. GNVQ at intermediate or advanced level is acceptable, provided a communication skills element is included. Subjects must include English, and 'practical' subjects are not accepted. There are no age restrictions and there is special provision for mature students aged 21 years or over.

The Institute sets a two-part examination for membership. Part I introduces the legal system and covers elementary law and practice, with a practical approach. Students normally study part-time over two years at one of over 120 colleges, or by correspondence course, but full-time study is possible. Part I papers are set at A-level standard. Part II (subject-for-subject exemptions for law graduates) requires candidates to take three 'substantive' law subjects, plus a specialist procedural paper. The law papers are set at degree level.

Fellows of the Institute must have successfully completed the Membership examination, have five years' qualifying employment in a legal office, and be over 25. There is a special route to qualification as a solicitor reserved for Member Fellows of the Institute. Their examination counts towards the academic stage of a solicitor's training. Fellows of the Institute are normally exempt from the Training Contract.

Legal accountants

The Institute of Legal Executives offers a scheme of training and qualification for finance staff employed in solicitors' offices. Students must normally have four passes at GCSE. A two-part Legal Accounts Examination is set – Part I covers general accounting principles and specialised aspects of solicitors' accounts, and legal background. Part II deals with four specialist financial/legal subjects. Completion of the exams gives accountancy membership of ILEX; at least five years' legal-accountancy experience entitles members to call themselves legal accountants.

Legal secretarial work

See in ADMINISTRATION, BUSINESS MANAGEMENT AND OFFICE WORK.

Further information

The Institute of Legal Executives.

Law costs draftsmen

Law costs draftsmen (draftsman is a generic term that includes men and women) are specialists in the field of legal costs in all areas of the law. There are many rules and regulations making the preparation of bills of costs time-consuming for practising lawyers. Law costs draftsmen are often appointed to deal with the processes involved in the quantification and justification of legal costs, thus leaving legal practitioners free to use their time more profitably.

There are three main areas of legal costs in which law costs draftsmen may become involved. Solicitors and own client costs (the costs a solicitor charges his or her client): a law costs draftsman may be instructed in the preparation of detailed bills to lodge at court and subsequently attend to argue the case (or to argue against costs claimed by another solicitor). Legal aid costs: the assessment is usually dealt with without attendance at court. Costs inter partes (payable to the successful party by the unsuccessful party): a detailed bill of costs is prepared and lodged. A hearing is appointed before a taxing officer.

Law costs draftsmen may be employed by firms of law costs draftsmen, firms of solicitors, government departments, local authorities or other legal departments. Many are also self-employed.

Recruitment and entry

The usual method of entry to the profession is via a solicitor's office where a law costs draftsman gains experience and knowledge of the law as well as of legal procedures.

Qualifications and training

Law costs draftsmen can take the examinations of the Association of Law Costs Draftsmen (ACLD). Membership of the ACLD is open to men and women who are employed as full-time costs draftsmen, dealing predominantly with the preparation and taxation (assessment) of legal costs. Normally entry is as a student member regardless of experience. Students follow a course of study, the content of which depends on the experience already gained in the profession, and sit the examination within five years. Experienced costs draftsmen can apply to sit the examination earlier. Successful completion of the examination and further employment for a continuous period of five years give a student the right to be an Associate Member of the ACLD. An Associate qualifies as a Fellow upon successful completion of a written examination and with eight years in practice.

Barristers' clerks/practice managers

A barristers' clerk is a member of one of the smallest professions. There are approximately 350 barristers' chambers in London and the provinces (1995), most of which are managed and administered by barristers' clerks. The success of the chambers can depend on them. The clerk or practice manager not only sees that the chambers are properly and efficiently managed, and so is effectively the office manager, but also (mostly) decides which briefs to accept, which of the barristers should have which brief, and negotiates the fees to be paid by solicitors and other professional intermediaries. The clerk can help to get a young barrister started by offering briefs to them. The senior clerk/practice manager is an influential member of chambers, has a say in the choice of barristers to join the chambers, and frequently earns more than the barristers. Juniors run errands, make tea, carry robes and books, as they learn. Some senior clerks still work on a the basis of a percentage of the fees earned but increasingly practice managers are now salaried, perhaps receiving a percentage of the fees as a bonus.

Competition for posts – there are only about 280 senior clerks in England and Wales – is considerable. There is no shortened route to becoming a barristers' clerk.

Qualifications and training

Most junior clerks are school-leavers with a good educational background. If they intend to qualify they must have a minimum of four GCSEs grades A–C, or equivalent. The training is mainly on-the-job with part-time study for the BTEC Diploma in Business and Finance.

Further information

The Institute of Barristers' Clerks.

Licensed conveyancers

All conveyancing – essentially the legal processes involved in transferring buildings and/or land from one owner to another and dealing with the financial transactions – was the sole responsibility of solicitors until 1987.

Under current legislation, it is now possible for other people to become conveyancers, known as licensed conveyancers. Banks, building societies (especially those providing mortgages), property developers and solicitors employ licensed conveyancers. Many licensed conveyancers practise on their own or in partnership. Once the Council for Licensed Conveyancers' examinations have been successfully completed and the practical training requirements undertaken, applicants may apply for a limited licence which would permit them to offer conveyancing services only as employed people. Once they have held a limited licence for a period of three years, they may then apply for a full licence, which permits them to offer conveyancing services directly to the public as the sole principal or as a partner in a firm of licensed conveyancers.

Qualifications and training

Anyone wishing to become a conveyancer must meet the training requirements of the Council for Licensed Conveyancers. The Council requires at least four GCSE passes, or equivalent, in English language and three other approved subjects at grades A, B or C. However, mature students over 25 may be accepted with relevant practical experience only.

The Council's examinations are in two parts – Foundation and Finals. The Foundation comprises three modules: module 1 – office practice and procedure; module 2 – conveyancing practice and procedure, both assessed assignments; module 3 – land law and law of contract. The Final examinations comprise three subjects: conveyancing law and practice, landlord and tenant, and accounts. Tuition is available on a part-time basis at a number of colleges and universities throughout the country, and the correspondence course is available direct from the Council for Licensed Conveyancers.

Candidates must also complete two years' practical experience in conveyancing with a licensed conveyancer or solicitor who is entitled to practise as a sole principal, or within a conveyancing department of a bank, building society, property developer or local authority. This can be achieved part-time or full-time before, after or while studying for the examinations.

Further information

The Council for Licensed Conveyancers.

Court work

Every court has to be staffed, and in the largest court houses, where up to 15 courts may be held at one time, the administration may employ up to 200 people.

In England and Wales, the senior staff who advise magistrates (justices and court clerks) are mostly qualified barristers and solicitors, or are partly qualified. Justices Clerks' Assistants have their own qualifications which can lead on to training to become a solicitor.

All courts employ office administrators and clerical/secretarial staff. They get all the papers on each case ready for the court, and clear the paper work after a decision has been made, answer queries from the public, and deal with fines (some courts have special accounts staff).

Civil and Crown Court staff are civil servants and part of the Lord Chancellor's Department. Unlike the Magistrates' Court the Chief Clerk does not have to be legally qualified, but is a higher or senior executive officer of the Civil Service. There are some exceptions, for instance at the Central Criminal Court. Many court clerks are qualified lawyers, although this is not a requirement for the post.

Recruitment and entry

In Magistrates' Courts junior staff are generally expected to have a GCSE or equivalent pass in English, although most have considerably more. Some posts need experience or qualifications, in e.g. accounts, computing, office administration. For County and Crown Courts, staff must have the relevant qualifications for administrative assistant, administrative officer or executive officer entry to the Civil Service. Vacancies are advertised at job centres and in the local press.

In Scotland, the Scottish Courts Administration is the government department responsible for administering the Supreme and Sheriff Courts, and the District Courts.

Further information

The Court Service, the Lord Chancellor's Department, local Crown or County Court or Probate Registry. In Scotland: Scottish Courts Administration

Patent work

Background – European Patent Office – patent agents – trade mark agents – patent examiners – patent officers

Background

The patent system gives a legal, 21-year monopoly on the use of a new invention, so that the patent owner gains some financial return on a new process or product, but in return the patent has to be published.

Rapid technological advance, intensifying world competition to be first in the field, and the difficulty of meeting everyone's needs in legislation make the patent system hard to operate and produces great tensions, understandable when high profits may be at stake. Patents are expensive; a simple, collapsible home work bench cost £500,000 in world patents and court actions in only six years. The system is inevitably complex and time consuming – it can take four-and-a-half years before a patent is granted. Early publication of a patent means many firms and inventors think they are giving competitors time to make the few design changes necessary to get round a patent. In electronics, innovation is now so fast and new developments spread so quickly that many manufacturers have given up patenting.

European Patent Office

Traditionally, patents were granted on a national, country-by-country basis, and every invention has, in the past, required a separate patent for each country, which meant multiple applications, different specifications, and language problems. However, owners of inventions normally wish to have their patent protected not only in the UK but also in other countries. The patent profession has therefore introduced international systems. The European Patent Convention treaty (signed in 1973 by 14 countries including the UK), set up a European Patent Office (EPO) which makes it possible to obtain patent coverage via a single application (and therefore a single search) and a single patent grant. The patentee decides how many countries to cover with one application, but it is at present an alternative system, existing side by side with national procedures. The headquarters of the European Patent Office is in Munich, with a branch office in the Hague and sub-offices in Berlin and Vienna. There are 17 member states at present including all the European Union states. The European patent system provides an alternative route to obtaining patent protection in the EPO member states.

European patent applications may be made in any one of the three official languages – English, French and German. Over half the applications to Munich are in the English language. UK patent agents now appear to have a larger share of European work than might have been expected because the use of English as the business language ensures that clients such as the Japanese and Americans use British agents rather than German or French. The number of European patent applications made in 1994 was 57,815, only slightly above the 1993 level. The number granted was 42,001.

At the end of 1994 there were 3,717 people employed by the EPO, of whom about 1,900 were technical examining staff. The European Patent Convention allowed certain qualified practitioners to represent clients before the EPO. There are now (1995) 5,500 European patent attorneys who are entitled to practise before the EPO. Most chartered patent attorneys are European patent attorneys.

Qualifications and training

The minimum qualifications required for a post as a technical examiner is an honours degree (first or second class) in science or engineering, plus a basic knowledge of French and German.

European patent attorneys need a university-level scientific or technical qualification (or equivalent), together with a minimum of three years' work experience under supervision, and success in the European Qualifying Examination. There are university and other courses available for the training of candidates for the examination. The European Patent Institute, the professional body set up as a result of the European Patent Convention, has details.

Patent agents

Patent agents are the experts who prepare and write the very detailed descriptions, called specifications, which form the basis of all applications for patents, registered designs and trademarks, and which must be submitted to show that an invention is completely new. Inventors can, of course, make their own applications, but the advantage of using a professional expert means few do.

Specifications are legal documents but the content is scientific and technological. They must be drafted in legal terms, but must be clear, concise and exact, leaving no loopholes or ambiguities and describing the invention in a way that gives the maximum possible protection. They must stand up to testing in court if necessary. In addition to drawing up the specifications, patent agents must also negotiate with and answer any objections to claims by the Patent Office examiners (*see below*) and possibly re-draft the specification.

British patent agents organise and supervise patent applications for as many countries as the client wants. They make direct application to the British and, if qualified to do so, the European Patent Office too. For other countries they work through local patent agents, who in turn ask British agents to make an application for them here. The local agent, whether British or foreign, has to revise specifications to meet local patent law, and translate them. British patent agents have to learn a great deal about patent law and procedures in a widening range of countries, since there is increasing emphasis on patenting on an international scale.

Most patent agents specialise to some extent, usually in a broad subject area like mechanical engineering or chemical processes.

Patent agents must make searches through patent records, advise clients on the chances of getting a patent, and whether it is worthwhile, and on the validity and risk of infringement of other people's patents. They advise on the terms of licensing agreements and are involved when patents are contested or there is an alleged infringement.

The work is mostly office and desk based, but a proportion of all patent agents' time is spent discussing and negotiating, both the clients and technical staff, and with officials. They may have to brief lawyers, and appear in court as expert witnesses. Young patent agents spend a high proportion of their time on patent searches.

It is a small profession and there are still only 1,350 currently fully qualified agents. Just over half are employed in private practice, offering their services to any company or individual needing advice in any of the areas of intellectual property, and the remainder work for industrial patent departments, or for the Ministry of Defence.

Most patent agents work in London, or other industrial centres, but some London firms have moved out into the home counties and the south coast towns. There are increasing opportunities to work abroad, especially in Europe.

Legislation permits anyone to practise in the field, but not to call themselves patent agents or registered trade mark agents unless they are registered.

Trade mark agents

There are about 500 people (1995) actively involved in trade mark work. A trade mark agent acts on behalf of and advises businesses primarily in matters relating to the protection of trade mark rights. The agent has to be an expert in trade mark law and practice in Britain and throughout the world. The majority of trade mark agents are also patent agents, approximately one-third are trade mark agents without the patent agency qualifications and a minority are solicitors. Since 1994 trade mark agents have been able to enter into partnership with patent agents, giving them similar career prospects to those of patent agents.

Firms of patent agents often employ specialist trade mark agents dealing with the protection and registration of related intellectual or industrial property rights such as designs, industrial copyright and trade marks. This is a difficult field, as once a trade mark is approved it may be renewed indefinitely. Registered designs are renewable five-yearly up to a maximum of twenty-five years. The product or service seeking registration has to be shown to be distinguishable from others. To register a trade mark there are many complex cases on which the case law is established. It is necessary to be highly skilled in presenting an argument to secure registration for borderline cases. Trade mark agents work in private practice (with trade mark or patent firms) or in large companies which have enough trade mark interests to need an agent to deal with them.

Recruitment and entry

For patent agents, entry is to a technical assistant post in a private practice, an industrial organisation or government department. Although organisations do advertise their technical assistant posts with careers advisory services and the national press, many recruit through speculative applications.

Normal entry is via a degree (usually first or second class honours) in science, engineering or a technological subject. This is a pre-requirement for becoming a European Patent Attorney (*see above*). The British Institute suggests that a broadly based and not too specialised course is most suitable – and it is now virtually impossible to start with the official minimum of five GCSE (or equivalent) passes and physics and chemistry A levels. Languages are increasingly useful, particularly French and German. Not all trainees are recruited straight after graduating; some work in, for example, research and development first.

Patent agents need a keen practical interest, and curiosity, in technological and scientific developments. They should have the kind of intelligence which can easily take in new and sometimes very advanced ideas in science and technology. They have to be capable of learning to write legally watertight prose, which means being able to think clearly, analytically and critically, reason logically, and be able to use the English language. They have to be able to negotiate and argue. Tidy-mindedness, accuracy and precision are needed.

The minimum educational requirements to enter the trade mark profession are GCSE (grades A–C) in five approved subjects and two A-levels, or their equivalents, in two approved subjects. Trade mark agents frequently begin their careers in private practice by joining a firm of trade mark agents or a firm of patent agents with a trade mark department. Graduates, particularly those with law degrees, may find it easier to secure trainee posts than non-graduates.

Qualifications and training

Patent agents have to be entered in the Register of Patent agents. They qualify via examinations set by the (British) Chartered Institute of Patent Agents (CIPA), while training on-the-job. Qualification generally takes between four and six years, although some people manage it in less than four years.

Nowadays, virtually all Chartered Patent Agents are also European Patent Attorneys, and trainees would usually be expected to pass the European Qualifying Examinations (EQE). Although EQE exams are set in English (as well as French and German), some of the materials for the papers may be in only one of these languages, so a good knowledge of French and German is essential.

Technical assistants have to spend quite a large part of their spare time studying – some help is given by a an informal group of CIPE members.

The Institute of Trade Mark Agents has its own qualifying examinations which consist of five Foundation Papers and two Advanced Papers, covering the principles of trade mark law and practice, design rights and copyright law, and basic English law. Trainees successfully completing these examinations are entered on to the Register of Trade Mark Agents and can be considered for corporate membership of the Institute. Graduates may be eligible for exemption in some Foundation Papers.

Patent examiners

Since 1990, the Patent Office has been an Executive Agency of the Department of Trade and Industry. Although this means staff are no longer civil servants there is no significant change in the nature of the work. However, the declining number of applications to the UK Office implies that either the Office will get smaller and/or that it will have to develop additional services. In 1991 the main office moved to Newport, relocating all the examiners. Only a small office now remains in London.

Examiners assess patent applications to see whether or not they are novel enough to justify awarding a patent. They search through earlier specifications and other published papers, prepare reports, interview patent agents (or the applicants), and, if there is a dispute of any kind, act for the Patent Office. They also write and index the shortened version of the specification for publication.

This is also mainly an office-based career, combining desk work with discussion and negotiation. Patent examiners usually specialise in one subject area, working in one of 26 specialist groups. UK-trained patent examiners can work for the European Patent Office. The UK has held a number of key posts, e.g. the vice-president responsible for examination and opposition, the principal legal-division director, and the secretary to the president.

Recruitment and entry

The UK Patent Office has no set numbers for annual recruitment. In 1994 there were 963 staff (patent examiners, trade marks examiners and design examiners). Vacancies are usually advertised in scientific and technical journals and the national press.

Qualifications and training

Entry requirements are good first or second class honours degrees in engineering, science or mathematics, and/or membership of a major professional institution in an appropriate field. Mathematics graduates should also have studied physics or a technology. A language (French or German) is useful for the UK Patent Office.

Training is in-house. All recruits undertake an initial training period of about one year working on actual cases to become familiar with the basic working of the patent law under the supervision of a senior examiner. Supervision of work continues for up to four more years.

Patent officers

Patent officers work for the Ministry of Defence and deal with patent work arising from the research, development and manufacturing activities carried out by, or on behalf of, government departments in the scientific, technological and engineering fields – they are, in effect, government patent agents. This includes arranging patent protection for Crown rights in new inventions and developments, assessing and settling claims for compensation for Crown use of patents, designs, processes and other types of industrial 'property', and general advisory work with government departments on the use of inventions. The staff of the patents directorate must keep totally up-to-date on government and related research and development and regularly visit research establishments. Numbers of patent officers are very small.

Further information

The Chartered Institute of Patent Agents, the Patent Office, the European Patent Office, The Institute of Trade Mark Agents.

Security and Protective Services

Contents

(CLCI: M – MAZ, QOT)

Background

Here the purpose is to provide the community with services to protect it against hazards ranging from fire to theft, and to help people involved when such events happen. Partly this is enforcing the law and keeping order. Most of these services are provided by the state, through the fire, police and prison services, as a legal responsibility, but private, commercial security organisations have been expanding.

Traditionally, these services have much in common, with each other and with the ARMED FORCES, in that they have similar, semi-military organisational patterns, with very formal hierarchical structures and traditional discipline, and uniforms are worn. However, within the formal framework, these organisations are developing modern management methods, making use of new technology, and (sometimes) taking into account the results of research in the behavioural and clinical sciences.

People working in these services see them as giving security, and as being worthwhile, since they help the community. The pension rights, the comradeship, and reasonable promotion prospects are attractive, and the work is often interesting and varied. However, there is shiftwork and relatively long hours, discipline, periods of boredom and tedium, routine chores, and such close ties to the job that, even when officially off duty, officers have to be ready to deal with an emergency. In all these careers too, the element of danger and risk may be exciting for the younger man or woman, but can become worrying when they marry and have family responsibilities.

The fire services

Working for the fire services – recruitment and entry – qualifications and training – further information

Coping with fire-fighting and fire safety is mainly the responsibility of local authorities, under the supervision of the Home and Scottish Offices. In all, there are some 64 fire authorities in the UK, mainly at county level. However, these are not the only organisations concerned with fire-fighting – others include the Ministry of Defence for the Army and the Air Force, the British Airport Authority's fire services, and some major firms, e.g. oil companies, have their own.

The main legal responsibility of the fire services is to fight fires, from the smallest domestic blaze in an over-heated frying pan, to major outbreaks in large factories, and obviously there are more of the former than of the latter. However, fire authorities must also see that there is a comprehensive system of fire safety in, for example, places of entertainment, public resorts and some kinds of residential accommodation, as well as under the Factories and Offices, Shops and Railway Premises Acts. Fire services also provide advisory services on fire prevention and spread, and escape methods.

Fire authorities can also use their fire brigades and equipment for emergencies other than fire-fighting, and of course they do. They deal with the tanker that crashes and pours an unnamed but toxic chemical across the high street; they cut and lift apart crashed trains or cars, deal with the consequences of floods, extract children from between railings, get cats down from trees, and cope when old buildings collapse and cranes topple over. Although they do not always charge for these services (except where the fire brigade may want to deter an adventurer from constantly repeating a mistake), the fire brigade can also be employed on a commercial basis, in emptying and filling swimming pools, water tanks and lakes, for instance.

The statistics are impressive. The number of fire and special service calls in England and Wales number about 988,000 a year (1994) (113,074 in Scotland in 1994–5). The fire authorities in England and Wales control about 1,800 fire stations, including two on the river in London, operating about 5,000 fire-fighting appliances (including pumps, turntable ladders, water and emergency tenders, and hose-laying lorries). In Scotland there are 251 stations operating 503 firefighting appliances.

The expertise demanded of the fire services increases steadily. Office and residential tower blocks, massive chemical plants, juggernaut tanker lorries, and modern materials (which produce toxic fumes on burning), present more and more new problems to be solved even as the number of hazards caused by lack of fire precautions in older buildings is slowly reduced. The whole of the country has been surveyed for fire risk, right down to the street and individual type of building. Each district is classified by degree of risk, and the services and personnel geared accordingly – high-risk areas include congested docks and concentrated heavy industry, while risks in non-forested rural areas are treated as relatively low. The services make increasing use of modern technology, from a computer-based information retrieval system on dangerous compounds to infra-red thermal cameras (to see through smoke) in remote monitoring and directing fire-fighting operations.

Working for the fire services

About 36,000 people work for the fire services in England and Wales whole-time (end 1994) (4,452 in Scotland in March 1995) and a further 15,000 (3,733 in Scotland) retained or as volunteers. (Retained fire fighters are trained in the same way as whole-time, but have a full-time job outside the fire service, and are called on to fight fires when needed). Most whole-time staff and virtually all retained staff are operational fire-fighters (of these 332 are women). There are over 1,500 control room staff (207 in Scotland) and about 1,180 are women (176 in Scotland).

Urban areas are mostly served by whole-time fire-fighters; however, most brigades, with the exception of London, also have retained fire-fighters. The number of retained fire-fighters employed by brigades vary from 13 in the West Midlands to 746 in Kent. In Scotland this varies from 103 in Fife to 586 in Strathclyde.

Almost all those working in the fire service are trained, operational fire-fighters – the numbers of purely administrative posts for fire service personnel are strictly limited to the senior officer levels, with most general administrative and clerical work done by local authority staff. There are, however, a number of specialist posts at officer level, in fire prevention, training, communications, transport, water supplies, and so on. Since every area faces different problems and hazards, practice varies from locality to locality, but in general the size of the staff of each station varies according to the number of appliances; the rule of thumb is that each appliance needs five personnel to crew it, but some 25 are needed to operate a pump at all times.

All calls for assistance come through to a control room, in the larger services a central control at brigade headquarters. While the message is being taken down, maps and detailed street indexes are consulted, and the charts which show which appliances are where, so particular stations can be alerted at the touch of a button. Even before a message is fully received, the appliance is manned with its engine running, ready to leave within a minute. Radio contact with the appliance gives the crew continuous information. After the fire, detailed reports must be prepared. Most brigades use computer-based control and information systems.

In between fire and other emergency calls, on-duty crews have other duties both inside and outside the station – inside they maintain the appliances, man the watch-room, keep the station clean, and carry out drills and exercises. They also have lectures and demonstrations, to maintain and improve fire-drill efficiency. Outside the station, fire-fighters spend time trying to improve fire prevention, visiting shops, offices, factories, cinemas, even homes, to recommend and advise, and giving lectures on fire precautions. At night, crews sleep between emergency calls, but on both day and night shifts an emergency call means an automatic reaction, to stop whatever they may be doing – eating, sleeping or station duties – and to reach the appliance as fast as possible, so that the pattern of fire-fighters working lives is totally unpredictable.

All fire-fighters have equal opportunities for promotion based on ability, not academic background on entry. All have to work their way up from junior fire-fighter and fire-fighter, through leading fire-fighter to officer, although for those with the right aptitudes it is possible to reach station officer by the mid-20s. Up to station officer promotion is by examination, thereafter by interview and selection.

Recruitment and entry

Recruitment to the service has been dropping in recent years, 1,082 people were recruited in England and Wales in 1994 (1,573 were recruited in 1990). One hundred and twenty-seven people were recruited in Scotland in 1994–5 (156 were recruited in 1990).

Although most people join the fire service in their twenties, it is possible to start at eighteen (junior entry for sixteen- and seventeen-year-olds is possible in a few brigades). There is no direct officer recruitment.

Formal academic qualifications are not set in England and Wales, although the level of competition is now such that passes at 16-plus in at least English, maths and a science are probably needed. In Scotland two S-grades are required, preferably in English and mathematics or a science. All recruits must be extremely fit physically, must be not less than 5' 6" or more than 6' 4" in height. Vision (without glasses) must be 6/6, 6/6 and applicants must be able to meet prescribed standards of health and fitness.

Qualifications and training

Fire-fighters are given thorough and extensive training. Every new recruit spends up to 16 weeks at training school. The courses combine lectures on everything from building construction through to first aid and fire-station work, with practical exercises in fire-fighting and emergencies, often in conditions which very realistically simulate the real thing. Drivers are specially trained, and must gain an HGV licence.

Fire-fighters go on studying and training throughout their careers, and promotion largely depends on completing the appropriate practical, and some written, examinations. Many fire-fighters study for membership of the Institution of Fire Engineers, although the examinations are not compulsory. Officers are given additional training in residential courses at the Fire Service College.

NVQ/SVQs for the Emergency Fire Service are available at level 2 in Fire-fighting and at level 3 in operations and supervision. A further operational qualification at level 4 and qualifications for control room staff and fire safety are being developed.

Further information

In the first instance, from Local Authorities' fire brigades (addresses in the telephone directory).

The Home Office Fire Department, the Fire and Emergency Planning Division of the Scottish Home Department, the British Airports Authority, or the Ministry of Defence.

The Police

Working in the police – recruitment and entry – qualifications and training – further information

The police, according to a particularly succinct definition, are responsible for saving people from the worst they can do to themselves and to each other. Their position and powers are balanced delicately on typically traditional British theories of the relations between the state and the police on the one hand, and the police and the courts on the other, while emphasising that the police are not an arm of the state and have never been 'recognised, either in law or by tradition, as a force distinct from the general body of citizens'.

A police officer, the official definition says, is not an employee or agent of either the local police authority or the central government, but is 'an independent holder of public office and exercises his powers as a constable, whether conferred by statute or by common law, by virtue of his office; he is an agent of the law of the land...'. Although all police officers can exercise their powers as constables anywhere in the country, therefore, as members of a disciplined body they are subject to the orders of superior officers. Constables may not take any active part in politics, to maintain impartiality, but they do not lose any of their constitutional rights as citizens – they can vote in elections and so on.

The police protect people and property, prevent and detect crime and look for the culprits, enforce laws of all kinds, control 'traffic' (people, cars, buses, etc.) in the street and other public places, deal with all kinds of emergencies and generally provide 'assistance', advice, and information. There are ordinary, everyday problems of the local community to solve, crowds of all kinds to control, and crises – from terrorist bombs and gas explosions through to missing children – to deal with. Deterrence – simply being around on the streets, in crowds, at events – is a major part of the job, as is a lot of patient backroom work, both planning and detecting. The police acquired both extra powers and extra rules – mainly giving suspects further rights – in 1985, and must now keep to tighter codes of practice.

It is an enormous job, and a difficult one, demanding hard decisions and exceptional tact, because maintaining law and order, and combating crime can so easily mean acting in ways which people see as infringing traditional personal freedoms. The police can never hope to prevent or detect 100% of all law breaking, so it is an endless balancing act and a hard battle to keep up, let alone improve, police effectiveness in a rapidly changing society, and be the fair and impartial police force the public expects. The 'rule of law' is only possible with the total support of the public for what the police do, and the police always have to be sensitive to public opinion. The problems get worse when the public has conflicting opinions.

The police have been under intense public scrutiny for some time now. Policing raises increasingly complex problems, to which it is correspondingly hard to find answers. Questions are raised on the way the police respond – to strikes, to inner-city disturbances – on their use of firearms, about their professionalism, the policing system generally, and the way police forces are organised. Many thousands of words have been written for and against community policing and relations with ethnic groups, on the accountability of the police to the community, on complaints procedures, on whether or not the police force has to introduce modern management methods, on police training, and so on. Lord Scarman analysed the principles of policing and how it should be carried out, back in 1981, but events have to some extent overtaken his report. The police, like everyone else, are having to learn to cope with a world of change, to be flexible, and have to be better trained, and educated, to cope.

The 43 separate police forces (England and Wales) divide the country between them, most covering relatively large areas (to give economies of scale). They range in size from London's Metropolitan Police of over 26,000 to mainly rural forces with under 1,000 officers. Each is independent, policing a county, or two or more 'joint' local authority areas. Mostly they are maintained by a police authority, which is a kind of local authority committee, but in London the Home Secretary is responsible for the Metropolitan Police. The Home and Scottish Offices nationally oversee police services generally, but they have no day-to-day involvement. They set guide-lines and make suggestions, approve the appointment of chief constables, make regulations on conditions of service, provide common services and do research, develop a planning/programming/budgeting system for the forces and for medium- and long-term planning of police resources.

But although each force is still completely autonomous and indeed often has a distinctive character of its own, co-operation between them has necessarily been increasing for many years. A major example is the regional crime squads, made up of teams of experienced detectives from several forces, which investigate major crimes which usually mean enquiries in more than one police area. They are supported by a network of regional criminal intelligence offices.

Some services are organised nationally, and centralisation of services is also increasing. The Metropolitan Police's Criminal Investigation Department (CID), helps, on request, any other police force in criminal investigations. The fraud squad is run jointly by the Metropolitan Police and the City of London Police, and the National Central Bureau handles

Interpol business for Britain. The Home Office's police department houses units like the scientific research and development branch, criminal records and the police national computer unit, the national fingerprint bureau, telecommunications, and the forensic science labs. Forces report all recordable offences to a national identification bureau.

Science and technology plays a major or increasing part, wherever feasible. Local forces are linked via terminals directly to the national computer with its complete file on vehicle registrations, and index to the fingerprint file. Computers are now being tried out in processing and analysing all the information collected on serious crimes, like murders. Police officers' personal radios are linked to increasingly sophisticated control systems in police headquarters. Forensic services are equipped with the latest automated equipment for scientific analysis, and molecular biology has just made a major new breakthrough, to give completely foolproof 'genetic fingerprinting'.

Working in the police

On the beat – station work – rural policing – patrol cars – criminal investigation – traffic departments – other units – promotion – civilians in the police forces – forensic science service – scientific research and development branch – traffic wardens

Between them, the regular police authorities in England and Wales employ (1994) around 123,743 police (including nearly 17,000 policewomen) and some 55,700 'civilians', including scenes of crimes officers and traffic wardens. Graduates now make up 7.7% of the police in England, Wales and Northern Ireland.

In Scotland (1995) there were 18,447 police officers (including 1,836 female officers) and 3,968 civilians.

Numbers of police officers will be increased over the next three years with 4,500 more officers in England and Wales and 500 in Scotland.

While there are a great many different jobs in the police force, most people spend a large part of their early years out of doors, on their feet, in all weathers, and/or behind the wheel of a car. More time may be spent in desk and office work as promotion comes, but for most police officers it is a very active life, with long and difficult hours. There is a lot of routine, report writing, and time spent in court, which means giving evidence. Almost all police work involves contact with people of all kinds. Police officers have to learn to accept that, even when off duty, many people will be wary of them.

Over 77% of all police men and women are constables. Most spend their working hours trying to see that ordinary, everyday life goes on as normally as possible in a particular area.

On the beat

After initial training, all police officers spend at least two years as probationer uniformed constables attached to a local station, and going out alone on the streets within a very short time, effectively learning on-the-job.

Most constables work as part of a 'unit' looking after an area, which may be a housing estate, a residential suburb, or a shopping centre. A typical unit beat is made up of two police officers, who work as a team with a back-up detective constable and a panda-car patrol team, all in touch with each other and with their station, via the radio. The unit has to know the area as well as possible, to know what usually happens and when, the regular pattern of activity in the neighbourhood, to know what is suspicious and what is not, to spot the unusual and out-of-the-ordinary. Where police forces use 'community' policing, constables are expected to become as closely involved as possible with the local people, to join in local activities and events, to help solve local problems which have little to do with policing (e.g. helping to raise money for a play area), and work with young people.

Beat constables are briefed daily, and are then given particular jobs to do. They have stolen cars to watch out for, and enquiries to make, such as seeing a witness for more information or showing someone stolen property that has been recovered.

At the end of these two years, constables can theoretically apply for other jobs within their force, although in practice, since changing jobs depends on vacancies, it may be much longer. Most policemen and women stay on the beat for several more years at least, and do other work in or from the local station.

Station work

Up to a dozen constables may be on a station shift at one time. Some go out on patrol (on foot, in a 'panda', or perhaps as a team in a van), some work on the enquiry desk, dealing with people who come in or telephone to report a crime or ask for help or information. One or more officers operate the radio links with their patrol constables, cars and force headquarters.

The collator looks after the station's information centre, with its walls covered in local maps and photographs, its card or computer-based indexes of all kinds of information, reference books, and computer terminals. The collator has to keep track of all reported crimes and incidents, missing cars, dogs, and children, and helps to build up evidence from information coming in all the time.

One or more police officers may specialise in liaison work with local schools.

Tutor-constables, experienced officers, are in charge of day-to-day on-the-job training of probationers.

Rural policing

Some experienced constables choose to become country policemen or women. They may look after a large area (and therefore have to use a car), which may include several villages, a length or two of major road, several large farms and estates. Rural police have their own police house with an office. They work mainly alone, under long-range supervision, and with rather more direct responsibility than the city constable. Many of them put down roots and stay with a district for some time. To be successful, the police officer has to build a close relationship with the local community.

Patrol cars

Constables can go from the beat to work in the 'panda' cars, patrolling the area also covered on foot by two resident constables, although some forces are now reducing the number of car patrols. Patrol cars can be sent out to incidents or to help a constable. Like the beat constable, the panda driver also makes calls and enquiries, looks out for anything suspicious or unusual, and sorts out accidents. From panda patrols, constables can go on to the larger area patrol cars with their driver-observer team, and work with both divisional headquarters as well as the local station.

Criminal investigation

Criminal investigation is another area of promotion for uniformed constables. Detective constables often start their careers, however, with the unit beat team (*above*). Here much of the work is patient, routine questioning, interviewing, collating, painstakingly collecting detailed evidence, trying to build a case from a mass of unrelated facts, and trying to find all the pieces in a complex jigsaw. Many cases are undramatic, straightforward thefts and minor crimes. Many forms have to be filled in and reports written.

Every detective works on a number of things at once. The work is all very time-consuming. Scene-of-crime work involves collecting evidence, interviewing witnesses and potential suspects and analysing the results, and working with the forensic experts. Detectives may work in criminal records.

Although every force has its own CID, they vary in size from 2,000 in London to about 100 in a small provincial force. From local CID, experienced detectives can go on to work in headquarters, or in a regional crime squad, or into a special unit. In regional crime squads there is an increasing range of specialised duties, for example intelligence officer, who deals with and organises the information coming into the squad, and selects 'target criminals'.

Traffic departments

Traffic departments employ quite large numbers. The work ranges from office-based planning to actually driving police cars. Traffic departments plan and operate the more complex traffic control systems, administer intelligence units which analyse traffic and accident information and identify and try to cure problems. They work closely with local authorities and government departments in planning or changing traffic schemes. They also operate the car and motorcycle traffic patrols which sort out traffic snarl-ups, cope with emergencies and accidents, stop dangerous drivers, breathalyse drunk drivers, and look out for dangerous, defective and unlicensed vehicles.

Other units

Smaller units (for which competition is always keen), include:

- river patrols;
- underwater search units (whose members are always trained divers);
- the mounted police, working mainly in crowd control at football matches, race meetings and demonstrations;
- mountain rescue teams;
- dog handlers, who look for missing children, track and trap suspects or escaped prisoners, do general search duties and patrolling, or specialise in hunting for drugs, explosives or buried bodies etc.

Promotion

Every police force has a strictly hierarchical structure – and the chief constables, who administer them (there is no central command), have been described as akin to feudal barons, often moulding their forces in a very personal way. All senior positions, right up to chief constable, are filled from within the ranks of the police themselves, but except for the most senior posts there is not much movement between forces.

Promotion is strictly on suitability and merit, on being the kind of police officer the interviewing board decides it needs for the particular job. There is no automatic promotion on age or length of service. Before promotion to sergeant or inspector, qualifying exams must be passed, but this does not in itself guarantee promotion. Although there are some technical, backroom jobs for more senior officers, the police emphasise that promotion is in terms of management, in being responsible for running a team of more junior officers, deploying them and equipment.

A uniformed sergeant leads a team of constables; an inspector in a sub-division is in charge of one or more sections, consisting of 10–15 constables and sergeants, responsible for seeing that they work together as a unit (but detective sergeants may work alone on some cases). A sub-divisional detective inspector is in charge of a team of detectives, but perhaps dealing directly with investigations where enquiries are particularly difficult or lengthy; a control room inspector is in charge of a shift of the constables dealing with emergency calls, and ensure that the right response is made.

All inspectors deal with day-to-day administration. Most senior officers are also given experience of specialist duties outside the main route of their career development – they may be seconded to the Police Research Services at the Home Office, or to the Inspectorate of Constabulary, for example.

Each year there is an accelerated promotion scheme for some 60 younger officers, at least a third of them usually graduates (*see* QUALIFICATIONS AND TRAINING *below*) who show the potential to rise quickly to inspector and above, and have passed the sergeants' exams at the first attempt.

Through this scheme it is possible to reach the rank of sergeant in three years, inspector in five years and chief inspector in seven years, subject to satisfactory performance.

Women police officers have been integrated into the force, with the same powers and responsibilities as men, since 1976. While duties such as searching prisoners may still be done by police officers of the same sex as the prisoner, many duties traditionally reserved for women officers (e.g. dealing with women and children in any kind of trouble) are now done by the best-qualified officer, regardless of sex. Women now theoretically compete for promotion on equal terms with men. In 1994, there were 239 women inspectors (17 in Scotland), and 96 in higher ranks (11 in Scotland) including 5 assistant chief constables. This is an increase on the 1991 figures. However at present only 2% of women (1% in Scotland) hold the rank of inspector or above, against 10% of men (6% in Scotland).

Civilians in the police forces

The numbers of civilians in the police forces are being increased with nearly 56,000 in 1994 (4,000 in Scotland) against 55,000 in 1991 (2,900 in Scotland).

The range of work they do is being extended to release police officers for operational duties. Many carry out administrative tasks such as preparing legal reports, processing accident reports and typing statements. Others run incident rooms, work in police control rooms and on station front desks. Many police authorities employ traffic wardens. There is also an increasing role for civilian specialists such as Scenes of Crime Officers and computer and telecommunications specialists.

Scenes of crime officers (SOCOs) visit scenes of crime to gather evidence to help investigating police officers determine how the crime was committed and by whom. They search for and collect physical evidence such as tools or weapons that might have been used in the crime, plus samples of clothing fibres, paint or metallic deposits, traces of blood and debris which they send to laboratories for analysis by forensic officers. They also detect and lift any fingerprints or palmprints from surfaces and take fingerprints of suspects, victims and bodies. Another part of their job is to take photographs at scenes of crime, at road traffic accidents and of suspects, victims and any exhibits or stolen property. Their work also includes preparing statements and giving evidence in court.

Forensic science service

The forensic science service employs mostly chemists and biologists. They help solve all kinds of crimes, examining and analysing a wide range of materials which might give a clue to the identity of the culprit, eliminate the innocent, or establish a major factor about the crime itself. The laboratory work involved is mainly chemical and biological. Other work includes investigating documents and inks, comparing, for instance, hairs and fibres, identifying blood groups from dried stains, and so on. Much of this is being automated. The laboratories are almost entirely regionally based at present (London has its own), but organisation and management are under review. The Aldermaston central laboratories do research in toxicology, biology and serology, and house the service's information centre which has a computer-based literature retrieval system.

Scientific research and development branch

The scientific research and development branch mainly studies ways in which modern technology can be used to improve police efficiency. Major projects include applying real-time computers to problems of, for instance, command and resource control and allocation, retrieving intelligence information and fingerprint comparison. The branch uses a wide range of statistical and mathematical model-building techniques, Small teams of scientists (under 50 in all), e.g. mathematicians, physicists, chemists, psychologists and engineers, work closely with police officers. Much of the work is contracted out.

Traffic wardens

Traffic wardens are employed by all police forces, and number about 5,000 country-wide. They mainly patrol the streets to see that parking and other restrictions are not being broken, and if they are, tell the drivers what they should (or should not) be doing and/or issue parking tickets. They also monitor schemes – such as one-way systems, controlled parking zones and yellow lines – to see if they are improving or impeding traffic flow. They watch out for stolen cars, check road-tax licences, and note licence numbers of cars, etc. which are clearly not safe to be on the roads. They sometimes do point duty if jams build up or traffic lights are out of action, supervise car pounds, and may control crossings when children are going in or out of a nearby school.

Recruitment and entry

Police officers

The minimum age of entry is 18½. There is no upper age limit in England and Wales; in Scotland the upper age limit is 40. Theoretically there are no formal educational entry requirements, but all candidates have to take an entry test.

A number of outstanding graduates (26 in 1994) are recruited each year under the accelerated promotion scheme for graduates (APSG) to attend the accelerated promotion course (APC).

The service employs about 650 graduates each year in total. Graduates can apply for the APSG during their first 12 months of service, if they have not been considered for it previously. It is possible to be reconsidered for APC on passing the promotion examinations for sergeant.

There is no longer any minimum height requirement for police officers. Most forces accept entrants who wear glasses or contact lenses, if their sight meets certain minimum standards, although standards vary from force to force. Good health and physical stamina are needed to work long and unusual hours, and to stay on one's feet for long periods.

Personal qualities are also very important. It is not possible to get in on educational and physical qualifications alone, and the rejection rate on personal characteristics and motivation is high. The police say they want people intelligent enough to be able to sum up situations quickly and efficiently, and who can make the 'right' decisions. They want well-balanced personalities, plenty of self-control, tact and level-headedness. Police recruits need to be objective and observant, to be able to keep their opinions to themselves, cope with people easily and firmly (a sense of humour helps) in all kinds of situations. They must be able to work in a team.

Civilian staff

Entry qualifications vary depending on the job. For many jobs there are no formal entry requirements; however, the scientific and technical specialists usually need at least A-levels or relevant technical/scientific qualifications.

Qualifications and training

Police officers

Training lasts for two years. New recruits start in a training centre going on to a modular training scheme which alternates practical on-the-job training, supervised by a tutor constable, with college courses. After that there may be additional training courses for specific jobs or groups. Anyone going into CID work, for example, has to go to a detective school, to study criminal law and methods of detective investigation.

The amount of training given is being increased steadily, with what are described as a 'carousel' of short courses for police officers of all ranks. The normal route to promotion as sergeant and inspector is via extremely stiff examinations.

The very demanding accelerated promotion course is run at the Bramshill Staff College. It has four phases which are flexible to meet the needs of the individuals selected for it.

Usually one third to a half of the members of each course are graduates selected through the APSG. Others are selected on the basis of suitability to reach the rank of inspector or above. Increasingly sophisticated courses (using, for instance, computer simulations) are given each year for those being promoted to intermediate, junior and senior command, all emphasising high-level administration.

Civilian staff

All civilian staff receive on-the-job training and those in specialist jobs usually receive extensive training and may be given time off to study by day-release or on a part-time basis for BTEC Higher Awards or degrees.

See also CENTRAL GOVERNMENT *and* THE LEGAL SYSTEM.

Further information

The Police Recruiting Department of the Home Office, the Police Division of the Scottish Home Department, or the headquarters of any individual force (refer to your local telephone directory).

The Prison Service

Working in the prison service – recruitment and entry – qualifications and training – further information

Prison staff have a job with two purposes: they serve the public by keeping in custody those committed by the courts, and they have a duty to look after prisoners with humanity and help them to lead law-abiding and useful lives in custody and after release. Long-term, the aim of the prison service is to concentrate increasingly on the latter, developing constructive methods of treatment and training to lead to prisoners' rehabilitation and reform.

Conditions within prisons vary considerably. Some are very overcrowded and conditions are far from ideal, whereas others, such as open prisons, have good conditions and facilities. Currently there are over 135 establishments of different types in England and Wales (22 in Scotland) with funding to increase the accommodation for a further 4,000 prisoners over the next three years. (Scotland now has funding for another prison to provide accommodation for another 500 prisoners.) This increase in accommodation will go a good way towards relieving overcrowding.

Working in the prison service

Prison officers' work is very varied. They supervise prisoners at work, in their cells, exercising and at recreation. An officer is also in charge of prisoners' training and rehabilitation, and is expected to help them sort out practical and other problems, make reports on any illness, on their conduct, and pass on to senior staff any special requests, or difficulties, and see that any problems, including psychiatric crises, have professional attention. Some officers are trained to help the prisoners they look after through group and other forms of counselling. They also have to deal with disruptive behaviour.

Prison officers are also in charge of receiving new prisoners. They run classification units which decide which prisons new prisoners should go to; and supervise workshops, visits by relatives and friends, and training. They escort prisoners to and from other prisons and guard gates and doors. In Scotland prison officers escort prisoners to and from court, but in England and Wales this work is now contracted out to private security organisations.

Officers may work in a variety of establishments ranging from open prisons, where the prisoners are serving sentences for non-violent offences and can reasonably be trusted not to escape, to top-security prisons, where prisoners are serving sentences for very serious offences. However, wherever an officer works, there is an element of stress and pressure in the job which must be recognised.

All prison officers in England and Wales enter at the basic grade and may be promoted through a series of supervisory grades into the governor grade. For those considered to be of exceptional ability there is an accelerated promotion scheme by which officers may reach Governor grade 4 in six years from entry. Competition for this scheme is fierce.

In Scotland a new staffing structure was introduced in 1994 and there is now open competition for many officer and management grade posts.

In England and Wales there is a hierarchy of governors, all of whom have different levels and areas of responsibility. In Scotland jobs now have titles relevant to the work involved. Each prison is run by a governor, but instead of having other governors of various grades, Scottish prisons have unit managers, estates managers, health centre managers etc. The Prison Governor is responsible for an entire prison including staff recruitment and the prison budget.

Governors/managers generally have administrative and managerial responsibility for part of a prison. They manage both staff and resources, supervise prisoners' progress, treatment, training and so on. They plan and organise work and training schedules, arrange for counselling, psychiatric treatment, educational programmes, entertainments and leisure activities. They look after the prisoners' records, deal with parole requests, disciplines, and other routines and procedures. It is possible to go on to work in regional management or administration, or to take on a training post. A very few people work for the prisons inspectorate.

The prison service also employs some specialists, most notably psychologists, but also some doctors and nurses for hospitals. Probation officers staff prison welfare offices. There are also jobs for caterers, and instructors for trades and other skills, and in physical education.

Over 30,000 people work in the prison service in England and Wales, including 24,000 prison officers (1994), and 4,324 in Scotland (1995).

Some prisons in England are now contracted out to private security organisations. These have their own structure and may not use the terms prison officer or governor. However, the work carried out is similar.

Recruitment and entry

There are no set educational entry requirements for prison officers. Selection is by aptitude test and interview. Entry age is 19½ to 49½ with a height requirement of 5'6" for men and 5'3" for women. Scottish requirements may vary – contact the Scottish Prison Service for up-to-date information. Applicants must be of good character and be able to provide references. Mobility is an important requirement and applicants must be willing to move home if necessary to take up an appointment. Candidates must be physically fit and have good health and eyesight.

There is currently an annual graduate recruitment campaign for direct entry to the Accelerated Promotion Scheme, together with an annual in-service competition.

Prison staff should be well-balanced, stable people. They need to carry out a range of duties from custodian to welfare worker and so should be caring, patient and assertive. They should have a realistic attitude towards and understanding of the causes of crime and develop skills to enable them to deal with prisoners tactfully and discreetly. A sense of humour is vital.

The entry requirements for contracted out prisons may be different from the prison service.

Qualifications and training

In England and Wales all entrants are given two weeks induction training, followed by a nine-week residential course. The course places considerable emphasis on interpersonal skills.

Scottish prison officers undertake a week's work in their allocated establishment then undergo a month of training at the Scottish Prison Service College near Falkirk. They must then satisfactorily complete a two-year probationary period.

The Accelerated Promotion Scheme involves a six-year programme which combines direct experience with specific residential training courses which cover the basic skills of prison work such as reception of prisoners, security and escort duty; interpersonal and social skills; and issues such as race relations, professional conduct and leadership. Those on the scheme progress through the grades of prison officer and principal officer to governor grade 5 where they will manage significant aspects of prison life. On completion of the scheme they progress to governor grade 2 where they could be in charge of running a prison with up to 700 prisoners and 300 staff.

Contracted out prisons have their own training systems.

Further information

The Prison Department of the Home Office or the Director of Human Resources, Scottish Prison Service .

Private security operations

Working in security – recruitment and entry – qualifications and training – further information

This is a growth industry, expanding annually and employing possibly 200,000 people (the two largest firms have 40,000 people between them). The industry is made up of a number of companies, offering highly sophisticated, nation-wide services, and small units, usually working on a local basis. Some firms specialise – in protecting precious metals, for instance, or in providing security equipment. Large-scale security now takes full advantage of all that modern technology can offer, guarding property with radios, electronic detection devices, closed-circuit television, and so on, often to give advanced warning of fire or flood as much as of a break-in.

The industry's mainstay is manned guarding, but many other services are provided, including delivery services for valuable packages, documents and cash in transit, advice and quotations on security systems, protection against industrial espionage, protection for people vulnerable to attack or kidnapping, and store detective services. Security services are used mainly by industrial and commercial firms which regularly handle anything valuable enough to warrant the cost of protecting it.

Working in security

Careers in security organisations do not have any formal structure. For security companies, as in all commercial firms, really efficient MANAGEMENT is essential. This is a business which has to be ready to change or develop the services it offers and to spot the changes coming. As less and less cash is moved around physically, for example, security firms will find less business in this. There are also posts in day-to-day administration, finance, personnel etc.

Most people in the industry work as guards, drivers or patrolmen, although there are some couriers, and a declining number of dog handlers. Technicians and engineers install and service alarm systems and all the other electronic and technological devices, as well as looking after the vans, cars and motorcycles.

Private investigators

Estimates of the number of private investigators vary and the closest approximation (1995) is between 3,000 and 5,000 working full time. The recent employment trend is marginally increasing by about 5–10%. Apart from specialists with specific technical/operational skills and principals of the larger agencies enjoying higher-than-average earnings, the majority make a reasonable, not unduly lavish, living. It is difficult to find work with worthwhile agencies without some prior background training, normally in POLICE or related work, the LEGAL SYSTEM (usually as a legal executive), the ARMED FORCES or industry, normally in MANAGEMENT SERVICES.

The work, according to one association, involves research, research and yet more research, plus checking research, some surveillance and very, very little glamour indeed. A highly developed instinctive sense, combined with disciplined analytical abilities, is crucial in order to achieve a reputation. It is advisable to begin with a very reputable agency before even considering freelance work. The main sectors are the corporate sector and the legal profession and the type of services offered include de-bugging and electronic safety devices, undercover/anti industrial espionage, infringements of patents, insurance claims, investigations into thefts and fraud, checking business bonafides, security and risk evaluations, debtor tracing, service of legal process, accident investigation and criminal defence work.

At present there is no legislative control over who can practise in this field. However, those whose work includes debt collection or credit referencing need to obtain a licence from the Office of Fair Trading.

Store detectives

Store detectives are mostly employed by larger retailers, although some shops use contract staff from security firms.

Recruitment and entry

There are some limited opportunities for school and college leavers. Companies prefer, where possible however, to recruit experienced people, especially those with the kinds of skills acquired in the police or armed forces. Recruits to a security firm are expected to have completely 'clean' records and the right kind of character. A successful career in the police or forces is considered to be a good indicator of these.

Qualifications and training

Security

No formal training is available. Larger companies now offer a reasonable level of training, particularly on legal responsibilities, the police, and relations with the community, and with the kind of equipment being used, as well as in emergency procedures.

NVQ/SVQs are available at level 2 in Security Guarding and Transporting Property under Guard.

The International Professional Security Association or IPSA (which includes the International Institute of Security) puts on a number of short and correspondence courses, some leading to membership of the Institute.

Private investigation

Most training is on-the-job combined with short courses in subjects such as surveillance. The Association of British Investigators and the Institute of Professional Investigators both run one-day seminars in relevant subjects. The Institute of Professional Investigators also runs a distance learning course. Loughborough University has a one-year part-time diploma in Investigative Management for those working in this field. Entry qualifications for this diploma are a degree or relevant professional qualification. NVQ/SVQs are available in Investigation at levels 3 and 4.

Store detectives

Guide lines on employer-based training for store detectives have been prepared by IPSA and the British Retailers Association.

Further information

The British Security Industry Association, the International Professional Security Association, the Association of British Investigators and the Institute of Professional Investigators.

Financial Careers

Contents

(CLCI: N – NAZ)

Background

Introduction – working in finance – recruitment and entry – qualifications and training

Introduction

Efficient financial management is a major pre-occupation for everyone nowadays. The government constantly tries to achieve an acceptable balance between what it must take in taxation and public expenditure; large numbers of families are buying their own homes and are therefore involved in the financial complexities of credit cards, mortgages, insurance; and a growing number of people are now dealing in shares too. Businesses, and indeed organisations of all kinds, have to manage their finances much more efficiently in today's economic conditions just to survive, let alone become more profitable (for commercial and industrial firms), or cost-effective (for organisations like local authorities, or charities). People and organisations alike are learning to use all the new and re-vamped financial services that are now being so aggressively sold to them.

All kinds of financial services, including banking, insurance, pension schemes, the stock markets, commodity trading, accounting and financial management generally, have been expanding for many years, but growth in the early 1990s was explosive. All companies must have their accounts kept and audited. Banking facilities, credit and insurance of risks are essential to both organisations and individuals. One commentator typified the role of finance in contemporary Britain by saying that, were Napoleon alive today, he would not have called us a nation of shopkeepers, but a nation of accountants. Financial institutions – pension schemes, insurance companies, investment and unit trusts – are a major force in the securities, owning a high proportion of all company shares, and having considerable influence on all areas of the country's economic life.

There is likely to be increasing competition and pressure on profitability in financial services in the future. What have been, until recently, very separate, different and clearly defined financial institutions – banks, building societies, insurance companies – offering quite different financial services, are now multi-faceted institutions, having moved into each other's markets. Banks have been competing with building societies for mortgage business and for deposit accounts. Banks are competing with accountants to provide computer-based financial information services – and the banks have the advantage of being able to give companies direct, on-line access to their very latest financial position. However, the banks themselves face greater competition too, from the building societies, from other (particularly the foreign) banks, from retailing firms competing on credit facilities. The result may be that eventually consumers could find that they are being offered all types of financial services – banking, credit facilities, savings schemes, insurance, mortgages, shares and so on – by a single high-street finance office. For the consumer this is also likely to mean more 'self-service' using automatic electronic equipment like the already familiar automatic cash dispensers, and home computers to check accounts and buy shares, etc.

All financial institutions have been shedding traditional attitudes and have, especially, become aggressively marketing-oriented. Financial organisations, and finance departments within companies and other organisations, were among the first to install large sophisticated 'mainframe' computers to record transactions and accounts – and without computers financial institutions would not have been able to expand so greatly. Current and future developments in finance also depend on even more sophisticated information technology. However, these systems are extremely costly, and with greater competition and tighter profit margins, all organisations are rationalising hard and extracting the greatest possible savings – fewer branch offices and fewer staff – from them.

However, financial institutions are still, and are likely to remain, labour-intensive, at least while services go on expanding and stay profitable. Numbers employed have risen steadily for over 25 years, with one or two relatively minor hiccups, although recruitment in some areas has reduced and redundancies have become a feature of financial services. While financial institutions want to keep numbers down as far as possible, they say that expanding services should counterbalance the effects of new technology. Independent observers suggest much depends on the extent to which financial institutions adopt the more advanced technological options, and the speed with which they do so. This, in turn, depends on the competitive pressures, how far financial institutions consider they must reduce their level of staffing to improve profit margins, how far other sectors (e.g. retail stores) are prepared to co-operate in, for instance, direct debiting, and on how easily the public accepts more 'new technology'.

Working in finance

Finance is a very wide field of employment. It includes the broad areas of banking (which breaks down into different kinds of services, such as retail and merchant banking), the insurance sector, pensions management, trade financing, building societies, the London Stock Exchange, and other finance houses. It ranges from national policy-making, as in the Treasury (*see* CENTRAL GOVERNMENT), to the financial management of industrial and commercial companies, and other organisations including local government, educational institutions, trade unions.

Career choice parallels this. For example, it is possible to be a financial expert in a financial organisation, an accountant in an accountancy practice or a banker in a bank. Alternatively, it is possible to be a financial expert in other kinds of organisation – a finance officer in local government, or a management accountant or treasurer in a hotel company, airline, retail store or TV company. It is also possible to choose to work for a financial institution, but not to specialise in finance – most employ lawyers, computer staff, personnel managers, public relations experts, and so on. Large financial institutions also use a great deal of research, and therefore employ specialists such as economists and statisticians. Independent organisations also provide financial information, often now 'on-line' to terminals on customers' desks.

The financial world has a relatively large number of managers and administrators – 17% of the total number of employees. In fact many institutions treat all, or most, employees interested in long-term careers as potential managers.

In the past, financial institutions have employed very large numbers of lower-grade clerical staff, many of them obviously directly involved in recording and calculating financial transactions (*see* SECRETARIAL, OFFICE AND CLERICAL WORK *in* ADMINISTRATION, BUSINESS MANAGEMENT AND OFFICE WORK). With the increase in the use of technology, this is changing.

The range of different kinds of financial institutions gives a choice between the very small and the very large, although generally the balance is moving towards larger organisations, mainly because economies of scale still apply, and size is essential to compete in a wide range of financial services.

However, even the largest (like the retail banks) are mostly broken down into smaller, local units. The scope for the individualist small business to develop is not as great as in some other areas of employment, although some independent financial consultants and analysts make a reasonable income.

Larger financial institutions tend to be fairly rigidly hierarchical organisations. Progress and promotion within them tend to be somewhat formalised and there is less movement between institutions than in most other sectors of employment, so 'first choice' can be very important. The traditional City (of London) is still the world's largest financial centre, and still dominates financial affairs in Britain. But in October 1986, when the London Stock Exchange de-regulated and went all-electronic, many traditions vanished almost overnight. The new computer-based dealing systems emptied the London Stock Exchange floor in weeks, with the markets now available on information screens. And so while people still work in City offices, most having something to do with money or trade, the 'City' is rapidly becoming a concept rather than a physical centre, with firms moving wherever buildings become available.

Some larger financial institutions, and some company head offices have also moved out of London altogether. It is now usual to site some functions, e.g. the bulk processing of accounts, out of London, while keeping a small core financial management team presence in the capital.

Recruitment and entry

The traditional method of entry, straight from school, is still quite common in the financial world, although the balance has swung quite sharply to graduate entry in many professions, e.g. accountancy, banking. Insurance companies, building societies and other larger institutions still take quite large numbers from those coming out with, preferably, two A levels/three H grades, although the 16 plus intake (with four or more GCSE/SCEs grades A–C/1–3, or equivalent) is still quite large. Graduate intake is rising. The larger institutions continue to take a number of 16-year-olds on Youth Credits/Youth Training programmes.

Instinct suggests that higher entry qualifications should mean better opportunities for promotion to senior management, but most large institutions deny this, and insist that entrants with A levels/H grades, at the very least, stand just as good a chance if they show aptitude. A good general level of education, with reasonable numeracy and use of English, though, is essential.

Other aptitudes are those which generally only develop after experience, for instance, problem solving in the context of complex financial situations. A logical and analytical mind capable of understanding legal and economic theory and practice as well as the intelligence to learn enough of the technicalities of any business are needed. Much financial work, especially at managerial level, is effectively decision-making, often dealing with large amounts of money, and in screen-based transactions, at speed. Although decisions are based on well-established criteria, an element of risk is always there, and the ability to judge risks and take decisions at the right moment is often a set of skills some people have and others do not. Attention to detail and painstaking care are important, but financial institutions are all now looking for people who will be capable of working in a highly competitive, heavily marketing-oriented environment.

Financial work often involves dealing with many different kinds of people, in negotiating, in communicating financial decisions, and in explaining complex financial matters, and this obviously requires tact and diplomacy as well as the ability to develop good working relations and to communicate clearly.

Qualifications and training

Formal education for financial careers has developed only slowly. It is still common to study for professional qualifications on a part-time basis, although there are exceptions. Most financial organisations have their own development and training schemes for all staff, usually supplemented by internal or 'association' courses, and these usually go up to management level. Further education colleges offer part-time (usually evening) courses.

An accountancy qualification is claimed to be one of the best passports to careers in almost all areas of finance, and in some it is almost essential. The emphasis on professional, and relatively narrow, qualifications in the separate financial specialisations – banking, insurance, actuarial work, etc. is still strong – although some professions now accept more broadly based qualifications such as GNVQ/GSVQs and the BTEC National and Higher National awards in business studies which have a broad financial bias. Some of the professions are introducing various levels of NVQ/SVQs (e.g. in building society work) which demonstrate specific work-related skills .

Accountancy and financial management

Background – working in professional accountancy and financial management – public practice accounting – accountants in industry and commerce – public sector accountancy – recruitment and entry – qualifications and training – professional bodies – related professional bodies – working overseas – further information – working as an accounting technician

Background

The work done by accountants has changed very considerably over the past 30 or so years. To begin with, they were only really responsible for seeing that the financial accounts of individuals or firms in business, or public bodies like local authorities, were recorded accurately and properly, under legislation passed to prevent fraud etc.

Company accounts still have to be formally audited by law, but in fact under 27,000 chartered accountants and 5,000 (1996) UK certified accountants hold practising certificates and can therefore audit accounts, and this is less than 25% and 2% of the membership of the respective member bodies.

Effectively, the profession has been virtually transformed, taking on far wider, more positive and greater responsibility in the general field of financial management and advice. Although not every financial manager is, or has to be, a qualified accountant, a great many are. The increasing complexity of the business world, the economic climate and all the rapid changes which now affect the financial state of any organisation, together with more intensive competition, mean that firms and other organisations have to monitor their performance much more closely in financial terms. They must plan their future operations more systematically and need sophisticated advice on how to handle their finances – when and how to invest, where best to go for credit, and how to present the best case, and so on.

Accountants have taken on this role and developed it successfully, although they face increasing competition from, for instance, banks, lawyers and management consultants.

Financial management, including management accounting, involves planning, budgeting, analysing and interpreting to control an organisation's financial affairs efficiently. Accountants design, develop, set up and manage modern and sophisticated financial and management accounting procedures and systems for their firms or clients. They have to be able to report accurately on what has happened to a company financially, not just once a year – more frequent monitoring is needed so profitability can be regularly analysed and measured, forecasts and plans made. This is done both for the company as a whole, for sectors of it and even for individual products. Marketing managers, for instance, look for regular reports on products to check that objectives are being achieved, or if not why not. Obviously, such systems have to be computer-based, and from the very start sophisticated financial management developed hand-in-hand with the technology, which accountants and accounting technicians must know how to use. Increasing use of computer technology is having a further effect on the whole working environment of all accountants.

Accountancy, as a profession, has expanded enormously in the last 35 years. With its widening role, numbers have risen from 25,000 to well over 223,000. However, the ever-changing economy has meant that recruitment in some areas has reduced and redundancies have been made – especially in public practice (industry, commerce and public service organisations are more stable). Nevertheless, the demand for high-level financial expertise is still considerable, especially in management accounting (much less in historical reporting), and employers want better calibre people with good experience of the business world, even in 'line' management.

Jobs are moving, probably in line with the general movement of work, into areas not traditionally employing professional accountants, e.g. retailing and distribution. Even the Civil Service, although cutting overall numbers, is recruiting more accountants.

Promotion prospects are getting tougher – in public practice, there are unlikely to be enough senior positions and 'top' partnerships to satisfy the numbers of able people competing for them, since up to two-thirds of all professional accountants are now under 45. However, in industry and commerce, the professionally trained and qualified accountant continues to dominate the financial functions, right up to director level. Accountants have had a fairly free run into general and top management until now, but other professionals, such as engineers, are being encouraged to develop their management skills and play a greater part in running companies, and so accountants may have face stiffer competition for top jobs in the future.

Career planning is becoming critical. Young accountants' career paths can now be set within two or three years of qualifying (in minimum time for the best start). Employers increasingly want finance staff, including accountants, with expertise and experience tailored to their interests, or to a particular function, and so specialisation is growing.

Working in professional accountancy and financial management

Accountancy traditionally divides into three different types of work – private practice, sometimes called public practice, industry and commerce, and public service. All organisations of any size employ accountants, and most have to use accountancy practices to advise them and/or audit their accounts. The intricacies of company law and taxation alone mean that anyone in business must have an accountant, and all companies and public bodies must have their accounts independently audited. So the qualified accountant can work for organisations in broadcasting and television, the press, football clubs, retail stores, construction, the oil industry, in fact any areas of business.

Many accountants also move away and/or up from strictly accounting work soon after, or sometimes even before they qualify. A professional accountancy qualification is a passport into financial work which is not strictly accounting (e.g. treasury function), into more general financial and senior management, into consultancy, into Stock Exchange work, into insurance and pension-broking, investment policy formation, operational research, systems analysis, tutoring etc.

Accountancy and financial management is mainly office- and desk-based work, but as much time is often spent talking to other people – listening, questioning, advising, discussing, reporting – as with a calculator or computer. However, many accountants and financial managers spend quite a high proportion of their time away from their own offices and desks. In public practice, clients' offices may be far from base, and audit teams may have to work in whatever corner can be found for them. Accountants and financial managers in industry, commerce and public authorities spend a significant amount of time moving around their organisations. In larger organisations they are generally expected to change jobs and move around regularly. Hours can be irregular, especially when it comes to the financial year end.

Public practice accounting

Public practice accounting employs most professional accountants, and the majority qualify via the Institute of Chartered Accountants in England and Wales (ICAEW) and the Institute of Chartered Accountants of Scotland (ICAS). Most of the rest qualify with the Chartered Association of Certified Accountants (ACCA) (*see* QUALIFICATIONS AND TRAINING *below*).

Accountancy firms vary in size from the very small to the very large. Small firms may have only one qualified principal, one or two trainees and a minimal staff of assistants ('technicians') and secretaries; large firms may have more than a dozen offices in different centres at home and overseas, over 2,200 trainees, a large number of young qualified staff, and managers to supervise the audit teams and head specialist departments, as well as partners with financial shares in the firm. The largest firms have people working full-time on planning, marketing, management consultancy and technical development.

The profession is increasingly dominated by about six multi-million pound 'firms', or rather partnerships (out of a total of about 19,000). They are increasingly being run as businesses, going for growth, rather than as practices. Current economic conditions also mean that accountancy practices must justify their services and costs, 'sell' themselves to customers, and keep costs down.

While audit is a secure business, since every company must have auditors, there is little or no scope for bringing in more clients, except by luring them away from other practices. Widening services is the only way to increase business, and many practices, particularly the larger firms, have greatly extended both their audit-related and wider financial services, only stopping short of actual market making and capital funding. Most larger organisations expect their auditors to check and comment on their financial and internal control systems as well as on their balance sheet, and many auditors go beyond this, to more general advice on financial problems. Even smaller practices are, in today's tough trading conditions, having to give their small business customers sophisticated advice on how to cope. The largest accountancy practices have 'diversified' further, forming their own management consultancies, and a number operate internationally.

Preparing and auditing accounts, including accounts for tax authorities, however, is still the main work of most accountancy practices. This means a lot of routine checking of balance sheets and 'books' (usually kept as computer-based records even by small firms and one-person businesses), examining and verifying financial statements, and so on. Standard routines have cut the time this takes, and computer-based audit routines are now used more extensively. Nearly all practices now have their own computer systems. This leaves auditors more time to look at firms' accounting procedures, systems and controls, and suggest improvements, new reporting routines, etc.

In public practice, accountants audit for and advise a wide variety of organisations and individuals in many different lines of business. Smaller practices generally deal with smaller local organisations, and traders (who may, nevertheless, include clients of considerable variety, from local writers to farms, garages, stores and builders), while the larger firms usually also have major industrial and commercial companies on their books.

In medium-to-large firms, audit staff work in teams, mostly going out to clients' offices in different parts of the country, even abroad (so the job can be rather more peripatetic than in industry), to check on their operation, to see if their accounts give a 'true and fair' view of the financial position of the organisation on a given date. The size and make-up of an audit team depend on the size and scope of the organisation being audited. It can be two, three or four people, it can be up to 50 or more. Audit teams generally consist mainly of staff in various stages of training, headed by an experienced accountant.

In smaller practices, auditing for individuals and very small businesses in the locality is more usually done in the office by one person, and often involves putting together the accounts first from a collection of bank statements, receipts, invoices etc.

Accountancy practices also act as executors and trustees, provide company secretarial and registration services or act as liquidators or receivers when companies become insolvent – a growth area during economic recession. They make financial investigations of all kinds: for example, when a client is considering buying a business or changing a partnership; preparing and verifying financial statements when a company issues a prospectus offering shares to the public; and generally providing management information, statistical advice and similar services.

A number of trainees leave their practices within a few years of qualifying, mostly to work in other practices, other financial services, into financial work in industry or commerce, other organisations (from broadcasting to charities) or into management consultancy. Some go on to be accountancy tutors, a few into financial journalism. Of those who stay, some continue to specialise in audit work, usually as a manager within a couple of years, some go into other divisions of the practice but most, especially in smaller firms, deal with the full range of the practice's services. A small percentage become partners in the larger firms.

Accountancy practices are now allowed to advertise, and the larger practices have taken on MARKETING managers, and some PUBLIC RELATIONS people too. (*See also* BUYING, SELLING AND RELATED SERVICES.) Of course all practices employ office staff.

Accountants in industry and commerce

Financial accounting – cost accounting – treasury management – tax management – management accounting – other functions – recruitment and entry

Industry and commerce and most other organisations employ trained financial staff, a high proportion of them qualified accountants. Financial staff – management accountants – are now crucial and integral members of an organisation's management team at all levels. While they may work in separate financial departments, they no longer do so at arm's length from the rest of the organisation, just recording what happened to it recently or administering financial transactions, but take part in all aspects of managerial decision-making, strategic forward planning and forecasting. Financial managers provide information on which decision-making and planning can be based, and performance measured and controlled; assess and evaluate financial information, plans and decisions; and actively look for ways to maximise profits and make the best use of available resources.

Central to all areas of financial management are increasingly sophisticated computer-based systems, which provide and analyse more complex financial information far faster than has ever been possible. Financial managers can give senior management a more accurate, speedy service and can show the details in a way that is meaningful to them. Their advice is stronger because they can process more data, using more sophisticated 'models'. All financial staff now have to be familiar with computerised systems and recruiters also look for people able to help improve and further develop these.

Financial or management accounting can be divided up into several different types of work. At various stages in their training and subsequent careers, accountants and other finance staff may work in just one of these and go on to specialise (and perhaps add extra qualifications), or they may move between them, or (in smaller organisations) combine them. Firms often have different ways of organising the functions – for instance, an accountant may be part of the project manager's team on a major construction contract, being responsible for all the records and controls to monitor and report on the project, reviewing its financial status and providing information for capital budgeting.

However the functions are divided, they have to maintain close liaison and information flows, and all financial functions are, in a sense, part of management accounting, since they all contribute the information on which it is based.

Financial accounting

Financial accounting deals with the routines of keeping financial records. The main tasks are operating accounts – more often now computerised accounting systems, and doing internal audits, but also include dealing with wages and salaries, paying accounts and sending out invoices, and coping with tax. Trainee accountants can expect to spend time carrying out the full range of basic accounting tasks and go on to, for instance, interpreting accounts; later to supervising, controlling and organising expenditure and income, etc. Their work includes compiling regular – monthly and yearly – management accounts as reports for directors.

Cost accounting

Cost accounting deals with the complex business of working out what particular operations, jobs, products really cost to produce, taking into account all the relevant factors and not just labour and materials, but all the 'overheads' and the less obvious costs too. It extends to budgeting and budgetary control, forecasting future needs and costs (for instance, looking ahead to rising or falling energy prices), monitoring expenditure to see that costs are not over-shooting, and providing reports, etc. for management accounting. It involves analysing and comparing costs, translating information from non-financial managers into financial terms and explaining financial information for them. Cost accounting uses computer systems extensively which in the most sophisticated firms can input and extract the necessary information into/from integrated computer-aided design and manufacturing (CAD/CAM) systems.

Treasury management

Treasury management is the financial 'housekeeping' function, which has recently become much more critical to those companies which take a much more positive and sophisticated line in managing their money. Tighter profit margins, high interest rates on borrowing and lending, fluctuations in currency exchange rates and new ways of exploiting the money markets have all contributed to create what is being called a 'new' profession.

Treasury managers see that receipts and credits are banked fast (four times, rather than twice a day, can save a major corporation up to £75,000 a year). They know exactly how much is in each bank account early enough in the day so that they can invest the balance overnight and see that all idle funds are earning. They avoid or minimise exchange losses on overseas contracts by, e.g. trading in financial 'options'. They negotiate the best possible charges with bankers and negotiate the best possible terms for capital borrowing. This involves projecting the firm's needs well ahead and predicting movements in interest rates. Treasury managers work on the principle that time is money, so ensure that debts and stocks (e.g. of components) are kept to a minimum, that terms of payment and discount rates are reviewed regularly, and that invoices go out fast once orders have been despatched.

Positive treasury management depends totally on efficient and rapid information and this has to mean the latest in IT systems so that advantage can be taken of all that the banks have to offer in real-time access to the very latest position on accounts. The largest firms with the most sophisticated and aggressive treasury managers even have their own dealing desks, monitoring share and currency prices on screen and trading direct with market makers. This is fast becoming the major role for large-company treasury staff.

Tax management

Tax management is sometimes a separate function, sometimes part of treasury management. Tax managers specialise in optimising a firm's fiscal structure, to ensure the company pays as little as is legal. Increasingly they have to cope with taxation on an international scale and with the very different tax laws of different countries – a 'world tax planner' database can, in ten minutes, give managers ten alternative ways to repatriate the maximum amount of cash, some of them via several countries. They look at the tax implications of new plans, changes in company structures, in fact of any major decision. They advise on the tax effect of performance goals, which includes pricing policies.

Management accounting

Management accounting collects, organises, collates and analyses information from all parts of the organisation, including all the financial departments. In larger organisations, this may be based on sophisticated, computer-based systems designed to maintain detailed and up-to-date records of all the firm's expenditure via internal costing systems backed up by comparative information from elsewhere. This makes it possible to make regular critical analyses of past and present financial performance, with projections for the future.

Management accountants monitor all the many and varied costs involved in making a product or providing a service, from raw materials and labour through to transport, administrative costs, overheads on buildings, and so on. They record and analyse sales trends. By constantly monitoring performance and efficiency, they can spot and report on problems, for instance why performance is not matching predictions, provide figures on which to base future pricing policies, and suggest ways of making economies by analysing costs and the financial implications of different production methods, rationalising the number of factories, or finding a new source of components. They may also provide the information which helps treasury management to anticipate and ensure funds for expansion, and generally provide expert assessments of the possible effects of events outside the company, such as expansion or merger plans of competing companies, new company or other legislation, and changes in taxation.

Individual accountants, or finance staff, do specific jobs within these broad fields and may move between them, particularly within large organisations, although many specialise in one aspect. They generally start with more mundane and routine tasks – keeping accounts, working on internal audits, costing and stock control, doing research such as making price comparisons of different brands and types of a particular product. From there the work becomes progressively more responsible – designing a new financial reporting system for a factory to improve the accuracy of the information coming through, evaluating tenders in terms of their potential contribution to profits, or examining the financial consequences of the firm's changeover from being labour intensive to high investment in advanced technological production, or working as part of a team rationalising and reorganising a company's warehouse depots within a region, for example. Budget control – making regular cost reports for a factory, working out why one set of costs have suddenly risen and what to do about it – is another typical area of responsibility.

Other functions

Finance departments, especially in larger organisations, will also have to prepare prospectuses for share issues. Finance departments may be responsible for managing pension funds and long-term investments; investigate prospective investments, and do the preparatory work on the possibility of taking over another company. In some, usually smaller, organisations, the financial controller may carry out the legal responsibilities of the COMPANY SECRETARY. (*See in* ADMINISTRATION, BUSINESS MANAGEMENT AND OFFICE WORK.) Promotion can be to financial control – of a small unit at first, later perhaps to large units, regional centres, or the whole organisation – and 'top' strategic planning.

Recruitment and entry

A qualification in accountancy is not absolutely essential. Especially in some functions – corporate treasurers, for example, may find a City-dealing/banking background more helpful – a broad-based business-cum-finance with IT qualification at degree level is increasingly useful. However, an accountancy qualification is an undoubted advantage. Accountants who want to work in industry or commerce can now train and qualify with any of the professional bodies.

The Chartered Institute of Management Accountants (CIMA) qualifications are specifically tailored to accounting as a management tool, but do not qualify in statutory audit work. Reports suggest that in future, organisations may prefer to recruit people who have trained in industry/commerce for the CIMA or ACCA qualifications rather than chartered accountants trained mainly in public practice.

Public sector accountancy

Local government – central government – other public authorities

In the public sector professional accountants are employed by local authorities, the Civil Service and organisations such as the National Health Service, the British Council, the National Audit Office and the Audit Commission. As elsewhere, the emphasis nowadays is on effective and efficient financial management as well as on auditing.

Local government

Local government employs accountants in some numbers (5,131 Chartered Institute of Public Finance Accountants (CIPFA) members alone in 1996). The work itself may seem similar to that of accountants and financial managers in industry or commerce, but it is done within a very different framework – administrative, economic, and political – and with different aims. With more competitive tendering and 'value for money' being a major pre-occupation – and the willingness and capacity of chargepayers to provide the finance – the aim is not to maximise profit, but to provide services for the community. The resources are never enough to meet the potential demands made upon them, with central government expecting local authorities to work within tighter and tighter 'cash limits'. Even so, local government spends billions of pounds each year on services to the public. Since every financial decision vitally affects both the economic and the social life of the community, local government too is demanding more and better financial management and information systems on which to make decisions.

While it is the elected members of the authority who are actually responsible for deciding what services to provide and what is needed to finance them – or how to allocate what they are permitted to spend with set cash limits – they must use the expertise of their financial officers to work out and implement their plans. Financial officers advise the authority, prepare annual budgets according to policy decided by the council and show, for example, how economies can be made, how capital can be raised and what the different options for expenditure are. They have to analyse and interpret the complexities of government financial legislation and regulations and work out the practical implications for their own authority.

The financial officers also set up and run financial control systems, administer revenue collection (of community charge and rents), manage any loan debts and supervise capital loans, pension fund investments, mortgage accounts, and so on. They see that government grants arrive and pay wages, bills, etc.

Again, most trainees start in audit work and routine work such as revenue collection, payments, payroll. They move on to problem solving and legal aspects (what to do when someone cannot pay their community charge), checking parts of the financial control system, or helping to develop new computer-based systems. They may work on separate assignments, for instance, estimates for a new sports centre or showing the financial benefits of restoring property against rebuilding. They may specialise in work on one area of an authority's services, e.g. housing, dealing with subsidies, preparing financial accounts etc.

Promotion is to increasingly responsible work and/or to 'group' accountant as a team leader and higher. Chief executives of local authorities are most often former finance officers.

Most local government finance officers start their careers in an authority, usually taking the examinations of CIPFA or ACCA and it is not easy for anyone qualified on the basis of training and experience in other areas to get in without CIPFA or ACCA membership. However, CIPFA qualified accountants are now being recruited in some numbers by other organisations, especially the NHS and public bodies generally, and by practices auditing and working with local authorities. Movement between authorities is also common. *See also* LOCAL GOVERNMENT.

Central government

Central government departments and agencies currently spend and collect an estimated £500 billion a year (1995). The government wants accountants who will 'play a vital part in the drive to improve financial and resource management', and to involve them fully in financial management and policy-making generally within government departments.

One of the main functions of the accountancy service is to develop, install and apply the measurement techniques of management accounting – budgetary control, performance indicators, expenditure statements, memorandum trading accounts, etc. to make people working in government more 'cost conscious' to achieve efficiency, effectiveness and economy.

Internal audit systems are also being developed in departments, not just to see that systems are working and are properly controlled, but also more widely to monitor operational efficiency and policy effectiveness.

Accountants are also used where government works with private firms – for instance, in pricing and negotiating government contracts and assessing appropriate rates of profit, making sure that potential contractors are financially viable.

They also help administer any government aid to industry, and see that legal requirements are met – by companies generally, by banks and insurance companies. In the Department of Energy they may work on oil and gas royalties, in industry on the impact of European financial legislation in the UK, and so on.

Accountants work in a range of departments and generally move between departments more often than other civil servants. Promotion prospects are being improved.

Training given in several departments is mainly for CIMA, ACCA and, to a lesser extent, CIPFA, but not normally ICAEW. *See also* CENTRAL GOVERNMENT.

Other public authorities

Other public authorities employing accountants, both as accountants and financial managers, include the National Health Service, the National Audit Office, the Audit Commission for Local Authorities (England and Wales), the Accounts Commission (Scotland) and the Northern Ireland Audit Office. Privatised services such as electricity, gas and water also employ accountants.

The National Health Service has always been a major employer of accountants and financial experts and accountants and finance staff work in district and regional health offices, and in individual hospitals and trusts. Finance teams have been involved in developing computer-based information systems used in generating budget and controlling spending – the NHS budget is over £30 billion a year – paying accounts, salaries, etc. and providing information for management. NHS spending priorities and budgeting are highly sensitive issues, and finance officers not only advise, monitor and control, but also have to take part in very difficult negotiations over what and how much to spend where.

Accountant training schemes for all professional bodies are organised mainly by regional authorities, although some districts and trusts also recruit direct. Both graduates and A level entrants are taken on. Staff are generally trained and qualify as accountants via CIPFA, or accounting technicians depending on basic qualifications. *See also* MANAGING THE HEALTH SERVICE.

The National Audit Office (NAO) gives independent information, advice and assurance to parliament on the expenditure, revenue and use of resources of the government, including international organisations to which the UK belongs (e.g. the UN). The 730 staff (1995), the majority of whom are qualified accountants, deal with anything from military contracts to university grants, agricultural subsidies to atomic energy. They also 'audit' the financial aspects of organisations like the Church Commissioners. Trainee NAO accountants train and qualify via ICAEW.

The Audit Commission for Local Authorities (England and Wales), the Accounts Commission (Scotland) and the Northern Ireland Audit Office audit accounts of local authorities and regional and district health authorities mostly using their own staff, although outside firms carry out some of the work. Training for the above is for CIPFA qualifications.

Electricity, gas and water are all now privatised and have to produce profits for shareholders. Services have to be made and kept cost-effective, and reconciling this with customer demand for efficiency and reasonable prices is difficult in today's economic conditions. These industries are also very capital-intensive, having to spend very large sums on new generating plant, sewerage treatment schemes, etc. All policy decisions and forward plans have to be made with information and advice from financial managers, who also work with engineers on new projects. They monitor expenditure, manage cash flows, supervise billing and accounts, work on revenue and capital accounting. *See also* WATER INDUSTRY *and the* ENERGY INDUSTRIES *in* THE MINING AND ENERGY INDUSTRIES.

Qualifying as an accountant

Recruitment and entry

Most people start as trainees in public practice, larger industrial or commercial companies, local and other public authorities, including the Civil Service. The great majority of trainees start straight from higher education, although it is possible to go through the technician-level route (*see below*), or start directly after A-levels. Recruitment policies, especially amongst the largest practices, are changing, mostly to cope with City competition for top-flight graduates. Firms are taking fewer, more carefully selected, new graduates and offering training packages (up to and including MBA) etc. – filling the 'body' gap with computers and accounting technicians (*see below*).

Entry qualifications for professional accountants in England and Wales are standardised at a minimum of five GCSE/SCEs (grades A–C/1–3) with two A-level/3 H grades. English and mathematics at GCSE/SCE level are not compulsory subjects for ICAEW qualifications, but most firms insist on it. CIPFA state that students must have English and mathematics at GCSE/SCE or equivalent (e.g. BTEC/SCOTVEC National, NVQ/SVQ level 3, Advanced

GNVQ/GSVQ) level. In Scotland, ICAS requires a degree (currently 98%). A degree is a strong advantage and the proportion of graduate entrants is rising, although unevenly between the professional bodies. By 1994/95, virtually 95% of the 4,082 ICAEW students registering training contracts were graduates (under 1% had HNDs). CIPFA entry is over 65% graduate, CIMA over 50%, and ACCA 40% (1995).

Competition for training places is extremely fierce, especially in the major public practices, and organisations with good training records. A traineeship is not a guarantee of a long-term job on qualification. Choice of practice can influence accountants' careers – training in a small, country practice is unlikely to lead to work with, or for, large corporations, for instance.

ICAEW had 2,127 authorised training offices in 1993/94 (but only 200 or so firms take students in any one year) while over 3,500 firms in 1995 registered with ACCA for training purposes. While over 62.3% of 1993/94 entry students found training in firms with over 100 partners, over 95% of them were graduates, as were 95% of the 12.8% of students in firms with between 21 and 100 partners. Firms with ten (or fewer) partners took just 20% of new students, but 67.5% of non-graduate entrants. ICAEW figures show a strong correlation between A-level grades, class of degree and pass rates for professional exams. A relatively high percentage cancel their training contracts or have them terminated.

Degree level. Degree subject is not crucial – about 80% of ICAEW entrants to the profession have degrees which are not apparently 'relevant'. Graduates with degrees in engineering, maths, law and classics all do well in ICAEW exams, and graduates with 'relevant' degrees only do better if they have firsts or upper seconds. A degree in, e.g. engineering, can be especially useful in industry and for anyone wanting to get into consultancy work eventually. A good degree – preferably a 2.1 – is a strong advantage, and larger employers especially also look for good A level/H grades and even good GCSE/SCE grades as well.

School leaver entry. School leaver entry for good training places in both public practice and industry/commerce often demands high A-level and GCSE/SCE grades. Numeracy is obviously essential, although high-level mathematical skills are not needed. It is more the ability to be able to 'make sense' of information in number form, to be able to 'think' numerically and be happy working with figures. Employers want people who are interested in the business and financial world. Accountants must also be able to work closely with others, to talk and listen to anyone with or for whom they may be working. The information which accountants must collect comes from sources ranging from the factory floor, other professionals (e.g. engineers), and top managers, and they must be able to explain clearly, effectively and quickly what they want and understand what their informants are saying. They have to develop the ability to make reasonably shrewd judgements of people they work with or for. They may need considerable persuasive skills to, for instance, get colleagues to understand the need for and adopt new reporting procedures. At more senior levels, they may work as part of a management team with production and marketing managers.

Computer training/experience at some stage is a must. Languages are increasingly valuable, especially to get into the international business of management consultancy.

Recruiters are increasingly looking for management potential from among their graduate entry – the qualities needed to take on responsibility for other staff within a relatively short period and learn to delegate, to be able to problem-solve and know how to decide on priorities, to make decisions of increasing importance, to be able to think for oneself but know when to ask for advice. Social skills are emphasised.

Qualifications and training

All the careers literature stresses that training and qualifying in accountancy is very tough and lengthy, even for graduates. Trainees have to be prepared to work for long-term aims. A professional qualification is essential for public practice and public authorities, and major industrial and commercial employers ask for accountancy qualifications for many posts in their finance departments.

ACCA and CIMA qualifications can both be studied for on a full-time basis at colleges throughout the UK and overseas. In these cases students usually obtain their practical experience after completing the examinations. However, for many students training is largely on-the-job with part-time study for professional qualifications, and all entrants, graduate or not, start with a period on the most basic work – for example, learning book-keeping and audit routines. Periods of study-leave are usually written in to ICAEW and ICAS training contracts and CIPFA training is shorter with block (three years) than with day release (four years). ACCA has Approved Training Schemes which include study leave, rotational training and financial assistance for participating students; employers offering the best package receive 'gold star' status. It is clearly worthwhile trying for schemes which give study time and formal tuition – some practices and firms put on their own study sessions, otherwise study has to be by evening or correspondence course. Some employers offer CIMA-approved 'Professional Development Programmes'.

Even with time off to study, getting through the exams takes a lot of every entrant's spare time – often after a long day on an audit – for the first three to five years. Firms are taking an increasingly dim view (and terminating contracts) of students who do not pass them in the shortest possible time, and are selecting recruits whose academic 'profiles' indicate that they are more likely to do so (ICEAW and CIPFA also set time limits on resits).

Entrants without a degree are normally required by CIPFA to do a foundation course at college, which is usually taken before starting the training period (although it is possible to do a preliminary period of training first), and some colleges expect students to have a provisional training place before accepting them.

All of the accounting bodies require trainees to gain a minimum of three years' relevant training, although for A-level/H grade entrants with CIPFA and ICAEW a four-year training period is the minimum.

Graduates normally have to do a three-year training. For both graduates and non-graduates, ICAEW, ICAS and CIPFA require formal training contracts; a period (at least three years) of approved relevant employment/experience is required for membership of other bodies. Graduates training with ICAEW, ICAS and CIPFA who do not have a relevant degree must take a foundation course and exams, but need not do so full-time.

Although most chartered accountants complete their training in practice with a firm of chartered accountants, there are now opportunities to 'train outside public practice' (TOPP) under the TOPP scheme. Those students who are already attracted to working in industry, commerce or the public sector can now study for their qualification with one of these organisations. In March 1995 there were 25 authorised TOPP offices training a total of 94 students.

Professional bodies

The profession has inherited six major accountancy bodies and several minor ones. The illogicality of this is generally recognised within the profession, but despite years of negotiation rationalisation seems as far away as ever. There is a growing consensus of opinion on education and training; the pattern of their examinations is similar, and all the professional bodies try to keep their examinations up-to-date on modern developments in accounting.

The major bodies are the three Institutes of Chartered Accountants, the Chartered Association of Certified Accountants, the Chartered Institute of Management Accountants, and the Chartered Institute of Public Finance and Accountancy.

The Institute of Chartered Accountants in England and Wales has, in 1996, over 108,000 members plus over 10,649 students. The Institute of Chartered Accountants of Scotland has, in 1996, over 14,000 members, but only about 60% work in Scotland, and 1,400 students. The third Institute of Chartered Accountants is for Ireland. About 50% of ICAEW members who responded to a ICAEW questionnaire work in public practice as partners or employees, 29% work in industry and commerce, 1% work in social services, 1% in government and 9% in other areas of finance. About half of all ICAS members work in commerce and industry.

The Chartered Association of Certified Accountants (ACCA) 28,997 (1996) UK members (total over 47,000 plus some 100,000 registered students), work in public practice (32%), industry (26%), commerce (25%), and the public sector (14%). ACCA entrants can train in, and move between, public practice and/or central/local government and industry/commerce.

The Chartered Institute of Management Accountants (CIMA) has 61% of its 39,000 membership in industry, with rising proportions in areas such as financial and business services (9%), transport and distribution (7%), national and local government (3%), and consultancy (5%). Over half the 57,000 registered students are in the UK. CIMA entrants train mainly in industrial and commercial firms, and the qualification is best suited to those certain they want a future in the business world (CIMA expects trainees to gain 'real' working experience in departments other than finance, e.g. marketing), and who are not concerned about training for public practice.

The Chartered Institute of Public Finance and Accountancy (CIPFA) – 1996 membership 12,368 plus 3,200 students – is mainly for accountants in local government (45% of members), although its qualifications are used by other public authorities – the NHS (nearly 10%), government and governmental bodies (4%), the water industry (3%), with small numbers working in gas/electricity audit firms and other organisations. Most entrants train in local authorities or other public bodies but in practice this does not restrict movement into other areas of accounting/financial work.

Degree level courses

Relevant degrees may exempt from first-stage professional foundation examinations, and other graduates may be given subject-for-subject exemptions – this varies between the professional bodies. Relevant degree courses are available in most universities. Exemptions for BTEC HND is on a subject-for-subject basis only.

First destinations in accountancy, 1994:

total graduating	*1,003*
destination unknown	54
overseas students	179
research, etc.	42
teacher training/other non-degree courses	85
believed unemployed 31 December	50
temporary work	37
permanent UK work	525
not available for employment	19
employers	
accountancy	357
banking/insurance/finance	24
other commerce	50
Civil Service	5
local government	17
public utilities and transport	14
oil & chemicals	5
engineering	5
other manufacturing	18
higher/further education	6
Armed Forces	5
entertainment, leisure	5
functions	
financial work	435
marketing, etc.	19
admin/operational management	16
management services	6
personnel, social, etc.	4

Note that there is a very high correlation between graduates in accountancy and those entering the accountancy profession.

Related professional bodies

Related professional qualifications include those of the Chartered Institute of Taxation which is the leading body in the UK concerned solely with all aspects of taxation. It has nearly 10,000 members (1996) plus over 3,500 registered students working within accountancy and law firms, in industry and commerce as well as acting as tax advisers for central government, banks and tax consultancy firms. The majority of members are either lawyers or accountants. The qualifying examinations of a number of appropriate professional bodies entitle students to a Certificate of Eligibility to enter the Institute's professional examination.

The Association of Taxation Technicians is one of two professional and educational bodies in the UK concerned solely with taxation. In 1996 it had 2,000 members and 3,500 registered students, working in accountants' and solicitors' practices, tax consultancy firms, banks and commercial and industrial concerns. Success in its examinations, together with practical experience, enables students to call themselves taxation technicians and to use the letters ATT. The Taxation Technicians examinations also mean that students can register with the Chartered Institute of Taxation and go on to take their qualification.

The Association of Corporate Treasurers (formed 1979) has 2,300 members and 1,400 students (1996). Entry to the Associate level examinations is usually with four GCSE passes including mathematics and English with qualified accountants being exempt from four out of the six papers. Equivalent qualifications such as GNVQ/GSVQs may be considered on an individual basis. Associates can proceed on to the membership level examinations to take modules in corporate financial management, advanced funding and risk management and treasury management.

Work overseas

Opportunities for accountants to work overseas are increasing, particularly in Western and Central Europe and other developed countries, such as the USA, Australia, New Zealand and Canada. China is potentially a large market for newly qualified accountants, although obviously those that can speak Mandarin will be at an advantage. While newly qualified accountants may find work abroad, more senior staff are now being seconded overseas at manager and partner level.

Further information

The Institute of Chartered Accountants in England and Wales (ICAEW), the Institute of Chartered Accountants of Scotland (ICAS), the Chartered Association of Certified Accountants (ACCA), the Chartered Institute of Management Accountants (CIMA), the Chartered Institute of Public Finance and Accountancy (CIPFA).

Working as an accounting technician

Accounting technicians have been a separately defined group for the past ten years and many thousands do this kind of work – as cashiers, book-keepers, ledger and payroll clerks, accounting assistants, audit clerks, costing clerks, accounts supervisors and even more senior staff. The 'accounting technician' label is designed to indicate competence and ability to take on responsible work. The Association of Accounting Technicians (AAT) is the professional body for its nearly 100,000 members and students worldwide.

Most qualified technicians work in the private sector, although estimates suggest that about 14% of AAT members work for local or public authorities. Accountancy practices, looking to cut their intake of increasingly expensive graduates, are using computers more in areas such as audit. Since the work can be done by audit 'technicians', this is likely to mean more opportunities for them – and shortages are already showing up.

There is no hard-and-fast job specification for technicians – the work they do varies from organisation to organisation. It ranges from the more routine, but still technical, work – such as audit – within an accounting practice or office, through to quite considerable responsibility for staff and/or systems. In industry and commerce, there is nothing to prevent people with technician qualifications gaining promotion to management positions.

Accounting technicians work as, for instance, audit clerks – checking records and bank reconciliations. They may be invoice clerks – checking invoices and arranging payments. They may prepare financial data to go into computer systems, prepare accounts, and work out how much cash is needed in any one month to pay contractors for work which has been done on a particular project. They may check VAT and other official financial returns. Accounting technicians go on to more technical aspects of auditing, keeping financial records, costing and budgeting, and usually become supervisors in larger organisations, planning and monitoring the work of more junior staff.

Recruitment and entry

The Association of Accounting Technicians (AAT), set up in 1980, was one of the first professional bodies to move to an NVQ-based vocational education and training scheme and is the only professional body accredited to award NVQs in accounting at levels 2, 3 and 4.

Entry is open access, although applicants are expected to have an interest in mathematics and a good command of English. The AAT provides interesting and varied opportunities for career development and job mobility. Recognition by the major chartered accountancy bodies also offers the opportunity to progress to chartered status.

Qualifications and training

The practical nature of the AATs Education and Training Scheme gives staff in accounting and finance the skills to succeed in today's employment market across all employment sectors. The qualification is available at more than 480 centres throughout the UK and is unit-based to provide maximum flexibility. Options available for training include day-release, part-time, evening classes, distance-learning study and work place assessment.

Students who have completed the Scheme and have one year's relevant work experience can become members of the AAT and use the designatory letters MAAT. Members continue to gain additional skills and to update current skills through a comprehensive Continuing Professional Development programme.

Further information

The Association of Accounting Technicians.

Banking

Background – retail banking/ clearing banks – merchant and investment banking – international banking – recruitment and entry – qualifications and training – the Bank of England – further information

Background

One dictionary defines a bank as 'an institution for keeping, lending and exchanging ... money', but this hardly describes the range and variety of contemporary British banking. The banking system has been, and still is, going through a series of real revolutions, especially for anyone who thinks banking is synonymous with traditionalism. Banks have broken out of their conventional moulds.

Review after review charts the radical changes that have transformed banking over the past 25 years – and are continuing to do so. The staid, genteel image has been swept away. Banks, which used to play down the fact that they are commercial businesses which have to be profitable, have become increasingly competitive, using both aggressive marketing and promotion to sell themselves and their services and the latest financial management methods.

The banking system is no longer split between different types of banks, but into different services. These are – retail banking, merchant and investment banking, central and regulatory banking (the Bank of England), and international banking.

Not only are banks moving into new areas of business, but distinguishing between the traditionally very different clearing, merchant and savings banks is becoming increasingly difficult. The difference today is between the banking functions, the type of services being offered, rather than between one type of bank and another, although every bank is trying to establish its own recognisable, individual image.

Much of the change has happened because other financial interests, notably building societies, began competing with clearing banks for traditional clearing bank customers. In fighting back, the clearing banks not only introduced completely new services, but also went into their new competitors' business, e.g. mortgages. As competition has opened up further, with de-regulation the larger clearing banks have moved into areas such as merchant and investment banking, estate agency, insurance and the stock market, either developing their own divisions or (more often) buying into existing businesses, becoming banking and financial 'conglomerates'.

However, technology is, of course, also instrumental in changing the face of banking, and many of the new services and other developments would have been impossible without it. For a long time banks were users of highly efficient huge main-frame accounting and transaction-processing systems, but in the last ten years they have brought in the now-familiar cash machines, and the less-obvious 'back office' electronic clearing, inter-bank communication and information systems, both internal, with terminals for cashiers, and for services – computerised cash-management for companies. The latest, more sophisticated automated teller machines can be programmed to provide a widening range of services; systems can handle and rapidly process transactions in a 100 different currencies at airports, the first 'home banking' systems have started, as have nationwide electronic 'cashless shopping' – officially 'electronic funds transfer at point of sale.'

More is in the pipeline. Branches will be further automated (with considerable implications for staffing), and huge sums are being spent on integrated data communications systems for the branch networks, to give at least 30 times the traffic volume of systems installed barely ten years ago, and to help e.g. 'target' customers for marketing projects. Home banking may really take off when a palm-sized terminal, a 'bank in your pocket', can be plugged into a telephone socket for direct access to accounts – in fact almost all key developments now projected depend on direct communication between customers and bank data systems, via a terminal.

The whole style of banking has been transformed, and with it many managerial roles and attitudes, and ways of organising work, with major implications for future careers. Bankers now have to combine the traditional virtues of stability, judgement etc., with modern managerial, especially marketing, and technological skills.

Retail banking/clearing banks

Retail banking is the most familiar, with high-street branch banks offering services for both the general public and business, large and small. In the UK the retail bank has four main functions: the transmission of money, normally electronically; a means of depositing and borrowing money, providing loan facilities to all types of customer; provision of banknotes and coins; and the provision of financial services.

The 'banks' involved are Barclays, National Westminster, the Midland and Lloyds–TSB – plus Coutts (owned by National Westminster), the three Scottish and two Northern Ireland banks, the Co-operative Bank, the Trustee Savings Bank (TSB), and the Girobank (now owned by Alliance and Leicester Building Society). Building societies too, offer personal-account services in many ways similar to those of the traditional domestic banks. Standard Chartered is now also a 'clearing bank', as yet without a major stake in the high street; Citibank, the first foreign UK clearer, has barely a dozen branches so far.

Until now, 'domestic' banking services have been synonymous with a multiplicity of high-street branches. In theory, rapidly developing automation, 'robot cashiers' which can provide cash, statements, information, perhaps even 'expert' advice, together with plastic-card payment for shopping, etc. make the traditional branch redundant. Automated teller machines can be installed almost anywhere. In practice, banks, recognising that personal customers matter most, have decided that 'human' contact between staff and customers is still important, and are now putting their automated machines etc. inside the branch. But while the branches are unlikely to go altogether, there will be fewer, and they are changing considerably.

The branch system is being reshaped, both to 'target' customer services more accurately and to save some of the high costs involved in automation and marketing etc. Each bank has a slightly different policy, but the main themes are the same – separating personal and business services, and providing different levels and types of service at different branches, instead of every branch providing all services to their catchment area. Each bank's branch network might have some small, very streamlined 'robot' centres; some larger branches provide a range of services for personal customers and small businesses, designed to attract customers with informal, open-plan, carpeted areas staffed by advisers/sales staff at ordinary desks; and the largest, area or 'key' offices, provide sophisticated services for larger business customers and manage the other branches. TSB has a fully automated branch, enabling customers to pay bills, and answering transaction queries.

The volume of work handled by the retail banks continues to expand. 'Cashless shopping' is expected to replace only some 10% of cheque volume in the short term. Automated teller machines (ATMs), while taking work from bank counters, encourage people to take cash out in smaller amounts, but more frequently, so increasing the work of up-dating accounts, and they produce more queries about balances. ATMs have, so far, increased the overall workload.

Credit card use – the banks had 25.7 million in circulation in December 1994 – is expected to rise rapidly, and further 'product diversification' is expected to increase business too, although with the introduction of card fees in the 1990s the actual number of cards in circulation decreased.

Clearing banks have in the past monopolised the transfer of money – from one account to another, mostly as cheques via a 'central clearing house', but they also (and increasingly) do this directly through the bank giro and other direct debiting methods – and other financial firms are competing with them here. They handle foreign exchange and discount bills for exports.

During the 1980s the banks moved into the house mortgage sector of loans and at one time they posed a serious threat to the traditional building societies (at the end of December 1994 lending stood at £108,000 million). However, they continue to fund new small businesses, finance firms exporting capital goods, and make medium- and long-term loans to industry, even keeping firms alive. Clearing banks give firms sophisticated financial information systems, based on systems which allow company treasurers direct, instant on-line access to the current state of all the company's bank balances. This, together with the need for banks to have much more sophisticated information themselves about what is happening to particular industrial sectors and firms, is paving the way for separate services to corporate and individual customers.

For personal customers, there are more and varied savings schemes, which is one way of fighting building societies for their depositors. Banks have long been involved in trustee and executor work (in which the bank will administers wills, trusts, etc.), and in investment services. They have also greatly extended both these and other services; trustee work now helps organise family trusts, and with tax problems. Investment services extend both to financial planning in general and unit trust investment, and into services to companies, for instance, administering pension funds, international investment and organising employees' savings schemes.

The number of full-time staff in the main clearers' branches in 1994 was around 288,000 (336,900 in 1990), and numbers working part-time increased to well over 50,000. However, in the 1990s, retail banking is going through a difficult period with high interest rates, an increasing number of companies going into receiverships and bankruptcies, and a growth in the number of mortgage repossessions, all of which inevitably affect their profitability. Clearing banks are therefore cutting branch staffing and making redundancies with possibly more planned for 1996. Future staffing projections are difficult to make but independent assessments suggest reductions in staffing of up to a third by the end of the century.

Working in retail banking

Most career opportunities are in retail banking. While individual banks may have diversified out of their traditional services, staff still normally specialise in one type of banking, since each is very different.

Banks of all kinds treat the majority of their long-term staff as 'bankers', and most managerial posts go to them. They also employ quite significant, and probably increasing, proportions of other professional staff – systems analysts and other computer experts, lawyers, economists, personnel managers, market researchers, marketing managers, public relations experts etc. Some of these are, however, wherever possible, 'home grown'. Studies suggest the hard distinctions between 'bankers' and 'specialists', particularly software designers, will blur, and managers will have to be as familiar with information technology as with traditional banking subjects. But specialisation in areas such as treasury management, leasing, money markets, and management services, dealing, plus staff management, has become more important.

The clearing banks start most of their career entrants, graduate or school-leaver, in a branch, and many spend all their working lives in them.

Traditionally, every 'career' banker in the clearing banks is a 'generalist', but this is changing as banks separate the services they provide for larger companies from the rest of their customers. The new breeds of managers normally specialise in either personal or corporate services, at a fairly early point in their careers.

Each branch has a considerable degree of independence, and the manager, at the top, is responsible for its profitability. Each branch has a range of staff at varying levels. All jobs in the branches cover a wide variety of tasks, and the 'mix' of tasks varies from bank to bank. Tasks have changed considerably over the past 25 years, and will go on so doing. While there is little evidence of wide deskilling, technology has cut the drudgery, and shifting skill requirements for individual tasks has become a near-continuous process. A continuing 'slow shift' away from junior clerical and technical/service functions is expected, towards more specialist, professional and managerial positions. Typically, though, new staff may start as remittance clerks – who check and sort cheques and other credits for electronic reading – or terminal operators, who key in data to bring customers' accounts and other records up to date (although in some banks this is done regionally). Next on the rung is dealing with standing orders, and cashiering. Foreign work – buying and selling currency, handling travellers' cheques, import-export documents, arranging trade finance, settling overseas accounts – follows. At this stage many people gain some supervisory experience – being in day-to-day charge of terminal operators and remittance clerks. The top clerical grades are securities work – seeing that loans are properly covered, and being a manager's clerk, taking on some of the routine work.

Depending on the size of the bank, senior positions normally include a chief cashier, loan officers, and assistant or junior managers who may look after particular accounts, or are responsible for office management. The manager has to see that the branch is run efficiently. Management can start in a small branch, with progression to larger places.

Many bank staff spend their days inside the bank, largely in desk work, but the manager and some other staff spend time out in the community, because they have to expand business and improve profitability.

The main route to promotion is still via the branch banks, although a rising proportion of staff go into specialist divisions direct, and increasingly, the route up is likely to divide between personal and corporate banking fairly early. Despite any accelerated promotion (usual for graduates and possible for school-leaver entrants who show potential), progress through the branches, learning the day-to-day work of the bank in branches in different settings (rural, small town, suburban, industrial estate, shopping centre and so on), and in branches of different sizes, still takes time.

In the new corporate-finance offices, career staff will gain experience as, for example, 'account executives' who will diagnose company needs and design and deliver services such as leasing, investment management, treasury management, insurance, and export and expansion financing.

All these can be interspersed both with experience of 'special' (e.g. credit finance), and head office departments such as economic intelligence, financial control, marketing and personnel, and with training, mostly on banks' own schemes.

Promotion depends largely on entry qualifications and abilities. Graduates can expect, for instance, to reach assistant manager in three to five years.

Career staff tend not to move between the clearing banks, although it is possible for staff to apply openly for some posts. The banks retain the right to send staff to jobs in different parts of the country, and all staff must be prepared to move.

As well as career staff, the clearing banks also employ large numbers of secretarial and office staff, computer staff (programmers, systems analysts, operators), and business machine operators.

Merchant and investment banking (including merchant banking divisions of clearing banks)

Traditionalist they may seem, but merchant banks have always been entrepreneurial, living by their wits and seizing new opportunities as they came along, thriving on change. They have long ceased to be merchants, and have been diversifying for some years out of their traditional business, although most still provide such services and keep up their prestigious international connections. This was originally mainly financing exports and international trade – through acceptance credits, for example; negotiating loans; and banking, loan business etc. for governments and international institutions. There is no real difference between merchant and investment banks.

Their principal role now is as arrangers of finance for the business community, and as intermediaries in the flow of savings into the finance of investment. They do this by assisting firms which are seeking funds for investment to sell shares, bonds and other forms of securities, and by managing the investments of financial institutions, notably pension funds.

As bankers and financial advisers to companies rather than individuals, other than very wealthy ones, they have become experts in all aspects of corporate finance, especially in capital issues, the high-profile take-overs, mergers, and company 'flotations', as well as advising companies on their financial 'structures', and generally acting as financial intermediaries. They provide venture capital for embryonic businesses and will assist with management buy-outs. They deal in bullion, organise medium- and long-term finance for major projects, trade in commodities, advise on shipping and insurance problems (some actually broking).

In order to carry out their role as intermediaries in the capital markets between savers and investors they own stockbroking and market-making firms through which shares and bonds are bought and sold. As managers of investments on behalf of savings and investment institutions their knowledge of the investment requirements of industry helps them to find appropriate ways to invest savers funds. Because of their international basis of operations they have also been active in enabling investors to spread their investments over a number of countries to diversify risk.

A major role for investment banks in recent years has been in the privatisation of public sector industry – as advisers to governments as vendors and to privatised firms, and as managers of the sale of shares to investors worldwide.

Throughout the world industry has been looking increasingly to the capital markets – as opposed to bank loans – as a source of finance. A number of major banks have therefore been aiming to expand their investment banking businesses, which has led to their acquisition of previously independent merchant banks.

Many international investment banks operate from London, which is, with New York, the leading world centre. All the leading merchant and investment banks, including the merchant banking subsidiaries of the clearing banks, are members of the London Investment Banking Association

Merchant banking employs relatively small numbers. Figures are hard to get, especially at a time of rapid change, but 'career' staff probably total under 25,000 (1995).

Working in merchant banking

Career staff are increasingly specialising in one area of the bank's business – banking, investment or funds management, corporate finance etc., or in a 'support' function, such as research or investment analysis. They may be part of a 'team' looking after the account of a single client, or providing information and advice on one area of investment, or actively looking for companies vulnerable to take over ('arbitrage'). As firms increase in size, complexity and international scope, they are having to re-think their internal managerial 'styles', putting in place more formal organisational structures instead of the fairly loose 'entrepreneurial' frameworks that had been traditional, and this is likely to change career patterns somewhat.

Much of the work is highly technical, and can be very intensive. Long hours may be necessary when putting together a 'bid' for a major company to a tight deadline. A first-time 'flotation' on the stock market can take up hundreds of hours of working time for the banker's team. Clients, and the Stock Exchange, expect very high standards of research and investigation, accuracy in preparing prospectuses, etc.

Banks expect their career staff to show entrepreneurial 'flair', to be creative in developing new business, managing their clients' positively – suggesting how they should invest, diversify etc., and spotting new opportunities. Promotion is generally much faster than in retail banking for those who rise to the challenge. It is, however, much less likely to be a job for a whole career.

International banking

Banks, both UK and those of other countries, have long operated overseas, providing traditional-style services both for individuals and companies – the latter largely funding trade and development, and transmitting funds. Since the 1960s the international banking scene has been growing, with more sophisticated, comprehensive worldwide services mainly for business customers, and aggressive marketing inroads into foreign financial centres. The competition for business is intense, and developing new financial services is crucial to success. British and foreign banks have combined in completely international consortia.

Banks operating internationally still finance trade (as well as handling documentation and advising on trading conditions), and overseas investments. But with the more recent boom in loan business, they are increasingly getting involved in the new global securities markets, particularly currency trading, and in issuing the commercial 'paper' which firms are now preferring to loans.

British banks operate abroad and one of the major British banks now has over 1,800 'branch' offices in around 60 countries While a high proportion of their staff are nationals of the countries concerned, they all recruit UK nationals.

The number of foreign banks with branches or offices in London has been rising for years – over 480 in 1995. Most (over 180) are European; 68 are US, 40 are Japanese, and 34 Arab. Only about half a dozen of the world's top 100 banks are not represented in London. The largest have bought into stock market firms or are building up their own securities trading departments, and use London as a base for trading international securities. Numbers employed are hard to estimate with all the recent developments, and individual banks vary in size from a handful running what is essentially only a 'listening post', up to one major US bank offering a full range of services with over 2,000 staff.

Working in international banking

Both UK banks with international divisions and overseas banks operating in the UK are changing in line with the whole financial sector, and the career opportunities vary from bank to bank, depending on size and range of services. Although some UK banks still run both domestic and corporate services overseas, branches in other countries mostly employ nationals.

Other UK and some overseas banks concentrate on providing sophisticated and comprehensive services for international corporate customers. Here the career opportunities are very similar to those in merchant banking, including currency trading, but mostly with greater emphasis on funding international trade.

Overseas banks in London may also try to exploit particular UK markets. Opportunities to work abroad for British banks are fairly limited, although all major clearing banks have overseas branches. However, these are mainly staffed by local people. It is possible to get into the career structure of overseas banks operating in London, and then gain promotion overseas. A number of banks also incorporate a secondment abroad as part of their graduate training programmes. A foreign language is obviously a real asset in this area of banking.

Recruitment and entry

Clearing banks – merchant and investment banks

Until a few years ago, banks recruited tens of thousands of school leavers each year for junior clerical positions. Now there are only limited opportunities for 16- or 17-year-olds.

Many vacancies today are for those with degrees, A-levels (or equivalent) and for experienced people to work part-time in branches during busy periods. Most permanent recruitment is now at graduate level. However, increasingly, banks consider personal qualities, experience and professional competence as important as formal educational qualifications. High standards of appearance and manners are important. Good interpersonal skills are vital as are integrity, initiative, pleasing personalities and sense of responsibility. While the characteristics traditionally associated with banking are still crucial, banking now needs people prepared to be flexible, adaptable, and with the potential to develop marketing skills. Clearing banks recruit the largest numbers.

Banks are becoming more flexible in their approach to applicants with vocational qualifications and GNVQ/GSVQs are becoming more widely accepted as alternatives to GCSE/SCEs and A-levels. A number of banks also offer their staff the chance to achieve NVQ/SVQs in banking (levels 2–4).

The few banks operating a Youth Training Scheme normally require no formal academic qualifications. For the limited number of junior clerical positions available, banks often ask for a range of GCSE/SCEs (A–C/1–3), including English and mathematics, as well as keyboard skills. Occasionally they may ask for A-levels or the equivalent.

Clearing banks

The clearing banks recruited about 1,000 graduates in 1994. They all want people with good degrees and, except for those who go into specialist divisions, the subject is immaterial. For specialist divisions, although any subject is usually accepted, law, economics, statistics, business studies and courses including banking subjects are particularly relevant. Again, banks recruit not just on academic ability, but are also looking for the right personal qualities, 'leadership, initiative, enthusiasm, the ability to adapt from theory to practice and ability to work as part of a team'.

Merchant banks

Merchant bank recruitment is normally not large. At least half their intake are already trained professional lawyers, accountants, etc. with experience elsewhere, and most of the balance are graduates. All banks are looking for expertise and high qualifications. Estimates of annual graduate intake vary, from about 120 to well over 200. A good degree in accountancy, law, business studies, maths or computer science is probably most useful, but one bank says high grades are more important than degree subject. Most recruitment is now for specific jobs, rather than to a graduate training 'pool'. Over 50% of intake is now from universities other than Oxbridge.

Self-confidence is essential as merchant bank staff have to deal with clients' top management very early in their careers. Merchant bankers live by the quality of their decision-making, and have to make decisions and give advice which may affect the futures of multi-million pound businesses, and even governments. Entrepreneurial instincts, marketing/'abrasive' skills, and a sharp, profit-seeking mind are quoted characteristics. Physical and temperamental stamina to take the pace are also needed.

Qualifications and training

Professional qualifications – the Pre-Associateship Route – associate examinations – the Lombard scheme

Training throughout banking is still largely on-the-job and in-house. The clearing banks operate their own, often highly sophisticated internal schemes, programmed learning systems and training centres, but they and the merchant banks release staff to study elsewhere if necessary, e.g. for an MBA.

Except in specialist departments, for example, for which specific skills or experience are needed, almost everyone aiming for a long-term career starts at the bottom, is taught each routine separately and then spends time practising it.

In clearing banks, even graduates start with six to nine months learning quite basic clerical work in a high-street branch. After that, most graduates and some others are given accelerated training, with additional courses, on management development programmes.

In overseas banks, training in systems also begins with routine work, learning the mechanics of finance and investment, and so on, gaining responsibility, but again normally with accelerated training, and higher-level work, for graduates. The first three years of any banking career should be seen as mainly training, very hard work and sometimes boring and frustrating. All young employees learn as junior members of a team, but at a pace set for each individual, depending largely on the level of entry/educational background and developing potential.

In merchant banking training is likely to be more individual, reflecting the high academic or professional qualifications of most entrants. Early years are likely to be arduous and competitive, although rewards will be substantial to those who meet the challenge.

Professional qualifications

While these are not compulsory, promotion past clerical grades may depend on gaining them. Some merchant banks now require entrants to take Securities Institute examinations. The Chartered Institute of Bankers (UK membership 82,000 in 1993 plus 18,000 overseas) provides a range of qualifications for those working in the financial services industry. The aim is to offer junior employees a thorough grounding in, for instance, balance sheets, securities, lending criteria and marketing strategy and can give basic advice to both personal and corporate customers on a range of broad financial matters. Future managers also need increasing technical knowledge, and modern marketing and administrative skills. Bank employees' need for a qualification with wider acceptance among employers, necessary under modern conditions of increasing job mobility, is taken into account. The Institute's examinations are not a 'licence to practise' but rather ones which provide foundations on which a banking career can be built, and together with internal bank training, give an objective yardstick by which employees can show their level of skill.

Certificate in Financial Services Practice

This provides a practical introduction to the financial services industry. It is for customer contact staff in banks and building societies. There are no entry qualifications and candidates are able to build their own programme from a range of modules. Students gaining the Certificate can progress to the final section of the Banking Certificate.

Banking Certificate

This is designed for those aiming at senior supervisory grades. It is generally a three-year course, which has a practical job-related syllabus. The Preliminary Section is open to all and provides a foundation for further study. Candidates with one or more A-levels/H-grades and a GCSE/SCE (grade A–C/1–3), or equivalent, in English or five years' relevant work experience may enter the Final Section direct. The Final Section covers economics, basic accountancy, banking, law, supervisory skills, lending, international business, customer services and marketing.

The Pre-Associateship Route

This is a 'fast track' for students with one or more A-levels/H grades and a GCSE/SCE (grade A–C/1–3) , or equivalent, in English. It is not a qualification in its own right but provides entry to the Associateship examinations. Candidates must pass the four subjects which comprise the economics, accountancy and law papers of the Banking Certificate plus one other from the Final Section, within a maximum of three consecutive attempts. Students with these academic qualifications on entry may, if they prefer, take the 2-year Final Section of the Banking Certificate.

Associateship examinations

Bankers aspiring to management will wish to continue their studies and achieve Associateship of The Chartered Institute of Bankers. The length of time required to complete will depend on the individual but, with good progress, should take about three years. Successful completion of the examinations, together with three years' banking service and three years' Institute membership, qualifies for the award of Associateship (ACIB). Entry requirements are either: the Banking Certificate, successful completion of the Pre-Associateship Route, a BTEC/SCOTVEC National Diploma/Certificate in Business or Finance or a recognised degree or professional qualification. Candidates take four core papers in law, accountancy, economics and management, and choose four papers from a wide range of options covering retail, corporate, international and trustee work.

The Lombard Scheme (post-Associate)

Associates of the Institute are eligible for consideration for the Lombard Scheme – an innovative programme involving selected universities and business schools and leading to the award of an MBA. Courses (typically three years part-time) include special banking electives, and on completion of these the Institute awards the designatory letters 'DipFS' (Financial Studies Diploma).

The Bank of England

The Bank of England's objective is to achieve a stable monetary and financial framework for the effective functioning and development of the UK economy. In pursuing this objective it has three core purposes:

– maintaining the integrity and value of the currency: this is based on the belief that monetary policy should be directed towards maintaining price stability, which is a necessary condition for achieving the wider economic goal of steady growth and employment. This is reflected in the Government's decision to set an inflation target of 2.5% as the objective of monetary policy. The Bank's role is to advise the Chancellor of the Exchequer on the level of interest rates which it considers necessary to achieve the inflation objective. The Bank publishes a quarterly Inflation Report, which forms the basis for the Bank's monetary policy advice to the Chancellor. The Bank is also responsible for the implementation of monetary policy decisions through its operations, mainly in the money market, but also in the gilt-edged and foreign exchange markets. The Bank manages the country's gold and foreign exchange reserves and can influence the exchange rate directly by intervening in the exchange markets to buy or sell sterling for foreign currencies. It also manages the government's borrowing operations. Like any bank, the Bank of England provides banking services to its customers, principally the government, the banking system and other central banks. It plays a key role in the principal payment and settlement systems and acts as bank of issue, producing and distributing 5.5 million bank notes each day (1996 figures).

– maintaining the stability of the financial system: the Bank has an important role in ensuring that banks and certain other City institutions are sound and well run. It has an explicit statutory responsibility for the supervision of banks and formal responsibility for supervising firms in the wholesale markets for sterling, foreign exchange and bullion. It also monitors links between different financial markets. In exceptional circumstances the Bank may provide lender of last resort financial support to banks in difficulty.

– seeking to ensure the effectiveness of the UK's financial markets: London is an international financial centre and the Bank works to ensure that it maintains this position, monitoring its development and identifying weaknesses and competitive threats. The Bank is also concerned that the City should provide efficient financial services to domestic industry. In situations where the market on its own is finding it difficult to resolve problems because of conflicting interests between the parties involved, the Bank can sometimes play a useful role in encouraging collective initiatives.

In February 1996, the Bank had a staff of 3,635, of which 790 were at the Printing Works in Debden, 280 were in the Registrar's Department in Gloucester and 160 worked at the five regional branches. Just under 65 members of staff were temporarily working for other organisations in the UK and abroad.

Recruitment and entry

Graduate

Graduate recruitment focuses in particular on those who are 'economically literate'. They are not recruited to work in a specific division or department of the Bank, but once recruited, their initial allocation will be based, as far as possible, on degree subject and personal preference. In the early years most graduates will undertake mainly analytical work and can expect to make career moves at three- to four-year intervals. Graduates must display the personal and intellectual qualities needed to move into senior managerial posts.

The Bank recruits between 25–35 graduates each year. It aims to recruit intellectual excellence and lively characters across all disciplines. The Bank's work is likely to appeal to those who are interested in the public policy aspects of monetary and financial management and who will enjoy the challenge of practical analytical work demanding high standards. Successful graduates will need to show strong intellectual and personal qualities.

The Bank also offers a small number of postgraduate studentships to final year undergraduate economists who want to undertake a Master's degree in economics and subsequently join the Bank.

Clerical

The Bank of England also recruits senior clerical staff who have obtained a range of GCSEs, or equivalent, including mathematics and English language, as well as at least two academic A-levels, or equivalent. New entrants will initially undertake clerical work, gaining practical experience in one or more areas. The choice, sequence and length of time spent in each area depend on vacancies and the qualifications, aptitudes and preferences of the individual. Progression is on merit and some senior clerical entrants go on to undertake analytical work. Senior clerical entrants are encouraged to undertake further study.

Junior clerical staff will normally have a range of GCSEs or equivalent, including mathematics and English language. New employees are generally employed initially on straightforward tasks, such as taking telephone messages and sorting out queries; processing documents and checking their accuracy; maintaining and updating vital databases using a variety of IT packages; recording and filing information both manually and on computer.

Word processor operators/junior secretaries must be 16 or over with a good range of GCSEs, or equivalent, including mathematics and English language, plus accurate keyboard skills of at least 35 words a minute. There is a full range of secretarial opportunities in the Bank.

Qualifications and training

Graduate

Graduates are recruited as trainee officials. The Bank of England offers a flexible programme of formal qualifications, training courses, development workshops, on-the-job training and seminars to ensure that trainee officials have the knowledge and skills to be successful in their initial job and in a variety of other areas of the Bank. The Bank encourages graduates to learn at least one other major European language.

Clerical

Much of the clerical staff training takes place on the job. As clerical staff progress, they are given the opportunity to expand their personal skills to enable them to undertake a wider range of jobs. A variety of training is available in-house. There is a choice of trainer-led courses or open and distance learning. Clerical staff decide with their supervisors which training best suits their needs.

Further information

The Banking Information Service, the Chartered Institute of Bankers, the Institute of Bankers in Scotland, the London Investment Banking Association, the Bank of England, and other individual banks.

Building societies

Working in building societies – recruitment and entry – qualifications and training – further information

Building societies have traditionally operated a relatively simple two-way financial service. First, they make it possible for people to invest their savings with a reasonable rate of return, good security, and relatively easy access to their money when they want it. These funds are then used to make long-term loans to members (most of whom are already savers) to buy houses (and land) and/or to build.

While this might continue to be their 'mainstream' business, building societies have been widening and improving their services – with automated teller machines commonplace – to customers for some time, and effectively competing with banks for deposit and current accounts. Changes in legislation and the financial climate have meant increased competition with retail banks.

Building societies are now diversifying into many areas of personal finance and investment. Many are offering a range of house-buying – from estate agency and surveying to conveyancing – and other financial services, including personal equity plans and pensions. They can hold and develop land for housing. They can, with approval, set up subsidiary companies (in banking, insurance broking, hire purchase, etc.), can make unsecured loans, and raise up to 50% of their funds from non-retail sources, subject to the Building Societies Commission's approval. However, 90%

of their commercial assets will still have to be in traditional mortgage loans.

As building societies, they will continue to be non-profit making and must invest any surplus funds in completely safe securities, but must use their funds as efficiently as possible. However, subject to complex rules and members' approval, they may now become public limited companies.

Many building societies (1996) are exploiting this legislation and have opted to lose their 'mutual' status and float on the London Stock Exchange (e.g. Abbey National, Cheltenham and Gloucester, Halifax, Woolwich). This enables them to offer full banking services to compete directly with banks. Other building societies, seeking to make themselves stronger in a more competitive field, have merged with banks or with other larger building societies.

Some 75% of home ownership is financed by a rapidly falling number of building societies (79 in 1995), making them a key factor in the lives of over two-thirds of households who are owner-occupiers (and over 40 million people have accounts with them). They are also moving fast towards the point of representing the largest concentration of financial assets in the country, with total 1994 assets nearing £301,011 million between about 96 societies (down from 726 in 1960, and 2,286 in 1900), although 45% of funds are held by the three largest.

The overall number of staff (end 1994) had increased to approximately 100,000 (including several thousand part-time) from 24,600 in the 1970s. The reasons for the mergers are likely to mean that societies will hold down staff numbers where possible, with help from technology, and rationalisation.

Working in building societies

This is largely an office- and desk-based career, with fairly straightforward administration and routine, which societies computerise as far as is economic. Most staff work in the branches – where they deal extensively with customers, both over their accounts and when negotiating home loans. They can go on to more specialised work in savings or mortgages, or into the various departments of head office – e.g. mortgage accounts, investment accounts, finance, mortgage securities, accountant, audit, administration, mortgage advances, mortgage administration, mortgage control, marketing, management services etc.

Building societies also employ specialists, such as surveyors, accountants, computer personnel, and these posts tend to make greater demands on personnel than branch management, which is fairly tightly controlled centrally. The new opportunities for expansion may result in demand for other specialists, as well as giving building-society staff opportunities to go into new areas – societies traditionally 'home grow' their own experts. Societies also employ e.g. secretaries, computer operators, cashiers etc. The gap between career and other staff is widening, especially in the larger societies.

Promotion is generally through progressively more responsible work in the branch system and/or head office departments, on a similar pattern to the clearing banks, starting with clerical work and up to branch and more senior management via the various departments. Managerial opportunities – and training – are greater with the larger societies. Promotion usually involves moving, from branch to branch or head office, or to another society.

Building-society management has been getting steadily more demanding, taking greater professionalism, as societies grew larger, with competition, and new technology. More home buyers at a time of high unemployment have lead to the need for more careful arrears management.

The new legislation intensifies the problems of strategic planning; decisions on whether or not to expand out of traditional business will involve complex planning of organisational, managerial and staffing structures. Marketing strategies, still relatively new to building societies, will have to become more sophisticated, and ways found to deal with greater and more intense competition and technology. Building societies work on very tight margins, and since they must, by law, maximise their investments, finance, especially functions such as corporate treasury, are also increasingly important.

Recruitment and entry

Traditionally entrants have started straight from school, but in future the societies may have to 'buy in' particular experience and expertise, and widen/raise the ability range of new intake. Although it may be possible to get into a society with less than the stated minimum qualifications of four GCSE/SCE (grades A–C/1–3) (including English and mathematics), prospects are generally better with two A levels/H Grades. Increasing numbers of graduates are being recruited. Building societies also take 'quite substantial numbers' each year onto YT programmes.

Qualifications and training

Training is largely still on-the-job, over three or four years, with some formal schemes and day-release for courses with larger societies, but most exam preparation still has to be by spare-time study. Some societies have accelerated training schemes for graduates, but reports suggest training for management is not yet matching the new demands being made on staff.

Professional qualifications

There are two professional qualifications relevant to people working in building societies:

– the Certificate in Financial Services Practice, which is a vocational examination for clerical staff who want to learn more about the way the industry operates. No entry qualifications are required for this certificate which is a recognised qualification in its own right. A good pass can lead on to the Associateship examinations.
– the Associate examination of the Chartered Institute of Bankers (the Chartered Building Societies Institute merged

with the CIB in 1993). CIB qualifications are not essential, but increasingly useful for promotion, and career staff are expected to take CIB, or other appropriate exams, e.g. ICSA, CIMA, ACCA.

Many building societies are now offering staff training leading to NVQ/SVQs in Building Society Services (levels 2,3,4). Some societies also offer NVQ/SVQs in other areas of work, such as clerical or secretarial administration, information technology, accounts, etc.

Further information

The Chartered Institute of Bankers, the Building Societies Association.

Insurance

The insurance business – working in insurance – general recruitment and entry – qualifications and training – the insurance specialists

The insurance business

Insurance deals in risks, but as a by-product, and offers a means of saving for many. It is a multi-million-pound business built on the law of averages, so that if a great many people pay relatively small sums of money to protect themselves financially against some kind of loss which is only going to happen to some (and relatively few) of them, then those who do suffer can be compensated, from the funds collected.

It may sound simple, but at the scale on which insurance companies work, the business is very complex. Insurers also have to make a profit, and they have to make sound investments, so that they can cover their liabilities if claims are made. This takes considerable expertise, to decide on the exact degree of risk for each policy, and then to set fair premiums and conditions to meet it. They have a combination of long-established principles, guide-lines and experience to work on, but it is still a form of gambling (using the law of averages) on a grand scale. Insurance cannot be too cautious, because if the premiums are too high or the conditions too strict, then people simply will not insure.

There is virtually no limit to the risks which can be insured against. It is possible to insure material possessions against the direct cash value of their loss, or to protect oneself or family against, for example, personal risks such as death or disablement. There are 'special' schemes such as those which enable parents to spread the cost of school fees. In general, however, there are eight generally accepted 'classes' of insurance: life (including industrial life assurance); property (including fire and theft); marine, aviation and transport; motor vehicle; personal accident and sickness; liability to third party (including employer's liability); pecuniary loss (including fidelity guarantee, credit and consequential loss insurance); and reinsurance of any of the above in which the original insurers reduce their risk by taking out an insurance with another insurance company for part of the total risk.

Insurance has a very marked effect on the country's economy. The 821 insurance companies (including, for example, subsidiaries of major banks, and some 160 overseas companies), are the largest single group of investors. This is a major source of financing for industry and commerce of all kinds, and in fact supplies some half of long-term capital needs. Insurance also contributes to Britain's 'invisible' earnings overseas.

Life assurance and general insurance differ greatly. Life is the only long-term insurance business, i.e. usually lasting ten years or more, and is the only form of business insuring against something that is inevitable – retirement or death. Other forms of insurance are taken out against risks which may not happen, and the premiums agreed at the start of the contract remain unchanged. Life insurance is generally, therefore, organised on rather different lines from more general activities.

New risks are being covered in non-life insurance all the time. Technology brings new kinds of cover: the British market first covered a satellite launching, of 'Early Bird', in 1965, including third-party risk against collision with other satellites. Insurers paid NASA to recover a satellite, and then re-sold it. Other 'modern' risks insured against include kidnapping, computer failure, North Sea oil-rig disasters, and nuclear reactor leaks. The scale of modern construction – massive dams, and tower blocks involving the use of, e.g. tower cranes – produces further insurance headaches. All of these involve completely new kinds of problem-solving for insurance assessors. A substantial proportion of the non-life market is in fire insurance, and again the hazards of new materials (both building and furnishing) and modern construction methods have added to the insurance problems which still include contending with the difficulties of older buildings which lack proper fire protection. Over half of all business in the non-life sector is concentrated among just ten major companies.

While insurance business has expanded steadily for many years, it is not always so easy to make a profit. The industry has had some difficult years in the 1980s and even worse years in the early 1990s, and good results are needed just to maintain, let alone increase, employment. Mergers and increasing use of computer-based systems (for accounting, policy renewal, premium collection and records generally, claims applications) also affect employment. More office technology – with branches being linked up to head office – almost certainly means fewer lower-grade clerical and data processing jobs, but numbers of specialist and professional staff are expected to stay at roughly present levels for the immediate future.

Insurance is a very varied industry, employing a relatively high proportion of specialists. They may work in any one of the three broad divisions of the insurance market: the insurance companies, Lloyd's underwriters, and brokers.

Working in insurance

Companies vary considerably in size and scope. Some specialise in one kind of insurance (over a quarter in life, alone); others do business in several types, and are known as composite companies. Company men and women are said to work either inside (for example, actuaries and underwriters) or outside (for example, sales staff and surveyors). Claims officials, for instance, may work inside and outside, though.

The work of a large insurance firm is divided between its area branches and head office. Branches are generally responsible for day-to-day business, which means finding and negotiating new contracts, calculating premiums and preparing policies, revising policies according to changing needs and conditions, and dealing with income, correspondence, and straightforward claims. The number of branches has been substantially reduced in recent years, following several mergers and the need to cut high staff costs; some have been replaced by small sub-branch offices but with only a handful of staff.

In head office, the division is between administration and underwriting departments. Head office deals with policy and guide-lines for deciding on risks, premiums, etc. in the specialist underwriting departments and claims. It also deals with investment management where company funds must be invested to give the highest yield consistent with security and with the fact that sufficient funds must always be available to meet claims and other company requirements. Reserves must be properly and safely invested – involving highly trained investment analysts. Otherwise, administration involves the functions found in any commercial firm, such as the secretary's office, accountant, personnel, publicity.

Most insurance companies are highly automated and computerised (one of the industry's main problems is to cut the large percentage of premium income, about a third, which goes in expenses, and automation is one way of cutting expenditure, particularly on labour). Most have had large data-processing departments for many years, and are moving with new office technology to the extent that most people entering the industry now will routinely use computers and computer terminals.

The underwriting departments are generally divided according to types of insurance carried by the company and to the degree of specialisation – one company may have a single fire and accident department, another may separate them. In addition, separate departments deal with overseas insurance and supervise branch management.

While every branch or department is largely made up of specialist staff, each also has a full complement of managerial and supervisory staff, mostly promoted from specialist insurance work.

General recruitment and entry

Insurance companies recruit at a number of levels, both direct from the education system, and amongst mature and experienced people, depending on need.

Overall recruitment has been fairly static lately, after some years at low levels (resulting from technological change, tight economic conditions, and very low levels of staff turnover) and redundancies. Recruitment has, however, increased in, most notably, life assurance. CII claims that the increased versatility possible with new technology, increasing complexity and diversity of insurance offered, is widening the range of job opportunities.

There are no rigid entry qualifications, but for people planning a long-term career, most insurance companies increasingly prefer graduates, although 18-year-olds with two A-level passes, or a BTEC National are considered. Major companies have YT programmes.

Graduate recruitment has been rising steadily with nearly half becoming trainee actuaries and most of the rest going into the 30 largest companies, and the six largest brokers. Any degree subject is acceptable for general insurance work, although obviously some are more useful e.g. behavioural sciences, business studies, economics, languages, law or mathematics; engineering or some sciences for underwriting, surveying or claims inspection in specialist fields. While a relatively high proportion of insurance companies still recruit for specific posts and are therefore looking for particular disciplines, more companies are now seeing graduate recruits as potential managers. Competition for graduate traineeships is rising.

Most companies also recruit for clerical and other support work, such as computer operating.

As well as qualities needed for any business-related career, insurance takes intelligence to master technical information and problems, the ability to explain complex matters in simple language, and to develop a sense of judgement – of risks, situations, and people.

Qualifications and training

Training is largely on-the-job and in-house, and most people, graduates included, spend some time learning via routine work. All the major life and composite insurance groups have extensive training schemes, both administrative and technical, ranging from induction courses for school-leavers to specialist training for senior management. CIIs 'College' provides comprehensive courses for the smaller companies unable to operate their own, including three-month and one-year full-time courses for associateship exams, and courses on more specialised aspects of insurance such as aviation underwriting. Training schemes and methods are improving, and some release for courses etc. is usual.

Professional qualification

Chartered Insurance Institute (1996 membership approximately 70,000) qualifications are now essential for promotion.

The Associateship (ACII) is for career professionals, including holders of the Certificate of Insurance Practice (CIP). It is the highest professional insurance qualification that can be gained by examination. A-level qualifications or equivalent (e.g. Scottish Highers, BTEC Nationals, NVQ/SVQ level 3, Advanced level GNVQ/GSVQ level 3) are required for anyone under 25 years old on the date of the examination. However, it is strongly recommended that candidates complete the CIP before entering the Associateship. Candidates over 25 who are employed or engaged in insurance do not need any qualifications to register for the examination.

Fellowship (FCII) is taken post-Associateship and is the highest level of professional qualification in insurance and requires a minimum of four years' experience, evidence of continuing professional development and a dissertation of 3,000–5,000 words to be submitted.

Other CII qualifications include the Certificate of Proficiency, and Certificate of Insurance Practice.

The Certificate of Proficiency is a basic qualification (six months' part-time study and two exam papers) for anyone who wants a broad understanding of insurance. There are no formal entry requirements. Completion of the Certificate provides essential knowledge for NVQ/SVQ level 2 in insurance. It is also a natural stepping stone to the Certificate of Insurance Practice.

The Certificate of Insurance Practice (CIP) is an examination designed for technicians and staff who require more than the Certificate of Proficiency but do not want to take the full Associateship examinations. Candidates under 21 years old need a minimum of four GCSE/SCEs (grades A–C/1–3) or equivalent (e.g. BTEC First, NVQ/SVQ level 2, GNVQ/GSVQ) or the Certificate of Proficiency or Financial Planning Certificate to enter the CIP.

The CII also has a series of examinations for those employed in the financial services field: the Financial Planning Certificate and the Advanced Financial Planning Certificate.

The insurance specialists

Adjusting – agency inspecting – agency work – branch management – claims work – insurance broking – Lloyd's – Lloyd's underwriters – Lloyd's staff – risk or insurance management – surveying – underwriting – other work – further information

The insurance world employs a very wide range of skills and training, and there are a number of very clearly defined specialist careers.

Adjusting

Adjusters are the industry's detectives. They are impartial and independent specialists, called in by an insurer, the broker, or the insured (or maybe all three) to apportion legal and financial liability in a claim which may be very large, or where the claim is not straightforward. Many claims are, of course, settled with comparative ease by the insurer's own claims officials (*see below*), and adjusters may not be needed. Some adjusters specialise in marine claims work, and are called average adjusters. They are experts on every kind of claim written on a marine policy – general, energy, cargo, loss of hire, builders' risks, ship repairs and liability. Those who deal with other kinds of loss are normally known as loss adjusters (they never, however, deal with life insurance claims).

The adjuster's importance lies in absolute impartiality, and they are therefore members of independent partnerships or firms, specialising solely in this and advisory work arising out of it. The adjuster may be involved in for example, establishing the cause of a fire, quantifying the damage and advising about repairs and rebuilding, policy coverage and liability under the policy. In reaching an adjustment the adjuster may help to compile a list of all the costs involved, and consults a wide range of other experts, including surveyors, lawyers, brokers and valuers, and the policy holder.

Adjusting is a very highly skilled profession, needing extensive experience. It is also a very small profession, although numbers have been increasing. Fully qualified loss adjusters number about 1,250 in the UK in 1996 (against 1,000 in 1991), plus over 1,100 in training. There are only 11 firms of members of the Association of Average Adjusters in the United Kingdom. Opinion generally is that the growth in numbers has levelled off, and it is most unlikely that it will increase again at least for the next few years.

Most adjusters are recruited from a related profession and already have professional qualifications in insurance, surveying, or accountancy. Although the formal minimum qualifications for loss adjusters are GCSE/SCE (grades A–C/1–3) and A levels/H Grades, the chance of an 18-year-old school-leaver being recruited as a trainee is extremely remote, although graduates are sometimes taken on. There are no minimum qualifications for average adjusters, although recruitment is increasingly at graduate level. Average adjusters need to be numerate, have an analytical mind and good communication skills. Fluency in foreign languages would be beneficial when bringing diverse international parties together to resolve a particular problem.

Professional qualifications are essential, and both professional bodies – the Chartered Institute of Loss Adjusters and the Association of Average Adjusters – require entrants to train with recognised firms.

The Chartered Institute of Loss Adjusters requires entrants to hold an approved professional qualification before attempting the professional examination. Candidates must normally have had two years' experience under supervision, before taking the examination. Five years in practice is required for election to Associate, but some qualifications (e.g. surveying) may cut this to three years.

The Association of Average Adjusters does not lay down any minimum educational standards for a candidate to sit its examinations, nor do the individual member firms have any rigid academic requirements. However, recruitment is increasingly at graduate level. A Practising Certificate is issued to anyone who has passed the qualifying examinations and spent a period of full-time service with a practising average adjuster. This period of service is not less than two years for those who already hold the Associateship diploma of the Chartered Insurance Institute in the Marine branch, or four years for those without such a diploma. In practice, a minimum of five years of practical study and theoretical study is usually necessary to satisfy the stringent examination requirements.

Agency inspecting

Inspectors are part supervisors, part specialists and part salesmen or women. They are a link between the people who deal with clients and the insurance company itself, and generally, therefore, work from a branch.

Insurance is 'sold' by a wide variety of different people, and about half is brought in by people who do not even work in insurance. They include solicitors, accountants, estate agents, and people who sell cars, who arrange insurance for their clients or customers when they buy a house or car. The other half comes through insurance brokers or the full-time home service agents. Some companies also employ direct-selling representatives.

Agency inspectors supervise a group of agents, deal on a regular basis with a group of insurance brokers, and also seek to bring in new business. They deal, either directly or through brokers, with local clients whose insurance needs are more complex than the agent normally deals with, tailoring the form of cover to the client's needs. Agency inspectors have to know a great deal about the terms and conditions on which insurance is offered. They assess 'insurability' of any risk, which means having to understand the potential hazards of particular materials or processes. They will often use an expert, such as a doctor on the medical viability of a client's life insurance, or a surveyor on the soundness of a building. Inspectors know what types of insurance their areas will produce. For instance, a residential area will produce mainly life policies, but agricultural, industrial, or port areas will give a different mix. Inspectors keep in touch with policy holders, deal with small claims, queries on accounts, and small surveys. They may also do some direct selling.

It is a job which needs extensive experience and technical knowledge. Most inspectors have normally worked for some time as branch clerks, and completed a professional qualification, and so usually become agents between the ages of 23 and 28, rarely before 21. Promotion is generally via branch management. In smaller branches the post of manager and senior inspector may be combined.

See GENERAL RECRUITMENT AND ENTRY *above*.

Agency work

The home service agents represent the insurance world to many British households, on whom they call frequently. They mostly canvas for and arrange life insurance, explain policies and conditions, deal with problems and personally collect premiums regularly, but also bring in more general fire and accident insurance, and the newer, more sophisticated forms of life insurance. Home-service agents can be unofficial social workers in their areas and develop personal relationships with families.

Agents are usually recruited either after a period of grounding as a branch-office clerk or after gaining experience of this kind of work in another area of employment. They must, however, develop a comprehensive knowledge of insurance and related business matters.

A few insurance companies also employ direct-selling representatives, again mainly in life assurance, using sophisticated marketing skills more usual in other areas of selling. Such sales representatives often sell in the wider field called financial planning, making up insurance 'packages' providing for estate duty, taxation, and company insurance as well as more conventional life cover. Direct sales people usually have experience in another occupation.

See GENERAL RECRUITMENT AND ENTRY *above*.

Branch management

Branch managers are in charge of all the 'teams' working within the branch and any satellite sub-branches (the trend is to fewer branches), working through their supervisors. These include the agency inspectors, underwriters, claims staff, and administration. The branch manager must see that the branch meets cash flow projections. The manager may become involved in, for example, a large new contract, or a claim where the negotiations run into problems. The manager has to see that all sections are running smoothly, including staffing and training. Most branch managers have come through, e.g. agency inspection.

Claims work

Claims are handled by teams of officials and assessors, who work 'inside' the company, and inspectors who work 'outside', assessing and investigating.

With the value of single insured losses rising steadily, this is very responsible work. It also takes great tact, as company reputation is dependent to some extent on the way in which claims are handled. Clients expect their insurance companies to settle claims fairly and efficiently, and since claims officials are the company's representative here, they must make decisions which are demonstrably reasonable, and cope with the personal distress which often goes with a claim.

In some companies, all claims are dealt with by one department in head office; in others, most are handled by claims departments attached to a branch office, or one claims department servicing a group of branches. Some companies use independent firms of loss adjusters (*see above*).

Claims inspectors investigate supposed insured losses and arrange settlement. Obviously the majority of claims are straightforward and need only straightforward checking, but a proportion give the inspector enough knotty problems to justify the claim of many that this is one of the most interesting aspects of insurance work. Probably the most demanding is settling claims under public liability policies which protect holders against legal liability to other people, as this can involve hard bargaining before a settlement is reached. Some claims may have to be investigated more fully, and may involve asking for and assessing reports from legal, medical and technical experts.

Claims officials need extensive legal and technical knowledge and must be able to assess the reports of experts who may have to be called in on claims. It is, of course, the claims official who may be the first to detect the possibility of crime or fraud. However, these are rare and claims officials are expected to co-operate fully with the policy holder and give help where needed.

See GENERAL RECRUITMENT AND ENTRY *above*.

Insurance broking

Brokers are independent professionals who advise on, arrange and negotiate individual policies or complete insurance packages for their clients looking for the best buy. The broker is therefore working for the customer. This may be an individual looking for the best deal for car insurance, through to large companies who have to insure factories and offices, machinery and computers, trucks and warehouses, and raw materials and finished goods in factories and in transit, against personal liability, as well as employees. Some brokers specialise in marine insurance, and aviation insurance.

Brokers must be able to give expert advice to clients on how to obtain favourable cover, and their knowledge of the insurance market must see that the initial plan takes into account the principles of insurability. Brokers must also have encyclopaedic knowledge of all sections of the market, and know how individual insurers work to get the best possible terms for the client. However, brokers are paid (with a percentage of the premium) by the underwriter and not by the client. Some arrange for fees to be paid by the client.

Insurance brokers provided a large proportion of the insurance market's income, accounting for almost half the total sales by insurance companies for life and general insurance business in 1994. The majority (96%) of Marine, Aviation and Transport (MAT) is sold via brokers (all business done at Lloyd's must be placed through approved brokers). In addition brokers sell 71% of commercial insurance (e.g. commercial motor) and 32% of personal insurance (e.g. private motor 49% and household 22%). About 73% of insured pension schemes and 40% of both personal pensions and ordinary life insurance are also sold by brokers.

Licensed brokerage firms number about 3,700, but the 1,300 member firms of the British Insurance and Investment Brokers Association (BIIBA) account for up to 90% of business and employ 56,000 staff. There are 260 broking firms (employing some 20,000 people) who are accredited to deal with Lloyd's underwriters (*see below*) and do most of the business. Firms range in size from the large London-based, employing up to 6,000, through those in major provincial centres employing 20 to 30, to the very small private firms with a single principal. Some brokers accept any kind of business, others specialise in one or more of the main branches of insurance, particularly reinsurance, and others in overseas business.

This is increasingly an international business, and is beginning to outgrow its more traditional, family-based attitudes.

Within the brokerage house are four main kinds of work –

- Account Executives obtain business and meet clients to discuss their insurance needs. They assess possible risks, how to cover them and how to reduce risks (of fire or burglary for example), so that the insurance will cost less.
- Placing brokers go to underwriters with a proposal, to find the best quotation for covering the particular risk. They know which insurance companies or Lloyd's syndicates are most likely to accept a particular risk, must be ready to discuss the risk (and so understand the problems and be well briefed), negotiate terms and take split-second decisions based on extensive experience.
- Claims brokers negotiate claims with the underwriter on behalf of the client.
- Technical specialists provide back-up to colleagues often checking policy wording and extent of cover. Some act as risk consultants and surveyors of industrial and consumer clients.

In very large firms brokers may even specialise within the jobs described above. On the other hand, in a small firm all the above jobs may be done by one person.

See GENERAL RECRUITMENT AND ENTRY *above*, but brokers have to be rather more 'entrepreneurial' than others in the industry. International business requires languages and brokers must understand the legal and financial systems of the countries they work with. The largest firms take, on average, ten graduates a year, plus computer specialists and school-leavers, mainly with A levels/H Grades. Some 60 brokers take around 150 trainees a year between them under a BIIBA-run Youth Credits Training programme, the majority of whom are employed.

Most larger brokerage houses provide training facilities, although some brokers begin their careers in insurance companies. BIIBA supports training in brokerage firms by offering a programme of training courses. No one can become a registered broker from 1997 without passing four specified CII examination papers (*see above*).

Lloyd's

Lloyd's is not an insurance company, but a society and corporation – an insurance market where individual underwriters do business in competition with each other. It is, traditionally, the centre of marine insurance and shipping intelligence, although marine insurance is now only 36.4% of business. Non-marine insurance makes up 43.4%, motor 12.2% and aviation 8%. Lloyd's has two main categories of investors – individual 'Names' (more properly described as underwriting members) and Corporate Names, who have been admitted to the market since the start of 1994 and now provide 31% of the underwriting capacity. The Names are allocated to syndicates, of which there are currently around 180.

Individual Names have unlimited liability and the Corporate Names have limited liability. For very many years all business was transacted face-to-face in the underwriting rooms, but as from 1 July 1996 all risks must be capable of being placed electronically.

Syndicates can now transact all classes of Lloyd's business, but still tend to specialise in specific areas. For 1993 (the last published year) Lloyd's total premium income including reinsurance was £8,605.5 million. The allocated capacity for 1996 was £9,582 million.

Lloyd's underwriters

Each syndicate is 'managed' by one of about 100 underwriting agencies (1996). Each employs its own professional underwriters and a number of other underwriting staff who are usually training or gaining experience as well as other staff including accounts staff.

While there are varying standards for educational entry to underwriting, it is becoming increasingly a graduate or post-A-level profession. Intake is small. Nobody can become an active underwriter in the Lloyd's market without having the full Associate of CII qualification (*see* QUALIFICATIONS AND TRAINING *above*).

Lloyd's staff

The Corporation of Lloyd's provides a supporting and administrative service for the syndicates with around 2,000 staff (1996). The larger departments are sited in Chatham, not London.

The departments include:

- A policy-signing office, which verifies the accuracy of policies, but increasingly is moving towards the origination and production of policies for the Lloyd's market. The department relies heavily on the use of IT.
- The Lloyd's Claims Office (LCO) handles the vast majority of non-motor claims in the Lloyd's market. Professional staff are expected to be qualified to the same level as their market counterparts.
- An agency department controls the network of about 1,500 Lloyd's agents and sub-agents worldwide, who settle claims, carry out surveys and provide shipping information
- it arranges arbitration following salvage of wrecked ships.
- An aviation department has a staff of qualified aircraft surveyors who investigate accidents and supervise repairs, and also provides a worldwide information service.

Other departments include international communications, membership services and the various components of the Regulatory Directorate. There is considerable demand for skilled computer staff in Systems and Operations Directorate and for appropriately qualified surveyors, engineers and catering staff in connection with support services.

Intake is quite small, and recruitment ranges from school-leavers to professionally qualified accountants and solicitors. There is a special graduate intake scheme (30 graduates a year) which commences at the beginning of each year.

Risk or insurance management

Risk, or insurance, managers are employed mainly by large companies and organisations whose need for insurance cover is large enough to warrant having staff to keep it under continuous review, to see that the extent of the cover is in reasonable relation to the cost, that insurance is adapted and altered to changing needs, and that short-term risks are covered.

Risk managers watch out for new risks within the company, and suggest ways of controlling or avoiding them, e.g. by removing possible causes of fires or accidents. They therefore get involved in safety work and training. It is a relatively new function, and similar to the work of the insurance broker, only on the inside rather than as an outside adviser. Some brokers offer risk management consultancy.

Normally via earlier and extensive experience in another other branch of insurance. *See* GENERAL QUALIFICATIONS AND TRAINING *above*.

Surveying

Surveying in the insurance world is not the same as professional surveying described under LAND USE PROFESSIONS. Insurance surveyors act as fact-finders for underwriters, who rely heavily on their technical reports, mostly in fire and accident insurance. A fire surveyor reports on buildings to be insured, showing how it is built, what materials were used, what machinery there is inside, what work goes on, whether there are fire escapes or not, what fire prevention and hazards there are. Burglary surveyors examine premises to see what the security arrangements are or are needed, and the contents being insured. Liability surveyors report on precautions against possible hazards and avoidance of unnecessary risk.

Insurance surveyors not only report on anything which may affect the insurance contract, but also recommend improvements which could be made and may even advise on appropriate precautions before buildings go up.

Surveyors are normally recruited from among 'inside' insurance staff who show aptitude, and have a 'technical' background (in e.g. engineering, science). They are trained inside the company and may be promoted to senior technical work or underwriting. Brokers' surveyors can combine broking with surveying.

Underwriting

Underwriters are experts in insurance itself. They decide whether a particular risk is insurable, and if so, on what terms and conditions to accept it. Premiums must be set in the light of some more generalised considerations – for example, they must provide a large enough aggregate to pay claims under the class of insurance concerned, cover their share of company overheads, contribute towards reserves and still leave a profit for the company. If premiums are too high or the terms too strict, the company loses business because people won't buy their policies, but if they too low the company will lose money. Policies must also be worded very precisely, especially in terms of the liabilities to be accepted and any special conditions or terms.

In some areas of insurance, especially life, fairly standard premiums are charged according to the risk (as assessed by the actuary), but some parts of particular proposals, for instance a client's medical record, are looked into and assessed by an underwriter. Where risks are unique or unusual, an underwriter has to rely on experience and judgement, based on as much factual and often technical information (such as the surveyor's report) as possible and using records and analyses of related cases.

Underwriters also decide on and organise reinsurance with other companies or underwriters for high risks or very heavy liabilities, what proportion to reinsure, with whom and on what terms.

Underwriters usually specialise in one particular branch of insurance, because they need to develop considerable expertise in the field and understand all the technicalities involved. For example in life assurance, underwriters need substantial medical background knowledge, and must be able to assess what kinds of medical history are average or high-risk, what occupations and age groups are at risk to what hazards, and so on. Marine underwriters (who may specialise in one aspect, such as hull, cargo or freight insurance) must know a great deal about ship construction and operation, the seas in which they operate and the cargoes they carry. Motor insurance takes both knowledge of the vehicles themselves and extremely detailed knowledge of the accident potential and therefore the driving habits of all classes and types of driver. Underwriters must also know about the legal implications of any class of insurance, be able to recognise and assess anything unusual about a proposal, and generally develop an 'underwriting flair' for detecting possible snags.

Company underwriters work along broad guide-lines set by company underwriting policy and have a great many statistics and actuarial reports to turn to. However, there are always new risks to be insured and technological and other developments mean that underwriters must continually make new assessments often based on their own personal knowledge of similar circumstances or parallel developments.

Underwriters often travel, since much insurance business is overseas.

See GENERAL RECRUITMENT AND ENTRY *and* LLOYD'S *above*.

Other work

Most insurance firms are very large organisations and have to employ large numbers of people in 'functions' other than those directly involved with insurance.

Computer staff

The industry has always taken full advantage of computer technology, and constantly looks for ways of exploiting new developments, often doing much of the necessary adaptations to insurance needs itself. Companies are at present developing real-time management information systems. They employ computing staff in some numbers, in e.g. programming, systems design, with structured promotion, possibly into management.

Investment management

Efficient investment of premiums is crucial if companies are to meet their commitment – the industry is the largest institutional investor on the London Stock Exchange. Investment managers aim for the highest rate of return that does not jeopardise security, and gives the liquidity needed to meet claims. Large numbers of experts are employed.

Estate and property management

Most companies invest heavily in property, and this has to be efficiently managed, valued, bought and sold, redeveloped and improved. Most property managers hold the professional qualifications of the Royal Institute of Chartered Surveyors.

Personnel management

Insurance is labour intensive, and demands efficient recruitment and development management, has major training commitments, and has to plan for the future.

Support staff

Processing clerks give a back-up service to underwriters, doing routine work like keeping records up to date, taking information from proposal forms to be used in preparing policy documents, photocopying, collecting statistical information. This usually means learning to use a computer terminal.

Underwriting clerks help to prepare quotations for proposals (often using reference books and computer terminals) and send out forms.

Claims clerks check that policies on which claims are being made are up to date and paid up, checking records, often via a computer terminal. Other clerical posts are in accounts, personnel and with brokers.

See GENERAL RECRUITMENT AND ENTRY *above*.

Further information

The Chartered Insurance Institute Careers Information Service, the British Insurance and Investment Brokers' Association, the Chartered Institute of Loss Adjusters, the Association of Average Adjusters, Lloyd's Training Centre, the Association of British Insurers and individual insurance companies.

Actuarial

Actuaries are the experts who minimise the financial risks in the life assurance business. They do so mainly via complex statistical analysis.

Actuaries decide the terms on which life policies can be issued, surrendered or changed (all of which must be kept constantly under review to keep pace with changing conditions). They do so by statistically analysing the life expectancy of different groups of people from known (but very complex) data drawn from a wide range of sources and made up of constantly changing factors – which affect how long people live (whether or not they smoke, or are overweight, or come from a particular area, for example), and how it changes with, for instance, medical and social developments.

They then calculate the funds which must be built up to cover the long-term liabilities. They also have to value their company's liabilities and assets in relation to the policies issued regularly, and decide what bonus distributions to make. This is more complex than it sounds – the number of policies at any one time is likely to be immense, and the terms extremely varied as they will have been issued at varying times and under varying conditions.

In each life assurance office, the actuary is legally responsible for certifying that the life funds are solvent (i.e. that sufficient assets are held to meet liabilities) to the Department of Trade and Industry. Few general managers of life offices are not actuaries.

Actuaries are generally responsible for overall planning, and deciding on and carrying out investment policy, since the expected investment return and the nature and value of assets are also part of their calculations. They supervise the underwriting of new policies and the design of types of contract especially in the field of pension schemes, advise on legal and tax questions (because actuarial calculations have to take account of these). Actuaries go on developing and refining actuarial techniques, including ways of using and improving computer systems.

The actuarial profession is relatively small but highly influential, with some 4,000 working in the UK (about 5,200 worldwide) in 1995, but has been growing steadily (from under 800 in the UK in 1955) and is expected to go on doing so. Demand for qualified actuaries continues to be high.

About two-thirds of actuaries still work in life assurance, or closely related areas such as employee-benefit work and pension fund management. The vast majority are employed by insurance companies (47%) or practise in consulting firms (40%) – 1995 figures. As well as the traditional areas where many actuaries are employed, the profession is taking a lead in extending actuarial work into new areas, such as long-term risks and rewards in capital planning projects.

According to figures in 1995, about 2% work in industry and commerce, 2% on the London Stock Exchange (giving investment advice, in research and investment analysis), around 2% for the government (down from nearly 3.5% in 1955) and 7% in other areas of employment – investment, insurance broking, merchant banking, academic work, computer development, for example.

In the CIVIL SERVICE, most actuaries work in the government actuary's department, a few in the DSS, the Home Office, the Ministry of Defence, and the statistician's department.

The government actuary's department deals mainly with national insurance and similar benefits, but also, because of cost and political sensitivity, with state pensions. The department acts as an independent adviser to the government, for instance reviewing financing of national insurance and industrial injuries schemes and examining the financial effect of major changes in them. This often involves fundamental studies of population projections, morbidity and similar statistical and demographic work. It reports on the financial effect of uprating benefit levels, for example, and advises the Reserve Pension Scheme and the Occupational Pensions Boards. It also does the actuarial work on pensions schemes for government employees and nationalised industries and scrutinises actuarial certificates submitted by insurance companies. Actuaries in government service have to take account of political and social as well as financial considerations.

About one-third of UK qualified actuaries work overseas. Most are based in Australia, New Zealand, Pakistan, India, South Africa and continental Europe. A UK actuarial qualification is recognised all over the world, increasing opportunities for actuaries overseas.

Recruitment and entry

Most recruits start as trainees in life offices. The Institute deliberately keeps its entry requirements flexible: the minimum is grade B at A-level in mathematics. However, most new actuaries have a first or upper-second class degree (mathematics, statistics, economics, science or business studies are preferred subjects). The most successful actuaries also have good oral communication skills and good written communication skills (GCSE English or equivalent is a requirement).

The Faculty (Scotland) requires three H-grades including maths at grade A and English, plus CSYS in two maths papers with grade A in one and at least grade B in a second. Provided the graduate has A-level maths, a degree in mathematics is not essential or even the best choice. Any degree subject, including a science, is acceptable. A combination of two or all three of maths, economics, and statistics is recommended.

The number of entrants is usually about 300 a year, for the UK, of which 84% in 1994 had first or second-class honours degrees.

Advanced GNVQ/GSVQs will be considered acceptable for entry requirements of the Institute and Faculty of Actuaries.

Qualifications and training

Training for actuarial work is long and tough. The average time taken to qualify is three to six years. Articled service is not required, but extensive practical experience is desirable to pass the examinations of the Institute of Actuaries or the (Scottish) Faculty of Actuaries. Most students therefore work in insurance offices or under a consultant.

Exemptions, even for 'relevant' degrees, are not extensive. City University, Heriot-Watt University, London (LSE), Kent University first-degree courses in actuarial science give the maximum. Actuarial options at Exeter University and Southampton University may also give some.

The professional nine-part examination (a joint examination for both professional bodies – *see below*) covers actuarial mathematics, economics and finance, statistics, investment and asset management, life assurance, general insurance and pensions. Pass rates are low. Graduates can gain exemptions for up to four parts, on a subject-for-subject basis. The one-year postgraduate diploma course at City University and Heriot-Watt University can lead to exemption from the first four subjects. Tuition is provided by the Actuarial Education Company on behalf of the Institute of Actuaries and the Faculty of Actuaries.

Professional bodies

There are few differences between the Institute of Actuaries, based in London and Oxford, and the Faculty of Actuaries, based in Edinburgh. Although the Faculty is much the smaller (907 Fellows in 1995, compared to the Institute's 4,017 in 1994), members of both professional bodies enjoy an equal professional status and from 1994 they set joint examinations.

Further Information

The Institute of Actuaries. The Faculty of Actuaries (Scotland).

Pensions management

Pensions Management developed following legislation which brought extensive growth of occupational pension schemes. Pension funds collectively have (1995) assets of approaching 300 billion, mostly held in securities, so managers are major investors.

Schemes have to be designed, negotiated and the funds' 'portfolios' managed and invested.

This is expert work, and employs actuaries, solicitors, accountants, pension consultants and brokers, investment managers (at least 2,000) and corporate treasurers as well as administrators. Pensions managers advise companies on the different forms of pension schemes available. They liaise with actuaries to look at the levels of funding required by both the company and its employees, now and in the future, and advise companies accordingly. They also advise on the best way to invest the funds.

They make sure that contributions from employees are collected and that this money is properly invested. They advise employees due for retirement on how they can have their pensions paid and they are also responsible for making sure that benefits are correctly paid out.

About one-quarter of the pensions managers work for insurance/assurance companies. Others work for private companies, public sector employers and trade unions which have their own pensions departments, and for pension consultants and consulting actuaries.

Recruitment and entry

Pensions companies recruit at a number of levels, both direct from the education system, and from among mature and experienced people, depending on need. Most employers in the pensions industry recruit for clerical and other support work, such as computer operating, as well as at the professional level. Overall recruitment has been fairly static lately, after some years at low levels and redundancies.

As a consequence of legislation, pensions has become a very complex subject. Employers therefore want to be sure that their staff are qualified and fully competent to deal with the work that is entrusted to them. Specialist pensions staff will usually be educated to degree or to at least the equivalent of A level standard before being recruited. Employers will then usually require staff to undertake one of the qualifications offered by the Pensions Management Institute (PMI).

As well as qualities needed for any business-related career, pensions takes intelligence to master the technical information and problems, the ability to explain complex matters in simple language and to develop a sense of judgement of situations and people. Pensions is essentially a 'people' industry, the hopes of other people's future happiness and prosperity are dependent on the skill, diligence and enthusiasm of the professional advisers in whose hands they have placed their trust.

Qualifications and training

Qualifications are awarded by the Pensions Management Institute. They set examinations covering the operation, management and administration of pension schemes. The nine papers are taken over a study period of several years. At least three years' relevant experience is also required for full membership. Entry qualifications are five GCSE/SCEs (grades A–C/1–3) and at least two A levels/H grades, passes to include English language and mathematics. The Institute is the awarding body for the NVQ/SVQ Qualification in Pensions Administration at level 4. It is designed for administrators of occupational pensions schemes and scheme administrators working in company schemes, public and private sector, insurance companies and consultancies.

Further information

The Pensions Management Institute.

Stock and other money/commodity markets and investment work

Of all the recent revolutions in the financial sector, the transformation of the London Stock Exchange has probably been the most radical. Long-established traditions have been overturned, and the City has secured its position as one of the three leading securities centres, sharing what is now virtually a single, global market with New York and Tokyo.

In October 1986, the London Stock Exchange ended the system of fixed commissions charged by brokers, removed restrictions on outside (and foreign) ownership of member firms, and abolished the demarcation between 'jobbers' and 'brokers' (*see below*). Simultaneously with this 'de-regulation' and restructuring, the Exchange introduced highly sophisticated new computer-based dealing, and information, systems. SEAQ (Stock Exchange Automated Quotation) displays 'instant' share trading information – buying/selling prices, volume of trading etc. – 'on screen' and records many deals within five minutes. Prices can be 'input' from anywhere in the British Isles. Anyone in the world with access to SEAQ's videotext information system can monitor, in 'real time', share quotations and dealings. SEAQ's success has been such that by the end of 1986, the traditional 'floor' of the London Stock Exchange was deserted, with almost all trading 'on screen' and via the telephone. Trading techniques have changed dramatically as a result.

For all its sharp new image, the London Stock Exchange is still the same market where companies and government raise funds by selling shares to investors, and where shares are traded between investors, on prices set by supply and demand. The government also uses the Exchange to 'sell' nationally owned firms to investors.

Since exchange control regulations ended in 1979, letting investors buy and sell shares in stocks and shares worldwide, the range of 'markets' being made, both on and outside the London Stock Exchange, has grown explosively. In 1995 a new market – AIM – was launched specifically for small and growing companies.

Trading in 'options' – paying for the right to buy or sell shares at a point in the future at a pre-fixed price – is a fast-developing way of investing with less risk without ever buying or selling a share. The London International Financial Futures Exchange (LIFFE), which further exploits options and 'futures' trading, and the London Eurobond (used to raise capital outside traditional markets) markets have been booming and by-passing the traditional lending by banks.

More developments are in the pipeline. SEAQ, which since 1987 only reports prices and trading on screen, so dealers must use the telephone to buy or sell, is to be upgraded to an all-electronic dealing system. Sharp-minded City firms, for the first time backed up by huge capital resources, will undoubtedly dream up new markets to 'make' more sophisticated 'paper lending' and services to offer.

The changes have brought major upheavals in the way the City is organised. The London Stock Exchange itself has had to strengthen its self-regulatory function. A completely new Securities and Investments Board (SIB) has been set up by the government to enforce codes of conduct and license investment businesses.

Exchange firms have gone through a major reorganisation, and more shake-ups are likely. The new competition demands far greater capital resources than old-style trading, while major UK and foreign banks, investment houses and other firms wanted to become Stock Exchange members but needed to buy in expertise. Almost all the old Stock Exchange members have therefore been taken over, mainly by large financial institutions. Even regional brokers have had to form larger groupings.

The majority are still like traditional stockbrokers, although they can buy shares on their own account and in some cases hold them for clients, but are now called 'agency brokers'. Market makers deal both with agency brokers and directly with institutional investors, can issue securities, and make markets work by buying and selling speculatively on their own accounts. Individual investors would normally deal with an agency broker, although all larger agency brokers also have institutional clients. While some of the larger market makers operate widely, many firms are choosing to offer specialised services. Smaller agency brokers mostly serve individual investors.

While only London Stock Exchange firms may deal on the London Stock Exchange itself, banks and other financial institutions form other markets, including LIFFE, the money markets, the Euro markets, and the foreign exchange market. Some markets include specialist firms, such as the foreign-exchange brokers, and the discount houses. Discount houses borrow surplus funds from the clearing banks 'on call' (giving the banks a source of interest for funds which can be easily available for customers) and investing them in government Treasury bill, commercial bills of exchange, and short-dated government bonds. They too are diversifying into other financial business.

The City is also the base for the commodity markets, which are centres, markets or exchanges where member brokers of particular dealing rings trade in supplies of materials – metals, cocoa, coffee, sugar, rubber, vegetable oils, wood etc. – traded internationally. The gold market handles bullion and other gold on offer. The markets play a major part in pricing these materials, and it is via them that producers sell and wholesalers, manufacturers and other customers buy their supplies. Prices change not only with supply and demand, but also with fluctuations in exchange rates. Investors also trade in commodities, using brokers to deal in 'forward' options, based on predictions of future trade and prices, without ever actually buying the commodity concerned. The goods often never even pass through the UK.

Commodity markets traditionally operate like the Stock Exchange. 'Trading' is via broker or dealer members of particular markets, on volatile, noisy open dealing floors, where traders shout prices at each other. Markets began switching to screen-based dealing systems even before the Stock Exchange. The London Commodities Exchange keeps prices up to date, like SEAQ, but also lets dealers 'call-up' prices on key-pads and then enter their bids and offers. *See also* SHIPBROKING *under* TRANSPORT INDUSTRY.

With the rapid growth and increasing complexity of financial markets, and availability of more sophisticated computer systems, a major growth area has been in market information, provided on screen and on line. While the London Stock Exchange has its own official system, independent companies offer dealers and investors a widening range of services. These cover not only prices, but also analyses and predictions of price movements in graphs and charts, and news likely to affect the markets.

Working in stock and other money/commodity markets and investment

Traders/ dealers/ market makers – sales staff (London Stock Exchange) – agency brokers (London Stock Exchange) – investment analysts and fund managers – commodity research – regulatory/ compliance officers – systems expert – management/ administration – recruitment and entry – qualification and training – further information

Employers include the London Stock Exchange member firms and other market firms, the dozen discount houses, investment and unit trusts investing on behalf of shareholders or subscribers (over 150 management groups), finance houses specialising in credit finance, and investment departments of large firms, pension funds etc.

The largest city firms and investment banks – financial 'conglomerates' – may be members of one, two, or several markets, with a co-ordinated 'presence' in London, New York and Tokyo. Smaller firms specialise. The sums handled by any one firm may be huge, but although the number of jobs has undoubtedly jumped recently, numbers employed in any one London Stock Exchange member firm, discount house or foreign-exchange broker is likely to be relatively small. Commodity houses (some doing both physical and futures trading, others specialising in futures) are also small.

London Stock Exchange member firms, under the new rules, can choose for themselves how to organise their trading operations, and the way jobs are designed will vary from firm to firm.

Working for a City firm may no longer mean working in the City. Electronic trading can be done from anywhere. While most firms are keeping their dealing operations in London, large integrated dealing rooms need a lot of space, so they are moving away from the traditional square mile. To save costs, the larger firms now also have out-of-town offices to house main-frame computers, and handle back-up administration, e.g. settlement and accounts. On account of the time differences between London, New York and Tokyo, shift work is increasing, and much longer hours are becoming the norm.

Traders/dealers/market makers

Large market making firms employ dealers/traders/market makers in teams, each specialising in 'market making' in different kinds of securities (banks, oils, chemicals), or types of trading (options etc.). In the main London Stock Exchange equity market, almost all traders now work entirely on the phone in computerised dealing rooms. Some trading on the LIFFE market, and commodity trading, is face-to-face.

Individual market makers use their experience and expert knowledge of the factors affecting share prices, and the way companies are performing, to make a profit on the difference between the price at which they sell and the price at which they buy – both of which they must now give clearly – and stick to – on information screens rather than verbally on the trading floor. Market makers have to do a lot of hard work on the securities being traded, what is likely to make the price of a security move, and who is likely to buy or sell them. The new trading conditions mean they must respond to what customers want, and work more closely with sales teams and research departments.

Dealers are also employed by agency brokers, and by banks and other financial institutions who also operate in the other financial markets. In merchant banks they specialise, dealing in 'straight' foreign change for immediate use, forward currency, 'swaps' etc. Just before the 'big bang', over a third of major institutional investment managers had their own in-house dealers, and numbers have probably increased since.

Commodity traders work for commodity firms, each dealing with up to 30 or 40 different commodities, but generally they specialise in one type of commodity. Commodity firms are usually quite small, ranging from around 20 to 30 to about 150 people. Floor traders are backed up by more senior traders monitoring prices etc. on VDUs, and phoning instructions to trading floors world-wide.

Sales staff (London Stock Exchange)

Market making firms can now offer large investors a direct service, for which they do not charge a commission. But firms' market makers do not normally deal directly with investors. Most have built up teams of sales staff who act as the link between market maker and institutional investor, not only arranging deals as the investors asks for them, but also trying to sell the client 'special offers'. Some firms also have teams of specialist, or research, sales staff who look after particular sectors and 'market' new ideas to clients. Sales teams work closely with the market makers. A market making firm may have as many sales staff as market makers.

Agency brokers (London Stock Exchange)

Firms not operating as market makers employ agency brokers in much the same way as pre 'big bang', although the environment has become much tougher. Most market making firms are likely to continue to offer their clients agency-broking services. Brokers must trade for their clients at best possible prices, and so may not always trade with their own market makers. Agency brokers work for the investor, institutional (pension funds, insurance companies, etc.), and individual. They buy and sell securities for their clients, using information screens to tell them what current prices are, and trying to better them. They also advise clients on what to buy and sell and when, and manage their investment 'portfolios' for them. Individual brokers usually look after a number of clients.

Investment analysts and fund managers

These work for any organisation which has large funds to manage, London Stock Exchange member firms, and other businesses providing advice and information on investment. Most so-called 'institutional' investors are in the financial sector – banks of all kinds, insurance companies, pension funds, investment and unit trusts, and so on. Many other large firms have investments large enough to warrant a professional department to look after them (some with over £2,000 million a year to invest).

Brokers, banks, business information services, financial consultants, etc. provide, or sell, expert information, analyse and advise on investment to their customers. Some 'manage' their clients' portfolios for them. London Stock Exchange market makers depend heavily on the back-up information provided by their investment analysts, usually being briefed by them before the dealing day starts.

Skilled investment means making money work and produce more money, regardless of how short or long a time it is available. Modern technology, and markets freed from many restrictions, make it much easier to make money on very short-term investment or lending. Some organisations, for instance banks and insurance companies, must keep a certain proportion of readily available funds, and so invest a proportion for only short periods, while some may go into medium and very long-term projects. Investment staff must know exactly where to invest, and for how long, to produce a return. They need very thorough knowledge of the markets, and extremely good intelligence on what can be earned on different securities, markets etc.

Investment departments, whether handling funds, providing on-screen or printed information services, or acting as advisers to those who do, store huge amounts of information, data about individual companies, about industries, about factors which may influence their growth or decline, etc. Analysts examine and question published figures, make their own investigations, break down, analyse and even re-calculate what they are given, and make their own projections of the future on a long- and short-term basis. They use an increasingly sophisticated range of computer-based information systems to keep them completely up to date on, for instance, exchange rates, company results, share prices. Analysts can move on to become fund managers, and this is the standard route.

Commodity research

Commodity Research in individual commodity houses is similar. Research departments gather information worldwide, from producing and trading countries, from traders and agents, and analyse it. They prepare reports, compile regular bulletins, and give personal briefings to traders.

Regulatory/compliance officers

Dismantling the old rules has not meant doing away with rules altogether, and events in several markets have proved the need for controls to protect investors, companies and City firms. The BANK OF ENGLAND (*see above*) has a major supervisory role, but the main emphasis is on self-regulation, through the Securities Investment Board (SIB), within a legal framework. SIB itself is delegating the task to 'Self-Regulatory Organisations' (SROs) which include, for example, the London Stock Exchange itself, and both SIB and the SROs, as well as the Bank, will have a fair number of staff monitoring and checking regulations. The London Stock Exchange and other firms subject to the new legislation have appointed their own 'compliance officers', to make sure that practices within the firm fully protect the investor. This is, however, mainly work for people who already have extensive experience of financial services, banking, the Stock Exchange etc.

Systems experts

The City and the markets are now totally committed not only to computers, but to the very latest in 'information technology' systems. For all this City firms need a wide range of experts with skills in information technology (*see* INFORMATION TECHNOLOGY AND COMPUTER WORK), able to assess, develop and manage whole systems for the firm's business (which means understanding it), and in specific computing skills – in, e.g. local area networking, linking up systems of all kinds, getting fast on-screen reaction times without overestimating capacity etc. Firms also use software houses with securities divisions to develop systems for them, and so employment opportunities have expanded among them also. However, most organisations and firms also have in-house computer support services.

Management/administration

With so much expansion and development, all firms in the investment business have grown in size and complexity, and most are now developing more rigorous corporate management, and administrative, systems. These 'back office' functions (plus computer support) can involve as many as a third of all employees. They range from all the usual corporate financial functions, but needing particularly strong and efficient settlement and accounting systems, usually including corporate treasury and tax specialists, through to far more systematic and high-level personnel management, training etc. Most large City firms now have to employ property specialists to manage and maintain buildings housing complex systems, and prepare for expansion.

Recruitment and entry

Entry is largely a matter of getting a first post, which for non-graduates often means starting in 'back office' administration. In recent years many firms, including large securities houses, have made staff redundant, or closed divisions completely. Although many people have found new positions within the industry, there are many skilled market makers, analysts, sales people etc. without jobs, as the level of recruitment depends very much on the activity and profitability of the securities markets.

For market making the right personality, a sharp and quick thinking mind and a flair for numbers are still most important. People are generally selected from back office and other clerical positions. Sales people and analysts are often recruited initially as graduate trainees. The subject of the degree is not always important, although maths, economics, statistics or accountancy may be favoured. Languages such as French, German or Spanish may also be highly beneficial in getting a position.

LIFFE employs 530 administrative staff (1994) and in 1995 is expected to recruit six graduates of any discipline under a Graduate Training Scheme. Vacancies are advertised in the national press.

Qualifications and training

Training is often in-house, and on the job, but it is increasingly becoming more formalised. Graduate trainees normally spend a number of months in several contrasting areas before they settle in one, e.g. analysis, sales, corporate finance. This gives them an all-round feel for the business and helps to identify their strengths. The following training/qualification requirements must be met.

The Securities and Futures Authority (SFA) is responsible for registering employees of its member firms who work in the field of securities/derivatives trading and advice. To be authorised to give investment advice it is necessary to be registered as a representative; to commit the firm in market dealings only it is necessary to be a registered trader. Mandatory examinations now exist to support this registration structure and the majority of firms will sponsor new employees for their training and examinations.

For floor traders who work on the market floors of exchanges such as LIFFE (London International Financial Futures Exchange), separate examinations exist. School leavers and graduates are also recruited as trainees to work on these markets. A period of practical experience under the supervision of a Registered Trader on the floor and the successful completion of the London Commodity Exchange's trading examinations are necessary in order to become a Registered Trader.

For those working in administration and support areas, SFA offers an increasingly popular non-mandatory Merit Award, made up of a number of modules such as the Foundation Certificate, an introduction to the workings of the financial services industry.

The Securities Industry Examinations, administered by SFA on behalf of the London Stock Exchange, has eight papers which may be taken individually. The Securities Industry Diploma is awarded to those with passes in any three papers. A number of training organisations offer a range of study methods for these examinations including day-time tuition and distance learning. The London Stock Exchange operates a Graduate Training Programme for graduates or final-year degree students and a Network Training Scheme for school leavers aged 17 or under.

The Investment Management Regulatory Organisation (IMRO) is the regulatory authority for investment management and asset management organisations, and has established a register for fund managers. Institutional fund managers are required to register, and the mandatory examination for them is the Investment Management Certificate (IMC), set by the Institute of Investment Management and Research (IIMR).

The IMC is the first examination leading to the IIMR qualification of the Associateship of the IIMR. The Associate examination consists of six papers set at university pass level, and normally this programme can be completed in two or three years. Tutorials and distance learning for these examinations are offered by a number of training organisations. Companies increasingly encourage trainee fund managers and analysts to study for the examinations.

The IIMR (formerly the Society of Investment Analysts) has a membership of 3,500 (2,500 qualified and 1,000 students – 1996). Minimum entry requirements for enrolment as a student member are five GCSE/SCE grade C or above, including mathematics and English. Applicants must be at least 18 years of age.

The Finance and Leasing Association offers Diploma and Higher Diploma examinations in finance.

For those dealing with credit management the Institute of Credit Management (over 8,000 members in 1996) has a two-stage examination, entry to which is with at least four GCSE/SCEs (grades A–C/1–3) including English and mathematics. However, students with business experience over the age of 21 may be accepted without formal qualifications. GNVQ/GSVQs are accepted for registration purposes. Examinations cover economics, law, accountancy, credit management, law of credit management, legal proceedings and insolvency. The institute also offers a preliminary certificate in credit management for those students who do not wish to pursue the full professional course. No entry qualifications are specified for this course.

Other relevant professional qualifications in the field include the Chartered Institute of Bankers, Chartered Insurance Institute, Institute of Actuaries (Finance Investment Certificate).

Further information

The Securities Institute, the London Stock Exchange, the Institute of Investment Management and Research, the London Commodity Exchange and other appropriate professional bodies.

Contents

Buying, Selling and Related Services

(CLCI: O – Oz)

Marketing (general)

Industry and commerce today are supposed to be marketing- rather than production-oriented. Crudely put, this reverses the traditional attitude which says 'make it first and then sell it', and is based on a near-automatic demand for goods and services. It is reasonably easy to sell a product or service in a market where there is little or no competition, and for a long while few firms in the industrialised world had any problems in selling their goods. Now conditions are different – competition is worldwide and getting tougher all the time – and UK firms have to become 'marketing-led'. That marketing has become recognised as crucial to companies' success is demonstrated by the inclusion of a section on marketing in a recent government White Paper on competitiveness.

Marketing, then, is not just modern jargon for selling – although selling is a major part of the marketing process and the two are often confused. There is a great deal more to marketing than selling. Marketing is a strategy rather than a direct activity. Marketing has to see that a firm produces the goods or services which will make the most profit, and having decided on the most profitable goods and services, uses its expertise to see that the profit made is as high as possible. The Chartered Institute of Marketing defines marketing as 'the management process responsible for identifying, anticipating and satisfying customer requirements profitably'.

A company's planning will include setting marketing objectives. As part of the planning, markets must be researched before any decision is made on what to produce, and so marketing has to find out as much as possible about potential markets. Marketing is used to find out what potential customers really want. Marketing looks to see if there is a gap in the market which a firm can fill, whether there is a market for a potential new product or service; and if so, tries to identify ('target') the people or organisations most likely to buy or use it.

One large company found that, of 600 ideas for new products, only 100 were serious candidates. Of these, only 57 reached the test-marketing stage, only 40 were launched nationally, and only 30 were commercially successful.

Marketing is not, though, only concerned with new products. Marketing keeps checks to see if a product or service is still selling well, evaluates consumer response, and tries to find out why, if a product is losing customers. Markets change, and nowadays change faster than ever before, and it is marketing that must watch out for, and even keep ahead of, changing demands, so that the firm can respond quickly and flexibly.

Marketing, then, has to match what the firm can make, or the service they can give, as closely as is practicable with the customers' identified needs, and work out and evaluate the possible profits. The price (and therefore the cost) of a product or service has to be pitched at the right level to give the best profit – higher cost and therefore lower sales volume, or vice versa perhaps – and to see that the product reaches sales outlets at the right time. Throughout a product's life, marketing has to go on trying to improve 'customer appeal' and profitability, look for ways to extend its life, see if there are ways of improving it or making manufacture cheaper and/or simpler and whether or not these are cost-effective. Sometimes marketing reviews the entire range of products or services.

Marketing therefore has to be closely involved with the firm's planning and entire strategy. Marketing has a complex and sometimes difficult role – it has to coordinate effort without actually being in direct control. What is often called the 'marketing mix' usually involves market research, product development and design, costing, production, packaging, sales promotion and market planning, distribution, advertising, merchandising and even after-sales servicing.

Ideally, a marketing manager would like to have the entire company marketing-'oriented', and may spend a lot of time trying to convince other managers of this – since all these activities are the responsibility of other departments within a firm, and even of other firms, such as the retailers who sell the company's products to the customer. Marketing also has to create and maintain strong links between them, both within the company and outside it, so that the marketing effort on a product, group of products, or service is as far as possible a team activity.

But however important all these elements may be, the most crucial is the nature, quality and design of the product itself. Good marketing starts before a product is even designed.

There are two types of marketing: consumer marketing and industrial marketing. Marketing strategies are different for consumer goods like soap powder and canned soups; products for industry such as machine tools or car parts; and services such as holiday packages, banking services, or insurance schemes. Within these broad groups, there may be quite different strategies for different types of product: for 'fast-moving consumer goods' (like butter, tea, and washing-up liquid) and consumer durables (TV and video sets, radios and washing machines).

In marketing consumer goods, the product is designed from the outset to attract a particular group of people, using information from market research to help define what it should be like, with product development, design and packaging adding their own distinctive 'styling' to the basic technical design, tailored to the purchasing patterns of the particular consumer group, and costed for that group's purchasing power. Distribution, sales promotion campaigns, promotional material, and briefing retailers, are all usually treated as part of the marketing 'chain'.

Marketing also has to ensure that there is an efficient after-sales service for consumers.

Services such as insurance or holidays are also designed to meet the needs of fairly tightly defined groups of consumers. Service industries such as banking have adopted modern marketing concepts, because they must now sell their services more widely. Part of the marketing role here is to 'educate' the consumer into wanting the service in the first place. Banks, for example, compete hard for the student market, because market research shows that customers, once caught, stay with their first bank. 'Package' deals, complete with smart 'styling' and offers, are designed each year for the young.

Industrial marketing sells goods and services to other companies or organisations. These may be 'one-off' products – a chemical plant, a dam, or a mainframe computer system – and the product is designed specifically for that customer. They may be finished goods – robot systems for car manufacturers, for example; they may be components – silicon chips, for instance – from a production line or assembly room. Whatever the product, industrial marketing has to stay abreast of developments not only within the area in which it is selling, but also (for instance) in the production methods of potential customers, to help predict future demands and open up new markets. Marketing has to see that the product meets exactly the customer's technical specifications, that delivery dates are kept, and problems solved quickly and efficiently. Industrial marketing advertises and promotes products somewhat differently from consumer-orientated marketing: promotion, for example, may involve demonstrating and displaying products at trade exhibitions.

Direct marketing is a growth industry – and closely linked to advertising. It targets potential customers by means of mail shots, catalogues, TV, radio and printed advertisements which ask an interested party to respond by telephoning or by completing a coupon. Direct marketing is expected to increase by over 30% in 1996.

The marketing 'function', then, varies from sector to sector. The Chartered Institute of Marketing's 25,000 members are divided: 28% financial and business services, 20% mechanical and engineering, 14% food, drink and textiles, 11% retail and hotels, 10% education and medical, 8% chemicals, metals and minerals, 5% transport and communication, 3% energy, water and fuel and 1% other.

Most firms have their own marketing departments, although some use independent consultancies, and some large advertising agencies offer marketing services. An organisation's marketing department is generally made up of a marketing director and a number of brand or market managers, each responsible either for a range of similar products or for a particular market, which may be an area (usual in export marketing) or a particular group of customers. The shape and structure of marketing departments change frequently, especially as product ranges change more often.

Marketing managers are responsible for company strategy on market research, advertising and sales. They coordinate all marketing and production activities. They must both try to improve the marketing of existing brands and develop new goods and services as these are introduced or the need for them identified. Within the overall strategy for the particular product or market, the manager must forecast income from its sales (deciding at the same time on the year's sales target and pricing policies, based on researching the market and its development). Generally s/he is responsible for the budget for the product or brand, and for deciding on the best 'mix' of marketing methods and resources to use. The brand manager then has to bring together and coordinate the various specialists needed to implement a marketing plan. This may mean organising particular parts of the plan with other departments, as well as deciding on, arranging contracts with, and supervising, an advertising agency and campaign for the product (for example).

Marketing managers spend a great deal of their time acquiring, assimilating and assessing information of all kinds. Most obviously this comes from market research, feedback from sales people, results of advertising audits, etc. However, other reports come from within the company, for example the management accounting monitoring system, from production. Since much of the information comes in number form – market research surveys, sales figures, costings – analysis is often statistical, using computers.

Marketing managers must also pass on information to others, again in the form of reports and statistics – feedback from sales staff, for example, to product design about particular features of a product, or from servicing staff to production about a recurring problem.

New entrants might begin as marketing assistants, perhaps looking after merchandising, the crucial but rather basic job of seeing that, for example, supermarkets put the product on the shelf in a prominent position (and don't leave it in a storeroom), and that special displays are assembled and put out in the store. Promotion to assistant brand manager and brand manager can be fairly fast – 'front-line' marketing managers are generally young. It is one of the toughest and most aggressive functions.

Progress upwards is via group brand management, marketing management and marketing directorship. Marketing is said to be one of the best routes into senior management, but marketing managers also move out, into consultancy, or starting their own businesses (using their skills to identify a profitable market gap).

Britain has lagged behind the rest of Western world in developing marketing techniques, and as an identifiable career marketing has a history of not much more than 35 years.

Recruitment and entry

It is unusual to start in marketing itself direct from school, but there are no hard-and-fast rules (and not all jobs advertised as 'marketing' are truly marketing jobs). Firms are recruiting new graduates directly for marketing traineeships in increasing numbers and the Chartered Institute of Marketing says that only graduates (of any discipline) are recruited directly into brand management, although other people transfer to brand management from other functions. Degree subject is probably not too important for marketing consumer goods, although the signs are that some business studies content or a postgraduate qualification could improve chances (competition for places is very fierce), but is no substitute for experience. For industrial marketing, a relevant engineering or science degree is needed. Fluent languages, and familiarity with the business life of the countries where they are spoken, are useful for export marketing. Trainees in all types of marketing are normally expected to spend a period 'on the road' as a sales representative, and sometimes a period in market research also.

More usually, though, employers want recruits for marketing with some form of business experience first, such as selling, sales administration, advertising, customer support, market research, although it could be, e.g. R&D. These are not formal routes into marketing, however.

Marketing demands the ability to communicate, both in writing and verbally, the ability to persuade, to explain, to sell ideas and to gain other people's cooperation. Marketing managers have to be intellectually capable of assessing complex information, and working out its implications for strategy. They have to be numerate enough to work with and be able to understand a mass of statistical material. They need self-confidence; it helps to be outgoing and fairly thick-skinned, to be happy working inside sizeable organisations with formal structures, and to have plenty of physical stamina.

Qualifications and training

It is possible to read for a degree, either in marketing or in business studies with a substantial marketing content, or a BTEC HND in business studies biased to marketing. There are now nearly 50 degrees in which marketing can be studied, either as a single subject or in combination with another. Examples include: Marketing with Languages, Marketing with Food Studies, Marketing with Leisure Studies, Marketing with Statistics, Marketing with Travel and Tourism.

Professional qualifications are increasingly useful. The Chartered Institute of Marketing (with a membership of 25,000 in 1996) provides the main qualification. The number of students currently studying for one of the Institute's qualifications is 30,000.

The Institute's minimum entry requirements for the certificate (minimum age 18) are four GCSE/SCE standard grade passes at A–C/1–3 (or equivalent) to include English and mathematics; and one pass at A-level/appropriate GNVQ/GSVQ Advanced Diploma or equivalent, or one year's full-time marketing experience: for the diploma, either the certificate or an approved BTEC/SCOTVEC higher national award, degree or postgraduate qualification with an approved marketing content.

The two-year certificate course covers: fundamentals of marketing, economics, principles and practice of selling, practice of marketing, statistics, business law, behavioural and financial aspects of marketing. The diploma covers: marketing management, communications, planning and control, financial services and international marketing. Over 160 universities and colleges give tuition for CIM certificate and diploma examinations. CIM also provides a wide range of training packages.

NVQs are in place at levels 3 and 4 – offered by the Chartered Institute of Marketing in conjunction with City & Guilds and by the RSA.

Further information

The Chartered Institute of Marketing.

Advertising

Advertising aims to attract attention, to create a particular and lasting image in the minds of consumers, and to persuade people to buy a particular product, to go on a particular holiday, to apply for a particular job, or not to smoke, for example. Most advertising is, by implication, also designed to inform, but some advertising is a great deal more informative than others – bus timetables, for instance.

Although, to most firms, advertising is a crucial part of the marketing 'mix', it is a relatively small part. Estimates say the cost of advertising makes up only about 10% of total marketing costs. But while it is only the tip of the marketing iceberg, it is a very visible, vocal and expensive one.

Advertising started out by selling 'hard' products to consumers, and although this still makes up a large part of the industry's income, other sectors, notably services (finance, leisure, holidays, etc.), are now major contributors. Government, political parties and charities all also use advertising as a means of getting their message across.

In 1994 total advertising expenditure in the UK amounted to £10.17 billion – an 8.5% increase in real terms on the previous year. As a percentage of Gross Domestic Product, advertising grew from 1.67% in 1993 to 1.76% in 1994 (but although the industry is now growing at a healthy rate across all sectors, this figure is below the record level of 1.96% reached in 1989).

The total expenditure (including direct mail) was spent in various ways, but with use of the press still dominating: 55.1% was spent in newspapers, magazines and business directories; 28.3% on television advertisements; 10.3% in direct mail; 3.4% on outdoor and transport facilities (posters, hoardings, etc.); 2.4% on radio advertising and 0.5% at cinemas. Retail and mail order were the heaviest sectors to use advertising, with food, cars, and financial services next. Lowest users were the agricultural and tobacco industries and charities.

Advertising projects a glamorous, creative and entertaining image, giving the impression that it is all rather fun. It may be all gloss and froth on the outside, but underneath it is a very commercial, competitive, tough business where profits are taken as seriously as anywhere else. Advertising has suffered as much as any other industry during the recent recession, even though company expenditure on advertising has actually been growing in real terms, with importers and UK companies in increasing competition; and some sectors have substantially increased their spending – car manufacturers for instance spent £440.8 million in 1994 against £283 million in 1988; office equipment suppliers, £228 million against £96.5 million.

Earlier efforts at becoming more businesslike and with better management and financial control, which are just as important as creative flair, have born fruit.

Advertising people are by nature optimists, but their expectations for the rest of the 1990s are well supported. More and more organisations are now convinced they must advertise regardless of trade conditions, and the explosion in all the kinds of media in which they can advertise – colour magazines, TV channels, radio stations, newspapers – means more intense competition for advertising. Nevertheless, the industry is maintaining tight financial controls, and some agencies did cut staff in spite of increased billings.

Working in advertising

The choice of employers is between

- firms which actually do the advertising – the advertising agencies which sell their services to advertisers;
- advertising departments of firms which do their own;
- service organisations – medium-sized and smaller agencies 'contract out' work: creative work to independent art or film studios; media planning and buying, and sometimes research; to account planning and other consultancies; to market research organisations; and to promotions houses;
- media firms which provide the advertising 'space' (newspaper and magazine publishers, television and other broadcasting organisations, etc.);
- companies which provide specialist services for advertising agencies or departments – market research firms, film units, and freelance artists and designers – where agencies or departments do not have their own;
- marketing departments in larger companies, where buying advertising is a major job.

Advertising people have to produce a profit for their agency. They do this by creating original, imaginative lively 'campaigns' with maximum impact – even in bread-and-butter areas like job ads and selling cleaning services or tools for industry. The creativity has to be geared to persuading people to buy something, within a budget, to meet a tight marketing strategy and sales target, often with impossible schedules. Computers are being used to 'target' consumers and their views ever more exactly, to improve services.

Advertising people work in teams, with endless discussions and meetings, and much negotiation. Attitudes may be informal and relaxed, but the pressure is often intense, hours can be long, and the crises frequent. An agency's character usually strongly reflects the personal style and ideas of the directors. The first job of an agency is to project a strong image of its own, and staff may be chosen to fit a particular mould as well as for their talents.

Advertising agencies and departments

These provide most of the career opportunities.

It is a small, fast-changing industry, with some 300 major agencies employing about 15,000, of whom 10,000 work in London; and around 300 smaller agencies with fewer than 3,000 jobs between them. The 'top twenty' agencies employ between 125 and 550 staff each, others usually less than 100. Most agencies are still in London, but with growing numbers in other major towns.

For over two decades, the same agencies have stayed at the top, and most are still American-owned. American dominance, though, is being increasingly and successfully challenged by a 'new wave' of British agencies – three are now in the top ten and one has topped the billings chart for several years. Every year sees agencies closing or merging, and new ones opening. New agencies are rarely started by anyone new to advertising, though – extensive experience of running another agency is usually crucial. Agencies 'pride themselves on the high quality of their staff'.

Information on who works for the advertising departments of major manufacturing and other companies is not collected, but estimates suggest they employ fewer than 1,000 people between them. The use of short-term contracts and freelance workers is increasing.

Agencies, and some advertising departments, plan, organise and run the 'campaigns' for particular products or organisations – agencies call their clients 'accounts'. Every campaign has to be carefully matched to the market for the product, so one manufacturer may use different agencies for different products because each agency has its own kind of market expertise. The campaign has to be planned closely with MARKETING (*see above*), or brand managers, because it must be linked into the 'brand image' which creates a common theme for packaging, displays, TV, newspaper and magazine advertisements.

Launching a new product takes one kind of campaign, concentrating on encouraging consumers to try it. Once a product is established, the formula may change to compete with other brands and keep up consumer interest. Advertising works through every available medium: newspapers, journals and magazines, TV and radio, posters, packaging, the cinema, shop displays, exhibitions, circulars and direct mailings. Agencies also produce all the myriad free- and cheap-offer coupons, promotional leaflets and so on which do so much for sales, but an estimated 60 separate sales promotion agencies now do much of this.

In some organisations which have products or services to advertise, the advertising department may do all or some of the work of the agency, but in others the brand or advertising manager will contract out most accounts, handling only small-scale work internally. S/he liaises closely with the agency to make sure that the advertising in the firm's name says the right things, at the right time, to the right people, at the right cost, and monitors the success of the campaign with them.

The larger the agency the greater the range of accounts they handle and the more services they offer. Smaller ones tend to specialise in particular markets. Some agencies have their own marketing and market research units, and offer sophisticated services on, e.g., product development or corporate image. Some employ their own writers and artists, others commission specialists from outside service houses for particular campaigns.

Advertising agencies are highly individualistic organisations, creating for themselves a very distinctive image, and 'selling' themselves on the basis of, e.g., strong creative, or marketing, expertise. Some are strongly hierarchical, others not. Broadly, they use a common set of terms to describe the various functions, although how far those functions are carried out by one, or several, people, usually depends on the size of the agency.

Account executives

Account executives (who with their assistants, make up about a quarter of the staff of the major agencies) each look after a group of accounts (perhaps three or four), and are the links with the clients.

The account executive must find out what the client is after, as much as possible about the product(s) and agree a budget with the client. Under the account executive, a team then plans and designs a campaign, using all the available expertise, from market researchers to designers.

When, and if, the client agrees the resulting 'presentation', the account executive must see that plans turn into reality, monitor progress and solve the inevitable problems. Once the campaign is launched, s/he must keep track of its effectiveness.

Account executives must be able to weld all the different people working on an account into an effective team, understanding all their different jobs. Account executives are leaders, organisers and negotiators, and need personality, drive, and physical and mental stamina.

Account planners

Account planners provide information on the consumer's point of view at each stage of the campaign. They use market and other kinds of research to define the target audience and present an analysis of consumer attitudes and needs to the client. The planner is responsible for writing the advertising strategy and then converting this into a creative brief. This involves working closely with the account executive and the creative department.

Creative staff

Creative staff are the copy- and scriptwriters, the artists and typographers.

Copywriters

Copywriters (at most 800 in the top 300 agencies), not only write the slogans, jingles and sharp headlines, but also the longer and more detailed sales brochures, the cheap-offer coupons, trade features and advertisements which are part of many campaigns. In some agencies copywriters may also write scripts for film and TV advertisements; in others the two roles are separate, because they take rather different skills.

Copywriters, it goes without saying, need a way with words, but it has to be a skill which persuades and doesn't only produce sharp prose (although one of today's most successful novelists was once a very sharp copywriter).

Art directors

Art directors – every agency has one – look after the all-important visual images.

Some agencies employ their own artists, graphic designers, illustrators and typographers (there are some 1,500 altogether in the top 300 agencies), or they may commission outside studios or freelance artists.

Television and film advertisements are generally made by independent film units, employing their own or freelance staff (including scriptwriters), but working under agency supervision.

The media staff

The media staff (about 1,200 of them in the main agencies), are researchers, planners and buyers. They specialise in knowing how best to use television, radio, posters, newspapers and magazines, depending on what is being advertised and to whom. They are expert at buying space and air or TV time at rates best suited to a particular client's product and budgets.

Media executives need business skills and must be expert in understanding and analysing complex statistics and pricing arrangements. All must become really skilled judges of the media.

The media department used to be just the place where orders were processed. Increasingly, campaigns are directed at specific groups and not at mass markets. Here a good media department can save large advertisers millions using people expert at negotiating with media owners.

Production departments

Production departments arrange for film and TV commercials to be made and for the production of artwork for press advertisements, posters, leaflets, showcards and so on (*see also* PRINTING *in* MANUFACTURING INDUSTRIES). Departments employ, or more usually commission, photographers, illustrators and typographers, and contract work to radio and film production teams.

Traffic or control departments

Traffic or control departments make sure that everything happens at the right time; for example, that copy, proofs and artwork are all delivered on time. The work demands accurate record-keeping, attention to detail and awareness of time and deadlines.

Other staff

Some large agencies also have their own MARKET RESEARCH departments (*see below*), and some also MARKETING departments (*above*). Most have information departments, but usually train their own staff to meet agency needs for information (e.g. desk surveys), rarely employing qualified librarians or information scientists. All employ 'service' staff, in finance, secretarial work (1,600 in the main agencies), personnel (in the largest agencies only) and computing.

Media advertising departments

They 'sell' space and air time to advertisers or agents. Publishers – of national and regional newspapers, magazines, trade and technical journals (totalling about 14,500 different publications) as mentioned earlier, carry more than half of all advertising. TV carries nearly one-third. The largest media advertising departments are, therefore, in the major newspaper and magazine/journal groups.

Advertising revenue is crucial to the profitability of newspapers, magazines, and TV companies. A national Sunday newspaper may derive as much as 60% of its revenue from advertising as opposed to 40% from sales. Similar figures for national dailies are 44% and 56% respectively; for regional weekly papers 92% and 8%. It can cost a client £48,000 to place a full page advert in a Sunday paper; nearly £8,000 for a colour page in a teenage magazine and from a few hundred pounds to over £50,000 for a 30-second spot at peak viewing time on TV, depending on the TV company and whether it is regional or national (1996 rates). Competition is fierce, and so considerable ingenuity and very sophisticated techniques are used to sell space. Sales staff may work on a single publication, or on a product or service, e.g. holidays, for a group of publications.

Recruitment and entry

There is no accepted, straightforward route into advertising, and it is rarely easy to get started. It is probably easier to start with an advertiser, a media firm selling advertising than to get into an agency, or even with a marketing department, and to make the necessary contacts in agencies by working with them.

Competition for jobs promotion has always been very intense. Agencies are reluctant to invest in untrained talent. A special kind of flair, or creative or organisational ability is needed to attract the attention of agencies, now interested only in the best of new talent. Every year at least ten graduates compete for each trainee position, and only 15 agencies have a regular recruitment programme. Advertising, though, needs a regular infusion of new talent and ideas 'to stand out in a noisy world', and is always looking for the right kind of creative or organisational ability, for people prepared to work very hard to tight schedules, within exact budgets, and who are ready to take advantage of any opportunities.

While academic qualifications are not important in themselves, a reasonable level of intelligence and good educational background are. Employers do therefore tend to choose graduates when recruiting the very few trainee account executives they take, which is at most four or five a year for even the largest agencies, an estimated 120 places, with most in the twenty largest. A degree is seen as evidence of a certain level of ability, although graduates are also expected to have the right personal qualities. The subject(s) studied is therefore relatively unimportant, except for creative artists, who are normally expected to have a degree in art and design, although a relevant BTEC award may be acceptable. Some kind of relevant student activity or vacation work experience may help in getting a first post. Applicants have to sell themselves hard.

While a degree is not absolutely essential (one agency regularly interviews some of its own junior staff for trainee executive places), a Higher award in business studies (preferably with advertising and marketing options), two A-levels, 3 Highers (or the equivalent in A- and AS-levels) are normally needed to get onto the career ladder.

Particular jobs within advertising require particular abilities, but in general, everyone needs the ability to persuade, some kind of creative talent, and business sense. Advertising also needs an intelligent and detailed interest in what motivates people, how they express their likes and dislikes, their buying habits, etc. It also takes the ability to work as part of a team, all of whose members tend to be fairly extrovert, self-confident people. Other qualities often quoted include imagination, ability to work under extreme pressures, and a mature approach.

Qualifications and training

No industry-wide formal training schemes as such exist. Most training is on the job with part-time study, although some agencies give their new entrants a period of planned training with regular moves between different jobs and departments.

Professional qualifications

The Communication, Advertising and Marketing Education Foundation (CAM) certificate and diploma sets the only formal qualifications. CAM qualifications are not essential, and agencies vary in the weight they attach to them, some encouraging entrants at all levels to study for CAM exams. Over 1,000 UK students registered for the examinations in 1996, divided between advertising, PR and 'other' work (sales, marketing and direct marketing). About 15% of registered advertising students work for agencies, and about 8% each for advertisers and advertising services. However, the influential Institute of Practitioners in Advertising has developed its own programme of training courses to cater for the training needs of the staff in its 245 member agencies.

The full CAM scheme can be covered in three years part-time (at one of 35 colleges in main centres or by correspondence course). The common certificate course in communication studies covers advertising, marketing, public relations, media, research and behavioural studies, sales promotion and direct marketing (each can be taken separately).

Entry qualifications are five GCSE passes at A–C/SCE S grades 1–3, including English, or equivalent, *plus* one year's relevant work experience *or* three GCSE/SCE passes as above with two A-levels/three H-grades *or* a BTEC/SCOTVEC HND in business studies *or* alternative qualifications recognised by CAM. All candidates must be 18 in order to register for the examinations.

The diploma which follows comprises three three-hour written examinations, one on each of management and strategy (compulsory), and two optional ones, consumer advertising and business-to-business advertising, so that students can choose options appropriate to their own professional needs.

Direct entry to the diploma is sometimes possible with an appropriate degree, BTEC Higher award or professional qualification.

Degree and diploma level courses

There are now: one degree in advertising management (at Bournemouth University), two in advertising and marketing (Lancaster University and London Institute) and one in communications, advertising and marketing (University of Ulster). Bournemouth also has a degree course in creative advertising.

There are four HND courses in advertising – at Falmouth College of Arts, the London Institute, West Hertfordshire College, Watford, and Wolverhampton University.

Other relevant qualifications and courses include BTEC/SCOTVEC HND in business studies with options in advertising and advertising design.

NVQs are in place at levels 3 and 4, offered by the CAM Foundation in conjunction with RSA and by the Chartered Institute of Marketing/City & Guilds.

Further information

The Communication, Advertising and Marketing Education Foundation, the Advertising Association, and the Institute of Practitioners in Advertising.

Market research

Market research is used to test public opinion on anything and everything from a new drink to TV programmes and political policies. First and foremost, it is one of marketing's most essential tools, developed, constantly refined and used to pinpoint as exactly as possible the groups of consumers most likely to buy a particular product, and how that product should be designed, packaged, priced and advertised for maximum sales.

While marketing commercial products – and services – obviously provides most market-research organisations with the largest part of their income, it is also used by a great many other organisations, to find out what the public thinks, or how they react, or would react to, for example, particular political policies or parties. Even more broadly, market-research techniques are used to find out basic facts and statistics for all kinds of other studies of people's behaviour, habits and attitudes. It is also used by those who formulate policy. A social survey, for example, will not lie dormant as a snapshot of a situation but be used for a purpose – in planning for particular social needs.

Market research people also compare their company's or client's share of the market with that of any competitors, and make regular retail audits, which log the movement of goods in and out of the shops.

Market research has actually expanded while other industries and professions have suffered – although it is still a small profession employing about 160,000 people (January 1996). Managers and decision-makers of all kinds now see the value of having relevant and current information. Market research is the vanguard of this and therefore is a relatively secure profession. It is also a young person's profession. The Market Research Society has a special group for its members under 30.

Market research organisations

There are two main kinds of market research organisation:

One is a department attached to another organisation, for example, large advertising agencies and manufacturers. Government, local authorities, and some other organisations have survey and/or research and intelligence units using market research techniques.

The other is the independent agency, which is generally quite small (most employ under 50 people, a few have only one or two staff, and a few over 500). Of just over 150 market-research agencies, the largest 30 account for 80% of annual commission. The broadest range of services come from the market research departments of large advertising agencies and the larger independent agencies, which generally provide many special survey services, and will take the nation's pulse on anything from censorship to motorway planning. Smaller agencies generally specialise, and there are a few specialist market audit companies. Market research departments within major firms generally concentrate on the company's own products, services and image generally, although they usually help in monitoring the effects of, for example, an advertising campaign designed by an outside agency.

Working in market research

The 1995 survey of Market Research Society members showed that 50% were then working for market-research suppliers, mainly agencies/consultancies. The society's membership is 53% female.

Market research work consists almost entirely of obtaining, collating and analysing information, much of it statistical, and then turning the results into a report either for the marketing department (some companies still have in-house market research departments, although the majority outsource to agencies) or for an external client.

The information is collected via two kinds of surveys:

The first, desk surveys, gather information from published sources such as the press, trade and other specialist papers, research documents, government publications, statistical reports and so on.

The second consists of field surveys, mostly carried out by interviews and questionnaires using standard random- and quote-sampling techniques, but perhaps also involving panel and group discussions, some in-depth interviews and interviews on the telephone. Telephone interviewing has become routine in some agencies. Most field surveys are large-scale or 'quantitative', but some involve intensive psychological probing of a few consumers, and are 'qualitative'. The Market Research Society points out that much more qualitative research is conducted than is generally realised. Leading market researchers expect to use 'viewdata' to collect information from consumers in their homes in future, predicting a 'slow death' for the familiar face-to-face interviewing techniques.

Market research also uses a considerable amount of research into consumer reaction to specific products via placement tests, pack-testing and test-marketing. The balance between the kinds of surveys used for any one piece of research varies – looking into the potential market for a new industrial product (e.g. a machine tool) is likely to involve more desk research, for example, than researching possible demand for a better disposable nappy. The field surveys will differ between them too – the market for the machine tool will be fairly restricted, and so most potential customers can be contacted and interviewed directly; surveying the nappy market has to be done by careful sampling of a much larger group of people.

Surveys have to be designed scientifically, to ensure, for example, that the sample chosen accurately represents those who buy thc product. Designing surveys is very exacting, and involves understanding thoroughly how people behave when they are asked questions, to eliminate any risk of bias and to find out what interviewees really think, rather than, for instance, what they think the interviewer wants to hear. At the other end, sophisticated statistical techniques and computer-based analyses are used to extract information from the raw results.

Surveys of this kind give manufacturers direct information on the type of people who buy, or are likely to buy, the company's products, how the company's share of the market compares with, and is related to, that of any competitors, and how it changes, for example in response to a new 'brand image'. Market research quantifies the existing state of any given market, potential changes in it, and forecasts of possible market trends.

Research executives

Research executives supervise projects and, in agencies, are the link with the client. The research executive plans and organises a project, briefs the people who organise the surveys and other research, supervises progress, and prepares and edits the final reports. Research assistants help to plan surveys and prepare questionnaires. They become market-research executives. The normal route thereafter is via group leader generally into management, but it is possible to move into, e.g., general marketing.

Specialist staff

Specialist staff, such as psychologists (*see in* SUPPLEMENTARY HEALTH PROFESSIONS *and* SOCIAL AND RELATED SERVICES), mathematicians, statisticians, and economists (*see* MATHEMATICS, STATISTICS AND ECONOMICS) and computer personnel (*see* INFORMATION TECHNOLOGY AND COMPUTING), help prepare research projects and surveys, and supervise collating and analysing results. They can move into management functions in some organisations.

Interviewing

Interviewing is generally a part-time occupation, done by people with good educational backgrounds, or by students, although some kinds of interview (for example, panel and group discussions) need trained psychologists.

Recruitment and entry

Recruitment is generally on a trainee basis, usually as a research assistant. Although there are no hard-and-fast rules, market research is largely a graduate occupation. Certainly, entry as a trainee research executive is largely restricted to those with degrees or HNDs. Annual entry is fairly low, due to the small size of the profession (no exact figures are available). Well over half of new graduate entrants are normally social scientists. Qualifications in economics, psychology, statistics and business studies are favoured by some employers. A significant proportion are engineers and scientists. Specialists are also recruited for particular posts, as in computing services.

Qualifications and training

Training is still largely informal and on-the-job, although the Market Research Society and the Industrial Marketing Research Association jointly run a range of short courses including a basic training course for new entrants.

The Market Research Society runs two kinds of training: the academic route, consisting of a certificate and diploma; and a vocational route in the form of NVQ/SVQs. Both routes are, however, workplace-based and rely heavily on obtaining practical experience. The certificate, which must be obtained before the diploma, may be acquired through distance-learning organised by De Montfort University. It is possible for some students on undergraduate courses in business studies or marketing, whose course includes relevant work experience, to obtain the certificate during their course rather than having to purchase the distance-learning package later. Both certificate and diploma cover behavioural aspects; statistics, sampling and analysis; market-research techniques and applications and case studies. It is stressed that all entrants should have a period of practical training under experienced supervision before they can be considered fully qualified. Some 75% of the Society's 5,500 members are graduates, over 10% (25% under 24) have the MRS diploma.

NVQ/SVQs are in place at levels 1, 3 and 4. Level 1 is for interviewers (telephone and face-to-face); level 3 for research executives, field managers and for 'purchasers' of market research, i.e. managers in client companies; level 4 is for research executives with higher responsibilities. NVQ/SVQs are offered by the Market Research Society in conjunction with the RSA and by the Chartered Institute of Marketing with City & Guilds.

Overseas opportunities

There are opportunities to work throughout the EU and in Eastern Europe where the UK is regarded as the leader in market research. Many agency directors specialising in overseas work are rarely at home!

Further information

The Market Research Society, the Industrial Marketing Research Association.

Public relations

Public relations is defined by the Institute of Public Relations as 'the planned and sustained effort to maintain goodwill and mutual understanding between an organisation and its public'.

Public relations complements advertising. Where advertising creates highly vocal and persuasive campaigns, actively promoting particular products or services, public relations is a rather more low-key, sustained activity. Public relations people (who may be called information communications or press officers) look after the general reputation of the organisation for which they work, although in large organisations some may deal only with a particular product or service.

All kinds of organisations employ public relations people – industrial and commercial firms, government departments (one of the largest users of PR!), hotels, travel agencies, universities and colleges, trade unions, publishers, banks and charities. This is demonstrated by the fact that the Institute of Public Relations (IPR), the industry's professional association, has the following special interest groups: charity and voluntary, construction industry, health and medical, technology and engineering, tourism and leisure, city and financial, government affairs and local government. Use of public relations expertise is growing, although it is all too often limited to reacting to events, particularly crises or problems, rather than being proactive and exploiting knowledge to shape opinion or influence what happens. But while many companies still fail to involve PR experts in crucial decision-making, surveys show that growth rates for public relations consultancy were between 30% and 50% each year between 1990 and 1995.

Public relations weathered the recession. Whereas approximately one-third of PR budgets were cut in the early 1990s, over one-third were increased. Job losses were mainly amongst those working for industrial firms, but were compensated for by expansion amongst the agencies.

PR remains a small profession, probably employing not many more than 37,000 in total (20,000 practitioners plus support staff).

Working in public relations

Ideally, public relations staff should see that an accurate picture of what the organisation is and does gets over to both the general public and particular groups which matter to the organisation – their shareholders and customers, or the community in which a factory is sited, for example. They must also see that people who need information about the organisation actually get it, and should also try to keep the organisation informed about what people outside are thinking about it.

Some public relations departments also look after internal communications, especially in companies which have factories and/or offices scattered about the country.

Obviously, public relations staff try to present their employers or clients in the best possible light, but the aim is, or should be, to explain the organisation's actions and decisions, not to conceal and excuse them, which is generally counterproductive. Public relations cannot substitute for good management.

The keynote of good public relations is a steady programme of positive publicity, deliberately designed to create and keep an informed public, who recognise the organisation and its products or services, have a favourable impression of it, and are likely to think of it first when they want that kind of product or service.

Public relations staff work through people like journalists, maintaining good contacts with them, sending out press releases and being available to answer questions. The public relations office must counter, at source, any misleading information or rumours, and see that complaints are properly settled.

Public relations staff advise on (for example) the 'visual image' which stamps an organisation's personality onto notepaper, sales and publicity material, transport and store fronts, and packaging, so that it is instantly recognisable.

In fact, public relations people expect to do anything that will help 'project' their organisation – preparing annual reports and careers literature, giving talks, organising promotional films and exhibitions, writing articles and speeches for managers, arranging press and other conferences, seeing that stands go into appropriate exhibitions, sponsoring events. They may produce house journals and newsletters, both internally and for more general circulation. They may be involved in lobbying politicians.

In agencies or consultancies account managers may be responsible for more than one client; otherwise the work is more or less the same from organisation to organisation.

It is a very varied life, but tends to be hectic with long and often irregular hours (45% of IPR members say they work 40–50 hours a week, 25% 50–70 hours). They spend much of their time in contact with other people, and the pressures can be considerable.

Public relations staff have to learn how to reach particular audiences through the mass media. This means knowing, in detail, how press, TV and radio work, and how to make the best use of them. They have to understand all the technicalities of printing, photographic, film and exhibition work, to make maximum impact and use resources economically.

Public relations experts work either in organisations or advertising agencies with PR departments, or in public relations consultancies. A growing number are self-employed.

Reflecting economic changes, more PR practitioners are now employed in the service sector and fewer in manufacturing industry. Over 50% of IPR members work for PR consultancies (of which there are over 2,000 including those owned by sole practitioners or by two or three people). Both central and local government have seen an increase in PR staff, and central government is now the largest single employer of PR practitioners.

Recruitment and entry

Since so many of the qualities needed for PR are developed only with experience and maturity, it is almost impossible to start straight from school, and not common even from higher education, although some larger organisations take trainees. Generally, it is much more usual to gain experience of the communications field elsewhere first, most often in journalism, marketing, or advertising, although there are signs that people with flair are now getting into PR earlier than has been traditional.

Whatever the route, and there is no fixed way in, wide experience is essential, of communications, and preferably also of an organisation's area of activity. Maturity is also needed. Academic qualifications are not, in themselves, crucial, but intelligence and a good educational background are, and a rising proportion of entrants have degrees.

Public relations needs the ability to get on well with anyone, to be persuasive, tactful, completely unflappable and able to stay calm and polite whatever the provocation. PR people must be able to explain almost anything to almost anybody clearly and simply. They need creativity, imagination, ingenuity, intuition and news sense linked to other journalistic skills, especially writing. They ought to be good organisers and planners. They have to be able to work under considerable pressure.

Qualifications and training

No general formal training arrangements exist. Some companies have their own internal schemes – 46% of IPR members say they have a training budget. The IPR runs well-attended short courses, seminars and one-day workshops.

Qualifications in PR work are optional, but since January 1992 IPR membership has been restricted to those who hold approved qualifications combined with a period of professional experience. The first qualification to be recognised was the IPR's own diploma. This is now administered by CAM (Communication, Advertising and Marketing Education Foundation).

The diploma may only be taken by students who have completed the first part of the CAM qualification, i.e. the common CAM certificate in Communication Studies which is run by 35 colleges and can also be obtained through distance learning (*see under* ADVERTISING *above*).

The diploma examinations contain three compulsory papers: management strategy, public relations practice and public relations management. Ten colleges and training centres run part-time courses and there is also a distance-learning route.

The IPR accepts other qualifications, including:

- degrees in public relations from the universities of Bournemouth, Exeter (the College of St Mark and St John, Plymouth), Central Lancashire, Leeds Metropolitan, Manchester Metropolitan, Napier and Stirling;
- the diploma in international public relations from West Hertfordshire College, Watford;
- the diploma in public relations from the Dublin Institute of Technology;
- NVQ/SVQs at level 4.

NVQ/SVQs

These are in place at levels 3 and 4, administered by the Chartered Institute of Marketing/City & Guilds and by CAM/RSA.

Further information

The Institute of Public Relations and CAM.

Buying, purchasing and supply

Buyers and purchasers are absolutely crucial to the viability of any retail organisation and to that of most industrial or commercial ones, and without real efficiency in these areas the efforts of others in marketing and management are largely wasted. Industry and commerce must sell if the country is to have reasonable living standards, and fortunately this kind of work has now lost its unattractive image. Graduates are continuing to enter the field in increasing numbers (12.5% of those in 1994 who entered employment directly went into purchasing, buying, marketing and selling) but show a marked preference for careers in marketing or buying.

Professional buyers and purchasers in industry and commerce today are expected to combine the skills of the behavioural scientist with those of the technologist. They must cope with both the technological changes affecting all products and the increasingly sophisticated selling strategies developed by marketing managers, which sales must put into effect in the field and to which buying and purchasing must develop equally sophisticated responses.

Maturity, both personal and in business judgement and experience, are hallmarks of the buyer, the purchaser and the salesman/woman. These are careers which may develop out of a less specialised start in industry or commerce, following several years' commercial experience, although many companies now recruit graduates direct to training programmes in purchasing, supply, buying and logistics.

People in purchasing and sales need drive and energy, numeracy, the ability to assimilate technical or other data quickly and easily, and later to communicate these again equally easily. They need to be able to work well in a team. Many positions require a thorough knowledge of computer-based systems. They must be ready to travel extensively (but not necessarily abroad), often living in less-than-ideal conditions, and be able to make personal contacts easily.

Efficient, expert purchasing or buying is very much more important in the viability of almost all organisations than is often realised. The Chartered Institute of Purchasing and Supply (CIPS) estimates that businesses spend an average 55% of their total production costs on buying goods and services (80% in some manufacturing companies). Only too frequently the organisations themselves fail to appreciate this importance. A recent CIPS survey revealed that 17% of managing and financial directors did not know what proportion of their total costs went on external goods and services.

It is reasonably obvious that the profits of shops and stores of all kinds depend heavily on the expertise of their buyers. But it is also true for manufacturing, where up to two-thirds of the cost of finished products may be in the materials and parts – every 1% saved by purchasing managers can increase gross profits by as much as 15%. Industry not only buys parts and materials, though. It also has to buy increasingly expensive new machinery, and almost all organisations now have sophisticated office equipment and computer systems.

With high and sometimes rising prices for fuels, raw materials and supplies of all kinds, the problems of purchasing or buying within tighter budgets, whether or not a profit has to be made, have increased tremendously for all organisations, although the scale of the problem is obviously greatest for the largest.

Every organisation, today, whether it is an insurance, manufacturing or construction company or a public-sector organisation, needs expert purchasers or buyers. Central and local government for example spend £150 billion on supplies; the National Health Service more than £4 billion on drugs, sophisticated electronic machinery, etc. every year.

'Purchasing' is the term industry uses, 'buying' is the retailing word, while other organisations often use 'supplies' and the Ministry of Defence 'procurement'. All use common techniques, and the demands of the job are similar. They are just as much part of the marketplace as selling and marketing, and need the same tough, expert commercial attitude.

Purchasing

Purchasing managers are now part of a wider profession which has grown considerably during the 1990s and is known as supply chain management – a term which is often interchanged with the terms, 'logistics management' or 'purchasing and supply'. The supply chain consists of all the stages of the process that get product to customer – from purchasing raw materials, through manufacture, storage, distribution, transport and selling. (*See* RETAILING AND DISTRIBUTION *and* WHOLESALING AND WAREHOUSING *below*; *also* LOGISTICS MANAGEMENT *below*.)

Purchasing is probably at its most complicated in manufacturing industry, where products such as cars are assembled from a great many different components, many made elsewhere. Purchasing managers may be involved right from the time when design engineers begin to specify the raw materials and the parts needed, starting to pinpoint possible suppliers and sorting out any problems on new designs with them, going back to the designers if their first specification will not work for any reason – perhaps cost.

A purchasing manager may consider several potential suppliers for a single item (looking at all their literature, samples, prices, asking for and assessing quotes, etc.) and any final contract will depend on achieving the best possible balance between technical specifications, the right delivery dates, and price. This can be multiplied several times when buying a component for cars, for instance. Obviously, the purchasing people discuss the specifications with the design engineers, and production managers – which requires an understanding of engineering problems. Their job is then to get the best possible commercial deal. They may 'buy forward' overseas to benefit from a change in exchange rates in their favour. They must know when and how to take advantage of capital allowances. They must know all the legal implications of negotiating and finalising contracts.

Purchasing must see that all the components for a particular product arrive at the right time. While components or raw materials arriving too late obviously hold up production, equally disastrous are purchases which arrive too early or in too large quantities: they tie up company money and valuable space and so affect overheads and therefore costings. Newspaper companies have the paper for tomorrow's editions delivered as late as possible. Keeping stock at the most cost-efficient levels is helped by computer-based stock control and manufacturing systems. Supermarkets order replacement stock from their own warehouses and in turn from suppliers (aided by instant analysis of sales from the tills via bar codes) as it is needed and not before.

Purchasing managers have to know a great deal about potential suppliers – their ability to produce the product required and their overall reliability and stability – since continuity of supply can be a vital factor. Some purchasing officers specialise in buying one kind of component, material or product.

A purchasing department in a large organisation can be responsible for a budget of several hundred million pounds a year, and have a staff running into hundreds. The problems of supply can result in major companies buying shares in supplier companies. Purchasing staff monitor tariffs, prices and other criteria worldwide, and most raw materials have to come from abroad. Purchasing managers may also buy materials for overseas contract work, and this often means purchasing materials and goods suitable for use in quite different environmental conditions, for example, concrete for construction in the Middle East.

Purchasing managers do not buy merely for today. When they are buying goods and services for their own organisations they must look to the long term, making decisions on the life of a computer system, for example, and taking into account the likely annual running and maintenance costs.

The responsibilities of purchasing managers in the public sector have changed dramatically. The introduction of compulsory competitive tendering under which they must contract out many of their services means that they are now involved in issuing tenders, evaluating bids and finally awarding contracts.

Buying

Buyers in retailing have to be expert forecasters. Retailing makes its entire profit and its reputation on the ability of its buyers to predict what will sell at a given point in time, and to acquire the products at the right time, and in the right quality and quantity. Buying too much or too many of a particular product not only means surplus stocks on the shelves and in store, but also leaves less shelf space for other lines which might have sold better. Too few or too little, and customers are lost again. Automatic stock control systems are, however, giving buyers faster, sharper analyses of what is selling best, and helping to cut down the basic routine in reordering.

Retail buying has achieved a popular reputation and status (often equal to the store manager's) so far, rather unfairly, denied to purchasing in other spheres.

Working in buying, purchasing and supply

The working day of a purchasing manager or buyer combines office-based work with a lot of time spent visiting suppliers. A great deal of time goes on negotiating, liaising inside the organisation with people for whom the purchasing/buying is being done, checking up and chasing suppliers. Detailed deskwork includes dealing with the complexities of contracts and understanding some contract law. Purchasing must keep up with technical changes in the firm's products, market and financial trends, monitoring contracts, watching for warning signals of problems or breaks in supply, and looking out for new price trends. Purchasing departments also contribute from all this to the information that management needs to plan and forecast. There can be a lot of pressure and regular crises to sort out. Buyers and purchasing officers travel a great deal, often overseas.

Purchasing officers and buyers have to become skilled negotiators and decision-makers, develop sound business and financial sense, and learn to make objective judgements of people and companies. They need to learn to forecast trends and how to acquire and assess complex information. Although not expected to be technical experts, in some organisations they need to acquire some knowledge of the technicalities of what they are buying. They have to liaise closely with colleagues within their own organisation and to create the right kind of personal relationship with suppliers' representatives. They need to be methodical and well organised, especially if they are involved in stock control.

Recruitment and entry

It has been usual to go into purchasing in industry from a related 'function', for instance selling, and this is invariably the rule still in retailing. However, more and more organisations, particularly the larger manufacturing companies, service industries and the public sector, now recruit trainee purchasers direct from school or, more usually, university, although time spent gaining experience elsewhere in an organisation is always an advantage.

Although smaller organisations may often not be too concerned about academic qualifications (apart from numeracy and English), the larger ones are increasingly demanding a good level of education, preferably at least to A-level, GNVQ/GSVQ Advanced, BTEC National or even Higher National Level award. (The proportion of A-level entrants is still small though.) An increasing number of graduates – about 25% of intake – are going into purchasing, especially where the work is technical and/or complex.

Qualifications and training

Many companies now recognise the need for key personnel to have relevant qualifications and skills training in the purchasing and supply chain management functions.

Trainees are often required to pursue the professional qualifications offered by the Chartered Institute of Purchasing and Supply and/or follow a programme of skills training designed by their company. There are now a number of first degrees in relevant areas with specialist options and one degree in purchasing and supply chain management (at the University of Glamorgan). For more experienced individuals a postgraduate course or NVQ/SVQs in purchasing may be more appropriate.

The Chartered Institute of Purchasing and Supply (1995 membership 23,500) is the professional body for all those engaged in purchasing and supply chain management, including materials management, logistics, project and contracts management, inventory management and distribution. The CIPS has been raising its own, and its members', status steadily over the past decade and provides a full range of training programmes to support this objective.

CIPS provides a foundation stage programme, dealing with essential business topics such as accounting, economics, management and statistics, but some 60% of entrants gain exemption by virtue of a previous relevant qualification such as a degree or HND in business studies or other professional qualification.

The Institute's professional stage includes compulsory papers on strategy, tactics and operations and a range of options to suit candidates' individual needs. Examinations through the use of case studies emphasise the importance of practical application of knowledge to work. Study may be completed through part-time or distance-learning routes.

For those with experience or who prefer a less academic route, NVQ/SVQs are available. Full membership of CIPS may be obtained by following either the professional qualification or the NVQ/SVQ route.

Minimum entry requirements for the professional qualification route are three GCSE/SCE passes at A–C/1–3 and three at H grade or two at A-level (or equivalent). There are exceptions for people over the age of 23 who may be accepted without academic qualifications if they have their employer's support. CIPS also provides a pre-foundation certificate course for which there are no entry requirements.

Further information

The Chartered Institute of Purchasing and Supply.

For qualifications and training in retail buying, *see under* RETAILING AND DISTRIBUTION *below*.

Direct marketing and mail order

Selling direct to the consumer, via direct mail, mail order catalogue, TV or radio, magazine or newspaper, to produce a direct response or order, is one of the fastest-growing ways of selling, and is also one with the greatest potential. Practitioners identify several reasons for this: social – working women with less time to shop, too busy to cope with the problems of parking near a shopping centre, yet with more money to spend; economic – the increasing cost of taking the car to shop; and technological – the possibility of consumers using a computer link to order goods straight from the screen.

Direct marketing accounts for 10.3% of total advertising revenue, demonstrating its importance. Direct sales, traditionally made from catalogues through a network of part-time agents, has grown to include those made by sizeable speciality firms such as book and record clubs and now includes a host of niche retailers (for example, Innovations and Kaleidoscope) operating through small catalogues distributed via national newspapers and magazines. Ninety per cent of general catalogue mail order work is done by four or five big companies such as Grattan and Littlewoods, mostly based in the North of England.

These companies must keep operating costs to a minimum, and thus were among the earliest to use computers, with screen-based customer accounts, and standardised response letters, etc. Even more crucial are sophisticated management techniques to provide good-quality, tested merchandise, at prices which must be accurately predicted to hold for the life of an expensive catalogue.

Buying is therefore one of the key roles, and the firms employ large teams. Efficient warehousing, stock control and order assembly are equally crucial. Correspondence clerks look after agents; and VDU operators, in fairly large numbers, do the order-processing. General administrators, as well as personnel, advertising (and promotion), accounting and computer personnel are also needed.

Training is largely in-house, although entrants are recommended to gain appropriate professional awards and NVQ/SVQs.

Retailing and distribution

Retailing and distribution are the nerve ends of marketing, since it is here that strategies stand or fall, at the checkout.

Retailing, however, is one of the industries worst affected by the present economic climate. In a period when people are afraid of being made redundant or are trapped in negative equity property situations, they spend less. Even though total retail turnover was £144.14 billion in 1994 analysts doubt that sales will ever again reach the levels of the 1980s. However, sales and turnover have increased in the retail industry since the early 1990s although the number of outlets has decreased. Turnover per member of staff has increased due to greater efficiency and improved technology.

In the consumer-led 1980s consumer spending rose. Retailers expanded, investing in new, larger or improved premises. The 1980s were also the decade of design, when about 75% of retailers redesigned their stores.

The trend to move out of town centres has continued in the 1990s as more retail parks combining superstores with cinemas and other leisure facilities opened. Smaller shops closed. The threat to high-street shopping continued to increase with the opening of regional centres, offering not only sport, leisure and supermarkets but also branches of department stores, chain stores and multiples under one roof. Some are still being constructed, although planning and greenbelt protection considerations have imposed an overall limit. It is anticipated that there will be one near every conurbation in the UK by the end of the century. It is interesting, however, that even though the large chains have meant death to many small shops, even they have not been able to leave the high street entirely. Some of the supermarket chains are opening new town-centre stores (1996) in response to customer demand. The Tesco chain is one notable example, opening new 'metro' stores in high streets, which stock a range of the most popular lines.

All this expansion costs money which companies had hoped to recoup in increased sales. Unfortunately, they found themselves faced simultaneously with declining sales and increasing overheads. (Staff wage demands went up, and rents and business rates increased.)

Recession has not affected retailers equally. Sales in household goods and those associated with house purchase (DIY goods) slumped, while food and clothing sales were less badly affected. Food retailers survived, with varying degrees of success, due to their guaranteed volume sales.

New tactics have constantly to be found to meet rising competition and costs in all areas, but especially on staff, premises and rates. Customer demand, for more flexible opening hours, for greater choice, better design, style and quality have to be met. Technology has been a major aid – supermarkets were hardly feasible until cheap and efficient pre-packaging was developed – and it is still making changes.

Retailers were slower than expected to use the latest computer and electronic technology, but laser-scanning checkouts are now in use in large supermarkets and in most other stores, even corner shops. These not only save time, but also allow automatic stock control, reordering and invoicing, so costly store space can be saved while fast-selling lines are ordered in time to prevent stock running out, and sales trends can be monitored and analysed daily. Sophisticated managerial methods and information systems quickly show through in company accounts: net profits for those without have risen at a much slower rate than costs. Even the family corner shop can have this kind of management information and calculate VAT, pay, stock control, etc. on relatively cheap micros.

Several 'electronic fund transfer' experiments, direct-debiting customers' accounts at the checkout terminal, are now also widespread. 'Teleshopping' via interactive TV viewdata and/or home computers is becoming available.

Technology has led to some staff losses, mainly at the unskilled end. The 1990s are the decade of cost-cutting, but firmly linked to this is the need for quality management.

Despite the trend to fewer, larger stores – the number of shops has been falling steadily, indeed, there were 29,000 fewer businesses in 1994 than in 1984 – well over 220,000 businesses are still operating through nearly 320,000 retail outlets, and the range and variety is still large. They still include many 'traditional'-style large chain and department stores, multiples and smaller specialist shops – antique shops, booksellers, butchers, bakers and chemists. The supermarkets, and their edge-of-town big-brother superstores and shopping centres, are an accepted part of life now.

But the retailing revolution which began with them and the 1960s boutiques, aggravated by recession, has entered a new and much more aggressive phase, as younger, pace-setting retailers swallow up chains and department stores which have failed to target new markets or adapt to changing consumer demand.

Retailers, according to one analyst, can now only succeed by closely identifying their customers, making sure they get the products they want and the stores are attractive to them. Even the most successful and largest chain store has been forced to rethink its winning formula, 'managing change', its chairman has said. Galleria or 'shops within shops', specialist 'satellite' stores, new product ranges and working more closely with suppliers to react faster to consumer demand, new store designs and promotions, and credit-card schemes are amongst the ways managers are responding now to the impact of even greater competition. 'Image' is crucial to success. Targeting markets more closely – in clothes, food, 'high-tech' equipment, financial services, everything for the home – means some store groups are now running several different, 'parallel' retail operations, to get target groups of customers to identify with them.

Increasing use is made of modern managerial methods: anticipating demand and regulating supply, determining optimum stock levels and mixes and controlling stock losses more accurately, reducing operating costs, looking endlessly for more economies in overheads, self service, fewer but larger stores, and cooperative buying. Optimum use of staff – with a high and rising use of part-timers, especially 16- to 20-year-olds still in education – plays a major part.

Some sectors, e.g. butchers, shoe shops, fishmongers and bakers, have changed very little in their trading methods, with more than 90% of sales accounted for by one kind of product. In others, especially grocery, clothing, 'high-tech' electronics (and photography), DIY, furniture and other consumer goods for the home, and pharmacies, innovation is now near-continuous, and trading styles transformed. Completely new chains, of health food and video shops and record/cassette stores, have burst onto the high street. Computer dealers have come, and many have already gone.

Retailing still employs (1996) about 2.4 million people (of whom 48% work part-time): over 10% of the working population. Male and female employment are at 38% and 62% respectively, but men predominate at management level. The British Retail Training Consortium estimates that by the year 2001, full-time employment will have decreased further; men will increasingly take part-time jobs, and more managerial positions will be created. (Women, they say, will take more of these positions.)

Employment is now concentrated in large multiples which account for less than 1% of retail businesses. Large multiples employ 46% of retailing employees and account for over 50% of turnover. There are still over 196,000 single-outlet retailers which provide 30% of jobs and account for 25% of turnover.

The retailing sectors

The range and variety of goods sold by stores expands steadily both with technological innovations – for example, it is estimated that, since the development of man-made fibres, the number of different types of cloth has increased to 400 from the basic four made from natural fibres – and from greater opportunities to import. Expertise in type of product is often essential.

Antiques and art, and bookselling

Dealing in antiques and art and bookselling traditionally demand expert knowledge, both of the entire field and usually also a section of it. Both have a different kind of image from other areas of retailing. Yet selling works of art, antiques or books is still commerce, and traders have to make a profit. They need a business sense, must know what is profitable to buy and what price will make a profit, as well as management skills just as other retailers. Caring too much for antiques, paintings, books, etc. can be a positive disadvantage, since it can be a strong disincentive to sell.

As in other areas of retailing, shelf or shop space is valuable, and the accent is always on good turnover of stock.

Antique dealing

In antique dealing, with an estimated 20,000 dealers, only 400 are members of the British Antique Dealers' Association, and the Fine Art Trade Guild has only 1,000 members. The field is divided between a fairly large number of medium- and small-sized dealers, and the large salerooms (dealing in both art and antiques). Interest in antiques and in handmade objects generally has grown considerably, both for their intrinsic interest and as investments. Increased interest in antiques notwithstanding, the antique world can provide a living for very few, and it takes considerable dedication to make a career. It is a very close-knit world. Many businesses are run by families, or have been set up by friends with interests in common, and dealers frequently sell to, and via, each other, so personal contacts count for a great deal. Learning is mainly by experience, preferably under an established dealer, and may involve starting as a clerk or in packing, although entrants now commonly have a fine art or art history degree.

Art

The art world is even more specialised. Dealing in art can be similar to antique dealing, but galleries which exhibit and sell works of art (as opposed to the art galleries, which are repositories) are slightly different. Most specialise in the work of a group of artists, frequently with some thread (of period, or school, for example) linking their work. In the past the gallery–artist relationship could be very paternalistic, but galleries (and indeed even the artists) have become far more businesslike, backing their aesthetic judgement with very commercial contracts. Like antiques, art is now sold on an international scale, with London as one of the major centres. For a few, therefore, travel is possible.

However, neither galleries nor dealers employ very many people, and opportunities are limited. Getting a first job usually involves sending a CV to numerous dealers. Luck or personal contact often play a part, but it makes sense to have in-depth knowledge of a particular subject as well as a broad background in art, normally via a first degree or similar course in history of art (although this is not necessarily accepted as a qualification). Some larger art dealers, particularly auction houses, now run regular training courses – a few last a year, but there are also shorter programmes. Training also involves gaining appropriate experience. There is also one degree course in Fine Art Valuation.

Bookselling

Booksellers face tremendous problems of rapidly rising costs (premises, books, staff) with an explosive annual increase in the number of books published, which makes stock-buying increasingly hazardous. The abolition in 1995 of the net book agreement, under which book prices were fixed, has led to greater competition, with some booksellers able to discount prices. However, sales have been rising quite sharply, lately, and larger firms have been controlling stock more tightly using computer-based systems.

Traditionally, bookselling was considered a rather erudite occupation, but modern conditions have forced the trade into a mould closer to the rest of retailing, with larger organisations, not necessarily only selling books. Many booksellers now rely on trade in things like stationery to maintain profitability, and use modern marketing methods. Specialist bookselling, of technical, business and scientific books, and for universities and other libraries, has expanded most. Some 2,195 firms (with over 3,790 bookshops) employ about 20,000 people. Stationers employ a further 28,000 in over 5,000 outlets, owned by 3,000 firms.

Antiquarian bookselling is also highly specialised, and has close links with antique dealing, with one important exception: thanks to the relatively small size of the printing industry and censorship up to the industrial revolution, the titles and editions of most books published are known and catalogued. Of an estimated 2,600 antiquarian and secondhand booksellers in the UK, 350 belong to the Antiquarian Booksellers Association. Many do not have shops at all, but deal entirely by post or in person, and many travel the auctions and salerooms with antique and art dealers, often making a steady profit from the never-ending demand for individual titles from overseas university libraries.

The best booksellers provide highly personalised services for their customers. They help anyone not sure of what they want and trace individual books, both new and secondhand, for others.

Opportunities for promotion are greatest in the chains and larger independents rather than in the bookshops with few staff. The level of subject expertise which most booksellers achieve is rarely as well rewarded in bookselling as it would be elsewhere. In larger organisations, of course, executive responsibility (as opposed to subject expertise) is generally more suitably rewarded.

Qualifications and training

Assistants learn on the job, starting fairly menial tasks: keeping shelves clean and tidy, filling out order forms and keeping records. Most booksellers encourage their staff to read the trade press and stay abreast of publishing trends, and also to study for the Booksellers' Association Diploma in Professional Bookselling, designed to meet the needs of bookshops of all types and sizes, which consists of study manuals for students to work through at their own pace.

No formal academic qualifications are needed, although most employers would expect new entrants to have a suitable educational background which should include some GCSE/Standard grade passes at A–C/1–3, normally including English and mathematics. School-leavers with A-levels and some graduates are recruited by the larger, specialised bookshops, especially those serving universities. One company, Waterstones, recruits graduates, refers to them all as booksellers rather than sales assistants and makes them responsible for their own sections and for ordering stock.

There is one postgraduate diploma course in antiquarian bookselling at University College, London – the only organised way of obtaining a formal training. The course is validated by the Antiquarian Booksellers' Association and may be studied over one year, full-time, or part-time over two years.

There is one first degree course in fine arts valuation, at the Southampton Institute.

NVQ/SVQs in bookselling may be introduced in the future.

Builders Merchants

See in THE CONSTRUCTION INDUSTRY.

Butchers and poulterers

The traditional sawdust-strewn shop is under threat, with only an estimated 15,563 shops remaining (down 6,000 in three years). Specialist butchers now sell under 40% of carcass meat, their market eroded by supermarkets and freezer centres, and consumers eating less meat. The major chains have been rationalising and merging, and are looking hard for ways to widen their appeal.

Trained butchers, though, are still needed by traditional shops, larger multiples and supermarkets (where the work is mainly pre-packaging). Promotion is into shop management, inspection, or meat buying for large organisations – retailers, large hotels and caterers, manufacturers producing cooked meat products, poultry producers, etc.

Qualifications and training

The national organisation is the Meat Training Council, which promotes training and is also the industry's examining body. It has developed modern apprenticeship schemes (under which all apprentices will have employed status) and linked to these, NVQ/SVQs at levels 2 and 3. Levels 3 and 4 are being developed.

Selling cars and other vehicles

Selling cars and other vehicles is not the only function of the retail motor industry. It also does maintenance, testing and repair (*see* ROAD TRANSPORT *in* THE TRANSPORT INDUSTRY), and sells tyres and other parts, and petroleum products.

Car sales staff work for dealers, and sell new and/or secondhand cars. Dealers selling new cars work closely with the manufacturer(s) with whom they have a dealership, often fitting into nationally designed marketing campaigns. Buying a car is the second largest purchase in many people's lives and so is a major event. Sales staff are expected to give them just as good service as they give anyone replacing their car annually. Sales staff have to be very convincing, and helpful. They may buy secondhand cars as well as selling them. To gain promotion, to sales manager and above, often means moving around. Competition for car sales is intense, and showrooms have been closed, but manufacturers still franchise nearly 7,000 dealers (down by just under 4,500 in four years).

Car sales are heavily affected by economic climate. Sales of new cars slumped from 14,958 in 1990 to 12,148 but picked up again – to 14,589 in 1993. *See* THE MOTOR INDUSTRY *in* THE MECHANICAL ENGINEERING INDUSTRY.

Qualifications and training

Most employers who can offer reasonable training and some prospects require a good standard of education shown by a good spread of GCSE/SCE standard grade passes at A–C/1–3 or above. There are some training programmes available through YT, and NVQs in vehicle selling are available at levels 2 and 3 (Chartered Institute of Marketing/City & Guilds, RSA or RTITB Services).

In the case of adult entrants, companies do look for some experience, although they also can attend manufacturers' courses. *See also* ROAD TRANSPORT *in* THE TRANSPORT INDUSTRY.

Chemists or (community) pharmacists

Over 7,500 chemists are in business, with some 12,800 outlets. About 15% are owned by the major multiples (the largest with over 1,000 branches). They employ about 87,000 people (over half part-time), of whom nearly 15,000 are qualified pharmacists and some are pharmacy technicians. Pharmacists may own their own shops, but more usually manage a pharmacy for someone else, or work for a multiple.

Although, on average, some 70% of independent pharmacies' turnover comes from dispensing drugs under contract to the NHS, most pharmacies also sell a wide range of other medical and related products, toiletries, cosmetics, and some a great many household and leisure products. Consumer spending on toiletries and 'over-the-counter' or non-prescription remedies doubled in the 1980s. Pharmacists have, then, to combine a professional with a business role.

While drug companies now pre-package most drugs and other medical supplies, the pharmacist still has a major part to play. Interpreting, clarifying, recording and checking the 400 million prescriptions they process every year, though, is still rather different from actually preparing and dispensing medicine, of which they now do little. Modern medicines, while more effective, are also more complex, potentially more dangerous, and more expensive. Pharmacists can expect to handle more complex forms of treatment, and with a rising proportion of older people, greater and more specialised advice and attention will be needed.

Community pharmacists spend an increasing proportion of their time talking to and advising patients on a wide variety of health-related matters. They sell non-prescription drugs and give advice on correct use and dosage of prescribed medicines. Patients are becoming more ready to accept pharmacists' advice on treatment of minor illnesses and injuries. The pharmacist is always careful, however, to refer patients to their GPs when necessary.

Qualifications and training

Pharmacists must qualify via a recognised degree course. *See in* SCIENTISTS AND TECHNICIANS IN THE HEALTH SERVICE.

Clothing and footwear

Clothing and footwear accounts for a fairly constant 6% of consumer expenditure. In 1995, the number of clothing and related stores was estimated at 51,319 with stores specialising in women's clothes outnumbering men's by nearly three to one, and including an estimated 10,144 footwear stores. Employment was at 264,000 against some 294,000 in 1992, nearly half part-time.

Ever since the 1960s fashion revolution this has been one of the most volatile retailing sectors, constantly changing in response to trends and coping with several trends and a great variety of styles at once. But profits are hard to earn. Small shops, often specialising in quite a narrow range of the very latest 'designer' wear, greatly outnumber the multiples, and men's outfitters have joined, and are even ahead of, the trends. The retail trade has become accustomed to a much more fashion-conscious buying public, a buying public which is surer of what it wants, and less ready to buy just anything.

For the trade, the skills it has always needed to make a success and profits are more important than ever. Crucial is the ability to predict trends, to see what will and will not sell, to find sources of supply at home and overseas, to keep costs down, and turnover up. For qualifications and training see the general section below.

Confectioners, newsagents and tobacconists

The number of outlets has stayed roughly static at about 48,000 for several years. The half-dozen or so multiples (most combining newsagency with bookselling) are steadily expanding and increasing their share of the market, to around 40–50%, and the number of owner-manager shops is falling. Between them they employ 215,000 people, well over half on a part-time basis.

Few independents can afford many full-time staff, so most openings are with multiples, where the size of operations gives considerable prospects for managers. The pace for owner-managers can be tough, but it is difficult not to make a fair profit at the moment – customer traffic is estimated at 38 million visits each week – and 'prime site' shops sell well when their owners have had enough six-and-a-half twelve-hour days a week. Total turnover for these businesses is running at £14.05 billion.

DIY and hardware stores

This £3.75 billion market is dominated by the nationally known DIY multiple retailers operating from supermarket-type retail outlets. Independent hardware/ironmongers/ DIY shops account for about 8,300 outlets. In addition, hardware products are available from approximately 2,000 department stores. Traditionally, independent shops are known for personal service and professional advice. This was the fastest-growing retail sector during the housing boom of the 1980s but suffered considerably in the slump of 1990–91. All retailers face aggressive competition and are having to improve training standards. Annual turnover is £5.03 billion.

Electrical consumer durables

Electrical consumer durables (radios, stereo systems, refrigerators, heaters and so on, account for an expanding proportion of consumer expenditure) are an example of an area of specialised selling which needs extensive knowledge of the goods being sold. In the past it has been easy to gain this experience in the shop, but formal training is becoming necessary as goods increase in technological sophistication and customers require advice on both their suitability for particular purposes and/or the use and care of particular items, as well as efficient repair services.

Some 16,000 outlets employ 87,000 people. After-sales service is essential, and so many thousands of skilled service and installation technicians and craftworkers are employed, although not necessarily at the point of sale. Some of the largest firms in distribution operate in this sector. Turnover is £7.51 billion. For service staff, *see* ELECTRICAL AND ELECTRONIC ENGINEERING.

Financial services

Retail banks and building societies have long had a presence in the high street, but have always managed to maintain a somewhat different 'image' from the rest of retailing, and have only lately begun to adopt sales-oriented marketing strategies. *See in* FINANCIAL CAREERS.

Florists

Florists not only sell flowers and plants, they also make up bouquets, wreaths, and decorative displays, both for individual customers and for many firms and other organisations with plant displays in offices, hotels, restaurants, at exhibitions, etc. While most florists work for retail shops – specialist or multiple store – some work for independent contractors, and go out to create and maintain displays, window boxes, etc. The total number of floristry outlets is 6,645, with a total number of 35,000 employees and an annual turnover of £1.27 billion.

Some people prefer to stay with display work, while others go on to become buyers, supervisors or managers, or start their own businesses.

Recruitment and entry

While no formal qualifications are required to obtain employment, employers may wish their trainees to attend part-time college courses, which have varying entry requirements according to the award chosen.

Most people start in a local florist, but some larger firms have traineeships, and the British Retail Florists Association runs YT schemes in some towns. A 'Saturday job' in a florists while still at school can be useful.

Qualifications and training

Training involves learning about plants and how to display and care for them. It also includes training in marketing, buying, financial and other retailing management techniques, and developing a business sense.

Most people learn while working, studying part-time for the examinations. It is, though, possible to study for them full-time over one or two years at a college of further education with periods of work experience in florists, or at a private school (but this can be very expensive).

The main qualifications are: City & Guilds 019 (three parts, plus an advanced, part 4 certificate in business procedures); BTEC First and National Diploma/Certificate or recognised private-school qualification. All the above can be followed by Society of Floristry diploma examinations, required for full membership of the Society.

Full-time BTEC First Certificate/Diploma courses are run by 20 colleges and a BTEC National Diploma is available at 17. There is one day-release SCOTVEC National Certificate course (at Clackmannan College of Further Education).

NVQ/SVQs are in place at levels 1 to 3.

Food sales

Food sales is the area of retailing where rationalisation has been greatest, but recent takeovers have been by large firms wanting to expand. The industry's 60,000 firms employ 854,00 people, but over half of them part-time, in 78,600 outlets. 74.5% of turnover is accounted for by multiple operators, but the five largest account for 60.5%. Specialist food stores still include, in addition to butchers (*see above*), greengrocers, bakers, fishmongers, dairies, and health-food stores, but their share of the market is down to 19%. Total turnover of all food sales is £144.14 billion.

To maintain profitability and retain market share, the large multiples are having to be both aggressively efficient – in financial control, purchasing, stock control and turnover, and staffing – and innovative in marketing, looking for new ways to attract customers, and diversifying out of food into household goods, etc. Smaller chains and independents are having to turn into up-market or convenience formats.

Qualifications and training

The Institute of Grocery Distribution is a training provider for the food and drink industry. It offers two core courses, the Diploma in Grocery Distribution and the Diploma in Grocery Marketing. The former is designed for young managers working in grocery retailing and the latter is typically attended by national account managers from the manufacturing sector. Other courses include an open learning commodity knowledge programme, a food safety training package and short seminars on various topics.

Franchises

A high proportion of franchise businesses are retail outlets – fast food, copy shops, etc. *See in* THE WORLD OF WORK.

Furniture and furnishing

This sector furnishes homes, offices, hotels, ships, aeroplanes, etc., and also leases, or sells to organisations which lease. The cost of furnishing is rising steadily, with fashions changing constantly. Customers often need expert help in making choices, and staff have to be aware of the latest developments. Some areas of retail furnishing come close to antique dealing, especially in department and larger furniture stores.

Over 14,600 outlets employ some 60,000 people. Eight firms take over a third of the market. Competition has grown, with multiples not traditionally selling furniture coming into the market, and prospects for young management trainees look reasonable, particularly in the growth area of kitchens. Total turnover is £4.70 billion.

See also MANUFACTURING INDUSTRIES *and* ART, CRAFT AND DESIGN.

Jewellery

Jewellery is one of the few retailing sectors still closely linked to the craft, some traders (still) selling their own work, although most retailers' workshops deal only with repairs. People buy jewellery for special occasions and are often willing to spend large amounts. The salesperson therefore has to know what is in stock, how it is made and how it functions, to satisfy the most discerning customers. Jewellery shops (a total of just over 8,000 with 33,000 employees) usually sell a range of products, silver and electroplated ware, luxury leather goods, and clocks and watches; some deal in gems and precious stones. Total turnover is £1.74 billion.

Qualifications and training

Training is done by employers, many of whom expect their staff to follow the National Association of Goldsmiths' Retail Jewellers' course. The course is in two sections. The first deals with salesmanship and product knowledge of the six main groups of merchandise: jewellery, watches, clocks, hollow ware, cutlery and flatware, and giftware, each group consisting of a large number of subdivisions. The preliminary examination leads to the award of a certificate. The second part, the diploma course, deals with: diamonds, gemstones, hallmarks, testing of metals, antique silver and old Sheffield plate, mechanical watches, display, marketing, repairs, valuations, law and security. The course lasts two years and is mainly followed through open-learning/correspondence courses, although some local colleges provide tuition. The allied Gemmological Association of Great Britain also offers a two-year correspondence course in gemmology, but this is more often taken by jewellery makers or valuation specialists. *See also* ART, CRAFT AND DESIGN.

NVQ/SVQs are not yet established.

Further information

The National Association of Goldsmiths.

The music trade

The music trade includes shops which sell musical instruments (from guitars and the latest electronic equipment for pop groups, through to wind, string and percussion for orchestral players), and piano showrooms, which have recently increased sales. Records and cassettes are sold by several thousand retail outlets, in many instances alongside hi-fi equipment, although this is now as often sold in stores selling electrical and electronic equipment for home use. Many music outlets are part of multiples.

Working in the music business generally demands a reasonable musical background, and a good knowledge of the products involved, preferably taking in all kinds of music. *See in* THE PERFORMING ARTS.

Opticians

Since deregulation in 1984, anyone can sell spectacles, although only ophthalmic opticians (or doctors) may issue prescriptions. Major chains still employ ophthalmic opticians and have most of their outlets managed by dispensing opticians. While sales have increased by over 5% since 1984, the number of outlets has risen by an estimated 12%, and the competition is considerable. The largest chain has nearly 500 outlets, and nearly 20% of the sight-testing market. *See in* SUPPLEMENTARY HEALTH PROFESSIONS.

Wine trade

The wine trade involves buying, importing, bottling, marketing and distribution of wine. It is now a particularly buoyant sector in the UK as more people drink wine on a regular basis rather than seeing it as a luxury. Some wine and spirit merchants manage the entire operation from vineyard to customer; others only sell. There are a number of retail chains in addition to discount warehouses, mail order suppliers and small specialist wine merchants. In addition, all the major supermarkets have wine sections.

The chains have a retail management structure which can lead from branch to regional management and specialist marketing jobs at head office.

Wine buyers have large responsibilities and must know the producers well. The buyers for large chains and supermarkets have considerable power and influence in negotiating prices.

There are no particular entry requirements, but most companies expect a good standard of education. Some companies employ graduates (any discipline) on management training schemes.

Specialist qualifications in product knowledge (as opposed to retailing) are offered by the Wine and Spirits Education Trust, which has certificate, higher certificate and diploma qualifications.

Further information

The Wine and Spirits Education Trust.

Other sectors

Other specialist sectors of retailing include sports equipment, garden centres, stationery and office machinery, and toys and games.

Working in retailing

Every shop and store is geared to one purpose, selling, so most people (except for office and display staff) who go into retailing spend some time selling, to gain experience of the point of the exercise, to learn about the stock and how to keep abreast of trends, how to handle money and cash registers, about stock and sales records and, above all, about good customer relations and the skills of selling.

Some people stay in selling and work their way up to supervisor, section, departmental, store, area, regional and more senior management. Others may, after a period of experience, move into either buying, merchandising, personnel and training, or other areas of administration. Generally, people spend less and less time actually selling, with promotion fastest for those who show the greatest aptitudes.

The most obvious career prospects are in larger group and chain stores, although smaller independent shops do still offer a different kind of career and working life.

Large multiples, with well over 1,000 stores, will have as many managers, but six to twelve times as many departmental heads and a total sales staff of some 30,000. They can offer structured experience, career progression and promotion within a large, and somewhat hierarchical, organisation. Smaller stores may have less to offer in breadth of experience, training or promotion, but individual responsibility may come earlier, the work at any one time may be more varied, and the managerial structures less formal. To gain experience and/or promotion may mean changing jobs, while major multiples may have to move staff from branch to branch and from town to town to give them appropriate training and promotion.

Management

Managers of departments or stores are responsible for day-to-day operations, within the guidelines of company policy, usually transmitted by a stream of daily memos, etc. Although major 'functions' like buying and some personnel management/recruitment may be centralised, the store or department manager still has considerable personal responsibility, and in a large store will have one or two assistants, plus office staff including someone to handle shopfloor staffing.

Managers must meet sales targets, using both established techniques and ingenuity to attract customers. They must prepare detailed reports on sales, progress, estimates and projections. They keep a check on their stocks, supervise sales staff and stockroom, see that goods are coming in as needed with no shortages, that the quality and quantity of goods is checked, that stock not 'moving' does not lock up shelf space, that price changes are made, etc. The manager has to see that the store or department is properly staffed to meet the number of customers normally expected at any one time or day – neither too many, nor too few – recruit as needed (and know where to find staff), supervise them and arrange any training. Managers must watch local trading conditions, and report to head office on what other stores are doing. They report on aspects of buying policy too. Managers are responsible for security and keeping down stock losses. They organise and monitor displays and window-dressing, sales promotion and local advertising, service where this is needed, and cleaning and maintaining the shop premises. They have to be ready to solve all kinds of problems on the spot. Many managers are quite young, still in their twenties.

Merchandising

Merchandising is a label given to several different jobs, but it is largely about seeing that stores are properly and fully stocked with the right 'mix' of products for what sells in the locality; watching and planning stock levels, and seeing that budgets are designed so as to minimise risks and maximise profits. Merchandisers monitor what is happening in individual stores of the group, both visiting them and analysing computer records of stock levels and sales: which colours and what sizes have sold best and which have not, and where? Some merchandising teams layout and stock new or revamped stores and get them working profitably. It is usually part of the route up for management trainees.

Sales promotion and display

Very professional display and presentation – shop window and interior displays – are essential to modern marketing techniques for retailing. They use a wide range of sophisticated artistic and advertising techniques to attract customers both to the store itself and to particular items of merchandise. Larger stores employ their own teams of trained artists, window-dressers, sign- and even copywriters. Smaller ones may combine the work with other tasks or employ agencies or freelance staff to do this. In all cases they have to work closely with marketing staff, to know what to promote and how it should be promoted, and with departmental sales to ensure that the displays will fit in and their purpose be appreciated. *See also* ADVERTISING *above, and* ART, CRAFT AND DESIGN.

Other staff

Some larger groups have technical departments, e.g. labs to test products, and so employ small teams of, e.g., scientists. Larger store groups employ relatively large numbers of administrative staff, including accountants, personnel managers, MANAGEMENT SERVICES (including computer staff), and general administration (*see also* ADMINISTRATION, BUSINESS MANAGEMENT AND OFFICE WORK). Large groups also have their own property and maintenance divisions, employing, e.g., SURVEYORS (*see in* LAND USE PROFESSIONS). All need supporting clerical staff. Service departments include transport and catering.

Recruitment and entry

It is not generally difficult to get a start somewhere (except in very popular areas like antique dealing), but competition is increasing for the best opportunities for training and promotion.

Retailers readily admit that distribution 'does not yet present the image of a modern employer, and so is not able to attract and hold the best of workers. The human and organisational challenges, and the opportunity for early management, which are the industry's greatest assets as an employer, are largely unappreciated by many who would find most satisfaction in grasping such opportunities' (*Management Training in the Distributive Trades*). Since that was written, unemployment has soared, and retailing can be more selective, although it is unlikely that attitudes among the young have changed much. According to the British Retail Consortium's 1995 Labour Market Report, they consider that a career in retailing is of a lower status than other economic areas, e.g. banking. 'It is therefore becoming increasingly important that the image of the retail industry is improved.' The report went on to highlight the need to attract managers and suggested that pay scales for sales assistants might need to be linked to training, qualifications or appraisals in order to reward skilled employees. Graduate training schemes with the major retailers, however, continue to attract large numbers of applicants.

Retailing is now recruiting fewer but better-qualified people for training as managers, and while this is mainly amongst school-leavers still, larger groups and stores expect to increase further their graduate recruitment, now recognising the need to recruit a larger number of graduates in the long term and to retain them. One large group alone takes several hundred. Over fifty major groups and stores are now known to recruit graduates regularly, and another thirty on an occasional basis.

Retailing needs entrants with some knowledge of modern managerial techniques, an understanding of the social and economic environment in which retailing operates, some knowledge of statistics and behavioural sciences, and ability to organise and operate modern communication systems in organisations which may have a large number of very widely scattered relatively small units.

With few exceptions (for example a degree in pharmacy is needed to become a retail/community pharmacist), educational qualifications are not the most important factor. However, a good educational background is likely to improve prospects of promotion.

It is estimated that some 10% of YT trainees are on programmes preparing them for employment in retailing. However, 'delivery' is largely at local level, and schemes clearly vary from store to store.

Qualification and training

Training arrangements within retailing used to be, with some notable exceptions, rather piecemeal and not particularly good. (Some large groups had fairly large-scale in-house training schemes.) Now (1996), 61% of employers spend more time on training. The last few years have seen a revolution in schemes offered, largely due to the efforts of the National Retail Training Council and the Distributive Occupational Standards Council. Now, NVQ/SVQs in retailing are available at levels 1 to 4, from operative level to supervision and management. (Offered by City & Guilds, RSA and SCOTVEC in partnership with the Distributive Occupational Standards Council.) Modern apprenticeships are also being introduced.

All YT trainees are expected to work towards national vocational qualifications in retailing, and many employers expect all their new entrants to do so.

Larger organisations, and stores selling goods which need a sound technical background and/or skills (e.g. butchers, electronic goods stores), have the best track records on training. A high proportion is in-house, and in smaller stores, often fairly informal. Larger stores have their own training schools. Some retailers give day- or other release to study for nationally recognised qualifications, but it cannot be assumed – even some large chain stores expect to keep their best, including graduate, recruits for life, and so see no need for them to gain outside qualifications, which they might need to change jobs. It may, then, be a sensible precaution to study for a professional or distribution qualification on a spare-time basis. Training for management – theoretically possible for everyone with ambition, appropriate personal qualities and reasonable educational background – is largely by a combination of varied experience in the stores and training sessions. It should include direct selling experience in several different departments, and experience in departments not directly involved in sales, e.g. merchandising, finance or personnel. Graduates starting out in most large retail organisations are generally placed on accelerated training courses, lasting between three and 18 months, with experience in junior supervisory posts coming within a very short period, and the possibility of a post as, e.g., assistant buyer or an equivalent function within two years of starting.

Some large retailers are now devising postgraduate training schemes in conjunction with higher education institutions which are responsible for the theoretical input to a manager's training, and some encourage their potential high fliers to study for an MBA.

Degree and Higher Diploma level courses

Degree courses in retailing are held at Abertay, Bournemouth, Dundee, Glasgow Caledonian, Loughborough, Manchester, Oxford Brookes, Surrey and Ulster Universities and at the London Institute (which also runs an HND course). Huddersfield University has a degree course in Marketing, Retail and Distribution.

Courses leading to Higher National awards in Distribution share some core content (work organisations, external environment, operational techniques and procedures) with other business and finance schemes, adding units in the distributive industry, distribution and the market environment, and resource management and control in distribution. The remaining option units are college-based, ones of particular relevance to retailing being merchandising, business and consumer law and the principles and practice of purchasing.

National Certificates and Diplomas (BTEC)

These courses share some core content (business-related skills, people in organisations, finance and the organisation in its environment) with other business and finance schemes. The remaining option units can be taken from a list including display, law relating to distribution, mail order, supervision principles and practice, buying principles, sales function and selling methods, storage and stock control. Entry requirements are as for all BTEC National awards.

First Certificate/Diploma awards (BTEC) contain a compulsory study of distribution and options which may include consumer legislation, food or hardware/DIY retailing, product design and packaging, selling methods and customer relations, buying, selling and presenting goods. Entry requirements are as for all BTEC First awards.

A Continuing Education Certificate in management studies (retailing) is also available.

SCOTVEC provides schemes/awards in distribution at National Certificate and Higher National level.

Further information

The Distributive Industries Training Trust.

Selling (including exporting)

Selling, as opposed to retail sales, is the interface between manufacturer, wholesaler retailer or customer. It is complementary to marketing, which deals with overall strategy for which selling provides the tactical army, although when selling a single plant to an engineering giant the two may well seem the same. The salesman or woman, company representative, or sales engineer sells a company's product or services to their consumers who may themselves resell it, or use it.

While a large number of salesmen and women sell products to retailers, an equally large number sell products, parts and components to other industrial and commercial concerns, and yet others sell plant and equipment and other services. It is, therefore, not one but increasingly a range of careers, since the skills and processes involved in selling cosmetics to the high-street chemist are rather different from those needed to sell a multi-million-pound chemical plant to a leading international company, or car components in Coventry. Sales staff frequently spend much of their working life within one of several broad areas; for instance, repeat consumer goods (food, stationery, cosmetics, etc.), consumer durables (home computers, television and video equipment, furniture, carpets), clothing, footwear, toys, industrial supplies (chemicals, bricks, components), capital equipment (office or factory), and services (print, business systems, financial services, packaging).

In principle, the more scientifically or technologically complex the products or services being sold, the more complex and lengthy the sales process.

An estimated 760,000 people work in sales, selling computers, pharmaceuticals, chemical plant, machine tools, vehicles, office equipment, steel, engines, space, print, paper, fuel and consumer goods to retailers, and services (for instance, time-sharing computer facilities). In manufacturing industry and in plant manufacture, the sales staff are often called sales engineers (probably over 50,000 people), about a fifth of whom probably are graduates or have an equivalent technological background. In principle, anyone who sells must be expert in the particular field, so the more sophisticated, complex or technologically advanced the product, plant or service, the higher the qualifications the sales staff will need. Pharmaceuticals are mostly sold by those with degrees in pharmacy, pharmacology, life sciences, or even medical sciences, and the more sophisticated and complex computers and computing services by graduates or people with equivalent qualifications and fully trained in the machines or services they are offering.

Whatever is sold, the sales force is a major point of contact between their own organisation and the customer, and the importance of this is recognised by reputable and responsible firms. Selling, in these terms, means rather more than gaining a signature on an agreement. Sales people have to build up a good working relationship with their clients. This often means that the sales staff must learn a great deal about the customer's business, and may be able to make constructive suggestions of new uses or possible modifications to the equipment or service they have sold. They must be able to assess what modifications or special needs the customer may have, and how best these may be met by their own company. The customers will want to know a great deal about the goods, equipment, or service they are buying; they may want advice on promotion of, for instance, certain consumer goods, or to tap the sales staffs' wider knowledge of current and future trends. In turn, a firm will expect its sales force to keep management informed of any market intelligence that reaches them, and to feed back customers' reactions on a wide range of issues.

Most sales staff, except perhaps those selling one-off or custom-built plant or equipment, or goods or services which have limited demand, each have their own clearly defined geographical areas, the size of which will largely depend on the number of customers, or potential customers, the firm has in the region. Within their own areas, sales staff are generally able to organise their own working times and methods, so long as they produce satisfactory results. Selling is a very peripatetic career, whatever the size of the area: small, and the salesman or women responsible for it gets to know it very well, and becomes a member of the working community; larger, and there is greater variation and more frequent surprises.

Selling overseas, exporting, to be successful, needs even greater expertise, especially with current levels of competition. Export sales staff need in-depth knowledge of the people to whom they are going to sell; they need to know and appreciate the effects of the environment in which they live and work, to understand and respect particular customers, and to be able to get on with people whose attitudes, thinking, etc. are very different from their own. Exporters must know how their products can be exploited in particular regions, do research into what will and will not sell, be prepared to modify their products to meet local needs, and understand export/import procedures and regulations for the UK and country of destination. While technical skills are crucial, to be able to sell, and communicate well, in the relevant language, is about as important. A recent survey showed a high proportion of firms admitting they had lost export orders because their sales teams did not have the right languages. With so much to learn first, it is rare to start in export sales, except for graduates with appropriate degrees, business training and experience. *See in* ADMINISTRATION, BUSINESS MANAGEMENT AND OFFICE WORK.

Most people who go into sales start in sales administration. Although some major firms put people into 'the field' straight away, a spell inside a firm to learn the business, about products, accounting/invoicing and systems, etc., is more common. For school-leavers, this may take a year or two, for graduates months.

Junior or trainee salesmen/women usually go on to more important field posts, in areas larger, or more densely populated (with customers, that is); some may then go into export sales. Others may later become supervisors, with the possibility of promotion to area or regional sales manager, to sales manager and even director. Some people may spend time in training, or in sales administration at middle-management level, or in sales promotion, research or recruitment. At the lower levels, particularly, and in the less complex forms of selling, staff turnover is generally high, so promotion can come quite rapidly for those who do well in the field.

Hours are often long and irregular, with time away from home, travelling, and much waiting about. Reports have to be written, orders made out and sent in to the office, and accounts recorded.

Recruitment and entry

Although sales staff are trained, not born, selling does demand certain personal qualities. It takes physical and mental stamina, even toughness; it means being resilient, not easily offended, and adaptable; it needs drive, initiative, self-confidence, and persistence. Sales people have to be good at working with others, always ready to meet new people and prepared to get on with all types. Salesmen/women have to be able to live in the middle of a situation, between the problems and demands of an employer wanting to sell, but perhaps having difficulties meeting schedules, and the customer, anxious about the scale of investment involved. Salespeople need to be able to keep up with what is new in their field, to stay abreast of technical change, to know what customers may want before they know it themselves. The ability to express, and sell, oneself well is essential. Appearance, dress and manner count.

Career prospects are best with a reasonable educational background: at least four GCSE/SCE standard grade passes at A–C/1–3. A national, higher national or advanced GNVQ/GSVQ award in business studies or a technical subject could be useful.

Exporting demands all these qualities and more: overseas buyers are generally said to respect tough negotiators, able to argue knowledgeably about the technical merits of their products, demonstrate real awareness of the customer's markets, and show persistence. It does not make sense to aim for exporting without a thorough understanding of the relevant part of the world plus complete business, technical, colloquial fluency in the appropriate language(s), and training in international trade procedures.

Qualifications and training

Most training is in-house, but is becoming more intensive and high-level. Length depends on the age and educational background of the trainee, and the technical sophistication or otherwise of the product being sold, and can vary from a few weeks to a year or more.

Training mostly aims at improving existing abilities: guiding and formalising techniques for established sound working relationships, learning tact and how to avoid antagonising buyers and how to act in difficult situations, maintaining goodwill, learning facts and figures about the product and specific markets for it, learning how to arrange to see the right people (and how to find out who they are in the first place) and knowing how to judge the most convenient times, acquiring background business skills to be able to assess markets and companies for sales potential, and so on. Sales staff have to learn how to make rapid decisions, and how to negotiate terms, such as price, performance and delivery, and to make them realistic.

Little formal training, and few widely accepted qualifications used to exist, but national qualifications have now been established. NVQs are in place at levels 2 and 3, and the Institute of Sales and Marketing Management has established specific schemes in cooperation with City & Guilds, leading to certificates at operational salesmanship and sales management levels.

The Operational Salesmanship Certificate covers salesmanship, organisation for selling, communication, and marketing practice. No formal entry requirements exist, but candidates must take an approved course. With two years' experience in selling and marketing, this gives associate membership of the Institute.

The Sales Management Certificate covers the sales manager's role, business planning and control, forecasting, planning and organising, controlling the sales operation, business and company law, product development, and distribution channels. With five years' practical experience, and two years in management, the certificate gives membership of the Institute.

Courses for both certificates are offered by numerous FE colleges and other approved centres.

The Chartered Institute of Marketing's Certificate of Sales Management is also relevant. Candidates may substitute a paper in the practice of sales management for practice of marketing. *See under* MARKETING (GENERAL) *above.*

Part 1 of the Institute of Export's professional exams is the Advanced Certificate in Overseas Trade, covering marketing, law relating to overseas trade, international trade and payments, and international physical distribution. The second part, the Diploma in Export Management, covers international marketing (export distribution), international marketing research and principles of management in export.

The Institute of Freight Forwarders' part 1 exam, the Advanced Certificate in Overseas Trade, covers marketing, law relating to overseas trade, international trade and payments, and international physical distribution. In order to gain professional membership of the Institute candidates who successfully complete this course must next study a series of distance-learning modules (combined with competence assessed in the workplace) in: transportation geography (compulsory) and three options from advanced customs, dangerous goods (surface), foreign languages for industry and commerce, insurance and carriage law. *See* FREIGHT FORWARDING *in* THE TRANSPORT INDUSTRY.

Napier University has a degree course in export studies and languages.

Several HND courses in business studies or marketing include export options. *See also* MARKETING (GENERAL) *above*.

There are NVQs at levels 2 and 3, run by the Chartered Institute of Marketing/City & Guilds, RSA and LCCI.

Further information

The above organisations.

Technical service

The technical sales service gives assistance and advice to a firm's customers, both actual and potential. This is an extension to, and back-up for, sales, and is primarily intended to retain customers, who have probably purchased something very expensive – a major computer system, chemical plant, control system, business machinery, etc. It is designed to see the customer gets the best use possible out of the purchase; makes sure problems are solved as quickly as possible, assesses the need for any modifications, trains the customer's staff to use and maintain the new purchase. Technical service may also be responsible for finding additional uses for a new product, for testing it, and for verifying quality. Technical service staff often act as troubleshooters, and so are always on call when problems happen.

Technical service teams are usually managed by experts, usually with appropriate degrees – in chemical engineering for plant manufacture, in chemistry for chemicals, in a physical or materials science for plastics, for example. *See also* SELLING *above*.

Wholesaling and warehousing

This is a field of employment which is often linked with retailing (*see the* RETAILING *sections above*), under the label of distribution, but is also closely connected to transport (*see* THE TRANSPORT INDUSTRY), with warehousing especially, which is often a part of road haulage businesses.

Wholesalers lost some of their trade when multiples started to do their own warehousing and distribution, but compensated by expanding and improving their services to independent retailers and to caterers.

Wholesaling and warehousing are becoming more highly sophisticated operations, and an essential part of the marketing chain. Modern systems are crucial, to help beat tight profit margins, rising costs and competition. New technology, computerised and automated warehouses give sophisticated stock control, and computer modelling is used to design the optimum distribution and warehousing system. Considerable expertise is needed to work out the optimum size and best location(s) for warehouses and/or depot chains, on the choice of freight methods, on delivery priorities, etc.

Wholesalers provide a service sited (geographically and quantitatively) halfway between the manufacturer and the next customer in the chain, so that the manufacturer only has to deliver to a set number of points. The wholesaler operating for a particular area serves a specific range of people. Wholesalers often specialise in particular types of goods: food and other grocery products, electrical goods, hardware, gardening equipment, jewellery, clocks and watches, etc. Some manufacturers wholesale their own products, and may offer a wholesaling service to others. In some industries, for instance publishing, distribution is generally on a national basis, and therefore a publisher's books are all warehoused together (although some regional distribution points have been set up).

The wholesaler acquires goods in bulk from manufacturers, breaks them down into smaller quantities, and resells them to customers, who may be retailers, contractors, other manufacturers, large organisations like local authorities, or industrial users. Stock may be made up of quite literally thousands of different products from hundreds of manufacturers. Wholesalers aim to provide a rapid delivery service, and also technical advice, the opportunity to inspect and compare similar products, and credit facilities for bulk purchases.

Wholesalers employ sales staff, both on trade counters and as representatives, buyers who maintain contact with manufacturers, accounts staff, and a high proportion of managerial staff, who often work their way up, although the large employers also take graduates. Some employers accept any degree subject, while others prefer relevant disciplines such as IT or operations management. Other jobs include storekeepers, order pickers (who must often be prepared to drive fork-lift trucks in the warehouses and stores), dispatch clerks, and van and lorry drivers.

Employment may be with manufacturers, with independent wholesalers in particular fields, with some retailers and retailer/manufacturers, and with transport firms in the freight business (*see* FREIGHT FORWARDING *in* THE TRANSPORT INDUSTRY).

Qualifications and training

For administration/management, qualifications are similar to those available in RETAILING (*see the sections above*). The Wholesaling Certificate is awarded under the auspices of the National Wholesale Training Council. NVQs are available in Wholesaling, Warehousing and Stores at levels 1 to 4. *See also* THE TRANSPORT INDUSTRY.

Further information

The National Wholesale Training Council.

Logistics management

The word logistics was first used to mean the planned movement of supplies and bodies from the battlefield, but since the late 1980s it is used to cover the management of an entire supply chain from the raw materials through to the point where the end-product is used or consumed. This supply chain embraces purchasing and supply, materials handling, materials management, production planning, production control, transport, storage, distribution, installation and servicing. It covers every company which manufactures goods or provides a service.

The overall aim of logistics management is to ensure that goods are in the right place, at the right time, in the right quantity, at the right price. As well as the operations already mentioned, logistics is fundamental within a company for forecasting, packaging, strategic management, property, quality, procurement, order-processing, inventory, storage, project management, reuse and recycling, information technology, warehousing, import and export.

Working in logistics

Although the logistics job market cannot be closely defined, the Institute of Logistics says there is a core figure of about 25,000 practising managers in the UK employed by around 2,000 organisations. These organisations range from the National Freight Consortium (Exel Logistics, BRS, Pickfords Removals and Lynx Express) employing thousands, to companies with a handful of logistics professionals.

Whatever the supply chain operations are called, this is a massive and expanding employment area. Recent job titles covering logistics management have been operations planning manager, warehouse manager, sales and operations planner, distribution and haulage manager, goods out manager, general manager (automation), depot manager, European controller, business development manager, contract manager and fleet manager. Running a vehicle fleet, for example, involves ensuring that adequate supplies of vehicles are available at all times to meet the needs of goods and personnel without having too many on standby.

A career in logistics could mean working for a manufacturer, a retailer, a specialist provider of logistics and distribution services, a logistics consultancy or in HM Forces.

There are jobs in the public sector with central government, local authorities and health services. Logistics management is still a new career title, so although the Health Service may in theory have only a few logistics posts, in practice it is an enormous supply chain operation involving a large number of patients, and covering food and medical supplies, ambulances, laundry, etc., and employing large numbers of personnel involved in logistics.

In the private sector, the food industry and retailing chains such as Marks & Spencer and Dixons have enormous supply chain operations. Privatised industries such as BT, British Steel, and water and electricity companies are expected to ensure that fewer people deliver a better service and produce dividends for shareholders. They need good logistics management.

Despite cutbacks in armed forces personnel, the military still need logistics experts to manage the supply lines and ensure that food, equipment, munitions, etc. are supplied wherever they are needed throughout the world.

Logistics personnel need to think tactically, be able to motivate others and to make things happen while still attending to the details.

Recruitment and entry

There are no well-defined career paths. Some companies will seek graduates with a specialist degree, usually MSc or MBA, while others will recruit graduates with a good first degree and then provide the specialist logistics education.

Qualifications and training

The last ten years has seen a growth in degree-level courses in logistics, transport and warehousing: transport and distribution at Huddersfield University, logistics at Aston University, etc. There are also a number of business degrees with optional modules in logistics. Many logistics courses include twelve months' industrial placement. Graduates of related disciplines such as geography, information technology, or engineering are also welcome in the profession.

Postgraduate masters courses leading to an MSc or MBA programme in logistics, distribution and supply chain management are also available. These include postgraduate courses at Cranfield, Plymouth, Huddersfield, Edinburgh, Cardiff and Birmingham Universities.

Professional

The Institute of Logistics has, in 1996, 12,422 members. It provides a Foundation in Logistics course for people at junior supervisory level, covering materials handling, warehouse management, inventory and transport.

A Professional Development Programme leads either to a Certificate in Logistics, for junior managers and senior supervisors involved with warehousing, transport, inventory and with operational planning and control; or to a Diploma in Logistics, suitable for graduate trainees and those already managing an operation. Both Certificate and Diploma courses cover managing people and physical and financial resources.

The Diploma also incorporates an extensive logistics management module with information about working relationships, the total supply chain and the development of logistics strategy with regard to company requirements and customer service levels.

An Advanced Diploma is under development on a Europe-wide basis. It is aimed at people working at a strategic level.

All courses are modular and include simulated or company-based projects. They can be taken on a distance-learning basis and at selected colleges.

There are no NVQs in logistics, but there are NVQs relevant to a career in logistics, such as those in transport, warehousing and import/export. *See also* THE TRANSPORT INDUSTRY; BUYING, PURCHASING AND SUPPLY (*above*); *and* WHOLESALING AND WAREHOUSING (*above*).

Further information

The Institute of Logistics.

Modelling

Models are used in advertising, promotional and sales campaigns, for clothes, for holidays, cars, and domestic products, such as toothpaste and cosmetics. Modelling is used to create illusions and so uses 'show-business' techniques, which means it is often mixed up with the entertainment world.

There are two different types of modelling: live and photographic. It is difficult to combine the two, because they often require quite different physical characteristics, but they do overlap.

Most live models work in the fashion business, either full-time for a fashion house, or on a free-lance basis.

In the fashion house, designers create clothes on the live model, cutting, pinning and draping the clothes as they go, which means long hours spent standing still. Models display the clothes to customers, who may be buyers for stores as well as better-off individuals, and show the clothes in regular, twice-yearly 'collections'. Freelance models work for fashion houses which do not employ their own, are taken on just for collections, work in fashion shows for larger stores, and also do promotional work – showing jewellery, and appearing at, for example, car shows and other exhibitions.

While the most popular photographic work is for the very glamorised fashion and other women's magazines, this provides work for only a very few, top models. The bread-and-butter work for most photographic models comes from mail order catalogues, holiday brochures, advertisements for toothpaste, cosmetics, and washing-up powders. A few models find some work on filmed TV commercials, but generally these are done by actors and actresses with Equity cards. Good feet and hands can be used in advertisements for shoes, jewellery, tights. Some models do only hand work.

Modelling really is a tough, physically demanding and exhausting life, except for the very few who get to the top, and it is very hard work. Most models spend much of their time standing, or rushing from one engagement to another, or changing clothes as fast as they can, or repairing their make-up. Much of their time is spent in hot, overcrowded, airless, and generally uncomfortable places. None of this is good for their appearance, on which their livelihood depends. Even so they must appear cool and unruffled – no sweat, and no goose pimples – calm, even arrogant, all the time. The way the fashion business is organised generally has photographic models huddled in winter clothes under hot lights in a stuffy studio in summer, and freezing near-naked on winter beaches in swimwear. There is rarely time to enjoy exotic locations.

Men are generally employed mainly as photographic models, but may also do fashion-show work.

There is marginally more work for fashion than for photographic models, at least at the top. Photographic models earn more, but have to pay for more of their own expenses, clothes, etc. Work lasts for as long as the model's face and figure looks young enough and fits in with the current trend. There is some modelling of clothes for older and larger people. Intelligent models use the time when they are working to make contacts for later on, for example, teaching in model schools, fashion consultancy, or in public relations in fashion houses or stores, or selling. It is extremely rare and difficult to get into acting via modelling, except for those who clearly have acting ability and 'star' quality anyway, and even they must get Equity cards.

Recruitment and entry

It is rare but not unknown for agencies or other employers to take on untrained models.

To become a model, body and face must match the current 'image'. Height and other measurements are usually crucial too; they do change, but a height of 1.72 metres and a standard size 10 or 12 is a generally accepted minimum standard for women and 1.83 metres for men. An 'interesting' appearance rather than conventional 'beauty' is the ideal, but photographic modelling probably demands a good facial bone structure. Models need to be well coordinated, able to move well even before training. They should usually have a flair for making any clothes they wear look good, and be able to adapt their appearance to different clothes, different fashions, and different conditions. They should have an interest in and ability to stay ahead of trends – in hair and make-up as well as clothes and accessories. Models need to be very healthy, and physically strong. They need intelligence and emotional stability to cope in a very tough business.

Reputable model schools will make a completely ruthless assessment of anyone's chances of gaining work as a model before accepting them, and do not accept for career training those who have no chance at all. If several reputable schools say that someone has no chance, it is sensible to accept their advice.

Qualifications and training

It is not essential to train as a model, and taking a course (which can be very expensive) is no guarantee of employment. However, a good modelling course does teach the techniques of both fashion and photographic modelling. All but one school in Britain are commercially run. It is crucial to go to a good and reputable school, the best of which are linked to a reputable agency. Good schools introduce their successful students to agencies and possible employers, and generally tell them, during the course, if they are not going to be successful, normally refunding part of the fee. Getting on the books of a reputable agency, such as one belonging to the Association of Model Agents is essential.

The course at the London College of Fashion (part of the London Institute) for which entry is three GCSE/SCE standard grade passes at A–C/1–3, lasts a year and is broader than most, including selling, business studies and fashion-sketching as well as modelling techniques. At a reputable commercial school the four- to six-week courses generally cover, in addition to modelling itself, individual tuition in make-up, skin care, hair-styling, exercises, movement and mime, dress sense, and basic techniques of posing for the camera. *See also* ART, CRAFT AND DESIGN *and the* RETAILING *sections above.*

Further information

Association of Model Agents.

Contents

Science Careers and the Physical Sciences

(CLCI: Q, QOB, QOF, QOX)

The sciences

The sciences explore the natural world in all its complexity and variety, probing ever more deeply into the make-up of both living and non-living things, from the smallest nuclear sub-particle to the giant supernova star, from the most minute microbe to the dinosaur.

In investigating the natural world, in endless experiment, careful observation and inspired speculation, scientists try to discover the reasons for what happens in the natural world, and the common patterns and underlying principles, attempting to set up a network of logically connected theories which represent current thinking about the natural world.

But science has a practical side too and, either deliberately or incidentally, plays a major part in solving problems, such as the causes of a crippling disease, or of a fault in a metal structure. Scientists may choose to work directly in 'applied' research, but more often than not more fundamental, 'pure' research work is needed first to solve practical problems of this kind – discovering how a particular part of the body works or a metal is made up, for instance, before it is possible to see what has gone wrong. Pure and applied work, therefore, do not always go into separate, watertight compartments, and most scientific discoveries, however theoretical and irrelevant, however speculative they may seem, sooner or later turn out to have some practical value, simply because science is about the real world.

The tools and techniques developed for scientific research, both the very exacting methods of experiment and testing, and the sophisticated equipment like electron microscopes, oscilloscopes and computers, have also found uses outside the lab – in industry, for example, in measuring chemicals as they go through a conversion process, or in hospitals, monitoring patients' conditions in intensive care.

Science stretches from the most abstract and theoretical thought (e.g. proving mathematically the existence of 'black holes' in space) to the most practical (e.g. developing a new moth-proofer for wool). And even scientific thinking and the rigorous and exact methods by which scientists observe, experiment, test, prove and quantify are now adapted for use outside the sciences, from archaeology to social sciences, and management.

Although it is common to talk and think about chemistry, biology, physics and mathematics, as separate 'branches' of scientific knowledge, 'real' science cannot be rigidly divided into such neat and watertight compartments. They are no more than convenient labels. There is no rule of nature which dictates the divisions between 'branches', and more often than not they have come about by accident. As a quick definition, we describe chemistry as the science of materials and change, biology as the science of life. But living things – plants, animals, people – are also materials, so here chemistry and biology meet and merge in a common interest in living materials – what is called 'biochemistry'.

Chemistry and physics also supply the rest of the scientific world with instruments, techniques, even ways of thought. For example, oceanographers use chemical techniques to analyse the make-up of sea water and any increase or fall in oxygen content as this can affect marine life. All scientific labs, whether technically working in chemistry, biology or physics have, for a long time now, been full of equipment developed by physicists.

There is no such person as 'the' scientist. 'Among scientists', wrote Nobel-Prize winner Sir Peter Medawar, 'are collectors e.g. geologists, classifiers e.g. zoologists, and compulsive tidiers-up of theories, ideas, etc; many are detectives by temperament, and many are explorers, some are artists and others are artisans'.

Britain needs more scientists to make advances in science and develop new technologies. However, the number of young people taking A-levels in Physics and Mathematics has declined in recent years and those completing A-levels in Chemistry are not increasing. The number of graduates in physics has stayed constant over the last seven years at 2,300 while the number of graduates in chemistry has risen by a third to 2,800. Given the current financial strictures on universities it is unlikely that there will be any further growth over the next five years.

As industry has recovered from the recession of the early 1990s these graduates are increasingly becoming in short supply. This is particularly reflected in a serious shortage of science teachers, especially physicists. This situation shows no sign of improvement. In 1994 there were 523 acceptances for 610 places to go on postgraduate courses for aspiring teachers.

Using science

Most scientists at least begin their careers in a particular 'branch' of science, as physicists or chemists, biologists or mathematicians. Many, though, are recruited more for their broad scientific training than for their specialist skills, and many will move on into jobs which cannot be easily labelled as, e.g. 'physicist'. Many work in multi-disciplinary 'teams' – in research labs, in design and development, in analytical work and control – and over the years their skills become more multi-disciplinary too.

Although there are many different types of scientists the main functions are:

Research

'Being a scientist' is generally equated with doing scientific research work, and most people who call themselves scientists probably do start their careers here, or in analytical work.

'Research' is mostly lab based, although some scientists, e.g. geophysicists, may spend more of their time 'in the field', while others eventually become scientific managers. Many scientists in all 'branches' spend some of their working time at a computer terminal.

Research ranges from the most abstract, working out on the theoretical frontiers of, for example, particle physics, to the most practical, largely working for, with, or in support of industry. There are still exciting discoveries to be made – like proving the existence of 'dark matter'. In the academic world they talk of 'pure' and 'applied' for either end of the spectrum, which generally means that 'pure' research is totally speculative, investigating something for its own sake, while 'applied' has a definite aim, which may or may not turn out to have a practical use. But what started off as pure research may, years later, become applied – superconductivity for example.

Many universities now work very closely with industry, and research on applied and industrial problems – in advanced fields like biotechnology for instance – can be just as taxing, and interesting, as more theoretical work. In industry, people tend to talk about 'product' directed research which looks at areas within a company's scope, e.g. chemicals or electronics, to see if there is anything new which could be developed and exploited. This can be exciting and challenging and even within the strict confines which companies set on this kind of research, scientists still do some pioneering.

Scientific research has very precise methods of working. Based on existing knowledge, scientists suggest theories or 'hypotheses' to begin to fill in the gaps in their knowledge of a particular area, and then by very exact observation, experiments and endless testing try to prove or disprove the theories, modify them, or come up with a new theory. It is challenging, time-consuming work but can be very stimulating and rewarding although often progress can be slow. Solving problems can be satisfying in itself; it can also be very creative theoretically and practically.

Science is becoming increasingly 'people' oriented and scientists can get the thrill and excitement of working as part of a team, contributing and benefiting from the exchange of information and knowledge, and this in turn can spark off new ideas and developments. The integration of different skills and personalities is vital in the advancement of new ideas.

Once there is something to show for all the hard work, researchers have to write up their results, present them at seminars and conferences, and get them published in the scientific journals, for other scientists to argue over, scrutinise, and compare with their own work.

Development

More scientists are employed to develop ideas than to research them. Development involves taking a discovery and developing it into a marketable product. Scientists working in development have to take account of the cost, safety and attractiveness to customers of their final products. Chemists work with chemical engineers to scale up their process from the test tube to a large scale plant. Materials scientists choose the best materials for each application, which often involves making a compromise between the best and the affordable. Development work involves considering all the options and taking a view on which is the optimum choice.

Analytical work

Scientific analysis and investigation are the basis for research and development but are also important for maintaining efficiency and quality. This can be to check that a drug is correctly formulated, in a pharmaceutical firm, and is part of quality control. It can be working in the health service to see what is wrong with a patient's blood; working for a police forensic science lab examining physical clues from a crime; or analysing food to see if it is infected with bacteria in a local government public analysts laboratory.

Production

The manufacturing industry recruits scientists and engineers to manage and supervise the manufacturing processes. *See in* engineering and manufacturing chapters.

Other science-based work

While not strictly scientific work, a number of occupations require a scientific training/background.

In schools, scientists rarely get a chance to do anything other than teaching, but in universities they can combine teaching with research work.

See also, e.g. PATENT WORK *in* THE LEGAL SYSTEM; MANAGEMENT SERVICES; LIBRARY AND INFORMATION WORK.

Non-scientific work

It is common to think of studying science in order to become a scientist of some kind. But science graduates do not have to become scientists. The pattern of recruitment of scientists by industry is changing and their value is recognised for other areas. The chemical industry, for example, now actively recruits chemists for areas like marketing specifically because of their knowledge of chemistry.

A higher proportion of people with science qualifications find work which 'uses' their degrees than do, say, philosophy graduates, and they have a wider choice of non-scientific work too, simply because they understand scientific 'language', can analyse and solve problems, and have to be very numerate. It is also easier to acquire technological skills from a science base, and so go into occupations when particular shortages emerge.

Partly because there has been a shortage of openings for research scientists, partly because other employers have become more interested in people with numerate, scientific backgrounds, increasing numbers of graduate scientists are working in non-scientific careers. A science degree can be treated as a non-vocational qualification and as the 'first employment' figures show for Chemistry and Physics graduates later in this chapter, and also for other science and engineering disciplines in other chapters, financial work, including accountancy, banking and insurance, management services and all kinds of commerce generally, are taking on science graduates.

Where scientists work

The main employers of scientists are government, industry and education but the proportion going into each varies according to discipline. If one analyses the 1993/94 first destination statistics for the science disciplines the percentages going into the various categories were as follows:

	Industry	Public Service	Education	Commerce	Misc
Physical Sciences	33.5	14.0	6.0	37.3	9.2
Biological Sciences	21.0	20.0	12.5	31.8	14.2
Mathematics	22.6	5.9	3.9	61.3	6.2

In industry scientists work in research and development, mainly in traditional science-based industries (making, for instance, drugs, processed food and drinks, or chemicals), but also in high-technology areas such as oil, biotechnology, materials, telecommunications and electronics. Others manage production or quality control and testing in a great many industries from electricity generating to brewing, or work in specialised, technical marketing, sales, purchasing in e.g. pharmaceuticals or the food industry. *See* MANUFACTURING INDUSTRIES.

The Public Service category includes central government departments, research establishments wholly or largely sponsored by the government and other publicly funded bodies e.g. the health authorities, and local government. Recruitment by the government has changed as many sections of departments and institutes have been hived off, transformed into independent agencies with government backing or privatised. The range of employment covers all scientific disciplines and is very varied, ranging from testing work on fire foams for the Home Office Scientific Development Group, and analysing pesticides for the Ministry of Agriculture Fisheries and Food, to working on underwater acoustical measurement at the Defence Evaluation Research Agency or vehicle pollution for the Transport Research Laboratory (TRL). In April 1996 TRL was privatised by a management buyout and converted into an independent non-profit making trust outside the Civil Service. The research councils (Engineering and Physical Sciences, Biotechnology and Biological, Medical, Natural Environment, and Particle Physics and Astronomy) employ scientists in their own research units as well as funding universities and other higher education institutions.

The numbers entering education and teaching science vary across the disciplines with higher numbers of biological scientists entering teaching than from the physical sciences or mathematics.

Opportunities for science technicians

In theory there are the 'professional' scientists and 'technician' scientists, but in practice the line between them is increasingly blurred, as some science graduates are going into what has been considered technician-level work.

Professional scientists would not get very much done if they had to do all the work needed to set up research experiments, constantly monitor drug production, operate quality control machinery, or do all the tests for a trial chemical. Nor would a science teacher, or university lecturer, do much teaching if he/she had to prepare all the frogs needed for dissection, or care for all the rats, rabbits and insects, or set up or make the equipment for an experiment.

Lab technicians, lab officers, assistants, scientific assistants – there are many different names and titles – are not 'dogsbodies' to fetch and carry or clean and sterilise test tubes. Although initially the work can be repetitive and routine it is skilled practical work and a very experienced technician will be in charge of much of the day-to-day work that goes on in the lab, and may also be doing full-scale research every bit as intellectually demanding as that of the lab's fully professional scientists.

Lab technicians prepare samples, build scientific equipment, check equipment for accuracy and reliability and use it to make measurements, carry out experiments, and record results. There are probably nearly as many different jobs for technicians as there are labs – scientific-glass blowers, Met Office weather forecasters, forensic science technicians analysing the blood, sweat and saliva taken from murder victims, technicians preparing microscopically thin sections and slices of rocks for geologists or animal tissue for zoologists. The list is endless.

In industry technicians also work in research labs, but more often in areas like quality control, where much of the work is analytical. Raw material, whether metal, sugar or plastic, coming into any factory has to examined and analysed to see that it is up to specification. Throughout production, of everything from cheese to paper, drugs to plastics, petrol and chemicals, lab technicians test and analyse regular samples, and make sure the mix is correct and has the right qualities.

Recruitment and entry

Graduate level

A degree in science is required. Entry for most degree courses is two or three A-levels/Higher grades plus two or three GCSE/SCEs, grades A–C/1–3. Advanced GNVQs and AS levels are usually acceptable in combination. Science A-levels/Highers may be specified. Some students begin by registering for an HND course and then transfer after two years to the second year of a degree course.

Technician level

Technician posts usually require a minimum of four GCSE/SCEs at grades A–C/1–3 for entry to BTEC/SCOTVEC national qualifications, or one A-level/Higher grade and three GCSEs at grades A–C/1–3 for entry to BTEC/SCOTVEC higher national awards.

With BTEC/SCOTVEC higher national qualifications it is possible to study for various qualifications of the professional scientific institutes and achieve professional scientist status.

Qualifications and training

Most professional scientists have studied for a degree in one of the basic sciences, or other pure and applied sciences, and some have also studied for a postgraduate qualification. No postgraduate qualification guarantees a job but in some areas it may facilitate entry depending on the course and discipline.

There are BTEC/SCOTVEC National Diplomas and Certificates and Higher National Diplomas and Certificate courses in Laboratory Sciences.

Professional institutes

There is no 'umbrella' professional body for all scientists in the way engineers have the Engineering Council (although there are the 'learned societies'), or any scientific registration board. Each 'branch' of science has its own professional body.

Further information

Professional Institutes listed below and in subsequent sections, the Institute of Science Technology, the Institute of Biomedical Sciences.

Chemistry

Almost all research in chemistry is of practical use to someone, somewhere. Any advance in chemistry – however disinterested in its applications the researcher may be – on, for instance, the structure of glass or the synthesis of compounds from plants, can have results which are useful. Whole industries have been built on chemistry and chemical research. They include agrochemicals (herbicides, fungicides, pesticides and fertilisers), cosmetics and toiletries, dyestuffs, plastics, paints, pharmaceuticals, veterinary health products, industrial chemicals, metal treatment chemicals, intermediates for synthetic textile fibre production, detergents, explosives, water treatment chemicals, disinfectants, household polishes and cleaners, chemicals for paper and fabric treatment, petrochemicals, etc. Chemical research made the petroleum industry the supplier of more than half the new materials used in the chemical industry – products made by separating and purifying crude oil include plastics, man-made fibres, drugs, solvents, detergents and fertilisers as well as fuels and lubricants. Research and Development (R & D) expenditure is high, particularly for pharmaceuticals, and, for the whole of the UK chemical industry expenditure is equivalent to about 6% of sales.

According to the Chemical Industries Association (the main trade/employer organisation in the industry with a membership of 230 companies), the chemical industry is Britain's 4th biggest manufacturing industry after food, drink and tobacco. Its latest employment figures suggest that 240,000 people were employed in the chemical industry in 1996. The largest company is Glaxo Wellcome. The pharmaceutical companies spent £2,540 million on R&D in 1994 while chemical companies spent £365 million and food companies £651 million. (Unilever, the largest food manufacturer, alone spent £543 million.)

The influence of chemistry extends well beyond the chemical industry. All manner of industries benefit if understanding the chemical characteristics of the materials being used can improve a product or make the production method more efficient, especially if this can also make the materials more suitable for the use to which they are being put. Chemists help to improve the qualities of fibres used in making textiles, work with metallurgists in reducing the 'fatigue' properties of metals by changing their crystal structures. There are applications for chemical research in work on electronic components needed for e.g. more advanced computing and IT systems, building materials, ceramics, food processing, and glass. Chemistry is fundamental to a lot of medical research in developing new chemical methods of treating or otherwise combating diseases.

In the future, the chemical industry faces difficulties and rising costs to deal with environmental issues both in terms of pollution by chemical plants and with some of its products. There is increasing concern about non-biodegradable plastics, recycling plastic waste, the effect of chlorofluorocarbons (CFCs) on the ozone layer, the level of nitrate in drinking water and the use of pesticides and fertilisers

There are always new substances to be found, developed and investigated and the Engineering and Physical Sciences Research Council (EPSRC) funds a number of 'special initiatives', e.g. protein research, and Interdisciplinary Research Centres (IRCs). IRCs include Surface Science (Liverpool University), Superconductivity (Cambridge University), Semiconductor Materials (Imperial College), Materials for High Performance Applications (Birmingham University), Polymer Science and Technology. (Durham, Leeds and Bradford Universities), Centre for Process Engineering (Imperial College), Opto-electronics (Southampton University), Biomedical Materials (QMW College, London).

The analytical techniques and equipment that chemists have developed for their own research are now widely used elsewhere – in other sciences (biochemistry and geochemistry, for example), in industry for analytical and quality control, in diagnostic work in the Health Service, in ensuring clean water, in local government labs, and in forensic labs, among many others.

Opportunities for professional chemists

Demand for chemistry graduates in terms of chemistry-related work has been fluctuating for many years now, and is almost impossible to predict. The chemical industry (and that includes agrochemicals and pharmaceuticals) still depends on a high rate of innovation – new products and better processes – and is, therefore, still research intensive; it is also affected by the economic situation. And so although the 'lead time' for new products and processes in chemicals etc. is long, recruitment of chemists both for research and other work varies from year to year and from sector to sector (*see* MANUFACTURING INDUSTRIES). Further, there are now far fewer posts in academic work in higher/further education, and in the public sector – the Civil Service, NHS, etc. However, as higher education has expanded the numbers graduating in chemistry have not risen as fast as other disciplines and there is still a severe shortage of school-teachers in chemistry. Teacher training applications for chemistry in 1995 were 527, down from 935 in 1991.

An estimated 60,000 or more professional chemists work in Britain, 29,659 of whom are members of the Royal Society of Chemistry (RSC). The RSC makes regular surveys of members, and the 1994 results are incorporated below based on replies by 16,755 members.

The range of work done by professional, normally graduate, chemists, includes:

Research and development

Research and development still employ the largest group of chemists. In 1994, 30% of chartered RSC members (just over half mainly as managers) were working in research and/or development (a figure which has remained constant for some years).

Many chemists still start their careers in the laboratory. Fundamental research, going ever deeper into the nature of matter and of chemical processes, is not limited to universities, although in industry speculative research happens only in larger companies heavily involved in chemicals and pharmaceuticals. Research usually means team work, and chemists work particularly closely with biochemists and physicists. In industry, and industrial research associations, most research is on possible new products, ways of improving existing ones, cheaper or more efficient raw materials, cheaper or more efficient routes to a new product, or replacing an existing product which may have some undesirable qualities.

Chemical research and development is not as routine as in some other industries, and may involve much more original thinking, inspiration and speculative work than some other kinds of industrial research, but the researcher is usually working to a tight plan and budget, and cannot investigate everything interesting that turns up. Development chemists turn a new reaction into a commercially viable process, check for unwanted side-effects (in e.g. pollution problems), and make sure that the qualities and process are the best possible, given available finances, potential profits, manufacturing methods, etc. Development work, which may be combined with research, involves a considerable amount of repetitive experimentation and testing. Some development chemists specialise in improving or designing new processes, for instance increasing the yield from a particular raw material, or finding a better catalyst for a reaction, and work closely with chemical engineers (*see* PROCESS ENGINEERING, BIOMEDICAL ENGINEERING AND MATERIALS SCIENCE).

Linked to R&D is formulation – formulation chemists work out a form for the product which is easy and economical to use, will store without breaking down or congealing, and can be safely packaged. In the pharmaceuticals industry formulation chemists work out the optimum composition of medicines, determining how much of the active ingredient (drug) there should be and what other compound in what proportions it will be mixed with.

Chemists also do research in government departments and government-financed research establishments. Many of these have seen considerable change over the two years 1994–6. Some have been privatised (sold to a private company or a consortium) and others have been contractorised (are managed by contractors on behalf of government).

Warren Spring Laboratory was sold by the Department of Trade and Industry to AEA Technology and moved to Harwell where it became the National Environmental Technology Centre. Its work includes the analysis of air pollution, and acid rain; materials recovery from contaminated land; pollution abatement especially relating to vehicle emissions; biological treatment of effluent and chemical spills; marine pollution particularly from oil in the North Sea and chemical analysis. Chemical scientists employed include analytical chemists, organic chemists, inorganic chemists, physical chemists, applied chemists, materials scientists and metallurgists. They work with mathematicians, statisticians, computer scientists; physicists, oceanographers and meteorologists; civil, mechanical chemical and biochemical engineers; and biologists, biotechnologists, environmental scientists, geologists and soil scientists.

The Laboratory of the Government Chemist (LGC), employing around 280 staff, has been bought by a consortium including its management and the Royal Society of Chemistry and the bank 3i. It continues to be the focal point for analytical science in government. These services are designed to protect the consumer and the environment improving animal and human health. Scientists analyse food, agricultural materials, toxic metals, and other hazardous materials of environmental interest, i.e. cosmetics, tobacco, drugs, etc. It develops new methods of analysis and the application of new techniques to provide more sensitive or more precise analytical results.

The MOD Directorate of Pricing and Quality Services, part of the Defence Engineering and Science Group, employs about 600 scientists and ensures that the complex equipment supplied to the armed services meets required quality and performance standards. Chemists are most likely to be employed in the materials laboratories working with paints, fuels, lubricants, plastics, explosives, metals, etc. The MOD Chemical and Biological Defence Establishment, a laboratory of the Defence Evaluation and Research Agency, is the UK centre for research to evaluate the hazard to the armed services and to develop protective measures against chemical or biological agents. Chemists here carry out research on vapour and particulate filtration, air purification and general pollution control, as well as investigating how toxic chemicals behave. They also work as members of United Nations detection and verification teams which investigate instances of biological or chemical warfare world-wide.

Other government departments and agencies employing chemists include the Patent Office, the Home Office Forensic laboratories, the British Museum's research laboratory, and the National Gallery (where they try to understand deterioration processes and especially the long-term effects of light, heat, humidity and atmospheric pollution, analysing old varnish and paint media using thin-layer and gas chromatography and infra-red analysis, and developing permanent picture varnish).

Analytical work

Analytical work employs (1994) about 13.4% of professional chemists (slightly more than in 1992), with a large proportion, about 55%, mainly as managers and administrators. Quality control employs 4.8% of professional chemists, almost all of them as managers and administrators.

In industry, analytical work and quality control involve continuous checking for purity, quality, correct proportions, and safety. Elsewhere, analytical work is done by e.g. local authority public analysts (there are 33 public analysts laboratories around the UK), the forensic services, and the Health Service. Much of this work is now fully automated, using all forms of chromatography and spectroscopy. The professional chemist manages and supervises, looks into problems, develops standards, and works out new techniques when needed. Larger industrial groups still have quite large laboratories working on longer-term problems.

Technical services

In technical services, chemists work as members of liaison teams which deal with industrial and commercial customers. The chemist makes up technical specifications, discusses and agrees solutions to customers problems and complaints, shows them how to make the best use of the firm's products, and generally gives technical back-up to sales and marketing.

Education

Education employs just 14.9% of chartered chemists (down from over 19% in 1986) – teaching pupils in schools, trainee technicians in technical college, or degree and postgraduate students in universities, where teaching is normally combined with research.

Other chemistry or science-related occupations

These include production in the chemical and allied industries, employing 3.1% of professional chemists.

About 9.5% of professional chemists have become general managers/administrators, and 4.0% work in sales/marketing.

Nearly 9% of professional chemists do 'other' (unspecified) scientific or technical work – mostly as managers or administrators.

About 6.1% work in 'other' services (e.g. health and safety, patents and information services), and 4.1% are consultants.

Where professional chemists work

According to the 1994 RSC survey, industry and commerce employ 41.4% of the professionally active members (over 21% of members are fully or partly retired, and 1.8% unemployed). The largest groups, not surprisingly, are in the chemical-related industries – 19.4% in pharmaceuticals (up from 14.5% in 1986), 8.7% on 'other' chemicals, 4.9% in plastics and polymers (slightly down), 3.7% in oil and allied products (a considerable decrease) and 3.4% in food and drink. Other important employment sectors include water supply 4.2%, detergents and soaps 1.6% and nuclear fuel 1.6%.

The Chemical Industries Association (CIA), which represents more than 230 companies, has published graduate recruitment figures for 1994 and predicted static recruitment in 1995 and 1996. Its report was more positive about recruitment for the rest of the decade. In 1994 their members who responded to a survey employed 93 new graduates with a first degree in chemistry, compared with 179 in 1990. It does not expect these recruitment levels to rise until 1997 at the earliest. These CIA members took on 41 chemists with a postgraduate degree in 1994 compared with 86 in 1990.

The 1994 RSC survey found that about 3.2% of professional chemists work in energy production, including over 1.6% in the nuclear fuel industry. Some 4.2% work for the water supply, river purification, sewage and waste disposal industry.

Some 5.6% of chemists work for central/local government and are employed in analytical, testing or service labs.

Research units, government or otherwise, employ 4.3% (slightly down). The NHS employs 1.2%.

As already described, most chemists work in R&D, or analytical work, but some are employed in production, general management, marketing and sales etc.

Education employs 11.8% in universities, 4.3% in schools and 2.1% in colleges of further education.

Opportunities for technician chemists

The work of chemistry-trained technicians is mainly as described in the general section on scientific careers, but the figures show a high proportion are clearly working in jobs virtually indistinguishable from those of professionals – about 40% work in a managerial or administrative capacity. The RSC 1994 survey showed that, for licentiates over 19% work in research and development, with about a third of them employed primarily as managers or administrators. More than 17% do analytical work, with over 25% employed mainly as managers or administrators. Another 14.4% work in quality control, about 70% of them as managers or administrators. Over 13% do other scientific or technical work, over half of them as managers or administrators.

Other types of work include – general management or administration (11%), marketing and sales (8.7%), education (1%), production (5.9%), other services, e.g. health and safety, patents, information work (3.7%).

Where technicians work

Some 65.9% work in industry or commerce. The largest group is in the chemically related industries – 14.5% in pharmaceutical industries (10.2% in water, sewage and river purification) 10.1% in 'other' chemicals, 5.7% in plastics and polymers (down over 0.7%), 6.2% in food and drink (up 1.5%), 4.6% in oil companies, 1.3% in cosmetics and toiletries. Other manufacturing industries employing significant proportions include electrical and electronics (2.3%), and paper and printing (3.1%).

Water, sewage and waste employ 10.2% – a growing figure reflecting increasing concern on environmental and pollution aspects, and nearly 3.7% work in energy supply.

In education, 3% work in schools, 1.2% in FE colleges, with 2.9% working for universities.

Some 3.1% work for central or local government analytical, testing or service labs, with another 4.3% working for research units, government or otherwise; 1.1% are employed in central or local government administration.

Studying chemistry

After school, chemistry can be studied at first-degree and technician level. Most professional chemists today read for degrees, but the route to qualification via professional examinations remains open (*see below*), and there is a significant technician-level entry.

As of 1994, of the number responding to the RSC survey: 4,321 members have doctorates (PhD); 666 masters degrees (MSc); 2,079 first degrees; 1,410 the Graduateship of the Royal Society of Chemistry (GRSC) or earlier qualifications; and 1,363 up to HNC/HND or part 1 (GRSC).

At first-degree level chemistry is taught at most universities, excluding only those with no science faculties. However, 'rationalisation' has resulted in some departments closing. At degree level chemistry deals more with concepts, theories, laws and basic principles than processes and techniques. Many courses take a more 'unified' modern approach to the traditional divisions of physical, organic and inorganic chemistry, although courses obviously still spend more time on types and groups of elements and compounds, their synthesis and the reactions involved.

Because it is such a vast subject, chemistry degree courses generally try to reflect this broad span, and to cover it as widely as possible, concentrating largely on fundamental principles, concepts and methods in the early years. However, because there is always something new happening in chemical research, most courses also respond quickly to the latest advances, and give students at least a glimpse of current research – usually via research projects in their final year. There is normally a strong emphasis on experimental work.

Some courses allow specialisation in such subjects as medicinal chemistry, colour chemistry, food chemistry, forensic, pharmaceutical, polymer, marine or materials chemistry. It is also possible to combine chemistry with a second subject, such as a second science, and some combinations of chemistry and physics are so closely integrated as to become a specialisation, chemical physics, in their own right.

The same degree of integration is possible with biology – biochemistry – and geology (geochemistry). There has been a growth of degree courses which include the study of a European language and a year in a chemical company or university in Europe. Chemistry can be studied with education for a teaching qualification, with materials or metallurgy, and with management, business studies or economics.

Some universities offer 'enhanced' chemistry courses leading to an MSc degree, which take a year longer but allow more in depth study of the subject and additional research experience.

'First destination' figures are (1994):

total graduating	*2,850*
research, etc.	1,161
teacher training	156
other training inc. law	69
believed unemployed 31 Dec	258
temporary work	120
overseas work	36
permanent UK work	901
employers	
chemicals	318
manufacturing industry	87
other commerce	164
accountancy	68

Civil Service	27
NHS/local government	37
higher/further ed.	27
functions	
scientific R&D	276
financial work	109
admin/ops management	89
marketing, etc.	96
scientific support	134
management services	40
personnel/social/medical	33

A-level chemistry and normally maths and another science are needed; 4,181 students were accepted for chemistry degree courses at universities in 1995 compared with 3,924 in 1990.

In 1994, 2,850 students graduated with first degrees in chemistry and 1,281 with higher degrees.

Professional qualification

The Royal Society of Chemistry (1995 membership 45,867) is the learned and professional body. Fellows and Members of the institute can use the designation Chartered Chemist (CChem). The normal route to satisfying the academic requirements for professional membership of the society is by means of a degree in chemistry which is accredited by the Society for either graduate or licentiate membership.

Most Chartered Chemists qualify via an approved first or second class honours degree and at least two years' relevant experience. The RSC has a long tradition of maintaining an alternative route through its own examinations but its graduateship examinations are being phased out and the last opportunity to take them will be in summer 1996. At the Licentiate level, a grade of professional membership corresponding in standard to a pass degree in chemistry, the RSC introduced its own examinations in 1995. Eighty-five students took the exam in that year and 66 passed.

Several Institutions offer a joint BSc/GRSC award through joint validation arrangements with the society.

Postgraduate study

Research, posts in higher education, and some other areas of work normally require a higher degree. However, there are research and/or academic posts for only very few of those who gain PhDs, and such a degree is not always a suitable preparation for other areas of work, although the chemical industry is now recognising the value of postgraduates. It is possible to avoid this 'trap' by finding work in industry, and combining this with part-time study for a higher degree. The majority of taught postgraduate courses (as opposed to research degrees) lead to MScs or diplomas and are very specialised. A recent innovation is the Masters in Research – MRes, a one year postgraduate course which aims to develop skills in research techniques. Funding for postgraduate study may be available from the Engineering and Physical Science Research Council (EPSRC). The Biotechnology and Biological Sciences Research Council and firms in the chemical, oil and pharmaceuticals industries also support chemical research though almost half postgraduate students receive no funding other than their own.

Technician level

Technician-level qualification is via BTEC or SCOTVEC awards.

Further information

The Royal Society of Chemistry (leaflets, etc.).

Physics

Physics, according to the dictionary, is the study of the properties of matter and energy. This is a very short definition for a subject which ranges so widely over the physical world, and tries to identify the laws which dictate the way it works, and how it is put together. It takes in space, time, motion, electricity, radiation, magnetism, heat, optics, sound, and mechanics. It studies the atom, and so extends from the level of invisible elementary and sub-nuclear and anti-particles right out to the entire universe. It takes in the most abstract of concepts, such as relativity, and the most practical, such as radiotherapy.

And so one physicist can be a very different kind of scientist from another. Some are theoretical physicists, for example, who use maths, logical thinking and intuition – even guess-work – to come up with possible new physical laws. Many physicists nowadays spend a lot of their time at computer terminals. Experimental physicists may spend a lot of time in the lab trying to prove the theoreticians right or wrong. Others find and develop applications of physics.

Despite the huge body of knowledge that physics has already accumulated, it is still developing new ideas and producing results, refining and revising theories in the light of new experimental data, and vice versa. The 'spin-off' from research in physics is phenomenal, and however theoretical the work may seem, it will inevitably have applications somewhere. Much of engineering depends on the laws of classical physics. Nuclear physics has applications in medicine and engineering. Low-temperature physics is the basis of a whole industry – cryogenics – which makes, for example, liquid helium for rocket fuels, and is also used in surgery. It is work in solid-state physics which results in so many more uses for electronics, and in the silicon chip – and is still producing results of enormous value. Opto-electronics has already produced the optical fibres now replacing copper cables in telephone transmission systems and is now producing many more integrated optical devices to replace electronic circuits for many purposes. The possibilities of lasers are equally extensive.

The laws of physics, physicists' research techniques and equipment are now also used in research in many other areas, from materials science and the biological sciences, to geology and archaeology. Co-operation between physicists and other scientists has resulted in whole new areas of study with 'names' of their own, like chemical physics, medical physics and geophysics. Astrophysics investigates the physical laws of the universe, out in space with the astronomers (*see* ASTRONOMY *in* EARTH AND SPACE SCIENCE).

Opportunities for Professional Physicists

There are probably around 30,000 physicists in the UK.

According to a survey published in 1992 (the latest available) by the Institute of Physics (IOP) based on replies received from 42% of its corporate members, in 1992, physicists were employed as follows (the 1990 figure is given in brackets):

Central or local government laboratory	136 (180)
Research institute	338 (448)
Hospital (non-teaching)	102 (122)
Communications	134 (152)
Electricity generation	141 (159)
Electrical & electronic equipment industry	368 (487)
Computer systems and applications	230 (256)
Aerospace industry	150 (161)
University	931 (1,093)
Technical College	84 (117)
School	264 (296)
Consultancy	132 (137)
General Management	219 (227)
R & D as manager/administrator	539 (666)
R & D not as manager/administrator	925 (1,175)
Other scientific or technical work as manager/administrator	199 (214)
Other scientific or technical work not as manager or administrator	196 (243)
Educational work as manager/ administrator	200 (258)
Educational work not as manager/ administrator	717 (881)

Categories with response rates of under 10 were not counted.

Industry

According to the IOP survey about 35–45% of physicists were employed in industry. This figure includes 37.7% industry, commercial company or trade association, 3.9% in the nationalised industries, public corporations and water authorities, and 4.4% working for the AEA Technology and associated companies.

A high proportion of physics graduates begin their careers in research and development (R&D), many of them in industry. While there is no 'physics' industry in the same sense as there is a 'chemical' industry, in many industrial sectors products depend on applications of physics. Electronics, aerospace, telecommunications and the defence industries tend to dominate the employment scene for physicists but there is also scope in the nuclear power, chemical, oil, plastics, photographic, paper, materials fibres, foods, metals, glass, and car industries. Within electronics growth areas are opto-electronics, and developing new semiconductor materials and devices and communication systems.

In electronics, for example, physicists work in multi-disciplinary teams, with e.g. electronic engineers, on new solid-state infra-red lasers for range-finder systems, on the next generation of semiconductor devices, and on improving production methods to meet the technical demands of new processes in making semiconductors.

In telecommunications and information technology now using radio frequency communications and opto-electronics, physicists work on developing networking systems and optical-fibre networks. One group works on methods for producing – growing – specialised compound semi-conductors from which are made the lasers and photo-diodes that make up the transmitters and receivers for fibre-optic communication links.

In heavier engineering, physicists do experimental work with mechanical engineers on turbine aerodynamics, on vibration and stress problems, and develop testing techniques. Physicists work on developing, for instance, new designs of circuit breakers for the electricity companies.

In the chemical industry, physicists work with chemists and biologists on designing new measuring techniques, and with engineers and polymer chemists on developing improved methods to make, for instance, coated films. They work with instrument engineers and computer scientists to improve process control systems for chemical plant.

They may do basic studies on materials – e.g. fatigue studies on polymers, or in economic methods for strengthening yarn fibres – or try to solve specific problems, overcoming technological problems which prevent advance in a particular field. They also study and measure such things as wear, investigate problems of noise (for example, in aircraft engines), and are generally involved in the design, construction and application of mechanical, optical and electronic instruments.

Particularly in industrial research, physicists generally develop expertise in the field in which they are working, and their original degree subject steadily becomes more irrelevant to their future careers. *See also* MANUFACTURING INDUSTRIES.

Where professional physicists work

Government and research councils

According to an IOP survey 10.3% of physicists work in the public sector. The publicly financed research laboratories have been hived off into agencies during the last few years and some have been privatised. The Defence Engineering and Science Group of the Civil Service including the Defence Evaluation and Research Agency is a major employer of physicists. The laboratories of the Department of Trade and Industry have been contracted out or privatised.

The National Physical Laboratory is now run for the government by a private company SERCO. It continues to serve as the national standards laboratory for measurement and calibration covering subjects like acoustics, atmospheric monitoring, fibre optics, lasers, radiometry, thermal conductivity, ultrasonics, etc. Research on materials aims to assist in the improvement of quality, design and reliability of products such as ceramics, corrosion and fracture prevention, and thermodynamic data. Other important areas include information technology, smart cards and the provision of physical and engineering data and nano-technology. Environmental protection work includes the development of spectroscopic techniques for the analysis of the atmosphere, and investigation into noise and its effect on hearing. At NPL they are co-operating with other European labs on standards – NPL is responsible for the calibration of humidity standards and screw-thread gauges for the oil industry, while Germany for example takes care of gear measurement. NPL employs about 750 staff. During the upheaval of a change in its management recruitment has been frozen, but now that its future is clear vacancies may well arise once more.

The Atomic Weapons Establishment at Aldermaston is now managed by a private consortium and AEA Technology (which included the United Kingdom Atomic Energy Authority) is being privatised. Culham laboratory is still engaged with a multi-national team in seeking ways to develop a practical nuclear fusion reactor.

The Defence Evaluation and Research Agency employs a large number of physicists to work, for example, on command information systems and electronics at Malvern or aircraft systems or structural materials at Farnborough. Physicists may work on research into Intelligent Knowledge Based Systems, underwater sonar and ocean science, the design of miniature microwave radars, research and development into surface waves, semi-conductor devices, development of detectors, optics and systems for imaging using thermal radiation, etc.

The Rutherford Appleton Laboratory and the Daresbury Laboratory are run by the Council for Central Laboratories of the Research Councils. Rutherford Appleton, employing 1,270 staff, houses the world's most powerful neutron source and high power lasers which are used for materials research. It is also concerned with space science and the building and testing of instruments for space experiments. Some of its scientists are working on particle physics and it has an extremely powerful Cray computer.

Daresbury Laboratory employs 500 people. Its research facilities include a synchrotron radiation source and it carries out research into the fabrication of tiny parts by electron etching. One of its research groups is working on surface transformations and interfaces.

Particle physics research is now largely concentrated at the European CERN laboratory at Geneva.

Other Government work covers patents, environmental pollution at the National Environmental Technology Centre at Harwell. Research at the Road Transport Laboratory, optical physics in the Scientific Development Group (part of the Home Office), food irradiation processes in the MAFF Food Safety Directorate.

See also CENTRAL GOVERNMENT. The Meteorological Office both employs physicists in atmospheric research and trains them in METEOROLOGY and there are opportunities in ASTRONOMY (*see in* EARTH AND SPACE SCIENCE).

The medical and health sector

The medical and health sector employs significant numbers of physicists. The IOP survey gives a figure of 3.1% of physicists going into the NHS.

Audiological scientists are concerned with investigation into hearing and balance disorders. The main responsibilities include diagnostic audiology, rehabilitation including hearing aid fitting, paediatric audiology i.e. assessing hearing loss in babies and young children, calibrating and monitoring equipment, and research and development. It is a small profession employing at the most about 100 audiologists, who will usually have an appropriate first degree in a subject like physics plus an MSc in Audiology. *See also* AUDIOLOGICAL SCIENCES *in* SCIENTISTS AND TECHNICIANS IN THE HEALTH SERVICE.

Modern medicine depends heavily on physics and technology and the medical physicist has an important role. The use of ionising radiations in radiotherapy, radioactive isotopes for diagnosis and observation, and ultrasonic radiation for treatment and diagnosis and the use of nuclear magnetic resonance for brain and body scans are well known. Current growth areas are the use of diagnostic imaging techniques laser treatment and fibre optics to assist keyhole surgery. *See also* MEDICAL PHYSICISTS *in* SCIENTISTS AND TECHNICIANS IN THE HEALTH SERVICE.

Radiation and health physics is the specialised multi-disciplinary branch of health and safety which deals with safe working practices in the use of ionising radiations. The major employers are the United Kingdom Atomic Energy Authority (UKAEA) and the electricity supply industry, British Nuclear Fuels, Amersham International, HM Inspectorate of Industrial Pollution (HMIP), MAFF and the MOD. *See also* BIOMEDICAL ENGINEERING *in* PROCESS ENGINEERING, BIOMEDICAL ENGINEERING AND MATERIALS SCIENCE.

Education

There is still a chronic shortage of physics teachers in schools, although this is partially masked by other scientists or mathematicians teaching physics.

Opportunities in higher education – to lecture and/or do research – have been decreasing and are likely to fall further.

Studying physics

Physics is studied mainly at degree level, although there are courses at higher-technician level too.

Degree courses

Following publication in 1990 of a report on *The Future Pattern of Higher Education in Physics*, physics departments have reduced the content of their single honours degree programmes. They have also developed enhanced programmes to provide a basis for more advanced work in physics whether this be in the field of research within higher education or within a work-based context.

Physics degree courses now do more to develop students' intellectual and imaginative powers, their understanding and judgement, their problem-solving skills, their ability to communicate, to see relationships within what they have learnt and also to see their field of study in a broader perspective. Departments have adopted a wider range of teaching and learning strategies including more small-group teaching and supported self-study.

The three-year programme leads to a BSc and its standard is the same as that for an honours degree in other subject areas. However, by reducing the content, the three-year programme may not be sufficient preparation for the more technically demanding careers, or for much research work leading to PhDs in physics, nor is it likely to be recognised as equivalent to first degrees in Europe which involved longer periods of study. Physics departments have therefore introduced four-year programmes leading to either an MSci, or an MPhys qualification. The fourth year of such courses has a core component of advanced physics, plus an optional component and a project component which in some cases is completed on a SOCRATES/ERASMUS scheme in another European country, attending a different university. Part of the optional component is sometimes in another discipline, appropriate to certain careers, such as a foreign language or management.

In 1996, 55 universities, including several in Scotland, are offering 'enhanced' courses.

Because physics is such a vast subject, almost all courses try to give the widest possible picture, starting with and concentrating on fundamental principles, and going on to more advanced theories and experimental work. Courses go through more advanced studies of 'classical' physics – e.g. mechanics, electricity and magnetism, structure and properties of matter, vibrations and waves, thermodynamics. They may also start early on areas of 'modern' physics, such as relativity, quantum mechanics, nuclear and atomic or particle physics, optics, and solid state, and will also cover e.g. thermal physics, electromagnetism. But because there is always something new happening in physics research, most courses also respond quickly to the latest advances, giving graduates at least a glimpse of current research – usually in the final year.

Because there is so much to cover, there are not usually quite so many choices as in some other subjects before the final year, but a chance to specialise to some extent may be given, perhaps in theoretical or experimental aspects, or to pick out a variety of topics. Specialisation in the final year(s) may include atomic physics, astrophysics, theoretical physics, solid state; the physics of materials, or of the atmosphere, oceans, and solid earth; applied and practical aspects such as health or medical physics, radiation physics, acoustics, optics, etc.

Some give the chance to study physics in relation to another science, e.g. biophysics or geophysics, or to study advanced spectroscopy or instrument design. Some courses allow earlier specialisation in physical electronics, which deals more with the scientific principles of electronics and with developing new devices than electronic engineering, and which at some places can be studied with microcomputer electronics. Physics may be studied 'with' a linked subject, e.g. laser technology, computing, or management science.

Some courses are called applied physics, concentrating on this in the later years of the course, and some include an industrial training period. Generally, applied physics courses start with the same basics as a 'normal' physics course, but move on to more technological aspects – options may include e.g. vacuum technology, applied solid state, microprocessors, macromolecules, applied acoustics, X-ray diffraction, and nuclear technology, energy in nature, human uses of energy, reactor physics, instrument physics, corrosion science, medical physics, computers in the lab, acoustics, optics.

Students are also thoroughly trained in the 'language' of physics, which means learning to use sophisticated mathematical methods, thinking and analysing mathematically. Most physics research nowadays uses computers, and students learn to use them, to process data for the computer, and interpret what comes out. Obviously, a great deal of time is spent in labs, learning the full range of modern experimental techniques, and ending in the final year with a small experimental project.

'First destinations' in physics (1994):

total graduating	*2,362*
research, etc.	817
teacher training	123
other training inc. law	82
believed unemployed 31 Dec	226
temporary work	97
permanent UK work	613
employers	
engineering industry	96
commerce	132
public utilities	27
accountancy	58
chemicals	25
Civil Service	54
other manufacturing	27
NHS/local government	38
HE/FE	32
functions	
scientific/eng. R&D	143
management services	108
financial work	94
admin/ops management	42
scientific/eng. support	28
marketing, etc.	31
personnel/social/medical	21
teaching/lecturing	14

Entry normally requires three A-levels or two A-levels and two AS levels, or equivalent qualifications including baccalaureate and advanced GNVQs. The most usual subject combinations are Physics and Maths, or Physics, Maths and Chemistry or Maths plus other subjects.

Professional qualification

The Institute of Physics (1995 membership 21,673) requires four to five years' (depending on degree class) appropriate postgraduate experience for full membership. The Institute has withdrawn its graduateship examination.

A 1995 IOP survey gives the qualifications of the Fellows, Members and Associate Members in full-time employment as:

HND/HNC & supplementary studies	87
Honours degree	12,102
Masters degree by exam or thesis	2,787
PhD	6,030

Postgraduate study

Most postgraduate MSc courses in physics specialise, for example, in medical physics, principles of instrument design, semi-conductor physics and technology, etc. Physics graduates can also do postgraduate study in another discipline – astronomy, astrophysics, computing and information technology, geophysics, engineering, for instance.

Research posts in higher education, and some other areas of work, normally require a PhD.

Some students receive funding for postgraduate study from the Engineering and Physical Science Research Council (EPSRC) or the Particle Physics and Astronomy Research Council (PPARC), some are funded by industrial firms and about half finance their studies themselves.

Technician-level qualification

Technician level qualification is via BTEC or SCOTVEC National and Higher National awards.

Foundation course

Several universities offer one-year foundation or bridging courses for those with non-standard or inappropriate entry qualifications.

Further information

The Institute of Physics (booklets).

Contents

Biological Sciences

(CLCI: QOD)

Background

The biological sciences, also referred to as life sciences or biological sciences, evolved very rapidly over the last fifty years from straightforward, descriptive natural history of living organisms (plants, animals and microbes), to a highly experimental study of the common principles and processes of life itself. At one end of the scale, biologists now probe into the most fundamental structures at sub-cellular and molecular levels; at the other, they investigate the ecology of complete animal and plant communities and habitats, the development of and interrelationships in those communities, the factors such as climate, ground conditions and human influence affecting them, and their conservation.

The biological sciences study the basic similarities and common features of living systems – for example, cells and cellular structure; how living organisms acquire and use energy through chemical changes; how they reproduce themselves, grow and develop. They treat life as a series of processes with characteristics to be observed, described and analysed, and study the origins of living organisms and how they develop.

The current emphases in biological research are genetics and biological engineering, microbes, plant science and productivity, developmental biology (gene expression, control of cell growth division and shape, pattern formation, and cell signalling), neurobiology and cognitive science, animal function, and the structure, function and engineering of large biological molecules.

Research in biological sciences at a molecular level only became possible with advances in chemistry and physics and with the development of technology such as the electron microscope, which can examine the fine detailed structure of plants and animal cells. Real understanding of the complex chemical composition and functioning of living cells was impossible until chemists had developed both the necessary theories, and the sophisticated experimental and analytical techniques needed to do the research. Physicists have contributed with new scientific techniques and ideas, developed as biophysics.

Biologically based processes have been in practical use for many centuries, for example, in fermenting yeast for bread-making and brewing, long before they were properly understood. Modern developments in the biological sciences have given many more ways in which they can be exploited. Biologists make regular contributions to medical advance, for instance helping to stop transplants being rejected, and work on controlling neurological disorders and pain. Agriculture, agricultural research, and the food-processing and food-preserving industries depend in many ways on biological work. So-called pure research almost always has practical value eventually; for example, biochemical research on how substances are transported across cell membranes helps to find ways of neutralising toxic substances.

Applied biological sciences are the basis for one of the major technologies of today which will become even more important in the future; biotechnology. Much existing industrial technology is based on exploiting mineral resources, which are non-renewable, using techniques from the physical and engineering sciences. As these resources become increasingly scarce, industrial systems will have to change over to biological resources which are renewable and use biological systems to manufacture with, in other words growing resources in laboratories. Estimates suggest that already over 40% of manufacturing output is biological in nature or origin. *See also* BIOTECHNOLOGY *in* MANUFACTURING INDUSTRIES.

Biological sciences are becoming even more widely applicable and interdisciplinary, as major research initiatives demonstrate. An example is the study of image interpretation which is how the human brain recovers useful information from a retinal image to guide a response to a changing scene, and detecting, discriminating and interpreting intensity changes, surface features, edges and two- and three-dimensional features. Such biological information is needed to underpin advances in engineering systems, such as designing high-resolution TV displays and developing 'intelligent' machines able to recognise and assemble components. This neuroscience initiative ranges from molecular and cellular biology to behavioural and psychological aspects, drawing on many scientific disciplines.

Branches of biological science

The biological sciences cover many interrelated subjects, and it is difficult to separate disciplines such as biochemistry from molecular biology. Traditionally the divisions were according to the kinds of organisms studied and the distinctions between them, but today emphasis is on the processes which living things have in common. The processes are interrelated to such an extent that the boundaries between them are indistinct. Research work increasingly crosses the traditional frontiers, and often takes multidisciplinary teams from many of the sciences, for example biochemists and molecular biologists, as well as crystallographers and computer graphics experts, might design new forms of enzymes which can function at higher temperatures or in more acid conditions.

Biologists who may describe themselves as physiologists or neurologists would use biochemical methods to find out how pain is passed to the brain and processed by it to produce a reaction to the pain. There are, conversely, chemists whose main interest is in the chemical changes which happen in biological systems, such as the brain. The difference between a physiologist and a zoologist, once they are well into their careers, may be difficult to define. In research on, say, cats' muscles, the physiologist is probably more interested in muscle systems generally and how they differ, what it is about cat muscles that enables them to jump so well, when dogs, for example, cannot. The zoologist, on the other hand, may be interested in what effect such muscle power has on a cat's development and life.

Traditionally, the main branches of biology studied particular types of living things – plants, animals, or microbes (living organisms which are too small to be seen without a microscope). These were then just descriptive sciences, concentrating on classifying different types of organisms, identifying the differences between them, and studying their anatomy and the way in which they function. With the recent rapid developments in studies at the level of individual cells, and the chemistry of the processes occurring within them, subjects like botany, zoology and microbiology have become much more experimental in their approach, and more concerned with basic biological principles.

The biological sciences now have many new branches which study particular aspects or levels of living systems, and the processes which occur within them and around them, regardless of the type of organism. While there always were biologists interested in physiology, or genetics (the study of inheritance), the developments in biochemical techniques have created a whole new subject, molecular genetics, which is fundamental to biological engineering. Other aspects of the biological sciences have also developed into studies in their own right, such as ecology, for example, which links biological and environmental sciences.

Human beings have long used applications of biology, but now scientists are developing ways of turning basic biological principles to practical use, in medical or industrial settings, in ways which may have many other applications.

Aquatic/marine and freshwater biology

Aquatic biology brings together the study of life in the seas and freshwater, from tiny algae and plankton to whales. It studies the special structure, development, physiology, and behaviour, and adaptations of aquatic organisms. Studying the ecology of sea life has its own special aspects, and involves studying related sciences, such as OCEANOGRAPHY (*see in* EARTH AND SPACE SCIENCES). Marine biologists work with other scientists in practical research, in developing artificial rearing and farming of sea creatures, looking for new sources of food amongst sea organisms, investigating how to conserve fish stocks, and solving the problems involved in pollution at sea, and waste disposal. The ecology of estuaries and coastal waters is important in seeing that they are properly managed, by understanding the basic properties and processes underlying these ecosystems, and the effect of human influence in building oil terminals or wave barriers.

Biochemistry

Biochemistry studies the way in which biological systems of all kinds are organised, and function, at molecular and atomic levels. This means that biochemists see all living things (animals, plants and microbes) in terms of their basic chemical substances and processes – and have demonstrated the basic similarities of life systems at these levels. Biochemists are interested in living cells and the molecules and chemical reactions which occur in physiological systems. For example, many of the chemical reactions by which the microbe yeast produces alcohol from sugar are almost identical with those by which muscles of mammals derive the energy needed for their movement, so biochemists study these chemical processes in microbes and mammals. Photosynthesis, the process by which plants produce carbohydrates from simple molecules using the energy of sunlight, is an important area of research in plant science and productivity.

Biochemistry began by identifying, analysing and synthesising the chemicals, such as complex proteins, which make up living cells. It then moved on to draw maps of cells and the place of each chemical within them, and to work out the major pathways by which chemical changes take place inside the cell, and the mechanism of different reactions. Biochemists mapped the 'metabolic pathways' which allow living cells to synthesise and break down, for example, sugars, fats and amino acids, and worked out how cells keep a balance between energy-producing and energy-demanding reactions. Once enough was known about the mechanisms of enzyme reactions, about their energy needs, and how enzymes worked in series in metabolic pathways, they went on to examine how the cell controls and regulates its own metabolism. This led to the solution of the problem of how giant molecules are copied accurately to reproduce themselves on cell division, how coded genetic messages contain the instruction on synthesising cells – to operate kidneys and muscles, nerves and brain, and how the nerve-cell network communicates with muscle or other nerve cells.

An important area of research at the moment is the study of 'prions' or chemically altered proteins in which the normally helical shape of a protein molecule straightens out. These prions are believed to be the agents responsible for the transmission of Creutzfeld Jacob's disease (CJD), and it is essential to find out how human beings develop this disease before any treatment can be developed. It is suspected that the prions pass from infected cows which have 'mad cow' disease in the human food chain to people who eat infected products from cows. Some researchers believe that proteins in animals and plants can be altered to form harmful prions and that this can be caused by the use of agricultural chemicals such as organophosphates, which are commonly in use to treat vegetable crops against disease, as well as in sheep dip, but may leave a residue which can then be consumed by humans.

Another area of research which is important at the moment is the development of chemical polymers, which are very long thin molecules of repeated units, and which are very important in the study of the transmission of electrical impulses as in the human nervous system; such polymers can be used to help to regenerate human nervous tissue which has been damaged.

The work of biochemists is, then, fundamental to understanding the basic processes of living systems, and crucial in any attempts to improve and exploit them. *See* CLINICAL BIOCHEMISTS *in* SCIENTISTS AND TECHNICIANS IN THE HEALTH SERVICE.

Biophysics

Biophysics applies the theories and techniques of physics to the study of living organisms and the molecules of which they are made.

Biophysicists study biological systems and processes, for example the structure of biological molecules and the bonds within them such as DNA, the genetic material. It was a physicist who predicted a key principle in our present understanding about the mechanisms of inheritance, long before it was proved experimentally, that a single genetic unit could not have more than a few thousand atoms, and that according to the laws of physics, the genetic unit must represent a code specification.

Biophysicists use many techniques and instruments for investigating structures and making fine measurements, such as X-ray crystallography, X-ray diffraction, electron microscopes, spectrometers and oscilloscopes, and computers to analyse data and display results.

Research in biophysics includes investigating the electrical, magnetic and mechanical properties of cells and tissues, and the methods of energy conversion that take place between a living organism and its environment, and within the organism itself. Biophysicists investigate and measure the structure and mechanisms of biological molecules such as enzymes, proteins and nucleic acids, and study the energy transfers within living systems such as the transmission of nerve signals for the reception and transfer of visual signals in the eye and the brain.

Botany or plant science

Botany has developed from a purely descriptive study of the morphology, anatomy and classification of living and fossil plant forms, into a much more experimental subject, increasingly called plant science. It studies plants of all kinds, from the so-called lower plants with the simplest structures, such as mosses, algae, and phytoplankton in the sea, through to the highest or complex forms, the flowering plants, such as trees or cacti. Some botanists specialise in particular groups of plants, such as mycologists, who study fungi. Botanists now study plants as biological systems, right down to the cellular level where their interests cross those of the molecular biologists, for example when studying the chemistry and physics of the photosynthesis process. Botanists study plants as sources of food and energy for animals and people, and their place in the natural environment. Plant ecology, also called physiological ecology, is the study of plant communities including the analysis of the movement of chemical substances and energy associated with the ecosystem, how plants have grown and developed in a particular habitat, and how they disperse elsewhere.

Botanists study how plants have evolved and breed new strains. They study plant growth, development, demography (studying factors determining the size of plant populations), reproduction, and the physiological and biochemical mechanisms involved. Botanists carry out research on particular groups of plants, for example to find out which kinds of trees would be suitable for coniferous plantings in a particular area, or the intensive culture of poplar trees for wood fibre. Botanists study the fixation of nitrogen from the air by lichens which can then be used by other living organisms to assess their contribution to the nitrogen economy of their environment.

Despite all the years of research, understanding of the fundamental processes involved in plant growth and development is in need of further work even to bring it to the level of understanding in comparable animal sciences. Interdisciplinary research in this area is important, to bring together biochemistry, genetics and molecular genetics, as well as botany. Once processes are understood, it will be possible to manipulate plant systems. To alter plants genetically to produce new and improved plants that food-hungry countries need, there is a lot of work to be done first on characterising plant genetic material. Botanists are using the techniques of biotechnology to produce saffron, which is a particularly valuable crop, commercially.

Study of the major plant processes, such as photosynthesis, are continuing. Understanding photosynthesis will make it possible to create even more efficient plant systems, and use photosynthetic systems for other uses, ultimately to reduce the dependence of human beings on non-renewable mineral resources. There is still much research needed into the basic processes of photosynthesis at the molecular level.

There is also research into the physiology and biochemistry of plant growth; for example, how plant metabolism is biochemically regulated, how plants take up and assimilate nitrates, the synthesis of plant growth-regulating substances, and the biochemical mechanisms underlying plant responses to their environment. There is also research into plant molecular genetics, into the classification and genetic diversity of plants, and into plant biophysics; for example, the structure, isolation and function of cell membrane systems, and the transport of nutrients through them.

Ecology

Ecologists study ecosystems which are made up of all the living organisms and their natural environment, and the ways in which they interact with each other and with the non-living world around them. Ecologists model the environment, and try to build a scientific picture of the natural world. They try to discover, for example, why there are particular population sizes of mice, foxes, and various kinds of plants in a certain ecosystem, what the factors and processes are which produce these sizes, and what factors change the numbers and the balance between them. Studying an ecosystem involves considering all the living things within it, how they are adapted to each other and to the environment, and their interaction with the geographical and geological surroundings including the climate and microclimates within the ecosystem.

In this way, ecologists use scientific methods to collect information, and statistical and mathematical techniques in measuring, weighing, counting, comparing and analysing. Investigating an ecosystem includes a study of the food chains or webs, and the flow of energy through it, starting with the plants which fix the sun's radiant energy in photosynthesis.

The environment is an enormously complicated interacting system that mankind is affecting as never before, and both plant and animal communities will be affected by the changes in the climate. The modelling and prediction of impacts on complex communities is an area of great interest in current research.

Genetics

Genetics studies how living organisms of all kinds, from the relatively simple (such as viruses, bacteria and fungi) to the most complex higher animals, including humans, acquire and pass on their own individual and distinctive characteristics from one generation to another. Genetics deals with the physical and chemical properties of genetic material and how the information it contains is expressed in the growth and development of the organism. Classical genetics began simply with experiments to show that, in sweet peas, it was possible to predict accurately the colours of the flowers which would develop in one generation of plants from knowing only the flower colour of the two plants which were parents to that generation. The experimental work led to practical applications such as improving wheat strains by selecting parent plants and developing generations of plants which have a higher yield of larger or heavier seeds, or which are resistant naturally to common diseases such as fungal infections, or which grow better in a particular climate, or breeding generations of plants which combine these inherited characteristics in appropriate combinations for a particular environment.

With the discovery of how DNA (the molecules which make up the genetic material) copies itself, genetics became more concerned with what actually happens inside living cells when new cells develop, the structure of the genetic material, and how the genetic information, for example colour of eyes, is transcribed and translated into the form of molecules which determine the colour of eyes in the offspring. Research in genetics has played a central part in formulating concepts which unify biology, and allow the exploitation of biological systems. The success of modern genetics has come from the analysis of genetic mechanisms within individual cells using sophisticated equipment and techniques from chemistry and physics to probe the structure and function of genetic material.

From this, geneticists have developed techniques to splice DNA molecules by isolating a length which represents the genetic material for a particular protein, and implanting it into a microbe so that it will be copied as though it belonged to the microbe. This area of research is microbial genetics and has important applications in biotechnology, as many different products, for example food proteins, can be made in large quantities by breeding genetically altered microbes.

Geneticists use similar experiments to identify and analyse the products of inheritance and the effect of changes in the DNA on them. These biological techniques, known as genetic engineering, are the basis of many biotechnology processes.

Genetic engineering makes minute artificial changes in the genetic material to alter the characteristics of the offspring; for example a ewe has now been bred in Scotland which produces milk containing an extra biochemical substance which can be used as a drug to treat a particular kind of liver disease. This is an economical way to produce this scarce drug. There are many important developments in this area, and a great deal of research is currently being undertaken.

The genetic material of animals has been modified by including human genes into the natural sequence of an animal's genetic material, and the new generation of animals bred by such techniques are called transgenic animals. A valuable example of a transgenic animal is a baboon with genes which cause it to have human-compatible bone marrow, which can then be used to transplant into people needing bone marrow because their own bone marrow is diseased and if not replaced would probably lead to death. Primates or higher mammals such as the baboon are most often used for such research, as their genetic material is most similar to that of humans. Another example of a transgenic mammal is the pig which can have its genetic material modified to produce human-compatible liver or human-compatible kidneys which can then be transplanted into humans. The pig is a useful mammal in this respect as it breeds quickly and grows fast so that the organs can be produced in a few months; but the pigs reared in this way must be free from all known diseases, and must be barren and the offspring of a single rearing. It may be possible to treat Altzheimers disease by similar techniques.

Genetic manipulation is now possible even with mammals, and in 1996 a flock of sheep has been bred in which each sheep is genetically identical, that is they are clones of each other.

Genetics has many applications; for example making it possible to diagnose genetically caused disease by identifying damaged or unusual genetic material in cell cultures or tissue samples in the foetus. These techniques raise difficult ethical questions, as parents can choose to reject a foetus which carries defective genetic material. Also there are ethical problems in using primates such as baboons as transgenic animals, and in any such baboon research, as they are evolutionarily threatened.

Genetic disease is thought to be apparent in 5% of the population by the age of 25, and clearly research can help avoid or control the passing of defective genetic material to subsequent generations, and forms the basis for genetic counselling, whereby prospective parents can be told the statistical probability of their offspring inheriting certain characteristics. There are many very serious genetic diseases, such as Duchenne muscular dystrophy and spinal muscular atrophy, where research is isolating the genes which are responsible and trying to find ways to reduce the effect of these genes, perhaps by replacing them with other genes. It may take many years to isolate a particular gene, such is the molecular complexity of the genetic material, and researchers use many sophisticated biochemical techniques as well as looking for clues such as genetic linkage where there are other characteristics which have a statistically significant tendency to be inherited together with the gene being studied. In the foreseeable future geneticists will have determined the sequence of all human genes, which will provide the information for the possibility of genetic engineering to analyse, ameliorate or avoid genetic diseases' being inherited.

Genetically altered fruit and vegetables are now being developed, and can be very useful in the human diet; for example, red bananas have extra vitamins so can supplement a deficient diet. Fruit can also be produced containing the antibiotic drug penicillin, which is normally produced from the fungus *Penicillium*, and this fruit can be an alternative way of administering this drug, for example to children.

Geneticists have developed 'genetic fingerprinting', which is able to identify each human being with absolute certainty by the structure of their DNA molecules. This technique is now used by forensic scientists (*see in* SECURITY AND PROTECTIVE SERVICES) in helping the police in murder investigations when only a tiny sample of blood from a suspect can give a genetic fingerprint which will implicate one particular human being in an incident. Micro-organisms can now be bred with specific characteristics, so that they are tailored for the control of specific pests or to dispose of waste such as oil slicks. Trees are being bred by modifying the genetic material so as to produce wood with specified characteristics; for example, straighter grain.

Another branch of genetics is population genetics, which involves studying changes, usually very long-term, in the genetic make-up of any group of individual living things that can interbreed, and their offspring, and the forces that can cause these changes. This has relevance to discussions on evolutionary theory; and as models of genetic change become more sophisticated, genetics will help to refine and develop ideas on how evolution happens. More practically, population genetics isolates, for example, what causes the prevalence of diseases to vary between different geographical areas.

Research also looks into possible genetic origins of disorders such as diabetes and schizophrenia, and studies agents producing genetic damage in relation to environmental hazards. Geneticists isolate weaknesses in pests which can be used to control them biologically.

Much research effort and resources are at the moment being put into the Human Genome Project, which expects to have completely mapped the human genetic material by the year 2006. This research has very wide applications – in that it will then be possible to manipulate human genetic material for very specific features – and thus may be used to eradicate genetic disease, or cause human breeding to occur or not occur for certain specified features. The ethical implications of such possibilities are vast, and government ethical committees are beginning to look at the controls which will be necessary in law to control such techniques as are available now and even more far-reaching possibilities which will be available in the near future.

Genetic testing is a very important service for prospective parents who may have themselves inherited the potential for a genetic disease even though the disease may not be manifest in them, when they are known as carriers of that disease. The parents can find out exactly what genes for known diseases they do carry, and can then be given an estimate of the statistical possibility of their children inheriting those diseases. For example, there is a specific gene for the disease tubular sclerosis which can be detected. Also a gene has been identified and located which predisposes those women which have it to breast cancer; but then there are thought to be other genes which affect the development of the disease, so there is not an 'all or nothing' response to the breast cancer gene. *See* GENETICISTS *in* SCIENTISTS AND TECHNICIANS IN THE HEALTH SERVICE.

Microbiology

Microbiology studies the smallest forms of life, the microbes, existing as single cells or organisms with only a small number of cells, so small that they cannot be seen without a microscope. Some examples of microbes are viruses, micro-algae, protozoa, bacteria, yeasts, and micro-fungi. Microbes are interesting as the most widely and diversely adapted of any living organisms, and microbiologists study their structure, metabolic processes, physiology, biochemistry, ecology, variation and genetics, as well as classifying them.

Bacteria are a particularly important group of microbes, as some have harmful effects such as causing disease, whereas others are useful as they produce important substances such as drugs or foods. The specialised study of bacteria and their processes is bacteriology.

However, microbes are important in their effect on larger organisms and in all living systems, both for good and for ill. Microbes have been used for centuries, to produce beer and bread, and to make yoghurt, and silage to feed farm animals, and they are being grown in attempts to produce a direct source of fats, proteins, and vitamins. New strains of microbes have been used in developing new enzymes, and organic chemicals. Microbes are used to recycle waste products and keep the soil fertile. Biotechnology is largely founded on the molecular genetics of a small group of bacterial species. However, micro-organisms can also do great damage; spoiling food, for example; attacking timbers or textiles; or damaging buildings, metal tools, pipelines, ships and aircraft through corrosion.

Current research is concentrating on the basic physiology of bacteria, filamentous fungi and yeasts, largely based on studies of their biochemistry and on their molecular genetics. There is much research to find organisms, microbes or enzyme activity likely to be useful. Learning more about microbes, what chemical changes they can bring about, and how to control and use them, should give many useful results such as controlling those microbes which cause food to spoil.

Another branch of microbiology is virology, which studies viruses, the smallest living things which can reproduce themselves only within specific kinds of bacteria and thus affect other living things. As viruses are also the simplest form of life which can reproduce itself using a genetic code, they are used to study the basic characteristics of living molecules. Virologists study the detailed make-up of virus particles, map how they reproduce themselves, observe and try to explain the changes a viral infection makes in cells, how viruses can become part of the hereditary material of a host cell, and what happens to viruses when the symptoms of an infection have gone. Virologists have developed very advanced vaccines to prevent some viral attacks, but much more research into viruses is needed.

There are many areas of employment for microbiologists, such as the hospital service, the Public Health Laboratory Service, environmental work such as pollution control, the agricultural industries, the pharmaceutical industry, the food and drink industry and the water industry.

Molecular biology/cell biology

Molecular biology specifically studies the three-dimensional structure, forms, physical properties, behaviour and mechanisms of molecules in all kinds of living systems, and their evolution, exploitation and ramification at higher levels of organisation. A survey of molecular biology in higher education shows the crucial importance of chemistry, and that not enough applicants have adequate chemistry for these studies.

The work of molecular biologists is critical to breakthroughs in genetic engineering. It can take years, even using computer-aided design systems, to build a three-dimensional model of an enzyme which genetic engineers want to alter to change the way in which it functions. An enzyme can be made up of as many as 1,000 amino acids arranged in a specific sequence of side chains arranged along a spine. Making changes to just one side chain can alter the enzyme's surface chemistry, and its properties. Modelling is needed to demonstrate the effects of each minute change.

Molecular biology is a key branch of the biological sciences, as its research will increase our understanding of diverse processes such as evolution, and the toxic effects of pollution cocktails. Molecular tools will allow advances to be made in the study of microbial organisms in the soil which affect the functions of plants. It is difficult to draw distinctions between biochemistry and molecular biology, and molecular biology and biophysics.

Cell biology or cytology is the study of cells and the structures within them at the molecular level. Cytologists study the function of parts of cells such as the membrane or mitochondria, the influence of chemical and physical factors on cells, and the growth and division of cells. One of the applications of cytology is studying abnormal cells, for example in cancer research.

Parasitology

Parasitology specialises in life forms which live on or in other living creatures; for example, plants such as mistletoe, animals such as tapeworms, or microbes. Interesting in their own right, they are important because they are involved in the transmission of so many serious diseases, and themselves cause illnesses, particularly in the third world. Parasitology often involves studying ecology too, because parasites occur in ecosystems and have different forms at various stages of their complex lifecycles. They can adapt their metabolisms to very different hosts and energy supplies. Parasites have developed very sophisticated ways of avoiding attempts to get rid of them, both by the host body's natural defences and by drugs.

Physiology

Physiology studies the systems by which all living things function – not just describing them, but probing how and why they function as they do, and researching into the underlying physical and chemical principles. Physiologists want to know how systems work; for example, how the heart beats; how a fertilised egg develops into an embryo; how bacteria, fish, birds, and humans obtain food and convert it into energy; how the body regulates its own growth, metabolism, and reproduction.

Physiologists are, like other biologists, interested in how the processes they study are regulated and controlled. They not only study organs and systems, such as the heart, or muscles, but also investigate processes at the level of individual cells; for example how cell membranes function, and how substances get through them. Here physiologists work closely with biochemists and pharmacologists.

While physiologists study the functional processes of all living organisms, in practice they are usually more interested in animals, and especially the higher vertebrates, including humans. A great deal of interest is centred on neurophysiology, physiology of the cardiovascular system, and electrophysiology.

Neurology or neurophysiology is a branch of physiology which investigates the nervous system and the way in which messages are passed through it, and has many applications in the treatment of diseases of the nervous system.

Toxicology

Toxicology is about the safety of medicines. It is concerned with the nature, mechanisms, and severity of adverse effects of toxins (poisons), drugs and radiation on biological systems, and especially on the human body and farm and domestic animals. Toxicology is related to pharmacology, but concentrates on the harmful effects of chemicals and radiation. It involves biochemistry, molecular biology and physiology.

Clinical toxicologists work with clinical pharmacologists in hospitals, dealing with patients who have been poisoned accidentally or deliberately. They also study the side-effects of drugs and the environmental effects of chemicals. Some toxicologists work for the regulatory bodies, doing toxicity testing on new products before they are licensed, and setting safety limits for the use of chemicals, such as the solvents used in different industries.

Toxicologists also work in industry studying the harmful side-effects of pharmaceuticals, food, and chemicals used in agriculture, and in the petroleum industries and in other industries using chemicals. Production and disposal of harmful substances must be monitored carefully to avoid contamination of the environment and danger to the health of employees.

Some toxicologists work in forensic laboratories to analyse which drugs or poisons have been responsible for a death. They will look for evidence as to which substances are involved, and then trace and isolate samples, which may be in very small quantities. The evidence must be recorded in detail for the police legal services to use in investigating crimes, and toxicologists often have to give their evidence in court.

A few toxicologists work in universities in teaching and in research; for example, investigating biochemical pathways of toxins and the mechanisms by which they exert harmful effects.

Zoology

Zoology today describes and classifies animals, as well as studying animal physiology, development, behaviour, and ecology. Studies of reproductive physiology can help in saving rarer species. Ecological studies in Africa have helped to decide which areas are suitable for animal parks and reserves, as part of a growing interest in improving the management of wild-animal communities. Studying patterns of fish migration may aid in conserving stock. Surveys of animal species are made to assess levels of pollution, and the effects of herbicides and pesticides on animal populations.

Insects are a group of animals of particular importance, and are studied by entomologists. Insect-pest resistance to chemical control is now a major problem. Entomologists are studying insect physiology and neurobiology as part of the drive to develop new pesticides which are based on the biology of chemicals that the insects themselves produce in their nerve cells. They also study the ultrasounds produced by insects.

Some examples of zoological research are: finding out how whales and dolphins avoid the bends when they surface after diving; parasitic infections in wild mammals; and the interaction between parasites and domestic birds. In studying animal development and behaviour, the work of zoologists and experimental psychologists overlap.

The biological sciences also include AGRICULTURE, HORTICULTURE and FORESTRY (*see in* LAND USE INDUSTRIES); Food science and BIOTECHNOLOGY (*see in* MANUFACTURING INDUSTRIES); and PSYCHOLOGY (*see in* SOCIAL AND RELATED SERVICES).

Opportunities for biologists

With biology probably the most popular of the sciences amongst school-leavers, output of graduates has risen steadily, outstripping the supply of jobs for which a degree in biological sciences is directly relevant. At the same time, the number of posts in schools, higher education and research organisations has fallen. To stay in biology-based careers, graduates take posts previously considered non-graduate, largely in university and Health Service laboratories, where nearly all entrants are now graduates. Those with higher degrees are more likely to find related work, but even some of these go into non-scientific employment.

There are never likely to be directly relevant jobs for all biology graduates, but numbers recruited for scientific work did pick up considerably over the last decade. The new public awareness of the importance of 'green' issues has contributed to the demand for biological qualifications. Competition for jobs is still very keen, however, and is likely to remain so. Much depends on the extent, and speed, that industry invests in, develops and exploits the latest biological advances, and on the funding universities and research establishments receive for relevant research.

Employers tend to differentiate between what are often termed 'harder' and 'softer' biological sciences. Biochemists and microbiologists have for some years been in greater demand than botanists or zoologists, particularly for research and development, and in analytical and other test laboratories. Research and development employs people with highly specific training working in teams, rather than general biologists, as the wide-ranging expertise needed is almost impossible for one scientist to gain.

Botanists and zoologists who have specialised in description and classification are at a disadvantage in the employment market, and cuts in more applied agricultural/horticultural research can only make this worse. Work on pest and disease control, and on producing better crops by the newer genetic methods such as cloning, is the exception, but needs a background of molecular biology.

Recent research confirms there will be future shortages of skilled manpower in certain specialist areas of the environmental sciences and in the molecular sciences.

Teaching

While the largest single group of working biologists is almost certainly in teaching, the proportion going into teaching has been falling steadily for some years. At secondary level this will continue for most of the 1990s, but primary-school recruitment could increase. Biological sciences graduates are well suited to primary teaching, where there is an increasing demand for the teaching of science as a core subject along with maths and English in the national curriculum. At secondary level a biological scientist who can also offer maths, physics or chemistry to A-level or Scottish Higher grade is more likely to get a place on a postgraduate training course for teaching.

In higher and further education, recruitment should increase by a small amount towards the end of the century with the planned provision of more places for students. The number of university posts in biological sciences which combine teaching with research is about 2,000 in total, but competition for posts is very severe and candidates would be expected to have a higher degree (PhD) as well as a number of publications.

Biological scientists with first degrees or Higher National Diplomas can apply for research assistant or research technician posts in higher education. There are fewer posts in biology in further education, although more students do study for GCSE exams and BTEC schemes in FE. A small number of biologists teach in agricultural and horticultural colleges, as well as schools of nursing, and colleges teaching physiotherapy, chiropody, or laboratory technology. *See also* EDUCATION AND TEACHING.

Civil Service, executive agencies and related bodies

The government has traditionally been a large employer of biologists. The Ministry of Agriculture, Fisheries and Food (MAFF) takes the largest numbers, both for research such as animal health, fisheries, pest control, and plant pathology, and also for advisory work in the Agricultural Development and Advisory Service. In Scotland these functions are provided by the Department of Agriculture and Fisheries and the Scottish Agricultural Colleges, and in Northern Ireland by the Department of Agriculture. Graduates usually have degrees in biology, biochemistry, botany or microbiology. *See* AGRICULTURE *in* LAND USE INDUSTRIES. The Central Science Laboratory of MAFF and the Horticultural Research Institute employ biologists, biological scienists, biotechnologists, botanists, biochemists and microbiologists. The National Resources Institute (an executive agency) provides scientific services to third-world countries aimed at sustaining the development of renewable natural resources.

The Ministry of Defence in its Defence Engineering and Science Group employs biologists, biochemists, microbiologists and biotechnologists, while the Defence Evaluation and Research Agency (DERA) takes mainly biochemists and physiologists, especially at the Chemical and Biological Defence Sector establishment at Porton Down, and for naval and aviation medicine.

The Department of Health employs biochemists and microbiologists. Biochemists and biotechnologists are employed by the Patent Office. (*See* PATENT WORK *in* THE LEGAL SYSTEM.) Some life scientists are employed by the Laboratory of the Government Chemist (LGC), now an executive agency. Biochemists, botanists, zoologists and microbiologists work for the Forensic Science Service (now an executive agency) or as forensic scientists for the police services in Scotland or the London area.

The British Museum employs biologists in the Natural History section, the Centre for Overseas Pest Research employs mainly zoologists and entomologists, the Tropical Products Institute takes on biologists with various specialisations, and the Forestry Commission takes small numbers of biologists. Some life scientists work for the Health and Safety Executive minimising injuries, death and disease arising from work. *See also in* CENTRAL GOVERNMENT.

Research councils

The main research council for biological work is the Biotechnology and Biological Sciences Research Council (BBSRC) which was formed in 1994 from the former Agricultural and Food Research Council and the biotechnology and biological sciences programmes of the former Science and Engineering Research Council. Research councils employ biological scientists, but research training and a higher degree are normally needed. The supply of biological sciences graduates far outstrips the demand in research and development. In recent years all the councils have had financial difficulties which have resulted in considerable reorganisation.

BBSRC supports over 7,000 scientists, postgraduates and support staff in universities and research institutes. The main scientific themes which are being investigated are biological molecules, how cells work, the genetics and development of organisms, plants and micro-organisms, animals, and the interface of biology with engineering, physics and maths.

A significant proportion of the scientists in agricultural research have degrees in biological subjects (including quite a large proportion of biochemists). They do directed research on improving quality and productivity of agricultural products working in some 30 or so research units. *See also* AGRICULTURE *in* LAND USE INDUSTRIES.

Many of the Medical Research Council's (MRC) 800 non-clinical staff are biologists (including about 180 biochemists and a number of microbiologists), working in one of about 50 units, many attached to hospitals or universities. Research ranges from very fundamental studies in molecular biology through to clinical work. *See also* THE MEDICAL AND DENTAL PROFESSIONS.

The Natural Environment Research Council (NERC) probably has about 200 biologists, including biochemists (out of a total of 1,400-plus scientists), although staff numbers have been falling for a long period. NERC predicts an increasing demand for skilled manpower in the environmental sciences as environmental issues continue to attract public attention and priority.

Biologists at NERC work mainly for the Institute of Terrestrial Ecology, but also for the British Antarctic Survey, the Institute of Oceanography, and the marine and freshwater biological units. Research into a wide range of areas is being supported, including detecting changes in, and modelling, environmental systems such as forests; the dispersal and spread of living organisms; the effects of fish-farming on the environment; the effects of pollution on seals; the feeding habits and population sizes of white whales; and biochemical studies of the processes in the cell nucleus and the relationship between the damage of genetic material and the development of cancer cells.

NERC points to skill shortages in molecular biology, and thus funding of research in this area will be supported. It also identifies new initiatives in biological sciences research in understanding pollutant pathways from land to water, and the study of wildlife diseases. Also a programme of research into Arctic terrestrial ecology has been started. *See in* CAREERS IN CONSERVATION AND THE ENVIRONMENT.

Other research organisations employing biologists include research associations serving individual industries (especially those mentioned below but mainly food); and commercially run contract organisations, some specialising in evaluation and testing of products such as drugs, others doing very advanced research in biotechnology. Privately funded research institutions specialise in particular fields – for example the charities which work on the causes, prevention and treatment of cancer – and these employ a number of biologists.

Hospital services

Hospital services employ graduate biologists, including a high proportion of biochemists, working in clinical specialisms such as virology, haematology, and endocrinology in medical laboratory work, mostly in hospital pathology laboratories. Graduates now go in on three levels; firstly as Chemical PATHOLOGISTS (*see in* SCIENTISTS AND TECHNICIANS IN THE HEALTH SERVICE), who are medical graduates and many of whom have a degree in medicine or a postgraduate clinical qualification such as Member of the Royal College of Pathologists. Secondly graduates enter as Clinical Scientists, with a variety of relevant degree subjects. These pathologists and scientists supervise and check diagnostic testing, carry out the more sophisticated analyses such as immunoassays or analyses using recombinant DNA technology, go over results with medical staff and research and develop better techniques. Thirdly there are MEDICAL LABORATORY SCIENTIFIC OFFICERS (*see in* SCIENTISTS AND TECHNICIANS IN THE HEALTH SERVICE) which is the main grade for new entrants. These are technical staff, providing the clinical biochemistry service in hospitals. Most Medical Laboratory Scientific Officers are now graduate entrants. These officers do the routine analyses of blood, urine and other samples from patients to determine the amounts of substances in the body fluids, such as glucose, proteins and ions (for example, sodium). Much of this is now computer-controlled and automated, but great skill is needed in recording and analysing results, and in detecting possible irregularities in samples.

Scientists specialising in cytology examine samples of human tissue under the microscope to look for abnormalities. Some scientific officers specialise in haematology, for example in regional Blood Transfusion Centres, where they test samples for incompatibility at transfusion, and investigate for defects such as diabetes or infectious organisms in blood samples. In teaching hospitals it is sometimes possible to get short-term contract research assistantships which may offer the chance to work towards a higher degree.The blood transfusion service also employs biologists, but mainly microbiologists.

Most medical research is done in MRC units, but there may be some opportunities to do work on, for example, the nature and mechanism of particular diseases, enzyme defects, epidemiology and disease control.

Clinical biochemists working in the hospital services also teach undergraduate medical students.

Geneticists are employed in advisory services as genetic counsellors to test for and detect hereditary diseases, malformations, cancer and infertility. They culture and study human tissues, and map human chromosomes.

Many public health laboratories are housed in hospitals. *See also* SCIENTISTS AND TECHNICIANS in the HEALTH SERVICE.

Industry

Industry employs biologists in some numbers, in traditional production as well as biotechnology. The industries needing biologists are mostly those which process biological materials, use biological agents to make a product, or make agricultural or medical products (agriculture, horticulture and fishing are also effectively biology-based industries). Some companies use the research, information and advisory services of research associations or contract research laboratories, such as the Flour Milling and Baking Research Association, the Campden Food and Drink Research Association, the Paint Research Association or the British Textile Technology Group. These recruit some life scientists, particularly microbiologists or biochemists.

The pharmaceutical industry is the largest employer of biological scientists for research and development, especially those who have specialised as microbiologists, biochemists, physiologists, and pharmacologists, but with some demand for people who have specialised in immunology, bacteriology, virology, toxicology and parasitology. They are needed mostly for applied research and development, working in multidisciplinary teams on the development and testing of new compounds, including a wide range of biologically based products from antibiotics and vaccines through to antibody diagnostic kits. Biological scientists also evaluate and test products, with some posts in quality control, and in developing production techniques. Pharmaceutical companies, particularly, recruit biologists for MARKETING, technical sales, and purchasing (*see in* BUYING AND SELLING AND RELATED SERVICES). *See also* PHARMACOLOGISTS AND PHARMACISTS *in* SCIENTISTS AND TECHNICIANS IN THE HEALTH SERVICE.

The food and drink industry (*see in* MANUFACTURING INDUSTRIES) (which includes dairies, breweries, and large food retailing chains) employs scientists, including biologists (mainly microbiologists and biochemists), some for research (on standards, preventing contamination, and new products), but mostly in product development, quality control and technical management. The brewing industry (*see in* MANUFACTURING INDUSTRIES) recruits a small number of biochemists and some microbiologists most years. Biochemists can work in areas other than research using their specific expertise in, for example, control of fermentation or food-processing plant, or in developing industrial processes, and can train in production management.

The CHEMICAL INDUSTRIES (*see in* MANUFACTURING INDUSTRIES) has always employed small numbers of biologists (including biochemists), largely in research and development on agrochemicals (insecticides, fungicides and weedkillers) and fertilisers, but chemical firms are also moving into biotechnology. Agrochemical firms also take on biology graduates for MARKETING (*see in* BUYING AND SELLING AND RELATED SERVICES) and Sales. Some biologists work in areas like environmental protection in the oil industry.

The WATER INDUSTRY (*see in* CAREERS IN CONSERVATION AND THE ENVIRONMENT) is responsible for water supply and sewage disposal through the regional water companies and for pollution control of rivers and coastal areas through the new Environment Agency (which includes the former National Rivers Authorities) and the River Purification Boards in Scotland. Biologists (including biochemists) are employed in aquatic biology, fishery administration and management, pollution control, weed and insect control, marine ecology, toxicity testing, and microbiology.

Overseas

Developing and other tropical countries still have major problems to solve in agriculture, forestry and health, for which biologists are employed. The majority of posts are either in government service or in overseas universities and are usually on a contract basis (*see* WORKING OVERSEAS). Some commercial organisations with interests overseas have research programmes on crop improvement and production. There may be short-term projects in countries too dependent on particular crops (sugar, for example) and which must diversify their economy to meet changing world markets.

AGRICULTURE and HORTICULTURE (*see in* LAND USE INDUSTRIES) have always taken small numbers of biologists, mostly for practical management, but a few for research and development. Now the success of plants developed by genetic engineering is creating new opportunities. Other possible growth areas include research to enhance, or find new uses for, plants which will grow in very dry conditions, which research work at Kew Gardens is investigating. Small numbers of biologists, especially those who have specialised in ecology, are finding CAREERS IN CONSERVATION AND THE ENVIRONMENT.

Biologists are just as well qualified as other scientists to go into areas such as LIBRARY INFORMATION AND WORK, PATENT WORK (*see in* THE LEGAL SYSTEM), and technical writing (*see in* MEDIA CAREERS). Some biological scientists go on to take professional training in other areas of commerce and industry.

Some technicians work in Physiological Measurement, training in the use of complex electronic equipment to measure characteristics in audiology, cardiology, neurophysiology and respiratory function. They usually entered directly from school, but some graduates become Physiological Measurement Technicians after a year's training on the job. *See* SCIENTISTS AND TECHNICIANS IN THE HEALTH SERVICE.

Studying biological sciences

First-degree courses offer the student increasing variety, which makes choice hard. Given that this is one of the most rapidly developing of the sciences at present, there is a strong argument for choosing flexible courses which allow students to defer any choice of specialisation for as long as possible, which can be as late as the end of the second year. Anyone intending to teach is generally advised to study as broadly as possible, but it is usual for anyone planning to do research to specialise at some stage, although there is an argument for joint honours in two biological subjects, given the interdisciplinary nature of much current research. To gain the best chance to do research in a specific area, it is advisable to choose a course in a university department doing advanced research in that field.

Although the boundaries between the traditional divisions of biology have become increasingly blurred, it is still common to specialise at some stage in a named branch of the biological sciences. There are various choices to make, such as whether to specialise in a branch of biology from the start of the course, or start with a broadly based introduction to biological sciences generally. Some courses continue broadly, but usually give a choice of topics for advanced study in the final year. In other courses, students are given a thorough grounding in the common aspects of the biological sciences, then go on to specialise in one or two of the traditional branches. To benefit from a degree in biological sciences, a sound background in chemistry and/or physics and a reasonable level of mathematical skill are necessary.

In 1993/94 there were 2,034 Biology, 134 Botany, 719 Zoology, 233 Genetics, 411 Microbiology, and 1,097 Biochemistry graduates.

Aquatic, marine and freshwater biology

Aquatic Biology/Marine Biology/Freshwater Biology is taught in first-degree courses at the following universities: Aberdeen, Buckingham, Glasgow, Liverpool, Newcastle, St Andrews, Stirling, Wales Aberystwyth, Wales Bangor, Wales Swansea. Plymouth University offers Fisheries Science.

Biochemistry

Because biochemistry requires a more thorough grounding in chemistry than other biological sciences, it is more usual to specialise from the start of the course, although it is possible to specialise after a year studying biology and/or chemistry. At some universities it is possible to study the applied options, e.g. industrial biochemistry, medical or clinical biochemistry, toxicology, and pharmaceutical biochemistry.

Graduates can convert to biochemistry after a degree in another subject via a postgraduate course. Most graduate biochemists go on to more advanced postgraduate study and specialise, i.e. in clinical, molecular, agricultural or analytical biochemistry, steroid endocrinology or biochemical pharmacology. Courses in biochemical engineering train biochemists in the engineering skills used by industry to exploit biological processes. Nutritional Biochemistry is available at Nottingham University.

Biophysics

Biophysics can be studied at East Anglia, Liverpool John Moores and East London universities; Molecular Biophysics at Leeds University.

Botany or plant biology/sciences

Botany is taught as a specialist honours subject at about 30 universities, and is a possible specialisation in many other courses in biological sciences. There is Plant Physiology at Lancaster and Aberystwyth; Marine Botany at Bangor; Molecular Plant Biology at Leeds; and Environmental Plant Science at Reading.

Ecology

Ecology forms part of most biological sciences courses, and is offered as a first-degree course at the following universities: Aberdeen, Anglia Polytechnic, Dundee, Sussex and Bangor.

Genetics

Genetics is available at about 20 universities. Dundee, London King's College and Sussex offer courses in Molecular Genetics, and Nottingham and University College London offer Human Genetics.

Microbiology

Microbiology is available either as a single honours course at about 45 universities, or it may be studied as a major option within a biological sciences degree. There are also degree courses in Environmental Microbiology at Aberdeen and Surrey; Microbial Biotechnology at Liverpool and Surrey; Food Microbiology at Nottingham; Virology at Warwick; and Medical Microbiology at Surrey and University College London.

Molecular biology/ cell biology

Molecular biology is available at Nottingham, Portsmouth and York universities; Cell biology is available at East Anglia, Essex, London King's College, London Queen Mary and Westfield, University College London, Manchester, St Andrews, and Aberystwyth.

Physiology

Physiology, Anatomical Science and Neuroscience are all available as separate degree studies.

Toxicology

Toxicology can be studied as a single degree subject or as a joint degree.

Zoology, or animal science

Zoology is available at most universities teaching biological sciences. More unusual courses are Developmental Biology at Glasgow; Entomology at London Imperial College; and Parasitology at both Glasgow and Imperial College.

Other related subjects

Other related subjects include Biometrics, which is the application of mathematics and statistics to biological problems.

Professional qualification

The Institute of Biology's graduate examinations are considered to be equivalent to an honours degree by most employers. The Institute's own examinations are in two parts: the first is divided between general biology and a special subject, with part 2 devoted entirely to the special subject. Courses leading to the Institute's own graduate examination are offered at about a dozen colleges in the UK, normally on a part-time basis. Corporate full membership of the Institute gives the status of Chartered Biologist (CBiol), which is recognised throughout the European Community.

Technician level

Technician-level qualification is via a BTEC/SCOTVEC Higher National award, which can also be the first stage to professional qualification (*above*) but well over a third go on to a degree. About 20 colleges of further and higher education offer BTEC Higher National Diploma courses in science (applied biology). Two sciences (preferably biology or chemistry) should have been studied with a pass in one.

Further information

The Institute of Biology, the Biochemical Society, the Association of Clinical Biochemists, the Society for General Microbiology and the Society for Applied Bacteriology, all of which produce booklets.

Contents

Mathematics, Statistics and Economics

(CLCI: QOG, QOJ, QOK)

Mathematics

Mathematics is a scientific 'language' or shorthand, describing complex situations relatively simply and precisely. It can be used as a tool to analyse and tackle all kinds of problems. It is a living and growing language. New mathematical techniques are being developed and refined all the time and, coupled with the use of sophisticated computers, make it possible to do research and solve real problems that would have been impossible only a few years ago.

Although it is common to talk about 'being' a mathematician, in fact most work employing people trained in mathematics actually applies mathematical skills to solving someone else's problems ranging from theoretical physics and life insurance to environmental studies. Increasingly organisations are turning to maths to predict and to solve problems, but mathematical skills are usually not sufficient in themselves. Mathematicians must also be able to communicate their results often to the mathematically semi-literate.

Opportunities for mathematicians

Theoretical mathematicians are primarily concerned with pure and abstract mathematical concepts and work mainly in universities, although some work for industrial research associations and government research establishments.

Many mathematicians work in industry in pharmaceutical research and development, and environmental research and monitoring, but there are rarely enough good mathematicians and statisticians to fill all the available jobs.

In industry, the main employers are research-intensive firms in, for example, aero-engineering, electronics and telecommunications, chemicals, and firms making and using large-scale power equipment. Mathematicians here work as members of R&D or design teams, and have to become fairly expert in the field in which they are working. They make theoretical predictions of what will happen to a particular engineering design under given conditions, help to calculate complex stresses, analyse what has happened in the experimental test bed or wind tunnel, or make mathematical models of the possible behaviour of a liquid as it is processed.

Examples include:

- a study of the breakdown of sewage by micro-organisms;
- models of polymer melt processing (e.g. film blowing);
- an analysis of how cracks in metals grow;
- predicting the aerodynamic performance of an aircraft wing;
- modelling the behaviour of a gas turbine.

Mathematicians in industry are expected to be flexible and arrive at a speedy solution to a problem.

In production, mathematicians work on machine and production scheduling, systematic stock provision, and developing new control systems.

Government departments and executive agencies employ a number of mathematicians. These include Horticulture Research International, the Office for National Statistics, Defence Engineering and Science Group, Defence Evaluation and Research Agency, Government Actuaries Department, Government Communications HQ (GCHQ), Home Office, Inland Revenue, Information Technology Services Agency, Patent Office, HM Treasury, and the Scottish Office. The mathematical range of work varies considerably from helping to model the atmosphere in the Meteorological Office, to working on analytical tasks, linear algebra, number theory or finite field theory at GCHQ. *See also* CENTRAL GOVERNMENT.

Organisations of all kinds use mathematicians to help solve complex organisational and business problems. Job titles can vary, and many people using mathematical techniques may not regard themselves primarily as mathematicians. Operational researchers for example might be using mathematical modelling to solve management and operational problems such as the optimum place to site a distribution depot (*see* OPERATIONAL RESEARCH *in* MANAGEMENT SERVICES). Computer applications engineers use mathematical models and develop computer systems to solve scientific and engineering problems (*see* INFORMATION TECHNOLOGY AND COMPUTER WORK). Actuaries use probability theory to assess the degree of risk and calculate life insurance policies (*see* ACTUARIAL *in* FINANCIAL CAREERS).

Mathematical skills are also important for other aspects of financial work such as taxation (*see in* CENTRAL GOVERNMENT), ACCOUNTANCY and INSURANCE (*see in* FINANCIAL CAREERS).

Many mathematicians combine their mathematical skills with teaching and work in universities, schools or colleges.

Qualifications and training

Degree courses

Mathematics is extensively studied for first degrees at almost all universities. A-levels should normally include maths, and universities often prefer two separate passes.

Mathematics at university can sometimes be quite abstract in the sense that pure mathematicians spend more of their time developing concepts and theories, and looking for underlying patterns which, for example, explain something about all prime numbers, rather than something about a single prime number, and instead of studying immediate applications to other subjects. However, mathematics also has many applications; and abstract mathematical ideas developed in one century or decade have a habit of turning into theories with a real existence – as wave equations accurately predicted radio waves.

Degree courses are on a different level from sixth-form studies, tackling complete theories rather than formulae and single patterns. Much time is spent on basic rules – axioms, theorems, etc. – using logical argument and intuition and even creative imagination, to devise and prove theorems, and then use these theorems to prove others.

The first year, and usually the second year too, is a broadly based study of what mathematicians see as the central and most important areas of maths. On most courses this still means roughly equal time to pure and applied maths, although the distinctions between them are becoming blurred, as topics like differential equations, probability theory and numerical analysis cross the boundary and are important in both. Mathematicians are always creating new links between what are often thought of as separate parts of maths; as one mathematician said, 'it is commonplace to start with a problem in analysis, turn it into topology, reduce it to algebra, and solve it by number theory'.

Central to most mathematics courses on the pure side are areas like algebra, and analysis, which continues calculus on a more theoretical level. Applied maths takes the ideas, theorems and techniques of pure maths and uses them to solve problems in the real world. Applied maths traditionally deals almost entirely with applications in other sciences, and in engineering technology, but today it is also applied in areas like OPERATIONAL RESEARCH (*see in* MANAGEMENT SERVICES), games theory, linear programming and 'catastrophe' theory, otherwise called the theory of discontinuous processes.

Most mathematics courses include at least some statistics, and for some a large part of applied maths is statistics and operational research, and most professional statisticians study maths. Statistics covers basic theories and techniques – of probability, for example. Courses generally include some computer science, and virtually all make use of computer packages for statistical analysis.

Maths is a very large subject, and most courses offer a considerable choice of topics to study. The range of subjects which can be combined with mathematics for joint honours is now very wide and includes education, computer science, operational research, economics, experimental psychology, and management sciences, as well as the more conventional combinations with physics, chemistry and so on, all providing a useful basis for many careers.

'First destination' in mathematics, 1994:

total graduating	*2,683*
overseas students	36
research, etc.	491
teacher training	279
law and Bar exams	11
other training	130
believed unemployed 31 December	217
temporary work	108
permanent UK work	1,000
employers	
engineering industry	42
commerce (not finance)	245
accountancy	239
banking/insurance	214
public utilities	42
oil, chemicals, etc.	18
Civil Service	42
higher/further education	19
local government	17
other manufacturing	21
functions	
management services	149
financial work	464
scientific/engineering R&D	44
administration/operational management	68
marketing, etc.	47
personnel/social, etc.	24
teaching/lecturing	21
scientific support	7

Note the very high number of mathematicians that go into financial work and management services.

While mathematics is primarily a graduate career, it is possible to work in a mathematical environment without a degree, and there are several useful qualifications at BTEC/SCOTVEC Higher National level which combine mathematics with statistics, computing or physics.

Professional body

The Institute of Mathematics and its Applications has a membership of about 6,000, with grades of individual membership ranging from student to chartered mathematician.

Further information

The Institute of Mathematics and its Applications.

Statistics

Statistics is very closely related to mathematics, and it is very difficult to separate them, because statistics relies heavily on mathematical techniques. Statistics is mostly used in analysing complex data, and therefore means knowing how to ask the right questions, and how to produce information which will help in decision-making and clear up problems of uncertainty.

Statistics can be used to test hypotheses, to plan experiments, to chart changes in experimental results, to produce indices. Statistics can be used in numerous ways:

- to provide an exact picture in number form of, for instance, the use of a particular street by traffic at different times of the day, showing the ratio of cars to commercial vehicles, which can help in planning new traffic systems;
- to give an accurate picture of voters' attitudes to a political policy using sophisticated 'sampling' techniques;
- to predict using probability theory;
- to monitor the level of pollution in rivers, check quality control standards in industry, and collect and interpret data on hospital admissions and treatment.

New fields are opening up in biometry and risk management.

Opportunities for statisticians

Statistical work is carried out in many organisations and research establishments, such as the Civil Service, the Health Service and large industrial and commercial concerns, particularly those involved in pharmaceutical research and development and environmental research and monitoring.

Over 600 professional statisticians (known collectively as the 'Statistician Group') work in 30 government departments and agencies. These include the Ministry of Agriculture; Fisheries and Food; Office for National Statistics (ONS); HM Customs and Excise; Defence Analytical Services Agency; Department for Education and Employment; Department of the Environment; Department of Social Security; Foreign and Commonwealth Office; Government Actuary's Department; Department of Health; Health and Safety Executive; Home Office; Inland Revenue; Overseas Development Administration; Department of Trade and Industry; Transport Research Laboratory; Department of Transport and HM Treasury. Increasing EC involvement could entail overseas travel, while international statistical work provides some opportunities to work abroad.

The Central Statistical Office merged on 1 April 1996 with the Office of Population Censuses and Surveys (OPCS) to form a new government agency and government department, the Office for National Statistics. The ONS maintains a central database of key economic and social statistics, drawn from the whole range of statistics produced by government, and produced to common classifications, definitions and standards. It advises the government on statistical issues and priorities.

A postgraduate qualification in statistics is an advantage for statisticians working in industry, particularly the pharmaceutical industry. Here statisticians analyse the results of experiments in chemistry, biology, pharmacy and toxicology, and on animals, to assess the effectiveness and safety of testing new drugs on humans.

Biometry is a new and growing field covering research and development in environmental fields, food science and medicine. Most statisticians in this field work for research institutes, or in the agrochemical or food industries. The largest employer is the Institute of Arable Crop Research and the Scottish Agricultural Statistics Service.

The Medical Research Council, the Public Health Laboratory Service and most large hospitals employ statisticians. Medical statisticians are largely concerned with monitoring aspects of the health service to predict future demand or to analyse drugs and disease.

Many statisticians also work in MANAGEMENT SERVICES and ACTUARIAL work (*see in* FINANCIAL CAREERS). *See also* MATHEMATICS *above*.

Recruitment and entry

Assistant Statisticians in the Civil Service are recruited with a first or second class honours degree containing a minimum of 25% formal statistical training, or a Graduate Diploma of the Royal Statistical Society, or a postgraduate qualification with at least 25% formal statistics, or equivalent qualification. The fast-stream recruitment scheme for those with exceptional ability is applicable for Assistant Statisticians and Trainee Statisticians.

Industry prefers statisticians to have a good honours degree or a postgraduate qualification, and there are rarely enough good statisticians to fill the available jobs.

Qualifications and training

There are a range of degree courses in or including statistics. In 1994 there were 274 graduates in statistics. Of these, 109 entered employment and 73 went on for further study. Of those entering employment, 7 went into the Civil Service and 65 went into commerce, banking, accountancy, etc. Of the 92 postgraduates in 1994, 18 went into research and development, 47 into management services and 9 into financial work.

Postgraduate courses in statistics, and specialist aspects such as biometry or medical statistics, are available.

Entry to the Royal Statistical Society's Ordinary Certificate examinations is possible with good GCSE/SCE passes or equivalent. The Higher Certificate follows on from the Ordinary Certificate and may be accepted for degree course entry, or for entry to the Society's Graduate Diploma, which is widely recognised as a degree equivalent.

Professional membership of the Society also requires appropriate experience; but it is possible for anyone to join as an ordinary Fellow and there are about 6,000 Fellows altogether.

The Institute of Statisticians merged with the Royal Statistical Society at the beginning of 1993, and all former Institute of Statisticians activities have now been taken over by the Royal Statistical Society.

Further information

The Royal Statistical Society.

Economics

Economics is based on the assumption that a society can never fully satisfy everybody, that however high living standards are, people will want to go on improving theirs, and that people's wants (as opposed to basic needs) – for food and clothing, houses and cars, holidays and entertainment, etc. – are unlimited. Given that resources are finite, this is clearly an impossible goal. Economists therefore say that resources are 'scarce', not because there is necessarily any apparent shortage now, but because the potential level of demand cannot be met. 'Resources' can mean finance, raw materials, goods of all kinds, services, even people.

And so economists study the way available resources are allocated, by individuals and collectively: by businesses, by industries, by local communities, by the nation (government), even by families. They study the way such choices are, and can be, made: how to decide who should have what; what to produce and in what quantities; the most economic way of providing goods and services, and the often wide-ranging effects of particular decisions.

Everyone makes economic decisions. Individuals may have to decide whether the cost of maintaining an ageing car is becoming so high that it would be more economic to buy a new one, and whether it is more economic to save up for it or to buy it on credit. Firms may have to decide, for example, at which point (if any) the cost of investment in new, automated machinery can be covered from extra sales and will improve profits, perhaps partly by cutting labour costs, or whether the price at which the goods would have to be sold would be uneconomic for the consumer.

Governments, of course, make major economic decisions, presumably based on their interpretation of voters' views, and on whether they believe they will achieve greater economic success and their political goals by following free-market, or centrally planned economic policies (or a mixture of both). One of the central economic problems of the 1990s is clearly whether it is possible to control inflation and unemployment at the same time, and if so, how.

Economists are not decision- or policy-makers, yet they assist in formulating policy. They are expert advisers, providing the information and analyses on which policy-makers can work. Just as they do not try to suggest any limits to consumer demand, so they do not tell governments or firms how to choose their priorities. Economists observe, chart and monitor the choices made, attempt to produce theories which explain economic behaviour and use them to analyse and attempt to predict the consequences of the choices made and what the alternatives are. They may also show how to achieve particular results.

Economics is a relatively young science, and the methods used are often still experimental with few agreed conclusions: not all the workings of economic systems are fully understood. Economists have to work on factual information and they are always trying to obtain better and more exact information on which to build a picture of what actually happens in the economy, or one part of it, or in a firm's business affairs. The number of facts and influences which economists can build into their models of the economy or the firm is almost limitless, and a major problem is the sheer complexity of economic systems. They begin with very simple models of what happens in an economic system and step by step add more proven facts to get closer to the real level of complexity. But it is difficult. In the sciences, a 'fact' (e.g. the speed of light), once established, stays constant. In economics, 'facts' may be variables and change frequently: a lower birth-rate and rising number of older people, for example, are changing some of the criteria for allocating resources in health and social services. It is not always easy to decide what all the factors are in analysing a given economic problem – such as whether or not reducing benefits would reduce numbers unemployed.

Economics also involves making assumptions about the way people behave, which is obviously not so easily mapped or predicted as the behaviour of an atom of hydrogen. Economists also need time to test their theories. As it is clearly impossible to create lab conditions to test economic theories, they must either wait for real events to prove them right or wrong or work on a period in the past and test them there.

Economists work, like scientists, by observing; by recording and analysing data; and by developing possible theories. They also build assumptions and try to work out logical consequences from their research. Economic analysis uses mathematical techniques extensively: theories can be expressed better in mathematical terms and their meaning worked out mathematically. Statistical analysis is used to make sense of the data collected and can help to decide the probability that certain economic events had particular causes – for instance, that increasing indirect taxes reduced consumption. Economists have to write up their results, sometimes in technical language for publication in academic journals and books, more often in language more readily understood by the lay reader, in reports for firms or government, for example. They may have to present a case personally and be able to make a case for their arguments. They work closely with administrators and with other specialists, particularly statisticians.

Opportunities for economists

Most professional economists combine research with teaching in a university. University economists can and do also act as advisers and consultants on economic affairs to outside bodies, some running their own intelligence units.

However, many economists work full-time as professional advisers, often in multidisciplinary teams under the generic title of 'economic intelligence unit' for a wide range of organisations. Most public bodies (e.g. the Bank of England), and major utilities (British Coal, British Gas, and British Telecom) have their own economic intelligence units. And so do the larger commercial and merchant banks (with staff ranging from three up to 40) and stockbrokers, where information systems and/or forecasting are needed to decide where investment should be made and sophisticated computer-based analysis used.

Larger industrial and commercial firms may employ economists to advise on, for example, the effects of government policies, or trade trends, or the implications of technological innovation; to make detailed forecasts on marketing, or the economic advantages or disadvantages of, for example, changing production methods or sites; or to provide intelligence reports and help analyse statistical data. Management consultants, CBI, the TUC and major unions also employ economists.

Economists can become economic journalists on newspapers and magazines, and on radio and television (*see in* MEDIA CAREERS) and in independent economic intelligence units, but numbers are small. Professional economists move around; from, for example, government service or journalism to academic life and back again.

The Government Economic Service, which gives expert advice to ministers and senior civil servants, employs about 500 economists (1996). The Service is centrally managed. Its staff work in nearly all the major departments and have the opportunity to transfer between them. The largest number (90) work in the Treasury.

Treasury economists prepare short- and medium-term projections on how the economy may develop, mostly using a large econometric model of it. They also analyse the consequences (in terms of the growth of the economy, inflation, unemployment, the balance of payments, etc.) of policy proposals (e.g. plans for public expenditure). Treasury economists advise on specific policy questions, including domestic monetary policy, fiscal policy, and the effects of taxation; and on international issues, including liaison with IMF, OECD and the EU. They also provide general briefings for ministers and other officials.

In the Department of Social Security a team of economists analyses and advises on the impact of the social security system on the labour market, and on issues concerning pensions and benefits. They analyse and review policies affecting particular groups of beneficiaries and assess and monitor the effects of social policies. They have made cohort studies of the unemployed and an econometric analysis of retirement. They advise on finance problems and assist in evaluating medical developments on a cost–benefit and cost-effectiveness basis.

In the Department of Trade and Industry, economists provide economic analysis and briefing on macroeconomic policy and current and future development in the UK and the world economy, particularly as they affect UK industry and commerce. They advise on a range of international economic questions including UK trade performance, EU issues, export promotion, and international trade policy, and on Eastern Europe. They also advise on regional and enterprise policies, on innovation and new technologies, on sectoral and company issues, and on competition, regulatory, consumer protection and privatisation issues.

The 30 Department of the Environment economists are concerned with a wide range of issues including environmental protection, housing, local government, the water industry, inner cities, and nature and the countryside. In the environmental protection area they advise on economic, efficient ways of allocating resources to reduce pollution in air, water and land (for example, through price incentives and market mechanisms). In housing they provide advice and analysis on demand for social housing and means of finance for greater effective consumer choice. In local government they advise and work on systems for distribution of local authority grants, local taxation systems, the community charge and the revenue support grant. Research officers (as opposed to economists) in the Civil Service may be involved both in economic and sociological research, and in industrial intelligence, and analyse and interpret data for policy-planning.

The newly formed Department for Education and Employment has 30 economists who work on a wide range of issues: from the general economics of training, and labour market analysis, of skills and trends; through evaluation of training programmes and monitoring of the Employment Service; to forecasting staying-on rates in education and demand for vocational training; or departmental strategy and international issues.

A further 40 economists work in the Overseas Development Administration, which manages British aid to 150 developing countries. About 40% of ODA economists work overseas.

International organisations such as the United Nations agencies, the World Bank, and the International Monetary Fund – which work extensively on the economic problems of developing countries – and the administrative offices and various organisations of the European Union, all employ economic advisers.

Work in other organisations is mainly in economic intelligence and/or forecasting, linked to the interests of the particular employer. Few employers do primary economic research on anything like the scale of the government economic service or the universities. The economist mostly forecasts and makes predictions on published or unpublished data from other sources, and in some organisations the work shades off into a form of economic public relations.

An economics degree is, of course, a good basis for careers in related areas like OPERATIONAL RESEARCH (*and other* MANAGEMENT SERVICES), ACCOUNTANCY, BANKING, INSURANCE, investment analysis, taxation (*see in* FINANCIAL CAREERS), MARKETING and MARKET RESEARCH (*see in* BUYING, SELLING AND RELATED SERVICES), or indeed any career for which an understanding of economic affairs is useful. (*See in* BUYING, SELLING AND RELATED SERVICES; *and in* FINANCIAL CAREERS.)

Qualifications and training

Economics is taught mainly at first- and higher-degree levels, but is also a significant element in a wide range of business studies and business-related professional training courses. *See in* ADMINISTRATION, BUSINESS MANAGEMENT AND OFFICE WORK.

Degree courses

Degree courses are offered by the majority of universities, either as a single honours subject, as the major subject after a broad introductory course in social sciences, in a two-subject degree course, or in modular programmes.

Some provide options within economics to give practical training for what may be considered related careers, e.g. integrating accountancy with economics to give some exemption from professional examinations, while others include less formal options in these subjects. Some courses are more rigorously mathematical or quantitatively based than others, some specialising extensively in mathematical economics, or econometrics, but it is possible to take options in econometrics as part of most economics degree courses. Many courses at the newer universities, the former polytechnics, strongly emphasise applied economics.

'First destinations' in economics, 1994:

total graduating	*2,837*
destination unknown	286
overseas students	360
research, etc.	374
teacher training/other non-degree courses	168
believed unemployed 31 December	208
temporary work	136
permanent UK work	1,118
not available for employment	131
employers	
accountancy	318
banking/insurance/finance	324
other commerce	181
Civil Service	30
local government	39
public utilities and transport	32
oil and chemicals	29
engineering	35
other manufacturing	48
higher/further education	14
Armed Forces	4
entertainment, leisure	17
functions	
financial work	647
marketing, etc.	107
administration/operational management	104
management services	80
personnel/social, etc.	23

Entry: Maths is the most common requirement at A-level. In October 1995, 4,685 students were accepted for university courses. The average A-level 'score' for entry was 20+ (or BBC–BCC). These figures refer to England, Wales and Northern Ireland. Since students in Scottish universities are admitted to faculties rather than departments, identical statistics are not kept. Average entry grades, however, were four or five Bs at Higher Grade.

Postgraduate study

A master's degree is becoming increasingly necessary to work as an economist with most organisations. The Government Economic Service sponsors a small number of non-economics graduates each year through postgraduate courses in economics.

Training for professional economists leads to specialisation in, for example, development studies, econometrics, fiscal studies, industrial or regional economics, economic statistics, or economics of education.

Further information

The Society of Business Economists, the Economist Management Group, HM Treasury.

Contents

Earth and Space Science

(CLCI: QOL, YAB)

Geoscience

Geology or geoscience is the study of the structure, evolution and dynamics of the Earth, and of the natural mineral and energy resources that it contains, from its beginnings to the present day. What happens to the Earth is largely controlled by changes deep inside it, and these obviously cannot be observed or recorded directly. However, what happens is recorded in the rocks which make up the Earth's crust, and so geologists or geoscientists study Earth's history using the crust as though it were a set of historical documents.

Geoscientists study the make-up, arrangement and origins of the rocks which form the Earth's crust, and the processes involved in the evolution of its present structure. To build a complete record of the sequence of events, they must disentangle what happened when rocks were originally formed, from later events which may have changed them.

To a geoscientist, all natural, non-living, solid material found in or at the Earth's surface is a 'rock' of some kind or another – peat and mud as well as granite and slate.

Geoscience involves much detective work, fitting hard-won evidence together, and theory-building and testing based on the evidence. The geological model of the Earth's history has grown enormously in the last two decades, from evidence confirming the theory of 'plate tectonics' and 'continental drift'. Geoscientists are sure that today's continents are drifting fragments of an ancient 'supercontinent', and that the outer layer of the Earth is made up of rigid plates in constant motion. They have plotted in detail the pattern of drift for the last 200 million years.

Geoscience is generally broken-down into clearly defined topics:

- *Physical geology* studies rock structures and processes which shape the Earth's surface: the work of gravity, the atmosphere, weathering, wind, water, ice, rivers, and the sea - the processes of denudation or erosion, and deposition or building up.
- *Petrology* studies the nature, make-up, textures and origins of igneous, metamorphic and sedimentary rocks, and of mineral ores.
- *Mineralogy* studies the make-up and physical characteristics (including crystal forms) of naturally formed substances with definite chemical compositions and definite atomic structures (minerals), e.g. diamond and graphite.
- *Sedimentology* studies the processes which form sedimentary rocks.
- *Stratigraphy* is the historical study of the rocks that make up the Earth's crust, their relationship to each other, their structure, how they are grouped chronologically, their lithology and the conditions involved in their formation, and their fossil contents.
- *Palaeontology* and *palaeobotany* trace the history of life on Earth and the structure and relationships between different kinds of organisms. Palaeontology studies them in fossil form.
- *Tectonics* and structural geology specialise in rock structures.
- *Geophysics* is the use of physical measurements of such as gravity, magnetism, electricity, radioactivity and seismic waves, to determine the physical structure of the Earth, and its age.
- *Geochemistry* is the study of the behaviour of the elements during igneous and sedimentary processes.

As with all subjects, there are applied aspects to geoscience. A very high percentage of the materials we use in everyday life, ranging from coal and cosmetics to wire and water, are derived either directly or indirectly from the Earth, and geological techniques are used to find them. Some of the most important applications are:

- Geophysical exploration (e.g., seismic surveying) to investigate subsurface structure, for oil, coal, and mineral exploration, and for large engineering projects.
- Engineering geology investigates and reports on the physical condition of sites for dams, roads, tunnels, etc. Geoscientists study the soil, slope stability, and drainage to predict whether the construction project will be manageable or catastrophic.
- Both hydrology and hydrogeology are concerned with the distribution and exploitation of naturally occurring water, and particularly underground water, supplies. Hydrology is mainly concerned with the physical and chemical processes involved, whereas the focus of hydrogeology is the geological factors that control the

distribution and extraction of groundwater supplies, and the potential pathways for groundwater contamination from surface sources of pollution. Applied studies of specific groundwater regimes by hydrogeologists often raise general scientific problems about the physical and chemical processes operating in the ground, which are then pursued by hydrologists.

Hydrogeology is an expanding field. Hydrogeologists play a vital role in the assessment of underground water resources, particularly in desert countries; and they play a significant role in determining the safety of landfill and nuclear waste disposal sites to prevent water seepage into rivers or the drinking water supply.

- Environmental geology encompasses waste disposal arrangements, pollution through seepage, and coastal erosion.
- Economic geology concentrates on aspects needed by mineral industries, the ore and other deposits, and their nature and origins. It includes, for example, assessing the economic values of particular reserves and the cost of mining them.

Some areas of study are related to hazard. For example,

- Seismology monitors faults in the Earth's crust and earthquakes. Observing the behaviour of the shock waves generated helps geophysicists to predict earthquakes more reliably.
- Volcanology is the study and measurement of active volcanoes. By monitoring the behaviour of volcanoes geoscientists can predict eruptions.

Opportunities for professional geoscientists

Opportunities in geoscience are very closely tied to the level of economic activity worldwide. Demand for professional geoscientists is erratic, and generally, so far as industry is concerned, tied to the availability of the enormous funds it takes to prospect, and whether or not companies think they can recover the cost and make a profit within a reasonable period. Projects therefore close down if oil or mineral prices fall, reopen when they improve. Because the hydrocarbons industry is the main employer of geoscientists, one of the most reliable indicators is the number of seismic field crews operating in the United States. (This statistic is published regularly in the scientific journal *Geophysics* published by the Society of Exploration Geophysicists). Political and other events also affect policy.

If the global economy continues to grow over the next few years, job prospects for geoscientists in the hydrocarbons industry should continue to pick up. This will continue to be the main field of employment for geoscientists, but growth areas for employment include the environmental field (e.g., planning, waste disposal, contaminated land) and water supply (groundwater resources, pollution, etc.). There are about 6,000 geoscientists employed in the UK, and about half are working abroad for UK-based companies.

Although the number of long-term, permanent posts abroad is now fairly small, most professional geoscientists still spend at least part of their working lives in the field, moving around the world a lot, in more and more remote areas, under difficult physical conditions. Generally this is in their earlier years, since promotion brings more desk- and office work. But in, for instance, oil exploration and production, the amount of fieldwork needed is falling, and more use is being made of the computerised data, obtained through satellite imagery, air photography, photogeology, airborne geophysics and remote-sensing techniques.

In the oil, mining and quarrying industries geoscientists work in exploration – surveying and surface-mapping in geologically promising areas of the world from the Arctic to the tropics, looking for new mineral deposits and working out the size of the reserves. In the oil industry, geoscientists analyse geological data and recommend which areas to bid for exploration licenses and then try to pinpoint the optimum place(s) to test drill. They log or analyse the material brought up by the test drills, decide whether to continue or abandon a test and, in production, work out where to site development wells. Geophysical, or seismic, surveying and well-logging is increasingly done by specialist service companies. Most oil firms have their own research labs, providing analytical services for their operating staff, and theoretical studies to improve ways of predicting where oil may be found.

In mining production geoscientists use core drillings to estimate the extent of the reserves, and suggest the most economic way to mine, and how to develop the mine safely. They map open pits and underground workings and update the maps daily; plan the development of the mine using three-dimensional pictures obtained from sampling the grade, composition and depth of the ore; and solve any day-to-day problems caused by faulting. Mining geologists work closely with mining engineers. The mining and quarrying industries are dominated by large multinational companies, and most opportunities are abroad.

In construction, engineering geologists work mostly for consulting civil engineers, specialist site investigation consultants, and the small number of construction firms specialising in foundation or ground engineering. In addition to examining sites to see if they are suitable for buildings, dams, tunnels, underground storage, etc., and checking on stability where slopes, etc. are involved, geoscientists also assess rocks and soils for use as construction materials.

The largest single employer in the UK is the British Geological Survey (BGS) which is responsible to government for the UK geological survey both onshore and offshore, and for providing a national geoscience information service. It employs (1996) 523 geoscientists, both on its own surveys, and under contract to other governments and industry.

Government departments or agencies employing geoscientists include the Department of the Environment, Building Research Establishment, and Department of Trade and Industry. Geoscientists are also employed at various institutes, such as the Institute of Oceanographic Sciences,

Institute of Hydrology and with bodies such as the British Antarctic Survey. The Transport Research Laboratory was privatised in 1996.

The water industry absorbs increasing numbers of geoscientists. Hydrogeologists are concerned with evaluating and extracting water from aquifers and avoiding groundwater contamination by waste, fertilisers and other pollutants. They also help to locate safe sites for the underground disposal of hazardous radiation waste, nuclear power stations and landfill sites. Hydrogeologists work for the British Geological Survey, water companies and the new Environmental Agency (Envage), created in 1996, which includes the former National Rivers Authority.

Hydrologists map and chart the distribution of water and disposition of sediments, and collect precipitation data. Their primary preoccupation is with surface water, and at the Institute of Hydrology they maintain the Surface Water Archive. Most organisations concerned with water supply will employ a small number of hydrologists. There are increasing opportunities in consultancy work for both hydrologists and hydrogeologists. *See also* CAREERS IN CONSERVATION AND THE ENVIRONMENT.

Other work for geoscientists includes teaching and lecturing, working in local government planning departments, or working with environmental bodies. A few geologists are employed in scientific museums.

Geoscience is generally thought of as an all-graduate profession, but over 3,500 technical staff work in geoscience. More than half work in the oil industry with the rest mainly employed by civil engineering firms, higher education or research institutes. A small number are employed in the mining and quarrying industry.

Technical jobs include well-logging activities; field acquisition and processing of geophysical data; preparing geological maps and sections; sampling and laboratory testing of rocks and soils; taking photos of microfossils, etc. All technical support work is carried out under supervision from a professional geoscientist.

Recruitment and entry

A degree in geology or geoscience is normally needed, and a growing number of employers prefer a higher degree as well. A relevant one-year taught Masters course is required by some companies for employment as an exploration seismologist, geochemist, micropalaeontologist, hydrogeologist or engineering geologist. At least 30% of geoscientists follow postgraduate courses leading to a Masters or PhD qualification.

However, geoscientists are not just scientists. They must be able to report results clearly and lucidly, both verbally and on paper. They have to be able to work with other people but must be self-sufficient and capable of standing up to tough physical conditions out in the field.

Qualifications and training

Degree level

Over 50 UK universities offer degree courses in geoscience. Some universities offer geoscience modules as part of a broader programme of study.

It is not usual to specialise to any great extent in any branch of geology, although on some courses it is possible to opt for an applied bias. There are some specialist courses in engineering geology, geochemistry, geophysics, and mining geology.

Traditionally A-levels or SCE Higher grade passes have been required, but other qualifications such as GNVQ/GSVQs may now be acceptable. 'Above-average' chemistry, good physics and adequate mathematics are preferred. Biology may also be useful. A- or AS-level geology is not required.

'First destination' statistics in geology in 1994 were:

total graduating	*887*
research/further study, etc.	267
teacher training	16
believed unemployed 31 December	81
temporary work	67
permanent overseas work	23
permanent UK work	247
employers	
oil, mining, etc.	32
commerce	57
manufacturing/engineering industry	34
local government	9
higher/further education	19
Civil Service	5
public utilities including transport	13
functions	
scientific/engineering R&D	34
management services	12
scientific support services	20
environmental planning	15
financial work	29
marketing, etc.	20
administration/operational management	25
personnel/social	14

Technician level

A BTEC HND course in Geological Technology is offered at the University of Luton, and an HND in Science (Industrial Geology) is available at Camborne School of Mines.

Postgraduate level

Almost all postgraduate courses provide for further specialisation, but it is possible to gain entry to these on the basis of a degree in a subject other than geology, e.g. chemistry, physics or engineering. They cover subjects such as engineering geology, geotechnical engineering, exploration geophysics, structural geology and rock mechanics, hydrogeology, engineering geology, micropalaeontology, geodesy, geotechnics, geochemistry, geophysics, marine geology and geophysics, mining geostatistics, petroleum geology, remote sensing, and image processing.

Professional body

The professional body is the Geological Society, which has absorbed the Institution of Geologists and is now a Chartered body, recognised by the Department of Trade and Industry as the designated authority for the Earth Sciences, under the terms of the EC Directive on Professional Qualifications.

Membership as a fellow normally requires a degree in geology or a related subject, and two years' geological experience thereafter. Chartered status requires a minimum of five years' approved postgraduate experience.

Further information

The Geological Society.

Geography

At degree level, geography is not just descriptive, but is far more analytical and interpretative. The main theme is relationships, or the interaction between human activities – economic, political and social – and the physical environment. Geography has extended its scope and content enormously over the past forty years, and developed in method and purpose. With increased pressure on resources and the environment it is more important than ever to understand how physical features have evolved and how they are affected by factors such as weather and human activity.

Geography courses have changed too. Traditionally, geography students specialised in human or physical geography, but today they have a wide-ranging and flexible choice of topics. The traditional divisions still exist, but the possible 'mix' is less rigid.

'Systematic' studies form a substantial proportion of most courses. Physical geography studies the Earth's natural features, their formation and how they change. It includes studies of atmosphere and climate, water resources and soils, etc., including the energy chain and the ecosystem, and their relevance to human society.

Human geography ranges widely over the interaction of people and the environment, and is increasingly concerned with human and social problems with a 'spatial' context – the conflicts caused by changes in transport policy, for instance. It covers economic geography, studying the geographical reasons for industrial development, trading patterns and long-term effects of development. Human geography has many modern aspects: land use and resource studies, urban geography (the patterns of towns and suburban development, decay and renewal), medical geography (where, for instance, geographers mapped the spread of diseases), and even recreational geography.

In what used to be called regional studies, particular places or areas with distinctive geographical 'identities' are examined, such as 'functional' regions, a city and the area it serves, an industrial region, or places with cultural and climatic identity. They are studied as living, changing, developing organisms.

Geography now uses scientific methods of collecting information and statistics, storing data and analysing it by computer, but still also works with maps, diagrams and photos.

Opportunities for geographers

Geography graduates go into an enormous range of occupational areas, but only a few enter careers where their subject area is relevant. There appear to be no significant differences between graduates with a BA or BSc in geography.

A high proportion of geography graduates go on to do research or further training. The popular belief is that geography graduates go into teaching. However, the first destination statistics show that only about 5% overall train to be teachers.

Relevant employment using geography covers SURVEYING (land, hydrographic and general practice), and CARTOGRAPHY (*see in* LAND USE PROFESSIONS); remote sensing (using remote sensing techniques to evaluate the Earth's resources); METEOROLOGY (*see below*); environmental management, hydrology, pollution, waste disposal and conservation (*see* GEOLOGY *above*); CAREERS IN CONSERVATION AND THE ENVIRONMENT; TOWN AND COUNTRY PLANNING (*in* LAND USE PROFESSIONS); and EDUCATION AND TEACHING.

Specialist careers are open to those with relevant postgraduate qualifications. For example, photogrammetrists use photogrammetric plotting instruments (which use stereoscopic viewing of photographs) to make reliable measurements to produce maps. Photogrammetrists work mainly for the Ordnance Survey and aerial survey companies.

The management of Geographical Information Systems (GIS) is a relatively new career area. It covers collecting and updating geographical data, integrating it into the existing databank, assessing how it is used and developing new applications. GIS allows the overlaying of data from various sources, e.g. vegetation, climate and 'land-use', species distribution, transport, demographic distribution, water and mineral resources, etc. which can be used for improving company operating efficiency, studying relationships between, for example, health-related information and poor housing, or planning future developments. GIS managers work for specialist computer companies.

Working 'in the environment', particularly conservation areas, is very popular, but competition is likely to be fierce and employers will look for relevant work experience. Geographers may be able to find work as countryside rangers or managers, nature reserve wardens or in advisory work. However, geographers are unlikely to get jobs in field survey or research work unless they have a relevant biological background or an appropriate postgraduate qualification.

Jobs in THE TRANSPORT INDUSTRY; distribution LOGISTICS MANAGEMENT (*in* BUYING, SELLING AND RELATED SERVICES) (getting the right quality and quantity of goods in the right condition to the right place at the right time); FREIGHT FORWARDING (*in* THE TRANSPORT INDUSTRY); THE TRAVEL INDUSTRY; and international trade may be of particular interest to geographers.

Studying geography

Geography, as a single honours subject, or in combination with another subject, or as part of a broader-based or modular scheme, is taught at most universities. It is possible to read for an arts, social science or science degree. The courses do not necessarily differ; usually it is the entry requirements and the subsidiary subjects studied which differentiate them.

First destination figures were in 1994:

	(BA)	(BSc)
total graduating	*1,501*	*1,180*
research/further study	171	174
teacher training	31	99
law and Bar exams	37	14
other training	92	61
believed unemployed 31 December	154	89
permanent employment (UK)	551	420
employers		
accountancy	58	40
banking and insurance	53	48
other commerce	168	122
local authorities	27	26
Civil Service	20	21
public utilities	40	26
engineering	25	14
oil, chemicals, etc.	12	9
other manufacturing	26	18
Armed Forces	18	18
higher/further education	18	13
functions		
financial work	102	80
administration/operational management	90	60
marketing, etc.	110	61
personnel/social	45	41
management services	20	15
environmental planning	10	16

Courses usually prefer A-level geography to have been studied.

Postgraduate study

Advanced courses in geography most frequently extend a specialised part of a first-degree course; this may be a region: for example, geography of Africa and the Middle East or polar studies. Or they may specialise in techniques, e.g. remote sensing, geographical information systems (GIS) or photogrammetry.

Further information

The Royal Geographical Society (leaflets on careers and degrees in geography).

Meteorology

Meteorology is technically the physics of the Earth's atmosphere, and a branch of geophysics – the science of the weather and forecasting is only an applied aspect of meteorology. There are a number of specialist branches:

- *Synoptic meteorologists*, the technical name for weather forecasters, plot data, use computer modelling techniques to simulate and interpret the developing weather patterns and provide weather forecasts.
- *Climatologists* study weather patterns, analyse past statistical records and advise on future climatic trends. Practical applications of their work include advising on the design of oil rigs, flood damage prevention or agricultural production.
- *Physical meteorologists* study the physical nature of the atmosphere including its chemical composition and acoustical, electrical and optical properties. They study radiation, turbulence, the boundary layer, precipitation, cloud physics, etc.
- *Dynamic meteorologists* study the physical laws related to air currents.

Meteorological research can take many forms. Internationally, the 'world climate research programme' is studying the mechanisms that influence climate, especially the interactions between the atmosphere and the other components of the climate system (e.g. oceans, sea-ice and land surfaces, dust and carbon dioxide).

Applied research plays an essential part in improving the ways that forecasting and climate models represent atmospheric phenomena. Recent research projects include testing and evaluating a new radiative transfer scheme for the Meteorological Office's weather and climate prediction model using data collected by C-130 aircraft; creating an improved urban air quality prediction model; and developing an interactive workstation data and product display system.

Meteorological research and forecasting go hand in hand, and both are done cooperatively, with the weather services of almost all countries working closely together. The global network of basic systems observes, collects, disseminates, stores and retrieves data. 'Systems' now range from the most modern satellites through 'radiosonde' instrument packages carried by balloons, to the more traditional weather ships, automatic weather stations, and the straightforward observations of ships at sea and of coastguards.

Methods of data collection are being improved all the time: for example SADIS (Satellite communications Dissemination System for aeronautical meteorological data) allows the distribution of new high-resolution global forecast upper-wind and temperature data, and collection and dissemination of aerodrome weather reports and forecasts.

The Meteorological Office was formally established as an Executive Agency within the Ministry of Defence in 1990 and is responsible to the Secretary of State for Defence. Its aim is to provide for UK military and civil users an effective, modern and efficient National Meteorological Service supplying a wide range of weather information. The daily general forecasts are a comparatively small part of the work. One of the main tasks is a weather service for the RAF, and another for shipping – helping them avoid hurricanes, for instance. Specialist weather information is sold commercially – for anything that flies, from pigeons to airlines: to the offshore oil and gas industries, to highway authorities (who want snow and ice warnings so they can grit roads), to gas and electricity companies (to anticipate changes in demand), to farms and other crop sprayers, to the construction industry, and even ice-cream makers.

All operational forecasting at the Meteorological Office is now based on a sophisticated numerical computer model that utilises surface and upper-air observational data from around the world. Improvements to operational models, automation of certain elements of forecasting and the development of medium-range, probability and oceanographic forecasting are currently being tested.

The range of services provided by the Meteorological Office is expanding rapidly as they become increasingly commercially oriented; producing site-specific forecasts for a wide range of road projects, sunburn forecasts, Open Road ice-warning services for local authorities, and a Metroute ship-routeing service.

Working in meteorology

Most meteorologists work for the Meteorological Office, which is an Executive Agency within the Ministry of Defence. In 1995 they employed the equivalent of 2,323 staff of whom about half work at headquarters. The remainder are dispersed at around 100 offices throughout the UK and a few overseas locations. During 1995 they recruited 55 new staff of whom 22 were graduates, the lowest number for many years. Staff numbers overall are decreasing in line with increased efficiency, closing of forecasting sites and development of computer-based systems. Meteorological Office staff are no longer employed at major airports since the Civil Aviation Authority introduced their Meteorological and aeronautical information retrieval system (MARS) in 1995. There is a Mobile Meteorological Unit which provides support for military exercises and UN operations.

A small number of meteorologists work in universities. In the private sector, meteorologists work for exploration companies, particularly those working in the offshore oil industry. Commercial airlines may employ meteorologists, and a few work for private forecasting and consultancy firms often specialising in marine work.

Scientific officers (normally graduates) in the Meteorological Office generally start with work in research, on computer and instrumental development, and then go on to weather forecasting. Forecasters prepare detailed forecasts from the computer output of charts and graphs. The intervention team of senior forecasters constantly monitors the basic data and computer analysis. Forecasters work at Bracknell or at civil and RAF airfields both in the UK and overseas. Those stationed on airfields may work exclusively for aircrew, while elsewhere general, or a range of special forecasts may be produced.

Junior grade staff make scheduled weather observations, code reports for transmission over international networks, plot data and generally help forecasters. Shiftwork is usual and staff may be stationed at any outstation located throughout the UK. Some work in research or in computing or instrumentation where shiftwork may not be necessary.

Recruitment and entry

Recruitment is as to the Scientific Civil Service.

At Scientific Officer (SO) level, candidates must have a degree in either meteorology, mathematics or physics (either as a single subject or in combination), computer science or electronics. Physical chemistry, oceanography, environmental science and geography may also be acceptable provided a candidate can show proven ability in mathematics and physics. An MSc in Meteorology is useful.

Assistant Scientific Officers (ASOs) need at least four passes at GCSE/SCEs grades A-C/1-3, or equivalent, and must include English language, mathematics and physics or a double science GCSE including physics. A levels/H grades are preferred in Mathematics, Physics, Statistics, Computer Studies or Electronics.

The 'Met' Office College runs specialist courses for R&D staff, forecasters and observers, lasting from three days to 18 weeks. Courses are also provided for technicians and computing staff. Emphasis is placed on continuation training throughout an individual's career.

Qualifications and training

Only Reading University offers a first degree course in meteorology as a single subject; however, related degrees are offered at University College, London in Physics with Climate Science, at Edinburgh in Physics and Meteorology and at East Anglia University. Postgraduate courses in meteorology, climatology and atmospheric sciences are offered at a number of universities.

Further information

The Meteorological Office.

Oceanography

Oceanography is a multidisciplinary field drawing on many scientific disciplines including physics, chemistry, mathematics, biology, geology, and geophysics. Oceanographers study the seas and oceans, the shoreline, coastal waters, estuaries, continental shelves and ocean depths.

Broadly speaking, physicists study how and why waves, tides and currents behave in the way they do, chemists investigate the composition and properties of seawater and the sediments on the seabed, and mathematicians use computer modelling to demonstrate processes at work in the ocean. Marine geology is linked closely with geology and geophysics – partly because ocean floors are important in studying how and why the Earth's outer layer moves ('plate tectonics'), and partly because valuable minerals lie on the sea floor and beneath it – and has developed as a separate discipline. Some oceanographers are primarily concerned with biological organisms living in the sea or along the shoreline and their relationship with their environment.

It can, however, be difficult to define the actual boundaries, and oceanographers often work in teams with scientists from other disciplines, and with engineers. Collecting information about the seas can also be very expensive, and so several countries may cooperate, using one fleet of ships and aircraft to gather data and record results. Increasingly, acoustics or remote-sensing techniques are used to collect information. Although some fieldwork is usually essential during the first few years of employment, many oceanographers are laboratory-based and carry out experiments using, e.g. physical models of estuaries in wave tanks.

Oceanographic research has practical value. A map of the sea floor can show telephone engineers where best to lay their cables; improved predictions on tidal movements and currents is useful for weather forecasting, for engineers designing oil rigs, for developing devices for generating electric power from sea waves, or for preventing and solving coastal erosion.

The seas and sea floors are increasingly important for minerals and for the food the seas can provide. Oceanographers study the conditions fish and algae need to thrive, and how to avoid killing them (or their food) with pollution. *See also* FISH FARMING *in* LAND USE INDUSTRIES.

Developing and improving instruments and equipment for use in oceanographic research is also important. Oceanographers have developed a remote-controlled corer which can be used to sample rocks and sediments under the sea at depths of up to 2,000m. Oceanographers are also involved in developing new underwater weapons, and improving sound equipment for detecting submarines.

Working in oceanography

Although the environment is now a high priority for everyone – the public, government, industry and commerce – there are comparatively few jobs in Britain for oceanographers. The NATURAL ENVIRONMENT RESEARCH COUNCIL (NERC) (*see in* CAREERS IN CONSERVATION AND THE ENVIRONMENT) is the largest employer and has two main oceanographic institutions:

- the Centre for Coastal and Marine Science (CCMS), which includes the Dunstaffnage Marine Laboratory at Oban, the Proudman Oceanographic Laboratory at Birkenhead and the Plymouth Marine Laboratory;
- Southampton Oceanography Centre, formed in April 1995 from the James Rennell Centre for Ocean Circulation, the former Institute of Oceanographic Sciences Deacon Laboratory, Research Vessel Services, and some departments of Southampton University.

The NERC Marine Science laboratories employ scientists, marine biologists, chemists and physicists as well as oceanographers.

NERC is also responsible for carrying out an increased amount of marine geological research at the British Geological Survey at Keyworth, and funds various research units, e.g. the Sea Mammal Research Unit at St Andrews university, the Centre for Global Atmospheric Modelling at Reading university and the Remote Sensing Applications Development Unit at Huntingdon.

Other employers of oceanographers include the Ministry of Agriculture Fisheries and Food (on fishery research), the Admiralty (on weapons research), the Royal Navy, the Scott Polar Research Institute in Cambridge, the water companies, pharmaceutical companies, and the new Environmental Agency (Envage), created in 1996, which includes the former National Rivers Authority. Consultancy work for the oil companies is increasing as more environmental legislation is introduced. Overseas, there are likely to be increasing opportunities in Europe, and the US has a large oceanographic research programme.

Recruitment and entry

A degree or postgraduate qualification in oceanography or a related discipline such as meteorology or marine science is the usual entry requirement, but there are also some opportunities for physics, chemistry, mathematics, geology and biology graduates to train or obtain work in oceanographic fields.

Qualifications and training

Oceanography can be studied as a first-degree subject at Bangor (University of Wales), Plymouth, Southampton, Liverpool and East Anglia Universities. Postgraduate courses are available at a number of universities.

Further information

Natural Environment Research Council, Southampton Oceanography Centre, Society for Underwater Technology.

Astronomy

There has been a major revolution in the science of astronomy over the last few decades. Observations of the universe have reached beyond the limits of optical observations to include detections in radio, X-rays, ultraviolet, infrared millimetre-waves and gamma-rays. Robotic spaceprobes have been sent to the far reaches of the solar system. Finally in 1992 an optical observatory was launched into Earth orbit, the Hubble Space Telescope. New discoveries are now flooding in, advancing our understanding of some of the most fundamental questions such as how our solar system was formed, how stars burn and how the entire universe began and evolved.

Astronomy is almost all pure research of the most original and fundamental kind – and working alongside the astronomers are people doing theoretical work, such as astrophysics.

The weather and atmospheric distortion in Britain make observational astronomy difficult, so the largest optical telescopes are now situated on the main peak of La Palma, the Roque de los Muchachos, in the Canary Islands. Developed jointly with other countries, the observatory has three reflecting telescopes which are available to British astronomers, including the 2.5-metre Isaac Newton telescope, which was moved from Herstmonceux in Sussex, and the 4.2-metre William Herschel telescope. In Hawaii, the UK runs an infrared telescope (UKIRT) and a 15-metre sub-millimetre-wave radio telescope (JCMT). In the search for knowledge about the universe all wavelength bands of the electromagnetic spectrum are equally important. Some of this radiation is completely absorbed by the Earth's atmosphere and it is necessary to put telescopes to detect X-rays, gamma-rays or the ultraviolet up into space. Long-wavelength radio waves easily penetrate the atmosphere, and to detect these the UK has giant radio telescopes at Jodrell Bank in Cheshire and in Cambridge. British astronomers use all these facilities and also use major telescopes abroad such as Siding Springs in Australia, and in South Africa, and elsewhere in the world. Competition is fierce to get observing time on any of the world's major telescopes.

In the UK, astronomers are based at either of the two Royal Observatories, the Royal Greenwich Observatory (RGO) in Cambridge or the Royal Observatory Edinburgh (ROE), or in one of a number of university departments. Both RGO and ROE are primarily concerned with developing and maintaining instrumentation for the overseas telescopes and are currently working on the new generation of 8-metre GEMINI telescopes which will become operational in 1999 (in Hawaii) and 2000 (in Chile). Current scientific work includes the astronomy-based public services (e.g. preparing astronomical almanacs), astrometric and astrophysical research (e.g. determining the distances to nearby stars or to more remote star clusters and galaxies and the quantitative chemical analysis of the spectra of these objects to determine the past history and future evolution of the universe). Both RGO and ROE also have a programme of astronomy education to schools and the general public.

Computer-controlled 'star machines', which extract and analyse data from astronomical observations on a level of sophistication not possible with 'manual' techniques, are as important as telescopes now to astronomers. Yet today's – and tomorrow's – telescopes are themselves only possible because of major technological advances in glass and mirror technology. Instrumentation took over in large observatories a long time ago, so professional astronomers need never actually look through a telescope themselves now. UKIRT and all the La Palma telescopes are now on-line and can be operated by remote control from the UK. Senior astronomers are as much 'project managers' of complex teams of scientists and equipment as they are research workers.

The RGO currently has (1996) around 110 staff of whom probably about 45 are professional astronomers, physicists, mathematicians, engineers, computing and instrumentation experts. There are 15 administrators, and about 50 technicians. The work is split between the astronomy group and the technology group.

Around 100 work at the Royal Observatory Edinburgh of whom about 35 are scientists, including astronomers. Other staff include engineers, technicians, photographers and administrators.

Everyone going into astronomy now is a graduate. While there are first-degree courses in astronomy and astrophysics (*see below*), it is generally suggested that intending astronomers should study physics and/or mathematics, largely because there are so few astronomy posts. However, an astronomy or astrophysics degree involves extensive mathematics and physics, and so graduates can go into a number of related fields, for example geodesy, upper-air research, rocket and satellite studies and, for those who have studied radio astronomy, telecommunications and electronics. The developing European space research programme may bring more technological posts.

Qualifications and training

First-degree courses are available at a number of universities either as separate subjects, or combined together, or in combination with physics. A few courses also combine them with mathematics, electronics or logic and philosophy. Astrophysics courses are more theoretical.

Entry normally requires very good grades in A-level maths and physics.

First destination statistics in astronomy were, in 1994:

total graduating	*76*
research/further study, etc.	28
teacher training	5
believed unemployed 31 December	8
temporary work	5
permanent overseas work	1
permanent UK work	18
employers	
education	1
industry and commerce	11
public service	1
miscellaneous	5

functions	
management services	4
scientific support services	1
environmental planning	–
financial work	1
marketing, etc.	2
administration/operational management	1
personnel/social	1
teaching	1
others	7

Of the twelve postgraduates entering employment 1993–94, eight obtained posts at universities.

Further information

The Royal Astronomical Society.

Space science and astronauts

Space science as an academic discipline is taught in combination with physics or technology at the Universities of Kent, Leicester, Salford, Southampton and at University College London.

Although opportunities for going into space are limited, the UK regularly has experiments on space missions; one of the most recent is Leicester University's wide field camera aboard the ROSAT X-ray satellite, an international collaboration between Germany, the UK and the USA.

Astronauts

There are basically two types of astronaut.

The first are the *Missions Scientists.* They are specialist scientists or engineers with postgraduate specialisms in subjects such as Medicine, Engineering Science, etc. The second type are *Pilots.* They have had training and usually a lot of experience and flying time in the military as jet pilots.

There is a third type of astronaut, who are usually specialists working for aerospace companies and who fly for just one mission to undertake particular research. They are know as 'payload specialists'.

Qualifications and training

The main requirements are a degree in maths, chemistry, physics, biology or engineering. Astronaut training requires a very stiff medical, especially for pilots (mission specialists have less strict medicals). There are also height restrictions (for the USA between 5ft 4 inches and 6ft 4 inches). Mainly USA nationals are accepted, unless there is some arrangement to take other nationals, for instance through the European Space Agency.

Applicants undergo intensive interviews and tests to assess their personality as well as their aptitude. If selected, there follows a year of training before the candidate can be considered an astronaut. They then have to wait to be selected for a mission.

Further information

NASA Astronaut programme. British Aerospace Space Systems.

Contents

General Engineering

(CLCI: R–RAB, ROD)

Engineering definitions

The term 'engineering' is constantly being redefined nowadays because the old traditional definitions of 'engineering' tended to play down the subject's originality and creative aspects, making it sound dull, repetitive and mechanical. They described it (rightly) as an applied subject using scientific principles but this implied (wrongly) that the 'principles' were discovered by others and the engineer simply took them over.

Now more emphasis is placed on using imagination and creativity, so a modern definition might be that engineering is concerned with designing practical solutions to real-life problems, and developing imaginative ideas into novel working products, devices, processes, structures, and systems which serve human needs. Moreover, the skills of the engineer cover a vast range of products – from tiny silicon chips to giant power stations, from static structures like dams to mobile machinery like cars, and include all kinds of industrial processes from refining oil and sugar to turning raw materials into anything from cakes to glue. Engineering, therefore, has influenced all aspects of modern life.

If the definition of the term 'engineering' is confused, then so is the meaning of the title 'engineer'. Strictly, 'engineer' means 'chartered' and 'incorporated engineer', but too many people still lump all engineers together, as manual workers in dirty overalls working deep inside oily machines. Even journalists still tend to write about 'engineers' on strike, when they usually mean the craft engineering worker or engineering technician members of a particular union – toolmakers, fitters, maintenance people, people on the assembly line – and not chartered or incorporated engineers. Leaving aside the fact that modern electronic technology is fast removing much of the muck from most machines, chartered and incorporated engineers work with their brains and imaginations rather than their hands.

Yet the lack of clear distinction between one kind of engineer and another is only a realistic picture of the position as it actually is in the real working world (with some exceptions, most notably construction) in Britain. The Engineering Council realistically accepts that there is no hard-and-fast line between the kind of work undertaken by those in the different grades, and the greater flexibility being promoted by employers and education/training initiatives alike mean that the distinctions are likely to blur even further.

Engineering, then, covers a very wide spectrum of activity indeed, from the most creative and cerebral to the most practical and repetitive.

Chartered engineers work at the most complex end of the spectrum, craftworkers at the most practical, but there is a very wide area in between where the role of chartered, incorporated engineer, engineering technician and craftworker is not so easily defined in practice. The divisions vary from branch to branch of engineering, and from industry to industry, to some extent depending on the complexity of the product being made or whatever is being built – it may even vary from firm to firm.

Some chartered engineers work on projects which take them to – or even beyond – the boundaries of existing knowledge, or put them in control of massive and/or potentially highly dangerous resources (e.g. nuclear power stations). But others may well be doing work which makes little demand on their professional skills. In one situation, the incorporated engineer may be doing the kind of work given to a chartered engineer in another, and vice versa; or the engineering technician may do work similar to craftworkers' elsewhere, and vice versa.

Moreover, graduate and other professionally qualified engineers have, according to surveys by the Engineering Council, been moving away from their traditional roles in research, development and design, into other functions.

In the 1995 Engineering Council *Survey of Professional Engineers and Technicians*, 12.1% of non-graduate engineers work in maintenance and repair compared with 3.0% of graduate engineers and 0.7% of postgraduate engineers.

Although this is an area not traditionally considered to need such a high level of qualification, nearly a quarter of those working in it have a degree. Conversely, incorporated engineers (15.6% of whom, according to the survey, are in any case graduates) are not excluded from professional-level work: just over 2.2% of incorporated engineers answering the questionnaire in 1995 worked in R&D, 8.7% in design and 4.7% in teaching.

The Engineering Council defines an engineer as 'one who acquires and uses scientific, technical and other pertinent knowledge and skills to create, operate or maintain safe, efficient systems, structures, machines, plant, processes and devices of practical and economic value'.

Chartered engineer

Chartered engineers are scientifically trained to solve problems, in a practical way. They design and develop devices (such as computers or machine tools), plant and processes (to refine petrol or produce beer), or structures (such as bridges and dams), which solve problems (as in extracting oil and gas from the North Sea), improve existing products (using microprocessors to build ever smaller but more powerful and sophisticated computers), or create new ones (such as space satellites).

They use exact scientific methods and their work is based on scientific principles: physical – as work in solid-state physics led eventually to the silicon chip; chemical – the basic principles for chemical engineering; and even biological – for genetic engineering and biotechnology. The solutions, machines, processes, etc. have to be designed so as to take account of all kinds of often conflicting technical, economic, commercial, social and even political factors. Where professional engineers work in actual manufacturing or construction, it is in a managerial capacity, which usually means working with a team of other people.

Employed according to their training and capability (which does not always happen), chartered engineers have to be able to use ingenuity, original thinking and judgement. They ought to be able to look ahead, foresee problems and plan to meet or forestall them. They must keep up to date with technological developments, and know how to take advantage of them, and how to manage change. They must learn how to negotiate – on contracts, for instance – to write reports, and to manage both people and resources.

The chartered engineer usually has a desk- and/or laboratory-based job, but is also normally involved in liaison and teamwork, with customers, with the company's marketing staff, with other engineers, and with support people. It will, usually, mean using and/or working on all kinds of computer-based systems. Many chartered engineers, though, make regular visits to the site or the factory floor, especially in their earliest years (when they may, as part of their training, actually work as a supervisor). Some – especially in large-scale construction – may work on site, as part of the 'resident' engineer's team, and later, perhaps, as resident engineer.

Chartered engineers can expect to move on from direct involvement in an engineering 'function' (*see below*) into management, especially if they have gained in-depth training and experience in, for instance, contract negotiation, or financial control. Technological sophistication and complexity, the vast scale of many engineering projects, and the financial investment involved, mean there are signs that more engineers are being groomed for senior, general management.

The Engineering Council's 1995 survey showed that over 85.7% of chartered engineers are now qualified to graduate level or above. The proportion of all engineers who are graduates rises from 54.7% of those over the age of 55, to 74.0% of those under 35.

The incorporated engineer and engineering technician

Incorporated engineer and engineering technician are really blanket terms referring to qualifications rather than job specifications for a wide variety of different occupations at varying skill levels between, and overlapping with, craftwork at one end and professional engineering at the other. Incorporated engineers are generally senior to engineering technicians (because they have more advanced-level technical qualifications and experience), but there is often some overlap in the kind of work they do, and the level of skills needed can vary from branch to branch of engineering.

Incorporated engineers normally hold the senior position in a team of technicians, as in the drawing office, usually under a chartered engineer, or give direct assistance to chartered engineers, for instance in R&D or project engineering. In production, the manager's functions may be subdivided, with someone of incorporated-engineer status (or a young chartered engineer) deputising in each of the functions. There is nothing to prevent an incorporated engineer moving up into more senior and even general managerial positions – and the indications are that a significant proportion do so – although there may be problems in gaining relevant experience early enough.

Engineering technicians often lead teams of craftworkers, in technical after-sales service, for example. They, too, can gain promotion to what is defined as incorporated-engineer-level work, and beyond.

Like chartered engineers, engineering technicians and incorporated engineers normally work within one branch of engineering, and further within one kind of occupation. There are a great many areas of work for engineering technicians and incorporated engineers, many now being computer-based jobs. Examples include:

- design/drawing office work – which ranges from preparing detailed scale drawings of components for individual products, to component and assembly design with responsibility for relevant engineering calculations, preparing materials and parts lists, and supervisory work;
- testing, for research and development or inspection – for example, setting up and even making test equipment, and then running the test programme;
- production – where technician engineers deputise for the production manager in larger firms;
- estimating – for example, costing standard components, or one-off projects;
- installing and 'running in' new equipment or plant;
- scheduling production – deciding when raw materials should be delivered, keeping checks on lists of materials, preparing information for production planning, and analysing the work content of orders;

- programming numerically controlled (automatic) machine tools – analysing what the machine is expected to do in a given operation, and then writing, checking and 'de-bugging' the specifications for the control tapes;
- maintaining and repairing machinery and other equipment and services – for example, in broadcasting or telecommunications;
- after-sales service or sales engineering – maintaining and repairing equipment, e.g. machine tools or computers, for customers;
- applications engineering – finding and promoting uses for a company's products, and working with a (chartered) project engineer on design, development and testing of new products or modifications.

Incorporated engineers are expected to show ingenuity, to be able to diagnose and solve problems, identify and analyse faults, use a variety of sophisticated tools and measuring devices and processes, be able to organise their own and others' work, understand the processes involved in making or building products, and be able to make technical reports, both verbally and in writing.

The engineering technician

The engineering technician 'specialises in a specific, normally practical, skill; technicians are expected to be able to understand the principles underlying the work they do; they must be able to read a complex engineering drawing and turn it into a practical reality; they must be able to order the right materials in the correct quantities to make a piece of equipment or machinery, plan the order in which the job is done, set it up and then carry it out, frequently to very high degrees of accuracy and precision; they must be able to solve basic problems. Promotion is to supervisory work, to quality control and inspection' (Engineering Council).

Examples of technicians' work include:

- machine shop crafts – toolmaking, turning (on a lathe), milling (where the component is fixed and the machine moves to produce flat or curved surfaces, slots, grooves, gears or cam-forms);
- jig-boring and grinding;
- electrical, electronic or mechanical fitting – assembling components which may need preparation to make them fit together and therefore need accurate measurement and marking, and use of hand tools;
- maintenance – of cars, electrical plant, electronic equipment, lifts, instruments, machine tools, etc;
- 'setting' machines for semi- or unskilled workers.

Engineering technicians traditionally work with a minimum of direction and supervision and are expected to be able to read and interpret complicated engineering drawings, and make the component or product or wiring system correctly from it. This means they must also be able to order the right materials in the correct quantities, plan for themselves the order in which the job is done, set it up, and then carry it out, very often to a high degree of accuracy and precision. They also solve basic problems.

Employment in engineering

A report on *The Labour Market in Engineering Manufacture* by the Engineering Training Authority in 1993 shows that the overall level of employment in the engineering industry declined dramatically during the recession of the early 1990s. – by approximately 15%. From October 1990 to April 1993 numbers employed in the industry fell by 279,000 to 1.59 million.

The overall decline in total employment masks the fact that employment at sites with less than 99 people had increased by 2.8%. Aerospace lost 30% of employees, down to 101,000, while instrument engineering only reduced by 12%, down to 58,000, and electrical engineering, electronics and data processing fell by 15% to 460,000. Motor vehicle manufacture lost 18% of employees, down to 199,000, and mechanical engineering 17% down to 428,000 employees.

Engineering employment fell most in the South East (-20%) and North West (-19%). Employment of engineers in East Anglia actually rose by 2%.

By occupation the employment of professional engineers increased by 9.0% to 104,000, but managerial staff reduced by 4%, to 124,000. Administrative staff were unchanged at 172,000. Craft employees declined by a further 5% from 1990 to 295,000 in 1993. Technicians, however, were the most seriously affected group recording a reduction in employment of 25% to 126,000. Engineering operators and assemblers, the largest occupational group, were also reduced in number by 16%, to 506,000.

The report estimates that 32% of those working in the industry are operators and assemblers, 19% are craftsmen/women, 11% work in a clerical or administrative capacity, 8% are technicians, 8% managers, 7% professional engineers and 5% supervisors.

Of these, women made up 6% of managers, 7% of supervisors, 5% of professional engineers, 24% of engineering operators and assemblers, 2% of craft employees, and 62% of administrative and clerical staff working in the engineering industry.

Most people going into engineering begin their working lives specialising in one of the so-called 'branches' (see later in this and subsequent chapters). They are employed in a number of sectors.

Industry

Industry, both manufacturing and other sectors such as construction, has traditionally employed the majority of engineers, but with the decline of manufacturing industry, the proportion has been falling for some time.

In 1995, 52.8% of chartered and 49.7% of incorporated engineers were working for industrial companies; a further 7.2% of chartered and 12.3% of incorporated engineers worked for public utilities (water, electricity, etc.).

In industry, they start out in one of several different types of work (*see* ENGINEERING FUNCTIONS *below*), although later many engineers change the area of engineering in which they work, and also their 'function'.

Local and central government

Local authorities are also major employers of engineers: 5.4% of all chartered engineers and over 7.4% of all technician engineers in 1995. They manage and organise road-building, planning, and maintenance; traffic systems (planning and organising e.g. new one-way systems, and all that goes with them, like islands, intersections); sewage and refuse disposal, and street cleaning; local-authority building and housing; building controls and inspection; parks, playing fields and cemeteries; sometimes public transport. *See also* LOCAL GOVERNMENT.

The Civil Service employs a sizeable number: in 1995, 2.1% of all chartered and 1.8% of incorporated engineers. They work in R&D, project management, construction and installation, and even (but less and less) production.

Civil and structural engineers work for several government departments including the Department of Transport, the Department of Health, the Foreign and Commonwealth Office and the Ministry of Agriculture Fisheries and Food. The work entails looking after building and construction projects and land. The Property Services Agency, which used to look after government buildings and land, has been privatised and is now owned by Tarmac Black and Beach. All contracts for the maintenance or building of government property are now subject to compulsory competitive tender.

Mechanical, electrical and electronic, and marine engineers, naval architects, etc. work for the Ministry of Defence, mainly on design and development, and increasingly they supervise defence contracts.

Education

Education employs some 6.6% of chartered engineers, 4.8% of incorporated engineers – several thousand perhaps. They work in universities and colleges of higher education, where they combine teaching with research, development, consultancy, etc., and in further education.

Other employers

Over 14.1% of chartered engineers are consultants, and 11.5% self-employed (for incorporated engineers the equivalents are 6.7% and 8.1%). The Armed Forces employ 1.7% of chartered, and 4.5% of incorporated engineers.

The future of engineering

Engineering as a career is changing. First, there are the effects of new technology itself, and of economic and industrial conditions. Second, but closely bound up with this, are the changes that engineers are making to their own futures.

Predicting future levels of employment for engineers is even more difficult than in those professions which have a more stable demand such as medicine and teaching. As are many occupations, engineering employment is affected by the varying economic situation and by government policies. It takes a minimum of seven years (average nine years) to become a chartered engineer, and this period is bound to cover a variety of economic situations.

Between 1989 and 1993 the number of undergraduates in engineering increased by 30%, and the number of students graduating each year went up to 17,000, while British industry went through a major recession. After the full employment of the late 1980s engineers suddenly found that more of them would need to seek jobs outside the engineering industry. As the recession has receded employment prospects for engineers have improved and shortages have arisen in some areas, notably radio frequency engineering, computers and optoelectronics, the automobile industry and biotechnology.

As industry has recovered, a shortage of technicians has become evident and a new scheme 'modern apprentices in engineering', with the specific aim of helping school-leavers aged 16–19 to enter the industry, started in 1995 offering three years of experience and training and leading to NVQ level 3 or above.

The Engineering Training Authority (EnTra) in partnership with the Training and Enterprise Councils (TECs), is promoting programmes to upgrade the skills of incorporated engineers and engineering technicians. There is an important growth in the number of employees gaining national vocational qualifications (NVQs), which span all levels of skill within the industry from craft level to management. Shortages of skilled people within electrical engineering and electronics, particularly in areas such as software engineering and radio frequency engineering, emerged during 1995.

Students with arts/social science A-levels can take a one-year 'conversion' course, often called a 'foundation course', in preparation for a degree or HND course in engineering, technology, or science/CDT teacher training. Access courses (full-time and part-time) leading on to engineering degree courses are also available for mature students (over 25) wishing to train to become engineers.

Radically changing technology, and the drive for greater efficiency and competitiveness, have already resulted in a steady change in the balance between skilled and unskilled workers. While the number of engineering operators declined by 94,000 between 1990 and 1993, technicians reduced by 41,000 and craftsmen and women by 17,000. Yet the number of professional engineers increased by 9,000 to 104,000, and administrators hardly changed at 172,000 people. Female employees also reduced in number, declines of 37% in female technicians and 26% in operators masking a 79% increase in craftswomen.

Given the rise in opportunities since 1993, it is unlikely that any job losses resulting from automation or other technological developments will adversely affect general career opportunities for skilled people overall, at least for the immediate future. Of course actual jobs, even for skilled engineers, will go as new technology makes them obsolete – as digital-electronic control systems and robots cut the number of production jobs dramatically even for technicians. Computer-aided design (CAD) is steadily automating away routine drawing-office work. Increased reliability is dramatically reducing opportunities in the maintenance of electronic equipment. But the increased efficiency made possible by new technologies looks set only to help ease skill shortages, and of course engineers also design, develop and make the new machinery and products, which makes them somewhat less vulnerable.

But the corollary is that even skilled engineers will need to be flexible both in their approach to what work they will do and in their training. The evidence says engineers will also need to have broader-based skills, to be multi-skilled, and to have skills which cross traditional barriers. A major example here is the growing need for integrated electromechanical skills (now being labelled 'mechatronics' by some), and of course 'information technology' – or 'engineering' – are complex amalgams of what have been treated as independent disciplines.

Engineers will need to have skills which will transfer, and there will have to be more systematic arrangements for updating and converting engineers' skills through continuing professional development, just as in all other sectors of employment, both for their personal futures and to make their employers more competitive. Industry is increasingly 'outsourcing' many of its functions, and more engineers are now self-employed than five years ago.

Jobs will go on changing in character with all kinds of new technology, as they have been for some time now. Sophisticated computer-based technology is now routinely in use throughout industry – in research and development, in design, in manufacture, in stores, in distribution, in administration, to be used by people of all skill levels, but with many more revolutionary developments, particularly in robotics, automation, and telecommunications to come. Other technologies have been developing, have come into use more quietly and are set to make even more dramatic changes.

The level and range of skills needed for specific jobs may change, and so may the levels of responsibility. In a fully automated cement factory, central control can be supervised by a single operator (in place of several technicians for less sophisticated systems), but automated machine tools tend to require higher-level skills: they have to be programmed, and the operator has to be able to react appropriately to problems.

Recruiters suggest they will in future be looking for higher-calibre people for engineering functions, right through from management level – to be able to get people working in teams and getting greater efficiency and productivity – through engineer grades, to craft levels, where high-level, flexible skills and the ability to tackle problems are of increasing importance.

In the longer term, however, early signs are that the demand for some technological skills in the UK could decline. Many industrial concerns now manufacture their products in South East Asia (especially Malaysia and Singapore), where the cost of skilled labour is lower. Another crucial factor is whether or not the next generation of computers and software will deliver effective 'expert' systems which will enable many people to do tasks of increasing technical sophistication without necessarily being a fully-qualified specialist engineer/technologist. When and if this happens, the skills needed will change yet again, probably to (even) more broadly-based intellectual training, and even greater emphasis on flexibility, adaptability, problem-solving and troubleshooting.

A changing profession

The engineering profession has been through a period of intense self-analysis and criticism. The Engineering Council made a major attempt to unify the profession during 1994 and 1995. The plan was to group the 42 Engineering Institutions into six 'colleges'. These were electrical, mechanical, civil, extraction and processing, transport, and institutions which were pan-disciplinary or concerned with support and services. The plan failed because the institutions valued their autonomy. Instead the engineering institutions brought about the replacement of the Engineering Council by another body with the same name but with different membership, reflecting the supremacy of the Engineering Institutions.

The new Engineering Council was formed on 1 January 1996 and consists of an elected senate of 54 members representing the Engineering Institutions, the different grades of membership and the Privy Council.

However, since being set up in 1981 the Engineering Council has done much to raise standards and promote the engineering profession. To encourage school-leavers to consider a career in engineering it has promoted visits by professional engineers to schools, nurtured the establishment of Engineers Clubs in schools and held a prestigious annual 'Young Engineers for Britain' competition. It has also conducted a vigorous 'Women into Science and Engineering' (WISE) campaign which has increased the numbers of women joining the profession. In 1994 a 'Top Flight' scheme was introduced with backing from government, to give bursaries of £500 to students on engineering degree courses who possess good A-level grades (two As and a B).

In its role of setting the standards for qualifications, education, and training of chartered engineers, incorporated engineers, and technicians, the Engineering Council produced a document *Standard Routes to Registration* which provided a unified framework for engineers in training, educational establishments and the Engineering Institutions to work to.

In setting new standards for qualification, etc., the Council kept a three-tier register, with the designations Chartered Engineer (CEng), Incorporated Engineer (IEng), and Engineering Technician (EngTech).

Each section has a three-stage registration. At each stage the standards must meet the Council's requirements, which include arrangements to assess training, accreditation of courses, etc. The stages are:

- *Stage 1* educational qualification – registers those who have passed an examination or other academic test in the principles of engineering.
- *Stage 2* training qualification – registers people who have been trained for the profession, or have held position(s) which have given such training. Entrants must have satisfied the stage 1 requirement.
- *Stage 3* experience – registers people who have gained responsible engineering experience, and have met both stage 1 and 2 requirements.

These clearly defined stages of registration are designed to put greater emphasis in future on training and experience.

For each section of the Register, this means:

Chartered Engineer (CEng)

The stage 1 main route is via an accredited enhanced honours BEng or an enhanced and extended MEng (*see* ENGINEERING COURSES, QUALIFICATIONS AND TRAINING *below*). Alternative routes are via EC part 2 examination, a part-accredited course or an accredited ordinary or unclassified degree plus extra engineering studies.

For stage 2, entrants must normally go through a two-year approved training programme (of which at least six months must be postgraduate), but other routes are possible, e.g. scientists and mathematicians can qualify if they complete a longer training or period of engineering experience at the appropriate level.

Stage 3 requires at least two years' responsible experience, and a professional review including a report and an interview. The minimum age for CEng is 25.

Although people with appropriate qualifications can apply direct to go on the professional register, they must be members of a nominated Chartered Engineering Institution to gain 'chartered' status.

Incorporated Engineer (IEng)

The stage 1 main route is via an accredited BTEC/SCOTVEC HNC/D (*see below*). Alternative routes are an equivalent qualification (e.g. City & Guilds) or an accredited ordinary or unclassified degree.

For stage 2, entrants must normally have had at least two years' approved training.

Stage 3 requires at least two years in a post of increasing responsibility. The minimum age is 23.

Engineering Technician (EngTech)

The stage 1 main route is via an accredited BTEC/SCOTVEC NC/D; alternative routes are an equivalent qualification, e.g. City & Guilds.

Stage 2 requires at least two years' approved training programme or scheme.

For stage 3, entrants must show competence in relevant skills and be responsible for work where proven techniques and procedures are used, but no time is set. The minimum age is 21.

By December 1995, there were some 197,426 chartered engineers; 54,075 registered incorporated engineers, and 15,716 engineering technicians on the Register. These numbers vary somewhat over the years. The CEng Register is stable, the IEng Register shows some sign of increase since 1989 and the EngTech Register is still falling.

Engineers are not legally required to join a professional institution or to be registered as such with the Engineering Council to practise/work as a professional. But chartered status may sharply improve promotion prospects, especially with major employers and for consultancy work. Many companies overseas, however, insist that qualified professional engineers are employed on their contracts. At present, though, many new graduates clearly do not join.

A European qualification, EurIng, has also been introduced through FEANI (the body representing the principal engineering bodies in more than 20 countries. As Britain becomes more integrated into Europe this qualification will inevitably become increasingly significant.

In 1995 the Engineering Council published *Competence and Commitment*. This report suggested increasing the qualifications required to attain Chartered Engineer, Incorporated Engineer and Engineering Technician status. Under these proposals the educational qualification for Chartered Engineer would become a masters degree, for Incorporated Engineer a degree and for Engineering Technicians a Higher National Certificate. It also proposed that Chartered Engineers seeking EurIng status should be fluent in a second European language up to A-level standard. If approved the new regulations will come into effect towards the end of 1996.

Further information

Engineering Council and individual engineering institutions (*see* sections following).

Engineering functions including production engineering

Careers in engineering divide in two ways – into branches (*see* following section) and into occupations or 'functions' which are common to all or most of the branches, although the proportions employed in the various functions vary from branch to branch.

The main engineering functions are design, research and development; production (which may be construction or manufacture), planning and management; commissioning, installation, maintenance and servicing. Terms used sometimes vary between industries and branches. Increasingly, especially where contracts are very large and complex – for multi-million-pound chemical or other plant, major civil engineering projects like dams, even defence projects (like the vertical take off plane) – 'project' engineers oversee them from start to finish. A high proportion of chartered and incorporated engineers become managers.

In industries where the product is technologically sophisticated – computers, or chemical plant – marketing and sales employ qualified engineers too.

Engineers and technicians do also go into engineering-related functions like purchasing, patent work and training. Some go on to become accountants, which is a useful stepping-stone into management consultancy, and finance generally has been showing greater interest in people with technological backgrounds lately. A few go into personnel work. The proportion of chartered engineers working in non-engineering functions had declined to 2.3% in 1995. The proportion of incorporated engineers working outside engineering has also declined, to 1.9% in 1995. Nearly 20% of chartered engineers and 15.7% of incorporated engineers are general managers, and 6.1% of chartered engineers and 2.9% of incorporated engineers have risen to chief executive of their business.

Engineering design

Engineering designers turn ideas into plans or specifications for a real product – its performance, shape and size, the materials from which it will be made, and so on. Engineering designers work on 'products' which range from a completely new bridge or dam (which is civil engineering), down to a new microprocessor, which is electronic engineering. Chemical engineers design new processes and plant to make a new detergent; naval architects design ships; mechanical engineers cars or machine tools. In some industries, e.g. aircraft, a completely new design is a comparatively rare event – although new modifications may be made, to take advantage of a new technical development (which could, perhaps, improve fuel consumption), to meet a competitor's design modification, or to improve materials. In other industries, like civil engineering, each new project usually means a completely new design.

'Design' is a word which implies 'creating' something that looks good. But in engineering, design has first and foremost to come up with a product that does the job for which it is intended, which actually works. Aesthetic appeal and visual impact may be built in, but the priority for this varies from product to product. In civil engineering, for example, a bridge or a dam is expected first and foremost to be strong enough for the traffic they must carry or the water held, but they are also expected to 'fit' aesthetically into the environment. Car designers must make a car's appearance appeal to the customer, but within the constraints of a vehicle that is fast, safe, fuel-efficient, and so on. Aesthetics barely rate in designing machine tools or electronic components.

The creativity of a design engineer lies in the ability to make critical judgements on what will be the best design in the circumstances. This means trying to balance the customer's ideal with the very many constraints set by technical, manufacturing, and marketing – including pricing – factors. A dam must meet specific stresses and strains for a given weight of water, taking into account all the factors of terrain, soil, etc., yet be technically possible to build with a minimum of materials of a given strength, at a price the customer will pay – and still fit into its surroundings.

To improve sales, a company's designers worked out a completely new set of principles for garden secateurs, giving them a more efficient hammer action with which even the least green-fingered cannot bruise plant stems, with few parts to rust or lose – and therefore also easier to manufacture – with a better grip and balance, and better-looking too. These designers worked to specifications set by marketing, who commissioned market research to survey gardeners' needs. They took into account all the manufacturing problems, and designed it to be as economical to produce in terms of time, labour, tools and machinery as they could. They ironed out problems which could have resulted in a part snapping under certain stresses by changing the material used, and made some modifications at the request of service staff. They discussed with packaging whether or not the standard box could be used or whether it needed strengthening, and how much this would cost.

Most engineering design offices handle very large amounts of information, much of it in number form. Here other departments may be involved: research and development may be asked for reports and tests on possible materials for a product and how they behave, if they need any strengthening, and if so how it can be done, and whether or not the material can be produced economically in the right amounts. Marketing researches customers and retailers and feeds back the information, and designers do their own searches of the technical literature, or get the library to do it.

Designers have to make a great many calculations, not only of sizes and shapes of both the finished product and the parts, but also of how best to achieve the result the customer wants in many other ways. A chemical engineer has to calculate how strong a chemical reactor vessel must be to withstand given pressures, for instance. The design process may involve several modifications, and all the other calculations then have to be rechecked. The final 'design' translates all these parameters into a tight specification, expressed in engineering and mathematical terms and with working drawings, etc., with the balance between all the factors right.

Reconciling all the conflicting demands, yet finding a satisfactory result, is not simple, but designers have computer-aided design (CAD) systems which handle the data and do most of the calculations, with VDUs on which they can see the design in three dimensions and considerable detail, so it can be modified using a light pen. These systems help designers to work out, for example, the best way to route pipes round an oil refinery, lay out electronic circuits, or the most aerodynamically efficient shape for a car.

CAD systems save the designers a great deal of time, cut the amount of testing that has to be done – in a wind-tunnel for example, on aerodynamic shaping – and so keep down costs. They drive automatic draughting machines and control parts of manufacture, e.g. cutting car body panels. CAD systems can give greater consistency, and the best design practices can be selected, coded and stored in the machine, to be adapted for the next related project. They cannot (yet) replace designers, but allow more sophisticated thinking, save valuable time, and give more time for making decisions.

Engineering designers work mostly in teams, consisting of qualified engineers supported by technicians, such as draughtsmen and women (who produce the final specifications in working drawings, again increasingly using CAD systems rather than drawing boards). Since most engineering products are complicated and have many parts, the design work is divided between them according to the complexity and sophistication of the design and the individual engineer's level of experience. They may work directly for a manufacturer, or work for (or be) a design consultant.

Qualifications and training

Engineering design work is technologically very sophisticated, and designers need a high level of engineering know-how; so at most levels it is usual to start by gaining a qualification in one of the branches of engineering.

At first-degree level the design content of all engineering degree courses is substantial, and some give considerable emphasis to design.

At technician-engineer and engineering-technician levels, design and/or draughtsmanship is most frequently a stream/option within BTEC courses, which can be linked to formal training as a draughtsman/woman or design technician with an employer.

There are a number of degree courses in Product Design.

Professional qualifications. Most design engineers usually qualify for membership of the professional body which covers their 'branch' of engineering. However, one body specialises in design: the Institution of Engineering Designers, with a membership (1996) of 4,779. The main route to qualification as a member of the Institution is with a BTEC HNC with two years' training and three years' experience in design or drawing office. The minimum age for membership was reduced in 1995 to 23 years. But a significant proportion qualify as associate members with a BTEC National plus two years' training and seven years' experience (including three years in design or drawing office). The minimum age of associate members is 27. In 1996 there were 3,094 full members, 223 associate members and 38 graduate members. The Institution can nominate suitably qualified engineering designers for chartered, incorporated or technician engineer status.

Further information

Institution of Engineering Designers (leaflets).

Research and development

These frequently go together for engineers. Most engineers who do research are employed in industry, where they work mainly on solving specific and actual problems which are often fairly routine. They support design (above), particularly in testing prototypes, and finding and/or testing new and/or cheaper materials. But often it is practical problem-solving on an existing range of products. Research engineers look for ways of using research done elsewhere in the company's products or processes; try to solve production problems – perhaps by modifying a tool – iron out snags in processes, or try to improve and simplify them, and so make them more efficient and cheaper. They may search for ways to cut fuel consumption, e.g. by using heat exchangers.

Chances to work on more fundamental problems, to use very advanced theoretical and experimental methods, are found mainly in universities (generally combined with teaching), or in government, research council laboratories, industrial research establishments or research associations. However, major efforts are underway to step up more industrially useful research in universities, via collaborative ventures with industry. The government White Paper *Realising Our Potential: A Strategy for Science, Engineering and Technology*, published in May 1993 led to the setting up of committees in each industrial sector to prioritise UK research.

Engineers in both universities and industry develop new equipment for science too. Much new scientific research depends on engineering developments – progress in particle and nuclear physics, for instance, usually follows closely on new, ever more sophisticated particle accelerators; astronomy and astrophysics depend on refinements in mirror technology, and highly sophisticated computer-based machines to record and analyse observations, as well as on space probes and satellites.

Engineering R&D is multidisciplinary teamwork, with engineers from more than one 'branch' working alongside and closely with materials specialists, physicists, chemists and even doctors (on e.g. medical equipment). They are supported by technicians whose work includes running experiments and tests, operating things like wind tunnels, test beds, building equipment, etc.

While much of the research that engineers do is still based on the traditional lab, a lot also goes on in 'labs' which look more like factory workshops or areas which have, or are, 'models' of real life: the river to be dammed, the wind tunnel, etc. Increasingly, though, both lab- and model-based research are being used especially in the early stages and on areas like wind-tunnel testing, computer modelling and simulation/emulation.

The majority of 1994 graduates in electrical and electronic engineering who went into employment (55%) entered research design or development work. Of graduate mechanical engineers who went into employment in 1994 64.1% entered the fields of research, design or development.

Qualifications and training

Virtually all engineers going into R&D are now graduates who generally read for a degree in an appropriate branch of engineering or (general) engineering science followed by research training for a higher degree.

Draughtsmanship

Draughtsmen and women produce the necessary drawings in any area of work which involves making or building anything.

It is common to think of draughtsmen and women as working only in the engineering industry, but construction in general and architecture in particular are amongst those employing many in their drawing offices; map-makers (*see* CARTOGRAPHY *in* LAND USE OF PROFESSIONS) also use draughtsmen and women trained in cartographic techniques.

This is, then, a 'function' and a career stage rather than a career in its own right. It is an area of work which has been changing for some years, but is doing so particularly rapidly just now, mainly with the introduction of computer-aided design (CAD) systems. (*See* Engineering design *above*).

CAD systems produce drawings in two or three dimensions, 'compiling' them either from data entered in 'real-time', or from information stored in a linked database. Drawings can be modified electronically, usually on a VDU screen using a 'light pen'. CAD is a viable proposition for most engineering firms and design practices, so they can produce both new and modified products, much faster than by traditional drawing methods. Firms can also improve their service – offering more elaborate drawings with tender documents, for example, or meeting demand for special features – with CAD systems. CAD automates drawing rather than design, which still needs an expert brain instructing/guiding the system, so it is drawing-office jobs that are most at risk.

Employers identify two levels of draughtsmanship. At the upper level, the incorporated engineer works directly under a chartered design (or other) engineer, and prepares 'general-arrangement' rather than detail drawings. They would also provide engineering designs outside the scope of established procedures, standards and codes of practice to a competitive level of cost and safety, quality and reliability. They may supervise the work of detail draughtsmen/women. Lower-level draughtsmen/women may work under an incorporated design engineer, probably doing component or part drawings from general-arrangement drawings prepared by the incorporated engineer, and probably qualified to BTEC National level (or equivalent).

(Technical changes in drawing materials, reprographics and microfilming have virtually eliminated tracing work.)

In engineering, CAD has automated 'pure' routine and repetitive drawing, so fewer draughtsmen/women, reliant on drawing rather than engineering skills, are now required.

Traditionally, the drawing office was the bright apprentice's route to professional qualification, standing, etc. The closing-off of the part-time route to professional qualification and the increased intake of young graduates with whom the draughtsmen/women had to compete for promotion, has altered this, rather than any automated system.

There has been a significant decrease in the numbers of draughtsmen/women employed in the engineering industry in recent years. Much of this fall is attributed to the parallel decline in firms' R&D activity, particularly in mechanical engineering.

In engineering, most draughtsmen/women work in machinery and machine tool manufacture, in 'other' mechanical engineering, and in vehicle manufacture. While electrical engineering employs substantial numbers, electronics tends to employ engineers rather than draughtsmen/women in design. Other sectors employing draughtsmen/women include metal goods manufacture, and marine engineering.

The other main area of employment for draughtsmen/women is construction (where they may have a somewhat broader job specification, which can include brief preparation through to account settlement). Professional surveyors, architects and cartographers, whether themselves in employment or in private practise, generally have drawing office staff.

Qualifications and training

There is no separate education or training for draughtsmen/women as such. Learning drawing office and CAD skills is part of technician-level training within a particular field of employment. The evidence suggests that in future it will be essential to gain a broadly based engineering (or building/construction) training which leans more heavily on basic engineering skills than on straightforward drawing ability.

Most draughtsmen/women in training are office- rather than college-based. College courses are taken on a release basis. Qualification should normally be via appropriate BTEC/SCOTVEC courses.

Draughtsmen/women need a solid background in the principles of the particular industry in which they are working and of the manufacturing and production processes through which the product must go, and the materials and components from which it will be made. Mathematical skills are very important, as is scientific/technological understanding, and an interest in how things are made. They must obviously understand the new computer-based systems with which they will work. Draughtsmen/women need imagination to help them understand what the designer intends and to visualise the finished product or construction, but actual drawing skills are not now crucial.

Further information

Engineering Training Authority (EnTra), Engineering Council, Institution of Engineering Designers, or from professional bodies with technician-level entry, or specific technician organisations in the areas in which draughtsmen/women work.

Production planning and management (including project engineering, construction, installation, inspection)

These are functions in which engineers plan, organise and control production in manufacturing industry – from sophisticated single aircraft through to mass-production of cars or home computers – or the site in civil or chemical engineering construction. There is some differentiation, as the following examples show.

Project engineers are increasingly put in charge of very large contracts, particularly in civil and chemical engineering, starting from the time when the contract is signed, through construction, installation, and commissioning, to the final handing over of the facility to the customer.

Production engineers are normally the people who plan and try to improve productivity, who see that the plant produces the right number of cars or cans of soup at the right quality, at the right cost, on time. Planning production means breaking down the manufacturing or construction process into stages, deciding (for mass-production) what the most efficient batch size is. They prepare flow charts and from them production plans and work schedules, which are at their most complicated when many different components have to come together in sub- and main-assemblies from different places (stores, machine shop, forge, etc.), with each part arriving at the right time. They have to work closely with other departments, such as purchasing and stores.

At the planning stage, too, production engineers work out, whether in the factory or out on the site, what plant, machinery and tools are needed (and if necessary have them made or purchased), estimate the people (numbers and types of skills), needed to produce the goods, and cost the operation.

Production engineers organise the assembly, product or flow lines; work out the machine loadings; arrange materials handling; and see that progress is monitored and controlled. They try all the time to improve on their systems: they may look for simpler (i.e. cheaper and faster) ways of making the product, more economical ways of using materials, or assess new machinery for viability. If new systems and equipment are purchased, they must be planned for, installed and run in. Different production methods may be needed, and incentive systems worked out, with management services staff.

Traditionally, production is part of the promotion ladder for skilled craftworkers and technicians, but simpler production lines (making biscuits, chocolate, etc.), often employ people (e.g. any graduate) who are not technologically trained at all, as part of their management training, but under the supervision of qualified engineers. The more complex and sophisticated the product and/or production process, the closer to the line or the site qualified engineers are employed, but scientists (usually physicists or chemists, depending on the product) are often 'converted' to production.

Inspection and quality control are part of the production process. Routine inspection is based on statistical sampling, and it is not only the finished product which has to be inspected, but everything that goes to making a particular product: the raw materials coming into a plant, or onto a construction site. Tests have to be made to see that processes have been completed properly, that there are no flaws in the material from which the product is made (possibly using sophisticated techniques like ultrasonic testing). Inspection and quality control teams are constantly trying to improve and if possible simplify their methods – if only to cut hold-ups in production. In science-based industries, quality control is a lab function.

Maintenance is a carefully organised programme of cleaning, inspection, testing, adjusting, and replacing parts, etc., designed to see that production is not interrupted any more than can be avoided. Maintenance must also solve any problems as fast as possible when machinery and equipment develop faults.

Maintenance is more an incorporated than a chartered engineer function, and the latter are generally only employed as managers, etc., where the machinery and/or equipment is particularly sophisticated, or where there can be problems of keeping major installations running continuously, e.g. nuclear power plant, and where there has to be a particularly large team of maintenance engineers.

Production engineering

The branch of engineering called production is not easy to separate from the production function or production management.

The professional production engineer is responsible for the efficient deployment of a manufacturer's resources, both human and material. The production engineer is the technological expert of the production team as well as a trained manager, and so the chartered engineer usually works where the product being made, or the machinery and equipment which is used to make it, is the most technologically sophisticated and complex.

In any manufacturing firm, production engineers plan and design new production facilities, revamp or revise existing equipment or arrangements, look for ways to improve production methods, speed production, cut costs, or counter new competition. Production engineers assess the potential and check the specifications of new machines and machine tools, and may manage any switch to automation or other use of computer-based technology. They plan the layout of production lines for maximum efficiency. Some production engineers design and produce new manufacturing equipment.

The production engineer is an expert in the economics as well as the technology of production, and must be able to justify changes or new machinery in terms of saved costs or improved production. Production engineers also deal with the problems of industrial relations on the shop floor, especially when systems are being changed.

Production engineers do also manage production facilities, especially early in their careers (many spend their first training periods working as foremen), but their special expertise is designed to take them into more senior posts reasonably quickly. But production in the UK still suffers from the poor image of engineering, and industry is short of them.

Incorporated engineers, working under the production engineer, control known manufacturing techniques and give detailed instructions to the workshops as well as, in many cases, supervising the work of skilled craftworkers.

Production engineering technicians provide support for the senior staff and work in specific areas of production.

Qualifications and training

First-degree level. It is not always called production engineering – there are numerous variants, including manufacturing systems engineering, industrial engineering, plant engineering, process engineering, product engineering, product design, manufacturing and business studies. Production engineering is also frequently taught as part of mechanical engineering courses. For production engineering, subjects studied include basic sciences, mathematics, engineering principles (many courses are common in their early years with mechanical engineering), and then extensive studies of production/manufacturing (examining production, processes, methods, machine tools, assemblies, accessories, etc.), planning and control (including automation), economics and economics of production, industrial relations and management sciences (e.g. work study and operational research).

Postgraduate level. At postgraduate level there are a number of courses leading to higher degrees and diplomas, but industrial experience and/or sponsorship is usually necessary.

Professional body. The professional body is now the Institution of Electrical Engineers. The Institution of Manufacturing Engineers (covering Production Engineers) merged with the Institution of Electrical Engineers in October 1991.

Further information

The Institution of Electrical Engineers and the Institution of Mechanical Engineers.

Engineering courses, qualifications and training

The term 'engineering' serves several purposes: it defines the career of engineering, the academic subject engineering, and the industries which employ engineering techniques. All too often the three are confused and the distinction between them blurs: the career is seen to follow on logically, and inevitably, from the academic study, and just as inevitably, as being pursued in the engineering industry.

In fact, engineering is an academic discipline in its own right, just like science and arts subjects. A career in engineering is no more the inevitable outcome of a degree course in engineering than a career as a mathematician or physicist is for graduates in those subjects.

Engineering Training Authority (EnTra)

Formed by the engineering industry, EnTra is responsible for setting standards of competence and training in engineering. As the Industry Training Organisation for the engineering sector, EnTra, is also the Industry Lead Body for engineering manufacture and has a key place in the government's National Training Framework. In this role it has defined the competencies required at various levels and in the many different roles within the industry to define the competence-based National Vocational Qualifications in collaboration with the National Council for Vocational Qualifications and the examining bodies including BTEC/SCOTVEC and the City & Guilds of London Institute.

Progression routes

For the past 20 or so years, education and training for engineering has become more rigidly stratified and divided between craft, technician and professional levels. However, progression routes have stayed open and even become more flexible with the development of NVQs which ensure a move towards a common view of standards of competence.

The commitment of NCVQ to base qualification on competency and to allow people to build on their competencies instead of having to meet rigid formal examination requirements, and so go step-by-step into different levels, is another indication of the importance put on an integrated coordinated approach to engineering training. The Engineering Council committed itself to preserve, and if possible supplement, the existing education 'bridges' (transfers between academic courses, e.g. from BTEC/SCOTVEC HNC/D to a degree) and 'ladders' ('bolt-on' modules taken during or after some training and experience).

Students graduating from part-accredited degree courses may gain CEng status by undertaking extra study to raise their formation to BEng equivalent, and people registered as IEng may go on to take Engineering Council part 2 exams to complete the academic requirement for CEng. It is also possible to be entered in different sections of the professional register at the same time. For example, someone qualified at stage 3 IEng may also be entered at stage 1 CEng if he or she has the appropriate qualifications.

The Engineering Council also sees 'due recognition of engineering talent, at whatever stage it can be identified, as an important contribution ... and is anxious that individuals who achieve a high standard of professional competence during their careers should not be handicapped by lack of early educational opportunities'. The mature-candidate route to registration does allow direct entry to stage 3 (at age 35) and says a conventional examination to satisfy stage 1 requirements would not be appropriate.

However, entry to chartered (as opposed to registered) status is still subject to the requirements of individual engineering institutions, and it is stressed that the 'burden of proof' on the individual is stringent.

Professional/graduate courses, education and training

For some time now, the great majority of professional engineers have started on the route to their careers with full-time or sandwich-based study for a degree in engineering. While an engineering degree course can be treated as a purely academic/intellectual education, giving the graduate a wide range of possible careers, in fact most engineering graduates do go on to become professional engineers.

Traditionally, engineering degree courses have been heavily academic and theoretical in bias. It is still certainly essential that every course gives a solid foundation of basic engineering sciences, i.e. thermodynamics, fluid dynamics, electrical science and technology, materials science, measurement principles, chemistry and mathematics. However, there has been growing pressure to make courses more 'relevant'. Hence the introduction of the Integrated Engineering Degree; the greater emphasis on developing design and problem-solving skills taught mainly through project work and incorporating only enough engineering science and mathematics as needed; and more time spent on fabrication and use of materials.

Courses also include relevant business techniques, again to be taught mainly via case studies and worked projects, so that engineers learn from the start to work within the limits of time (schedules), cost market factors and budgets, to work with others and cope with the problems of relationships in industry.

The Integrated Engineering Degree (IED) is offered at the universities of Aberdeen, Wales (Cardiff), Luton, Manchester Metropolitan, Nottingham Trent, Portsmouth, Reading, Sheffield Hallam, Staffordshire and Sunderland.

There is, though, no general agreement on what should go into an engineering degree course. As a result, engineering departments have become much more 'creative' in their syllabus design, bringing increasing variety and diversity into degree courses. But by no means all employers want engineering students taught 'management' on a first-degree course, for example – they prefer graduates who are fully trained in fundamental sciences, basic skills and practices on a degree course, leaving management training until they have had reasonable work experience.

There has also been a significant growth in the number of combined engineering and European Studies or language degree courses.

Way back in 1980 the Finniston report demanded that as many students as possible should gain their initial industrial experience via a sandwich-based degree course, and failing that, for departments to have well-equipped workshops where students could learn to use the very latest in computer-controlled machine tools. In fact, a mix of experience of real working life in factories and learning to use machinery in a university workshop, where the student is not constrained by the production line, has to be valuable.

The Engineering Council has laid down firm guidelines on what it requires for accreditation of degree courses in its policy statement (Standards and Routes to Registration – SARTOR). The guidelines tidy up the confusion of new terminology – between so-called 'enhanced' and 'extended' courses, for example – which resulted from the response to the 'Dainton' initiative which set up 'extended' courses in a few universities.

Engineering Council recommendations can be summarised as follows:

- All courses should adopt an integrated approach to theoretical and practical teaching related to the needs of industry.
- Such courses will be known as 'enhanced' (but not necessarily 'extended'). 'Enhanced' means remodelled courses which are in line with the subject content described below. 'Extended' courses should be broad courses, i.e. not an in-depth study of a specialist area. All extended courses, incorporate a major design project, mainly after a two-year course in common with the 'enhanced' course (preferably after assessment, which should include performance on the engineering applications elements), but with the possibility of either direct entry, or transfer after a year only.
- Accredited degree courses should be designated as Bachelor of Engineering (BEng) or if 'extended' MEng, and the Engineering Council 'strongly discourages' the use of these titles for other courses.
- BEng courses must be of honours standard and classified to gain accreditation for stage 1 of the chartered register when they graduate. All Chartered Engineers are entitled to apply for the title of European Engineer (EurIng).
- MEng courses need not be classified, but anyone gaining an MEng should be capable of at least a second class BEng.
- Subject content: at least two-thirds of the content of accredited courses should be on engineering subjects. All students should be introduced to good engineering practice and be involved in a 'significant' amount of relevant, individually assessed, project work.

Courses are expected to have the following features ('enhancement'):

- Technical content in appropriate depth and breadth, emphasising fundamentals and including relevant maths and sciences.
- Application of scientific and engineering principles to the solution of practical problems of engineering systems and processes; emphasis on the relevance of theory and analysis (including training in developing and using theoretical models from which the behaviour of the physical world can be predicted). Courses should embody and integrate theoretical, practical and project work.
- Introduction to good engineering practice, and the properties, behaviour, fabrication and use of relevant materials and components.

- Design studies (including manufacturing, reliability, maintainability, quality assurance and economic aspects): 'Engineering should be taught in the context of design, so that design is a continuous thread running through the teaching ... exposing the student to a proper mixture of analysis, synthesis, conceptual design and other wider issues.'
- Emphasis on methods of practical problem-solving using the latest technology, excluding obsolete methods and topics.
- Technical decision-making and its commercial implementation; use of technical information services; relevant government legislation; management and industrial relations principles; engineers' responsibility to the profession, the community and the environment.
- Specific measures, e.g. teaching methods, to encourage students to find out and learn for themselves, e.g. communication skills, oral and written expression, and a critical approach to problem-solving, with appropriate methods of examination and assessment.
- Significant industrial involvement in the preparation of the course.

Some honours degree courses, which do not include sufficient engineering content to be fully accredited by the Engineering Council, are 'part-accredited'. Graduates from these courses will have to undertake further studies after graduation in order to reach the minimum academic standard required for Chartered Engineer status. One way to achieve this is by taking the Engineering Council's own examinations.

Ordinary and unclassified degree courses in engineering not accredited for direct entry to stage 1 of the chartered engineers' register are suitable qualifications for stage 1 of the incorporated engineers' section.

It must be made clear that Engineering Council requirements are a minimum. Individual engineering institutions are still free to ask for still-higher standards. The Institution of Electrical Engineers, for example, insists that applicants for membership have at least the equivalent of a second-class honours degree.

Engineering at degree level is taught by universities, but only a very few other colleges. Over 17,000 students began their studies for first degrees in engineering and technology and more than 5,600 commenced studies for a postgraduate courses in this area in 1994 (this compares favourably with 1989 when 11,000 first-degree and 4,500 postgraduate students commenced their studies in engineering in UK universities). Another 46,489 registered in further education for the first year of a BTEC course in engineering, 14,676 for studies in the built environment and 27,536 for computing and information services in 1995.

Entry to engineering degree courses normally requires A-levels in maths and at least one science (physics or chemistry as appropriate) or equivalent.

Students with A-levels in arts/social science subjects can take a one-year 'foundation' course, designed to give them the maths and physics needed for entry to an engineering degree (or HND), at a number of higher education institutions.

Alternative professional examinations to a degree

The Engineering Council is responsible for administering the direct-entry examinations in engineering. The Council is continuing the examinations in roughly their present form but suitably 'enhanced' with course and project work, design, etc., to bring them into line with the requirements for degree courses. Entry to courses for these examinations for professional qualification is still possible direct from school (via the same qualifications as for entry to a degree course), or an appropriate technician-level course with credit-standard results. But this two-part examination is the minimum requirement for registration as a professional engineer, and may not meet the requirements of some individual institutions; additional study may be necessary (*see* individual sections following) for chartered status.

Postgraduate study

More graduate engineers now go on to further academic study and training (14.7% in 1994 compared with 8.1% in 1989). Although engineers' interest in postgraduate study is increasing, it still lags well behind that of scientists, 28% of whom went on to postgraduate study in 1994. A high proportion of those postgraduate students studying engineering full-time in universities and colleges (47% in 1994) come from overseas. However, many engineers return to postgraduate study after a period in employment.

Graduate engineers can choose to go on, or return, to further study for a variety of purposes. They can decide to train for research, normally by completing a three-year PhD. Five universities – Brunel, Cardiff, Swansea, UMIST and Warwick – offer Doctorate in Engineering (EngD) degrees which include industrial experience as well as research. Engineers can choose to do a one-year full-time course either to specialise in one area of their first-degree subject, or to 'convert' their basic engineering training to another area (e.g. chemical engineering to biotechnology, broad-based electronics to software engineering), or add on extra skills, e.g. management. They can take a one year Master of Research (MRes) course to increase their research skills as a precursor to PhD studies or a career in research. They can return to study to upgrade or update their original training.

The Engineering and Physical Sciences Research Council (EPSRC) gives grants for postgraduate study in engineering. *See* STUDENT FINANCIAL SUPPORT.

Further information

The Engineering Council (which publishes a definitive list of accredited courses), Engineering and Physical Sciences Research Council (for postgraduate awards).

Incorporated-engineer courses, education and training

The main courses for incorporated engineers are those leading to BTEC and SCOTVEC Higher National Diplomas and Certificates, although as indicated earlier, ordinary and unclassified degree courses do no longer qualify for chartered status without additional study, and so may progressively become incorporated engineer qualifications too.

Courses (part-time only for HNC, full-time, sandwich-based or part-time for HND) for BTEC and SCOTVEC Higher awards are taught at the new universities (England and Wales), central institutions (Scotland), and larger FE colleges. As for all other BTEC courses, HND/C in all branches of engineering are now unit-based and modular and take into account developments in technologies, evolving needs of employers and professional recognition.

The number of people registered for BTEC Higher awards in all branches of engineering in 1995 was 16,246 of whom 7,351 were registered for HND courses in engineering and 8,895 registered for HNC courses. The great majority of people who study engineering for an award at this level specialise in a branch of engineering rather than general engineering. Entry to HND/C is as for all BTEC Higher awards, if via A-level, with the pass in maths or physics, and the other studied to A-level.

SCOTVEC general engineering (HND only) is built around mechanical, plant and production engineering, training for relatively senior work. Design and industrial studies are integral, and final-year options include agricultural engineering and offshore petroleum technology. Entry is as for all SCOTVEC higher awards, the H grades to include maths and physics or engineering.

Engineering-technician courses, education and training

As for incorporated engineers, engineering technicians used mainly to come through from skilled craft level, but direct entry routes to engineering-technician training and qualification have been developing for some years now. In line with modern training developments, skill-specific NVQs have been developed by the Engineering Training Authority with the emphasis being put on modular-based training demonstrating skill and competence rather than time-serving. There are NVQ level 3 qualifications in six areas: engineering machining, joining materials by welding, engineering assembly, engineering material processing, engineering finishing, and installing and commissioning. Each NVQ consists of five core units and further technical units. Most have a range of specialisms within them. Engineering assembly, for example, includes fitting; vehicle body building and assembly; and electronic equipment testing, inspection, assembly and fitting.

There are also numerous level 1 and 2 NVQs in such subjects as welding, machining, electronics manufacture, and high pressure aluminium diecasting, which are for engineering operators of all ages in these areas and can also be appropriate for those wishing to progress to higher levels.

The main courses for engineering technicians are those leading to BTEC National Diplomas and Certificates, and SCOTVEC National Certificates.

BTEC courses (part-time only for National Certificates, normally two-year full-time or three-year sandwich-based for National Diplomas) and SCOTVEC courses for National Certificates are taught by many FE colleges.

Some 19,803 people registered for BTEC National awards in engineering in 1995 with 9,028 registered on National Diploma courses and 10,774 for National Certificate courses, a considerable drop from 1985 when 34,000 registered with about 31% (1985–86) studying for diplomas. BTEC First engineering courses are available too.

Craft courses, education and training

Gaining engineering skills has traditionally meant a three- or four-year apprenticeship, straight from school at 16, learning on the job but with release to study at college on craft courses, usually for City & Guilds awards. The engineering apprenticeship system has a history going back a hundred or more years, and has survived many attempts to modernise it, but in the 1980s and early 1990s it went into decline. In 1995, however, it was given a boost by the introduction of 'Modern Apprentice' schemes.

Engineering craft training schemes, courses and qualifications are designed cooperatively by the EnTra, City & Guilds, FE and industry. EnTra has completely revised craft training. Training is now standards- and competency-based, and increasingly 'modular' with far less emphasis on rigid patterns and periods of training, and no artificial time-serving requirement. Most trainees still start before their seventeenth birthday, and usually complete normal training by the time they are 20.

First-year training in basic engineering skills involves 46 weeks (shorter for trainees who have successfully completed an acceptable technical/practical option at school or on a YT scheme), off-the-job in a training centre, with day- or block-release to study, normally for City & Guilds exams. Thereafter, trainees are taught specific craft skills on a 'modular' basis, the choice of modules depending on company need and the trainee's potential. Time spent on each module depends on progress, content, availability of training opportunities. Each trainee takes either two stage 2 modules or one stage 2 and one stage 3 module as a minimum. Extra 'endorsement' modules can be added at any time. All trainees should have day- or block-release to continue to study for City & Guilds exams.

Entry to craft traineeships is now generally set at a minimum of three suitable subjects (e.g. maths, physical science, English) at GCSE (any grade), or equivalent, plus (for preference) one or more practical subjects (e.g. technical drawing, CDT, metalwork, woodwork) but employers are likely to prefer rather more. Entry is also possible via a YT scheme.

Further information

The Engineering Training Authority.

The branches of engineering

Most engineers qualify initially in a 'branch' of engineering, and careers literature tends to emphasise the divisions between them. But these 'branches' evolved by historical accident, and in the real working world the distinctions are much less hard-and-fast. In a fast-changing technological environment they can look rather artificial. All the major growth points in engineering R&D are interdisciplinary, and the trends in modern technology increasingly mean a cross- or interdisciplinary or 'systems' approach to problems, so the distinctions between them are blurring even further. Machinery – conventionally designed by mechanical engineers – is now being given sophisticated electronic, frequently computer-based, control systems which must be closely integrated into the design. One result is a growing demand for people skilled in electronic/mechanical engineering, which one group of academics has labelled 'mechatronics'. The conversion of electronic systems using copper wire to those employing glass fibre and laser beams has led to increased employment in optoelectronics, and developments in computing such as multimedia, and the increased use of the Internet and other telecommunications systems have further advanced electronics computing and 'software engineering', which are now essential ingredients for all branches.

Engineers also change their specialisations during their career, often because they find themselves applying their initial skills in a different industry. They mostly work in multidisciplinary teams, alongside engineers from 'other' disciplines, and often with scientists too.

Some branches of engineering:

- Aeronautical engineering includes the design of aeroplane structures and wings, guided weapons, and structures which may be subject to high winds or ocean currents, etc. *See* THE AEROSPACE INDUSTRY *in* THE AEROSPACE, NAVAL ARCHITECTURE, MARINE ENGINEERING AND SHIPBUILDING INDUSTRIES.
- Agricultural engineering covers design, production and maintenance of farm machinery and buildings, plus aspects like irrigation, soil erosion and drainage. *See in* LAND USE INDUSTRIES.
- Chemical engineering is the design, installation, operation and maintenance of plant for large scale processes in oil, chemical, pharmaceutical and allied industries. *See in* PROCESS ENGINEERING, BIOMEDICAL ENGINEERING AND MATERIALS SCIENCE.
- Civil engineering involves the design and construction of roads, bridges, railways, tunnels, dams, harbours, airports, large buildings, etc. *See* THE CONSTRUCTION INDUSTRY.
- Electrical and electronic engineering split into heavy-current (electrical machinery, generating stations and distribution systems) and light-current (telecommunications, control systems, computers, etc.). *See* ELECTRICAL AND ELECTRONIC ENGINEERING.
- Energy engineering is the design, manufacture and management of energy plant in the coal, oil, gas, electricity and nuclear industries, etc. *See* THE MINING AND ENERGY INDUSTRIES.
- Marine engineering deals with the design, manufacture and operation of engines and machinery in ships. *See in* THE AEROSPACE, NAVAL ARCHITECTURE, MARINE ENGINEERING AND SHIPBUILDING INDUSTRIES.
- Mechanical engineering covers the design, development, manufacture, operation and maintenance of plant, machinery and mechanical products. *See in* THE MECHANICAL ENGINEERING INDUSTRY.
- Municipal engineering involves the design and construction of public works for local authorities, and other public bodies. *See* THE CONSTRUCTION INDUSTRY.
- Naval architecture is the design and construction of all types of vessels and floating structures. *See in* THE AEROSPACE, NAVAL ARCHITECTURE, MARINE ENGINEERING AND SHIPBUILDING INDUSTRIES.
- Production engineering is the planning, managing and maintenance of manufacturing processes. *See* PRODUCTION ENGINEERING *above*.
- Structural engineering is the design, construction and maintenance of all types of structures, buildings, and dams. *See* THE CONSTRUCTION INDUSTRY.

Contents

Process Engineering, Biomedical Engineering and Materials Science

(CLCI: QOS, RAG, RAM)

Chemical or process engineering

Increasingly chemical engineering is called process engineering, since for many years chemical engineering has treated all kinds of materials, not just chemicals. Even the 'processes' need not involve chemical changes but can be any kind of physical transformation. They are, though, mostly large-scale.

Chemical engineers design, construct, commission, control and operate plant and equipment capable of yielding a steadily widening range of products. They turn crude oil into petrol and plastics, concentrate sulphuric acid and sugar, convert minerals into fertilisers and iron into steel, desalinate water, refine copper and aluminium, produce drugs and paper, and treat waste. They are even involved in producing energy from atomic reactions.

Biochemical engineering, which processes biological rather than other materials, is a branch of chemical engineering. It combines traditional fermentation techniques with the principles used in chemical engineering to produce pharmaceuticals like antibiotics and vitamins, some foodstuffs, in brewing and, increasingly, in treating waste products. It links closely with BIOTECHNOLOGY (*see in* MANUFACTURING INDUSTRIES).

But whatever the material treated or product being made, the fundamental principles and problems are similar: the equipment used to concentrate sulphuric acid is very like that used by refiners to concentrate sugars. The central problem is to apply laboratory techniques to the large-scale of a commercially viable plant; usually this is via an intermediate stage called a 'pilot' plant. This helps to diagnose problems inherent in the 'scaling up' process. The chemical engineer cannot simply enlarge the laboratory equipment: a giant reactor vessel cannot be shaken like a test tube, so other ways of getting a proper mix of materials are employed. Similarly, separating, filtering, distillation, heat exchange etc., become much more complex operations on a large scale, which means being expert on both the theory and the practical side of gas, liquid and fluid flow, heat and mass transfer, temperature measurement, and control. Ways – transport systems – have to be found to get raw 'feedstock' and intermediate and end products to flow evenly through a sequence of 'unit' operations. Plant cannot be made of glass, but must be built of materials to withstand extreme temperatures, high pressures, corrosion etc.

Traditionally, processes and plant were designed as a series of separate but linked 'unit' operations; the unit operation is still the basis of most processes. Now, however, the computer – both as a design tool and as the basis for automatic control systems for the processes themselves – makes 'continuous' processes more common. Chemical engineers therefore try to design 'all through' processes and plant with control systems fully integrated into them. The real expertise in chemical engineering lies in designing processes and plant which work economically to produce as much as possible of any given product at the least possible cost. It is also important to waste as little as possible of the raw feedstock and energy used.

A chemical engineer may have to find a marketable use for a by-product of distillation or a new process where the existing one has become too expensive, or has unwanted effects on the environment. The petrochemical industry can find a use for every single fraction of the end-products of a barrel of crude oil, for example, and can change the balance between products (more petrol, less domestic heating fuel and petrochemicals for plastics, for instance) to match changing market demand. Computers aid substantially in designing processes and systems which give optimum performance and efficiency. Some of the most difficult problems have been solved via a single computer program; others, previously thought too complex ever to be solved, can now be analysed.

Chemical engineering involves complex problem-solving using logical and mathematical techniques, and finding answers in which economics is often just as important as technology. Chemical engineers more often than not work as members of a team.

Working in chemical engineering

Development and design

Design engineers turn the data produced at pilot-plant stage into plans for full-scale equipment. This may mean working on an entire process or plant; calculating temperatures, pressures and flow rates for individual units; designing the pipework, valves and pumps that transport materials from operation to operation. Some design engineers specialise in the detailed design of the sophisticated, mostly computer-aided control systems.

Manufacturing and production

Chemical plant is extremely expensive, and even to recoup the cost – let alone make a profit – plant must run continuously (twenty-four hours a day, seven days a week if possible). The plant manager's job of controlling raw materials, fuel supplies, energy consumption, maintenance, staffing and labour relations is crucial. Plant engineers 'trouble shoot', check equipment performance and look for ways to improve efficiency.

Research

Projects range from the most theoretical study of basic phenomena to practical work on full-scale plant. It may involve developing new techniques and processes for new products (liquid fuel from coal for example); designing and evaluating pilot plant (and producing data from which profit forecasts can be made); looking for methods to cut down the impurities in a product, and technical service work.

Other activities

These include instrumentation and control, plant construction and installation, quality control, maintenance and servicing, technician engineers. An increasing number of chemical engineers are also employed in technical marketing, sales, purchasing, general administration and higher education.

Specialist chemical engineers are usually part of OPERATIONAL RESEARCH and WORK STUDY AND ORGANISATION AND METHOD teams (*see in* MANAGEMENT SERVICES) in the chemical industry, and may also work in computing. There are additional opportunities in PATENT WORK (*see in* THE LEGAL SYSTEM).

Nearly three-quarters of recent first-degree graduates in chemical engineering found employment in engineering research, design and development. Not all chemical engineers, however, are employed directly in the chemical industry. There are opportunities in the oil industry – from extraction to refining and petrochemical production; fuel industries – including nuclear fuels, gas production and distribution, coal processing; food and drink manufacture – especially where traditional fermentation methods are used in process plant, e.g. brewing; mining and quarrying; ceramics and glass; paper and printing; electrical and electronics and textiles.

Recruitment and entry

While it is possible to become a chemical engineer via a degree in chemistry, physical sciences or mechanical engineering followed by postgraduate training in chemical engineering, a first degree in chemical engineering is preferable. Chemical engineers need training which integrates and closely dovetails relevant theoretical principles and practical training from chemistry and engineering. In 1994, 1,400 students started first degree courses in chemical engineering.

To become a Corporate Member of the Institution of Chemical Engineers usually requires at least four years approved industrial training and professional engineering experience after completion of a first degree (the minimum age for election to membership of the institution is 25 years).

Postgraduate training in chemical engineering for graduates in other, but related, subjects is available at a number of universities. Graduates in chemical engineering can go on to specialise, for instance, in biochemical engineering, biotechnology, integrated design of chemical plant, plant engineering in the process industry, and desalination technology.

Qualifications and training

Entry to most chemical engineering degrees is with chemistry, maths and physics at A-level/H grade but other subject combinations are possible for entry to some courses. Appropriate equivalent qualifications may also be acceptable. A number of industrial and professional organisations offer sponsorship opportunities to students taking first degree courses in this subject.

Chemical engineering is a more self-contained branch of engineering than most others with much less in common ground with the rest. It is, then, rather more important to be sure of a strong interest in chemical engineering since there is less chance of transferring into other areas of engineering, though chemical engineering is just as good a basic discipline for careers in many areas outside professional engineering.

BTEC Higher National Certificate (and Diploma courses) are available at a number of colleges.

The Chemical Industries Association (CIA) has implemented APBPI/SVQ schemes in Process Operations (Chemical and Pharmaceutical) Levels 1-3; Process Operations Technical Support (Chemical and Pharmaceuticals) Level 3; Laboratory Operations (Chemical and Pharmaceutical) Levels 1-4; and Process Engineering Maintenance Levels 1-3.

Further information

The Institution of Chemical Engineers.

Biomedical engineering

In biomedical engineering, biological and physical sciences come together in a highly interdisciplinary way to solve all kinds of practical medical problems. Although scientists and engineers have been designing and producing devices, instruments, equipment etc. for use in medicine for over a hundred years, biomedical engineering has only relatively recently been recognised as a discipline in its own right.

Biomedical engineers design 'prosthetic' devices and materials to replace, support or repair parts of the body which have been lost or damaged by trauma or disease. Many are now in everyday use – cardiac pacemakers and valves, joint replacements, and kidney dialysis machines, for example. Work on refining and improving them, however, is continual. Prostheses, particularly those which go inside the body, must be extremely reliable – maintenance and repair are impossible once they are in place yet they must stand up to very hard wear, be made of materials that the body will tolerate, and must often be extremely small.

Biomedical engineering also develops instruments of increasing complexity and sophistication. They measure, analyse, monitor, diagnose, and even operate. In the clinical laboratory, elaborate and intricate machinery, computer-controlled, accurately and exactly measures and analyses body fluids, like blood, often doing many tests at the same time, separating samples, and so on. Doppler measurement of blood velocity has opened up research into an ever-wider range of uses for ultrasonics for both monitoring and diagnosis.

In monitoring, biomedical engineers have produced a wide range of equipment which can watch patients continuously, in intensive care, under surgery, or even in day-to-day life, and can be programmed to signal crucial changes. Ultrasonic scanning has replaced X-rays in monitoring the developing foetus more efficiently and less dangerously than X-rays. Instruments will soon monitor the body's ions and molecules so that eventually closed-loop control and treatment in anaesthetics, dialysis, intensive care and post-operative recovery may be possible.

In diagnosis, equipment in common use includes the whole-body ultrasonic scanner (linked to computer-based analysis of multiple readings which would take a lifetime to calculate manually). Nuclear magnetic resonance techniques have been developed for even more sophisticated imaging. Delicate, hairline tubes and optical fibres can take miniature instruments in to explore and even operate inside the body on, for instance, lung, heart or vein unreachable by other means. Use of biosensors and cheap, disposable diagnostic 'kits' (increasingly making use of developments in biotechnology) is expected to grow rapidly. Simple enough to use at home, the readings from such kits can be transmitted automatically via the phone to the monitoring hospital.

Surgeons can have scalpels which seal blood vessels as fast as they are cut. Lasers are almost routine in some forms of surgery, and scientists have devised a 'weapon' which combines the power and penetration of radiation therapy with the pin-point precision of the surgical laser.

Biomedical engineering is developing computer programs to analyse the information collected by the new medical instrumentation or see what can be discovered from the case histories of many patients with a particular disease – its epidemiology, or the success rates of specific forms of treatment, for instance. Computer programs have been designed which can begin the process of asking a patient about the symptoms which have brought them to the doctor or hospital.

Research and development in biomedical engineering is often extremely expensive, and so can be the resulting equipment. Much of the R&D is done to meet a specific need in a particular hospital or unit, and only if and when it is successful is it developed for wider use and commercial sale – if investment can be found.

Advances in biomedical engineering depend not only on developments in the technologies which go to create devices and techniques, but also on complete understanding of how the body works and the medical problems which researchers are trying to solve, and on other basic sciences. There are strong links between bioengineering and MATERIALS SCIENCE AND TECHNOLOGY (*see below*).

Working in biomedical engineering

The numbers employed are relatively small. There is no clearly defined career structure or a formal educational ladder. Rarely does any one person have all the necessary expertise on a project, so there has to be close team work and collaboration between, for example, the scientists, engineers, and the medical people, and through this scientists and engineers often gain the extra skills they need.

Most people working in this field are in universities, medical schools or universities, some in non-teaching hospitals, a few in the Department of Health, some in research organisations and firms (some specialist medical equipment manufacturers and others for whom this is a small part of a business mainly concerned with scientific instruments or even electronics).

There are opportunities for non-graduates at Medical Technical Officer grade in the NHS and in universities.

Qualifications and training

Many people enter professional-level biomedical engineering after qualifying in another subject, usually via a degree. Almost any branch of engineering is useful, but electronic engineering, mechanical engineering, materials science, medicine, physics, computer science, or a life science – especially physiology – are particularly useful. Many Biological Engineering Society members originally qualified as engineers.

There are a few degree courses which include biomedical engineering disciplines – with mechanical engineering at Brunel and University College, London and with electronic engineering at Aberdeen, Kent and Salford universities. A comprehensive list of first degree courses is available from the Biological Engineering Society.

Graduates, particularly those with specific degrees, may enter biomedical engineering without further formal training. A number of post-graduate courses are available in specialisations such as bioengineering, biomedical engineering and biomedical instrumentation.

The Biological Engineering Society has various grades of membership. Suitably qualified and experienced members can be nominated for registration as chartered engineers, incorporated engineers and engineering technicians.

Further information

The Biological Engineering Society.

Materials science and technology

Materials science includes ceramics, glass and refractories technology, metallurgy and plastics and polymers.

Most materials, whether metal, ceramic or polymer, have the same kind of microstructure. All are made up of innumerable fine crystals, and the differences between materials are due to the myriad different shapes, types, and size of crystals, the different structures which link up the crystals, and the impurities and defects in them. Creating new materials for particular purposes and adapting and improving materials to more exacting specifications are often only possible because materials scientists and technologists now know how to manipulate and create new crystal structures to meet demand. New composite materials combining the best characteristics of metals and polymers, or bonding them together efficiently, often for the first time, are needed and are being developed. Many modern technological advances would be impossible without new and better materials. The silicon chip would have been impossible without a detailed understanding of the structure of materials, and further research on electronic materials, such as 'super lattices', will bring more novel devices. Modern medicine demands materials which will survive and work in the body – in heart valves, hip joints etc.

The process is two-way: on one hand, design engineers need materials to meet more exacting specifications, for instance to withstand greater stress or higher temperature; to be more flexible to mould; to keep their shape and size under intensive radiation; or to replace materials which have become too scarce or expensive to use. On the other, research can result in new materials and by-products for which new uses can be found, and may even make possible advances in other areas of technology. Sometimes uses may be found for a new discovery – a plastic made by bacterial fermentation using sugar or other renewable material (as substrate), for instance, turns out to be 'biodegradable', and so possibly usable for controlled or slow release of drugs or agrochemicals, or as sutures or temporary implants. Polymer, sturdier and easier to join, could replace glass in optical fibres in future.

Ceramics looks set to become a real high-tech 'wonder' material with the discovery that copper-oxide ceramics are superconductors. It is the second-largest group of man-made engineering material already, and the ceramics can be such good heat resisters that they are used on the outside of space shuttles, in rocket nozzles, and nuclear fuel elements. Ceramics can cut steel at high speed and are used to line bullet-proof vests. Glasses and ceramics are being tried out for use in gas turbines, fuel-burning devices, hard-wearing jibs, and high-temperature chemical plant where existing metallic materials are near the limit of their performance. Ceramic engines for aircraft and cars are a real possibility.

But research also looks for new and better ways of working with and on materials. Areas of current interest include improving manufacturing methods using, for instance, 'near-net shaping' – making castings from powered metals instead of solid shapes to cut waste and the number of manufacturing stages; improving surface and joining technology – increasing heat and wear resistance of tools by coating them with ceramics; and assurance of product performance, e.g. using automated methods to create new materials, new ways of evaluating materials, and of assessing their likely operational life. Materials and methods of joining them have to be bettered constantly to cope with more difficult environments – from oil rigs in the North Sea to shuttles in space.

In academic study and research, 'materials' is increasingly treated as one subject, based on common scientific principles and benefiting considerably from a logical, collective study of all solids. However, integrated study of materials is still relatively young, and it is still common to think in terms of the individual branches:

– *metallurgy*, dealing with metals from their extraction from ores. Chemical metallurgy covers refining, mineral dressing, preparing ore concentrates; metal forming or process metallurgy covers shaping by casting, rolling, forging, drawing; physical metallurgy covers structure and physical properties of metals including their behaviour under stress and temperature.
– *ceramics*, dealing with products that range from the output of the traditional clay-based industry – building bricks, pipes, domestic china and pottery – to the many industrial ceramics used because of their physical hardness, their heat and chemical resistance or their bonding reaction.
– *glass*, dealing with the results of 20th-century research, and the completely new products and production processes that have been developed by glass technologists.
– *polymers*, dealing with chemicals whose feedstock is crude oil (for example, acetylene, benzene, butadiene, ethylene, propylene and ammonia), and which are variously combined, with ancillary materials such as heat and light stabilisers, anti-oxidants and pigments, to form bulk synthetic resins and polymers.

Working in materials science

Most metallurgists and ceramic, glass and polymer technologists work in their 'parent' industries – metallurgists in metal production, etc. Significant and rising numbers work for firms making other materials, especially as 'composite' material production increases, and for the larger customer firms which use metals, plastics, glass, etc. in large quantities, particularly in sectors like electronics, aerospace, car making, chemicals and plastics, electricity generation, and gas.

Demand for people with a broader materials training is increasing, and gives graduates greater flexibility. Degree courses have increased their treatment of design and other engineering topics so that the materials specialist can more readily participate as part of an engineering team.

Many materials experts are employed in research and development, often as members of multidisciplinary teams with other materials specialists (e.g. polymer technologists in the steel industry trying to improve plastic coatings) and scientists, especially chemists. R&D ranges from the development of new materials for particular purposes, through working on new products or improved versions of old ones, to finding ways of making production more efficient, faster and less wasteful.

Materials specialists are not confined to R&D laboratories. There are many opportunities in production – senior managers of steel mills may be metallurgists, for example. There are also many opportunities in engineering design, where materials specialists ensure the materials specified are right for the particular product and its manufacturing process. Here a materials specialist may have to satisfy the specifications required by mechanical, chemical, production and design engineers.

Various factors affect employment for materials specialists. Recession, competition from overseas producers (both of materials and of the products, such as cars, from which they are made), and increasing competition from other materials (especially plastics), have adversely affected the metal industries and especially steel, aluminium and glass.

Qualifications and training

Metallurgy and materials of all kinds are studied at higher diploma, degree and postgraduate levels. Some courses stress scientific aspects, whereas others emphasise the engineering design aspects of the subject. The latter type of course may benefit materials specialists hoping to participate as members of an engineering team. A few universities specialise in polymers or ceramics.

Entry requirements are usually with mathematics and physics or chemistry at A-level/H grade.

See also MANUFACTURING.

The professional body is The Institute of Materials. As a Chartered Engineering Institution, it is authorised by the Engineering Council to accredit appropriate degree courses in materials for those seeking Chartered Engineer status. Successful completion of an accredited higher diploma course satisfies the academic requirement for registration as an Incorporated Engineer.

Training, on-the-job with release for college study, leads to BTEC/SCOTVEC National Diploma awards in Metallurgical Studies and Metals Technology.

NVQs at levels 1 to 3 are available. The British Polymer Training Association, Steel Training and various ceramic training organisations have developed schemes to cover aspects of rubber and plastics production. Twelve aspects of plastics production are included such as: injection moulding, thermoforming, FRP laminating at Levels 1 and 2. Rubber processes include: retreading tyres, vulcanising and assembly at Levels 1 and 2. There are also administration, customer services, wholesaling, warehousing and store at Level 2. Open centres around the country offer a variety of courses including: Supervisory Management (MCI) Polymer Processing Technology Award and Developing Polymer Products.

Further information

The Institute of Materials (Education Department).

Contents

The Aerospace, Naval Architecture, Marine Engineering and Shipbuilding Industries

(CLCI: RAC, RAV, ROF)

The aerospace industry

In the UK, the aerospace industry makes not only civil and military aircraft and engines and avionic equipment and systems for them, but also guided weapons and missiles, hovercraft, and space gadgetry. The cost of aircraft manufacturer and of the crucial research and development, on which expenditure is probably higher than in any other industry, has been soaring for years. The large-scale manufacturers have been meeting the problems with cross-national cooperative venturers – e.g. the European Airbus, and the multi-role combat Tornado – but lately smaller countries have been trying to develop aerospace businesses as a 'spearhead' technology giving access to huge markets, increasing the competition still further.

The UK, despite considerable rationalisation over the past few years, is still the third largest aerospace industry in the world after the US and France. Germany is close behind in fourth place. Turnover on UK civil and military aircraft grew by 12.3% a year during the 1980s, peaking in 1990 at £12,000 billion. This decade has seen a steady decline, which reached a turnover of £10.2 billion in 1993. Exports of civil aviation products are running at around 75% while exports of military products are in the region of 55%. Aeroengines have the highest export ration with 80% of them being exported. The UK relies more heavily on exports than the French or German aerospace industries both of which are more reliant on their domestic markets. Of the three aircraft manufacturers which account for virtually all Western production of aircraft, UK companies have a 25% stake in one, the European Airbus consortium, as well as being major suppliers to the two American manufacturers, Boeing and McDonnell Douglas. Rolls Royce has more than quadrupled its share of the world market for jet engines since 1987.

Long-term planning is necessary in the aerospace industry as there is a typical 10–15 year life cycle for aerospace products. Airlines have no option but to replace their ageing fleets with newer jets that are more efficient and economic to fly, but which, and what kind, they require is determined by the mix between business travel, tourism and freight, between long hauls and shorter journeys.

Despite government plans to trim defence expenditure, and the phenomenal cost of modern defence equipment, European (including British) aerospace firms are collaborating together on several major new ventures, including the design and construction of a new vertical takeoff fighter. On the commercial side, manufacturers are currently developing improved versions of earlier aircraft, and working on completely new generations of airliners, across the full range from 'jumbo' jet through to 100-seat or less, including so-called commuter and regional jet and turboprop types. All are designed to cut operating costs, improve payload performance, and extend the range. All will incorporate very advanced technology – and bring down fuel consumption. New aircraft have more efficient engines, make extensive use of advanced lightweight materials, more refined aerodynamics, less weight, and sophisticated fuel management systems, from accurate electronic control of engine settings to on-board computers which can calculate the most economical route from moment to moment, e.g. avoiding cross winds where possible. On-board computers and electronic cockpit control and coloured cathode ray tube displays instead of vast arrays of instrument dials for the crew make them easier and safer to fly. Environmental considerations are increasingly important and manufacturers also have to build, as economically as possible, quieter and less atmospherically polluting aero-engines.

To fill order books and factories, aircraft manufacturers constantly try to talk customers and governments into new projects – and governments into funding their immensely expensive development. Aircraft manufacturers depend greatly on being able to raise huge sums for investment, and can never be absolutely certain of sales, so there is always an element of insecurity.

In the late 1980s the main aircraft and aero-engine manufacturers in the civil sector were confidently forecasting huge increases in sales into the 21st century as airlines replace their ageing fleets. Boeing predicted that world traffic would grow at an average annual rate of 5.4% and thought the 1990s would be the best decade it had ever had.

In 1989, huge aircraft contracts were placed, order books were very healthy and it looked as though the problem for the industry would be expanding output to cope with demand. This resulted in a backlog of orders which helped to maintain and support production in the early 1990s. While the defence markets began to decline in 1991 the civil aviation market continued to grow until well into 1992 and has not declined significantly since. Military aerospace turnover in the UK is running at around £5.5 billion and civil turnover at £5.0 billion. Cutbacks in the defence and military markets were caused by the recession, the easing of East–West tensions and the Gulf war. The future order-book is very sensitive to projected increases in airline traffic and in 1996 this looks promising. Early in 1996 British Airways placed a large order for new aircraft and China ordered $2 billion worth of aircraft from Airbus Industrie. Such large orders will have a long-term knock-on effect in the sale of spare parts.

The outlook on the military side too is less gloomy than it was in the early 1990s. The defence equipment industry has declined following the developments in central and eastern Europe and the disintegration of the Warsaw Pact. Also, the rising cost of military aircraft places strains on defence budgets and some countries, like Belgium, have decided to update their existing fighter aircraft rather than join a consortium developing a new military jet. In 1996, however, British Aerospace were teaming up with McDonnell Douglas to design and build a replacement for the Harrier and F16 Eagle. It will be a supersonic jet steered by its engine and with vertical takeoff capability. Lockheed Martin and Boeing were also competing. Britain has also committed itself to developing and puchasing the 'Eurofighter'. During the difficult trading conditions of the early 1990s many companies have diversified into other businesses outside aerospace. British Aerospace, for example has diversified into car manufacture, ammunition production, telecommunications and information technology.

Employment prospects in the industry have declined during the first few years of this decade with a 30% reduction in manpower from 144,000 to 101,000. Considerable rationalisation has taken place and several hitherto important aerospace sites have been closed. The worst is probably now passed. Rolls Royce was ninth and British Aerospace 15th in the R&D spending league in 1994 with budgets of £218 million and £99 million respectively but these figures were down from £253 million and £168 million respectively spent in 1993.

Britain's aerospace industry makes a wide range of aircraft from crop-sprayers to wide-bodied jets, from jet trainers to fighters. British Aerospace is the industry's main linchpin, and is one of the world's most innovative hi-tech companies, engaged in the design, development, manufacture and marketing of a wide range of products from micro-electronic sub-systems to aircraft, missiles and satellites. The BAe Group has been restructured around several divisions as follows:

Aerostructures, employing 4,000 people at Chadderton, Filton and Prestwick is assembling fuselages for RJ aircraft and wing sub-assemblies for Airbus. It manufactures aircraft components, advanced composite materials and spares.

Airbus, in which BAe is a 20% partner, employs 4,000 people. It designs and produces wings and components for Airbus Industrie products such as the long-range A330, the wide bodied A300 and the single aisle A319 jet. They are developing a large military transport aircraft and researching advanced supersonic travel.

Avro, with 1,800 employees, assembles, markets and supports its range of regional jet aircraft which seat between 70 and 130 people. It is merging with French Aerospatiale and Alenia.

Jetstream, with 2,000 employees, designs and manufactures and provides customer service for the Jetstream turboprop aircraft. Again this is a joint venture with Aerospaciale and Alenia.

British Aerospace Systems and Equipment with 1,000 employees produces inertial navigation systems, digital terrain systems, naval gunfire controls, flight data recorders, secure message handling systems, radomes and motion sensors.

Dynamics, with 2,500 employees, designs and manufactures guided weapons such as the Rapier 2000, ALARM, Sea Skua and ASRAM (short-range air to air missile).

Military Aircraft Division with 15,000 employees is by far the largest. Its role is to design, develop produce and market combat aircraft, training aircraft and military systems on a worldwide basis. It is developing the next generation of Euro-fighter, the Harrier, Hawk, Tornado, Gripen and T45 Goshawk.

Royal Ordnance, with 4,800 employees, manufactures small arms, large guns, ammunition rocket motors and armoured vehicles.

Short Brothers of Northern Ireland make turboprops for the short-haul market and regional jet aircraft. Westland, the helicopter maker, has benefited from the North Sea oil industry providing aircraft to transport supplies and individuals offshore. They have also recently received orders from Saudi Arabia. Westland also makes hovercraft.

Space is an important source of income now for the UK industry, which provides satellites for telecommunications, weather forecasting, remote sensing and defence purposes. BAe Dynamics and GEC-Marconi manufacture spacecraft and satellites. .

Rolls Royce has a workforce of 38,000 of which 21,000 are employed in their Aerospace Group based at Derby, Bristol, Glasgow and Ansty. Britain's Aero engine manufacturer, and one of the world's big three, it has fought fiercely to increase its share of the estimated £3.6 billion market. Development costs have forced engine manufacturers into collaborative programmes, e.g. Tornados RB199 and the EJ200 for the new fighter and the V2500 for large commercial aircraft – huge technological advances are needed to meet the required performance. New engines for civil aircraft can now cost £1,000 million to develop, and for military the figure is even higher.

Employment in the industry

Numbers employed in aerospace are (1993) around 101,000 against 144,000 in 1990, a fall of 30%. Future employment depends primarily on orders but the level of government funding, the volume of defence cuts and the return to growth in passenger traffic all have their effect. In 1995 BAe employed around 45,000 people of whom 24,000 were employed in the defence companies and 21,000 in the commercial aircraft companies.

Aircraft, aero-engines, satellites, etc., have to be built individually. Parts, e.g. wings or noses or frames, may be built in different locations, even different countries, and then transported to yet another factory for final assembly. BAe, for example, builds Airbus wings for assembly in France and Germany.

While production is difficult to automate fully, manufacturers employ the most technologically advanced techniques and machinery feasible, including robots – often specially developed by the companies themselves. Computer-based systems are used wherever possible, from computer-aided design and manufacture (CAD/CAM), through to systems for handling – storing and retrieving – the 22,000 different parts needed to build, for instance, a Tornado, and the latest in flexible manufacturing systems and numerically controlled machines. Parts made in composite materials, which start out as powder/granules, can be formed and bonded using mass production techniques, so there will be less and less 'metal bashing' and welding/riveting, etc. in the future.

But building aircraft is still a skilled business, and even using the most modern equipment available, the industry still employs comparatively large numbers of people trained to use sophisticated, modern machines and techniques.

The proportion of highly skilled people employed at both professional/graduate and technician level is inevitably high across the full spectrum of 'functions', and not just in R & D. Developing, designing, building and marketing/selling end products as complex, costly and technologically advanced as high-performance aircraft and space equipment take multi-disciplinary teams of experts of all kinds, and aeronautical engineers are only part of them.

The electronics and computer-based equipment going into commercial aircraft, for example, is now at least a third of the total cost and considerably higher for military and space craft. While some aeronautical engineers are trained specialists in these 'avionic' systems, developing and designing them also involves electronic and control engineers, and computer scientists.

Engineering designers may work on structures or on electronic and avionic systems. But they may also be involved in developing computer-aided design systems and methods, in developing and designing database and information retrieval and transmission systems for CAD/CAM systems, or in design support – dealing with design standards and procedures. Designers may have to solve particular problems, produce prototype models, design laboratory tests, analyse data, and write reports.

Production management is a complex business of co-ordinating both manufacture and assembly of specific aircraft, and each area of manufacturing – wing skin panels for example – i.e. 'project' and 'product centre' management.

Aircraft manufacturers also design and develop their own advanced manufacturing technology and systems both for making many of the components and parts, and for assembly. This can involve, for example, developing the new processes needed when metals are replaced by plastic or carbon fibre composites. Efficient production depends heavily on work/method study, which has to live with continual changes, preparing optimum factory layouts and production flow lines, deciding on work packages and monitoring output.

Production engineering works out how to produce and/or assemble components, designs (and has made) tools, etc. and plans manufacturing sequences and processes.

Quality assurance in aircraft manufacture has to meet legal standards and control throughout all phases of manufacture, assembly and testing, starting with the materials and parts made by other companies as well as the machines used in manufacturing, through to the point of delivery. Monitoring for defects throughout manufacturing, and preventing them happening again, is part of the function. Test programmes and equipment have to be designed and produced.

Production employs mainly aeronautical, mechanical/production, and electrical/electronic engineers, some scientists (e.g. physics graduates in production of opto-electronic sensing devices); most manufacturers involve people with business qualifications too.

The British Aerospace commercial aircraft companies organise their staff into cross-disciplinary teams with individual graduate jobs falling into the following main areas:

- Structural Engineering, where graduates may be investigating the best balance between the conflicting demands of low weight, minimum cost and structural integrity; using techniques to predict the dynamics of stress; and investigating the risks of structural fatigue and fracture.
- Aerodynamics, where graduates help to find answers to how to create aircraft with good flight and load-carrying characteristics, that are safe and economic for airlines to operate and comfortable for passengers – for example, analysing acoustics to minimise engine noise or applying flight control principles to achieve stable flight. Advanced computer techniques are used to derive theories which are then tested in ground and flight trials.
- Systems Engineering, where graduates deal with problems in flight deck display systems, automated control systems, navigation systems, communication systems, hydraulic and pneumatic systems, and all systems affecting passengers and crew. Engineers of all disciplines have to work closely with staff in marketing, design, production and customer support departments, and with the equipment suppliers and regulatory bodies.
- Manufacturing Engineering, where graduates produce manufacturing and purchase specifications, oversee production, design automation and materials handling systems and work with production staff from shop floor up to senior managers.

Commercial functions and support services deal almost routinely with huge sums and long-term sales. They all have a significant technical/technological content which makes an engineering/science background as useful as commercial training. Pre-planning market research, attempting to predict needs decades ahead, takes considerable experience of the aircraft business. Sales engineers monitor and analyse the airline business, traffic and revenue predictions, prepare sales material, visit airlines and take part in sales presentations. The battle for an airline's business, which can have a dramatic effect on the success of an aircraft and so company profits, is fierce and very sophisticated. Negotiating contracts is a highly technical business with significant legal content. Finance has to evaluate and control projects with multi-million cash-flows which can last 20 years or more. Reliable and competitive estimating on design, development and manufacturing costs can make a considerable difference to the commercial viability of an aircraft, as can purchasing. All commercial functions make extensive use of computer systems to provide and manage data quickly and accurately, and companies do their own development work on these.

Recruitment and entry

In a highly sophisticated business, the small number of firms are always looking for high-calibre people at all levels, although the numbers are never very large. Since the industry has major ups and downs, the number fluctuates enormously. For example, in good years of the late 1980s British Aerospace recruited over 500 graduates each year and took about a third of the 590 aeronautical engineers who graduated annually. In bad years jobs can be thin on the ground. In 1996, British Aerospace is planning a graduate intake of around 200. Demand is for graduates to work in engineering design, research, technical manufacturing, testing and trial, customer support and commercial departments. Disciplines in most demand are electronic, electrical, mechanical and aeronautical engineering, computer science, physics, maths and materials science.

School-leavers with at least four GCSE/SCEs (grades A–C/1–3), or equivalent passes, including mathematics and physics or another appropriate science, are recruited for technician training. Appropriate GCSE/SCEs are also preferred for craft-level training.

Qualifications and training

Some of the larger companies offer a small number of sponsorships to read for appropriate engineering-type degrees (not necessarily aeronautical), but most professional staff enter as graduates. (*See* AERONAUTICAL ENGINEERING *below*.)

Technician/craft training is largely in-company, on-the-job and in training centres, with release to study for appropriate BTEC and City & Guilds awards.

Further information

The Society of British Aerospace Companies and aircraft manufacturers.

Aeronautical engineering

This is one of the most technologically advanced branches of engineering, often involving quite original research and high-level development work in solving design problems. Real technological 'leaps' may be needed, to exploit new materials (e.g. lithium) and make further technological breakthroughs.

Designing and building civil and military aircraft is not only technologically demanding, aeronautical engineers must also meet customers' other, often tight, specifications. It is, for example, pointless producing a technological miracle (e.g. Concorde), if it cannot be operated economically. New civil aircraft must meet market requirements: they must be capable of carrying a certain number of passengers, at certain altitudes, at certain speeds, over certain distances; they must be as economic as possible in their use of fuel; they must be straightforward to maintain, and above all, safe to fly. Increasingly airports are insisting on quiet aircraft which do not cause an environmental problem and protests from local communities.

It is not a simple job to make an aircraft completely safe and also ensure that it is profitable to operate. Planes must be structurally strong, and comfortable for passengers and crew, but also as light and as aerodynamically streamlined as possible – all of which cause design conflicts and make decisions difficult, with no room for error. Military aircraft, loaded with armaments and electronic equipment, demanding higher speeds and manoeuvrability and flexibility, are even more difficult to design.

Fortunately, computer-aided design now helps to solve many problems, and its sophistication also makes possible substantial improvements in wing design to give better aerodynamic efficiency, for example. CAD also helps to cut design costs, because less time has to be spent in wind-tunnel testing for example, and also makes the whole design process faster.

Professional aeronautical engineers usually specialise in one of the main aspects of aeronautical design. These are aerodynamic systems – hydraulic, fuel, pneumatic – and avionics, which involves designing the very sophisticated navigational, communication and radar systems which are now based on airborne minicomputers. Aeronautical engineers are more usually employed in R&D and design, less in production and related functions than other engineers. There is more team work, liaison and consultation in aeronautical R&D/design than in other branches of engineering.

Incorporated engineers and engineering technicians work in design or project work (e.g. as draughtsmen or women), in jig and tool or layout offices, as planning or project engineer in a production office, as inspectors or supervisors who need technical knowledge.

Aeronautical engineers work mainly in the aerospace industry (*see above*) but some aeronautical engineers work for firms designing/manufacturing other vehicles where aerodynamic principles are useful, e.g. hovercraft, high-speed and linear motor systems, and even the auto industry, although generally the very exacting techniques of aeronautical engineering are too expensive for other industries.

Quite a few aeronautical engineers work for airline companies. Professionals work with manufacturers on plans for the next generation of aircraft, and manage and administer (and try to improve) the airline's service and repair operations. The servicing and repair is actually done by technicians and craft workers. (*See also* CIVIL AVIATION *in* THE TRANSPORT INDUSTRY).

Aeronautical engineers are also employed by the Ministry of Defence at the Defence Evaluation and Research Agency laboratory at Farnborough and the RAF (*see* ARMED FORCES).

Qualifications and training

Professional aeronautical engineers normally have a first degree course in aeronautical engineering, although it is possible to convert to aeronautical engineering at postgraduate level from, e.g. mechanical engineering or electronics. Degree courses are Engineering Council (EC) accredited and are offered by the following universities.

Bath: Aeronautical Engineering BEng (3/4), specialising in aeronautical engineering, option to include French or German. Aeronautical Systems Design and Manufacture MEng (4 yrs).

Belfast: Aeronautical Engineering BEng/MEng (3/4 yrs) in air transportation, advanced aerodynamics, stability and control, aircraft production.

Bristol: Aeronautical MEng (4 yrs) in fluid mechanics, aerodynamics, astronautics, languages, major design project, major research project. Aeronautical Engineering with study in continental Europe MEng (4 yrs).

Bristol University of the West of England: Aerospace Manufacturing Engineering BEng/MEng (3/4 yrs).

Cambridge. Aeronautical Engineering MEng (4 yrs).

City (London): Aeronautical engineering BEng (3/4 yrs), MEng (4/5 yrs), BSc/MEng, common first six terms, options include aerodynamics, aircraft structures and propulsion: Air-transport engineering BEng (3 yrs) includes airline economics and administration.

Coventry: Aerospace Systems Engineering BEng (3/4 yrs), 1st year in common with other BEng degrees, engineering, aerospace science, advanced manufacturing techniques, industrial placement in European/UK aerospace company, individual project drawing.

Glasgow: Aeronautical engineering (4 yrs) course partly in common with other branches of engineering, choice of options in final year: Avionics BEng (4 yrs) entry via aero or electronics engineering.

Hertfordshire: Aerospace Systems Engineering BEng/MEng (3/4 yrs). Aerospace Engineering BEng/MEng (3/4 yrs).

Kingston: Aeronautical Engineering BEng (4 yr sandwich with industrial placement), design-based including flight dynamics, lightweight structures, aircraft power plant, aerodynamics, aeronautics.

London Imperial: Aeronautical Engineering M Eng (4 yrs), specialising in aeronautical or fluid and structural mechanics

London QMW: Aeronautical Engineering BEng (3 yrs) available with French, Spanish and German. BSc Eng. Aerospace Materials Technology BEng (3 yrs). Avionics BEng (3 yrs).

Loughborough: Aeronautical Engineering BEng (3 yrs). MEng and Diploma in Industrial Studies (4 yr thick sandwich course).

Manchester: Aerospace Engineering BEng/MEng (3/4 yrs) also offer an integrated European programme. Aerospace Engineering with Systems MEng (4 yrs). Aerospace Materials Engineering MEng (4 yrs).

North East Wales Institute of Higher Education: Aeronautical Engineering BEng (4 yrs).

Salford: Aeronautical Engineering BEng (3 yrs). Aeronautical Systems BEng (3 yrs).

Southampton: Aeronautics & Astronautics BEng (3 yrs)/MEng (4 yrs). Aerospace Systems Engineering BEng/MEng (3/4 yrs).

Entry to degree courses in aeronautical engineering normally requires three A levels (or five Scottish H grades) including maths, physics (physical or engineering science).

Some candidates offer advanced GNVQs as part of the entry requirements, backed up by an additional A level.

After graduating, professional aeronautical engineers normally complete their practical training on the job. Membership of a professional body and registration as a chartered engineer is optional.

The Royal Aeronautical Society has approximately 16,500 members in 1996, of whom 7,500 are full 'corporate' members. The Society accepts EC academic-entry standards and the guidelines of SARTOR for the formation of an engineer.

The Society of Licensed Aircraft Engineers, whose members worked mainly in civil aircraft maintenance and air worthiness, merged with the Royal Aeronautical Society in 1987.

The Royal Aeronautical Society has in 1996 2,000 incorporated engineers and 800 technicians as members, who must have at least a BTEC/SCOTVEC Higher National award or City & Guilds FTC, plus at least six years' experience.

Further information

The Royal Aeronautical Society.

Naval architecture and marine engineering

Naval architecture, shipbuilding and marine engineering cover between them the expertise used in designing, building, repairing and operating ships.

Shipbuilding is a complex problem in engineering design and production, but traditionally the 'ship' and the 'engine' have been treated separately, although 'they have common and overlapping interests requiring a common identity of thought and purpose for their common pursuit'.

Ships have to be designed to meet the tight specifications of their owners – to carry a certain cargo, to have a certain capacity, to travel in particular seas and dock at specific ports, to sail at set speeds, and to be built to budget and schedule. Technical considerations include stability, vibration, hydrodynamics, and fuel and general operating economy. Giant tankers have one set of manoeuvrability problems, naval vessels another. Particular cargoes need special care – eliminating all fire risks for crude oil and chemicals, for instance.

Naval architects plan, design, build, and when required, rebuild the ship and its components, excluding the machinery. In theory, they are trained to design and construct every kind of vessel or system which move just above, on, or under the sea. These include merchant ships, warships, submarines and underwater vehicles down to yachts and other small craft. Some design the unconventional, e.g. hovercraft and hydrofoil, and naval architects are involved in designing offshore drilling platforms and semi-submersibles.

Naval architects need to have an understanding of many branches of engineering and must be at the forefront of high technology areas such as computer-aided engineering and information technology. They play a key role as project leaders and specialists and must utilise effectively the services provided by scientists, engineers, sea-going and business people of many kinds, lawyers and accountants.

The traditional marine engineer designs, constructs, operates and maintains the ships' machinery, both main propulsion and auxiliary engines, in ships ranging from cruise liners, naval vessels, container ships, tankers and ferries to the support vessels and specialised craft of the offshore industry. The Royal Navy also offers a career as a marine engineer (*see* ARMED FORCES).

Naval architects and marine engineers must, obviously, work closely together, not only on how a ship is to be powered and on the new and very sophisticated control systems the vessel is likely to have, but also on piping, pumping systems, electrical generating and supply systems, refrigeration, air conditioning, and, importantly, to ensure that the international and national laws on safety and the protection of the environment are complied with.

Working as naval architects and marine engineers

Both naval architects and marine engineers have been suffering from the problems of the industry (*see* THE SHIPBUILDING INDUSTRY *below*).

Professional naval architects are relatively few in number with only about 4,500 qualified people. A relatively small proportion of these work in the shipbuilding and repair industry itself, as designers and/or managers, and some work for oil-rig fabricators and operators. Some work for ship-owning companies which have their own marine technical departments where they not only design ships, but also solve problems in e.g. cargo handling.

Others work for one of the several firms of marine consultants employing naval architects and marine engineers. They may specialise in one or more of shipyard management and marine consultancy, shipbuilding and ship repair, ports and harbour works, defence, off-shore and fisheries work. They provide services including market research, contract research, production technology, equipment specification and supply, planning and organisation, operating systems and training. Clients may include government departments, major international companies and overseas government agencies. They may work alongside other graduates in various branches of engineering, marine science, oceanography, computing and mathematics.

Some work for Government departments or specialise in work for the Royal Navy. For example, Devonport Royal Dockyard does refit, repair, maintenance and modernisation of the surface warships, submarines (conventional and nuclear) and auxiliary vessels of the Royal Navy. It has specialist expertise in weapon system engineering, nuclear engineering and structural fabrication. Inevitably, the contraction in the armed services has hit naval work and in order to survive it now competes for high technology business outside the Royal Navy.

Some naval architects are employed by small craft and yacht builders and equipment manufacturers.

Lloyd's Register of Shipping and the Department of Trade both recruit naval architects and marine engineers as ship surveyors. Lloyd's surveyors assess ships' structural strength, while those working for the Department of Trade mainly enforce safety regulations, but both have research sections. Surveyors may also work for firms of consultants specialising in particular areas of the shipping industry, dealing with strandings, collisions, machinery failures, fires, explosions, towage, providing expert witnesses in cases of litigation or carrying out surveys to ensure vessels meet international and national standards.

A few naval architects do research mainly in universities and at BMT Cortec (*see below*). A few naval architects teach at higher education establishments.

Professional marine engineers work for the same range of employers, and also as consultants for marine equipment manufacturers. They also go to sea as ships' engineering officers and are employed by ship owners as superintendents.

The offshore industry has led to the development of a unique industry employing individuals from virtually every engineering discipline. Much of the work is at the forefront of technology, requiring ingenuity, inventiveness and sound engineering common sense. The combined efforts of marine engineers, naval architects, mechanical engineers, metallurgists, structural and civil engineers, chemical engineers and those proficient in electrical and electronics and control engineering are necessary to design, construct and operate the plant to exploit the offshore oil and gas.

Technicians and technician engineers within the industry work in design (drawing offices), and in supervisory/managerial capacities.

Qualifications and training

Naval architecture and marine engineering can be studied at professional/degree, technician and craft ('technical') level.

The professional bodies are:

The Royal Institution of Naval Architects

The Royal Institution of Naval Architects (1995 membership about 5,000 of whom some 3,100 are chartered) advises study of a broad range of GCSE (or equivalent) subjects including mathematics, physics and English. These studies should lead to qualifications satisfying the entry requirements for either an accredited degree (BEng) course if CEng status is sought or an accredited BTEC/SCOTVEC (National Certificate/HNC in Engineering) course for EngTech/IEng.

Entry to BEng courses normally requires three A level/five Scottish Highers or a mixture of Advanced GNVQs and an A level. BTEC and SCOTVEC certificates and diplomas may be considered for entry to accredited BEng courses.

The Institute of Marine Engineers

The Institute of Marine Engineers (1995 has 10,233 members, a third overseas, about two-thirds chartered) accepts Engineering Council examinations Parts I and II, or Department of Transport Extra First Class Certificate of Competency as meeting the academic requirement for membership, as well as an accredited degree in engineering, but practical training and responsible experience are also required.

There is also a 'Mature' Candidate Route (MCR) for those over 35 who have had experience involving superior responsibility for at least five years in the design or execution of important work in maritime engineering.

Its membership spans the whole range of maritime engineering disciplines including marine engineering, naval architecture, offshore/subsea engineering and structural, mechanical, civil and electrical engineering with marine applications.

It is an Authorised Body of the Engineering Council and members are entitled to be registered as Chartered Engineers (CEng), Incorporated Engineers (IEng) or Engineering Technicians (EngTech) depending on level of achievement. CEng members may be eligible to register through the Institute with the European Federation of National Engineering Associations (FEANI) and thus obtain the title European Engineer (EurIng).

The Institution of Mechanical Engineers

The Institution of Mechanical Engineers has marine engineer members.

Degree courses

Degree courses traditionally specialise in naval architecture or marine engineering, although it is possible to combine them. Marine engineering is closely allied to mechanical engineering.

The main UK universities specialising in Naval Architecture/Ship Science are Glasgow, Newcastle, Southampton, Strathclyde and University College, London, offering BEng and MEng degrees.

Southampton IHE has a degree in Yacht and Power Craft Design BEng/MEng.

There are various degree courses in Offshore/Ocean/Marine Engineering at the following universities:

Heriot Watt: Offshore Engineering with chemical and Process Engineering BEng (4 yrs), Offshore Engineering with Civil Engineering BEng (4 yrs).

Liverpool: Civil and Maritime Engineering MEng (4 yrs).

Liverpool John Moores: Maritime Studies BSc (3 yrs).

Newcastle: Marine Technology MEng (4 yrs full time or 5 yrs sandwich).

Robert Gordon University: Mechanical and Offshore Engineering BEng (4 yrs).

Surrey: Mechanical Engineering with Offshore and Maritime Engineering, BEng/MEng (3/4 yrs).

BTEC/SCOTVEC

There are Marine Engineering BTEC/SCOTVEC HND courses at:

Liverpool John Moores University; South West University; University of Plymouth; South Mersey College; South Tyneside College; Southampton IHE; Glasgow College of Nautical Studies.

There are HND courses in Naval Architecture, and Yacht Manufacturing Technology and Marine Industries Management, at Southampton IHE. Courses are in the process of change so for the latest position contact BTEC. Distance learning packages are being developed and implemented.

Vocational qualifications

NVQ/SVQs are being developed based on industry standard and will be delivered through BTEC programmes and other awarding bodies.

Craft-level qualifications

City & Guilds qualifications for the industry are: Shipbuilding Craft Studies (scheme 2410); Shipbuilding Competencies (scheme 2420); Marine Craft Fitting (scheme 2430); Marine Craft Competencies (scheme 2440); Yacht and Boat Building and Ship Joinery Craft Studies (scheme 2450); Marine Plumbing and Coppersmiths' Work (scheme 2480).

The principal UK marine training colleges are:

Anniesland College, Glasgow (2440); Belfast Institute of Further Education (2410, 2420); Berkshire College of Agriculture (2440); Cornwall College (2450); East Yorkshire College of Further Education (2440); Furness College (2410); Guernsey College of Further Education (2450); Highbury College of Technology, Portsmouth (2410, 2420); Isle of

Wight College (2450); Kidderminster College of Further Education (2450); North Devon College (2420); Selby Tertiary College ((2420); Pembrokeshire College (2440); Plymouth College (2480); Southampton Technical College (2440, 2450); Wirral Metropolitan College (2450); Worcester College of Technology (2440).

See also MANUFACTURING INDUSTRIES, ARMED FORCES and THE TRANSPORT INDUSTRY.

Further information

The Royal Institution of Naval Architecture and the Institute of Marine Engineers (both publish careers booklets).

The shipbuilding industry

The headlines tell most of the story – 'battle to keep shipbuilding afloat', 'yards get close to the rocks', 'crunchtime looms for yards', are typical. Part of the UK's industrial tradition, shipbuilding is, across most of the world, in the deepest possible trouble. As in other 'traditional' industries, the advantages are with low-cost developing countries like South Korea.

The decline stems from a variety of factors: uncompetitive pricing, insufficient flexibility, long delivery dates, poor productivity, and individualism rather than cooperation, leading to yard closure and rationalisation.

Shipbuilding in the UK currently employs 50,000 people and has a turnover of £2 billion annually. While shipbuilding is not doing well in the UK, ship repair is a big business which has increased considerably in recent years. There are three yards building warships, two building conventional ships and one producing special vessels for the North Sea oil business.

The yards still building and repairing large vessels are Vosper Thorneycroft, Yarrows, VSEL, Harland and Wolff, and Kvarner Gowan. In addition Rosyth and Davenport are government owned but managed by private contractors. Despite the reduction in defence spending Vosper Thorneycroft received an order for seven minesweepers from the Royal Navy in 1994. which will provide several years work.

There are 60 smaller shipyards in the UK working on fishing vessels, small ferries, yachts and similar sized boats.

The whole industry has had to modernise in every way, to improve management, marketing, design, production methods, etc. and many traditional methods have to go. Ships are still built individually, and indeed are increasingly 'customised'. Computers are used – for example, to produce a specification from the customers' requirements (e.g. speed, cargo capacity, draught and weight), to plan production more efficiently, to calculate the size and shape of each part, to guide flame-cutters – or lasers – burning out shapes in steel plate, and some welding. Modular construction systems, using standard sections which can be pre-assembled, have developed.

Most forecasters agree that the market will improve in the late 1990s, when shipowners will have to begin replacing about half the present world fleet. The oil companies will need to replace existing tankers and this market is expected to remain reasonably buoyant. For many years there has been a surplus of tankers lying idle or acting as floating storage vessels, but to put these back into full service again and get them up and running would mean astronomical repair bills of six or seven figures including the cost of modifications to meet the new legislation which insists on double skinned vessels. The tanker disaster at Milford Haven in 1996 will increase pressure for such developments.

However, the upturn in orders does not necessarily mean better times for UK shipbuilders. There is no law which says British shipping companies must give work to British shipbuilders. Instead British yards will tender for contracts alongside foreign competitors and will only get the work if their quotes are reasonable. P&O's new QEII ship was built abroad. All cruise ships built during the past few years and those on order have been and will be built by four major shipyards in Germany, France, Helsinki, Turku and Trieste.

The now streamlined UK shipping industry is in a slightly better position to compete than a few years ago.

Employment in shipbuilding

Whatever happens to the industry, and however far it is modernised, it will still need a high proportion of manual and skilled craft workers. The traditional narrow skill bases, however, have changed, to increase productivity. The emphasis has been on working towards a 'system' rather than craft-based skills. The traditional groupings – of metalworking, outfitting, engineering crafts, and woodworking – still exist but today's engineers are much more flexible and able to complete a broader range of tasks than their predecessors.

Boatbuilding employs rather more woodworking and outfitting trades and fewer metalworkers, and there is also a significant proportion of jobs for glass-reinforced plastic laminators.

Technicians will be increasingly important in the industry in the future. While many will continue to work in the traditional areas of draughting, estimating, and planning, a growing proportion will work in the increasingly complex production control and supervision.

Traditionally the industry employs relatively small numbers of professional engineers and technologists, and these are mainly mechanical and production engineers, marine engineers, some electrical engineers, and metallurgists, and some naval architects. Most engineers and technologists work in production, planning and management, and in design.

Only a few now work in research and development. British Maritime Technology (BMT) at Teddington, and its subsidiary BMT Defence Services at Bath, are independent research and technology organisations. They employ around 500 people, mostly naval architects, marine engineers and mechanical engineers. BMT carries out consultancy, research and design work for the industry. BMT was created through the merger of British Ship Research Association with British Maritime Technology. Staff work on projects ranging from the safety of ferries through to 'tomorrow's ship'. BMT provides eight scholarships every year for students to study naval architecture or marine engineering and has its own graduate training scheme which is accredited by the relevant engineering institutions.

Recruitment and entry

The view of the whole industry is that it is 'currently seeking young men and women of the education and calibre necessary to carry change forward into the next century'.

Graduate/professional level

Mainly engineers (naval architecture, marine, mechanical, electrical, electronic, systems, and production), but also computer scientists, mathematicians, and some physicists. There are occasional vacancies for people with particular qualifications to do research for BMT and BMT Defence Services.

Craft-/technician-level levels of recruitment are difficult to predict. A rising proportion of any vacancies are likely to be for technician-level (with at least four GCSE or equivalent passes) rather than craft training.

Qualifications and training

Training is company-based. Graduate/professional level training is needed for professional status, as is experience in as many different parts of the industry as possible.

Craft apprentices and technician trainees are similarly given fully integrated training, leading to City & Guilds and BTEC awards.

Further information

From employers.

The Mechanical Engineering Industry

Contents

(CLCI: RAE, RAX, ROK, ROZ, SAM)

Mechanical engineering

Mechanical engineering applies basic scientific/engineering principles to designing, developing, manufacturing, installing, operating and maintaining machinery of all kinds. Mechanical engineering is not just about completely mechanical systems – levers, inclined planes, pulleys, wheels, axles, screws – although some or all of these may be involved. The same principles are used in designing and developing (etc.) any kind of moving machinery, whatever actually makes it move or work – gas or steam (turbines), electricity, petrol, compressed air, or hydraulics – or even if it is manually operated.

'Machinery' stretches from dentists' drills to giant cranes, and includes cars, turbines, refrigerators, and machine tools. Modern mechanical engineers have a wide brief. Their knowledge extends across the subject's traditional boundaries into areas more commonly associated with other disciplines. They must stay abreast of electronic technology, learning, for instance, about the new kinds of control systems which go into moving machinery, whether it is a gas turbine or sewing machine.

Whatever the machinery, common mechanical principles are involved, common types of components – gears, wheels, bearings – are used, and common problems have to be solved. Stresses and strains in structures and between moving parts must be calculated; appropriate materials of the right strengths, etc., chosen; tolerances allowed for. Vibration, lubrication (tribology), noise, and weight-support must be considered.

Mechanical engineers also plan complete plants and factories, choose and supervise installation of equipment, develop operating systems and manufacturing processes, and organise and administer whole plants, etc. Mechanical engineers design and manufacture the equipment used to process and refine basic materials into metals and plastics, and the machine tools which shape them. Here mechanical engineering meets production engineering.

Accepting that most systems are now designed, made and operated by multidisciplinary teams, mechanical engineers work increasingly closely with other engineers, e.g. electrical/electronic engineers in the development and design of equipment which is 'electromechanical' and/or computer-based, but see themselves in a pivotal role in such teams, and as interfacing with other technologies.

Working in mechanical engineering

Mechanical engineers work in most industrial sectors and in a wide range of functions.

Professional engineers

The Institution of Mechanical Engineers 1994 survey of members gives the following percentages for numbers of professional engineers employed in the different functions:

The largest group, 26%, work in engineering development and design. Manufacturing and production planning and management takes the next largest group, just 14% with a further 8% working in maintenance and servicing, 3% on quality control and standards, and 7% in instrumentation and control. Just 5% work in construction and installation (including testing and commissioning) of new plant and machinery, 7% work as consultants, 6% in marketing and technical sales. Only 3% do research. Some 5% have moved into general administration (more than half of all mechanical engineers are believed to become managers within a few years of graduating, and most do so eventually); 5% work in the educational field, and 3% are in management services.

Mechanical engineers work in most industries and throughout most sectors.

By type of employer, chartered mechanicals work mainly for industrial or commercial organisations: nearly 63% in 1994. Of the rest, 13% work for nationalised industries, UKAEA, etc., plus 4% for central government (including research councils); 6% work for educational establishments (mostly universities); some 6% are principals or partners of consulting practises and another 4% are self-employed.

Incorporated engineers and engineering technicians

Incorporated engineers and engineering technicians work throughout industry in support functions, mostly in production, assembly, machine shops, testing and quality control and design, but also in marketing. Technicians also work on installation, maintenance, etc.

The fundamental nature of incorporated engineer posts is such as to demand a practical approach and a detailed understanding of technology as well as an awareness of the business management, safety, social and economic context of the work. Considerable overlap exists between the skills and responsibilities of chartered and incorporated engineers. Their work may be in such fields as design, research and development, manufacture, quality assurance and testing, sales, or education and training.

Craftworkers

Craftworkers in mechanical engineering are toolmakers, fitters, machinists, mechanics, etc. They are employed not only in manufacturing, but also in service industries for maintenance, as e.g. garage mechanics.

Qualifications and training

Graduate level

Most degree courses concentrate on the broad basic principles of mechanical engineering, but have also now to include increasingly large elements of, for instance, electrical/ electronic engineering. Guidelines of the Institution of Mechanical Engineers (IMechE) expect courses to cover basic materials, solid mechanics, dynamics and control, fluid mechanics and thermodynamics. Alongside, IMechE wants included the principles and applications of manufacturing systems, measurement and instrumentation, electrical power and machines, electronics and microprocessors, and computer-aided engineering. Maths, statistics and computing are studied to a level needed to underpin the engineering subject, and with a bias to application. Materials, manufacture and design should be 'woven' into courses. Design has to be treated in its widest sense, from identification of need, through concept evaluation to manufacturing method.

Most degree courses give a choice of options in the final year(s), which range from advanced work in areas such as control, energy conversion, applied mechanics, fluid mechanics, reactor engineering, tribology, and auto engineering, through to 'broadening' studies like human factors in engineering, languages and environmental engineering.

Some degree courses are offered as sandwich courses providing the opportunity for students to gain industrial experience as well as knowledge. Many firms in the engineering industry offer sponsorship to students of mechanical engineering degree and HND courses.

'First destination' figures (1994) were:

total graduating	*2,934*
permanent employment	1,126
short-term employment	135
further academic study	347
teacher training	23
other training (including law)	44
overseas employment	21
overseas students leaving UK	571
believed unemployed 31 December	276
employers	
engineering	582
oil, chemicals, etc.	73
public utilities (including transport)	90
other manufacturing	80
armed forces	26
Civil Service	27
commerce	97
accountancy/banking	42
local authorities	16
HE/FE	34
functions	
administration/operational management	71
research design development	739
scientific and engineering support	50
planning construction	11
marketing, etc.	39
management services	38
financial work	41
legal work	1
security/medical	26

Professional qualification. The Institution of Mechanical Engineers (1996 total membership 77,806 including 47,599 chartered) requires an accredited degree (but also accepts EC examinations) to meet the academic requirements for corporate membership. The Institution also accepts a pass or ordinary result from an honours course.

The training requirement must also be met, and this (including career-directed experience) must be in line with the Institution's aims and objectives; no actual period is now specified but candidates for chartered engineer status must be at least 25.

In addition to attaining the minimum academic requirements engineers must complete a period of training and experience in a responsible job. This is usually achieved through the 'monitored professional development scheme': the student engineer works for four years (normally two years' professional training then two years' planned career development) under the general supervision of a principal industrial mentor (who must be a chartered engineer).

Incorporated engineer

Incorporated engineer registration at Stage 1 (education), is via BTEC or SCOTVEC Higher National Diploma or an appropriate Higher National Certificate.

It is possible to bias BTEC courses to aeronautical or automotive engineering, refrigeration and air-conditioning, marine engineering, or fuel technology, and a wide range of units can be put together to give many different specialisations.

SCOTVEC provides an HNC course in mechanical/ production engineering.

Professional qualification. The Institution of Mechanical Incorporated Engineers was formed in 1988 by an amalgamation of The Institution of Mechanical and General Technician Engineers and The Institution of Technician Engineers in Mechanical Engineering. It announced in 1996 that it intends to merge with the Institution of Incorporated

Electrical and Instrumentation Engineers (IIEIE). This will become the largest engineering institution for incorporated engineers.

The minimum academic requirement for corporate membership and registration with the Engineering Council as an Incorporated Engineer is BTEC HND or appropriate HNC, two years' practical training and at least three years' engineering experience of which two should be at Incorporated Engineer level; minimum age is 23. The Engineering Council, however, has announced its intention to increase the academic requirement to an ordinary degree during 1996.

Engineering technician

Qualification is via BTEC or SCOTVEC National awards.

BTEC National Certificate and Diploma engineering courses must have a common core of basic engineering skills, but the two required 'applications/technology' units can be biased to mechanical/production engineering, as can some or all of the optional four (Certificate), 10.5 (Diploma) units.

Under current guidelines courses are expected to have a minimum core of essential units; these include mathematics to level 2, engineering science to level 3, with level-2 courses in manufacturing technology and in engineering drawing and design. Other units are chosen according to the needs of particular groups or of individual students – examples of possible additional units include level-3 manufacturing technology, control of manufacture, electrical science, mechanical science, mathematics, engineering drawing and design, and project work. The diploma course is intended to be broader than the certificate.

Entry requirements are as for all BTEC National awards.

SCOTVEC's National Certificate courses can include a substantial number of modules in mechanical, production and related areas of engineering. Entry is as for all SCOTVEC National Certificate courses.

Professional qualification. The Institution of Mechanical Incorporated Engineers' requirements for Associate Membership and registration with the Engineering Council, are an appropriate BTEC/SCOTVEC National award, two years' training and at least one year's experience at an Engineering Technician level; minimum age is 21.

Craft level

Craft-level qualifications are set by City & Guilds.

Further information

The Institution of Mechanical Engineers, The Institution of Mechanical Incorporated Engineers.

The motor industry

The motor industry, which makes, sells and services cars and commercial vehicles (coaches, goods vehicles, buses, tractors and off-the-road vehicles, taxis, trailers and caravans) is the largest employer in the manufacturing sector and has staged a remarkable recovery since the mid-1980s, following a long period of decline dating back to the early 1970s. The quality, reliability, safety, economy and comfort of vehicles has been radically improved, and the industry has introduced the latest technology in design, engineering and manufacturing, and continued to invest heavily in plant and equipment.

In 1995 the UK motor industry produced 1.47 million cars (7% more than in 1993) and 228,000 commercial vehicles (an increase of 18% on the previous year). Exports totalled £12 billion – greater than any other manufacturing sector. Exports included cars worth £5 billion, commercial vehicles worth £576 million and parts and accessories valued at £5.7 billion.

The industry as a whole has been moving for many years towards greater and greater concentrations of production and control, mainly to give greater economies of scale, but also to make the necessary investment a viable proposition. Manufacturing cars, trucks and vans costs a great deal of money. This is not just in research and development – although more is now being spent on R&D and design, since innovation is one of the ways of fighting the intense competition. Investment is needed to install highly automated plant and equipment and to buy components to produce large numbers of vehicles as fast and as economically as possible. The UK motor industry has benefited by considerable investment, mostly by the Japanese (Nissan, Toyota and Honda in particular), but also by Ford, General Motors (Vauxhall), and Peugeot. The effect of this trend was a dramatic surge in car exports.

Recession hit the industry hard in the early 1990s. Daf, the truck manufacturer, became insolvent and was rescued by a management buyout. Rover was bought by British Aerospace and, after a joint venture with Honda, has now been taken over by BMW.

During 1995, the market for vehicles recovered. Toyota announced that it will double capacity at its plant at Burnaston, near Derby. Honda increased its production at Swindon by a third. Ford increased production of light vehicles by 18% and invested in its engine plant at Bridgend in South Wales to double its capacity. Ford also increased production of diesels at Dagenham.

The industry and its suppliers consist of six distinct major elements:

- Full-line vehicle assemblers such as Rover and the international companies with production facilities in Britain. Some are also large-scale producers of components and sub-assemblies.
- Specialist vehicle producers of such as high-value cars, e.g. Rolls Royce (now owned by Vickers).
- Large international component companies; typically, large multiproduct companies with production facilities in several countries. Some are British-owned, others foreign-based.
- Medium-sized component companies. Some are independent, others part of international companies.

- Small component companies either supplying direct to vehicle companies or more usually supplying to component producers.
- Large suppliers of materials and intermediate items such as steel, aluminium, glass, plastics, synthetic rubber, paint and ball bearings.

The number of separate companies producing vehicles and their components at national, European and international level has fallen sharply over the years as a result of mergers and closures. The majority of car makers these days are international companies, manufacturing in several countries, or having close links – in a 'vast web' of joint ventures – with companies in other countries. Car manufacturers fight each other across the world for a viable share of the global, as well as regional and local, markets.

Jaguar cars became part of the Ford group at the end of 1989. The British car industry is now down to a relatively small number of major companies: Rover, Ford (which also produces Jaguar and Aston Martin cars), General Motors (Vauxhall), Rolls Royce, Nissan, Honda and Toyota currently account for about 98% of total production. The Japanese have invested heavily in the UK, and in 1994 they made 333,000 cars here – 23% of the UK production. Nissan were building more than 200,000 cars a year in 1994 at their Sunderland plant. Toyota manufactured 85,500 cars at Burnaston in 1994 and plan to take this up to 200,000 a year by 1999. Honda built 43,000 cars at its Swindon plant in 1994, a rise of a third over the previous year.

These figures compare with Ford, which produced 300,000 cars in the UK; Rover, 463,000 cars and Vauxhall 250,500 cars in 1994.

In 1994 the production of commercial vehicles moved ahead even better than cars, increasing by 17.8% on the previous year. Ford were the largest producer by a long way with 150,000 vehicles. Rover produced 24,200 vehicles and Vauxhall 13,300 vehicles. The Japanese manufacturers were not active competitors in this market.

According to the Society for Motor Manufacturers and Traders there were 331,000 employees dependent upon car manufacture in 1996. Job losses caused by increased efficiency had been offset by increases in employment with new arrivals such as Toyota and Honda.

The market is fiercely competitive with profit margins being squeezed, and this in turn affects the components industry. The car market is fairly homogeneous, but the component sector is characterised by a multiplicity of companies of different sizes and functions. The three biggest companies are GKN (forgings, castings, pressings, chassis, body and transmission parts), Lucas (chassis and powertrain systems, electronics and electrical products and wiring) and Turner and Newall (producing brake linings, pistons, gaskets and con-rods) but there are still hundreds of little-known specialists making everything from plastic mouldings to nuts, bolts and washers. They provide around half the 15,000 or so components that go into the final products. However, component suppliers in the last decade have had to rationalise while improving product quality and developing more complex components, and this leaves the vehicle makers increasingly in the role of assemblers. The component makers have been investing heavily to rectify the £1 billion trade deficit in components which existed in 1990 and to persuade vehicle makers to buy British parts.

Dramatic cost-cutting, increased productivity, and more frequent, innovative, sharply styled and engineered new models are central to economic recovery, meeting competition, and expanding. The introduction of partnerships between manufacturers and suppliers, improved logistics and just-in-time deliveries has improved efficiency and reduced the number of suppliers.

Manufacturers are still seeking new materials, new shapes, new power units, new fuels, new suspension systems, new brakes and anti-skid devices, new ways to reduce atmospheric pollution and vehicle noise and so increase efficiency, comfort, convenience and usefulness.

Car design used to be based on a four- to seven-year production life with only a limited amount of change possible at the mid-cycle point. With modern computer-assisted design techniques and integrated manufacturing systems these times are reducing, allowing manufacturers to respond much more quickly to market needs. There is no shortage of bright new technological ideas for cars, but manufacturers have to be sure they are what the customer wants. In future, on-board microprocessors may automatically adjust seats and mirrors and control suspension, decrease fuel consumption by anticipating bumps, avoid wheelspin and skidding, start or switch on wiper systems and lights automatically, display information on a 'need to know' basis, and use electronic navigational aids to guide the driver to their destination. Cars will be increasingly 'customised'.

In the factories and on the production lines there has been a significant technical revolution in the way vehicles are built, the way the workmanship is checked and the quality of the product before it reaches the customer. Machines, robots, controls and systems are firmly in place. Most of the industry is extensively automated and computer-controlled and some areas of production nearly fully automated. Flexible manufacture, with lines capable of building several different models, and completely 'customised' short runs (e.g. for a hire fleet), is in operation. It is now commonplace to have automatic body assembly and robot welding, driverless robo-tugs transferring components, microcomputer-controlled systems checking every electrical wiring loom, instrument and lamp assembly before installation, etc.

Employment in the industry

Recent estimates indicate that 846,000 jobs are dependent on the British motor industry in 1996, of which, 331,000 are dependent on manufacturing at various levels. According to the Society of Motor Manufacturers and Traders (SMMT) job losses caused by increased productivity are being offset by the influx of firms from abroad and an increase in output.

The industry employs the following:

- Graduate design engineers translate experimental research and development into technological advances for vehicles of the future. Creative styling ideas are combined with engineering skills to produce detailed, accurate visual interpretations, deciding size and shape and the materials to be used. Although there has been an increase in R&D and design, much of this is done on a multinational basis, so the actual numbers involved in the UK are quite small. Research, development and design is multidisciplinary teamwork, mainly for engineers, some scientists, and supporting technicians (e.g. in the drawing office, testing).
- Graduate development engineers turn designs into the products and are responsible for building, testing and modifying prototype modes. They assess individual components and complete vehicles against standards governing cost, performance and safety.
- Graduate production engineers prepare flow charts and work schedules to plan and organise the manufacturing process, and liaise with other departments as well as keeping in touch with the latest developments in automated machinery and computer-controlled manufacturing.
- Graduates are employed in quality assurance, marketing and sales. The commercial functions of marketing and product planning – finding out what mass-market customers will buy in several years' time and analysing competing firms' plans – go together in the automobile industry, and so marketing managers are often qualified engineers. Sales teams liaise with dealers, or work on sales to, e.g. hire-car fleets or firms which buy cars in large numbers for employees. Customer services, mainly employing engineers, set standards for dealer facilities, develop marketing programmes on service facilities, etc.

  With components being such a major element in a car's cost, the scale of orders is huge, and purchasing is a crucial function in ensuring secure, economically-priced supplies of parts which meet new technological specifications. In financial management sophisticated budgetary and inventory and other financial control systems are used.
- Technician engineers work alongside the professional engineers in manufacturing, quality control, new product development and production engineering.
- Craftsmen and craftswomen – electricians work on installation, maintenance and repair of production or control equipment; toolsetters in production change tools and settings on computerised, numerically controlled machines; fitters/mechanics ensure vehicle mechanical parts are in good order; patternmakers produce patterns for cast components for the vehicle; body makers produce sheet metal components used for prototypes and production models; clay modellers use traditional skills to sculpt replicas of vehicles from sketches or drawings.

Promotion in the industry is largely from within, for people with extensive experience of the industry. A high proportion of today's top managers started as engineering apprentices in the industry.

Recruitment and entry

The combined effects of recession and labour-saving investment cut recruitment in the early 1990s but in 1996 there was a significant upturn. Ford were seeking 180 graduate trainees and Lucas Industries had been forecasting an intake of about 80 graduates, in 1996 and GKN about 30 graduates.

The main requirement in the motor industry is for mechanical/production (including automobile), manufacturing and electrical/electronic engineers, computer-aided engineering, and computer/systems scientists, with occasional requirement for aeronautical engineers. Up to half of all vacancies are, however, in non-technical functions, and open to graduates in any discipline.

School-leavers are recruited for craft- and technician-level training in comparatively small numbers.

Qualifications and training

Training is based mainly on individual firms.

Professional/graduate level normally pre-entry via a degree. Some manufacturers offer sponsorships for engineers. Firms provide training for professional engineering qualifications, and the larger ones have developed postgraduate training schemes with universities to cover, e.g., car electronics, mathematical modelling, and aerodynamics.

Technician engineers need a BTEC/SCOTVEC Higher National Certificate or Diploma and follow a broad-based training course.

Craftworkers usually have GCSE/SCEs with passes in maths, technical and practical subjects. They may study for City & Guilds, or BTEC awards.

Further information

The Society of Motor Manufacturers and Traders.

Machine tools

Machine tools are an essential part of the production process, but for many companies they have not proved to be very profitable and in the face of severe competition the British machine tool industry, with 250 firms, has had to contract and rationalise. It now accounts for less than 3% of world production, compared with 9% 25 years ago and largely consists of independent small to medium-sized companies producing high-quality, advanced machines in relatively small numbers.

The emphasis is on specialisation, and high investment is necessary to ensure speed, accuracy and reliability for customers. Computer-controlled production is changing the industry, and one major development, just in time (JIT) production, involves the complete integration of technical and business systems. Essentially this means that the products are manufactured only when orders come in, and this needs a very flexible manufacturing system with sophisticated control systems which can make several different products and versions of the same product.

Most factory operations, however, are less sophisticated, although use of computer numeric control (CNC) machine tools are increasing. The introduction of computer integrated manufacturing (CIM), which includes accounts, engineering design, parts specifications and lists, materials, machine tool and management data control, has improved efficiency in recent years.

Other new developments in machine-tool design include improvements in cutting tools with carbide, ceramics and composites supplementing or replacing conventional cutting materials; 3-D laser machining for flat sheet metal; and monitoring sensors which can detect tool breakage or exceptional tool wear.

Employment in the industry

The numbers employed have been falling steadily in the machine tool industry for many years, from 18,000 in 1991 to 12,000 in 1996.

The industry is moving towards more and more customisation to meet individual customer requirements and, to provide this high-quality service, machine tool manufacturers must have high-quality labour. Increased automation means that more skilled technicians are needed to use and maintain the equipment and fewer operatives are required on the shop floor.

Most of the professionals, who work mainly in production and other managerial functions, are engineers – mostly mechanical, some electrical, with a rising proportion of electronic/systems (especially where microelectronic controls are being incorporated in products or used in production) – and some materials scientists and metallurgists. There is a limited amount of research and development work, often done by industry-funded research associations.

Qualifications and training

The main graduate requirement is for mechanical and manufacturing/production engineers, electronic/systems engineers, and some electrical engineers.

Technician engineers need a BTEC/SCOTVEC Higher National Certificate or Diploma and follow a broad-based training course.

Craftworkers usually have GCSE/SCEs or equivalent with passes in maths, technical and practical subjects. They may study for City & Guilds, or BTEC awards.

Further information

The Machine Tool Technology Association.

Instrument manufacture

Instruments are the precision tools used in scientific laboratories, the measuring and control systems used in industry, the surgeon's tools, watches and clocks of all kinds, and photographic equipment. The industry's products are almost all ideal candidates for electronic, microprocessor control, especially industrial control systems, automatic testing equipment, and medical instruments for monitoring patients in intensive care. As a result, many products now count as electronic, and the sector is rapidly on its way to joining the capital equipment sector of the electronics industry. The Scientific Instruments Research Association provides contract research for firms within this industry and those outside it which need its expertise. (*See* ELECTRICAL AND ELECTRONICS ENGINEERING.)

Metal manufacturing and the steel industry

The industry both produces crude metals from mineral ores, and manufactures semi-finished and finished products, ranging from iron castings through to plates, wire rods and bars, light steel sections and hot-rolled bars, bright-steel bars, hot- and cold-rolled strip, sheets, tubes and pipes, and special products such as high-speed tool and magnetic steels.

The industry is largely dominated by iron- and steelmaking, and manufacture of iron and steel products. The rest of the industry is very small by comparison. It includes aluminium and aluminium-alloy production. The industry also produces copper, brass and other copper alloys, and 'other' base metals. They include smelting and refining lead, zinc, magnesium and titanium, and manufacturing their alloys as well as finished products from them.

The industry now depends almost entirely on imported ores, although a few are still mined in Britain. Remaining domestic ores, though, are too low-grade for iron and steel production to compete with imports, which at present come mainly from Canada and Sweden. One effect of this is that metal production is now largely concentrated near major deep-water terminals.

The steel industry

Steel production in Britain has undergone massive changes since the uneasy days of the 1970s. Dramatic increases in energy prices worldwide then changed forever any expectation that the industry could survive and remain competitive without strict attention to cost reductions, the elimination of excess capacity and improved performance. An increasingly critical worldwide steel market, served by modern steelmaking facilities in both established and developing economies, has since come to demand very high standards in product quality and customer service.

Britain's steel industry in the 1990s is dominated, in terms of size, by British Steel plc. Making about three-quarters of the nation's steel, its business consists principally of the bulk steels used for consumer products, transport, construction, food and drink packaging and for the engineering industry and large capital projects. The company also makes stainless steel, but alloy and special engineering steels are produced by a number of more specialised firms, who also make a wide variety of the smaller steel products, including rods, bars and wire.

British Steel plc, now one of the lowest-cost producers in the world, was privatised in 1988 (it was formerly the nationalised British Steel Corporation). Its activities are concentrated on four major sites: Port Talbot and Llanwern in South Wales, and Scunthorpe and Teesside. The company's stainless steel making is based in Sheffield and it also makes tubes and pipes in the East Midlands and the North-East as well as operating other Welsh plants engaged in applying metallic, paint and plastic coatings to sheet steel.

British Steel has made intensive efforts to match and surpass the efficiency of its competitors and is currently the world's fourth largest manufacturer of crude steel. Substantial improvements in yield, labour productivity and energy efficiency have combined with advanced techniques and working practices to drive costs down – cost reduction is a constant management preoccupation. At the same time, research efforts have focused on meeting the increasing demands from customers for improved steel products, establishing new uses for steel and competing against alternative materials. The company spent £29 million on research in 1994.

These developments have inevitably been associated with major reductions in numbers employed – down to 39,000 in 1995. However, a measure of the productivity advances achieved is seen in the fact that British Steel was making more steel by the end of the 1980s than at the beginning of the decade, with less than a third the number of employees.

Employment in the steel industry

Approximately 35,000 people are employed by British Steel in the UK and a further 4,000 working overseas. In recent years British Steel has concentrated its production efforts on fewer, more efficient sites. This has resulted in a smaller total number of employees, but has enabled the company to establish a position as one of the most productive and profitable steel companies in the world. New working practices continue to be introduced, such as a continuing drive for improvement through the use of Total Quality Programmes, which ensure that all employees contribute to improving product and customer service quality. The restructuring of craft jobs and greater use of teamwork are leading to a highly skilled workforce.

Production

Jobs in production involve a vast range of activities from primary processes, such as work in the coke ovens and blast furnaces, through steelmaking in basic oxygen furnaces and electric arc furnaces, to the rolling and finishing of steel, including the applications of special coatings such as tin plating, or the painting of steel. These are all high-technology activities, producing materials to meet the customers' technical specifications to exacting quality standards.

Metallurgical and technical services

Metallurgical and technical services work closely with production to ensure the quality of the products and that the customer is given the right material for the job, at the right time and at a competitive price. The metallurgical characteristics of the steel are monitored using advanced automated technology at every stage of the process. This allows the steel to be produced to precise specifications and for problems in the production process to be anticipated early and corrected.

Engineering

The engineering function is responsible for the plant and machinery used to produce steel. This involves a wide range of jobs covering electrical, electronic, mechanical and control engineering. Steel is a capital-intensive industry, and spending on research and development at British Steel is currently £36 million per year. Capital expenditure in 1995 was £129 million. The engineering function is responsible for managing that spending, to ensure that complex plant runs to maximum efficiency, avoiding costly stoppages and maintaining product quality, with the objective of improving yield and economising in the use of raw materials, energy and manpower.

Research laboratories

British Steel has a number of central research laboratories. Swindon, in Rotherham, concentrates on general and special steel product research, Welsh laboratories at Port Talbot specialise in research on the manufacture, development and use of flat-rolled steel, and Teesside in the north-east of England has extensive pilot plant facilities to focus on process and engineering research.

Information technology

British Steel is at the forefront of information technology, with some 600 RPP (relative processing power) of installed computer centre capacity operating 24 hours a day, 365 days a year. There are also minicomputers and thousands of microcomputers which need careful planning and tight organisation across the business. Some of the computing capacity and expertise is sold to companies outside British Steel. The IT function is split into four main areas: Information Systems, Computer Centre Operations, Telecommunications, and Operational Research. Each is geared to improving the quality of business information available to customers and the business as a whole. Every major business within British Steel has an IT department.

Commercial, sales and marketing

The commercial area covers sales and marketing activities across the company. Steel is a volatile market, where product availability and price can fluctuate dramatically. In the marketing area there is a strong emphasis on developing new opportunities for steel products. Nearly half of the sales are to export markets, with British Steel products being sold throughout the world.

Supplies and transport production planning and control

The supplies and transport production planning and control function involves the bulk purchase of vast quantities of raw materials and energy, and shipping and transport to tight deadlines with limited resources. The production planning and control activities in the steelworks act as a link between the sales function and production departments, programming several hundred orders each week, through all the stages of manufacture, to meet the customers' delivery requirements. This in turn determines the overall level of works activity and thus the need for raw materials and other supplies. The purchase of key raw materials is handled centrally in order to negotiate the best prices and to manage the logistics of moving large quantities of materials within, and exporting from the country.

Steel stockholding

British Steel's UK and overseas distribution activities are combined into a single business, British Steel Distribution, which has employees working in over 200 locations around the world to provide stockholding and processing services to customers in more than 20 countries. In the UK and Ireland British Steel Distribution is the largest steel stockholder, with locations varying in size from a handful of people to hundreds.

Finance

Finance in British Steel can be broadly divided into the following activities:

Management accounting is the focal point for company budgets and strategic plans. Accountants in close touch with other functions prepare business plans and monitor performance against budget to prompt actions for improvement.

Financial accounting handles all types of statutory company records and manages the main accounting operations and credit control of the company. Internal audit involves the review of systems and control to ensure the effective operation of each area of the business.

Specialist services involve taxation, mergers and acquisitions and treasury operations.

Recruitment and entry

Promotion within British Steel is based upon merit and is open to both school-leaver and graduate trainee entrants. A large proportion of British Steel's senior managers are graduates, but this is by no means exclusively so, and there can be opportunities to study for a degree whilst working for the company.

Approximately 100 graduates are recruited each year, the majority with science or engineering background, but a significant number with other degrees. The company also sponsors around 60 students each year whilst at university, and returning sponsored students provide a significant proportion of the graduate intake.

School-leavers are recruited locally by each division and works.

Qualifications and training

Training within British Steel is organised locally by the various divisions and works. Commitment to the development of the workforce has resulted in 21 National Training Awards being won by the company, and 15 regional commendations. Over 1,600 managers attend training courses at the company's residential management training college at Ashorne Hill each year, and accreditation of the training has been received from the Institutions of Electrical Engineers, Mechanical Engineers and Chemical Engineers. Managers in all functions are encouraged to become professionally qualified in their own disciplines. There is an accelerated management development programme which is run in conjunction with Warwick University Business School and leads to an MBA by distance-learning. This programme trains over 20 young managers each year.

Further information

British Steel plc.

The cast metals industry

The industry is involved with the development of many new applications for cast metal components and the introduction of new materials such as metal composites. Whilst the industry is still involved with the production of traditional cast metals components such as machine tool parts, engine blocks, crank shafts, and consumer parts such as bells, many foundries now produce parts for computers, modern aircraft engines and modern capital equipment.

The industry is bullish about the future, expecting the output of cast metal components at its 650 foundries to increase from 1.4 million tonnes in 1996 to 1.7 million tonnes by the year 2000. Foundry 2000, a project sponsored by the Department of Trade and Industry, is helping the industry to focus on its technology, marketing and human resources needs to compete with suppliers overseas.

Over the last few years the industry has become more automated. The definitions of the shapes to be cast are now produced by computer and available on disk to the equipment forming those shapes in the foundry. Manpower needs are more for people conversant with modern technology than for the unskilled.

Many changes have taken place within the requirements for cast metal components, and new techniques introduced have been aimed at producing better-quality components which have been designed to reduce their weight penalty. The design of cast metal components has now been enhanced with the development of solidification modelling programmes which enable the designer and the cast metals technician to design a component which will have the required physical properties with a minimum of defects. Finite element analysis is also carried out by computer programmes which again assist in the development of components.

The industry has come to terms with the Environmental Act, which requires foundries to register their production processes.

The number of castings produced in aluminium, magnesium and iron is increasing while those manufactured in steel are declining. The industry has now developed a much broader base for its castings, many of which find their way into the export market.

The two research associations which undertake contract research and development work for the industry, the British Casting Industries Research Association (Alvechurch) and Casting Technology International (Sheffield), decided to merge in March 1996.

Recruitment and entry

The industry still employs over 30,000 people, of whom possibly up to 40% are at the operative level. These operatives include moulders, coremakers, dressers and inspectors.

Qualifications and training

Most material, metallurgical and production engineering degrees have cast metal units within them. There are no specific degrees related solely towards cast metals technology.

Further Education colleges at Sandwell and Chesterfield offer BTEC courses in materials technology. Those at St Helens, Coventry, Falkirk and Charles Keene College, Leicester, all offer BTEC courses in patternmaking and technician work within the industry. The Institute of British Foundrymen, with 2,000 members, has developed NVQs to levels 1 and 2 and is currently (1996) developing level-3 qualifications with EnTra, the Engineering Training Authority (*see in* GENERAL ENGINEERING).

There are City & Guilds courses available for both foundry craft and patternmaking. National Vocational Qualifications are now being introduced and implemented.

Professional body

The Professional Institute for the industry is the Institute of British Foundrymen, which was granted a Royal Charter in 1921 and is an Institution Affiliate of the Engineering Council.

The Institute has Fellowship (FIBF), Member (MIBF), Associate Member, Associate and student grades. It can also nominate members for registration with the Engineering Council as Chartered Engineer (CEng), Incorporated Engineer (IEng), and Engineering Technician (EngTech). The grades for which members are nominated will depend upon their academic qualifications and experience.

The Institute has now introduced its own training programmes and has a continuing professional development.

Further Information

The Institute of British Foundrymen.

Contents

Electrical and Electronic Engineering

(CLCI: RAK–RAL)

Electrical and electronic engineering

Based on common physical principles, both electrical and electronic engineering make use of electric currents and devices, and modern industrial societies are largely dependent on the results, from the power which provides heat, light and energy through to electronic instruments, computers, telephones and electronic control systems.

Much of what we do, and how we do it, is being transformed by electronics and the power of information technology which enables information to be stored, analysed, transmitted and received. Electrical engineering and electronics influence almost every part of our lives whether at home in the kitchen, using the vast range of domestic appliances and gadgets, or in home entertainment using hi-fi/videos/TVs/computer games, or in the office, where use of the Internet, fax machines, databases, spreadsheets and word processing are essential ingredients of everyday life.

The electrical and electronic industry can be divided into five main groups, some of which are dealt with more appropriately in other chapters:

1. Energy and power

This involves the production and distribution of electricity to railways, factories, offices, homes, hospitals and schools, as well as the manufacture of the power-generation equipment, including turbines and boilers, involved in these processes. (*See* ELECTRICITY SUPPLY *in* THE MINING AND ENERGY INDUSTRIES.)

2. Contracting and building services

Services such as lighting, heating, ventilation, refrigeration, lifts and escalators. (*See* BUILDING SERVICES ENGINEER.)

3. Transport

The manufacture, operation and maintenance of trains, ships, aircraft and road vehicles. Also the design, installation and production, testing and maintenance of electric railways and battery-driven vehicles. (*See* THE TRANSPORT INDUSTRY *and* AEROSPACE, NAVAL ARCHITECTURE, MARINE ENGINEERING AND THE SHIPBUILDING INDUSTRIES.)

4. Electronics

The Federation of Electronic Industries divide electronics into five sectors: information and communications technology, defence and public- sector projects, components, electronic equipment and office products and manufacturing.

Information technology and telecommunications

Information technology is the use of computers and telephone systems to capture, process and distribute information. That information can be in several forms: the written word, drawings and photographs, audio or video. Multimedia techniques, the use of which is growing rapidly, allow computers and telephone systems to handle several of these media at the same time. During the 1990s there has been a strong move away from large 'mainframe' computers to large numbers of computers linked by networks of telephone systems. The Internet and the World Wide Web are such systems which subscribers can use to access information and to send messages by electronic mail.

Telephone companies around the world, and especially in Europe and North America, which were often owned by governments in the past, are now becoming free of government control. In the UK more than 100 companies, including BT, Mercury, Vodaphone, Cellnet, Orange, Energis and those which provide cable television services, have licences to provide telephone network services. Mobile telephones have seen major growth, and each of the service suppliers is increasing the number of their clients in a highly competitive market. BT, which still maintains a dominant position with over 90% of the market, is fighting to maintain market share by providing an ever-increasing range of services.

The number of television channels which can be directly accessed in the home has risen and the opportunity to view programmes broadcast in other countries has become a reality.

All of these developments have provided employment for electronic engineers, especially in the areas of optoelectronics, radio frequency and digital electronics. It is almost certain that the number of firms in the telecommunication services industry will reduce over the next decade through takeovers and mergers because even with an industry growing as fast as this one competition is so high that not all the current players could possibly survive. Already there are signs that BT and Cable and Wireless, two of the major international firms, will merge.

These engineers are also employed by the government at the Government Communications Headquarters and within the Armed Services, for example within the Royal Signals Regiment, to send secure messages or attempt to intercept those of an enemy.

Many large companies including banks, rail transport providers, news and information providers such as Reuters also employ electronic engineers to maintain and develop their own networks.

Telecommunications equipment

All of the developments discussed in the previous paragraphs have led to increased demand for telecommunications equipment. The design, development, manufacture and installation of telecommunications equipment, including telephone systems, digital exchanges and networks, transatlantic optical cables, aerials and waveguides, decoders and satellites, is the second major area of employment for electronic engineers. Firms such as GPT, Racal, Philips, Nortel and BICC Cables are busily manufacturing telecommunications equipment, and all employ electronic engineers to design, develop, manufacture, test and maintain their products. Communication by satellite has also increased, and companies such as Matra Marconi which manufacture telecommunication satellites have full order books in 1996.

Computers

Every aspect of our lives is now influenced in some way by computers. The retailer's till, the cash machine in the bank, navigation of ships and aircraft, the control of defence systems, the operation of manufacturing and processing plant, education and training, office work, administration and publishing – these are just some examples which demonstrate the ubiquitous penetration of computers into everything that we do.

As computers became cheaper and more powerful, the early 1990s were bad times for the major computer manufacturers. IBM and Digital made huge losses and had to adapt to fast-changing technologies and commercial situations. Currently there are numerous manufacturers which build and market personal computers by simply buying in the parts and putting them together. Intel has become a dominant supplier of processors and Microsoft a major supplier of software for such systems. ICL, Fujitsu, Hewlett Packard, Dell, Packard Bell and Mitsubishi (owner of Apple) are among the major computer manufacturers of the mid-1990s. They all employ electronic engineers to design their systems, in manufacture and testing, and to provide the essential after-sales service which the customers demand. The provision of software has become more profitable than hardware (computers) and many firms in the computer industry are much more concerned than they were with software. Electronic engineers who also have computer programming skills are particularly in demand. (*See also* INFORMATION TECHNOLOGY AND COMPUTER WORK.)

Components and electronic devices

The basic building blocks of electronic equipment are the components. They include integrated circuits, memory devices, transistors, resistors and capacitances. They also include all the equipment needed to connect the various parts of a piece of electronic equipment together: connectors and cables, printed circuit boards and related devices. Manufacturers of components and devices employ electronic engineers for their design, development, production, testing and marketing. They include such companies as Texas Instruments, Smiths Industries, GEC Alsthom and Motorola.

Advances in electronic and optoelectronic devices, including the design of new types of semiconductor devices and integrated circuits, will maintain the momentum and open up many new areas of application and radically change existing ones in the next century.

5. Measurement, control and automation

There are numerous situations where it is necessary to sense what is happening, relay that information to a computer, use the software installed in it to decide what should be done and send a signal which initiates action. The control of manufacturing and processing plant, defence systems, the navigation of ships and aircraft and many other situations all need control and automation equipment. In hospital wards, for example, the breathing, pulse and temperature of several patients can be monitored by a nurse from a central control desk. Electronic engineers are also employed to design and develop such systems, sometimes as consultants who devise systems to meet specific needs, sometimes as employees of equipment manufacturers, and also within industries which use the equipment for their own purposes.

Electronic equipment and office products

In parallel with these developments there has been a growth in the use of electronic equipment in the office and at home. Fax machines and text scanners, photocopiers and electronic timing devices, electronic locks and entertainment systems – these have all been gaining ground. In the field of medical equipment electronics is making a major contribution. Ultrasonic and NMR (nuclear magnetic resonance) scanners and imaging devices, the use of lasers and ancillary equipment in surgery are all examples of the steady march of electronic equipment into new areas.

Manufacturing

Modern manufacturing and processing plant is capital-intensive and employs fewer operatives. Measuring and weighing, changing the speed or flow, monitoring temperatures and pressures, ensuring that raw materials do not run out: these are all systems which are electronically controlled in the production environment. Computer-assisted manufacturing systems where lathes, drills and other forming machinery is controlled by computer and robots – which complete repetitive processes such as welding, drilling and painting as well as carrying parts around the factory – are all examples of electronics in industry. All manufacturing industry, from producers of foods and detergents to makers of aeroplanes and turbines, needs the skills which only electronic engineers can offer.

See below and also BIOMEDICAL ENGINEERING *in* BIOLOGICAL AND PROCESS ENGINEERING AND MATERIALS SCIENCE; *and* INFORMATION TECHNOLOGY AND COMPUTER WORK.

Working in electrical and electronic engineering

The range of work and employment is extensive and widening steadily.

Professional engineers

The Institution of Electrical Engineers regularly surveys its members. 1995 figures show that research, development and design employ the largest proportion of electrical and electronic engineers. In the private sector, 35.1% were working in development and design, 2.6% in research. In the public sector, only 14.1% were working in development and design with just 8.8% doing research only.

The figures show that the proportion doing just research is relatively small, although the dividing line between research and development is very fine in such an advanced field. Some, but by no means all, of the theoretical work which produces new ideas is done by scientists. Electrical and electronic engineers may do research work that is fundamental and basic if needed to develop particular products – they may then have to study the structure and properties of materials, for instance. These engineers take the ideas and do further work to develop them into safe, economic and marketable products and systems. Electrical and electronic engineers in research and development, and design, work in teams, often with other engineers, and scientists, e.g. computer scientists, physicists and materials scientists.

In research, development and design, the kind of work involved in the 'heavy' electrical end differs somewhat from the 'light' electronic. There is rather less really advanced research and development work at the 'heavy' end, on generators and motors, switchgear, power transmission lines and equipment, transformers, lighting and heating equipment, and traction equipment. There is, however, research into new methods of generating electricity, e.g. using wind (technological versions of the windmill) and sea waves. Development concentrates to some extent on improving existing equipment and systems, on solving and preventing causes of breakdown, and improving efficiency. The electricity supply companies do most of the research, design and development in the generating field. *See* THE ENERGY INDUSTRIES *in* THE MINING AND ENERGY INDUSTRIES.

Designing a new power station is a one-off project. Electrical engineers also develop and design new components for, e.g. a new design of car, especially if it is to be battery-driven, or small motors for a host of uses. Some research is done in universities, in industrial research associations, and in government, especially Ministry of Defence, establishments. ERA Technology is the research association which undertakes contract research for the electricity industry.

Electronic engineers work on new systems, devices, etc. for computers, telecommunications, broadcasting, radar, satellite systems, etc. They are employed by both the manufacturers, electronics firms of all kinds, and by the larger users, such as BT, broadcasting organisations, the Civil Service and the Armed Forces.

In production, electrical and electronic engineers plan, manage, and troubleshoot. Production may mean being a member of the management team of a power station, supervising the assembly of a cathedral-sized generator, or controlling the production of printed-circuit boards. With more industries installing sophisticated automated production systems, recruitment of electronic engineers has increased. In the private sector, 15.1% of chartered engineers worked in production in 1995 (an increase from 1986 when only 5.4% of chartered engineers worked in production), with another 3.1% in quality control, and 3.8% in maintenance and servicing. In the public sector, some 3.4% worked in production, 1.8% in quality control, and 9.8% in maintenance and servicing.

Construction and installation work includes, for professional engineers, being on the management team, building a new power station or a major new telecommunications facility. Some 5.3% of electrical/electronic engineers working in the private sector, and only 6.0% in the public sector, were employed in construction and installation in 1995.

Marketing and selling some of the highly sophisticated equipment produced in the electrical and electronic industries, and large-scale generating, transmission and computing equipment often requires people who have a good technological understanding of what they are selling. In the private sector, some 8.7% were doing this kind of work, 1.9% in the public sector.

Many electrical and electronic engineers move up and out into general management – some 15.1% of those working in the private sector and 19.6% in the public sector. Another 10.5% of engineers working in the private sector had become consultants, 5.3% in the public sector.

Some electrical/electronic engineers teach/lecture, mainly in universities, and FE colleges – 25.3% of those working in the public sector, but 0.7% in private-sector employment.

In terms of where they work, in 1995, of the fully qualified and experienced chartered engineers, the largest group, 54.8%, were employed in private industry or commerce. The second largest group, 7.5%, worked for nationalised industries or public corporations. Central and local government employed 5%. Universities employ 5.8%, and 1.7% teach in colleges of further education. An increasing number, now 7.3%, are self-employed, 4.3% in consulting practice. The Armed Forces employ 2.4%. About 1% work for each of the UKAEA and associated companies, and 0.9% in the health authorities. In 1995 2.9% were unemployed (a major improvement from the 4.6% recorded in 1992).

In 1995, 22.6% of all chartered electrical and electronic engineers worked in electronic or telecommunications equipment development or manufacture, 6.7% were working in electricity generation or distribution. The proportion working in electrical machinery or equipment development or manufacture fell further, to 4.0%. There were 6.5% working on control systems and instrumentation; 6.9% working in broadcasting, telecommunications, etc. and some 3.3% working in building services. Some 3.4% were employed in chemical or allied manufacture or processing; 10.0% worked in 'all other' development, manufacturing or processes. A few were working in transport (4.9%), research organisations (2.1%), and 'other' engineering services (4.3%).

For incorporated engineers and technician engineers, there has always been steady demand. The range of occupations is extensive and immensely varied, and many posts carry considerable responsibility in both the private sector and the public sector. The Institute of Electronic and Electrical Incorporated Engineers' members have 'full, unsupervised managerial responsibility for budgets and long-range planning with full control over senior staff'. Many 'undertake long- and short-term planning and supervision of projects and decisions on work programmes, with budgetary control ...'. Almost half 'plan, conduct and co-ordinate projects of some complexity, are responsible for technical matters, work to general objectives and priorities, and supervise qualified and other staff'.

Qualifications and training

Professional engineer

First-degree courses are taught by almost all universities with engineering facilities. Some universities offer degree courses in electrical engineering and six run courses in electrical power systems and engineering. More than 80 universities have courses in electronics engineering. Many universities offer combined degree courses in electrical and electronic engineering. Other related degree courses include those in control engineering, digital systems engineering, electromechanical engineering, communications/telecommunications engineering and electronic design engineering. The courses are offered at the bachelors degree (BEng) level including three years of study and at the masters degree level (MEng) with four years at university. In Scotland the degree courses are a year longer. Many of the newer universities also offer HND courses.

Some of the courses are offered on a sandwich basis and include periods of industrial experience of at least one calendar year. Some offer this experience abroad. A considerable proportion (more than one in five) of undergraduate students in these subjects are sponsored by employers through their degree courses or HNDs.

In many courses students commence their studies with a broadly based scheme covering the fundamentals of both electrical and electronic engineering, and choose their specialisms through a range of options later in the course.

First destination figures (electrical/electronic) for 1994 were:

total graduating	*5,227*
research, etc.	676
teacher training	49
other training including law	64
believed unemployed 31 December	330
temporary work	163
overseas students leaving UK	798
permanent UK work	2,072
employers	
chemicals, oil, etc.	44
other manufacturing	87
engineering	965
communications/transport, etc.	263
other commerce	268
accountancy	18
Civil Service	58
NHS/local government	26
higher/further education	52
armed forces	16
functions	
engineering/scientific R&D	1,104
engineering/scientific support	154
financial work	35
administration/operational management	88
marketing, etc.	67
management services	340
personnel/social/medical	31

A very high proportion of electrical/electronic engineering graduates go into employment related to their degree discipline. Entry requirements normally include A-levels in maths and physics or equivalent.

The number of postgraduate courses in electrical and electronic engineering has risen considerably in recent years. Some help graduates who have read related subjects (e.g. applied physical sciences or physics), to convert to electrical and/or electronic engineering at postgraduate level. Graduates in electrical and electronic engineering often use postgraduate courses, especially diplomas and masters' degrees, to specialise in one area of their subject such as telecommunications or integrated circuits.

Professional qualifications are awarded by:

The Institution of Electrical Engineers (IEE), total 1995 membership 134,714 of whom 60,712 are corporate members (chartered engineers) and 74,002 are non-corporate members (including associate members, student members and trainees). At least a second-class award on an accredited honours degree in electrical/electronic engineering is required for corporate membership. Candidates with a minimum standard of a second-class honours degree from a course which has not been accredited by the IEE are eligible to apply to join as Associates after they have demonstrated their application to the practice of electrical/manufacturing engineering over a period of not less than two years. Graduates who gain a lower-class degree can meet the requirement by passing set examinations at second-class standard after at least five years' working experience, or by gaining a master's degree. All entrants must have at least two years' industrial training and two years' career development in a responsible position, and pass a professional test.

(The Institution of Electronic and Radio Engineers (IERE) amalgamated with the IEE in October 1988. The Institution of Manufacturing Engineers and the Institution of Electrical Engineers merged in October 1991).

Incorporated engineer

BTEC Higher National Diploma/Certificate in engineering with specialisation in electrical, electronic, communications, etc. It is possible to study electrical and/or electronic engineering, and a wide range of units can be put together to give many different specialisations, in, e.g., communications or telecommunications engineering.

Entry is as for all BTEC Higher awards via A-levels; maths and physics studied with a pass in one.

SCOTVEC sets both HNC and HND courses in electrical/electronic engineering, with a wide range of options at level 5.

Professional qualifications. Since 1990, when the Institution of Electrical and Electronics Incorporated Engineers and the Society of Electronics and Radio Technicians were amalgamated to form the Institution of Electronics and Electrical Incorporated, this has become the largest professional body for incorporated and technician engineers, with a membership of over 27,000 (1995). Discussions are underway early in 1996 to merge with the Institute of Incorporated Mechanical Engineers, which has 8,000 members.

Minimum requirement for membership is BTEC HNC (in a coherent group of units with at least six units at level 4/5 including at least four with a 'substantial' electrical/electronic engineering content; at least two at level 5, one related to electrical/electronic engineering; and at least one full maths unit at level 3). The requirement is an HND in appropriate subjects, or an equivalent, and so people seeking to qualify via an HNC will normally have to gain supplementary units. The Institution publishes a list of approved training schemes.

Engineering technician

Qualification is via a BTEC National award or a SCOTVEC National Certificate.

BTEC National Certificate and Diploma engineering courses must have a common core of basic engineering skills. The programme in electrical engineering has specialised options for, e.g., general electrical technicians, practical electrical technicians biased to electrical services, technicians in illuminating engineering, electrical draughtsman, technicians in electricity supply, and maintenance technicians; other programmes are in electronics and telecommunications, in audio and TV servicing, etc. The various programmes share many common courses, and students can switch from e.g. telecommunications to electrical engineering, at various levels. At Certificate level, electrical technicians should, for example, study both light- and heavy-current applications. Courses in all these subjects are available at many centres throughout the country. Entry requirements are as for all BTEC National courses.

SCOTVEC's National Certificate courses can include a large proportion of modules in electrical/electronic engineering and/or related subjects. Entry is as for all SCOTVEC National Certificate courses.

Professional qualifications can be with the Institution of Electronics and Electrical Incorporated Engineers (*see also* Incorporated engineer level *above*). IEEIE accepts, for associate membership, BTEC National awards in electrical engineering, electronics, telecommunications, and building services (electrical). The award must be in a coherent group of units at pass standard with at least three relevant level-3 units, two electrical/electronic-related.

Craft level

Qualifications are set by City & Guilds, which tries to provide for the many and varied needs within the various industries.

Further information

The Institution of Electrical Engineers, which publishes a range of leaflets and booklets on careers in electrical and electronic engineering; the Institution of Electronics and Electrical Incorporated Engineers.

Electronics and communication systems

The provision of good and reliable communications services forms an integral part of economic and business development in all industrialised countries. Communications provide the practical systems by which information is transmitted, as distinct from the systems which provide the information – traditionally, the letter carrier as distinct from the letter writer. *See* THE POST OFFICE *in* ADMINISTRATION, BUSINESS MANAGEMENT AND OFFICE WORK.

For centuries, information transmission was a slow business, and it is really only in the last hundred years that faster systems have been developed. Yet now it is feasible, quite literally, to move information with the speed of light, from one side of the globe to the other in fractions of a second.

During this century, electronic engineers have built up a telecommunications phone network to link every household, or provide access for them to the network, and in so doing have created the relatively new fields of satellite communications, optical fibre transmission, computer-controlled telephone exchanges and networks, advanced modulation methods, speech-processing and cellular radio systems. These enabling technologies have led to the creation of new products and services such as mobile communications, high-speed data and facsimile transmission, radiopaging and direct satellite-to-home TV.

Worldwide, totally integrated, computerised communications, broadcasting and information networks are now a reality. Computers can be plugged directly into the public telephone network, and exchange data with anywhere in the world. Offices can be linked up, for video conferencing; sales staff can transmit orders from hand-held computers down-line to office computers; and many office workers can now work from home. Television screens carry 'teletext' – viewdata systems like Oracle and Ceefax. Networks, like the Internet, allow data terminals in EC countries access to databases storing scientific, technical, medical, legal and business information. 'Interactive', two-way systems, allow customers to order directly and instantaneously what they see on the screen and to 'call up' their bank statement. Electricity and gas meters can be 'read' remotely.

Satellites allow remote-sensing of features on the Earth's surface, such as wave heights in the North Sea and the production of various crops by farmers; an analysis of weather patterns and the movement of armed forces. They give vastly improved radio-telephone links between ships, aircraft and their land bases. Astronomers can remotely control telescopes across the world via satellites. Firms and private individuals can have their own dish aerials or terrestrial cables and use special business satellite systems or optical cables to carry data rapidly across continents and seas, or receive broadcast information directly into the home.

Optical cables have produced a revolution in the communications business. A 'cable' of very pure glass as thin as human hair can transmit impulses of light instead of radio waves, using light-emitting diodes or laser beams, and can carry far more information than conventional copper cables, or even satellite links. A single fibre with a core only one-tenth of a millimetre in diameter can carry 8,000 telephone conversations simultaneously. The first optical fibre transatlantic cable carried 40,000 telephone conversations, and the first cable across the Pacific Ocean carries 600,000. Optical fibres now circuit the globe and are immune from electromagnetic interference, need less boosting and therefore fewer repeaters, and are very hard to tap. They can also carry voice, picture and other data along the same cabling. They are in many homes carrying not only telephone calls, but data, television 'electronic' mail and newspapers. Existing copper cable networks will become obsolete. Fibres are appearing in other areas too: aircraft communication, and control systems of such as the London Underground railway.

Telecommunications

While straightforward telephone systems are still the mainstay, 'telecommunications' increasingly means much wider communication systems, as a result of the technological advances already described. 'Telecommunications' now means data transmission networks of all kinds and it has become commonplace for businesses to communicate with each other via the telephone system and transmit voice, text, graphics, pictures or data.

British Telecom was established as a public corporation in 1981 and became a public limited company in 1984. It subsequently changed its name to BT and in 1995 had a turnover of £13.89 billion. As a global telecommunications services provider it has been forming alliances with other telecommunications companies in Portugal and Germany and has a 20% stake in MCI, a US telephone operator. The industry's regulatory body – the Office of Telecommunications (Oftel), which monitors and administers the holders of telecommunication licences, has been driving down charges for telephone services to increase competition. Initially this dramatically reduced the staffing at BT and career opportunities but in 1996 it was seeking 500 new recruits, most of them engineers.

Evaluation of apparatus to be connected to the networks is the responsibility of the British Approvals Board for Telecommunications (BABT).

Value-added services and applications are growing, including managed networks, database services and the specific application of advanced telecoms to other sectors like banking or medicine. The convergence of computers and telecommunications offer considerable scope for development. Most big companies have sophisticated telecommunication requirements and employ their own telecom engineers or consultants, while software systems are increasingly used to solve telecom problems.

Manufacturing covers a vast range of products from expensive computer-controlled telephone switches to small handsets for mobile communications. Optical fibres, opto-electronic devices, modems, earth stations, multiplexers, specialised application circuitry, real-time computers, repeaters and regenerators and cordless phones are some of these. All require the skills and expertise of electrical and electronic engineers and the ability to use computing tools is an advantage.

A high proportion of the work involved in developing and introducing telecommunications systems, initially, is done by manufacturers, and there are exciting career prospects developing new systems and software. However, once installed, modern, high-technology communication systems do not need very large numbers of people to operate or maintain them. All-electronic communication systems need little maintenance, and the main opportunities are for a relatively small proportion of very highly skilled managers, capable of sophisticated decision-making, flexible and responsive to what is a very volatile business, and for marketing experts.

BT

BT continues to dominate the telecommunications industry both in terms of purchasing equipment and systems as well as the provision of services. As a public service provider it still has around 90% of the domestic telephone market. It has had a radical structural reorganisation and is now organised in three divisions which relate directly to its customer base:

- *Personal Communications*, who provide the core services of phone and fax for its 20 million domestic customers;
- *National Business Communications*, who provide similar core services to the corporate market including videoconferencing, direct-dial satellite service for ships and in-flight calls for aircraft, and distribution of live coverage of horse and greyhound racing to high-street betting shops over Europe's largest private satellite TV service, etc.; and
- *Global Communications*, which handles all of its international business.

In addition to these divisions, *Network and Systems* department operates and maintains the telecommunications networks required to supply the businesses which the three divisions provide. It employs numerous engineers in network engineering, to design, build, install and maintain BT's extensive networks. The *Group Business Management* department decides and implements business strategy, supporting the 1,500 different products BT provides to its three market sectors. It has a *research laboratory* at Martlesham, near Ipswich and spent £271 million on research and development in 1995. In recent years its researchers have kept it ahead of the competition by introducing a range of novel products and services which the many other operators did not have the technological muscle to develop.

About 60% of its research and development spending is used to improve the network performance and develop new customer services. The other 40% goes on more longer-term work, often in collaboration with equipment manufacturers in the electrical and electronic business, with universities and colleges, and in major advanced collaborative programmes in the UK and Europe.

BT currently (1996) has 110,000 employees, 100,000 fewer than in 1991. It is virtually impossible to describe all the available jobs in what is now a hugely diverse operation. Work in areas such as finance, marketing, purchasing and personnel is now very similar to that in any other large-scale, capital-intensive, business. However, there are some special employment features and BT recruits at various levels.

Graduate level

Seventy percent of BT of their graduates have engineering or science degrees, with the most relevant being in communications, computing, electrical/electronic, general engineering, materials, physics, power, computer software and systems engineering, although other engineering disciplines are also relevant. Graduates are employed in the following.

- *Research and technology*. Current R&D is on transmission methods such as satellite communications and submarine cables, developing open networks, and developing 'expert' systems of software.
- *Network systems*. Network engineers design and construct the connections within the system. There are the connections between the customers' equipment and the network, and there are the connections between one switching centre and another. 'Switching' is accomplished by software which decides the route a signal will take through the network.
- *Systems engineering* (sales). Graduates act as the technical support to a sales team running a national account customer. They look at the needs of the customer, and design and commission a new system tailored to customer needs.
- *Network and strategic planning*. Graduates plan the networks for the public telephone system and for private systems, including telex and data transmission. The networks are constantly developing and responding to new technology.
- *Operational engineering management*. Graduates are responsible for anything from installing business systems to running a repair service centre. They manage between twelve and 25 staff.

In 1996 BT expected to recruit 300 graduates in engineering or related disciplines, most of them electronic or software engineers. Graduates are also recruited for marketing, finance and human resources management.

School-leaver level

Telecommunication Officers do much of the day-to-day work. In planning, they help to forecast the volume of 'traffic' both short- and long-term, using computer-aided and statistical methods to study population trends, commercial and industrial developments, etc. In customer service they monitor reliability and quality, deal with customers' problems and complaints, queries on bills, etc. Telecommunications, commercial, and sales support officers can gain promotion to junior management dealing with letters and committee papers, supervising clerical staff, helping with policy formulation, or general administration. All A-level entrants, including trainee programmers and systems analysts, as well as graduates, are treated as future managers.

BTs *telephone technicians* work in three main areas:

- *Installation and maintenance*. Installing new telephone lines at customers' premises involves climbing ladders and telegraph poles, cleating the wire to the outside of the building and installing sockets and wiring inside. Repairs and maintenance involves fault-finding and testing. This can be done remotely from the exchange but can also involve visiting customers' premises and repairing and testing underground and overhead cables.
- *Cable jointing*. This involves installing and repairing cable between the exchange and customers' premises.

Most work is underground, but some of the work is on overhead lines.

- *Internal construction.* Installation work within a telephone exchange or a number of exchange satellites.

BT's technician engineering workforce is expected to shrink over the next five years.

Technicians and mechanics are also needed to maintain BT's fleet of vehicles and carry out servicing and repairs at their transport workshops. BT also crews cable-laying ships.

The number of telephonists employed has decreased.

Qualifications and training

Graduates with appropriate degrees are recruited and have one- or two- year training periods. They are encouraged to study for professional qualifications and to achieve Chartered Engineer status. They may be sent on courses, e.g. BT runs an MSc course in telecommunications engineering for employees at its Martlesham site, given by lecturers from London University.

School-leavers are recruited as:

- *technical and commercial trainee* (age 16 – 41). Entry requirements as for entry to BTEC/SCOTVEC courses, usually four GCSE/SCEs grades A–C/1–3, or equivalent. A-level/Higher, GNVQ level 3 passes or equivalent needed as trainee programmer/analysts, for junior management, or as telecommunication officers. A driving licence is an advantage.
- *technician IIB* (age 16–58). No academic or vocational qualifications are required but applicants must pass aptitude tests of numeracy, mechanical appreciation and manual dexterity. Some experience of electrical, electronic, communications, scientific, mechanical, civil, craft or similar disciplines is desirable. 16-year-olds are more likely to enter as craft trainees.
- *craft trainee.* No academic or vocational qualifications are required but applicants must pass aptitude tests of numeracy, mechanical appreciation and dexterity. Some young people entering as craft trainees have GCSE/SCE grades.

Mercury

Mercury, with a turnover of £1.2 billion employed around 8,500 staff in 1995. It is a subsidiary of the global telecommunications company Cable and Wireless. They recruit around 30 graduates each year into engineering, information systems, marketing, finance and human resources. In operations, graduates handle projects, drawing up a specification for part of an 'intelligent network', developing a database to monitor the submarine cable system, or preparing a capital expenditure proposal for a trunk network development, etc. In the regions, graduates may be employed in network planning and installation, network management, network maintenance, customer planning and installation and customer maintenance.

Further information

BT and Mercury.

Measurement, control and automation

Measurement and control are closely linked because control systems operate by continuously monitoring, or measuring, the difference between the actual and the required value of each parameter or variable concerned (such as the speed of flow of a liquid, or the temperature in a building, or the pressure in a reactor) and, also continuously, as a result of this 'feedback', taking action to make any necessary correction. Measurement also depends on accurate and reliable instruments, both where they are used in control systems and in devices used solely for measuring; for instance industrial, laboratory and scientific instruments for research of all kinds, and those used in clinical diagnosis.

Even windmills used the basic principles of control, but real development came with the Second World War, when electromechanical ('wired') control systems were adopted to increase the speed and accuracy of training and firing guns to combat rockets, to steer radar and searchlights following highly manoeuvrable aircraft, and to guide naval vessels automatically onto submarine tracks. Computers and microprocessors have brought increasingly sophisticated, fast and efficient control systems, and made it feasible to automate many more activities, and to 'manage' all kinds of services, such as the heating system for a hospital complex, to both improve conditions and save energy. Future advances will be machines capable of learning from experience and adapting themselves to new and changing conditions.

Control systems are used in particular machines – automatic pilots, telescopes, radar trackers, generating equipment, gas turbines, and machine tools – and in production processes, particularly in chemicals, food and textile manufacture, where accurate, high-speed and sensitive control saves labour, raw materials, and energy. Sophisticated central heating systems and grain dryers use automatic control. Continuous crop production is possible in computer-controlled environments that provide plants with their optimum growing conditions automatically. Medical diagnosis and treatment uses control technology.

It is not only manufacturing industry, though, which must increasingly be automated and controlled; banks, the retail sector, newspaper publishing and transport are some of the other businesses which are making increasing use of automation. Computer control will spread too into the home, saving fuel, allowing appliances to be switched on and off via telephone commands.

Working in control engineering

Most control engineers are employed by firms making the machinery, equipment and systems in which control systems are installed – for defence, navigation, signalling, air-traffic control, computing, communications and so on. Chemical engineers who have specialised in control systems are employed by chemical-plant manufacturers. Large manufacturers, especially in process industries, employ their own – to identify areas where new control equipment can be used profitably; monitor the design and manufacture of the system; help with installation; supervise maintenance, and troubleshoot.

Professional control engineers can work in:

- Research into developing more sophisticated principles of measurement and new approaches to automatic control. This can involve finding out first which measurement will produce the information needed, or what controls will give a particular result, often using mathematical modelling.
- Design and development of new systems and instrumentation, modifying, adapting and upgrading systems and sub-systems, and looking for new applications.
- Instrument manufacture or production, installation and maintenance – complex and sophisticated control and instrumentation systems, often costing many hundreds of thousands of pounds, need very careful maintenance and fast, well-organised repair systems, or a lot of money could be lost.
- Marketing/sales – sophisticated systems need professional engineers to sell them.

People with first-degree and postgraduate qualifications in control engineering are in considerable demand, but many employers still 'grow their own' control engineers by training new graduates from almost any branch of engineering or even maths or physics.

Incorporated engineers and technician engineers solve problems in measurement and control instrumentation using established techniques and principles; provide suitable instrumentation, either by ordering or by adapting existing devices; produce sketch drawings of details so that craftworkers can construct 'one-off' devices for special applications; compile schedules of routine procedures for instrument craftworkers; and see that calibration of electrical and physical parameters is done correctly and recorded.

Craftworkers are also employed. Skilled production, installation, and maintenance craftworkers can gain promotion to, e.g. prototype production, supervisory posts.

Qualifications and training

For a first degree, although it is a multidisciplinary subject, control engineering is most often studied as a specialised option or aspect of electrical and electronic engineering, e.g. control systems, the theory and practice of feedback and measurement, instrumentation, communication and information theory, and design of computer systems, logic and hardware as well as programming and systems analysis. A few courses take a 'systems' approach, training control engineers to design control systems and strategies for almost any process. There are BEng degrees in Control Engineering at more than 20 universities. It is also possible to combine control with another engineering subject, which may mean specialising in control systems within that branch (notably chemical) or with related subjects such as computing.

Professional qualification

The (Chartered) Institute of Measurement and Control normally requires a degree in science or engineering for corporate membership (plus four years' experience), but will accept EC part 2 (in set papers). Total membership of the Institute of Measurement and Control in 1996 is 5,155. A total of 1,594 members are chartered, 884 are incorporated and 91 are engineering technicians.

Incorporated engineer

Qualification is normally via a BTEC Higher National award or a SCOTVEC HNC.

BTEC HND/C engineering. Programmes have core units in analytical instrumentation, process sampling systems, fault diagnosis, and process control or control engineering, with additional units chosen from use of computers, electronic instrumentation systems, further analytical instrumentation, monitoring systems and sequential control, data-handling, industrial relations and work study, and college-devised units for local needs.

Entry is as for all BTEC Higher awards via a relevant National award, a GNVQ level 3 or A-levels; maths and physics should have been studied with a pass in one.

SCOTVEC sets an HNC course in industrial instrumentation and process control. Entry is as for all SCOTVEC Higher awards.

The Institute of Measurement and Control accepts HNC/D, plus five years' experience for Licentiate (TEng) membership.

Engineering technician

Qualification is via BTEC National awards and SCOTVEC National Certificate.

SCOTVEC's National Certificate allows choice of modules which can bias a course to industrial measurement and control. Entry is as for all SCOTVEC National Certificate courses.

The Institution of Measurement and Control accepts a BTEC National (plus five years' experience) for Associateship.

Craft level

Qualification is via City & Guilds awards.

Further information

Institute of Measurement and Control.

Contents

The Mining and Energy Industries

(CLCI: RAN, ROB)

Mining, prospecting and quarrying

Background – exploration and prospecting – mining, drilling and quarrying operations – processing – employment in the industry – mining and mineral engineering courses

Background

The raw materials which come from the ground or the sea bed heat homes, fuel vehicles and machinery, and build houses. They are turned into metals and plastics, synthetic fibres, chemicals and fertilisers, jewellery and mugs, glass and cement. A growing population ensures that, even without any new uses being found for these materials, or any rise in standards of living, the world uses more mineral ores, chemical deposits, crude oil, sand, stone and salt every year. The underground reserves of some raw materials – not only crude oil, but also aluminium and tin, silver and gold, tungsten and zinc – are dwindling fast. Britain could once produce most of the iron ore it needed – today it is all imported. The only long-term reserves in the UK are coal – Britain still mines some tin and industrial minerals, but off-shore oils and gas will be used up quite quickly.

Prospectors have to search further afield, into ever more remote and inhospitable areas of the globe, and experience increasingly difficult conditions. The oil industry, for example, now works the North Sea and frozen Alaska. Mining and oil companies have to mine deeper, use more sophisticated ways of finding reserves (such as surveys made by satellites), new methods to extract, for instance, tar oil from sand, to refine poorer grades of ore and develop new machinery. Soon it will be worthwhile trying to find and recover metal ores from under the sea, despite the huge technological problems involved, as oil and gas are now brought up from under the sea bed, first of all from the strange, manganese-rich 'nodules' which lie on the ocean floor. New reserves will become increasingly difficult and more expensive to develop – financially and in terms of cost regarding the high amounts of energy needed, dealing with the environmental problems, etc.

The astronomical costs and massive technological problems mean that only large, multi-national, international or state-owned companies, or consortia (groups), can afford to prospect for minerals or other reserves, and to spend the finance required for extraction. Many oil fields and ore reserves are known, but will not be exploited unless or until the price of the product reaches an economic level to initiate mining or drilling. Economic price often includes the cost of developing new technology. The Athabasca tar sands in Canada were known for many years, but only the 1973 explosion of oil prices made it more cost-effective to develop machinery for squeezing the oil out. Mines, wells and quarries open and close with market trends; whole regions develop and collapse through economic trends in the industry.

Government control is also crucial: it may take a stake in any company or set a level of tax which can be either advantageous or detrimental to growth. These are factors which companies take into account when deciding whether or not to prospect and/or exploit minerals etc. Many mineable reserves on land are now located in third world countries – putting the developed world at a disadvantage in that field.

The industry is dominated by international companies: several major international oil companies (which have also diversified into mining, other areas of the energy business, chemicals etc.), and about 20 mining companies, plus national organisations, e.g. Middle Eastern oil companies, which dominate production of oil worldwide. In general, smaller companies provide mainly specialist services, such as geological/geophysical surveying.

The coal industry

British Coal has now been privatised; there are now only a few mines left in the UK. RJB (UK) Ltd in Doncaster handles 80% of output. Long-term prospects for coal are theoretically bright with enough identifiable reserves to last at least 300 years, and probably longer with improvements in coal mining technology. Coal will, at some stage, have to provide some replacement for crude oil.

Although Britain produces more than 91 million tonnes of coal the industry has to compete with imports from open-cast Australian and third world mines, whose production costs are lower than those of British pits. This means there is emphasis on greater productivity and lower costs; computer monitoring and control of machines and operations; and flexible working patterns for miners are new working practices.

Colliery manpower has fallen dramatically, from 239,000 in 1977/78 down to less than 57,300, the last figure available before privatisation in 1990/91. Over the same period productivity more than doubled. More recent statistics are unavailable. However, recruitment is achieved by two routes, via the colliery and by employment with contract companies employed by the mines.

The oil and gas industry

In 1994, Western Europe accounted for 1.6% of the world 'proven' crude oil reserves. Confidence in the industry has risen since the price slump of 1986 when companies were abandoning exploration plans and over 40 off-shore rigs in the North Sea stood idle. The world now uses nine times more oil every day than in 1945 and almost 50% more than in 1970. By 1994 there were 68 off-shore and three on-shore fields producing 126 million tonnes of crude oil, with more under development. Similar expansion is taking place in gas fields. Technology involved in every aspect of production has changed considerably along with patterns of supply. The big concern in later years has been to balance the desire for energy with the desire for a clean environment.

Other mining and quarries

The most important non-ferrous metal mined is tin, but the fortunes of this small industry too are decided by prices and markets, and only two (of six) mines survived the 1985–6 failure of London's tin market. In 1996 only one tin mine remains – South Crofty in Cornwall. The future beyond 1996 is still uncertain.

Britain is a major producer of clays, fuller's earth, salt, fluorspar, gypsum, and anhydrite, but again they are very small industries. ECCI is the largest producer of china clay in the world and supplies white international minerals to the paper, ceramics, paint, rubber and plastics industry; 88% of the output is exported. The industry has a high level of research development with £15 million being spent annually. ECCI Europe recruits a wide range of employees including mining, chemical, mineral and electrical engineers. They also require commercial, marketing, accountancy skills and have opportunities for skilled operational jobs including explosive experts, HGV drivers and heavy plant operators.

Quarries also produce a range of materials, such as sand, gravel, slate, chalk, clay, granite and limestone, which are used either in construction, or in manufacturing, e.g. ceramics. Some quarries also prepare materials for use, for example dressing or coating stone, making lime, or mixing aggregates for cement. Some quarrying firms produce and deliver ready-mix cement, others have extended into slag and crushed-concrete recovery. The industry is very capital-intensive and highly automated.

Whatever a company is bringing up from the ground, whether oil, ore, coal, sand or gravel, there are three clear stages in the process: exploration and prospecting; mining, drilling or quarrying; and processing. Some companies carry out all three stages (and market the product too), but in prospecting particularly, it is now common for one set of specialist firms to do the geophysical survey work involved, and to interpret the data, another to develop and manage the mine or oil reserve. The emphasis on team work is strong, but the different stages employ different combinations of experts and skills.

Exploration and prospecting

Exploration and prospecting covers finding where the materials are in the ground or sea bed, finding out how much there is there and of what quality, what problems there are in getting at it, how much it will cost to extract, and if it is economic to do so given the quality of the material and the state of the market. Prospecting is a highly sophisticated business, using the most advanced geophysical techniques and computers to collect, record and analyse the data.

Geologists are employed by oil-logging companies. Even major quarrying companies have their own small teams of geologists. When recruiting, some survey companies train their own seismologists, taking on not only geologists and geophysicists, but also physics graduates, mathematicians and people qualified in computing. Most are trained on-the-job at e.g. data processing centres, and then go on to field crews. (*See also* GEOLOGY *in* EARTH AND SPACE SCIENCE.)

Land surveyors and hydrographic surveyors are employed in prospecting to locate shot points and the levels between them, scout and direct and, off-shore, do hydrographic surveys based on radio positioning systems and acoustic sensors.

Electronic engineers and technicians do instrument work and computer maintenance. Mining and drilling engineering teams do test drilling under the instructions of geologists. Mining engineers and minerals or petroleum engineers help assess potential mines or wells. Civil, electrical and mechanical engineers plan and cost the plant and equipment, allowing for e.g. power and water supplies, construction, and roads to get to the site. A few cartographers are needed.

Mining, drilling and quarrying operations

If and when a mine, oil reserve or quarry is developed, geologists and mining or petroleum engineers work together initially, although the mining/petroleum engineer is usually in charge at this stage. Geologists work out where mining/drilling should begin, and how to produce the best grades of ore or oil incurring little waste. Mining engineers then plan mine development and oversee operations, so that the ore is recovered logically, economically, and safely. This means seeing that shafts are properly supported, ventilated, blasted etc. Petroleum engineers decide whether wells are economic, and prepare the development plans.

Mining and drilling operations use very advanced technology. A North Sea oil rig is a major advance in naval architecture/civil/structural engineering technology. Half of all ore production comes from 150 giant, highly automated mines, some 80% of them open cast. The new privatised coal mines operate some of the most technologically advanced equipment there is.

Mining operations are normally controlled by mining engineers. All British Colliery managers and many more senior management staff within the coal industry are qualified mining engineers (*see* MINING AND MINERAL ENGINEERING COURSES *below*). Individual colliery managers have considerable freedom to decide (subject to the requirements of mining law) how best to manage their pits in order to meet agreed objectives. They are responsible for production, mine safety, and a supporting staff of mining engineers including under-managers, electrical and mechanical engineers, mining surveyors, etc. as well as underground, surface workers and office staff. They need considerable managerial as well as engineering skills.

The design, construction, installation, operation and maintenance of machinery in mines require the skills of mechanical and electrical engineers who often deal with very complex installations, including complex high-pressure hydraulic equipment. Engineers also take charge of the large mine service centres which overhaul, recondition and repair equipment. Mining companies also employ mining surveyors.

Oil production is controlled by petroleum engineers, who are the senior managers. Production or drilling engineers (including superintendents, production and workover/wireline supervisors) may divide their time between exploration and on-shore services. They control the wells and rigs, planning and budgeting drilling operations, appointing and supervising drilling and service contractors, looking after the engineering aspects of choosing new equipment and drilling systems.

Like mining, oil drilling operations need quite large supporting professional staff, usually made up of electrical/electronic engineers and mechanical engineers, who design, construct, install and maintain machinery, from high-pressure hydraulic equipment, to electronic remote-control and monitoring gear, oil rig and platform equipment, pipelines, and associated machinery, e.g. turbines and rotary drills. They are supported by electrical/electronic, instrument and mechanical-engineering technicians.

Mining and oil production also employs geologists – to help in planning and monitoring developments through regular drilling and logging and assessing the cores which come up – to see which is the best area to develop next.

All mines, quarries, and oil operations also need supervisory and technical staff, as well as skilled workers. In a mine, for example, they include: deputies, who supervise the work of an underground mining district; overmen, who are in charge of several districts; the under-manager, responsible to the manager for the whole colliery; electricians; fitters; and the people who actually operate the sophisticated mining machinery.

On wells and drilling rigs the drilling superintendents and 'toolpushers', drillers and crewmen (including the derrickman, rig crewmen, roustabouts and crane operators) set up mobile rigs and permanent drilling platforms. Once a platform is in production, the production engineers are supported by production operators and assistants, including workover/hoist crewmen, wireline operators and technical assistants, all shore-based.

Oil wells, particularly in more remote areas and certainly at sea, must also have their own support services, giving employment to cooks, stewards, clerks, storemen, radio operators, helicopter pilots and, for off-shore operations, sailors to man supply vessels, and experts like divers.

Processing

Processing ore, coal, or oil, after extraction, is the third operation. Here mineral technologists, extractive metallurgists, and chemical engineers take over, using all kinds of methods to sort, separate, extract or purify the raw material. Separating useful raw materials from unwanted soil, rock, sand, etc. with which they may be mixed becomes more of a technological/scientific problem as firms are forced to extract from the more difficult reserves such as Athabasca, where the sands themselves are mined and then processed to extract the oil. Chemical engineers are employed by oil refineries, either in works management (in charge of a tar or coking plant), general management or in engineering services. An alternative is technical advice to management, evaluating, designing and improving processes.

Oil from wells is normally transported in crude or semi-refined form to refineries closer to the markets, where breaking it down into petrol, heating fuels, the chemicals from which plastics are made, and so on, is a chemical process, managed and designed by chemical engineers. Quarrying firms also prepare their materials, dressing and coating stone, making lime, or mixing cements.

Processing can require plant and machinery every bit as sophisticated as that used for mining, quarrying or drilling, but much of it is highly automated. Most of the jobs involved are therefore technical, in quality control, in monitoring the processes and machinery, in laboratories where checks and some research and development are done.

Within the next few decades, supplies of oil and natural gas are expected to begin to decline. Collieries are therefore developing processes for turning coal into the many oil-based products, such as petrol and chemical feedstocks, upon which modern civilisation depends. In addition, British Gas is developing ways of making substitute natural gas from coal.

Management skills, in an industry where the sheer scale of the operations, the size of the investments involved, and the level of technology needed, as well as the risks of all kinds, and the physical problems are enormous, have to be of the highest order. Most top managers are mining or petroleum engineers, but finance, marketing, purchasing, planning, research and development, etc., are also very important functions. Coal companies and the major internationals are staffed by experts with appropriate qualifications.

Employment in the industry

The pattern of employment for qualified people within the industry is continually changing. While many continue to work for prospecting and mining companies, more are likely to work for companies which specialise in developing and managing mines for other organisations (for instance, the government of a developing country, or a semi-government agency), or for companies offering specialist services (e.g. survey work), or developing particular treatment processes.

Professional mining engineers work in prospecting and surveying, in test drilling, designing and planning both underground and open cast workings, sinking shafts and making them safe – from gas, dust, and flood – with ventilation and pumps. Mining engineers manage mines once they are operating. Most mining engineers become managers.

British-trained engineers are employed by international, mainly metal, mining companies. Here mining engineers usually begin in mine management, but can go on to planning, assessing new projects, dealing with contractual or financial work, or investigating and starting new technological developments. Some go on to consultancy work, or mining finance. Only a few work in research and development.

Mining overseas is likely to mean working in increasingly harsh conditions, as the less remote mines are worked out.

As well as employing appropriately qualified engineers, the industry also employs scientists in research and development, scientific control, etc. Most large firms also require a relatively large proportion of operational research experts and computer personnel, etc.

Promotion within the industry is generally from producing mine to consulting engineering or a mining finance house. The managers of British mines will, as required by law, have begun their careers at the bottom, as rank and file mineworkers – working their way up and obtaining the statutory qualifications enabling them to become supervisors (deputies and overmen), undermanagers and managers.

In most mining/oil companies, the head office employs experienced mining engineers in complex problem-solving and trouble-shooting, finding ways of improving performance, considering new projects, planning new mines, dealing with the financial and contractual aspects of developing new areas, and investigating and initiating technological development. All skilled miners may seek the qualifications required for promotion to supervisory and management posts.

In Britain, the jobs and careers are at all levels, from the mine face, the quarry floor, and the oil rig, right up to top management.

Britain's oil industry employs only about 100,000, consequently in any one year the total of job opportunities is limited. However, while there are unlikely to be any real increases in the number of jobs, the proportion of professionally qualified personnel will certainly be higher. Oil companies are therefore increasingly looking for skilled people with open minds, intellectual integrity and the ability to adapt their career paths to the changing demands and patterns of the oil business. Exploration is a costly process, particularly off-shore or in remote sites. Teams include geologists, geophysicists, petroleum engineers and drilling engineers. Planners, economists and computer staff are also involved in every stage.

Nearly half of those working directly for the industry are probably crewmen, production operators and their assistants, radio operators, divers, etc., maintenance technicians and craft workers, and several thousand are support staff like cooks, store men, etc.

In quarrying, the number of jobs has been falling steadily for some years. Ball and china clay, sand and gravel, and limestone and lime account for over half of all jobs. The decline in numbers has been greatest amongst operatives (who include HGV drivers, shot firers and laboratory workers), but they still make up an estimated 50% or more of all workers. A relatively small proportion of craft workers (under 14%) mainly maintain plant and vehicles, with some bricklayers, carpenters, plumbers, etc.

Managers and supervisors make up most of the rest of those employed, with only very small numbers of sales/marketing people, scientists, technologists, and technicians. The largest groups employ geologists, their own drilling crews, and mechanical and electrical engineers, both to work on the design and planning of new projects, and to manage and develop new vehicles and plant.

Overseas the number of permanent posts for UK nationals is shrinking all the time, as governments insist that more jobs and career posts go to their own nationals. This means that work overseas is now mostly limited to professional and other highly skilled occupations for which local people have not yet been trained, and is likely to be short-term contract work, in planning, engineering design, prospecting and surveying, not in mine management or supervision. Virtually all work at technician level or below is now done by local people.

Anyone working for an international oil or mining company must expect to spend at least the first part of their working lives moving regularly from place to place. However, with the increasing use of computer-based exploration methods and more off-shore operations, people like geologists will in future probably spend less time in the field, more at desks with computer terminals. Engineers will be more involved in the design and development of new equipment and processes, and then in office-based planning and management.

Even so, the early years in mining or the oil industry, even for professionals and graduates, will include time spent in the hottest and coldest, wettest and driest, most uncomfortable and remotest spots in the world, sometimes alone, and in some degree of danger.

Recruitment and entry

The modern mining, oil and quarrying industry needs progressively more brain and less brawn. Even the modern miner, although still working in very difficult conditions, no longer wields pick and shovel, but operates highly sophisticated machinery, which has to be expertly controlled and understood. All companies try constantly to cut employee numbers. Mechanisation and automation help towards this, continually reducing the number of jobs at the mine or quarry face.

The mining and quarrying industry recruits scientists and technologists, mainly geologists, mining engineers, some metallurgists, civil, electrical and mechanical engineers and surveyors. Automating mines, putting mine information systems on-line, using computer-based systems in exploration, are all increasing demand for, e.g. electronic/systems engineers and computing experts.

In the oil industry the main opportunities for graduates are with the major oil companies, but for oil exploration/production the main demand is for specific qualifications (as above). Few other graduate entrants find work directly in exploration/production but they can work in the commercial functions such as marketing, finance, personnel etc.

Qualifications and training

In quarrying, training has never been developed to any great extent. Doncaster College provides BTEC Higher National courses in minerals processing and materials reclamation, minerals surveying, and quarrying. Camborne School of Mines run HNDs in mining and minerals engineering, industrial geology, minerals surveying and resource management and environmental science with technology.

In the oil industry a number of the oil companies provide industrial training places for students following college-based sandwich courses in a range of disciplines including engineering, applied sciences, computer sciences and business studies. There are limited opportunities for pre-university training for those with good A-level/Higher grade or equivalent passes. Some companies offer summer vacation training to students from full-time degree courses.

Firms generally recruit for other work from people with relevant qualifications, training and/or experience. Some oil companies recruit school-leavers with four GCSE level or equivalent passes at 16-plus including maths, a science and English for craft/technician training in instrument and electrical engineering, process work and maintenance. Most oil companies are now participating in YT in both technical and clerical areas.

The oil exploration/production industry does not have any comprehensive industry-wide training schemes. Every company has its own training programme, which will vary with levels of demand for skills, which at present are low in exploration/production.

The industry has a drilling and production technology training centre (at Montrose in Scotland), which puts on a range of short courses (some for graduates), but most students are company sponsored.

Divers must now legally have a valid certificate of competence and approved training. Four centres (at Falmouth, Fort William, Fort Bowland, and Diver Training School, Exmouth) provide approved training. Students are mainly sponsored. Private students are accepted but courses are very expensive. The minimum age is 18.

Mining and mineral engineering courses

Mining and mineral engineering deal with all aspects of extracting ores and other minerals and materials from the ground.

Mining engineers study not only mining operations such as drilling and blasting, support and excavation, but also the origin and nature of ore deposits, structural geology, and applied geophysics. It also involves studying mechanisation and automatic control (since automated mining machinery is now some of the most sophisticated around), power supply and transmission, transportation, ventilation and air-conditioning, etc. Basic engineering and geological principles, management, organisation and economics are also taught.

Minerals engineering and technology cover similar ground, but also deals with the treatment of mined ores by chemical and physical processes, to separate valuable minerals from others and from the rocks and soil.

Diploma, first degree and postgraduate courses in mining and related subjects are offered at four institutions: the universities of Leeds, Nottingham and London (Imperial College) and Camborne School of Mines in Cornwall.

Related courses are in engineering mechanics, excavation engineering, mineral process design, production management, coal preparation and ore dressing.

Camborne School of Mines trains engineers for the whole world and particularly for metal mines overseas, including gold, copper, tin, zinc and lead mines.

The school runs courses which form a closely-knit matrix which allows students to specialise in one area, from geology, mining engineering, minerals engineering, environmental science and technology, and minerals surveying and resource management. There are 12 degree options currently running (1996) and a range of MSc courses.

Professional bodies

The Institution of Mining Engineers (membership about 3,500) requires all candidates for full membership either to have a degree or to have passed EC examinations, and at least two years' training plus two years' appropriate experience in the industry. The institution has also associate membership for Incorporated Engineers, for which the entry requirements are an appropriate HNC or its equivalent, and at least five years' appropriate experience including two years' practical training.

The Institution of Mining and Metallurgy (membership 4,500 plus) requires all entrants to be of graduate standard, with either an appropriate degree in science or technology, or EC examinations; at least two years' training and two years in a position of professional responsibility is also required.

(Both institutions accept as members anyone working in mining or an allied industry – not just qualified mining engineers but those qualified in other professions, for example other branches of engineering and surveying, and research scientists.)

The Institution of Mining Electrical and Mechanical Engineers (total membership 2,500) requires candidates for corporate membership normally to have had appropriate training and at least five years' engineering experience and four years' employment in a responsible position. Membership is also open at different grades (with appropriate training and experience) to incorporated engineers, engineering technicians and those at craft level.

Further information
The above institutions.

The energy industries

Modern, developed economies, with their associated high standard of living, grew as a result of, and have been underpinned by, a cheap and plentiful supply of energy. This is required for everything from industrial power through transport to domestic heating. Until the 1973 oil crisis, cheap and plentiful energy was virtually taken for granted.

It is now over 20 years since that first oil crisis, and the energy business is once again in a state of change. Since 1973 oil prices have variously plunged and rallied affected by a range of global factors and events, from recession to, most recently, the Gulf War. Energy use has not risen as was expected in the 1960s, mainly due to the recession which oil price rises helped to cause, and partly due to some conservation and better energy management. Predicting the future of the energy business, whether use will rise or fall and what structural changes there will be between the various sources, appears to be impossible even for experts, not least because political and environmental issues, particularly post-Chernobyl, are major factors.

But just for developing countries to industrialise and modernise, world demand for energy is expected to triple by the end of century. Demand grows as economies develop, but the old days of swift growth have probably gone forever. However, focus on efficient operations and considerable advances in technology have helped to reduce offshore costs by up to 50% per barrel of oil.

Oil's share of world energy consumption is now falling. While oil will have to go on being the main transport fuel for some time (despite Brazil's 'green gas'), it will be used for electricity production and by industry less, so proven reserves are now predicted to last well into the next century. In the world, oil still accounts for 37.5% of energy consumption, solid fuels 25.38%, natural gas 20.1%, nuclear energy 6.7%, and hydro-electric power 7.5%.

Conservation and more expert energy management are supposed to be the main 'sources' of energy for the next 20 years. In the UK, the government is attempting to persuade users to 'save' the 20% of consumption which it estimates is wasted annually.

Research into alternative, renewable sources – from wind, wave, sun, dung – of energy continue, although it seems less urgent than in the crisis years of the 1970s. The enormous investment involved may just not give a good enough return, so that developing commercially viable alternative sources is still some way off. Wind energy is one of the main areas of renewable energy potential. In 1995, generation by wind energy projects in the UK was up 10% on 1994 and the government wants to see energy generated from non fossil fuel obligations double in the new few years.

Current research programmes, including projects to assess wind energy potential and the possibility of siting large numbers of wind-turbines off-shore, are in progress. In 1996 there were 29 wind farms in operation, and 13 more were either under or awaiting construction.

OSPREY (Ocean Swell Powered Renewable Energy) is also gathering pace. This is a new design which may hold the key to energy production from waves on a commercial scale.

Biofuels make use of carbon fixed from the atmosphere during plant growth and geothermal energy exploits the rise in temperature which is found as the earth's crust is penetrated. However, although this energy may be considered renewable, it is in fact mined. Solar power uses mirrors to concentrate the light; successful prototypes producing between 1 and 10 Mw have been built in Spain, Sicily and California.

All these resources have potential both in terms of energy and employment prospects. Numbers employed are estimated at 2,200.

Since energy is such an essential commodity, long-term opportunities in these industries must continue. But the number of jobs is predicted to go on falling as the utilities push for greater productivity and efficiency, through more automation and sophisticated control and monitoring systems, etc. The greatest job losses are likely to be in manual, semi-skilled and craft work. While there are unlikely to be any real increase in the number of skilled and professional level jobs, the proportion will certainly be higher, and the demands made of managers, etc., more exacting.

Coal is a major source of energy, but it is predominantly a mining industry (*see* THE COAL INDUSTRY *above*).

Electricity supply

Generating companies – operations – markets – research – employment in the industry – recruitment and entry – qualifications and training – further information

The industry generates, transmits, distributes, and sells energy as electricity. It is one of the largest industries in the UK. The Bill to privatise the state-owned electricity supply industry received royal assent in 1989. Privatisation has changed the structure of the industry radically.

Generating companies

The industry is made up of seven generating companies within three distinct geographical areas: National Power, PowerGen and Nuclear Electric in England and Wales, Scottish Nuclear, Scottish Power and Scottish Hydro-Electric in Scotland, and Northern Ireland Electricity. Of these Nuclear Electric, Scottish Nuclear and the NIE remain state-owned, although plans are in progress to privatise the NIE and link their supply by an undersea cable to the Scottish system in 1996. Between them they produce 90% of the electricity available in the UK. Of the remaining 10%, 4% is contributed by imports from Electricité de France. Most of the remaining 6% comes from auto-generators – companies which produce electricity wholly or primarily for their own use. Prominent in the latter are the UK Atomic Energy Authority (UKAEA) and British Nuclear Fuels (BNLF).

Overall the companies are looking to reduce manpower. Since National Power took over from the CEGB in 1990, employees are down nearly 10,000 to just under 17,200 with productivity up by 50%.

The old area boards were first privatised in 1990/91 although they are still in the process of change in 1996 and recently Scottish Power have taken over MANWEB and NorthWest Water have taken over NORWEB. Between them, via a holding company, they own the National Grid Company (NGC) which owns the main transmission system in England and Wales. In Scotland, Scottish Power and Scottish Hydro-Electric Suppliers offer terms to all customers in their authorised areas. In principle, customers can choose their suppliers, but at present only those with a maximum demand above 1 Mw are able to do so.

Operations

In the new regime, customers buy electricity from suppliers; suppliers purchase electricity through a wholesale electricity market – the 'pool'. Sales and purchases of electricity in the 'pool' are made by participating generators and suppliers according to a set of rules which govern the markets operation, and the calculation of payments due to generators and payments due from suppliers. Competition in generation is facilitated by the pooling system. Generators sell their output under special 'pool' trading arrangements which effectively establish 'spot' electricity trading prices on a half-hourly basis.

Markets

Final energy consumption grew by just 2% over the last two decades. The growth of electricity consumption was 38%. The low growth of total usage reflects a substantial degree of substitution in favour of more efficient and convenient fuels. The growth of electricity has also been assisted by the continuing development of applications for which there is no practical substitute.

Electricity counts for just over 15% of final total energy consumption, considerably behind that of petroleum. The electricity industry supplied over 26 million customers in 1995. The largest sector is 'domestic' which accounts for over 90% of the total, the 'services' sector (includes commercial and public administration) is 7%, industrial and fuel is 1%, and agricultural is 1%.

Research

EA Technology Ltd, based at Capenhurst, is part of the Electricity Association, and supports the electricity industry through a range of research projects and technical services. Two-thirds of the research programme is associated with the utilisation of electricity in industry, agriculture, commerce and the home. Another third of resources are employed in research aimed at reducing the costs of distributing electricity. In research and development, engineers and scientists (with technicians), work in interdisciplinary teams. The centre employs some 100 graduate researchers, a high proportion of whom hold postgraduate qualifications in various disciplines.

Employment in the industry

Electricity is one of the largest industries in the UK, directly employing some 109,914 people. Professional engineers, mainly electrical engineers, some mechanical, mostly work in the power stations. Under 400 people are needed to run a power station. Under a charge engineer, who controls the power station plant, professional engineers work on shift teams – as desk engineers in the control room, on plant operation (in charge of shutting down, taking off, or putting on plant as needed to meet demand, reporting faults, etc.), or in charge of maintenance teams.

Electrical engineers also look after the maintenance of transmission lines, cables and transforming stations. Systems operation engineers staff control centres, where they see that the right amount of electricity is being generated, that the system is not being overloaded, and that the most economical plant is in use, maintaining voltage and frequency etc. They have to keep track of what is happening to the weather, popular TV programmes, and anything else that helps them to predict sudden changes in demand.

Electrical engineers also specialise in commercial applications, negotiating and planning supplies with larger customers, such as industrial firms or hospitals, and evaluating both the technical and economic aspects and problems. They also look for ways to improve electricity use, and for new uses in e.g. industrial processes, where they may work with engineers designing new factory plant, or heating/ventilating systems for buildings.

Teams of electrical, mechanical and civil engineers plan, develop, and supervise construction of new power stations, generating equipment, and transmission. Engineers design new system control facilities (using CAD systems). Back-up teams of technician engineers include draughtsmen and women.

Technician-level work includes support work for professional engineers in power stations and design, draughting, developing and operating distribution networks, supervising industrial and craft workers, negotiating and planning customer supplies, and working on ways of using electricity in new industrial processes.

Craft workers are employed in all the companies. Some work on the mechanical side – with boilers, turbines, pumps, valves and so on – and others do electrical work on generators and transformers, switchgear, and so on. Electrical fitters install transformers and switchgear in substations, and linesmen add new overhead lines and inspect, check and renew lines where needed. Electricians, fitters, meter mechanics and cable jointers work on the distribution system, and connect or repair supply systems for customers. Meter mechanics and testers clean, overhaul, repair, adjust and test several thousand meters a year.

Administrative staff include accountants and accounts staff, personnel staff, legal staff, people to look after and negotiate wayleaves for the transmission systems and manage estates, customer relations staff, sales people (for REC shops), secretarial and clerical staff. Promotion to senior posts and management is from within the companies.

Recruitment and entry

The industry recruits right across the 16 to 21-plus age-range, and at all levels of school/higher and further qualification.

Qualifications and training

For professional-level work within the industry, it is usual now to complete an appropriate degree course prior to entry. The industry recruits across a wide range of disciplines; Engineering (utilisation/distribution), Computer Programming/Systems Analysis, Administration, Accountancy, Human Resources Management/Personnel, Appliance Marketing, Energy Marketing, Telecommunications, Power Purchasing, Customer contracts and tariffs, Law, Forecasting. Graduates undertake training in the work place and at various purpose built training centres throughout the country. Training is up to two years and can lead to professional qualifications.

The industry trains extensively at all levels, and training schemes are regularly reviewed and updated. Companies aim to produce flexible and multi-skilled employees who are capable of high productivity levels.

Most training schemes lead to NVQ/SVQs at level 3 or higher or those of professional status. There are also new Modern Apprenticeships in place. They fully support schemes which encourage full participation by women in the work environment.

Further information

Electricity Training Association which is the lead body for the electricity sector.

The gas industry

Gas became a re-vitalised source of energy with the discovery of natural gas in the North Sea in the mid-1960s, although by then the industry had already used a great deal of initiative to modernise itself. British Gas is a major energy supplier in Britain and is currently active in 45 countries overseas.

The company is the sixth largest in Britain, serving 8 million customers. Manpower has been reduced by 10,000 through voluntary redundancy and in 1994 the total number of employees was 60,800. It went through massive restructuring in 1994 and the trading operations are now split into several autonomous Business Units: Public Gas Supply, Business Gas, Retail & Service and TransCo. Since privatisation there has been heavy investment in Exploration and Production. Gas demand is projected to rise by 40% by 2005.

UK gas business–trading

This includes the distribution and marketing of gas, the sale of gas appliances through some 670 sales centres, as well as servicing, billing, meter reading and 24-hour safety cover.

The Gas Business has won an average of 250,000 new customers every year for the past 12 years. The company is one of the most advanced users of IT in Europe and spends some £160m a year in this area. It helps develop its own software and has since privatisation spun off two wholly owned computer companies to market this. It is also developing a programme to utilise some 500 acres of gas land throughout the country, including a £1 billion mixed development project in Greenwich, London. A Venture Capital company has been set up to support new companies developing ideas related to the gas business.

A fast changing company supplying the competitive energy market, British Gas places great importance on training, spending some £36 million a year on developing its workforce. British Gas also runs an active community programme spending some £10 million a year supporting education, the arts, environmental protection and charities.

Exploration and Production

Exploration and Production, building on 30 years of company experience, is exploring for and producing gas and oil in some 20 countries throughout the world. It has around 1,300 employees and has headquarters offices in Reading, Berkshire, and Houston, Texas, USA. A significant gas discovery has been made in UK waters and gas sales began in 1994 from the wholly owned Morecambe field. There has also been a major oil discovery in the Gulf of Suez. It is producing gas in the US and oil in Russia, as well as Tunisia and Gabon in Africa. Development of the three British Gas operated Armada fields scheduled for 1997 has now been approved.

Global Gas

Global Gas seeks business opportunities for the company both at home and overseas, through starting up new ventures or by acquisition. It seeks to develop gas systems in parts of the world where these are under-developed – as currently in Tunisia and Turkey – and purchasing established systems.

Global Gas is responsible for Canada's largest natural gas company, serving a million customers there and has interests in gas and energy service companies in Germany, France, Spain, Portugal and Italy. It has recently won a major contract to supply gas to Tunisia. The Technology Transfer section is active in around 30 countries and markets the company's expertise and technology. Global Gas is also actively marketing power generation skills and is currently involved in around six projects at home and abroad. Citigen, 50% owned by British Gas, markets Combined Heat and Power, providing electricity, heating and air-conditioning from gas. It has a major contract to supply the City of London Corporation.

Group services and research

Group Services serves all Business Units and provides public relations, personnel support and a legal service. They include a major financial and treasury operation to support the company worldwide. Research and Technology is responsible for an £80 million a year research and development programme, helping every area of the business off-shore and on-shore. Research has led to the development of the first natural gas heavy goods vehicle launched in May 1994.

Recruitment and entry

In 1994, British Gas employed 32,283 in UK Gas Business–Trading, 2,202 in Exploration and Production and around 1,300 in Global and Power Generation. They run a graduate development programme and professional training forms the basis for management careers.

Qualifications and training

Gas distribution and service engineers

The company recruits around 400 young people as craft apprentices (some 10% of whom recently have been female). These are age 16 to 18 and preferably have good GCSE/SCE grades, or equivalent, in maths, science, English or a practical subject. They embark on a four-year City & Guilds qualification with on-the-job training and when qualified, successful apprentices have the prospect of promotion and further training. They look after some 300,000 km of pipeline and the equipment which controls its pressure and flow, and also qualify to install and service the wide range of appliances used in homes, offices and factories.

Commercial trainees

British Gas recruits around 200 young people aged 16 to 18 to follow careers in commerce each year. Entrants should have good GCSE/SCE grades, or equivalent, at 16 or A-level/Higher/BTEC/SCOTVEC National Certificate at 18. Trainees follow a programme which includes both personal and academic development, attaining professional skills in a range of business careers.

Graduates

The company takes a varying number of graduates every year, currently around 150. Around two-thirds of those sought will have engineering or scientific qualifications but the others can come from any other discipline.

Graduates joining the company begin a two-year training process including general management training, to familiarise them with all aspects of the business. The company also pays for further studies for relevant qualifications such as the Institute of Supplies qualifications, accountancy etc., as well as having its own national management training centre.

Further information

Graduate and Professional Recruitment, British Gas, 100 Rochester Row, London SW1P 1JP. Apprentice and Commercial Trainees – details of openings from the Personnel Recruitment Manager at the nearest Regional headquarters (under 'Gas' in telephone directories).

The oil industry

The industry only partly comes under energy supply, even though some 90% of refinery output (over 92 million tonnes in 1994) is converted into fuel of one kind or another. The rest is turned into raw material, feedstock, for the petrochemical industry, into lubricating oils, bitumen, etc.

The oil industry charts its modern beginnings from 1859 when Colonel Edwin Drake discovered oil in Pennsylvania, USA. From a single product, Kerosene, which was in immediate demand, there was soon a growing product range from a number of refinery processes which today includes products from lubricants to paints, plastics, and man-made fibres. Oil companies built their profitability on involvement in all aspects of oil production, right from exploration and crude oil production (*see* MINING, PROSPECTING AND QUARRYING above) through to refining and transportation, marketing, research, and petrochemical production (*see* CHEMICAL INDUSTRIES *in* MANUFACTURING INDUSTRIES).

In Britain, North Sea Oil progress has been remarkable. In little more than a decade production more than matched domestic demand and placed the UK among the world's top five producers. From an almost standing start in 1975 UK off-shore oil production peaked in 1985 at over 110 million tonnes. By 1994 UK off-shore oil production reached 114.38 million tonnes. The future of the oil industry, and oil as a basis for fuels and energy, is full of uncertainties. While supplies for Britain are secure for the life-span of the North Sea fields (estimated at 56 years at present production rates), oil output worldwide will before long decline, and use of oil will probably have to be progressively concentrated in premium uses like road transport, where economic replacement fuels are more difficult to find. On present estimates, though, the oil industry will survive well into the next century.

Employment in the industry

Oil refining is a highly automated process. A typical refinery employs no more than 750 people, although distribution, marketing, etc., even excluding exploration and crude production, employ many more. Oil refining is basically a chemical engineering process, and the same types of technologies and qualified people are employed in, for example, process design and supervision, technological control and development, laboratory and pilot-plant research, construction project work and maintenance, instrument engineering, and engineering research.

Chemists, chemical and mechanical engineers, instrument engineers, some electrical engineers, physicists and metallurgists/materials scientists, and supporting technicians and operators work in testing and quality control, plant control (and automated systems), development and processing, maintenance, instrumentation and safety.

Marketing and distributing petroleum products is a very complex operation, and can be extremely competitive. Oil companies employ graduates, including engineers and scientists, in administration, distribution, marketing, personnel, planning and technical services, economic forecasting and market research.

Qualifications and training

See above under MINING, PROSPECTING AND QUARRYING.

Further information

The Institute of Petroleum.

Fuel technology

'Fuels' traditionally meant those coming from conventional sources and, more specifically, fossil fuels like coal and oil. Today, the subject covers the whole spectrum of energy including nuclear power, energy policy and management.

Fuel technologists are still working on the more efficient and economic use of energy, and on new sources of energy and fuel, including substitute natural gas from coal, wind- and sea-power, and the possibility of unlimited, safe energy created by harnessing nuclear fusion. Such research, however, employs scientists, engineers and technologists in multidisciplinary teams, rather than fuel technologists *per se*. Research is fundamental into materials and the laws which govern their behaviour, for example, and is applied where, in addition to finding replacements, synthetic or otherwise, for hydrocarbons, more sophisticated methods of controlling, utilising, conserving and recovering fuels already in use are needed. Research also has to solve specific technological problems for fuel suppliers, appliance manufacturers and consumers.

Fuel technology deals with the preparation of raw (fossil) materials, processing both natural and derived fuels (converted by carbonisation, gasification, hydrogenation, distillation, reaction and so on) for solid liquid or gaseous fuels, and recovery of by-products. It involves designing and developing whole systems, processes, plant and equipment, e.g. boilers, heat-exchangers and pumps, and burners, ranging in size from the giant boilers for massive power stations, down to domestic boilers. Control systems of increasing sophistication are now an essential part of energy supply and systems. Fuel technologists have to see that the right kinds of fuel are produced to meet specific demands, in the correct amounts and at the appropriate cost. They also solve technical and economic problems in transporting fuels, according to bulk, weight, state (liquid, solid, gaseous) and safety.

Energy management is an expanding area of work, but except in organisations where the problems are extremely complex, does not necessarily involve expert fuel technologists.

Fuel technologists also work in design offices, factories and laboratories. They operate as part of a project team involved in designing and constructing new power plants. Their work involves meeting customers in consultancy, technical marketing, sales and servicing.

It is usual to specialise in a particular branch of fuel engineering. The gas industry, for instance, employs specialised gas engineers to work on distribution, in contracting, appliance and industrial gas-burning equipment manufacture, in exploration, and in areas of advanced technology. Electricity supply normally employs electrical engineers.

Studying fuel/energy engineering/technology

At one time it looked as though fuel and energy would expand as a first degree subject in its own right, but this has not happened to any real extent. Relevant degree courses include chemical process engineering, chemical engineering, fuel & energy engineering, fuel & combustion science, mechanical engineering with energy option, nuclear engineering, natural gas engineering, fuel technology and engineering technology.

There are taught postgraduate courses in fuel and energy related subjects such as environmental management, energy studies and technology. Further training may be available through employers.

The Institute of Energy (membership about 5,000) has membership grades for Incorporated-engineers with a relevant BTEC/SCOTVEC Higher National award plus appropriate training experience. *See also* relevant industries *in* MANUFACTURING INDUSTRIES.

Further information

The Institute of Energy.

The nuclear industry

During the early 1950s, nuclear energy was considered to be a sustainable, inexpensive and clean energy resource which could replace conventional fossil fuels. However, although nuclear power stations produce fewer greenhouse gases than thermal stations they do present potential risks in other areas, especially radioactive waste disposal and contamination accidents.

Not surprisingly nuclear power stations have not expanded at the rate expected in the pioneering days. A series of disasters and scares have made the public extremely suspicious of new developments. Current thinking (1996) is that no new nuclear power stations are to be built for the foreseeable future; the whole Nuclear Power Programme has been frozen after the Hinckley Point 'C' Inquiry in 1994–5. France is the largest user of nuclear energy whereas the UK's use is relatively small.

Nuclear reaction or fission is the essence of nuclear energy and the whole industry has many aspects and career opportunities. The mining of uranium and the subsequent milling of uranium from uranium ore to prepare it for further processing begins the fission chain. Uranium is then processed further and purified for the nuclear fuel manufacture process. Geologists, mining engineers and chemists are all required for these processes.

Nuclear sciences cover an enormous range of industries, not just power or weaponry. Medical treatment has improved significantly from this new technology. Radioisotopes provide the medical profession with diagnostic techniques and have made significant impact on the way disease is diagnosed and treated. Nuclear instrument manufacturing makes reactor control instruments and radiation-detection and monitoring devices. The disposal of radioactive waste employs a whole section of industry in the packaging and disposal of these materials from spent reactor fuel to protective clothing. However, nuclear sciences have had their greatest impact in the field of energy.

There are many different fields to work in, including nuclear weapons. The majority of employees are nuclear physicists, nuclear engineers, physics technicians, metallurgy technicians, power plant maintenance workers, geologists, chemists, miners and drillers, and research workers. Although considerable emphasis is being placed on the environmental aspects of this industry, little employment growth is anticipated for nuclear engineers. Employment prospects for nuclear engineers will, however, remain reasonable as there are comparatively few courses and small numbers of graduates.

Manufacturing Industries

Contents

(CLCI: QON, S–SOZ)

Background to manufacturing

Britain's manufacturing industry still makes most of the things that are used every day, from pins to plates, and pens to cars, for sale to the ordinary 'consumer'. It produces food, such as bread and baked beans, and drinks, such as beer, orange squash and instant coffee, and what are called consumer durables, e.g. furniture and bicycles. Industry makes products which other industries need to make other things, for instance the components for cars; bricks and cement for the construction industry; steel tubes; and raw plastics. Some of these are called 'capital' goods, expensive items like machine tools and cranes, aircraft and trucks, and mainframe computers, which mean heavy investment for the customer. Industry makes very ordinary things, like soap powder, in very large quantities; it makes 'one-off' products like generators; it makes things which it has made for centuries, like glass and leather goods, and new things like silicon chips, lasers, optical fibres, space satellites and robots.

Manufacturers of consumer goods and capital goods are particularly vulnerable in recession because consumers can defer replacement of goods such as the car, fridge, etc., and companies defer investment plans until the economy improves.

However, overall long-term trends are discernible despite the fluctuations caused by periods of recession. The shape of British manufacturing industry has changed permanently: many traditional, 'heavy' industries like shipbuilding are shadows of their former selves, and the future now appears to be mainly to be with high-value-added industries and products where high technology is critical to success. Investment in new technology and increased automation has definitely invigorated some key sectors, and many companies have improved their effectiveness by refocusing their efforts towards higher-value-added and more specialised products where they can be internationally competitive.

Footloose industries

During the 1980s and 1990s there has been a growing trend for new industries to locate on the edge of large urban areas on industrial estates. These were termed 'footloose industries' as their location is not tied to the source of bulky raw materials. These industries include: electronics, computing, food-processing, clothing, ceramics, and associated activities such as carriers, packaging and distribution. All these industries are dependent upon the road network for supply of raw materials and distribution of finished goods. Consequently they are usually situated very close to major motorway junctions.

New technology

New technology is at the heart of manufacturing, and the success of the UK manufacturing industry in the future will probably hinge on its ability to develop and exploit five key technologies:

- Aerospace technology including satellite communications: space-based applications are already an industry worth around $30 billion worldwide.
- Pharmaceuticals: as the population ages the demand for pharmaceuticals and diagnostic medical equipment is likely to soar, while third-world population increases will ensure continued growth in demand for vaccines, pharmaceuticals and primary healthcare.
- Materials technology: where the trend is towards lighter, stronger materials tailored specifically to their end-use. The demands of the electronics and space industries combined with the pressure for new environmentally friendly materials is likely to increase activity in this area.
- Biotechnology: growth has been slower than predicted although some useful products have emerged, from biodegradable bottles through to Aids diagnostic kits and pest-resistant crops.

- Information and communications technology: the increasing use of integrated services digital networks (ISDN) through optical networks and satellite communications, and the development of the link between telecommunications and information technology, have greatly increased international exchange of information.

The manufacturing industry can be divided into the following sectors: aerospace industry; biotechnology; ceramics, glass and other mineral products; chemical industry; electrical and electronic engineering; energy; food and drink; mechanical engineering; metal manufacturing; packaging; paper-making; plastics processing; printing; shipbuilding; textile; clothing and related industries; timber and furniture; and the vehicle industry. Some of these are dealt with in this chapter: others are covered elsewhere.

To produce wealth, companies must invest in research and development and produce new cost-effective and environmentally safe products. Firms need to make sophisticated analyses of potential markets, to discover as exactly as possible what customers want of a particular product, and what new products they will buy. They must stay aware of what new technological developments can do to their business, both in their own products and in manufacturing methods.

Firms have to assess their competitors accurately, and decide if competing in a market is the best policy or whether an income is better made by, e.g. innovating and/or going for related products which will fill a gap in what the market wants. They have to develop a flexible, adaptable strategy for the company, a strategy which can respond to unexpected changes and new developments, and be changed radically if need be. They must work out the most efficient and effective methods of manufacturing, distributing and selling products which are better designed, and more reliable and efficient. Investment in research and development, innovation and design, is essential to compete effectively.

Being successful demands a much greater and more sophisticated understanding of how success is achieved. This means developing and integrating strategies, and making sure these are carried through in decision-making. It needs efficient and effective planning, and constant, and tighter control and monitoring of all aspects of the business. Reliable delivery, product quality, design and volume flexibility, and price, are all crucial.

Making an income from manufacturing is a team effort, with all departments and parts of the company, however it is organised, working closely together, and communicating with each other efficiently, all the time. It demands a lot of intelligent thinking and expertise from a great many people; an enormous amount of information which is well organised and analysed; a great many skills which are cerebral as well as practical; and a great deal of efficient planning and careful decision-making to which many people, not just the production manager and board of directors, contribute. Manufacturing industry needs a highly skilled and well-trained workforce.

Antipathy to manufacturing industry runs deep in our society. Industry is held in low esteem and so attracts too little of the country's talent and other resources. Manufacturing industry tends to be associated in many people's minds with heavy industry, declining markets and work which is dull and boring. Industry too is identified as the source of environmental problems, rather than the solution to them. This view must change. Future living standards, the quality of life and career prospects in the UK depend on having a successful manufacturing industry.

Production work

Production is the core of any manufacturing company, but the methods used by a company vary from sector to sector, from product to product.

Some products, particularly in chemicals and food, can be made in a series of continuous linked processes which are relatively straightforward to automate fully. The plant may be smelly and noisy and look like a tangle of pipes going in all directions, connecting huge containers in which chemicals are separated or mixed, crude oil 'cracked' and food stuffs treated while valves and pipes eject steam and vapour, but automation usually means there are relatively few people around. They monitor the dials and lights in central, ultra-modern control rooms, check the plant, or maintain systems and machinery.

Other forms of continuous processing are different – the massive sets of linked machinery and equipment on which, for instance, sheet glass is made by 'floating' the liquid mixture on molten metal, or the half-mile sets of rollers through which a sludge is turned into paper.

Cars are among items produced and assembled on a series of continuously moving mass-production and assembly lines. Most lines are now automated, with fewer and fewer hands putting lids on bottles, welding or painting, or working on the car body, the cake or the biscuit. 'Flexible' manufacturing systems enable firms to switch the lines to different versions of the same product, or even to a different product.

Yet other items and components are made on individual machines or at a bench. Many hundreds of parts and components, some large, some minuscule, may go to make up a single product, although for many products microelectronics means fewer and fewer parts and components (which in turn cuts costs because it reduces the number of operations and people needed). Metal parts start as strip, sheet, tube or pre-formed blanks, and are formed (forged, cast, stamped or pressed out, moulded or fabricated), machined (milled, turned, ground, planed, shaped and drilled) to tolerances of many-thousandths of a cm to give the keyways, rings, grooves, hollows, etc., they may need to fit them into other parts, and smoothed to a fine finish, each part going through several processes. Plastics are extruded, moulded, trimmed, bonded, etc.

Computer control means that a machine will do one of any number of different jobs, and do them much faster and more exactly – with less waste. In integrated systems, the machine's instructions are generated when the product is designed, and put into action when orders go through the computer system.

Lasers are being used increasingly in plant, to cut metals, plastics, and even pasta accurately, or to measure, weld, or drill, or control quality.

In assembly, on a line, bench or floor, the various parts and components are brought together, possibly in sub-assemblies first, and then built into the finished product. Most finished products must be packaged in some way, ready for distribution. Packaging may be the final stage of a production line, or may be a separate operation, increasingly automated.

Quality control has to make sure that raw materials and components coming in are as ordered, in the right quantities and quality. All the way through production, checks, tests, and regular monitoring are carried out: for quality and to see specifications are being met. At some stages, for some products, a simple visual check may be enough; and in some factories work done by robots is checked by computers using TV cameras without any need for human inspectors. For others, or at other stages, there may have to be more sophisticated checks: samples to be analysed chemically in labs; welds or other joins under X-ray or by radiography or ultrasonics, for example. Finished products are usually fully tested to ensure that they are working properly. Automated, and highly sophisticated, testing and analytical equipment is increasingly used throughout industry.

Production is supported by several departments/ functions, although what they do and how they are organised depends on the manufacturing strategy.

Before production can begin, detailed instructions, which may still be drawings, or programs, have to be prepared – or computer generated – for the factory to work from.

Production has to be planned and schedules drawn up. This ranges from time-and-motion studies, through to producing factory layouts and production lines. As technology continues to develop ever more rapidly, production engineers are constantly re-evaluating the most cost-effective way of producing and assembling components. They also design any special tools, jigs etc. needed for production, and these are usually made in the company's own toolroom.

The raw materials, components, processes and labour that go into the product must all be costed, again increasingly using information generated by computer. Purchasing has to buy materials, components, equipment, services. Stores keep production supplied as needed with raw materials, components, etc. The more complex the product, the greater the need for precise and effective stores management. Too many or too much of any part or material raises costs unnecessarily and can be as expensive as not having the needed components at all. Computer control of stores both increases efficiency and can reduce costs by monitoring stocks and their movement more exactly.

Maintenance and repair workshops keep the factory's plant and machinery operating, both by regular, planned servicing, trying to avoid breakdowns, and by dealing with breakdowns. Some, mostly more sophisticated, equipment is serviced and repaired by the manufacturers or by independent service companies.

Transport and distribution departments transfer a company's product either to warehouses, or direct to the customers. Some manufacturers install and commission equipment on customers' premises, and may also maintain and service it for them on a long-term basis.

There is an increasing tendency for companies to 'outsource', i.e. to contract out services such as transport, distribution and computing. Such services still need to be 'managed' by someone in the company who keeps an eye on the contract and ensures its delivery meets the requirements, though the actual work is another organisation's direct responsibility.

Most companies will also have a need to exercise the functions of human resource development (training and personnel work); sales and marketing of their products; cost and management accounting; purchasing of materials; and general administration. These may be carried out by a specialist in that function in the larger companies, but in smaller organisations, the tasks may be incorporated into the work of more general managers. All manufacturing companies, however, will require some form of production management.

Production manager

The production manager oversees the activities associated with production. Targets have to be met, resources and quality controlled, production processes scheduled, coordinated and organised. The production manager is also concerned with labour relations and discipline. The production manager will often be a production engineer. *See* production engineering in GENERAL ENGINEERING; *and* LOGISTICS MANAGEMENT *in* BUYING, SELLING AND RELATED SERVICES.

Qualifications and training

There are no minimum qualifications for production management, but for direct entry into production supervision a degree is usually required. This can be in any discipline, although for high-technology areas, degrees in technical subjects, mathematics or science are preferred.

The professional body for production management is the Institute of Management. They run programmes themselves (the Competent Manager Programme) and they accredit programmes run by over 150 other institutions throughout the UK and overseas. These programmes lead to National Vocational Qualification, at levels 3, 4 and 5; Certificates and Diplomas including the IM Certificate in Supervisory Management (NVQ 3) which is aimed at those on the first rung of the management ladder; and the IM Certificate and Diploma in Management. For candidates on the Competent Manager Programme, the Certificate is taken with an Open University Certificate in Management Studies, and the Diploma with an Open University Diploma in Management Studies.

The Certificate leads automatically to Associate Membership, the Diploma, with appropriate experience, to full Membership of the Institute.

Further information

Institute of Management.

Biotechnology

This is not a particularly new subject or industry, since brewing can be described as biotechnology. However, it first became a modern technology in the 1940s with new fast-fermentation techniques to produce, e.g. antibiotics and steroids. Oil companies have been trying since the late 1950s to exploit the fact that yeasts thrive on the waxy fraction of some crude oils, multiplying to make a protein-rich animal feed and raising the quality of the oil fraction itself.

The present phase of development began in the mid-1970s with the discovery that living organisms can be modified genetically to make substances not known in nature or too scarce to be used commercially, and to modify and improve existing substances. Biotechnology is not, though, based on a single, clearly identified product like the silicon chip. Biotechnology involves processes whereby living organisms are 'cosseted' so that they grow and multiply efficiently, to the point where they can yield a product: beer, penicillin, interferon, hormones.

Biotechnology is not a branch of biological science. Biotechnology is a convenient label to use for the application of fundamental biological research in industrial processes – and eventually it will be used by many different, often existing, industries (food, agriculture, chemical, pharmaceutical, medical, etc.), not by a new, or separate 'biotechnology' industry. It has become a major interest in the scientific and industrial world because the right discoveries and ideas from the frontiers of 'bioscience' can be turned into practical processes, process aids, and routes to new products and devices, which industry can exploit for a profit. Although there have been considerable successes already, the long-term future is still not absolutely certain.

A growing range of products are already being made, or are in the pipeline. Genetically engineered insulin is already improving treatment of diabetes, and a human growth hormone is available for children who lack it. Examples of other health care products being developed, or on doctors' list of priorities, are: simple, cheap tests and genetic 'probes' to diagnose heredity diseases, and viral, bacterial and parasitic infections; infection-free blood products; better vaccines for whooping cough and measles; a cheap substitute for breast milk that is better for babies than cows' milk; and drugs 'engineered' so that tumours can be targeted accurately, and normal cells not damaged.

In an agricultural application of biotechnology a 'cocktail' of enzymes and microbes has been developed to boost farmers' silage production. Inoculating plant roots with mycorrhizal fungi can increase yields and improve resistance to disease. Genetic engineering linked to plant tissue culture is having a major effect on crops of all kinds, and vegetables, tomatoes and fruit, as well as wheat, will all soon be 'designed' to meet consumer taste, ease of harvesting, packaging, and transport, etc.

Biotechnology has made significant advances in all aspects of life.

Clothing and textile industries have benefited considerably from the use of biotechnology. Tencel, a new fabric, has been successfully launched; Cellusoft has been developed to prevent piling and fading; the enzyme mixture Denimax produces denim fade without damage to fabric or machinery. Fashion, also, has benefited from the transformation of fabrics available. Biopolishing improves the looks and the drapability of cotton in addition to man-made fabrics. Biostoning helps to artificially age denim.

Biotechnology is not the result of research in any one area of biology but is multidisciplinary. Molecular biology and the well-publicised techniques of genetic engineering recombinant DNA technology are certainly central. Other priority areas are biocatalysis, including immobilised enzymes and cells; plant genetics and biochemistry; and large-scale growth of mammalian and plant cells.

To exploit biological processes, technology is needed – and 'scaling up' from the lab to an industrial process is a major problem (*see* CHEMICAL OR PROCESS ENGINEERING *in* BIOLOGICAL AND PROCESS ENGINEERING AND MATERIALS SCIENCE) – as well as science. Examples include fermentation technology (especially new reactor design and microbial physiology), new concepts in 'downstream' processing, and the control aspects: sensors and bioelectronics generally. Specialised 'backup' technologies are major growth points for better separation and purification of products like proteins, and for faster speeds and greater purity.

Once a dream for the future, biotechnology is now a hard, commercial business, and one with considerable potential for growth.. The largest companies, especially in chemicals/pharmaceuticals and food, are heavily involved. Healthcare, closely followed by products for agriculture and 'synthetic' food, are likely to dominate well into the next millennium. Later will come the large-scale development of new ways of treating wastes, especially the highly toxic ones, and replacing energy-intensive chemical processes. Biotechnology began with small-scale plant, making high-value products, but firms are expected to try to shift to increasingly larger plants for lower-value products at high production rates.

It has been estimated that there are more than 70,000 companies in the UK who could benefit, including: chemicals, textiles, food, paper, leather, oil and gas extraction, and mining.

Companies are developing products such as:

- ecology-conscious insecticides which do not kill bees because dosage rates are 20–100 times less than for conventional chemicals, and they are physically less volatile;

- (bio)polymers or plastics which are biodegradable and non-allergic; using microbes which, when fed on starch, sugars or gases, excrete long-chain molecules;
- non-woven fabrics 'grown' from microfungal hyphae to make better simulated leather, filter fabrics, and materials for medical use (e.g. wet-wipes), fabrics with better wet-strength, flexural rigidity, abrasion resistance and tensile/tear strength;
- biological methods of pest control which cost 1% of chemicals now used in forests;
- microbes that 'eat' metals, e.g. lead, from the surface of precious metal catalysts, so they do not have to be expensively recycled.

Biotechnology takes huge, and long-term investment, and until low-cost products can be made in bulk, it will not be a major money-spinner – or major job creator. The lead time between discovery and full production is lengthy, many good ideas will not be commercially viable, and companies have a tough time surviving. International oil and chemical companies have already suffered badly once, when they tried to develop markets for single-cell protein products. The cattle feed produced (from bacterium grown on carbon from methanol), is 75% protein (10% richer than fish meal, and contaminant free, but much more expensive). Firms need an early success, a cash 'flywheel' to survive and protect them against the near-inevitable crises. Costs are high, and it is still hard to find products which can compete with more conventional ones. Biotechnology, said one commentator, demands very good science, an earthy business approach (and the ability to pick commercially viable products) and enthusiastic marketing.

Efficient, and cost-effective techniques of 'harvesting', and deciding on the best growing mediums, are crucial – and of course full-scale production is very different to producing materials in the lab. Getting new products and processes from the lab to commercial production means going through 'scale-up' in the same way as in CHEMICAL OR PROCESS ENGINEERING (*in* BIOLOGICAL AND PROCESS ENGINEERING AND MATERIALS SCIENCE) but with some rather different but just as difficult problems to solve. Success in the biotechnology business depends on perfecting the processes of separating (from nutrient broth and bacterial cells) and purification (cleaning up products after fermentation). Firms which can develop this process technology are at least as, likely to be profitable as the 'high profile' cloners.

Organisations which are estimated to be involved in biotechnology (approximately half are research organisations, the others being equipment and product manufacturers) range from major petrochemical, pharmaceutical and food conglomerates to the many 'new biotechnology' firms which specialise in cloning, etc., the largest of which employ several hundred people. Some 'companies' are based on universities, but funded mainly by industrial contracts. Some larger, e.g. chemical, firms have had people working in what is now called biotechnology for many years, and have sizeable research teams. Some firms are contract research companies only, some do their own research and then go on to manufacture, some firms buy research from a contract research company or fund university-based research. Some very small firms specialise in making the biochemical materials, e.g. peptides, which researchers need. Another 'spin-off' area is making the highly sophisticated, computer-based and automated equipment used throughout the biotechnology business from research to production.

Recruitment and entry

There are no accurate, up-to-date figures on how many people are working in biotechnology, especially as biotechnology work may also be done as part of R&D under other names, and products may be manufactured as part of 'normal' pharmaceutical output. In addition to those with specific qualifications in biotechnology, biochemists, microbiologists and biochemical engineers are examples of many other specialists working in this field.

In such a high-tech area, scientists and engineers are employed not only in basic R&D and other lab-based projects, but also to work on technical feasibility studies, market assessments, and business development. In other words to be both technically skilled and able to help 'commercialise' biotechnology.

While many managers are scientists/engineers too, the financial demands of the business, and problems of marketing, should give some employment for other high-calibre people.

Laboratory trainees or apprentices are likely to be recruited with good GCSE/SCEs including subjects such as maths, science and technology, and there may be an opportunity to study for further qualifications. Important subjects for would-be entrants are biology, chemistry, maths and/or physics at A-level.

Qualifications and training

Various degree and postgraduate qualifications are available in biotechnology and related disciplines. For example, there is an MSc in Plant Biotechnology at London, Wye College. A first degree in Biotechnology in Agriculture with European Studies is a slightly unusual variant at Nottingham University and the University of Abertay in Dundee offers three variations: Plant and Animal Cell Biotechnology, Microbial Biotechnology, and Environmental Biotechnology, as first degrees. Other possibilities include Medical Biotechnology (University of East London), Process Biotechnology, and Molecular Genetics, or Business and Biotechnology (Sheffield Hallam University) as well as Biotechnology alone. The number of degree courses has increased in recent years. In addition, all biochemistry degree courses will include modules on biotechnology and genetic engineering.

See also degree courses in other disciplines in appropriate science and manufacturing sections.

Further information

The Bioindustry Association, the Biochemical Society.

Ceramics, glass and other mineral products

Based on the ancient, traditionally clay-based industry, modern ceramics and related products form the second largest group of factory-produced engineering materials (*see also* MATERIALS SCIENCE AND TECHNOLOGY *in* BIOLOGICAL AND PROCESS ENGINEERING AND MATERIALS SCIENCE).

The new industrial classification divides these into three main groups: building materials and abrasives, ceramic and refractory goods, glass and glassware. Employment levels in the industry as in other industries fell considerably during the 1980s and early 1990s, partly because of recession and intense competition, and in some parts of the sector because of automation. Some sectors, e.g. building materials and flat glass, were relatively straightforward to automate, while others, particularly ceramics, have found it far more difficult. All, though, have adopted sophisticated electrical/electronic systems.

Most industries in the sector are traditionally craft-based, with operatives and craftworkers making up well over two-thirds of all employees. Where plant is fully mechanised or automated, the numbers employed have fallen sharply. Automation and other modern technologies generally mean that some other jobs become more technical, but the proportion of technicians employed is still relatively small. The proportion of scientists and technologists is also small.

Building materials and abrasives

Manufacture of most building materials is now highly mechanised, and in some sectors, fully automated. Economy of scale is a major feature, with a few, very large, firms in each sector. This is particularly true in the brick-making industry. Tied to peaks and troughs in the construction industry, firms have both rationalised hard and marketed bricks and traditional products aggressively to compete with materials like concrete and sheet glass.

Modern, continuous-process factories have replaced a high proportion of traditional brickyards. From preparation of raw clay through to firing, these are operated by centralised, push-button controls. Bricks, etc. move from process to process, and through processes, such as firing, on or by automated conveyors, on mechanised 'cars', or on fork-lift trucks, so eliminating most heavy manual work.

Cement and cement product manufacture, also a continuous and closely controlled, highly automated process, is dominated by a few firms. Also tied to the state of the construction industry, the sector faces a growing threat from cheap imports. Limestone, chalk and clay (or power station ash) are crushed, turned into slurry, screened and mixed, fired in kilns to form clinker, ground and mixed. The whole process is controlled from a single, central, control room, and different grades and mixes can be produced easily to meet customer specifications. Production and maintenance is increasingly teamwork, with less and less demarcation between jobs. As large companies, cement manufacturers need efficient managerial and administrative staff, if only in small numbers. The industry employs only limited numbers of technicians, scientists and technologists.

A wide range of products are made from pre-cast concrete, from floor, walling and roof units for industrialised building, through to street and garden 'furniture' (such as street light standards) to pipes and tiles. The firms involved are closely linked in to quarrying and concrete-making on one side, and the construction industry on the other, and some firms have interests in at least one of these. Some firms are subsidiaries of large contractors, and may erect and mix their own products, or assemble multistorey car parks, for example.

Production work is in several stages – moulding, mixing, metal reinforcing, mould assembly and filling, stripping and finishing, etc. – but only metal reinforcing is a specialised job. Pipes and tiles are mostly machine made, but some fittings may be handmade by craftworkers. Cast stone (generally a concrete filling faced with reconstructed stone or coloured concrete) is made in much the same way as cast concrete, although the stone-maker is probably more skilled than the concrete-mould-maker. The industry also employs draughtsmen/women to design moulds. Civil and structural engineers are employed in design and production.

The abrasives industry shapes natural abrasives into grindstones, grinds natural and synthetic abrasives, coats cloth and paper with abrasives, and makes abrasive bonded wheels. The industry is completely mechanised, so production employs mainly semi-skilled machine operators. Qualified engineers and technologists manage production, and work on design of, e.g. special machinery. Research and development employs technologists and, e.g. chemists to work on adhesives.

Employment in the industry

Plant in the sector can be operated with minimal numbers of operators and craftworkers, who mainly control, maintain and repair plant, and drive fork-lift trucks, etc. The opportunities for, e.g. skilled moulders to hand-make bricks, etc. are now very limited. Comparatively small numbers of technicians work in process control, and quality assessment, developing/improving products and manufacturing systems, with scientists, technologists and engineers, who also manage the plants. Managerial and administrative staff include sales and marketing people, reflecting the industry's need to promote products more efficiently.

Ceramic and refractory goods

The familiar 'domestic' porcelain and china – the tableware, vases and ornaments made in bone china and earthenware – make up some 60% of output. Two firms produce most of the tableware. Ceramic tiles, sinks, baths, and 'sanitary ware' are also made for the home.

But the industry also produces less obvious things. It makes electrical accessories such as fuses, switch bases and sockets; a wide range of giant insulators for use in power stations and on pylons, etc. in the electricity distribution network; and ceramic burners for the newest gas-fired industrial furnaces (cutting fuel costs by two-thirds). It produces pre-formed ceramic cores for aircraft components, porous ceramics for filtering and aerating, laser guides, artificial hip joints, tips for plough shares, sensors for boiler controls, and refractory moulds for precision casting work.

Ceramics are predicted to be one of the materials of the future – car firms are replacing some engine parts at present made of metal with ceramics, and a new ceramic alloy, sialon, is being used for cutting and welding. Lately ceramics have proved to be the best bet for superconducting materials which can work at normal temperatures, putting them in the lead to replace (amongst other things) silicon microchips in computers.

Although a difficult industry to mechanise, let alone automate, investment in new technology is being made. The potter's wheel is a fairly rare sight, but hand production is still common. Some products, e.g. glazed tiles, are now made on production lines which are now being automated, but generally it is still only possible to mechanise/automate some stages. Clay preparation has been automated for some time, and automated glazing machines are now being introduced. Products with fairly simple shapes – cups, saucers and plates – can be made on semi-automatic machines, although they still need skilled operators (and cup handles have to be put on separately), and some decorating can be partly automated too. Sophisticated electronic control systems, however, have been installed with the new gas- and electricity-fired kilns. Things with more complicated shapes, though, from basins and sanitaryware to china figures, still have to be cast in moulds by hand.

Employment in the industry

The industry is still labour-intensive, most people working in production, mainly as operatives. Most production staff generally work in one of the four main processes – making, firing, glazing and decorating – and warehousing and despatch. The skill content of the work varies with individual processes.

Larger companies usually have their own design departments, where trained designers create new 'shapes' – for cups, plates, bathroom ware, etc. – and/or new patterns for new or standard shapes. The modeller carves a solid clay or plaster model of any new shapes, and from this makes a set of master moulds, or cases. These are used by mould-makers to make working moulds (they can only be used some 70–80 times so new ones are always needed), and this is one of the few skilled crafts.

In production, the clay is prepared semi-automatically, under supervision of a trained slipmaker. The slipmaker assesses the quality of the clay and liquid slip, and has to see that the quantities of raw materials are exactly right, and that they are blended and filtered properly. Making the shapes involves either operating a machine and finishing the shape, or casting more complex pieces, removing them from the moulds and finishing by smoothing and e.g. punching bolt holes in sanitary ware. Things like ceramic bullet-proof vests are formed by 1,000-ton presses.

When the basic shapes have been dried and checked for defects, they are fired, glazed, fired again, decorated, and fired yet again. In firing, mechanised and automated trucks and trolleys move shapes automatically through continuous ovens. Even so, loading and unloading the kilns and operating the kiln controls is skilled work for kiln attendants, who must know what physical and chemical changes are involved in firing and what temperatures and times are needed. They work in shifts because kilns cannot be shut down overnight.

Glazing is done by either dipping or spraying. Some decorations are added before glazing, others after. While some decorations are put on by machines, some tableware is still hand-decorated (with gold bands, for example) and figures, etc., have to be hand-painted, which is skilled work.

The industry employs a significant number of technologists, scientists and technicians, in technical and ceramic development, laboratory work, and quality control. Much R&D goes into improved processes and lower firing temperatures.

The increasing amount of plant and machinery means opportunities for electrical and mechanical engineering craftworkers and technicians, both for maintenance and in designing new equipment. The industry expects to employ more electronic and systems engineers, able to cope with modern control systems.

Pottery firms traditionally employ only a relatively small number of administrative staff, but they face the same complex business problems as the rest of industry, and so now need people with greater expertise to cope with them. Marketing/sales and Purchasing raw materials (*see* BUYING, SELLING AND RELATED SERVICES) and ACCOUNTANCY (*see in* FINANCIAL CAREERS), etc. are all involved.

Most supervisory staff are promoted from within their own departments, and may go on to become managers, although some form of technical or professional qualification is normally needed.

Recruitment and entry

At professional/graduate level firms need engineers, ceramic technologists, scientists and applied designers but recruit in relatively small numbers, although the major firms try to maintain a regular intake for long-term management development. Recruitment is with appropriate degrees – or A-levels/H grades – for technological and administrative functions. Examples might be: Development Technologist in Fine China, Technical Services Engineer in Refractories, Product Co-ordinator in Giftware, or Trainee Works Manager in Brick Manufacture. It is still common to work up through the industry. Designers are normally recruited with a degree in Art and Design (*see in* ART, CRAFT AND DESIGN).

School-leavers with good grades at GCSE/SCE are recruited for training as, e.g. modellers, design assistants or decorators, lithographers, drawing office staff, technical assistants (sciences needed), electricians, mechanical fitters, mouldmakers and casters, (kiln) bricklayers, trainee quarry engineers and so on, depending on the industry sector involved.

Junior technologists, trainee technical managers and assistant managers may be recruited after A-levels/ Scottish Highers, or GNVQ.

Qualifications and training

Relevant degrees include Ceramic Science and Engineering (University of Sheffield), Ceramic Technology (Staffordshire University). There is a BTEC Higher National Diploma in Ceramic Technology at Staffordshire University.

See MATERIALS SCIENCE AND TECHNOLOGY (*in* BIOLOGICAL AND PROCESS ENGINEERING AND MATERIALS SCIENCE) for various degrees and other courses in materials engineering/science/technology. *See* ART, CRAFT AND DESIGN for various degrees and other courses in ceramic design and three-dimensional design.

The professional body is the Institute of Ceramics.

National Vocational Qualifications. Any trainee can expect to receive standards-based training leading to National Vocational Qualifications. Examples at NVQ level 2 might be 'Decorating by Hand' (taken by a trainee in a company making tableware, perhaps) or in 'Forming by Hand' or 'Forming by Machine' (taken by a trainee in a tile manufacturing company). Other NVQ units not specific to the industry could be added depending on the personal career path. For example, a trainee with craft skills who moved into an engineering and maintenance role might add to their ceramic NVQ, A level 2 in Engineering. Certificates obtained as a result are usually awarded by City & Guilds. Examples include Industrial Ceramics (068) and Ceramics Technicians (072).

The lead body for the industry is the Association for Ceramic Training and Development. There are three Industry Training Organisations each of which is responsible for training within its own sector. Work is currently being done on developing NVQs for supervisors and graduate entrants at management level. The Institute of Clay Technology offers sponsorship for students who want to take ceramics as a career.

Further information

The Association for Ceramic Training and Development.

Glass manufacture

Glass is both a very traditional and a modern material. It still has many traditional uses: in windows, as bottles, jars, vases and glasses to drink from. It is extensively used in industrial plant, as lenses; and for scientific and laboratory work glass has become a cabling material, as optical fibre, for faster and more efficient telecommunication and data transmission. Controlled-release glass – which dissolves in any fluid at a predetermined rate – will deliver, e.g., drugs and insecticides over a long period. Increasingly coated glasses are being used for a variety of applications, e.g. heat retention/reflection and protection of electronic data sources.

Recession, and tough competition from overseas, have brought some problems of declining demand to the industry. Additionally there has been competition from the plastics industry for the bottle/container market – making containers for food and drink accounts for about a third of all glass sales. Other sectors, such as the window-replacement market, have faced fewer problems.

To produce glass, raw materials, in the right quantities for the particular product, are mixed and then melted in very-high-temperature furnaces until they vitrify. Furnaces range from large, continuous, automated melting tanks to small clay pots. The viscous glass is formed by casting, pressing, blowing, drawing (into fibres, sheets or tubes), extruding, rolling or floating. After forming it is annealed in a special oven. All window and mirror glass is produced using a very sophisticated, modern process which involves 'floating' the viscous glass on a bed of liquid metal.

Most bottles are blown by complex automated or semi-automated machines, turning out over 450 a minute, and electric light bulb envelopes are also produced this way at over 2,000 a minute. Even stemmed drinking glasses can be made by a combination of machine blowing and pressing; and, e.g. oven-to-table ware, washing machine windows, and some scientific glasses are now also produced on automated machines. Machines also make ampoules for the pharmaceutical industry, safety glass, and vacuum ware. Glass fibre is spun or drawn.

Glass is still 'blown' and hand-pressed in the traditional way by craftworkers, but only to make fine and ornamental products, lead-crystal tableware, special pieces for scientific use, and things like aircraft runway lights. Increasingly, new methods of manufacture are being introduced in all sectors of the industry.

Employment in the industry

Numbers decreased significantly over the past ten years or so. A high but falling proportion of employees are operatives: traditionally they included batch mixers, furnace workers, machine operators and setters, optical grinders, some hand-forming operatives, and inspectors. In large-scale production, though, the divisions between the separate jobs are going, and workers who look after mixing raw materials, melting and forming the glass are all becoming 'glass-making operatives' or 'glass process workers'. Craftworkers include glassformers, engravers, decorators, maintenance and electrical craftworkers.

The industry employs a small but rising proportion of technicians, and just a few hundred scientists (including chemists) and technologists (glass and fuel) in research and development laboratories which have made major breakthroughs in new products and processes. Mechanical and electrical/electronic (including control/instrument) engineers are also employed, mainly in production and developing more sophisticated new machinery.

Firms making containers, such as bottles and jars, drinking glasses, or fine glassware, have their own design departments, staffed by industrial designers and artists. Even bulk-produced bottles have to be carefully designed, and redesigned if a customer wants to make changes. Distinctive appearance is not the only factor: the bottle or jar must hold a particular quantity of a product economically and in a way that doesn't damage it, it must be easy to fill with the product (normally automatically) and be tailored to the manufacturer's particular production line, packaging and transport facilities, and so on. It must be economic to make.

Recruitment and entry

For professional-level functions and management training the larger manufacturers recruit graduates over a wide range of disciplines, but especially in science and engineering (any disciplines for administrative functions).

School-leavers with good grades at GCSE/SCE are recruited for technician training and apprenticeships and commercial/administrative work. Competence-based training leads to NVQs.

Qualifications and training

One degree course is available: Glass Science and Engineering at the University of Sheffield.

See ART, CRAFT AND DESIGN for various degrees and other courses in Design and Three Dimensional Design in Glass. *See* MATERIALS SCIENCE AND TECHNOLOGY (*in* BIOLOGICAL AND PROCESS ENGINEERING AND MATERIALS SCIENCE) for various degrees and other courses in materials engineering/science/technology.

Training is largely industry-based, monitored via the voluntary training organisation Glass Training Limited. They have developed an 'Integrated Graduate Development Scheme' (leading to an MSc degree in Management and Glass Technology). A range of new or updated NVQ/SVQs at levels 1–3 are currently in preparation.

Craftworkers also train on the job, and may study by release for various City & Guilds qualifications: examples include Glass Manufacture and Processing (Scheme 065) and Glass Manufacture (Scheme 069).

Further information

The British Glass Manufacturers' Federation, or Glass Training Ltd, separate organisations based at the same address.

Chemical industries

According to the Chemical Industries Association (the main trade/employer organisation in the industry with a membership of 230 companies), the chemical industry is Britain's fourth biggest manufacturing industry after food, drink and tobacco. Its latest employment figures suggest that 240,000 people were employed in the chemical industry in 1996. The largest company in this group is Glaxo Wellcome. The pharmaceutical companies spent £2.45 billion on R&D in 1994, while chemical companies spent £365 million and food companies £651 million.

The UK chemical industry has over 1,000 companies. They range in size from the five major internationals – whose interests stretch across several chemical groups, from oil refineries and petrochemical plants, through to drug, paint and other consumer products – to quite small specialist companies. Few companies, except perhaps in pharmaceuticals or industrial gases, specialise narrowly, although competitive conditions have now forced companies to look carefully at their product base and concentrate on product areas in which they have market strength, economies of scale, or specific expertise.

Much of what is made goes to other firms to be turned into something else; for instance, the oil-based 'feedstock' chemicals such as ethylene, propylene and benzene, are made into solvents, plastics and synthetic resins, synthetic fibres and detergents. The industry produces chemicals such as oxygen and sulphuric acid and oxides which also go into fertilisers, and paint. Pharmaceuticals is part of the chemicals sector, making antibiotics, vaccines, anaesthetics, and many other medicines. The industry also makes cosmetics, perfumes, detergents and soap, dyes and pigments, polishes and glues, explosives and fireworks, weedkillers, pesticides, and disinfectants. Chemical and pharmaceutical companies increasingly use biotechnology techniques in production processes.

Chemicals were the success story of British industry from the end of the Second World War until the early 1970s. Competition on an international scale has always been intense and was met by investing heavily in progressively larger, more efficient, but hugely expensive plant which has to be run at full capacity on a 24 hour basis to be profitable. The rate of technological change, in plant, process and feedstock, has been huge, making much of the industry very capital-intensive. Research and development are crucial to success.

In the late 1970s, demand stubbornly refused to meet predictions, and by 1981 recession brought real crisis to chemicals. Growth stopped altogether. Home customer demand collapsed as the recession knocked out traditional markets like textiles and vehicles, and competitiveness was lost, particularly against US companies. Over-capacity has been acute in some products and some sectors, both in the UK and on a European and worldwide basis, with resultant closures.

The UK industry, however, has fought back – some companies with fairly spectacular success (but at a heavy price in jobs), despite predictions of contraction. As with steel, shipbuilding and vehicles, chemicals have had to cope with the 'migration' of 'commodity' chemical production from developed to developing countries. Newly industrialising countries – Brazil, South Korea, Saudi Arabia and Taiwan – are developing their own petrochemical industries and competing successfully. Canada has become a major producer/exporter, and Scandinavian companies are operating more in Europe.

Chemicals has long been an international industry. Most large companies plan their production and marketing strategies globally, and locate major plants where they can most easily satisfy demand within broad markets, such as

Western Europe, or the US. Major chemical producers cooperate by operating networks of plants, each making an assortment of products supplied on a supranational basis to, for example, the whole European market, so allowing maximum use of plant capacity. Firms have rationalised by swapping plants, so that fewer companies make each major petrochemical, and letting companies get out of product areas where they are weakest. Those staying in the particular market have had to grow even larger to stay competitive.

The European, including the UK, industry has had to change strategy. Marketing and finance managers analyse markets, costs, and profits in great detail, and they are now much more closely involved in decisions on what to produce, where and in what quantities. The industry cannot now depend on simply building new, ever-larger, more advanced plant to churn out commodity chemicals provided by R&D – no new massive petrochemical plants are planned for the foreseeable future except to replace old with more cost-effective capacity. Chemical companies have also turned to high-value-added, specialist products which can give a profit on much smaller quantities (which means developing automated batch-processing systems).

In the future, the chemical industry faces difficulties and rising costs to deal with environmental issues both in terms of pollution by chemical plants and with some of its products. There is increasing concern about non-biodegradable plastics, recycling plastic waste, the effect of chlorofluorocarbons (CFCs) on the ozone layer, the level of nitrate in drinking water and the use of pesticides and fertilisers.

Pharmaceuticals

Pharmaceuticals is one of the strongest sectors of UK industry, although growth is expected to be slower than in the past. The UK is the fourth-largest exporting country, and the base for about 12% of the huge sums spent worldwide on research and development (and predicted to stay that way). The 150-plus pharmaceutical firms account for about 17% of chemical industry sales, and 9% of exports. The small number of large companies (including several multinationals), though, produce most of the output.

The pharmaceutical industry expects to find answers to many of the world's most-difficult-to-cure diseases in the next ten years, and to improve the way many others are treated. But it has to spend more resources on research and in development (more on the latter than the former today) than most other industries (except aerospace and electronics). It is taking on more difficult problems, and researching deep into living cells to find causes for, and so cures to, disease. It involves a lot more basic research than other industries do these days (with molecular biology and biotechnology increasingly providing the breakthroughs).

Computers, plotting even the most complex molecular structures and displaying them three-dimensionally on screen, are helping researchers to 'target' new medicines. Even so, one new drug can involve synthesising and testing over 10,000 different substances. It takes more time, is more expensive and needs ever more sophisticated methods and equipment. Taking ten to twelve years to develop, the cost of a new drug is astronomical.

Only a small proportion of newly synthesised compounds ever come to the market – testing, trials and so on – see to that – but profitability has also to be predicted, and these days marketing takes a close look at potential products much earlier.

Employment in chemicals

Overall numbers have been falling steeply since 1979, and were down to approximately 290,000 by 1996. Some sectors however have increased their numbers. In 1996 the number of people directly employed in the pharmaceutical sector of the chemical industry was 90,000, having steadily risen from the 1988 total of 80,000. However, the number is likely to reduce as a result of an increased number of mergers in a drive for ever greater efficiency.

With research and development (R&D) so crucial to many sectors of the industry, a relatively high proportion of employees work in R&D – the figure is as high as 20% (17,800 people) in sectors like pharmaceuticals, and at similar levels in e.g. agrochemicals and specialised organics. R&D expenditure has nearly doubled in the past ten years.

Research and development is a multidisciplinary activity in which chemists seldom work in isolation from other scientists: biochemists, pharmacologists, pharmacists, microbiologists, computer scientists, agricultural scientists, physicists and mathematicians are examples of the various disciplines which may be involved in any major project. Much of the research is carried out on an international scale, involving academic institutions and governments as well as production companies. Complex development projects may last many years.

Development in technical departments takes the research scientists' new compound and works out how to turn it into a product which can be produced economically, how it should be done, from what raw materials, etc. In other laboratories, scientists and technicians test new processes and try to iron out problems in existing ones on small-scale versions of the full chemical plant. (Actual design and construction of chemical plant is done by Chemical engineers working for specialist construction companies). (*See in* BIOLOGICAL AND PROCESS ENGINEERING AND MATERIALS SCIENCE).

Professional/graduate engineers and scientists manage production units, run quality control laboratories, etc. In large, continuous-process plants, producing basic commodity chemicals, plastics, or fertilisers in very large quantities, the plant is largely automated, running 24 hours a day, seven days a week.

Plants are staffed by small shift teams (3–4 people), each looking after one sizeable section, under a senior controller, and shift supervisor. Plant operators, under a plant controller who monitors the control room instrument panel for the section, check what is happening in the plant itself, take readings, make adjustments, take samples for testing, clean out pipes, shut down faulty equipment, etc., but are largely there to cope on the rare occasions when a serious breakdown occurs.

In firms which make medicines, inks, paints or cosmetics, a continuous production line takes raw material through a series of automated processes, but some production, e.g. pharmaceuticals, still has to use single machines: 'cookers', tablet-makers and blenders, making items in stages; and electro-mechanical methods, operated by semi-skilled workers. Bottles are filled with tablets, tubs with face creams, cans with paint, and the bottles, etc., put into packages on production lines, again increasingly automated, but still employing operators in some places, if only to monitor output.

Mechanical, electrical and instrument craftworkers maintain and service plants. The routine work of testing whatever is being produced in the plant is done by scientific/laboratory technicians, under a professional/graduate scientist.

In management/administration, the industry is a large employer of computing staff, and people trained in MANAGEMENT SERVICES. In some sectors, e.g. pharmaceuticals, selling employs people with qualifications in appropriate subjects, e.g. life sciences, even medical sciences. Firms also employ scientists, e.g. pharmacists in the pharmaceutical industry, in advising on and dealing with statutory product regulations.

Recruitment and entry

The industry recruits at all age levels. The main recruitment points into the chemical industry are for graduates and postgraduates. Relatively few are taken on with A-levels/HND/HNC. Generally low levels of recruitment have probably pushed up the quoted minimum entry requirements

The industry is a graduate recruiter in all disciplines, with some emphasis on scientists and engineers (mainly chemical, but also mechanical, electrical/control), computer scientists and mathematicians, but numbers recruited are not extensive. Even the largest UK-based multinational recruits around 200 graduates in total each year (and has 5,000-plus applications). The number of sponsorships to read for appropriate degrees (mainly in engineering), is comparatively small, although this could change.

Laboratory Trainees/Apprentices are recruited with good GCSE/SCEs including subjects such as mathematics, science and technology. Clerical trainees are recruited with good GCSE/SCEs including subjects such as English, mathematics and business studies. There are some additional opportunities for school-leavers with A-levels/H grades, or appropriate BTEC/SCOTVEC qualifications, to join laboratory, financial and sales training schemes. Those wishing to work on the biological side of the pharmaceutical industry should study science at GCSE Level and biology and chemistry at A-level or equivalent.

Qualifications and training

Training is carried out by individual firms.

Professional engineers and scientists normally read for degrees in appropriate subjects prior to entry, but they and other graduate entrants are generally given appropriate training for any relevant professional qualification, e.g. in accountancy. Biological science graduates (biology, biochemistry, pharmacology, pharmacy, microbiology) are recruited by the pharmaceutical industry at first-degree and PhD levels.

The Chemical Industry Association along with the Pharmaceutical Industry offer three NVQ areas. The CIA/ABPI NVQ/SVQ schemes are based on Process Operations (Chemical and Pharmaceutical) levels 1–3. Technical and Support level 3, Laboratory Operation levels 1–4. The training is organised mainly on the job, and people are assessed in the workplace on real jobs and everyday tasks. The competence schemes may be combined with release to study at local colleges. These training arrangements lead to NVQs for craft engineers, process operators and laboratory technicians. Modern apprenticeships are available.

Further information

The Chemical Industry Association (Training Information Officer), and the Association of the British Pharmaceutical Industry (Health Industry Information Officer).

Food and drink manufacturing

Food and drink is one of the largest manufacturing industries. In 1994 it produced (along with tobacco) approximately 14% of total UK manufacturing output. It makes a wide range of products: bread and biscuits, chocolates and other sweets, sausages and pies, milk and milk products, canned, frozen and dried fruit and vegetables, soups, sugars and jams, orange squash and beer, savoury snacks and potato crisps, etc.

The industry is highly rationalised and streamlined. Production is mostly concentrated in a few large 'conglomerate' companies, many of whom diversified out of fairly narrow, craft-based specialities – bread, flour, fish, chocolates. Beer, biscuits and snack foods, soft drinks and frozen food are examples of the products produced mainly by a few very large companies. However, the industry has several thousand small firms, and numerous small independent breweries.

For years the industry has been squeezed between rising produce prices and operating costs and increasingly aggressive supermarkets, locked in a discount war with each other. Food manufacturers are having to fight harder for sales. In a static market, manufacturers' success depends more and more on clever marketing, on being able to spot a trend in food sales, and react to it faster than competitors, as well as constantly improving productivity and efficiency.

The food industry responds sharply to consumer demand, and particularly to the demand for 'healthy' high-fibre, low-salt, sugar- and fat-free products, as well as better-quality and more varied 'convenience' food products. But the population is no longer rising; the market is static, and UK consumers are generally getting as much to eat as they need, so significant overall growth in demand is unlikely.

Diversification, for food and drink firms, also means 'vertical integration', to increase efficiency as well as profits. Larger brewers are just as much pub operators and even hoteliers and caterers, as beer makers.

Exports of manufactured foods and soft drinks account for only about 8% of total output, but the industry provides about 20% of the food and drink processing output of the EU. Within the UK, food and drink is the largest item in the household budget. Total consumer expenditure in this area is nearly a quarter of total consumer spending.

Scientific and technological developments have been extensively exploited – from large-scale processing and preservation techniques to the use of modern packaging materials.

Mass food production demands both very high standards and maximum efficiency. Quality has to be checked continuously from the arrival of new raw materials through to finished products, via batteries of scientific tests and sample tasting, which have to interrupt production as little as possible.

The industry uses all the latest production methods, including automated production lines, for economies of scale. New technology can mean batch-production lines even more efficient than existing continuous lines, and 'intelligent' robots which can be reprogrammed rapidly to allow frequent line changeovers, for several products to come from the same production line.

The largest firms are also investing in BIOTECHNOLOGY, (*see in* MANUFACTURING INDUSTRIES) e.g. producing mycoprotein from plant starch as a fibrous edible fungus which can be used to make palatable imitations of poultry meat.

Brewing is a major section of the industry, and an example of considerable capital expenditure and high technology. Technical brewers control the biochemical processes, and may specialise in a particular aspect of the process. Brewing engineers control production and maintenance, as well as some of the more specialist functions such as process control, project engineering, packaging development or energy management. More beer is consumed in the EU than anywhere else except for Australia and New Zealand. However, increased automation has resulted in a fall in numbers employed; opportunities are limited for technical brewers but do exist for brewing scientists in research and development, quality control, brewing engineering, sales, marketing, personnel and distribution.

Employment in the industry

The industry employs about 10% of the total workforce in manufacturing industry. Already highly automated (it is one of the largest microelectronics users in production), manufacturing and processing food and drink products employs fewer and fewer people. A rising proportion of work in production (including packaging) is in process control, and in quality control and inspection – in an industry where not only consistently high quality and 'freshness' but also absolute hygiene and cleanliness are essential.

Process workers

Process workers control the production lines and process plant, mainly watching for problems, checking that instruments are reading correctly ,and adjusting controls where necessary. Fewer and fewer people mix, flavour, shape, cook, decorate, package or bottle any food by hand.

Technicians

Technicians and other control staff carry out the frequent quality tests and checks – of moisture and salt content in butter for instance; to make sure raw materials meet requirements, and to see items are bacteria-free, for example – and provide the controls and figures needed by both operatives and management.

Engineers

Production employs engineers. Designing, developing and implementing new high-technology processing plant has extended the range of disciplines needed, and further increased the numbers of chemical/process engineers, systems designers, electronic engineers with systems design/instrumentation, in addition to the mechanical and electrical engineers traditionally employed. Maintenance teams look after the machinery and equipment.

Specialists

Some industries traditionally have their own specialists – for example, beer-making is controlled by qualified technical brewers who ensure consistency and quality of the product; however, the raw materials, such as hops and barley, may vary from batch to batch, and 'troubleshoot' when process operators have problems they cannot solve.

Not every brewery is fully automated, or is likely to be; and many smaller firms cater for people who want their food and drink produced in more traditional ways. A growing number of independent and small brewers make 'real ale'. While traditional 'corner shop' bakeries still fight for survival, in-store bakeries and fresh-baked-bread stores are doing well. Some dairy firms still make butter, cheese and yoghurt in traditional ways. Opportunities still exist, therefore, to become craft-based bakers, brewers, butter- and cheesemakers, etc.

Food scientists, food technologists, nutrition experts and dietitians

What goes into the food and drink, and how products are mixed and made, are largely controlled by food scientists and technologists. Mass food production demands both very high standards and maximum efficiency. Most of those people who have qualifications in food science/technology are employed in the food industry, retailing or environmental health/food premises inspection. The industry also employs nutrition experts, and some dietitians who work mostly for firms making specialist dietetic products (although the majority of dietitians work in the Health Service).

Production is supported by work in experimental kitchens and control laboratories. Here new products, from health foods and exotic-looking ice-cream desserts to chocolate bars and soups, are developed. Food scientists and technologists, dietitians, home economists (*see in* HOTELS AND CATERING), chemists, microbiologists (*see in* BIOLOGICAL SCIENCES) and laboratory technicians (*see in* SCIENCE CAREERS AND THE PHYSICAL SCIENCES), find ways of improving existing products, processes and packaging, and exploiting new ideas. Market research provides valuable information about customer preferences.

A few larger firms have more advanced experimental units, working on the possibilities of exploiting BIOTECHNOLOGY (*see in* MANUFACTURING INDUSTRIES) in making new products (particularly pre-prepared meals), replacement/cheaper food products, or in improving the flavour. Brewers are already genetically 'engineering' their yeasts by constructing industrial strains that improve fermenting efficiency and give better control over flavour. There is little fundamental research except in the largest companies, but some 'troubleshooting' and problem-solving. Purchasing the various raw materials and packaging materials has to be of such high standard in the right quantities at the best possible price that it is often supervised by food scientists or technologists.

Universities, plus a number of other colleges, do research in food science/technology, on topics ranging from the physiology of yeasts, and applications of protein engineering, through the effects of farming and processing methods on trout, to prison and army feeding, and the use of food waste.

Other essential elements of the food and drink manufacturing industry include marketing through merchandising, distribution and scheduling – often using computer-based systems for route planning, etc., and sales reporting – and transport.

Recruitment and entry

Long-term, career opportunities in the industry are largely restricted to reasonably well-qualified school-leavers, graduates and technologists, and people already professionally qualified. There are also opportunities for school-leavers with fewer qualifications.

Professional level

In technical areas (for research, product and process development, production control, plant engineering, ingredients technology), and in other management areas (for production supervision/management, purchasing, marketing, market research and management services) the industry recruits in quite small numbers, but across a broad spectrum of disciplines, including food science and technology; engineering, agricultural science (*see in* LAND USE INDUSTRIES) and veterinary science (*see in* WORK WITH ANIMALS). Graduates with degrees in any subjects are recruited for various administrative functions.

Technician Level

Technicians are recruited for training usually with at least a reasonable number of good GCSE/SCE grades, including some sciences, and there are opportunities for entrants with A-levels/H grades or appropriate BTEC/SCOTVEC qualifications.

Craft level

Trainees are recruited mainly for training in engineering skills. Competence-based training leading to NVQ is organised by a number of companies.

Qualifications and training

Training is divided between sectors, each having its own voluntary organisation, and is provided mainly by the larger groups and firms.

Professional bodies

The Institute of Food Science and Technology (1996 membership about 3,500) requires a relevant degree or equivalent for professional members (1,800 in 1996). Candidates following the BTEC Higher route must also obtain IFST's graduate diploma. All entrants to professional membership must also have at least three to six years' relevant experience (depending on initial qualification). Approximately 200 a year join IFST.

The British Dietetic Association. BDA is not a qualifying body, but members must have a recognised dietetic qualification, which has to be a degree in dietetics or nutrition.

Graduates and others recruited into technical brewing prepare for the Associate and Diploma membership qualifications of the Institute of Brewing through part-time study.

Degree level

There are a range of food-oriented degree courses ranging from food manufacture and food marketing to food science and food technology. A few sectors have specialist degrees, e.g. Brewing and Distilling at Heriot Watt University. Nutrition can be studied with an emphasis on biochemistry, physiology, biology or catering, and there are a number of dietetics courses. Other appropriate degree courses include biochemistry, biotechnology, microbiology, engineering (various fields) and business/management.

Entry to many of these courses is with chemistry plus other sciences at A-level/H grade.

Postgraduate level

In food sciences/technology, there are 'conversion' courses for graduates in related subjects, and more advanced specialist courses at a number of universities and colleges. A postgraduate qualification in food control, awarded by the Institute of Food Science and Technology, is useful for senior posts in industry. In dietetics, graduates who have studied a related subject (including enough human biochemistry and physiology) can qualify via a two-year diploma course at Glasgow: Queen's College, or Leeds.

BTEC/SCOTVEC Higher National Certificate/Diploma level

Numerous full-time Higher Diploma and part-time Higher Certificate courses are available in Food Science, Food Development and Production, and Technology of Food. They are all science-based. It is possible to take options in, e.g. dairy, bakery, and other specialist technologies, as well as quality control. A relevant HND qualifies for Licentiate membership of the Institute of Food Science and Technology (*see above*).

Technicians

Technicians can obtain NVQs at L 1-4 covering Drink Manufacturing, Drink Laboratory Competence, and Baking Technology, or study for various national certificates or diplomas in food technology. Food technology courses train in basic sciences, food processing and preservation, and include elements of business studies. There are also GNVQs in Manufacturing (Food) and Science (Food Science) at Intermediate and Advanced Level.

Craft level

Craftworkers train on the job and by day-release for various City & Guilds awards and NVQs.

Further information

Institute of Brewing, British Dietetic Association, and the Institute of Food Science and Technology.

Packaging

UK manufacturers' sales of packaging materials amount to approximately £9 billion each year. The packaging industry is wide-ranging, producing pouches, bags, sacks, cans, bottles, cartons, jars, tubes, drums and aerosols from paper, board, plastics, aluminium, tinplate, glass and polymer film. It comprises three different groupings:

- raw materials manufacturers, who produce the primary materials used in packaging;
- convertors, who convert the materials into packaging forms such as pouches, bags, sacks, etc.;
- packer/fillers, who bring together the pack and the product.

Nearly three-quarters of all packaging is used by the food and drinks industry, so although, like every other business, packaging is affected by growth and recession, it never reaches the depths of recession experienced by others such as producers of consumer durables or luxury goods. It is also an indicator of economic performance, in that forward orders for cases (brown boxes used for transit packaging) usually reflect an upturn or downturn in the economy two or three months before it actually occurs.

The prime purpose of packaging is to contain and protect. It protects against the atmosphere, which can damage food; it protects against the knocks and shocks of transport systems; it keeps things clean and sterile – for example pharmaceuticals; it deters tamperers; and it allows difficult-to-handle products such as liquids to be moved from point of manufacture to point of use. It also has to provide information on use and potential hazards of the product contained, information on weight or volume and contents, and by what date it is best to use the product.

In the retail environment, where brands compete against each other on the supermarket shelves, the pack is often the 'silent salesman'. Packer/ fillers are constantly on the lookout for new ideas and new designs, whether three-dimensional or graphic. And now, more than ever before, users are anxious to encourage packages that conserve resources and meet environmental demands.

Many packages have to be packed automatically, so there is an enormous engineering effort put in by machinery manufacturers into filling-, weighing- and checking-equipment; and into wrapping-, cartoning- and case-packing-machinery. Computer systems play a vital role in production control, flexibility of product change, and speed of operation. Printing equipment is continuously being updated to convert plastics, paper, board and foils into attractive flexible packaging, cartons and labels.

Employment in the industry

A wide range of companies make packaging materials and equipment – from multinationals to small or medium-sized firms. Packaging technologists and buyers are also employed by packaging users such as food, chemicals, cosmetics and pharmaceutical producers. Employees include research and development technologists, designers, production technicians, quality controllers, buyers, and marketing, technical sales and service personnel.

Recruitment and entry

Companies recruit at all levels of skill in a wide range of disciplines.

Graduates are recruited with degrees in engineering, packaging technology, chemistry, materials sciences, food technology, testing and control engineering and graphic and three-dimensional design for specialist functions. Graduates of any discipline may go into business and marketing.

School-leavers are recruited mainly for technical and sales training; entry is usually with at least four good GCSE/SCEs.

Qualifications and training

Degree courses exist in packaging technology and design, sometimes in conjunction with the more general study of graphic media. For example, Surrey Institute of Art and Design offers a BA in Packaging Design. Sheffield Hallam

University has the first-degree course most closely related to packaging, according to the Institute of Packaging.

There is an MSc in Packaging Technology jointly run at Brunel University West London and Loughborough University.

There are also a few relevant BTEC Higher National Diploma-level courses. These may be described as HND in Design (Packaging) or HND in Printing, Publishing and Packaging or some similar title. *See also* PRINTING (*in* MANUFACTURING INDUSTRIES) *and* ART, CRAFT AND DESIGN for other appropriate courses.

Part-time courses are available for people already working in the industry, leading to the membership diploma qualifying examination and the Institute of Packaging Diploma. The Institute also provides an Open Learning Course in Packaging Technology, which has the same outcomes. It also runs a ten-day Packaging Principles and Practice course, which earns a credit exemption from paper 1 of the exam, as well as a twice-yearly three-day school to enable people to fill gaps in their knowledge and prepare for the exams.

Further information

The Institute of Packaging.

Paper-making

Paper has been made here for over 500 years, and has been essential to the spread of knowledge and development of civilisation, but new uses are still being found for it each day. It is used for writing, and for many kinds of printing, such as of reports, books and pictures, newspapers and magazines, pamphlets and posters. It is used for packaging, from paper bags and wrapping materials to cartons and corrugated cases. Business uses it for typewriting and photocopying, for pressure-sensitive uses such as carbonless copying paper and for thermal uses such as fax-machine rolls. It is also used for health and hygiene applications, for wall boarding, for wall coverings, for internal fittings for vehicles, industrial filters – and of course for bank notes. All these are produced by a wide range of industries categorised as paper and board converters or as printers.

There are several sectors of the industry, given the differences in making and marketing different grades of paper and board. For example, board is made differently from, and sold to a different market from, tissue paper. It is probably helpful to think of six main areas: newsprint, soft tissues, paper for printing and writing, packaging paper, corrugated case materials, and board.

There are 99 paper mills in the UK, employing around 24,000 people. They produced 5.8 million tonnes in 1994, 4.6 million of which were used in Britain. Production is concentrated in certain areas of the country where it developed first, historically (partly due to the need for good water supplies) – Lancashire. the West Country, central Scotland and the north of Kent – but has spread more widely in recent times.

A new paper and board mill may cost as much as £250 million, using machines backed by advanced control system technology and computers. Such plant is designed to optimise the use of raw materials and minimise the consumption of energy through advanced combined heat and power systems. For example, UK Paper plc at the beginning of 1996 was recycling 150,000 tonnes of waste paper and making widespread use of combined heat and power (CHP) systems. Energy accounts for between 5% and 40% of costs, according to what grade of paper is being produced.

Waste paper provides the greatest source of raw materials (57%) with imported woodpulp (31%), the balance being made up by home-produced pulp from UK trees (12%). All the woodpulp comes from natural, renewable sources. These are mostly from managed forests whose economics are greatly dependent on paper-making, and where pulp is derived from sawmill waste and thinnings with few other economic uses. Imported woodpulp, however, is costly and variable in price, depending on the exchange rate between sterling and the currency of the exporting country. Hence the concern in the industry to maximise the use of home-grown timber and home-produced waste paper. In 1994 newsprint manufactured in the UK had a 74% recycled content – a record figure.

Paper-making is an internationally competitive business. More than half the capacity of British paper mills is owned by companies based overseas, while British-based companies in turn have overseas subsidiaries. In 1994, according to the Paper Federation, approximately 60% of the 11.6 million tonnes of paper and board consumed in Britain were imported, while 1.3 of the 5.8 million tonnes produced here were exported.

Employment in the industry

About 20,000 people are employed by paper-makers in membership of the Federation, according to information from the Paper Federation, of whom 14,063 were manual employees and 6,406 staff employees in 1996. The numbers employed had fallen by 37% since 1985. Demand for paper and board is closely related to economic growth since the products are used in all areas of economic life.

The work involves running the mainly large-scale machines or the sophisticated equipment to control the movement of materials and products within the mill. There has always been a lot of shift-working. The industry is capital-intensive and the plant must be utilised 24 hours a day for technological and financial reasons.

The workforce in the mills falls into three groups:

- Process employees involved in direct manufacturing, from the point at which new materials reach the plant to the point at which finished paper and board are sent off.
- Maintenance employees, who repair and maintain the machinery, equipment, power supply and buildings.

These are usually engineering craftspeople supported by semi-skilled grades.

- Staff involved in management, research, development, administration, sales and clerical work. Technical and scientific staff ensure the maintenance of quality and environmental standards, together with development of improved techniques and methods. Whilst many of the essential administrative and managerial skills may be applicable in any industry, there is a tendency for promotion in the paper industry to be mainly from within.

Recruitment and entry

Only a few dozen new people will be recruited each year. While many of the larger firms recruit small numbers of graduates for commercial functions, the main needs of the industry are for scientists and technologists – engineers from various disciplines, chemists, physicists, materials scientists. Many of these will have had some particular relevant training.

Research and development leading to scientific and technological advances are important in an industry particularly concerned with energy conservation and environmental issues. But a total of only 740 scientific and technical staff were employed in federated mills in 1995, according to the Paper Federation, along with 674 professional and administrative staff, and 1,000 senior and functional managers.

School-leavers may not require formal qualifications to train in process work, although there will be opportunities for those with good grades at GCSE/SCE to join production and engineering training schemes.

Qualifications and training

UMIST (Manchester) runs several degree courses in Paper Science including combined degrees with Management, French or German. There is also a postgraduate research school. By the year 2000 it is planned to develop a Centre of Excellence to support the paper industry at UMIST, with links to Robert Gordon University (Aberdeen) (which runs an HND in Applied Science with Paper Technology), Bury College and the University of Wales at Bangor.

The professional body is the Paper Federation. There is a 'Craftsman Education and Training Scheme' which awards Technical Diplomas designed to multi-skill the maintenance engineering employees. There are also NVQ/SVQs at levels 2 and 3. Awards are made by the Paper Education and Training Council (the industry training organisation) jointly with City & Guilds in the case of NVQs, or with SCOTVEC for SVQs. A modern apprenticeship scheme was launched in 1995.

Further information

The Paper Federation (formerly the British Paper and Board Industry Federation).

Plastics processing

The industry takes its raw materials (a huge range of different raw plastics and plastic-based 'composites') from the CHEMICAL INDUSTRIES (*see above*) and turns them into an ever-widening range of industrial equipment, components for other manufacturing industries, and everyday consumer products such as kitchen utensils, cling-film and floor coverings. The industry's customers cover the whole spectrum of manufacturing and service industries, with main sales to firms in motor vehicles, domestic electrical appliances, telecommunications, buildings and toys – in fact nearly everyone in the modern world is a customer of the industry.

The industry uses a wide range of production processes, mostly based on heating the raw granules or powder that have come from the makers. Moulding is the most usual, and injection-moulding (forcing the hot material through a small hole into a shaped mould) is the most common; typical products range from computer housings to buckets and buttons. In blow-moulding a split mould is clamped round a pipe of plastic, and compressed air is forced in, expanding the plastic to fit the mould; typical products include bottles and fuel tanks. In the extrusion process hot plastic is forced through a nozzle or 'die'; typical products include pipes and window frame sections. Sheet materials such as bags and 'cling-film' are created by the blown-film process, packaging cartons are made by vacuum formings, and products such as road cones and bollards are made by rotational moulding. All processes are mechanised, and increasingly automated.

Future developments will include the increasing production of biological polymers, especially man-made proteins that may soon compete with plastics and rubbers in specialist applications.

Employment in the industry

Total numbers employed have fallen. Many firms are small, with under 50 employees each.

- *Process operatives* operate machinery and maintain the quality of production. Some products have to be further shaped or specially finished. A process operator may control one machine, or several automated machines, although some need more than one operator. Machines take time to heat up and may therefore be operated around the clock, which means shiftwork. Promotion opportunities exist to instruction, inspection, supervision and managerial work.
- *Craft engineers* use practical skills to install and maintain machinery, or perhaps work in the toolroom on mould design, proving, making and repair.

- *Engineering technicians* work in a variety of roles typically in maintenance, design, production planning, safety, materials selection and 'troubleshooting'.
- *Plastics technicians* may work in processing, quality assurance, technical sales, materials testing, and design and development.
- *Scientists and technologists* work in research and development, particularly on uses for advanced plastics, engineering design, quality control, etc. Many go on to management.

Recruitment and entry

At professional/graduate level the industry recruits a small number of polymer and materials scientists/technologists, chemists, physicists, and engineers. The Institute of Materials offers a scholarship of £1,000 to a first-year student at each of the accredited materials departments. Graduates from materials technology degree courses are in demand, and even during the recession of the early 1990s there was a low level of graduate unemployment

At school-leaver level there are opportunities for those with at least four GCSE/SCEs, including mathematics, English language and a science, for technician-level training. Craft engineers usually require at least three good GCSE/SCEs.

Qualifications and training

Various degree courses are available in Polymer Chemistry, Polymer Engineering, Polymer Science and Polymer Technology. *See* MATERIALS SCIENCE AND TECHNOLOGY (*in* BIOLOGICAL AND PROCESS ENGINEERING AND MATERIALS SCIENCE) for closely-related degree courses in Materials Science/Technology.

Various part-time certificate and full-time diploma courses are available at HND level in Science (Polymer Technology).

National Vocational Qualifications at levels 1, 2, 3 and 4 are available, and there are also relevant GNVQs (two years full-time) in science and engineering. Level-2 competencies include for example, injection-, compression- and blow-moulding, thermoforming, and the conversion of plastic film. Level 3 involves for example, competence in polymer-processing technology and the development of polymer products as well as supervisory management and engineering maintenance.

Training is largely-industry based, under the British Polymer Training Association. Training is provided to NVQ standards in engineering skills and in polymer technology. The BPTA are responding to declining numbers of school-leavers by providing 'multi-skill' training programmes for existing staff.

Further information

The British Polymer Training Association, the Plastics and Rubber Institute, Institute of Materials.

Printing

Printing 'produces' books; local and national newspapers, periodicals and magazines of all kinds; greetings cards; brochures and pamphlets; posters; banknotes; stamps; cheque books; office and computer stationery; packaging; wallpaper; airline tickets; forms; credit cards; etc. Only in the newspaper industry, and less often there now, are the printers part of the same organisation as the people who provide the raw materials – the manuscript, or 'copy', for books, periodicals, etc., the artwork for posters.

The printing industry has passed through a major technological revolution, based on new film and photographic techniques, on electronics and the computer and microprocessor. Setting type in 'hot metal' letters and printing on a letterpress machine from the raised surface of the type – processes which have not basically changed (despite mechanisation) since Caxton – are now rapidly on their way to becoming a thing of the past, except in some specialised work.

Most type is now 'set' on film, and printed by very fast offset litho machines. Keyboard operators work at typesetting computer terminals to 'input' the copy, together with coded instructions on choice of type and page layout. The 'compositor' can read and check the copy on the screen, move it around, correct and edit it. Pages and illustrations are then assembled on film, and the film image transferred to final printing plates. After printing, copy can be stored on disks so that any publication can be revised on a VDU screen in a fraction of the time needed for conventional 'resetting'. Increasingly, the originators of the text – the author, the journalist, the advertising staff – 'input' their own copy, either direct into the computer, or onto disk from where it can be 'converted' automatically to drive the computer-based setting machine.

New technology means the industry operates in an increasingly international market: film and computer data can be shipped from country to country, and computer-to-computer links make it possible to set and print where it is most economic for the customer. Photocopying, 'instant-print' shops, and 'desktop' computer-based systems which make it easy for firms to do their own printing are creating more competition. Longer-term, though, the industry expects demand for printed matter to increase rather than decline as a result of new technology, as it did when, for example, television reached virtually every home.

Some printing companies operate as 'general printers' by offering a wide range of services (from mail order coupons to catalogues), but many specialise: either in producing particular products, (cartons, stationery, labels, printing on metal (e.g. beer cans and metal badges), books, high-quality colour printing for brochures or cards or fine art reproduction, newspapers, and 'security printing' (banknotes and bond issues); or in providing one particular service to other companies, such as 'origination' (the stages from typesetting to plate-making) or print-finishing and bookbinding.

Employment in the industry

The printing industry is the UK's sixth largest industry, with people employed in 10,000 companies excluding newspaper printing. About £85 is spent annually per head of population in the UK on books, magazines and newspapers, and the value of sales is put at £9 billion per year by the British Printing Industries Federation (BPIF).

Employment, however, has been falling for some years. In 1990 the BPIF estimated that numbers (excluding those employed in the newspaper industry) were down to 168,000 from 315,000 in 1975. Further reductions have continued throughout the 1990s.

The impact of new technology brought about drastic changes in the industry in the last decade. The effect was most dramatic on national newspapers, where most journalists now directly input their own copy, as they already did on local papers.

Occupations may be generally divided into pre-press department (e.g. keying or scanning copy into the computer and manipulating it, using desktop publishing software usually to produce the required image, as well as planning layout and plate-making where necessary); printing (the actual setting up of the presses and printing of the text, pictures, etc., as well as maintenance of the equipment and checking quality of the product); converting/finishing (working mainly on machinery to turn printed pages into books, cartons, magazines, etc., cutting and trimming, folding, stitching, sticking and so on); and production control (organising the work of others, setting priorities and liaising with other departments). More commercially orientated activities are estimating (taking details of customers' requirements and working out the costs and price of the job) and account and sales executives.

Firms may also employ their own GRAPHIC DESIGN TEAM (*see in* ART, CRAFT AND DESIGN) and typographers, technical authors and copywriters, buyers, and advertising and sales staff.

Recruitment and entry

Recruitment is still at very low level, although machine printing has proved to be a skill-shortage area. BPIF is trying to encourage firms to recruit more graduates and A-level leavers.

Graduates are recruited only in small numbers, some with specialist printing qualifications (*see below*), but people with degrees in virtually any subject may be recruited for a wide range of functions, including production, marketing, finance, personnel.

School/college-leavers with A-levels/H grades or appropriate GNVQ qualifications may be recruited as management trainees, starting in functions such as estimating or sales. The recommended minimum requirements for entry to the various skilled printing jobs are usually good GCSE/SCEs in English, mathematics and science/technology; and many companies look for people who have got some basic skills in printing from attending a full-time college course leading to Foundation or Intermediate GNVQ. Good colour vision is essential for most jobs. There are also opportunities for administrative training in areas such as estimation, production planning, processing or quality control.

Qualifications and training

The rate of technological and other change in the industry means that all entrants need better and more sophisticated preparation and training. Training in the industry is strongly supported and encouraged by the British Printing Industries Federation, which is the industry training organisation (ITO), and the unions. Independent reports have described the industry's modernised craft-training schemes as a model for other industries. The flexibility of the new skills-training agreements is allowing firms to provide retraining for the existing workforce, and newly recruited adults, on an 'unprecedented scale'. A number of introductory courses are run at colleges throughout the country.

Relevant degrees included (in 1996): Printing and Packaging Technology: West Herts College, Watford; Printing Management: London College of Printing and Distributive Trades; Printing Technology (combined studies option): Manchester Metropolitan University.

BTEC/SCOTVEC Higher National Certificate/Diploma level included (in 1996): Printing Administration and Production: Napier University; Printing: Universities of Manchester, Nottingham; Printing, Publishing and Packaging: West Herts College; Printing Management and Production: Glasgow College of Building and Printing; Printing (Planning and Production): London College of Printing and Distributive Trades.

See ART, CRAFT AND DESIGN for various degrees and other courses in graphic design, including typography.

National Vocational Qualifications

The industry has a fully worked out NVQ framework, covering level 2–5 (levels 4 and 5 being supervisory and management) and divided into commercial, production, and management areas. There are NVQs for every key printing occupation. Print production is available in five specialisms: pre-press, press, print-finishing, mechanised bookbinding, and carton manufacture. For example, at level 2 in print-finishing, competence is required in five units – three core units covering, as usual, health and safety, effective working relationships, and maintenance of equipment, and two optional units from: setting and operating, cutting, folding, binding, and enhancing equipment. Print commercial covers estimating, buying, production planning and control, and customer services. The British Printing Industry Federation offers a customised package of support at every stage.

A modern apprenticeship scheme is available to anyone between 16 and 22 who is in full-time employment in the industry. It leads to NVQ level 3.

Further information

The Institute of Printing and the British Printing Industries Federation (BPIF) and the Scottish Print Employers Federation (SPEF).

Textile, clothing and related industries

This closely linked group of industries historically used natural resources – cotton, wool, leather, etc. – to make a great variety of products ranging from clothes and shoes, rope, twine and net, through carpets and other furnishings, to lace and furs. These traditional industries have been suffering just because they have long histories, and because of competition from cheap-labour countries.

The relative buoyancy of the late 1960s and early 1970s, mainly based on cheap synthetic fibres, masked the growing problems, but the industries were badly placed to take advantage of new developments, which still required heavy inputs of labour. Textiles and clothing were among the first industries to be set up in developing countries, where costs are low, and where for the most part industry is low-technology and low-investment.

The politics of the UK and of the EU were in favour of free trade, leading to a steady increase in the amount of clothing and footwear being manufactured in the low-cost countries of Asia and Eastern Europe.

Despite decline, this is still a major group of industries. The market for products at home and overseas is worth billions of pounds and, for the time being at least, employs around 400,000 people in total. Although unlikely to remain so labour-intensive for very long, paradoxically the viability of the industries' recovery is threatened by skill shortages. High-quality products, produced using highly sophisticated machinery needs a highly skilled workforce through from shop floor to top management. This type of production creates high-quality and high-value products.

The industry divides along very traditional lines. Modern technology, and the changing shape of the industry, make old classifications very dated, to the extent that 'textiles' is often used when both (traditional) clothing and textiles are being discussed. However, the industries still have employers, in line with the traditional divisions, and the facts and figures come from them. Rationalising the industries into larger groupings earlier meant 'vertical' integration – of textile with clothing firms mainly – but today large groups believe in decentralising as far as possible, so textile and clothing divisions and factories still keep the characteristics of their own sectors. The knitting (and lace) industry does not, though, fit neatly into either, since so often it makes up the fabric at the same time as it turns them into end-products like sweaters and shirts. The knitting sector is not traditionally part of the clothing industry, and is still treated as part of textiles.

The clothing industry

The clothing industry is large, complex and fragmented, with a comparatively large number of very small firms, despite steady rationalisation and mergers which have been underway for some years now. It includes the *'haute couture'* houses, wholesale manufacturers, and the rapidly falling number of 'bespoke' (made-to-measure) tailors. It is traditionally divided between, at one end, firms which are very design- and fashion-conscious, making good-quality, high-value garments in relatively small quantities; and at the other, those supplying volume markets with larger production runs, although this is changing as wholesale manufacturers try to take advantage of the 'designer' trend, and have to switch to shorter runs of more varied up-to-the-minute fashion goods. Firms generally specialise – making some form of men's, women's or children's outerwear (suits, coats, raincoats, anoraks), sportswear, baby clothes, dresses, skirts, blouses, shirts, ties, uniforms, underwear/nightwear etc. Woven clothing represented the largest proportion (about a third) of total output in 1995, followed by knitted goods (13%).

The clothing and textile industries together represent 1.4% of our gross domestic product and is the fifth largest manufacturing sector in the UK with a turnover from clothing exports of £2.5 billion in 1996. Of this, 8% was due to British designers, and worth £160m.

The future of the industry depends on companies taking advantage of their closeness to UK and European markets, becoming much more flexible and responding quickly to changing fashion and demands, and doing more to lead and influence market patterns; upgrading their marketing, improving use of designers, and concentrating more on specialist or high-value-added merchandise, or market outlets. UK retailers are pushing for an efficient home industry which can get the latest fashion idea to them far faster than firms the other side of the world, making clothes which project a sharp, recognisable 'designer' image for the individual retailer. Non-price competition – in terms of increased quality, effective supply and distribution networks, innovation, and the development and efficient use of human resources – have resulted from a demand for quality.

Productivity has been steadily rising (approximately 65% between 1986 and 1993), with heavy investment in new technology and methods, and a major training programme. One firm can now produce 3,000 suits a week with 370 people against 4–500 a week with 300 people in the past. New, faster equipment is being installed at all stages from materials handling, preparation and cutting through to garment construction, sewing, finishing and pressing – the industry even has robots, to pick single piles of garment parts from a stack, and place them exactly where needed, for example. Garments are handled mechanically as they pass from stage to stage; cutters have had fast, electrically operated shears and machine band knives for some time, but laser cutters are now a reality; bulk quantities can be die cut; sewing machines are electronically controlled. Computers, from customers' measurements, automatically prepare 'lays' for cutting, and pattern-cutting can be automated too. Computerised stock control, costing, and ticket-printing systems are also helping to improve efficiency.

Employment in the clothing industry

This is a labour-intensive industry, but numbers employed have been falling in recent years, and productivity increasing, in line with the rest of the manufacturing sector. There are about 140,000 employees today in clothing companies compared with over 255,500 during the early 1980s (and over 500,000 in 1951). In 1996 about 80% were operatives, and the rest were involved in administrative and technical jobs; 99% were employed by small to medium-sized enterprises.

Skilled work. The great majority of people in the industry work on the shop floor in wholesale manufacturing. Most are skilled (sewing) machinists. They may work on complete garments, but more usually on one part of it, or they operate the special machines which, e.g. overlock or embroider. Most machinists become skilled in five or six different machining jobs. Sample machinists help designers, do trials for specifications and quotations, etc. Pressing is the other main skilled work in this area of production. Promotion may be to garment examining, supervising, training, etc. Skills such as machining or pressing can be used in any clothing company, and in some others, such as those manufacturing soft furnishings.

The numbers in other skilled work are rather smaller, although the proportion is probably rising. The work includes: pattern technicians, or design pattern cutters – who turn designers' drawings into production-line patterns; lay planners – who are generally experienced cutters and work out in detail the most economical method of placing patterns on the cloth (although with computerisation, the job involves loading the information into the machine, making calculations and working out the lay on a VDU screen); cutters – using traditional knives, dies, and computerised, including laser, cutters; pattern-makers – the people who do the marking or fixing, putting together all the different pieces for a garment and marking the stitch lines; and hand sewers. Traditional hand-craft tailoring is obviously a skill needing years of training, whereas handling a computerised cutter or another machine process can be learned more quickly.

A relatively recent innovation has been to employ machinists in groups, enabling them to 'make-through' individual garments using several machines to balance production, thereby increasing their skills and flexibility. Workers with these skills usually stand rather than sit at their machines.

Promotion is to supervisory work, organising a section or department, including quality control and training. In bespoke tailoring and dress-making there is more emphasis on hand work, although automation is being introduced here too wherever possible. The cutter both drafts the pattern onto the cloth and measures the customer, and may supervise the sewing, which is done partly by machine, partly by hand. Most workshops, except in the multiple retailers still making-to-measure, are small, with close teamwork. Some experienced bespoke cutters and tailors go into manufacturing as, e.g. pattern-cutters or cutting-room managers.

Engineering. The growing sophistication of the machinery means the industry needs increasing numbers of technicians and engineers to design/develop, install, maintain and service them. Some machines also have to be adapted to do different jobs. Some clothing firms employ their own maintenance staff, especially for the large numbers of sewing machines, while other, more sophisticated, machinery may be serviced by the manufacturers, for whom maintenance staff then work.

Design and product development. Not all firms have their own professional designers, although the numbers employed are increasing as the demand for branded production (own label) increases (*see* ART, CRAFT AND DESIGN). Designers must also understand technical issues and the production process, be able to make up patterns, and know something about the market and different sales techniques. Except in the smallest companies, designers will be part of a product development team, which usually means working alongside fabric buyers, pattern-cutters, machinists (to make up the sample garments), pattern-makers and graders (to work out how the cloth should be cut and prepare patterns) as well as lay planners (*see below*).

In common with other industries there will also be opportunities in marketing and sales.

Managerial/ administrative work. An estimated one in ten employees are managers. While there are clearly defined functions to fill, with so many smaller firms one person may do more than one job, and the areas of responsibility are rarely clear cut. Production managers are still mainly promoted from the shop floor and supervisory work, but some, mostly larger, firms now take on production assistants specially to train as managers.

Commercial functions – finance, marketing and sales – are increasingly important for the industry. In BUYING, PURCHASING AND SUPPLY (*see in* BUYING, SELLING AND RELATED SERVICES) firms have support and backup from textile companies and fibre-makers with whom they work closely. It is a skilled job to know what materials will be in fashion some time ahead, and which will be suitable – including in quality and cost – for the designs.

Young executives are generally given experience of several functions. Promotion is largely from within the industry, and it is still common for people to work their way up. Business acumen, entrepreneurial flair and ambition are still frequently more highly rated by existing managers than formal qualifications. Reports suggest, though, that firms need to develop more sophisticated managerial skills, and the industry seems to be recognising this.

Recruitment and entry

While numbers employed may have fallen, the industry – with aggressive PR help from the Industry Training Organisation – needs to recruit people of the calibre essential to run a modern industry fighting for market share. The shortages are not restricted to high-level skills: in many areas there are desperate shortages of machinists.

It is suggested that the industry needs at least 500 new junior executives a year (including A-level entrants as well as graduates), for production management and technology, design and design management, marketing, and sales management, particularly. Specialist qualifications are not essential, but are supported with grants, sponsorships, etc.

Engineering technicians are trained on the job, often with day-release to support the attainment of NVQs. Others also receive training leading to NVQs. By 1995, about 21% of clothing manufacturers had introduced NVQ/Competence-based training (far more than in the associated textile industry), according to a survey by Staffordshire TEC.

Qualifications and training

The level and quality of graduate and professional training is being steadily improved with the support of CFI International (formerly the Clothing and Footwear Institute).

Degree level. Examples of relevant degree titles include: Clothing Engineering and Management, Clothing Industry Management, Clothing Management and Technology, Textiles with Clothing Studies, Clothing Engineering (combined with Management Studies). Such courses are offered by universities, including in 1996 UMIST, Heriot-Watt, Manchester Metropolitan, Ulster, and Nottingham; and by the London College of Fashion (part of the London Institute).

BTEC/SCOTVEC Higher National Certificate/Diploma level. Colleges offering relevant awards at this level included (in 1996): Belfast College of Technology, Jacob Kramer College: Leeds, Kent Institute of Art and Design, London College of Fashion, Manchester Metropolitan University, Nottingham Trent University, and Cardonald College. Examples of relevant course titles include: Clothing Technology with Design, Clothing Machine Engineering, and Clothing Manufacture. About 80 UK colleges offer various training courses on clothing manufacture, fashion and textiles.

See ART, CRAFT AND DESIGN for various degrees and other courses in fashion.

National Vocational Qualifications. Training, on the job with release for college study, leads to NVQ awards at levels 2 and 3 in Clothing. Craftworkers such as machinists and pressers train on the job, sometimes with day-release, some after preliminary training in (larger) firms' own training schools. The first NVQ/SVQs were aimed at operatives in stitching, forming, and cutting (e.g. NVQ levels 1 and 2 Manufacturing Products from Textiles, and Handicraft Tailoring) and the broad-based Product Development (Apparel) level 3 for the needs of pattern/garment technicians, lay-planners, and graders, which offers a bridge between manufacturing and design. Other, more general NVQs, e.g. in Training and Development, recognise needs common to all industries and workplaces.

A modern apprenticeship is being developed, resulting in a variety of qualifications including Product Development/Engineering.

Further information

CAPITB Trust, the officially recognised industry training organisation and the industry's lead body.

The footwear industry

The footwear industry is fighting against intense foreign competition: in 1996, more than 75% of the market consists of imported products, with Italy and the Far East as the leading suppliers. For survival, the British shoe industry must stay out of products like trainers, and concentrate on making shoes in the latest fashion, however quickly it changes, therefore beating importers, who cannot possibly get their products into the market fast enough. In addition, a move up-market has secured sales. Firms have to be able to make a wide variety of well-styled shoes, in short runs. This means having innovative designers, and flexible, up-to-date manufacturing equipment, and concentrating on the export market. However, there is still room to succeed if the product is good; and there have been notable successes in recent years..

Shoemaking, though, is very difficult to automate, and is still at the stage of putting electronics into individual machines rather than setting up automated lines. Computerised, numerically controlled stitching machines mean one operator can do the work done by four on traditional equipment, and computer-controlled conveyor belts speed the leather shapes round the machinists. A robot has been developed to check that 'uppers' are properly glued to soles, and another can pick and place leather. Computer-aided design is being developed, but it needs highly sophisticated software to get over the problem of converting a three-dimensional design on a last into a two-dimensional pattern. CAD/CAM systems could automate last-and mould-making, but cutting the leather still needs human skills.

The number of firms has been falling for some years and, although many of the smaller, family businesses have been forced out by the competition, few are very large, and most are both manufacturers and retailers. There are 88 manufacturers who employ more than 100 people and these are centred around the East Midlands, Lancashire, the South West and Norwich. Many specialise in one kind of product: women's or children's shoes, or boots, for instance.

Employment in the industry

Numbers employed have been falling since 1970 to under 80,000 in 1991 and 30,000 in 1996, even though the industry remains labour-intensive. However, there are around 10,000 jobs created indirectly through associated supplies. Yet the industry is competing favourably and has the added advantage of being close to the largest footwear market in the world: the European Union.

Most people working in the industry are semi-skilled operatives, who then move up into more skilled trades, and into supervisory work. Shoemaking is a skilled craft. The pattern-cutter drafts out the separate pieces which will make up the pattern for the shoe. From this is produced a sample, and then the pattern-maker produces grades patterns for the various sizes. As many as 30 pieces may be needed for a single shoe. Many of the processes, such as clicking or cutting the uppers, are skilled work, even though shoes may be cut with a hydraulic press rather than by hand. Preparing the pieces for stitching may involve as many as 40 or 50 separate operations. Soles and other 'bottom components' are generally made by specialist firms, but joined to uppers by the shoe manufacturer.

However, the increasingly sophisticated production processes mean some aspects of production are now treated as technician-level work. The industry also employs technologists and technicians in research and development, as well as production control. Most firms employ their own designers, who have to work closely with production. (*See* ART, CRAFT AND DESIGN.) Expert management, marketing, finance, etc., are as crucial to shoemakers as any other industry.

Recruitment and entry

Traditionally, the industry recruits people for work as semi-skilled operatives, but there are now more schemes for young people with good school-leaving qualifications to train as technicians. Firms also recruit some school-leavers with A-levels and graduates for management training in both production and commercial functions.

Qualifications and training

The industry has always trained extensively, especially at operative/craft, and now also at technician, levels. On-the-job training is combined with release to study for national awards.

Degree and postgraduate level. Footwear Design: De Montfort University and Cordwainers College (London). MA in Footwear Design in conjunction with SATRA Footwear Technology Centre.

BTEC Higher National Certificate level (part-time/block-release). Footwear: Accrington and Rossendale College.

Technician level. Training, on the job with release for college study, leads to the BTEC National Certificate in Footwear: courses are available at Accrington and Rossendale College, Kendal College of FE, and Wellingborough College. Full-time BTEC National Diploma courses in Footwear are available at Accrington and Rossendale College, Cordwainers College (London), South Fields College of FE (Leicester) and Wellingborough College.

A BTEC National Diploma course in Footwear Design is available at Cordwainers College (London).

Craft level. Craftworkers also train on-the-job, and may study by release for City & Guilds Footwear Manufacture Operatives Scheme awards (454). An NVQ level 2 has been developed for footwear operatives. Level 3 has passed a feasibility study. along with a Modern Apprenticeship. The professional body is CFI International (formerly the Clothing and Footwear Institute).

Further information

CFI International, and the British Footwear Association.

Leather and leather goods manufacture

Some firms specialise in preparing leather, some in making leather goods, some do both.

Leather manufacturers tan and dress the hides and skins, and prepare them as heavy, light and fancy leathers, for boots and shoes, gloves and handbags, clothing and upholstery, saddlery and industrial use. Leather is produced from animal skins and hides, using different manufacturing agents depending on the kind of leather being produced. A chemically based industry, the processes are based on chemical interactions, which include tanning agents, dyes, fat liquors and finishes, on the skins.

The industry uses as much automatic and semi-automatic machinery as possible. However, the processes have to be constantly adjusted to allow for variations in the quality of the skins and/or the requirements of a particular product, making full automation difficult. The industry has been affected by environmental and waste management issues – for example, they have moved away from using solvents to aqueous finishes.

Leather goods include luggage and bags of all kinds, saddles, fancy goods, etc. The industry keeps the same name although a large number of its products are made of synthetic materials, often made to simulate leather, rather than leather itself. The industry divides between a small number of large firms making a range of products using very modern machinery and production methods, and a very large number of quite small firms who specialise in particular products, e.g. saddlery and harnesses, and quality leather goods, using traditional craft methods still.

Employment in the industry

UK employment is around 15–20,000. In addition there are many jobs in the chemical industries that supply finishes, dyes, etc. The leather industry employs a relatively high proportion of scientific, technological and technician-level staff, not only in production and control, but also in the commercial functions, particularly buying and selling, with a fairly high proportion of executives holding appropriate qualifications. Research posts are few, though.

The leather goods industry also employs quite large numbers of craftworkers, particularly for products like saddles which are still hand-made. Even a simple saddle takes the equivalent of three working days to make. Other skilled work includes designing fancy goods, bridle and other hand-stitching. In mass-production, goods are usually produced by bench assembly, which includes a considerable amount of machining and machine-sewing. Engineers, technicians, and tool- and jig-makers are also employed.

Recruitment and entry

For junior executive/technological/scientific work, the industry recruits a small number of trainees annually, and usually sends them to study full-time (*see below*).

For technician-level, entry is with at least four good grades at GCSE/SCE. Leather-goods designers need similar minimum entry qualifications. Apprentice saddlemakers usually require some good GCSE/SCEs.

Qualifications and training

Technological/scientific training is generally via a degree (for leather manufacture this is normally in chemistry, chemical engineering, or other science-based subjects).

Leather technology is now taught at Nene College, Northampton, which is the only college offering courses in this subject. Courses include a BSc and MSc in Leather Technology and MPhil and PhD courses.

BTEC Higher National Diploma and National Certificate courses are offered in Science (Leather Technology). Open-learning courses lead to City & Guilds which offer Craft (scheme 457), and Operative (scheme 456) awards. BTEC Certificate of Achievement which is a Foundation Year for a degree.

There is an NVQ level 2 Leather Technology.

For saddlery, training on the job lasts some five years. Training in other leather goods manufacture is also on the job (with release to study for City & Guilds scheme 470) but takes rather less time.

Further information

National Leathersellers Centre (Nene College) and British Leather Goods Manufacturers Association.

Textile manufacture

Textile manufacture turns raw cotton, wool, linen, cellulose and synthetic fibres first into yarns, and then into fabrics. It produces fabrics for woven cloth, knitted goods, carpets, lace, and the growing industrial-fabric 'non-wovens' market. It has changed from a labour-intensive, craft industry, into a capital-intensive (its machinery is now very expensive), highly automated one in a very short space of time. Some textiles are still produced traditionally, however, by for example the small number of mill workers and home weavers of the Harris Tweed industry on the Outer Hebrides. Other firms still make traditional lace, but on increasingly high-tech machinery. It accounted for about 2% of UK manufacturing output in 1995 – a little less than the clothing industry it contributes to.

The industry is being forced to be more design and fashion conscious. It is investing in new technology still further, innovating, and spending more on R&D. It is, however, totally dependent on shrewd management and manufacturing decision-making – going into making fabrics, etc. for more than the traditional single (summer or winter) season, to help even out the peaks and troughs, for example.

The textile 'industry' is still, in fact, several industries, even though the largest groups extend both out to synthetic-fibre production (technically part of the CHEMICAL INDUSTRIES; *see above*) and out into clothing manufacture, and across other sectors too. Wool, worsted and knitting are still distinguishable from the Lancashire, cotton-based, sector, for technological and technical as well as historical reasons. Until the early 1970s, the industry was still made up of a great many small, specialised operations – spinning, weaving, knitting, dyeing, finishing, etc. The industry went through a tough period of rationalisation which resulted in a small number of vertically integrated mega-groups, and a spate of takeovers which merged three of these. Central control, however, is no longer in vogue, and the emphasis has shifted to local profit centres and management motivation. But by contrast, many of the companies in the knitting (and lace) industry are still small, family-type businesses, with under 100 employees each.

The technological changes are little short of revolutionary. Reports which one day insist robots cannot possibly handle cloth are confounded the next. But innovation is not confined to automation. In weaving, for example, the 'weft' is no longer taken between the 'warp' by shuttles, but can be guided by jets of air or water. 'Friction', instead of traditional 'rotary' spinning doubles the rate at which machines can produce yarns. Modern machinery can produce textiles and knitted fabrics in much more sophisticated and interesting patterns, faster.

Various research centres within the industry have recently united to form the British Textiles Technology Group, offering test and analytical services on all kinds of textile products, processes and equipment.

Employment in the industry

The largest sector is knitting, followed by woollen and worsted and cotton. Increased productivity is likely to bring employment down still further, but the speed of the fall is dependent on levels of investment, and on how strongly the industry manages to combat imports and increase exports.

'Process' workers, controlling an ever larger number of highly sophisticated, automated machines, still make up a high proportion of people employed, although it is falling. Knitting operatives, for instance, increasingly control eight, twelve, or banks of up to 40 high-precision machines. They keep them supplied with fibre or yarn, adjusting them, watching for faults, etc., whatever the process, from spinning through to weaving or knitting. While lace-making is still skilled work, the complex machines controlled by pattern cards are now also being replaced by computer-controlled machines, operated via VDU screens and keyboards. The draughtsmen/women and designers are still crucial, though.

Technicians. The industry has a rising proportion of jobs for technicians. Technicians work in product and process development. They may be in charge of particular production sectors. They also work in quality control. In yarn and fibre production, they check machines to see that they are set and running properly, service and maintain them, install and adjust new machines, supervise machine operators. In bleaching, dyeing, finishing, etc., they work out the recipes for chemicals or colours for different fabrics, work out machine settings (temperature, speed, pressure, timing), supervise dye-mixing, and test to see that the fabric has been properly treated, for flame resistance, for example. Technicians and mechanics keep the sophisticated electronic, computer-controlled machinery operating smoothly.

Designers. Designers are employed in increasing numbers, although still mainly by the larger, and specialist (e.g. lace) companies. *See* ART, CRAFT AND DESIGN.

Textile technologists. Textile technologists work as production managers/controllers (which includes quality control), general managers, or technical officers/advisers, in research and development – (working on, e.g. new machinery, computer-control methods (especially in dyeing and colouring), improving fibre characteristic such as strength and durability, etc. – and in marketing.

Recruitment and entry

Although the industry is never likely to recruit in huge numbers again, it is clearly looking for its share of higher-calibre people at all levels. Recruitment is fragmented between sectors, and tends to be locally based.

The industry recruits graduates with appropriate degrees (*see below*), but may take small numbers of e.g. chemists, mechanical/production engineers, electronic/systems engineers, and people with business-related degrees, especially for sales and marketing.

Technicians normally require good GCSE/SCEs, including mathematics and a science subject, with increasing recruitment at 18-plus with A-level/H grade passes.

No formal qualifications stated for craft level, but appropriate GCSE/SCE grades are an advantage.

Qualifications and training

Much of the training is industry-based and supported by various training bodies serving the main centres of the industry.

Degree level. Technologists in scientific and engineering disciplines normally qualify pre-entry. A number of degree courses are designed specially for the industry, but there are very few sponsorship opportunities for students taking textile-related courses. Entry to many courses is with science subjects at A-level/H grade. Examples of relevant degree titles include Textile Chemistry, Textile Management, Textile Manufacture, Textile Science and Technology: Textile Studies, Textiles with Clothing Studies, Applied Chemistry (Colour/Materials), Manufacturing Computing (Textiles),Textile and Knitwear Technology, Textile Technology Management Studies.

See ART, CRAFT AND DESIGN for various degrees and other courses in textile design.

BTEC/SCOTVEC Higher National Certificate/Diploma levels exist in similar subjects, as well as, for example, Business and Finance (Textile Marketing).

The professional body is the Textile Institute, with 50% of members working in textile manufacturing. Students completing certain degree courses may be also be eligible for chartered membership of the institute (CText ATI).

Technician Level. Training, on the job with release for college study, leads to NVQs in Textiles or in Science.

Craftworkers. Craftworkers also train on the job, and may study by release for various City & Guilds qualifications and NVQs

Further information

British Textile Confederation, the Textile Institute, and the sector training organisations, e.g. the Confederation of British Wool Textiles Ltd., and the Knitting and Lace Industries Training Resources Agency.

Timber and furniture

Wood is still a staple material for many industries such as paper-making, furniture-making, and construction. Although more modern alternatives may be longer-lasting and less liable to decay, wood is still popular for many uses, and it is often only cost which is the problem. Britain imports over 90% of timber and wood products used.

The timber trade

This is now a national rather than a locally based industry, after extensive restructuring: larger and stronger groups are nationally, or regionally, based. Timber and other wood materials are imported on huge bulk carriers, and so have to be discharged at specially built timber terminals. Some importing companies are now involved also in manufacturing end-products, mainly components for the building industry, such as wood flooring, sawn fencing, veneers, plywood and chipboard, wooden doors and window frames, greenhouses and sheds.

Timber agents, of whom there are several hundred, represent overseas suppliers in this country, and use their expert knowledge and marketing intelligence to sell the shipper's output to importers. They also help both shipper and importer to make arrangements for delivery, which includes arranging insurance, documentation, chartering and financing. Importers buy timber from overseas suppliers either via agents or directly. They normally sell to merchants or direct to wood-using customers or through their own merchanting outlets, but sometimes to each other. They carry stocks of a wide range of wood materials of varying species and in numerous grades and dimensions. Most companies therefore have sizeable yards, and have their own sawmills, drying kilns, chemical treatment plants and fabricating shops.

Merchants buy from importers, not only handling the raw wood, but also stocking a wide range of wood products. Merchants may be multi-purpose building merchants, but they may serve a wide range of customers, and may operate sawmills and wood treatment plant too. Modern machinery, especially powered equipment (increasingly computer-controlled), and new glues and stapling equipment, have revolutionised timber preparation.

Employment in the industry
Current estimates suggest some 55,000 to 60,000 are employed in the industry in 1996, against some 99,000 in 1973. The major proportion of the industry is now involved in trade counter, shop, or yard/warehouse sales work. Sawmills are becoming highly mechanised, and do not require large numbers. Those that are recruited, however, must become fully skilled – skills includes wood machining, maintenance (including sharpening and generally caring for industrial saws) and fitting, preservation and kiln work. Promotion opportunities include sales, supervisory and yard management. Staff in sales, buying, and general management all have to be skilled in timber technology.

Recruitment and entry
Junior executive staff are expected to have good grades in at least four GCSE/SCEs. A small but growing proportion are recruited with higher qualifications, including appropriate degrees (*see below*). Senior positions are usually filled by internal promotion.

Timber agents are not normally recruited direct from school/college: most are recruited from people already working in the trade, and who are fully experienced and qualified.

There are no formal minimum entry requirements for craft wood machinists and timber yard staff, but good GCSE/SCEs are an advantage.

Qualifications and training
Degree level. Forest Products Technology: Buckinghamshire College of HE (a college of Brunel University); Wood Science: University of Wales, Bangor.

Technician level. Institute of Wood Science courses at selected colleges of FE/HE, usually by block-release.

Craft level. Training is industry-based: a complete training system covering all aspects of the industry has been developed by the voluntary organisation Timberstart. NVQs have been developed jointly by City & Guilds and Timber Trades Federation. Modern Apprenticeships give automatic entry to technician level leading to technician-level qualification.

Further information
Timberstart (Timber Trade Federation).

Furniture

Furniture is mainly produced in factories using a number of modern manufacturing processes and materials, e.g. wood, plastics and metals. Each part of the process is carried out by a different group of people, all of whom are skilled workers.

The majority of manufacturers concentrate on a particular product, e.g. cabinetmaking or chairmaking, or in a specialised area of the market, e.g. kitchen, office or pine furniture. The skills required will vary depending on the type of product the manufacturer specialises in.

It is estimated that there are between 1,200 and 1,300 manufacturers in the UK, ranging in size from small family firms employing less than 25 people, to large organisations employing over 650 staff. In addition to this there are a great many craft workshops making furniture by hand using traditional skills.

Employment in the industry
An estimated 85,000 people work in the industry (1996). Craft skills recognised in the industry include:

- Wood machining – cutting and shaping the wood, usually by operating a number of different machines to saw, plane, mortise, route, drill or turn the components. The wood machinist has to be able to follow drawings and work accurately.
- Veneering – covering exterior surfaces with a thin layer of expensive wood, e.g. walnut or mahogany. Veneers have to be selected according to specification, jointed to form the correct size, design and shape, then applied to the 'core' material, e.g. a dining room table or cabinet.
- Cabinetmaking – fitting and assembling furniture, ensuring doors hang correctly and drawers fit and run smoothly, etc. Cabinetmakers in large firms may only work on one or two stages, while in smaller organisations they may complete the entire assembly process. Some may specialise, e.g. as chairmakers.
- Polishing and finishing – adding the final staining and surface touches to furniture, often using high speed industrial spray guns. There is, however, still a need for workers who can complete this process using handskills.

Craft skills associated with upholstered furniture making include fabric cutting, machine sewing, and upholstering (building up the shape of the chair or settee using a variety of filling materials, then covering and adding accessories such as buttons and fringes).

Skilled technicians are required to set and maintain machines, and sometimes to program them. Other skilled workers produce and sharpen tools, make jigs and create prototypes. There are also opportunities for experienced supervisors and charge hands.

Recruitment and entry
The industry recruits a small number of qualified people for production and management each year. School-leavers wishing to enter the industry may require good GCSE/SCEs in design/CDT, mathematics, English language and a science.

Qualifications and training

Training is largely industry-based, although it is possible to follow a full-time college course prior to entering the industry.

Degree and postgraduate level. Furniture Manufacture and Innovation: London Guildhall University; Furniture Production: Buckinghamshire College of HE (Part of Brunel

University) BSc Furniture Production, BA Fine Craft, BA Furniture Restoration, MA Furniture Making and Design.

BTEC/ SCOTVEC Higher National Certificate/ Diploma-level Furniture Studies. Furniture (Production option): London Guildhall University; Furniture: London College of Furniture/London Guildhall University.

See ART, CRAFT AND DESIGN for various degrees and other courses in furniture design.

BTEC/ SCOTVEC National level. Full-time National Diploma courses in Furniture are available at Basford Hall College of FE (Nottingham) and London College of Furniture (now part of London Guildhall University). There are numerous SCOTVEC National Certificate modules in Furniture Manufacture.

The industry runs a three year apprenticeship scheme leading to the appropriate craft area. NVQ/SVQs are normally a mix of on-the-job training and college courses, although these are being phased out.

Further information

British Furniture Manufacturers (BFM) National Training Executive.

The Construction Industry

Contents

(CLCI: U, UD, UF, UJ, UN)

The construction industry

The construction industry is an amalgam of what was traditionally two separate sectors – building, which conventionally means roofed structures, and civil engineering, which is the heavier end of construction, of roads, bridges, canals, docks, and so on. Nowadays the distinction is blurred, mainly because many large buildings, like office blocks, are built on civil engineering principles, using concrete or steel frames and foundations. Parts of the industry, particularly the large-scale end, make increasing use of advanced technology, highly mechanised methods and industrialised techniques; but in house-building, which one commentator rather aptly described as a 'cottage' industry, it is still very much craft-based, although highly skilled.

It can be an exciting industry in which to work, with new and challenging problems to be solved daily. People carp about the cost of the Channel Tunnel, but it remains a magnificent feat of engineering. And it is intensely satisfying for someone engaged in construction to look, for instance, on the Dartford Bridge which eases traffic flow, a new hospital, a flood relief scheme, or a waste-derived fuel plant, and to be able to say, 'I helped to design or to build that'. In few professions is it given to one to leave behind such concrete results of one's efforts.

The nature of the industry is constantly evolving. After the war, priorities included rural water supplies and housing. Massive tower blocks were constructed and prefabrication came in. Motorways began to evolve. Then it was fashionable to build vast office blocks and supermarkets. Now the water companies are providing a tremendous amount of work, meeting tough environmental standards so that drinking water is improved in quality. The ring main around London is substantially longer than the Channel Tunnel and there is talk of water being distributed from Northumberland to Yorkshire. Leaks are being stopped, new waste water pipes put in and old sewerage replaced. Pollution control and water treatment are ongoing processes and heavy users of capital. Sea outfalls are being improved. Anglian Water, for example, has a £21 million scheme to clean up the waters along the coast: part of its Operation Clearwater initiative to bring the sea up to European bathing water directive standards. They have removed five ancient short sea outfalls which discharged virtually untreated sewage into the North Sea. These have been replaced by a single 1½-mile-long sea outfall, a new connecting sewer, a sewage treatment plant, pumping stations and backup storm tanks.

Unfortunately, this massive and complex industry is very vulnerable to the economic climate – to the availability of finance, to interest rates and so on – so it is one of the first to be affected by changes in the economy, and usually suffers badly in recession. Harsh winters have an equally devastating effect.

The industry has great difficulty in achieving the even flow of output so necessary for maximum profitability. It is not easy to plan or manage efficiently. As a result, upturns in production tend to be unexpected, and frequently bring shortages, particularly of skilled people. It is hardly surprising that the construction industry holds the record for bankruptcies.

Construction had not had a really good year since the 1973 oil crisis, until 1987, when the industry boomed, particularly in the commercial sector. Fuelled by relaxation of credit rules, removal of planning constraints and a generally bullish economic mood, contractors benefited from the favourable market conditions. The end of the boom in 1989 and poor economic conditions saw companies struggling to maintain growth, being forced to cut back activity and even go into liquidation.

Prospects for the industry in both the housing and commercial markets, at least in the short term, look bleak. Civil engineering accounts for around one-fifth of total construction in Great Britain. In their quarterly survey of civil engineering workload trends, published in January 1996, the Federation of Civil Engineering Contractors (FCEC) remarked on the low level of invitations to tender for future work. FCEC Director General John Hackett said that a succession of recent government announcements and actions by public sector clients had created a situation of considerable uncertainty and concern over the outlook for civil engineering later that year. Looking at immediate prospects for civil engineering, the Federation welcomed a slight increase in the percentage of firms reporting order books fuller than the year before. But for every firm with more orders there were two with order books less full than in January 1994. More orders for water and sewerage works were not making up for the decline in orders for the transport infrastructure works, particularly roads, that provided the greater part of civil engineering workload. There would be more work later in the year on the first Design, Finance and Operate road schemes, but that would not make up for the cuts in public spending, not even in 1997.

That same month (January 1996) the Building Employers Federation reported a fourth successive quarterly fall in construction output and a decline in new enquiries. The construction downturn, they added, was becoming more geographically widespread, with Yorkshire as the only region to report a marginal improvement in output during the quarter. Public-sector housing and non-housing repair and maintenance appeared to have suffered the largest setbacks. The commercial sector – the only sector to report an improvement during the quarter – continued to grow consistently but modestly. Shops and offices had provided the main engines for growth in the last six months.

Overseas, the story is more cheerful. British contractors have been notably successful in the intensely competitive international market. In 1994 they won new overseas business worth £3.8 billion, a 14% increase on 1993. They are currently active in over 100 different countries, usually operating through local subsidiaries or agents. While North America is our most valuable market, the areas of greatest recent growth have been the European Union, the Middle East and Hong Kong. Career opportunities overseas for British nationals are, however, limited, as most construction work is undertaken and supervised by local personnel.

The industry has been modernising its business methods, and developing more positive and sophisticated marketing – a major factor in house-building recovery. Long-established contract and organisational working methods, and the rigid divisions and demarcations between architect, engineer and building contractor are being abandoned in favour of a range of possible contract arrangements to give greater efficiency, tighter control, and speed. Improving productivity is another priority.

Construction companies

The construction industry consists of some 606,000 firms (source: BASRA/CFR 'Workload Mix and Occupations September 1995'). General builders, building and civil engineering contractors and civil engineers account for 42% of these. The majority consist of general builders with fewer than eight employees. The survey analysis shows that in 1993, the total turnover of the industry was £65 billion. The turnover of the largest general contractors and civil engineers totalled £25.8 billion, which compares with a turnover of £28.7 billion reported by 80 of the largest construction companies in their annual accounts for that year.

Only 58,406 firms came within the scope of the CITB in 1993/94. Some are too small, and certain categories, such as electricians and plumbers, are no longer in scope. Of the total, 53,568 consisted of small employers (up to 13 employees), 4,375 medium employers (14–114 employees), and 463 large employers (over 114 employees). When you consider the size of the firm, however, the number of employees is to some extent irrelevant, as today so much work is subcontracted.

Firms range from a few giant internationals, with up to 40,000 employees, capable of building airports, complete harbours and dockyards, oil refineries, large housing estates, etc., down to the very many, small 'jobbing' or specialist firms.

Much construction work is carried out by private contractors, of whom growing numbers are self-employed. Since 1985 the number of private contractors across the range of trades has increased considerably, though not in every trade.

	1985	1993
General builders	64,475	70,765
Building and civil engineering contractors	3,623	6,264
Civil engineers	2,662	4,070
Plumbers	14,934	13,880
Carpenters and joiners	10,949	13,302
Painters	14,662	9,774
Roofers	5,818	6,891
Plasterers	4,019	6,891
Glaziers	4,387	6,599
Demolition contractors	559	708
Scaffolding specialists	966	1,645
Reinforced concrete specialists	515	729
Heating and ventilating engineers	8,461	9,355
Electrical contractors	15,449	20,589
Asphalt and tar sprayers	856	1,071
Plant hirers	3,664	5,567
Flooring contractors	1,400	2,248
Constructional engineers	1,560	2,375
Insulating specialists	1,308	1,147
Suspended ceiling specialists	842	1,597
Floor and wall-tiling specialists	1,167	1,492
Miscellaneous	2,549	11,490
All trades	167,825	195,107

Public-sector building

In describing employment in the construction industry, the part played by the public sector, including the health service, must not be forgotten. However, local authorities today normally hive off their responsibilities for the building of housing to housing associations.

Until recently the Property Services Agency (part of the Department of the Environment) provided, managed, maintained and furnished property used by the government at home and abroad. It also had new buildings designed (either by PSA staff or, and increasingly, by private consultants) and supervised construction by private contracts. From 1 April 1996, departments have taken over responsibility for the property they occupy and, if they wish to construct new buildings, will have to tender in competition with the private sector.

From the same date, a new central agency, PACE (Property Advisers to the Civil Estate) was set up to:

- coordinate government's activity in the property market;
- promote inter-departmental estate rationalisation;
- offer 'intelligent client' support (on repayment terms) to departments which cannot economically provide them in-house; and
- provide department with off-the-shelf advice and support.

Research and development

Research and development for the industry is done mainly by the Building Research Establishment, although it works primarily for the government. Much of its work is on building methods designed to cut heating costs, and the practical implications of changes in building regulations. It has a staff of several hundred.

How the industry works

A building, whether it is a house, an office block or a bridge, is not something that is bought new every day. For most organisations and individuals it happens only rarely, and is a very expensive business. Moreover, building projects are 'one-off' products – they are all different in some way and need different teams of experts to design and build them. Many of today's projects demand greater expertise, both in the technicalities of the building and in better understanding of the client's business. The customer, whether novice or experienced in buying buildings, has to find the best team for the particular job, which with today's high costs must be completed as economically, efficiently, and as fast as possible – and be safe.

A changing industry, fighting for work and profit, is having to change its working methods. The failure of some building systems and prefabrication processes alone has brought a major rethink of the selection and management processes, right back to the start of a project.

The traditional way of working was for a company (industrial or commercial), local authority, government department or individual to appoint or commission a designer: an architect for a building or complex of buildings; a civil engineer for a bridge, dam or power station; a chemical engineer for some kinds of industrial plant. The architect or engineer might put together a design team if the project was a complex one – an architect designing a tower block would need structural and building services engineers; a civil engineer designing a bridge might have architects on the team. The designer would recommend a quantity surveyor to the customer. The quantity surveyor advised on, e.g., materials and systems (as well as itemising materials and work, and making up the 'bills of quantity' on which contractors tender). The designer had to get planning consent for the building, invite tenders from building or civil engineering contractors (based on the quantity surveyor's bill of quantities), advise the client which to accept, and then supervise the project on behalf of the owner.

It is a hierarchical structure, with an architect or civil engineer in charge. The work proceeds in set stages, starting with a long period on design, preparation of specifications and bills of quantity, getting planning permission, and putting work out to tender, before any construction can start.

Some organisations are such large customers of the construction industry that they have always employed permanent staff to manage their construction work, building repair and maintenance, instead of commissioning. Here the responsible 'manager' is often a qualified engineer – who may be called a works superintendent or a clerk of works – or they may be a surveyor.

Clerks of works or their equivalent are also employed by other organisations with long-term and continuing maintenance and building programmes; for example, commercial and industrial firms and universities. For one-off projects or short-term development on a fairly large scale, the client (or the architect) may appoint a clerk of works for the duration of the contract.

Patterns of working have been changing for some years. Building nuclear power stations, or airports, are so specialised that engineers, construction firms, and other experts have put together permanent teams to bid for complete contracts, through from initial design to final delivery. Different methods of managing projects are now, however, being used more widely to give greater efficiency, better use of professional skills, and speed.

Management contracting, or project management, is increasingly used, particularly for large and complex projects, where the design has to build in construction methods and materials from the beginning, where changes are possible (e.g. in renovating an older building), and where speed is vital. A firm of management contractors may take on the entire project, putting together a specialist design team on which the demands of the client and the project are paramount (and not, say, the aesthetic aspirations alone of the architect). Each stage of the building can go to a specialist subcontractor, still chosen by competitive tender, working under contract to the management contractor (whose construction companies agree not to bid). Clients may, though, choose to commission their own architects and employ a management contractor just to control the building work. Using management contractors means greater flexibility, an earlier start to building, and built-in systems for solving inevitable problems. Management contracting, however, changes quite radically the traditional roles of professionals involved in construction.

Design-and-build is increasingly common, even for the largest contracts. Whereas in the past, the potential employer would engage a consulting engineer, who would specify exactly what was wanted, the argument has been put forward that contractors have experience in knowing what is economical to build and the best methods of construction.

Today the potential employer may engage a firm of contractors who either have their own design department or employ a consulting engineer.

Even more recent management systems are known as design, build and finance (as in the case of the Channel Tunnel) or design, build, finance and operate (in the case of trunk roads).

Management contracting, and variants of it, affect the building contractor, and bring contractors into projects earlier. While larger contractors, particularly, make increasing use of marketing experts and sales teams to help them gain contracts, they still have to put in a competitive tender.

Estimating staff, working with, e.g., the planning engineer, buyers, plant specialists (advising on machinery needed), soil lab technician (providing data for planning foundations), etc., work out each operation, what it involves in time, materials and labour. Then they cost it, putting in a tender pitched low enough to gain the contract, high enough not to make a loss. If the contract is gained, the planning engineers/site planners and contract manager prepare a detailed plan (for which the latest analytical, graphical and computer-based systems are used), making as economical use as possible of materials, equipment and labour.

The contract manager plans, manages, monitors and controls actual building operations, usually handling several contracts at once. Site managers – on a large site there maybe several, each with assistant managers in charge of sections – report to the contract manager. For very large contracts, however, a project manager may be in sole charge. Site managers are directly responsible for progress and day-to-day building work. They, too, are involved right from the planning stage, when methods and sequences of the operations are decided, through decisions on schedules, choice of plant, organising the site and site services (access, water, drainage, safety, etc.). They have to make sure other section managers and subcontractors are kept informed, that materials and equipment arrive on time, and that the sequence of work is kept on schedule.

The buyers are crucial to profitability, since at least half the money tied up in a building contract is in materials. Their problems and responsibilities are similar to those met by purchasing and buying officers in any industry. The buyers help prepare the initial tender, and they in turn put out to tender materials and work to be subcontracted. They must find the specified materials, in the right quantities (with as little waste as possible), at the right time (too early and it is in the way and tying up capital, too late and expensive workers stand idle).

When construction begins, site managers recruit the skilled and semi-skilled workers needed, helped perhaps, by personnel staff. Some general and craft foremen and supervisors, and craft- and tradesmen, may be permanent employees. The builder's contracts surveyors constantly measure and value the work in progress, keep accurate records, make site surveys before the work starts, and agree ground levels. The surveyors check subcontractors' bills and prepare accounts for the clients.

Larger firms have their headquarters, regional and even overseas offices; employees are then generally divided into office and site staff. Most professional staff spend much of their time on deskwork, negotiating, etc., although surveyors and engineers have field and site responsibilities. On larger projects, a bewildering number and variety of people may be involved, working for several different firms, some of them independent consultants, some subcontractors. Professionals, technicians, and skilled workers have to get on together, and understand the technical aspects of one another's work.

In addition to the professional and other construction jobs outlined above, a large construction company may also employ marketing staff, personnel and training officers, accountants and accounts staff, and supporting clerical workers.

Except for staff whose work ties them to the office, work in the industry is extremely hard and physically demanding. On site it is an occupation for younger people, and a high proportion of even skilled workers look for indoor work as they grow older. Since every project only lasts so long (although it can be years), on-site work means moving around from place to place, and for everybody regular new projects make life somewhat different from work where there is greater continuity.

Working in the industry

Professional and managerial staff – civil/structural engineers – building services engineers – other engineers – building control surveyors/inspectors – surveyors – architects – engineering geologists – builders merchants – technicians – craftworkers

Construction employs about 1.25 million people. General builders, building and civil engineering contractors account for 42% of firms in the industry, which total about 258,000. Of these, general builders with fewer than eight employees are the majority with 230,000. Main contractors with more than 115 employees account for 33% of the total turnover but only 9% of total employment.

The total turnover of the industry is £65 billion (1995) of which £6.7 billion is subcontracted to labour only, £15.6 billion subcontracted to other contractors, and £36 billion undertaken by own employees. General and civil contractors accounted for 68% of the turnover of the industry in 1993. Self-employment and small specialist subcontractors are expected to continue to be a key element in the labour and process markets. Public-sector employment in construction has continued to fall steadily.

The industry recognises a general decline in the demand for unskilled workers, while the numbers of specialist building trades can be expected to increase. Technical developments also affect demand for particular trades. For instance, use of timber frame in house-building (which is not as popular as it was) changes the pattern of skills. With timber-frame building there are reportedly fewer trades to be coordinated, labour content is less and there is less dependence on labour. As a result, trade supervision is reduced (but rigorous control must be exercised) and fewer wet trades are used. It cuts demand for bricklayers and associated wet trades, e.g. plasterers. Trades likely to benefit are non-manual occupations – because timber frame requires more detailing/design than traditional methods.

Professional and managerial staff

Professional and managerial staff employed in the UK construction industry include architects, quantity surveyors, building surveyors, chartered civil engineers, chartered structural engineers, other professional engineers and incorporated engineers, plus managerial staff. In addition there are large numbers of technicians of various grades.

The majority of professional and managerial staff, whatever their original qualifications, not unexpectedly work for the relatively small number of larger combined building/civil engineering contractors, general building firms, and specialist civil engineering contractors. A small number work for the few large heating and ventilating firms, and a similar proportion for a rather larger number of electrical contractors (many of these are engineers qualified in heating/ventilating, and electrical/electronic engineers respectively). Just a few work for plant hirers.

Management in the industry, particularly of larger firms, is now more sophisticated and professional, using the modern techniques now employed in other industries. The type and number of managerial posts depend to a large extent on the size of the firm. In larger firms there are separate departments, and therefore managers, assistant managers, etc., for estimating and tendering, contract planning and management, site and project management, material and plant control and purchase, and drawing-office, and in some of the largest, design. An increasing number have marketing departments and managers. The largest companies also have managers who are not necessarily directly concerned with construction, e.g. personnel and finance. Managerial staff are also employed in the contracting organisations.

There is no single route into construction management. In civil engineering, many managers are chartered civil/structural engineers, but in building it is still just as common for managers to come up from supervisory and technician-level work as from the ranks of professionals. However, the proportion and number of technologically trained people going straight into professional and junior managerial posts is probably increasing, and the industry is certainly looking for more people with relevant qualifications for management.

Civil/structural engineers

Engineers are mostly civils and structurals, with some qualified in building services and electrical engineering. They account for more than 65% of professional staff employed in the industry. They work for combined building and civil engineering contractors, and for civil engineering contractors and consultants. The proportion working for general building firms is smaller, but probably rising. While civil/structural engineers employed by construction firms may do any work for which they are qualified, construction firms do not usually do much designing themselves, and normally employ consultant engineers for this. Most engineers work in, for example, contract preparation, planning and management, and in site management in the construction industry itself. *See* CIVIL AND STRUCTURAL ENGINEERING *below*.

In the past, civil engineers who worked for local authorities effectively became municipal engineers with a fairly wide remit. However, with the coming of compulsory competitive tendering (CCT), councils are no longer employing so many engineers directly. By 1997 all their engineering work must be subcontracted. What has happened, in many cases, is that civil engineers formerly employed by local councils have set up their own consultancies, which compete for a wide variety of construction work. *See also in* LOCAL GOVERNMENT.

Building services engineers

Building services engineers look at the environmental needs of buildings as a coherent problem, solving them by using engineering principles. Building services engineers plan and design mechanical, electrical/electronic, and electro-mechanical systems. These range from the commonplace heating and ventilating systems, plumbing and lighting, through the increasing use of air-conditioning in larger buildings, to the sophisticated systems needed by some industries to create particular kinds of environment. These include refrigeration for food storage, low-temperature areas for liquefying gases and other industrial processes, dust-free 'clean' rooms for firms manufacturing electronic equipment or involved in the production of compact discs, special ventilation to clear factory fumes, and sprinkler systems to douse fires.

Such systems have to be both efficient and economic, to give comfortable, hygienic and safe conditions. Building services engineers often need to know a great deal about other aspects of advanced building technology – to design and construct air-conditioning and heating systems for glass-clad buildings for example – or they may have to be very well briefed on a product to be stored, or on industrial processes which a building will house. They may influence the design of a new building – to get service piping, ducts, cables, etc. in a central 'core', and access for maintenance. Building services engineers also work on the development of new systems such as solar heating.

However, many engineers who actually work on building services still think of themselves as electrical, mechanical, or whatever their original specialisation was.

The professional organisation for building services engineers is the Chartered Institution of Building Services Engineers (CIBSE). A BTEC/SCOTVEC NC, together with a combination of practical training and experience, qualifies the holder to become a Licentiate of the CIBSE.

The holder may then register with the Engineering Council and use the letters 'EngTech, LCIBSE' after his or her name.

There are also a number of accredited degree programmes nationally which lead to Graduate Membership and fulfil the academic requirements for Chartered Engineer status (CEng). Those wishing to progress to registration as Chartered Engineers must complete further training and gain suitable experience in the field of building service engineering, the final stage of which is in the form of a Professional Competence Review.

Alternatively, school-leavers may enter into an apprenticeship as a student engineering technician. They join either a firm's own scheme or one operated by BEST (Building Engineering Services Training Ltd), on behalf of the Heating and Ventilating Contractors Association (HVCA). The successful apprentice obtains a BTEC/SCOTVEC NC in a building services engineering subject and NVQ/SVQs to at least level 3.

Further information

Careers literature is available from both the CIBSE and the HVCA.

Other engineers

Mechanical engineers research, design and produce much of the highly sophisticated machinery and equipment used in construction now, e.g. lift manufacture, heavy plant installation, power generation, and hydraulic and compressed-air services. *Electrical engineers* work for both general and specialist contractors, on electrical distribution and protection, control systems, power generation generally, etc.

Building control surveyors/inspectors

Building control surveyors are responsible for ensuring that buildings conform to regulations on public health, safety, energy conservation, and access for disabled persons. Building regulation approval is also required when structural changes are made to existing buildings, such as adding a kitchen extension to a private dwelling. Building control surveyors work indoors, checking plans, and outdoors in all weather, making site visits, to ensure that foundations are safe, walls put up correctly, ventilation adequate, and so on. A head for heights is necessary, as at times it may be necessary to climb on to scaffolding to inspect a roof.

Building control surveyors are employed mainly by local authorities and by the National House Building Council (NHBC). In local government, the building survey team is also responsible for dangerous structures and demolitions within the town or city, and often, in conjunction with the Fire Brigade, for fire protection.

The NHBC was set up some 60 years ago as the self-regulatory body of the house-building industry. The majority of new homes built each year in the UK are subject to NHBC warranty and insurance. Builder members have to operate according to a set of rules and standards. The NHBC's 400-strong field staff monitor new homes under construction, visiting sites to ensure that all construction practices conform with the NHBC's prescribed minimum standards. The builder then has an obligation to rectify any defects reported.

Qualifications and training

Minimum entry standards for student membership of the Institute of Building Control are five GCSEs (A–C), including maths, a science and a subject demonstrating use of English. Many building control employers, however, only recruit trainees with A-levels or degrees. Non-graduate entrants normally obtain a BTEC HNC/D in Building Studies by day- or block-release, followed by professional examinations set by the Institute. Applicants with degrees in building-related topics are eligible for exemption from some stages.

Surveyors

Surveyors are employed in quite large numbers in the industry with combined building and civil engineering contractors, for general building firms and a relatively small proportion for purely civil engineering contractors. Contractors' surveyors mostly measure work in progress and cost, although the work they do is changing. Only on very large-scale civil engineering projects do they do any land surveying as such (most people with qualifications in building or civil engineering learnt basic surveying, and on smaller projects general foremen or site engineers do the necessary survey work).

Building Surveyors in particular offer professional advice on many areas relating to the occupation and construction of property ranging from the design of large modern structures to facilities management. They are also involved in building control areas, contract administration and budget control, planned maintenance, project management, and building conservation, and act as planning supervisors.

The professional organisation for Building Surveyors is the Royal Institution of Chartered Surveyors (RICS) and approximately 10% of the overall 90,000 membership are Chartered Building Surveyors. The RICS is the foremost property organisation and has members worldwide. *See also in* LAND USE PROFESSIONS.

Architects

The industry employs comparatively few architects, who work mainly for general building firms or building and civil engineering contractors, although a number of smaller specialist (e.g. renovation) firms have builders and architects in partnership. Organisations with large-scale building operations, such as the NHS, also employ architectural staff, who work closely with other departments involved in construction. *See also in* LAND USE PROFESSIONS.

Engineering geologists

Engineering geologists carry out site investigations for building and civil engineering projects of all kinds. Any structure, be it foundations for a building, a bridge, a dam, a tunnel or a mine, has an impact upon the ground below. In its turn, the ground itself has an impact upon the structure. If a road is being built, and a cutting is necessary, then the engineering geologist looks at the geology and the properties of the rocks, to enable the slope to be designed to the correct angle so that the cutting is stable.

Engineering geologists work with planners to advise on the implications of planning decisions. One does not want, for instance, to build a large housing estate on top of useful mineral resources nor locate a waste disposal site above an aquifer providing drinking water. They are also concerned with the assessment of geological hazards such as landslides or ground subsidence due to shrinkage of clay soils in very dry weather.

In their work they use maps, reports, aerial photographs and satellite imagery as necessary, drill boreholes to check ground conditions and collect soil and rock samples. The samples are then tested for their physical, mechanical and sometimes chemical properties. In some cases geophysical surveys are carried out.

Qualifications and training

A first degree in either geology or civil engineering is advisable, followed by a master's degree in engineering geology. Without the latter, it is increasingly difficult to get a job. Some 50–70 postgraduates complete MSc courses each year and the majority do find relevant posts. The Engineering Group of the Geological Society encourages all engineering geologists to work towards chartered status (CGeol).

Further information

The Engineering Group of the Geological Society.

Builders' merchants

Builders' merchants supply the industry with materials of all kinds. To operate successfully, builders' merchants must understand the way in which both the construction industry and producers operate, they must keep up with new products and materials and new construction methods. They have to cope with the industry's periods of expansion and contraction, keeping producers informed of future demand and avoiding both shortages and overstocking in their own warehouses. Many builders' merchants now also cater for the general public, with the growth in 'do-it-yourself', which now accounts for about 24% of turnover.

Builders' merchants provide technical and cost information for building firms, deliver materials (often on schedules agreed in advance), and have showrooms for both the trade and public up and down the country. There are 6,500 firms altogether, as follows:

- builders' merchants 3900
- decorators' merchants 600
- plumbers' merchants 1000
- timber merchants 400
- other merchants 150

Ten major firms are responsible for about 60% of the turnover. The biggest firm, Wolseley Centers [sic], has some 450 branches in the UK and about 4,500 employees. Some firms are one-man businesses. The average firm employs about six or seven, and a larger outlet perhaps 20.

As a form of retailer, the builders' merchant is increasingly using self-service and pre-packaging. Some firms specialise in 'heavy' goods (bricks, cement and so on) and others in 'light' (pipes, baths, taps, etc.), but recession in building means merchants must sell as many items as possible, and more firms now combine both. There are some special firms, such as bulk cementmakers and suppliers, and the architectural ironmongers who specialise in the supply of door and window fittings, handles, knobs, locks, and so on.

Builders' merchants are like warehouses. Selling, to both the trade and the public, off the counter and for advance schedules, is obviously most important, but it has to be supported by efficient purchasing, stock control and warehousing, estimating and costing, financial management, computer programming, and in some firms even making and assembling components, and producing designs and technical drawings. Some firms make up fireplaces or assemble plumbing equipment, for example.

Efficient distribution is also crucial. Palletisation and packaging of bulk materials now facilitate the mechanised handling of products and the loading of builders' collecting vehicles, while crane lorries are generally used for site deliveries.

The Builders Merchants Federation, with a membership of about 400, whose turnover totals about £6.5 billion, has approval to run a modern apprenticeship scheme which will deliver training to NVQ level 3 over about three years.

Further information

Builders Merchants Federation.

Technicians

There are some 60,000 technicians, draughtsmen/women, and foremen in the construction industry. Most work for the larger firms, the combined building and civil engineering contractors, but an increasing number/proportion work for general building firms. A relatively high proportion of draughtsmen/women work for specialist constructional engineering firms, or for firms of heating and ventilating engineers.

Most foremen and supervisory staff work their way up from craft levels through trade foremen (with on-site responsibility for all craftworkers, apprentices and labourers in their own trade). They will have had extensive experience in their own trades, must be able to solve problems and be good at explaining. General foremen have to know a fair amount about all the trades on the site as well as the one in which they were trained.

Draughtsmen/women prepare detailed working drawings and plans for everything; from diagrams showing geological structures, plotting features of bridges or road routes, through to structural steelwork and concrete, and to drawings of individual installations, such as central heating, for subcontractors.

The other main group of technicians work for surveyors and/or in surveying departments, particularly quantity surveying, where they do contract work: costings and compiling tenders, final accounts, etc. They may do land surveying, soil testing, manage plant and equipment on site, do site investigation, or manage traffic. Larger firms, especially in civil engineering, use technicians in laboratory work, in testing and specifying concrete mixes and so on. In some of these areas there is more scope in working for civil engineering consultants.

People get into technician-level work by a number of different routes, in the past mostly from craftwork, but increasingly direct from school or FE college. Technician-level work is still a possible route into management, and professional qualification, although it is getting more difficult.

Craftworkers

Craftworkers still form the backbone of the industry. Most work for general building firms and building and civil engineering contractors, a relatively small proportion for purely civil engineering firms and the rest for specialist firms and subcontractors. Local authorities, property companies, and some industrial and commercial firms employ craftworkers to do maintenance work, and some building. Whether the work is on a massive housing estate, or repair and conversion for a small local jobbing builder, the work within each craft or trade is more or less the same.

The industry has some 19 or more recognised crafts and trades. They include: carpenters/joiners; electricians; painters; bricklayers; plumbers; heating/ventilating engineers; plasterers; mechanical equipment operators, roof slaters/tilers; glaziers; floor/wall tilers; masons; paviours; steel erectors and sheeters.

Fully qualified craftworkers are trained to work on their own, or as part of a small team. They are responsible for the quality of their own work, and for planning it. Craftsmen and women work to technical drawings or notes, must measure very accurately, and be able to work well with their hands.

Qualified craftworkers may be promoted to foreman and supervisor, and from there can go on to management, although the route up is becoming tougher, especially in larger organisations. They may also become, e.g., sales representatives, building inspectors, or craft instructors. Recently, many more have become self-employed, working part of their time directly for clients, part for building firms, as work is available.

Recruitment and entry

The industry recruits at all levels. The recession has led to less recruitment but, if the industry is to become and stay profitable, it must increase the proportion of skilled managers. Hence the need for more professionally trained and graduate and technician staff.

Professional-level engineers of all kinds, and architects, normally complete a full-time or sandwich-based degree or degree-equivalent course before entry. It is increasingly common for building technologists and surveyors to do the same, although they can also start out in the industry. *See* BUILDING TECHNOLOGY *below*.

Technicians training in architectural work, building, or surveying normally start at either 16 or 17 (with at least four GCSE or equivalent passes at 16-plus) or 18-plus (having studied two A-level subjects and passed in one, or equivalent) and train on the job with release to study for qualifications, although they can opt for a full-time or sandwich-based course first.

Craft and trade skills. Although the outlook for the construction industry has not been rosy in recent years, there are skill shortages.

Qualifications and training

The main training agent for the construction industry is the Construction Industry Training Board (CITB) through its two-year schemes; the remaining training is carried out at further education colleges.

The CITB deals with the development of training at all levels from managerial and supervisory levels through to craft and general work. In 1994/95 the CITB Field Service recruited 9,178 youth trainees, and the total number in training as at 31 March 1995 was 10,987. Because the number of school-leavers wishing to enter the construction industry continued to fall, the CITB pioneered a full-time craft construction course in FE colleges. The CITB continues to work as a managing agent for the provision of youth new-entrant training through TECs and LECs, and has developed a modern apprenticeship scheme; 42 trainees were signed up in January 1995 in a prototype scheme run conjointly between the CITB and Manchester TEC.

While CITB supports training at all levels, and throughout the industry, running its own training centres, etc., the Board's main effort goes into new-entrant training.

Professional/graduate training

The industry, mostly in the largest firms, mainly provides the all-round training and experience needed for professional qualification for civil, mechanical and electrical engineers, surveyors, etc. CITB provides off-the-job training, for new graduate entrants and management, etc., at its national centres.

Technician and craft level

New-entrant training: CITB is primary YT managing agent for the whole construction industry, and this is the preferred route for new entrants, at operative, craft and technician level. Trainees may be employed or not employed. There are various different methods of entry, depending on the training agreement entered.

Some schemes have specific entry requirements, e.g. the electricians scheme: good GCSE or equivalent passes at 16-plus in English, maths, and a science are recommended as the minimum for success in the exams. All applicants are required to take selection and aptitude tests.

Electrical contracting industry trainees go into employment from the start of their scheme. On other schemes the aim is to have trainees in employment by the end of the first year. Trainees may be registered under formal agreements, according to industry sector.

Schemes cover the basic training for all building/construction trades, skills, technician-level work and clerical work. Schemes are tailored to the needs of the particular sector/skills, but all combine off-the-job training with work experience and training on the job. Technicians continue into a third year of training, and some craft/mechanic/operative schemes allow trainees who have done well to go on to technician-level training.

BTEC courses

BTEC Continuing Education Diploma, designed to help technicians to make the transition from 'middle' to 'senior' management and for many disciplines, offers the chance to move towards chartered status.

BTEC Higher National Certificates and Diplomas, are intended to develop the reasoning of 'how, why, where, and when' to use a particular approach to tackling a problem, and an appreciation of the economic, legislative and contractual constraints within which the technician has to operate. Most higher national courses include coverage of 'management skills', both company and personal, required to work effectively at a 'middle-management' level. The certificate is normally studied two years part-time with day-release, the diploma two years full-time plus work experience, or three years sandwich.

BTEC National Certificates and Diplomas develop the technical skills appropriate to particular areas of study and the ways in which problems are approached. Courses for building, building services and civil engineering technicians also include applied science and the mathematics needed to support it. Land administration courses provide an introduction to the economic and legislative constraints that have an influence on technical decisions, whilst surveying and cartography courses include applied technology and the graphics/mathematics support necessary to make it effective. The certificate is normally studied two years part-time with day-release, the diploma two years full-time plus work experience. Entry requirements are as for all BTEC nationals but GCSE-level-equivalent passes should include some relevant subjects.

BTEC First Certificates and Diplomas provide a grounding in communications, science and mathematics together with a broad introduction to construction. The certificate is studied one year with day release, the diploma one year full-time plus work experience.

National vocational qualifications

NVQs are replacing the traditional craft certifications and are available at levels 1–4.

Further information

The Construction Industry Training Board Careers Advisory Service.

Building technology

Building technologists work mainly for the larger general building contractors in the building/construction industry. Very few work for non-building firms. Firms manufacturing building equipment, especially of the more sophisticated 'industrial' kind, also employ technologists, and some work for property developers. Building technologists are employed in the public sector, a high proportion of them in local government, relatively few in central government. A significant proportion work for consultancies, and quite a few teach.

They work in management, often as general managers or project managers. Others become surveyors, or quantity surveyors. Smaller numbers work in estimating; design; property development, maintenance and management; site supervision, quality control, production planning and control. A few work in training, work study, purchasing, and sales. Comparatively few work in research and development (R&D).

Qualifications and training

The use of modern technologies in the construction industry means the building technologist must learn much more about the fundamental sciences. Modern building techniques depend heavily on the right, and often new, materials, so materials science and technology is part of building courses. Structural and environmental engineering are major subjects of study. Surveying, building economics, contract work, and managerial and site-control techniques are also taught.

At professional level, it is increasingly useful to study for a degree. The construction industry would like to recruit more specialist graduates, and a variety of university and polytechnic degree courses are offered throughout the country. Relevant three- and four-year courses leading to BA or BSc degrees include: building; building economics and quantity surveying; building technology; building linked to architecture; planning and environmental studies; building construction and management; building surveying including a building production option.

Managers in construction and building technology may belong to one of three bodies: the Royal Institution of Chartered Surveyors (RICS), the Chartered Institute of

Building (CIOB), and the Association of Building Engineers (ABE).

Broadly based, the CIOB created a route to professional status for construction technicians. Membership is divided into three levels: professional level; higher technician and technician level; and for those undergoing training/practical experience. The institute has a membership of 33,000 and is the qualifying association for the building industry. Its exams are taken in June by some 3,500 candidates at centres in the UK and overseas at higher-technician and degree level, and are designed to produce the general practitioner in building.

The Institute recognises appropriate exempting qualifications. Building technicians at higher level qualify via BTEC and SCOTVEC Higher National awards. Entry is as for all BTEC Higher National awards; if via A-levels, the pass should be in maths or a science, with the other studied to A-level.

Building technicians at the lower level qualify via BTEC/SCOTVEC National awards. National Certificate/ Diploma courses are given at over 160 colleges countrywide. Entry is as for all BTEC National awards, with GCSE/SCE grades normally including maths, applied science and English language. Craft-level qualifications are those set by City & Guilds and will eventually be replaced by NVQ/SVQs available to level 4.

The principal route to professional menbership of the Association of Building Engineers (formerly the Incorporated Association of Architects and Surveyors) is by way of an accredited construction-related classified honours degree. Admission to the Associate Member (senior technician) class is open to candidates having not less than two years approved work place experience who hold an academic qualification of a standard not less than that of an appropriate BTEC or SCOTVEC Higher National Award.

Further information

The Chartered Institute of Building, the Association of Building Engineers (careers booklets and leaflets), and the Construction Industry Training Board.

Civil and structural engineering

These disciplines underpin the design and construction of many different kinds of structures. They include road and railway systems (including bridges, flyovers and tunnels), airports, harbours, docks and canals, dams and barrages, coastal protection systems, sports stadia, irrigation systems, and structures and systems for services such as water, gas, sewerage and electricity, and for mining. Traditionally, civil engineering dealt only with unroofed structures, but civil engineering principles and techniques have to be used in designing and constructing very large buildings which need very deep foundations and steel or stressed-concrete frames. This has led civil engineers to be closely involved right from the design stage in projects like the Sydney Opera House and the Lloyd's building in the City of London.

Many civil engineering structures today are increasingly massive in scale, and get more adventurous all the time, which means extremely complex problems have to be solved. The Channel Tunnel is probably one of the most ambitious civil engineering projects ever undertaken.

Civil engineering has a number of sub-branches, and most civil engineers eventually develop their expertise in one of these and/or in working in particular areas of construction. But it is usual to qualify and gain plenty of broad-based experience before specialising. The main sub-branches:

- Structural engineers deal with stresses and strains, and ensure that structures are safe. They have to learn about structural materials and mechanics, local and national regulations, and British Standards specifications in just about the full range of civil engineering construction work.
- Municipal engineers work for local authorities and are legally responsible for, e.g., planning, highways, sewerage, lighting, building and housing, traffic engineering, transport, parks, playing fields, cemeteries, building control, cleansing and refuse collection. However, much of the work is now subcontracted under compulsory competitive tendering.
- Water engineers either specialise in water conservation and work on the construction of dams, water towers, pumping stations and supply, or work for the National Rivers Authority (NRA) or other water companies, or help to develop hydroelectric schemes.
- Public health engineers specialise in designing, constructing and maintaining sewage and waste treatment and disposal systems, sanitation, heating, lighting and ventilating (*see also* Building Services Engineers *under* WORKING IN THE INDUSTRY *above*).
- Highway and traffic engineers deal mainly with road and bridge design, construction, planning and maintenance, but increasingly also with traffic-control systems and planning.

The civil engineering design process must be based on extensive information about the site and the way it relates to and affects the surrounding area. This often involves younger engineers in making ground and soil surveys. Accurate measurement for all projects is crucial. Roads, bridges and tunnels built from both ends must meet exactly in the middle; complex road intersections must be fitted into the smallest possible site.

Every large project involves laboratory analysis (of soil and rock samples, for instance), model-testing and computer simulation and analysis both before the designers start work and throughout the process. A great many calculations have to go into working out forces and stresses; resistance to wind and water (or other pressures); and choice of materials, etc. Computer-aided design systems now play a major part: most of the routine drawing work is done on computer-driven plotters.

Designers look for an optimum solution, which takes into account economy, safety and environmental factors as well as more obvious design criteria. They use computer-based analysis for this, too. The size and sophistication of modern structures, and the new techniques and materials available to them, mean that civil engineers depend increasingly on close cooperation with other experts.

In any case, civil engineers have to work very closely with everyone else concerned in the project, from the authority or firm commissioning it (which means politicians, planners and other officials) to the contractor and architects, building managers, and surveyors.

Once the design is complete, materials, etc., have to be specified in detail, costings made, tenders put out, and contractors briefed. On site, professional engineers are responsible for 'setting-out' and general preparation (such as seeing that safety precautions are taken), and go on – as 'resident' (increasingly 'project') engineer – to monitor and supervise, organising the work so that people, materials and machines are there as needed, and that work is kept on schedule (often just as difficult in a busy city centre as in the depths of a vast desert); anticipating and solving the inevitable day-to-day problems; and trying to see that normal activity in the area can go on with minimal interruption.

Although civil engineering is a huge area of knowledge, there are just three professional qualifications – these are Chartered engineer, Incorporated engineer, and engineering technician. The majority of civil engineers work in or close to their branch of engineering.

Chartered engineers

Chartered engineers work in construction and installation work, as consultants, and in development and design (for consultants or contractors) and a few are involved in research work, mostly in research stations, but with some posts in industry. Examples of their work include problems of corrosion, or the strength of water-retaining structures.

Some chartered engineers have become general administrators or managers. Others work in maintenance and servicing, teach or lecture. Very small percentages are employed in manufacturing and production, quality control, management services, or marketing and sales.

Not surprisingly, most work in the civil engineering industry, also in building, municipal engineering, water supply and transport. Employers include local authorities, independent engineering consulting practices, civil engineering contractors, central government, public corporations, and nationalised industries.

A few work for manufacturers who design and build large industrial plant (e.g. power stations, or chemical and petrochemical complexes). There is structural design work for a few in, e.g., the aircraft and steel industries. Civil engineers have always moved around a lot in their work, but recent recession has pushed firms into greater efforts than ever to obtain contracts abroad. This provides opportunities for civil engineers to spend some time overseas, though most of the work is undertaken and supervised by local personnel.

Incorporated engineers and engineering technicians

Teamwork, say the professional institutions, is the keystone of civil engineering. Chartered engineers depend considerably on the support of incorporated engineers and engineering technicians.

They work in design offices, as draughtsmen and women (now more often than not using computer-driven equipment), preparing general arrangement and layout drawings, and detail structural elements, working details and schedules, formwork and other temporary works.

They help to make calculations; select materials, components, and plant; collect technical data on different construction methods, etc.; make routine specification clauses and decide on quantities; work out the best way to organise a construction project; look after safety measures, and so on.

On site, incorporated engineers and engineering technicians provide the support in, e.g., project management and site supervision, with possible promotion to clerk of works, site agent, contract work, etc. Incorporated engineers, as in all branches of engineering, are expected to be able to exercise independent technical judgement, assume personal responsibility to management level, and carry out technical duties.

Qualifications and training

Chartered engineers

The normal route to becoming a chartered civil engineer is an accredited honours degree in civil engineering followed by appropriate training and experience with an employer approved for training.

After an appropriate period of professional experience they may apply to take the Chartered Professional Review (CPR). After passing CPR the candidate may become a Member of the Institution of Civil Engineers (MICE). The Institution will then register the successful candidate as a Chartered Engineer (CEng).

Entry requirements for a degree in civil engineering are usually A-levels/H grades in maths, physics and another subject. Relevant first-degree courses (many with specialist options) in civil/structural engineering of usually three or four years' duration lead to BSc/BEng/MEng, and are available at universities throughout the country

'First destination' figures for civil engineering graduates are (1994):

total graduating	*1,739*
research/further study	223
believed unemployed 31 December	154
permanent UK employment	774
employers	
Civil Service	7
HM Forces	15
local government	50
education	13
engineering and allied industry	27

building/civil engineering and architecture	462
public utilities	45
commerce	90
functions	
engineering R&D	82
administration/operations management	22
scientific/engineering support	21
environmental planning	494
buying, marketing and selling	13
management services	34
financial work	37

Postgraduate studies higher-degree/diploma courses in advanced civil and/or structural engineering are offered at a number of universities, but most postgraduate courses are designed to give graduates more specialised training.

Incorporated engineers

Training for incorporated engineer is normally via a BTEC or SCOTVEC Higher National award, taken on a full-time/sandwich or part-time basis. BTEC HNC/HND courses in civil engineering studies, together with training and a professional review/examination of the Institution of Civil Engineers, Institution of Structural Engineers, or the Institute of Highway Incorporated Engineers lead to qualification as an incorporated engineer. Entry requirements to the HND course is with one suitable A-level/H grade (normally maths or physics) or with BTEC/SCOTVEC Certificate/Diploma. HND courses (two years full-time/three years sandwich) and HNC courses (two years part-time) are available at colleges throughout the country.

The Institution of Structural Engineers has associate membership for incorporated engineers with qualifications equivalent to a BTEC Higher National award in appropriate subjects, plus experience in a responsible post.

Engineering-technician qualification is normally via BTEC/SCOTVEC National Certificate/Diploma course in civil engineering studies with workplace training during and after the course and professional interview/examination of the Institution of Civil Engineers or the Institute of Highway Incorporated Engineers. Entry is with four GCSE/S grades (typically maths, science, English, and a foreign language). Full-time/sandwich/part-time courses are available at colleges throughout the country. BTEC First National awards: *see* WORKING IN THE INDUSTRY *above*.

NVQ/SVQs to level 5 in construction are being introduced.

Professional bodies include – The Institution of Civil Engineers, Institution of Structural Engineers, Institute of Highways Incorporated Engineers.

Further information

The Civil Engineering Careers Service, Engineering Training Authority, and above professional bodies.

Contents

Land Use Professions

(CLCI: UB, UH, UL, UM, US, UT)

Background

The roles of the professions involved in creating, improving, managing and maintaining an environment for people to live, work, and play in seemed to be clearly defined and firmly fixed. The architect was often seen as aloof from the commercial/profit motive, concerned solely with style, taste, and aesthetics. Developing new kinds of structures was left to the civil/structural engineer, and costing the project to the surveyor. But the modern property and construction business now uses professionals rather more interchangeably than the careers literature suggests, particularly in managing a project, in controlling and managing building, rebuilding and renovation. Clients decide for themselves whom to put in overall charge.

Competition is increasing between the professions, especially between architects, surveyors, and today's sophisticated and highly qualified building managers (*see* THE CONSTRUCTION INDUSTRY). As a result, the architectural code of practice has been revised to allow architects to have a direct interest in property development companies, manufacturing and contracting. However, building may have become too complex technologically and too commercialised for architects to keep their assumed automatic leadership of the building professions. Given, though, the modern problems of large-scale building – ensuring safety; giving maximum benefit for cost; reducing energy costs; designing buildings which use, and can be used for, modern technology – commentators think it is crucial that these professions should move more closely together, and should all learn the same basic skills.

Architecture

Architects design buildings of all kinds. They can be 'one-off' houses, but are more usually a number of homes for a new estate. They may be single office blocks or stores, or complete shopping centres and precincts, office complexes or city centres. They may be single factories or warehouses or complete industrial estates. They may be hospitals or sports centres, schools or town halls, theatres or colleges. Architects also 'design' conversions, extensions and modernisations of older buildings, creating flats from family houses or historic warehouses; updating hotels; and turning churches or mills into homes; old factories into sets of small offices, workshops and studios; and large old-fashioned cinemas into complexes of smaller ones.

Design is not just a matter of sketching a three-dimensional drawing of a building or group of buildings so that they will look good aesthetically, fit into the surroundings, be interesting or startling, impress the critics, or project an impressive image for the owners. The design has to be practical in all sorts of ways. The architect has to produce a structurally sound building, and so, on larger projects, will work closely with engineers skilled in working out how this is to be done. Being practical also means not choosing materials for their appearance alone, because these can dictate what can and cannot be done, taking into account qualities such as strength, and length of life, and cost.

Then the building should work for the people who are going to use it, which should mean much consultation, finding out about and taking into account the different ways in which people live. Buildings being designed now must take greater account of energy-saving. Costs and budgets are all important, and the final design is inevitably a compromise between frequently conflicting demands of aesthetics and practicality within the confines of a set, and often tight, budget.

The architect's job does not end when the drawings and plans are accepted by the customer. Traditionally, the architect then becomes a manager to see that paper drawings become a brick-and-concrete reality. The architect's office must gain planning permission, and prepare and negotiate contracts, using detailed working drawings, specifications and estimates. The architect may still be in charge when building starts, overseeing work on site, inspecting it as it progresses, giving instructions, discussing problems and certifying that payments can be made when agreed stages of construction are completed.

Working in architecture

Architecture is a broadly based profession including in-house company architecture; private practice; central-government and local-authority architecture; co-operatives; and lecturing and teaching. There are also many related areas such as publishing and journalism, interior design, town planning and property development.

British architectural training is highly regarded, and the profession offers many opportunities for British architects to work overseas. A knowledge of languages is becoming an increasingly important asset.

The Architects' Journal workload survey for the third quarter of 1995 showed only small relief from the continuing downturn in prospects. In recent years architects have been hit by the recession in the construction industry and a cut in public-sector spending.

Work in private housing was sharply down, countered by a rise in retail work, and a firming up in office work. A large proportion of retail work consisted of refurbishment (30%). A gleam of hope was afforded by the fact that new commissions were 14% higher than at the same time in the previous year. The leisure sector was said to look healthy, with a continued rise in new commissions, whereas there was a 58% fall in health-sector work.

There were about 24,000 architects in the 1995 workforce, of whom 5% were not working, 10% working part-time and 85% full-time. The RIBA survey on 'Architects' Employment and Earnings 1995' showed 72% of full-time architects to be in private practice, 9% in private in-house, 6% in central government, and 13% with local authorities. Private practices range in size from one or two principals working alone, or with a few assistants, to very large offices with a staff of 51-plus. Some multiprofessional building design groups are more than 500-strong, but architects may make up only a third of the staff, the rest being civil, structural and service engineers, quantity surveyors, and interior, graphic and product designers, plus technical support staff.

While some architects do work on their own, it is more usual to be a member of a team, each team handling a particular project. The team may consist solely of architects or may be multidisciplinary, depending on the project, and its complexity obviously determines the size of the team. The team will include qualified architects of varying experience, under a team leader, and may also include newly qualified architects completing their training, as well as architectural technologists.

Design work is generally split between members of the team, with the easier items going to the juniors who gain their experience this way. Most architects now expect to make use of computer-aided design systems. The technology has given architects a whole new freedom: to clad a building entirely in glass or cover a vast area with a roof supported only on the perimeter. This is a career which combines artistic design with a hard practical technological output and administration/management of building operations. It combines the office-based work, increasingly on VDU screen instead of drawing-board, and deskwork dealing with reports, estimates, specifications, etc., with the climbing around in the mud and apparent chaos of working on a building site. It involves endless meetings and discussion with clients, other experts, planners, builders and so on.

Recruitment and entry

A person may not use the title 'architect' until he or she has completed the statutory qualifications and training, and registered with the Architects Registration Council of the UK. Once qualified, most young architects go into employment, either in private practice or with an employer, since starting a practice requires financial resources and plenty of experience of the business as well as the professional side of architecture.

Prospective architects need to be numerate, and to combine creativity and imagination with the ability to absorb, understand and use very technical data. They need to be logically and analytically minded, to be able to plan buildings, and also to deal with the design and construction process. This takes administrative potential and some business skills.

Qualifications and training

While architecture is, for most people, a vocational training for a specific career, it is also an interesting subject for study in its own right. Degree courses have been broadened, and while they are still strongly design-based, and primarily studio-taught, studying aesthetics and architectural history in depth, courses have also to give plenty of time to building science and technology, and the construction process. Schools train students to use computer-aided design. Courses also cover the environmental setting of architectural design, via urban planning and the planning process, and behavioural and social sciences.

Architecture is usually studied almost entirely full-time, although many schools offer part-time courses. Most schools of architecture have two-part structures to give a first degree in architecture after three years, and a postgraduate award after a further two. There are 38 schools of architecture in the UK with courses that are recognised by the RIBA.

Entry to a degree course at architectural college or university is generally straight from school, after A-levels/H grades. Minimum entry requirements are at least five GCSEs and two A-levels or the Scottish equivalent. English language, mathematics and a science are usually compulsory, with other subjects drawn from a mix of arts and sciences, or via BTEC/SCOTVEC National Certificate/Diploma in building studies.

An Advanced GNVQ/GSVQ in Art and Design or the Built Environment may be acceptable at some universities, but additional GCSE or A-levels may be required. RIBA recommends that GNVQs are combined with A-levels because the qualification has 'yet to achieve a tried and tested status, as it is very early days in their development'.

To qualify as an architect takes a minimum of seven years. However, this can be spread over a longer period through part-time and day-release courses. Salaried work experience is an integral part of the architect's training, and it is during this intensely practical period that an architectural student can gain firsthand experience of the long-term career opportunities. No one can practise as an architect in the UK until they have obtained the statutory educational and professional qualifications. Students must have passed, or gained exemption from, Parts 1, 2 and 3 of the RIBA (Royal Institute of British Architects) Examinations in Architecture.

They must also have spent a minimum of two years working in an architectural office.

RIBA sets its own examinations, but all architects must, by law, register with the Architects' Registration Council of the United Kingdom (ARCUK), and the RIBA examinations are only one of the qualifications (which include those from overseas schools) recognised by the Council. Both ARCUK and RIBA list schools and courses they approve.

'First destination' figures for graduates are (1994):

total graduating	*473*
total employment	264
research/academic study	28
teacher training	2
Law Society and Bar exams	1
other training	27
believed to be unemployed at 31 December	30
employers	
architecture, etc.	159
local authorities	19
commerce, banking, etc.	8
Civil Service	2
functions	
environmental planning	186

Architectural technologists

Architectural technologists work closely with fellow professionals, including architects, on building projects. They are concerned with the technological aspects of building design and construction, from the initial client briefing to completion of the project. They work in architectural practices, in local authority planning offices, in central government, and for building contractors and housing associations. Many set up in practice either on their own or in partnership with architects or other members of the construction industry.

The work varies, depending on where they work. It may, for example, include office or project management, inspection and certification of construction work, site inspection and quality control. Architectural technologists are experts at the application of computer-aided design (CAD) techniques and may also make design presentations. In some posts they undertake land and building surveying, the collection and analysis of technical data, the selection and specification of materials, and feasibility studies.

The architectural technologist generally works as part of a design team, so a willingness to deal and work with other people is an essential ingredient of the job. An ability to visualise objects in three dimensions is an asset. The architectural technologist needs to be a good communicator and to possess a methodical, practical and enquiring mind.

The demand for skilled architectural technologists has continued to grow throughout the building, design and architectural professions. For well-qualified and experienced architectural technologists it can be a job with considerable responsibility.

Recruitment and entry

There are various different ways in which one may become an architectural technologist. Some will become trainees on leaving school and study for appropriate qualifications. Others will obtain higher qualifications before seeking a post.

Qualifications and training

There are various routes to membership of the British Institute of Architectural Technologists. Associate membership requires a degree or HND/HNC or higher-level NVQ/SVQ in Architectural Technology or in another technology-based environment subject. Full membership requires the completion of a two-year practice qualification (i.e. a diary), and attending a formal interview arranged by the institutions is an asset.

Useful subjects to study at GCSE include maths, sciences, technology, art and English. After GCSE the following choices are available:

1 A/AS-levels in science and technology subjects, followed by a degree in architectural technology or a related subject, or HNC/HND in building studies with architectural options;
2 BTEC NC/ND in building studies, followed by either a degree in architectural technology or related subject, or HNC/HND in building studies with architectural options;
3 GNVQ in the built environment (advanced level), followed by the degree or HNC/HND as above;
4 Finding employment and studying for higher-level NVQ/SVQs. It is projected that registration for level 4 NVQ/SVQ in architectural technology will begin late in 1996.

Minimum entry requirements for a BTEC/SCOTVEC ND are four GCSEs, or the Scottish equivalent, including mathematics and physics, chemistry or general science, and English (or a written English subject). Some colleges will accept students with lesser qualifications, if they are satisfied that the applicant has the potential to complete the course. A-levels/H grades, particularly maths and science, may allow entry onto an intermediate 'bridge' course or to recognised degree courses.

Further information

The Architects' Registration Council of the United Kingdom, Royal Institute of British Architects (leaflets and a list of recognised schools), the Royal Incorporation of Architects in Scotland, British Institute of Architectural Technologists (leaflets and directory of approved courses).

Cartography

This is 'the art, science and technology of making maps' of all types, as well as plans, charts, sections, three-dimensional models and globes, together 'with their study as scientific documents and works of art'. Map-making has become both easier and more innovative by the continuing adoption of modern technologies of all kinds. Map-makers routinely use aerial surveys, environmental remote sensing, seismic sensing methods, and satellite observation to give them better, more interesting and more accurate information. Computer-based techniques, including Geographic Information Systems (GIS), mean maps can be prepared automatically, and therefore more accurately, with better quality, and faster. The greater use of reprographic techniques, colour, infrared and false-colour photography, three-dimensional graphic techniques, etc., coupled with the employment of improved printing methods, also computer-controlled, give the cartographer increased freedom in the preparation of effective media of communication.

This also means that maps can be much more sophisticated, and provide more and different information – in cartographic jargon, 'spatial variations and relationships'. Map-makers can show the contours of the seabeds (crucial for the North Sea oil industry), or the results of, e.g., infrared satellite photography, which can be used to map cities or mineral resources. Synoptic surveys of magnetic differences give aeromagnetic and gravity maps. Maps illustrate statistical variation in graphic form, e.g., patterns of unemployment, population differences, areas of industrial use, or the distribution of particular animals. Photographs of the moon and planets are also turned into maps.

Working in cartography

The profession is small. Estimates suggest that there are not many more than 3,500 posts in the UK for suitably fully qualified staff. It is a two-tier occupation:

Cartographers (they may also be called editors or mapping and charting officers) research and then analyse and evaluate cartographic, geographic, photographic or statistical information for authenticity, accuracy, etc., and then 'edit' it in line with agreed specification.

Cartographic draughtsmen/women actually produce the map, chart or equivalent. The work may still involve hand-drawing, but increasingly the information is stored in computers programmed to produce the particular map required. They organise the graphic processing and map design, and produce final documents for printing.

Employers

While the list of organisations employing cartographic staff is quite long, few employ more than a handful.

Government departments are the major employers of cartographic staff (nearly 2,000 cartographic/recording draughtsmen/women alone). The largest is Ordnance Survey, but they also include Ministry of Defence units and departments, the Meteorological Office, the Hydrographic Office, the Departments of the Environment and Transport, the Ministry of Agriculture, and the Directorate of Military Survey. NERC employs cartographers in the British Geological Survey, the Institute of Oceanographic Sciences, and its information services. Other national-body employers include British Telecom, British Coal, British Gas, the Civil Aviation Authority, and the Forestry Commission.

Local-authority architect and planning departments employ cartographers to produce maps, plans and other illustrative materials. Most university geography departments employ cartographic technicians, where they may experiment with and design and produce visual aids.

Commercial employers include about 25 map printers/publishers and cartographic companies; some dozen land, sea and air survey companies; the larger civil engineering contractors; oil and other exploration companies; and a few service organisations (e.g. the AA and RAC).

Digital or computer-assisted cartography has opened up opportunities for cartographic staff to go into R&D, sales, machine operating, software engineering/programming, etc. At least 20 companies are employing qualified cartographic staff.

Recruitment and entry

Competition is stiff for the comparatively few vacancies, and limits on public expenditure have cut job numbers. Cartographers are normally expected to have a relevant degree and/or appropriate postgraduate training. Cartographic draughtsmen/women are traditionally trained on the job with day-release to study, but the availability of full-time pre-entry courses has cut the number of training places. *See also* CENTRAL GOVERNMENT.

Qualifications and training

At two levels:

Cartographers normally have a relevant degree in, e.g., geography or surveying, or a postgraduate diploma. Specialist first-degree courses at, e.g. Glasgow (topographical science BSc); Newcastle (surveying science BSc); Swansea (geography BA/BSc including options in topographic science/cartography); East London (surveying and mapping sciences BSc); Kingston (geographical and information systems); Oxford Brookes (modular BA/BSc in cartography and another subject).

Some cartographic training is included in university geography courses at Aberdeen, Edinburgh, Glasgow, Hull, Keele, Leeds, Leicester, London: UCL, Portsmouth, Kingston and Luton.

Postgraduate qualifications: Glasgow (diploma in cartography, and geoinformation technology); Swansea (diploma in topographic science).

Cartographic draughtsmen/women normally qualify via the BTEC/SCOTVEC award in land use and surveying (*see* SURVEYING *below*).

Further information

The British Cartographic Society.

Housing management

Most professional housing managers work for local authorities, which between them still (1994) own about 20% of the country's housing stock, although quite a few are employed by non-profitmaking housing associations and trusts, and by some property companies owning flats, or their managing agents.

A large local authority may have over 60,000 houses and/or individual flats to let, maintain and improve, and housing demands expert management. Housing departments have to advise the authority on housing policy under strict cash and political restrictions (local authorities' capital expenditure on housing in 1994/95 was £1.54 billion, with £1.59 billion capital receipts): e.g. monitoring and assessing need and how best to cope with it; preparing or revising any new-housing programme; deciding where and how to renew and renovate old property; consulting with architects and other authority staff in planning and designing new or renovated property; and looking for ways to improve life on estates with major problems in high-stress urban areas. Efficient management is essential both to meet the needs of the community and to make best use of declining resources.

Housing departments may manage not only rented accommodation, but also authority-owned shops and community halls and sheltered housing, and appoint and supervise wardens, caretakers and estate staff. They cope with all the practicalities of day-to-day running of housing: organising rent collection and dealing with arrears; interviewing people who need housing and helping the homeless; allocating and letting houses; visiting people to assess their housing needs or to see if property needs repairing (and organising the work); and finding ways to involve tenants in running estates or blocks of flats.

Most are involved in housing welfare and liaise with social services, and many provide housing advisory services, and coordinate housing association activities. Many do some research. A proportion administer house purchase schemes, and grants.

A local-authority housing department administering 70,000 or more properties (the average is about 11,000) may have a staff of around 650, of whom some 250 will be professional staff. In large authorities it is common to specialise, in e.g. housing advice or rent accounting (most authorities now use computers for this). Although the work is mainly office-based, contact with tenants and the public is a major part of the work for everyone.

Housing associations are growing in number. By 1994/95 some 3,000 were registered. As well as providing flats and houses and bed spaces in hostels, many run sheltered housing, mainly for older people. They may own a group of a dozen almshouses, and in 1994/95 twelve housing associations had more than 10,000 homes housing an average of 15,000 people. The managerial responsibilities and opportunities are therefore similar to those of a district authority. Property companies, and property managing agents, usually employ people qualified in SURVEYING (*see in* LAND USE PROFESSIONS).

Recruitment and entry

Usually as an administrative trainee in a housing department/association, either with a degree or post A-level. *See also in* LOCAL GOVERNMENT. Since 1995 it has also been possible to enter into a modern apprenticeship.

Qualifications and training

Some posts do not require formal qualifications, whilst others require relevant examination passes, e.g. Accountancy or Public Administration. Training is available on a variety of levels for a wide selection of staff. BTEC National Certificates in Housing Studies and in Public Administration are available.

The Chartered Institute of Housing is the representative body for staff in all areas of housing work and in 1996 has nearly 13,000 members. The Institute has implemented a new Professional Qualification from 1991. This allows both graduates and non-graduates to study on a day-release basis at a local college. Non-graduates study for the BTEC/SCOTVEC Higher National Certificate in Housing Studies over a two-year period (entry at minimum age of 18 years, with three GCSE passes A–C, and at least one A-level pass or equivalent, such as an Advanced GNVQ in the Built Environoment). Alternatively a BTEC/SCOTVEC National Certificate in Housing Studies or BTEC/SCOTVEC National Certificate or Diploma in Business and Finance, Distribution Studies or Public Administration; or, a National Certificate or Diploma of any other BTEC/SCOTVEC title together with appropriate work experience and completion of a conversion programme. Students who are over the age of 21 and have relevant work experience but do not fulfil the above requirements may be considered as exceptional entrants. Graduates study on the Graduate Foundation course for one year.

Both groups go on to study for the Professional Diploma over a two-year period. Alongside their college studies students are required to complete a series of work-based assessments: The Test of Professional Practice (TPP) Parts 1 and 2. Alternatively individuals may complete a recognised course which, along with the equivalent to TPP 1 and 2, allows them to become professionally qualified and join the Institute as Corporate members.

Courses, both full- and part-time, from BTEC/SCOTVEC to graduate and postgraduate courses, are available at colleges and universities throughout the country.

The following centres offer full-time undergraduate courses: Heriot-Watt/Edinburgh College of Art, University of Salford, Sheffield Hallam University, University of Ulster, University of Greenwich, University of Westminster, Liverpool John Moores University, University of the West of England (Bristol), University of Central England in Birmingham, Cardiff Institute of Higher Education.

The following centres offer full-time postgraduate courses: University of Central England in Birmingham, Heriot-Watt/Edinburgh College of Art, University of Salford, University of Stirling, London School of Economics,

University of Northumbria, Oxford Brookes University, Sheffield Hallam University, Cardiff University of Wales, University of the West of England (Bristol).

Twenty institutions offer part-time postgraduate courses. The Chartered Institute of Housing will provide a list.

Further information

The Chartered Institute of Housing.

Landscape architecture

This has developed, from the centuries-old skills of landscaping gardens and parklands, into a broader discipline which designs environments: city centres, motorways, industrial estates and housing schemes. The intention is to integrate essential construction into the natural landscape to create a harmonious setting, or to bring nature into the built environment.

Landscape architects, or designers, then try to create pleasant surroundings for people to live, work and play in. They turn the industrial scars of the past into parks and leisure areas, create attractive settings for new housing estates, shopping precincts, pedestrianised town centres and office developments, and tuck factory sites behind trees and green banks. They help to blend new roads into the existing landscape.

Landscape is rather more than arranging plants, trees and lawns to make a setting look attractive. It has to be very practical too. It is, for instance, no use creating a beautiful path which meanders through shrubs across a housing estate if it doubles the distance to the bus stop, and helps create hiding places for muggers. Other safety factors must also be taken into account, such as finding ways to prevent people crossing roads at dangerous places without using ugly barriers: cobblestone hillocks which are impossible to walk on do the job just as well.

The rules of perspective, balance of shape and colour, and so on, form the framework for creativity and imagination, but the 'art' of landscaping is, in fact, just as much a science and technology. The science is not only horticultural (landscape architects obviously have to take into account what plants will flourish where), but has to include geology and soil science, to understand how local ground and weather conditions may affect the reshaping of the land and the health of plants. Technology has to include materials and construction: what methods and materials can and should be used, to achieve particular effects, and to stand up to particular levels of use. Landscape architects have to take into account the way people use their environment; create surroundings in which the people using them will feel at ease; allow for small children; combat vandalism; etc. Of course schemes must fit into tight budgets, and be carefully costed, and this has to include the cost of maintenance (with complex problems to solve, e.g. whether initially expensive but long-lasting shrubs are better value than bedding plants which have to be changed with the seasons).

Landscape architects work closely with other experts – planners and architects, civil engineers and builders, and gardeners – as well as customers. Ideally, the landscape architect starts work at the earliest stages of a project, alongside the planner and the architect. They can then suggest, perhaps, an adjustment to the line of a road or the positioning of a building to improve landscaping possibilities.

As well as preparing drawings, plans and detailed schedules, the landscape architect has to produce estimates, collect tenders, supervise the work as it is done, see that the right trees and shrubs are properly planted in the right places, and arrange long-term maintenance.

Landscaping is a relatively young profession, and may develop in various ways. Some people, for instance, work as landscape managers, caring long-term for an area and its landscaping, and may also administer grants to improve the environment. Here it may link with administering leisure (*see in* PROFESSIONAL SPORT AND THE RECREATION AND LEISURE INDUSTRIES) and/or CONSERVATION (*see in* CAREERS IN CONSERVATION AND THE ENVIRONMENT).

Landscape scientists provide scientific data on soils and pollution, analyse these, and give advice on the best way to minimise the impact on the environment of development proposals. They also advise on reclamation techniques. Their work may include contract specification and supervision.

Recruitment and entry

It is now usual to start by going through a full-time or sandwich-based course, or courses, rather than training on the job. Landscape design needs strong creative design potential and imagination, linked to interest in and sensitivity to land, trees, and plants, in terms of their shapes and form. Entrants should also be interested in architecture, and in creating surroundings that people will enjoy. Designers have to be able to absorb and use scientific and technical (construction) data, with some drawing/draughting ability. Designers have to be able to work within a team. Some business sense is useful.

Minimum entry requirement is two A-level passes, normally including English, maths and/or a science, and GCSE passes in history, geography, or a language, or equivalent.There are obvious advantages to studying a 'relevant' subject at A-level, e.g. geography, art or biology. The Landscape Institute does not concern itself with entry to degree courses. It is up to individual universities to decide whether they will accept an Advanced GNVQ in the Built Environment, Art and Design, or Science.

This is a small profession. About 50% of people work for authorities such as the Department of Transport, local councils, and new towns; the remainder work for design and architectural practices, are self-employed, or work for contractors or developers.

Appreciation of the changes and improvements landscape architects can make is growing. There should be scope for expansion, especially as landscaping is a natural area for job-creation, but public expenditure cuts do not help.

Qualifications and training

There are two main routes for landscape architects/designers:

1 Landscape architecture/design first-degree courses: at Heriot-Watt, Sheffield, Leeds, Greenwich and Manchester Metropolitan universities; Cheltenham and Gloucester College of Higher Education.
2 First-degree courses in, e.g., agriculture, architecture, art/design, engineering, geography, geology, horticulture, or planning, followed by a postgraduate course (full- or part-time).

Graduates must then complete the Landscape Institute's professional practice examination (Part 4) in order to become fully professionally qualified.

There are several undergraduate landscape management courses, the pioneer being the four-year sandwich at Reading University leading to the BSc (Hons) in Landscape Management. An MSc in Landscape Ecology, Design and Management is available at Wye College.

Qualification for landscape scientists is achieved by means of an appropriate first degree, followed by a higher degree or some relevant experience or a combination of both.

Further information

The Landscape Institute.

Town and country planning

The main aim of planning, often called 'town and country' planning, is to attempt to keep some kind of balance between all the conflicting and competing demands made on the land in a relatively small and fairly overcrowded island. Space has to be found for homes, offices, factories, roads, schools, hospitals, and reservoirs, yet land must be reserved for agriculture, and for recreation and leisure. Coal must be mined, but the English countryside must be preserved. Someone has to live with the power station or the airport. Planning has to try to protect the environment from overdevelopment and physical damage, and from projects which may spoil an area of natural beauty or destroy an historic building; to prevent social problems, and yet allow for a reasonable level of new growth, and regeneration for decaying areas.

Planning can be controversial: at one extreme people often object to any official interference, at the other are those who believe the planners usually know best, with the majority generally accepting the need for planning in principle, but often quarrelling with the effects of planning decisions in their own neighbourhoods, especially when it brings, for example, a new motorway.

Policy on planning changes all the time, sometimes dramatically, sometimes more quietly. At present there is a strong swing away from rigid and long-term plans, to an attempt at broad 'strategies' which can allow for unforeseen and unforeseeable social and economic changes and developments, and some looser decision-making. Strategic planning is being scaled down.

Planning is mostly done by local authorities (*see* LOCAL GOVERNMENT) – the county and district councils – with the Department of the Environment as adviser, coordinator and adjudicator in disputes and appeals, responsible for national policy, and for deciding on national needs.

County planning offices work continuously on a so-called 'structure' plan for the county. This sets out, in written form rather than as a map or plan, broad policy guidelines, some of which are dictated by national plans, such as for new motorways, some by local needs, for instance to cope with a high level of empty space. Structure plans set out the main priorities for conservation, redevelopment or improvement, examine levels of industrial and/or office development, and show the possible consequences of major projects like power stations, mines, reservoirs, and hospitals. For example, new housing estates and industrial developments both involve building new roads or improving old ones, and providing extra main services of all kinds. Conversely, a new motorway may attract new businesses and land, and premises must be allocated for them. If new industrial development is allowed, should there be space for extra housing too, or should the new firms be expected to recruit from people already living in the locality? Authorities can decide to have a period of consolidation if they have grown rapidly for a while, but have to be sure they have allowed for more employers if the population is rising.

District council planners, who should work closely with county authorities on structure plans, and perhaps with neighbouring districts (on, for example, roads), turn the guidelines of the 'structure' into a detailed plan, pinpointing proposed conservation areas, earmarking places for redevelopment or improvement, showing where industry can be sited, and the exact routes of new roads.

In the now-abolished metropolitan county areas, structure and local plans have been replaced by new unitary development plans, prepared and adopted by the London borough, and metropolitan district, planning authorities. They cover both general policies and detailed proposals for land use and development control.

District councils also process applications for planning permission, usually submitted by architects on behalf of clients, to build new offices, rebuild (for instance) a cinema, or extend existing factories or houses.

Working in planning

The profession is not very large – the Royal Town Planning Institute has 13,500 corporate members (1996). Most professional planners (obviously) work for county and district councils, and a small number work for the Department of the Environment. Since the mid-1980s there has been a considerable growth in the number of planners working as planning consultants in the private sector. Up to 20% of RTPI's corporate membership works in this sector for over

1,250 firms. A further small number of planners work for e.g. property developers.

In county authorities planners work almost entirely on policy and strategy. In districts the work is more varied and detailed. Here planners may work on policy and strategy with county planners, but they may also work on the detailed local plan, or may guide planning applications through all the legal procedures, which includes making recommendations to the planning committee, and may include a public inquiry.

Work on structure and local plans involves a lot of detailed research before reports can be written or plans prepared or revised. Planners have to know a great deal about their county or district: anything and everything that could affect its physical development in the future. They collect data through the other departments of their own councils, through and from other organisations such as the Department of the Environment, local transport organisations, the area or district health authority, and the chamber of commerce, from library research, and through local surveys.

They must know, for example, whether the area's population is growing or declining in numbers; whether it is changing in any way, for instance, which local industries are not likely to recover fully when recession ends; whether more older people are retiring to the district or there are more young families. The former will need greater health provision and social services, the latter schools, and either would want different leisure facilities.

Planners watch local industry and commerce to see what is expanding or declining, and try to match future employment needs (as shown by their population studies) to the known plans of business. They investigate what may be causing any industries or commercial activities to decline, and want to know whether more people are travelling to work outside the area (and also changing the pattern of rush-hour travel). They ask questions about the use of, say, swimming pools or football pitches, to see if recreation provision is about right or needs changing. They try to decide whether anything could affect where and when people shop in the district, and whether therefore existing shopping centres are large enough, or have enough parking facilities.

In county planning departments, the information collected is fed into computers which put it all together to make a 'model' of the region, and how it will probably develop if the data is complete and accurate. The computer can be used to suggest several possible strategies, with the benefits and disadvantages of each, and to pinpoint unforeseen problems. But collecting and analysing information, and decision-making, are complicated, and tend to be long and drawn-out. People and organisations, from local residents through to the Department of the Environment, must be consulted; planning committees have to deliberate, and objectors be given the chance to have their views properly heard and considered, perhaps at a public inquiry. Planning must be done within the framework of planning law, and to a tight budget. Stitching new developments, new road schemes and even improvements into the fabric of the existing environment has to be done with care, and there are always many problems to solve.

Professional planners

Professional planning staff put up plans and recommendations to the council's planning committee, determine which analysis of the future to accept, carry out all the legal steps, act as negotiators, write reports, and see that detailed plans are prepared. They generally work in 'project' teams. This is mainly an office-based job, but with much time spent in meetings and discussions, and in visits. Planners work closely with other experts – such as architects, economists, computer staff, statisticians, surveyors, sociologists – and other departments of the local authority (leisure and recreation, roads, etc.) to see that the right information is collected and that it is properly analysed. Promotion is to team leader, and senior managerial posts, but with under 500 planning authorities, the chances of a 'top' job are rather limited.

Planning technicians

Planning technicians collect, collate and analyse planning information for the professional staff, and help present information, policies and ideas as effectively as possible. They organise surveys, compile statistical and other information from reports. They maintain the detailed written records all planning departments must keep. This includes maps and plans, and making limited revisions to them, producing extracts from, and enlargements or reductions of maps for (say) simple site plans or diagrams, as well as photographic and written reports and records. They keep photographic and written records of listed buildings in the area. They record and check planning applications, deal with enquiries, prepare plans for committees and inquiries, and write more straightforward reports. They produce leaflets and set up exhibitions to help keep the public informed, and work up sketch layouts.

Other planning support staff

Planning administrators and planning enforcement officers are also involved in the planning process. Administrators may be employed in both the public and private sector. Enforcement officers work for a planning authority.

Recruitment and entry

It is theoretically possible to get into a first planning post with a degree in a subject other than planning. But competition for posts – and some scaling-down in funding for postgraduate training – means that graduates in planning are now preferred, also for the knowledge and skills acquired in their education.

Professional planners

Professional planners must be able to understand, absorb and assess all kinds of information, much of it highly technical and complex, and much in statistical form. They must be sympathetic to and understand the social and personal needs of the people who live and work in the area, and deal patiently with people facing the disruption of redevelopment, but with a sense of realism. They have to be observant, imaginative with a strong visual sense, but capable of detailed, patient research. They must be able to work as part of a team, be good at negotiating, and able to cope in difficult situations. They must be prepared to take responsibility for hard decisions, based on careful judgement. Administrative ability is useful.

Planning technicians

Planning technicians are competent practitioners in their own right and play a strong technical supportive role to that of the Chartered Town Planner. Although the technician may have less responsibility for the formulation of policy, design and plan, he/she may often need greater skills in certain aspects of the planning process than does the professional. Technicians are generally recruited as trainees from school or college with at least four GCSE level A–C or equivalent passes at 16-plus including maths, and a subject requiring a facility in written English.

Qualifications and training

For *professional planning* it makes sense to study for a degree in planning. It is advisable to look for an RTPI-accredited course as this is part of the qualification to become a Chartered Town Planner. The RTPI does not specify particular qualifications for entry to an RTPI-accredited undergraduate course. Individual universities may accept an Advanced GNVQ in the Built Environment, or Art and Design, or Business. Planning takes in information from a wide range of different subjects – architecture; engineering; surveying; geology; geography; local government and planning law; demography; and social, including behavioural, sciences – studied in an integrated way. Planning courses are designed to train in technological, design and communication skills, and demonstrate the legal, economic and social implications.

RTPI-accredited undergraduate courses are at the Universities of Belfast, Central England, West of England, Wales (Cardiff), Coventry, Dundee, Heriot-Watt, Strathclyde, London (UCL), Westminster, South Bank, Manchester, Newcastle upon Tyne, Nottingham, Oxford Brookes, and Sheffield. It is possible to study first for a degree in a related subject (e.g. geography, economics, architecture, civil engineering, estate management, sociology, law, statistics or surveying) and go on to full-time postgraduate training, but the grant support for postgraduate courses has been scaled down very sharply. It is possible to study part-time, but students should have a first post in a planning department.

RTPI-accredited postgraduate courses are at: Belfast, Central England, West of England, Wales (Cardiff), Dublin, Heriot-Watt, Strathclyde, Leeds Metropolitan, Liverpool, Liverpool John Moores, London (UCL), Westminster, South Bank, Manchester, Newcastle, Nottingham, Oxford Brookes, Reading, Sheffield, Sheffield Hallam. There is also a distance-learning course offered by a consortium of planning schools together with the Open University.

For *planning technicians* courses have been established in a number of colleges throughout the country to enable students to qualify for BTEC Certificates in Land Administration (or in Scotland, the SCOTVEC Certificate in Planning). These courses are normally run on a two-year part-time basis for the BTEC Certificate, with a further two years' part-time study for the BTEC Higher Certificate (Scotland, SCOTVEC Higher Certificate in Planning). Entrants to BTEC courses require at least four GCSE level A–C or equivalent passes at 16-plus including maths, and a subject requiring a facility in written English. NVQ/SVQs are being developed for planning staff, i.e. for technical staff, enforcement officers and planning administrators. *See also* SURVEYING *below*.

Further information

Royal Town Planning Institute, the Society of Town Planning Technicians.

Surveying

General practice – building – rural practice – land and hydrographic – minerals – quantity – planning and development – marine resource management – archaeological – technical

Surveying is not a single profession, but a group of interlinked and overlapping careers with broadly common interests: the land, the sea, and their resources. The resources range from minerals, such as coal and tin, deep inside the earth and under the seabed, to the 'resources' people put on the land, such as buildings of all kinds and installations like harbours and mines. Surveyors map and measure, manage, value and sell, develop, maintain, and advise. Surveying is commonly divided into a number of clearly defined branches, but with subdivisions within them. It is a changing and developing area of employment. The various titles used can be confusing: insurance surveying, for instance, is not generally included with the branches of surveying described here but is usually treated as part of INSURANCE (*see in* FINANCIAL CAREERS).

Confusion is often compounded because larger surveying practices may want to offer their clients as broad a range of services as possible, and may therefore employ surveyors from several different branches (and some may be qualified and/or experienced in more than one), depending on the character of the area (urban, rural, port, etc.), the type of industry and/or commerce the area has, and so on. In the high street, the surveyor's practice may be known as 'the estate agent', or 'auctioneer', even though this may be only part of what the practice actually does, but an estate agency is not necessarily part of a surveyor's practice – it may now be owned by, for example, a bank, or an insurance company. Some practices are 'multidisciplinary', employing surveyors, architects, engineers, etc.

Surveyors are also extensively employed by local authorities, by the Civil Service, by construction companies, and by firms, other organisations and individuals with interests in land, property, agriculture, mines, etc.

The profession is large and growing, with getting on for 75,000 chartered surveyors. Most surveyors specialise fairly early on, but people do change the type of work they do, especially on the basis of a broadly based qualification. The differences, though, are considerable between the working lives of different types of surveyor. The land surveyor is out of doors most of the time, often in pioneering conditions, while the quantity surveyor is office-based, though spending a good deal of time on site as well. Most surveyors work with other people, but some, like quantity surveyors, work mostly with other experts – architects, engineers and builders – while others, such as estate agents or agricultural surveyors, spend more time negotiating with, or advising, clients.

Surveyors today have highly competitive, even aggressive, instincts, and are steadily widening the range of work they do and the services they can offer (the profession has been described as 'volatile and arguably dynamic'). They take on, and compete for, work such as (building/construction) project management, budgetary control, property development, and giving expert advice in planning. Valuation and estate surveying are increasingly important when property is a major area of investment. Surveyors manage property interests for major pension funds, and are managing directors of some of the largest property developers. Chartered surveyors now hold all the senior non-military managerial posts in Ordnance Survey.

Surveying, like most other professions, has been gaining and changing with new technology for some years; Geographical Information Systems (GIS) capable of handling many layers of map, geological, and demographic information, quickly and in combination, allow flexible processing of data to address different issues as they arise in the life of a project. These systems allow efficient storage of spatial information which can be interrogated more rapidly and effectively than information held on paper maps and manual records. With the speed and ease which computers bring to the handling of geographical data, spatial information, already a key resource in the 1990s, is likely to grow.

General practice surveying

General practice surveying is still the largest division – RICS membership (including students) in general practice is (1996) some 36,000. It is itself divided into a number of subspecialisations:

Estate agents

Estate agents negotiate the sale, purchase or lease/letting of any type of land or buildings, not only houses, but factories, farms, offices, etc. as well. They provide support services, for example arranging and advising on mortgages, spelling out the legal position on letting, and suggesting what the price or rent might be for a given property.

They may also manage property – flats, houses or office blocks – for the owners, although some property companies employ their own housing managers, who are frequently qualified surveyors, as do the largest housing associations. (Local authorities also employ housing managers for their residential estates, but they are not usually qualified surveyors.)

Estate agents are often also auctioneers, and may be valuers. Auctioneers normally qualify also as valuers, so it is usual to be qualified in at least two of these three. A larger firm of estate agents may employ different people: as property sales negotiators (dealing directly with sellers and buyers, and usually specialising in houses or industrial/commercial property), as valuers, and as auctioneers. An estate agency practice managing property may also employ, for example, building surveyors (*see below*).

Estate agency can be a tough, aggressive business, and has become more so in current competition, as the financial-services sector moves in. Negotiators can suffer 'burn out' and consequently few stay at the front end past forty, and need to be well-prepared and qualified for the equally difficult, but different, job of management if they are to survive in the business.

Traditionally it is a very fragmented sector. In 1994, The National Association of Estate Agents estimated that there were 12,580 outlets, compared with 13,600 in 1992 and 15,000 in 1988. (The housing market collapse of 1989 resulted in branch closures, redundancies, job losses and heavy financial operating losses.) 1995 was likely to show further shrinkage. Some analysts suggested that the sector needed to lose around 20% more outlets (leaving about 10,000) to balance supply and demand.

Ballpark figures for the end of 1994 suggested the following breakdown of outlet ownership:

Corporates	4,000 handling 50% of residential sales
Small independent chains	8,000 handling 40% of residential sales
Single offices	500 handling 10% of residential sales

(Corporates are defined as outlets owned by banks, building societies, insurance companies, other big institutions or large, specialist estate agency chains.)

A 1995 KEY NOTE: *Report on Estate Agency* shows the major corporate estate agents at the end of 1995 to be:

Agency	Number of branches
Hambro Country Wide plc	747
Halifax Property Services	620
Royal Insurance Life Estates Ltd	430
Black Horse Agencies Ltd	341
General Accident Property Services	340
National Homes Network	204
Legal and General Estate Agencies	200
Woolwich Property Services	184
Reed Rains	144

TEAM Association Estate Agencies	143
Connell Estate Agents	140
Arun Estates	124
TSB Property Services	112

The RICS has about 14,000 members in agency practice, ISVA 7,500, and NAEA about 9,000.

Auctioneers

Auctioneers organise and run the sale by auction of property of all kinds – houses, industrial and commercial buildings, farms and other estates – land, and the contents of houses, farms, and factories. In farming areas they also sell cattle, sheep, pigs, and machinery. Handling the sale is only part of an auctioneer's work – they have to know a lot about values, recommend reserve prices, have the items grouped into lots, and catalogued. Some firms specialise entirely in auctioneering, and even in selling particular types of property, while others combine auctioneering with estate agency or rural practice (*see below*). Very few, mainly London, art salerooms employ art experts who may specialise in valuing 'chattels', such as silver or paintings.

Valuers

Valuers are also called valuation surveyors or even just surveyors. They have to decide just how much a property (which may be land, buildings or contents), is worth at the time of valuation – which may be when it is for sale, when a sale or purchase is contemplated, for the rating authority, or for insurance, accounting or death duties.

Valuers do not only look at the property itself and its condition, but also compare it with similar property in the area and at the potential for improvement or development. For houses, the neighbourhood is important – the amenities, such as shops, schools, parks and swimming pools; whether it is noisy; whether any local nuisance is bad enough to affect the value; whether public transport is close enough for convenience yet not close enough to be intrusive. Planned motorways or new housing estates may affect valuation, as may a conservation or development area. There is always an element of inspired guesswork: whether the area could become fashionable, for instance. Equally important factors have to be taken into account when valuing industrial sites or offices.

Valuers work for estate agents, in private practice, and for commercial firms and property developers. They also work for local authorities, and for Inland Revenue's valuation office, which values property for tax and also makes rating assessments, and acts for other government departments when they acquire or sell land and buildings, and for local authorities too when government money is involved.

Building surveying

Building surveyors look after the structural well-being of buildings of all kinds, 'managing' maintenance and repair, and regular checks on their condition. They also frequently take charge of improvements, renovation and extension of buildings, an expanding field of work as it becomes more economic and environmentally acceptable to convert old buildings of all kinds for new uses. Here they frequently supervise the building work, having prepared plans, measured and specified the work to be done. It is building surveyors who make structural surveys for people (or their building societies) wanting to buy houses.

Some building surveyors are self-employed practitioners (or work for another surveyor who is); some work for large property owners (who are not only property companies as such, but also include firms such as banks, and hotels or store chains, who have premises all over the country), for government departments, or for firms which manage property on behalf of the owners. For them, they set up and run maintenance programmes, which have to be properly costed, and also prepare plans for, specify and supervise work on conversions and improvements for them.

Rural practice surveying

Rural practice surveying encompasses the disciplines of agricultural surveying and land agency. Individual *land agents* traditionally managed large estates as employees of the owners, and over 300 still do.

They care for the land itself, the buildings, woodlands, and estate roads, and deal with tenants, and fishing and other game rights. In the past they also ran the 'home' (as opposed to tenant) farms. More large estates, including those owned by pension funds and other financial institutions, are now run by firms of land agents, who may also be rural practice surveyors.

While farms themselves may be run by people qualified in agriculture (and some rural practice surveyors start out in agriculture), land agents now deal mainly with the business management of farms, advising, for example, on ways of making a better income out of land – for example, by converting part to a country park or caravan site – on the design and development of farm buildings, and the management and development of commercial woodlands. They look after stocktaking valuations, and negotiate claims when there is a compulsory purchase. Rural practice surveyors/land agents are expected to help solve many of the current problems being faced by AGRICULTURE (*see in* LAND USE INDUSTRIES).

About half the 2,000 or more rural practice surveyors in private practice are livestock auctioneers; many of the rest are also involved in estate agency, valuation and other auctioneering, but of country and farm properties, and agricultural machinery. Several hundred work for the Ministry of Agriculture's advisory services – on siting, layout, design and construction of farm buildings, drainage, land reclamation, as well as managing some government-run land, handling applications for grants, and advising planning authorities on the implications of proposals on agricultural land.

Land and hydrographic surveying

Land and hydrographic surveying are two distinct specialisations, but both measure, plot and map.

Land surveyors

Land surveyors measure and plot the earth's physical features to provide the data from which cartographers make maps, civil engineers lay out new roads or other major works, planners prepare a new development, and on which the boundaries of estates are settled.

They employ ultra-modern equipment, such as aerial photography, satellite surveying and automatic measuring instruments (which use laser beams as light source and transfer measurements to computer memory at the press of a button). With the help of these the problems of recording every change in the shape of the land, plotting exactly the route of a road or river, accurately locating buildings in relation to each other, checking the acreage of a wood, or measuring exactly the minute annual movements of the earth's crust, have been made somewhat easier, giving clients a better service. Distances, vegetation, and weather still mean that surveyors need resourcefulness, determination and plenty of experience, though.

Land surveyors may be self-employed in private practice (or work for such a practice), or work for consulting engineers, for large construction companies, aerial survey firms, or for the government's surveying departments: Ordnance Survey, the Ministry of Defence mapping and charting establishment, and the Directorate of Overseas Surveys. The Directorate sends experienced surveyors to work mainly in developing countries. In fact, about half of all land surveyors are generally working overseas at any one time – mapping the last few unsurveyed areas, mostly in the Middle East, Africa, the Caribbean and the Pacific.

Hydrographic surveyors

Hydrographic surveyors 'map' the seas, rivers and other inland waterways, harbours and ports, producing charts which show, for instance, the varying depths of the seabed, hazards (like wrecks), tides and currents. Like land surveyors, they have modern, technological equipment, including infrared, microwave and laser-ranging instruments to compute distances and, for instance, the exact position of an oil rig; and sonar, echo-sounders, etc. for underwater exploration.

North Sea oil and gas exploration, and supertankers drawing twice as much water as they used to, have increased considerably the work of hydrographic surveyors. Much of the North Sea had not been surveyed at all. Where charts existed they were totally inadequate to plot accurately where, for example, the offshore boundaries are, to plan and route oil and gas pipelines, to build new terminals with the necessary channels for tankers, or locate production sites.

Most hydrographic surveyors are in the Royal Navy, since it is the British Admiralty charts produced by the Navy's hydrographic department which are used worldwide, but there are some posts in the government's central survey branch, and with the steady increase in exploration for underwater resources (not only oil and gas but, in future, other ores also), more opportunities in exploration and survey firms. Nevertheless, it is still a very small group – probably less than 200 in all.

Minerals surveying

Minerals surveyors map deposits of mineable minerals, such as coal, metal ores, salt, and phosphates, and building materials such as sand, gravel and aggregates, etc. They make detailed surveys of concession areas, and make and maintain plans of mine workings. The job includes responsibility for mine safety, stability problems stemming from mine operations, and for solving environmental problems. Minerals surveyors also value deposits, manage concessions, and advise on pricing policies and rates for leasing, and deal with legal aspects.

In Britain, the major employer is British Coal, but there are some posts in local council planning offices, and water companies. Inland Revenue's valuation office employs a few in the valuation of surface and underground minerals, mineral-bearing land and damage from subsidence. The main opportunities to work in areas like metal mining are overseas, with some international firms recruiting surveyors in the UK.

Quantity surveying

Quantity surveyors are cost experts. Largely because they closely monitor soaring construction bills and so can make projects viable and profitable, it is a division of surveying that has expanded rapidly in the last ten years (over 30,000 qualified RICS members and students), and is rapidly developing, too. The typical quantity surveyor is now a very powerful figure in the construction world with financial muscle, who is extending the role into the fields of contracting, civil and industrial engineering, services consultancy and project management and control. A commentator said, 'In today's competitive world, quantity surveyors are as commercial and as quick-footed as anyone in the property industry.'

All this is developing out of their traditional work of seeing that a building project is finished within budget and on time, looking after both overall and detailed cost-control through preconstruction and construction. But the traditional working methods meant that, however good they were as cost managers, quantity surveyors could not always control other parts of the design/construction team – with buildings only too often late and way over budget. By becoming project managers (*see* THE CONSTRUCTION INDUSTRIES), working directly for the customer (and not just one of a team) and in control, quantity surveyors can provide realistic cost, time and quality targets and see they are kept. Quantity surveyors, brought into a project early enough, can evaluate the development, prepare several different costing options, and find one that is going to be cost-effective. Because projects may be viable only if built fast, a skilled quantity surveyor can look into, compare and assess construction methods, to come up with the most efficient. 'Design-and-build' or package-deal contracts also give quantity surveyors a place as client or employer's representative. Quantity surveyors may make economic analyses of competing designs.

Information technology has made this possible. Much of the traditional, and very lengthy, nuts-and-bolts data collection, estimating, costing and tender documenting work of quantity surveying is now done by computer, faster, to give much more accurate information from the earliest days of a project. Information flows can be constantly and more accurately monitored and controlled. Old 'crisis-management' methods and on-site problems can now be eliminated using such systems. Customers can also take a longer-term view of the real cost of buildings and their maintenance.

Not all quantity surveyors will be able, or want, to move into these new high-profile roles. And while project management teams may be quantity-surveyor led, they have to include other experts, e.g. construction managers and process engineers, who can fully understand what the design team is doing. Many, probably most, will continue to monitor costs on a more mundane level, responsible for advising designers on costings, controlling the computer-based process of turning finished design drawings and plans into a detailed breakdown of materials, labour and equipment and working out how much it will cost to build. Quantity surveyors draw up building contracts, decide/advise on tendering methods. They monitor the budget throughout construction, checking and agreeing contractors' and suppliers' invoices, monthly, negotiating on pricing 'variations', and the final account.

Some 55% of the 21,000 qualified and practising quantity surveyors work (1996) in private practices, many of which are increasingly multidisciplinary, including architects, engineers, etc. as part of a team. Practices are employed by e.g. architects, contractors, property-owning clients, for the length of a contract. About 19% work for construction companies, construction managers, and consultant civil engineers, 18% for government departments or local councils, and 8% for other commercial and industrial firms. In each case they do their costings, etc., negotiating on their behalf with the 'other side'.

Planning and development surveying

These surveyors try to inject economic realism into planning, and aim to show what is possible in terms of given resources, and what the alternative uses of the resources might be. They may, for example, show how an extensive plan for a shopping precinct may be modified to allow funds for a sports centre elsewhere, or the difference in costs and advantages to renovating existing factories against a brand-new industrial site. They investigate to see that the investment decision is the right one – Will a new shopping centre attract enough shoppers to justify the rents? Is there the demand for, and the groups to use, a new leisure centre?

Some development planners provide factual information for others to use and interpret. Some analyse and use it themselves as an equal member of the planning team in a district council; others work on strategic planning in counties. They work for the Department of the Environment, advising on planning policies, acting as assessors in public inquiries. Some work for firms of planning consultants while others go into general surveying practice, providing a service to clients in the development business – suggesting projects, and advising on development proposals and planning procedures. Some work for property developers or construction companies, where they can become project managers on individual developments.

Marine resource management surveying

A chartered surveyor qualified in this field is concerned with the management of resources linked to the sea. The sea, and the coastline in particular, is being more intensively used, and the need for effective management has become increasingly important. The chartered surveyor in marine resource management is charged with finding solutions to the problems associated with intensity of use and the conflicts which arise as a result. Increased awareness of the importance of marine resources and the requirement for effective management will create a greater demand for this type of surveyor. They will be employed at all levels of management, from private practice to international agencies such as the United Nations, and will be instrumental in developing policies which will ensure the continued good management of marine resources.

Archaeological surveying

The archaeological surveyor is concerned essentially with the past and must be capable of interpreting and recording the various features of past ages as the work of excavation progresses. To be able to give graphical record of the evidence of the past is an essential attribute. Necessary skills include elementary land surveying, a knowledge of trigonometry, and the ability to plot ground plans and vertical section in comprehensible relationship. Naturally, a knowledge of the elements of archaeology is required, all the more so as the archaeological surveyor may be called upon to produce detailed drawings of artefacts unearthed by excavation. The domain of the archaeological surveyor is restricted, as one of a relatively small band. Services will be sought by various bodies concerned with the past both at home and abroad. *See also* ARCHAEOLOGY *IN* HISTORICAL AND RELATED WORK.

Technical surveying

Some of the less demanding areas of professional surveyors' work is frequently done by 'technicians' – a term which refers to a level of qualification rather than a job specification. The dividing line between professional and technician is not hard-and-fast, though, and many technician-level posts are highly specialist and still carry considerable responsibility, although mostly they work under supervision from a professional surveyor (or architect, or engineer). Technician-level careers range through all the branches of surveying. Examples of the work they do include the following:

In *general practice* the estate agent's negotiator is generally trained to technician level, and the valuer and estate manager will be similarly-qualified assistants.

In *building surveying* they may be the people who actually climb about the attics to look for dry rot. They may prepare the detailed plans and specifications for repairs or improvements, organise the work, and deal with the day-to-day business on tenders and contracts, checking accounts.

In a *local council* a building inspector is technician-level, and so may be a site manager in construction.

In *land surveying* the 'technician' is generally an assistant, actually carrying out the measuring, and maintaining records.

In *quantity surveying* assistants 'take off' the measurements and items from the architect's or engineer's specifications and drawings, and list them as materials, processes, and labour. They 'work up' (i.e. work out) the quantities, areas, and volumes measured in taking off, and describe them in standardised units. Much of the work is now computer-based. They are site measurers of materials and labour used and the amount of work done.

Photogrammetric technicians prepare, under supervision, maps, photomaps, elevation drawings and digital data for a computer information store, by interpreting and measuring photographs. They have to give the information to the required scale, and put it into an appropriate format.

Recruitment and entry

Entry divides between professional and technician levels.

Professional

Generally speaking the academic component is an accredited degree or equivalent qualification in a relevant discipline. However, the minimum requirement for student entry (age 16) to ISVA is five GCSEs (A–C), including English language and mathematics, or various equivalents such as a suitable ND or NC.

Technical

It is possible to start work as a trainee technical surveyor at 16-plus with at least four GCSE/SCEs (including maths and science), but it is more usual to start at 18-plus with GCSE/SCEs plus two A-levels/H grades.

All surveyors (and their assistants) need numeracy, for measurement, valuation, and costing, but the level needed varies. Land surveyors are the most mathematical, but in all branches surveyors must be able to extract the story the figures tell, and explain it to others. Surveyors need to be accurate and exact, able to work to high tolerances, and have a practical approach to problems. They have to be able to absorb and understand a lot of different kinds of information – finance and patterns of investment, land and property markets, etc. included; to know a lot about the problems and practices of architects, planners, and engineers; to understand building technology and the construction industry and keep abreast of developments; they may need to know a lot about agriculture or forestry, to stay abreast of industrial and commercial change – and the new kinds of accommodation they need – and monitor social developments like where and how people want to live. They must have a sound business sense, and increasingly all kinds of managerial skills, in the public sector (to see that rate- or taxpayers get value for money) no less than in private practice or commercial employment – although the commercial pressures are obviously greater in the private sector – and be able to get on with other people, work in teams, and cooperate closely with other professionals.

Qualifications and training

Divides between professional level and technician level.

Professional level

Academic standard for entry to the RICS as a student is five GCSE/SCEs grade A–C/1–3 including English and mathematics, plus two A-levels/four H grades. Two AS-levels will be accepted in place of one of the A-level passes required. With the right A-levels (or equivalent) it is possible to do an accredited degree (such as a BSc in building surveying or BSc in estate management), or a shorter BTEC HNC/D course in a relevant subject, (this offers advanced entry to a degree or diploma course usually at second-year level). An Advanced GNVQ/GSVQ may allow candidates to enrol on an RICS-accredited degree course.

All candidates then go on to take the Institution's Assessment of Professional Competence (APC). The professional competence element consists of two years' practical experience under the guidance of a chartered surveyor.

Normally at least one year of this practical experience must be gained after an accredited degree or diploma. A record of experience is submitted to RICS for approval, and towards the end of the second or third years the candidate will undergo a final assessment. A list of accredited degrees may be obtained from the RICS.

Technician level

Entry as a student member is with enrolment or pass in BTEC/SCOTVEC NC or HNC/D.

To become a full member of the Society of Surveying Technicians (SST) candidates must hold BTEC/SCOTVEC HNC/D, and pass a Joint Test of Competence (JTC) which is operated jointly by the RICS and SST.

As a full member of SST it is possible to progress to membership of RICS via a special bridging arrangement unique to the society: full members may apply to sit the RICS direct membership examination at age 30, compared with a minimum age of 35 for non-members.

Professional bodies

Despite some mergers, there are still a number of professional bodies. Usual minimum academic qualifications for student entry to these are four GCSE/SCEs A–C/1–3 to include maths, science, and a subject demonstrating use of English. Trainees normally undertake courses leading to BTEC/

SCOTVEC NC or diploma. Those with GCSE/SCEs plus two A-level/H grade passes may be considered for full-time or part-time study leading to a degree or HND, and then take the institution's professional examination. Full membership normally requires a degree or equivalent in an approved discipline.

Royal Institution of Chartered Surveyors (RICS), is the main professional body, with a membership (1996) of over 93,000 including students.

ISVA (the professional society for valuers and auctioneers) has 80% of its members in estate agency/auctioneering but specialises in valuing, etc. of fine art and 'chattels', industrial plant/machinery, etc. (1996 membership 7,000).

Association of Building Engineers (ABE) (formerly the *Incorporated Association of Architects and Surveyors* [IAAS]) had a 1995 membership figure of about 4,500. Membership includes architects, and surveyors in building, fire, land, quantity, security, and valuation, town planners, and engineers.

Architects and Surveyors Institute (ASI) was formed in 1989, with an amalgamation of the Construction Surveyors Institute and Faculty of Architects (1996 membership about 5,500). Surveying applicants must have successfully completed all three stages of the Institute's examinations; partial exemptions will be granted to holders of other recognised qualifications. Applications from architects may only be considered if their names are registered with the Architects Registration Council of the United Kingdom.

National Association of Estate Agents is the professional organisation for independent and corporate estate agents and has about 9,500 members throughout the UK. To qualify for membership, candidates must demonstrate a thorough knowledge of estate agency practice and property law and must agree to abide by the NAEA's Code of Professional Ethics. The NAEA runs both in-house and distance-learning educational courses for estate agents at all levels, and awards professional qualifications.

A National Assessment Centre for NVQ/SVQs has been established at the NAEA, Warwick, for level 3 and 4 qualifications, using peripatetic assessment and verification. Level 3 is available in Selling Residential Property (distance-learning pack available) and Customer Service. Level 4 is available in Managing Residential Estate Agency. In addition, the Core Skill areas of Communication, Information Technology and the Application of Number are available as 'add-on' or 'free-standing' units.

Most of the main corporate estate agents are members of the Residential Estate Agency Training and Education Association (REATA).

Many local TECs provide opportunities for young people to take part in a modern apprenticeship, leading to level-3 NVQ.

Society of Surveying Technicians (SST) 1996 membership 5,500.

Chartered Institute of Building. Surveyors working for construction firms frequently take CIOB examinations.

Further information

The professional and other bodies cited above.

Contents

Land Use Industries

(CLCI: W–WAH, RAD)

Background

Britain is a relatively small island, and its land resources limited. Agriculture, roads, housing, leisure, industry and commerce, nature itself, compete for space, and planners have to try to arbitrate between the competing interests. Making the environment produce an income inevitably produces conflicts between, for example, immediate profit and producing resources like food, and the longer-term interests of conservation and preservation of landscapes and natural life. It means constant dilemmas in the working lives of many. Farmers have been constantly exhorted to produce more cheap food but are castigated for trying to do so at the expense of, for example, century-old trees and hedgerows.

Work in this sector is changing just as much as in other industries and areas of employment. Conservation management, for example, has become an integral part of everyday farming, with the creation of environmentally sensitive areas covering 15% of UK land.

The traditional skills used in growing crops and keeping animals are still needed. But technology of all kinds, the computer, scientific techniques, modern business methods, expert financial management, sophisticated marketing, efficient planning and decision-making techniques are as essential to the farmer as to the bank or the electronics firm. Higher levels of skills and expertise, better training, closer teamwork are needed to make a success of all enterprises. Technology, the drive for higher productivity, fewer and larger enterprises in farming and competitive economic conditions also change the nature of work – more managers, technologists and technically skilled staff, but fewer semi- and unskilled – and this is combined with an overall decline in the total number of jobs.

The land and the environment can provide a wide range of different types of work, from the very scientific to the most practical, from the aesthetic to the commercial. By definition, working in these sectors frequently involves working out of doors, with all its obvious pleasures and disadvantages. In many jobs there is at least some element of practical work, and most deal with the physical and material, although some have a creative element too.

Despite the steady takeover of land by homes, industry, roads, etc., over 77% of Britain's land area is still used productively – to grow food and flowers, wool and timber. These essential crop-producing industries have been and are still going through both a scientific/technological and a managerial/marketing revolution. As a result, long-established and traditional ways of working the land have changed. Crop growers have had to become technologically and scientifically minded and astute managers. The men and women who work for them have had to become increasingly skilled too – and they are now technicians who can cope with very sophisticated machinery, and the scientific methods used to produce larger and more intensive yields of everything from lambs to peas, poultry to wheat, pot plants to pigs, rainbow trout to trees.

While the majority of jobs are on the land itself, in the very practical, hard work which, despite modern science and technology, is still farming, horticulture, gardening, forestry and fishing, there are related occupations. These include the advisory services (*see below and also in* CENTRAL GOVERNMENT), teaching (*see* EDUCATION AND TEACHING), scientific research and technology. They usually require specialist training to degree level.

Agricultural production too needs a rather better intellectual and educational background than has been traditional in order to understand, operate and adapt to scientific and technological equipment and techniques, and to exploit modern marketing methods. Modern, sophisticated equipment has considerably reduced much of the heavier, backbreaking drudgery of work on the land; animals, birds, and some crops are more often cared for under cover in clean, hygienic conditions. The weather, though, is still a major factor to cope with, and hours are still more often than not long and irregular.

Agriculture

Dairy farming – sheep farming – arable farming – poultry farming – deer farming – working in agriculture

The agricultural industry has become a victim of its own efficiency and productivity. In Britain and Europe, at least, the industry is producing more food than can be sold while EC quotas on output threaten profitability.

Farming occupies almost 80% of the land areas of the British Isles, and in 1993 its contribution to the Gross Domestic Product was £7.6bn or 1.4% of total GDP. Fifty years ago Britain's farms produced about a third of the food for 48 million people. By 1994 they were producing three-fifths of the nation's food and exporting some, too. This was the result of investing heavily in science and technology: developing high-yield crops, sophisticated breeding techniques for both livestock and crop plants, feeding the soil, feeding animals better, improving seed germination and fertilisers, controlling pests and diseases, improving drainage and irrigation, and developing sophisticated machinery and intensive methods generally. But this has meant a huge and largely uncalculated increase in the use of resources.

This has also been achieved with a massive drop in the numbers of people working on the land: from about 800,000 in 1967 to 528,000 in 1994 (including farmers, partners and directors, regular full- and part-time employees and casual workers). This represents about 2.2% of the total workforce. The farming industry provides more than 15% of employment in rural areas – in some parts of the country much more.

High levels of productivity have led to surpluses, and in 1988/89 a number of grant schemes were introduced to encourage farmers to seek other sources of revenue rather than produce surpluses. Modern farming methods have changed the face of the land, often dramatically, and there are now far fewer but much larger farms.

Officially there are still (1994) some 244,253 'statistically significant' farming units in Britain. Of these, 153,426 are in England, 28,404 in Northern Ireland, 29,910 in Wales, and 32,513 in Scotland. Only 1,944 UK holdings have an agricultural area of 700 hectares and over. The greatest number, 41,880, have 50–100 hectares, followed by 36,943 with 10–20 hectares, while 14,135 farm less than two hectares. The trend towards fewer but larger units continues. Many farms are company-owned and run.

Farming is a business, and any profit farmers make depends increasingly on their business skills and efficiency, on a relentless drive to maximise performance. This depends as much on being able to ride the vagaries of the money markets and interest rates to make the best use of fast-declining support systems, as on more traditional farming skills. Figures released by the Ministry of Agriculture, Fisheries and Food (MAFF) in February 1996 revealed that farmers earned £1 billion more in 1995 than in 1994. This was partly because of the long, hot summer.

The Annual Report for 1995 of the National Farmers' Union (NFU) stated that British agriculture, with the regrettable exception of poultry and egg producers, had consolidated and improved its position. However, public misunderstanding about BSE had caused severe problems to the beef market. Live animal exports remained a high-profile issue during the year.

Farmers are increasingly using computers in managing their farms and employ management accountants, land agents, etc. to help them plan their finances and business generally. An arable farmer may, for example, have to decide whether it is efficient to lock up £1 million in harvesting and other machinery which may only be used for a few weeks each year, to be able to clear land quickly (so that another crop can be sown) with fewer workers. The benefits of economies of scale have had farmers cooperating: in building common grain stores so they can dry, store and ship their grain more cheaply and efficiently, for example. They have also moved 'down-line' from just growing food into the middle-man business of getting produce to the right places and then selling it.

Farmers will, in future, have to be even more inventive, and fast-thinking, to make a living. They can no longer simply increase output with intensive farming to improve profits, but must look for 'added-value' products and services. 'Diversification' is the order of the day.

Some are going into low-chemical-input, organic farming, to exploit the growing market for 'natural' foods. It is estimated that 14,000 hectares (an average of 24 hectares per farm) utilises organic farming methods. A further 4,100 hectares (average of 7 hectares per farm) is in the transition stage. Some are turning to (even more) unusual 'crops' – the list of experiments includes deer, llamas and goats (for their fleece), willows (for cheap fuel), sunflowers (for oil), durum 'spaghetti' wheat, edible snails. Farmers are being encouraged to grow more timber, to turn land over to recreational use, and to provide more holiday accommodation.

What farmers produce depends on an increasingly complex balance between acreage, soil type and weather – and therefore locality – quotas, availability of markets, and which product will bring in the best income. Officially, there are six different types of farming – arable, dairy, horticultural, livestock, pigs and poultry, and mixed – and although the trend has been to specialisation, there may be all kinds of reasons now for one kind of farm to go into another type of farming. An arable farmer, for example, may fatten beef cattle on potatoes which are too small or badly damaged to sell. If the potatoes are being grown for a crisps manufacturer, they may be a type which needs irrigation, and once an irrigation system is installed, other crops may become viable, and so on. Rape, from which margarine is made, has been popular with farmers because it is easier to grow than sugar beet and can be harvested by the same combines as bring in cereals.

Grazing livestock farms, dairy, hill, upland or lowland livestock production make up 60% of UK farm businesses; cereal and general cropping 20%; intensive livestock 4%; and horticultural holdings 5%. The West of England, with its higher rainfall, has better dairy pasture than the rest of the country.

Dairy farming

Dairy farming is the largest sector of the industry, but is in long-term decline. There are 39,904 dairy farms in the UK (1996 figures; 42,306 in 1990), less than a third of the 1965 figure. The fall in milk producers is expected to continue by a further 25% by the end of the century. The UK dairy herd now stands at 2.71 million dairy cows, and the average size of dairy herds in England and Wales is 70 animals. Average yields have risen, but although dairy cows are bred for maximum milk output, at least half of a cow's yield depends on the stockman or woman's skill in caring for and feeding her. Any break in routine can upset production, and feeding has to be carefully balanced and regulated.

Most dairy farms are highly mechanised, and most cows are milked in highly sophisticated and automated parlours, and even fed by machine. Dairy farming is very closely linked to milk marketing, processing and distribution. The Milk Marketing Board was abolished in 1995, and has been replaced by several different bulk milk purchasers (*see* FOOD AND DRINK SCIENTISTS AND MANUFACTURING *in* MANUFACTURING INDUSTRIES), which buy from some 31,510 registered producers in England and Wales.

Dual-purpose breeding, mainly of Friesians but also using Charolais and Limousin sires, means at least 66% of beef produced now comes from dairy cattle. Beef cattle and pigs are commonly weaned early and intensively fattened over shorter and shorter periods and as economically as possible, and to give the kind of meat consumers want, in indoor units which specialise in either breeding or fattening for market. Expert breeding – for the right kind of flesh and maximum numbers – accurate feeding, and meticulous care to keep them healthy (pigs particularly are disease prone) are crucial.

Sheep farming

Sheep are the sole 'crop' of specialist upland farms. On lowland farms they are not often more than a minor part of the stock and the units are smaller and intensive. Sheep can live in the open all the year round, so that as yet there are no permanent indoor units, the sheep generally roaming freely over what may be very rough country in the hills, or moved from pasture to pasture on lowland farms. To improve production, however, ewes either have lambs more often, or earlier, or are bred to have twins or triplets, which means lambing under cover and more work for shepherds. MAFF statistics show that the total number of sheep and lambs (20.2 million) in 1995 was similar to the previous year.

Arable farming

Arable crops are grown mainly in eastern and central-southern England and eastern Scotland. The crops grown (cereals and so on) need larger acreages than other forms of farming. Following the reduction in the set-aside requirement for 1995, the total area under crops increased that year by almost 2% to 3.87 million hectares. The area under cereals was nearly 2.7 million hectares, an increase of 4% compared with June 1994. The area of fodder crops fell by 6% with a 19% drop in the area of field beans. There was a further large increase (13%) in the area of maize grown, which now accounts for around 30% of the total area of fodder crops. The area of oilseed rape fell by 8%. This crop area had been affected by penalties on subsidy payments resulting from plantings greater than the allowed areas in 1994. The NFU forecast was that the 1995 cereals harvest at some 21.67 million tonnes would be 8.7% up on the 1994 outcome. The wheat yield, estimated at 7.66 tonnes per hectare was the second highest on record – bettered only in 1984. Whatever the crop, the annual cycle of ploughing, cultivating, sowing and harvesting is similar from farm to farm.

Poultry farming

Poultry, for both meat and eggs, developed in less than 20 years from a sideline to an industry producing some 874,000 tonnes of meat in 1985 (1936–38 output was only 90,000) and in 1990 this reached over a million tonnes. In 1993 British shoppers bought almost £1.5 billion worth of poultry meat a year and £1.1 billion worth of eggs a year. Chickens make up most poultry production, but turkeys, produced year round, and ducks, make up a growing proportion.

Laying birds, producing eggs for sale and for hatcheries; the hatcheries; and broiler fattening, are all separate operations. Some poultry producers maintain laying birds, hatcheries and broiler production, but usually they specialise, broiler firms buying-in many thousands of chicks from egg producers, some also 'contracting-out' broiler-bird fattening to farmers who return them for killing, cleaning, plucking and packing. All operations are now highly automated, even industrialised, and bear little resemblance to traditional methods of poultry care. Over 95% of laying birds and broilers are handled intensively indoors, under deep-litter or battery systems. Laying birds live under artificial light to stimulate production. Feeding, watering and egg collection are mostly automated, but hygiene, ventilation and heating need great care, and cleaning has to be extremely efficient. Systems are constantly being improved and refined.

Approximately 800 million dozen eggs were produced in the UK for human consumption in 1993, and 14 million dozen were exported to other European Union countries.

Deer farming

There has been accelerated growth of the deer farming industry, and a growing need for professional management of wild deer in commercial forestry and in agriculture. Owners of park deer are anxious to improve the profitability of their herds by increasing venison production and live sales.

Working in agriculture

Farmers, tenant-farmers and farm managers – supervisory staff – skilled farm workers – stockmen/stockwomen – arable and mixed farms – working with machinery – farm secretaries – agricultural scientists – soil scientists – agricultural advisory services – agricultural research – agricultural contractors – farriers/blacksmiths – other work

Fewer and fewer people gain their income from the land, and numbers have been falling steadily. By the end of 1985, only 364,000 people were employed full-time (a further 252,000 were working part-time, seasonally or on a casual basis). Provisional MAFF census figures for June 1995 showed the total labour force (full- and part-time), including farmers and their wives/husbands, to be 428,100. Salaried managers were 6,800 (the same as in 1993) and total other family and hired workers 191,600.

Farmers, tenant-farmers and farm managers

Farmers, tenant-farmers and farm managers are today expert in both farming techniques and business methods, and have to be skilled managers. They have to organise work on the farm and supervise staff, do their own purchasing – of feedstuffs and fertilisers which can cost several thousand pounds. They have to market their produce, which may range from the traditional methods of taking stock to market to agreeing major contracts with food processors and producers. They must assess and plan progress, decide on investment – in stock, equipment, etc. – negotiate with the bank, see that the farm is maintained properly, and so on. Paperwork – records, tax, applications for support, correspondence, orders – is as extensive as in any other business. Most farmers still also spend a high proportion of their time actually working on the land: only on the largest company-owned estates is farm management almost entirely administrative.

Supervisory staff

Supervisory staff are employed on the largest farms and holdings. They may be in charge of, for instance, a number of poultry or pig units, or larger dairy herds where several stockmen/women are employed.

Skilled farmworkers

Skilled farmworkers mostly specialise in the work they do, whether they work on a specialist or a mixed farm. But while there are fewer and fewer general farmworkers, most people working on the farm expect to help out with almost anything when necessary: the pig stockman may take charge of the baler at harvest time, or plough a field. Most farmworkers are trained to drive or operate machinery, help with farm and equipment repairs, etc.

Stockmen/stockwomen

Stockmen/stockwomen care for animals – dairy herds, beef cattle, pigs, poultry, or sheep – each in their own special units. They look after larger and larger units: 20,000 poultry, a flock of 1,400 ewes, 2,000 pigs, or a herd of 200 cows. Except for shepherds, whose lives are still very hardy, they work mostly indoors, under artificially controlled, almost laboratory-like conditions, and mostly alone with only a large number of birds or animals for company, although shepherds have their dogs. Feeding and watering is mostly automatic, but stockmen and stockwomen must take great care to see that feeds are measured and mixed correctly, that all the equipment – feeding, ventilation and so on – is working properly, and that bedding is changed; and they must keep everything very clean, since hygiene is essential. Since most farm animals, especially under intensive conditions, are vulnerable to disease and do not react well to any break in routines, they have to be watched carefully for signs of trouble; dipped, injected, clipped, and inseminated at exactly the right times, and cared for when progeny arrive.

Stockmen and stockwomen are both midwives and nurses for sick animals. They must keep careful records, of weight increase and food intake, for instance, to monitor costs and efficiency, and dairymen and women must watch each cow's milk output. They must have animals ready for market when prices are best, and know just when to replace dairy cows – and have replacements available. Under intensive conditions, one electricity failure, one sick animal, can mean a major financial disaster if not caught in time, so stockmen and stockwomen carry considerable responsibility. Hours are long and irregular, since animals must be cared for round the clock, and cows milked, seven days a week.

Arable and mixed farms

On arable and mixed farms the job includes working the land: ploughing; fertilising; sowing; making hay and silage; harvesting wheat and barley, rape, potatoes, cabbage and cauliflower, beet and peas.

Working with machinery

Working with machinery is obviously now a large part of any farming career. On an arable farm, tractors plough, cultivate, drill seed, apply fertiliser, and spray, and most have combine harvesters. Other kinds of machinery include hedge trimmers and ditch graders, and the highly specialised machines, e.g. pea-viners, for harvesting different kinds of crops. The rough-terrain fork-lift truck is a firm favourite. Fixed equipment ranges from large grain-drying and storage plant to complex computerised milking parlours and feed-mixers.

Most farmworkers will use tractors and other machinery as part of their work, but larger farms may employ people mainly as tractor/harvester drivers, and the largest employ their own mechanics.

Farm secretaries

Farm secretaries are important in the farm economy, to cope with the extensive records, books, orders, forms, correspondence, etc. efficiently. Most large farms employ full-time secretarial help, but many use peripatetic farm secretaries, who travel from farm to farm. Some secretaries are self-employed, some work for agencies.

Agricultural scientists

Agricultural scientists are not scientifically qualified farmers, but research workers, advisers and so on.

They have made an enormous contribution to the increased productivity of the agricultural and horticultural industries in the past 40 years. This has largely been the result of extensive research: into improving crop yields, into new ways of growing crops, into making soils more fertile (e.g. greatly improved fertilisers), matching crops more closely to soil types, finding better ways of controlling pests and making crops disease-resistant, breeding fruit trees and bushes which can be harvested mechanically, improving animal stock through genetic studies.

The direction of R&D in agriculture is now changing, partly as a result of its own success – which has brought over-production – and partly due to financial cutbacks. More 'straightforward' research, on, e.g., arable crops and animal diseases and production, is being cut back, and more complex, 'modern' interdisciplinary studies, on, e.g., the molecular biology of crops and livestock, 'genetic engineering', will expand. Seeds are being improved with work in plant biochemistry and genetics; 'cloning' is producing plants with the most useful characteristics; more highly selective pesticides are being made by biocatalytic syntheses and isomer separation; new complex 'plant growth regulators' promise major improvements in crop yields, plants that are easier to manage and tailored to fit their purpose and available growing space, and even to open up new markets – miniature carrots, for instance, as health-food snacks.

Soil scientists

Soil is a vital natural resource, from which most of our basic food, fibre and timber are produced. It is also a highly complex material. All the time chemical, physical and biological processes are taking place. These, in their turn, are influenced by climatic and human factors.

Soil scientists study the properties of soil. They also apply this fundamental information to the solution of problems such as pollution control, crop production, and the reduction of soil degradation.

Soil scientists are employed in a number of research institutes and organisations, four being of particular interest: the Soil Survey and Land Research Centre at Silsoe; the Macaulay Land Use Research Institute in Aberdeen; the BBSRC-supported Institute of Arable Crops Research at Rothamsted; and the Institute of Grassland and Environmental Research. Research into soil-related topics also goes on in certain ADAS R&D centres. For all these posts, it is increasingly necessary to have a higher degree.

A few opportunities occur in education (universities and colleges of agriculture and horticulture), government departments and agencies, local government departments, industry and commerce, with major civil engineering companies, and the water industry.

Many professional soil scientists work overseas. Some are in higher education, perhaps via VSO. Others go out as experts (under the auspices of the Overseas Development Administration) to developing countries in need of assistance in projects concerned with increasing food production.

Soil science is, however, a relatively small profession. Most soil scientists are members of the British Society of Soil Science, which has 1,000 members.

Agricultural advisory services

ADAS (the Agricultural Development Advisory Service) became an Agency in April 1992 within the Ministry of Agriculture, Fisheries and Food. It is responsible for providing a range of scientific, technical, veterinary, and professional advice services for agricultural and associated industries, as well as to the government, and to individuals and corporate groups concerned with the countryside. Most of the advice services are fee-paying although in some areas, such as advice on conservation services, it is free. To back up the consultancy services, ADAS undertakes research and development on a large scale.

In Scotland these services are provided by the Department of Agriculture and Fisheries, the Scottish Agricultural Colleges and sectors of the state veterinary service.

In Northern Ireland, the Department of Agriculture has its own advisory and scientific service. These bodies are also responsible for advising the government on agricultural policy.

ADAS has around 2,500 staff, the majority of whom are scientists and professionals. Many ADAS consultants are based in seven consultancy centres, three statutory centres and five research centres. Some consultants are field-based.

Graduates are recruited for research, to the inspectorate, or to the advisory side. Consultants should normally have an honours degree in the appropriate specialism for the chosen area of work. There are over 30 of these, ranging from agricultural engineering and agronomy to structural engineering and wildlife and storage biology. They also include less obvious disciplines such as architecture, ergonomics, building design, and cartography.

In addition to the graduate-level staff, there are some scientific grades, whose duties are to assist with the running of experiments. Scientific officers require a minimum of HND, and assistant scientific officers four GCSEs, including maths and a science.

Large commercial organisations and manufacturers which supply the industry with seed, feedstuffs, equipment, and so on, also employ qualified advisory staff, but the service they provide is rather more limited. *See also* CAREERS IN CONSERVATION AND THE ENVIRONMENT; *and* CENTRAL GOVERNMENT.

Agricultural research

Agricultural research is conducted under the umbrella of the Biotechnology and Biological Sciences Research Council (BBSRC). This was established by Royal Charter in 1994, by the incorporation of the former Agricultural and Food Research Council with the biotechnology and biological sciences programmes of the former Science and Engineering Research Council. It is a non-departmental public body principally funded by the Department of Trade and Industry (DTI) through the Science Budget.

Its three main purposes are:

1 to promote and support high quality basic, strategic and applied research and related postgraduate training relating to the understanding and exploitation of biological systems;
2 to advance knowledge and technology and to provide trained scientists and engineers, to meet the needs of users and beneficiaries (including the agriculture, bioprocessing, chemical, food, healthcare, pharmaceutical and biotechnological-related industries), thereby contributing to the economic competitiveness of the United Kingdom and the quality of life;
3 to provide advice, disseminate knowledge and promote public understanding in the fields of biotechnology and the biological sciences.

The Council fosters multidisciplinary approaches, so there are opportunities for contributions from chemists, physicists, agricultural scientists and engineers, as well as biologists.

The BBSRC currently supports research in nine research institutes and in four Interdisciplinary Research Centres, and several smaller units and groups within universities. The institutes sponsored by the BBSRC derive, on average, half their income from the BBSRC, a significant proportion from the Ministry of Agriculture, Fisheries and Food (MAFF) by means of research commissioned on a customer/contractor basis, and the balance from various government departments, the European Commission, grant-awarding bodies and industry.

Most agricultural research is very practical – the most fundamental is in areas like growth and genetics – and in industry is likely to be concerned with the development or improvement of specific products. It usually involves both lab work and field and farm tests and trials, and yields, weights, output, etc., all have to be recorded and analysed statistically.

Agricultural contractors

Agricultural contractors provide services for farmers, generally on an occasional basis, especially at seasons when there is extra work or for work where the equipment may only be used for, e.g., harvesting, although some farmers now use contractors regularly for work such as hedging, ditching and drainage. Contractors employ managers and experienced workers, who have to be prepared to work in different places, often from day to day.

Farriers/blacksmiths

Farriers/blacksmiths number about 1,700 countrywide. Smaller farmers, who do not usually employ their own mechanics, use blacksmiths to do running repairs, e.g. straightening damaged ploughs, welding on machinery, joining broken chains, and most farriers do this as well as shoeing horses. In some areas, the numbers of riding schools, stables and racing stables make it possible to specialise in shoeing/farrier's work. Some horse trainers, and one or two brewery firms, employ their own farriers.

Other work

In industry, large farm-supply manufacturers also employ specialist graduates in marketing and sales. Food companies purchasing large quantities of produce, e.g. cereals for bread, etc., or vegetables for freezing, take agricultural scientists to train as buyers.

For overseas, agricultural scientists with a background of tropical agriculture are recruited by the Overseas Development Administration for the British aid programme to developing countries and by some large companies for managerial and technical work on their crop operations in other countries. *See also* WORKING OVERSEAS.

Teaching posts are mainly in agricultural colleges but with a small number of posts in universities.

Recruitment and entry

Opportunities, and routes in, vary.

Farmers

Anyone wanting to be a farmer has first to acquire a farm. This is – at least at present – very difficult, with few farms or smallholdings to rent, and so the chances of becoming a tenant-farmer – the traditional way to start – are very slim. Two-thirds of all farms are owner-farmed. To buy and stock even the smallest farm, which is less and less viable economically, means having considerable capital. Inheriting is the only certain way now. It does not make sense in today's conditions to try farming without gaining proper training (*see below*) and experience first.

Farm managers

Farm managers generally need an appropriate farming qualification, farming experience, and increasingly a management/business qualification as well. Although the number of managers' posts has not fallen lately, competition for vacancies is considerable. Managers are not usually taken on under the age of about 30.

Farm work

While it is possible to find a job on a farm, for young people intending to make a career in farming the best route is via a training scheme and/or FE course (*below*).

A high proportion of entrants to farming have no formal educational qualifications, but it is becoming increasingly important to have some exam passes at 16-plus to make promotion to responsible positions easier, and better qualifications are now an increasing advantage.

Qualifications and training

Profitable farming needs better-trained and highly skilled people who are able to adopt, adapt to, and make full use of new techniques and systems. Farmers are increasingly demanding high technical, supervisory and operator skills. Farmers themselves generally train via agricultural college, taking national awards.

For school-leavers entering farmwork below 18 years of age the usual route is via the YT Preferred National Scheme of one or two years' duration depending on age. No formal academic qualifications are required.

YT combines experience in the workplace with day/block release at college. All trainees work toward completion of units of National and Scottish Vocational Qualifications (NVQ/SVQs) at level 1 leading to the award of the Preliminary Certificate in Agriculture.

Those not undergoing YT should still receive on-the-job training and aim to complete NVQ/SVQ units for the Preliminary Certificate in the first two years. In some cases, modern apprenticeships are possible.

These units cover different work areas in detail: health and safety, driving a tractor, operating tractor-drawn machinery, repair and maintenance of farm buildings and equipment, looking after farm animals, feeding livestock, etc. On completion of level 1 trainees go on to work toward NVQ level 2, which is more advanced and covers areas such as dairy, beef, sheep, pig and goat production, estate management, etc. and leads to craft status. Level 3 NVQs deal with more complex skills.

In Scotland trainees follow a similar pattern of training in SVQ units at levels 1 and 2 via SCOTVEC National Certificate modules.

Agriculture/Agricultural degrees

Most degree courses in agriculture are biased to scientific aspects; few include any practical farming, and all begin with a substantial grounding in biological sciences, chemistry, some physics and mathematics. There is a wide range of different kinds of courses, but at a relatively small number of institutions. While there are many different course titles, it is generally possible at any one university to put off finally choosing a particular specialisation until the end of the first year. Undergraduate and postgraduate courses in agriculture and related disciplines include:

Universities: Aberdeen, Aberystwyth, Belfast, Bangor, Cambridge, de Montfort, Edinburgh, Glasgow, Leeds, London (Wye), Newcastle-upon-Tyne, Nottingham, Oxford, Plymouth, Queen's (Belfast), Reading, Strathclyde.

Colleges: Writtle, Harper Adams, Royal Agricultural College, Scottish Agricultural College and Silsoe.

'First destination' figures (agriculture/agricultural sciences) are, for 1993–94:

total graduating	653
research/further study, etc.	98
teacher training	11
other training	28
believed unemployed Dec 31	56
temporary work	41
permanent overseas work	18
permanent UK work	265
employers	
agriculture, etc.	94
commerce	42
industry other than chemicals	29
Civil Service	8
chemicals	8
local government	18
higher/further education	21
functions	
administration/operational management	104
marketing, etc.	34
scientific R&D	27
financial work	12
medical/personnel/social	237
scientific support services	13
teaching/lecturing	7
management services	4

A few higher-degree and diploma courses both allow those who have graduated in agricultural sciences to continue their studies to a more advanced level, and give graduates with suitable degrees in related disciplines the opportunity to convert to an applied specialisation in this area.

Agriculture and agricultural science degree courses are intended as preparation for scientific/advisory work and not to train farmers or farm managers, although intending farmers can and do take them. Anyone intending to farm or do related work should try to gain a year's practical experience before entry.

Soil science degrees

There are two training routes for soil scientists. One can either take a degree in soil science, or one which includes a substantial element of soil science, at the universities of Aberdeen, Newcastle or Reading, or take an appropriate first degree in pure or applied sciences, followed by an MSc, MPhil, PhD or postgraduate diploma in soil science.

BTEC awards

Schemes have a strong scientific base to support the production technology areas. All schemes include crop and animal production, mechanisation, management and marketing, but specialisation is also possible.

The Higher National Diploma is an advanced three-year sandwich-based course, primarily preparing for practical farming at a senior level or for work in an industry related to agricultural or ancillary professions. Specialised courses include arable or poultry husbandry, agricultural marketing, business administration and animal management/equine science.

Entry requirements are five GCSE passes including English and two maths/science subjects plus a science subject at A-level, or, a BTEC national in an appropriate subject (specially designed two-year HND schemes are planned for students who have a National Diploma in a similar subject area).

The National Diploma is a three-year sandwich-based course with a choice of either general agriculture or specialisation in, e.g., dairy technology, poultry husbandry, pig production or horse management. Entry requirements are four GCSE or equivalent passes at 16-plus including English and two maths/science subjects, plus at least twelve months' practical farming experience (which may be a YT year).

The First Diploma is a full-time course available at some colleges of agriculture and horticulture, aimed at school-leavers who wish to proceed onto the National Diploma, but do not have the full academic qualifications to do so without further study. It may or may not be residential, and completion of the course satisfies the requirement for pre-college industrial experience.

National Certificates

National Certificates in Agriculture (NCA) are one-year full-time courses in general agriculture available at most agricultural colleges. Students are normally required to have reached the age of 18 by 1 September in the year of entry. Candidates should note that demand far exceeds places, therefore a good general education, preferably at GCSE level or equivalent, is required, plus at least one year's practical experience (YT year may also qualify). These courses provide a sound basic training for those wishing to work in practical farming.

Sparsholt College, Hampshire, now offers a one-year course leading to the NEB Advanced National Certificate in Deer Management.

Other qualifications

Farriers are required (by law) to go through a four-year full-time training with an approved training farrier, including residential training at Hereford Technical College school of farriery.

Entrants spend a trial period of up to 12 weeks with a trainer, followed by written and practical exams with interview at Hereford. The diploma exam of the Worshipful Company of Farriers must be passed to become a registered farrier.

Further information

CETAC Warwickshire Careers Service, BTEC, East Anglian Regional Advisory Council for Further Education (Directory of Courses in Land-based Industries), the Farriery Training Service and the British Society of Soil Science.

Fishing

The waters around the UK have traditionally provided some of the richest fishing grounds in the world. However, sustainable fishing is essentially dependent on the successful management of fish stocks, and so EU quotas are increasingly stringent and further conservation measures are being introduced. The fishing industry, therefore, has had to adapt to many changing circumstances in recent years. Total landings of fish and shellfish in 1994 were about 640,000 tonnes.

There are around 9,500 fishing vessels in the UK fleet ranging from very small day boats, operating from beaches and harbours around the coast, through to the largest trawlers and purse seiners mainly operated from Scottish fishing ports such as Peterhead and Lerwick.

The small day boats use pots (creels), lines and fixed nets to catch a wide variety of fish and shellfish close to the coastline. Medium-sized vessels use various sorts of trawls and seines, which are towed along the seabed, to take major species such as cod, haddock, and plaice from the North Sea, the west and north of Scotland, the Irish Sea and the Channel. The latest, most efficient purse seiners can catch several hundred tonnes of herring and mackerel in one haul and hold the fish in refrigerated seawater tanks until it can be discharged ashore or to other vessels known as 'klondykers'.

Working in the fishing industry

In 1994 about 16,000 or so people were going to sea regularly, against 18,500 in 1973, but the number of part-time, mainly seasonal skippers and crews, has remained fairly static since 1986 at about 5,000. Owners have economised by reducing crews, but the impact of technology, quotas and more efficient fishing methods has served to reduce the number of people required. The number of fishing boats in operation also affects the onshore employment opportunities, and for every fisherman at sea there are between three and five people working onshore, as, for example, fish salespeople, and in boat-building, ship-repairing, fish gear manufacture and similar supporting sectors.

Fishing combines seagoing with food hunting and gathering, together with various levels of food processing. Fishing is still very hard and dangerous, but the industry talks of greater comfort, sophisticated electronic equipment for navigation and locating fish, and efficient fishing gear, which turns deckhands into 'technicians'. While fishing is underway, work can be continuous and round-the-clock, with every hand working shifts of up to 18 hours. On some boats, particularly the smaller ones, much of the work is done on deck. On larger ships, however, much of the processing is carried out below, and only while 'shooting' the net and hauling it in again are crews exposed to the weather. On smaller vessels, which may still be very modern and have highly sophisticated gear on board, crews must sort and stow the fish once it is hauled in, and wash down decks. Larger vessels usually carry one or more designated engineers and a cook who will also perform other general duties. On smaller boats, particularly those which operate on a day-trip basis, all duties tend to be shared out between the crew. *See* WORKING AT SEA *in* THE TRANSPORT INDUSTRY.

Fishing vessels use a variety of methods to catch fish, and many boats are designed to operate in a multipurpose role depending on seasonal factors and quota restrictions. Bottom-trawling, where a net is dragged along the seabed behind one or between two vessels, can be used to catch ground fish such as cod, haddock or plaice. Midwater-trawling, where the net is towed off the seabed, is used to catch shoaling species such as mackerel, herring and sprats. Seine net boats which herd fish into the net by means of long ropes, operate mainly in sandy areas free of seabed obstructions, while purse seiners are able to surround shoals of pelagic fish with a wall of netting and then close the bottom edges together like a zip fastener.

Inshore fishing boats are generally small, and use a greater variety of gears, including trawls, pots, gill nets, lines and dredges.

The stocks of fish in the North Sea and other traditional fishing grounds are subject to intense fishing pressure from all European fishing nations. Therefore fisheries management, with the objective of ensuring the continuing long-term health of fish stocks for commercial fishing, is organised through a system of Total Allowable Catches (TACs) and national quotas. Regulations on mesh sizes and minimum landing sizes are also in place to protect young fish.

Ashore, managers, administrative and clerical staff work for the owners or vessel agencies, harbours and market authorities. The fish-processing industry covers a very wide range of different companies varying from simple sorting and packing operations to producers of ready-to-cook meals. Fish in various retail and catering forms also features as one of the products marketed by the national frozen-food companies. Export markets are becoming more and more important to the UK fish catchers and processors.

Recruitment and training

Although the number of regularly employed fishermen/women is tending to decrease, the industry must still continue to recruit. The usual route of entry for young people is via one of twelve area-based Group Training Associations, who either coordinate through others or operate their own Youth Training, or (in Scotland) Skillseekers schemes. In 1994/95, 156 trainees were taken on compared to the 1989/90 figure of 280. Most of those who go into the industry have grown up in fishing ports or have family fishing connections, but there is nothing to prevent anyone from another part of the country from entering the industry. All fishermen/women must be good 'seamen', able to do many different tasks, and to react in an emergency. Good health, stamina and the ability to work in a team are obviously essential. All recruits must undergo statutory one-day training courses in sea survival, fire-fighting and first aid before going to sea.

The industry recruits small numbers of school-leavers and graduates with appropriate qualifications for administrative/managerial work – including the main commercial 'functions' – in both fishing and fish-processing companies. The food-processing industry provides opportunities in a wide range of occupational areas, including production work, sales and marketing, buying, product research and development, and is currently facing a shortage of food technologists.

Qualifications and training

Training is organised by the Sea Fish Industry Authority Training Council, mainly through its network of twelve group training associations. The Authority has a sophisticated 'flume' tank at its base in Hull which is used for testing model trawls and for training fishermen in gear technology through its courses organised via the group training associations.

New entrant fishermen/women on Youth Training or Skillseeker schemes enrol on programmes which lead to achievement of competent deckhands in Fishing Vessel Operations NVQ/SVQ level 2. The modern apprenticeship scheme which has been developed and introduced in 1995 is designed to allow new entrants to achieve NVQ/SVQ level 3 qualifications in either a deck or an engineering capacity.

By law, fishing vessels above a certain size and operating in prescribed areas must carry certificated ('ticketed') deck officers and engineers in line with a manning formula established by the Marine Safety Agency. With the recent development of competence-based vocational qualifications up to and including NVQ/SVQ level 4, with help from the industry, the Merchant Navy Training Board and the Marine Safety Agency of the Department of Transport, it is hoped that these new qualifications will eventually replace the 'ticket' qualifications currently prescribed for deck and engineer officers. These qualifications are being piloted at the present time alongside the existing statutory 'ticket' courses and will provide the future route by which a young person can work his or her way up to become mate, engineer, or even a skipper.

In 1994, 350 fishermen attended approved college courses leading to recognised certificates of competency. Formal college courses are supplemented by alternative methods of study. These include open-learning, which has proved a cost-effective route to a qualification for some fishermen without access to local college facilities.

Seafish Training, through its network of group training associations, also runs short courses, and in 1994 some 800 fishermen attended various in-port courses in a range of skills, including radio communications, helicopter rescue techniques and net-mending. In addition 1,700 fishermen attended statutory one-day safety courses in survival, fire-fighting, and first aid.

See also WORKING AT SEA *in* THE TRANSPORT INDUSTRY.

Further information

Sea Fish Industry Authority.

Fish farming

Some sea-creatures, e.g. oysters, have been 'farmed' under water for centuries, but as accessible stocks of naturally bred fish decrease, fish cultivation is increasing. The technology is well advanced, and only the problem of getting the cost–price equation right holds back development. Even so, in 1994, the value of the fish and shellfish farming industry was estimated at approximately £250 million.

Government-funded research has, for over 25 years, been trying to solve the problems of hatching and raising fish species from eggs under controlled conditions. They have been successful with sole and turbot, amongst others. There is now less research on fish farming funded by the government, as the application of techniques is felt to be more appropriately carried out (and funded) by the industry.

There is a certain amount of research into salmon farming still being carried out by the Marine Laboratory at Aberdeen and the Freshwater Fisheries laboratory at Pitlochry. Disease studies, especially in farmed salmon, continue.

To date, trout and salmon farming have been most successful. Output of trout in England, Wales and Northern Ireland was nearly 15,000 tonnes in 1994, and salmon 64,067 (compared with about 28,000 tonnes in 1990). According to the Ministry of Agriculture, Fisheries and Food, the number of people employed in the fish and shellfish farming industry in 1994 is estimated to be 3,000.

There are 802 registered fish-farming sites in England and Wales, and most still rear fish for stocking rivers and lakes for sport. Scotland has 658 registered sites (324 shellfish, 262 Atlantic salmon and 72 rainbow trout) and Northern Ireland 26. The number of jobs is still fairly small, but numbers are increasing. Most farms are small, owner-run businesses, although a number of frozen-food manufacturers and other large organisations have farms, particularly where heat and/or water is a by-product (e.g. electricity generation) or where fish can be used to test artificial feeds. The largest employers are the bigger Scottish salmon farms, with a limited number of posts within the National Rivers Authority. Government departments, the Sea Fish Industry Authority, and a number of trusts are others.

Fisheries management

Many of the jobs in fisheries are effectively 'policing', and dealing with the public (i.e. anglers), as water bailiff. The National Rivers Authority employs fisheries staff in a number of roles. Fisheries inspectors/bailiffs enforce fisheries legislation, check licences, perform fisheries management operations, etc. Fisheries scientists investigate fish populations, fish health, fish mortalities; (Area) Fisheries officers supervise the inspectors and are in charge of operations within regions.

On intensive fish farms, the jobs include managing fish farms/hatcheries; caring for the fish, from hatchery through to harvesting, constantly monitoring them and their environmental conditions, checking for disease, giving regular and exact feeds, etc. As with any intensive farming, any accident, disease, etc., can have catastrophic effects. Skilled marketing and commercial management are crucial functions. Most research jobs are in government, or research association labs, a few with pharmaceutical and feed companies. Fish farms are usually sited in remote areas, so weather, isolation, etc. are factors to take into account. Fish must be tended seven days a week, all year round, whatever the weather.

Recruitment and entry

Many of those keen to enter fisheries have undertaken a biological course, usually to first-degree level, some are still at school and others (ex-servicemen in particular) are seeking new careers.

Most of the positions for qualified staff go to biologists with specialist postgraduate training or fisheries experience. Prospective candidates who can reinforce their biological knowledge with other relevant skills will be viewed most favourably by employers. Skills might include:

- engineering training and experience, particularly agricultural or marine engineering;
- livestock husbandry experience, with evidence of inborn understanding of animals, show by good stockmen;
- a general agricultural training, including such skills as bricklaying, erection of concrete structures or laying concrete, plumbing and electrics, together with a general aptitude to make things work in a farming environment.

A full driving licence is almost essential. Generally it is advisable to obtain the highest qualifications before seeking permanent employment in the fisheries field.

The Institute of Fisheries Management (IFM) has identified five entry points to the industry:

1 *Hatchery workers/assistants.* A general interest in fisheries and previous experience of fishing methods, dealing with anglers and police work is useful for water bailiff positions. The Certificate of the IFM will almost always secure an interview.

2 *Head bailiff or hatchery manager/keeper.* Experience of working at point 1 is the major requirement. For technical assistant posts GCSE/SCE or A-levels/H grades or equivalent are normally required, and further qualifications an advantage.

3 *Assistant fisheries officers/biologists/research scientists.* Experience in a relevant post at point 2 or a degree in a biological subject coupled with other relevant experience. Postgraduate experience is particularly useful for research posts.

4 *Fisheries officers/ biologists/ research scientists.* Experience in a relevant post at point 3 or a higher university degree in a biological subject coupled with a number of years' involvement in the fisheries field. The Diploma of the IFM is a distinct advantage for entry points 2–4.

5 *Principal fisheries/ recreation/ scientific officer or equivalent.* A university degree coupled with several years of working in a relevant post at point 4 is a minimum requirement.

Qualifications and training

There are few opportunities, but they are expanding.

The Institute of Fisheries Management runs a correspondence course for its certificate exam, and success in this can lead to their diploma exam (two-year course).

Relevant BTEC ND, HND, SCOTVEC certificates and short courses are available at: Sparsholt College, Barony Agricultural College, Merrist Wood, Brooksby College, Lews Castle College, North Atlantic Fisheries College.

Relevant first-degree and postgraduate courses are available at the following universities: England – Buckingham, Hull, Lancaster, Liverpool, King's College London, Queen Mary and Westfield London, Newcastle, Norwich, Nottingham, Plymouth, Portsmouth, Reading, Cranfield (Silsoe), Sparsholt College; Scotland – Aberdeen, Edinburgh, Heriot-Watt, Stirling; Wales – Aberystwyth, Bangor, Swansea, School of Ocean Science (Menai Bridge), UWIST (Cardiff).

NVQs in Fish Husbandry to level 2 are available.

Further information

The Institute of Fisheries Management.

Forestry

Although Britain has doubled its forest area this century, it grows proportionately fewer trees than most European countries, and still (1994) imports 85% of timber used. The proportion of home-grown timber produced is increasing: in 1994 woodland covered 2.39 million hectares, about 10% of total land area, up from 8.5% in 1978. Government policy aims for steady expansion of tree cover. Productive forests cover more than two million hectares, about 46% at present owned and managed by the Forestry Commission, and the rest private. Woodland also represents a promising alternative for use of agricultural land. New planting is expected to rise steadily, with the major contribution from the private sector.

Since 1979 over one-third of a million hectares of new woodland have been planted in Great Britain. For the year ending 31 March 1995, the Forestry Commission provided grants for private planting for over 24,000 hectares. Since the introduction of the broadleaves policy in 1985, there has been a significant increase in the planting of broadleaf and mixed woodland. New planting with broadleaves has risen from 656 hectares in 1985 to over 10,000 hectares in 1995 and now accounts for over half of new planting. The mixture is 40% broadleaf to 60% conifers.

The emphasis nowadays is on multipurpose forestry.

The Forestry Commission encourages public access and welcomes more than 50 million day visitors to its forests each year to enjoy a range of leisure and recreational pursuits. Public recreational facilities owned and managed by the Forestry Commission include 29 camping and caravan sites, 630 picnic places, 752 forest walks and forest nature trails, 29 visitor centres, 22 arboreta and forest gardens, 11 forest drives, and 174 forest cabins and holiday houses. It also offers 163 cycle trails, 87 horse trails and 31 wildlife hides.

In 1989 a joint initiative between the Forestry Commission and the Countryside Commission to create community forests on the outskirts of major cities and towns in England and Wales has so far led to the establishment of twelve designated community forest areas.

The state-owned Forestry Commission fulfils two distinct roles:

1 As the Forestry Authority it acts as adviser on government forestry policy and undertakes functions such as research, technical advice, plant health, the control of tree-felling and the administration of grant aid for the private sector.
2 The Forestry Enterprise, an agency of the Forestry Commission, acts as a trading body primarily responsible for the management of Commission forests, but with other functions such as the protection and enhancement of the environment and the provision of recreational facilities.

The Commission produces and markets timber; provides recreational facilities; encourages private forestry and offers grants; does research and development work; and trains.

For private owners, the Commission provides a technical advisory service, financial grants, and schemes for planned management.

The Commission coordinates the country's forestry research through a forestry research coordination committee. The Commission itself works mainly on practical problems – e.g. methods of improving trees and sites to increase the volume of wood produced and improving some properties of wood for major future markets, new methods of propagating and growing broadleaved and coniferous trees (e.g. enclosing seedlings in plastic tubes), machinery development, and use of forest produce.

Basic research is more limited and is mainly concentrated in tree health, forest hydrology, tree genetics, pests and disease control.

The Commission has two main research stations, one near Farnham (Surrey), the other at Roslin, near Edinburgh.

Working in forestry

The Forestry Commission's latest employment survey (1993/94) shows there were around 35,000 jobs within the forestry industry with more than half in England. Of these, 40% were in the haulage of timber and primary wood-processing activity. There was an overall decrease in jobs compared with a similar survey in 1989, primarily due to increased efficiency.

Work-years (whole job equivalent):

	England	Wales	Scotland	GB
Forestry Commission	2,570	1,270	2,810	6,650
Private estates	7,525	1,100	2,125	10,750
Management companies	735	125	1,050	1,910
Timber-harvesting companies	2,135	515	1,645	4,295
Wood-processing	6,445	1,740	3,030	11,215
Total	19,410	4,750	10,660	34,820

The wood-processing industry has been revitalised over the past decade. Production has risen since 1979 from 4.7 million cubic metres to 7.7 million cubic metres a year in 1994. It is expected to rise further to nearly 9 million cubic metres a year by 2000.

Employers other than the Forestry Commission include private landowners (especially in Scotland), cooperative forestry societies, local authorities, and commercial firms, particularly contractors who provide tree-care services, and some timber merchants.

Other agencies involved in forestry, such as the Ministry of Agriculture (which encourages shelter plantings), conservation bodies such as English Heritage, and the Department of the Environment (*see* CAREERS IN CONSERVATION AND THE ENVIRONMENT), do not employ forestry officers as such.

Within the Forestry Commission, aside from general care of woodlands, the work involves seed-collection; preparing land for tree-planting; raising and planting trees for afforestation and replanting; tree-thinning, which involves marking and sometimes felling and transporting timber, fire protection; and road work – the Commission builds and maintains its own roads.

The work is highly mechanised, and some sophisticated machinery can be used even deep in the forests. A high proportion of forest staff work in such remote areas that the Forestry Commission provides not just houses but complete 'forest villages', managed by Commission-employed estate officers.

In forestry work, the main jobs are as follows:

- *Forest workers*: mainly manual work, or operating machines, in fencing, planting, draining, weeding, pruning, felling and nursery work. Workers can become forest craftsmen, and gain promotion to ranger or foreman.
- *Wildlife rangers*: protect and conserve the forests and forest wildlife, control pests, create and keep up habitats for birds, animals, etc., and act as guides for the public. It is a round-the-clock job.
- *Foresters*: technical, on-site supervisors, planning, measuring and controlling work programmes, estimating costs, setting piecework rates, controlling and protecting forest property, etc. They mainly look after planting, tree care and felling, but also liaise with other landowners and people using the forests. Some do more specialist work, e.g. wildlife conservation, research, training forest workers, work study, etc.
- *Forest officers*: district forest, or 'junior' managers do work similar to foresters at a more senior level, administer grants and felling licences, some going into recreation management, R&D, training, etc. They may be promoted to district and senior forest officers: senior management. The 'top' managers are the conservators.
- *Scientists*, with relevant qualifications, are employed in research, with some forest officers, etc.
- *Mechanical engineers* are in charge of the Commission's wide range of sophisticated mechanical equipment and vehicles. The Commission's mechanical engineers are charged with servicing and repairing machines while maintaining a consistently high level of availability of equipment over the wide range in use in Commission forests. They select, inspect and run workshops in the forest districts, and a few assess possible new equipment, deal with safety, etc.
- *Civil engineers* look after all the Commission's civil engineering works, supervising and organising maintenance of roads and bridges, car parks, water supplies, tip reclamation, etc., and a few are in R&D, planning, etc.
- *Clerks of works* supervise construction, improvement and maintenance of houses, offices, and farm and other buildings.
- *Land agents* manage the Commission's estate – buying, selling and letting land and buildings, etc., looking after wayleaves, grazings and holdings, and managing some commercial operations, e.g. camping and caravan sites.

The Commission also employs a few cartographic draughtsmen/women, and landscape architects (for both, *see in* LAND USE PROFESSIONS). Other employers include the National Parks, the water and electricity companies, forest contractors, some local authorities (*see in* LOCAL GOVERNMENT), and large private owners, who may be investment funds, etc.

Other work with trees

Forestry nowadays takes a multipurpose approach. 'Arboriculture' produces, plants and manages trees to make, and keep, the environment attractive, although arboriculturalists do help to manage woodlands of all kinds, and forestry and arboriculture do overlap.

Tree specialists are employed in the commercial sector, and by LOCAL GOVERNMENT. Producing trees – from seeds or vegetatively – is done mainly by nurseries, of which only some specialise in trees (*see* HORTICULTURE *below*). Some nurseries, independent commercial teams, and local authorities supply and plant trees. Tree surgeons do remedial work, repair damage, and trim and fell trees; they are mostly independent contractors, but some work for local authorities. Some large organisations, mainly local authorities, have enough trees in their care to employ professional tree specialists to manage them.

Recruitment and entry

Most private owners would want people as well-qualified as does the Forestry Commission. Competition at all levels of entry is considerable, so high standards are required.

The structure of forestry education and training has been designed and developed to meet the industry's needs, to provide formal recognition of technical and managerial competence and to encourage upward mobility for those with exceptional ability. The point of entry within the industry will depend on academic and/or vocational qualifications.

Forestry workers

No academic qualifications are required to start as a forest worker either with the Forestry Commission or in the private sector, although a reasonable level of literacy and numeracy is essential. There are very few direct openings and work is often in remote places, but good opportunities exist for those who are prepared to undertake contract work on a self-employed basis. Progression to forest craftsman or forest machine operator is common and is achieved usually by a combination of in-service training and college attendance by block-release.

Forest supervisors and managers

Forest supervisors and managers usually require either BTEC HND in Forestry, BTEC ND in Forestry (or Scottish equivalents), BSc degree in Forestry, City & Guilds Phase IV certificate in Forestry or SCOTVEC equivalent. A full driving licence is also essential.

People with these qualifications usually commence their career as Technical Managers/Supervisors, known in the industry as Foresters.

Other specialisms

Scientists will normally have a relevant degree, but some may be 'technically qualified' experimentalists with relevant experience.

Assistant scientific officers are recruited with at least four GCSE/SCEs or equivalent passes at 16-plus.

Engineers, clerks of works, land agents, etc. should have relevant qualifications and several years' practical experience.

In the Forestry Commission and some other large employers, opportunities also exist for those who wish to specialise in activities such as wildlife conservation, training or research. Subsequent progression within the industry is based on merit, and high calibre graduates can expect more rapid promotion to responsible posts, but there are no longer artificial barriers for those with lower-level qualifications. Wildlife rangers do not need any formal qualifications, but must have some relevant previous experience (vacancies are few and far between). Recruitment is on a local basis.

Qualifications and training

The National Preferred Youth Training Scheme is now firmly established within the forestry industry as an appropriate foundation for employment and entry to higher-level vocational qualifications. The scheme is aimed at school-leavers and lasts for two years, for those eligible for YT places. The scheme prepares young people for the working environment and at the same time allows them to learn specific skills. The YT programme enables trainees to gain vocational qualification NVQ/SVQs as either units or awards at levels 1 and 2. Proficiency test certification is often a part of the vocational qualifications training programme.

Entry is also possible after a full-time one-year BTEC first diploma or a SCOTVEC one- or two-year national certificate course.

City & Guilds courses for the National Certificate in Forestry are available either full or part-time at a number of colleges. In 1996 revised and extended vocational qualification NVQ/SVQs became available spanning levels 2, 3 and 4. At levels 2 and 3 the awards are functionally based to maximise access to them. The new awards allow for career progression through workplace-based assessment for new entrants and existing employees.

The Forestry Commission run their own short in-service training courses, and similar courses for the private sector are provided by Instructors registered with the Forestry Training Council. The Forestry and Arboriculture Safety and Training Council (FASTCO) provide a number of short skill courses according to local demand.

BTEC/SCOTVEC Diploma courses

Three-year sandwich courses lead to a National Diploma, or Higher National Diploma in Forestry. Minimum entry qualifications for ND are normally four GCSE passes in maths, English, a science subject and one other. Entry to HND requires an additional A-level/H grade. Vocational qualifications and relevant experience may also be acceptable, and candidates should check with individual colleges. ND courses are available at a selected number of colleges. HND courses are available at Newton Rigg in Cumbria (also leading to NVQ level 4) and at Inverness College in Scotland.

Degree-level courses

Degrees in forestry involve the study of biological characteristics of tree and forest growth, forests as 'raw material' for the timber industry, and the role trees and forests play in ecology and rural economy, as well as forest management.

BSc degree-level courses in forestry or forestry-related subjects are available at only three universities now: Aberdeen (Forestry) (those with good A-levels/H grades may be exempt from the first year); Edinburgh (Ecological Science and Forestry, or Agriculture, Forestry and Rural Economy);

and the University College of North Wales at Bangor (Forestry; Agroforestry; Soils and Forest Science; Wood Science and Forestry; and Wood Science).

Wood science courses are for those who wish to follow a career orientated to the wood-using industries. Provision on the above courses is made for a sandwich year to gain practical forestry experience.

'First destination' figures (forestry) are (1994):

total graduating	*60*
research/further study, etc.	3
training	6
believed unemployed Dec 31	6
temporary work	5
permanent overseas work	2
permanent UK work	29
employers	
forestry, agriculture, etc.	11
commerce	6
Civil Service	0
industry	0
local government	4
functions	
administration/operational management	17
scientific R&D	1
financial work	0
medical/personnel/social	0
scientific support services	2
environmental planning	1

Entry: A-level requirements vary from course to course, but two, preferably three, sciences are normally needed, with chemistry most frequently named; the other(s) from biological subjects, physics or maths. A year's practical farming experience may be required or an advantage.

NVQ/SVQs

NVQs at levels 1 and 2 and SVQs at levels 1, 2 and 3 are now available. Other level-3 and level-4 courses are being developed.

Professional qualifications

The National Diploma in Forestry (NDF) is considered equivalent to an ordinary degree. It is offered by the Central Forestry Examination Board and is for experienced forestry staff. The Institute of Chartered Foresters (ICF) offers chartered status by examination to professional foresters with two or more years' experience in approved practice. It is a two-part exam, and exemption may be obtained from some or all of Part 1 by possession of other forestry qualifications. Part 2 is taken by all candidates and tests professional competence.

Further information

The Forestry Commission, the Forestry Training Council, the Royal Forestry Societies, the Arboricultural Association.

Horticulture

Commercial horticulture – working in commercial horticulture – amenity horticulture

The industry divides into two. 'Commercial' horticulture produces crops – ranging from lettuces to cut flowers in market gardens, nurseries and greenhouses. 'Amenity' horticulture is traditionally 'aesthetic', using plants to create an attractive environment, but it extends increasingly into the wider role of landscape management and providing outdoor recreational and leisure facilities.

Horticulture is all too often equated with labouring on the land, or at best skilled craft-level 'gardening'. In fact, the main career prospects are in management which, while it requires a solid scientific/technical background, also takes expert business skills, the ability to handle people, and especially, for the commercial sector, MARKETING (*see in* BUYING, SELLING AND RELATED SERVICES).

Commercial horticulture

Growers produce a wide range of crops: top and soft fruit, vegetables and salads, mushrooms, cut flowers, pot plants, bulbs, ornamental trees, shrubs, roses and herbaceous and bedding plants. In 1994, a MAFF census showed that vegetables were grown on 10,118 holdings in the UK, covering 126,760 hectares; orchards and soft fruits on 6,932 holdings, covering 43,822 hectares; nursery stock, bulbs and flowers on 4,697 holdings, covering 14,174 hectares; and glasshouses on 5,704 holdings, covering 2,262 hectares.

Different crops are grown in different parts of the country, according to soil and weather conditions, and holdings range in size from those growing, for example, large acres of bulbs or flowers in Lincolnshire, or daffodils in the Scilly Isles, through apple orchards in the South-East and raspberries in Scotland, to smaller, intensive units specialising in tomatoes, cucumbers, etc. under glass. Field vegetables, though, are now grown widely throughout the country often, as are root crops in eastern England, on a very large scale, using methods similar to arable farming.

An expanding part of the industry caters for the country's very many gardeners. Nurseries specialise in producing seeds, or propagating and/or raising shrubs, roses, alpine plants, trees, etc. for amateur gardeners and for local authorities, landscape gardeners, firms and other organisations with parks, and for public gardens, town centres, etc. Garden centres are an important part of this business.

Profitability is hard to maintain in the face of high fuel and fertiliser bills, intense competition from overseas growers, and changing consumer demand. Even to stay in business takes greater technical and marketing expertise every year. Like farmers, growers are trying to maintain and improve profitability with more scientific methods of propagating, growing and feeding crops, and controlling pests and diseases. A small number of firms are already exploiting tissue culture and the cloning techniques of MOLECULAR BIOLOGY to produce plants.

Harvesting is mechanised – only flowering plants are now processed entirely by hand; heating and ventilating is automatically controlled in greenhouses, and watering is semi-automatically controlled. More crops are grown under plastic to extend the growing season, and each acre may now carry three or four crops a year, which means work in the fields also has to go on year-round. Improving profitability also means working closely with food-processing firms, and some crops, like peas, are processed in the fields. Marketing perishable produce is very difficult, and producers try all kinds of methods, including forming cooperatives and allowing customers to pick their own fruit.

Working in commercial horticulture

Commercial horticulture employs some 75,000 people, 30,000 of whom work in garden centres.

Growers and managers

Growers and managers for major horticultural producers are today expert in both the scientific horticultural techniques and business methods, and have to be skilled managers and marketers. They organise work on the holding and supervise staff, and do their own purchasing: of seeds, perhaps seedlings, and fertilisers which can cost several thousand pounds. They market their produce, and this may range from sending crops to market in the traditional way, to agreeing major contracts with food processors and producers. They must assess and plan progress, decide on investment in equipment, etc., negotiate with the bank, see that the holding is maintained properly, and so on. Paperwork – records, tax, applications for support, correspondence, orders – is as extensive as in any other business.

Skilled horticultural workers

Each type of crop, from fruit grown on trees through to tomatoes, cucumbers, or pot plants, is generally grown on a specialist holding, and demands expert care and attention. Most skilled workers therefore specialise, both in particular types of crop – ornamental plants, bulbs, fruit, salad, or greenhouse crops for example – and, on larger holdings, in particular stages of the operation. They may have to understand complex new biological techniques.

People who are making a full-time career of horticulture need spend only a relatively short period doing routine work on the land – or in the greenhouse – itself. This is because some of those working in commercial horticulture are part-time or seasonal workers, taken on as and when needed, particularly for setting cuttings or planting out, or harvesting, grading and packing, or when deliveries are being made to freezer or other food-processing firms, or to garden centres.

Once trainees have learnt the techniques of soil treatment and preparation, propagating, pricking-out and potting-on or planting-out, or pruning and pollinating, for example, and have enough experience, they can be promoted quite quickly. They may go on to technical work – deciding when to irrigate or apply fertilisers, and setting up equipment – and/or to supervisory work – in charge of a particular operation, like propagating or packaging, and responsible for the workers, keeping records, checking quality, etc.

Research and development

Research and development employs scientists – to develop the new propagating methods, new breeds of plants, more efficient fertilisers, better methods of controlling pests and diseases, etc. Engineers develop improved control and irrigation systems, harvesting equipment. Most research is done by specialist research stations, some larger and specialist firms and manufacturers. ADAS employs horticultural advisers. *See also* BIOLOGICAL SCIENCES.

Other opportunities

Opportunities are not, though, all with the growers and garden centres. Large customers, such as supermarkets, employ experienced staff in inspecting crops, purchasing, crop-estimating, and organising crop-processing.

Amenity horticulture

This is traditionally large-scale gardening, groundsmanship, etc. It is increasingly being treated as part of the recreation and leisure industry (*see* PROFESSIONAL SPORT AND THE RECREATION AND LEISURE INDUSTRIES), as much of the work involves managing and caring for parks, and areas which are used recreationally.

Employers include local and national authorities managing parks, public gardens and other landscaped areas; landscaping contractors; the National Trust, which maintains older larger gardens; and commercial firms who undertake maintenance and management on contract. Large private estates/gardens, particularly those belonging to historic houses, employ professional gardeners.

About 80,000 people are believed to be employed in this sector, and although many more trees and shrubs are being planted and areas landscaped, cuts in public expenditure and high costs, combined with mechanisation, are keeping down the number of jobs.

Local-authority parks departments have almost disappeared since the introduction of compulsory competitive tendering (CCT), under which the work is subcontracted to firms and individuals who compete for the contract. Contractors often have their own tree and plant nurseries.

More senior, managerial staff deal with more than just the horticultural work. They may be involved in developing the use of grounds, etc. for recreation, and managing facilities such as tennis courts, cafes, allotments or concert areas. They have to see that buildings, paths, etc. are maintained and cleaned, that rubbish is collected, and parks patrolled. But they may also be responsible for conservation, perhaps for making part of a formal park into a more natural habitat, or ensuring that developers do not destroy or damage woodland or specimen trees, for example.

Recruitment and entry

Becoming a grower is possible, but it can be difficult and very expensive to acquire enough land and equip it to grow crops for which only a large acreage is economic, since very little land is now available for rent. Some specialist markets – for herbs or a particular species of plants for gardeners – which need very little land, are possibilities. A few people are exploiting the new ways of propagating plants, which need little space (but quite sophisticated equipment). Proper training (*see below*) and experience are needed.

Managers are increasingly recruited with appropriate higher qualifications, at degree or HND level, plus experience, although it is possible to gain promotion from skilled and supervisory work.

For school-leavers entering horticultural work below 18 years of age there are now modern apprenticeships in amenity horticulture, and NVQ/SVQs in several different aspects of horticulture to be obtained while undergoing training. No formal academic qualifications are required.

Qualifications and training

For both amenity and commercial horticulture, it is probable that most managers will in future have gained a post-A-level, or equivalent, qualification. Both sectors of horticulture need better-trained and highly skilled people who are able to adopt, adapt to, and make full use of new techniques and systems, at all levels from operator, through technical and supervisory, to managerial.

Degree courses

Horticulture degree courses are intended to prepare for scientific/advisory careers and not to train growers or managers, although growers/managers increasingly take them. Anyone intending to go into the industry or do related work should gain a year's practical experience before entry.

Other qualifications

Include BTEC/SCOTVEC certificates and diplomas, and NVQ/SVQs in horticulture. *See also* GROUND MAINTENANCE/GROUNDSMANSHIP and other jobs *in* PROFESSIONAL SPORT AND THE RECREATION AND LEISURE INDUSTRIES.

A further nationally recognised qualification is the Royal Horticultural Society's General Examination in Horticulture. Courses are available on a part-time basis, usually over one or two years at about 80 centres. Correspondence courses are also available. The standard of knowledge required is equivalent to GCSE level in science. The RHS Diploma is a new award, a step up from the RHS General Examination in Horticulture, and a qualification recognised for Associate Membership of the Institute of Horticulture. For those wishing to proceed to the Master of Horticulture (RHS) award, it is essential.

The Kew Diploma (a qualification recognised, with three years' post-study experience, for Corporate Membership of the Institute of Horticulture) offers a broad-based training in amenity horticulture. Students must have obtained four GCSEs and two A-levels (or equivalent), one of which is a science. They must also have had two years' practical experience.

The National Trust offer eight training opportunities each year in amenity horticulture. Individuals, six of whom are under 20 years of age, and two under 35, are recruited in September and employed at specially selected Trust gardens for three years. They work towards NVQ level 3/BTEC National Diploma.

Courses for people with disabilities are offered at various specialist centres. Further details are available from disablement resettlement officers or from CETAC.

Further information

CETAC Warwickshire Careers Service, Institute of Leisure and Amenity Management, Institute of Horticulture, National Trust National Co-ordinator (Bodmin).

Agricultural engineering

Agricultural engineering is one of the several technologies and sciences on which the post-Second World War revolution in agriculture has been based. It is an interdisciplinary study which applies engineering principles to the needs and problems of the industry. It needs a fully integrated training in the theory and practice of both engineering and agriculture, horticulture and forestry.

Mechanisation and automation have been central to increasing food production and making it more efficient and cost-effective both in Britain and overseas in developing countries. Every stage in crop and livestock production can be made more effective and economic using more sophisticated and complex equipment, but still more efficient systems and equipment are needed, even in developing countries, where high technology is not appropriate.

Firms making agricultural machinery and equipment suffered quite badly from recession, and EU cutbacks in agricultural output will continue to affect them.

Agricultural engineers now have to develop and design buildings, machines and equipment which take account of the realities of the farming business. Demand for agricultural engineers, though, is unlikely to fall.

Working in agricultural engineering

Collectively, their activities cover a broad technical and administrative spectrum including the biological sciences. The three main areas of work for agricultural engineers are:

- Designing, developing, producing and marketing agricultural vehicles and machinery of all kinds – tractors and harvesters for farms, horticultural holdings, and forestry operations – based on mechanical engineering principles.

- Planning, designing and laying out farm and horticultural buildings which incorporate advanced control systems: milking parlours, glass houses, crop dryers, and buildings where poultry or pigs (for example) are reared intensively. This involves environmental control engineering.
- Field engineering of systems for, e.g., irrigation, drainage, roads and water supplies, which depend on civil engineering principles. Soil conservation, land clearance and reclamation – planning, designing and managing soil and water resources efficiently – increasingly involve agricultural engineers.

Agricultural engineers must work closely with others. With farmers, for instance, to understand what they want, such as tractors which cope with anything farmworkers do with them; with breeders of easier-to-harvest plants, on harvesting machines; and with civil engineers, on irrigation systems.

This is not a highly structured area of employment, and there are no hard-and-fast divisions between the work of professionals and technicians or between technicians and mechanics.

There are many posts for both professional and technician engineers overseas, especially in developing countries, and particularly for field engineers. Agricultural engineers enjoy a wide range of job opportunities for career development; these include Manufacturing; Research, Design and Development; Consultancy; Advisory; Marketing and Sales; and Teaching.

Manufacturing

The industry spans a wide range of products and company sizes, from multinational to local workshops. Surveys suggest there are 1,000 companies engaged in manufacturing agricultural equipment in the UK, 90% of which employ fewer than 20 people. In total, 35,000 are employed in this sector.

Research, design and development

This is often industry-linked or sponsored and takes place in one of the five major centres: Silsoe College and the Silsoe Research Institute; the Scottish Centre at Penicuik; Newcastle University; Harper-Adams College in Shropshire; and BBSRC research centres.

The research work carried out by industry is usually of a rather less fundamental nature than that of the Research Institutes and universities and may in many cases be development work on the range of machines manufactured by the company. Smaller companies contract-out their work to a research institute or university department, and this trend has led to the employment of research officers, particularly by the universities, on a contract basis for work on a specific project.

Advisory

Advisory work covers work for the Ministry of Agriculture, Fisheries and Food, ADAS and the Food and Agricultural Organisation, e.g. on suitable systems and machines for particular situations.

Consultancy

The attraction of consultancy work is the potential variety of work and opportunities for travel and seemingly high rates of remuneration. It is normally quite specialised, open to those with qualifications at degree/postgraduate level and considerable field experience. Success in this area may depend on professional contacts and reputation in the industry.

Marketing and sales

To be effective in selling and promoting products, services and ideas, a thorough understanding is required of the marketing environment and the characteristics of the customers which the organisation services.

Teaching

Teaching can offer a satisfying career at many differing levels from teaching craft skills to 16- and 17-year-olds, to teaching in a college or university. In general the teacher must possess qualifications and experience to a higher level than that which his pupils are hoping to achieve. Many posts also demand some form of teaching qualification.

Incorporated engineers and engineering technicians

They are also employed in R&D and development as support staff, but more often in manufacture, advisory work, technical writing and sales, demonstrating and also field engineering. They also work in distribution, in management or at foreman level and on installation of, for example, field systems, grain dryers and automatic feeders.

Craftworkers

Mechanics (rather than technicians or professional engineers) look after maintenance and repair – crucial when animals' lives or the survival of crops may be dependent on very sophisticated control systems. On the land, mechanics are generally employed only on the largest farm or horticultural units where there is enough machinery to use their time economically, and therefore they must be able to service and repair a variety of different kinds of machinery.

There is other work for dealers, manufacturers and contractors.

Recruitment and entry

While it is possible to train and qualify in agricultural engineering straight from school, a significant proportion of people become agricultural engineers – professional, technician or craftworkers – after training and experience in a related occupation, e.g. mechanical engineering or agriculture.

Qualifications and training

Age	Qualifications	Courses available	Level of registration available after training and experience
16	none	YT/Craft apprentice; City & Guilds 015	-
16	GCSE; S grades	BTEC/ SCOTVEC dip	Engineering Technician
18	one or two A-levels or H grades	BTEC/ SCOTVEC HNC/D	Incorporated Engineer
18	three A-levels; four H grades	BSc/BEng	Chartered Engineer

Professional body

The Institution of Agricultural Engineers (2,000 membership) has a rising percentage of professional members: over 60% are academically qualified to be chartered, incorporated or technician engineers, and Institution members can register. The top corporate grade of fellow requires a degree plus eight years' appropriate experience, including full-time training.

Degree level

Demand for graduate agricultural engineers is relatively small. For first degrees, only four courses are available at:

- Cranfield/Silsoe: agricultural engineering with final-year specialisation in machinery engineering, environmental control or field engineering;
- Harper-Adams: agricultural engineering, includes farm and industrial placements;
- Writtle College, Chelmsford: BEng Agricultural Engineering and BSc Agricultural Engineering with Business Management.

Entry to all three is with A-level passes in physics (or engineering science) and mathematics, or via technician-level awards at credit standard plus appropriate industrial experience.

Postgraduate courses

MSc/diploma postgraduate conversion courses are available after a degree in agriculture or engineering at the above universities.

BTEC/SCOTVEC courses

Incorporated engineer qualifications are now BTEC/SCOTVEC Higher National awards. Engineering technician qualifications are now BTEC and SCOTVEC National Diploma awards.

HND/C and national diploma courses are available at a number of colleges. The names of the courses frequently change to reflect changes in the specialisation. However, they all include terms such as 'Agricultural Engineering', 'Rural Engineering', 'Mechanisation', etc.

Entry is as for all BTEC Nationals; with 16-plus, passes should include maths and a physical science. Pre-entry experience (e.g. on a YT scheme) is useful. Alternatively, the BTEC National Diploma course in farm mechanisation is agriculture-based. It can be taken at Chippenham: Lackham College of Agriculture; or at the Berkshire College of Agriculture. Entry is as all BTEC Nationals (with 16-plus, passes to include maths and a physical science), plus twelve months' experience in the industry (e.g. on a nationally preferred YT scheme). SCOTVEC's National Certificate with agricultural-engineering modules can be taken at Outridge College of Agriculture, Elmwood College of Agriculture and Technical College, Barony College of Agriculture; and Clinterty College of Agriculture.

City & Guilds courses

City & Guilds has qualifications for mechanics:

National Certificate in agriculture specialises in farm machinery and mechanisation (entry with one or two years' experience).

Scheme 015 teaches basic knowledge of agricultural machinery and workshop processes and of maintenance and repair of farm tractors, implements and machinery, complementing industrial experience by introducing a wider range of practice and problems than is normally met in daily work.

Scheme 018 gives more specialised training in tractors, power units and mechanisms, or machinery maintenance and repair. No specific entrance requirement, but some colleges prefer students to have done first-year engineering. Available at a number of colleges across the country, courses last three years day- or block-release, but can be taken full-time.

Vocational qualifications

NVQ/SVQs are being introduced and will eventually replace the above craft-level awards.

Further information

Institution of Agricultural Engineers.

Work with Animals

Contents

(CLCI: WAL–WAM)

Opportunities for working with animals are not very numerous, and most involves a great deal of heavy and messy or dirty labour. The number of posts is comparatively small.

Veterinary surgeon

Caring for animals – preventing and treating diseases, and treating injuries – is the most obvious purpose of veterinary science. However, veterinary scientists also look for ways of improving conditions for animals, and work with other scientists to develop more efficient methods of animal husbandry and stockbreeding.

Of some 14,700 active veterinary surgeons on the register of the Royal College of Veterinary Surgeons, approximately 10,100 practise their profession in the UK. At present, the demand for veterinary surgeons exceeds supply and there has been an increase in the number now admitted to veterinary schools.

Eighty four per cent work in private practice, a high proportion looking after 'small animals' (i.e. pets) including almost all the vets who work in towns. If they work in the country they may look after pets too, but most of their 'patients' are farm animals – which can include even fish. In some areas practices may choose to specialise – in looking after (race)horses in the Newmarket area, for example. Vets in private practice are self-employed, but newly qualified vets are employed by the practices, as assistants, on a salaried basis. They may later be able to purchase a share in the practice or set up on their own. Three animal-welfare organisations also have their own clinics and hospitals, and employ some 230 vets.

On the farm, as much time is spent trying to prevent disease – through regular testing and inoculations – as in curing it, and in helping to 'manage' the animal stock, keeping them healthy and productive, checking on possible health reasons for failure to put on flesh or lay eggs, for example. Modern vets may have efficient, modern drugs to use, and scientific equipment. Farms may be cleaner and more hygienic than in the past, but animals still give birth or become ill at the most inconvenient times, the work can still be extremely messy, and animals still tend to bite or kick anyone trying to help them. Hours can be long and irregular in all practices.

Over 700 vets work in government service, in the Ministry of Agriculture, Fisheries and Food (which employs the largest number, 498), the Northern Ireland Ministry of Agriculture (142), the Department of Agriculture for Scotland, the Home Office, the Ministry of Defence and the Overseas Development Administration (4). Government vets deal with government regulations and schemes to control and improve health standards for farm animals, run schemes designed to prevent and control notifiable diseases (e.g. foot-and-mouth disease in cattle), tuberculin test cattle, campaign to get rid of warble fly, and inspect animals both on the land and in markets. They also work in laboratories on the causes of diseases, identifying them from the carcasses and organs sent in by other vets. They do field investigations into outbreaks of disease among farm animals, advise on treatment and decide what needs to be done to prevent outbreaks spreading. They also monitor disease, providing information, advice, etc. for farmers.

There are 455 vets working in research, in universities (where they also teach). Research in university veterinary schools is mostly on the clinical side, with some work on, for example, parasitology and pathology. But veterinarians also work on teams doing research in animal husbandry in agriculture departments, where research is more usually in areas like genetics linked to improving breeds (e.g. for meat production), or on better methods of nutrition, as well as in parasite control and basic animal physiology. Government supports a number of institutions where, as well as research and laboratory investigations being carried out, some biological products are made, for example, tuberculin and S19 vaccine to control brucellosis.

There are 420 vets working in research in government-financed research establishments, and in firms in industries linked to farming, such as feedstuff manufacturers, pharmaceutical companies, and firms making equipment used both for indoor feeding of animals and poultry and control of their environment.

Many veterinarians find work overseas, and a UK veterinary qualification enables any UK citizen to practise anywhere in the European Union. Contract appointments in developing countries are found through the Overseas Development Administration.

Small numbers are employed full-time by cattle breeders, horse breeders, racing stables, zoos and safari parks, and by the Army where The Royal Army Veterinary Corps looks after the Army's horses and dogs.

Qualifications and training

All courses are at degree level. Courses last five years except at Cambridge where the course is six years. The first two years cover basic sciences, such as biology, chemistry, anatomy, physiology, pathology and biochemistry, with some genetics and microbiology. The final years concentrate on veterinary science, medicine and surgery with integrated studies in animal husbandry, pharmacology, public health, etc.

There are only six veterinary schools (some 400 places; about 12 applications per place), at Bristol, Cambridge, Edinburgh, Glasgow, Liverpool, and London (Royal Veterinary College) Universities.

To practise as veterinary surgeons, graduates must register with the Royal College of Veterinary Surgeons.

Entry requirements are three science GCE A-levels, to include chemistry and one or two other science subjects from maths, physics and biology (exact requirements vary from college to college). Usual entry grades are AAA or AAB. Advanced GNVQ is unlikely to be acceptable.

Courses cover animal anatomy, physiology, biochemistry; pharmacology, pathology, microbiology, parasitology, bacteriology; animal health and husbandry; clinical medicine and surgery; reproduction; and veterinary public health.

Prospective vets not only need the intelligence to study at an advanced level, but personal qualities which include an interest in and an intelligent concern for animals, and the ability to gain the confidence of both owners and animals.

Further information

The Royal College of Veterinary Surgeons, British Veterinary Association.

Veterinary nurse

Veterinary nurses work mainly for veterinary surgeons in town and country practices, veterinary hospitals, etc. They work mostly with 'small animals' – pets – although the scope of possible work may get wider in future.

Veterinary nurses care for animals recovering from operations or other treatment, collect and analyse specimens, help in the surgery, clean and sterilise instruments and other equipment, clear and clean up the surgery and accommodation for animals. They may be allowed to do some simple treatment, e.g. removing thorns, etc., and in future nurses may be able to run clinics carrying out routine operations and vaccinations.

New legislation means that everyone who describes themselves as a veterinary nurse will have to be registered with the Royal College of Veterinary Surgeons, for which they must be qualified. The RCVS has over 4,000 qualified veterinary nurses.

It is not possible to use veterinary nursing qualifications as a route to becoming a vet other than as a basis for applying for a place at a university veterinary school. Few practices are large enough to offer nurses any significant promotion prospects.

Recruitment and entry

Entry is via a formal training, and examination scheme (*below*), which must be with an approved centre. Competition for training places is considerable, and it is useful to have had a holiday job or done voluntary work in a veterinary practice, which is also a way of being on the spot when training places come up.

The British Veterinary Nursing Association runs an employment register which puts prospective trainees, and qualified veterinary nurses, in touch with prospective employers.

Qualifications and training

The veterinary nursing scheme is run by the Royal College of Veterinary Surgeons in association with the British Veterinary Nursing Association (BVNA). To gain the qualification, trainees must enrol with the RCVS, and work full-time in an approved training centre (or centres) – mainly veterinary practices – for at least two years. Practical tuition is provided 'on the job'. Trainees can gain the necessary theoretical background studying on their own, but a number of agricultural colleges run full-time or modular courses and there are around two dozen part-time courses at local colleges of further education. The two-stage exams may be taken whenever the trainee is ready, but no one can be registered until the two years are up.

Training includes the study of anatomy; physiology; first aid and nursing; husbandry and dietary requirements; theatre practice; kennel and hospital management; quarantine procedures; laboratory techniques; anaesthesia; dispensing; radiography and darkroom techniques.

Minimum entry requirements are four GCSE passes at C or above, to include English language, and a physical or biological science or maths, or equivalent qualifications. The applicant must be at least 17. Many entrants have better qualifications than this, even including appropriate A-level passes.

A pre-veterinary nursing course has been introduced with no set entry qualifications.

A new two-year diploma course in veterinary nursing has been launched for those in full-time practice: Advanced Veterinary Nursing (Surgical).

Further information

The Royal College of Veterinary Surgeons, and the British Veterinary Nursing Association (sae required by the latter).

Animal research and animal technicians

Animal research ranges from work on breeding farm animals which will produce more or better meat, or wool, through to controlling diseases and pests which affect farm animals, formulating improved feedstuffs, or working out the conditions under which animals will reach maturity most economically. (*See also* zoologist *in* BIOLOGICAL SCIENCES). Animals are also used extensively in many other areas of scientific research.

Animal technicians

Animal technicians care for animals where they are used in laboratories or field research centres for research (scientific, veterinary or medical), or in schools, universities, etc. for teaching. The use of animals in scientific experiments is a controversial area, but without such research many advances in medicine, nutrition, pharmaceuticals, agriculture and other disciplines would be impossible (unless technological advances come up with alternatives).

Animal technicians provide high standards of animal care. They ensure that the animal cages are kept clean and that the animals are properly fed and watered. Temperature, lighting, humidity, etc. have to be strictly controlled and are subject to a government code of practice. Animals have to be cared for seven days a week, every week of the year. Regular overtime is a routine part of an animal technician's work. Animals under experiment require close observation and special care. Animal technicians may have to maintain records of the animals' condition for the scientist doing research. At the end of the experiment they may have to kill animals humanely and prepare them for an autopsy.

Eighty per cent of animals used in experiments are rats and mice although other species (guinea pigs, rabbits, monkeys, dogs and cats) may be used occasionally.

All research and animal breeding laboratories are inspected and registered by the Home Office. Senior animal technicians, sometimes called animal technologists, may help with the experiments, e.g. by taking blood samples, giving injections, administering anaesthetics or performing minor surgery. To do this they must be highly qualified and be personally licensed by the Home Office. Very senior animal technologists may also be the statutory Named Person responsible for day-to-day care of animals as required by law, or animal facility managers.

There are estimated to be between 3,200 and 4,000 animal technicians in Great Britain working for pharmaceutical companies, contract research laboratories, animal breeders, educational establishments and government research laboratories. Animal technicians can and do work abroad, in Europe, the USA and developing countries.

Recruitment and entry

Entry requirements vary depending on the employer. It is usual to have at least three to five GCSE or equivalent passes including English, a biological subject, and mathematics and/or a physical science. This may be relaxed for individuals with special aptitude for animal care.

Qualifications and training

Training is on-the-job, with release to study for a Certificate in Laboratory Animal Technology awarded by the Institute of Animal Technology (IAT). A Certificate in Laboratory Animal Husbandry may be awarded for partial success in the Laboratory Animal Technology examinations. The IAT also sets Membership and Fellowship examinations.

BTEC/SCOTVEC National and Higher certificates covering animal technology can lead to exemption from some sections of the Institute of Animal Technology examinations.

Further information

The Institute of Animal Technology.

Animal welfare

RSPCA/SSPCA – The People's Dispensary for Sick Animals

Quite a few organisations and charities deal with animal welfare, ranging from the prevention of cruelty through to treatment of sick animals, but the number of full-time employees is relatively small.

RSPCA/SSPCA inspector

The RSPCA, the largest, and which operates in England and Wales, employs about 300 uniformed inspectors with additional staff in the animal hospitals and wildlife rehabilitation centres. There are ten regions, each with its own regional communication centre where telephone lines are open to the public 24 hours a day, seven days a week. All inspectors are in contact with their regional headquarters via mobile telephones. In addition to the above staff there are about 40 market inspectors who work on a part-time basis in cattle markets.

The Scottish equivalent (SSPCA) employs 96 trained staff with 47 uniformed inspectors, 23 staff at their ten animal welfare centres and 26 staff engaged in education, administration and publicity. It does not employ any veterinary staff.

A large part of inspectors' work is investigating allegations of cruelty, and ensuring that the law relating to animals is complied with, but the RSPCA/SSPCA tries to help any animal (and its owner) in difficulty, and the problems are many.

Law enforcement work

The principal laws are the Protection of Animals Act 1911 and the Protection of Animals (Scotland) Act of 1912, but other laws cover animals in transit, animal welfare and the protection of birds and pets. All complaints are investigated, but inspectors have no powers to force entry or remove an animal without permission, however bad the situation and suffering. The inspector decides what action to take, for instance educating an owner or starting court proceedings, but relatively few cases result in prosecution.

Inspection

Each inspector has a designated area of between 50 and 2,000 square miles, depending on whether it is an urban or rural area, and they try to ensure that all establishments selling or dealing with animals, e.g. pet shops, zoos, kennels, and slaughterhouses, comply with regulations.

Welfare

Inspectors ensure that any abandoned, mistreated or unwanted animal receives the appropriate care, or, in certain circumstances, is humanely killed.

Recruitment and entry

No formal academic qualifications are required, but a reasonable standard of education is expected. Applicants must hold a full, clean, current driving licence. The RSPCA requires applicants to swim 50 metres fully clothed and a high proportion of entrants are mature people, many with an Armed Service background.

The SSPCA prefers applicants to have gained previous experience working with farm animals. An increasing number of applicants have attended agricultural college.

The minimum age of entry is 22 years for the RSPCA and 25 years for the SSPCA. Competition for vacancies is extremely intense.

Qualifications and training

Training lasts six or seven months, depending on the body, and mostly takes place in Edinburgh or Horsham. The RSPCA is currently reviewing its training course and the length may be reduced. Trainees have to pass written examinations in subjects like the law relating to animal welfare; animal injury and disease; humane slaughter; the work of animal clinics, hospitals and homes; report writing; and animal first aid.

Further information

The RSPCA and SSPCA.

The People's Dispensary for Sick Animals

The People's Dispensary for Sick Animals (PDSA) is a registered charity, has 48 veterinary centres, and employs around 180 vets, and about 250 veterinary nurses. Blue Cross is similar but much smaller. They both operate in a similar way to veterinary practices.

Other work with animals

Kennels and catteries – pet shop assistant – canine beautician/ dog-groomer – pet behavioural consultant – animal trainer – guide dog trainer/ mobility instructor – trainer of hearing dogs for the deaf – dog handler – gamekeeper – horse riding, racing and hunting – Royal Society for the Protection of Birds – zoos and wildlife 'safari' parks – animal therapist

Kennels and catteries

Kennels, catteries and pet shops employ people to look after dogs, cats and other domestic pets. Some kennels board and quarantine animals on a fairly large scale, some specialise in breeding and showing, or are racing (greyhounds only) or hunt kennels. There are also quarantine kennels approved by the Ministry of Agriculture, Fisheries and Food, and kennels maintained by animal welfare organisations such as the RSPCA/SSPCA, Guide Dogs for the Blind Association and National Canine Defence League. The work is hard, involving long and irregular hours, spent cleaning, feeding, exercising, training and grooming the animals, caring for litters, staying up late when puppies are born, looking after sick or post-operative dogs, and travelling to and from shows or races. Most staff live in.

Entry requirements vary from nothing formal to four GCSE/SCEs (grades A–C/1–3) for national diploma courses in animal care. Some of the private schools ask for GCSE/SCEs in English, biology and mathematics. Opportunities for promotion are few, since most kennels are owner-managed, but animal technician exams (*see* ANIMAL RESEARCH AND ANIMAL TECHNICIANS *above*) may help in finding more responsible posts.

Pet shop assistant

Pet ownership is growing steadily, and in 1990 a market intelligence survey found that 58% of households had pets, the most popular being dogs, cats and goldfish. In the UK in 1996 there were over 3,500 pet shops and 600 specialist aquatic centres employing over 15,000 people. Most pet shops are privately owned and managed, but pet superstores are on the increase and some garden centres have pet and aquatic centres. A licence to operate a pet shop has to be obtained from the local authority. Under the Pet Animals Act 1951 local authorities are empowered to use their discretion in setting certain conditions before granting the licence. Environmental health officers inspect premises and use standards produced by the Pet Care Trust which became a registered charity on 1 January 1996.

The main qualification is a City & Guilds course in Pet Store Management which can be obtained through distance-learning. The course leads to an examination consisting of two written papers taken at a City & Guilds approved centre or at the Pet Care Trust Training Centre in Bedford.

Canine beautician/dog-groomer

There has been increased demand for the services of dog beauticians, who are concerned with dog-grooming, clipping and trimming. Opportunities for full-time work are limited and vary according to area and local demand. Many establishments such as boarding kennels, breeding kennels, or pet shops now offer this as an additional service, but most groomers become self-employed.

There are three methods of training: on the job at a grooming establishment, through YT or through a full-time course at a private fee-paying centre. There is a City & Guilds certificate in dog-grooming. A list of approved training centres may be obtained from the Pet Care Trust.

The Animal Care Industry Lead Body is working on NVQs at level 3 in separate branches of animal care: Animal Training; Animal Welfare and Management; Pet Retailing and Dog-grooming. These should be in place by September 1996. Levels 1 and 2 in grooming care, already in existence, are being reviewed.

Pet behavioural consultant

Most consultants are based in a veterinary practice, taking referrals both from the practice and from other veterinary practices. Most of the work is with cats and dogs – dealing with canine aggression, pets soiling houses, etc.

There are no specific entry requirements, but animal psychologists and pet behavioural consultants would normally have a first degree in veterinary science, biology, zoology or psychology and have had a lot of experience in handling animals.

Animal trainer

Animal trainers train dogs – both in general obedience and for specific purposes. Dogs are now, for instance, trained to sniff out conditions such as dry rot. Trainers have a variety of backgrounds. There is an organisation, the British Institute of Professional Dog Trainers, which can provide further information.

Guide dog trainer/mobility instructor

The Guide Dogs for the Blind Association employs 1,100 staff in both dog-handling and administrative capacities. Kennel staff carry out all aspects of kennel work (cleaning, grooming and feeding, and looking after dogs/puppies). Kennel staff are recruited at 18 and must be educated to GCSE standard or equivalent with passes in English and mathematics. Guide Dog Trainers are responsible for introducing young adult dogs to basic guiding skills. They are also recruited from the age of 18 and must be educated to GCSE standard or equivalent in English, maths and science.

Guide Dog Mobility Instructors commence at 18 years or above and must have a minimum of five passes at GCSE or equivalent in English, maths, science and, ideally, a social science. Guide Dog Mobility Instructors train visually impaired people to achieve independence through the use of guide dogs. Training is given to all staff, who are required to pass City & Guilds examinations as a condition of continued employment.

Employment is mainly at the Guide Dogs for the Blind regional training centres – Bolton, Exeter, Forfar, Leamington Spa, Middlesbrough, Redbridge and Wokingham – and at the breeding centre in Tollgate, Warwickshire. There are smaller support centres at Belfast, Cardiff, Larkhall, Maidstone and Nottingham. The Association has a stiff selection procedure, and there is usually a waiting list of suitable candidates.

Trainer of hearing dogs for the deaf

Hearing dogs are trained to react to sounds such as alarm clocks, crying babies, door bells, etc. and to lead their owners to the source of the sound. Trainers train dog and owner to work together in partnership.

Applicants for posts as trainers do not need to have any specified examination passes but should be educated to GCSE standard. They must also have some previous experience of work with dogs, even if only training their own dogs in obedience. Many successful applicants have previously worked as veterinary nurses, although this type of experience is not essential. Voluntary work at veterinary centres and some kind of voluntary service in the community are also seen as relevant. There is a minimum age of 18 and a clean driving licence is required.

Training is carried out at the organisation's residential centre in Oxfordshire – and includes training in signing.

Further information

Hearing Dogs for the Deaf.

Dog handler

THE ARMED FORCES and the POLICE (*see in* SECURITY AND PROTECTIVE SERVICES) all employ dogs, but handlers are usually chosen from people already in the service, and trained by them.

Gamekeeper

Gamekeepers work for game management firms as well as private landowners who want to hold shoots. Estimates suggest as many as 5,000 are employed.

Shooting is increasingly popular, and is one of the most rapidly growing sports. Gamekeepers and their assistants rear game, whether it be grouse, pheasant, partridge, duck or, mainly in Scotland, deer, using the most sophisticated breeding methods; they protect birds, deer, etc. from vermin and poachers (poaching is big business) and maintain covers. Some protect and manage salmon rivers and trout streams.

Many gamekeepers are developing wider responsibilities in countryside activities, especially where game management firms have related interests.

The best way into the job is to gain experience by approaching local gamekeepers for beating jobs. Traditionally keepers are trained 'on the job' but there is a one-year gamekeeping/waterkeeping training course at Sparsholt College in Hampshire. The subject matter is predominantly gamekeeping-related, but the waterkeeping has been included for those who may work on an estate which has a sport fishery interest. Students have to be at least 17 and have completed a relevant twelve-month pre-college practical period or Youth Training Game course. There are also BTEC First and National Diplomas in Game, Wildlife and Habitat Management and an HND in Wild Life Management. *See in* CAREERS IN CONSERVATION AND THE ENVIRONMENT. Short courses are offered by the Game Conservancy Council.

Horse riding, racing and hunting

Competition stables – hunt stables – livery stables – riding schools – polo – bloodstock agencies – transport agencies – other opportunities

These are popular leisure activities, and so provide a number of openings, in riding, instructing and in caring for the animals (working as a groom). Many jobs are in racing – *see in* PROFESSIONAL SPORT AND THE RECREATION AND LEISURE INDUSTRIES.

Competition stables

Owners of show horses and jumpers employ both professional riders and staff to maintain the horses, and in both there is a considerable amount of exercising and training. Fewer professional riders are employed in jumping and the season is longer, so it is difficult to combine this with hunt work. A considerable amount of travel and 'living rough' is involved.

Hunt stables

Hunt stables employ hunt 'servants', who work up from 'strapper' to second horseman; second horseman to second whipper-in; second whip to whip and then to 'carrying horn' as professional huntsman. Grooms are employed on a seasonal basis only during the hunting season from October to March. The best opportunities are with a well-established hunt with continuity of mastership and therefore security of employment (preferably under a professional huntsman rather than an amateur). Some private stables with hunters also employ grooms. Some allow grooms to hunt, and to ride in hunter trials, shows and similar events, as well as exercising. Most require some experience, because usually only one groom is needed.

Livery stables

These look after horses for those owners who do not have their own stables.

Riding schools

Only 700 of the estimated 2,400 riding schools are approved by the British Horse Society (some so-called 'schools' are no more than hiring stables). A fair number of instructors are employed, but competition for jobs is considerable.

Qualified instructors teach ('school') both riders (children and adults) and horses. Hours are long, and usually include evenings and weekends, for both teaching and going to shows, gymkhanas, etc. Qualified instructors with experience can become stable managers.

Some schools let their instructors ride in shows and other events, and may give a potential show rider or jumper facilities for training and practice and time off to attend events. It is, however, exceptionally difficult (and expensive) to become a successful show jumper, even with the facilities of working in a stable or school.

The BHS publishes a Register of qualified instructors – approved establishments, in general, must employ instructors who are registered.

Seasonal work includes helping with pony-trekking holidays (some 150 approved centres), as an instructor, guide or groom.

Polo

Polo is largely an amateur sport played in the summer from April to September. Polo teams are usually stabled at centres where polo is played, although the employer of stable staff is generally the owner and not the centre. With only some 200 professional player/riders in Britain (most come from the Argentine, bringing trained ponies), most of the available work is for grooms. Some polo players tour overseas and grooms accompany them.

Bloodstock agencies

Most stables breed horses, but the bloodstock agencies, where horses are bred as a business, employ about 400 people. Most of the work involved is in selling, buying and leasing horses for stud, and in valuing, insurance and maintaining pedigrees, although the studs do employ people to look after the horses. Most of these jobs normally demand considerable experience of horses and of racing.

A top stud can command a fee running into six figures, so stud, mare and foal can expect the most expert care and attention. There are two main types of stud: public and private. The stud year has three phases. February to July is the official breeding season when mares visit stallions on public studs. Foals are generally born from mid-January until June; and from the end of July to October the yearlings are prepared for the auction sales. Breeding-stock sales take place in November and December.

Transport agencies

Transport agencies specialise in moving race and show horses, polo ponies and bloodstock mares and foals around the world. Horses travel by road, air and sea as far as Australia and Argentina. The work involves both caring for the horses and handling an enormous amount of paperwork.

Other opportunities

It is possible to ride horses (and care for them) in THE ARMED FORCES (mostly in ceremonials only), and the mounted POLICE (*see in* SECURITY AND PROTECTIVE SERVICES). Both also employ VETERINARY SURGEONS (*above*), farriers and saddlers.

Recruitment and entry

Entry is normally right at the bottom, but reasonable career prospects should be available in a well-run stables or school giving proper on-the-job training. Competition for jobs in the best stables and schools is stiff, but it is possible to start via a YT scheme. Potential instructors should always check the British Horse Society or Association of British Riding Schools' lists of approved riding establishments.

Trainee instructors should have a good general education with at least four GCSEs or equivalent passes, and preferably some kind of backup qualification, in e.g. business studies, secretarial work, or farming. No formal entry requirements are set for grooms.

Qualifications and training

The main qualifications are set by the following.

The British Horse Society (BHS) runs exams at centres throughout the country for all persons who work with horses including:

- Instructors: 3-stage qualification, the (final) certificate includes stable management as well as horsemanship and teaching. Entrants to the first, assistant instructor's exam must be 17½ and, if under 18, have four GCSEs or equivalent passes including English. The BHS issues an International Equestrian Passport to instructors who have passed its examinations. This enables them to obtain work in 27 schools which are members of the International Group for Qualifications in Training Horse and Rider.
- Grooms: horse knowledge and care exams go through four stages to the stable manager's certificate.

The Association of British Riding Schools (ABRS) has preliminary horse care and riding certificates at levels 1 and 2 and groom's certificate and diploma (which prepare for stable management). No formal qualifications are required. The qualifications may be obtained while in full-time employment or through YT. The ABRS also awards a teaching certificate. No formal entry requirements are stipulated but candidates must be a least 19 and have teaching experience.

A few colleges run courses for BHS/ABRS exams, combined with general education, secretarial studies and/or home economics; others, which usually encompass BHS exams, lead to National Examinations Board or BTEC certificates.

The National Pony Society sets examinations in horse care and management, and in stud work, both of which offer optional training in equitation. Syllabuses have recently been revised to allow them to award NVQs.

NVQs are in place in the horse industry at levels 1–4. They include specialist NVQs (levels 1–3) in racehorse care and management, awarded by the Racing and Thoroughbred Training Board.

The two-year YT programme has become a major route of entry to a career in the horse industry. However, the list of college courses offering qualifications in horse management, etc. is now very extensive, covering more than 30 colleges, with courses from national certificate up to degree level. Degrees and HNDs in equine or horse studies are offered by 17 higher education institutions.

See also horse racing *in* PROFESSIONAL SPORT AND THE RECREATION AND LEISURE INDUSTRIES; and farriery *under* AGRICULTURE *in* LAND USE INDUSTRIES.

Further information

The Association of British Riding Schools, British Horse Society, National Stud, National Pony Society.

The Royal Society for the Protection of Birds

The RSPB is Europe's largest wildlife conservation charity. It leads the way in the effective conservation of birds and makes a positive contribution to a better environment.

There are a variety of career opportunities within the organisation, covering all aspects of conservation work, as well as the support and service functions at the Head Office in Sandy, Bedfordshire.

A degree or professional qualification is required for specialist positions together with experience in a relevant field. A keen interest in ornithology and conservation is important.

The RSPB also operates a voluntary wardening scheme in England, Scotland and Wales.

Zoos and wildlife 'safari' parks

These are the main opportunities to work with wild animals in Britain.

There are about 150 zoos, wildlife parks, bird gardens and aquaria, of which the Zoological Society of London is the largest and most important, although superb work is also being done in some provincial zoos and country wildlife parks. Steeply rising costs, and some resulting fall in the number of visitors, are causing zoos severe financial problems. This has resulted in some redundancies.

The London Zoo provides some indication of the kinds of careers and jobs available today. The Society's permanent staff is down to 150, of whom about 50 are keepers (as against nearly 300 in 1992). The staff not employed as keepers work on construction, maintenance, gardening, and general and public services; in the shops, in scientific departments, in the library, and in administration. About 100 work in catering, but this is now run by private contractors. However, the Society, like other zoos and wildlife parks, employs a fair number of seasonal staff in the summer.

There are three areas of work: research, conservation and education. Employees fall into the following categories:

- a curator, who manages the animal collection and captive breeding project;

- assistants, who keep the stud book up to date and 'manage' particular animal groups (every zoo species throughout the world has a worldwide family tree which is kept up to date by a designated zoo);
- scientists, who work in the institute on reproduction, genetics, pathology, biology, or wildlife diseases;
- education officers, who run education programmes for schools and interpret the collection for the public through information panels and lectures, and who run a scheme for 140 volunteers;
- conservation officers involved with overseas conservation projects, plus field staff, who may be British people on an attachment with the zoo to do research, or who may be 'local' people;
- editorial staff for the zoological publications;
- three veterinary surgeons;
- administrative staff such as personnel, marketing and accounts;
- technicians, including animal technicians working in the laboratories;
- keepers, who may become highly expert in caring for and breeding particular groups of animals, although everyone starts with 'mucking out';
- gardeners, plumbers, electricians, sign designers, cashiers, etc.

There are occasional short-contract research studentships and fellowships.

Provincial zoos employ similar grades of staff although they have even fewer posts for graduates.

Wildlife parks both bring in staff who have trained initially in zoos, and also employ animal experts from other fields; for example, staff trained in safari work overseas, on contract to provide and manage the animal exhibits.

Recruitment and entry

The number of vacancies at any level is always small.

For professional posts, a good honours degree in one of the biological sciences or veterinary science is needed. Education officers should have a degree in biological science and a teaching qualification. Library and senior administrative staff are also generally graduates with appropriate degrees.

For technician posts, competition is keen, and candidates for junior posts should have at least four GCSEs or equivalent in appropriate subjects. For intermediate posts at least two A-level science passes in biology and usually chemistry, plus one other, are looked for; and for senior posts applicants should have an HNC in applied biology or membership of the Institute of Medical Laboratory Sciences or Institute of Science Technology.

Animal technicians do not need such high educational qualifications, although candidates should preferably have four GCSE passes, or equivalent, and some previous experience with laboratory animals. They should be sensible, humane and conscientious. Hospital technicians should either be registered veterinary nurses by examination or have a suitable alternative qualification.

Keepers are often recruited as seasonal staff from the age of 16, with at least five GCSE or equivalent passes, including English, maths and biology. Most start in seasonal employment from Easter until the late summer, and the best get any vacancies on the permanent staff. They should be sensible and interested in animals.

Qualifications and training

Professional staff and senior technicians are recruited from amongst people who already have appropriate qualifications.

Other technicians are encouraged/expected to complete professional qualifications.

Keepers have to complete a two-year correspondence course leading to City & Guilds in animal management to become qualified; promotion is based on acquiring this qualification, coupled with length of service, up to senior keeper grade.

Further information

The Federation of Zoological Gardens of Great Britain and Ireland, which has 55 member zoos; the Association of British Wild Animal Keepers.

See also under MUSEUM WORK *in* HISTORICAL AND RELATED WORK; *and* CAREERS IN CONSERVATION AND THE ENVIRONMENT.

Animal therapist

Some chiropractors and physiotherapists specialise in work with animals. They must first qualify through one of the recognised training (degree) courses for the professions before taking postgraduate courses to qualify them to work with animals. It is an offence to treat animals except on referral from a veterinary surgeon.

Further information

The Association of Chartered Physiotherapists in Animal Therapy, and the McTimoney Chiropractic group.

Careers in Conservation and the Environment

Contents

(CLCI: WAR)

Background

'The range of work directly involved in conservation, of both the natural environment and the heritage of the past, and studying, caring for and protecting the environment is relatively limited, although it is generally accepted that mankind and its advancing technology has violently disturbed the environment and compelled mankind itself to achieve some form of tolerance to crowded, ugly and noisy surroundings, dirty skies and polluted waters' (the Natural Environment Research Council).

Conservation aims at preserving as much as possible of the natural landscape which remains unspoilt, reclaiming derelict land, caring for and preserving the countryside as well as buildings and areas of historic interest, including churches, palaces, houses, monuments, and ancient town centres. Much of what is preserved in this way is used positively to provide recreation and leisure facilities, and in AGRICULTURE and FORESTRY (*see* LAND USE INDUSTRIES). Conservation work on buildings and artefacts is dealt with in HISTORICAL AND RELATED WORK.

Planning authorities are mainly directly responsible for deciding what should and should not be preserved, but most of the bodies described here are represented on planning bodies, and make a strong input to decision-making.

The main opportunities for work in the organisations described below are for people with appropriate qualifications and/or experience:

- Scientists and people in the LAND USE PROFESSIONS (surveying, land agency, architecture, landscape architecture, etc.) may be managers, conservation advisers, fieldworkers, or doing research.
- Most conservation organisations look after resources themselves, and employ wardens, rangers, gamekeepers, and other ground staff.
- Managers, marketing, and market research staff are also employed by many organisations.

Working for statutory bodies

There are a number of statutory bodies concerned with conservation and the environment.

English Nature (formerly the Nature Conservancy Council for England)

English Nature advises the government on nature conservation in England and on how policies may affect nature conservation, i.e. the ecological consequences of changes in land use and other ways in which society has an impact on the countryside. It also has UK and international responsibilities.

English Nature maintains and manages about 180 national nature reserves, and it identifies and notifies Sites of Special Scientific Interest (SSSIs), currently about 4,000. Local authorities have to consult English Nature about developments that may affect the SSSIs.

English Nature advises and gives help to anyone actively concerned with the natural environment and commissions and supports relevant research, largely via the Natural Environment Research Council (NERC).

It employs around 600 permanent staff including a mixture of scientists, conservators, specialists, administrators and people with particular professional qualifications such as land agents and cartographers.

Scientists are generally recruited as assistant conservation officers. They identify, survey and assess suitable scientific habitats with a high conservation interest, liaise with their owners, and work with planning authorities and conservation bodies. Assistant conservation officers would be expected to have at least a good first degree in biology, botany, zoology, geology or geography, plus possibly an MSc in conservation or ecology. Previous experience and voluntary work are important. Competition for all posts is very stiff.

Every nature reserve employs site managers to patrol reserves and enforce by-laws, deal with general maintenance and conservation, advise and control the public, monitor what happens on the reserve, keep scientific and other records, write reports, supervise and organise voluntary wardens and other estate staff, service scientific research work, and liaise with local landowners and scientific staff.

Site managers (formerly known as wardens) have to be over 26 and good all-round naturalists with skills in estate work and forestry, able to undertake basic scientific survey work, maintain vehicles and have a full driving licence. Vacancies are extremely infrequent and competition is fierce. There are no minimum entry requirements and site managers have a variety of backgrounds. Experience in conservation, most often as a voluntary warden, is desirable.

Estate workers, who hedge, ditch, fell, reed-cut, operate and maintain machinery, and help with maintenance, may become site managers. Estate workers are recruited locally, but vacancies are fairly rare.

Qualifications and training

Training for all levels of work is provided directly by the employer and by distance-learning methods or attendance at short courses run either in-house or at colleges and field centres. The Countryside Commission sponsors many such courses. NVQ/SVQs in Environmental Conservation (Landscape and Ecosystems) are in place at levels 2 to 4. New GNVQ courses in Land and Environment (Intermediate and Advanced levels) are being piloted from September 1996.

English Nature also recruits staff direct for clerical and administrative duties (entry requirements usually the same as described under CIVIL SERVICE *in* CENTRAL GOVERNMENT). The work covers land agency, accounting, library services as well as general administration.

Scottish Natural Heritage

Scottish Natural Heritage was formed by merging the Nature Conservancy for Scotland with the Countryside Commission for Scotland in April 1992. The work is comparable to that for English Nature – managing reserves, selecting SSSIs, conservation, research and education. Staff numbers are around 460 and include biologists, ecologists, geologists, landscape architects and planners, archaeologists and cartographers, amongst others.

Countryside Council for Wales

In April 1991 the Council took over the duties of the Countryside Commission in Wales and Nature Conservancy Council in Wales. It is responsible for providing advice on conservation to central and local government, and voluntary organisations.

Wales has three national nature reserves and a variety of protected habitats – dunes, estuaries, offshore islands, etc.

Staff employed are similar to those for Scottish Natural Heritage.

The Countryside Commission for England

The Countryside Commission aims to promote understanding of the countryside and countryside issues, give policy advice on conservation and recreational provision and technical advice on managing the countryside. It does research to establish facts on landscape shape and leisure patterns, and experimental work to develop and demonstrate new techniques in conservation or recreation management. It is responsible for designating areas of outstanding landscape, development control and distributing grants but it does not own or manage land other than for experimental purposes. It supports national parks, footpaths and bridleways through grants and advice and advises national and local government.

The Commission has 250 staff, half employed at Cheltenham and the rest in seven regional offices. It operates in three divisions: Resources, Operations and Policy. It now has greater independence and recruits direct rather than through the Civil Service. Specialist staff employed include graduates with life sciences, planning, landscape architecture or economics degrees.

National parks

There are ten national parks in England and Wales, each with its own board or committee. In England the Countryside Commission is responsible for the general management and welfare of the national parks, but each board is autonomous and responsible for planning, buying new land, and administration. In Wales the general management is the responsibility of the Countryside Council for Wales.

Staff numbers vary from over 191 full-time plus 93 part-time staff in one large park down to 40 in the smallest. Part-time figures include seasonal staff who tend to be employed year after year. It is anticipated that the number of jobs will fall over the next few years. There are openings for scientists, planners, surveyors, recreation managers, ecologists, naturalists, foresters, soil scientists and for a whole range of executive, clerical and manual staff.

During the summer a small number of new part-time staff may be needed. Such work can provide valuable experience for applying for permanent posts.

Forestry Commission

Forestry employs about 35,000 people mainly working for the Forestry Commission and the private estates. Over half of these are in England with a third in Scotland and the remainder in Wales. More than half work in forests and nearly 40% in haulage of timber and primary wood processing activities. Just under 10% are engaged in non-forest activities such as management, research and increasingly, recreation and conservation. *See* FORESTRY *in* LAND USE INDUSTRIES.

Further information

Bodies mentioned above.

Environmental control

Environmental control can mean several different things. It is used, for example, to describe control of the environment in buildings, i.e. heating, ventilating and air-conditioning; this is building services engineering (*see in* THE CONSTRUCTION INDUSTRY). However, in this chapter environmental control brings together jobs which deal with protecting the environment from pollution, and restoring and repairing the results of past pollution and neglect.

Overall responsibility for improving environmental conditions, for ensuring that decisions do not result in damage, for controlling organisations or individuals to prevent pollution, and for promoting measures to clean up the environment, lies with central and local government.

Central government sets guidelines and legislation, and coordinates environmental control within the framework of planning. Local government deals primarily with the detailed aspects of environmental protection, for example, clean air, noise abatement, monitoring background radiation, methane monitoring of landfill sites, refuse disposal and recycling of waste products. The 1990 Environmental Protection Act has increased local government responsibilities for the implementation and enforcement of air pollution aspects. However, some aspects of direct control come under central government, e.g. the Alkali Inspectorate of the Health and Safety Executive, which enforces control of industrial emission of harmful substances into the air.

Development of new environmental technologies is rapid, and there is an increasing move away from simple 'end-of-pipe' pollution control to more extensive waste minimisation and recycling techniques. This development means that environmental responsibilities are likely to spread further through the workforce and become an integral part of the production process.

Recruitment and entry

Overall nearly 400,000 people are estimated to be in jobs associated directly or indirectly with environmental conservation. Over 12,000 are in full-time landscaping and wildlife conservation, more than 100,000 in pollution control and the waste management industry while the regulatory agencies employ over 14,000. About 30,000 environmental management jobs exist in the polluting industries and around 70,000 work in providing equipment for controlling air and water pollution and supplying services for waste management.

Many of the posts which deal with control of environmental pollution are largely administrative, and involve monitoring and enforcing statutory control measures, such as the Environmental Protection Act. These are the responsibility of CENTRAL GOVERNMENT (*see* Health and Safety Commission/Executive *in* the Department of the Environment *under* GOVERNMENT DEPARTMENTS), or LOCAL GOVERNMENT, mainly environmental health departments. Backing up the administrators are specialists such as the chemists of the Laboratory of the Government Chemist.

Qualifications and training

At graduate level science and engineering are the preferred disciplines, rather than 'environmental specialisms'. This is not to say that courses in environmental science are irrelevant, but there is such a large number of these, developed in response to student demand (rather than, dare one say, the needs of employers?) and having different slants and emphasis, that prospective students must study the course content very carefully. Some are science-based with a strong emphasis on environmental chemistry, pollution studies and environmental monitoring. Others are biased towards countryside management and yet others have a strong ecological and geographical content. There are a number of postgraduate courses in environmental management which cover subjects like environmental legislation, environmental technology, environmental planning and policy, environmental economics, water pollution studies, solid waste disposal, air pollution studies and radioactive pollution studies.

Central and local government

Department of the Environment

The Department of the Environment (DoE) has overall, central control of land use, planning, and related areas. The department has divisions dealing directly with countryside planning and management, and land-reclamation units. Protection schemes are actually carried out by local authorities, but departmental engineers do help them. The headquarters of its Executive Agency, the Planning Inspectorate, is at Bristol and is one of the largest employers of planners in the country. (It handles about 25,000 planning appeals every year in addition to several public enquiries.)

DoE has lost some of its direct involvement in conservation since the listing of listed buildings, management of royal parks and palaces, and administration of state-owned historic buildings and ancient monuments are now the responsibility of either the Department of National Heritage or Historic Scotland (an Executive Agency of the Scottish Office, which looks after 330 properties).

The Countryside and Wildlife Division is responsible for conservation and enhancement of the countryside and liaises closely with the statutory bodies dealt with already. It employs some specialist staff as Wildlife Inspectors who are responsible for regulating the import and export of birds and animals and for bird registration. The Rural Development Division is responsible for effects of policy on rural development and liaises closely with the national parks administrations and with local authorities.

The DoE is also responsible for most aspects of pollution control through its Environment Agency, established in April 1996 (*see below*).

The Environment Agency

The Environment Agency (for England and Wales) is one of the most powerful environmental regulators in the world. It was formed by merging the former Her Majesty's Inspectorate of Pollution (HMIP), the Waste Regulation Authorities and the National Rivers Authority in order to combine the regulation of land, air and water (making it much easier for industry, and others, to deal with one regulator rather than three).

Its functions include advising the Environment Secretary on the government's national air strategy, providing guidance to local authorities on their local air quality management plans and regulating over 2,000 industrial processes with the greatest polluting potential.

The agency is also responsible for regulating the disposal of radioactive waste at more than 8,000 sites and of controlled waste (household, commercial and industrial) at 8,000 waste management sites and involving 70,000 carriers and implementing the Government's waste management strategy. (*See* WASTE MANAGEMENT *below*.)

Responsibilities for the water environment include preserving and improving the quality of rivers, estuaries and coastal waters (including 100,000 water discharge consents and regulation of over 6,000 sewage works); conserving water resources through 50,000 licensed abstractions (anyone from a water company to a local farmer who wishes to draw water from a river must have an Agency licence to do so); supervising flood defences; maintaining and improving salmon, trout, eel and freshwater fisheries (issuing over a million angling licences – these too are compulsory); conserving nearly 40 million hectares of water, some of which is used for recreational purposes; and maintaining and improving non-marine navigation (the Agency licenses about 40,000 boats).

It also regulates the management and remediation of contaminated land designated as special sites and liaises with its counterparts internationally, particularly in EU countries to help develop consistent environmental policies.

The Environment Agency employs approximately 9,000 staff, who are based in eight Regional and 26 Area Offices. Work varies slightly between different regions. For example, two of the eight Regions have no EU designated bathing beaches or sea defence responsibilities and some have more industrial processes to regulate than others. However, staff employed fall into the following major categories:

Pollution Inspectors, who regulate complex industrial processes, ranging from paper incinerators and pharmaceutical manufacturers to power stations and petroleum refineries. They have degrees in chemical or mechanical engineering, chemistry, physics or the environmental sciences.

Water quality teams, who set limits for discharges (any waste water discharged into the environment, including from water company sewage treatment works); monitor pollution from land-based sources up to three miles out to sea; and take samples from bathing beaches. *Officers* have degree or equivalent qualifications in chemistry, biology, biochemistry, and environmental science. *Water resources officers* monitor river flows, groundwater levels, rainfall and climate. They regulate water abstraction, balancing environmental needs with those of the public and of industry. Qualifications are as for water quality officers. Some engineers and scientists with an MSc in hydrology or hydrogeology are also employed.

Waste regulation officers, who used to work for County Councils (and who transferred to the new agency on its creation), issue licences for the safe handling, storage, treatment, disposal and transport of waste. (*See* WASTE MANAGEMENT *below*.) They play a key role in delivering the national waste strategy. Qualifications are as for water quality officers except that some officers may have planning qualifications or other local authority backgrounds.

The Department of National Heritage

The Department is responsible for the arts, libraries, galleries, tourism and heritage in England, together with some national responsibilities. Some of its various Executive Agencies are directly concerned with the environment, for example, the Historic Royal Palaces Agency, administering five palaces (*see* HISTORICAL AND RELATED WORK) and the Royal Parks Agency, which has responsibility for London's nine royal parks plus some open spaces such as Parliament Square. Staff in the royal parks now work for private contractors and include gardeners and other horticultural staff and gamekeepers. Staff in the Royal Palaces Agency include gardeners and conservation specialists.

Energy

The Energy section within the Department of Trade and Industry is responsible for the nation's energy policy and liaises closely with the energy supply industries – oil, gas, electricity, nuclear – and those involved in the exploitation of the UK's natural energy resources such as coal and offshore oil and gas. It has conservation responsibilities for the environment. *See also* CENTRAL GOVERNMENT.

Overseas Development Agency

The Overseas Development Administration (ODA) is concerned with providing aid to help developing countries, particularly with the management of renewable natural resources, farming, forestry, fisheries, and the implementation of agricultural systems (crop utilisation, pest control, etc.). It has a Natural Resources Institute in Kent which employs 470 staff. *See* Foreign and Commonwealth Office *under* GOVERNMENT DEPARTMENTS *in* CENTRAL GOVERNMENT.

Ministry of Agriculture, Fisheries and Food

The concerns of the Ministry of Agriculture, Fisheries and Food (MAFF) include some conservation of the marine and freshwater environments, and environmental protection. It is responsible, for instance, for the protection of the coastline against erosion – a responsibility given to it since much coastal land is owned by farmers. Most of the openings for environmental scientists are with the Agricultural Development and Advisory Service (ADAS), which became a joint Agency of MAFF and the Welsh Office in April 1992 and is based in Oxford. It employs 2,320 staff. Examples of their work include studying the effects of pesticides on wildlife and investigating suspected wildlife poisoning incidents. ADAS also provides technical information and advice to farmers

MAFF runs a Central Laboratory, formed from a merger between its former food science laboratories and the ADAS Central Sciences Laboratory. In 1996 it relocated to a single site in Rydale, North Yorkshire. Staff also work for the Directorate of Fisheries Research laboratories at Lowestoft, Burnham-on-Crouch, Conwy and Weymouth, on the effects of marine pollution. Their environmental protection work involves chemists, biologists and geologists studying problems arising from the disposal of radioactive, industrial and domestic wastes.

The Food Safety and Pesticides Safety Directorates, which have obvious environmental impact, are executive agencies of MAFF.

See also CENTRAL GOVERNMENT *and* LAND USE INDUSTRIES.

Transport Research Foundation

The Transport Research Foundation, formerly the Transport and Road Research Laboratory, was privatised by a management buyout to form a 'non-profit distributing company' in April 1996. It has various groups including the Vehicles Group, which develops methods of making vehicles less damaging to the environment in terms of air pollution, noise, vibration and general nuisance. The main research group is at Crowthorne in Berkshire with a smaller branch near Edinburgh.

Local authorities

Local authorities bear much of the burden of conservation in practice. The ten national parks, for example, are administered by local planning authorities, who look after the parks' landscapes and safeguard public access to them. Local authorities also provide, equip and manage their own country parks of 25 acres or more where the use is mainly for leisure.

They have some responsibility for seeing that derelict land is reclaimed; they preserve and plant trees, provide parking and picnic areas, and work with English Heritage and other bodies to preserve and maintain listed buildings, etc. *See also* LOCAL GOVERNMENT.

Local authorities have important environmental roles in towns as well as the countryside and they are responsible for rubbish collection and recycling. They have increased statutory responsibilities under the 1990 Environmental Protection Act for controlling and implementing government policy on environmental pollution in their areas.

A number of local authorities have appointed environmental education officers.

Further information

Government departments and local authorities.

The Natural Environment Research Council

The Natural Environment Research Council (NERC) encourages, plans and carries out research in the biological and physical sciences relating to the natural environment and its resources. The work is aimed at advancing understanding of the nature and processes of the environment, the relationship between people and their surroundings, and their impact on each other.

NERC is one of the government's five autonomous Research Councils. Two-thirds of its funding comes through the Department for Education and Employment with the remainder earned from commissioned research, conducted on behalf of UK government departments, overseas governments, industry and UN agencies. NERC carries out research and training through its own and other grant-aided institutes, and by awards to universities and other higher education institutions.

The main fields of research are, broadly:

- the solid earth – its structure, physical properties and processes, minerals, bulk materials and fossil fuels (geology, geophysics and geochemistry);
- the seas and inland waters – their characteristics and living and mineral resources (physical, chemical and biological oceanography, marine ecology, hydrology and freshwater ecology);
- the terrestrial environment – structure, interactions and productivity of plant and animal populations and communities (terrestrial ecology and soil science);
- the atmosphere – its structure and interactions;
- the Antarctic environment – interdisciplinary studies of its physical and biological properties.

Increasing use is being made of a sophisticated computer technique, called Geographic Information Systems (GIS). GIS allows the overlaying of data from various sources, e.g. species distribution, vegetation, climate and land-use, to produce a comprehensive picture of the environment.

Research institutes

NERC used to have three directorates which carried out environmental research: the Earth Sciences Directorate, the Marine Atmospheric Sciences Directorate and the Terrestrial and Freshwater Sciences Directorate. These were disbanded in 1995, and although the same work is done, it is now carried out by 20 institutes on 40 different sites.

One such institute is the British Geological Survey, which prepares and constantly revises the geological database on the UK, collecting, interpreting and correlating available data, but about 70% of its research programme is work commissioned by government departments, e.g. surveying for mineral resources, environmental mapping, assessing the hydrocarbon potential on- and offshore. Although funding on basic research has been cut, some regional surveys have been maintained, and BGS is working on a computerised databank from which thematic maps can be generated interactively. BGS does work like making a report on the geological background to the Abbeystead methane explosion, produces maps to help developers on mining and ground stability, and also does work overseas, e.g. geotechnical studies in Cyprus, and looking at ways to improve groundwater yield in Africa and South Asia.

The marine surveys groups in BGS make geological maps of the British continental shelf and the Marine Operations group collect the geophysical and geological samples needed for the preparation of the maps. BGS employs 523 (1996) geoscientists, both on its own surveys, and under contract to other governments and industry.

Work done by other institutes includes:

Marine sciences, where the range of research includes the effects of ocean turbulence, developing ways of collecting data using remote sensing by satellite, studying what happens in underwater sediments to make clearer the potential impact of effluent on it, the feeding habits of inshore fish, working out why farmed salmon get certain diseases, and the effect of detergents on fish gills. Current major programmes are concerned with interactions between the oceans and the atmosphere, in the context of global warming and climate change. Research in oceanographic science, coordinating the UK contribution to the international study of ocean circulation, is conducted principally by Southampton University.

In atmospheric sciences, much of the research is done in the Antarctic, studying the global climate at one end of the scale and how water droplets and ice particles develop at the other, as well as problems like the greenhouse effect, acid rain, the depletion of the ozone layer, and nuclear winter.

In terrestrial and freshwater sciences, the main programmes include forest and woodland ecology, land resources and use, aquatic ecosystem management, human impact on the hydrological cycle, land surface water balance, environmental pollution, population and community ecology and virology.

British Antarctic Survey

The British Antarctic Survey (BAS) has three permanent stations in the Antarctic plus a summer station and employs 420 staff, of whom many are scientists. BAS also employs builders, cooks, mechanics, medical staff and pilots for the Antarctic stations.

The British Antarctic Survey does work in all the above areas: studying the hard continent under the ice and mapping it, probing into the 100,000-year-old ice sheet and studying its history, making meteorological measurements and exploring the upper atmosphere, and studying the food chain in the southern ocean and especially krill, birds and seals.

Expenditure on Antarctic research has recently been doubled. A new ice-strengthened ship, the RRS *James Clark Ross*, provides the basis for studying marine sciences, and a new airstrip in the Antarctic will allow easier access of field scientists and their deployment in Antarctica. There are five aircraft which operate from the bases in the summer.

Recruitment and entry

Staff employed directly by NERC and by the institutes number about 3,000 and include some 1,500 scientists on permanent contract. Others are employed on short-term contract, especially to work in the Antarctic (about 50 a year).

Scientists from almost every discipline are employed. Recent contract posts advertised include ones for a marine biologist, a seabird ecologist, electronics engineers, radar engineer, plant population biologist, and plant physiologist. Staff would be expected to have good degrees plus preferably a higher degree in an appropriate subject. NERC also employs nearly 325 people in scientific services – computing, radiocarbon dating, and on the research vessels (about 75 shore-based staff and over 100 seafarers) and about 220 HQ staff.

The number of staff recruited and the disciplines depend entirely on individual vacancies and what research, especially contract work, is currently underway. Competition is stiff, especially for short-term BAS contracts. Structure, grading and recruitment method is as for the Civil Service (*see* CENTRAL GOVERNMENT), although some posts may be filled by individual institutes.

On the support side there are some openings in administration and some engineering opportunities for those with workshop experience and appropriate qualifications.

Qualifications and training

While NERC provides grants for postgraduate study, staff recruited on permanent/fixed-term contracts are normally expected to have an appropriate scientific qualification (structure and grading as for the Civil Service – *see* CENTRAL GOVERNMENT). Further training mainly consists of short courses run by NERC, e.g. in computing.

Further information

NERC and other bodies mentioned above. Although there is no longer any central body governing the research institutes, enquiries about career prospects in the above areas may be sent to NERC headquarters at Swindon, and will be forwarded to the appropriate institute.

Working in industry

Seeing that industrial plant meets current legislation, and does not pollute the environment with waste chemicals, gases or smoke, has to be built into new plant or equipment, which makes it part of the work of the *design engineer*. seeing that plant operates properly, and does not accidentally pollute its surroundings, and upgrading existing plant, is part of the responsibility of the *production engineer*.

The concept of Integrated Pollution Control, for the more highly polluting plants and processes, is practised in the UK, and legislation has been introduced in England and Wales which aims to:

- prevent pollution at source;
- minimise risk to health and the environment;
- encourage the best solution for the environment as a whole;
- ensure that the 'polluter pays'.

An increasing number of firms employ environmental control specialists, to see that company policy is kept in line with legislation and public pressure, costing it, turning public interest to commercial advantage, and trying to save costs. For many firms, however, this is more likely to be just part of the work of the most suitable person. Other firms will call in specialists when needed, either consultants or the technical teams from equipment manufacturers. *See also* MANUFACTURING INDUSTRIES.

The number of scientists and planners employed by industry on environmental issues has grown in recent years, but few companies employ many. Among the largest are the Dow Chemical Company, National Power, ICI Agrochemicals Research Station and ICI's Environmental Laboratory.

Employment in industry is likely to increase with growing public awareness and concern with environmental problems and 'green' issues. Moreover, environmental management has become very important for all businesses, with new environmental legislation and environmental audits taking place.

Recruitment and entry

Environmental management issues are mainly the responsibility of senior and middle management, and staff include plant chemists, chief scientists and technical/plant directors with science and engineering degrees. Supervisors and operatives are involved with the sampling and monitoring of waste streams and collating of environmental data. These staff require few pre-entry qualifications although further study is encouraged for City & Guilds examinations.

The voluntary sector

Voluntary organisations are numerous, but have few full-time jobs to offer except for the National Trust (*see below and in* HISTORICAL AND RELATED WORK).

Of the others, the Civic Trust and the British Trust for Conservation Volunteers (BTCV) are two of the largest. The Civic Trust encourages high-quality architecture and planning, and tries to preserve buildings of aesthetic and historic interest, to protect the countryside, to eliminate and prevent ugliness, and to encourage public interest. It also is concerned with the restoration of canals. It supports and assists local civic and amenity trusts and has initiated hundreds of schemes. The British Trust for Conservation Volunteers employs about 215 full-time staff throughout the UK and trains over 50,000 volunteers a year to carry out environmental work. Most field officers working for the BTCV have a degree. The BTCV also has a trading company which sells trees, handbooks, specialist tools, protective clothing and other merchandise by mail order. This employs 80 full-time staff.

The Field Studies Council is an educational charity which promotes 'environmental understanding for all'. It has ten residential and day centres delivering short fieldwork courses. The Council also runs a small research centre specialising in the effects of oil pollution. Teaching staff (between two and four at each centre) must have an honours degree in an environmental subject, and preferably a teaching qualification too. The research centre recruits graduates in chemistry, mathematics, biochemistry and physics.

Other national societies, completely dependent on voluntary support, include the Councils for the Protection of Rural England, Wales and Scotland; the British Trust for Ornithology; the Commons, Open Spaces and Footpaths Preservation Society; the Ramblers' Association; the Royal Society for Nature Conservation; the Society for the Protection of Ancient Buildings; the Ancient Monuments Society; the Victorian Society. There are a lot of opportunities to gain valuable work experience through voluntary work for these bodies – especially on site management tasks, both on rural and city sites. However, there are usually only a few full-time posts with these organisations and these are mainly for administrative/secretarial staff.

Some organisations are international, e.g. the World Wide Fund for Nature (WWF), employing a full-time staff of about 225; Friends of the Earth (FoE); and Greenpeace (about 100 employees). Fundraising and press and publicity work are important aspects of their activities.

Qualifications and training

With such a diversity of work and employers, and the high level of competition for the few posts, no clear route in exists, and there is no specific training.

A relevant qualification, especially a good science degree – physics, mathematics, engineering science, zoology, biology, environmental science, geology or chemistry, oceanography, forestry, etc. – combined with plenty of voluntary, spare-time work in the chosen area of conservation, probably gives the best chance.

The National Trust

The National Trust acquires land and buildings of national and historic interest and improves and protects them. It owns, or controls, large areas of land throughout the UK,

1,000 scheduled ancient monuments, over 200 historic houses, 160 gardens, 50 or so nature reserves and parks, and even entire villages and islands. It is the country's largest single private landowner. It is extensively involved in improving the environment and, in addition, protects 550 miles of coast and owns 590,000 acres of countryside.

The Trust, whose income is from voluntary contributions, legacies, grants and visitors' entry fees, employs many specialists with professional qualifications and experience. These include land agents, cartographers, archaeologists, foresters, gardeners, wardens, architects, etc.

The National Trust has 3,000 full-time employees. It also provides YT training for school-leavers in amenity horticulture, forestry and countryside management (about 40 a year).

Competition is extremely fierce for posts.

Further information

The Environment Council and the organisations mentioned above.

Waste management

Waste is a sensitive and often emotive issue to which there is no easy solution. The main options in waste management are recycling, recovery of resources such as materials (recycled construction waste, for example, such as crushed concrete, can be used again and at the same time minimise waste for disposal and conserve natural resources like sand and gravel which would have to be extracted) or the production of energy and finally, disposal. In the UK, waste is jointly managed by local government (in the form of county planning authorities which formulate policy and have waste management departments to deal with disposal and district councils which collect domestic waste), national government (the regulatory authority) and private industry (the contractors).

National policy on waste is strongly influenced by the EU, which has developed policies through a number of directives, in particular, the 1989 Strategy for Waste Management and the 1991 Waste Framework Directive. These established a hierarchy: the first priority should be to minimise and prevent waste, the second to reuse, recycle and recover, the third to optimise final disposal. The main thrust of EU policy is to minimise the production of waste through increased use of clean technologies, to reuse, and to use disposal, particularly where landfill is used, only as a last resort. Member states are also required to be as self-sufficient as possible and minimise the transportation of waste. EU policy has led directly to UK legislation. The original Control of Pollution Act has been superseded by the 1990 Environmental Protection Act.

Also in 1990, the Town and Country Planning Act laid a duty on planning authorities (mainly county councils) to prepare local waste plans, which must be made available to the public before being adopted. Then came a DoE consultation paper in 1992 which said that only in exceptional circumstances, where for instance it requires special treatment, should waste be transported out of a region.

The government has set a target of recycling half the country's recyclable household waste – equivalent to 25% of all household waste – by the year 2000.

Local authorities must consider the different means of waste management at their disposal and endeavour to use the most efficient where possible. Technology is leading to progress (although landfill is still much used). It is now possible to use high-technology methods such as anaerobic digestion (which produces biogas for use as fuel from organic waste) and gasification (conversion of organic waste to gas by partial combustion at high temperature) and to create energy from waste incineration by the mass-burn incineration of waste and use of the heat to generate electricity. Low-technology methods include sorting, reclaiming and aerobic composting. However, even though incinerators are vastly more efficient than some other methods, planning authorities have to give careful consideration to their siting. (No one wishes to live near one!)

'Special' waste, defined in legislation as hazardous, presents particular problems. Strict controls must be observed and its movement notified to waste authorities. 'Difficult' waste, including clinical waste, sewage and sludge, presents its own problems. Public opinion is now against the idea of spreading sludge on agricultural land, and sea disposal must cease under the EU Community Urban Waste Water Treatment Directive by 1998.

Local authorities are responsible for the disposal of waste, but this is usually contracted out to private firms. Prior to April 1996 they were also the regulatory authorities, but this function has now passed to the Environment Agency, whose waste regulation officers licence waste disposal, treatment, transport and storage (*see* Environment Agency *under* CENTRAL AND LOCAL GOVERNMENT *above*). They issue licences for car breakers and scrapyards in addition to incinerators and landfill sites. They also advise industry on methods of safe waste disposal and encourage minimisation, and must be consulted by local councils on all new development close to landfills.

Recruitment and entry

At present (1996) most waste regulation officers previously worked in local authorities where their duties were very similar. They and their former colleagues in local authorities' waste management departments have varied backgrounds. Many are graduates in chemistry, biochemistry or engineering; others hold HNDs or other technical qualifications; some are former planners.

Qualifications and training

Postgraduate courses in waste management are available at Central Lancashire, Luton and Sunderland universities. There is also an Open University degree in pollution control which has relevant content.

Most people acquire their specific expertise in waste management once in employment. Training is supervised by the Waste Management Industry Training and Advisory Board, the lead body, which has, in conjunction with City & Guilds, devised NVQs. There are NVQs in Regulating Waste Management at levels 3 and 4, in Transfer Operations (Inert Waste) at level 3, Treatment Operations (Inert Waste) at level 3, Managing Landfill Operation (Biodegradable Waste), Managing Incineration Operations (Special Waste), Managing Landfill Operation (Special Waste), Managing Transfer Operations (Special Waste) and Managing Treatment Operations (Special Waste) all at level 4.

The water industry

The water industry in England and Wales went through a major reorganisation in 1989 when the former ten regional authorities were privatised. Thus, they joined the 28 statutory water companies in the private sector. The newly privatised companies are water supply and sewerage companies whereas the former statutory water companies were involved only in water supply. Since 1989 there have been a number of mergers and takeovers among the statutory companies and they have now been reduced to about 22, giving a total of 32 companies involved in water supply and sewerage treatment in England and Wales.

In Scotland water supply and sewerage is dealt with by three public water authorities (North, East and West Scotland) and in Northern Ireland these functions are the responsibility of the Department of the Environment (NI).

The industry provides a continuous, reliable and high standard of service with a very high quality of water to 99% of the population in Great Britain. The volume of water used per day is 20,360 megalitres.

The industry also provides sewage treatment services for about 96% of the population of Great Britain.

Costs are high of making sure that the system can meet consumer demand for water; meeting European Community and UK requirements with regard to water quality; and effluent discharge and other consents in order to protect and improve the water environment. A total of £28 billion will have been invested in capital expenditure programmes in the period 1991 to 2000.

The water industry was one of the few to increase its recruitment during the recession.

The main organisations in the industry in England and Wales, and their activities, are:

Water service companies

Ten water and sewerage undertakers with the same boundaries as the former Regional Water Authorities. Their interests are promoted by a Water Services Association which employs 34 people at its head office.

Water companies

Twenty-two companies, all of them originally statutory companies, but some of which have now converted to plc status. They supply about 25% of the drinking water in England and Wales. The Water Companies Association looks after their interests.

The Environment Agency

(*See under* CENTRAL AND LOCAL GOVERNMENT *above*) has regulatory responsibilities which include regulating the water industry.

The Office of Water Services (OFWAT)

The economic regulator of the water industry. It is a government agency responsible for making sure that the water industry in England and Wales provides customers with a good quality and efficient service at a fair price. OFWAT is independent of the industry and has set up regional Customer Service Committees. They have a duty to investigate many types of customer complaints about water and sewerage companies and have a wider role in looking after the interests of water consumers in their area by keeping under review, and discussing with the companies, the services they provide.

Drinking Water Inspectorate (DWI)

Created in 1990 to carry out a technical audit of the Water Services Companies and Statutory Water Companies to determine whether they are complying with regulatory requirements. The DWI's assessment is based on an examination of water quality determinations carried out by the companies.

British Waterways

Created by the Transport Act 1962, it is responsible for almost 2,000 miles of canals used mainly for recreational purposes, but with some commercial use. It has 2,400 employees. *See also* THE TRANSPORT INDUSTRY.

River Purification Boards

In Scotland the pollution control functions are the responsibility of seven River Purification Boards.

Department of Environment for Northern Ireland (DOENI)

DOENI is responsible for the supply and distribution of water and for the provision and maintenance of sewerage services.

A number of organisations are involved in research relating to water, and the main participants are:

The Water Research Centre (WRc)

Having two laboratories at Medmenham and Swindon, it carries out research on sewerage and waste water treatment, drinking water treatment, environmental protection, instrumentation, water mains and sewers. It is a private company employing about 400 staff. WRc Medmenham recruits mainly biology and chemistry graduates plus the occasional toxicologists, ecologists and postgraduates qualified in waste management. WRc Swindon recruits graduate biochemists, chemists, chemical engineers, physicists, materials scientists and engineers.

Working in the water industry

In England and Wales the Water Service Companies employ 37,418 people and the water companies an additional 6,210 people. In Scotland the industry employs 6,653 people and in Northern Ireland 2,418 people.

Numbers of staff working for individual Water Service Companies vary considerably. In 1995 the ten Water Services Companies employed: Anglian Water Services Ltd (4,815), Northumbrian Water Ltd (1,377), North West Water Ltd (5,471), Severn Trent Water Ltd (6,531), Southern Water Services Ltd (2,371), South West Water Services Ltd (2,084), Thames Water Utilities Ltd (6,485), Dwr Cymru Cyfyngedig (3,329), Wessex Water Services Ltd (1,582), and Yorkshire Water Services Ltd (3,373).

In recent years there has been a very marked improvement in efficiency and a very substantial investment in instrumentation control and automation.

There is a high proportion of professionally qualified staff in managerial and administrative posts, including engineering and scientific posts, finance, accounting, personnel, etc.

Civil, mechanical and electrical engineers, and scientists, are employed in the design, construction and management of water treatment, storage and distribution systems, and in the design, construction, operation and management of sewerage systems and sewage works.

Technicians work as laboratory technicians and supervise and monitor systems. Craft and operative workers are employed in running pumping stations and treatment plant, inspecting and maintaining equipment, looking after rivers and other water channels. Pipe-laying and construction work are often done by contractors.

The water industry overseas

The activities covered are the same as in the UK, but the organisations vary considerably.

The UK overseas aid programme is operated by the Overseas Development Administration (ODA) and contributes to water and sanitation projects in some 40 developing countries. Charity organisations such as the UK water industry's 'Water Aid' have also carried out a range of projects.

Many UK contractors, consulting engineers and firms producing water supply equipment export a range of goods and services. About 1,600 members of the Chartered Institution of Water and Environmental Management work as consultants overseas.

Recruitment and entry

Recruitment is carried out directly by the companies and organisations.

Because of the very wide range of duties, responsibilities and work within water companies and the regulatory authorities the industry recruits staff with a very wide range of qualifications.

Graduates are required with degrees in civil, mechanical, electrical and electronic engineering, quantity surveying, land management, biochemistry, chemistry, biology, mathematics, economics, computing, geology, microbiology, physics, etc.; non-graduates for technical posts should have Higher National Certificates and National Certificates.

Qualifications and training

There are few specific national qualifications for the water industry.

Water Training International provides training at all levels within the industry.

The lead institution in the industry is the Chartered Institution of Water and Environmental Management, which currently has 11,800 members. Admission to the corporate grade of membership is by honours degree and a professional review which requires the submission of a technical paper and an interview before three members of the institution. The grade of Graduate is available as a holding grade for graduates with insufficient experience and training. In addition, there are grades of Associate and Affiliate for personnel with Higher National Certificate and National Certificate, respectively. There is also a Student grade open to people engaged either full- or part-time on courses of study approved by the Institute.

Further information

Chartered Institution of Water and Environmental Management; the Water Services Association; individual water companies.

The Transport Industry

Contents

(CLCI: Y–YAZ, RAE)

Background

Transport systems that give people the freedom to travel and for goods to be transported throughout the world are a central feature of our lives. Efficient transport is crucial to economic growth. While life today would be unimaginable without transport, advanced communication systems could cut demand as they give people the opportunity to work from home with a computer, telephone and modem.

The transport industry is large and complex. Achieving efficient, cheap passenger transport systems has proved hard. Attempts to plan and develop integrated, cooperative transport, never too successful except in a few cases, are still proving difficult. Deregulation, with increasing competition between commercially owned bodies, is being tried, with fewer state owned organisations and less involvement for local authorities. Most transport operations now work hard to make a profit from the services they provide. Competition is both between sectors, and between operators in the separate sectors – air transport ended long-distance sea transport for passengers, while road transport systems take business from rail. All passenger services are competing with the car as well as each other and new innovations like the Channel Tunnel, financed and built entirely by the private sector, have changed the scenario even more. In some urban areas, trams are being reintroduced, such as the Manchester Metrolink, in an effort to ease traffic congestion. There is also the major issue of pollution and experiments are under way with electrically and gas powered forms of public transport.

Transport systems are not, therefore, easy to manage. They are also costly, even if fuel prices are low. Transport systems are usually labour-intensive, and they use very expensive hardware – aircraft, ships, railway rolling stock, freightliners, even buses, which have to be planned for and ordered well in advance of need.

Most national and international transport firms have widely distributed bases, and even local transport organisations have to manage systems that are widely scattered and on the move most of the time. Just keeping track of them and staying in touch is a major problem, although technology is making this easier. Many transport systems run seven days a week, all year round, and some round the clock too.

The problems, then, range from the need for high-level strategic forward planning at one extreme, to solving the daily problems of moving people and goods around at the other. Operating transport systems in today's economic and competitive conditions takes increasing managerial, marketing and financial expertise, and greater technological skills. Transport fleets and systems have to be managed and operated with increasing efficiency and great control. For instance, many transport fleets now have computerised systems which can analyse routes to give the best routes for speed and economic fuel consumption.

Transport organisations fall into two different types. First are the organisations which specialise mainly in providing a transport service, although some have also diversified into other, related sectors like hotels. They range in size from major national and international companies down to the one person operation. Second, are the organisations in other sectors which have their own transport, mainly road, systems which they need to do their own business – examples are the Royal Mail with vans, trains and even aircraft to carry mail, British Telecom which needs vans and trucks mainly for its engineers, and brewing, oil and chemical companies who must move their own products from production plant to warehouse and retailer.

The transport industry is also generally taken to include the ports where ships dock and airports. The transport industry uses a range of services from fuel suppliers through to specialist freight or air forwarders.

All transport operations, whether by independent carriers like the railways or in transport sections of manufacturing or other companies, involve a similar series of operations. Goods or people have to be loaded onto the vehicle being used to transport them (which means having somewhere to do this). They are then transported as efficiently, directly, cheaply and safely as is cost-effective to their destination, where they are unloaded.

Transport services by definition involve managing a fleet of vehicles – deciding which planes, buses or trucks to buy, possibly having special vehicles designed and developed, maintaining and repairing them, planning their replacement, fuelling them (which includes buying the fuel and seeing it is safely stored), etc.

Transport services operate 24 hours a day and involve both complex planning and scheduling and large numbers of people. Consider, for example, the problems involved in keeping a supermarket supplied with fresh food. Most transport services meet regular problems which must be solved rapidly and efficiently such as vehicle breakdowns, traffic congestion, accidents, bad weather or people and goods in the wrong places. For longer-distance passenger services catering and sleeping accommodation may have to be provided.

Working in transport

Approximately 872,000 (1995) people now work in the transport industry, down from a peak of well over one million in 1979. While recession had a major effect, the industry has also been restructuring and attempting to cut staffing levels permanently, with some help from new technology and the effects of privatisation in some areas

The Chartered Institute of Transport (CIT) identifies a number of functions common to all transport operations. These are planning, policy and financial control, operations and management, physical distribution management, technology, research and education, and social and environmental aspects.

Specific areas of work

Management and administration

Directly managing and administering a fleet or facility (e.g. an airport, port, railway station, bus or freight depot) on a day-to-day basis. Specific specialist jobs include scheduling and timetabling. The work includes commercial functions common to all businesses such as finance, marketing, personnel management, though dealing with the particular needs of a transport firm.

Engineering

Designing and developing systems and vehicles, maintenance and repair at all levels, from managerial through technician to craft, etc.

Operating transport systems

As driver, pilot, ship's officer, sailor, etc.

Supporting work

Includes air traffic control, marine pilotage.

Related work

Transport and traffic planning, etc. in LOCAL GOVERNMENT and the Civil Service, where they have direct responsibility for traffic. TRAVEL AGENCY and TOUR OPERATING (*see in* THE TRAVEL INDUSTRY), FREIGHT FORWARDING (*see below*).

Recruitment and entry

Normally directly into a transport operation, for training in a specific function – in administration as clerk or management trainee, engineering, or working on the transport system itself.

Entry is possible from a variety of different educational backgrounds, but CIT believes it crucial that the industry recruits a rising number of people with a 'high standard of general and vocational education and practical experience'.

Qualifications and training

Depends to some extent on sector and function, but is mainly on-the-job and part-time, with some few opportunities for pre-entry qualification.

Professional qualifications are essential requirements for transport managers, as EU regulations demand certain standards of competence demonstrated by the Certificate of Professional Competence.

The Chartered Institute of Transport, founded early in the century, has (1996) a membership of over 20,000, some 9,000 of them based overseas. Full membership needs an approved relevant degree, or completion of the Institute's qualifying exams. These are broadly based (and now include management and marketing) but provide for some specialisation in a branch of transport. Minimum qualification for entry to these is at least five GCSE or equivalent passes (including English language and maths). Other qualifications may also be accepted and advice about these can be obtained from the CIT.

The Institute of Transport Administration, founded 1944, has a membership (1996) of 4,000 (down from 5,000 in 1986). Seventy-four per cent of these work in road transport (as owner operators or fleet managers). They have introduced a system of management training leading to a Certificate in Transport Administration (NVQ/SVQ Level 3).The exam consists of six modules and is available at many colleges through the country. It is also available through the Transport Tutorial Association (based at the Chartered Institute of Transport) as a distance learning package. By December 1996, a NVQ/SVQ Level 4 Diploma in Transport will be in place. Exemptions for these qualifications are available on application to IOTA.

IOTA particularly recommends the degree courses at the Universities of Central England, Loughborough, Salford and Plymouth.

Degree courses

Universities – Aston (transport management), Cardiff (international transport), Central England (environmental planning), Huddersfield (transport and distribution), Loughborough (transport management and planning), Plymouth (transport), Ulster (transport): Institutes of HE – Southampton (International Transport).

Postgraduate and post-experience courses

Universities – Cardiff, Cranfield, Huddersfield, Leeds, Liverpool John Moores (Maritime), London: Guildhall, Imperial and University College Loughborough (Airport Planning), Newcastle, Plymouth, Salford, Southampton, Westminster; Institutes of HE – Swansea.

BTEC/SCOTVEC Higher awards can be taken with transport administration at a number of universities and other colleges. Most give at least some exemptions from CIT exams.

Civil aviation

The airline industry – the airlines – working in airlines

The airline industry

Civil aviation is the fastest growing area of the transport industry. The number of passengers carried on international scheduled services has increased by 50% and the number of charter passengers has doubled to over 20 million per year. This has put considerable pressure on the air traffic control systems and this is now one of the main priorities in air transport. Safety and security is another priority, and a costly one: governments and hijackers both create political crises. Air travel is still the safest form of transport and is getting safer all the time. Over the last ten years, there has been one passenger fatality (on UK airlines) for every 2.2 billion miles flown.

The airlines also have to consider the cost of maintaining and replacing ageing aircraft and face the constant problem of fluctuation in oil prices.

Transport is a complex and difficult business to manage, with very high, and rising fixed capital and running costs, and problems in predicting traffic levels far enough ahead to have the right numbers and types of planes, ground facilities, and staff, available. Competition is intensifying, with airlines merging to create 'mega carriers'. They now have no option but to be heavily marketing oriented, and customers will no longer tolerate poor service.

Passengers make up the bulk of air traffic, with the air freight business accounting for the rest.

The airline business is made up of the airlines themselves, the supervisory Civil Aviation Authority, the airports, and other support services.

The airlines

There are approximately 30 airlines operating in the UK. Over 40 other firms have air transport licences, and a great many other firms run smaller flying operations, including over 100 air-taxi firms, crop sprayers, charter companies (who work for, e.g., the POST OFFICE), air survey companies, and helicopter services, for, e.g., the North Sea oil and gas rigs. Some organisations have their own, fairly small, flying operations, e.g. the POLICE and the Search and Rescue services.

The aviation industry as a whole is becoming more deregulated which means more competition between airlines which in turn leads to new innovations within the industry and more competitive services and fares.

The number of passengers entering and leaving Britain is increasing all the time: in 1994 there were over 95 million passenger movements by air in the UK.

British Airways is one of the world's largest carriers, and the major UK employer within the industry. It covers some 169 destinations in 80 countries. A further 33 points in Europe and North Africa are served by the airline's franchise partners CityFlyer Express, GB Airways, Loganair, Maersk Air and Manx Airlines (Europe). It has partners in Europe (Deutsche BA and TAT European Airlines) and interests in USAir, USAir Express and Quantas. BA has a fleet of 190 planes, including seven Concordes. British Airways and partners employ over 53,000 (1996) staff (up from 48,000 in 1992) and is currently on a recruiting drive after very low recruitment for some years.

Other major airlines in the UK include: Britannia (part of the Thomson group), the UK's second largest airline and the world's biggest charter airline carrying 8 million passengers from 17 UK airports to more than 100 destinations worldwide. They operate 24 aircraft, leasing extra planes at peak season. British Midland employs 3,900 staff and is the UK's second largest scheduled service airline with over 1,000 flights a week, carrying over 5 million passengers in 1995. It has a fleet of 35 aircraft. Virgin Atlantic started in 1984 and flies from Heathrow and Gatwick to destinations in the USA, Hong Kong and Tokyo. Virgin employs approximately 3,100 staff.

Working in airlines

Airline staff can be divided between aircrew and ground staff. Considerably more people are employed on the ground than in the air.

Flying staff

Flying is possible for only a small proportion of people in the civil aviation business, probably well under 20% of the total.

Everyone who flies, from senior pilot to the most junior member of the cabin crew, has to work irregular hours, although the number of hours they can spend in the air is strictly controlled. On long-haul routes they usually have enforced stopover rest periods abroad, although it might only be a single night with no time for sightseeing, etc. They may have to go through several time zones on one flight. On short-haul routes they may be on four (or more) consecutive flights without even leaving the plane, and be home again most nights.

Pilots: 12,000 people hold commercial licences and British Airways employs about 3,000 of them. Until a few years ago most civil airline pilots were men because women were not accepted for training by British Airways. This has now changed and opportunities are equal but BALPA (the pilot's union) say that of their 8,000 membership, just over 1% are women. The British Women Pilots Association at Rochester airport have 250 members and membership is open to those who fly as a profession or hobby.

In the airlines, most planes are flown by just a captain and co-pilot; only older, long-range planes need a third person in the cabin (a flight engineer or third pilot). The pilots spend less and less of their time 'flying' in the traditional sense. Instead they concentrate on managing flight in the most efficient way, using state of the art computers to control and monitor the aircraft and to marshal its many resources. This is not to say that the pilot's role is diminished. The captains and co-pilots still have to make vital decisions to guarantee the safe operation of their aircraft. They must still be experts in flight planning and have all the flying skills ready to 'go manual' should the need arise.

Once in the air, the crew has many tasks to complete. Continual checks have to be made on the aircraft's technical performance, fuel load and position – as well as outside factors such as weather conditions and air traffic.

Contact with the ground must be maintained and any instructions received must be acted upon promptly and accurately.

Every airline has its own system, and the larger the airline the greater the range of opportunities, although promotion may come faster in a smaller airline. In British Airways, newly appointed second officers, once trained, start on short-haul routes as co-pilots. The chance to transfer to long-range aircraft (still as co-pilot) does not come for at least five years. On present agreements, etc., promotion to probationary captain is unlikely to come until mid career, retirement is normally by 55, and means going back to short-haul routes and planes. Airline pilots can try for senior managerial positions on the ground.

Other opportunities for pilots are in the air-taxi and charter business, flying helicopters, or smaller executive jets. They take people to business meetings or sports events, carry mail or urgent cargoes, schedule-fly helicopters to and from North Sea oil rigs or fly reporters around. There is some aerial survey work and photography and crop spraying. Some experienced pilots work as instructors.

Smaller planes have increasingly complex systems too: navigational aids and autopilots, but there is still more manual flying than in an airliner.

Test pilots are usually ex-military pilots and/or instructors who are recruited directly by the aviation and aerospace industry. They have had considerable experience of flying in all conditions and may even have taken part in display flying (e.g. Red Arrows).

Recruitment and entry

British Airways has a cadet pilot training scheme (1996). Only British Midland has been known to sponsor pilots in the past. Virgin Atlantic has never offered sponsored training.

Entry requirements (for BA) are at least seven GCSE passes (including English language, maths and a science) and two A-levels, ideally in maths and physics (or equivalent). Candidates have to be extremely fit (and get through a stiff CAA medical), be between 5' 2" and 6' 3" in height (the minimum height requirement has been lowered by 2" to promote more equal opportunities for women and ethnic minorities) with weight in proportion to height. They must have good eyesight (but spectacles accepted), hearing and good hand to eye coordination.

Age range is between 18 and 28 (at time of application so candidates might be 29 when they start training). Candidates must be a European Economic Area Citizen with an unrestricted worldwide passport. They must be fluent in English with a clear speaking voice and be able to work as part of a team.

Stringent aptitude tests are set – BA does not expect more than one in ten of those interviewed to pass them. Tests are computer-based as well as written and there is an assessment based on the interview and some group activities.

Recruitment is open to both men and women and BA are keen to recruit more women in line with their equal opportunities policy. The lowering of the height restriction should encourage more applications from women.

For British Midland, candidates should be aged between 18 and 25 in the year in which the course commences. Minimum qualifications are 5 GCSEs or equivalent to include maths, english and a science. All interviewing, aptitude testing and shortlisting is done for British Midland by the Oxford Air Training School in Oxford.

All potential pilot cadets must be able to pay close attention to detail, particularly with figures. They must be calm under pressure, even when managing a number of tasks simultaneously. They must have good spatial awareness and the ability to interpret maps and 3D displays.

Qualifications and training

All commercial pilots have to gain the Civil Aviation Authority's commercial pilot's licence and instrument rating, and to have trained for this at a CAA approved school or college. Training is now available via BA and sometimes British Midland, with the alternative of training privately which is extremely expensive.

The British Airways training scheme begins with 70 weeks' basic training, which is at the British Aerospace Training College in Prestwick or the Oxford Air Training School. In addition to the basic licence, trainees are expected to gain the airline transport pilot's licence.

Typically, the BA course begins in the classroom with 8 weeks training in basic aviation theory and practice. Successful students then begin flight training in a light, single engine two-seater trainer in order to gain the CAA Private Pilot's Licence.

After that, time is spent flying sometimes alone or with fellow cadets who will fly together as pilot and co-pilot, learning to work as a flight deck crew.

Having mastered light aircraft, the cadets progress to larger, twin engine aircraft with more sophisticated systems. Training in flying using instruments starts.

After much more study and practice, cadets start flying in controlled airspace, joining normal commercial air traffic and flying into major airports. They then sit the CAA

Instrument Rating exam. Final training is then given on the ground, using flight simulators to practise on larger jet aircraft from the fleet. The course finishes with final exams and general flying tests and the completion of the Commercial Pilot's Licence.

British Airways estimate that the cost of training, accommodation and exams during the course is over £60,000. Twenty-five per cent of this is repaid from the pilot's salary once they start work. The pilot must work for British Airways for at least five years to avoid repaying any more.

British Midland require candidates to pay the first £10,000 of their training and this is deducted from their salary once they start work, over a period of three years.

Basic training is also available at two other CAA approved colleges, but costs over £56,000 (1996) for the 54-week course. These are Air Service Training Ltd in Perth and the Oxford Air Training School. Entry requirements are as above. Air Service Training Ltd also offers a two-year full-time HND in Aviation with Business Studies validated by SCOTVEC and the CAA.

It is also still possible to start with a private pilot's licence, and build up the required 700 hours' flying time (possibly as an assistant flying instructor), then take the CAA tests. However, the sophistication of modern airliners makes it doubtful if airlines will accept this as it probably means not getting any time in airliner simulators.

Some people take the American or Canadian Commercial Pilot's Licence which is cheaper and then fly abroad to build up the necessary 700 hours. They then convert the foreign licence to a British licence. The cost would be about half that of a course in the UK.

There is also an NVQ/SVQ in Piloting Transport Aircraft Level 4.

Cabin crew

Cabin crew (no longer known as stewards and stewardesses) look after passengers' safety and comfort while they are in the aircraft. They check stores, see that blankets, cushions and so on are available, welcome passengers on board and make them comfortable, look after children travelling alone, answer questions, and try to calm people who are worried by flying, taking particular care of travellers with problems. They sell duty free goods, serve drinks and meals, etc., and make announcements. The work is physically, and sometimes emotionally, demanding. There is always a lot to do and little time to relax. Cabin crew have to work in very confined space (and a big jet may have a cabin crew of up to 14), in close contact with a lot of people.

Promotion can be to Cabin Services Manager or purser, responsible for what is at present treated as one of the major ways of winning the battle to attract passengers. However, a high proportion of staff are recruited on temporary contracts, for the summer season only. The industry is estimated to employ about 9,000 aircabin crew in all, most by the larger airlines.

Recruitment and entry

Cabin crew are expected to have a good educational background, to at least GCSE or equivalent standard, with reasonable, conversational fluency in at least one European language. The age on entry is from about 20 to 35, although this varies according to the airline. Catering, nursing or first aid qualifications are desirable and experience in a public contact job is very useful. Cabin crew must be able to continually strike up and maintain a relationship with total strangers, so personality counts a great deal. Airlines no longer look for the old-fashioned, stereotyped 'stewardess' although some may want the glossy executive image to attract business customers. Nowadays they want their cabin crew to make passengers feel at ease. Both men and women are encouraged to apply. Cabin crew have to be friendly and outgoing, good at being reassuring and organising people tactfully. They must be able to stay calm and organised whatever happens. They should have common sense. It does not help to be clumsy or awkward. Many airlines have height and weight restrictions. Good health, plenty of stamina and energy are essential, as is the ability to swim (Virgin Atlantic specify a minimum of 25 yards). Normal eyesight is essential and contact lenses and glasses are acceptable. British Midland and Virgin Atlantic prefer contact lenses to be worn.

For UK airlines, applicants must be from the UK or EU. Applications by Austrian, Finnish, Swedish, Norwegian and Icelandic nationals are also considered.

Some airlines recruit support cabin crew, doing the same work as cabin staff, but on a part-time basis and with no promotion.

Selection (for BA) is in three parts and each stage must be passed successfully. The first stage lasts three hours and all candidates are brought together to be assessed for their personality and aptitude for airline work. There are some written tests.

The second stage is an in-depth interview and the requirements for height and weight are checked.

The third stage is a thorough medical and language test. References are taken up at this point before an offer of employment is made.

Qualifications and training

At BA, trainees receive a study pack to work on before commencing training.

The training programme is held at a special centre near Heathrow Airport. It includes lectures, group activities, presentations covering all aspects of the work and training in areas such as customer service, sales techniques, first aid, emergency and survival procedures, currency exchange, passenger care and special diets. Applicants must successfully complete the course which includes written exams.

There then follows a period of six months, on-the-job assessment once flying duties commence.

There are planned NVQs/SVQs available in Cabin Crew Level 2, 4.

Ground staff

Engineering – flight operations – airport services – commercial management – air traffic control and services

On the ground a number of services are needed to keep planes flying and passengers and freight processed smoothly. Airlines employ a wide range of skilled and other people, most of them working at or near airports, and mostly working on a shift basis, to cover all the hours when planes are landing and taking off, and to ensure that the planes are maintained, repaired, loaded, etc.

Engineering

Engineering divisions of airlines do three things.

First, they (or an independent servicing contractor) maintain, service and overhaul planes, replace parts or whole engines, strip a plane down, and update systems. The technological sophistication of commercial airliners, with their many millions of parts and advanced avionic, electronic and computerised control systems make this a very exacting job. There are many different systems and moving parts. All the instruments and electrical installations, hydraulics and pneumatics, fuselage, wings, control surfaces and undercarriage, as well as the engine, have to be carefully checked and tested, often by equipment every bit as sophisticated as the plane itself, each on a separate schedule. Fault finding is equally complex. All planes have pre-departure checks and if they are on the ground for any length of time, a short maintenance or non-urgent repair which has been waiting for a suitable moment gets done.

This is round the clock shift work. Every part of every job, even tightening nuts and bolts, has to be double-checked, inspected and certified. With such complex systems, maintenance engineers generally specialise, for instance in avionics (landing aids, autopilots, navigation systems, etc.).

Second, aircraft manufacturers do not design and build hugely expensive planes without consulting their customers, the airlines. An airline's (professional) engineers are generally in on the ground floor on the next generation of airliners, first discussing the planes they want and then detailed specification, new equipment or improved engine and aerodynamic design (to use less fuel, for example). Airline engineers may decide they want some custom-built modifications to the production model and work out the specification. Airlines' professional engineers may do some R&D alongside the manufacturer, for instance in improving engine performance.

Finally, airline engineers also search for ways to reduce servicing costs, improve reliability, look into problems, and develop, e.g., improved engine control monitoring systems, and try to improve workshop turn-round times.

Airline engineering divisions (and specialist maintenance companies) of any size employ engineers with a range of skills – BA employs 9,300 (1996). They include craft workers (sheet metal work, avionics, engine/mainframe, carpentry, painting, etc.) and technicians.

BA's technical workshops are split into three sections.

Mechanical workshops undertake a wide range of work including the overhaul of hydraulic and pneumatic components, undercarriages, flying controls and other airframe mechanical components.

Avionic workshops work on the entire range of electrical instruments, radio/radar and avionics components, servicing and repairing.

Engine maintenance involves work on jet engines, auxiliary power units and items such as fuel pumps and control units. Work is undertaken for other airlines.

Most airlines also have fairly sizeable fleets of vans, lorries, fork-lift trucks, tankers, etc., and these have to be driven and maintained.

Recruitment and entry

Airlines generally recruit across the range of educational qualifications for engineers, mostly for apprenticeships.

BA recruit graduates with any engineering degree (except civil or chemical) to train to become Engineering Business Professionals. This not only involves training towards Chartered Engineer status but also business training in order to progress to management and to be able to handle BA's external engineering customers successfully.

Technician apprenticeships: four GCSEs at grade C or equivalent including maths, English language and physics (or combined science or physics with chemistry). Candidates must be capable of achieving BTEC/SCOTVEC qualifications. Age 16–20 (up to 21 with British Midland).

British Midland occasionally sponsor licensed engineers training at the Oxford Air Training School in Oxford. This is a three-year course for applicants aged 18-plus and they must be qualified to BTEC/SCOTVEC Advanced standard.

Craft apprenticeships may also be available: entry requirements are GCSE or equivalent passes at 16-plus in maths, science, English language and evidence of practical ability. Britannia recruit both craft and technician apprentices.

Qualified tradespeople are also recruited between the ages of 22 and 55.

Qualifications and training

Larger airlines train their own engineers.

Technician and craft training is given in appropriate skills, leading to, e.g., BTEC/SCOTVEC awards.

Qualified tradespeople undergo further training and may achieve Aircraft Engineer status.

NVQs/SVQs are available in Aircraft Maintenance Engineering (Mechanical and Avionic) Level 3.

Flight operations

Airline flight operations deal with the very complex business of moving many thousands of people around the world on as few planes as possible. It involves having the right types and size of plane in the right place at the right time, in a fully operational condition, and with crews (who have had their legal rest times) ready to fly them. It is an enormous planning operation, although computers make it easier. Passenger and freight schedules have to be produced many months ahead and flight operations have to work out as accurately as they can the number of flights that can be filled, or at least flown economically, at different times of the year, using available aircraft as profitably as possible. However, schedules often have to be changed, when an aircraft breaks down, when weather conditions make flying impossible or aircraft have to be diverted.

Day-to-day direction and control of aircraft movement mean close team work between flight operations, generally managed by qualified aircraft captains, maintenance and crew control. It takes experts and computers to work out flight schedules, crew itineraries, and maintenance programmes.

Flight planners, using computers, select the most economic routes, and optimum operating heights for each flight, depending on weather conditions, time of day and hazards – e.g. defence exercises. They may calculate the fuel needed, take-off and landing weights, although these are often now computer generated, for aircrew and load control. They have to see that aircrews have their flight plans, which include weather forecasts, payload information, and any special instructions from air traffic control.

Operations staff/assistants monitor aircraft movements, send, receive and log other movement messages (e.g. diversions and rewritings), keep logs of air-to-ground messages, compile weight and balance data – and, with increasing computerisation, print out flight information and keep control of operations sheets, brief crews, deal with loading diagrams, update weather reports, and maintain daily records.

Airport services

Airline ground staff, known as Customer Service or Passenger Service Agents (they used to be known as ground stewards and stewardesses) look after passengers, answer flight and general enquiries, deal with computerised check-in procedures, help passengers who need it through control points, check boarding passes, prepare cargo documents for customs, check that everything and everyone is on the plane.

Ramp agents (BA) load and unload passenger baggage, freight and mail, clean aircraft inside and out (and sometimes de-ice them), sort luggage in the baggage hall, help in the departure hall, take disabled passengers to and from planes, take meals to the aircraft, etc.

Britannia recruit Movement Control and Ramp Assistants.

Commercial management

Airline commercial management depends on and employs the same functions as any other commercial organisation, including finance, marketing, personnel, management services, public relations, etc. Senior managers are responsible for strategy, route planning and developing charter work. The industry is estimated to have at most 4,000 mainly in technical, operational or marketing. Promotion to management is mainly from within.

All the usual jobs have to be done, with the addition of reservations sales staff who make flight or cargo reservations. Airlines are mostly fully computerised, so there is demand for people with appropriate computing expertise as well as secretaries and clerical staff.

Other job titles include Revenue Processing Clerks who deal with the documentation and accounting for tickets (BA employ 1,000).

Britannia employ operations staff in movement control, crew planning, route planning and crew records.

Recruitment and entry

Customer Service or Passenger Service Agents usually have to be at least 20 at time of application (BA). Britannia has an age range of 18–35. Applicants should be educated to GCSE standard with passes in maths, English and geography, and a knowledge of another language is desirable. Keyboard skills are useful. BA have a minimum height restriction of 5' 0" with weight in proportion to height and Britannia's is 5' 2". At least 18 months' experience in a public contact job is essential.

Willingness to work shifts is important.

Graduates (in any discipline) are recruited in small numbers for management training. BA recruit in the following areas: Business Planning, Engineering, Finance, General Management, Pensions, Purchasing.

For most commercial posts, airlines want at least GCSE or equivalent standard education including English and maths. A minimum age of between 18 and 20 is usual especially in jobs with customer contact where maturity is important. It helps to live within commuting distance of an airport and to have your own transport, especially if you are working shifts. Staff whose work involves contact with the public are expected to have a warm, friendly manner, be smart, talk clearly and preferably have a second language and have experience of similar work. Secretarial and clerical staff are recruited fully trained.

It is worth noting that as airlines receive so many speculative applications, many only hold CVs on file for three months.

Further information

From individual airlines. Aviation Training Association.

Air traffic control and services

The Civil Aviation Authority was set up to regulate the safety of those who fly for profit or pleasure. It runs air traffic services (*below*) and also licenses UK aircrew, air traffic controllers and maintenance engineers. It is also responsible for safety in the air and airworthiness regulations. All planes operating in the UK must come up to CAA standards. The CAA can ask for foreign-made aircraft to be modified if they do not meet the British Standards. With UK manufactured aircraft, the CAA will advise from the start.

All 220 aircraft operators in Britain have to abide by the same standards, whether they are large airlines or only use one plane as an air-taxi, in order to qualify for their Air Operator's Certificate.

It is responsible for airport development, and generally regulates and supervises all aspects of the industry. Through the licensing system it has considerable effect on the industry.

The main area of employment, however, is in air traffic control.

Air traffic over Britain and some of the surrounding sea areas is controlled by the National Air Traffic Services (NATS), run jointly by the Civil Aviation Authority and the Ministry of Defence. They operate an intricate network of countrywide communications including radar equipment, computer-assisted control, navigational aids, and so on, keeping aircraft movements over Britain under continuous surveillance.

Air Traffic Controllers (known as ATCOs) have to keep air traffic moving without snarl-ups or accidents through what is almost impossibly crowded air space. They are in charge, and pilots must obey them. The electronic equipment they use to do this has visual radar displays showing aircraft positions, track, height and number; radar and landing systems which can pierce fog and bring an aircraft down 'blind'; computers which analyse facts and figures at speed – all of which helps to make the work more manageable but never easy. Planes get faster and larger, the amount of traffic is increasing steadily, and one controller may have to handle up to 100 aircraft an hour. Even with the electronic assistance, air traffic control still depends on control tower and pilot talking to each other.

Pilot and controller have to work in three dimensions, and so air space has to be divided into manageable territories, both horizontally and vertically.

One group of controllers operates the 'en route' services which keep all aircraft, whether commercial, military or private, in transit along the imaginary airways, separated from each other (1,000 feet vertically, five nautical miles horizontally), even if one is a slow, light aircraft and the other an Air Force fighter jet. Each controller watches a 'cube' of airways, and passes the planes on from one centre to the next, or to the approach controllers.

Approach controllers fit incoming planes into the other traffic coming into the airport, 'sequencing them down' (perhaps through a waiting stack of planes), and filtering planes taking off up into the airways. Aerodrome controllers guide in-bound planes on the last stages of landing, give them clearance, course and heights, direct them to unloading areas, and make sure the runways are kept clear.

Air traffic control is a very difficult and stressful job, which gets harder when the airways are busy. A traffic controller must watch a display screen covered in complex and changing patterns and figures, take in new information all the time, and listen and talk to pilots (whose English may not be perfect), all at once. Also at the same time, he or she must make very fast decisions and react rapidly to new situations, such as changing weather conditions or emergencies.

Controllers work from the two major control centres at West Drayton, near Heathrow, and Prestwick in Scotland. They are also based at the London airports – Heathrow, Gatwick, Stansted and London City – as well as Aberdeen, Belfast, Edinburgh, Glasgow, Prestwick, Birmingham, Manchester, Cardiff and Sumburgh (Shetland). They are also at some military airfields. The West Drayton Control Centre is run jointly with the RAF. (The West Drayton Centre is due to be relocated to Swanwick in Hampshire in 1997.)

NATS employs (1996) about 1,700 people in air traffic control (down from 2,600 in 1986).

Air traffic control radar, computers, air-to-ground communication systems and visual display units must all work at maximum efficiency, since it is extremely difficult for controllers to work without them. NATS therefore employs its own engineers, both technicians for day-to-day maintenance, and graduate professionals for field management, development and installation.

Recruitment and entry

The CAA expects to recruit about 92 air traffic control officer cadets a year (1996), down from 240 per year in 1992. Assistants are recruited locally and it is still possible to retrain as an air traffic controller from being an assistant, although there are age limits.

CAA cadet entry is with five GCSEs or equivalent passes (including English and maths) plus two A-levels/three H grades or a BTEC/SCOTVEC Advanced qualification. There are no set subjects for A-levels/H grades and BTEC/SCOTVEC qualifications. Age limits are at least 18 and under 27 on the date of application (up to 34 for experienced RAF personnel). A high level of physical fitness is needed, and eyesight (normal colour vision) and hearing have to be very good (the eyesight test is higher than that required for a driving licence). Ability to concentrate, to retain essential facts, to make decisions and act firmly and stay totally calm whatever happens are all essential.

Candidates must be able to work in the UK and have to undergo security clearance.

Eighty per cent of all ATCOs work shifts so candidates must be aware of the shift work involved in a service that is operational 24 hours a day.

Selection is in two stages. First there is a day-long programme where some preliminary selection tests are given and candidates have a chance to find out about the job.

After the first stage, successful candidates are invited for interview. If the interview is successful then a medical is given and must be passed before a job offer is made.

Employing airports each have their own requirements, some take only trained and experienced controllers, but some recruit trainees (the minimum entry requirement is likely to be five GCSEs or equivalent passes including English, maths, science).

NATS recruits only qualified air traffic engineers, who must have an IEE (Institute of Electrical Engineers) accredited Honours degree at 2:2 or above.

Qualifications and training

CAA air traffic control training lasts two years, starting at the air traffic control college (Bournemouth), and interspersed with practical work at control centres and airports, plus 15 hours' 'introduction to flying'. Specialist training in, e.g. programming, management, etc. is available for experienced officers.

Some employing airports train on the job, and at the air traffic control college or with a training company. A CAA licence is required.

Engineers are given training to keep them up-to-date, and may be released to study part time for additional qualifications.

Other work

The rest of CAA's responsibilities employ people who are normally already qualified on recruitment in, for example, accountancy, economics, law, engineering, science, and some posts require previous experience in the industry, e.g. in accident investigation. There are over 7,500 employees in all.

Further information

The Civil Aviation Authority.

Airports

Airports are very much more complex places than, say, railway stations, and need expert management. More people go through them, more services are housed there – for passengers, for the airlines, for air traffic control, immigration, freight handling, catering, car parking, etc.

Although the country has some 200 working airports, the largest 30 or so deal with most of the traffic, and provide most work.

BAA plc (formerly the British Airports Authority) owns and manages seven airports, including the two largest – Heathrow (51.7m passengers per year) and Gatwick (21.2m) – as well as Stansted (3.3m), Glasgow (5.6m), Edinburgh (3.1m) and Aberdeen (2.2m) (all 1994 figures). In March 1991, the government abolished most of its traffic distribution rules which had restricted certain airlines using Heathrow and it is anticipated that about three-quarters of a million passengers will be switched to Heathrow. Planning for the possible development of Terminal 5 at Heathrow continues and this could lead to Heathrow handling an extra 30m passengers a year. These seven airports handle between them about 75% of passengers and 85% of freight. The Civil Aviation Authority manages operations at several other airports and has just acquired the freehold of Southampton airport.

Twenty or so other airports, including Manchester (14.6m passengers), the third largest, are managed by local authorities. The London City Airport in London Docklands, which is privately owned, has recently been extended which will increase the range of aircraft able to operate there.

Working in airports

Several thousand people work in a large airport, but only a small proportion are airport administrators or other employees. In March 1991, the Queen opened a new passenger terminal at Stansted, taking the airport's annual capacity up to eight million passengers, although the recession has obviously hindered further expansion. There is also pressure to provide further capacity in the South-East with the proposed fifth terminal at Heathrow Airport.

An airport is like a small town, with the airport managers providing the accommodation for airline service staff and air traffic control (as above), immigration authorities, freight handling companies, caterers, banks, shop concessionaires, and so on. Services like security are provided by specialist firms on contract.

Airports are administered and managed by staff employed by BAA, the CAA, or a local authority. Although the teams running them may be small, the job is a major one, which ranges from having the land and buildings available to cope with the level of traffic through developing and installing highly sophisticated systems for planes, passengers and freight, to ensuring the airport runs efficiently and economically.

BAA is now a commercially owned organisation, and has changed quite considerably over the past few years. It has extended its operations into developing and managing airports in the UK and overseas, opened three new hotels at Heathrow, Gatwick and Stansted and expanded as a land and property developer. It also has interests in air cargo and freight forwarding. Each of its airports is run as a subsidiary company, so most BAA employees are employed to work at one airport only. Currently it also has a small headquarters staff whose work includes forecasting future demand for air travel, planning short- and long-term airport development, deciding on and commissioning the latest electronic and communication systems like the automatic train which connects two terminal buildings at Gatwick. Property and commercial management involves dealing with both tenants in the airport and contractors, from the airlines themselves to the shops and banks in terminal buildings.

Airport managers have to make enough space available for customs and immigration; provide for huge quantities of volatile fuel to be stored safely ready for use; provide fire and other safety and security services; build and operate baggage and cargo handling facilities.

On the airports themselves, terminals are administered by terminal officers with teams of traffic officers.

They may be in charge of, for instance, the 'aprons', help to organise arrivals and departures, allocate aircraft to stands, log their arrival and departure, and how long they stay.

Traffic duty officers have to see that passengers and their baggage are in the right places at the right time, that baggage is moving properly on conveyors, that lifts and escalators are working, etc.

Professional engineers plan, design, and supervise construction, maintenance, etc. of e.g. terminals, runways, transport systems; design and manage installation and maintenance, etc. of computer controlled communications, information and other electronic systems, automated equipment for, e.g. baggage handling, etc.

Some engineering, maintenance staff work full-time in the airports, clearing runways, maintaining landing aids, repairing conveyors, escalators, etc.

Every airport has its own FIRE SERVICE (*see* THE FIRE SERVICES *in* SECURITY AND PROTECTIVE SERVICES) especially trained to deal with aircraft emergencies and routine work like defrosting runways.

Information desks have to be staffed, and flight arrival and departure indicators kept up to date, people paged. Nurses and nursery nurses are also employed.

Recruitment and entry

Most airport staff are recruited from among people either with relevant qualifications, e.g. in accountancy, engineering, surveying, etc., or with some previous experience. BAA recruits very few staff at the time of writing except for additional seasonal staff during the summer and other peak times. They say that new technology has reduced the need for permanent staff.

However, in 1996, BAA at Heathrow Airport, known as Heathrow Airport Ltd (HAL), have advertised vacancies for trainees in airport services and engineering training. Recruitment is aimed at a slightly older age than school-leavers (although they are considered). Minimum requirements are GCSEs or equivalent in maths, English, CDT and a science. Other qualifications such as GNVQs or HNCs will be considered.

There are planned NVQs/SVQs in Airport Operations Level 3 and 4. If these are accepted, there are plans for the Level 3 to form the basis of a 16-plus airport operations apprentice scheme and for Level 4 as a post-A-level training scheme.

Further information

BAA, the Civil Aviation Authority, and local authority airports.

Railways

Introduction – privatisation

Introduction

Railways are an important part of the transport infrastructure of the UK. The past few years have seen a rapid change in the structure and operation of British Railways. Apart from the construction of the Channel Tunnel, providing a fast and easy link to Europe, there have also been new modern light railway systems built such as the metro system in Newcastle. The railway system is also undergoing privatisation.

Rail is Britain's most energy efficient means of land transport. Trains are efficient as they consume 40% less energy than cars per passenger kilometre and 80% less energy than lorries for each tonne kilometre of freight. Trains are also being improved all the time with a new type of engine being tried out on the InterCity 125 trains which uses 20% less fuel and produces less smoke.

Trains also have an excellent safety record which means they are suited to carrying dangerous goods such as chemicals. They also take up little land: a high-speed railway line can offer the same capacity as a motorway while occupying one-third the amount of land. A modern suburban railway or metro can carry 70,000 passengers per hour on a single track whereas a bus system operating on congested roads can only carry 10,000 passengers per hour.

Carrying freight is also more efficient by rail as an average freight train is the equivalent of 50 lorry journeys and Britain's largest freight train can keep up to 185 lorries off the road.

There is still lively debate about the future of the railways in view of the process of change and privatisation as well as the environmental issues involved.

New developments are continuing and include the new Heathrow Express project with BR in partnership with BAA plc to provide a link, expected to open in 1998, between Paddington and Heathrow Airport. Seventeen new stations have also been opened in the past year.

Privatisation

In 1992, the Government published its formal proposals for the privatisation of British Rail, among which were the following:

- The whole of the track and infrastructure would become the responsibility of Railtrack, a new track authority.
- All passenger services would be managed and operated by the private sector through a system of franchising.
- Freight and parcels operations would be transferred entirely to the private sector.
- Private companies would have the right to purchase or lease stations.

This White Paper became the Railways Act 1993 and in April 1994 British Rail ceased to be a national railway owning tracks and running trains.

Privatisation of the railways has already happened in other countries such as Argentina, Chile, Japan and New Zealand. Privatisation is not new to Britain as in 1923 there were over 100 private companies running the railways.

The British Railways Board still exists as an administrative centre and is overseeing the privatisation process as well as monitoring the current operations and performance of the train operating companies. It is still responsible for the companies that have not yet been sold. There is no central recruitment through the British Railways Board as all the companies are recruiting separately.

There is also a new Rail Regulator established by the Railways Act of 1993 to grant licences to railway operators and to approve and register the granting of an access right to track, station and depots and to guard the rail users' interests. The Rail Regulator establishes the best way for the railways to be structured and developed in the long term.

There is a separate Rail Industry Training Council (RITC) which is responsible for all the NVQ/SVQs and training within the rail industry.

The principal elements of the railway system are: Central Services; Railtrack; British Rail Infrastructure Services; British Rail Telecommunications; Passenger Trains (25 train operating companies); European Passenger Services; Rail Express Systems; Rolling Stock Leasing Companies (three); Freight Operating Companies (three); Railfreight Distribution; Freightliner; Union Railways; Miscellaneous.

Central Services

This is part of the British Railways Board and comprises a number of businesses providing a variety of support and development services to train operators, Rail Track and British Rail Infrastructure Services. These include research and development, train engineering companies and the travel and rail marketing company. All businesses will eventually be sold.

In 1994 there were 100,264 staff still working for British Railways Board and its subsidiaries (down from 131,430 in 1991) and the number will continue to decrease. It is not known how many staff are working for the privatised companies.

Railtrack

Almost the whole operational railway infrastructure was transferred to Railtrack which is owned by the government. It is due to be privatised in 1996.

Railtrack now owns 10, 275 miles of track, 2,506 passenger stations, over 40,000 bridges, viaducts and tunnels and over 9,000 level crossings.

The company is responsible for selling trains to train operators, managing the allocation of train paths and compiling the working timetable as well as operating the rail network overall, which includes all the signalling and maintenance and safety work (this includes maintaining and renewing the railway infrastructure).

Railtrack also operates 14 large mainline stations and leases stations and depots to the passenger train operating companies (*see below*).

Railtrack's income comes from the charges paid by passenger and freight train operators for access to its rail network and mainline stations. It also makes money by leasing stations and maintenance depots to train operators and also from letting shops and arches to businesses.

Railtrack is to be floated on the Stock Exchange in 1996.

Railtrack employs mainly engineering and signalling staff and still runs a graduate recruitment programme.

British Rail Infrastructure Services

Following the establishment of Railtrack, the maintenance of its assets became the responsibility of a new body, split into a number of regional units and known as British Rail Infrastructure Services. The units reflect a separation between major renewal work and routine maintenance. There are therefore seven Infrastructure Units and six Track Renewal Units. Seven infrastructure design and engineering units have already been sold.

British Rail Telecommunications (BRT)

Formed from the old signalling and telecommunications function of British Rail, it was sold to the Racal group of companies in December 1994. BRT provides the signalling infrastructure to Railtrack, much of which consists of fibre optic telecommunications systems for automatic signalling and telephone communications. BRT owns 20 locomotives of which only five are maintained to be serviceable, the rest being used for spares, and a small number of specialist rail vehicles. BRT employ linesmen and signalling engineers as well as support staff. They also recruit signals/telecoms technicians with 4 GCSEs grades including maths, English and science. Drivers are usually hired from Railtrack. There are NVQ/SVQs Level 2 available in Signal operations.

Train Operating Companies (TOCs)

The passenger network has been split up into 25 units for privatisation known as Train Operating Companies (TOCs). InterCity, Network SouthEast and Regional Railways no longer exist.

The areas they cover are as follows:

Anglia Railway Train Services Ltd.

Local services in East Anglia and InterCity services from Liverpool Street to Harwich International Port, Ipswich and Norwich.

Cardiff Railway Co. Ltd.

South Wales Valleys with Cardiff Queen Street as the hub.

Central Trains Ltd.

Local and inter-urban services across central England and Wales.

Chiltern Railways Co. Ltd.

All services from Marylebone to Aylesbury, High Wycombe, Banbury and Birmingham.

CrossCountry Trains Ltd.

InterCity and other services linking Scotland and the North of England with South Wales, the West Country and the South Coast via Birmingham.

InterCity East Coast Ltd.

InterCity services from King's Cross to Humberside, West Yorkshire, North-east England and Scotland.

Gatwick Express Railway Co. Ltd.

Victoria to Gatwick Airport.

Great Eastern Railway Ltd.

Services from Liverpool Street to destinations in Essex and Suffolk.

Great Western Trains Co. Ltd.
InterCity services from Paddington to South Wales and the West of England.

Island Line Ltd.
Ryde Pier Head to Shanklin, Isle of Wight.

LTS Rail Ltd.
Fenchurch Street to Tilbury, Southend and Shoeburyness.

Merseyrail Electrics Ltd.
Local electric services radiating from central Liverpool to Southport, Ormskirk, the Wirral and Chester.

Midland Main Line Ltd.
InterCity services from St Pancras to Leicester, Nottingham, Derby and Sheffield.

Network SouthCentral Ltd.
Services from Victoria, Charing Cross and London Bridge to Surrey, Sussex and Hampshire.

Regional Railways North East Ltd.
Local and inter-urban services in Yorkshire, Humberside, across the Pennines and throughout North-east England.

North London Railways Ltd.
Euston to Northampton services with branches to Bedford and St Albans, and the North London Line orbital route.

North West Regional Railways Ltd.
Local and inter-urban services throughout North-west England and North Wales.

Scotrail Railways Ltd.
All local and inter-urban services within Scotland and overnight Sleeper services between Scotland and Euston.

The South Eastern Train Co. Ltd.
From Charing Cross, Cannon Street, Victoria to all stations in Kent and some destinations in Sussex.

South Wales and West Railway Ltd.
Local and inter-urban service within South Wales (other than the Valley Lines) and the West of England, some services being extended to Manchester, Liverpool, North Wales, Brighton and Waterloo.

South West Trains Ltd.
Services from Waterloo to Surrey, Hampshire, Dorset, Wiltshire, Somerset and Devon.

Thameslink Rail Ltd.
Services from Bedford to Brighton via King's Cross Thameslink, the City of London, East Croydon and Gatwick Airport.

Thames Trains Ltd.
Services from Paddington, via the Thames Valley, to Oxford, Banbury, Stratford-upon-Avon, Hereford, Newbury and Bedwyn. Also Reading to Basingstoke and Reading to Gatwick Airport via Guildford.

West Anglia Great Northern Railways Ltd.
Services from King's Cross, Moorgate and Liverpool Street to Hertford, Stansted Airport, Cambridge, King's Lynn and Peterborough.

InterCity West Coast Ltd.
InterCity services from Euston to the West Midlands, North Wales, Manchester, Liverpool, Cumbria and Glasgow.

In December 1994, three TOCs were sold to private operators, South West Trains to Stagecoach Holdings, Great Western Trains to Great Western Holdings Ltd and LTS Rail to Enterprise Rail Ltd, the last two being management buyout teams.

Train crews and some station staff will be employed by the TOCs. The service provided by each of the companies varies according to the contract under which they operate. They all provide information services to passengers, sell tickets and provide local timetables (taken from the Railtrack National Timetable). They may also buy in services such as on-board catering from private companies.

Flying Scotsman Railways took over the former Special Trains Unit from BR in April 1995. The company operates excursion and special trains under the Waterman Railways name. The company owns a variety of coaching stock as well as several 'preserved' diesel and electric locomotives based on preservation sites throughout the UK.

Train staff are usually employees of Flying Scotsman or Waterman Railways, drivers are employees of RES (*see below*). Several other companies operate trains for the enthusiast, tourism or business market, hiring in stock and staff from either Waterman or the various TOCs.

Drivers and conductors are obviously still needed by TOCs and there is a minimum age of 18. Some companies offer special training schemes for young people.

Most TOCs do not set minimum qualifications but will set an aptitude test. Staff join as trainees and are then selected for driver or conductor training according to their preference and aptitude.

Drivers must be physically fit and there are tests for alcohol and drugs for all applicants. There is an upper age for driver recruitment of 46.

There are NVQ/SVQs Level 2 available in driving and shunting.

Station assistants are also recruited by the operating companies and are involved in general duties to keep a station running efficiently. This could include helping passengers, dealing with enquiries, making announcements.

Training is provided by each TOC.

An NVQ/SVQ 2 is available in Passenger Services.

European Passenger Services (EPS)

EPS is a subsidiary of BR, still government-owned (operating together with SNCF/French railways and SNCB/Belgium railways).

EPS operates the Eurostar service which commenced in Autumn 1994. The service goes to Paris and Brussels via the Channel Tunnel. EPS also operates direct connecting services to Waterloo from other parts of the country and in future will operate direct Eurostar services from all over the country, and this will incorporate a sleeper service for overnight trains.

All UK staff are based at the new International Terminal at Waterloo station.

At present the journey time between London and Paris is three hours with higher speeds on the French side.

EPS has been sold to the London and Continental Railway Company.

There are two grades of staff recruited by EPS.

Train managers are responsible for the comfort and safety of the passengers as well as dealing with general customer queries. They are responsible for seating and catering facilities and very occasionally would have to drive the train. EPS recruit train managers, who must be over 21, and have conversational French or Flemish (additional foreign languages would obviously be useful). They travel with the train throughout the journey. Each train has a train manager, catering staff, immigration staff and from time to time Transport Police.

Customer Service Agents are based in the passenger lounges and operate very much like airline passenger service agents. They check in passengers and answer queries. Customer Service agents are recruited at 18 plus with some experience dealing with the public and conversational French.

Immigration staff have their own office on board the train. Catering is contracted out to the Cross Channel Catering Company and the cooking is done by another company, SAS, who deliver direct to the train.

Drivers are recruited from experienced BR drivers. They have to undergo extra training to learn the European regulations and signalling systems. They will also gain experience on a driving simulator. They have to learn French and this involves a period living in France with a family. They also have to undergo medical and personality tests including alcohol and drug tests.

Rail Express Systems (RES)

RES owns and operates its own locomotives and rolling stock. It is the only company to hold a nationwide operating certificate for its locomotives. It is therefore the only company to be able to provide locomotives and crews to the private sector excursion market. The main customer for RES is Royal Mail.

RES carries approximately 24% of all Royal Mail trains and is an integral part of the UK mail system. RES operates 60 trains daily for the Post Office, 24 of these being Travelling Post Offices on which mail is sorted on the move.

A new fleet of trains is being built as well as a new Royal Mail facility at Willesden in north-west London which will be the centre of operations for RES. Train staff (except guards) on the postal trains are Royal Mail employees. RES hires out train crews and locomotives to other operators.

RES has responsibility for maintaining and operating the Royal Train although the coaching still remains the property of BRB.

RES was sold to North and South Railways Ltd, a consortium led by Wisconsin Central Transportation Corporation (an American railroad operator) in December 1995.

Rolling Stock Leasing Companies (ROSCOs)

The TOCs are only operating companies and all the trains are leased from ROSCOs. The whole of the BR passenger train stock was divided into three and passed to the private sector in November 1995. Together they own or lease around 11,000 vehicles. The three companies are Angel Train Contracts, Eversholt Leasing and Porterbrook Leasing.

Freight Operating Companies (FOCs)

Seven ex-British Rail freight sectors have been divided into three along geographical lines.

Mainline Freight (formerly Trainload Freight South) operates in the Midlands and South of England. They own locomotives and employ drivers. Mainline's main serving depots are at Stewarts Lane (London) and Toton (Sheffield), where many of their locomotives are serviced. Staff employed by Mainline include diesel fitters and specialist electricians involved with the day-to-day servicing of the locomotives. Heavy repairs are usually contracted out to major works such as at Crewe.

Loadhaul (formerly Trainload Freight West) is very similar to Mainline but is based in the north-east of England with headquarters in Doncaster.

Transrail (formerly Trainload Freight West) has bases at Motherwell, Bescot, Cardiff and headquarters at Crewe and covers the west of England, Wales and Scotland.

Although in geographical areas, the companies are in competition with each other and so when contracts come up for renewal there may be further business opportunities. For example, Loadhaul has carried coal from the Potteries to South Wales, both areas being deep in Trainsrail territory. However, the companies may also cooperate with one another when for instance a locomotive fails. These companies will eventually be sold to one buyer.

Railfreight Distribution (RfD)

This company handles international freight via the Channel Tunnel as well as general freight haulage between large distribution depots. The type of freight carried includes china clay from Cornwall to Italy and motor cars from the Midlands to France and Italy. RfD employs drivers and distribution depot staff throughout the country and has agents on the continent.

Railfreight Distribution has not yet been privatised.

Freightliner
This used to be part of Railfreight Distribution and has been separated and is being run by the British Railways Board prior to privatisation. It operates container trains between ports and freightliner terminals operating on the freightliner train and terminal network. It also has its own storage and maintenance facilities along with its own locomotives and staff. Railtrack provides the guards for the trains.

Union Railways
This is now a government-owned company set up to finalise the route of the high-speed line from London to the Channel Tunnel. The Channel Tunnel Link will be built and operated by a private sector consortium at an estimated cost of £2.6 billion. A London terminus at St Pancras was selected in 1994, following which details of the 67-mile route were announced by Union Railways.

Two consortia are bidding for the Channel Tunnel Railway Link contract. Construction is expected to start in 1997, with the approval of the necessary legislation bill and completion is estimated to take place in 2002.

Other companies
National Power, ARC and Foster-Yeoman own and operate American/Canadian-built Class 59 locomotives hauling their own, or leased wagons. The train crews for ARC and Foster-Yeoman are hired in, National Power is training its own drivers and crews and will cease buying in personnel when sufficient numbers are certified.

National Power is based at Ferrybridge near Leeds and ARC and Foster-Yeoman are operated jointly as Mendip Rail with bases at Whatley and Merehead in Somerset.

The fourth company operating its own locomotives on a regular basis is Hunslet-Barclay of Kilmarnock. This company provides a pool of refurbished, ex-BR Class 20 locomotives to haul the annual vegetation control trains (weedkillers). The drivers are normally hired from BR and/or Railtrack for the area in which the train is working. The trains are operated by either Nomix-Chipman or Shering Chemicals who provide their own staff. The weedkiller trains are contracted by Railtrack.

There are two other private operators. British Nuclear Fuels Ltd operating Direct Rail Services are in the process of purchasing their own locomotives from British Rail in order to run trains independently of BR staff. RFS Industries was a company formed by ex-BR employees to purchase the locomotive works at York and Doncaster. They refurbished trains for industrial use, most notably supplying locomotives during the building of the Channel Tunnel. RFS was wound up in 1995 and Tarmac took over the locomotives, which are now being refurbished for BNFL.

Red Star Parcels
This is now owned by a management team and operates a parcels collection and delivery service throughout the UK. They use road transport or buy space on trains. They own no locomotives or rolling stock of their own and employ reception clerks and road vehicle drivers as part of the company.

British Rail Property Board
This is still in operation and manages BR property as well as providing services to companies such as Railtrack and European Passenger Services. It handles the sale of former railway sites as well as advising on restoration of historic railway buildings such as the frontage of St Pancras station and the viaduct at Leader foot in the Scottish Borders.

Numbers of staff
It is difficult to estimate total numbers of staff. In 1995 the British Railways Board employed 100,264 staff (down from 130,000 in 1992). In 1976, nearly a quarter of a million staff worked throughout British Rail.

It is not known how many staff work for the individual companies, although there are 17,000 train drivers throughout the system (down from 20,350 in 1986).

NVQs/SVQs are being developed by the Rail Industry Training Council (RITC).

Further information
Railtrack, Training Operating Companies and individual companies.

Road Transport

Passenger transport – road haulage – repair sector – other sectors – working in the industry

Road transport rapidly became the most popular way of travelling and transporting goods, and has a major impact on all aspects of life out of all proportion to its age. In 1996, 25.2 million vehicles were licensed to go on the roads (up by over 5 million in only five years), of which 21.2 million are cars. Eighty-five per cent of passenger mileage is by car and taxi, only 6% by bus and coach. There are 2.2 million company cars, 2 million light goods vehicles, 580,000 other goods vehicles and 720,000 motorcycles, scooters and mopeds. Thirty-five million people currently hold driving licences.

The length of public roads in the UK increased by 5% between 1984 and 1994 and the length of motorways increased by 15%, making the road system more comprehensive. Motorways and trunk roads cover 6,000 miles throughout England. The Highways Agency manages over £1¾ billion per year for the national road building and improvement programme.

Road transport is a very fragmented industry. The road system is provided by the government, so unlike the railways the industry does not have among its costs expensive building and maintenance of any permanent way. It is possible to start up in road transport rather more cheaply than other forms of transport, and the one-person business is fairly common.

Road transport divides into two main sectors, passenger transport and road haulage.

Passenger transport

Bus and coach services suffer from the same, severe, problems as the railways in that they have to compete with the greater convenience of cars. They also have to contend with the fact that the more cars there are on the roads, the more difficult it is to run efficient and cost-effective services which bring in customers. Fewer passengers mean higher unit costs and so higher fares, and the total effect is a downward spiral of provision.

In 1986, the bus and coach industry was almost completely deregulated. This was the biggest shake-up in over 50 years. For the first time since 1930, anyone who wants to operate a bus service whether it is one bus on one (short or long) route or a fleet serving many, can do so, just by buying the vehicles, satisfying safety regulations and hiring drivers with PCV licences (Passenger Carrying Licence).

There are now (1996) over 2,000 bus and coach companies employing over 150,000 people using approximately 5,000 vehicles. The situation in the bus and coach transport sector is evolving all the time with larger groups and companies emerging and many smaller operators coming and going.

Taxis and minicabs provide a more personal service and there are around 58,000 licensed taxis in England and Wales, 18,000 of these being in London.

In addition there are 52,000 private hire vehicles and at least 40,000 minicabs in London alone. They can now (under government legislation) provide shared ride services at separate fares. They can also run regular local services, and can tender in competition with bus operators for services being subsidised by local authorities.

Taxis ply for hire on the streets, must legally accept any fare, and generally do the shorter journeys.

Minicabs may be booked for an immediate journey or in advance. The work is usually more varied and journeys are generally longer, often to an airport or mainline station.

Both taxis and minicabs are run by firms owning fleets of cars and/or taxis, and employ drivers full- or part-time. Many operate a kind of franchise system, where the driver in effect hires the cab or car from the owner, paying the owner an agreed proportion of the takings. Many taxi drivers, and many minicab drivers now, are self-employed, although they may work for a particular firm, or belong to a co-operative, which provides a central radio-controlled booking system.

Car hire is an expanding business with over 160 firms but they tend to employ few staff. Some employ extra seasonal staff when required.

Car leasing is also a growing area. Firms lease fleets of cars from a leasing company instead of buying company cars for employees who have to travel for the company or as a 'perk' for management. After the lease has expired, the cars are returned (and sold into the second-hand market) and a lease is agreed for a new fleet of cars.

Road haulage

The road haulage industry ranges from huge container trucks traversing Europe, the Middle East and sometimes Africa, down to the local delivery van. This further subdivides. The largest group consists of firms which are purely road haulage operators, carrying other people's goods, etc. from one place to another. The other is made up of industrial, commercial and other organisations which prefer to operate their own vehicle fleets (although quite a few firms have their fleets run by a specialist contractor). Firms which operate, or have operated for them, their own fleets range from manufacturers (of bread, flour, electrical goods), through petrol and chemical companies with their tanker fleets, to the Post Office (delivery vans mainly) and British Telecom (installation and maintenance vehicles).

Road haulage has expanded almost continuously since the Second World War, and now (1996) carries over 80% of goods traffic. However, the actual number of goods vehicles licensed has not risen very much – largely because the size and capacity of vehicles have increased steadily, so about 78% of the traffic is now carried in vehicles of over 25 tonnes. International road haulage has grown fast – some 23 million tonnes a year are carried in and out of the UK, with France the main destination.

Road haulage suffers very badly during recession – largely, say commentators, because current marketing and selling techniques are ignored, and managerial competence and efficiency vary so widely, but properly managed firms survive and do reasonably well.

In terms of size, the industry is very pyramid shaped. Some 90% of firms have five or fewer vehicles. Road haulage is an industry of small privately owned businesses. There were 121,000 operators in 1995 owning 403,000 heavy good vehicles.

Repair sector

An important part of the industry is repairing both commercial vehicles and cars. Most firms that have fleets of any size (e.g. the Post Office, British Telecom) have their own repair workshops, but firms with only a few vehicles, and the vast majority of car owners, expect to use a garage for servicing and repairs.

There are approximately 25,000 garages in the UK and in 1995 it was estimated that 182,000 employees were employed in the maintenance and repair industry.

Other sectors

Other sectors which involve work related to road transport include driving schools, car dealing and distribution, and managing parking facilities (dominated by one firm whose management team includes 40 SURVEYORS (*see in* LAND USE PROFESSIONS) and site negotiators).

Working in the industry

Managerial, professional and supervisory staff – engineers – drivers – driving instructors and examiners – vehicle mechanics and technicians

Road transport is labour-intensive, mainly at the operating end, and since every vehicle needs at least one person to drive it, it is difficult to find ways of cutting staff past a certain level without cutting services too. Passenger transport is steadily cutting out the bus conductor, simpler to maintain cars and trucks mean fewer workshop staff are needed, and numbers of managers, clerical staff have never been large. A high proportion of those working in the industry are operatives: drivers, craft workers, forklift truck operators, porters, packers, etc. The percentage of managers, professional, commercial, sales and clerical staff is rising, if only because the number of workshop staff and drivers, etc. is being trimmed so hard.

Working in the industry is often strenuous, hectic and demanding (even for managers) and often (as one graduate entrant said) with 'baffling but stimulating logistic problems to solve'. Business goes on round the clock, seven days a week, so shift work is necessary and managerial staff as well as drivers may have to be mobile for career development.

Managerial, professional and supervisory staff

Managerial, professional and supervisory staff probably make up only about one in twenty of those working in the industry, mainly because there are so many small firms. Many firms are run by a single owner-manager.

The operations or transport manager is an important part of the team. In road haulage, they need to know how to organise the loading and delivery schedules of a fleet of vehicles. This involves an increasing use of computer and information technology to plan load, delivery pattern, routes, collections and runs. In public transport they need to be able to handle vehicle scheduling, service timetabling, crew rostering and other management responsibilities. The key task nowadays is squeezing maximum efficiency from the available resources.

Among the most professional managers are probably those running distribution services for, e.g. large supermarkets, major manufacturers and other retailers – their costs can be some 3.5% of prices charged, and on turnovers of £1,000 million or more this is a substantial sum. Effective and efficient distribution can save a great deal of money, and involves some sharp operational decision-making, as just an hour's delay per vehicle per day, it is said, would mean £1 million a year to a major food manufacturer.

Distribution has become capital- and energy-intensive, and has always been labour-intensive. Managers may have to use computer controlled systems to organise routine operations and try to cut delivery cycles to a minimum. While distribution managers do not have to make a direct profit, their operations must be cost-effective and they may have to compete for their own firm's business with outside contractors.

Many of the managerial jobs are in line management, especially in independent contractors and passenger firms. Large firms are increasingly pushing as much responsibility as possible down into garages and depots. Each is usually a semi-independent unit, with its own administrative and clerical staff. The work is routine transport administration, managing people, making schedules and timetables work, planning routes, allocating people to jobs (and loads to trucks), dealing with all the (usually extensive) paperwork and complex legal regulations, costing contracts, seeing that buses and trucks are properly maintained and serviced and so spend the maximum time on the road. Some managers specialise as, e.g. service or parts/stores.

In larger organisations, promotion is to managerial and professional posts at district, regional and national levels. Work will include planning, for instance forecasting demand, setting timetables or schedules, fares or charges, planning routes, developing new business. Larger firms employ people in MARKETING, PURCHASING (*see in* BUYING, SELLING AND RELATED SERVICES) and FINANCIAL CAREERS, but the industry employs comparatively few specialist managers in PERSONNEL or MANAGEMENT SERVICES (*see in* ADMINISTRATION, BUSINESS MANAGEMENT AND OFFICE WORK). Many firms use computers in some form now, though, the larger firms quite sophisticated systems.

Engineers

Engineers are employed in a professional capacity by comparatively few organisations, although they may be taken on as general managers. Transport services with 'metro' systems (London, Glasgow and Newcastle) employ the largest numbers, in multidisciplinary teams, especially where new rail systems (e.g. for London docklands) have opened. Most of the work is, however, maintenance and improvement – CIVIL ENGINEERS (*see in* THE CONSTRUCTION INDUSTRY) work on stations, bridges, etc., ELECTRICAL/ELECTRONIC ENGINEERS (*see in* ELECTRICAL AND ELECTRONIC ENGINEERING) on, e.g. signalling, power generation and communication networks.

Mechanical engineers may also be employed to organise and manage fleet development, vehicle maintenance and overhaul, etc. for larger firms, but overall numbers are comparatively small (in the hundreds).

Supervisory staff in the industry are mainly garage and workshop supervisors and foremen fitters, PCV inspectors, office and depot supervisors, and chargehands.

Recruitment and entry

A high proportion of managers, administrators, supervisors, etc. work their way up from clerical work or driving. Direct entry to administrative work, with the possibility of managerial training, is mainly for school-leavers at 18-plus with GCSEs and A-levels (or equivalent), or a BTEC/SCOTVEC award. Only the largest organisations specifically recruit graduate trainees. In passenger transport, this is done mainly by London Regional Transport.

Older people may be recruited, but may be asked for a certificate of professional competence (*below*) pre-entry.

Qualifications and training

Formal management training is only given by larger companies, although the amount of training being done throughout the industry is rising. All managers must now (under EC rules) have a certificate of professional competence (awarded on the basis of a written test set by the RSA or an exempting professional qualification). It is useful to gain a relevant qualification, e.g. of the Chartered Institute of Transport (*see* WORKING IN TRANSPORT *above*), or gain the qualifying exams of the Institute of Road Transport Engineers.

Drivers

Drivers make up well over half of all operatives in the industry. These are the bus and coach (and some train) drivers in passenger transport, van and truck drivers in the haulage business.

Bus and coach drivers work either within a restricted town or country area, or on long-distance routes either on mainland Britain, or on European coach tours. There is taxi or hire-car driving.

Haulage drivers may drive vans for local deliveries and collections, deliver for large stores. They may collect milk from farms, doing a regular daily run, or take petrol from depot to petrol stations, ferry builders' materials to and from suppliers and yards, carry bulk goods from manufacturer to warehouse, or food from warehouse to supermarket.

The job is rarely just driving. Bus and coach drivers now also collect fares, and cope with passenger problems, etc. Delivery and haulage drivers must load and deliver goods, make sure their vehicles are properly and safely loaded, must be able to couple and uncouple trailers, operate tipping gear, or tail lifts, etc. They must all keep their vehicle's documentation in order, make detailed reports, be able to check their vehicles and recognise faults, and be able to find their way through complex transport and freight regulations in other countries. Most driving jobs mean irregular hours and shiftworking, but actual hours on the road are strictly limited. Driving is an active, outdoor life, for a practical person.

NVQs/SVQs are available in: Assistant in Road Haulage and Distribution Operations Level 1; Bus and Coach Driving Instruction (formerly entitled PSV Driving Instruction) Level 3; Bus and Coach Driving Customer Care Level 2; Organising Road Transport Operation Level 2; Storing Goods for Distribution by Road Level 2; Transporting Goods by Road Level 2; there is also a planned Level 5 in Senior Management (Road Haulage).

Recruitment and entry

Since it is not possible to hold a PCV (Passenger Carrying Vehicle) for buses and coaches, taxi or LGV (commercial vehicle) licence under the age of 21 (and in practice employers prefer 25 because the insurance is cheaper), the main entry requirement is age. The ARMED FORCES train under 21s. Some companies will take on trainees at 18 plus to drive minibuses on certain routes.

Other qualifications include physical fitness (but strength is no longer so important, as the latest commercial vehicles are easier to drive), good sight (but glasses can be worn), the ability to concentrate, reasonable literacy and numeracy, and practical/mechanical aptitude.

Qualifications and training

Larger passenger transport companies and road haulage firms train, in their own schools, and the larger ones may use driving simulators.

The LGV licence is in two categories: Category C, driving rigid vehicles over 7.5 tonnes; Category C and E, driving articulated lorries or lorries with a trailer.

Courses last between one and two weeks and include tests of mechanics, securing loads, the highway code, driving and manoeuvring.

There are NVQs/SVQs available in some of these areas.

Taxi drivers have to gain a local licence, and the regulations for these can be strict. Before a licence is granted, drivers have to pass a special driving test, and also a test of knowledge of the area concerned; in large cities like London, this can take between a year and four years. Some firms run training schemes, and in London there are a few schools.

Driving instructors and examiners

Driving instruction and examination are closely linked to driving. However, although instructors must be good drivers, they must also be able to teach both practical skills and road sense/rules to people from all walks of life, so they must have a lot of patience as well. Costs keep the bulk of all driving instructors on the road. It is teaching by example and practice, although instructors have to make sure that their pupils are learning the highway code. The hours can be unsociable since most people have to learn to drive during the evening or at weekends. Work can be seasonal as demand for lessons is highest during the summer months. Instructors must know where they can take their pupils to give them appropriate driving experience, arrange driving tests, keep efficient paper work (including a diary) and self-employed instructors have to keep their own accounts. There are around 33,000 approved driving instructors in the UK.

Most instructors spend a relatively short time working for a school before becoming self-employed. Large transport firms and training associations employ instructors to teach for passenger (PCV) and large goods vehicle licences (LGV).

Driving examiners are civil servants, working for the Department of Transport. After initial training, the examiners work in teams, under the supervision of a senior examiner, at one of several hundred test centres throughout the country. Each examiner takes eight or nine examinations daily, and is solely responsible for deciding whether or not to pass or fail a driver.

There are 1.8 million driving tests every year for cars, motorcycles, bus and lorry driving.

Recruitment and entry

Driving instructors must have held a full and clean driver's licence for four years of the preceding six, and must pass the Driving Standards Agency (part of the Department of Transport) driving instructor's examination. It is not possible to become an instructor younger than 21, and in practice schools prefer to recruit at 25 plus, when the insurance premium is lower.

Some schools recruit people with 'Trainee Licences' which are given by the DoT to give them a chance to gain practical experience. Trainee Licence holders must have passed the written and driving parts of the Register Qualifying examination (*see below*). Personal qualities, such as patience and ability to keep calm, are important.

Driving examiners must be at least 28 years of age, have at least eight years' driving experience on several different types of vehicle and have had particularly wide experience in the preceding five years (e.g. as a driving instructor). They must know the highway code extremely well, are expected to have an active interest in motoring, traffic, road sense and safety problems, and some mechanical knowledge of the vehicles with which they are familiar. Selection is by competitive exams and interview followed by a special driving test except where the applicant holds an approved instructor's licence.

Qualifications and training

To become a qualified instructor, you must register with the Driving Standards Agency as an Approved Driving Instructor (ADI) or a licensed trainee.

Instructors must pass an examination and practical test of driving and a practical test to show you can instruct. Qualification must be gained within two years after the examination has been taken. It is possible to study for these at an instructors' school (one- to three-week intensive courses) but standards vary. The Driving Standards Agency has a list of qualified tutors and training schools. It is possible to prepare for the written test by using a distance learning pack. Once the test has been passed, the registration must be reviewed every four years and the instructor may be tested (whenever required) to see that he or she is still fit to remain on the register.

Examiners are trained after recruitment, but must pass a further test.

Vehicle mechanics and technicians

Mechanics/technicians are employed in substantial numbers by every road vehicle fleet operator, and in independent garages.

The job is becoming increasingly technical as car systems get more sophisticated and automatic diagnostic systems are introduced, especially in, e.g. auto-electrical work where fault diagnosis, car tuning, in-car entertainment systems and fitting accessories are increasingly complex. However, while the newest cars and trucks need less frequent checks and are mechanically simpler to repair, many older cars, which inevitably need more work on them, will be on the road for years to come.

Most mechanics/technicians specialise in light or heavy goods vehicles, motorcycles or performance cars, coach building, crash repairs or electrical/electronic systems. There is nothing to prevent good mechanics/technicians from adding to their skills and changing to another specialised area. After basic training most continue to add to their skills.

Some, for example, become highly skilled technicians who diagnose what is wrong and specify what has to be done (the actual work is then done by workshop staff with more limited skills).

Others may specialise as reception engineers, the link between garage and customer, finding out what the customer wants, estimating the cost, telling the workshop about the job and organising the collection and payment with the owner.

They may become supervisors and go on to management, perhaps running a garage of their own.

Recruitment and entry

The number of trainee posts has decreased, due to new technology, and there is a demand for technician trainees, who need higher qualifications and will do additional technical training. Auto-electricians are more in demand due to the advanced electronic components in modern cars.

While no formal entry requirements are set, the mechanic training programmes will probably want at least some GCSE or equivalent passes at 16-plus, especially maths and a science. Applicants will have to pass an aptitude test. Technician training will require at least four GCSEs (grade C and above) or equivalent in order to take further BTEC/SCOTVEC qualifications. Some trainees are accepted having completed BTEC/SCOTVEC Advanced full-time at college. Many of the new performance cars require this level of training, i.e. BMW, SAAB, etc. Vehicle systems are changing, so mechanics and technicians have to be capable of keeping up with developing technologies. Practical aptitude for dealing with machinery and electrical and electronic systems is needed, as well as reasonable physical fitness. Mechanics/technicians have to appreciate the care needed to ensure vehicles are safe to drive.

There are some Youth Training programmes available run by Centrex, training groups or individual firms.

Qualifications and training

Training programmes/apprenticeships for school-leavers can last between two and four years, including release to study to NVQ Level 2 or 3 via City & Guilds or BTEC/SCOTVEC awards. The training is modular, which lets trainees take tests in individual skills when they are ready.

NVQs/SVQs available are: Maintaining PCVs (Body Trades) Levels 1,2,3; Maintaining PCVs (Electrical) Levels 1,2,3; Maintaining PCVs (Mechanical) Levels 1,2,3; Vehicle Body Fitting Level 2; Vehicle Body Repair Level 3; Vehicle Mechanical and Electronic Systems Maintenance and Repair (Heavy Vehicles) Level 3; Vehicle Mechanical and Electronic System Maintenance and Repair (Light Vehicles) Level 3 (Heavy Vehicles); Vehicle Mechanical and Electronic Systems – Unit Replacement Level 2; Vehicles Refinishing Level 3.

See also RETAILING *in* BUYING, SELLING AND RELATED SERVICES.

Further information

The Institute of Road Transport Engineers, Bus and Coach Training Ltd, Driving Standards Agency, the Road Haulage Association, Road Haulage and Distribution Training Council Ltd, Centrex and individual transport firms.

Sea and inland waterways

The Merchant Navy – working at sea – cruise liners and ferries – pilots, coastguards and lighthouse keepers – working on shore – working in the ports – inland waterways

It is common to think of all occupations that involve the sea and waterways together, probably because the skills involved in driving ships are similar whatever purposes the ships themselves may have. The choice is between three distinct careers – the defence forces, mainly the ROYAL NAVY (*see* THE ARMED FORCES), the FISHING industry (*see in* LAND USE INDUSTRIES), and in providing passenger and freight services through the Merchant Navy. While only the Merchant Navy is dealt with here, as transport, all three have very many common features. Also dealt with here are the support services, such as ports and pilotage.

The Merchant Navy

Merchant ships of many different nations are plying the world's oceans, every day, 365 days of the year. They carry all kinds of cargo, as well as passengers. They make an essential contribution to world trade and economy.

Before the Second World War, 40% of the world's merchant fleet was UK registered. Today it is about 3%. However, there has been a turnaround in recent years despite the fact that companies will still 'flag out' to register vessels in other countries that offer tax advantages. The privatisation of ports has made the industry competitive. The terminal facilities for shipping services have undergone drastic change over the last 20 years and the growth in passenger shipping and luxury cruises has improved prospects in the Merchant Navy. However, most of the job opportunities are for skilled, trained people so the outlook for the basic seafarer is not so good, as many companies will employ cheaper foreign labour.

The British Merchant Navy remains a significant force in international shipping.

Ships are now technologically sophisticated. The bridge is enclosed and the deck officer controls the ship through banks of instrument panels similar to the flightdeck of an airliner. The ship is not steered in the traditional sense at all, it is controlled automatically. Deck officers do not 'ring down' any more to the engine room – they just press a button. Sensitive electronic controls are needed to give these 'juggernauts' the necessary manoeuvrability. Deck officers navigate, monitor instruments and control the ship rather like airline pilots.

Among the instrument banks are satellite-linked radar and radio navigation aids and the officer on watch has their own VDU to perform the necessary calculations such as checking on speed against load and weather conditions, to ensure the ship gets to port on schedule. The officer can input navigation changes and call up all kinds of information, for instance a detailed analysis of fuel consumption. Ship-to-shore communications use satellite systems, so that ships can be in continuous touch with the company's offices and with ports en route. From the satellite data, ships can obtain weather charts which will enable the ship to save time and fuel.

Ownership of merchant shipping varies according to type. Foreign going cargo liners and container ships are mostly operated by large groups, provide worldwide networks of scheduled cargo and container services as well as being in the passenger and holiday cruise liner business. Foreign going tramp ships, on the other hand, are operated by private owners, some with large fleets, but many owning only a small number of ships, some even only one. Most of the tanker fleet is owned and operated by the oil companies themselves, with a few major independent British tanker owners.

Working at sea

Deck officers – engineers – radio/electronics officers – seamen – catering and other crew

The number of people, and particularly seamen, employed in the merchant fleet fell dramatically, partly as a result of lower staffing requirements for today's ships, but mainly due to the recession linked to 'flagging out', which allows shipping lines to recruit crews of any nationality at the lowest going rates. In 1939, merchant seamen numbered 150,000 – now they number 30,200.

It is interesting to look at the make-up of the current fleet:

	1984	1994
UK Officers	15,200	7,600
Foreign Officers	0	1,500
UK Ratings	17,500	9,600
Foreign Rating	5,200	5,200
Cadets	500	700
Total	38,400	24,600

In response to the massive fall in seafarers, especially at cadet level, the government launched a scheme called the Merchant Shipping Act in 1988. Among other schemes to help existing seaman was a scheme to assist recruitment of young merchant navy cadets. The scheme aims to recruit about 350 new cadet officers each year. There are therefore opportunities at Deck and Engineer Officer level for those willing to train in engineering or other technical areas (an increasing number of officers being women). It is far more difficult to find employment as a rating due to cheaper foreign labour.

Technologically advanced ships have changed long seagoing traditions. For instance, as one deck officer on watch (with a cadet) can 'handle' the ship, control its speed and direction from the bridge, engineer officers do not now need to keep round the clock 'watches', so halving the number of engineer officers a ship needs to carry. As a result, new ships' complements get smaller and smaller, down below the 23 which only recently was said to be the absolute minimum.

Going to sea in the merchant navy is, then, a mixture of the traditional and the new. However much the ships are improved, the sea and the elements stay the same, and they are still as dangerous and hostile as ever, just as capable of sinking a container ship or a cross channel ferry, the *Titanic* or a tea clipper. They must still to be treated with great respect and caution. The way the sea behaves is still not properly understood, or the effects of some developments in ship size and structure. The sailor's life style, though, has improved, with comfortable cabins, good food, TV and video and in some cases swimming pools. The isolation is still there (and with faster turn-around times a higher proportion of each voyage is spent at sea), although married couples may be able to sail together.

Deck officers

Deck officers' work has become much more technical. They have to be able to manage advanced automated systems and computerised information and communication networks. Ships' masters and deck officers must do rather more than get the ship from port A to port B. They are now expected to be involved in the commercial management of the ship, work to an annual budget and use their information systems and flexible communications to meet their financial targets and improve their ships' profitability. They may negotiate the finer details of charters on the spot, for example, send the latest information to head office via satellite, use the satellite to find and exploit 'spot' fuel prices at ports on the way, use the computer to calculate weather-to-fuel-to-load ratios to the best advantage, find ways of speeding turn-around times, etc. The shipping industry now treats ships' masters and officers as a management team, with similar responsibilities to a production management team in industry and of course they also manage a team of seamen.

Engineers

Engineers also have technologically advanced equipment to monitor and solve problems, including routine maintenance and emergency repairs. Today's engine room is clean, well lit and ventilated. They basically look after the ships' engines as well as any other mechanical and electronic equipment on the ship. Some companies recruit Dual Certificates Officers who qualify as deck and Engineering Officers. This is due to that fact that the line between deck and engineering officer is becoming blurred as the use of new technology in ships increases.

Radio/electronics officers

Radio/electronics officers use sophisticated communication and electronic equipment, radio telephones, satellite links, radar and other navigating equipment, the ship's own closed circuit TV and sonar (for depth sounding) apparatus, data transmission systems and printers, etc. While radio officers maintain much of the equipment, on the most highly automated ships there may be enough work for an electronics officer also. Some shipping companies employ their own radio officers, but most now have contracts with one of the marine radio companies which both install the equipment and supply a radio officer.

Seamen

Seamen now work both on deck and in the engine room, doing whatever job may be needed at the time.

On deck, ratings keep watch the same as naval ratings, steer, load and unload cargo, patrol the ship and perform standby duties, which usually means maintenance work or cleaning. In port, crew may also have to clean out holds or tanks ready for a new cargo.

In the engine room, ratings look after, operate, maintain and where possible repair machinery, etc., monitor instruments, look after stores, watch keep.

The number of ratings a ship carries depends to some extent on how much maintenance (e.g. painting) the company decides to have done while the ship is at sea. There are rarely, though, now more than nine to a dozen, including bosun and bosun's mate on a cargo liner, petty officers on a container ship. Depending on the type of ship or cargo (which may include passengers), a ship may also carry a carpenter, one or two mechanic fitters, an electrician and a refrigeration engineer.

Catering and other crew

Every ship carries its own catering crew, small on a tanker or cargo ship with a small crew to feed, much larger on cruise liners where the senior catering officer may be called a hotel services manager. On larger ships, the job is often split with the purser, who generally looks after the passengers' comfort and entertainment, provides a banking service, deals with customs and immigration, and handles all the ship's accounts, leaving the catering officer to organise stores, see menus and meals are prepared, manage dining rooms and services, etc.

CRUISE LINERS and FERRIES (*see below*) carry additional civilian staff.

Recruitment and entry

Recruitment is healthy at the officer level and there is often a shortage of recruits with the required qualifications. Once qualified and experienced, UK nationals can compete for work on foreign registered ships. There are 27 shipping companies who are currently recruiting.

Deck and engineer officers normally start as sponsored cadets at between 16 and 19½. Some companies have no fixed upper age limit but it is usually up to 25. Minimum entry requirements are four or five GCSE passes including maths, English and a physical science (or equivalent) – some companies offer faster training with maths and/or physics A-levels or H grades (or BTEC/SCOTVEC); preference is usually given to those with mathematics qualifications.

Dual Certificate Officers must have a minimum of four GCSEs grades A–C or equivalent. Subjects must include maths, physics and English. Candidates for the dual qualification must be good all-rounders who must have an interest in engineering but are prepared to be flexible. They are recruited up to 19½ years old.

For officer training, candidates must be physically fit and must have good eyesight (without glasses). They must pass the Department of Transport's eyesight test.

Those who cannot get the required qualifications as above may be able to apply for training for the Short Sea Restricted licence that is in operation within the European trading area. The requirements for this are three GCSEs grades A–C including maths, a science and preferably a language

There is no advantage to starting with a degree.

Radio/electronics officers are generally only recruited once fully trained (*see below*), and many are recruited by equipment manufacturers rather than shipping companies.

Junior deck, engine room and catering ratings entry is by company sponsorship and normally takes place through the National Sea Training College at Gravesend. No academic qualifications are set formally, but companies will normally expect maths and English to at least GCSE grades E/F standard or equivalent level. The age range for recruitment is 16–18. Applicants must have good health and eyesight.

Qualifications and training

To work on UK registered vessels in particular grades, all seagoing officers and ratings have to gain statutory certificates of competency and pass the relevant Department of Transport examinations. Computerised large ships need more highly skilled and trained people. Training is still largely based at sea, via company training schemes but longer periods are being spent at shore colleges, and the pattern of training is now more in line with other industries. The number of colleges training for the sea has been cut substantially.

P & O describe the typical training programme as follows. Deck Officers start their training with a four-week residential course at nautical college designed to prepare the cadet for life at sea. The course includes shipboard familiarisation, safety and survival at sea and the structure of the shipping industry. It includes a fire fighting course and instruction towards the Certificate of Proficiency in Survival Craft (CPSC examination).

A period of up to ten months at sea then follows. The cadet will work under the guidance of the Staff Captain of the ship and will spend some time working alongside the deck crew to gain some first hand experience. Cadets will also understudy officers on the bridge and learn the practice and theory of keeping a safe navigational watch. The cadet will also undertake some academic work towards the National Diploma in Nautical Science.

After the work experience, another year is spent at a nautical college learning subjects including marine operations, marine transportation, navigation and maths. Exams are then taken to lead to the award of the BTEC National Diploma in Nautical Science.

Another period at sea follows for up to ten months to gain further practical experience.

Then there are two more terms at college with studies leading toward Part 1 of the HND in Nautical Science.

Once candidates obtain their BTEC in Nautical Science, successfully complete Part 1 of the HND and pass a Department of Transport oral and signals examination, they will be awarded the Class 3 Certificate of Competency which completes the cadetship.

A cadet with A-levels/H grades receives accelerated training.

The Junior Deck Officer is now a qualified Navigating Officer and goes back to sea for another period after which he or she will return to college to complete the HND and gain a Class 2 Certificate of Competency.

After further experience at sea and further Department of Transport Oral exams the Deck Officer receives the Class 1 Certificate of Competency and becomes a Master Mariner.

Engineering officer cadets start with a one-year full-time course in engineering as well as the basics for life at sea.

The engineering cadet then goes to sea for up to one year to gain theoretical and practical knowledge under the supervision of the Chief Engineer Officer. The cadet will follow a correspondence course set by the college for the National Diploma in Marine Engineering. As with Deck Officer training, there will be the opportunity to get involved in the work of the departments to understand how the ship functions.

Then follow two years of training studying for the Higher National Diploma.

The Junior Engineer goes back to sea before returning to college to gain the motor, steam or combined Class 2 Certificate of Competency.

A further qualifying period at sea leads to the Class 1 (Chief Engineer) Certificate of Competency. The award of the HND gives exemptions to some of these exams.

As with the Deck Officer, the possession of A-levels/H grades accelerates the training.

Dual Certificate Training takes 18 months longer than Deck or Engineering Training.

As an alternative, colleges now offer a full-time two-year BTEC/SCOTVEC National Diploma in maritime technology,which is more broadly based, and gives students the option of going on to the HND in nautical studies or marine engineering, or to try for shore-based employment in marine related work, e.g. port operations, ship broking, freight forwarding/ship agency, offshore agency, etc. The colleges try to arrange industrial training afloat. Entry requirements as for other BTEC/SCOTVEC courses above.

Engineering officers can read for a degree, and it is possible to read for a degree in nautical studies pre-entry, but there is no advantage to starting with this – a degree is more useful as a post-experience qualification.

Radio/electronics officers now only study via a three-year course leading to a BTEC/SCOTVEC National and Higher National Diploma in maritime telecommunications (at a college belonging to AMERC – the Association of Marine Electronics and Radio Colleges) and the Department of Transport maritime radio communications general certificate (which requires six months' sea-going experience), which can be followed by a six-month course for the electronics navigational maintenance certificate. Minimum entry requirements are four GCSE or equivalent passes including maths, a physics subject, and English, but direct entry to the BTEC/SCOTVEC Higher is possible with maths and physics studied to A-level and a pass in either (or a BTEC/SCOTVEC).

Junior deck, engine-room and catering ratings entrants spend up to three months at the National Sea Training College in Gravesend. They must then do at least 12 months at sea. Entrants have to pass Department of Transport exams but cannot be certificated until they are 18 years old.

NVQs/SVQs are available in: Merchant Vessel Engineering Level 3,4; Merchant Vessel Operations Level 2,3,4.

Nautical colleges

Deck Officer Studies: Aberdeen, Blackpool, Liverpool CC, Glasgow College of Nautical Studies, Lowestoft, South Tyneside, Southampton and Stromness.

HND or equivalent (Classes 1, 2 and 3): Aberdeen, Kilkeel, Liverpool John Moores, Southampton IHE.

Maritime Studies: Blackpool, Liverpool CC, Glasgow College of Nautical Studies, South Tyneside, Southampton IHE.

HND Maritime Studies, Marine Operations, Nautical Science: Liverpool CC, Glasgow College of Nautical Studies, Liverpool John Moores, Plymouth, South Tyneside, Southampton IHE.

Degrees Maritime Studies: Cardiff, Glasgow College of Nautical Studies C, Liverpool John Moores, Plymouth, Southampton IHE.

Master Mariner Studies: Glasgow College of Nautical Studies, Liverpool John Moores.

Marine Engineering degrees: Glasgow Heriot-Watt, Liverpool John Moores, University College London, Newcastle, Plymouth, Robert Gordon, Southampton, Strathclyde, Surrey.

Further information

Chamber of Shipping, local Merchant Navy Establishment offices, the Department of Transport (for regulations), individual shipping lines.

Cruise liners and ferries

Before airline travel became generally available, the main way of travelling abroad was by ship. In the 1960s, travel by ship declined in popularity. However, ships and, in particular, cruises on a purpose built cruise ship are becoming an established part of the tourism industry and increasing in popularity.

Modern cruise ships are like holiday resorts. Apart from being a large hotel, ships may have swimming pools, health and fitness suites, cinemas and even gardens. Cruise liners are designed to carry as many passengers as a large hotel.

The biggest cruise ship in the world is the *Majesty of the Seas* which can carry over 2,000 passengers and over 800 crew.

The *QE2* is smaller but more luxurious. Cunard, who run the *QE2*, own the most ships with P&O coming second (another UK company). Due to the popularity and success of cruising (P&O carried over 35,000 passengers on 35 cruises in 1994) a new liner, the *Oriana* was introduced in 1995 and can carry up to 2,736 passengers.

Safety has become top priority and some cruises now have voyage event recorders on the ridge of their ships (rather like black boxes in aircraft).

There are certain countries that tend to specialise in running cruise liners, such as the USA, UK, Norway, Italy, Holland and Greece. The most popular areas for cruising are in the Caribbean and Mediterranean. The majority of cruise ship passengers are from the USA (over 60%).

A hotel needs many types of staff and if you include the extra services offered on board a cruise liner, there is a demand for various types of staff with different skills and abilities.

P&O list staff required as doctors, nursing officers, pursers, entertainment officers (who must also have their own act), chefs, bakers and confectioners, butchers, printers, nursery nurses, and bar staff.

There are companies who buy the concession to run their business on board cruise liners. For example, Steiner run hairdressing salons on ships.

Other possible jobs are: hotel jobs such as cleaner, receptionist, hotel manager; entertainment staff such as singers, musicians, children's entertainers; beauty therapists, gym and sports instructors; maintenance work such as plumbing and carpentry. Some cruise ships employ gardeners!

There are also office jobs available such as cashiers, secretaries and administrators. Sometimes a large ship publishes a newspaper or newsletter and employs journalists. Photographers who may process their own film or have a team of photo processors to help them can also find employment.

Many different nationalities are employed.

In addition there are the technical, Merchant Navy staff needed to keep the ship running such as engineers, deck officers, etc. They will always be the senior staff on any cruise liner.

Ferries employ roughly the same type of staff employed on cruise liners and can be seen as a mini version of a cruise ship. There will be shops, hotel and catering services (depending on the length of the crossing). There will also be the Merchant Navy crew. The ferry market has expanded, due in many respects to the improvements being made by the ferry operators themselves.

The freight business is growing, especially into Europe. P&O ferries managed to improve business between Dover and Calais by 25% in 1994–95, despite the Channel Tunnel. Now that the Shuttle is fully operational it may make things more difficult.

Safety continues to be an important issue for all ferry companies following the loss of the *Estonia* and a major review of safety was carried out in 1995.

Recruitment and training

Most jobs on cruise liners are never advertised as recruitment is done by speculative enquiries or word of mouth although there are a few specialist recruitment agencies. Some professional publications may carry specialist vacancies, such as the *Stage* for entertainers.

Work is often offered on a contract basis (usually 6–9 months). Hours are usually very flexible, depending on what needs to be done so there is rarely any guaranteed free time.

Further information

Cruise liner and ferry companies.

Pilots, coastguards and lighthouse keepers

These are safety services. Historically, they help ships in coastal waters avoid dangerous rocks, etc., and guide them into port. Despite all the new technology on ships, these services are still essential, especially for the huge tankers and container ships.

The Lighthouse Service now has both lighthouses and lightships that are almost fully automated and so no new staff are being recruited. There may, however, still be some opportunities to work on installation, maintenance and repair.

Trinity House plans to complete the automation process of the remaining lighthouses in two years' time. There are still manned lighthouses in the UK. Eight are in England and Wales, three in Ireland and 11 in Scotland (of which five are offshore). By 1998 all 348 will be automated.

Pilots navigate larger ships through coastal waters, estuaries and rivers into ports, and help them to berth safely, using their detailed knowledge of the area and their training in inshore navigation.

The pilot service has been reorganised and all pilots are employed by individual harbour authorities. According to the Act, 'competent' harbour authorities can employ pilots on whatever terms they decide will suit them best, or to sub-contract the service.

The Port of London Authority (which covers some of the east coast as well as the Thames) is the biggest but employs only 120 pilots (90 at sea and 30 for the rivers).

In April 1994, the Marine Emergencies Organisation became an Executive Agency known as the Coastguard Agency. It consists of the former HM Coastguard and the Marine Pollution Control Unit (MPCU).

The Coastguard Agency (still known as the Coastguard Service) initiates, directs and coordinates (civil) marine search and rescue action around the coast, and over 1,000 miles out to sea. It is an Emergency Service, keeping a 24-hour watch, by radio on the international maritime distress frequencies and through the '999' service, from 21 strategic sites around the UK coastline.

The service is organised in six 'Search and Rescue' regions: North and East Scotland; Eastern; South Eastern; South Western; West of Scotland; Northern Ireland.

Each is run by a regional controller based at a maritime rescue coordination centre (MRCC), with each region divided into sub-centres (MRSCs). All the centres are staffed around the clock with officers keeping constant watch on international distress frequencies. The Search and Rescue capability (SAR), has been upgraded with advanced communication systems, so that coastguards have information on the location of the caller immediately, cutting search time dramatically. All MRCCs have search planning computers which can resolve difficult problems quickly and accurately. The Coastguard is often the first to discover pollution on the coastline or at sea and reports this to the Marine Pollution Control Unit. They may also be the first on the scene and offer initial assistance where possible.

The Coastguard Service is staffed by 470 (1996) regular officers and some 3,500 part-time Auxiliary Coastguards as a local back-up network. The number of auxiliary coastguards has been cut from 6,500 in 1992. This has led some communities to set up their own voluntary schemes.

Each year, the Coastguard handle just under 7,000 incidents including offshore and cliff rescues.

All full-time coastguards must do shift work (watchkeeping periods normally last 12 hours), and be prepared to work anywhere in the UK. Promotion depends on passing a qualifying examination (which must be passed on the second attempt to stay in the service).

The Marine Pollution Control Unit (MPCU) has responsibility within the Coastguard for planning and operating counter pollution measures at sea when spilled oil or other dangerous substances from ships threaten the UK coast, important fishers or concentration of marine wildlife. It also offers advice and assistance to local authorities who are responsible for dealing with shore pollution as well as harbour authorities who deal with spills within ports and harbours. The Marine Emergency Operations room is based in the Coastguard's headquarters in Southampton. The MPCU has special aircraft fitted with remote sensing equipment that detects oil slicks on the surface. It has a fleet of seven DC3 aircraft which are equipped to spray polluted water with the necessary dispersant. The MPCU employs a specialist team of 11 people, bringing in outside help when necessary.

Recruitment and entry

The job of pilot is highly sought after as it offers the opportunity to work in shipping but yet to work reasonably regular hours compared to the average merchant seaman's life which could mean being away from home for six months at a stretch. Recruits must have a Master's certificate (Foreign going) which means they probably will have undergone officer cadet training and have substantial 'sea time' under their belt. This will mean 10–12 years' sea-going experience, so they are unlikely to be under 35. The usual recruit is someone with perhaps a young family who wants to 'settle down'.

Coastguards are expected to have three GCSE or equivalent passes including maths, English language and one other academic subject, and six years' practical marine experience or three years' operational experience in SAR coordination. The age limits are 27–40. Entrants are expected to be (and stay) very fit, have good sight and hearing, and be able to cope with sudden emergencies and stressful situations. A valid driving licence is also needed. Training lasts for six weeks and is at the Coastguard Training Centre at Highcliffe, Dorset.

Further information

The Coastguard Agency; individual harbour authorities.

Working on shore

Shore-based marine work includes working for shipping companies. These are commercial organisations like any other – they manage ships and their crews, cargoes and passengers. An estimated 10,000 managers and professional staff work for the companies ashore.

At senior managerial level, of course, the problems are strategic – possibly whether to stay in the business at all, whether or not to stay under the British flag, to lay up, or scrap ships, how to stay 'afloat', whether or not to risk investing, how to be cost-effective.

Managing ships is an expert, technical business, making sure that the right ships are in the right places at the right times and are operated as cost-effectively as possible.

Maintenance, refitting and repairs have to be organised with minimal disruption to schedules and at the lowest possible cost. Management has to find the yards which can do particular jobs most efficiently and cheaply, and may find it more economic to fly out gangs to do some routine work while a ship is still at sea or finish off a refit while the ship sails from yard to pick-up port. Ships have to be fuelled and stocked where it is most economic, and crew rosters have to take account of leave and training periods ashore.

Shore managers are the people masters and chief engineers report to, while at sea and when they return to their home port. Managerial staff are usually people with seagoing or equivalent qualifications and experience – in marine engineering, telecommunications, etc., although shipping lines employ people for general administrative work too.

Some shipping companies design their own ships, and so employ NAVAL ARCHITECTS (*see in* THE AEROSPACE, NAVAL ARCHITECTURE, MARINE ENGINEERING AND SHIPBUILDING INDUSTRIES), DRAUGHTSMEN/WOMEN (*see in* GENERAL ENGINEERING), etc. When firms buy 'off the shelf', or use independent (consulting) naval architects/marine engineers, they must still have a few technically qualified people to decide what is needed and to assess tenders, both for new ships and for maintenance and refitting.

Freight organising, to fill ships' holds and tanks or bring in passengers, is a marketing operation with its own slant.

In freight work, this involves finding exporting firms, providing the service customers want at the right price, having ships where cargoes are, being 'slick' at getting cargoes (usually containers) on and off ships, through harbours, and arranging collection and delivery. Cruise companies work rather more like TOUR OPERATORS (*see in* THE TRAVEL INDUSTRY), although it is their own 'hotel' accommodation they are selling.

Traffic managers – for freight, ferry/hovercraft, other passenger ships – mastermind operations. They or their staff have to liaise with port authorities for berths to co-ordinate sailings. Much depends on the company's port offices and agents, who must see that 'cargo' and ship come together at the right moment, do all the complex paper work, although most of this (e.g. preparing manifests) is computerised, get clearances, arrange loading and unloading at each end, see the ship has berths where and when needed, that tugs and pilots are available to bring ships in, and take them out again. They must ensure that freight or passengers are speeded through port areas and customs and that parking is available for trucks or cars, etc.

Cargo staff have to work closely with the people who manage the ships, and feed back into managers changes in customers' needs. The job can be complex, with many problems to solve, such as whether or not it is worth taking on a cargo from port A to port B if no cargo is in prospect at port B, whether or not a ship can take a 'dirty' (e.g. ore) cargo and have its holds cleaned fast and well enough to take on a waiting food cargo, how to crate an unusual cargo, whether or not containers can be off-loaded at remote, foreign ports.

Selling and buying cargo space in ships is not always done directly between shipping firm and clients. Independent SHIPBROKERS work from the Stock Exchange in London (*see* FINANCIAL CAREERS), both acting as go-betweens between owners and merchants and their chartering agents. Shipbrokers also buy and sell ships on behalf of owners.

See also FREIGHT FORWARDING *below*.

Recruitment and entry

Fleet managers are generally recruited from among sea-going officers who have the right aptitudes. On the commercial side, and for general administration, entry is still possible at 16 plus with reasonable GCSE or equivalent passes, to start in clerical work. Promotion prospects into management are probably better with A-levels, and some larger groups sometimes recruit graduates as trainee managers.

Qualifications and training

Training for most commercial work in the shipping business is largely on-the-job, with release to study (or by distance learning) for appropriate qualifications (*see* BUSINESS STUDIES *in* ADMINISTRATION, BUSINESS MANAGEMENT AND OFFICE WORK).

Working in the Ports

The ports have been going through considerable transformation and large-scale modernisation for some years, bringing in efficient, technological freight handling methods both to deal with conventional forms of freight, for bulk handling, and as part of continuing development of integrated containerised and 'roll-on, roll-off' systems, as well as improving port layout, and berthing facilities that these larger ships need. Reducing staffing levels is also a major consideration. The size and cost of improvement schemes have been considerable – Felixstowe's container terminal (built 1986), for example, cost £42 million. All ports (except one) have been privatised and so are subject to market forces. The growth in container freight services has meant that highly advanced equipment is now involved in the unloading of ships. The labour force is much smaller and the 'new age' ports such as Felixstowe have taken trade away from the traditional ports

All British ports must now compete with others in the EC and they now have a potential competitor in the Channel Tunnel just when new ferry capacity is being developed at several ports. The changing balance of UK trade is demonstrated by the fact that most recent developments have been on the east and south-east, Europe-facing ports and the ports from which ships traditionally sailed west to America, and which served the industrial areas of Wales, have declined most. The largest port (in terms of tonnes handled) is the Sullom Voe oil terminal.

Although some 300 places have port/harbour facilities, the number handling freight/oil in the size and quantity to provide employment is much smaller. Associated British Ports owns and operates 19 major ports – about a fifth of total capacity. Trusts control and manage about seven major ports, local authorities many small ports but also two large ones and the Orkney/Shetland oil ports. Most oil tanker terminals are owned by the oil companies and serve specific refineries.

No official figures have been given for the ports recently, but numbers of employees are certainly well down from 130,000 in the 1960s to 60,000 in 1983. The abolition of the Dock Labour scheme (which laid down a very rigid structure for the employment of workers) in 1989 has contributed to the decline in numbers. The ports are no longer 'labour-intensive' as the new, mechanised container ports require fewer but more highly skilled workers.

Ports employ a full range of managerial, administrative, technical and manual workers, but numbers working for each are now comparatively small.

A high proportion of managers are engineers, mainly civil, but also mechanical and electrical. Professional staff employed include mechanical engineers who design, specify, commission, and maintain port equipment from cranes of all sizes including massive container carriers, vehicles (buses, road sweepers, fuel tankers), lock-gate and bridge controls, conveyors and elevators, roll-on/roll-off linkspans, pumping stations, floating craft machinery, etc. Electrical engineers deal with electrical/electronic controls for, e.g., cranes, roll-on/roll-off berths, grain silos, pumping stations, petrol/chemical terminals, lighting systems, electronic control, radio communication and navigational aids. Civil engineers develop installations and container berth complexes, and associated structures (berths, locks, dock gates, sea-walls, jetties, roads, bridges, transit sheds, grain silos, etc.).

See also ACCOUNTANCY *in* FINANCIAL CAREERS, LEGAL STAFF *in* THE LEGAL SYSTEM *and* SURVEYORS *in* THE CONSTRUCTION INDUSTRY.

Recruitment and entry

Engineers are generally recruited with appropriate qualifications (*see* the engineering chapters). Ports just recruit to fill vacancies from among suitably qualified people.

Qualifications and training

NVQ/SVQs are available in: Marine Operations (Harbour based) Level 2; Marine Operations (Shore based) Level 3; Cargo Operations Level 1 and 2 are also planned.

There is a new degree in Shipping Operations and Management at Southampton Institute, taught in English, entirely at the University of Alicante in Spain.

Further information

Individual port authorities, British Ports Industry Training Ltd.

Inland waterways

Canals, rivers and other inland waterways are popular for leisure activities such as boating, fishing, etc. and their use is increasing all the time. Some freight is still carried and efforts are being made to increase this. Some canals are being re-opened and restored. In 1994, the first new stretch of canal built in Britain since 1905 was opened, a new 3.5 kilometre section on the Aire and Calder Navigation.

Inland, some 2,500 miles of rivers, canals, etc. are navigable, about 2,000 of them owned by British Waterways (formally the British Waterways Board), and the rest by local authorities and private companies. About 400 miles of the waterways under BW's control are in use commercially, mostly on 'canalised' rivers, and freight is also carried on, e.g., the Thames. Some 1,200 miles are maintained for recreational and amenity use, and BW also control about 90 reservoirs (which supply water for the canals), many of them also used for sailing, fishing, etc.

Both recreational and commercial facilities are being improved and developed, for example waterway walks have been opened, to encourage the use of the canals for tourism and leisure. There are now three in existence, along the Grand Union, the Kennet and Avon and the Oxford Canals. The development of tourism is also being encouraged with BW developing links with the hire boat industry and with tourist boards. There are now even hotel and restaurant boats and barges, where every luxury is provided.

BW carries freight, hires out canal boats, issues licences for all boats using the waterways, sells water for industrial and agricultural use, and provides docks, warehousing and terminal services. BW issued 29,767 boat licences in 1995.

British Waterways is the largest employer (1,630 staff in 1996) and there are other freight handlers, boat hire companies (such as Hoseasons) and companies providing marina and other river and canalside facilities.

BW has five head office departments: Environmental and Scientific Services, Technical Services, Waterway Development and Waterway Environment Services. There is also a team of managers in each of its five regions: Scottish, North West, North East, Midlands/South West and Southern.

Recruitment and entry

Apart from the commercial jobs found in any company, the specialist departments employ: engineers (civil, water, mining and bridge), SURVEYORS working with technicians, craftworkers, etc. to maintain and develop the waterways and installations (docks, warehouse, reservoirs, etc., and SURVEYORS and BUILDING INSPECTORS (*see in* LAND USE PROFESSIONS) to manage the extensive land holding and building other than those directly linked to the waterways, negotiating purchases, sales, selling water, etc. Environmental experts are also employed to work on particular projects, for example the design, research and installation of special deer ramps to allow deer to escape from canals should they fall in.

BW does not produce any careers literature and staff are recruited as vacancies arrise. No formal training schemes are offered. Vacancies are advertised in the local or national press and where appropriate in the relevant professional journals or through the Careers Service.

Freight forwarding

Firms also make an income out of matching people's transport needs to the most suitable form of transport, whether the cargo is people or goods. The industry employs people who have expert knowledge of the transport business.

Freight forwarders are experts at finding the best way of getting goods from the UK to anywhere in the world, and vice versa, in good condition, and at an economic cost. 'Best' has to be a balance between how quickly the goods are needed, how valuable they are, how much they weigh, what shape and size they are, how easily the goods can be damaged. Valuable freight that does not weigh too much, expensive fruit which damages easily and goes off quickly, racehorses, medicine and machinery needed in a hurry, might have to go by air. Other goods may go by sea, perhaps in containers, perhaps in bulk.

Freight has to be shifted from the factory, warehouse, market garden to the air or sea port, by road and/or rail, and similar arrangements made at the other end. Items may have to be stored for short or long periods at some stage in their journey.

Freight forwarders have to keep themselves up to date on what is happening in the transport business. Which carriers are most efficient, which ports have what facilities and fastest turn-rounds, and what ships they can 'service'. They have to be expert in getting cargoes packed correctly for each type of transport and in complexities of custom and excise requirements, licences, regulations and other documentation, and insurance, not just for the UK, but for other countries too.

Freight forwarders often provide a 'door-to-door' service and can negotiate bulk discounts with the transport companies. They are particularly expert at minimising delays, which can be costly, in getting goods customs clearance, for instance. They can keep customers up to date on changes in customs requirements or rates charged, new freight services, etc.

Around 1,100 companies are members of the Institute of Freight Forwarders which is incorporated within the British International Freight Association. They range in size from single office operations to major national and international companies with widely spread offices and representatives. There are other freight operators within the industry but not all come up to the standard required by the institute. Over 50% of import and export firms use freight forwarders to improve efficiency and cut costs and the most successful freight forwarders are quick to spot new opportunities when markets fall off.

Many freight forwarding companies specialise, or have specialist divisions/departments in transporting goods by air or sea, in different types of freight, and/or in transporting to and/or from particular parts of the world. Firms have offices, or representatives, permanently at air and/or sea ports in the UK and other countries, air freight companies normally have offices at the major airports. Many freight forwarding companies have their own warehousing and packaging facilities, and may have some transport, especially where airfreighting is involved.

Much of the work involved in freight forwarding is clerical/administrative, and most people start with basic routine, although computerised systems are now very important. Clerks deal with choosing routes and carriers; rates and schedules; telex, fax and telephoning; documentation (commercial, customs, transport, warehouse); getting freight through customs (this involves a lot of paperwork); finance (credit control, preparing invoices, quotations and tariffs, accounts). Experienced, trained, freight forwarders will deal with the negotiating and supervisory activities. Many firms also employ sales staff. Firms may also send experienced staff to overseas offices. Promotion is normally based on merit rather than age and staff will progress to, e.g., section leader, department, warehouse or branch manager and to senior management. Freight forwarders also employ warehouse staff – managers, clerks, drivers (vans, trucks, forklift trucks), packers, porters etc. *See also* SHIPBROKING *under* FINANCIAL CAREERS.

Recruitment and entry

There is no formal entry route. Most people start at the bottom, usually with at least four GCSE or equivalent passes including English, maths, geography – higher qualifications are likely to help gain expertise and promotion faster. Languages are very useful. There are A-level/graduate traineeships with larger firms. Personal characteristics are said to count considerably, particularly the ability to communication easily and clearly, especially on the telephone, and ability to cope with complex documentation, regulations, currency, etc.

Qualifications and training

Mainly on the job, learning from more experienced staff. Formal training schemes including those run in conjunction with the IFF/BIFA. There are some Youth Training programmes, the main programme being Freight Train (UK) Ltd which offers training with cargo, forwarding and shipping companies at 11 locations throughout the UK. The NVQ/SVQ for Forwarders is in International Trade and Services at Levels 2, 3 and 4.

There is also a correspondence course run through the IFF, the Advanced Certificate in Overseas Trade. This covers principles of marketing, law, international trade and payments and international physical distribution.

Some people enter after completing a degree or diploma with a freight-related option. There are many of these available.

The Institute of Freight Forwarders/British International Freight Association sets the examinations for membership, as well as organising training courses for the industry. The IFF qualifications can be gained by correspondence.

Further information

British International Freight Association (incorporating the Institute of Freight Forwarders), Freight Train UK (Ltd).

Appendix 1: Useful Addresses

Accountancy

The Chartered Association of Certified Accountants
29 Lincoln's Inn Fields
London WC2A 3EE
0171 242 6855/Fax: 0171 831 8054

The Chartered Association of Certified Accountants – Scottish Branch
2 Woodside Place
Glasgow G3 7QF
0141 331 1046

The Chartered Institute of Management Accountants
63 Portland Place
London W1N 4AB
0171 637 2311

The Chartered Institute of Public Finance and Accountancy
3 Robert Street
London WC2N 6BH
0171 543 5600/Fax: 0171 543 5700

Government Accountancy Service
Management Unit Room G08
HM Treasury
Allington Towers
19 Allington Street
London SWIE 5EB
0171 270 1748

The Institute of Chartered Accountants in England and Wales
PO Box 433
Chartered Accountants' Hall
Moorgate Place
London EC2P 2BJ
0171 920 8100

The Institute of Chartered Accountants of Scotland
27 Queen Street
Edinburgh EH2 1LA
0131 225 5673/Fax: 0131 479 4872

The Association of Accounting Technicians
154 Clerkenwell Street
London EC1R 5AD
0171 837 8600/Fax: 0171 837 6970

Actuary

The Faculty of Actuaries
44 Thistle Street
Edinburgh EH2 1EN
0131 220 4555/Fax: 0131 220 2280

Government Actuary's Department
22 Kingsway
London WC2B 6LE
0171 242 6828

The Institute of Actuaries
Actuarial Education Service
Napier House
4 Worcester Street
Oxford OX1 2AW
01865 794144/Fax: 01865 794094

Acupuncture *see* **Alternative Medicine**

ADAS
Oxford Spires Business Park
The Boulevard
Kidlington
Oxon OX5 1NZ
01865 842742

ADSET (Association for Database Services in Education and Training)
Chancery House, 4a Dalkeith Place
Kettering
Northamptonshire NN16 0BS
01536 410500

National Institute of **Adult Continuing Education** (NIACE)
21 De Montfort Street
Leicester LE1 7GE
01533 551451

Advertising

The Advertising Association
Abford House
15 Wilton Road
London SW1V 1NJ
0171 828 4831

Communication, Advertising and Marketing Foundation
Abford House
15 Wilton Road
London SW1V 1NJ
0171 828 7506

Institute of Practitioners in Advertising
44 Belgrave square
London SW1X 8QS
0171 235 7020

Royal **Aeronautical** Society
4 Hamilton Place
London W1V 0BQ
0171 499 3515

British **Aerospace** Flying College Ltd
Prestwick International Airport
Ayrshire KA9 2RW
01292 671022

AGCAS *see* **CSU**

Agriculture

British Agricultural and Garden Machinery Association
14–16 Church Street
Rickmansworth
Hertfordshire WD3 1RQ
01923 720241

Institution of Agricultural Engineers
West End Road
Silsoe
Bedford MK45 4DU
01525 861096

Ministry of Agriculture, Fisheries and Food (*MAFF*)
Nobel House
17 Smith Square
London SW1 3JR
0171 238 5598

Air Service Training Limited
Perth Aerodrome
Perth PH2 6NP
01738 552311

Oxford **Air Training** School
CSE Aviation Ltd
Oxford Airport
Kidlington
Oxford OX5 1RA
01865 841234

Airlift Book Company
8 The Arena
Mollison Avenue,
Enfield
Middlesex EN3 7NJ
0181 804 0400

Airlines

Britannia Airways Ltd
Head Office
London Luton Airport
Bedfordshire LU2 9ND
01582 424155

British Airways plc
Recruitment and Selection
Meadowbank
PO Box 59
Hounslow TW5 9QX
0181 564 1013

British Midland
Donington Hall
Castle Donington
Derby DE74 2SB

Virgin Atlantic Airways Ltd
Old Bright Road
Lowfield Heath
Crawley
West Sussex RH11 OPR
01293 747811/747914

British Airports Authority
Head Office
130 Wilton Road
London SW1V 1LQ
0171 834 9449

Alternative Medicine

The Anglo–European College of Chiropractic
13–15 Parkwood Road
Boscombe
Bournemouth
Dorset BH5 2DF
01202 436200

The Anthroposophical Society
Rudolf Steiner House,
35 Park Road
London NW1 6XT
0171 723 4400

Association of Tisserand Aromatherapists
65 Church Road
Hove,
East Sussex BN3 2BD
01273 772479

The British Acupuncture Association and Register
34 Alderney Street
London SW1V 4EU
0171 834 1012

British Association of Psychotherapists
37 Mapesbury Road
London NW2 4HJ
0181 452 9823

British College of Naturopathy and Osteopathy
6 Netherhall Gardens
London NW3 5RR
0171 435 6464

British Homeopathic Association
27a Devonshire Street
London W1N 1RJ
0171 935 2163

British Psycho-Analytical Society
Mansfield House
63 New Cavendish Street
London W1M 7RD
0171–580 4952

British School of Reflex Zone Therapy of the Feet
97 Oakington Avenue,
Wembley Park
London HA9 8HY
0181 908 2201

Council for Acupuncture
179 Gloucester Place
London NW1 6DX
0171 724 5756

General Council and Register of Osteopaths
56 London Road
Reading
Berkshire RG1 48Q
01734 576585

Institute for Complementary Medicine
PO Box 194
London SE16 1QZ
0171 237 5165

International College of Oriental Medicine
Green Hedges House
Green Hedges Avenue
East Grinstead
Sussex RH19 1DZ
01542 313106/7

McTimoney Chiropractic Group
14 Park End street
Oxford OX1 1HH

National College of Hypnotherapy and Psychotherapy
12 Cross Street
Nelson
Lancashire
01282 699378

The Society for Teachers of the Alexander Technique
20 London House,
266 Fulham Road
London SW10 9EL
0171 351 0828

Centre for Alternative Technology
Machynlleth
Powys SY20 9AZ
01654 703743

Animals

Association of British Riding Schools
Queens Chambers
38–40 Queen street
Penzance
Cornwall TR18 4BH
01736 69440

Association of British Wild Animal Keepers
12 Tackley Road
Eastville
Bristol BS5 6BQ

Association of Chartered Physiotherapists in Animal Therapy
Five Acres
Kenyon lane
Lowton
Warrington WA3 1LQ

British Horse Society
Stoneleigh
Kenilworth
Warwickshire CV8 2LR
01203 696697

Guide Dogs for the Blind Association
Hillfields
Burghfield Common
Reading
Berks RG7 3YG
01734 835555

Hearing Dogs for the Deaf Training Centre
London Road
Lewknor
Oxford OX9 5RY
01844 353898

Institute of Animal Technology
5 South Parade
Summertown
Oxford OX2 7JL

National Pony Society
102 High Street
Alton
Hants GU34 1EN
01420 88333

People's Dispensary for Sick Animals
Whitechapel Way
Priorslee
Telford
Shropshire TF2 9PQ
01952 290999

Pet Care Trust
Bedford Business Centre
170 Mile Road
Bedford MK42 9TW

Royal Society for the Prevention of Cruelty to Animals
Enquiry Department
Causeway
Horsham
West Sussex RH12 1HG
01403 264181

Royal Society for the Protection of Birds
The Lodge
Sandy
Bedfordshire SG19 2DL
01767 680551

Scottish Society for the Prevention of Cruelty to Animals
Braehead Mains
603 Queensferry Road
Edinburgh EH4 6EA
0131 339 0222

Royal **Anthropological** Institute of Great Britain and Ireland
50 Fitzroy Street
London W1P 5HS
0171 387 0455/Fax: 0171 383 4235

British **Antique** Dealers' Association
20 Rutland Gate
London SW7 1BD
0171 589 4128

Society of **Apothecaries**
Apothecaries Hall
Black Friars Lane
London EC4V 6EJ

Arboricultural Association
Ampfield House
Ampfield
Romsey
Hants SO51 9PA
01794 68717

Council for British **Archaeology**
Bowes Morrell House
111 Walmgate
York YO1 2UA
01904 671417

Architecture

Architects Registration Council of the UK
The Registrar
73 Hallam Street
London W1N 6EE
0171 580 5861

Architects and Surveyors Institute
15 St Mary Street
Chippenham
Wiltshire SN15 3WD
01249 444505

Royal Incorporation of Architects in Scotland
15 Rutland Square
Edinburgh EH1 2BE
0131–229 7205

Royal Institute of British Architects
66 Portland Place
London W1N 4AD
0171 580 5533

Royal Institute of British Architects (Publications Department)
39 Moreland Street
London EC1V 1BB
0171 251 0791 (*for priced publications*)

British Institute of Architectural Technologists
397 City Road
London EC1 1NE
0171 278 2206

Society of **Archivists**
Information House
20–24 Old Street
London EC1V 9AP
0171 253 5087

ARELS *Association of Recognised English Language Services*
2 Pontypool Place
Valentine Place
London SE1 8QF

British Association of **Art Therapists**
11a Richmond Road
Brighton
East Sussex BN2 3RL

Arts Council of Great Britain
14 Great Peter Street
London SW1P 3NQ
0171 333 0100

Arts and Entertainment Training Council
Glyde House
Glydegate
Bradford
West Yorkshire BD5 0BQ
01274 738800

Arts Training South
Centre for Continuing Education
University of Sussex
Falmer Brighton BN1 9RG

Associated Examining Board
Stag Hill House
Guildford
Surrey GU2 5XJ
Telephone: 01483 506506/Fax: 01483 300152

Association of Commonwealth Universities (*ACU*)
John Foster House
36 Gordon Square
London WC1H 0PE
0171 387 8572

Astronomy

Royal Astronomical Society
Burlington House
Piccadilly
London W1V 0NL

Audiology

British Association of Audiological Scientists
80 Brighton Road
Reading RG6 1PS

British Society of Audiology
80 Brighton Road
Reading RG6 1PS
01734 660622

Society of Hearing Aid Audiologists
Bridle Croft
Burgh Heath Road
Epsom
Surrey KT17 4LF
01372 725348

The Society of **Authors**
84 Drayton Gardens
London SW10 9SB
0171 373 6642

Aviation Training Association
125 London Road
High Wycombe
Bucks HP11 1BT
01494 445262

BACIE
35 Harbour Exchange Square
Off Marsh Wall
London E14 9GE

Society for Applied **Bacteriology**
PO Box 510
Harrold
Bedford MK43 7YU
01234 720047

British **Ballet** Organisation
Woolborough House
39 Lonsdale Road
London SW13 9OP
0181 748 1241

Banking

The Bank of England
Threadneedle Street
London EC2R 8AH
0171 601 4411/Fax: 0171 601 5460

The Banking Information Service
10 Lombard Street
London EC3V 9AT
0171 398 0066/Fax: 0171 283 9655

The Chartered Institute of Bankers
Emmanuel House
4/9 Burgate Lane
Canterbury
Kent CT1 2XJ
01227 762600

The Chartered Institute of Bankers in Scotland
19 Rutland Square
Edinburgh EH1 2DE
0131 229 9869

London Investment Banking Association (*changed from The British Merchant Banking Association*)
6 Frederick's Place
London EC2R 8BT
0171 796 3606/Fax: 0171 796 4345

The Institute of **Barristers' Clerks**
4A Essex Court
Temple
London EC4Y 9AJ
0171 353 2699

Institute of **Baths and Recreation** Management
36 Sherrard Street
Melton Mowbray
Leicestershire LE13 1XJ

BBC
Broadcasting House
London W1A 1AA
0181 231 9236

BBC Educational Developments (Distribution)
PO Box 50
Wetherby
West Yorkshire LS23 7EZ
01937 844774

BBC Educational Information
White City
201 Wood Lane
London W12 7TS
0181 746 1111

Beauty

British Association of Beauty Therapy and Cosmetology Ltd (*BABTAC*) Confederation of Beauty Therapy and Cosmetology (*CIBTAC*)
Parabola House
Parabola Road
Cheltenham
Gloucestershire GL50 3AH
01242 5720284

Federation of Holistic Therapists
38A Portsmouth Road
Southampton SO19 9AD
01703 422695

Health and Beauty Therapy Training Board
PO Box 21
Bognor Regis
West Sussex PO22 7PS
01243 860339

Institute of Electrolysis
138 Downs Barn Boulevard
Downs Barn
Milton Keynes MK14 7RP
01908 695297

International Health and Beauty Council *see* Vocational Training Charitable Trust/Vocational Awards International

International Therapy Examination Council
James House
Oakelbrook Mill
Newent
Gloucestershire GL18 1HD
01531 821875

Vocational Training Charitable Trust/Vocational Awards International
46 Aldwick Road
Bognor Regis
West Sussex PO21 2PN
01243 842064

BECTU Training
111 Wardour Street
London W1V 4AY
0171 437 8506

Betting Office Licensees Association Ltd
Francis House
Francis Street
London SW1P 1DE

BFI *see under* **Film**

Biblios PDS Ltd
Star Road
Partridge Green
West Sussex RH13 8LD

Bingo Association of Great Britain
4 St James Court
Wilderspool Causeway
Warrington
Cheshire WA4 6PS

Institute of **Biochemical Science**
12 Coldbath Square
London EC1R 5HL
0171 436 4946

Biochemical Society
59 Portland Place
London W1N 3AJ
0171 580 5530/Fax: 0171 637 7626

Association of Clinical Biochemists
2 Carlton House Terrace
London SW1Y 5AF
0171 930 3333

BioIndustry Association
14/15 Belgrave Square
London SW1X 8PS
0171 245 9911/Fax: 0171 235 4759

Biological Engineering Society
The Royal College of Surgeons
31–43 Lincon's Inn Fields
London WC2A 3PN
0171 242 7750

Institute of **Biology**
20–22 Queensberry Place
London SW7 2DZ
0171 581 8333

Biophysical Society
c/o Dr Hunter
Department of Chemistry
University of Manchester
Oxford Road
Manchester
0161 275 4712

Biotechnology

Biotechnology and Biological Sciences Research Council
Polaris House
North Star Avenue
Swindon SN2 1UH
01793 413201

Biotechnology in Europe Manpower Education and Training (*BEMET*)
Department of Life Science
Nottingham Trent University
Clifton
Nottingham NG11 8NS
0115 948 6628

National Centre for Biotechnology Education
University of Reading
Whiteknights
PO Box 228
Reading RG6 2AJ

Book House Training Centre
45 East Hill
Wandsworth
London SW18 2QZ
0181 874 2718

Booksellers

Antiquarian Booksellers' Association
Sackville House
40 Piccadilly
London W1V 9PA
0171 439 3118

Booksellers' Association of Great Britain
272 Vauxhall Bridge Road
London SW1V 1BB
0171 834 5477

Provincial Booksellers Fairs Association
The Old Coach House
16 Melbourn Street
Royston
Herts SG8 7BZ
01763 248400

BP Educational Services
PO Box 934
Poole
Dorset BH17 7BR
01202 669940

Brewers and Licensed Retailers Association
42 Portman Square
London SW1V 4EU
0171 486 4831

Institute of **Brewing**
33 Clarges Street
London W1Y 8EE
0171 499 8144

British Academy (BA) Humanities Research Board
Studentship Office, Block 1, Spur 15
Government Buildings
Honeypot Lane
Stanmore
Middlesex HA7 1AZ
0181 951 5188

British Antarctic Survey
High Cross
Madingley Road
Cambridge CB3 OET
01223 61188

British Chambers of Commerce
Certification Unit
Westwood House
Westwood Business Park
Coventry CV4 8HS
01203 695 688

British Council
10 Spring Gardens
London SW1A 2BN
0171 930 8466

British Council
Medlock Street
Manchester M15 4AA
0161 957 7000

British Gas
High Holborn
London
0171 242 0789

see also telephone directories for regional office addresses

British Hospitality Association
Queens House
55–56 Lincoln's Inn Fields
London WX2A 3BH
0171 404 7744/Fax: 0171 404 7799

British Ports Industry Training Ltd
PO Box 555
Bury St Edmunds
Suffolk IP28 6QG

British Waterways
Willow Grange
Church Road
Watford WD1 3QA
01923 226081

Scottish **Broadcast** and Film Training Ltd
4 Park Gardens
Glasgow G3 7YE
0141 332 2201

Building

Association of Building Engineers
Jubilee House
Billing Brook Road
Weston Favell
Northampton NN3 8NW
01604 404121/Fax: 01604 784220

Chartered Institute of Building
Englemere
Kings Ride
Ascot
Berkshire SL5 3BJ
01344 874545

Chartered Institution of Building Services Engineers
Delta House
222 Balham High Road
London SW12 9BS
0181 675 5211

Institute of Building Control
21 High Street
Ewell
Epsom
Surrey KT17 1SB
0181 393 6860

Building Societies Association
3 Savile Row
London W1X 1AF
0171 437 0655

BUNAC (*The British Universities North America Club*)
16 Bowling Green Lane
London EC1R 0BD
0171 251 3472

Bus and Coach Training Ltd
Regency House
43 High Street
Rickmansworth
Herts WD3 1ET
01923 896607

Business

Association of Business Schools (ABS)
344/354 Gray's Inn Road
London WC1X 8BP
0171 837 1899

Association of Masters in Business Administration (AMBA)
15 Duncan Terrace
London N1 8BZ
0171 837 3375

Business Links (Department of Trade and Industry)
national enquiries on freeline 0800 500200

Business and Technology Education Council
Central House
Upper Woburn Place
London WC1H 0HH
0171 413 8400/Fax: 0171–387 6068

Ivor Spencer School for **Butler** Administrators/Personal Assistants
12 Little Bournes
Alleyn Park
Dulwich
London SE21 8SE
0181 766 7321

Cambridge Market Intelligence (CMI)
London House
Parkgate Road
London SW11 4NQ
0171 924 7117

Cardiology

Cardiac Society
Cardiac Department
John Radcliffe Hospital
Oxford OX3 9DU
01865 220050

Careers

Career Development Loans
Freepost
Newcastle upon Tyne X
NE85 1BR
0800 585 505 (9–9 M–F)

Careers Europe
Ground Floor
Equity Chambers
40 Piccadilly
Bradford
BD1 3NN
01274 757529

Institute of Careers Guidance
27a Lower High Street
Stourbridge
West Midlands DY8 1TA
01384 376464

The National Association of Careers and Guidance Teachers
Portland House
4 Bridge Street
Usk
Gwent NP5 1BG
01291 672985/Fax: 01291 672090

British **Cartographic** Society
c/o Department of Cartography
Oxford Brookes University
Headington
Oxford OX3 0BP
01865 741111

CASCAiD Ltd
West Annex County Hall
Glenfield
Leicester LE3 8YZ
0116 2656690
(*moving end 1996 to Loughborough University*)

CBI
Centrepoint
103 New Oxford Street
London WC1A 1DU
0171 379 7400

Central Bureau
Seymour Mews House
Seymour Mews
London W1H 9PE
0171 486 5101

Centre for the Development of Vocational Training
(*CEDEFOPP*)
Bundesallee 22
D–10717
Berlin
Germany

Centrex (*formerly the RTITB*)
Centrex Training and Conference Centre
High Ercall
Telford
Shropshire TF6 6RB
01952 770441

Centrex (Scotland)
Hardie Road
Deans
Livingston
West Lothian EH54 8AR
01506 414011

CEPEC Ltd
Lilly House
13 Hanover Square
London W1R 9HD
0171 629 2266

The Association for **Ceramic** Training and Development
St James House
Webberley Lane
Longton
Stoke–on–Trent ST3 1RJ
01782 597016/Fax: 01782 597015

CETAC
(Careers Education and Training for Agriculture and Countryside)
c/o Warwickshire Careers Service
10 Northgate Street
Warwick CV34 4SR
01926 412427

Chamber of Shipping
Merchant Navy Training Board
Carthusian Court
Carthusian Street
London EC1M 6EB
0171 417 8400

Institute of **Charity Fundraising** Managers
Market Tower
1 Nine Elms Road
London SW8 5NQ
0171 627 3436/Fax: 0171 827 3508

Charles Letts *see under* **Letts**

The Institute of **Chartered Secretaries** and Administrators
16 Park Crescent
London W1N 4AH
0171 580 4741

Institution of **Chemical Engineers**
Schools Liaison Service
Davis Building
165–171 Railway Terrace
Rugby
Warwickshire CV21 3HQ
01788 578214 ext 213

Chemical Industries Association
Kings Building
Smith Square
London SW1P 3JJ
0171 834 3399/0171 932 0505

The Royal Society of **Chemistry**
Burlington House
Picadilly
London W1V OBN
0171 437 8656

Chiropodist *see* **Podiatrists**

Christian Aid
PO Box 100
London SE1 7RT
0171 620 4444

Christians Abroad
1 Stockwell Green
London SW9 9HB
0171 737 7811

Churches

Baptist Union of Great Britain
Baptist House
PO Box 44
129 Broadway
Didcot
Oxfordshire OX11 8RT
01235 512077

Catholic Church (*England and Wales*)
Diocesan Vocations Service of England and Wales
39 Ecceleston square
London SW1V 1BX
0171 630 8220

Catholic Church (*Scotland*)
Scottish National Vocations Office
2 Chesters Road
Bearsden
Glasgow G61 4AG
0141 943 1995

Church of England
Advisory Board of Ministry
Church House
Great Smith Street
Westminister
London SW1P 3NZ
0171 222 9011

Church of Scotland
Department of Education
121 George Street
Edinburgh EH2 4YN
0131 225 5722

CIIR (*Catholic Institute for International Relations*)
Overseas Programme
Unit 3 Canterbury Yard
190a New North Road
Islington
London N1 7BJ
0171 354 0883

Elim Pentecostal Church
Ministerial Training and Selection Board
Elim Bible College
London Road
Nantwich
Cheshire CW5 6LW
01270 610 800

Methodist Church
1 Central Buildings
Westminster
London SW1H 9NH
0171 222 8010

United Reformed Churches
Ministries and Training Committees
86 Tavistock Place
London WC1H 9RT

CITB
Construction Careers Services
Bircham Newton Training Centre
Kings Lynn
Norfolk PE31 6RH
01553 776677

CITB - Scotland
4 Edison Street
Hillington
Glasgow G52 4XN
0141 810 3044

City & Guilds
1 Giltspur Street
London EC1A 9DD
0171 294 2468/Fax: 0171 294 2400

Civil Aviation Authority
National Air Traffic Control Services
CAA House
45–59 Kingsway
London WC2B 6TE
0171 832 6696

Civil Engineering Careers Service
1–7 Great George Street
London SW1P 3AA
0171–222 7722

Institution of Civil Engineering Surveyors
26 Market Street
Altringham
Cheshire WA14 1PF

Institute of **Clerks of Works**
41 The Mall
London W5 3TJ
0181–579 2917

Clothing

CAPITB Trust
80 Richardson Lane
Pudsey
Leeds LS28 6BN
0113 239 3355

Kingscourt Training and Business Advisers (Clothing)
80 Richardshow Lane
Pudsey
Leeds LS28 6BN
0113 239 3355/Fax: 0113 256 8029

Coal

RJB (UK) Ltd
Coal Investments plc
Harworth Park Blyth Road
Harworth
Doncaster DN11 8DB
01302 751751

Coastguard Agency
Spring Place 105 Commercial Road
Southampton SO15 1EG
01703 329100

COIC (*Careers and Occupational Information Centre*)
Moorfoot
Sheffield S1 4PQ
01142 594563/4/9

COIC (*distribution and Newscheck mailing list*)
PO Box 348
Bristol BS99 7FE
01179 777199

COIC (*Employment department*)
E455
Moorfoot
Sheffield
S1 4RQ
01142 594576

COIC number for microDOORS enquiries is 0114 2593906

COIC **Scotland**
247 St John's Road
Corstophine
Edinburgh EH12 7XD
0131 334 0353

Committee of Scottish Higher Education Principals *see* **COSHEP**

Committee of Vice–Chancellors and Principals of the Universities *see* **CVCP**

Composers Guild of Great Britain
34 Hanway Street
London W1P 9DE
0171 436 0007

Computing

British Computer Society (*BCS*)
1 Sanford Street
Swindon
SN1 1HJ
01793 417417/Fax: 01793 480270

Institute for the Management of Information Systems (*IDPM*)
IDPM House
Edgington Way
Ruxley Corner
Sidcup
Kent DA14 5HR
0181 308 0747/Fax: 0181 308 0604

Information Technology Industry Training Organisation
16 Berners Street
London W1P 3DD
0171 580 6677/Fax: 0171 580 5577

The National Computing Centre
Oxford House
Oxford Road
Manchester M1 7ED
0161 228 6333/Fax: 0161 228 2579

Computing Services and Software Association (*CSSA*)
Hanover House
73/74 High Holborn
London WC1V 6LE
0171 405 2171/Fax: 0171 404 4119

Confederation of British Industry *see* CBI

Conservation (environment)

British Trust for Conservation Volunteers
36 St Mary's Street
Wallingford
Oxfordshire OX10 9NY
01491 839766

Council for National Parks
246 Lavender Hill
London SW11 1L
0171 924 4077

Conservation (historic)

Institute of Paper Conservation
Leigh Lodge
Leigh
Worcestershire W6 5LB
01886 832323

United Kingdom Institute for Conservation of Historic Works
6 Whitehorse Mews
Westminster Bridge Road
London SE1 7QD
0171 620 3371

Contributions Agency
Department of Social Security
Overseas Contributions
Longbenton
Newcastle Upon Tyne NE98 1YX

The Council for Licensed **Conveyancers**
16 Glebe Road
Chelmsford
Essex CM1 1QG
01245 349599/Fax: 01245 348380

Council for the Accreditation of **Correspondence Colleges**
27 Marylebone Road
London NW1 5JS
0171 935 5391

COSHEP
St Andrews House
141 West Nile Street
Glasgow G12 2RN
0141 353 1880

British Association for **Counselling**
1 Regent Place
Rugby CV21 2PJ
01788 78328

Countryside Commission
John Dower House
Crescent Place
Cheltenham
Gloucestershire GL50 3RA
01604 781848

Countryside Council for Wales
Plas Penros
Bangor
Gwynedd LL57 2LQ
01248 370444

CRAC/Hobsons Publishing PLC
Bateman Street
Cambridge CB2 1LZ
01223 354551/464334

Crafts Council
44A Pentonville Road
London N1 9BY
0171 278 7700

British **Crop Protection** Council
Bear Farm
Binfield
Bracknell
Berkshire RG12 3QE
01734 341998

Crown Prosecution Service
Recruitment Branch
50 Ludgate Hill
London EC4M 7EX
0171 273 8000

CSU
Armstrong House
Oxford Road
Manchester M1 7ED
0161 236 8677/Fax: 0161 236 8541

Customs and Excise
London Recruitment Unit 3rd Floor
Thomas Paine House
Angel Square
Torrens Street
Islington
London EC14 1TA
0171 865 3194/3199

CVCP
29 Tavistock Square
London WC1H 9EZ
0171 387 9231

Cytogenetics
Association of Clinical **Cytogenetics**
Cytogenetics Unit
Regional Maternity Hospital
Edgbaston
Birmingham B15 2TG

Dalebank Books
Arden Lodge
Savile Park Road
Halifax HX1 2XR

Dance

ADiTi
The National Organisation of South Asian Dance
Willowfield Street
Bradford BD7 2AH
01274 522059

British Council for Ballroom Dancing Ltd
240 Merton Road
South Wimbledon
London SW19 1EQ
0181 545 0085

The Council for Dance Education and Training (UK)
Riverside Studios
Crisp Road
London W6 9RL
0181 741 5084

Dance UK
Crisp Road
London W6 9RL
0181 741 1932

Imperial Society of Teachers of Dancing
Euston Hall
Birkenhead Street
London WC1H 8BE
0171 837 9967

International Dance Teachers' Association
76 Bennett Road
Brighton BN2 5JL
01273 685652

National Resource Centre for Dance
University of Surrey
Guildford
Surrey GU2 5XH
01483 509316

Royal Academy of Dancing
36 Battersea Square
London SW11 3RA
0171 223 0091

Dance Therapy
Association for Dance Movement Therapy
Hertfordshire College of Art and Design
7 Hatfield Road
St Albans
Hertfordshire AL1 3RS
01727 45544

Daphne Jackson Memorial Fellowships Trust
Department of Physics
University of Surrey
Guildford
Surrey GU2 5XH
01483 259166.

Defence Engineering and Science Group
DESG Recruitment Office
Pinesgate East
Lower Bristol Road
Bath BA1 5AB
01225 449106

Dentistry

British Dental Association
64 Wimpole Street
London W1M 8AL
0171 935 0875

General Dental Council
37 Wimpole Street
London W1M 8DQ
0171 486 2171

British Dental Hygienists Association
13 The Ridge
Yatton
Bristol BS19 4DQ
01934 876389

British Association of Dental Nurses
110 London Street
Fleetwood
Lancashire FY7 6EU
01253 778631

Dental Technicians Education and Training Advisory Board
5 Oxford Court
St. James Road
Brackley,
Northants NN13 TXY
01280 702600

British Association of Dental Therapists
The Dental Auxiliary School
The London Hospital Medical College,
36 New Road
London E1 2AX
0171 377 7634

Department for Education and Employment
Management Development Unit
Castle View House
East Lane
Runcorn WA7 2DN
01928 794133

Department for Education and Employment
Publications Centre
PO Box 2193
London E15 2EU
0181 533 2000/Fax: 0181 533 7700

Department for Education and Employment
Sanctuary Buildings
Great Smith Street
London SWlP 3BT
0171 925 5555

Department for Education and Employment
(Awards)
Mowden Hall
Staindrop Road
Darlington
Co. Durham DL3 9BG
01235 460155.

Department for Education for Northern Ireland
Rathgael House
Balloo Road
Bangor
Co Down BT19 7PR
01247 279279/Fax: 01247 279100

Department of Health
Skipton House
80 London Road
London SE1 6LW
0171 972 2000

Department of National Heritage
2–4 Cockspur Street
London SWlY 5DH
0171 211 2036

Department for National Savings
Charles House
375 Kensington High Street
London W14 8QH
0171 605 9300

Design Council/Young Designers Centre
28 Haymarket
London SW1Y 4SU

Society of **Designer Craftsmen**
24 Rivington Street
London EC2A 3DU
0171 739 3663

Chartered Society of **Designers**
29 Bedford Square
London WC1B 3EG
0171 631 1510

DfEE *see* **Department for Education and Employment**

British **Dietetic** Association
Elizabeth House
22 Suffolk Street
Queensway
Birmingham B1 1LS
0121 643 5483

British **Display** Society
70A Crayford High Street
Dartford
Kent DA1 4EF
01322 555755

Distribution

Distributive Industries Training Trust
5 Bridge Street
Bishop's Stortford
Hertfordshire CM23 2JU
01279 506125

Federation of Wholesale Distributors
Third Floor
Sun Alliance House
26 Gildredge Road
Eastbourne
East Sussex BN21 1HD
01323 24952

Institute of Grocery Distribution
Grange Lane
Letchmore Heath
Watford
Herts WD2 8D
01923 857141

Scottish Distributive Industries training Council
The Beta Centre
University of Stirling Innovation Park
Stirling FK9 4NF
01786 451661

Dogs *see* **Animals**

Drama

Conference of Drama Schools
c/o Central School of Speech and Drama
Embassy Theatre
Eton Avenue
London NW3 3HY
0171 722 8183

National Council for Drama Training
5 Tavistock Place
London WC1H 9SS
0171 837 3650

Production and Casting Report
PO Box 100
Broadstairs
Kent
01843 860885

Driving Standards Agency
Stanley House
Talbot Street
Nottingham NG1 5GU
0115 955 7600

East Anglia Regional Advisory Council for Further Education
2 Looms Lane
Bury St Edmunds
Suffolk IP33 1HE

ECCTIS 2000 Ltd
Oriel House
Oriel Road
Cheltenham
Gloucestershire GL50 1XP
01242 252627

Economic Group Management Unit
HM Treasury
Room 46/2
Parliament Street
London SW1P 3AG
0171 270 5622

Economic and Social Research Council
Polaris House
North Star Avenue
Swindon SN2 1UJ
01793 413000/Fax: 01793 413001

Economist Intelligence Unit
15 Regent Street
London SW1V 4LR
0171 830 1000

Scottish Council for **Educational Technology**
74 Victoria Crescent Road
Glasgow G12 9JN
0141 357 0340

Institution of **Electrical Engineers**
Schools Education and Liaison Section
Michael Faraday House
Six Hills Way
Stevenage
Hertfordshire SG1 2AY
01438 313311

Electricity Training Association
30 Millbank
London SW1P 4RD
0171 963 5859/Fax: 0171 963 5999

Institution of **Electronics and Electrical Incorporated Engineers**
Savoy Hill House
Savoy Hill
London WC2R 0BS
0171 836 3357

British Institute of **Embalmers**
21C Station Road
Knowle
Solihull B93 0HL
01564 778991

The Institute for **Employment Research**
University of Warwick
Coventry CV4 7AL
01203 523523

Employment Service
Overseas Placing Unit
Level 2
Rockingham House
123 West Street
Sheffield S1 4ER
01142 596051

Employment Studies
Institute of Employment Studies
Mantell Building
University of Sussex
Falmer
Brighton
East Sussex BN1 9RF
01273 686751

Engineering

Engineering Construction Industry Training Board
Blue Court
Church Lane
Kings Langley
Hertfordshire WD4 8JP
01923 260000

Engineering Council
10 Maltravers Street
London WC2R 3ER
0171 240 7891

Institution of Engineering Designers
Courtleigh
Westbury Leigh
Westbury
Wiltshire BA13 3TA
01373 822801

Engineering and Physical Sciences Research Council (*EPSRC*)
Polaris House
North Star Avenue
Swindon SN2 1ET
01793 444000

Engineering Training Authority
(Engineering Careers Information Service ECIS)
41 Clarendon Road
Watford
Hertfordshire WD1 1HS
01800 282167

Women's Engineering Society
Imperial College
Imperial College Road
London SW7 2BV
0171 589 5111

Institution of Engineers and Shipbuilders of Scotland
1 Atlantic Quay
Bloomfield
Glasgow G2 8JE
0141 245 3721

English Nature
Northminster House
Peterborough PE1 1UA
01733 340345

Environment

Department of the Environment
Room C6/07
2 Marsham Street
London SW1P 3EB
0171 276 6098

Environment Agency
Rivers House
Waterside Drive
Aztec West
Almondsbury
Bristol BS12 4UD
01454 624 400

Environment Council
80 York Way
London SW1W 9RP
0171 824 8411

Chartered Institute of Environmental Health
Chadwick Court
15 Hatfields
London SE1 8DJ
0171 928 6006

Institute of Environmental Sciences
14 Princes Gate
London SW7 1PU
0181 766 6755

Equal Opportunities Commission
Overseas House
Quay Street
Manchester M3 3HN
0161 833 9244

British Actors' **Equity** Associaton
Guild House
Upper St Martin's Lane
London WC2H 9EG
0171 379 6000/Fax: 0171 379 7001

ERASMUS
University of Kent
Canterbury
CT2 7PD
01227 762712

EURES, Employment Service Overseas Placing Unit
Level 4
Skills House
3–7 Holy Green
Off the Moor
Sheffield SW1 4AQ
0114 259 6051

European addresses *see also chapter on* **Working Overseas**

Europe

Commission of the European Communities
8 Storey's Gate
London SW1A 3AT
0171 973 1992

Commission of the European Communities
Rue de la Loi 200
B–1049
Brussels
Belgium

Commission of the European Communities
Office for Official Publications of the European Communities
L-2985 Luxembourg.

Council of British Schools in the European Community
c/o The British School of Brussels
Chaussee de Louvain
Teruren
Belgium 3080

European Parliament
UK Information Office of the European Parliament
2 Queen Anne's Gate
London SW1H 9AA
0171 227 4300

European Passenger Services
EPS House
Floor 2
Waterloo Station
London SE1 8SE

Institute of European Trade and Technology
29 Frogmorton Street
London EC2N 2AT
0171 628 3723

Institute of Export
64 Clifton Street
London EC2A 4HB

Export Credits Guarantee Department
PO Box 2200
2 Exchange Tower
Harbour Exchange Square
London E14 9GS
0171 512 7000

Fabric Care Research Association Ltd
Forest House Laboratories
Knaresborough Road
Harrogate
North Yorkshire HG2 7LZ
01423 885977

Farriery Training Service
Farriers Registration Council
PO Box 49
East of England Showground
Peterborough
Cambridgeshire PE2 0GU
01733 394848

Federation of Recruitment and Employment Services Ltd (*FRES*)
36–38 Mortimer Street
London W1N 7RB
0171 323 4300

British **Film** Institute
21 Stephen Street
London W1P 1PL
0171 255 1444

Fire

Defence Fire Service Headquarters
Building 44
1 Site
Royal Air Force
High Wycombe
Buckinghamshire HP14 4UE
01494 496235

The Home Office Fire Department
50 Queen Anne's Gate
London SW1H 9AT
0171 273 2416/Fax: 0171 273 2568

London Fire and Civil Defence Authority
Albert Embankment
London SE1 7SD
0171 582 3811

(*Scotland*)
The Scottish Office
Home Department
The Fire and Emergency Planning Division
St Andrew's House
Regent Road
Edinburgh EH1 3DG
0131 244 5400/Fax: 0131 244 2819

Fish

Seafish Industry Authority
Seafish House
St Andrews Dock
Hull HU3 4QE
01482 27837

Institute of Fisheries Management
22 Rushworth Avenue
West Bridgford
Nottingham NG2 7LF
01159 822317

Floristry Training Council
Roebuck House
Newbury Road
Hermitage
Near Newbury
Berkshire RG16 9RZ
01635 200465

Institute of **Food Science and Technology**
5 Cambridge Court
210 Shepherd's Bush Road
London W6 7NI
0171 603 6316

British **Footwear** Association
5 Portland Place
London W1N 3AA
0171 580 8687

Foreign and Commonwealth Office
Recruitment Section
4 Central Buildings
Matthew Parker Street
London SWlH 9NL
0171 210 0417/8

Forensic Science Society
18A Mount Parade
Harrogate
Yorkshire HG1 1BX
01423 506068

Forestry Commission
231 Corstorphine Road
Edinburgh EH12 7AT
0131 334 0303

British **Franchise** Association
Thames View
Newtown Road
Henley–on–Thames
Oxon RG9 lHG
01491 578049

Freight

British International Freight Association (*incorporating the Institute of Freight Forwarders*)
Redfern House
Browells Lane
Feltham
Middlesex TW13 7EP
0181 844 2266

Freight Train UK Ltd
Atlas house
Central Way
Feltham
Middlesex TW14 0UV
0181 751 3004

Fulbright Commission
62 Doughty Street
London WC1N 2LS
0171 404 6994

Funeral Directors

British Institute of Funeral Directors
146A High Street
Tonbridge
Kent TN9 1BB
01732 770332

National Association of Funeral Directors
618 Warwick Road
Solihull
West Midlands B91 1AA
0121 711 1343

British **Furniture** Manufacturers Association
High Wycombe
01494 523021

Further Education

Further Education Development Agency
Unit 3
Citadel Place
Tinworth Street
London SE11 5EH
0171 962 1280

Scottish Further Education Unit (*SFEU*)
Jordanhill Campus
University of Strathclyde
Sothbrae Drive
Edinburgh EH4 2LF
0131 332 2335

Future Prospects
Newland
Near Ulverston
Cumbria LA12 7QG
01229 588166/Fax: 01229 588225

Institution of **Gas Engineers**
17 Grosvenor Crescent
London SW1X 7ES
0171 245 9811

Genealogy

Association of Genealogists and Record Agents
29 Badgers Close
Horsham
West Sussex RH12 5RU

Society of Genealogists
14 Charterhouse buildings
Goswell Road
London EC1M 7BA
0171 252 8799

Royal **Geographical** Society
1 Kensington Gore
London SW7 2AR
0171 589 5466

Geological

British Geological Survey
Kingsley Dunham Centre
Keyworth
Nottingham NG12 5GG
0115 936 3100

Geological Society
Burlington House
Piccadilly
London W1V 0JV
0171 434 9944

Glass

British Glass Manufacturers' Federation
BGMC Building
Northumberland Road
Sheffield S10 2UA

Glass Training Ltd
BGMC Building
Northumberland Road
Sheffield S10 2UA
0114 266 1494/9263/Fax: 0114 266 0738

National Association of **Goldsmiths**
78A Luke Street
London EC2A 4PY
0171 613 4445

Government

Government Communications Headquarters
The Recruitment Office Room A/1108
Priors Road
Cheltenham
Gloucestershire GL52 5AJ
01242 232912/ 3

Government Economic Service
Economists Group Management Unit
HM Treasury
Parliament Street
London SWlP 3AG
0171 270 5622/5073/4581

Government Information Service
Marketing, Recruitment and Training Division
Cabinet Office (OPS)
Ashley House
2 Monck Street
London SW1P 2BQ
0171 276 2714

Graduate and Schools Liason Branch
Room 127/2
Cabinet Office (OPSS)
Horse Guards Road
London SW1P 3AL
0171 270 5750/5696/5697

Graduate Management Admissions Council
Educational Testing Service
PO Box 6108
Princeton NJ 08541- 6103
USA

Association of **Graduate Recruiters**
Sheraton House
Castle Park
Cambridge CB3 0AX
01223 356720

British Institute of **Graphologists**
4th Floor
Bell Court House
11 Bloomfield Street
London EC2M 7AY
0171 277 1474

Institute of **Groundsmanship**
19–23 Church Street
1, Agora
Wolverton
Milton Keynes MK12 5LG
01908 312511

GTI
6 Hithercroft Court
Lupton Road
Wallingford
Oxfordshire OX10 9TB
01491 826262

GTTR (*Graduate Teacher Training Registry*)
PO Box 239
Cheltenham
Gloucestershire GL50 3SL
01242 225868

The **Guardian**
Human Resources Department
119 Farringdon Road
London EC1R 3ER
0171 239 9536

Hairdressing Council
12 David House
45 High Street
London SE25 6HJ
01891 517317

Hairdressing Training Board
3 Chequer Road
Doncaster DN1 2AA
01302 342837

Health and Safety Executive
St Hughs House
Stanley Precinct
Bootle
Merseyside L20 3QY
0151 951 4000

Health and Safety Executive
Rose Court
2 Southwark Bridge Road
London SE1 9HF
0171 717 6000

Health Education Authority
Hamilton House
Mabledon Place
London WC1H 0TX
0171 383 3833

Institute of **Health Record Information and Management**
c/o Warrington Community Health Care NHS Trust
Winwick Hospital,
Warrington
Cheshire WA2 8RR
01925 639772

Health Service Careers
PO Box 204
London SE99 7UW

Institute of **Health Services Management**
39 Chalton Street
London NW1 1JD
0171 388 2626

Heating and Ventilating Contractors' Association
Old Mansion House
Eamont Bridge
Penrith
Cumbria CA10 2BX
01768 64771

HEIST
The Grange
Beckett Park Campus
Leeds LS6 3QS
01132 833184

Institute of **Heraldic and Genealogical Studies**
79–82 Northgate
Canterbury
Kent CT1 1BA
01227 768664

HESA *see* **Higher Education Statistics Agency**

Higher Education

Higher Education Advice and Planning Service
200 Greyhound Road
London W14 9RY
0171 385 3377

Higher Education Funding Council for England
Northavon House
Coldharbour Lane
Bristol BS16 1QD
01179 317317

Higher Education Statistics Agency
18 Royal Crescent
Cheltenham GL50 3DA
01242 255577/Fax: 01242 232648

Higher Still Development Unit
PO Box 12754
Holyrood Road
Edinburgh EH8 8ZA
0131 557 6810/Fax: 0131 557 6083

Scottish Higher Education Funding Council
Donaldson House
97 Haymarket Terrace
Edinburgh EH12 5HD
0131 313 6500

Historic Buildings and Monuments Commission for England
Fortress House
23 Savile Row
London W1X 2HE
0171 973 3000

Historic Scotland
Longmore House
Salisbury Place
Edinburgh EH9 1SH
0131 668 8600

Historical Association
59a Kennington Park Road
London SE11 4JH
0171 735 3901

HMSO Publications Centre
PO Box 276
London SW8 5DT
0171 873 0011

Hodder & Stoughton Educational (Hodder Headline)
338 Euston Road
London NW1 0YS
0171 873 6000

Institute of **Home Economics**
21 Portland Place
London W1N 3HF
0171 436 5677

Home Office Recruitment Section
Personnel Management Division
Room 214 Home Office
Grenadier House
99–105 Horseferry Road
London SWlP 2DD
0171 217 0056

Horses *see* **Animals**

Horticultural Therapy
Goulds Ground
Vallis Way
Frome
Somerset BA11 3DW
01373 464782

Horticulture

Horticulture Research International
Central Office
Wellesbourne
Warwick CV35 9EF
01789 470382

Institute of Horticulture
14–15 Belgrave Square
London SW1X 8PS
0171 976 5951

Hotel and Catering International Management Association
191 Trinity Road
London SW17 7HN
0181 672 4251

Hotel and Catering Training Company
Third Floor
International House
High Street
London W5 5DB
0181 579 2400/Fax: 0181 840 6217

Chartered Institute of **Housing**
Octavia House
Westwood Business Park
Westwood Way
Coventry CV4 8JP
01203 694433

Association of **Illustrators**
29 Bedford Square
London WC1B 3EG
0171 831 7377

Immigration and Nationality Department
Recruitment Section
Room 804
Apollo House
36 Wellesley Road
Croydon CR9 3RR
0181 760 8242

Society of **Indexers**
16 Green Road
Birchington
Kent CT7 9JZ

Industrial Society
Robert Hyde House
48 Bryanston Square
London W1H 7LN
0171 262 2401

Institute of **Information Scientists**
44–45 Museum Street
London WC1A 1LY
0171 831 8001

Inland Revenue
Recruitment and Employee Relations
3rd Floor Mowbray House
PO Box 55
Castle Meadow Road
Nottingham NG2 lBE
0115 974 0588/0603

Inland Revenue
EU Unit
Room 20
Somerset House
London WC2R 1LB
0171 438 6420

The British Institute of **Innkeeping**
Wessex House
80 Park Street
Camberley
Surrey GU15 3YT
01276 684449

Institute of Freight Forwarders *see* **British International Freight Association**

Insurance

The Association of Average Adjusters
200 Aldersgate Street
London EC1A 4JJ
0171 956 0099/Fax: 0171 956 0161

The Association of British Insurers
51 Gresham Street
London EC2V 7HQ
0171 600 3333/Fax: 0171 696 8999

The British Insurance and Investment Brokers' Association
BIIBA House
14 Bevis Marks
London EC3A 7NT
0171 623 9043/Fax: 0171 626 9676

The Chartered Institute of Loss Adjusters
Manfield House
376 Strand
London WC2R 0LR
0171 240 1496/Fax: 0171 836 0340

The Chartered Insurance Institute
Careers Department
31 Hillcrest Road
London E18 2JP
0181 530 6243/Fax: 0171 417 0563

International Baccalaureate Examinations Office
Pascal Close
St.Mellons
Cardiff
South Glamorgan CR3 0YP
01222 770770

International Institute of Sports Therapies *see* **Vocational Awards International Ltd.**

ISCO
12–18 Princess Way
Camberley
Surrey GU15 3SP
01276 21188

ISIS
56 Buckingham Gate
London SW1E 6AG
0171 630 8795

Jewish Educational Bureau
8 Westcombe Avenue
Leeds
West Yorkshire LS8 2BS
01532 663613

JIIG–CAL Careers Research Centre
University of Edinburgh
5 Buccleuch Place
Edinburgh EH8 9LW
0131 650 4310

Jobsearch UK
50–56 Portman Road
Reading
Berkshire RG30 1BA
01734 490060

Journalists

National Council for the Training of Journalists
Latton Bush Centre
Southern Way
Harlow
Essex CM18 7BL
01279 430009

National Union of Journalists
Acorn House
314 Gray's Inn Road
London WC1X 8DP
0171 278 7916

Kogan Page
120 Pentonville Road
London N1 9JN
0171 278 0433

Labour Party
John Smith House
150 Walworth Road
London SE17 1JT
0171 701 1234

HM **Land Registry**
32 Lincoln's Inn Fields
London WC2A 3PH
0171 917 8888

Landscape Institute
6–7 Barnard Mews
London SW11 1QU
0171 738 9166

Languages

Association Internationale des Interpretès de Conferences (*AIIC*)
British Isles Region
12 Vicars Road
London NW5 4NL
0171 284 3112

Centre for Information on Language Teaching and Research
20 Bedfordbury
London WC2N 4LB
0171 379 5110

Institute of Translation and Interpreting
377 City Road
London EC1V 1NA
0171 713 7600

Larousse Plc
Annanndale Street
Edinburgh EH7 4AZ
0131 557 4571

LASER Advisory Council
Chenies House
21 Bedford Square
London WC1B 3HH
0171 637 3073

Law

The Association of Law Costs Draftsmen
Church Cottage
Church Lane
Stuston
Diss
Norfolk IP21 4AG
Tel/Fax: 01379 741404

The Association of Magisterial Officers
35 High Street
Crawley
West Sussex RH10 1BQ
01293 547515

The Court Service Headquarters
Southside
105 Victoria Street
London SW1 6QT
0171 210 1775

Lawyers

Faculty of Advocates
Parliament House
Edinburgh EH1 1RF
0131 226 5071/Fax: 0131 225 3642

The General Council of the Bar of England and Wales
3 Bedford Row
London WC1R 4DB
0171 242 0082

The Law Society
Careers Office
227–228 Strand
London WC2R 1BA
0171 242 1222/Fax: 0171 583 5531

Law Society of Northern Ireland
98 Victoria Street
Belfast BT1 3JZ
01232 231614

Law Society of Scotland
26 Drumsheugh Gardens
Edinburgh EH3 7YR
0131 226 7411/Fax: 0131 225 2934

British **Leather** Confederation
Leather Trade House
Kings Park Road
Moulton Park
Northampton NN3 1JD
01604 494131

Government **Legal Service**
Recruitment Team
Queen Anne's Chambers
28 Broadway,
London SWIH 9JS
0171 210 3304

The Institute of **Legal Executives**
Kempston Manor
Kempston
Bedford
Bedfordshire MK42 7AB
01234 841000

Institute of **Leisure and Amenity Management**
Education and Training Unit
ILAM House
Lower Basildon
Reading
Berkshire RG8 9NE
01491 874222

Charles **Letts** and Co Ltd
Parkgate Road
London SW11
0171 407 8891

Liberal Democrats
4 Cowley Street
London SW1P 3NB
0171 222 7999

The **Library** Association
7 Ridgmount Street
London WC1A 1LY
0171 636 7543/Fax: 0171 436 7218
Email: info@la–hq.org.uk

Institution of **Lighting Engineers**
Lennox House
9 Lawford Road
Rugby
Warwickshire CV21 2DZ
01788 576492

Institute of **Linguists**
24A Highbury Grove
London N5 2DQ
0171 359 7445

Livewire
Hawthorn House
Forth Banks
Newcastle upon Tyne NE1 5SJ
0191 261 5584

Livewire Cymru
Freepost
Holywell CH8 7YL

Livewire Northern Ireland
Freepost
Belfast BT15 1BR

Livewire Scotland
PO Box 2
Penicuik
Midlothian EH26 0NR
01968 679915

Lloyd's Training Centre
Lloyd's of London
One Lime Street
London EC3M 2HA
0171 327 6513/Fax: 0171 327 6273

Local Government Management Board
Local Government Opportunities Section
4th Floor
Arndale House
Arndale Centre
Luton LU1 2TS
01582 451166

Institute of **Logistics and Distribution Management**
Douglas House
Queens Square
Corby
Northants NN17 1PL
01536 205500

London Chamber of Commerce and Industry
Marlowe House
Station Road
Sidcup
Kent DA15 7BJ
0181 302 0261/Fax: 0181 302 4169

London Commodity Exchange
1 Commodity Quay
St Katharine's Docks
London E1 9AX
0171 481 2080

London International Financial Futures Exchange
(*LIFFE*)
1 Cannon Bridge
London EC4R 3XX
0171 623 0444

Lord Chancellor's Department
Selborne House
54–60 Victoria Street
London SW1E 6QW
0171 210 8500/Fax: 0171 210 8549

Lord Chancellor's Department
Personnel Management Division
Rochester House
33 Greycoat Street
London SW1P 2QF
0171 210 1308

Macmillan Publishers Ltd
4 Little Essex Street
London WC2R 3LF
0171 836 6633

MAFF *see* **Agriculture**

Management

Institute of Administrative Management
40 Chatsworth Parade
Petts Wood
Kent BR5 1RW
01689 875555

Institute of Management
2 Savoy Court
Strand
London WC2R OEZ.
0171 497 0580

Institute of Management
Management House
Cottingham Road
Corby
Northants NN17 1TT
01536 204222/Fax: 01536 201 561

Association for Management Education and Training in Scotland (AMETS)
The Cottrell Building
University of Stirling
Stirling
FK9 4LA
01786 450906

Management Books 2000
Cowlcomb House
Cowlcomb Hill
Chalford
Gloucestershire GL6 8HP
01285 760722

Management Consultancies Association Ltd
11 West Halkin Street
London SW1X 8JL
0171 235 3897

Institute of **Management Consultants**
32 Hatton Gardens
London EC1N 8DL
0171 243 2140

Manpower plc
66 Chiltern Street
London W1X 1PR
0171 244 6688

British **Marine Industries Federation**
Meadlake Place
Thorpelea Road
Egham
Surrey TW20 8HE
01784 473377

Market Research Society
15 Northburgh Street
London EC1V OAH
0171 490 4911

Marketing

Chartered Institute of Marketing
Moor Hall
Cookham
Maidenhead
Berkshire SL6 9QH
01628 524922

Direct Marketing Association
Haymarket House
1 Oxendon Street
London SW1Y 4EE
0171 321 2525

Industrial Marketing Research Association
11 Bird Street
Lichfield
Staffordshire

Institute of **Materials**
1 Carlton House Terrace
London SW1Y 5DB
0171 839 4071

Mathematics

Institute of Mathematics and its Applications
16 Nelson Street
Southend–on–Sea
Essex SS1 1EF
01702 354020

Mathematical Association
259 London Road
Leicester LE2 3BE
0116 270 3877

MBA & GMAT Advice Centre
PasTest
Egerton House
Egerton Court
Parkgate Estate
Knutsford
Cheshire WA16 8DX
01565 755 266/Fax: 01565 650 264

Institute of **Measurement and Control**
87 Gower Street
London WC1E 6AA
0171 387 4949

Meat Training Council
PO Box 141
Winterhill House
Snowdon Drive
Milton Keynes MK6 1YY
01908 231062

Institution of **Mechanical Engineers**
Northgate Avenue
Bury St Edmunds
Suffolk IP32 6BN
01284 763277

Medical

British Medical Association
BMA House
Tavistock Square
London WC1H 8JP
0171 587 4499

General Medical Council
178–202 Great Portland Street
London W1N 6JE
0171 580 7642

Medical Research Council
20 Park Crescent
London W1N 4AL
0171 636 5422

Scottish Council for Postgraduate Medical Education
12 Queen Street
Edinburgh EH2 1JE
0131 225 4365

Association of **Medical Secretaries, Practice Administrators and Receptionists**
Tavistock House North
Tavistock Square
London WC1H 9LN
0171 387 6005

Meteorological

Meteorological Office
Personnel Department(Recruitment)
Room 604
London Road
Bracknell
Berks RG12 2SZ
01344 856032/33/34/38

Royal Meteorological Society
104 Oxford Road
Reading
Berkshire RG1 7LJ
01734 568500

Society for General **Microbiology**
Marlborough House
Basingstoke Road
Spencers Wood
Reading RG7 1AE
01734 885577

Midlands Examining Group
Syndicate Buildings
1 Hills Road
Cambridge CB1 2EU
01223 553311

Ministerial Selection and Training Board

Elim Pentecostal Church *see under* **Churches**

Ministry of Defence
Defence Evaluation and Research Agency (*DERA*)
Graduate Recruitment Office
DERA Portsdown
Portsmouth
Hampshire PO6 4AA
01645 346800

Association of **Model Agents**
St Catherine's Mews
Milner Street
London SW3 2PX
0171 584 6466

Money markets

The Institute of Investment Management & Research
(*was Society of Investment Analysts*)
211–213 High Street
Bromley
Kent BR1 1NY
0181 464 0811/Fax: 0181 313 0587

The London Commodity Exchange
1 Commodity Quay
St Katharine's Docks
London E1 9AX
0171 481 2080

The London International Financial Futures Exchange
1 Cannon Bridge
London EC4R 3XX
0171 623 0444

Institute of the **Motor Industry**
Fanshaws
Brickendon
Hertford SG13 8PQ
01992 511521

Museums

Museums Association
42 Clerkenwell Close
London EC1R 0PA
0171 608 2933

Museums and Galleries Commission
16 Queen Anne's Gate
London SW1H 9AA
0171 233 4200

Museums Training Institute
Kershaw House
55 Well Street
Bradford BD1 5PS
01274 391056

Music

Directorate of Naval Recruiting
Royal Marines School of Music
Canada Road
Deal
Kent CT14 7EH
01304 362121

RAF School of Music
Royal Air Force
Uxbridge
Middlesex UB10 0RZ
01895 237144 ext 6345

Royal Military School of Music
Kneller Hall
Kneller Road
Twickenham
Middlesex TW2 7DU
0181 898 5533

Royal School of Church Music
Addington Place
Gravel Hill
Croydon
Surrey CR9 5AD
0181 654 7676

Music Industries Association
Grove Court
Hatfield Road
Slough
Berks SL1 1QU
01753 511550

The Music Publishers' Association Ltd
3rd Floor Strandgate
18–20 York Buildings
London WC2N 6JU
0171 839 7779

Music Therapy

Association of Professional Music Therapists
Chestnut Cottage
38 Pierce Lane
Fulbourn
Cambridge CB1 5DL
01223 880377

British Society for Music Therapy
25 Rosslyn Avenue
East Barnet
Herts EN4 8DH
0181 368 8879

Institute of **Musical Instrument Technology**
134 Crouch Hill
London N8 9DX
0181 888 3003

Musicians

Incorporated Society of Musicians
10 Stratford Place
London W1N 9AE
0171 629 4413

Musicians Union
60–62 Clapham Road
London SW9 0JJ
0171 582 5566

NARIC *see* **National Academic Recognition Information Centre**

NASA Astronaut Program
Mail Code AHX
Johnson Space Center
Houston
Texas TX77058
USA

National Academic Recognition Information Centre
The British Council
Medlock Street
Manchester M15 4AA
0161 957 7065/Fax: 0161-957 7561

National Council for Vocational Qualifications
222 Euston Road
London NW1 2BZ
0171 387 9898/Fax: 0171 387 0978

National Council for Voluntary Organisations
8 All Saints Street
Regent's Wharf
London N1 9RL
0171 713 6161

National Foundation for Educational Research (*NFER*)
The Mere
Upton Park
Slough
Berkshire SL1 2DQ

National Institute for Careers Education and Counselling (*NICEC*)
Sheraton House
Castle Park
Cambridge CB3 0AX

National Trust
36 Queen Anne's Gate
London SW1H 9AS
0171 222 5097

National Trust for Scotland
5 Charlotte Square
Edinburgh
Lothian EH2 4DU
0131 226 5922

National Union of Students
461 Holloway Road
London N7 6LJ
0171 272 8900

Natural Environment Research Council
Polaris House
North Star Avenue
Swindon
Wiltshire SN2 1EU
01793 411500

Naval Architects
Royal Institution of Naval Architects
10 Upper Belgrave Street
London SW1X 8BQ
0171 235 4622

NBS CATCH
PO Box 21
Edinburgh EH2 1NT
0131 226 7999

NERC *see* **Natural Environment Research Council**

Newspaper Society
74–77 Great Russell Street
London WC1B 3DA
0171 636 7014

British Institute of **Non–Destructive Testing**
1 Spencer Parade
Northampton NN1 5AA
01604 30124

Northern Examinations and Assessment Board
Devas Street
Manchester M15 6EX
0161 953 1180

Northern Ireland Office
Old Admiralty Building
London SW1A 2AZ
and
Northern Ireland Civil Service Commission
Rosepark House
Upper Newtonards Road
Belfast BT4 3NR
01232 520400

Nursery Nurse

The Council for Awards in Children's Care and Education
8 Chequer Street
St Albans
Hertfordshire AL1 3XZ
01727 847636/Fax: 01727 867609

Nursing, Midwifery and Health Visiting

English National Board for Nursing, Midwifery and Health Visiting
PO Box 2EN
London W1A 2EN
0171 391 6200

National Board for Nursing, Midwifery and Health Visiting for Northern Ireland
RAC House
79 Chichester Street
Belfast BT1 4JR
01232 246333

Nurses and Midwives Central Clearing House
NMCCH
ENB
PO Box 9017
London W1A 0XA
0171 391 6291

Scottish National Board for Nursing, Midwifery and Health Visiting
22 Queen Street
Edinburgh EH2 1JX
0131 226 7371 ext 254

Welsh National Board for Nursing, Midwifery and Health Visiting
Floor 13
Pearl Assurance House
Greyfriars Road
Cardiff CF1 3AG
01222 395535

NUS *see* **National Union of Students**

British Examining Board in **Occupational Hygiene**
Suite 2
Georgian House
Great Northern Road
Derby DE1 1LT
01332 298087

British Association and College of **Occupational Therapists**
6/8 Marshalsea Road
London SE1 1HL
0171 357 6480

Institute of **Oceanographic Sciences**
Southampton OceanographyCentre
Empress Dock
Southampton SO1 3ZH
01703 595000

Office of Fair Trading
Field House
Bream's Buildings
London EC4A 1PR

Office of Population Censuses and Surveys
St Catherine's House
10 Kingsway
London WC2B 6JP
0171 242 0262

OFSTED
Alexandra House
33 Kingsway
London WC2B 6SE
0171 421 6800

Open College
Customer Services
Freepost
St Paul's
781 Wilmslow Road
Didsbury
Manchester M20 8RW
0161 434 0007

Open University
PO Box 71
Milton Keynes
Buckinghamshire MK7 6AG
01908 653231

British Association of **Operating Department Assistants**
70A Crayford High Street
Dartford
Kent DA1 4EF
01322 555755

Operational Research Society
Seymour House
12 Edward Street
Birminham B1 2RX
0121 233 9300

General **Optical** Council
41 Harley Street
London W1N 2DJ
0171 580 3898

Opticians

Association of British Dispensing Opticians
6 Hurlingham Business Park
Sulivan Road
London SW6 3DU
0171 736 0088

Federation of Ophthalmic and Dispensing Opticians
113 Eastbourne Mews
London W2 6LQ
0171 258 0240

The College of **Optometrists**
10 Knaresborough Place
London SW5 0TG
0171 373 7765

Ordnance Survey Recruitment
Romsey Road
Maybush
Southampton SO9 4DH
01703 792000

British **Orthoptic** Society
Tavistock House North
Tavistock Square,
London WC1H 9HX
0171 387 7992

Overseas Development Administration (*ODA*)
Overseas Appointments and Contracts Dept
Abercrombie House
Eaglesham Road
East Kilbride
Glasgow G75 8EA
01355 843309

OXFAM
274 Banbury Road
Oxford OX2 7DZ
01865 311311

Oxford and Cambridge Schools Examination Board
(part of the University of Cambridge Local Examinations Syndicate) *See* **Oxford and Cambridge Examinations and Assessment Council**

Institute of **Packaging**
Sysonby Lodge
Nottingham Road
Melton Mowbray,
Leicestershire LE13 ONU
01664 500055/Fax: 01664 64164

PACT (Producers Alliance for Cinema and TV)
Gordon House
Greencoat Place
London SW1P 1PH
0171 233 6000

Paper Federation
Papermakers House
Rivenhall Road
Swindon SN5 7BD
01793 886086/Fax: 01793 886182

Particle Physics and Astronomy Research Council
(PPARC)
Polaris House
North Star Avenue
Swindon SN2 1ET
01793 442000

Patents

The Chartered Institute of Patent Agents
Staple Inn Buildings
High Holborn
London WC1V 7PZ
0171 405 9450/Fax: 0171 430 0471

Patent Office
Marketing and Information Directorate
Cardiff Road
Newport
Gwent NP9 1RH
01633 814000

Penguin Books Ltd
Bath Road
Harmondsworth
Middlesex UB7 0DA
0181 899 4000
or
27 Wrights Lane
London W8 5TZ

Pensions Management Institute
PMI House
4–10 Artillery Lane
London E1 7LS
0171 247 1452/Fax: 0171 375 0603

Periodicals Training Council
Queens House
55–56 Lincolns Inn Fields
London WC2A 3LJ
0171 836 8798

Institute of **Personnel and Development**
IPD House
Camp Road
London SW19 4UX
0181 971 9000

Institute of **Petroleum**
61 New Cavendish Street
London W1M 8AR
0171 467 7100

Pharmaceutical

The Association of the British Pharmaceutical Industry
12 Whitehall
London SW1A 2DY
0171 930 3477/Fax: 0171 747 1411

National Pharmaceutical Association
Mallinson House
38–42 St Peters Street
St Albans
Hertfordshire AL1 3NP
01727 832161

Royal Pharmaceutical Society of Great Britain
1 Lambeth High Street
London SE1 7JN
0171 735 9141

British **Pharmacological** Society
16 Angel Gate
City Road
London EC1V 2PT
0171 417 0111/2/3

Phonographic Industry Ltd
25 Savile Row
London W1X 1AA
0171 287 4422

Photography

Association of Fashion, Advertising and Editorial Photographers
9–10 Domingo Street
London EC1Y OTA
0171 608 1441

British Institute of Professional Photography
1 Amwell End
Ware
Hertfordshire SG12 9HN
01920 464011

Professional Photographic Laboratories Association
Peel Place
50 Carver Street
Hockley
Birmingham B1 3AS

Royal Photographic Society
National Centre
Milsom Street
Bath BA1 1DN

Central Council of **Physical Recreation**
Francis House
Francis Street
London SW1P 1DE
0171 828 3163/4

Institute of Physical Science and Hospital Physicists' Association
2 Low Ousegate
York YO1 1QU
01904 610821

Institute of **Physics**
Education Department
76 Portland Place
London W1N 4AA
0171 470 4800

Physiological Society
Publications and Administration Office
PO Box 506
Oxford OX1 3XE
01865 798498

Chartered Society of **Physiotherapy**
14 Bedford Row
London WC1R 4ED
0171 242 1941

Association of British **Picture Restorers**
Station Avenue
Kew TW9 3QA
0181 948 5644

Pitman Training Group
154 Southampton Row
London WC1B 5AX
0171 278 6877

Institution of **Plant Engineers**
77 Great Peter Street
London SW1P 2EZ
0171 233 2855

Institute of **Plumbing**
64 Station Lane
Hornchurch RM12 6NB
01402 472791

Society of Chiropodists and **Podiatrists**
53 Welbeck Street
London W1M 7HE
0171 486 3381

Police (England and Wales)

Home Office Police Department
Publicity Section
Room 133
50 Queen Anne's Gate
London SE1H 9AT
0171 273 3773

Police (Scotland)

The Scottish Office
Home Department Police Division
St Andrew's House
Regent Road
Edinburgh EH1 3DG
0131 244 5400

Policy Studies Institute
100 Park Village East
London NW1 3SR
0171 387 2171

British **Polymer Training Association**
Coppice House
Halesfield 7
Telford
Shropshire TF7 4NA
01952 587020

Post Office Training and Development Group
Coton House Management Centre
Coton House
Rugby
Warwickshire CV23 0AA
01788 574111 (*for management training only; otherwise contact the Personnel Manager at the nearest Post Office or sorting office*)

Powers International
525 Fulham Road
London SW6
0171 385 8855

Prince's Scottish Youth Business Trust
Mercantile Chambers 6th Floor
53 Bothwell Street
Glasgow G2 6TS

Prince's Youth Business Trust
5 Cleveland Place
London SW1Y 6JJ
0171 321 6500

Print

British Printing Industries Federation
11 Bedford Row
London WC1R 4DD
0171 242 6904/Fax: 0171 405 7784

Scottish Print Employers Federation
48 Palmerston Place
Edinburgh EH12 5DE
0131 220 4353

Prisons

England and Wales Prison Service
Cleland House
Page Street
London SW1P 4LN
0171 217 6437

Scottish Prison Service
Communications Branch
Room 322
Carlton House
5 Redheughs Road
Edinburgh EH12 9HW
0131 244 8401

Private Investigators

Association of British Investigators
ABI House
10 Bonner Hill Road
Kingston–upon–Thames
Surrey KT1 3EP
0181 546 3368

The Institute of Professional Investigators
31A Wellington Street
St Johns
Blackburn BB1 8AF
01254 680072

Probation Service Division
Home Office
50 Queen Anne's Gate
London SW1H 9AT
0171 273 3241/Fax: 0171 273 3944

Council for **Professions Supplementary to Medicine**
184 Kennington Park Road
London SE11 4BY
0171 582 08666

Project North East
Hawthorne House
Forth Banks
Newcastle upon Tyne NE1 3SG
0191 261 5584

British Association of **Prosthetists and Orthotists**
c/o Dunoon General Hospital
Dunoon
Argyl, PA23 7RL
01369 706366

Psychology

Association of Educational Psychologists
3 Sunderland Road
Gilesgate
Durham DH1 2LH
0191 384 9512/Fax: 0191 386 5287

The British Psychological Society
St Andrew's House
48 Princess Road East
Leicester LE1 7DR
0116 254 9568/Fax: 0116 247 0787

Royal Institute of **Public Health and Hygiene**
28 Portland Place
London W1N 4DE
0171 580 2731

Public Record Office
Ruskin Avenue
Kew
Richmond
Surrey TW9 4DU
0181 876 3444

Institute of **Public Relations**
1 Great James Street
London WC1N 3DA
0171 253 5151

Publishers' Association
19 Bedford Square
London WC1B 3JH
0171 580 6321

Chartered Institute of **Purchasing and Supply**
Easton House
Easton on the Hill
Stamford
Lincolnshire PE9 3NZ
01780 56777

Commission for **Racial Equality**
Elliot House
10–12 Allington Street
London SW1E 5EH
0171–828 7022

Radio

Association of Independent Radio Companies
Radio House
46 Westbourne Grove
London W2 5HS
0171 727 2646

The Radio Authority
Holbrook House
14 Great Queen Street
London WC2B 5DG
0171 430 2724

Society and College of **Radiographers**
14 Upper Wimpole Street
London W1M 8BN
0171 935 5726

Railtrack PLC
Room 445
40 Bernard street
London WC1N 1BY
0171 344 7108 (*graduate recruitment*)

Railway Industry Training Council
Euston House
24 Eversholt Street
London NW1 1DZ
0171 320 0436

Raleigh International
Raleigh House
27 Parsons Green Lane,
London SW6 4HZ
0171 371 8585

Association of Professional **Recording** Services Ltd
2 Windsor Square
Silver Street
Reading RG1 2TH
01628 756218

Recreation Managers Association of Great Britain
Recreation House
7 Burkinshaw Avenue
Rawmarsh
Rotherham
South Yorkshire S62 7QZ
01709 522463

Recruitment and Assessment Services
Alencon Link
Basingstoke RG21 7JB
01256 29222

Reed Information Services
Windsor Court
East Grinstead House
East Grinstead
West Sussex RH19 1XA

Institute of **Refrigeration**
Kelvin House
76 Mill Lane
Carshalton
Surrey SM5 2JR
0181 647 7033

British Association of **Removers**
3 Churchill Court
58 Station Road
North Harrow
Middlesex HA2 7SA
0181 861 3331

National **Retail Training Council**
Bedford House
69–79 Fulham High Street
London SW16 3JW
0171 371 7673

Institute of **Revenue Rating and Valuation**
41 Doughty Street
London WC1N 2LF
0171 831 3505

Road Haulage Association Ltd
Roadway House
35 Monument Hill
Weybridge Surrey KT13 8RN
01932 841515

Road Haulage and Distribution Training Council Ltd
Suite C
Shenley Hall
Rectory Lane
Shenley
Radlett
Hertfordshire WD7 9AN
01923 858461

Institute of **Road Transport Engineers**
22 Greencoat Place
London SW1P 1PR
0171 630 1111

Institute of **Roofing**
24 Weymouth Street
London W1N 3FA
0171 405 9884

Routledge
11 New Fetter Lane
London EC4P 4EE
0171 583 9855

RSA Examinations Board
Progress House
Westwood Business Park
Westwood Way,
Coventry CV4 8HS
Telephone: 01203 470033/Fax: 01203 468080

Salvation Army
Territorial Headquarters
c/o William Booth Memorial Training College
Denmark Hill
London SE5 8BQ
0171 7331191

School Curriculum and Assessment Authority
Customer Services
Newcombe House
45 Notting Hill Gate
London W11 3JB
0171 229 1234

Science Policy Research Unit
Mantell Building
University of Sussex
Falmer
Brighton
East Sussex BN1 9RF
01273 686758

Institute of **Science Technology**
22 Bore Street
Lichfield
Staffordshire WS13 6LP
01543 251346

Scottish Certificate of Education Examination Board
Ironmills Road
Dalkeith
Midlothian EH22 1LE
0131 663 6601

Scottish Consultative Council on the Curriculum
Information and Marketing Services
Gardyne Road
Dundee DD5 1NY
01382 455053

Scottish Examinations Board
15 Ironmills Road
Dalkeith
Midlothian EH22 1LE
0131 663 6601/Fax: 0131 654 2664

Scottish Further Education Unit *(SFEU)*
Argyll Court
The Castle Business Park
Stirling FK9 4TY
01786 892000

Scottish Natural Heritage
12 Hope Terrace
Edinburgh EH9 2AS
0130 447 4784

Scottish Office
Recruitment Unit
Room 110
16 Waterloo Place
Edinburgh EH1 3DN
0131 244 3964

Scottish Office Education Department
New St Andrews House
St James Centre
Edinburgh EH1 3TG
0131 556 8400/4544

Scottish Office Education Students' Awards Branch
Room 107
Gyleview House
3 Redheughs Rigg
Edinburgh EH12 9HH
0131 224 5823

Scottish Office Personnel Department Recruitment Services
16 Waterloo Place
Edinburgh EH1 3DN

Scottish Universities Council on Entrance
12 The Links
St Andrews
Fife KY16 9JB
01334 72406

Scottish Vocational Education Council
Hanover House
24, Douglas Street
Glasgow G2 7NQ
Telephone: 0141 248 7900/Fax: 0141–242 2244

International Professional **Security** Association
IPSA House
3 Dendy Road
Paignton
Devon TQ4 5DB
01803 554849

Institute of **Shorthand Writers**
61 Carey Street
London WC1 2IU
0171 405 9884

Skills and Enterprise Network
Department for Education and Employment
Room W801
Moorfoot
Sheffield S1 4PQ
0114 259 4075 LMQR Enquiries

Skillset
124 Horseferry Road
London SW1P 2TX
0171 306 8585

Skillshare Africa
3 Belvoir Street
Leicester LE1 6SL
0116 254 0517

Small Firms Service
Carlyle House
Carlyle Road
Cambridge CB4 3DN
0800 222999 (*Freephone*)

Department of **Social Security**
Personnel, 7th Floor
The Adelphi
1–11 John Adams Street
London WC2N 6HT
0171 96Z 8174

Social work

Central Council for Education and Training in Social Work (*CCETSW*)
Derbyshire House
St Chad's Street
London WC1H 8AD
0171 278 2455/Fax: 0171 278 2934

Central Council for Education and Training in Social Work
The Registry, 3rd Floor
Caledonia House
223–231 Pentonville Road
London N1 9NG
0171 837 3999/Fax: 0171 837 3736

Central Council for Education and Training in Social Work Scottish Office
78–80 George Street
Edinburgh EH2 3BU
0131 220 0093

Social Work Admissions System (SWAS)
Fulton House
Jessop Avenue
Cheltenham
Gloucestershire GL50 3SH
01242 225977

Sociology

The British Sociological Association
Unit 3G
Mountjoy Research Centre
Stockton Road
Durham DH1 3UR
0191 383 0839

Southern Examining Group
Stag Hill House
Guildford
Surrey GU2 5XJ
01483 506506/Fax: 01483 300152

Royal College of **Speech and Language Therapists**
7 Bath Place
Rivington Street
London EC2A 3DR
0171 613 3885

Sport

British Amateur Weightlifting Association
131 Hurst Street
Oxford OX4 1HE
01865 200339

British Boxing Board of Control
Jack Peterson House
52a Borough High Street
London SE1 1XW
0171 403 5879

British Cycling Federation
c/o National Cycling Centre
Stuart Street
Manchester M11 4DQ
0161 230 2301

British Darts Organisation Ltd
Page's Lane
Muswell Hill
London N10 1PS
0181 883 5544

British Horseracing Board
42 Portman square
London W1H 0EN
0171 396 0011

British Institute of Professional Dog Trainers
Bowstone Gate
Disley
Cheshire
SK12 2AW
01663 762772

British Mountaineering Council
Crawford House
Precinct Centre
Booth Street East
Manchester M13 9RZ
0161 273 5835

British Racing School
Snailwell Road
Newmarket
Suffolk CB8 7NU
01638 665103

English Basketball Association
48 Bradford Road
Stanningley
Leeds LS28 6DF
0113 2361166

The Exercise Association of Great Britain
Unit 4, Angel Gate
City Road
London EC1V 2PT
0171 278 0811

Football Association
16 Lancaster Gate
London W2 3LW
0171 402 7151

Institute of Professional Sport
Francis House
Francis Street
London SW1P 1DE
0171 828 3163

Institute of Sport and Recreation Management
Giffard House
36–38 Sherrard Street
Melton Mowbray
Leicestershire LE13 1XJ
01664 65531

Keep Fit Association
Francis House
Francis Street
London SW1P 1DE
0171 233 8898

Lawn Tennis Association
The Queens Club
Barons Court
West Kensington
London W14 9EG
0171 381 7000

Motorcycle Sport
ACU House
Wood Street
Rugby CV21 2YX
01788 540096

National Association for Outdoor Education
12 St Andrews Street
Penrith
Cumbria
01768 65113

National Coaching Foundation
114 Cardigan Road
Headingley
Leeds
LS6 3BJ
0113 2744802

PGA European Tour
Wentworth Drive
Virginia Water
Surrey GU25 4LX
01344 842881

The Physical Education Association of Great Britain
Francis House
Francis Street
London SW1P 1DE
0171 828 9229

Professional Golfers' Association
Apollo House
The Belfry
Sutton Coldfield
West Midlands B76 9PT
01675 470333

RAC Motor Sports Association
Motor Sports House
Riverside Park
Colnbrook
Slough SL30 0HG
01753 681736

Rugby Football League
Red Hall
Red Hall Lane
Leeds LS1 8NB
0113 2624637

Rugby Union
Whitton Road
Twickenham TW1 1DZ
0181 892 8161

Scottish Sports Council
Caledonia House
South Gyle
Edinburgh EH12 9DQ
0131 317 7200

World Professional Billiards and Snooker Association
27 Oakfield Road
Bristol BS8 2AT
0117 9744491

Sports Council
16 Upper Woburn Place
London WC1H 0QP
0171 388 1277

Sports Council for Northern Ireland
House of Sport
Upper Malone Road
Belfast BT9 5LA
01232 381222

Sports Council for Wales
Information Centre
Welsh Institute of Sport
Sophia Gardens
Cardiff CF1 9SW
01222 397571

Statistics

Government Statistical Service
Room 1820
Central Statistical Office
Millbank Tower
London SWlP 4QQ
0171 217 4369/4222

Royal Statistical Society
12 Errol Street
London EC1Y 8LX
0171 638 8998

The London **Stock Exchange**
Resourcing Centre
Stock Exchange Tower
Old Broad Street
London EC2N 1HP
0171 797 1000

Institution of **Structural Engineers**
11 Upper Belgrave Street
London SW1X 8BH
0171 235 4535

Student Awards Agency for Scotland
Gyleview House
3 Redheughs Rigg
Edinburgh EH12 9HH
0131 244 5823/Fax: 0131 244 5887

Student Loans Company Ltd
100 Bothwell Street
Glasgow G2 7JD
0141 306 2000

Students *see also* **National Union of Students**

Society of **Surveying Technicians**
Surveyor Court
Westwood Way
Coventry CV4 8JE
01203 694757

Surveyors

Royal Institution of Chartered Surveyors
Surveyor Court
Westwood Way
Coventry CV4 8JE
01203 694757
and
Great George Street
Parliament Square
London SW1P 3AD
0171 222 7000

Royal Institution of Chartered Surveyors (Scotland)
9 Manor Place
Edinburgh EH3 7DN
0131 225 7078

Association of **Taxation Technicians**
12 Upper Belgrave Street
London SW1X 8BB
0171–235 2544

Teaching

Association of University Teachers (*AUT*)
United House
9 Pembridge Road
London W11 3JY
0171 221 4370

National Association of Teachers of Further and Higher Education (*NATFHE*)
27 Britannia Street
London WC1X 9JP
0171 837 3636

National Union of Teachers (*NUT*)
Hamilton House
Mabledon Place
London WC1H 9BD
0171 383 5752

Teacher Training Agency
Portland House
Stag Place
London SW1A 5TT
0171 925 5880

Teachers Education Admissions (*TEACH Scotland*)
PO Box 165
Edinburgh EH8 8AT
0131 558 6170

Television

Channel 4
124 Horseferry Road
London SW1 P 2TX
0171 396 4444

CYFLE
Gronant
Penrallt Isaf
Caernarfon
Gwynedd LL55 1NW
01286 671000

ft2
4th Floor
5 Dean Street
London W1V 5RN
0171 734 5141

Independent Television Commission (*ITC*)
33 Foley Street
London W1P 7LB
0171 255 3000

Independent Television Network Centre
200 Gray's Inn Road
London WC1X 8HF
0171 843 8000

TEMPUS (UK)
Information office
R&D Building
The University
Canterbury
Kent CT2 7PD

Textile Institute
10 Blackfriars Street
Manchester M3 5DR
0161 834 8457

Textile Services Association
7 Churchill Court
58 Station Road
North Harrow
Middlesex HA2 7SA
0181 863 7755

Theatre

Association of British Theatre Technicians
47 Bermondsey Street
London SE1 3XT

Independent Theatre Council
4 Baden Place
Crosby Row
London SE1 1YW
0171 403 1727

Tourism *see* **Travel**

Town Planning

Royal Town Planning Institute
26 Portland Place
London W1N 4BE
0171 636 9107

Royal Town Planning Institute Scotland
46 Northumberland Street
Edinburgh EH3 6JF
0131–558 1855

British Toxicological Society
c/o Institute of Biology
20–22 Queensberry Place
London SW7 2DZ
0171 581 8333

Trade & Industry

Department of Trade and Industry (*DTI*)
Ashdown House
123 Victoria Street
London SW1 6RB
0171 215 5000

Department of Trade and Industry (*DTI*)
European Division
Kingsgate House
66–74 Victoria Street
London SW1E 6SW
0171 215 5000

Department of Trade and Industry (*DTI*)
Recruitment Unit
1 Victoria Street
London SWlH OET
0171 215 S316

The Institute of **Trade Mark Agents**
Canterbury House
2–6 Sydenham Road
Croydon
Surrey CR0 9XE
0181 686 2052/Fax: 0181 680 5723

Trades Union Congress
Congress House
Great Russell Street
London WC1B 3LS
0171 636 4030

Institute of **Trading Standards Administration**
4–5 Hadleigh Business Centre
351 London Road
Hadleigh
Essex SS7 2BT
01702 559922

Transport

Chartered Institute of Transport
80 Portland Place
London W1N 4DP
0171 636 9952

Department of Transport
Recruitment Section Floor 4/02
Great Minster House
76 Marsham Street
London SWlP 4DR
0171 271 5351/5346

Institute of Transport Administration
32 Palmerston Road
Southampton SO14 1LL
01703 631380

Travel

British Tourist Authority/English Tourist Board
Thames Tower
Blacks Road
Hammersmith
London W6 9EL
0181 846 9000

Institute of Travel and Tourism
113 Victoria Street
St Albans
Hertfordshire AL1 3TJ
01727 854395

London Tourist Board and Convention Bureau
26 Grosvenor Gardens
London SW1A 0DU
0171 730 3450

Travel Training Company
The Cornerstone
The Broadway
Woking
Surrey GU21 5AR
01483 727321

HM **Treasury**
Personnel and Support Directorate
5th Floor
Allington Towers
19 Allington Street
London SW1E 5EB
0171 270 1539

Institute of **Trichologists**
228 Stockwell Road
Brixton
London SW9 9SU
0171 733 2056

Trotman & Company Ltd
12 Hill Rise
Richmond
Surrey TW10 6UA
0181–332 2132

UCAS
Fulton House
Jessop Avenue
Cheltenham GL50 3SH
01242 227788 (*applicants*)/222444 (*other enquiries*)

UK Information Office of the European Parliament
2 Queen Anne's Gate
London SW1H 9AA
0171 227 4300

UK Council for Overseas Students Affairs (UKCOSA)
9–17 St Albans Place
London N1 0NX
0171 226 3762

UN Association for International Service
Hunter House
57 Goodramgate
York YO1 2LS
01904 647799

UN Information Centre
Millbank Tower
21st Floor
21–24 Millbank
London SW1P 4QH
0171 630 1981

Understanding British Industry (UBI)
Sun Alliance House
New Inn Hall Street
Oxford OX1 2QE
01865 722585

Society for **Underwater Technology**
76 Mark Lane
London EC3R 7JN
0171 481 0750

Universities and Colleges Admissions Services (UCAS)
PO Box 67
Cheltenham
Gloucestershire GL50 3SH
01242 222444

University of Cambridge Local Examination Syndicate
See **Oxford and Cambridge Examinations and Assessment Council**

University of London Examinations and Assessment Council
Stewart House
32 Russell Square
London WC1B 5DN
0171 331 4000

University of Oxford Delegacy of Local Examinations
(part of the University of Cambridge Local Examinations Syndicate) *See* **Oxford and Cambridge Examinations and Assessment Council**

Vacation Work Publications
9 Park End Street
Oxford OX1 1HJ
01865 241978

Incorporated Society of **Valuers and Auctioneers**
3 Cadogan Gate
London SW1X 0AS
0171 235 2282

British **Veterinary Nursing Association**
The Seedbed Centre
Coldharbour Road
Harlow
Essex CM19 5AF
01279 450567

Royal College of **Veterinary Surgeons**
32 Belgrave Square
London SW1X 8QP
0171 235 4971

Vocational Awards International (*includes its subsidiary organisations, IHBC, IIHHT and IIST*)
46 Aldwick Road
Bognor Regis
West Sussex PO21 2PN
01243 842064

Voluntary Service Overseas (*VSO*)
317 Putney Bridge Road
London SW15 2PN
0181 780 2266

Water

Chartered Institution of Water and Environmental Management
15 John Street
London WC1N 2EB
0171 831 3100

Water Companies Association
1 Queen Anne's Gate
London SW1H 9BT
0171 222 0644

Water Research Centre plc
Henley Road
Medmenham
Marlow
Buckinghamshire SL7 2HD
01491 571531

Water Services Association
1 Queen Anne's Gate
London SW1H 9BT
0171 957 4567

Wellcome Institute
183 Euston Road
London NW1 2BE
0171 611 8505

Welsh Joint Education Committee
245 Western Avenue
Cardiff
South Glamorgan CF5 2YX
01222 265000

Welsh Office
Personnel and Management Division
Welsh Office
Cathays Park
Cardiff CF1 3NQ
01222 825111

Welsh Office Education Department
FHE1 Division
3rd Floor
Cathays Park
Cardiff CF1 3NQ
01222 825831

Wine and Spirits Education Trust
Five Kings House
1 Queen Street Place
London EC4R 1QS

Workers' Educational Association (*WEA*)
Temple House
9 Upper Berkeley Street
London W1H 8BY
0171 402 5608

London and Central **YMCA**
Training and Development Department
112 Great Russell Street
London WC1B 3NQ
0171 580 2989

National Federation of **Zoological Gardens of Great Britain**
Zoological Gardens
Regents Park
London NW1 4RY
0171 722 3333

Appendix 2: Bibliography

Contents

This *Encyclopedia* can, in a single volume, give only a broad sketch of what is happening across the spectrum of employment. Sources for further information are listed in the relevant chapters and a few chapters such as Special Needs and Job Search already have a detailed bibliography at the end. Below is an additional brief selected guide to books and other material available.

When using careers publications it is essential to use the most up-to-date edition and, if this is more than about 18 months to two years old, treat it with caution. Many items can be consulted in public reference libraries and careers offices. Most items are priced publications with prices ranging from below one pound to over one hundred pounds, so check the current price.

Many of the publications can be obtained from the major careers publishers/distributors – Trotmans, Hobsons (Biblios), Kogan Page and Future Prospects. Addresses of these and other publishers are given in APPENDIX 1.

General information: reference

CIOLA Directory 1996/97

An excellent source of where to obtain further information. Written and edited by Careers Information Officers and other careers specialists. Published Hobsons. Annual. 1996.

General information: careers encyclopedias

Careers encyclopedias in general fall into three categories. The easiest to use are those in alphabetical order of jobs and occupations, and probably the best in this category are the JIIG-Cal (Job Ideas and Information Generator Computer Assisted Learning) *Jobfile* and the CASCAiD *Careers Guide*, which are comprehensive, readable and well researched. Both encyclopedias developed as by-products to computer-generated careers systems and over the years have made considerable efforts to make each entry clear and user-friendly. The main drawback to both encyclopedias is that they tend to deal with each job in isolation. Alphabetical encyclopedias like the *Careers Guide* and *Jobfile* are much easier to update than classified encyclopedias. The *Penguin Careers Guide* is also alphabetical in approach, but uses broader alphabetical categories which often bring together a number of jobs or careers. While this usually makes good sense, it does make the information in that encyclopedia slightly more difficult to access quickly.

Some encyclopedias cover jobs and occupations in classified order. The most usual classification is the Careers Library Classification Index (CLCI) developed by the Careers and Occupational Information Centre (COIC) and used in *Occupations*, where related careers are grouped together. The CLCI approach was adopted for restructuring the last edition of this *Encyclopedia* (SEE APPENDIX 3).

The third category of careers encyclopedia is this one, which has a much wider remit with a number of detailed articles on career-related topics covering aspects like the world of work, vocational preparation and qualifications as well as a very thorough coverage of occupational areas and surveys of employment. This edition includes more new general articles and it is probably closest to the dictionary definition of an encyclopedia. It is unique.

Careers Guide (CASCAiD Ltd)

Developed originally by Leicestershire Careers Service to complement CASCAiD's computer programs it is now useful in its own right. CASCAiD Ltd is now wholly owned by Loughborough University. The Careers Guide 1996/97 incorporates substantial changes. It now contains information on about 650 jobs ranging from unskilled to professional level covering all jobs in the Kudos, Adult Directions and CareerQuest computer programs. It is now intended for people of all ages who are choosing or changing occupations, and for their advisers. The clear summaries cover work activities, personal qualities and skills, lifestyle, employment options, entry routes and training, qualifications and adult opportunities, further reading and addresses. Training and entry routes, qualifications, addresses and references for every career are checked and, if necessary, amended annually. Other material is revised, rewritten, deleted as and when appropriate. New or substantially revised descriptions are validated by relevant bodies and/or practitioners. Published by CASCAiD Ltd in conjunction with Hobsons, and Biblios will handle all orders and distribution. Annual. Next edition due September 1997.

Jobfile

Compiled from information contained in the Jobfile of the JIIG-Cal Computer Assisted Careers Education and Guidance System. The computer printouts form the basis of the book, and each job profile has a brief description of what it involves, together with details of any skills and/or qualifications required, plus notes on other relevant features. It contains information on 659 jobs or careers covering all occupational levels. Contains a very detailed alphabetical index and a CLCI index as well as its own JIIG-CAL index. It has considerable cross-referencing both in the indexes and in the job profiles. Typeface and layout have been greatly improved in recent editions. Published Hodder & Stoughton. Annual. Current edition published October 1996.

Occupations

Careers encyclopedia which deals in a traditional way with around 600 jobs and careers of all types, from unskilled to professional work. The articles are arranged in CLCI order and selected jobs are covered within each category. Each job is dealt with under a series of standardised headings. It is much more detailed than the alphabetical encyclopedias listed above, and by using the subject approach is able to show relationships between different careers. It contains a good alphabetical index. Although a revised edition is published each year in November, not every article will have been revised although 'the revision process ensures that the accuracy of information in all articles is checked at least every three years and that changes are made as necessary'. Published COIC. Current edition *Occupations 97* was published in November 1996.

Penguin Careers Guide

By Anna Alston and Anne Daniel. Consultant editor Ruth Miller. Previously called *Equal Opportunities* it still retains detailed information on the position of women for each career area covered and opportunities for career breaks. It also contains some interesting preliminary pages covering the balance of sexes in employment and training, and education. It also deals with sex discrimination legislation. Covers over 300 jobs and careers in alphabetical order concentrating on those which need formal training or which lead to the widest range of options. Primarily aimed at young people 14–20 but can be used by the older age group. Penguin. 10th Edition March 1996. Paperback. Updated approximately every 4 years.

General information: leaflets and booklets

Job outlines

One-hundred and fifty leaflets on individual jobs or career areas. Updated irregularly and quality is a bit variable. Currently (May 1996) there is a question mark about their future and certainly they are not in COICs portfolio for 1996.

Career Info sheets and Guidelines

Career Info sheets are a series of 115 leaflets covering careers from Accountancy to Youth and Community Work. Leaflets include some unusual areas such as Commodity Dealing and The Wine Trade. Available also as a bound book either direct from ISCO or through Hobsons. Updated irregularly.

The Guidelines are a series of 30 leaflets covering aspects such as option choice, study skills and higher education. Published Independent Schools Careers Organisation (ISCO) 1995.

Working in ... series

Over 40 titles covering a wide range of career ideas. Lively in style, including short profiles of people in work, illustrated and in colour. Published COIC. One-third updated or replaced every three years.

AGCAS Careers Information booklets

Series of about 60 booklets written for undergraduates but also useful for those considering higher education. Some more informative and detailed than others. Published AGCAS. In theory updated biennially but in practice more irregular.

Casebooks

A series of A4-size booklets giving an overview of various career areas, i.e. Management, IT, Supplies Management, Science, Engineering, Law, etc. Contains detailed profiles.

Primarily written for graduates, but there are some general ones: Equal Opportunities, Working Women, Ethnic Minority Students, Mature Students, and Disabilities. There is also a Casebook written specifically for sixth-formers, and a science and technology one for Key Stages 3 & 4. Published Hobsons. Updated annually.

Bulletins
COIC publishes *Newscheck* nine times a year, which reviews new literature, as does ISCO in its termly *CareerScope* magazine. Both publications also print articles and snippets bringing careers information up to date.

Offbeat Careers
Covers a range of unusual jobs. Published Kogan Page 1995.

General information: statistics

Annual Abstract of Statistics
Contains 350 tables giving data for about 10 years covering nearly every aspect of economic, social and industrial life. Published HMSO.

Education Statistics for the UK
Covers variety of topics. Published HMSO.

DfEE Statistical Bulletins
Cover variety of topics including *First Known Destinations of First Degree Graduates*. Free. Published DfEE Statistics Branch, Darlington.

Scottish Office Statistical Bulletins
Cover a variety of topics such as FE, Universities and Student Awards including first-destination statistics of graduates and diplomats from HE courses in Scotland. Published Scottish Office.

University Statistics
Statistics on students, finance and staff in HE including first destinations. Published by the Higher Education Statistics Agency (HESA).

UCAS Statistical Summary
Covers applicants to HE through UCAS. Published UCAS Research and Statistics Department (01242 225920). Second edition published 1996 will cover 1994–95 entry.

Statistical Quarterly
Analyses advertisements in *Prospects Today* and lists by type of employer, work, location, number of vacancies and salaries. Published by CSU Publications. (CSU also publish destination statistics based on information supplied by HESA.)

What do Graduates Do?
First-destinations statistics. Contains pie charts and general information. Data given in percentages rather than numerically. Also appears as a sub-section in *The Job Book* (Hobsons). Published CSU and obtainable Hobsons. Annual.

Labour market and manpower information

Labour Market Quarterly, Labour Market & Skill Trends
and other publications from the Skills and Enterprise Network. Publications of the Institute of Employment Studies Institute of Employment Research, Policy Studies Unit, Confederation of British Industry (CBI).

Mature entrants

There are a number of books aimed at adults and dealing with guidance and career change. These include:

Directory of Guidance Provision for Adults in the UK
Essential reference book listing where to find educational and careers guidance for adults. Lists services available throughout the UK and gives times of opening, facilities provided and charging criteria (where appropriate). Published ADSET (Association for Database Services in Education and Training). 1996.

Build Your Own Rainbow
A workbook for career and life management by B. Hopson and M. Scally, who are both experts in this field. Contains exercises designed to help develop your personal skills, aptitudes and ambitions. Used by the Open University. Copyright Lifeskills International; published Management Books 2000. Also obtainable Trotman. New edition 1996.

What Color is Your Parachute?
A practical manual for job-hunters and career-changers by Richard Bolles. Although this is an American publication and obviously contains material and references which are not applicable in the UK, it is a useful self-help book, particularly the chapters dealing with self-analysis. Published Tenspeed Press in the USA. Annual. Obtainable Trotman.

Second Chances
A comprehensive guide to education and training courses for adults at all levels. Published COIC. Edition due November. 1996.

Changing Course
By Maggie Smith. Useful DIY career- and life-planning publication. Copyright Lifeskills Communications and published by Management Books 2000.

Careers choice

Decisions at . . .13/14, 15/16, 17/18
Series of books covering choices at various ages and the options available. Published Hobsons. Updated irregularly. Bit dated in style.

13+ Pathways to Success
A very clear guide to choosing GCSEs, and Part One GNVQs. Magazine-style format. Teachers' notes available separately. 1996 edition. Published Hobsons.

14+ Pathways to Success
Designed specifically for Year 10 students. Magazine-style format. Teachers' notes available separately. Published Hobsons September 1996.

Which A-levels
In *Student Helpbook* series but published in large-format. Useful. Published Hobsons 1996.

Jobs and Careers after A levels
A much needed book on post-A-level opportunities by Beryl Dixon. Published Hobsons 1994.

Sixth Form Casebook
Twenty pages covering employment and higher education issues written by Katherine Lea. Also contains a few sixth-form and a large number of graduate case studies. Published Hobsons. Annual. Current edition summer 1996.

The Job Book
Useful information on jobs, companies, training courses and higher education. Published Hobsons. Annual. Current edition September 1996.

Various GNVQ/GSVQ/Vocational qualifications books:

Getting into Vocational Qualifications
Katherine Lea. Published Trotman 1995. New edition due 1997.

GNVQ: is it for you?
Published Hobsons. 3rd edition by Mike Duckenfield due May 1996.

All you Need to Know About GNVQs
Janet Gibson. Published Kogan Page. 1996.

All treat the subject slightly differently, but the clearest is still the Trotman book (although this editor may be biased!).

Working and studying overseas

The chapter in the *CIOLA Directory* lists a large number of useful publications. Consider particularly:

Getting into Europe
Aimed at careers advisers, etc. and covers ways in which young people can study and work in Europe. Published Trotmans. 1995.

SOCRATES-ERASMUS UK Guide
The best guide to programmes on studying in Europe. Updated annually. Published ISCO.

The European Choice: A Guide to Opportunities for HE in Europe
Free from DfEE Publications Office.

Working in the European Union
4th Edition by W. H. Archer and A. J. Raban. A practical tool for graduates. Readable. Published by European Commission/Hobsons.

Study Abroad
Published UNESCO (in English, French and Spanish) 1993.

European Education Yearbook 95/96
(undergraduate/postgraduate/diplomas/languages). Published Nexus.

Directory of Jobs and Careers Abroad
Guide to permanent career opportunities abroad in a wide range of countries but also has information on voluntary work. Contains a lot of useful addresses including specialist recruitment agencies both in the UK and abroad, and overseas address lists of British companies. Published Vacation Work.

Work Your Way Around The World
Lots of information and advice. Published Vacation Work. 1995.

(Vacation Work publish a range of other useful directories covering specific countries and topics.)

Qualifications

See also previous section on career choice.

British Qualifications
Comprehensive guide to qualifications awarded by higher education institutions and professional institutions and associations. Published Kogan Page. 26th Edition 1995. Also available Trotman.

British Vocational Qualifications
Massive comprehensive listing of approved NVQ/SVQs and their certification bodies. Published Kogan Page. 1995. Gives addresses of all Lead Bodies and Industry Training Organisations.

Review of Qualifications for 16–19 Year Olds
By Sir Ron Dearing. Published SCAA. 700 pages. 1996.

Which Subject? Which Career?

Covers the education system in the UK and academic and vocational changes in qualifications. Also contains an A–Z of careers, but this is much more limited than the alphabetical encyclopedias already listed. Published Consumers' Association in association with Hobsons. New edition March 1996.

Further and higher education: courses

University and College Entrance: The Official Guide

Essential reading, for anyone applying to higher education. Annual. Published UCAS with the *Independent* and Letts. Obtainable Trotman. The new 97 Entrance Guide includes StudyLink UK, the official CD-ROM multimedia guide to HE.

COSHEP/UCAS Entrance Guide to Higher Education in Scotland 1997

Annual. Now published UCAS but main supplier John Smith and Son (Glasgow), 57 St Vincent Street, Glasgow G2 5TB (0141 221 7472).

British University and College Courses

An essential guide for overseas students. Published Trotmans annually. Current edition June 1996.

Compendium of Higher Education (2 volumes)

Also includes degree, HND and professional courses outside the UCAS system. Published LASER. Also obtainable Trotmans.

Directory of Further Education/Directory of Higher Education (2 volumes)

Very detailed directory listing full-time, part-time, day-release, block-release and evening classes in all subjects and at all levels from City & Guilds courses and A-levels up to first degrees. The one on further education is the more useful. Published Hobsons. Annual.

UCAS Handbook

Essential reading for all applicants through UCAS. Published UCAS. Annual.

Handbook of Initial Teacher Training

Covers teacher-training courses including BEd and postgraduate and courses under the School-Centre Teacher Training Scheme and the Licensed Teachers' Scheme. Annual. Obtainable Trotmans September.

Higher education: guides (undergraduate)

How to Complete Your UCAS Form

Written by Tony Higgins of UCAS. Clearly laid out. Published Trotman. Revised annually.

Getting Into ... series

Useful series covering a wide variety of topics and subjects: getting into ... University and College; Oxford and Cambridge; Art and Design; Medical School; Psychology; Law; Accountancy, Business Studies and Economics; Computing; Engineering; Languages; Media; Nursing; Teaching; Veterinary Science. Published Trotman. Irregular, so check for latest edition.

The Complete Degree Course Offers for Entry to Higher Education

By Brian Heap. Summary of course choice and admissions procedures. Survey of grades required for individual courses. Published Trotman. Annual. Next edition due April. Also available on CD-ROM.

Degree Course Guides

Thirty-five guides covering the major areas of first-degree study in Britain. They look at the similarities and differences between courses. Published biennially, with half the set being updated each year. Published Hobsons.

Which Degree?

Four Volumes: Arts, Humanities and Languages; Engineering, Technology and Geography; Sciences, Medicine and Mathematics; Social Sciences, Business and Education. Lists courses and gives the basic details for each course. Saves wading through prospectuses to draw up a shortlist. Published Hobsons. Annual.

Which University?

Profiles of Institutions. Also on CD-ROM. Annual. Published Hobsons.

How to Choose your Higher National Diploma Course

Edited by Eric Whittington. A comprehensive guide to HND courses. Published Trotman. 3rd Edition 1996.

Higher education: student life, sponsorship and finance

Student Helpbook series

Published Hobsons at irregular intervals covering ... *A Year Off... A Year On*; *Pay your Way as a Student*; *Student Life: A Survival Guide.*

Push Guide to Which University

Independent and irreverent look at universities. Also available on CD. Annual. Obtainable through Trotman.

The Student Book 97

By Klaus Boehm and Jenny Lees-Spalding. A fat paperback covering how to apply to higher education and what it's really like. Usually published annually by Macmillan. Next edition probably due April 1997. Available through Trotman.

The Potter Guide to Higher Education

Describes each institution, covering the social life, the environment, accommodation provision and cost, balance of courses, travel and access. Very useful. Published Dalebank Books. Distributed Biblios PDS Ltd. Annual.

Students' Money Matters 3rd edition

Covers how much higher education costs (accommodation, food, travel, books, etc.) and where you can get the money to cover it (grants, loans, access funds, sponsorship, banks, scholarships, earning money through work, etc.), and budgeting. Published Trotman 1995.

Sponsorship for Students

Originally published by COIC but now taken over by Hobsons. The coverage of general information has increased to compensate for the fewer sponsorship opportunities around. Annual.

Higher education: guides (postgraduate)

How to Choose your Postgraduate Course

Gives general guidance in question-and-answer format. Well researched by Beryl Dixon. Published Trotman. 1996.

Guide to Business Schools 1996/97

This is essential reading for anyone considering financing themselves. Includes general chapters on choosing and financing your MBA, school profiles and a schools directory covering the UK, and selected schools in the rest of Europe, North America and the world. It also has a number of useful appendices including starting dates, multiple-choice questions representative of the GMAT, list of MBAs by Distance and Open Learning. Published with the Association of MBAs (AMBA) by Pitman. 12th Edition 1996.

Which MBA? A Critical Guide to the World's Best Programmes

By George Bickerstaffe. A well established publication which covers what an MBA is, how companies view it and how to choose a course. It compares the world's 'best' business schools, and its very detailed listings cover schools in Europe including those in the UK, many North American schools, and some schools in the rest of the world. Includes tables comparing and contrasting various aspects such as GMAT scores, fees, average starting salaries, etc. Published in the UK by the Economist Intelligence Unit in association with Addison-Wesley Publishing Company. 8th Edition 1996.

Directory of Graduate Studies

Guide to over 11,500 full-time and part-time postgraduate research and taught programmes in the UK. Published Hobsons. Annual. The Directory is also on CD-ROM and there is a condensed Students Guide with single-line listings.

Graduate employment

Skills for Graduates in the 21st Century

Interesting but glossy and contains a limited amount of information. Published Association of Graduate Recruiters.

See also various series published by AGCAS and Hobsons Casebooks (mentioned above), and Cambridge Market Intelligence series and GTI Careers Journals mentioned below.

Cambridge Market Intelligence

Publish a series called *Ivanhoe Guides*, which are very detailed books aimed at undergraduates and covering various professions such as *Information Systems*, *Insurance*, *Pensions Management*, *Actuaries*, and *Chartered Patent Agents*.

GTI

Publish a series of journals for graduates covering City and Finance; Civil and Structural Engineering; Construction and Building Services; Engineering; Engineering Construction Industry; Food and Drink; Law; Property; Quantity Surveying; and Water and Environment. Annual. The Law one comes out in March; the others in October.

Occupational books

Trotmans

New inexpensive Question and Answer Series covers a wide range of careers. The style and format is attractive and easy to read and many have been written by professional careers writers. So far there are around 40 books including *Armed Forces*, *Art and Design*, *Complementary Medicine*, *Environment and Nature Conservation*, *Modelling*, and *Music*.

Kogan Page Ltd

Publishes an extensive and useful *Careers* series of slim paperback books on individual careers. These are updated irregularly so older titles will contain out-of-date information. Recent titles include *Careers in Journalism* (7th edition 1996) and *Careers in Teaching* (6th edition 1996).

There are hundreds of specialist publications covering particular careers or courses. These may be published in a careers series, but quite often they are not written as careers literature at all. Handbooks, Directories and Yearbooks are valuable sources of information. For example, the *UK Biotechnology Handbook* published by the BioIndustry Association is a comprehensive directory including detailed company profiles of all the major companies operating in this sector as well as relevant academic institutions and government agencies and review articles. The *Music Education Directory* is a guide to 'credible' music education throughout the UK which is published annually by the BPI (British Phonographic Industry).

Careers books also appear occasionally from publishers who may not be noted for producing careers material – for example, *Inside the Music Business* is a Blueprint book published by Routledge in 1995. It is worth looking round if you are researching a particular career area, and if you are unable to find anything, contact the professional bodies for suggestions on where to look for more information.

Multimedia

In theory, the most up-to-date careers information should be on computer databases, but this obviously depends on how frequently information is checked and revised. Schools, Colleges, TEC/LECs, and Careers Offices may have access to one or more databases. Most of them are now available on CD-ROM. The *CIOLA Directory* contains a very useful chapter on interactive software.

The most useful computer resources are:

Adult Directions, Kudos and CareerQuest
Published CASCAiD Ltd.

ECCTIS plus
Provides information on around 80,000 courses leading to nationally recognised qualifications in universities and in HE and FE colleges.

JIIG-CAL Explorer, Headlight, Jobscope, Pathfinder, Skillcheck
Published JIIG-CAL.

MicroDOORS
An interactive occupational database covering about 1,000 job titles but 'becoming dated and increasingly unsuitable' (Trevor Tucknutt, COIC). Published at present by COIC but they are trying to find private providers to deliver it by a licensing arrangement.

National Database of Vocational Qualifications
Published by NCVQ.

CD-ROM versions are available of:

- *Careers Europe*
- *Choosing Higher Education Courses* (CHEC2)(Careersoft)
- *CIOLA Directory* (Hobsons)
- *Complete Degree Course Offers* (Trotman)
- *ECCTIS 2000*
- *Gradscope* (Software Solutions)
- *Job Book* (Hobsons)
- *Potter Guide to HE* (on ECCTIS CD)
- *PROSPECT HE*
- *PUSH CD Which University*
- *StudyLink UK* – official guide to HE courses (UCAS)
- *Which University* (Hobsons)

Internet information

Hobsons Publishing material is now on the Internet at http://www.hobsons.co.uk
Trotmans is now on the Internet at http://www.trotman.co.uk

Appendix 3: Careers Library Classification Index (CLCI)

ARMED FORCES

B General information
BAB Royal Navy, Royal Marines
BAF Army
BAL Royal Air Force
BAP Other countries
BAZ Others not specified

ADMINISTRATION, BUSINESS, CLERICAL AND MANAGEMENT

C General information
CAB Civil Service
CAC European Commission
CAG Local government administration and clerical work
CAL Health service administration
CAM Public services administration
CAP Business Management
CAS Personnel management and industrial relations
CAT Clerical and secretarial work
CAV Computer work
COB Politics
COD Management services
COF Operational research
COP Trading standards and consumer protection
COT Occupational safety and hygiene
COZ Others not specified

ART AND DESIGN

E General information
EB Fine art
ED Graphic art, design and illustration
EG Industrial and craft design
EJ Fashion and clothing design
EP Surface and two-dimensional design
ET Interior design and display
EV Photography
EZ Others not specified

TEACHING AND CULTURAL ACTIVITIES

F General information
FAB Teaching and teacher support
FAC Journalism and writing
FAD Publishing
FAE Museum and art gallery work
FAF Library and information work
FAG Historical and related work
FAH Archaeology
FAL Languages, work with
FAM Religion and church work
FAP Training officers and industrial training work
FAZ Others not specified

ENTERTAINMENT AND LEISURE

G General information
GAB Theatre and drama
GAD Music
GAF Dance
GAG Sport and outdoor pursuits
GAJ Sport and recreational management and support staff
GAK Betting and gaming
GAL Radio, television, films and video work
GAN Cinema and entertainment work
GAT Arts technical and support work
GAV Arts administration
GAX Travel and tourism
GAZ Others not specified

CATERING AND OTHER SERVICES

I General information
IB Hotel, catering and institutional management
IC Catering and domestic work
ID Home economics and consumer studies
IG Laundry and dry cleaning
IJ Cleaning, caretaking and attendant work
IK Beauty culture